Physiology of Behavior

twelfth edition
global edition

NEIL R. CARLSON
University of Massachusetts, Amherst

MELISSA A. BIRKETT
Northern Arizona University

PEARSON

Boston   Columbus   Indianapolis   New York City   San Francisco
Amsterdam   Cape Town   Dubai   London   Madrid   Milan   Munich   Paris   Montréal   Toronto
Delhi   Mexico City   São Paulo   Sydney   Hong Kong   Seoul   Singapore   Taipei   Tokyo

VP, Product Development: *Dickson Musslewhite*
Senior Acquisitions Editor: *Amber Chow*
Editorial Assistant: *Stephany Harrington*
Director, Content Strategy and Development: *Brita Nordin*
Development Editor: *Thomas Finn*
Director, Project Management Services: *Lisa Iarkowski*
Project Team Lead: *Denise Forlow*
Project Manager: *Shelly Kupperman*
Project Manager, Global Edition: *Sudipto Roy*
Senior Acquisitions Editor, Global Edition: *Sandhya Ghoshal*
Senior Project Editor, Global Edition: *Daniel Luiz*
Manager, Media Production, Global Edition: *M. Vikram Kumar*
Senior Manufacturing Controller, Production, Global Edition: *Trudy Kimber*
Program Team Lead: *Amber Mackey*
Program Manager: *Cecilia Turner*

Director of Field Marketing: *Jonathan Cottrell*
Senior Product Marketing Manager: *Lindsey Prudhomme Gill*
Executive Field Marketing Manager: *Kate Stewart*
Marketing Assistant, Field Marketing: *Amy Pfund*
Marketing Assistant, Product Marketing: *Frank Alarcon*
Operations Manager: *Mary Fischer*
Operations Specialist: *Carol Melville*
Associate Director of Design: *Blair Brown*
Interior Design: *Kathryn Foot*
Cover Design: *Lumina Datamatics, Inc.*
Cover Art: © *allnow/Shutterstock*
Associate Digital Product Manager: *Christopher Fegan*
Digital Studio Project Manager: *Pamela Weldin*
Digital Studio Team Lead: *Peggy Bliss*
Full-Service Project Management and Composition: *Cenveo® Publisher Services*

Acknowledgments of third party content appear on page 702, which constitutes an extension of this copyright page.

Chapter Opener captions: Ch. 1: The human nervous system contains billions of neurons; Ch. 2: Neurons are the cells of the nervous system that are specialized for communication; Ch. 3: The structures of the human nervous system are made up of billions of neurons that make trillions of synapses; Ch. 4: Cross-section of the vagus nerve of the peripheral nervous system; Ch. 5: Neurons in the cortex labeled with a fluorescent dye; Ch. 6: Cross-section of a retina. Photoreceptor cells are visible at the top of the image; Ch. 7: Confocal microscopy image of neurons (green) and glia (red) in the vestibular pathway; Ch 8: Cross-section of the cerebellum; Ch. 9: Cross-section of the hypothalamus of a mouse; Ch. 10: Cross-section of the pituitary gland (left) attached to the hypothalamus (right); Ch. 11: Example of pyramidal neurons found in the hippocampus; Ch. 12: Color-enhanced transmission electron micrograph of portions of two adipose cells and associated connective tissue in a rat; Ch. 13: New neurons in the mouse hippocampus are labeled with green fluorescence; Ch. 14: Scanning electron microscope image of a neuron in the cortex; Ch. 15: Neurons derived from mouse embryonic stem cells. Tyrosine hydroxylase (TH, a dopamine-synthesizing enzyme) is labeled in red; TH-containing neurons degenerate in Parkinson's disease; green labels a protein that's found in all neurons; blue labels the nuclei of all cells; Ch. 16: Neurons in the mouse hippocampus; Ch. 17: Cross-section of the adrenal medulla; Ch. 18: Neurons in the CA1 region of the hippocampus from a transgenic mouse stained for the CB1 cannabinoid receptor (red) and cell nuclei (blue).

Pearson Education Limited
Edinburgh Gate
Harlow
Essex CM20 2JE
England

and Associated Companies throughout the world

Visit us on the World Wide Web at:
www.pearsonglobaleditions.com

© Pearson Education Limited 2017

ISBN 10: 1-292-15810-7
ISBN 13: 978-1-292-15810-5

British Library Cataloguing-in-Publication Data
A catalogue record for this book is available from the British Library.

10 9 8 7 6 5 4 3
20 19 18

Typeset in Palatino LT Pro by Cenveo® Publisher Services

Printed by CPI Group (UK) Ltd, Croydon CR0 4YY

Brief Contents

Contents

5 Methods and Strategies of Research 132

6 Vision 163

7 Audition, the Body Senses, and the Chemical Senses 202

8 Control of Movement 245

9 Sleep and Biological Rhythms 275

10 Reproductive Behavior 310

11 Emotion 344

12 Ingestive Behavior 380

13 Learning and Memory 419

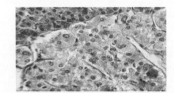

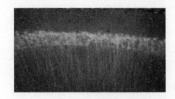

Preface

I wrote the first edition of *Physiology of Behavior* over thirty years ago. When I did so, I had no idea I would someday be writing the twelfth edition. I'm still having fun, so I hope to do a few more. The interesting work coming out of my colleagues' laboratories—a result of their creativity and hard work—has given me something new to say with each edition. Because there was so much for me to learn, I enjoyed writing this edition just as much as the first one. That is what makes writing new editions interesting: learning something new and then trying to find a way to convey the information to the reader.

In this edition, Melissa Birkett joined the team and contributed to the review of the chapter structure and the addition of new pedagogical features, which include learning objectives and revised thought questions. Her work on this book helped to focus the content around critical concepts and provide ways for readers to more consistently self-assess their understanding of behavioral neuroscience. She also worked to implement the new online resources that complement the content of the text and contributed to the ongoing reassessment of research contained in this edition. Together, we drew upon our teaching and experience working with students to create a comprehensive and accessible guide for students of behavioral neuroscience.

The first part of the book is concerned with foundations of behavioral neuroscience: the history of the field, the structure and functions of neurons, neuroanatomy, psychopharmacology, and research methods. The second part is concerned with inputs and outputs that guide behavior: the sensory systems and the motor system. The third part deals with classes of species-typical behavior: sleep, reproduction, emotional behavior, and ingestion. The chapter on reproductive behavior includes parental behavior as well as courting and mating. The chapter on emotion includes a discussion of fear, anger and aggression, communication of emotions, and feelings of emotions. The chapter on ingestive behavior includes the neural and metabolic bases of drinking and eating. The fourth part of the book explores learning, including research on synaptic plasticity, the neural mechanisms that are responsible for perceptual learning and stimulus-response learning (including classical and operant conditioning), human amnesia, and the role of the hippocampal formation in relational learning. The final part of the book examines the neural basis of human communication and neurological, mental, and behavioral disorders. The latter topic is covered in three chapters; the first discusses schizophrenia and the affective disorders; the second discusses stress, anxiety, and neurodevelopmental disorders; and the third discusses substance abuse.

Each chapter begins with a *Case Study*, which describes the experience of people whose lives are impacted by an important issue in neuroscience. Other case studies are included within the text of the chapters. *Learning Objectives* to guide your reading are now found at the beginning of each major section of the text. The learning objectives can help you identify and understand the key points from each section and are also summarized at the end of each section. *Thought Questions* are also located at the end of each section and are designed to stimulate your thinking about what you have learned. *Chapter Review Questions* conclude each chapter. They provide useful reviews of each chapter and a more comprehensive opportunity to test your understanding. *Critical Concepts* features have been added to each chapter, with goals of highlighting important topics in neuroscience and providing opportunities to explore them in greater depth.

New to This Edition

The research reported in this edition reflects both the enormous advances made in research methods and the discoveries these methods have revealed. In neuroscience, as soon as a new method is developed in one laboratory, it is adopted by other laboratories and applied to a wide range of problems. Researchers are combining techniques that converge upon the solution to a problem and use many methods, often in collaboration with other laboratories.

The art in this book continues to evolve. For this twelfth edition, the art has been updated to give the book a fresh, modern, cohesive feel, as well as to keep up with the latest findings and studies in the field. We have always striven to be as up to date and as accurate as possible. We hope the new art in this edition reflects that ongoing effort.

Great effort was also put forth in this edition to make the content more accessible, engaging, and easier for students to understand. We made every attempt to create more scaffolding within each chapter, grouping and reorganizing material so that readers can better identify important concepts and also better see how those concepts relate to each other in more comprehensive patterns. In addition to those organizational revisions, we also, of course, tried to update the literature to stay atop the latest trends and findings in the field.

You'll notice that the chapters contain new headings and subheadings, as well as learning objectives. These are some of the most significant structural changes to the new edition. The subheadings in each chapter correspond with the newly developed learning objectives and are associated with a learning objective summary for each section. We believe that this approach will help the reader to more easily identify main themes and concepts.

The following list summarizes some of the updates new to this edition.

Chapter 1

A new case study reflecting an application of neuroscience research was added to open the chapter.

An emphasis on neuroplasticity as an important theme in neuroscience was added.

New content on contemporary developments in the field of neuroscience was added.

A new section including information about ethical considerations in research with human participants was added.

A summary of new research in support of strategies for learning (along with practical suggestions for readers) was added.

Chapter 4

A new case study was added to the beginning of the chapter, including information about bath salts.

Additional content addressing organization of the field of pharmacology was added.

Chapter 5

Information about deep brain stimulation techniques and application was added.

Chapter 6

The beginning of the chapter was reorganized to provide an introduction to sensation and perception.

The structure of this chapter was rearranged to better align with the format of subsequent chapters.

New content was added to provide an overview of the visual pathway.

The topic of blindsight was added to this chapter.

Chapter 7

A new case study was added to the beginning of the chapter, highlighting the experience of congenital lack of pain receptors.

Information about the application of mirror box therapy for phantom limb pain was added.

Chapter 9

Revised sleep stage scoring guideline information was added.

A description of hypnic jerks is now included.

Research on the experience of lucid dreaming was added.

Additional research on regional cerebral blood flow in slow wave sleep was added.

Information about interventions for insomnia is now included.

Chapter 10

This chapter now includes a discussion of the terms *sex, gender,* and *intersex.*

Additional research about prenatal environment and sexual orientation is now included.

New research about the relationship between testosterone and anticipation of sexual activity is now included.

Chapter 11

A new case study describing the effects of amygdala damage is included.

Additional information about serotonin, progesterone, and aggression has been added.

Details about the use of anabolic steroids have been added.

New information about research on thin slice assessment of emotion is now included.

Chapter 12

New case studies describing interventions for eating disorders have been added to the chapter.

Information about the risk of mortality in anorexia nervosa has been added.

New research on satiety signals has been added.

Additional information about the endocrine response to bariatric surgery has been added.

Research about brain changes associated with eating disorder interventions has been added.

New research about environmental factors related to eating is now included.

Chapter 13

New research on motor learning has been added.

Additional information about neurogenesis has been added.

New research on spatial memory and the hippocampus is now included.

Chapter 14

A new section describing brain regions involved in learning more than one language has been added.

New research on aphasia and American Sign Language is now included.

Chapter 15

A new case study describing interventions for traumatic brain injury has been added.

New information on chronic traumatic encephalopathy has been added.

New research on interventions in Down syndrome is now included.

Details about the prevalence of epilepsy and brain tumors are now included.

New information about the application of deep brain stimulation is included.

Chapter 16

The case study at the beginning of the chapter was revised to reflect the experience of schizophrenia in a young adult.

New research describing brain changes in schizophrenia has been added.

Details about symptom progression and prevalence of hallucination type in schizophrenia are now included.

New information about interventions for schizophrenia is included.

Risk and protective factors in schizophrenia are now included.

New research on the use of ketamine in treatment-resistant depression is included.

Chapter 17

A new case study describing the experience of a panic attack in a young adult is now included at the beginning of the chapter.

The chapter has been reorganized to reflect overlapping content in stress and anxiety disorders, and neurodevelopmental disorders.

The content of the chapter has been updated to reflect changes in *Diagnostic and Statistical Manual for Mental Disorders (5th ed.)*.

New research on stress and immune suppression has been added.

New information about treatment for posttraumatic stress disorder has been added.

Research describing brain changes associated with ADHD is now included.

New information about interventions for autism spectrum disorder is now included.

Details about the prevalence for PTSD and comorbidity of PTSD and TBI are now included.

Information about stress resilience has been added.

Information about pharmacological intervention to treat and prevent PTSD has been added.

Information about a cross-cultural comparison of social anxiety has been added.

Chapter 18

The opening case study of this chapter has been updated to reflect trends in opiate abuse.

The content of the chapter has been updated to reflect changes in *Diagnostic and Statistical Manual for Mental Disorders (5th ed.)*.

New information about interventions for substance abuse has been added.

Details about abstinence rates following substance abuse treatment have been added.

New research about adolescent THC exposure and risk of schizophrenia is now included.

Instructor's Manual Each chapter includes an Integrated Teaching Outline with teaching objectives, lecture material, demonstrations and activities, videos, suggested readings, web resources, and information about other supplements. An appendix contains a set of student handouts. The Instructor's Manual is available online at www.pearsonglobaleditions.com/carlson.

Test Bank Includes over 2,500 thoroughly reviewed multiple-choice, completion, short answer, and essay questions, each with answer justification, page references, difficulty rating, and skill type designation. The Test Bank is also available in Pearson *MyTest*, a powerful online assessment software program. Instructors can easily create and print quizzes and exams as well as author new questions online for maximum flexibility. Both the Test Bank and MyTest are available online at www.pearsonglobaleditions.com/carlson.

Enhanced Lecture PowerPoint Slides with Embedded Videos The enhanced lecture PowerPoints offer detailed outlines of key points for each chapter supported by selected visuals from the textbook, and include the videos featured in the text. *Standard Lecture* PowerPoints without embedded videos are also available. A separate *Art and Figure* version of these presentations contains all art from the textbook for which Pearson has been granted electronic permissions. Available for download on the Instructor's Resource Center at www.pearsonglobaleditions.com/carlson.

Acknowledgments

We would like to thank the many colleagues and reviewers who have provided invaluable time, expertise, and resources to making this the best book it can be.

John Agnew, Walden University

MaryBeth Ahlum, Nebraska Wesleyan University

Mark Basham, Regis University

Lora Becker, University of Evansville

Jessica Bodoh-Creed, California State University, Los Angeles

Melissa Burns-Cusato, Centre College

Giuseppe Cataldo, Queens College-CUNY

Cynthia Cimino, University of South Florida

Ann Cohen, University of Pittsburgh

Deborah Conway, Community College of Allegheny County

Patricia Costello, Walden University

Traci Craig, University of Idaho

Joseph DeBold, Tufts University

David Devonis, Graceland University

Jeannie DiClementi, Indiana–Purdue Fort Wayne

Nick Dominello, Holy Family University

William Dragon, Cornell College

Michael Dudley, Southern Illinois University Edwardsville

Jean Egan, Asnuntuck Community College

Marie-Joelle Estrada, University of Rochester

Claire Etaugh, Bradley University

Rebecca Foushee, Fontbonne University

Mary Fraser, Menlo College

Joseph Green, The Ohio State University, Lima

John C. Hallock, Pima Community College

Julie Hanauer, Suffolk County Community College

Dr. Euriel Merrick, South University

Brian Piper, Husson University School of Pharmacy

Trisha Prunty, Lindenwood University-Belleville

Several colleagues have reviewed previous editions of this book and made excellent suggestions for improvement. We thank:

Massimo Bardi, Marshall University

Kyle Baumbauer, Texas A&M University

Lora Becker, University of Evansville

Annie Cardell, Mountain State University

James Cherry, Boston University

Gary Dunbar, Central Michigan University

Walter Isaac, Georgia College & State University

Eric Jackson, University of New Mexico

Karen Jennings, Keene State College

Linda Lockwood, Metropolitan State College of Denver

Christopher May, Carroll University

Khaleel Razak, University of California, Riverside

Christian Reich, Ramapo College of New Jersey

Christopher Sletten, University of North Florida

Alicia Swan, Southern Illinois University

Lorey Takahashi, University of Hawaii

Sheralee Tershner, Western New England University

Charles Trimbach, Roger Williams University

Steve Weinert, Cuyamaca College

Erin Young, Texas A&M University

We also want to thank the people involved in the editing and production of this book: Amber Chow, senior acquisitions editor; Cecilia Turner, program manager; Stephany Harrington, editorial assistant; and Shelly Kupperman, project manager. Thomas Finn, freelance development editor, made numerous invaluable contributions to preparing the content and format for this edition of the book. Finally, Neil thanks his wife Mary for her support and Melissa thanks her family for their support.

Please write to tell us what you like and dislike about the book at: nrc@psych.umass.edu.

Pearson would like to thank the following people for their work on the Global Edition:

Contributors:

Dr. Manish Goyal, All India Institute of Medical Sciences, Bhubaneswar

Dr. Sushil Chandra Mahapatra, All India Institute of Medical Sciences, Bhubaneswar

Dr. Yogesh Singh, All India Institute of Medical Sciences, Rishikesh

Reviewers:

Dr. Chi Wai Lee, The University of Hong Kong

Dr. Dilip Murthy, Universiti Malaysia Sabah

Chapter 1
Introduction

Chapter Outline

Learning Objectives

LO 1.1 Explain the importance of generalization and reduction in behavioral neuroscience research.

LO 1.2 Summarize contributions to the modern field of behavioral neuroscience made by individuals involved in philosophy, physiology, or other disciplines.

LO 1.3 Describe the role of natural selection in the evolution of behavioral traits.

LO 1.4 Identify factors involved in the evolution of large brains in humans.

LO 1.5 Outline reasons for the use of animals in behavioral neuroscience research.

LO 1.6 Discuss ethical considerations in research with human participants.

LO 1.7 Identify careers in behavioral neuroscience.

LO 1.8 Describe effective learning strategies for studying behavioral neuroscience.

Jeremiah is a 53-year-old lawyer. When he was just seven years old, he experienced a stroke while playing baseball. Although most strokes occur in older adults, unfortunately they can affect anyone, even children. A stroke occurs when a part of the brain is deprived of blood flow and oxygen (you will read more about strokes, cerebrovascular accidents, in Chapter 15). As a result of damage to the left side of his brain, Jeremiah lost all sensation on the right side of his body and had limited ability to use his right arm or leg. He received some rehabilitation immediately following the stroke and learned to walk with the assistance of a cane. He had to learn to write with his left hand because the fine motor movements proved too difficult for him to continue writing with his right hand.

He was never able to regain full movement of the right side of his body, however, and so despite the progress he made, Jeremiah fell frequently. More than forty years after his stroke, he still fell nearly 150 times a year, resulting in multiple injuries including bone fractures in his hand, foot, and hip. Jeremiah's ongoing struggles over a span of four decades prompted him to seek a new treatment to improve his balance, coordination, and fine motor skills. Remarkably, after only two weeks of training for his right hand, and three weeks for his right leg, Jeremiah's balance improved and he was once again able to write his name with his right hand. What happened in Jeremiah's brain that allowed this drastic improvement?

Jeremiah received a form of therapy called constraint-induced movement (CI) therapy. The therapy is based on the idea that stroke-induced paralysis is due to disuse of the limb and fewer cells in the brain being devoted to the limb's movement. To reteach the brain to engage in behaviors once again, the therapy involves intensive physical activity using the affected parts of the body. For example, Jeremiah spent hours each day working to move his affected limbs, doing things like picking up a pencil, stacking blocks, and clipping clothespins to a yardstick. To force Jeremiah to work with his weaker, right hand, therapists used mitts to cover his left hand. Such incremental training, or shaping, of the affected body part "rewires" the brain, allowing it to "relearn" basic functions and processes. This kind of "rewiring" of the brain is known to neuroscientists as plasticity, or the ability of the brain to change over time. Due to the plasticity of the brain, Jeremiah, after hours of intensive practice, was able to regain much of his motor control that had been lost decades before during the stroke he suffered as a child (Doidge, 2007).

*****

Until nearly the beginning of the twenty-first century, most researchers believed that the brain was not capable of change in adulthood. Several pioneering neuroscientists suggested the cells and connections of the adult brain are in fact flexible, or plastic, and attempted to change beliefs about the brain that had been held for more than a century. It was not an easy process. Though equipped with revolutionary new data, the researchers were criticized for years, their data and methods questioned. Eventually, the data accumulated and even the strongest critics began to retract their statements and accept the data demonstrating neural changes in the adult brain, including the presence of new cells in some regions of the brain.

Today, we know the adult brain forms connections between the cells in the brain, called **neurons,** throughout a lifetime. This change in understanding about the brain has been met with optimism and excitement. Therapies for brain injury and mental illness have been developed based on understanding about lifelong brain changes. Dozens of researchers are also making new discoveries every year about **neurogenesis,** the generation of new neurons.

This story of the change in how we understand the brain, and the potential benefits of that understanding, illustrates many of the important principles you will encounter throughout this book. Behavioral neuroscience is a dynamic and ever-changing field. As you read this book, consider not only the facts it contains, but also the process of obtaining those facts, the numerous and dedicated scientists responsible for conducting the research, and the exciting possibility that there is still much to learn about the brain and the nervous system.

The last frontier in this world—and perhaps the greatest one—lies within us. The human nervous system makes possible all that we can do, all that we can know, and all that we can experience. Its complexity is immense, and the task of studying it and understanding it dwarfs all previous explorations our species has undertaken.

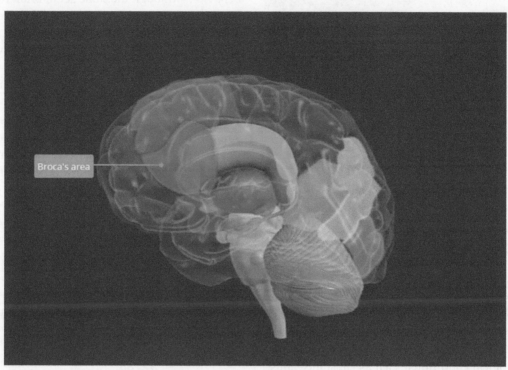

This figure depicts Broca's area, a region important in speech production that was discovered through pioneering studies of brain functions described in this chapter.

Foundations of Behavioral Neuroscience

Behavioral neuroscience was formerly known as *physiological psychology*, and it is still sometimes referred to by that name. In fact, the first psychology textbook, written by Wilhelm Wundt in the late nineteenth century, was titled *Principles of Physiological Psychology*. In recent years, the explosion of information from experimental biology, chemistry, animal behavior, psychology, computer science, and other fields has contributed to creating the diverse interdisciplinary field of behavioral neuroscience. This united effort is due to the realization that the ultimate function of the nervous system is behavior.

When we ask our students what they think the ultimate function of the brain is, they often say "thinking," or "logical reasoning," or "perceiving," or "remembering things." The nervous system does perform these functions, but they support the primary one: control of movement. (Note that movement includes speech and other forms of communication, an important category of human behavior.) The basic function of perception is to inform us of what is happening in our environment so that our behaviors will be adaptive and useful: Perception without the ability to act would be useless. Once perceptual abilities evolved, they could be used for purposes other than guiding behavior. For example, we can enjoy a beautiful sunset or a great work of art without our perception causing us to do anything in particular. And thinking can often take place without causing any overt behavior. However, the *ability to think* evolved because it permits us to perform complex behaviors that accomplish useful self-preserving goals. And whereas reminiscing about things that happened in our past can be an enjoyable pastime, the ability to learn and remember evolved—again—because it permitted our ancestors to profit from experience and perform behaviors that were useful to them.

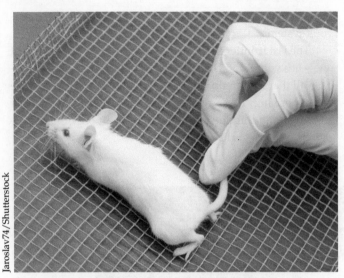

The study of nest-building behavior in mice shows that the same mechanisms can be activated by different parts of the brain.

The growing field of behavioral neuroscience has been formed by scientists who have combined the experimental methods of psychology with those of physiology and have applied them to the issues that concern researchers in many different fields. Research in neuroscience includes topics in perceptual processes, control of movement, sleep and waking, reproductive behaviors, ingestive behaviors, emotional behaviors, learning, and language. In recent years we have begun to study the neuroscience underlying human pathological conditions, such as substance abuse and neurological and mental disorders. These topics are discussed in subsequent chapters of this book.

The Goals of Research

LO 1.1   Explain the importance of generalization and reduction in behavioral neuroscience research.

The goal of all scientists is to explain the phenomena they study. But what do we mean by *explain?* Scientific explanation takes two forms: generalization and reduction. **Generalization** refers to explanations as examples of general laws, which are revealed through experiments. **Reduction** refers to explanations of complex phenomena in terms of simpler ones.

The task of the behavioral neuroscientist is to explain behavior by studying the physiological processes that control it. But behavioral neuroscientists cannot simply be reductionists. It is not enough to observe behaviors and correlate them with physiological events that occur at the same time. We must also understand the function of a given behavior. For example, mice, like many other mammals, often build nests. Behavioral observations show

that mice will build nests under two conditions: when the air temperature is low and when the animal is pregnant. A nonpregnant mouse will build a nest only if the temperature is cool, whereas a pregnant mouse will build one regardless of the temperature. The same behavior occurs for different reasons. In fact, nest-building behavior is controlled by two different physiological mechanisms. Nest building can be studied as a behavior related to the process of temperature regulation, or it can be studied in the context of parental behavior. Although the same set of brain mechanisms will control the movements that a mouse makes in building a nest in both cases, these mechanisms will be activated by different parts of the brain. One part receives information from the body's temperature detectors, and the other part is influenced by hormones that are present in the body during pregnancy.

Sometimes, physiological mechanisms can tell us something about psychological processes such as language, memory or mood. For example, damage to a particular part of the brain can cause very specific impairments in a person's language abilities. The nature of these impairments suggests how these abilities are organized. When the damage involves a brain region that is important in analyzing speech sounds, it also produces deficits in spelling. This finding suggests that the ability to recognize a spoken word and the ability to spell it call on related brain mechanisms. Damage to another region of the brain can produce extreme difficulty in reading unfamiliar words by sounding them out, but it does not impair the person's ability to read words with which he or she is already familiar. This finding suggests that reading comprehension can take two routes: one that is related to speech sounds and another that is primarily a matter of visual recognition of whole words.

In practice, the research efforts of behavioral neuroscientists involve both forms of explanation: generalization and reduction. Ideas for experiments are stimulated by the investigator's knowledge both of psychological generalizations about behavior and of physiological mechanisms. A good behavioral neuroscientist must therefore be an expert in the study of behavior *and* the study of physiology.

Biological Roots of Behavioral Neuroscience

LO 1.2   Summarize contributions to the modern field of behavioral neuroscience made by individuals involved in philosophy, physiology, or other disciplines.

From the earliest historical times, human beings have believed that they possess something intangible that animates them: a mind, or a soul, or a spirit. We each also have a physical body, with muscles that move it and sensory organs

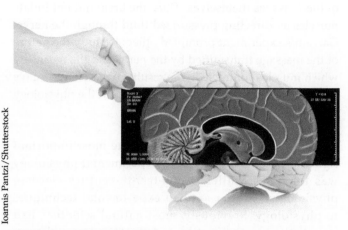

Most neuroscientists believe that once we understand the workings of the human body, we will be able to explain how we perceive, how we think, how we remember, and how we behave.

such as eyes and ears that perceive information about the world around us. Within our bodies the nervous system plays a central role, receiving information from the sensory organs and controlling the movements of the muscles. But what role does the mind play? Does it *control* the nervous system? Is it a *part of* the nervous system? Is it physical and tangible, like the rest of the body, or is it a spirit that will always remain hidden?

This puzzle has historically been called the *mind–body question*. Philosophers have been trying to answer it for many centuries, and more recently scientists have taken up the task. Basically, people have followed two different approaches: dualism and monism. **Dualism** is a belief in the dual nature of reality. Mind and body are separate; the body is made of ordinary matter, but the mind is not. **Monism** is a belief that everything in the universe consists of matter and energy and that the mind is a phenomenon produced by the workings of the nervous system.

Mere speculation about the nature of the mind can get us only so far. If we could answer the mind–body question simply by thinking about it, philosophers would have done so long ago. Behavioral neuroscientists, on the other hand, take an empirical, monistic approach to the study of human nature. Most neuroscientists believe that once we understand the workings of the human body—and, in particular, the workings of the nervous system—the mind–body question will be resolved. We will be able to explain how we perceive, how we think, how we remember, and how we behave. We will even be able to explain the nature of our own self-awareness. This section explores some of the important discoveries of the past that contributed to today's field of behavioral neuroscience.

ANCIENT WORLD   Study of (or speculations about) the physiology of behavior has its roots in antiquity. A papyrus

scroll from approximately 1700 B.C.E. contains surgical records of head injuries and the oldest surviving descriptions of the brain, cerebrospinal fluid, meninges, and skull (Feldman and Goodrich, 1999).

Because its movement was necessary for life and because emotions caused it to beat more strongly, ancient Egyptian, Indian, and Chinese cultures considered the heart to be the seat of thought and emotions. The ancient Greeks did too, but Hippocrates (460–370 B.C.E.) concluded that this role should be assigned to the brain.

Not all ancient Greek scholars agreed with Hippocrates. Aristotle did not; he thought the brain served to cool the passions of the heart. But Galen (130–200 C.E.), who had the greatest respect for Aristotle, thought enough of the brain to dissect and study the brains of cattle, sheep, pigs, cats, dogs, weasels, monkeys, and apes (Finger, 1994), and concluded that Aristotle's theory about the brain's role was "utterly absurd, since in that case Nature would not have placed the encephalon [brain] so far from the heart, . . . and she would not have attached the sources of all the senses [the sensory nerves] to it" (Galen, 1968 translation, p. 387). (See Figure 1.1.)

SEVENTEENTH CENTURY   Philosophers and physiologists in the 1600s contributed greatly to the foundations of today's behavioral neuroscience. The French philosopher René Descartes' speculations concerning the roles of the mind and brain in the control of behavior provide a good starting point in the modern history of behavioral neuroscience. To Descartes, animals were mechanical devices; their behavior was controlled by environmental stimuli. His view of the human body was much the same: It was a machine. As

Figure 1.1 Galen (130–200 C.E.)

Descartes observed, some movements of the human body were automatic and involuntary. For example, if a person's finger touched a hot object, the arm would immediately withdraw from the source of stimulation. Reactions like this did not require participation of the mind; they occurred automatically. Descartes called these actions **reflexes.** (See Figure 1.2.)

Like most philosophers of his time, Descartes was a dualist and believed that each person possessed a mind—a uniquely human attribute that was not subject to the laws of the universe. But his thinking differed from that of his predecessors in one important way: He was the first to suggest that a link exists between the human mind and its purely physical housing, the brain. He believed that the mind controlled the movements of the body, while the body, through its sense organs, supplied the mind with information about what was happening in the environment. In particular, he hypothesized that this interaction took place in the pineal body, a small organ situated on top of the brain stem, buried beneath the cerebral hemispheres. He noted that the brain contained hollow chambers (the *ventricles*) that were filled with fluid, and he hypothesized that this fluid was under pressure. When the mind decided to perform an action, it tilted the pineal body in a particular direction like a little joystick, causing fluid to flow from the brain into the appropriate set of nerves. This flow of fluid caused muscles to inflate and move.

However, it did not take long for biologists to disprove Descartes' belief about the brain using pressurized fluid to control behavior. Luigi Galvani, a seventeenth-century Italian physiologist, found that electrical stimulation of a frog's nerve caused contraction of the muscle to which it was attached. Contraction occurred even when the nerve and muscle were detached from the rest of the body, so

the ability of the muscle to contract and the ability of the nerve to send a message to the muscle were characteristics of these tissues themselves. Thus, the brain did not inflate muscles by directing pressurized fluid through the nerve. Galvani's experiment prompted others to study the nature of the message transmitted by the nerve and the means by which muscles contracted. The results of these efforts gave rise to an accumulation of knowledge about the physiology of behavior.

NINETEENTH CENTURY One of the most important figures in the development of experimental physiology was Johannes Müller, a nineteenth-century German physiologist. Müller applied experimental techniques to physiology. Previously, most natural scientists had been limited to observation and classification. Although these activities are essential, Müller insisted that major advances in our understanding of the workings of the body would be achieved only by experimentally removing or isolating animals' organs, testing their responses to various chemicals, and otherwise altering the environment to see how the organs responded. His most important contribution to the study of the physiology of behavior was his **doctrine of specific nerve energies.** Müller observed that although all nerves carry the same basic message—an electrical impulse—we perceive the messages of different nerves in different ways. For example, messages carried by the optic nerves produce sensations of visual images, and those carried by the auditory nerves produce sensations of sounds. How can different sensations arise from the same basic message?

The answer is that the messages occur in different channels. The portion of the brain that receives messages from the optic nerves interprets the activity as visual stimulation, even if the nerves are actually stimulated mechanically. (For example, when we rub our eyes, we see flashes of light.) Because different parts of the brain receive messages from different nerves, the brain must be functionally divided: Some parts perform some functions, while other parts perform others.

Müller's advocacy of experimentation and the logical deductions from his doctrine of specific nerve energies set the stage for performing experiments directly on the brain. Pierre Flourens, a nineteenth-century French physiologist, did just that. Flourens removed various parts of animals' brains and observed their behavior. By seeing what the animal could no longer do, he could infer the function of the missing portion of the brain. This method is called **experimental ablation.** Flourens claimed to have discovered the regions of the brain that control heart rate and breathing, purposeful movements, and visual and auditory reflexes.

Soon after Flourens performed his experiments, Paul Broca, a French surgeon, applied the principle

Figure 1.2 Descartes' Model

Descartes believed that the "soul" (what we now call the mind) controls the movements of the muscles through its influence on the pineal body. According to his theory, the eyes sent visual information to the brain, where it could be examined by the soul. When the soul decided to act, it would tilt the pineal body (labeled H in the diagram), which would divert pressurized fluid through nerves to the appropriate muscles.

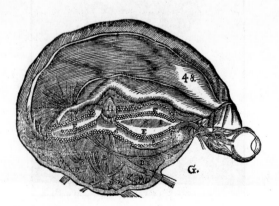

of experimental ablation to the human brain. He did not intentionally remove parts of human brains to see how they worked but observed the behavior of people whose brains had been damaged by strokes. In 1861, he performed an autopsy on the brain of a man who had had a stroke that resulted in the loss of the ability to speak. Broca's observations led him to conclude that a portion of the cerebral cortex on the front part of the left side of the brain performs functions that are necessary for speech. This came to be known as Broca's area (see Figure 1.3). Other physicians soon obtained evidence supporting his conclusions. As you will learn in Chapter 14, the control of speech is not localized to only one particular region of the brain. Speech requires many different functions, which are organized throughout the brain. Nonetheless, the method of experimental ablation remains important to our understanding of the brains of both humans and laboratory animals.

As mentioned earlier, Luigi Galvani used electricity to demonstrate that muscles contain the source of the energy that powers their contractions. In 1870, German physiologists Gustav Fritsch and Eduard Hitzig used electrical stimulation as a tool for understanding the physiology of the brain. They applied weak electrical current to the exposed surface of a dog's brain and observed the effects of the stimulation. They found that stimulation of different portions of a specific region of the brain caused contraction of specific muscles on the opposite side of the body. We now refer to this region as the *primary motor cortex,* and we know that nerve cells there communicate directly with those that cause muscular contractions. We also know that other regions of the brain communicate with the primary motor cortex and thus control behaviors. For example, the region that Broca found necessary for speech communicates with,

and controls, the portion of the primary motor cortex that controls the muscles of the lips, tongue, and throat, which we use to speak.

German physicist and physiologist Hermann von Helmholtz devised a mathematical formulation of the law of conservation of energy; invented the ophthalmoscope (used to examine the retina of the eye); devised an important and influential theory of color vision and color blindness; and studied audition, music, and many physiological processes. Helmholtz was the first scientist to attempt to measure the speed of conduction through nerves. Scientists had previously believed that such conduction was identical to the conduction that occurs in wires, traveling at approximately the speed of light. But Helmholtz found that neural conduction was much slower—only about 90 feet per second. This measurement proved that neural conduction was more than a simple electrical message, as we will see in Chapter 2.

Jan Purkinje, a Czech physiologist, studied both the central and peripheral nervous systems. He discovered Purkinje fibers—neurons terminating on cardiac cells responsible for controlling contractions of the heart. He also investigated neurons in the brain, describing Purkinje cells in the cerebellum and conducting studies of the visual system. Interestingly, he was also the first to describe the individuality of fingerprints (Bhattacharyya, 2011).

Late in the nineteenth century, Spanish anatomist Ramon Santiago y Cajal used the Golgi staining technique (described in Chapter 5) to examine individual neurons of the brain. His drawings of neurons (made under magnification from a microscope) from the brain, spinal cord, and retina depicted the detailed structures of these cells for the first time. Santiago y Cajal proposed that the nervous system consisted of billions of discrete, individual neurons, in opposition to the predominant idea of the time that the nervous system was a continuous network. In 1906, he was awarded the Nobel Prize for his work describing the structure of the nervous system.

CONTEMPORARY RESEARCH Twentieth-century developments in experimental physiology included many important inventions, such as sensitive amplifiers to detect weak electrical signals, neurochemical techniques to analyze chemical changes within and between cells, and histological techniques to visualize cells and their constituents. These and many other important developments are discussed in detail in subsequent chapters.

Briefly, highlights in contributions to neuroscience during the twentieth century include discoveries ranging from the electrical and chemical messages used by neurons, to the circuits and brain structures involved in a wide variety of behaviors, such as the mirror neuron system for coordinating social behavior (described in Chapter 8). Other developments contributed to new

Figure 1.3 Broca's Area

This region of the brain is named for French surgeon Paul Broca, who discovered that damage to a part of the left side of the brain disrupted a person's ability to speak.

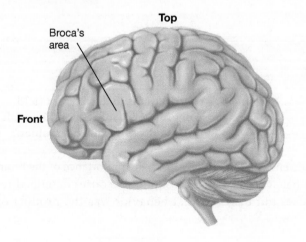

Broca's area

Top

Front

brain-based treatments for disorders such as depression and schizophrenia.

The twenty-first century has already witnessed several important advances and discoveries. As researchers continue to refine their understanding of the structures and functions of the brain, new discoveries about pathways and circuits abound. For example, the 2014 Nobel Prize was awarded to John O'Keefe, May-Britt Moser, and Edvard Moser for work on spatial positioning systems in the brain (often called the brain's global positioning system, or GPS). New advances in technology enabled treatments for severe depression and Parkinson's disease using deep brain stimulation techniques (see Chapters 15 and 16). The development of optogenetics provided researchers with the ability to selectively activate single neurons and observe changes in behavior—using light! (See Chapter 5.)

As behavioral neuroscience continues to progress as an interdisciplinary field, efforts such as the European Human Brain Project, which is working to develop a computer simulation of the brain, and the Brain Research through Advancing Innovative Neurotechnologies (BRAIN) initiative in the United States will continue to bring together groups of researchers from biology, chemistry, engineering, psychology, physiology, and other fields. Behavioral neuroscience, after all, has its roots—and its future—in interdisciplinary research.

DIVERSITY IN NEUROSCIENCE Neuroscience is a diverse, interdisciplinary field whose researchers work around the globe. The *Society for Neuroscience* was founded in 1969, with 500 members committed to developing a professional organization for scientists and physicians devoted to understanding the brain and nervous system. This international organization now has approximately 40,000 members from over 90 different countries. Reviewing the list of Nobel Prizes related to neuroscience research in Table 1.1, you'll notice the names of men and women from several different countries. The field is striving to increase diversity through inclusivity of women and underrepresented groups in the sciences.

Table 1.1 Selected Nobel Prizes for Research Related to Neuroscience

Year	Recipients (Country)	Field of Study
1906	Camillo Golgi (Italy) and Santiago Ramon y Cajal (Spain)	Structure of the nervous system
1963	Sir John Carew Eccles (Australia), Sir Alan Lloyd Hodgkin (U.K.), and Sir Andrew Fielding Huxley (U.K.)	Ionic mechanisms of nerve cell membrane
1970	Julius Axelrod (U.S.), Sir Bernard Katz (Germany, U.S.), and Ulf Svante von Euler (Sweden)	Neurotransmitters
1979	David Hubel (Canada, U.S.), Torsten Wiesel (Sweden, U.S.), and Roger Sperry (U.S.)	Functions of the nervous system
2000	Arvid Carlsson (Sweden), Paul Greengard (U.S.), and Eric Kandel (U.S.)	Neural communication
2014	John O'Keefe (U.S. U.K.), Edvard I. Moser (Norway), and May-Britt Moser (Norway)	Spatial positioning system in the brain

Section Review

Foundations of Behavioral Neuroscience

LO 1.1 Explain the importance of generalization and reduction in behavioral neuroscience research.

To explain the results of behavioral neuroscience research, generalization can be used to reveal general laws of behavior. Reduction can be used to explain complex phenomena in terms of simpler ones.

LO 1.2 Summarize contributions to the modern field of behavioral neuroscience made by individuals involved in philosophy, physiology, or other disciplines.

Ancient scholars disagreed on the importance of the brain in behavior. French philosopher Descartes described reflexes but believed that behavior was the product of pressurized fluid causing muscles to contract. Müller proposed the doctrine of specific nerve energies while Flourens and Broca studied brain region functions using ablation. Galvani discovered that nerves convey electrical messages and von Helmholtz refined that understanding to begin to account for chemical communication between cells. Purkinje and Santiago y Cajal studied the structures and functions of specific sets of neurons.

Thought Question

Recent advances such as the Brain Activity Map Project and the Human Brain Project have been considered by some as stepping stones toward artificial intelligence. There is a possibility that future machines may mimic some functions of the human brain. What do you think of the possible implications of such developments with respect to the advancement of human race? Can computers have self-awareness and consciousness?

Natural Selection and Evolution

Following the tradition of Müller and von Helmholtz, other biologists continued to observe, classify, and think about what they saw, and some of them arrived at valuable conclusions. The most important of these scientists was Charles Darwin. (See Figure 1.4.) Darwin formulated the principles of *natural selection* and *evolution*, which revolutionized biology.

Functionalism and the Inheritance of Traits

LO 1.3 **Describe the role of natural selection in the evolution of behavioral traits.**

Darwin's theory emphasized that all of an organism's characteristics—its structure, its coloration, its behavior—have

---

Figure 1.4 Charles Darwin (1809–1882)

Darwin's theory of evolution revolutionized biology and strongly influenced early psychologists.

(North Wind Picture Archives.)

functional significance. For example, the strong talons and sharp beaks that eagles possess permit the birds to catch and eat prey. Caterpillars that eat green leaves are themselves green, and their color makes it difficult for birds to see them against their usual background. Mother mice construct nests, which keep their offspring warm and out of harm's way. The behavior itself is not inherited. What *is* inherited is a structure—the brain—that causes the behavior to occur. Thus, Darwin's theory gave rise to **functionalism,** a belief that characteristics of living organisms perform useful functions. So, to understand the physiological basis of various behaviors, we must first understand what these behaviors accomplish. We must therefore understand something about the natural history of the species being studied so that the behaviors can be seen in context.

To understand the workings of something as complex as a nervous system, we should know what its functions are. Organisms of today are the result of a long series of changes due to genetic variability. Strictly speaking, we cannot say that any physiological mechanisms of living organisms have a *purpose*. But they do have *functions*, and these we can try to determine. For example, the forelimb structures shown in Figure 1.5 are adapted for different functions in different species of mammals. Adaptations also occur in brain structures. For example, male songbirds such as the white crowned sparrow possess highly developed brain structures (the *robust nucleus of the archistriatum, high vocal center,* and *Area X)* that differ from some of their close, nonsongbird relatives. The songbirds' unique structures allow them to learn and produce songs in response to complex social and environmental stimuli. The function of male song behavior in these species is to attract a mate and deter rivals. The nonsongbirds lack these brain structures and their associated functions (Beecher and Brenowitz, 2005). Among the various songbirds, in species in which only the males sing, males have larger song brain structures compared to females. In species in which both sexes sing duets, there is no difference between the size of the structures in males and females (Brenowitz, 1997).

Darwin formulated his theory of evolution to explain the means by which species acquired their adaptive characteristics.

Figure 1.5 Bones of the Forelimb

The figure shows the bones of (a) human, (b) bat, (c) whale, (d) dog. Through the process of natural selection, these bones have been adapted to suit many different functions.

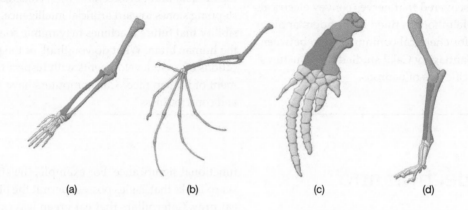

(a)   (b)   (c)   (d)

The cornerstone of this theory is the principle of **natural selection.** Darwin noted that members of a species were not all identical and that some of the differences they exhibited were inherited by their offspring. If an individual's characteristics permit it to reproduce more successfully, some of the individual's offspring will inherit the favorable characteristics and will themselves produce more offspring. As a result, the characteristics will become more prevalent in that species. He observed that animal breeders were able to develop strains that possessed particular traits by mating together only animals that possessed the desired traits. If *artificial selection,* controlled by animal breeders, could produce so many varieties of dogs, cats, and livestock, perhaps *natural selection* could be responsible for the development of species. In natural selection, it was the natural environment, not the hand of the animal breeder, that shaped the process of evolution.

Darwin and his fellow scientists knew nothing about the mechanism by which the principle of natural selection works. In fact, the principles of molecular genetics were not discovered until the middle of the twentieth century. Briefly, here is how the process works: Every sexually reproducing multicellular organism consists of a large number of cells, each of which contains chromosomes. Chromosomes are large, complex molecules that contain the recipes for producing the proteins that cells need to grow and to perform their functions. In essence, the chromosomes contain the blueprints for the construction (that is, the embryological development) of a particular member of a particular species. If the plans are altered, a different organism is produced.

The plans do get altered from time to time; mutations occur. **Mutations** are accidental changes in the chromosomes of sperm or eggs that join together and develop into new organisms. For example, a random mutation of a chromosome in a cell of an animal's testis or ovary could produce a mutation that affects that animal's offspring. Most mutations are deleterious; the offspring either fails to survive or survives with some sort of defect. However, a small percentage of mutations are beneficial and confer a **selective advantage** to the organism that possesses them. That is, the animal is more likely than other members of its species to live long enough to reproduce and hence to pass on its chromosomes to its own offspring. Many different kinds of traits can confer a selective advantage: resistance to a particular disease, the ability to digest new kinds of food, more effective weapons for defense or for procurement of prey, and even a more attractive appearance to members of the other sex (after all, one must reproduce to pass on one's chromosomes).

The traits that can be altered by mutations are physical ones; chromosomes make proteins, which affect the structure and chemistry of cells. But the *effects* of these physical alterations can be seen in an animal's behavior. Thus, the process of natural selection can act on behavior indirectly. For example, if a particular mutation results in changes in the brain that cause a small animal to change its behavior and freeze when it perceives a novel stimulus, that animal is more likely to escape undetected when a predator passes nearby. This tendency makes the animal more likely to survive and produce offspring, thus passing on its genes to future generations.

Other mutations are not immediately favorable, but because they do not put their possessors at a disadvantage, they are inherited by at least some members of the species. As a result of thousands of such mutations, the members of a particular species possess a variety of genes and are all at least somewhat different from one another. Variety is a definite advantage for a species. Different environments provide optimal habitats for different kinds of organisms. When the environment changes, species must adapt or run

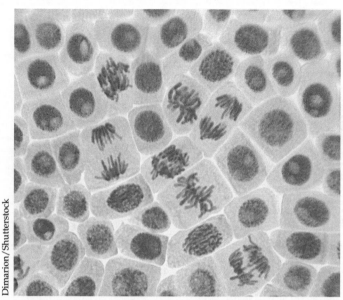

Mutations are accidental changes in the chromosomes of sperm or eggs that join together and develop into new organisms.

the risk of becoming extinct. If some members of the species possess assortments of genes that provide characteristics permitting them to adapt to the new environment, their offspring will survive, and the species will continue.

An understanding of the principle of natural selection plays some role in the thinking of every scientist who undertakes research in behavioral neuroscience. Some researchers explicitly consider the genetic mechanisms of various behaviors and the physiological processes on which these behaviors depend. Others are concerned with comparative aspects of behavior and its physiological basis; they compare the nervous systems of animals from a variety of species to make hypotheses about the evolution of brain structure and the behavioral capacities that correspond to this evolutionary development. But even though many researchers are not directly involved with the problem of evolution, the principle of natural selection guides the thinking of behavioral neuroscientists. We ask ourselves what the selective advantage of a particular trait might be. We think about how nature might have used a physiological mechanism that already existed to perform more complex functions in more complex organisms. When we entertain hypotheses, we ask ourselves whether a particular explanation makes sense in an evolutionary perspective.

Evolution of Large Brains

LO 1.4 Identify factors involved in the evolution of large brains in humans.

To *evolve* means to develop gradually. The process of **evolution** is a gradual change in the structure and physiology of plant and animal species as a result of natural selection. New species evolve when organisms develop novel characteristics that can take advantage of unexploited opportunities in the environment.

Appearance of the earliest humans can be traced back to the Cenozoic period when tropical forests covered much of the land areas. In these forests our most direct ancestors, the primates, evolved. The first primates were small and preyed on insects and small cold-blooded vertebrates such as lizards and frogs. They had grasping hands that permitted them to climb about in small branches of the forest. Over time, larger species developed, with larger, forward-facing eyes (and the brains to analyze what the eyes saw), which facilitated moving among the trees and the capture of prey.

The evolution of fruit-bearing trees provided an opportunity for fruit-eating primates. In fact, the original advantage of color vision (and the associated sensory regions of the brain) was probably the ability to discriminate ripe fruit from green leaves and eat the fruit before it spoiled—or some other animals got to it first. And because fruit is such a nutritious form of food, its availability provided an opportunity that could be exploited by larger primates, which were able to travel farther in quest of food.

The first *hominids* (humanlike apes) appeared in Africa. They appeared not in dense tropical forests but in drier woodlands and in the savanna. Our fruit-eating ancestors continued to eat fruit, but they evolved characteristics that enabled them to gather roots and tubers as well, to hunt and kill game, and to defend themselves against other predators. They made tools that could be used to hunt, produce clothing, and construct dwellings; they discovered the many uses of fire; they domesticated dogs, which greatly increased their ability to hunt and helped warn of attacks by predators; and they developed the ability to communicate symbolically, by means of spoken words.

Figure 1.6 shows the primate family tree. Our closest living relatives—the only hominids besides ourselves who have survived—are the chimpanzees, gorillas, and orangutans. DNA analysis shows that genetically, there is very little difference between these four species. For example, humans and chimpanzees share almost 99 percent of their DNA.

The first hominid to leave Africa did so around 1.7 million years ago. This species, *Homo erectus* ("upright man"), scattered across Europe and Asia. One branch of *Homo erectus* appears to have been the ancestor of *Homo neanderthalis,* which inhabited Western Europe between 120,000 and 30,000 years ago. Neanderthals resembled modern humans. They made tools out of stone and wood and discovered the use of fire. Our own species, *Homo sapiens,* evolved in East Africa around 100,000 years ago. Some of our ancestors migrated to other parts of Africa and out of Africa to Asia, Polynesia, Australia, Europe, and the Americas (see Figure 1.7).

Figure 1.6 Evolution of Primate Species

(Redrawn from Lewin, R. *Human Evolution: An Illustrated Introduction,* 3rd ed. Boston: Blackwell Scientific Publications, 1993. Reprinted with permission by Blackwell Science Ltd.)

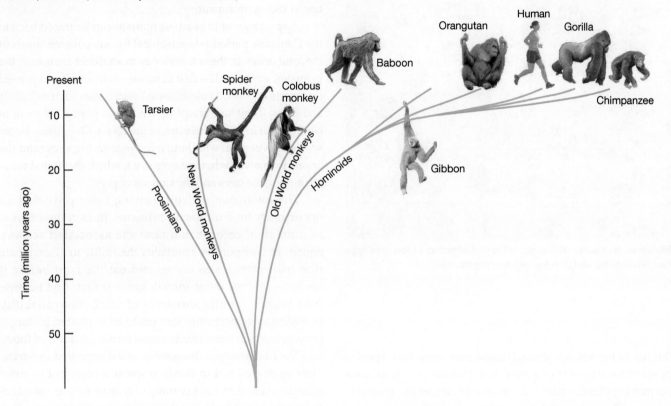

Humans possessed several characteristics that enabled them to compete with other species. Their agile hands enabled them to make and use tools. Their excellent color vision helped them to spot ripe fruit, game animals, and dangerous predators. Their mastery of fire enabled them to cook food, provide warmth, and frighten nocturnal

Figure 1.7 Migration of *Homo sapiens*

The figure shows proposed migration routes of *Homo sapiens* after evolution of the species in East Africa.

(Redrawn with permission from Cavalli-Sforza, L. L. Genes, peoples and languages. *Scientific American,* Nov. 1991, p. 75.)

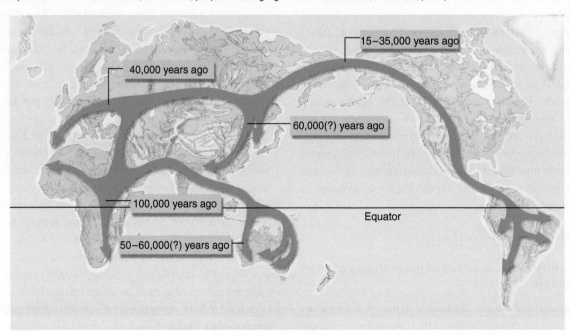

predators. Their upright posture and bipedalism (ability to walk using two rear limbs) made it possible for them to walk long distances efficiently, with their eyes far enough from the ground to see long distances across the plains. Bipedalism also permitted them to carry tools and food with them, which meant that they could bring fruit, roots, and pieces of meat back to their tribe. Their linguistic abilities enabled them to combine the collective knowledge of all the members of the tribe, to make plans, to pass information on to subsequent generations, and to form complex civilizations that established their status as the dominant species. All of these characteristics required a larger brain.

A large brain requires a large skull, and an upright posture limits the size of a woman's birth canal. A newborn baby's head is about as large as it can safely be. As it is, the birth of a baby is much more arduous than the birth of mammals with proportionally smaller heads, including those of our closest primate relatives. Because a baby's brain is not large or complex enough to perform the physical and intellectual abilities of an adult, the brain must continue to grow after the baby is born. In fact, all mammals (and all birds, for that matter) require parental care for a period of time while the nervous system develops. The fact that young mammals (particularly young humans) are guaranteed to be exposed to the adults who care for them means that a period of apprenticeship is possible. Consequently, the evolutionary process did not have to produce a brain that consisted solely of specialized circuits of neurons that performed specialized tasks. Instead, it could simply produce a larger brain with an abundance of neural circuits that could be modified by experience. Adults would nourish and protect their offspring and provide them with the skills they would need as adults. Some specialized circuits were necessary, of course (for example, those involved in analyzing the complex sounds we use for speech), but, by and large, the brain is a general-purpose, programmable computer.

How does the human brain compare with the brains of other animals? In absolute size, our brains are dwarfed by those of elephants or whales. However, we might expect such large animals to have large brains to match their large bodies. Indeed, the human brain makes up 2.3 percent of our total body weight, while the elephant brain makes up only 0.2 percent of the animal's total body weight, which makes our brains seem very large in comparison. However, the shrew, which weighs only 7.5 grams (g), has a brain that weighs 0.25 g, or 3.3 percent of its total body weight. The shrew brain is much less complex than the human brain, so something is wrong with this comparison.

The answer is that although bigger bodies require bigger brains, the size of the brain does not have to go up proportionally with that of the body. For example, larger muscles do not require more nerve cells to control them. What counts, as far as intellectual ability goes, is having a brain with plenty of neurons that are not committed to moving muscles or analyzing sensory information—neurons that are available for behavior, learning, remembering, reasoning, and making plans. Besides varying in size, brains also vary in the number of neurons found in each gram of tissue. Herculano-Houzel et al. (2007) compared the weight of the brains of several species of rodents and primates with the number of neurons that each brain contained. They found that primate brains—especially large ones—contain many more neurons per gram than rodent brains do (see Figure 1.8).

What types of genetic changes were responsible for the evolution of the human brain? This question will be addressed in more detail in Chapter 3, but evidence suggests that the most important principle is a slowing of the process of brain development, allowing more time for growth. As we will see, the prenatal period of cell division in the brain is prolonged in humans, which results in a brain that weighs an average of 350 g and contains approximately 100 billion neurons. After birth the brain continues to grow. Production of new neurons almost ceases, but those that are already present grow and establish connections with each other, and other brain cells, which protect and support neurons, begin to proliferate. Not until late adolescence does the human brain reach its adult size of approximately 1,400 g—about four times the weight of a newborn's brain. This prolongation of maturation is known as **neoteny** (roughly translated as "extended youth"). The mature human head and brain retain some infantile characteristics, including their disproportionate size relative to the rest of the body.

Figure 1.8 Comparison of Mammalian Brains

Species with more complex behaviors have brains with more neurons that are available for behavior, learning, remembering, reasoning, and making plans. Primate brains—especially large ones—contain many more neurons per gram than rodent brains and many more neurons in the cortex. Source: Herculano-Houzet, S., Marino, L. Brain Behav Evol 1998;51 230–238.

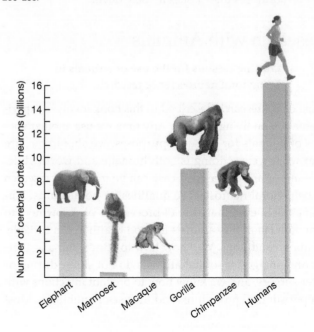

Section Review

Natural Selection and Evolution

LO 1.3 **Describe the role of natural selection in the evolution of behavioral traits.**

Natural selection is the process responsible for evolution of structures with specific functions. Members of a species possess a variety of structures. If the structures permit an individual to reproduce more successfully, its offspring will also have these structures and they will become more prevalent in the population. An example of inherited structures responsible for behavior is the set of brain structures responsible for male song behavior in some species of songbirds.

LO 1.4 **Identify factors involved in the evolution of large brains in humans.**

The evolution of specialized structures responsible for functions such as color vision, fine motor control, complex vision, and language required a larger brain. The size of a human brain at birth is limited by the size of the birth canal. Additional brain development occurs after birth and throughout an extended period of development and parental care in humans. Primate brains contain many more neurons per gram than other species. These additional cells are responsible for behavior, learning, remembering, reasoning, and making plans.

Thought Question

A recent paper by Kavoi & Jameela (2011) reported that a part of the brain responsible for olfaction, the olfactory bulb, is larger in dogs than humans, even after accounting for differences in overall brain size. Using the principles of natural or artificial selection, hypothesize how dogs came to have this larger structure in their brain and predict how it might impact their behavior.

Ethical Issues in Research with Humans and Other Animals

This book contains many facts about what is currently known about the structure and function of the nervous system. Where do these facts come from? They are the result of carefully designed experiments that can include computer simulations, individual cells, and often humans and other animals. Neuroscience research involving humans and animals is subject to important ethical considerations. This section addresses these issues in more detail.

Research with Animals

LO 1.5 **Outline reasons for the use of animals in behavioral neuroscience research.**

Most of the research described in this book involves experimentation on living animals. Any time we use another species of animals for our own purposes, we should be sure that what we are doing is both humane and worthwhile. It is important that a good case can be made that research in behavioral neuroscience qualifies on both counts. Humane treatment is a matter of procedure. We know how to maintain laboratory animals in good health in comfortable, sanitary conditions. We know how to administer anesthetics and analgesics so that animals do not suffer during or after surgery, and we know how to prevent infections with proper surgical procedures and the use of antibiotics. Most industrially developed societies have very strict regulations about the care of animals and require approval of the experimental procedures that are used on them. There is no excuse for mistreating animals in our care. In fact, the vast majority of laboratory animals *are* treated humanely.

Whether an experiment is *worthwhile* can be difficult to say. We use animals for many purposes. We eat their meat and eggs, and we drink their milk; we turn their hides into leather; we extract insulin and other hormones from their organs to treat people's diseases; we train them to do useful work on farms or to entertain us. Even having a pet is a form of exploitation; it is we—not they—who decide that they will live in our homes. The fact is we have been using other animals throughout the history of our species.

Pet owning has the potential to cause much more suffering among animals than scientific research does. Pet owners are not required to receive permission from a board of experts that includes a veterinarian to house their pets, nor are they subject to periodic inspections to be sure that their home is clean and sanitary, that their pets have enough space to exercise properly, or that their pets' diets are appropriate. Scientific researchers are.

In the United States, any institution that receives federal research funding to use animals in research is required to have an *Institutional Animal Care and Use Committee* (IACUC). The IACUC is typically composed of a veterinarian, scientists who work with animals, nonscientist members, and community members not affiliated with the institution. This group reviews all proposals for research involving animals, with the

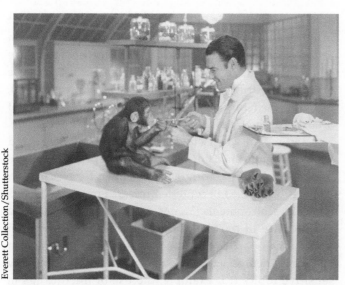

Everett Collection/Shutterstock

Research with laboratory animals has produced important discoveries about the possible causes or potential treatments of neurological and mental disorders.

intent of ensuring humane and ethical treatment of all animals involved. Even noninvasive research with animals (such as field work or observational studies) must pass review and be approved by the IACUC. This approval process ensures not only the welfare of the animals, but also that the research is compliant with local, state, and federal regulations.

The disproportionate amount of concern that animal rights activists show toward the use of animals in research and education is puzzling, particularly because this is the one *indispensable* use of animals. We *can* survive without eating animals, we *can* live without hunting, we *can* do without furs; but without using animals for research and for training future researchers, we *cannot* make progress in understanding and treating diseases. In not too many years scientists will probably have developed a vaccine that will prevent the further spread of diseases such as ebola, malaria, or AIDS. Even diseases that we have already conquered would take new victims if drug companies could no longer use animals to develop and test new treatments. If they were deprived of animals, these companies could no longer extract hormones used to treat human diseases, and they could not prepare many of the vaccines we now use to prevent disease.

Our species is beset by medical, psychological, and behavioral problems, many of which can be solved only through biological research. Let us consider some of the major neurological disorders. Strokes, such as the one experienced by Jeremiah at the beginning of this chapter, are caused by bleeding or obstruction of a blood vessel within the brain, and often leave people partly paralyzed, unable to read, write, or converse with their friends and family. Basic

research on the means by which nerve cells communicate with each other has led to important discoveries about the causes of the death of brain cells. This research was not directed toward a specific practical goal; the potential benefits actually came as a surprise to the investigators.

Experiments based on these results have shown that if a blood vessel leading to the brain is blocked for a few minutes, the part of the brain that is nourished by that vessel will die. However, the brain damage can be prevented by first administering a drug that interferes with a particular kind of neural communication. This research is important, because it may lead to medical treatments that can help to reduce the brain damage caused by strokes. But it involves operating on a laboratory animal, such as a rat, and pinching off a blood vessel. (The animals are anesthetized.) Some of the animals will sustain brain damage, and all will be euthanized so that their brains can be examined. However, you will probably agree that research like this is just as legitimate as using animals for food.

As you will learn later in this book, research with laboratory animals has produced important discoveries about the possible causes or potential treatments of neurological and mental disorders, including Parkinson's disease, schizophrenia, bipolar disorder, anxiety disorders, obsessive-compulsive disorder, anorexia nervosa, obesity, and substance abuse. Although much progress has been made, these problems persist, and they cause much human suffering. Unless we continue our research with laboratory animals, they will not be solved.

Some people have suggested that instead of using laboratory animals in our research, we could use tissue cultures or computers. While these techniques can be used to pursue some research questions, unfortunately, tissue cultures or computers are not substitutes for complex, living organisms. We have no way to study behavioral problems such as substance abuse in tissue cultures, nor can we program a computer to simulate the workings of an animal's nervous system. (If we could, that would mean we already had all the answers.)

Research with Humans

LO 1.6 **Discuss ethical considerations in research with human participants.**

Not all neuroscience research is conducted with animal models. Much of what we currently understand about the brain and behavior is the result of research with human participants. Much like animal research, research with human volunteers is essential to advancing our knowledge of the brain in health and disease. Also similar to animal research, work with human participants is subject to strict regulation and must be reviewed and approved by a board of experts and lay people. The *Institutional Review Board* (IRB)

Figure 1.9 Behavioral Neuroscience Research with Human Participants

Researchers work with volunteers to learn more about the brain mechanisms responsible for functions such as emotion, learning, memory, and behavior.

functions similarly to the IACUC to ensure ethical treatment of volunteers in research (see Figure 1.9).

In addition to humane research conditions, research with human participants must also include informed consent and precautions to protect the identity of the participants. **Informed consent** describes the process in which researchers must inform any potential participant about the nature of the study, how any data will be collected and stored, and what the anticipated benefits and costs of participating will

be. Only after obtaining this information can the participant make an informed decision about whether to participate in a study. Violating the informed consent process can have ethical, legal, and financial consequences. In 2010, the case of *Havasupai Tribe v. Arizona Board of Regents* was settled, including the return of biological samples and a payment of $700,000 to the Havasupai tribe after six years of dispute. The settlement was issued in response to a vague and incomplete informed consent process that resulted in the use of blood samples originally intended for research on diabetes being used in contested research involving factors related to schizophrenia (Van Assche et al., 2013). Protecting the identity of participants is crucial for all research with human participants, and particularly important in behavioral neuroscience research investigating potentially sensitive topics (for example, the use of illicit drugs in studies of brain changes in substance abuse and treatment development).

An emerging interdisciplinary field, **neuroethics,** is devoted to better understanding implications of and developing best practices in ethics for neuroscience research with human participants. A 2014 report from a panel of national experts explored the ethical challenges of neuroscience research by investigating (1) neuroimaging and brain privacy; (2) dementia, personality, and changed preferences; (3) cognitive enhancement and justice; and (4) deep brain stimulation research and the ethically difficult history of psychosurgery (Presidential Commission for the Study of Bioethical Issues, 2014). The panel recommendations included integrating ethics and science through education at all levels.

Section Review

Ethical Issues in Research with Humans and Other Animals

LO 1.5 Outline reasons for the use of animals in behavioral neuroscience research.

Animals are used in behavioral neuroscience research to improve understanding of the nervous system and develop treatments for disease and injury. Animal models are used when it is not possible or it is inappropriate to conduct research with human participants and when cell models or computer programs cannot simulate the complexity of the nervous system.

LO 1.6 Discuss ethical considerations in research with human participants.

Ethical considerations for research involving human participants include protections such as informed consent and

confidentiality. The field of neuroethics is devoted to better understanding implications of and developing best practices in ethics for neuroscience research with human participants.

Thought Question

Behavioral neuroscience research presents unique ethical considerations. For example, the development of drugs to enhance attention and learning, the refinement of imaging techniques to reveal a person's mood or beliefs, or new tests to reveal the likelihood of a person to engage in aggressive behavior all present challenging ethical dilemmas. Select one of the examples above and identify the ethical challenge and suggest whether this research should be conducted and why. If it is conducted, what precautions should be in place to protect the rights of participants?

The Future of Neuroscience: Careers and Strategies for Learning

What is behavioral neuroscience, and what do behavioral neuroscientists do? What are the best ways to learn more about this diverse and exciting field? By the time you finish this book, you will have a much richer answer to these questions. The next section will describe the field—and careers open to those who specialize in it. Likewise we want to provide you with some strategies to help you learn as you read and study this fascinating discipline.

Careers in Neuroscience

LO 1.7   Identify careers in behavioral neuroscience.

Behavioral neuroscience belongs to a larger field that is simply called *neuroscience*. Neuroscientists concern themselves with all aspects of the nervous system: its anatomy, chemistry, physiology, development, and functioning. The research of neuroscientists ranges from the study of molecular genetics to the study of social behavior. **Behavioral neuroscientists** study all behavioral phenomena that can be observed in humans and animals. They attempt to understand the physiology of behavior: the role of the nervous system, interacting with the rest of the body (especially the endocrine system, which secretes hormones), in controlling behavior. They study such topics as sensory processes, sleep, emotional behavior, ingestive behavior, aggressive behavior, sexual behavior, parental behavior, and learning and memory. They also study animal models of disorders that afflict humans, such as anxiety, depression, obsessions and compulsions, phobias, and schizophrenia. Although the original name for the field described in this book was *physiological psychology*, several other terms are now in general use, such as *biological psychology*, *biopsychology*, *psychobiology*, and—the most common one—*behavioral neuroscience*.

Two other fields often overlap with that of behavioral neuroscience: *neurology* and *cognitive neuroscience*. Neurologists are physicians who diagnose and treat diseases of the nervous system. Most neurologists are solely involved in the practice of medicine, but some engage in research. They study the behavior of people whose brains have been damaged by natural causes, using advanced brain-imaging techniques to study the activity of various regions of the brain as a person participates in various behaviors. This research is also carried out by cognitive neuroscientists—researchers with a Ph.D. (usually in psychology) and specialized training in the principles and procedures of neurology.

Most professional behavioral neuroscientists have received a Ph.D. from a graduate program in psychology or from an interdisciplinary program. Programs can include faculty members from departments such as psychology, biology, chemistry, biochemistry, or computer science. Most professional behavioral neuroscientists are employed by colleges and universities, where they are engaged in teaching and research. Others are employed by institutions devoted to research—for example, in laboratories owned and operated by national governments or by private philanthropic organizations. A few work in industry, usually for pharmaceutical companies that are interested in assessing the effects of drugs on behavior.

To become a professor or independent researcher, one must receive a doctorate—usually a Ph.D., although some people turn to research after receiving an M.D. Most behavioral neuroscientists spend two years or more in a postdoctoral position after completing their graduate degree, working in the laboratory of a senior scientist to gain more research experience. During this time they write articles describing their research findings and submit them for publication in scientific journals. These publications are an important factor in obtaining an independent position.

Not all people who are engaged in neuroscience research have doctoral degrees. Research technicians with bachelor's or master's level degrees perform essential—and intellectually rewarding—services working with senior scientists. Technicians can continue to gain experience and education on the job, enabling them to assume responsibility for managing and completing projects independently. (See Figure 1.10.)

Strategies for Learning

LO 1.8   Describe effective learning strategies for studying behavioral neuroscience.

The brain is a complicated organ. After all, it is responsible for all our abilities and all our complexities. Scientists have been studying this organ for many years and (especially in recent years) have been learning a lot about how it works. It is impossible to summarize this progress in a few simple sentences; therefore, this book contains a lot of information. We have tried to organize this information logically, telling you what you need to know in the order in which you need to know it. (To understand some things, you sometimes need to understand other things first.) We have also tried to write as clearly as possible, making examples as simple and as vivid as we can. Still, you cannot expect to master the information in this book by simply giving it a passive read; you will have to do some work.

Learning about behavioral neuroscience involves much more than memorizing facts. Of course, there *are* facts to be memorized: names of parts of the nervous system, names of chemicals and drugs, scientific terms for particular phenomena and procedures used to investigate them, and so

Figure 1.10 Pursuing a Research Career in Neuroscience

What kinds of training are required for a career in neuroscience? Where do neuroscientists work? Explore this timeline to learn more.

Time Period	Description	
High school	Students interested in neuroscience may take courses in biology, chemistry, psychology, or other sciences in high school. 	
College	Students interested in neuroscience may study biology, chemistry, psychology, neuroscience, or other related areas. Some students work as research assistants in laboratories and develop mentored relationships with researchers. College graduates interested in neuroscience can work as research technicians or assistants. 	
Graduate Training	Students can pursue advanced graduate training for one or more years after college. Graduate training typically involves advanced course work and more independent research. Graduate students are expected to conduct research (with the guidance of a research mentor) and disseminate the results of their work. After completing a graduate program, individuals may teach in a secondary or postsecondary institution, conduct research, or work in industry. 	
Postgraduate Training	Postgraduate positions are more independent and often involve additional training in specialized research areas or with specialized research techniques. After completing postgraduate training, individuals may teach in a secondary or postsecondary institution, conduct research, or work in industry. 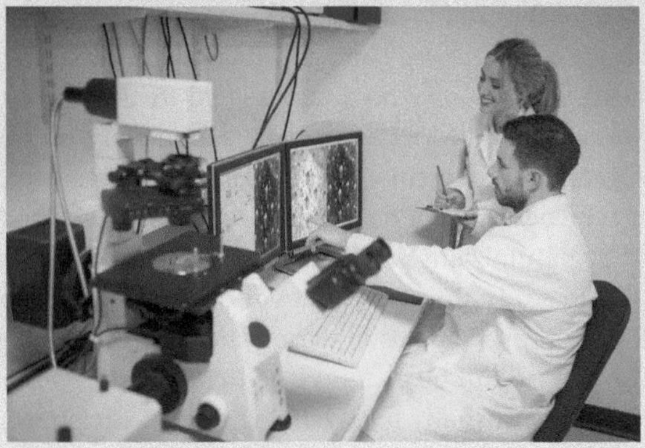	

on. But the quest for information is nowhere near completed; we know only a small fraction of what we have to learn. And almost certainly, many of the "facts" that we now accept will someday be shown to be incorrect. If all you do is learn facts, where will you be when these facts are revised?

Our goal is to offer some practical advice about studying. You have been studying throughout your academic career, and you have undoubtedly learned some useful strategies along the way. Even if you have developed efficient and effective study skills, at least consider the possibility that there might be some ways to improve them. This section is intended to provide you with suggestions to maximize your learning about behavioral neuroscience. These suggestions are supported by empirical research on learning.

- Take notes that organize information into meaningful groups. Linking new information to prior knowledge is an important means for learning. To do this will require actively thinking about the new information at hand and finding ways to link it to your current understanding. This is an active and involved process that will take some time and effort. Highlighting or underlining without combining the information into your own notes is passive and does not facilitate learning and retention the way that writing or typing your own notes does. Previous research has demonstrated the highlighting and underlining alone do not improve test scores, and in some cases may be detrimental to learning (Dunlosky et al., 2013).

- Teach yourself by teaching someone else. After reading a section or chapter, consider how you would teach the information to someone else—a classmate, a friend, or maybe a curious family member. This activity will help you to think about the most important aspects of the section. Nestojko et al. (2014) found that students who prepared to teach others about the content of a complex reading assignment performed better on a later test than students who had prepared themselves for a test on the reading.

- Study in the environment you will be tested in. State dependent learning theory says that information learned in one environment is most readily recalled in the same environment. The rationale behind this performance boosting effect of environment is that the context (e.g., the color of the walls, the seat, the people around you) provides important cues that help you recall what was previously learned in that environment. If you're *not* able to study in the same environment as you will be tested, you can try to incorporate as many of the same elements as possible (e.g., use the same computer, pens, procedure for note taking, etc.) *or* you can study in many different environments (e.g., at home, in the student union, in your residence hall) so that you will not become dependent on any one single cue or set of cues when you are tested. In an interesting test of state dependent learning, Godden & Baddeley (1975) tested college student scuba divers on information they read while underwater or on land. Students recalled information learned underwater best in an underwater test. The students performed most poorly on the tests of information in a different context (for example, information learned underwater but tested on land).

- Study with the absolute minimum of distractions. Your brain works best when it focuses on one challenging task (like learning about neuroscience!) at a time (Hattie & Yates, 2014). Turn off televisions, social media, and phones whenever possible, and try to study in a quiet environment. Lee et al. (2012) assigned college students learning about science, history, and politics to three groups: reading in silence, reading with a TV show playing in the background that students could ignore, and reading with a TV show playing in the background that students would later be tested on so that they would be sure to pay attention to both the TV show and their assigned study material. Students were instructed to read and answer multiple choice questions. As you might expect, students who tried to read and pay attention to the TV show performed the worst on the test.

- Spread out your study sessions. Studying new information in two shorter but separated sessions leads to more effective recall than studying in one long session. Don't cram. Instead, plan to study something new once, then study it again a different day before being asked to recall or apply it on a final test or assignment. Though you should plan your own study sessions around your schedule and based on assignment or test due dates in your class, some cognitive spacing has already been built into this book for you. While there is no "one size fits all" time period for spacing out reading and study sessions, one to several days is a good rule of thumb (Carpenter et al., 2012).

- Study the most challenging topic first or last. Classic studies in psychology revealed that when people were asked to learn long lists of words, the first words learned (the *primacy effect*) and the last words learned (the *recency effect*) were the most likely to be recalled. The same principles can hold true for learning about behavioral neuroscience. For example, if you are reading about the cortex, the thalamus, and the meninges in Chapter 3, and you already know most of the parts of the meninges, but are not feeling confident about your understanding of the cortex and thalamus, plan to study the cortex first, then the meninges and finally the thalamus information.

- Use mnemonics. Mnemonics are short-cuts for help-ing retain new information. For example, you could try *story chaining* by inventing a short story to link together discrepant items; *method of loci* to use images of physical locations enabling you to position items along an imagi-nary walk; and *acrostics* to use a word to represent a list (such as FPOT for the lobes of the cortex: **f**rontal, **p**ari-etal, **o**ccipital, **t**emporal) (Hattie and Yates, 2014).

How this book is organized.

- The text, animations, interactives, and illustrations are integrated as closely as possible. In our experience, one of the most frustrating aspects of reading some books is not knowing when to look at an illustration. Here ev-erything is presented to you as you need it.
- Each chapter begins with a case study that profiles a person's real-life experience, a list of learning objectives, and a figure of the brain. The case studies are meant to personalize and make more relatable the concepts we will discuss in the chapter. The learning objectives are there to help you focus on the key ideas included in the chapter,

and the figure of the brain will help orient you in the regions of the brain relevant in that particular chapter.

- You will notice that some words in the text are *italicized*, and others are printed in **boldface**. *Italics* mean that either the word is being stressed for emphasis or it is a new term. Terms in **bold** are key terms that are part of the vocabulary of the behavioral neuroscientist and you will see many of these terms used again in later chapters.
- At the end of each section, you will find two different types of review activities: section reviews and thought ques-tions. The section reviews will remind you of key points from the chapter and the thought questions will challenge you to apply what you have learned to a new context or to expand your thinking on a relevant topic. Finally, there are Chapter Review Questions at the end of each chapter to help you assess your understanding of the concepts.

Now that you have a sense of what the field of behav-ioral neuroscience entails, welcome to the rest of this book! The next chapter starts with the structure and functions of neurons, the most important elements of the nervous system.

Section Review

The Future of Neuroscience: Careers and Strategies for Learning

LO 1.7 Identify careers in behavioral neuroscience.
Researchers work in the fields of general neuroscience, behavioral neuroscience, and cognitive neuroscience. Neurologists are physicians who specialize in the nervous system. Individuals pursuing careers in neuroscience work in academia and industry and often pursue graduate education.

LO 1.8 Describe effective learning strategies for studying behavioral neuroscience.
Active strategies for learning are most effective. Taking notes, practicing teaching or sharing information with another person, making sure your study and test-taking environment share some common features, studying with

as few distractions as possible, spacing out your study sessions, carefully planning when to study challenging material, and using mnemonics whenever possible can en-hance your learning.

Thought Question

What is it like to work as a neuroscientist today? What kinds of training do careers in neuroscience require? What kinds of activities do neuroscientists engage in on the job? Conduct an online search and locate a job advertisement for a position in neuroscience. Read the job description and qualifications carefully. What qualifications are re-quired for the job? Why do you think these experiences or this training is required? What kinds of responsibilities and activities will the person in this position engage in?

Chapter Review Questions

1. Explain the goals of behavioral neuroscience research.
2. Describe the biological roots of behavioral neuroscience.
3. Describe the role of natural selection in the evolution of behavioral traits.
4. Explain the evolution of the human species and a large brain.

5. What measures may be adopted for preventing ethical misconduct in neuroscience research involving human participants?
6. Describe the scope and various disciplines and fields un-der the umbrella of behavioral neuroscience research.
7. Describe the various types of learning strategies and styles and their importance in maximizing your learn-ing about behavioral neuroscience.

Chapter 2
Structure and Functions of Cells of the Nervous System

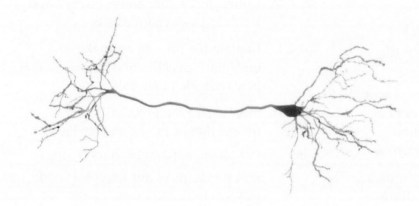

Chapter Outline

Learning Objectives

LO 2.1 Contrast the location of the central and peripheral nervous systems.

LO 2.2 Describe the structures of a neuron, including their general function.

LO 2.3 Differentiate functions of supporting cells of the central and peripheral nervous systems.

LO 2.4 Discuss the features and importance of the blood–brain barrier.

LO 2.5 Compare neural communication in a withdrawal reflex with and without inhibition of the reflex.

LO 2.6 Contrast the changes in electrical potential within a neuron when it is experiencing resting potential, hyperpolarization, depolarization, and an action potential.

LO 2.7 Summarize the contributions of diffusion, electrostatic pressure, and the sodium–potassium pump to establishing membrane potential.

LO 2.8 Summarize the series of ion movements during the action potential.

LO 2.9 Describe the propagation of an action potential.

LO 2.10 Describe the structures and functions of presynaptic cells that are involved in synaptic communication.

LO 2.11 Describe the process of neurotransmitter release.

LO 2.12 Contrast ionotropic and metabotropic receptors.

LO 2.13 Compare the functions of EPSPs and IPSPs in postsynaptic cells.

LO 2.14 Explain the roles of reuptake and enzymatic deactivation in terminating postsynaptic potentials.

LO 2.15 Summarize the process of neural integration of EPSPs and IPSPs.

LO 2.16 Differentiate between the locations and functions of autoreceptors and postsynaptic receptors.

LO 2.17 Identify synapses other than those involved in neural integration.

LO 2.18 Describe examples of nonsynaptic communication.

Kathryn was getting desperate. She had always been healthy and active, eating wisely and keeping fit with sports and regular exercise. She went to the gym almost every day for cardio classes and swimming. But several months prior she began having trouble keeping up with her usual schedule. At first, she found herself getting tired toward the end of her exercise classes. Her arms, particularly, seemed to get heavy. Then when she entered the pool and started swimming, she found that it was hard to lift her arms over her head. She did not have any other symptoms, so she told herself that she needed more sleep.

Over the next few weeks, however, things only got worse. Her exercise classes were more and more difficult to complete. Her instructor became concerned and suggested that Kathryn see her doctor. She made an appointment, but her doctor could find nothing wrong with her. She was not sick, showed no signs of an infection, and seemed to be generally healthy. Her doctor asked how things were going at work. Kathryn explained that she had been

experiencing a particularly stressful month at her job. Kathryn and her physician agreed that increased stress could be the cause of her problem. The doctor did not prescribe any medication, but asked Kathryn to make another appointment if she did not feel better soon.

She did feel better for a while, but then all of a sudden her symptoms got worse. She quit going to the gym and found that she even had difficulty finishing a day's work. One afternoon she tried to look up at the clock on the wall and realized that she could hardly see— her eyelids were drooping, and her head felt as if it weighed a hundred pounds. Just then, one of her supervisors came over to her and asked her to fill him in on the progress she had been making on a new project. As she talked, she found herself getting weaker and weaker. It even felt as if breathing seemed to take a lot of effort. She managed to finish the interview, but immediately afterward she went home.

She called her physician, who arranged for her to go to the hospital to be seen by a neurologist. The neurologist listened to a description of Kathryn's symptoms and examined her briefly. The neurologist thought she might know what was wrong. She prepared an injection and gave it to Kathryn. She started questioning Kathryn about her job. Kathryn answered slowly, her voice almost a whisper. As the questions continued, she realized that it was getting easier and easier to talk. She straightened her back and took a deep breath. She stood up and raised her arms above her head. "Look," she said, her excitement growing. "I can do this again. I've got my strength back! What did you give me? Am I cured?"

*****

All we are capable of doing—perceive, think, learn, remember, act—is made possible by the integrated activity of the cells of the nervous system. To understand how the nervous system controls behavior, we must first understand its parts—the cells that compose it. In Kathryn's case, the cells of her nervous system were not functioning appropriately, leading to her symptoms of fatigue. Kathryn was diagnosed with *myasthenia gravis*. The term literally means "grave muscle weakness." It is an uncommon disorder, but most experts believe that many mild cases go undiagnosed. Although there are drug treatments, unfortunately no cure has yet been found for it.

Myasthenia gravis is an autoimmune disease. For unknown reasons the immune system breaks down proteins in the nervous system that allow cells to receive messages. Understanding the structure and function of the cells of the nervous system allowed the neurologist to diagnose and treat Kathryn. Kathryn's case highlights many of the key aspects you will learn about in this chapter, including communication within and between cells of the nervous system. To learn more about the specific cells involved in myasthenia gravis, look ahead to the section on acetylcholine in *Termination of Postsynaptic Potentials.*

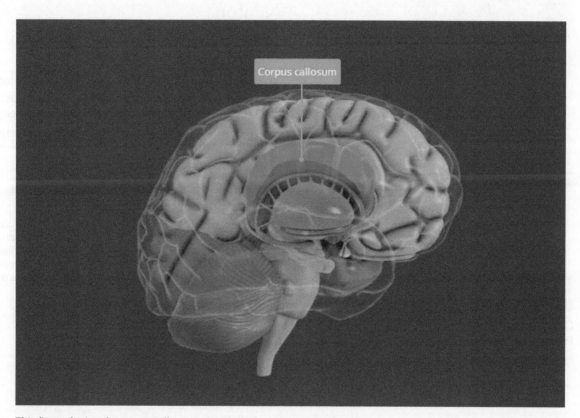

This figure depicts the corpus callosum, a band of white matter composed of many axons crossing between the right and left hemisphere of the brain. In this chapter you'll learn about the importance of axons in neural communication.

Cells of the Nervous System

There are billions of nerve cells, or *neurons*, in the human nervous system. Because this chapter deals with cells, you need not be familiar with the structure of the entire nervous system, which is presented in Chapter 3. However, you do need to know that the nervous system consists of two basic divisions: the central nervous system and the peripheral nervous system.

The Nervous System: An Overview

LO 2.1 **Contrast the location of the central and peripheral nervous systems.**

The **central nervous system (CNS)** consists of the parts that are encased by the bones of the skull and spinal column: the brain and the spinal cord. The **peripheral nervous system (PNS)** is found outside these bones and consists of the nerves and most of the sensory organs. (See Figure 2.1.)

Figure 2.1 The Central and Peripheral Nervous Systems

The central nervous system includes the brain and spinal cord. The peripheral nervous system includes all of the nerves that relay information between the central nervous system and the rest of the body.

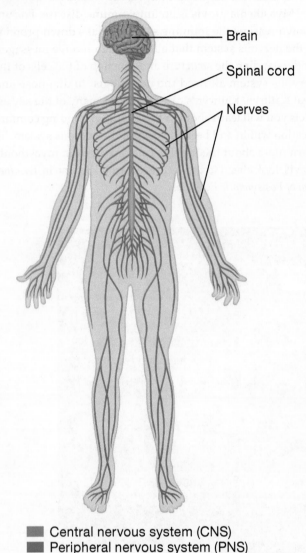

- ■ Central nervous system (CNS)
- ■ Peripheral nervous system (PNS)

of muscles, which are controlled by **motor neurons** in the PNS. And in between sensory neurons and motor neurons are the **interneurons**—neurons that lie entirely within the CNS. *Local interneurons* form circuits with nearby neurons and analyze small pieces of information. *Relay interneurons* connect circuits of local interneurons in one region of the brain with those in other regions. Through these connections, circuits of neurons throughout the brain perform functions essential to tasks such as perceiving, learning, remembering, deciding, and controlling complex behaviors. (See Figure 2.2.)

This section is devoted to a description of the most important cells of the nervous system—neurons and their supporting cells—and to the blood–brain barrier, which provides neurons in the CNS with chemical isolation from the rest of the body.

Neurons

LO 2.2 **Describe the structures of a neuron, including their general function.**

The neuron is the information-processing and information-transmitting element of the nervous system. Neurons come in many shapes and varieties, according to the specialized jobs they perform. Most neurons have, in one form or another, the

Figure 2.2 Sensory, Motor, and Interneurons

These three types of neurons relay information between the central and peripheral nervous systems. In this example, the person sees the glass of water and sensory nerves relay the sensory information toward the central nervous system. The motor output from the central nervous system allows the person to lift the glass to take a drink.

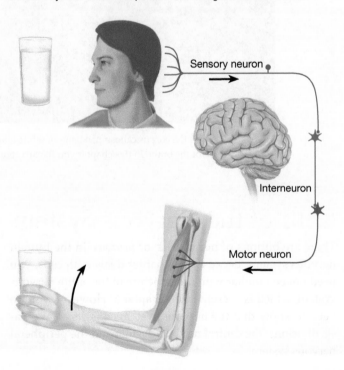

The CNS communicates with the rest of the body through **nerves** attached to the brain and to the spinal cord. Nerves are bundles of thousands of individual neurons, all wrapped in a tough, protective membrane. Under a microscope, nerves look something like telephone cables, with their bundles of wires. Like the individual wires in a telephone cable, nerve fibers transmit messages through the nerve, from a sense organ to the brain or from the brain to a muscle or gland.

Information, in the form of light, sound waves, odors, tastes, or contact with objects, is gathered from the environment by specialized cells of the PNS called **sensory neurons.** Movements are accomplished by the contraction following four structures or regions: (1) cell body, or soma; (2) dendrites; (3) axon; and (4) terminal buttons.

SOMA The **soma** (cell body) contains the nucleus and much of the machinery that provides for the life processes of the cell. (See Figure 2.3.) Its shape varies considerably in different kinds of neurons.

DENDRITES *Dendron* is the Greek word for tree, and the branched **dendrites** of the neuron look very much like trees (look again at Figure 2.3). Neurons communicate with one another and dendrites serve as important receivers of these messages. Dendrites function much like antennas to receive messages from other neurons. Just like an antenna can receive a message over a distance (think of an antenna that detects radio or Wi-Fi signals) dendrites receive neural messages that are transmitted across the **synapse,** a small space between the terminal buttons (described later) of the sending cell and a portion of the somatic or dendritic membrane of the receiving cell. Communication at a synapse proceeds in one direction: from the terminal button to the membrane of the other cell. (Like many general rules, this one has some exceptions. As we will see in Chapter 4, some synapses pass information in both directions.)

AXON The **axon** is a long, slender tube, often covered by a *myelin sheath.* (The myelin sheath is described later.) The outer surface of the axon carries information from the cell body to the terminal buttons and functions much like an electrical cord carrying an electrical message from an outlet to an appliance (look again at Figure 2.3). However, the basic message the axon carries is called an *action potential*. This function of an action potential is an important one and will be described in more detail later in the chapter. For now, know that an action potential is a brief electrical event that starts at the end of the axon next to the cell body and travels toward the terminal buttons. The action potential is like a brief pulse; in any given axon the action potential is always of the same size and duration. When it reaches a point where the axon branches, it splits but does not diminish in size. Each branch receives a *full-strength* action potential. Like dendrites, axons and their branches come in different shapes.

TERMINAL BUTTONS Most axons divide and branch many times. At the ends of the branches are little knobs called **terminal buttons.** Terminal buttons have a very special function: When an action potential traveling down the axon reaches them, they secrete a chemical called a **neurotransmitter.** This chemical (there are many different ones in the CNS) either excites or inhibits the receiving cell and thus helps to determine whether an action potential occurs in its axon. In this way, terminal buttons function like spray bottles by releasing chemicals into the synapse. Details of this process will be described later in this chapter.

An individual neuron receives information from the terminal buttons of axons of other neurons—and the terminal buttons of its axons form synapses with other neurons. A neuron may receive information from dozens or even hundreds of other neurons, each of which can form a large number of synaptic connections with it. Figure 2.4 illustrates the nature of these connections. As you can see, terminal buttons can form synapses on the membrane of the dendrites or the soma.

Axons can be extremely long relative to their diameter and the size of the soma. For example, the longest axon in a human stretches from the foot to a region located in the base of the brain. Because terminal buttons need some items that can be produced only in the soma; there must be a system that can transport these items rapidly and efficiently *within* the axon (like a subway system). This process is separate from the movement of the action potential along the surface of the axon. Instead, **axoplasmic transport** is an active process that propels substances along microtubule "tracks" that run inside the length of the axon. Movement from the soma to the terminal buttons is called **anterograde** axoplasmic transport. (*Antero-* means "toward the front.") This form of transport is accomplished by molecules of a protein called *kinesin*. In the cell body, kinesin molecules, which resemble a pair of legs and feet, attach to the item being transported down the axon. The kinesin molecule then walks down a microtubule, carrying the cargo to its destination (Yildiz et al., 2004). Energy is supplied by ATP molecules produced by the mitochondria. (See Figure 2.5.) Another protein, *dynein*, carries substances from the terminal buttons to the soma, a process known as **retrograde** axoplasmic transport. Anterograde axoplasmic transport is remarkably fast: up to 500 millimeters (mm) per day. Retrograde axoplasmic transport is about half as fast as anterograde transport.

Figure 2.3 Parts of a Neuron

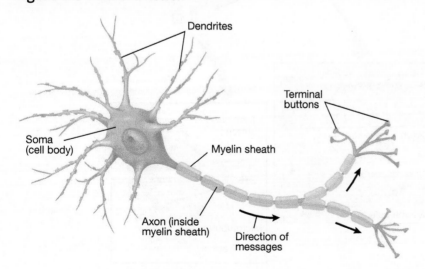

Dendrites

Terminal buttons

Soma (cell body)

Myelin sheath

Axon (inside myelin sheath)

Direction of messages

Figure 2.4 Overview of Structure and Synaptic Connections Between Neurons

The arrows represent the directions of the flow of information.

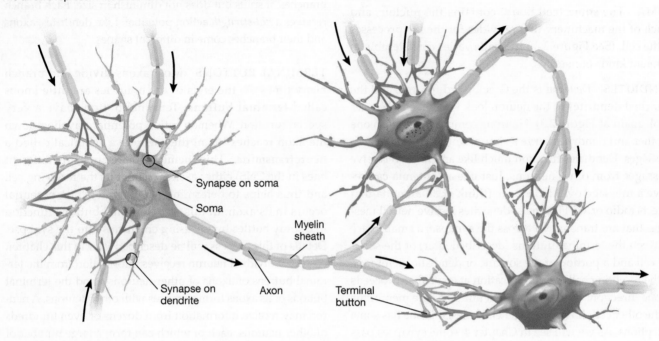

Synapse on soma

Soma

Synapse on dendrite

Axon

Myelin sheath

Terminal button

Figure 2.5 Axoplasmic Transport

This figure shows how kinesin molecules transport cargo along the cytoskeleton from the soma to the terminal button. Another protein, dynein, carries cargo from the terminal buttons to the soma.

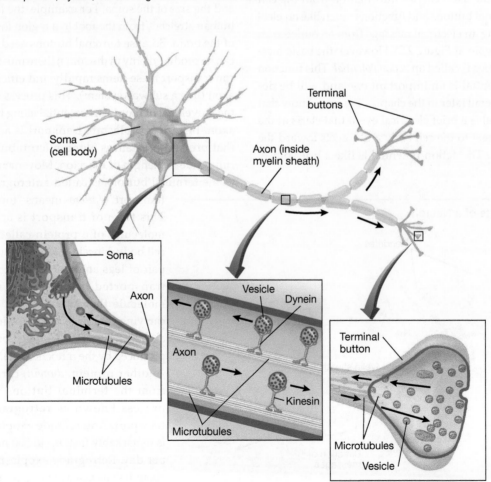

Soma (cell body)

Axon (inside myelin sheath)

Terminal buttons

Soma

Axon

Microtubules

Vesicle

Dynein

Axon

Kinesin

Microtubules

Terminal button

Microtubules

Vesicle

Figure 2.6 Internal Structures of a Neuron

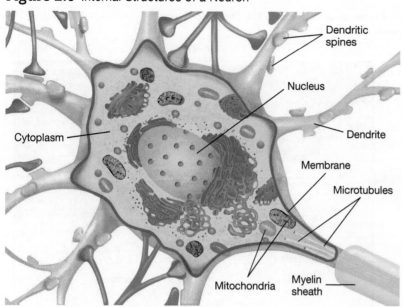

Dendritic spines

Nucleus

Cytoplasm

Dendrite

Membrane

Microtubules

Mitochondria

Myelin sheath

OTHER CELL STRUCTURES Figure 2.6 illustrates the internal structure of a typical neuron.

Much like your skin, the cell **membrane** defines the boundary of the neuron. It consists of a double layer of lipid (fatlike) molecules. Embedded in the membrane are a variety of protein molecules that have special functions. Some proteins detect substances outside the cell (such as hormones) and pass information about the presence of these substances to the interior of the cell. Other proteins control access to the interior of the cell, permitting some substances to enter but barring others. Still other proteins act as transporters, actively carrying certain molecules into or out of the cell. Because the proteins that are found in the membrane of the neuron are especially important in the transmission of information, their characteristics will be discussed in more detail later in this chapter.

The interior of the neuron contains a matrix of strands of protein. Much like the bones of your skeletal system, this matrix, called the **cytoskeleton,** gives the neuron its shape. The cytoskeleton is made of three kinds of protein strands, linked to each other and forming a cohesive mass. The thickest of these strands, **microtubules,** are bundles of thirteen protein filaments arranged around a hollow core.

Cytoplasm is complex and varies considerably across types of cells, but it can most easily be characterized as a jellylike, semiliquid substance that fills the space outlined by the membrane. It contains small, specialized structures, just as the human body contains specialized organs. The generic term for these structures is *organelle,* "little organ." The most important organelles are described next.

The **nucleus** of the cell is a round or oval structure found in the soma. The nucleus is enclosed by the nuclear membrane. The nucleolus and the chromosomes reside inside the nucleus. The **nucleolus** is responsible for the production of **ribosomes,** small structures that are involved in protein synthesis. The **chromosomes,** which consist of long strands of **deoxyribonucleic acid (DNA),** contain the organism's genetic information. When they are active, portions of the chromosomes **(genes)** cause production of another complex molecule, **messenger ribonucleic acid (mRNA),** which receives a copy of the information stored at that location. The mRNA leaves the nuclear membrane and attaches to ribosomes. (See Figure 2.7.)

Proteins are produced through a two-step process. In the first step of the process, *transcription,* information from DNA (which cannot leave the nucleus) is transcribed into a portable form: mRNA. mRNA takes this information to the ribosomes for the second step of the process: *translation.* During translation, the ribosomes use the information from the mRNA and create proteins.

To help you remember the complicated process of protein production, compare it to making a cake from a top-secret recipe. Imagine that the recipe for the cake is found in a rare cookbook in a library and you cannot remove the cookbook from the library. You can go into the library and take a picture of the recipe with the camera on your cell phone. Now you have the information in a new, more portable form. Next, you take the picture of the recipe home with you to your kitchen. There, you use the recipe information to assemble raw ingredients like flour, eggs, and milk into the cake. In this example, the cookbook locked in the library is like the DNA stored in the nucleus. The process of photographing the cookbook and removing the recipe information from the library represents transcription of information from DNA locked in the nucleus to a new, more portable form of information, mRNA. Taking the photo home and using the information it contains to assemble raw materials into a final product represents translation as the mRNA leave the nucleus and take information to the ribosomes, which the ribosomes then use to create proteins.

Proteins are important in cell functions. In addition to providing structure, proteins serve as **enzymes,** which direct the chemical processes of a cell by controlling chemical reactions. Enzymes are special protein molecules that act as catalysts; that is, they cause a chemical reaction to take place without becoming a part of the final product themselves. Because cells contain the ingredients needed to synthesize an enormous variety of compounds, the ones that cells actually do produce depend primarily on the particular enzymes that are present. Furthermore, there are enzymes that break molecules apart as well as enzymes that put them

Figure 2.7 Protein Synthesis

When a gene is active, a copy of the information is made onto a molecule of messenger RNA. The mRNA leaves the nucleus and attaches to a ribosome, where the protein is produced.

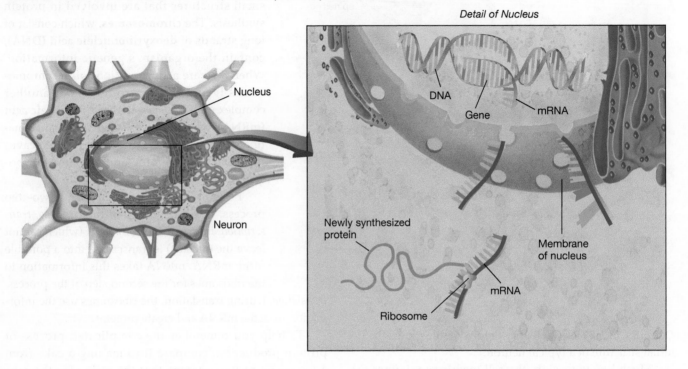

together; the enzymes that are present in a particular region of a cell thus determine which molecules remain intact.

Cells also contain an endomembrane system (a network of internal membranes) comprised of endoplasmic reticulum, Golgi apparatus, and lysosomes. The **endoplasmic reticulum** appears in two forms: rough and smooth. Both types consist of parallel layers of the same membrane that encloses the cell. Rough endoplasmic reticulum contains ribosomes. The protein produced by the ribosomes that are attached to the rough endoplasmic reticulum is destined to be transported out of the cell or used in the membrane. Unattached ribosomes are also distributed around the cytoplasm; the unattached variety appears to produce protein for use within the neuron. Smooth endoplasmic reticulum provides channels for the segregation of molecules involved in various cellular processes. Lipid (fatlike) molecules are also produced here. The **Golgi apparatus** is a special form of smooth endoplasmic reticulum. Some complex molecules, made up of simpler individual molecules, are assembled here. The Golgi apparatus also serves as a wrapping or packaging agent. For example, secretory cells (such as those that release hormones) wrap their product in a membrane produced by the Golgi apparatus. When the cell secretes its product, it uses a process called **exocytosis.** In exocytosis, the membrane-wrapped product migrates to the inside of the outer membrane of the cell, fuses with the membrane, and bursts, spilling its

contents into the fluid surrounding the cell. As we will see, neurons communicate with one another by secreting chemicals by this means. We will describe the process of exocytosis in more detail later in this chapter. The Golgi apparatus also produces **lysosomes,** small sacs that contain enzymes that break down substances no longer needed by the cell. These products are then recycled or excreted from the cell.

Mitochondria (singular: mitochondrion) are shaped like oval beads and are formed from a double membrane. The inner membrane is wrinkled, and the wrinkles make up a set of shelves (*cristae*) that fill the inside of the bead. Mitochondria perform a vital role in the economy of the cell; many of the biochemical steps that are involved in the extraction of energy from the breakdown of nutrients take place on the cristae, controlled by enzymes located there. Most cell biologists believe that many eons ago, mitochondria were free-living organisms that came to "infect" larger cells. Because the mitochondria could extract energy more efficiently than the cells they infected, the mitochondria became useful to the cells and eventually became a permanent part of them. Cells provide mitochondria with nutrients, and mitochondria provide cells with a special molecule—**adenosine triphosphate (ATP)**—that cells use as their immediate source of energy. Because of their role in generating usable energy, mitochondria can be considered the "power plants" of neurons.

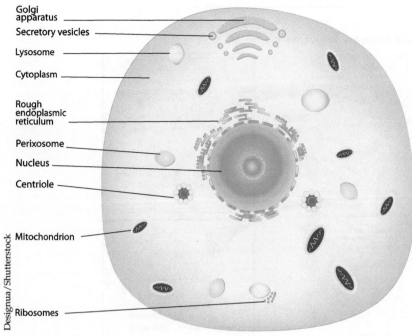

Golgi apparatus

Secretory vesicles

Lysosome

Cytoplasm

Rough endoplasmic reticulum

Perixosome

Nucleus

Centriole

Mitochondrion

Ribosomes

Designua/Shutterstock

Structure of a typical animal cell.

Supporting Cells

LO 2.3 **Differentiate functions of supporting cells of the central and peripheral nervous systems.**

Neurons constitute only about half the volume of the CNS. The rest consists of a variety of supporting cells. Because neurons have a very high rate of metabolism but have no means of storing nutrients, they must constantly be supplied with nutrients and oxygen or they will quickly die. Thus, the role played by the cells that support and protect neurons is very important to our existence.

SUPPORTING CELLS OF THE CENTRAL NERVOUS SYSTEM The most important supporting cells of the central nervous system are the *neuroglia*, or "nerve glue." **Glia** (also called *glial cells*) do indeed glue the CNS together, but they do much more than that. Neurons lead a very sheltered existence; they are buffered physically and chemically from the rest of the body by the glial cells. Glial cells surround neurons and hold them in place, controlling their supply of nutrients and some of the chemicals they need to exchange messages with other neurons; they insulate neurons from one another so that neural messages do not get scrambled; and they even act as housekeepers, destroying and removing the carcasses of neurons that are killed by disease or injury.

There are several types of glial cells, each of which plays a special role in the CNS. The three most important types are *astrocytes, oligodendrocytes,* and *microglia.*

Astrocytes **Astrocyte** means "star cell," and this name accurately describes the shape of these cells. Astrocytes provide physical support to neurons and clean up debris within the brain. They produce some chemicals that neurons need to fulfill their functions. They help to control the chemical

composition of the fluid surrounding neurons by actively taking up or releasing substances whose concentrations must be kept within critical levels. Finally, astrocytes are involved in providing nourishment to neurons.

Some of the astrocyte's processes (the arms of the star) are wrapped around blood vessels; other processes are wrapped around parts of neurons, so the somatic and dendritic membranes of neurons are largely surrounded by astrocytes. This arrangement suggested to the Italian histologist Camillo Golgi (1844–1926) that astrocytes supplied neurons with nutrients from the capillaries and disposed of their waste products (Golgi, 1903). He thought that nutrients passed from capillaries to the cytoplasm of the astrocytes and then through the cytoplasm to the neurons.

Recent evidence suggests that Golgi was right: Although neurons receive some glucose directly from capillaries, they receive most of their nutrients from astrocytes. Astrocytes receive glucose from capillaries and break it down to *lactate,* the chemical produced during the first step of glucose metabolism. They then release lactate into the extracellular fluid that surrounds neurons, and neurons take up the lactate, transport it to their mitochondria, and use it for energy (Tsacopoulos & Magistretti, 1996; Brown et al., 2004; Pellerin et al., 2007). Apparently, this process provides neurons with a fuel that they can metabolize even more rapidly than glucose. In addition, astrocytes store a small amount of a carbohydrate called *glycogen* that can be broken down to glucose and then to lactate when the metabolic rate of neurons in their vicinity is especially high. (See Figure 2.8.)

Besides transporting chemicals to neurons, astrocytes serve as the matrix that holds neurons in place—the "nerve glue," so to speak. These cells also surround and isolate synapses, limiting the dispersion of neurotransmitters that are released by the terminal buttons.

When cells in the central nervous system die, certain kinds of astrocytes take up the task of cleaning away the debris. These cells are able to travel around the CNS; they extend and retract their processes (*pseudopodia,* or "false feet") and glide about the way amoebas do. When these astrocytes contact a piece of debris from a dead neuron, they push themselves against it, finally engulfing and digesting it. We call this process **phagocytosis.** If there is a considerable amount of injured tissue to be cleaned up, astrocytes will divide and produce enough new cells to do the task. Once the dead tissue has been broken down, a framework of astrocytes will be left to fill in the vacant area, and a specialized kind of astrocyte will form scar tissue, walling off the area.

Oligodendrocytes The principal function of **oligodendrocytes** is to provide support to axons and to produce the

Figure 2.8 Structure and Location of Astrocytes

The processes of astrocytes surround capillaries and neurons of the central nervous system.

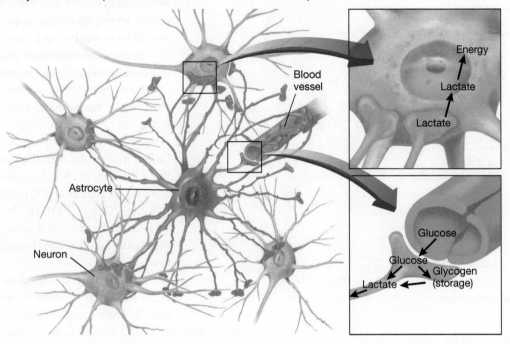

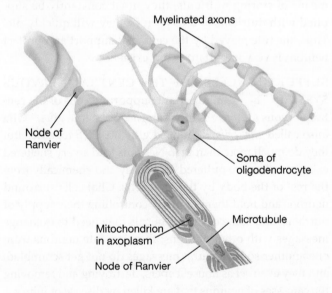

myelin sheath, which insulates most axons from one another. (Very small axons are not myelinated and lack this sheath.) Myelin, 80 percent lipid and 20 percent protein, is produced by the oligodendrocytes in the form of a tube surrounding the axon. This tube does not form a continuous sheath; rather, it consists of a series of segments, each approximately 1 mm long, with a small (1–2 μm) portion of uncoated axon between the segments. (A *micrometer,* abbreviated μm, is one-millionth of a meter, or one-thousandth of a millimeter.) The bare portion of axon is called a **node of Ranvier,** after the person who discovered it. The myelinated axon, then, resembles a string of elongated beads. (Actually, the beads are *very much* elongated—their length is approximately 80 times their width.)

A given oligodendrocyte produces up to 50 segments of myelin. During the development of the CNS, oligodendrocytes form processes shaped something like canoe paddles. Each of these paddle-shaped processes then wraps itself many times around a segment of an axon and, while doing so, produces layers of myelin. Each paddle thus becomes a segment of an axon's myelin sheath. (See Figure 2.9.)

Microglia As their name indicates, **microglia** are the smallest of the glial cells. Like some types of astrocytes, they act as phagocytes, engulfing and breaking down dead and dying neurons. But, in addition, they serve as one of the representatives of the immune system in the brain, protecting the brain from invading microorganisms. They are primarily responsible for the inflammatory reaction in response to brain damage.

Figure 2.9 Oligodendrocyte

An oligodendrocyte forms the myelin that surrounds many axons in the central nervous system. Each cell forms segments of myelin for several adjacent axons.

SUPPORTING CELLS OF THE PERIPHERAL NERVOUS SYSTEM In the central nervous system the oligodendrocytes support axons and produce myelin. In the peripheral nervous system the **Schwann cells** perform the same functions. Most axons in the PNS are myelinated. The myelin sheath occurs in segments, as it does in the CNS; each segment consists of a single Schwann cell wrapped many times around the axon. In the CNS the oligodendrocytes grow a

Figure 2.10 Formation of Myelin

In the peripheral nervous system, an entire Schwann cell tightly wraps itself many times around an individual axon and forms one segment of the myelin sheath.

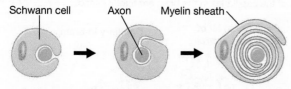

Schwann cell   Axon   Myelin sheath

number of paddle-shaped processes that wrap around a number of axons. In the PNS a Schwann cell provides myelin for only one axon, and the entire Schwann cell—not merely a part of it—surrounds the axon. (See Figure 2.10.)

Schwann cells also differ from their CNS counterparts, the oligodendrocytes, in an important way. As we saw, a nerve consists of a bundle of many myelinated axons, all covered in a sheath of tough, elastic connective tissue. If damage occurs to such a nerve, Schwann cells aid in the digestion of the dead and dying axons. Then the Schwann cells arrange themselves in a series of cylinders that act as guides for regrowth of the axons. The distal portions of the severed axons die, but the stump of each severed axon grows sprouts, which then spread in all directions. If one of these sprouts encounters a cylinder provided by a Schwann cell, the sprout will grow through the tube quickly (at a rate of up to 3–4 mm a day), while the other, nonproductive sprouts wither away. If the cut ends of the nerve are still located close enough to each other, the axons will reestablish connections with the muscles and sense organs they previously served.

Unfortunately, the glial cells of the CNS are not as cooperative as the supporting cells of the PNS. If axons in the brain or spinal cord are damaged, new sprouts will form, as in the PNS. However, the budding axons encounter scar tissue produced by the astrocytes, and they cannot penetrate this barrier. Even if the sprouts could get through, the axons would not reestablish their original connections without guidance similar to that provided by the Schwann cells of the PNS. During development, axons have two modes of growth. The first mode causes them to elongate so that they reach their target, which could be as far away as the other end of the brain or spinal cord. Schwann cells provide this signal to injured axons. The second mode causes axons to stop elongating and begin sprouting terminal buttons because they have reached their target. Liuzzi and Lasek (1987) found that even when astrocytes do not produce scar tissue, they appear to produce a chemical signal that instructs regenerating axons to begin the second mode of growth: to stop elongating and start sprouting terminal buttons. Thus, the difference in the regenerative properties of axons in the CNS and the PNS results from differences in the characteristics of the supporting cells, not from differences in the axons.

There is another difference between oligodendrocytes of the CNS and Schwann cells of the PNS: the chemical composition of the myelin protein they produce. The immune system of someone with *multiple sclerosis* attacks only the myelin protein produced by oligodendrocytes; thus, the myelin of the PNS is spared. The following case of Dr. C. illustrates the brain changes and symptoms that result from this disorder.

One evening, after dinner with her spouse at her favorite restaurant, Dr. C. stumbled and almost fell. She realized that she had been ignoring some symptoms that she should have recognized.

The next day she consulted with one of her colleagues, who agreed that her own tentative diagnosis was probably correct: Her symptoms fit those of multiple sclerosis. She had occasionally experienced double vision, sometimes felt unsteady on her feet, and noticed tingling sensations in her right hand. None of these symptoms was serious, and they lasted for only a short while, so she ignored them—or perhaps denied to herself that they were important.

Dr. C. had been afflicted with multiple sclerosis for more than two decades when she died of a heart attack. A few weeks after Dr. C.'s death, a group of medical students and neurological residents gathered in an autopsy room at the medical school. Dr. D., the school's neuropathologist, displayed a stainless-steel tray on which were lying a brain and a spinal cord. "These belonged to Dr. C.," he said. "Several years ago she donated her organs to the medical school." Everyone looked at the brain more intently, knowing that it had belonged to a skilled physician and teacher whom they all knew by reputation, if not personally.

Dr. D. showed the students MRI scans clipped on the wall. He pointed out some white spots that appeared on one scan. "This scan clearly shows some white-matter lesions, but they are gone on the next one, taken six months later. And here is another one, but it's gone on the next scan. The immune system attacked the myelin sheaths in a particular region, and then glial cells cleaned up the debris. The MRI doesn't show the lesions then, but the axons can no longer conduct their messages."

He put on a pair of gloves, picked up Dr. C.'s brain, and cut it in several slices. He picked one up. "Here, see this?" He pointed out a spot of discoloration in a band of white matter. "This is a sclerotic plaque—a patch that feels harder than the surrounding tissue. There are many of them, located throughout the brain and spinal cord, which is why the disease is called multiple sclerosis."

Dr. D. put the spinal cord down and said, "Who can tell me the basis of this disorder?"

One of the students spoke up. "It's an autoimmune disease. The immune system gets sensitized to the body's own myelin protein and periodically attacks it, causing a variety of different neurological symptoms. Some say that a childhood viral illness somehow causes the immune system to start seeing the protein as foreign."

"That's right," said Dr. D. "The primary criterion for the diagnosis of multiple sclerosis is the presence of neurological symptoms that repeatedly come and go over time. The symptoms don't all occur at once, and they can be caused only by damage to several different parts of the nervous system, which means that they can't be the result of a stroke."

The Blood–Brain Barrier

LO 2.4 **Discuss the features and importance of the blood–brain barrier.**

Over one hundred years ago, Paul Ehrlich discovered that if a blue dye is injected into an animal's bloodstream, all tissues except the brain and spinal cord will be tinted blue. However, if the same dye is injected into the fluid-filled ventricles of the brain, the blue color will spread throughout the CNS (Bradbury, 1979). This experiment demonstrates that a barrier exists between the blood and the fluid that surrounds the cells of the brain: the **blood–brain barrier.**

Some substances can cross the blood–brain barrier; others cannot. Thus, it is *selectively permeable.* In most of the body the cells that line the capillaries do not fit together absolutely tightly. Small gaps are found between them that permit the free exchange of most substances between the blood and the fluid outside the capillaries that surrounds the cells of the body. In the CNS the capillaries lack these gaps; therefore, many substances cannot leave the blood. Thus, the walls of the capillaries in the brain constitute the blood–brain barrier. (See Figure 2.11.) Other substances must be actively transported through the capillary walls by special proteins. For example, glucose transporters bring the brain its fuel, and other transporters rid the brain of toxic waste products (Rubin & Staddon, 1999; Zlokovic, 2008).

What is the function of the blood–brain barrier? As we will see, transmission of messages from place to place in the

Figure 2.11 The Blood–Brain Barrier

This figure shows that (a) the cells that form the walls of the capillaries in the body outside the brain have gaps that permit the free passage of substances into and out of the blood, and (b) the cells that form the walls of the capillaries in the brain are tightly joined.

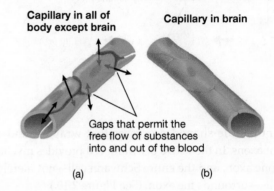

Capillary in all of body except brain

Capillary in brain

Gaps that permit the free flow of substances into and out of the blood

(a) (b)

brain depends on a delicate balance between substances within neurons and those in the extracellular fluid that surrounds them. If the composition of the extracellular fluid is changed even slightly, the transmission of these messages will be disrupted, which means that brain functions will be disrupted. The presence of the blood–brain barrier makes it easier to regulate the composition of this fluid. In addition, many of the foods that we eat contain chemicals that would interfere with the transmission of information between neurons. The blood–brain barrier prevents these chemicals from reaching the brain.

The blood–brain barrier is not uniform throughout the nervous system. In several places the barrier is relatively permeable, allowing substances that are excluded elsewhere to cross freely. For example, the **area postrema** is a part of the brain that controls vomiting. The blood–brain barrier is much weaker there, permitting neurons in this region to detect the presence of toxic substances in the blood. (A barrier around the area postrema prevents substances from diffusing from this region into the rest of the brain.) A poison that enters the circulatory system from the stomach can thus stimulate the area postrema to initiate vomiting. If the organism is lucky, the poison can be expelled from the stomach before causing too much damage.

Section Review

Cells of the Nervous System

LO 2.1 **Contrast the location of the central and peripheral nervous systems.**

The central nervous system is located in the brain and spinal cord. The peripheral nervous system is outside the brain and spinal cord. The PNS communicates with the CNS via nerves that relay sensory and motor information between the brain and spinal cord, and the rest of the body.

LO 2.2 **Describe the structures of a neuron, including their general function.**

Neurons include four basic structures: the soma, dendrites, axon, and terminal buttons. The soma contains the nucleus and many of the organelles. The dendrites are branched structures attached to the soma that receive messages from other neurons. The axon is a long thin extension of the soma that conveys an electrical message to the terminal buttons. The terminal buttons are extensions of the axon that receive an electrical message and convert it to a chemical message by releasing neurotransmitters into the synapse. Other important structures include the cell membrane, cytoskeleton, and cytoplasm for providing shape and support to the cell, as well as serving additional functions. Internal organelles help the cell survive and include the nucleus, endoplasmic reticulum, Golgi apparatus, and mitochondria.

LO 2.3 **Differentiate functions of supporting cells of the central and peripheral nervous systems.**

In the CNS, astrocytes, oligodendrocytes, and microglia support neurons by creating an environment conducive to neuronal function, providing a myelin sheath, and activating immune responses. In the PNS, Schwann cells provide myelin and assist with neural regeneration.

LO 2.4 **Discuss the features and importance of the blood–brain barrier.**

The blood–brain barrier protects the CNS, selectively permitting only some substances to enter. The barrier is made of capillary walls and helps regulate the composition of fluids in the brain, protecting neuronal transmission. The blood–brain barrier is more permeable in the area postrema, permitting neurons in this region to detect the presence of toxic substances in the blood.

Thought Question

While the blood–brain barrier is effective in preventing pathogens from entering the brain, it can also prevent therapeutic molecules from entering. Development of drug molecules that target sites in the brain is often complicated by the difficulty of getting the molecules past the blood–brain barrier. Crossing the blood–brain barrier is considered a key obstacle in developing drugs to treat diseases such as Alzheimer's and Parkinson's. Imagine that you have been selected to research techniques to enhance drug delivery across the blood–brain barrier. What strategies might you test and why?

Communication Within a Neuron

This section describes the nature of communication *within* a neuron—the way an action potential is sent from the cell body down the axon to the terminal buttons, informing them to release some neurotransmitter. The details of synaptic transmission—the communication between neurons—will be described in the next section. As we will see in this section, an action potential consists of a series of alterations in the membrane of the axon that permit small charged particles called *ions* to move between the interior of the axon and the fluid surrounding it. These ion exchanges produce electrical currents.

Neural Communication: An Overview

LO 2.5 **Compare neural communication in a withdrawal reflex with and without inhibition of the reflex.**

Before we begin our discussion of the action potential, let's step back and see how neurons can interact to produce a useful behavior. We begin by examining a simple assembly of three neurons and a muscle that controls a withdrawal reflex. In the next two figures (and in subsequent figures that illustrate simple neural circuits), neurons are depicted in shorthand fashion as several-sided stars. The points of these stars represent dendrites, and only one or two terminal buttons are shown at the end of the axon. The sensory neuron in this example detects painful stimuli. When its dendrites are stimulated by a noxious stimulus (such as contact with a hot object), it sends messages down the axon to the terminal buttons, which are located in the spinal cord. (See Figure 2.12.) The terminal buttons of the sensory neuron release a neurotransmitter that excites the interneuron, causing it to send messages down its axon. The terminal buttons of the interneuron release a neurotransmitter that excites the motor neuron, which sends messages down its axon. The axon of the motor neuron joins a nerve and travels to a muscle. When the terminal buttons of the motor neuron release their neurotransmitter, the muscle cells contract, causing the hand to move away from the hot object.

So far, all of the synapses have had excitatory effects. Now let us complicate matters a bit to see the effect of inhibitory synapses. Suppose you have removed a hot drink from the microwave. As you pick up the cup, the heat from

Figure 2.12 A Withdrawal Reflex

The figure shows a simple example of a useful function of the nervous system. The painful stimulus causes the hand to pull away from the hot iron.

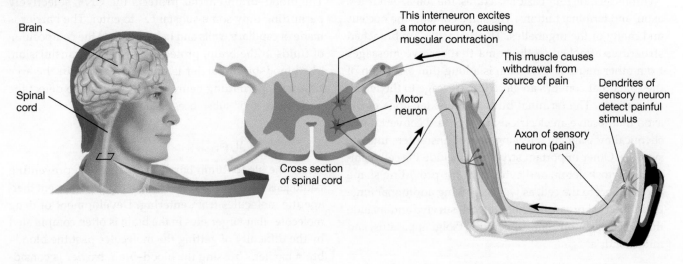

Brain

Spinal cord

Cross section of spinal cord

This interneuron excites a motor neuron, causing muscular contraction

Motor neuron

This muscle causes withdrawal from source of pain

Dendrites of sensory neuron detect painful stimulus

Axon of sensory neuron (pain)

the drink burns your hand. The pain caused by the heat triggers a withdrawal reflex that tends to make you drop the cup. Yet you manage to keep hold of it long enough to get to a table and put it down. What prevented your withdrawal reflex from making you drop the cup on the floor?

The pain from the hot cup increases the activity of excitatory synapses on the motor neurons, which tends to cause the hand to pull away from the cup. However, this excitation is counteracted by *inhibition*, supplied by another source: the brain. The brain contains neural circuits that recognize what a disaster it would be if you dropped the cup on the floor. These neural circuits send information to the spinal cord that prevents the withdrawal reflex from making you drop the cup.

Figure 2.13 shows how this information reaches the spinal cord. As you can see, an axon from a neuron in the brain reaches the spinal cord, where its terminal buttons form synapses with an inhibitory interneuron. When the neuron in the brain becomes active, its terminal buttons excite this inhibitory interneuron. The interneuron releases an inhibitory neurotransmitter, which *decreases* the activity of the motor neuron, blocking the withdrawal reflex. This circuit provides an example of a contest between two competing tendencies: to drop the cup and to hold onto it.

Figure 2.13 The Role of Inhibition

Inhibitory signals arising from the brain can prevent the withdrawal reflex from causing the person to drop the cup.

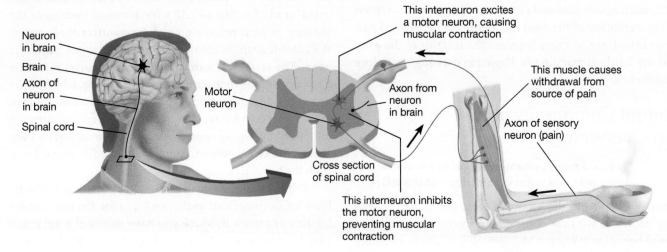

Neuron in brain

Brain

Axon of neuron in brain

Spinal cord

Motor neuron

Cross section of spinal cord

Axon from neuron in brain

This interneuron excites a motor neuron, causing muscular contraction

This muscle causes withdrawal from source of pain

Axon of sensory neuron (pain)

This interneuron inhibits the motor neuron, preventing muscular contraction

Of course, reflexes are more complicated than this description, and the mechanisms that inhibit them are even more so. Thousands of neurons are involved in this process. The neurons shown in Figure 2.13 represent many others: Dozens of sensory neurons detect the hot object, hundreds of interneurons are stimulated by their activity, hundreds of motor neurons produce the contraction—and thousands of neurons in the brain must become active if the reflex is to be inhibited. Yet this simple model provides an overview of the process of neural communication, which is described in more detail later in this chapter.

Measuring Electrical Potentials of Axons

LO 2.6 **Contrast the changes in electrical potential within a neuron when it is experiencing resting potential, hyperpolarization, depolarization, and an action potential.**

Next, we will examine the nature of the message that is conducted along the axon. This message can be measured as an electrical event. Researchers have developed electrical recording techniques using very small sensors called *microelectrodes* that can be inserted into a neuron to record changes in electrical activity across the axon membrane (see Chapter 5). When inserted into an axon at rest, the microelectrode will detect a negative charge inside the membrane. Most neurons are approximately 70 units, or –70 mV, more negatively charged *inside* the axon compared to outside. Any difference in charge (positive or negative) across the membrane is called the **membrane potential.** When the neuron is at rest and not involved in communicating with any other neurons, the membrane potential remains at approximately –70mV. This is called the neuron's **resting potential.**

In the nervous system, neurons receive messages from other neurons; however, it is possible to artificially simulate messages by applying electrical charge to neurons. If a negative charge is applied, the inside of the axon can become *more* negative (for example, –80 mV). When the inside of an axon becomes more negative relative to the outside, it is **hyperpolarized.** If a positive charge is applied, the inside of the axon can become more positive (for example, –50mV is less negative and therefore more positive than a resting potential of –70mV). When the inside of the axon becomes more positive, the neuron is **depolarized.** Each neuron has a **threshold of excitation,** or a set point, for depolarization to trigger the main electrical event in an axon—the **action potential.** The action potential is a burst of rapid depolarization followed by hyperpolarization. This spread of depolarization followed by hyperpolarization begins at the point where the soma meets the axon and propagates like a wave all the way to the end of the terminal buttons, informing the terminal buttons to release neurotransmitters into the synapse. The following sections will detail the events contributing to the action potential.

Before examining the steps of the action potential in detail, let's briefly look at a very unlikely key player and research participant—the squid. How is a squid related to research on action potentials? Nature has provided the neuroscientist with the giant squid axon (the giant axon of a squid, not the axon of a giant squid!). This axon is about 0.5 mm in diameter, which is hundreds of times larger than the largest mammalian axon, making it an easy-to-work-with model for studying electrical activity in an axon. Much of what is currently known about electrical potentials in the axon came from studies of the giant squid axon.

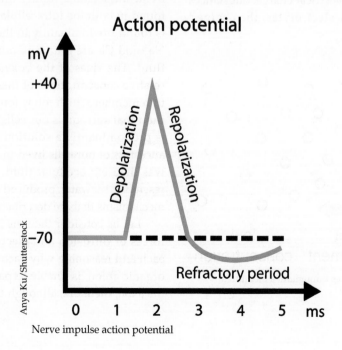

Nerve impulse action potential

The Membrane Potential

LO 2.7 **Summarize the contributions of diffusion, electrostatic pressure, and the sodium–potassium pump to establishing membrane potential.**

To understand what causes the action potential to occur, we must first understand the reasons for the existence of the membrane potential. This electrical charge is the result of a balance between two opposing forces: *diffusion* and *electrostatic pressure*.

THE FORCE OF DIFFUSION When a spoonful of sugar is carefully poured into a container of water, it settles to the bottom. After a time the sugar dissolves, but it remains close to the bottom of the container. After a much longer time (probably several days) the molecules of sugar distribute themselves evenly throughout the water, even if no one stirs the liquid. The process whereby molecules distribute themselves evenly throughout the medium in which they are dissolved is called **diffusion.**

When there are no forces or barriers to prevent them from doing so, molecules will diffuse from regions of high concentration to regions of low concentration. Molecules are constantly in motion, and their rate of movement is proportional to the temperature. Only at absolute zero [0 K (kelvin) = –273.15°C = –459.7°F] do molecules cease their random movement. At all other temperatures they move about, colliding and veering off in different directions, thus pushing one another away. The result of these collisions in the example of sugar and water is to force sugar molecules upward (and to force water molecules downward), away from the regions in which they are most concentrated.

THE FORCE OF ELECTROSTATIC PRESSURE When some substances are dissolved in water, they split into two parts, each with an opposing electrical charge. Substances with this property are called **electrolytes;** the charged

high   net   low
concentration movement concentration

Molecules evenly distribute themselves throughout a medium in which they are dissolved.

particles into which they decompose are called **ions.** Ions are of two basic types: *Cations* have a positive charge, and *anions* have a negative charge. For example, when sodium chloride (NaCl, table salt) is dissolved in water, many of the molecules split into sodium cations (Na^+) and chloride anions (Cl^-).

Particles with the same kind of charge repel each other (+ repels +, and – repels –), but particles with different charges are attracted to each other (+ and – attract). Thus, anions repel anions, cations repel cations, but anions and cations attract each other. The force exerted by this attraction or repulsion is called **electrostatic pressure.** Just as the force of diffusion moves molecules from regions of high concentration to regions of low concentration, electrostatic pressure moves ions from place to place: Cations are pushed away from regions with an excess of cations, and anions are pushed away from regions with an excess of anions. (See Figure 2.14.)

IONS IN THE EXTRACELLULAR AND INTRACELLULAR FLUID The fluid within cells **(intracellular fluid)** and the fluid surrounding them **(extracellular fluid)** contain different ions. The forces of diffusion and electrostatic pressure contributed by these ions give rise to the membrane potential. Because the membrane potential is produced by a balance between the forces of diffusion and electrostatic pressure, understanding what produces this potential requires that we know the concentration of the various ions in the extracellular and intracellular fluids.

There are several important ions in these fluids. These include: organic anions (symbolized by A^-), chloride ions (Cl^-), sodium ions (Na^+), and potassium ions (K^+). Organic anions—negatively charged proteins and intermediate products of the cell's metabolic processes—are found only in the intracellular fluid. Although the other three ions are found in both the intracellular and extracellular fluids, K^+ is found predominantly in the intracellular fluid, whereas Na^+ and Cl^- are found predominantly in the extracellular fluid. The sizes of the boxes in Figure 2.15 indicate the relative concentrations of these four ions. The easiest way to remember which ion is found where is to recall that the fluid that surrounds our cells is similar to seawater, which is predominantly a solution of salt, NaCl. The primitive ancestors of our cells lived in the ocean; thus, the seawater was their extracellular fluid. Our extracellular fluid thus resembles seawater, produced and maintained by regulatory mechanisms that are described in Chapter 12.

Let us consider the ions in Figure 2.15, examining the forces of diffusion and electrostatic pressure exerted on each and reasoning why each is located where it is. A^-, the organic anion, is unable to pass through the membrane of the axon; therefore, although the presence of this ion within

Pearson Education Ltd.

Figure 2.14 The Force of Electrostatic Pressure

Ions evenly distribute themselves throughout a medium.

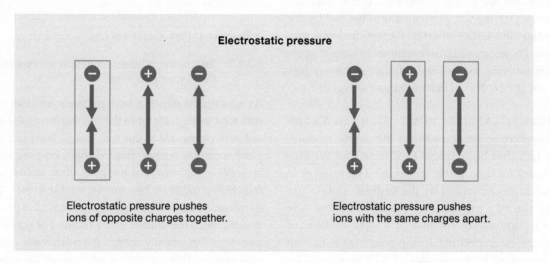

Electrostatic pressure pushes ions of opposite charges together.

Electrostatic pressure pushes ions with the same charges apart.

the cell contributes to the membrane potential, it is located where it is because the membrane is impermeable to it.

The potassium ion K⁺ is concentrated within the axon; thus, the force of diffusion tends to push it out of the cell. However, the outside of the cell is charged positively with respect to the inside, so electrostatic pressure tends to force this cation inside. Thus, the two opposing forces balance, and potassium ions tend to remain where they are. (Refer again to Figure 2.15.)

The chloride ion Cl⁻ is in greatest concentration outside the axon. The force of diffusion pushes this ion inward. However, because the inside of the axon is negatively charged, electrostatic pressure pushes this anion outward.

Figure 2.15 Control of the Membrane Potential

The figure shows the relative concentration of some important ions inside and outside the neuron and the forces acting on them.

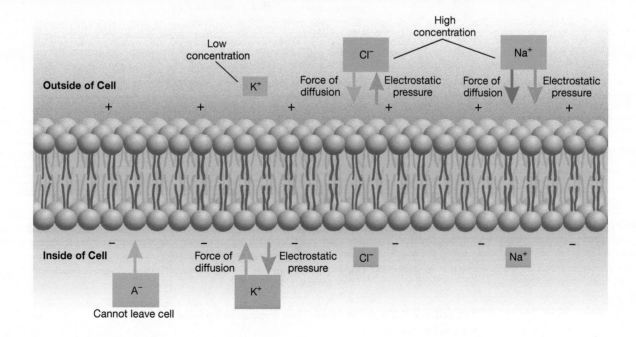

Again, two opposing forces balance each other. (Look again at Figure 2.15.)

The sodium ion Na^+ is also in greatest concentration outside the axon, so it, like Cl^-, is pushed into the cell by the force of diffusion. But unlike chloride, the sodium ion is *positively* charged. Therefore, electrostatic pressure does *not* prevent Na^+ from entering the cell; indeed, the negative charge inside the axon *attracts* Na^+. (Look once more at Figure 2.15.)

THE SODIUM–POTASSIUM PUMP How can Na^+ remain in greatest concentration in the extracellular fluid, despite the fact that both forces (diffusion and electrostatic pressure) tend to push it inside? The answer is this: Another force, provided by the **sodium–potassium pump,** continuously pushes Na^+ out of the axon. The sodium–potassium pump consists of a large number of protein molecules embedded in the membrane, driven by energy provided by molecules of ATP produced by the mitochondria. These molecules, known as sodium-potassium transporters, exchange Na^+ for K^+, pushing three sodium ions out for every two potassium ions they push in.

Because the membrane is not very permeable to Na^+, sodium–potassium transporters very effectively keep the intracellular concentration of Na^+ low. By transporting K^+ into the cell, they also increase the intracellular concentration of K^+ a small amount. The membrane is approximately 100 times more permeable to K^+ than to Na^+, so the increase is slight, but, as we will see when we study the process of neural inhibition later in this chapter, it is very important. The transporters that make up the sodium–potassium pump use considerable energy: up to 40 percent of a neuron's metabolic resources. Neurons, muscle cells, glia—in fact, most cells of the body—have sodium–potassium transporters in their membrane.

The Action Potential

LO 2.8 Summarize the series of ion movements during the action potential.

As we saw, the forces of both diffusion and electrostatic pressure tend to push Na^+ into the cell. However, the membrane is not very permeable to this ion, and sodium–potassium transporters continuously pump out Na^+, keeping the intracellular level of Na^+ low. But imagine what would happen if the membrane suddenly became permeable to Na^+. The forces of diffusion and electrostatic pressure would cause Na^+ to rush into the cell. This sudden influx (inflow) of positively charged ions would drastically change the membrane potential by depolarization. This is precisely what causes the action potential: A brief increase in the permeability of the membrane to Na^+ (allowing these ions to rush into the cell) is immediately followed by a transient increase in the permeability of the membrane to K^+ (allowing these ions to rush out of the cell). What is responsible for these transient increases in permeability?

We already saw that one type of protein molecule embedded in the membrane—the sodium–potassium transporter—actively pumps sodium ions out of the cell and pumps potassium ions into it. Another type of protein molecule provides an opening that permits ions to enter or leave the cells. These molecules provide **ion channels,** which contain passages ("pores") that can open or close. When an ion channel is open, specific ions can flow through the

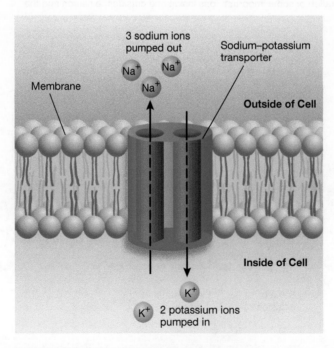

THE SODIUM–POTASSIUM PUMP These transporters are found in the cell membrane.

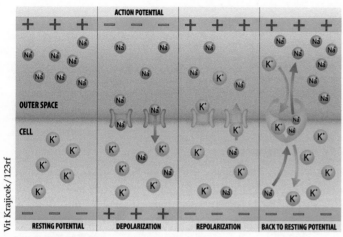

Nerve impulse action potential in neuron.

Next, voltage-dependent potassium channels begin to open, allowing potassium to leave the cell. These potassium channels are less sensitive than voltage-dependent sodium channels. That is, they require a greater level of depolarization before they begin to open, and they begin to open later than the sodium channels. Remember that the interior of the cell is *positively* charged, so K⁺ is driven out of the cell by diffusion and by electrostatic pressure. At about this time (1 millisecond [msec] after they open), the sodium channels become *refractory*—the channels become blocked and cannot open again until the membrane once more reaches the resting potential. (See Figure 2.17.)

The steps involved in generating an action potential are summarized here:

1. As soon as the threshold of excitation is reached, the sodium channels in the membrane open, and Na⁺ rushes in, propelled by the forces of diffusion and electrostatic pressure. The opening of these channels is triggered by reduction of the membrane potential (depolarization); they open at the point at which an action potential begins: the threshold of excitation. Because these channels are opened by changes in the membrane potential, they are called voltage-dependent ion channels. The influx of positively charged sodium ions produces a rapid change in the membrane potential, from –70 mV to +40 mV.

2. The membrane of the axon contains voltage-dependent potassium channels, but these channels are less sensitive than voltage-dependent sodium channels. That is, they require a greater level of depolarization before they begin to open. Thus, they begin to open later than the sodium channels.

3. At about the time the action potential reaches its peak (in approximately 1 msec), the sodium channels become

pore and thus can enter or leave the cell. (See Figure 2.16.) Neural membranes contain thousands of ion channels. For example, each sodium channel can admit up to 100 million ions per second when it is open. Thus, the permeability of a membrane to a particular ion at a given moment is determined by the number of ion channels that are open.

The action potential consists of a series of changes in opening and closing of ion channels and the resulting distribution of ions. First, the membrane potential must reach the threshold of excitation. Then, sodium channels in the membrane open, and Na⁺ rushes in, propelled by the forces of diffusion and electrostatic pressure. The sodium channels are called **voltage-dependent ion channels** because they are only opened by changes in the membrane potential. At this point, the interior of the cell starts to become much more positive.

Figure 2.16 Ion Channels

When ion channels are open, ions can pass through them, entering or leaving the cell.

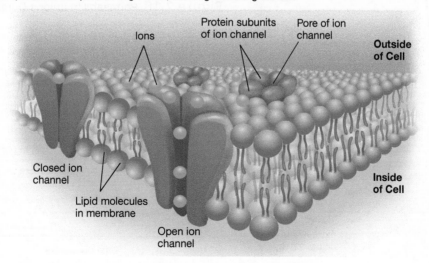

refractory—the channels become blocked and cannot open again until the membrane once more reaches the resting potential. At this time, no more Na⁺ can enter the cell.

4. By now, the voltage-dependent potassium channels in the membrane are open, letting K⁺ ions move freely through the membrane. At this time, the inside of the axon is *positively* charged, so K⁺ is driven out of the cell by diffusion and by electrostatic pressure. This outflow of cations causes the membrane potential to return toward its normal value. As it does so, the potassium channels begin to close again.

5. Once the membrane potential returns to normal, the sodium channels reset so that another depolarization can cause them to open again.

6. The membrane actually overshoots its resting value (–70 mV) and only gradually returns to normal as the potassium channels finally close. Eventually, sodium–potassium transporters remove the Na⁺ ions that leaked in and retrieve the K⁺ ions that leaked out.

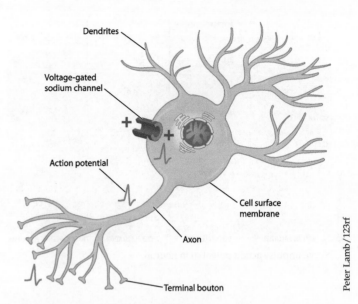

Development of an action potential in a nerve cell through the action of a voltage-gated sodium channel in the cell body.

Figure 2.18 illustrates the changes in permeability of the membrane to sodium and potassium ions during the action potential.

How much ionic flow is there? The increased permeability of the membrane to Na⁺ is brief, and diffusion over any appreciable distance takes some time. Thus, when we say, "Na⁺ rushes in," we do not mean that the axoplasm becomes flooded with Na⁺. At the peak of the action potential a very thin layer of fluid immediately inside the axon becomes full of newly arrived Na⁺ ions; this amount is indeed enough to reverse the membrane potential. However, not enough time has elapsed for these ions to fill the entire axon. Before that event can take place, the Na⁺ channels close, and K⁺ starts flowing out.

Figure 2.17 Ion Movements During the Action Potential

The image at the top shows the opening of sodium channels at the threshold of excitation, their refractory condition at the peak of the action potential, and their resetting when the membrane potential returns to resting potential.

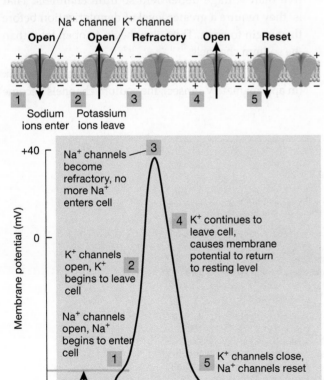

Figure 2.18 Permeability to Ions During the Action Potential

The graph shows changes in the permeability of the membrane of an axon to Na⁺ and K⁺ during the action potential.

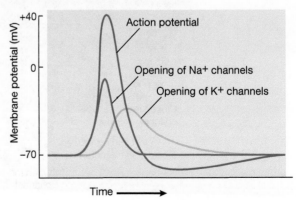

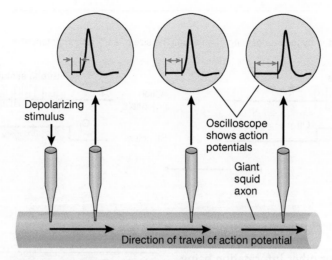

Depolarizing stimulus

Oscilloscope shows action potentials

Giant squid axon

Direction of travel of action potential

CONDUCTION OF AN ACTION POTENTIAL When an action potential is triggered, its size remains undiminished as it travels down the axon. The speed of conduction can be calculated from the delay between the stimulus and the action potential.

Experiments have shown that an action potential temporarily increases the number of Na^+ ions inside the giant squid axon by 0.0003 percent. Although the concentration just inside the membrane is high, the total number of ions entering the cell is very small relative to the number already there. This means that, on a short-term basis, sodium–potassium transporters are not very important. The few Na^+ ions that manage to leak in diffuse into the rest of the axoplasm, and the slight increase in Na^+ concentration is hardly noticeable. However, sodium–potassium transporters are important on a *long-term* basis. Without the activity of sodium–potassium transporters, the concentration of sodium ions in the axoplasm would eventually increase enough that the axon would no longer be able to function.

Conduction of the Action Potential

LO 2.9 Describe the propagation of an action potential.

Moving from a basic description of the resting membrane potential and the production of the action potential, let's next consider the movement of the message down the axon, or *conduction of the action potential*. To study this phenomenon, we again make use of the giant squid axon. We attach an electrical stimulator to an electrode at one end of the axon and place recording electrodes at different distances from the stimulating electrode. Then we apply a depolarizing stimulus to the end of the axon and trigger an action potential. We record the action potential from each of the electrodes, one after the other. Thus, we see that the action potential is conducted down the axon. As the action potential travels, it remains constant in size.

This experiment establishes a basic law of axonal conduction: the **all-or-none law.** This law states that an action potential either occurs or does not occur, and, once triggered, it is transmitted down the axon to its end. An action potential always remains the *exact* same size, without growing or diminishing. And when an action potential reaches a point where the axon branches, it splits but does not diminish in size. An axon will transmit an action potential in either direction, or even in both directions, if it is started in the middle of the axon's length. However, because action potentials in living animals start at the end attached to the soma, axons normally carry one-way traffic.

The strength of a muscular contraction can vary from very weak to very forceful, and the strength of a stimulus, like light detected by the neurons in the eye, can vary from barely detectable to very intense. Action potentials in axons control the strength of muscular contractions and represent the intensity of a physical stimulus. But if action potentials are all-or-none events and every action potential is exactly the same size, how can they represent information that can vary in a continuous fashion, such as strong to weak muscle contraction, or bright to dim light? The answer is surprising: Variable information is represented by an axon's *rate of firing action potentials*. A high rate of firing causes a strong muscular contraction, and a strong stimulus (such as a bright light) causes a high rate of firing in axons that serve the eyes. For example, an axon might respond to a dim light such as a candle by firing 10 identical action potentials in a unit of time (a low rate of firing). The same axon might respond to a bright floodlight by firing 100 identical action potentials in the same unit of time (a high rate of firing). The **rate law** refers to the principle that variations

Figure 2.19 The Rate Law

The strength of a stimulus is represented by the rate of firing of an axon. The size of each action potential is always constant.

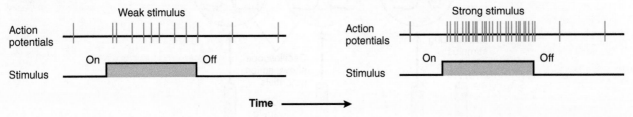

in the intensity of a stimulus or other information being transmitted in an axon are represented by variations in the rate at which the axon fires (see Figure 2.19). By analogy, imagine that every time you clap your hands, the sound occurs at the exact same volume. To show your enthusiasm for a great performance you might clap your hands very quickly for 30 seconds (a high rate of firing). To show your response to a performance you didn't enjoy as much, you might only clap your hands a few times, slowly, for 30 seconds (a low rate of firing). You are using the same method of communication (clapping, or in the case of a neuron, firing action potentials), but you are varying the rate to convey different messages.

Recall that all but the smallest axons in mammalian nervous systems are myelinated; segments of the axons are covered by a myelin sheath produced by the oligodendrocytes of the CNS or the Schwann cells of the PNS. These segments are separated by portions of naked axon, the nodes of Ranvier. Conduction of an action potential in a myelinated axon is somewhat different from conduction in an unmyelinated axon.

Schwann cells and the oligodendrocytes of the CNS wrap tightly around the axon, leaving no measurable extracellular fluid between them and the axon. The only place where a myelinated axon comes into contact with the extracellular fluid is at a node of Ranvier, where the axon is exposed to the extracellular fluid. In the myelinated areas there can be no inward flow of Na⁺ when the sodium channels open because there is no extracellular sodium. The axon conducts the electrical disturbance from the action potential to the next node of Ranvier. The disturbance is conducted passively, the way an electrical signal is conducted through an insulated cable. The disturbance gets smaller as it passes down the axon, but it is still large enough to trigger a new action potential at the next node. This decrease in the size of the disturbance is called *decremental conduction*. The action potential gets retriggered, or repeated, at each node of Ranvier, and the electrical disturbance that results is conducted decrementally along the myelinated area to the next node. Transmission of this

Figure 2.20 Saltatory Conduction

The figure shows propagation of an action potential down a myelinated axon.

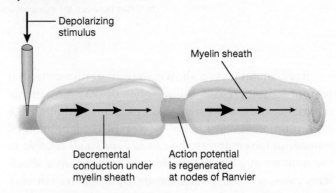

message, hopping from node to node, is called **saltatory conduction**. (See Figure 2.20.)

Saltatory conduction confers two advantages. The first is economic. Sodium ions enter axons during action potentials, and these ions must eventually be removed. Sodium–potassium transporters must be located along the entire length of unmyelinated axons because Na⁺ enters everywhere. However, because Na⁺ can enter myelinated axons only at the nodes of Ranvier, much less gets in, and consequently much less has to be pumped out again. Therefore, myelinated axons expend much less energy to maintain their sodium balance.

The second advantage to myelin is speed. Conduction of an action potential is faster in a myelinated axon because the transmission between the nodes is very fast. Increased speed enables an animal to react faster and (undoubtedly) to think faster. One of the ways to increase the speed of conduction is to increase size. Because it is so large, the unmyelinated squid axon, with a diameter of 500 μm, achieves a conduction velocity of approximately 35 m/sec (meters per second). However, a myelinated cat axon achieves the same speed with a diameter of a mere 6 μm. The fastest myelinated axon, 20 μm in diameter, can conduct action potentials at a speedy 120 m/sec, or 432 km/h (kilometers per hour). At that speed a signal can get from one end of an axon to the other without much delay.

Section Review

Communication Within a Neuron

LO 2.5 Compare neural communication in a withdrawal reflex with and without inhibition of the reflex.

A simple withdrawal reflex is made up of a sensory neuron that detects the stimulus, a spinal interneuron that excites a motor neuron, and a motor neuron that causes the withdrawal behavior. This reflex can be inhibited by input from the brain that can prevent the withdrawal behavior by inhibiting the motor neuron.

LO 2.6 Contrast the changes in electrical potential within a neuron when it is experiencing resting potential, hyperpolarization, depolarization, and an action potential.

Resting potential in most neurons is approximately –70 mV, or 70 units (mV) more negative inside the neuron compared to outside it. Hyperpolarization occurs when the inside of the neuron becomes more negative (for example, –100mV) and depolarization occurs when the inside of the cell becomes more positive (for example +20mV). An action potential occurs when a neuron is depolarized beyond its threshold of excitation. An action potential is a burst of depolarization followed by hyperpolarization that proceeds like a wave along the axon, starting at the point where the axon meets the soma and proceeding to the terminal buttons.

LO 2.7 Summarize the contributions of diffusion, electrostatic pressure, and the sodium–potassium pump to establishing membrane potential.

The difference in charge between the inside and the outside of the axonal membrane is generated by the force of diffusion, electrostatic pressure, and the activity of sodium–potassium pumps. The force of diffusion describes the process by which molecules distribute themselves evenly throughout the medium they are dissolved in. Electrostatic pressure describes the phenomenon in which like charges repel and opposite charges are attracted to each other. The sodium–potassium pump helps maintain the resting membrane potential by pumping three sodium ions out and two potassium ions into the cell with each molecule of ATP.

LO 2.8 Summarize the series of ion movements during the action potential.

After reaching the threshold of excitation, the voltage-gated sodium channels open, allowing sodium to enter the cell. Sodium's movement into the cell is driven by the forces of diffusion and electrostatic pressure. This depolarizes the axonal membrane. After approximately 1 msec, the sodium channels become refractory. The positive charge inside the cell opens voltage-gated potassium channels. Potassium exits the cell due to the force of diffusion and electrostatic pressure due to the now positive charge on the inside of the cell. As potassium exits and diffuses away from the cell, the cell becomes hyperpolarized and eventually becomes even more negatively charged inside the cell than resting potential. The potassium channels close, halting exit of potassium ions out of the cell. The sodium–potassium pumps become active, moving three sodium ions out of the cell and two potassium ions in.

LO 2.9 Describe the propagation of an action potential.

After initiating at the point where the axon joins the soma, the action potential propagates toward the terminal buttons according to the all-or-none law. The all-or-none law states that an action potential either occurs or does not occur, and, once triggered, it is transmitted down the axon to its end. In an unmyelinated axon, the action potential proceeds along the axon but is subject to decremental conduction. In a myelinated axon, the action potential in conducted via salutatory conduction, which speeds the message, reduces decremental conduction, and renews the action potential at the nodes of Ranvier. To vary the strength of the message conveyed by the action potential, the rate law explains that although each action potential event is identical, a stronger message can be conveyed by firing action potentials at a higher rate.

Thought Question

Have you ever received a local anesthetic to relieve pain from an injury or during a painful procedure, like having a cavity filled? Local anesthetics such as Novocaine or Lidocaine (and even cocaine) produce their numbing effects by blocking sodium channels along the axons of sensory neurons. Explain how blocking these channels could block sensory function in these neurons.

Communication Between Neurons

Now that you have encountered information about the basic structure of neurons and the nature of the action potential, it is time to examine the ways in which neurons can communicate with each other. These communications make it possible for circuits of neurons to gather sensory information, make plans, and initiate behaviors.

The primary means of communication between neurons is *synaptic transmission*—the transmission of messages from one neuron to another across a synapse. As we saw, these messages are carried by neurotransmitters, released by terminal buttons of the sending, or *presynaptic* cell. These chemicals diffuse across the fluid-filled gap between the terminal buttons and the membranes of the neurons with which they form synapses, called the *postsynaptic* cell. Neurotransmitters then produce **postsynaptic potentials**—brief depolarizations or hyperpolarizations—that increase or decrease the rate of firing of the axon of the postsynaptic neuron.

Neurotransmitters exert their effects on cells by attaching to a particular region of a receptor molecule called the **binding site.** A molecule of the chemical fits into the binding site the way a key fits into a lock: The shape of the binding site and the shape of the molecule of the neurotransmitter are complementary. A chemical that attaches to a binding site is called a **ligand.** Neurotransmitters are naturally occurring ligands, produced and released by neurons. But other chemicals found in nature (primarily in plants or in the poisonous venoms of animals) can serve as ligands too. In addition, artificial ligands can be produced in the laboratory. These chemicals are discussed in Chapter 4, which deals with drugs and their effects.

Structure of Synapses

LO 2.10 **Describe the structures and functions of presynaptic cells that are involved in synaptic communication.**

Synapses are junctions between the terminal buttons at the ends of the axonal branches of one neuron and the membrane of another. Many synapses occur on the smooth surface of a dendrite or on **dendritic spines**—small protrusions that stud the dendrites of several types of large neurons in the brain. Some synapses can occur on the soma and on other axons. (See Figure 2.21.)

Let's examine a representative synapse in more detail. The **presynaptic membrane,** located at the end of the terminal button, faces the **postsynaptic membrane,** located on the neuron that receives the message. These two membranes face each other across the **synaptic cleft,** a gap that varies in size from synapse to synapse but is usually around 20 nm wide. (A nanometer, nm, is one billionth of a meter.) The synaptic cleft contains extracellular fluid, through which the neurotransmitter diffuses. A meshwork of filaments crosses the synaptic cleft and keeps the presynaptic and postsynaptic membranes in alignment.

As you can see in Figure 2.22, two prominent structures are located in the cytoplasm of the terminal button: mitochondria and synaptic vesicles. We also see microtubules, which are responsible for transporting material between the soma and terminal button. The presence of mitochondria implies that the terminal button needs energy to perform its functions. **Synaptic vesicles** are small, rounded objects in the shape of spheres or ovoids. (The term *vesicle* means "little bladder.") A given terminal button can contain from a few hundred to nearly a million synaptic vesicles. (See Figure 2.22.)

Figure 2.21 Types of Synapses

Axodendritic synapses can occur on the smooth surface of a dendrite (a) or on dendritic spines (b). Axoaxonic synapses consist of synapses between two terminal buttons (c).

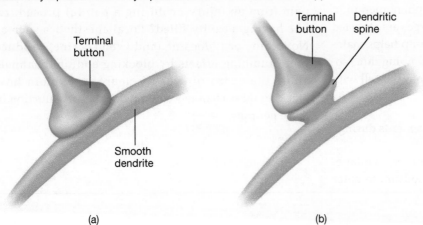
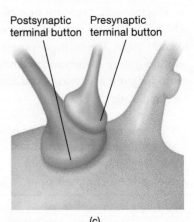

(a)   (b)   (c)

Figure 2.22 Details of a Synapse

This figure displays the structures of the synapse that are involved in synaptic communication.

Detail of Synapse

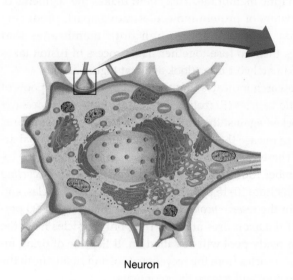

Neuron

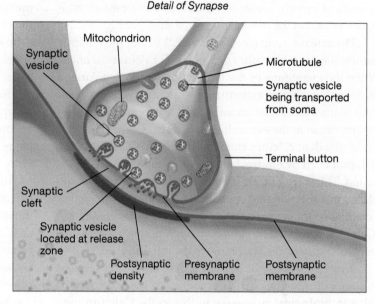

Mitochondrion

Synaptic vesicle

Microtubule

Synaptic vesicle being transported from soma

Terminal button

Synaptic cleft

Synaptic vesicle located at release zone

Postsynaptic density

Presynaptic membrane

Postsynaptic membrane

Many terminal buttons contain two types of synaptic vesicles: large and small. Small synaptic vesicles (found in all terminal buttons) contain molecules of the neurotransmitter. They range in number from a few dozen to several hundred. The membrane of small synaptic vesicles consists of approximately 10,000 lipid molecules into which are inserted about 200 protein molecules. *Transport proteins* fill vesicles with the neurotransmitter, and *trafficking proteins* are involved in the release of neurotransmitters and recycling of the vesicles. Synaptic vesicles are found in greatest numbers around the part of the presynaptic membrane that faces the synaptic cleft—near the **release zone,** the region from which the neurotransmitter is released. In many terminal buttons we see a scattering of large, dense-core synaptic vesicles. These vesicles contain one of a number of different peptides, the functions of which are described later in this chapter.

Small synaptic vesicles are produced in the Golgi apparatus located in the soma and are carried by fast axoplasmic transport to the terminal button. As we will see, some are also produced from recycled material in the terminal button. Large synaptic vesicles are produced only in the soma and are transported through the axoplasm to the terminal buttons.

Release of Neurotransmitters

LO 2.11 Describe the process of neurotransmitter release.

When action potentials are conducted down an axon (and down all of its branches), something happens inside all of the terminal buttons: A number of small synaptic vesicles located just inside the presynaptic membrane fuse with the membrane and then break open, spilling their contents into the synaptic cleft. Figure 2.23 shows a portion of a frog's

neuromuscular junction—the synapse between a terminal button and a muscle fiber. The axon has just been stimulated, and synaptic vesicles in the terminal button are in the process of releasing the neurotransmitters. Note that some vesicles are fused with the presynaptic membrane, forming the shape of an omega (Ω).

How does an action potential cause synaptic vesicles to release neurotransmitters? The process begins when a

Figure 2.23 Cross Section of Synapse

The photograph from an electron microscope shows a cross section of a synapse. The omega-shaped figures are synaptic vesicles fusing with the presynaptic membranes of terminal buttons that form synapses with frog muscle.

(From Heuser, J. E., in *Society for Neuroscience Symposia, Vol. II*, edited by W. M. Cowan and J. A. Ferrendelli. Bethesda, MD: Society for Neuroscience, 1977. Reprinted with permission.)

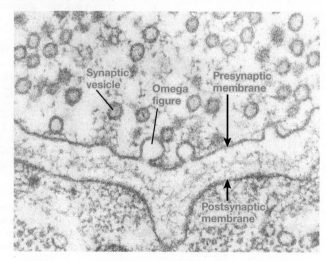

Synaptic vesicle

Omega figure

Presynaptic membrane

Postsynaptic membrane

population of synaptic vesicles becomes "docked" against the presynaptic membrane, ready to release their neurotransmitter into the synaptic cleft. Docking is accomplished when clusters of protein molecules attach to other protein molecules located in the presynaptic membrane (see Figure 2.24).

The release zone (see Figure 2.22) of the presynaptic membrane contains voltage-dependent calcium channels. When the membrane of the terminal button is depolarized by an arriving action potential, the calcium channels open. Like sodium ions, calcium ions (Ca^{2+}) are located in highest concentration in the extracellular fluid. Thus, when the voltage-dependent calcium channels open, Ca^{2+} flows into the cell, propelled by electrostatic pressure and the force of diffusion. The entry of Ca^{2+} is an essential step; if neurons are placed in a solution that contains no calcium ions, an action potential no longer causes the release of a neurotransmitter. (Calcium transporters, similar in operation to sodium–potassium transporters, later remove the intracellular Ca^{2+}.)

As we will see later in this chapter and in subsequent chapters of this book, calcium ions play many important roles in biological processes within cells. Calcium ions can bind with various types of proteins, changing their characteristics. Some of the calcium ions that enter the terminal button bind with the clusters of protein molecules that join the membrane of the synaptic vesicles with the presynaptic membrane. This event makes the segments of the clusters of protein molecules move apart, producing a *fusion pore*—a hole through both membranes that enables them to fuse together. The process of fusion takes approximately 0.1 msec (look again at Figure 2.24).

Research indicates that there are three distinct pools of synaptic vesicles (Rizzoli & Betz, 2005). *Release-ready vesicles* are docked against the inside of the presynaptic membrane, ready to release their contents when an action potential arrives. These vesicles constitute less than 1 percent of the total number found in the terminal. Vesicles in the *recycling pool* constitute 10–15 percent of the total pool of vesicles, and those in the *reserve pool* make up the remaining 85–90 percent. If the axon fires at a low rate, only vesicles from the release-ready pool will be called on. If the rate of firing increases, vesicles from the recycling pool and finally from the reserve pool will release their contents.

What happens to the membrane of the synaptic vesicles after they have broken open and released the

---

Figure 2.24 Release of a Neurotransmitter

An action potential opens calcium channels, which allow calcium ions to enter and bind with the protein embedded in the membrane of synaptic vesicles docked at the release zone. The fusion pores open, and the neurotransmitter is released into the synaptic cleft.

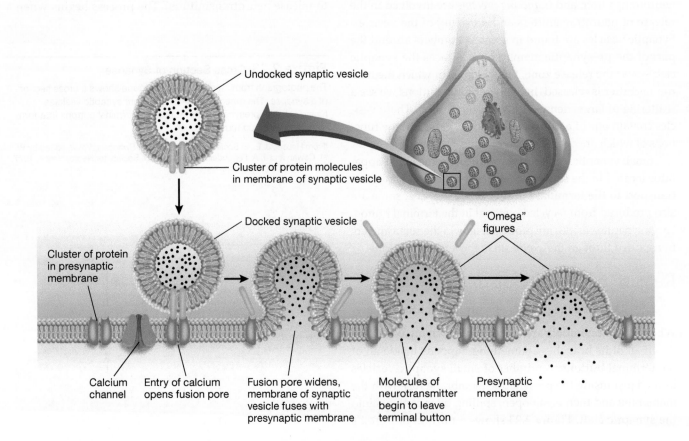

neurotransmitter they contain? It appears that many vesicles in the ready-release pool use a process known as *kiss and run.* These synaptic vesicles release most or all of their neurotransmitter, the fusion pore closes, and the vesicles break away from the presynaptic membrane and get filled with neurotransmitter again. Other vesicles (primarily those in the recycling pool) merge and recycle and consequently lose their identity. The membranes of these vesicles merge with the presynaptic membrane. Little buds of membrane then pinch off into the cytoplasm and become synaptic vesicles. The appropriate proteins are inserted into the membrane of these vesicles, and the vesicles are filled with molecules of the neurotransmitter. The membranes of vesicles in the reserve pool are recycled through a process of *bulk endocytosis.* (*Endocytosis* means "the process of entering a cell.") Large pieces of the membrane of the terminal button fold inward, break off, and enter the cytoplasm. New vesicles are formed from small buds that break off of these pieces of membrane. The recycling process takes less than a second for the readily releasable pool, a few seconds for the recycling pool, and a few minutes for the reserve pool (see Figure 2.25).

Figure 2.25 Recycling of the Membrane of Synaptic Vesicles

After the synaptic vesicles have released a neurotransmitter into the synaptic cleft, the following takes place: In "kiss and run," a vesicle fuses with the presynaptic membrane, releases the neurotransmitter, reseals, leaves the docking site, becomes refilled with the neurotransmitter, and mixes with other vesicles in the terminal button. In "merge and recycle," the vesicle completely fuses with the postsynaptic membrane, losing its identity. Extra membrane from fused vesicles pinches off into the cytoplasm and forms vesicles, which are filled with the neurotransmitter. The membranes of vesicles in the reserve pool are recycled through a process of bulk endocytosis. Large pieces of the membrane of the terminal button fold inward, break off, and enter the cytoplasm. New vesicles are formed from small buds that break off of these pieces of membrane.

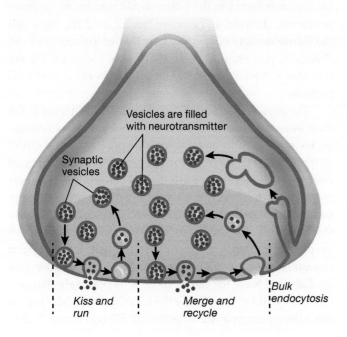

Activation of Receptors

LO 2.12 Contrast ionotropic and metabotropic receptors.

How do molecules of a neurotransmitter produce a depolarization or hyperpolarization in the postsynaptic membrane? They do so by diffusing across the synaptic cleft and attaching to the binding sites of special protein molecules located in the postsynaptic membrane, called **postsynaptic receptors.** Once binding occurs, the postsynaptic receptors open **neurotransmitter-dependent ion channels,** which permit the passage of specific ions into or out of the cell. Thus, the presence of the neurotransmitter in the synaptic cleft allows particular ions to pass through the membrane, changing the local membrane potential. Notice that neurotransmitter molecules cannot enter into the postsynaptic cell—only ions can enter the cell through ion channels.

Neurotransmitters open ion channels by at least two different methods, direct and indirect. The direct method is simpler, so we will describe it first. Figure 2.26 illustrates a neurotransmitter-dependent ion channel that is equipped with its own binding site. When a molecule of the appropriate neurotransmitter attaches to it, the ion channel opens. The formal name for this combination receptor/ion channel is an **ionotropic receptor.**

Ionotropic receptors were first discovered in the organ that produces electrical current in *Torpedo,* the electric ray, where they occur in great number. (The electric ray is a fish that generates a powerful electrical current, not some kind of Star Wars weapon.) These receptors, which are sensitive

---

Figure 2.26 Ionotropic Receptors

The ion channel opens when a molecule of neurotransmitter attaches to the binding site. For purposes of clarity the drawing is schematic; molecules of neurotransmitters are actually much larger than individual ions.

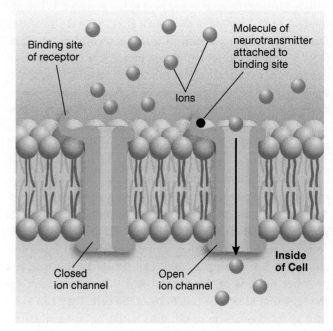

Figure 2.27 Metabotropic Receptors

When a molecule of neurotransmitter binds with a receptor, a G protein activates an enzyme, which produces a second messenger (represented by black arrows) that opens nearby ion channels.

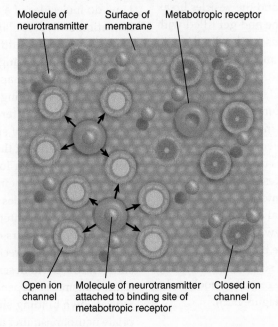

Molecule of neurotransmitter | Surface of membrane | Metabotropic receptor

Open ion channel | Molecule of neurotransmitter attached to binding site of metabotropic receptor | Closed ion channel

to a neurotransmitter called *acetylcholine*, contain sodium channels. When these channels are open, sodium ions enter the cell and depolarize the membrane.

The indirect method is more complicated. Ligand binding to some receptors does not open ion channels directly but instead starts a chain of chemical events. These receptors are called **metabotropic receptors** because they involve steps that require that the cell expend metabolic energy. Metabotropic receptors are located in close proximity to another protein attached to the membrane—a **G protein.** When a molecule of the neurotransmitter binds with a metabotropic receptor, the receptor activates a G protein situated inside the membrane next to the receptor. When activated, the G protein activates an enzyme that stimulates the production of a chemical called a **second messenger.** (The neurotransmitter is the first messenger.) Molecules of the second messenger travel through the cytoplasm, attach themselves to nearby ion channels, and cause them to open. Compared with postsynaptic potentials produced by ionotropic receptors, those produced by metabotropic receptors take longer to begin and last longer. (See Figure 2.27.)

The original second messenger to be discovered was *cyclic AMP*, a chemical that is synthesized from ATP. Since then, several other second messengers have been discovered. As you will see in later chapters, second messengers play an important role in both synaptic and nonsynaptic communication. And they can do more than open ion channels. For example, they can travel to the nucleus or other regions of the neuron and initiate biochemical changes that affect the functions of the cell. They can even turn specific genes on or off, thus initiating or terminating production of particular proteins.

Postsynaptic Potentials

LO 2.13 Compare the functions of EPSPs and IPSPs in postsynaptic cells.

As we mentioned earlier, postsynaptic potentials can be either depolarizing (excitatory) or hyperpolarizing (inhibitory). What determines the nature of the postsynaptic potential at a particular synapse is not the neurotransmitter itself. Instead, it is determined by the characteristics of the postsynaptic receptors—more specifically, *by the particular type of ion channel they open.*

There are four major types of neurotransmitter-dependent ion channels found in the postsynaptic membrane: sodium, potassium, chloride, and calcium (see Figure 2.28). Although the figure depicts only directly activated (ionotropic) ion channels, you should know that many ion channels are activated indirectly, by metabotropic receptors coupled to G proteins.

The neurotransmitter-dependent sodium channel is the most important source of excitatory postsynaptic potentials. As we saw, sodium–potassium transporters keep sodium outside the cell, waiting for the forces of diffusion and electrostatic pressure to push it in. When sodium channels are opened, the result is a depolarization—an **excitatory postsynaptic potential (EPSP)** (see Figure 2.28a). We also saw that sodium–potassium transporters maintain a small surplus of potassium ions inside the cell. If potassium channels open, some of these cations will follow this gradient and leave the cell. Because K+ is positively charged, its efflux will hyperpolarize the membrane, producing an **inhibitory postsynaptic potential (IPSP)** (see Figure 2.28b).

Figure 2.28 Ionic Movements During Postsynaptic Potentials

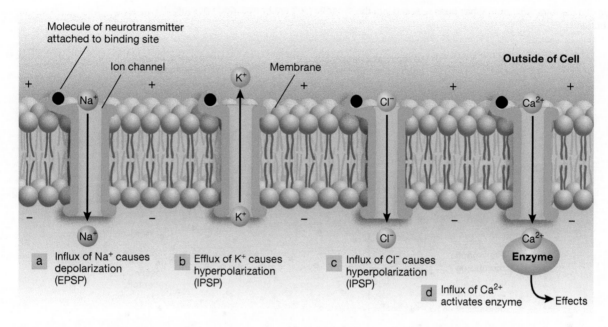

a Influx of Na$^+$ causes depolarization (EPSP)

b Efflux of K$^+$ causes hyperpolarization (IPSP)

c Influx of Cl$^-$ causes hyperpolarization (IPSP)

d Influx of Ca^{2+} activates enzyme

At many synapses, inhibitory neurotransmitters open the chloride channels, instead of (or in addition to) potassium channels. The effect of opening chloride channels depends on the membrane potential of the neuron. If the membrane is at the resting potential, nothing happens, because (as we saw earlier) the forces of diffusion and electrostatic pressure balance perfectly for the chloride ion. However, if the membrane potential has already been depolarized by the activity of excitatory synapses located nearby, then the opening of chloride channels will permit Cl$^-$ to enter the cell. The influx of anions (negatively charged ions) will bring the membrane potential back to its normal resting condition. Thus, the opening of chloride channels serves to neutralize EPSPs (see Figure 2.28c).

The fourth type of neurotransmitter-dependent ion channel is the calcium channel. Calcium ions (Ca^{2+}), being positively charged and being located in highest concentration outside the cell, act like sodium ions; that is, the opening of calcium channels depolarizes the membrane, producing EPSPs. But calcium does even more. As we saw earlier in this chapter, the entry of calcium into the terminal button triggers the migration of synaptic vesicles and the release of the neurotransmitter. In the dendrites of the postsynaptic cell, calcium binds with and activates special enzymes. These enzymes have a variety of effects, including the production of biochemical and structural changes in the postsynaptic neuron. As we will see in Chapter 13, one of the ways in which learning affects the connections between neurons involves changes in dendritic spines initiated by the opening of calcium channels (see Figure 2.28d).

Termination of Postsynaptic Potentials

LO 2.14 **Explain the roles of reuptake and enzymatic deactivation in terminating postsynaptic potentials.**

Postsynaptic potentials are brief depolarizations or hyperpolarizations caused by the activation of postsynaptic receptors with molecules of a neurotransmitter. They are kept brief by two mechanisms: reuptake and enzymatic deactivation.

REUPTAKE The postsynaptic potentials produced by most neurotransmitters are terminated by **reuptake.** This process is simply an extremely rapid removal of neurotransmitter from the synaptic cleft by the terminal button. The neurotransmitter does not return in the vesicles that get pinched off the membrane of the terminal button. Instead, the membrane contains special transporter molecules that draw on the cell's energy reserves to force molecules of the neurotransmitter from the synaptic cleft directly into the cytoplasm—just as sodium–potassium transporters move Na$^+$ and K$^+$ across the membrane. When an action potential arrives, the terminal button releases a small amount of neurotransmitter into the synaptic cleft and then takes it back, giving the postsynaptic receptors only a brief exposure to the neurotransmitter. (See Figure 2.29.)

ENZYMATIC DEACTIVATION **Enzymatic deactivation** is accomplished by an enzyme that destroys molecules of the neurotransmitter. Postsynaptic potentials are terminated in this way for **acetylcholine (ACh)** and for neurotransmitters that consist of peptide molecules. Transmission at synapses on muscle fibers and at some synapses between neurons in the CNS is mediated by ACh. Postsynaptic potentials

Figure 2.29 Reuptake

Molecules of a neurotransmitter that has been released into the synaptic cleft are transported back into the terminal button.

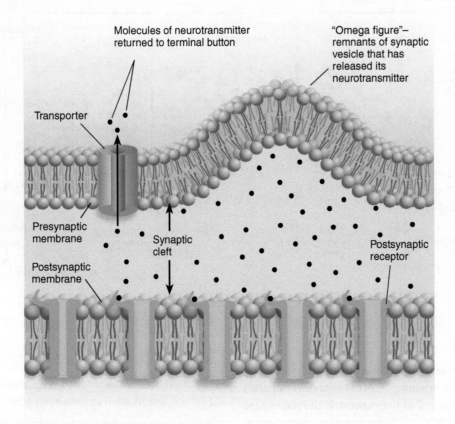

produced by ACh are short lived because the postsynaptic membrane at these synapses contains an enzyme called **acetylcholinesterase (AChE)**. AChE destroys ACh by breaking it into its constituents: choline and acetate. Because neither of these substances is capable of activating postsynaptic receptors, the postsynaptic potential is terminated once the molecules of ACh are broken apart. AChE is an extremely energetic destroyer of ACh; one molecule of AChE will break apart more than 5,000 molecules of ACh each second.

You will recall that Kathryn, the woman featured in the case study that opened this chapter, suffered from progressive muscular weakness. As her neurologist discovered, Kathryn had myasthenia gravis, a disease in which the immune system destroys ACh receptors, reducing the amount of information conveyed from the ACh system to the muscles, thereby producing muscle weakness. Her physician administered Kathryn a drug that blocks AChE. The result of administering this drug was to increase the amount of ACh available in the synapse (because it was not broken down by AChE). Although she still lacked a large number of ACh receptors, the increased ACh in the synapse sufficiently flooded her remaining ACh receptors and amplified the message to her muscles. As a result, Kathryn's ACh system could once again convey messages to her muscles and her muscle weakness was reversed.

Effects of Postsynaptic Potentials: Neural Integration

LO 2.15 Summarize the process of neural integration of EPSPs and IPSPs.

We have seen how neurons are interconnected by means of synapses, how action potentials trigger the release of neurotransmitters, and how these chemicals initiate excitatory or inhibitory postsynaptic potentials. Excitatory postsynaptic potentials increase the likelihood that the postsynaptic neuron will fire; inhibitory postsynaptic potentials decrease this likelihood. (Remember, "firing" refers to the occurrence of an action potential.) Thus, the rate at which an axon fires is determined by the relative activity of the excitatory and inhibitory synapses on the soma and dendrites of that cell. If there are no active excitatory synapses or if the activity of inhibitory synapses is particularly high, that rate could be close to zero.

Let's look at the elements of this process. The interaction of the effects of excitatory and inhibitory synapses on a particular neuron is called **neural integration.** The rate at which a neuron fires is controlled by the relative activity of the excitatory and inhibitory synapses on its dendrites and soma. If the activity of excitatory synapses goes up, the rate of firing will go up. If the activity of inhibitory synapses goes up, the rate of firing will go down.

Figure 2.30 illustrates the effects of excitatory and inhibitory synapses on a postsynaptic neuron. The top panel shows what happens when several excitatory synapses become active. The release of a neurotransmitter produces depolarizing EPSPs in the dendrites of the neuron. These EPSPs (represented in red) are then transmitted down the dendrites, across the soma, to the *axon hillock* located at the base of the axon. If the depolarization is still strong enough when it reaches this point, the axon will fire (see Figure 2.30a).

Let's consider what would happen if, at the same time, inhibitory synapses also become active. Inhibitory postsynaptic potentials are hyperpolarizing—they bring the membrane potential away from the threshold of excitation. Thus, they tend to cancel the effects of excitatory postsynaptic potentials.

Note that *neural* inhibition (that is, an inhibitory postsynaptic potential) does not always produce *behavioral* inhibition. For example, suppose a group of neurons inhibits a particular movement. If these neurons are inhibited, they will no longer suppress the behavior. Thus, inhibition of the inhibitory neurons makes the behavior more likely to occur. Of course, the same is true for neural excitation. *Excitation* of neurons that *inhibit* a behavior suppresses that behavior. For example, when we are dreaming, a particular set of inhibitory neurons in the brain becomes active and prevents

When we are dreaming, a particular set of inhibitory neurons in the brain becomes active and prevents us from getting up and acting out our dreams.

us from getting up and acting out our dreams. (As we will see in Chapter 9, if these neurons are damaged, people *will* act out their dreams.) Neurons are elements in complex circuits; without knowing the details of these circuits, one

Hung Chung Chih/Shutterstock

Figure 2.30 Neural Integration

(a) If several excitatory synapses are active at the same time, the EPSPs they produce (shown in red) summate as they travel toward the axon, and the axon fires. (b) If several inhibitory synapses are active at the same time, the IPSPs they produce (shown in blue) diminish the size of the EPSPs and prevent the axon from firing.

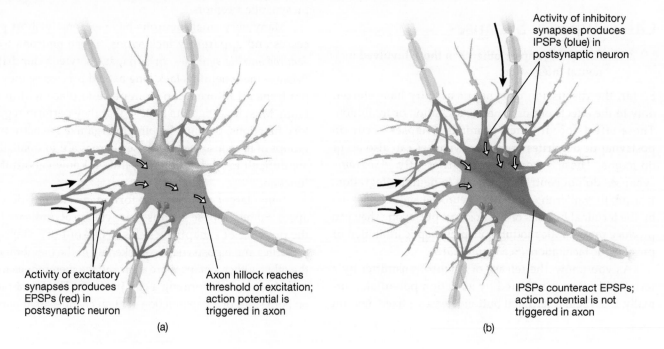

Activity of excitatory synapses produces EPSPs (red) in postsynaptic neuron

Axon hillock reaches threshold of excitation; action potential is triggered in axon

(a)

Activity of inhibitory synapses produces IPSPs (blue) in postsynaptic neuron

IPSPs counteract EPSPs; action potential is not triggered in axon

(b)

cannot predict the effects of the excitation or inhibition of one set of neurons on an organism's behavior.

Autoreceptors

LO 2.16 **Differentiate between the locations and functions of autoreceptors and postsynaptic receptors.**

Postsynaptic receptors detect the presence of a neurotransmitter in the synaptic cleft and initiate excitatory or inhibitory postsynaptic potentials. But the postsynaptic membrane is not the only location of receptors that respond to neurotransmitters. Many neurons also possess receptors that respond to the neurotransmitter that *they themselves* release, called **autoreceptors.**

Autoreceptors can be located on the membrane of any part of the cell, but in this discussion we will consider those located on the terminal button. In most cases these autoreceptors do not control ion channels. Thus, when stimulated by a molecule of the neurotransmitter, autoreceptors do not produce changes in the membrane potential of the terminal button. Instead, they regulate internal processes, including the synthesis and release of the neurotransmitter. (As you may have guessed, autoreceptors are metabotropic; the control they exert on these processes is accomplished through G proteins and second messengers.) In most cases the effects of autoreceptor activation are inhibitory; that is, the presence of the neurotransmitter in the extracellular fluid in the vicinity of the neuron causes a decrease in the rate of synthesis or release of the neurotransmitter. Most investigators believe that autoreceptors are part of a regulatory system that controls the amount of neurotransmitter that is released. If too much is released, the autoreceptors inhibit both production and release; if not enough is released, the rates of production and release go up.

Other Types of Synapses

LO 2.17 **Identify synapses other than those involved in neural integration.**

So far, the discussion of synaptic activity has referred only to the effects of postsynaptic excitation or inhibition. These effects occur when terminal synapses occur on postsynaptic dendrites or somas. Synapses can also occur on axons. These synapses work differently. *Axoaxonic* synapses do not contribute directly to neural integration. Instead, they alter the amount of neurotransmitter released by the terminal buttons of the postsynaptic axon. They can produce presynaptic modulation: presynaptic inhibition or presynaptic facilitation. (See Figure 2.31.)

As you know, the release of a neurotransmitter by a terminal button is initiated by an action potential. Normally, a particular terminal button releases a fixed amount

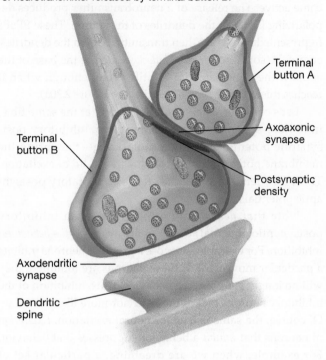

Figure 2.31 An Axoaxonic Synapse

The activity of terminal button A can increase or decrease the amount of neurotransmitter released by terminal button B.

Terminal button A

Axoaxonic synapse

Postsynaptic density

Terminal button B

Axodendritic synapse

Dendritic spine

of neurotransmitter each time an action potential arrives. However, the release of a neurotransmitter can be modulated by the activity of axoaxonic synapses. If the activity of the axoaxonic synapse decreases the release of the neurotransmitter, the effect is called **presynaptic inhibition.** If it increases the release, it is called **presynaptic facilitation.** By the way, as we will see in Chapter 4, the active ingredient in marijuana exerts its effects on the brain by binding with presynaptic receptors.

Many very small neurons have extremely short processes and apparently lack axons. These neurons form *dendrodendritic synapses,* or synapses between dendrites. Because these neurons lack long axonal processes, they do not transmit information from place to place within the brain. Most investigators believe that they perform regulatory functions, perhaps helping to organize the activity of groups of neurons. Because these neurons are so small, they are difficult to study; therefore, little is known about their function.

Some larger neurons also form dendrodendritic synapses. Some of these synapses are chemical, indicated by the presence of synaptic vesicles in one of the juxtaposed dendrites and a postsynaptic thickening in the membrane of the other. Other synapses are *electrical*; the membranes meet and almost touch, forming a **gap junction.** The membranes on both sides of a gap junction contain channels that permit ions to diffuse from one cell to another. Thus, changes in the membrane potential of one neuron induce changes in the membrane of the other. Although most gap junctions in vertebrate synapses are dendrodendritic, gap junctions at postsynaptic dendrites and somas can also occur. Gap junctions are common in invertebrates; their function in the vertebrate nervous system is not known.

Other Forms of Chemical Communication

LO 2.18 Describe examples of nonsynaptic communication.

Neurotransmitters are released by terminal buttons of neurons and bind with receptors in the membrane of another cell located a very short distance away. The communication at each synapse is private. **Neuromodulators** are chemicals released by neurons that travel farther and are dispersed more widely than are neurotransmitters. Most neuromodulators are **peptides,** chains of amino acids. Neuromodulators are secreted in larger amounts and diffuse for longer distances, modulating the activity of many neurons in a particular part of the brain. For example, neuromodulators affect general behavioral states such as vigilance, fearfulness, and sensitivity to pain. Chapter 4 discusses the most important neurotransmitters and neuromodulators.

Hormones are secreted by cells of **endocrine glands** or by cells located in various organs, such as the stomach, the intestines, the kidneys, and the brain. Cells that secrete hormones release these chemicals into the extracellular fluid. The hormones are then distributed to the rest of the body through the bloodstream. Hormones affect the activity of cells (including neurons) that contain specialized receptors located either on the surface of their membrane or deep within their nuclei. Cells that contain receptors for a particular hormone are referred to as **target cells** for that hormone; only these cells respond to its presence. Many neurons contain hormone receptors, and hormones are able to affect behavior by stimulating the receptors and changing the activity of these neurons. For example, a sex hormone, testosterone, increases the aggressiveness of most male mammals.

Peptide hormones exert their effects on target cells by stimulating metabotropic receptors located in the membrane. The second messenger that is generated travels to the nucleus of the cell, where it initiates changes in the cell's physiological processes. **Steroid** hormones consist of very small fat-soluble molecules. Examples of steroid hormones include the sex hormones secreted by the ovaries and testes and the hormones secreted by the adrenal cortex. Because steroid hormones are soluble in lipids, they pass easily through the cell membrane. They travel to the nucleus, where they

Figure 2.32 Action of Steroid Hormones

Steroid hormones affect their target cells by means of specialized receptors in the nucleus. Once a receptor binds with a molecule of a steroid hormone, it causes genetic mechanisms to initiate protein synthesis.

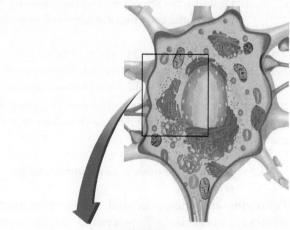

Detail of Cell

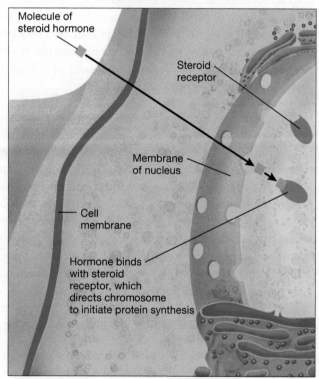

attach themselves to receptors located there. The receptors, stimulated by the hormone, then direct the machinery of the cell to alter its protein production. (See Figure 2.32.)

In the past few years, investigators have discovered the presence of steroid receptors in terminal buttons and around the postsynaptic membrane of some neurons. These steroid receptors influence synaptic transmission, and they do so rapidly. Exactly how they work is still not known.

Section Review

Communication Between Neurons

LO 2.10 Describe the structures and functions of presynaptic cells that are involved in synaptic communication.

Presynaptic cells contain synaptic vesicles filled with neurotransmitters. Transport proteins fill vesicles with the neurotransmitters, and trafficking proteins are involved in the release of neurotransmitters and recycling of the vesicles. The presynaptic membrane faces the postsynaptic membrane across the synaptic cleft.

LO 2.11 Describe the process of neurotransmitter release.

Following an action potential, a neurotransmitter is released from vesicles in the presynaptic cell that move and dock with the terminal membrane. Docking and creation of a fusion pore is triggered by the influx of calcium ions. The neurotransmitter is released into the synaptic cleft through the fusion pore. Following release, the membranes of the vesicles are recycled and return to the pool of available vesicles for future neurotransmitter release.

LO 2.12 Contrast ionotropic and metabotropic receptors.

Ionotropic receptors open ion channels in direct response to the binding of a ligand. Metabotropic receptors can indirectly open ion channels through the use of a G protein. Metabotropic receptors can also activate a second messenger system that can travel to the nucleus or other regions of the neuron and initiate biochemical changes that affect the functions of the cell. Second messengers can also turn specific genes on or off, thus initiating or terminating production of particular proteins.

LO 2.13 Compare the functions of EPSPs and IPSPs in postsynaptic cells.

In the postsynaptic cell, an EPSP is a depolarization resulting from the entry of sodium or calcium ions into the cell through a neurotransmitter-dependent ion channel. In the dendrites of the postsynaptic cell, calcium can also bind with enzymes that have a variety of effects. An IPSP is a hyperpolarization resulting from the exit of potassium ions from or the entry of chloride ions into the cell through a neurotransmitter-dependent ion channel.

LO 2.14 Explain the roles of reuptake and enzymatic deactivation in terminating postsynaptic potentials.

Postsynaptic potentials can be terminated by removing a neurotransmitter from the synapse through reuptake transporters or through breakdown by enzymatic deactivation.

LO 2.15 Summarize the process of neural integration of EPSPs and IPSPs.

Neurons receive multiple subthreshold EPSPs and IPSPs. The neuron integrates these messages. If the integrated messages result in depolarization beyond the threshold of excitation for the cell, the neuron will fire an action potential. If the messages are IPSPs or do not reach the threshold of excitation, the neuron will not fire an action potential.

LO 2.16 Differentiate between the locations and functions of autoreceptors and postsynaptic receptors.

Postynaptic receptors are located on the postsynaptic membrane and serve to relay a message to the postsynaptic cell. Postsynaptic receptors can be ionotropic or metabotropic. Autoreceptors are metabotropic receptors located on the presynaptic membrane that help regulate the amount of neurotransmitter that is released.

LO 2.17 Identify synapses other than those involved in neural integration.

Other types of synapses include axoaxonic or dendrodendritic synapses and gap junctions.

LO 2.18 Describe examples of nonsynaptic communication.

Neuromodulators are chemicals released by neurons that travel farther and are dispersed more widely than are neurotransmitters. Hormones are secreted by cells of endocrine glands or by cells located in various organs. The hormones are then distributed to the rest of the body through the bloodstream.

Thought Question

Many drugs that change behavior produce their effects by interacting with receptor sites or reuptake sites. For example, some antidepressant drugs and stimulant drugs block the reuptake of neurotransmitters. Describe the effect of blocking reuptake at the synapse. Will the amount of neurotransmitter available in the synapse increase, decrease, or stay the same? Explain your answer.

Chapter Review Questions

1. Name and describe the parts of a neuron and explain their functions.

2. Describe the contribution of the sodium–potassium pump in the maintenance of resting membrane potential.

3. Explain the physiological basis of the refractory period in neurons.

4. Describe axoplasmic transport. Distinguish between anterograde and retrograde axoplasmic transport.

5. Describe the structure of synapses, the release of the neurotransmitter, and the activation of postsynaptic receptors.

6. Explain postsynaptic potentials: the ionic movements that cause them, the processes that terminate them, and their integration.

7. Describe the regulation of the effects of the neurotransmitters by autoreceptors, presynaptic inhibition, presynaptic facilitation, and nonsynaptic communication.

Chapter 3
Structure of the Nervous System

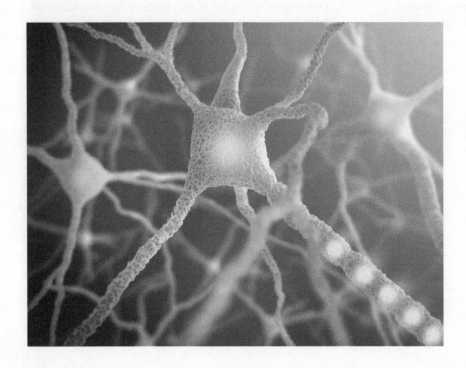

Chapter Outline

Learning Objectives

LO 3.1 Apply anatomical terms to the nervous system.

LO 3.2 Differentiate the locations of the three layers of the meninges.

LO 3.3 Describe the locations and functions of CSF within the ventricular system.

LO 3.4 Summarize the process of human brain development from ectoderm plate, to neural tube, to three interconnected chambers.

LO 3.5 Explain how prenatal development contributes to the development of complex human brains.

LO 3.6 Provide examples of how genetic change, personal experience, and neurogenesis can influence postnatal brain development.

LO 3.7 Identify the structures and functions of the forebrain, including the telencephalon and diencephalon.

LO 3.8 Identify the location and functions of the structures of the mesencephalon.

LO 3.9 Contrast the locations and functions of the structures of the metencephalon and myelencephalon.

LO 3.10 Describe the structure and functions of the spinal cord.

LO 3.11 Identify the functions of the cranial nerves.

LO 3.12 Differentiate between the functions of afferent and efferent axons of the spinal nerves.

LO 3.13 Compare the functions and locations of the sympathetic and parasympathetic divisions of the autonomic nervous system.

Ryan, a first year college student, had suffered from occasional seizures since childhood. His neurologist prescribed a medication to control the seizures, but lately the medication wasn't helping—his seizures were becoming more frequent. His doctor increased the dose of the medication, but the seizures persisted, and the drug made it difficult for Ryan to concentrate on his studies. He was afraid that he would have to drop out of school.

He made an appointment with his neurologist and asked whether another drug was available that might work better and not affect his ability to concentrate. "No," said the neurologist, "you're taking the best medication we have right now. But I want to send you to Dr. L., a neurosurgeon at the medical school. I think you might be a good candidate for seizure surgery."

Ryan had a focal-seizure disorder. His problems were caused by a localized region of the brain that contained some scar tissue. Periodically, this region would irritate the surrounding areas, triggering seizures—uncontrolled, sustained firing of cerebral neurons that resulted in cognitive disruption and, sometimes, uncontrolled movements. Ryan's scar tissue was probably a result of brain damage that occurred when he was born. Dr. L. ordered some tests that indicated that the seizure focus was located in the left side of his brain, in a region known as the medial temporal lobe.

Ryan was surprised to learn that he would remain awake during his surgery. In fact, he would be called on to provide information that the surgeon would need to remove a region of his brain that included the seizure focus. As you might expect, he

was nervous when he was wheeled into the surgery, but after the anesthesiologist gave him a sedative, Ryan relaxed and thought to himself, "This won't be too bad."

In preparation for the surgery, Ryan's scalp was shaved. Dr. L. marked Ryan's scalp where incisions would be made and then gave him several injections of a local anesthetic. Then he cut the scalp and injected some more anesthetic. Finally, he used a drill and a saw to remove a piece of skull. He then cut and folded back the thick membrane that covers the brain, exposing the surface of the brain.

When removing a seizure focus, the surgeon wants to cut away all the abnormal tissue while sparing brain tissue that performs important functions, such as the comprehension and production of speech. For this reason, Dr. L. began stimulating parts of the brain to determine which regions he could safely remove. To do so, he placed a metal probe against the surface of Ryan's brain and pressed a pedal that delivered a weak electrical current. The stimulation disrupts the firing patterns of the neurons located near the probe, preventing them from carrying out their normal functions. Dr. L. found that stimulating parts of the temporal lobe disrupted Ryan's ability to understand what he was saying. When he removed the part of the brain containing the seizure focus, he was careful not to damage these regions.

The operation was successful. Ryan continued to take his medication but at a much lower dose. His seizures disappeared, and he found it easier to concentrate in class. He went on to have a very successful college career.

*****

Ryan's story illustrates the importance of understanding the structures and functions of the nervous system. The overall goal of neuroscience research is to understand how the brain works. To understand the results of this research, you must be acquainted with the basic structure of the nervous system. This chapter contains only *some* of the large body of information about nervous system structures and their associated functions. In Chapter 2, you learned about the smallest units of the nervous system: neurons and supporting cells. In this chapter, you'll learn about larger structures of the nervous system that are made up of neurons. The first section begins with the basic structures of the nervous system, and the second section discusses how the nervous system develops. Then the third and fourth sections detail the central and peripheral nervous systems, respectively. The figure here presents an overview of the lobes of the cortex and the cranial and spinal nerves of the central nervous system, which are described in this chapter.

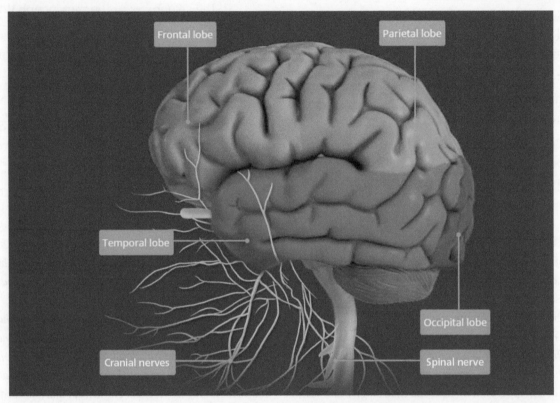

An overview of the lobes of the cortex, as well as the cranial and spinal nerves.

Basic Features of the Nervous System

The nervous system consists of the brain and spinal cord, which make up the *central nervous system (CNS)*, and the cranial nerves, spinal nerves, and peripheral ganglia, which constitute the *peripheral nervous system (PNS)*. The CNS is encased in bone: The brain is covered by the skull, and the spinal cord is contained within the vertebral column. Figure 3.1 illustrates the relationship of the brain and spinal cord to the rest of the body. The brain is made up of neurons, glia, and other supporting cells. It is the most protected organ of the body, encased in a tough, bony skull and floating in a pool of **cerebrospinal fluid (CSF).** The brain receives a copious supply of blood and is chemically guarded by the blood–brain barrier.

The brain receives approximately 20 percent of the blood flow from the heart, and it receives it continuously. Other parts of the body, such as the skeletal muscles or digestive system, receive varying quantities of blood, depending on their needs, relative to those of other regions. But the brain always receives its share. The brain can store only a small amount of its fuel (primarily glucose), and it cannot temporarily extract energy without oxygen, as the muscles can; therefore, a consistent blood supply is essential. A 1-second interruption of the blood flow to the brain uses up much of the dissolved oxygen; a 6-second interruption produces unconsciousness. Permanent damage begins within a few minutes.

Figure 3.1 The Nervous System

The figures show the relation of the nervous system to the rest of the body.

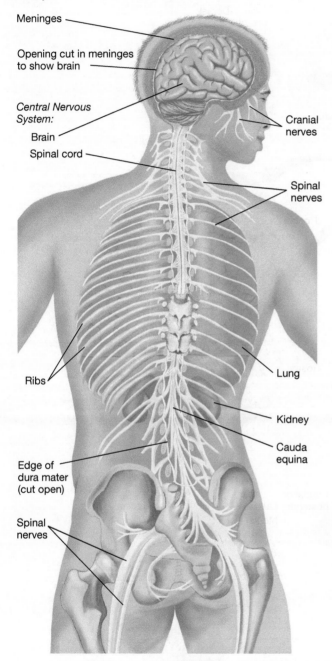

Meninges

Opening cut in meninges to show brain

Central Nervous System:

Brain

Spinal cord

Cranial nerves

Spinal nerves

Ribs

Lung

Kidney

Cauda equina

Edge of dura mater (cut open)

Spinal nerves

Anatomical Directions

LO 3.1 Apply anatomical terms to the nervous system.

Before beginning a detailed description of the nervous system, let's discuss the terms that are used to describe it. The gross anatomy of the brain was described long ago, and everything that could be seen without the aid of a microscope was given a name. Early anatomists named most brain structures according to their similarity to commonplace objects: amygdala, or "almond-shaped object"; hippocampus, or

"sea horse"; genu, or "knee"; cortex, or "tree bark"; pons, or "bridge"; uncus, or "hook," to give a few examples. Throughout this book we will sometimes translate the names of anatomical terms when they're introduced, because the translation can make the terms more memorable. For example, knowing that *cortex* means "bark" will help you to remember that the cortex is the outer layer of the brain.

When describing features of a structure as complex as the brain, we need to use terms denoting directions. Directions in the nervous system are normally described relative to the **neuraxis,** an imaginary line drawn through the length of the central nervous system, from the lower end of the spinal cord up to the front of the brain. For simplicity's sake, let us consider an animal with a straight neuraxis. Figure 3.2b shows an alligator and two humans. This alligator is laid out in a linear fashion; we can draw a straight line that starts between its eyes and continues down the center of its spinal cord. The front end is **anterior,** and the tail is **posterior.** The terms **rostral** (toward the nose and mouth) and **caudal** (toward the tail) are also employed, especially when referring specifically to the brain. The top of the head and the back are part of the **dorsal** surface, while the **ventral** (front) surface faces the ground. (*Dorsum* means "back," and *ventrum* means "belly.") These directions are somewhat more complicated in the human; because we stand upright, our neuraxis bends, so the top of the head is perpendicular to the back. (You will also encounter the terms *superior* and *inferior.* In referring to the brain, *superior* means "above," and *inferior* means "below." For example, the *superior colliculi* are located above the *inferior colliculi.*) The frontal views of both the alligator and the human illustrate the terms **lateral** and **medial:** toward the side and toward the middle, respectively.

Two other useful terms are *ipsilateral* and *contralateral.* **Ipsilateral** refers to structures on the same side of the body. If we say that the olfactory bulb projects axons to the *ipsilateral* hemisphere, we mean that axons originating in the left olfactory bulb terminate in the left hemisphere and axons originating in the right olfactory bulb terminate in the right hemisphere. **Contralateral** refers to structures on opposite sides of the body. If we say that a particular region of the left cerebral cortex controls movements of the *contralateral* hand, we mean that the region controls movements of the right hand.

To see what is in the nervous system, we have to cut it open; to be able to convey information about what we find, we slice it in a standard way. Figure 3.2a and 3.3 show the planes of the human nervous system. We can slice the nervous system in three ways:

1. Transversely, like slicing a loaf of bread, giving us **cross sections** (also known as **frontal sections** when referring to the brain). A transverse cut to the middle of the brain would divide the brain into front and back halves.

2. Parallel to the ground, giving us **horizontal sections.** A parallel cut to the middle of the brain would result in cutting off the upper half of the brain.

Figure 3.2 Anatomical Directions and Planes

The figures show (a) planes of section as they pertain to the nervous system and (b) side and frontal views illustrating the anatomical terms described in this section.

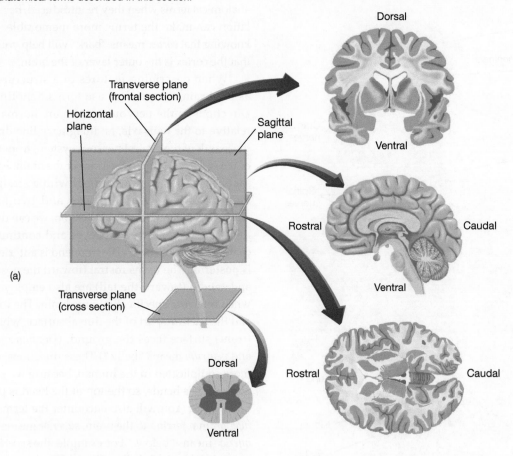

(a)

Transverse plane (frontal section)

Horizontal plane

Sagittal plane

Dorsal

Ventral

Rostral

Caudal

Ventral

Transverse plane (cross section)

Dorsal

Ventral

Rostral

Caudal

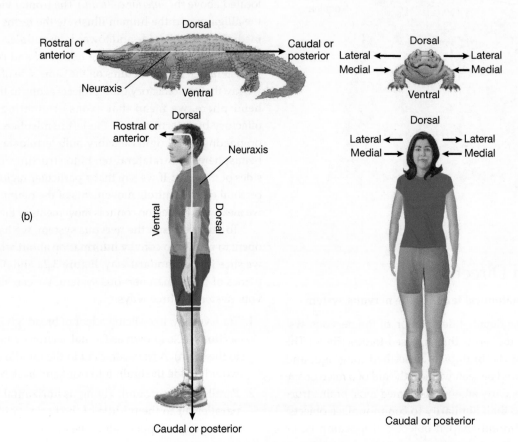

(b)

Dorsal

Rostral or anterior

Caudal or posterior

Neuraxis

Ventral

Dorsal

Lateral

Lateral

Medial

Medial

Ventral

Dorsal

Rostral or anterior

Neuraxis

Ventral

Dorsal

Caudal or posterior

Dorsal

Lateral

Lateral

Medial

Medial

Caudal or posterior

Figure 3.3 Brain Sections

This figure shows a three dimensional view of planes of sections as they pertain to the human brain

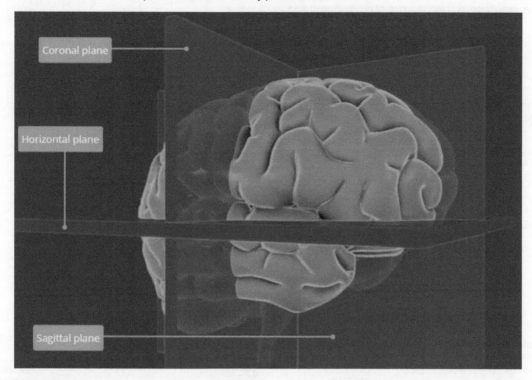

3. Perpendicular to the ground and parallel to the neur-axis, giving us **sagittal sections.** The **midsagittal plane** divides the brain into two symmetrical right and left halves. The sagittal sections in Figures 3.2a and 3.3 are in the midsagittal plane.

Note that because of our upright posture, cross sections of the spinal cord are parallel to the ground. (See Figure 3.2a.)

Meninges

LO 3.2 **Differentiate the locations of the three layers of the meninges.**

The entire nervous system—brain, spinal cord, cranial and spinal nerves, and peripheral ganglia—is covered by tough connective tissue. The protective sheaths around the brain and spinal cord are referred to as the **meninges** (singular: *meninx,* the Greek word for "membrane"). The meninges consist of three layers. The outer layer, called **dura mater,** is durable, thick, tough, and flexible but unstretchable. The middle layer of the meninges, the **arachnoid membrane,** gets its name from the weblike appearance of the *arachnoid trabeculae* that protrude from it (from the Greek *arachne,* meaning "spider"; *trabecula* means "track"). The arachnoid membrane, soft and spongy, lies beneath the dura mater. Closely attached to the brain and spinal cord, and following every surface convolution, is the **pia mater**. The smaller surface blood vessels of the brain and spinal cord are contained within this layer. Between the pia mater and arachnoid membrane is a gap called the **subarachnoid space.** This space is filled with cerebrospinal fluid (CSF).

The peripheral nervous system is covered with two layers of meninges. The middle layer (arachnoid membrane), with its associated pool of CSF, covers only the brain and spinal cord. Outside the central nervous system, the outer and inner layers (dura mater and pia mater) fuse and form a sheath that covers the spinal and cranial nerves and the peripheral ganglia.

The Ventricular System and Production of CSF

LO 3.3 **Describe the locations and functions of CSF within the ventricular system.**

The ventricular system of the brain consists of a series of hollow, interconnected chambers called **ventricles** ("little bellies"), which are filled with CSF. (See Figure 3.4.) The largest chambers are the **lateral ventricles,** which are connected to the **third ventricle.** The third ventricle is located at the midline of the brain; its walls divide the surrounding part of the brain into symmetrical halves. A bridge of neural tissue called the *massa intermedia* crosses through the middle of the third ventricle and serves as a convenient reference point. The **cerebral aqueduct,** a long tube, connects the third ventricle to the **fourth ventricle.** The lateral ventricles constitute the first and second ventricles, but they are never referred to as such.

The ventricles are more than vacant spaces in the brain; they serve the very important function of producing and containing CSF. CSF is manufactured by special tissue with an especially rich blood supply called the **choroid**

Figure 3.4 The Ventricular System of the Brain

The figure shows (a) a lateral view of the left side of the brain, (b) a frontal view, (c) a dorsal view, and (d) the production, circulation, and reabsorption of cerebrospinal fluid.

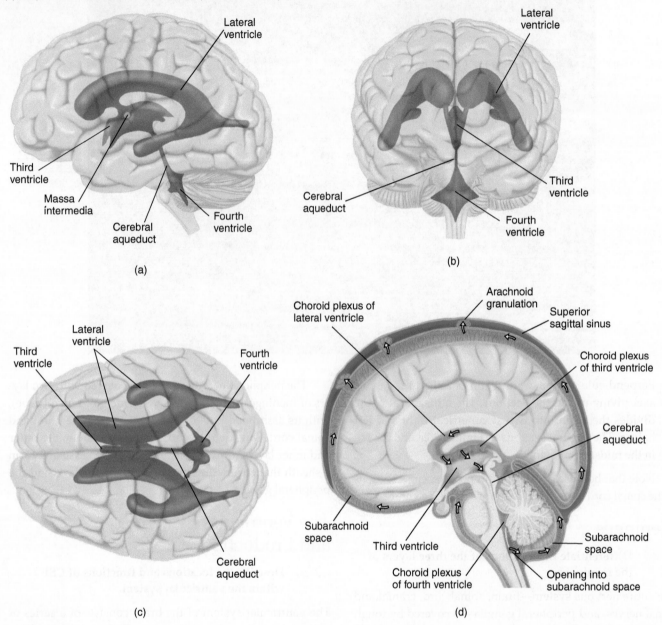

plexus, which protrudes into all four of the ventricles. CSF is produced continuously; the total volume of CSF is approximately 125 ml, and the half-life (the time it takes for half of the CSF present in the ventricular system to be replaced by fresh fluid) is about three hours. Therefore, several times this amount is produced by the choroid plexus each day. The continuous production of CSF means that there must be a mechanism for its removal.

Cerebrospinal fluid produced by the choroid plexus of the lateral ventricles flows into the third ventricle. More CSF is produced in this ventricle, which then flows through the cerebral aqueduct to the fourth ventricle, where still more CSF is produced. The CSF leaves the fourth ventricle through small openings that connect with

the subarachnoid space surrounding the brain. The CSF then flows through the subarachnoid space around the CNS, where it is reabsorbed into the blood supply through the **arachnoid granulations.** These pouch-shaped structures protrude into the **superior sagittal sinus,** a blood vessel that drains into the veins serving the brain.

The brain is very soft and jellylike. The considerable weight of a human brain (approximately 1,400 g), along with its delicate construction, necessitates that it be protected from shock. A human brain cannot even support its own weight well; it is difficult to remove and handle a fresh brain from a recently deceased human without damaging it.

Fortunately, the intact brain within a living human is well protected. It floats in a bath of CSF contained within the subarachnoid space. Because the brain is completely immersed in liquid, its net weight is reduced to approximately 80 g; thus, pressure on the base of the brain is considerably diminished. The CSF surrounding the brain and spinal cord also reduces the shock to the CNS that would be caused by sudden head movement.

Occasionally, the flow of CSF is interrupted at some point in its route of passage. For example, a brain tumor growing in the midbrain may push against the cerebral aqueduct, blocking the flow of CSF, or an infant may be born with a cerebral aqueduct that is too small to accommodate a normal flow of CSF. This occlusion results in greatly increased pressure within the ventricles, because the choroid plexus continues to produce CSF. The walls of the ventricles then expand and produce a condition known as **obstructive hydrocephalus** (*hydrocephalus* literally means "water-head"). If the obstruction remains and if nothing is done to reverse the increased intracerebral pressure, blood vessels will be occluded, and permanent—perhaps fatal—brain damage will occur. Fortunately, a surgeon can usually operate on the person, drilling a hole through the skull and inserting a shunt tube into one of the ventricles. The tube is then placed beneath the skin and connected to a pressure relief valve that is implanted in the abdominal cavity. When the pressure in the ventricles becomes excessive, the valve permits the CSF to escape into the abdomen, where it is eventually reabsorbed into the blood supply. (See Figure 3.5.)

Figure 3.5 Hydrocephalus in an Infant

A surgeon places a shunt tube in a lateral ventricle, which permits cerebrospinal fluid to escape to the abdominal cavity, where it is absorbed into the blood supply. A pressure valve regulates the flow of CSF through the shunt.

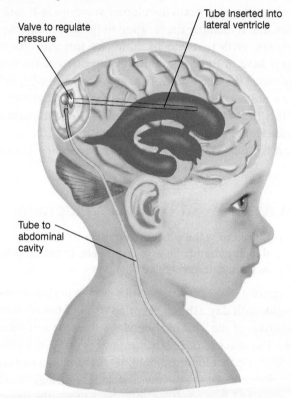

Valve to regulate pressure

Tube inserted into lateral ventricle

Tube to abdominal cavity

Section Review

Basic Features of the Nervous System

LO 3.1 Apply anatomical terms to the nervous system.

Anterior and rostral refer to the front of the nervous system; posterior and caudal refer to the back. Dorsal refers to top of the brain, head and the back; ventral refers to the "belly" side of the nervous system. Superior means above; inferior, below. Medial refers to a position along the midline; lateral, to the side. A frontal section is the result of a transverse cut; a horizontal section is the result of a cut parallel to the ground, and a sagittal section results from a cut that is perpendicular to the ground and parallel to the neuraxis in the human brain.

LO 3.2 Differentiate the locations of the three layers of the meninges.

The dura mater is the outer layer of the meninges. The arachnoid membrane is the middle layer of the meninges. The pia mater is the inner layer of the meninges.

LO 3.3 Describe the locations and functions of CSF within the ventricular system.

CSF is generated by the choroid plexus, lining the ventricles. CSF flows from the lateral ventricles, to the third ventricle, through the cerebral aqueduct, and to the fourth ventricle. CSF then flows into the subarachnoid space and is reabsorbed into the blood. CSF functions to protect the brain by distributing its weight and absorbing shock.

Thought Question

When studying the brain, many neuroscientists use a reference tool called a brain atlas. Just like a road atlas can help you find your way to a new location, a brain atlas can help a researcher find a location in the brain. Instead of using compass directions like north, south, east and west, a brain atlas uses anatomical directions, like anterior and posterior. Practice using anatomical terms by writing directions for navigating from the center of the brain to the cortex located at the most anterior point of the brain and the ventral surface of the brain to the most caudal point in the cortex.

Development of the Nervous System

Although the brain is complicated, an understanding of the basic features of brain development can make it easier to learn and remember the location of the most important structures. With that end in mind, we introduce these features here in the context of development of the central nervous system. The CNS begins early in embryonic life as a hollow tube and maintains this basic shape even after it is fully developed. During development, parts of the tube elongate, pockets and folds form, and the tissue around the tube thickens until the brain reaches its final form.

An Overview of Brain Development

LO 3.4 **Summarize the process of human brain development from ectoderm plate, to neural tube, to three interconnected chambers.**

Development of the human nervous system begins around the eighteenth day after conception. Part of the *ectoderm* (outer layer) of the back of the embryo thickens and forms a plate. The edges of this plate form ridges that curl toward each other along a longitudinal line, running in a rostral–caudal direction. By the twenty-first day these ridges touch each other and fuse together, forming a tube—the **neural tube**—which gives rise to the brain and spinal cord. The top part of the ridges break away from the neural tube and become the ganglia of the autonomic nervous system, described later in this chapter. (See Figure 3.6.)

By the twenty-eighth day of development the neural tube is closed, and its rostral end has developed three interconnected chambers. These chambers become ventricles, and the tissue that surrounds them becomes the three major parts of the brain: the forebrain, the midbrain, and the hindbrain. (See Figures 3.7a and 3.7c.) As development progresses, the rostral chamber (the forebrain) divides into three separate parts, which become the two lateral ventricles and the third ventricle. The region around the lateral ventricles becomes the telencephalon ("end brain"), and the region around the third ventricle becomes the diencephalon ("interbrain"). (See Figures 3.7b and 3.7d.) In its final form, the chamber inside the midbrain (mesencephalon) becomes narrow, forming the cerebral aqueduct, and two structures develop in the hindbrain: the metencephalon ("afterbrain") and the myelencephalon ("marrowbrain"). (See Figure 3.7e.)

Table 3.1 summarizes the terms introduced here and mentions some of the major structures found in each part of the brain. The colors in the table match those in Figure 3.7. These structures will be described in the remainder of the chapter.

Figure 3.6 Neural Plate Development

The figure shows development of the neural plate into the neural tube, which gives rise to the brain and spinal cord. *Left:* Dorsal views. *Right:* Cross section at levels indicated by dashed lines.

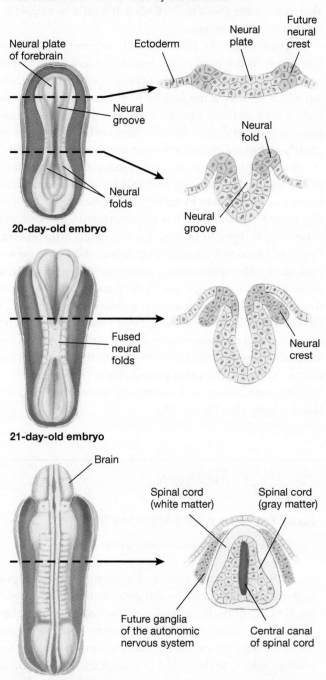

Prenatal Brain Development

LO 3.5 **Explain how prenatal development contributes to the development of complex human brains.**

Brain development begins with a thin tube and ends with a structure weighing approximately 1,400 g (about 3 lb)

Figure 3.7 Brain Development

This schematic outline of brain development shows its relation to the ventricles. Views (a) and (c) show early development. Views (b) and (d) show later development. View (e) shows a lateral view of the left side of a semitransparent human brain with the brain stem "ghosted in." The colors of all figures denote corresponding regions.

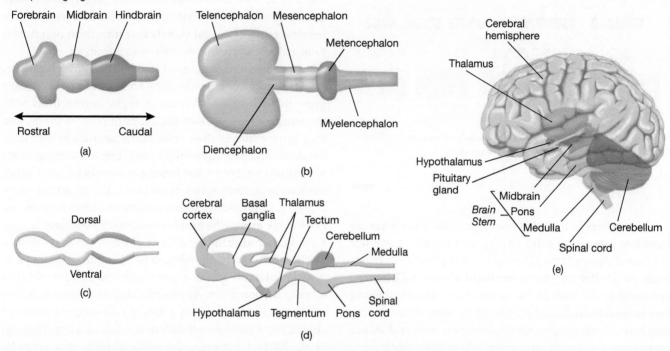

Table 3.1 Anatomical Subdivisions of the Brain

Major Division	Ventricle	Subdivision	Principal Structures
Forebrain	Lateral	Telencephalon	Cerebral cortex
			Basal ganglia
			Limbic system
	Third	Diencephalon	Thalamus
			Hypothalamus
Midbrain	Cerebral aqueduct	Mesencephalon	Tectum Tegmentum
Hindbrain	Fourth	Metencephalon	Cerebellum
			Pons
		Myelencephalon	Medulla oblongata

and consisting of hundreds of billions of cells. Where do these cells come from, and what controls their growth?

Let's consider the development of the cerebral cortex, about which most is known. The principles described here are similar to the ones that apply to development of other regions of the brain. (For details of this process, see Cooper, 2008, and Rakic, 2009.) The **cerebral cortex,** approximately 3 mm thick, surrounds the cerebral hemispheres. Corrected for body size, the cerebral cortex is larger in humans than in any other species. As we will see later in this book, circuits of neurons in the cerebral cortex play a vital role in perception, cognition, and control of movement.

Stem cells that line the inside of the neural tube give rise to the cells of the CNS. The cerebral cortex develops from the inside out. That is, the first cells to be produced migrate a short distance and establish the first—and deepest—layer. The next wave of newborn cells passes through the first layer and forms the second one—and so on, until all six layers of the cerebral cortex are laid down. The last cells to be produced must pass through all the cells born before them.

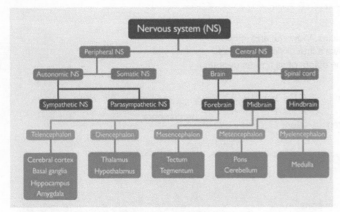

The CNS develops from a plate of cells to a hollow tube and maintains this basic shape even after it is fully developed.

The stem cells that give rise to the cells of the brain are known as **progenitor cells.** (A *progenitor* is a direct ancestor of a line of descendants.) During the first phase of development, progenitor cells in the **ventricular zone (VZ),** located just outside the wall of the neural tube, divide, making new progenitor cells and increasing the size of the ventricular zone. Some progenitor cells migrate a short distance away from the ventricular zone, where they continue to divide into more progenitor cells and establish the **subventricular zone (SVZ).** This phase is referred to as **symmetrical division,** because the division of each progenitor cell produces two new progenitor cells. This form of division increases the size of the ventricular and subventricular zones. Then, seven weeks after conception, progenitor cells receive a signal to begin a period of **asymmetrical division.** During this phase, progenitor cells form two different kinds of cells as they divide: another progenitor cell and a brain cell.

The first brain cells produced through asymmetrical division are **radial glia.** The cell bodies of radial glia remain close to the wall of the neural tube, in the VZ and SVZ, but they extend fibers radially outward from the ventricular zone, like spokes in a wheel. These fibers end in cuplike feet that attach to the pia mater, located at the outer surface of what becomes the cerebral cortex. As the cortex becomes thicker, the fibers of the radial glia grow longer and maintain their connections with the pia mater. (See Figure 3.8.)

The period of asymmetrical division lasts about three months. Because the human cerebral cortex contains about 100 billion neurons, there are about one billion neurons migrating along radial glial fibers on a given day. The migration path of the earliest neurons is the shortest and takes about one day. The neurons that produce the last, outermost layer have to pass through five layers of neurons, and their migration takes about two weeks. The end of cortical

development occurs when the progenitor cells receive a chemical signal that causes them to die—a phenomenon known as **apoptosis** (literally, a "falling away"). Molecules of the chemical that conveys this signal bind with receptors that activate killer genes within the cells. (All cells have these genes, but only certain cells possess the receptors that respond to the chemical signals that turn them on.) At this time, radial glia are transformed into astrocytes.

Once neurons have migrated to their final locations, they begin forming connections with other neurons. They grow dendrites, which form synaptic connections with the terminal buttons from the axons of other neurons, and they grow axons of their own. Some neurons extend their dendrites and axons laterally, connecting adjacent columns of neurons or even establishing connections with other neurons in distant regions of the brain. The growth of axons is guided by physical and chemical factors. Once the growing ends of the axons (the *growth cones*) reach their targets, they form numerous branches. Each of these branches finds a vacant place on the membrane of the appropriate type of postsynaptic cell, grows a terminal button, and establishes a synaptic connection. Apparently, different types of cells— or even different parts of a single cell—secrete different chemicals, which attract different types of axons (Benson et al., 2001). Of course, the establishment of a synaptic connection also requires effort on the part of the postsynaptic cell; this cell must contribute its parts of the synapse, including the postsynaptic receptors. The chemical signals that the cells exchange to tell one another to establish these connections are just now being discovered.

The ventricular zone gives rise to more neurons than are needed. In fact, these neurons must compete to survive. The axons of approximately 50 percent of these neurons do not find vacant postsynaptic cells of the right type with which to form synaptic connections, so they die by apoptosis. This phenomenon (sometimes called "pruning"), too, involves a chemical signal; when a presynaptic neuron establishes synaptic connections, it receives a signal from the postsynaptic cell that permits it to survive. The neurons that come too late do not find any available space and therefore do not receive this life-sustaining signal. This scheme might seem wasteful, but apparently the evolutionary process found that the safest strategy was to produce too many neurons and let them fight to establish synaptic connections rather than trying to produce exactly the right number of each type of neuron.

DEVELOPMENT OF COMPLEX BRAINS   As we saw in Chapter 1, the human brain is larger than that of any other large animal when corrected for body size—more than three times larger than that of a chimpanzee, our closest relative. What types of genetic changes are required to produce a large brain?

Figure 3.8 Cortical Development

This cross section through the cerebral cortex shows it early in its development. The radially oriented fibers of glial cells help to guide the migration of newly formed neurons from the ventricular zone to their final resting place in the cerebral cortex. Each successive wave of neurons passes neurons that migrated earlier, so the most recently formed neurons occupy layers closer to the cortical surface.

(Adapted from Rakic, P., A small step for the cell, a giant leap for mankind: A hypothesis of neocortical expansion during evolution, *Trends in Neuroscience*, 1995, *18*, 383–388.)

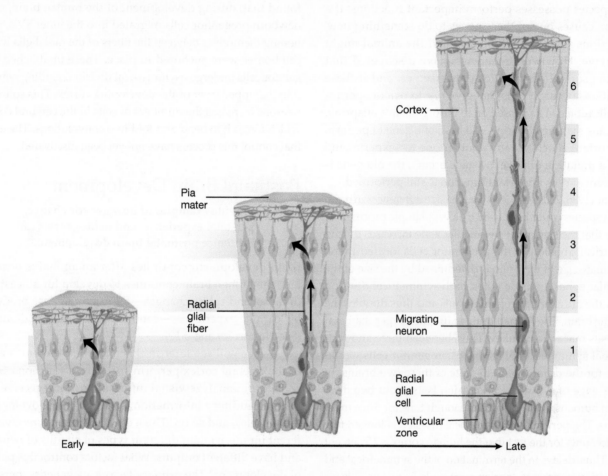

Pia mater

Radial glial fiber

Cortex

Migrating neuron

Radial glial cell

Ventricular zone

6
5
4
3
2
1

Early ⟶ Late

Figure 3.9 Refining Neural Connections: Overproduction and Refinement

Experience shapes brain architecture by early overproduction of neurons, followed by later apoptosis and refinement of synaptic connections based on learning and exposure to stimuli.

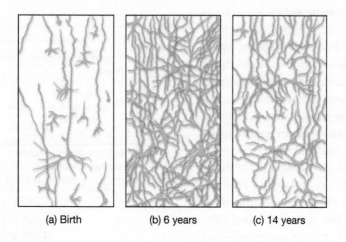

(a) Birth   (b) 6 years   (c) 14 years

The brains of the earliest vertebrates were smaller and less complex than those of later animals. The evolutionary process brought about genetic changes that were responsible for the development of more complex brains, with more parts and more interconnections. An important factor in the evolution of more complex brains is genetic duplication (Allman, 1999). As Lewis (1992) noted, most of the genes that a species possesses perform important functions. If a mutation causes one of these genes to do something new, the previous function will be lost, and the animal might not survive. However, geneticists have discovered that genes can sometimes duplicate themselves, and if these duplications occur in cells that give rise to ova or sperms, the duplication can be passed on to the organism's offspring. This means that the offspring will have one gene to perform the important functions and another one to "experiment" with. If a mutation of the extra gene occurs, the old gene is still present and its important function is still performed.

Rakic (1988, 2009) suggests that the size differences in brain between species could be caused by a very simple process. We just saw that the size of the ventricular zone increases during symmetrical division of the progenitor cells located there. The ultimate size of the brain is determined by the size of the ventricular zone. As Rakic notes, each symmetrical division doubles the number of progenitor cells and thus doubles the size of the brain. The human brain is 10 times larger than that of a rhesus macaque monkey. Thus, between three and four additional symmetrical divisions of progenitor cells would account for the difference in the size of these two brains. In fact, the stage of symmetrical division lasts about two days longer in humans, which provides enough time for three more divisions. The period of asymmetrical division is longer, too, which accounts for the fact that the human cortex is 15 percent thicker. Thus, delays in the termination of the symmetrical and asymmetrical periods of development could be responsible for the increased size of the human brain. A few simple mutations of the genes that control the timing of brain development could be responsible for these delays.

Small mammals such as rodents have brains with a relatively smooth outer surface, which limits the size of the cerebral cortex that cover them. Larger brains, especially those of the larger primates, have convoluted brains—brains with a surface covered by grooves and bulges. Convolutions greatly increase the surface area of the cerebral cortex, which means that the cortex of a convoluted brain contains many more neurons than that of a smooth brain. The increased number of neurons in the convoluted human cerebral cortex makes possible the complex circuitry found in our brains.

Two studies appear to have discovered an important aspect of the process responsible for the development of convoluted brains. The subventricular zone of convoluted brains is much thicker than that of smooth brains. In fact, this zone can be divided into two parts, the inner SVZ and the outer SVZ. (The inner SVZ is located closer to the wall of the neural tube, and the outer SVZ is located closer to the surface of the brain.)

In smooth-brained animals such as rodents, all of the cells of the brain derive from progenitor cells located in the ventricular and subventricular zones. Because the cell bodies of the radial glia that develop from the progenitor cells are locked in place, the surface of the developing cortex remains more or less parallel to the wall of the neural tube, which means that it will remain smooth. Fietz et al. (2010) and Hansen et al. (2010) found that, during development of the human brain, some newborn progenitor cells migrated into the inner SVZ, positioning themselves between the fibers of the radial glia whose cell bodies were anchored in place. These unattached progenitor cells undergo asymmetrical division, sending neurons into the upper layer of the developing cortex. This source of neurons increases the numbers of cells in the cerebral cortex, which forces it to bend and fold into convolutions. The genes that control this process have not yet been discovered.

Postnatal Brain Development

LO 3.6 Provide examples of how genetic change, personal experience, and neurogenesis can influence postnatal brain development.

Brain development continues after an animal is born. In fact, the human brain continues to develop for at least two decades, and subtle changes—for example those produced by learning experiences—continue to occur throughout life. (See Figures 3.9 and 3.10)

As we will see later in this chapter, different regions of the cerebral cortex perform specialized functions. Some receive and analyze visual information, some receive and analyze auditory information, some control movement of the muscles, and so on. Thus, different regions receive different inputs, contain different types of circuits of neurons, and have different outputs. What factors control this pattern of development? The primary factors are genetics, personal experience, and a process known as neurogenesis.

Some of the specialization is undoubtedly programmed genetically. The neurons produced by the asymmetrical division of a particular progenitor cell all follow a particular radial glial fiber, so they end up more or less above the

Figure 3.10 Pre and Postnatal Brain Development
Brain development begins during the prenatal period and extends through adulthood.

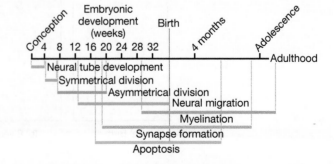

progenitor cell. Thus, if the progenitor cells in different regions of the developing brain are themselves different, the neurons they produce will reflect these differences.

Experience also affects brain development. For example, one cue for depth perception arises from the fact that each eye gets a slightly different view of the world (Poggio & Poggio, 1984). This form of depth perception, *stereopsis*, is the kind obtained from a stereoscope or a three-dimensional movie. The particular neural circuits that are necessary for stereopsis, which are located in the cerebral cortex, will not develop unless an infant has experience viewing objects with both eyes during a critical period early in life. If an infant's eyes do not move together properly—if they are not directed toward the same place in the environment (that is, if the eyes are "crossed")—the infant never develops stereoscopic vision, even if the eye movements are later corrected by surgery on the eye muscles. This critical period occurs sometime between one and three years of age (Banks et al., 1975). Similar phenomena have been studied in laboratory animals and have confirmed that sensory input affects the connections established between cortical neurons.

Evidence indicates that a certain amount of neural rewiring can be accomplished even in the adult brain. For example, after a person's arm has been amputated, the region of the cerebral cortex that previously analyzed sensory information from the missing limb soon begins analyzing information from adjacent regions of the body, such as the stump of the arm, the trunk, or the face. In fact, the person becomes more sensitive to touch in these regions after the changes in the cortex take place (Elbert et al., 1994; Kew et al., 1994; Yang et al., 1994). In addition, musicians who play stringed instruments have a larger cortical region devoted to analysis of sensory information from the fingers of the left hand (which they use to press the strings), and when a blind person who can read Braille touches objects with his or her fingertips, an enlarged region of the cerebral cortex is activated (Elbert et al., 1995; Sadato et al., 1996).

For many years, researchers believed that neurogenesis—production of new neurons—could not take place in the fully developed brain. However, many studies have shown this belief to be incorrect—the adult brain contains some stem cells (similar to the progenitor cells that give rise to the cells of the developing brain) that can divide and produce neurons. Detection of newly produced cells is done by administering a small amount of a radioactive form of one of the nucleotide bases that cells use to produce the DNA that is needed for neurogenesis. The next day, the animals' brains are removed and examined with methods described in Chapter 5. Such studies have found evidence for neurogenesis in two parts of the adult brain: the hippocampus, primarily involved in learning, and the olfactory bulb, involved in the sense of smell (Doetsch & Hen, 2005). Evidence indicates that exposure to new odors can increase the survival rate of new neurons in the olfactory bulbs, and training on a learning task can enhance neurogenesis in the hippocampus. (See Figure 3.11.) Chapter 13 has more to say about the role of neurogenesis in learning. In addition, as we will see in Chapter 16, depression or exposure to stress can suppress neurogenesis in the hippocampus, and drugs that reduce stress and depression can reinstate neurogenesis. Unfortunately, there is no evidence that growth of new neurons can repair the effects of brain damage, such as that caused by head injury or strokes.

Figure 3.11 Neurogenesis in the Adult Brain

Neurogenesis has been demonstrated in the adult brain in the olfactory bulb and the hippocampus.

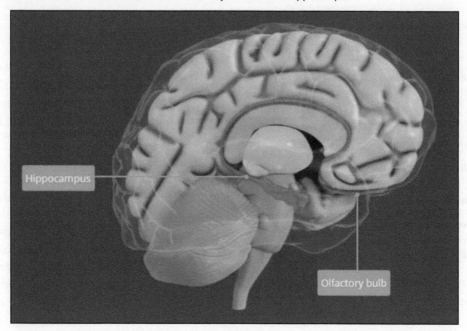

Section Review

Development of the Nervous System

LO 3.4 Summarize the process of human brain development from ectoderm plate, to neural tube, to three interconnected chambers.

The ectoderm begins to develop at approximately embryonic day 18. As more cells are added to the neural plate, the edges of the plate begin to curl together, forming the neural tube at approximately embryonic day 20. The neural tube fuses together at approximately embryonic day 28. The tube then begins to develop three interconnected chambers that will become the forebrain, midbrain, and hindbrain in the fully developed brain.

LO 3.5 Explain how prenatal development contributes to the development of complex human brains.

The development of complex human brains begins during prenatal development. The cerebral cortex of humans develops from the inside out, as progenitor cells from the ventricular system move into their final positions in the cortex. Initial brain cell development occurs during a period of symmetrical division, followed by period of asymmetrical division when the embryo is seven weeks old. Asymmetrical division lasts for approximately three months and produces radial glia, which help to establish the cortex. Once neurons have migrated to their final locations, they begin forming connections with other neurons. The axons of approximately 50 percent of the new neurons do not form synaptic connections, so they die by apoptosis. Larger brains, especially those of the larger primates, are convoluted. Convolutions greatly increase the surface area of the cerebral cortex, which means that the cortex of a convoluted brain contains many more neurons than that of a smooth brain. The increased number of neurons in the convoluted human cerebral cortex makes possible the complex circuitry found in our brains.

LO 3.6 Provide examples of how genetic change, personal experience, and neurogenesis can influence postnatal brain development.

Genetically, if the progenitor cells in different regions of the developing brain are themselves different, the neurons they produce will reflect these differences. Experience viewing objects with both eyes contributes to the development of brain regions involved in stereopsis and is an example of how personal experience can influence postnatal brain development. Another example of the effect of experience on postnatal brain development is when a person who can read Braille touches objects with his or her fingertips, an enlarged region of the cerebral cortex is activated. Finally, new neurons are produced in the hippocampus and olfactory bulb throughout the lifespan.

Thought Question

Many health care providers recommend that women consume folic acid (a B vitamin) before and during a pregnancy to reduce the risk of birth defects related to development of the nervous system. Insufficient folic acid can contribute to problems in neural tube development including spina bifida (problems of spinal cord development) or anencephaly (problems of brain development). Which parts of the developing nervous system might be most affected by spina bifida or anencephaly? How early in pregnancy might a neural tube defect occur? (Hint: What is the age of an embryo when the neural tube develops?)

Structure and Function of the Central Nervous System

The Forebrain

LO 3.7 Identify the structures and functions of the forebrain, including the telencephalon and diencephalon.

As we saw, the **forebrain** develops from the rostral end of the neural tube. Its two major components are the telencephalon and the diencephalon. (See Figure 3.12.)

TELENCEPHALON The telencephalon includes most of the two symmetrical **cerebral hemispheres** that make up the cerebrum. The cerebral hemispheres are covered by the cerebral cortex and contain the limbic system and the basal ganglia. The latter two sets of structures are primarily in the **subcortical regions** of the brain—those located deep within it, beneath the cerebral cortex.

Cerebral Cortex As we saw previously, the cerebral cortex surrounds the cerebral hemispheres like the bark of a tree. In humans the cerebral cortex is greatly convoluted; these convolutions, consisting of **sulci** (small grooves), **fissures** (large grooves), and **gyri** (bulges between adjacent sulci or fissures), greatly enlarge the surface area of the cortex, compared with a smooth brain of the same size. In fact, two-thirds of the surface of the cortex is hidden in the grooves; thus, the presence of these convolutions triples the area of

Figure 3.12 Forebrain

The forebrain is the most dorsal division of the brain. The forebrain consists of the telencephalon and the diencephalon.

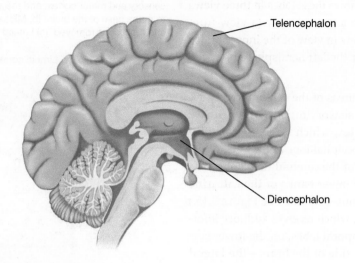

the cerebral cortex. The total surface area is approximately 2,360 cm² (2.5 ft.²), and the thickness is approximately 3 mm. The cerebral cortex consists mostly of glia and the cell bodies, dendrites, and interconnecting axons of neurons. Because cell bodies predominate, giving the cerebral cortex a grayish tan appearance, it is referred to as *gray matter*. (See Figure 3.13.) Beneath the cerebral cortex run millions of axons that connect the neurons of the cerebral cortex with those located elsewhere in the brain. The large concentration of myelin gives this tissue an opaque white appearance—hence the term *white matter*.

Lobes of the Cerebral Cortex   Discussing the various regions of the cerebral cortex is easier if we have names for them. In fact, the cerebral cortex is divided into four areas, or *lobes*, named for the bones of the skull that cover them: the frontal lobe, parietal lobe, temporal lobe, and occipital lobe. The brain contains two of each lobe, one in each hemisphere. The **frontal lobe** (the "front") includes everything in front of the central sulcus. The **parietal lobe** (the "wall") is located on the side of the cerebral hemisphere, just behind the central sulcus, caudal to the frontal lobe. The **temporal lobe** (the "temple") juts forward from the base of the brain,

Figure 3.13 Cross Section of Human Brain

This brain slice shows fissures and gyri and the layer of cerebral cortex that follows these convolutions.

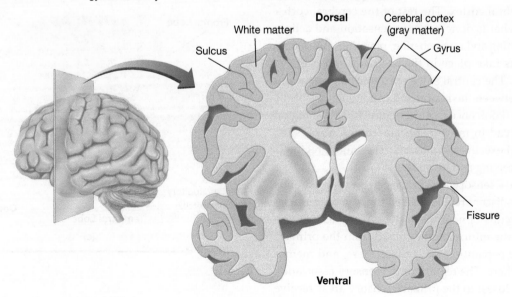

ventral to the frontal and parietal lobes. The **occipital lobe** (from the Latin *ob*, "in back of," and *caput*, "head") lies at the very back of the brain, caudal to the parietal and temporal lobes. Figure 3.14 shows these lobes in three views of the cerebral hemispheres: a ventral view (a view from the bottom), a midsagittal view (a view of the inner surface of the right hemisphere after the left hemisphere has been removed), and a lateral view.

SENSORY CORTEX Three areas of the cerebral cortex receive information from the sensory organs. The **primary visual cortex**, or **striate cortex**, which receives visual information, is located in the occipital lobe at the back of the brain, on the inner surfaces of the cerebral hemispheres—primarily on the upper and lower banks of the **calcarine fissure**. (*Calcarine* means "spur-shaped." See Figure 3.15.) The **primary auditory cortex**, which receives auditory information, is located in the temporal lobes, on the lower surface of a deep fissure in the side of the brain—the **lateral fissure**. (See the inset in Figure 3.15.) The **primary somatosensory cortex**, a vertical strip of cortex just caudal to the **central sulcus** in the parietal lobe, receives information from the body senses. As Figure 3.15 shows, different regions of the primary somatosensory cortex receive information from different regions of the body. In addition, the base of the somatosensory cortex and a portion of the **insular cortex**, which is normally hidden from view by the frontal and temporal lobes, receive information concerning taste.

With the exception of olfaction (smell) and gustation (taste), sensory information from the body or the environment is sent to primary sensory cortex of the contralateral hemisphere. Thus, the primary somatosensory cortex of the left hemisphere learns what the right hand is holding, the left primary visual cortex learns what is happening toward the person's right, and so on.

SENSORY ASSOCIATION CORTEX The regions of primary sensory and motor cortex occupy only a small part of the cerebral cortex. The rest of the cerebral cortex accomplishes what is done between sensation and action: perceiving, learning and remembering, planning, and acting. These processes take place in the *association areas* of the cerebral cortex. The central sulcus provides an important dividing line between the rostral and caudal regions of the cerebral cortex. (Look once more at Figure 3.15.) The rostral region is involved in movement-related activities, such as planning and executing behaviors. The caudal region is involved in perceiving and learning.

Each primary sensory area of the cerebral cortex sends information to adjacent regions, called the **sensory association cortex**. Circuits of neurons in the sensory association cortex analyze the information received from the primary sensory cortex; perception takes place there, and memories are stored there. The regions of the sensory association cortex located closest to the primary sensory areas receive

Figure 3.14 The Four Lobes of the Cerebral Cortex

The two symmetrical hemispheres of the cortex are divided into four lobes. This figure shows the location of the four lobes, the primary sensory and motor cortex, and the association cortex. (a) Ventral view, from the base of the brain. (b) Midsagittal view, with the cerebellum and brain stem removed. (c) Lateral view.

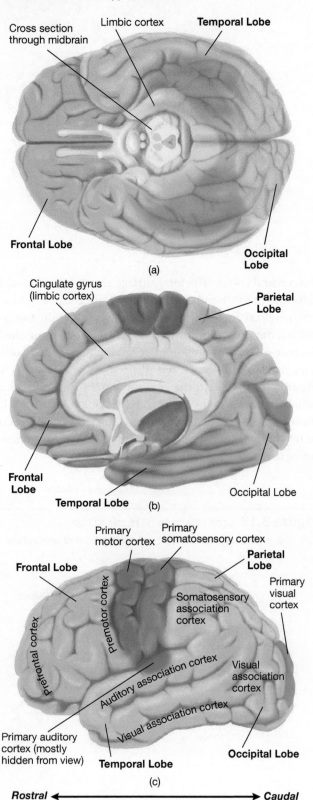

information from only one sensory system. For example, the region closest to the primary visual cortex analyzes visual information and stores visual memories. Regions of the sensory association cortex located far from the primary sensory areas receive information from more than one sensory system; thus, they are involved in several kinds of perceptions and memories. These regions make it possible to integrate information from more than one sensory system. For example, we can learn the connection between the sight of a particular face and the sound of a particular voice. (Look again at Figure 3.15.)

If people sustain damage to the somatosensory association cortex, their deficits are related to somatosensation and to the environment in general; for example, they may have difficulty perceiving the shapes of objects that they can touch but not see, they may be unable to name parts of their bodies (see the following case of Mr. M.), or they may have trouble drawing maps or following them. Destruction of the primary visual cortex causes blindness. However, although people who sustain damage to the visual association cortex will not become blind, they may be unable to recognize objects by sight. People who sustain damage to the auditory association cortex may have difficulty perceiving speech or even producing meaningful speech of their own. People who sustain damage to regions of the association cortex at the junction of the three posterior lobes, where the somatosensory, visual, and auditory functions overlap, may have difficulty reading or writing.

Mr. M., a city bus driver, stopped to let a passenger climb board. The passenger asked him a question, and Mr. M. suddenly realized that he didn't understand what she was saying. He could hear her, but her words made no sense. He opened his mouth to reply. He made some sounds, but the look on the woman's face told him that she couldn't understand what he was trying to say. He turned off the engine and looked around at the passengers and tried to tell them to get some help. Although he was unable to say anything, they understood that something was wrong, and one of them called an ambulance.

An MRI scan showed that Mr. M. had sustained an intracerebral hemorrhage—a kind of stroke caused by rupture of blood vessels in the brain. The stroke had damaged his left parietal lobe. Mr. M. gradually regained the ability to talk and understand the speech of others, but some deficits remained. A neurologist examined Mr. M. several weeks after his stroke. The dialogue went something like this:

Figure 3.15 The Primary Sensory Regions of the Brain

The figure shows a lateral view of the left side of a human brain and part of the inner surface of the right side. The inset shows a cutaway of part of the frontal lobe of the left hemisphere, permitting us to see the primary auditory cortex on the dorsal surface of the temporal lobe, which forms the ventral bank of the lateral fissure.

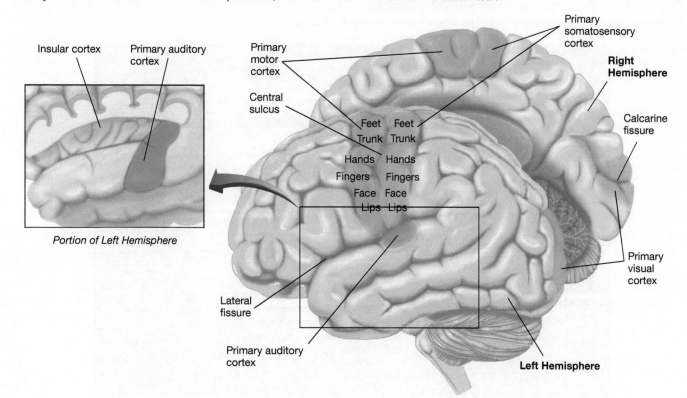

"Show me your hand."

"My hand . . . my hand." Looks at his arms, then touches his left forearm.

"Show me your chin."

"My chin." Looks at his arms, looks down, puts his hand on his abdomen.

"Show me your right elbow."

"My right . . ." (points to the right with his right thumb) "elbow." Looks up and down his right arm, finally touches his right shoulder.

Mr. M. could understand that the physician was asking him to point out parts of his body and could repeat the names of the body parts when he heard them, but he could not identify which body parts these names referred to. This strange deficit, which sometimes follows damage to the left parietal lobe, is called *autotopagnosia,* or "poor knowledge of one's own topography. The parietal lobes are involved with space: the right primarily with external space and the left with one's body and personal space. You will learn more about disorders such as this one in Chapter 14, which deals with brain mechanisms of language.

Motor Cortex   The region of the cerebral cortex that is most directly involved in the control of movement is the **primary motor cortex,** located just in front of the primary somatosensory cortex. Neurons in different parts of the primary motor cortex are connected to muscles in different parts of the body. The connections, like those of the sensory regions of the cerebral cortex, are contralateral; the left primary motor cortex controls the right side of the body and vice versa. Thus, if a surgeon places an electrode on the surface of the primary motor cortex and stimulates the neurons there with a weak electrical current, the result will be movement of a particular part of the body. Moving the electrode to a different spot will cause a different part of the body to move. (Look again at Figure 3.15.) You can think of the strip of primary motor cortex as the keyboard of a piano, with each key controlling a different movement. (We will see shortly who the "player" of this piano is.)

Motor Association Cortex   Just as regions of the sensory association cortex of the posterior part of the brain are involved in perceiving and remembering, the frontal association cortex is involved in the planning and execution of movements. The **motor association cortex** (also known as the *premotor cortex*) is located just rostral to the primary motor cortex. This region controls the primary motor cortex; thus, it directly controls behavior. If the primary motor cortex is the keyboard of the piano, then the motor association cortex is the piano player. The rest of the frontal lobe, rostral to the motor association cortex, is known as the **prefrontal cortex.** This region of the brain is less involved with the control of movement and more involved in formulating plans and strategies. (See Figure 3.16.)

Figure 3.16 Role of Cortical Regions in Motor Control

The motor, premotor, and prefrontal cortex all contribute to motor control in the cortex.

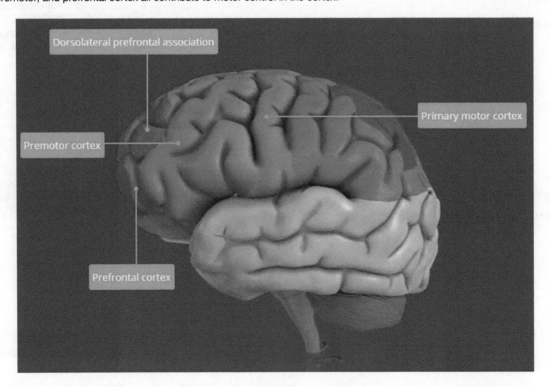

Lateralization in the Cerebral Cortex   Although the two cerebral hemispheres cooperate with each other, they do not perform identical functions. Some functions are *lateralized*—located primarily on one side of the brain. In general, the left hemisphere participates in the *analysis* of information—the extraction of the elements that make up the whole of an experience. This ability makes the left hemisphere particularly good at recognizing *serial events*—events whose elements occur one after the other—and controlling sequences of behavior. (In a few people, the functions of the left and right hemispheres are reversed.) The serial functions that are performed by the left hemisphere include verbal activities, such as talking, understanding the speech of other people, reading, and writing. These abilities are disrupted by damage to the various regions of the left hemisphere. (We will say more about language and the brain in Chapter 14.)

In contrast, the right hemisphere is specialized for *synthesis;* it is particularly good at putting isolated elements together to perceive things as a whole. For example, our ability to draw sketches (especially of three-dimensional objects), read maps, and construct complex objects out of smaller elements depends heavily on circuits of neurons that are located in the right hemisphere. Damage to the right hemisphere disrupts these abilities.

As we go about our daily lives we are not aware of the fact that each hemisphere perceives the world differently. Although the two cerebral hemispheres perform somewhat different functions, our perceptions and our memories are unified. This unity is accomplished by the **corpus callosum,** a large band of axons that connects corresponding parts of the cerebral cortex of the left and right hemispheres: The left and right temporal lobes are connected, the left and right parietal lobes are connected, and so on. Because of the corpus callosum, each region of the association cortex knows what is happening in the corresponding region of the opposite side of the brain. The corpus callosum also makes a few asymmetrical connections that link different regions of the two hemispheres. Figure 3.17 shows the bundles of axons that constitute the corpus callosum, obtained by means of *diffusion tensor imaging,* a special scanning method described in Chapter 5.

Limbic System   Figure 3.18 shows a *midsagittal* view of the brain. The brain (and part of the spinal cord) has been sliced down the middle, dividing it into its two symmetrical halves. The left half has been removed, so we see the inner surface of the right half. The cerebral cortex that covers most of the surface of the cerebral hemispheres (including the frontal, parietal, occipital, and temporal lobes) is called the **neocortex** ("new" cortex, because it is of relatively recent evolutionary origin). Another form of cerebral cortex, the **limbic cortex,** is located around the medial edge of the cerebral hemispheres (*limbus* means "border"). The **cingulate gyrus,** an important region of

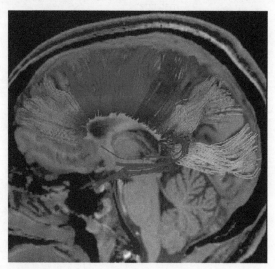

Figure 3.17 Bundles of Axons in the Corpus Callosum

This figure, obtained by means of diffusion tensor imaging, shows bundles of axons in the corpus callosum that serve different regions of the cerebral cortex.

(From Hofer, S., and Frahm, J. Topography of the human corpus callosum revisited—comprehensive fiber tractography using diffusion tensor magnetic resonance imaging. *NeuroImage*, 2006, 32, 989–994. Reprinted with permission.)

the limbic cortex, can be seen in this figure. In addition, if you look back at the top two drawings of Figure 3.14, you will see that the limbic cortex occupies the regions in the center of the brain that have not been colored in.

A neuroanatomist, Papez (1937), suggested that a set of interconnected brain structures formed a circuit whose primary function was motivation and emotion. This system included several regions of the limbic cortex and a set of interconnected structures surrounding the core of the forebrain. A physiologist, MacLean (1949), expanded the system to include other structures and coined the term **limbic system.** Besides the limbic cortex, the most important parts of the limbic system are the **hippocampus** ("sea horse") and the **amygdala** ("almond"), located next to the lateral ventricle in the temporal lobe. The **fornix** ("arch") is a bundle of axons that connects the hippocampus with other regions of the brain, including the **mammillary** ("breast-shaped") **bodies,** protrusions on the base of the brain that contain parts of the hypothalamus. (See Figure 3.19.)

MacLean noted that the evolution of this system, which includes the first and simplest form of cerebral cortex, appears to have coincided with the development of emotional responses. As you will see in Chapter 13, we now know that parts of the limbic system (notably, the hippocampal formation and the region of limbic cortex that surrounds it) are involved in learning and memory. The amygdala and some regions of the limbic cortex are specifically involved in emotions: feelings and expressions of emotions, emotional memories, and recognition of the signs of emotions in other people.

Figure 3.18 The Midsagittal View of the Brain and Part of the Spinal Cord

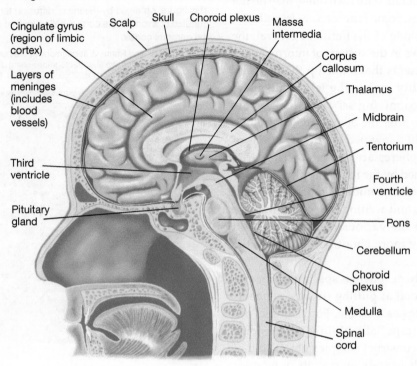

Cingulate gyrus (region of limbic cortex)
Scalp
Skull
Choroid plexus
Massa intermedia
Corpus callosum
Thalamus
Midbrain
Tentorium
Fourth ventricle
Pons
Cerebellum
Choroid plexus
Medulla
Spinal cord
Layers of meninges (includes blood vessels)
Third ventricle
Pituitary gland

Figure 3.19 The Major Components of the Limbic System

All of the left hemisphere except for the limbic system has been removed.

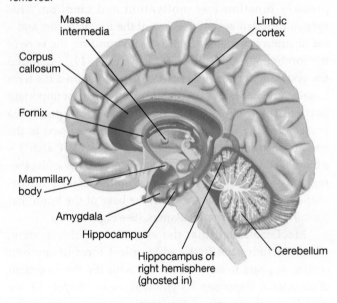

Massa intermedia
Limbic cortex
Corpus callosum
Fornix
Mammillary body
Amygdala
Hippocampus
Hippocampus of right hemisphere (ghosted in)
Cerebellum

Basal Ganglia The **basal ganglia** are a collection of *nuclei* below the cortex in the forebrain, which lie beneath the anterior portion of the lateral ventricles. Nuclei are groups of neurons of similar shape. (The word *nucleus* can refer to the inner portion of an atom, to the structure of a cell that contains the chromosomes, and—as in this case—to a collection of neurons located within the brain.) The major parts of the basal ganglia are the *caudate nucleus*, the *putamen*, and the *globus pallidus* (the "nucleus with a tail," the "shell," and the "pale globe"). (See Figure 3.20.) The basal ganglia are involved in the control of movement. For example, Parkinson's disease is caused by degeneration of certain neurons located in the midbrain that send axons to the caudate nucleus and the putamen. The symptoms of this disease are weakness, tremors, rigidity of the limbs, poor balance, and difficulty in initiating movements.

DIENCEPHALON The second major division of the forebrain, the **diencephalon,** is situated between the telencephalon and the mesencephalon; it surrounds the third ventricle. Its two most important structures are the thalamus and the hypothalamus. (See Figure 3.20.)

Thalamus The **thalamus** (from the Greek *thalamos,* "inner chamber") makes up the dorsal part of the diencephalon. It is situated near the middle of the cerebral hemispheres, immediately medial and caudal to the basal ganglia. The thalamus has two lobes, connected by a bridge of gray matter called the *massa intermedia,* which pierces the middle of the third ventricle. (Look again at Figure 3.20.) The massa intermedia is probably not an important structure, because it is absent in the brains of many people. However, it serves as a useful reference point in looking at diagrams of the brain.

Most neural input to the cerebral cortex is received from the thalamus; indeed, much of the cortical surface can be

Figure 3.20 The Basal Ganglia and Diencephalon

The basal ganglia and diencephalon (thalamus and hypothalamus) are ghosted in a semitransparent brain.

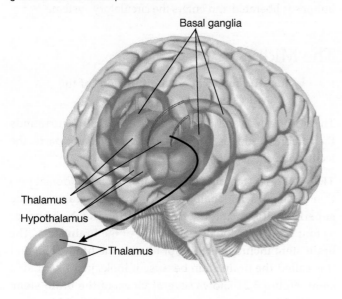

Basal ganglia

Thalamus

Hypothalamus

Thalamus

divided into regions that receive projections from specific parts of the thalamus. **Projection fibers** are sets of axons that arise from cell bodies located in one region of the brain and synapses on neurons located within other regions (that is, they *project to* these other regions).

The thalamus is divided into several nuclei. Some thalamic nuclei receive sensory information from the sensory systems. The neurons in these nuclei then relay the sensory information to specific sensory projection areas of the cerebral cortex. For example, the **lateral geniculate nucleus** receives information from the eye and sends axons to the primary visual cortex, and the **medial geniculate nucleus** receives information from the inner ear and sends axons to the primary auditory cortex. Other thalamic nuclei project to specific regions of the cerebral cortex, but they do not relay sensory information. For example, the **ventrolateral nucleus** receives information from the cerebellum and projects it to the primary motor cortex. Still other nuclei receive information from one region of the cerebral cortex and relay it to another region. And as we will see in Chapter 9, several nuclei are involved in controlling the general excitability of the cerebral cortex. To accomplish this task, these nuclei have widespread projections to all cortical regions.

Hypothalamus   As its name implies, the **hypothalamus** lies at the base of the brain, under the thalamus. Although the hypothalamus is a relatively small structure, it is an important one. It controls the autonomic nervous system and the endocrine system and organizes behaviors related to survival of the species—the so-called four *F* 's: fighting, feeding, fleeing, and mating.

The hypothalamus is situated on both sides of the ventral portion of the third ventricle. The hypothalamus is a complex structure, containing many nuclei and fiber tracts. Figure 3.21 indicates its location and size. Note that the pituitary gland is attached to the base of the hypothalamus via the pituitary stalk. Just in front of the pituitary stalk is the **optic chiasm,** where half of the axons in the optic nerves (from the eyes) cross from one side of the brain to the other. The role of the hypothalamus in the control of the four *F* 's (and other behaviors, such as drinking and sleeping) will be considered in several chapters later in this book.

Much of the endocrine system is controlled by hormones produced by cells in the hypothalamus. A special

Figure 3.21 A Midsagittal View of Part of the Brain

This view shows the hypothalamus. It is situated on the far side of the wall of the third ventricle, inside the right hemisphere.

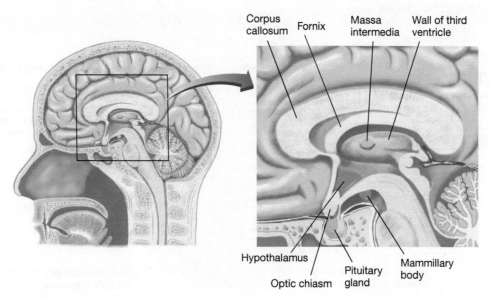

Corpus callosum   Fornix   Massa intermedia   Wall of third ventricle

Hypothalamus

Optic chiasm   Pituitary gland   Mammillary body

system of blood vessels directly connects the hypothalamus with the **anterior pituitary gland.** (See Figure 3.22.) The hypothalamic hormones are secreted by specialized neurons called **neurosecretory cells,** located near the base of the pituitary stalk. These hormones stimulate the anterior pituitary gland to secrete its hormones. For example, *gonadotropin-releasing hormone* causes the anterior pituitary gland to secrete the *gonadotropic hormones,* which play a role in reproductive physiology and behavior.

Most of the hormones secreted by the anterior pituitary gland control other endocrine glands. Because of this function, the anterior pituitary gland has been called the body's "master gland." For example, the gonadotropic hormones stimulate the gonads (ovaries and testes) to release male or female sex hormones. These hormones affect cells throughout the body, including some in the brain. Two other anterior pituitary hormones—prolactin and somatotropic hormone (growth hormone)—do not control other glands but act as the final messenger. The behavioral effects of many of the anterior pituitary hormones are discussed in later chapters.

The hypothalamus also produces the hormones of the **posterior pituitary gland** and controls their secretion. These hormones include oxytocin, which stimulates ejection of milk and uterine contractions at the time of childbirth, and vasopressin, which regulates urine output by the kidneys. They are produced by neurons in the hypothalamus whose axons travel down the pituitary stalk and terminate in the posterior pituitary gland. The hormones are carried in vesicles through the axoplasm of these neurons and collect in the terminal buttons in the posterior pituitary gland. When these axons fire, the hormone contained within their terminal buttons is liberated and enters the circulatory system.

The Midbrain

LO 3.8 **Identify the location and functions of the structures of the mesencephalon.**

The **midbrain** (also called the **mesencephalon**) surrounds the cerebral aqueduct and consists of two major parts: the tectum and the tegmentum. (See Figure 3.23.)

TECTUM The **tectum** ("roof") is located in the dorsal portion of the mesencephalon. Its principal structures are the **superior colliculi** and the **inferior colliculi,** which appear as four bumps on the dorsal surface of the **brain stem.** The brain stem includes the midbrain and the hindbrain, and it is called the brain stem because it looks just like that: a stem. Figure 3.24 shows several views of the brain stem: lateral and posterior views of the brain stem inside a semitransparent brain, an enlarged view of the brain stem with part of the cerebellum cut away to reveal the inside of the fourth ventricle, and a cross section through the midbrain. The inferior colliculi are a part of the auditory system. The superior colliculi are part of the visual system. In mammals they are primarily involved in visual reflexes and reactions to moving stimuli.

Figure 3.22 The Pituitary Gland

Hormones released by the neurosecretory cells in the hypothalamus enter capillaries and are conveyed to the anterior pituitary gland, where they control its secretion of hormones. The hormones of the posterior pituitary gland are produced in the hypothalamus and carried there in vesicles by means of axoplasmic transport.

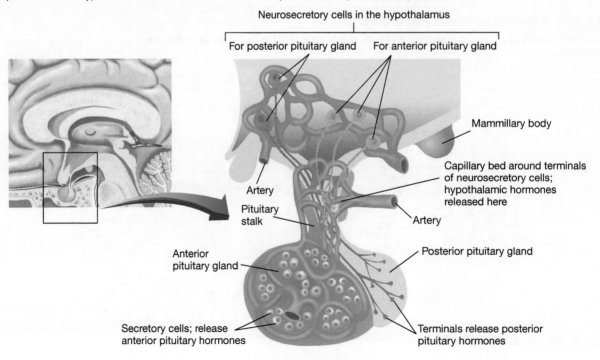

Figure 3.23 Midbrain

The midbrain, or mesencephalon, is the middle division of the brain, located dorsal to the hindbrain and ventral to the forebrain.

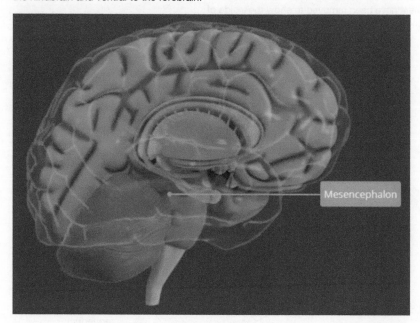

TEGMENTUM The **tegmentum** ("covering") consists of the portion of the mesencephalon beneath the tectum. It includes the rostral end of the reticular formation, several nuclei controlling eye movements, the periaqueductal gray matter, the red nucleus, the substantia nigra, and the ventral tegmental area. (See Figures 3.23 and 3.24d.)

The **reticular formation** is a large structure consisting of many nuclei (over ninety in all). It is also characterized by a diffuse, interconnected network of neurons with complex dendritic and axonal processes. (*Reticulum* means "little net"; early anatomists were struck by the netlike appearance of the reticular formation.) The reticular formation occupies the core of the brain stem, from the lower border of the medulla to the upper border of the midbrain. (Look again at Figures 3.23 and 3.24d.) The reticular formation receives sensory information by means of various pathways and projects axons to the cerebral cortex, thalamus, and spinal cord. It plays a role in sleep and arousal, attention, muscle tone, movement, and various vital reflexes. Its functions will be described more fully in later chapters.

The **periaqueductal gray matter** is so called because it consists mostly of cell bodies of neurons ("gray matter," as contrasted with the "white matter" of axon bundles) that surround the cerebral aqueduct as it travels from the third to the fourth ventricle. The periaqueductal gray matter contains neural circuits that control sequences of movements that constitute species-typical behaviors, such as fighting and mating. As we will see in Chapter 7, opiates such as morphine decrease an organism's sensitivity to pain by stimulating receptors on neurons located in this region.

The **red nucleus** and **substantia nigra** ("black substance") are important components of the motor system. A bundle of axons that arises from the red nucleus constitutes one of the two major fiber systems that bring motor information from the cerebral cortex and cerebellum to the spinal cord. The substantia nigra contains neurons whose axons project to the caudate nucleus and putamen, parts of the basal ganglia. As we will see in Chapter 4, degeneration of these neurons causes Parkinson's disease.

The Hindbrain

LO 3.9 **Contrast the locations and functions of the structures of the metencephalon and myelencephalon.**

The **hindbrain,** which surrounds the fourth ventricle, consists of two major divisions: the metencephalon and the myelencephalon.

METENCEPHALON The metencephalon consists of the cerebellum and the pons. The cerebellum is critical in coordinating movements while the pons is important in sleep/wake regulation.

Cerebellum The **cerebellum** ("little brain"), with its two hemispheres, resembles a miniature version of the cerebrum. It is covered by the **cerebellar cortex** and has a set of **deep cerebellar nuclei.** These nuclei receive projections from the cerebellar cortex and themselves send projections out of the cerebellum to other parts of the brain. Each hemisphere of the cerebellum is attached to the dorsal surface of the pons by bundles of axons: the superior, middle, and inferior **cerebellar peduncles** ("little feet"). (See Figure 3.24c.)

Damage to the cerebellum impairs standing, walking, or performance of coordinated movements. (A virtuoso pianist or other performing musician owes much to his or her cerebellum.) The cerebellum receives visual, auditory, vestibular, and somatosensory information, and it also receives information about individual muscle movements being directed by the brain. The cerebellum integrates this information and modifies the motor outflow, exerting a coordinating and smoothing effect on the movements. Cerebellar damage results in jerky, poorly coordinated, exaggerated movements; extensive cerebellar damage makes it impossible even to stand. Chapter 8 discusses the anatomy and functions of the cerebellum in more detail.

Pons The **pons,** a large bulge in the brain stem, lies between the mesencephalon and medulla oblongata, immediately ventral to the cerebellum. *Pons* means "bridge," but it does not really look like one. The pons contains, in its core, a portion of the reticular formation, including some nuclei that appear to be important in sleep and arousal. It also

Figure 3.24 The Cerebellum and the Brain Stem

This figure shows (a) a lateral view of a semitransparent brain, showing the cerebellum and brain stem ghosted in, (b) a view from the back of the brain, and (c) a dorsal view of the brain stem. The left hemisphere of the cerebellum and part of the right hemisphere have been removed to show the inside of the fourth ventricle and the cerebellar peduncles. Part (d) shows a cross section of the midbrain.

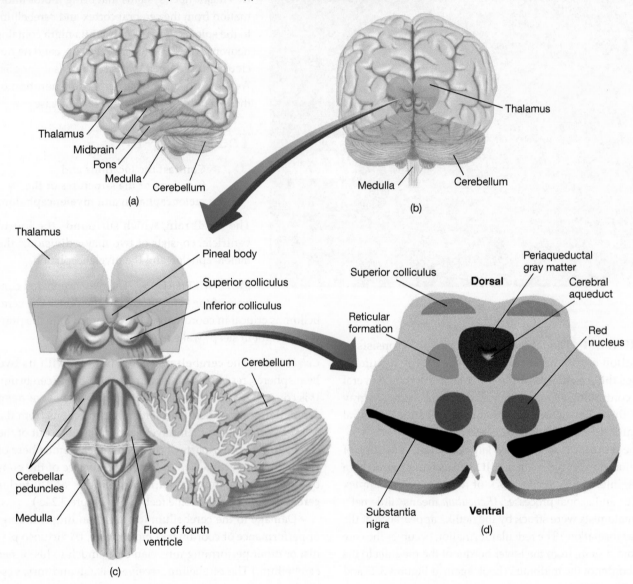

contains a large nucleus that relays information from the cerebral cortex to the cerebellum.

MYELENCEPHALON The myelencephalon contains one major structure, the **medulla oblongata** (literally, "oblong marrow"), usually just called the *medulla.* This structure is the most caudal portion of the brain stem; its lower border is the rostral end of the spinal cord. (Refer again to Figure 3.24c.) The medulla contains part of the reticular formation, including nuclei that control vital functions such as regulation of the cardiovascular system, respiration, and skeletal muscle tone.

The Spinal Cord

LO 3.10 Describe the structure and functions of the spinal cord.

The **spinal cord** is a long, conical structure, approximately as thick as your little finger. The principal functions of the spinal cord are to distribute motor fibers to the effector organs of the body (glands and muscles) and to collect somatosensory information to be passed on to the brain. The spinal cord also has a certain degree of autonomy from the brain; various reflexive control circuits (some of which are described in Chapter 8) are located there.

The spinal cord is protected by the vertebral column, which is composed of twenty-four individual vertebrae of the *cervical* (neck), *thoracic* (chest), and *lumbar* (lower back) regions and the fused vertebrae that make up the *sacral* and *coccygeal* portions of the column (located in the pelvic region). The spinal cord passes through a hole in each of the vertebrae (the *spinal foramens*). Figure 3.25 illustrates the divisions and structures of the spinal cord and vertebral column. The spinal cord is only about two-thirds as long as the vertebral column; the rest of the space is filled by a mass of **spinal roots** composing the **cauda equina** ("horse's tail").

Early in embryological development the vertebral column and spinal cord are the same length. As development progresses, the vertebral column grows faster than the spinal cord. This differential growth rate causes the spinal roots to be displaced downward; the most caudal roots travel the farthest before they emerge through openings between the vertebrae and thus compose the cauda equina. To produce the **caudal block** that is sometimes used in pelvic surgery or childbirth, a local anesthetic can be injected into the CSF contained within the sac of dura mater surrounding the cauda equina. The drug blocks conduction in the axons of the cauda equina.

Figure 3.26a shows a portion of the spinal cord, with the layers of the meninges that wrap it. Small bundles of fibers emerge from each side of the spinal cord in two straight lines along its dorsolateral and ventrolateral surfaces. Groups of

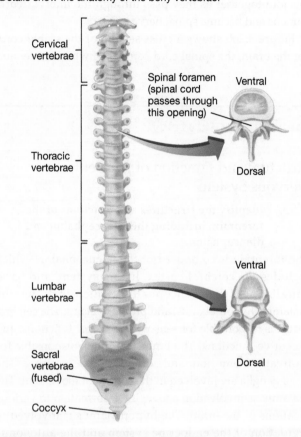

Figure 3.25 Ventral View of the Spinal Column
Details show the anatomy of the bony vertebrae.

Figure 3.26 Ventral View of the Spinal Cord
The figure shows (a) a portion of the spinal cord, showing the layers of the meninges and the relationship of the spinal cord to the vertebral column; and (b) a cross section through the spinal cord. Ascending tracts are shown in blue; descending tracts are shown in red.

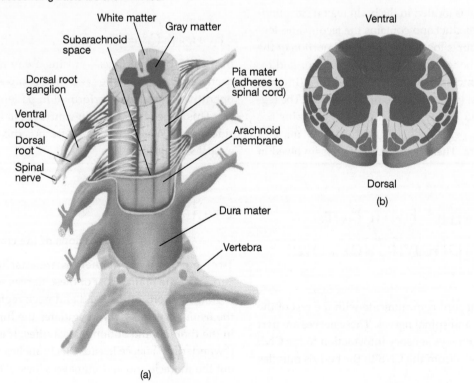

these bundles fuse together and become the thirty-one paired sets of **dorsal roots** and **ventral roots.** The dorsal and ventral roots join together as they pass through the intervertebral foramens and become spinal nerves.

Figure 3.26b shows a cross section of the spinal cord. Like the brain, the spinal cord consists of white matter and gray matter. Unlike the brain's, the spinal cord's white matter (consisting of ascending and descending bundles of myelinated axons) is on the outside; the gray matter (mostly neural cell bodies and short, unmyelinated axons) is on the inside. In Figure 3.26b, ascending tracts are indicated in blue; descending tracts are indicated in red.

Section Review

Structure and Function of the Central Nervous System

LO 3.7   Identify the structures and functions of the forebrain, including the telencephalon and diencephalon.

The forebrain is composed of the telencephalon, which includes the cerebral cortex, limbic system, and basal ganglia, and the diencephalon, which includes the thalamus, hypothalamus, and pituitary gland. The cerebral cortex is responsible for sensory and motor functions, and executive functions. The limbic system is responsible for motivation, emotion, and some forms of learning. The basal ganglia are involved in the control of movement. The thalamus is involved in conveying information to various locations of the brain. The hypothalamus is involved in regulation of the endocrine system and the autonomic nervous system. The pituitary gland is also involved in regulation of the endocrine system.

LO 3.8   Identify the location and functions of the structures of the mesencephalon.

The mesencephalon is located in the brain region surrounding the cerebral aqueduct and contains the tectum and tegmentum. The tectum is located in the dorsal portion of the mesencephalon. The tectum contains the superior and inferior colliculi, which are involved in auditory (inferior colliculi) and visual (superior colliculi) processing. The tegmentum is located below the tectum and contains the reticular formation, periaqueductal gray matter, red nucleus, and substantia nigra. The reticular formation is involved in sensory processing, sleep, attention, muscle tone, movement, and reflexes. The periaqueductal gray matter is involved in species-typical behavior and pain perception. The red nucleus and substantia nigra are involved in motor control.

LO 3.9   Contrast the locations and functions of the structures of the metencephalon and myelencephalon.

The metencephalon and myelencephalon surround the fourth ventricle. The metencephalon contains the cerebellum, which is involved in balance and coordinated movements, and the pons, which is involved in receiving information from the cortex and sleep regulation. The myelencephalon contains the medulla oblongata, which is involved in regulating vital functions.

LO 3.10   Describe the structure and functions of the spinal cord.

The spinal cord is contained within the vertebral column and functions to relay sensory information to the brain from the body, relay motor information from the brain to the body, and coordinate reflexive behaviors.

Thought Question

In the 1950s, lobotomies—cutting away most of the connections to and from the prefrontal cortex—were common operative procedures performed in patients with psychosis. This procedure became controversial due to serious side-effects. What deleterious effects is this kind of surgery expected to produce?

Structure and Function of the Peripheral Nervous System

The brain and spinal cord communicate with the rest of the body via the cranial and spinal nerves. These nerves are part of the PNS, which conveys sensory information to the CNS and conveys messages from the CNS to the body's muscles and glands.

Cranial Nerves

LO 3.11   Identify the functions of the cranial nerves.

Twelve pairs of **cranial nerves** are attached to the ventral surface of the brain. Most of these nerves serve sensory and motor functions of the head and neck region. One of them, the *tenth,* or **vagus nerve,** regulates the functions of organs in the thoracic and abdominal cavities. It is called the *vagus* ("wandering") nerve because its branches wander throughout the thoracic and abdominal cavities. (The word *vagabond* has the same root.) Figure 3.27 presents a view of the base of the brain and illustrates the cranial nerves and the structures they serve. Note that efferent (motor) fibers are drawn in red and that afferent (sensory) fibers are drawn in blue.

As we mentioned in the previous section, cell bodies of sensory nerve fibers that enter the brain and spinal cord (except for the visual system) are located outside the central nervous system. Somatosensory information (and the sense of taste) is received via the cranial nerves. Olfactory information is received via the **olfactory bulbs,** which receive information from the olfactory receptors in the nose. The olfactory bulbs are complex structures that contain a considerable amount of neural circuitry; actually, they are part of the brain. Sensory mechanisms are described in more detail in Chapters 6 and 7.

Spinal Nerves

LO 3.12 Differentiate between the functions of afferent and efferent axons of the spinal nerves.

The **spinal nerves** begin at the junction of the dorsal and ventral roots of the spinal cord. The nerves leave the vertebral column and travel to the muscles or sensory receptors they innervate (or supply), branching repeatedly as they go. Branches of spinal nerves often follow blood vessels, especially those branches that innervate skeletal muscles.

Now let us consider the pathways by which sensory information enters the spinal cord and motor information leaves it. The cell bodies of all axons that bring sensory information into the brain and spinal cord are located

Figure 3.27 The Cranial Nerves

The twelve pairs of cranial nerves serve regions in the head, neck, and thoracic and abdominal cavities.

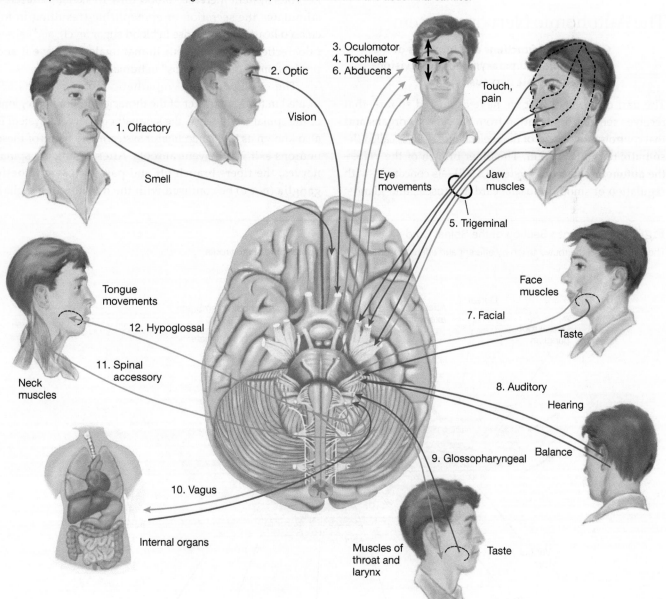

outside the CNS. (The sole exception is the visual system; the retina of the eye is actually a part of the brain.) These incoming axons are referred to as **afferent axons,** meaning that the direction of information is inward, toward the CNS. The cell bodies that give rise to the axons that bring somatosensory information to the spinal cord reside in the **dorsal root ganglia,** rounded swellings of the dorsal root. (See Figure 3.28.) The axonal stalk divides close to the cell body, sending one limb into the spinal cord and the other limb out to the sensory organ. Note that all of the axons in the dorsal root convey somatosensory information.

Cell bodies that give rise to the ventral root are located within the gray matter of the spinal cord. The axons of these neurons leave the spinal cord via a ventral root, which joins a dorsal root to make a spinal nerve. The axons that leave the spinal cord through the ventral roots control muscles and glands. They are referred to as **efferent axons,** meaning that the direction of information is outward, away from the CNS.

The Autonomic Nervous System

LO 3.13 **Compare the functions and locations of the sympathetic and parasympathetic divisions of the autonomic nervous system.**

The part of the PNS that we have discussed so far—that receives sensory information from the sensory organs and that controls movements of the skeletal muscles—is called the **somatic nervous system.** The other branch of the PNS—the **autonomic nervous system (ANS)**—is concerned with regulation of smooth muscle, cardiac muscle, and glands.

(*Autonomic* means "self-governing.") Smooth muscle is found in the skin (associated with hair follicles), in blood vessels, in the eyes (controlling pupil size and accommodation of the lens), and in the walls and sphincters of the gut, gallbladder, and urinary bladder. Merely describing the organs innervated by the ANS suggests the function of this system: regulation of "vegetative processes" in the body.

The ANS consists of two anatomically separate systems: the *sympathetic division* and the *parasympathetic division*. With few exceptions, organs of the body are innervated by both of these subdivisions, and each has a different effect. For example, the sympathetic division speeds the heart rate, whereas the parasympathetic division slows it.

SYMPATHETIC DIVISION OF THE ANS The **sympathetic division** is most involved in activities associated with expenditure of energy from reserves that are stored in the body. For example, when an organism is excited, the sympathetic nervous system increases blood flow to skeletal muscles, stimulates the secretion of epinephrine (resulting in increased heart rate and a rise in blood sugar level), and causes piloerection (erection of fur in mammals that have it and production of "goose bumps" in humans).

The cell bodies of sympathetic motor neurons are located in the gray matter of the thoracic and lumbar regions of the spinal cord (hence, the sympathetic nervous system is also known as the *thoracolumbar system*). The fibers of these neurons exit via the ventral roots. After joining the spinal nerves, the fibers branch off and pass into **sympathetic ganglia** (not to be confused with the dorsal root ganglia).

Figure 3.28 Cross Section of the Spinal Cord

The figure shows the routes taken by afferent and efferent axons through the dorsal and ventral roots.

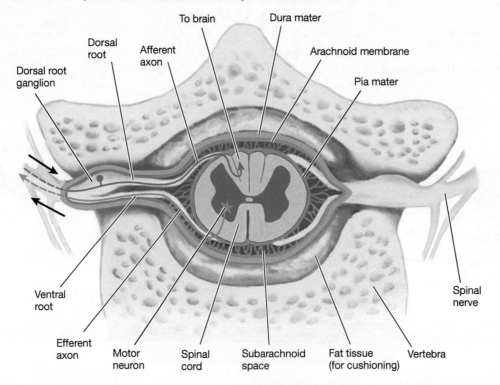

Figure 3.29 shows the relationship of these ganglia to the spinal cord. Note that individual sympathetic ganglia are connected to the neighboring ganglia above and below, thus forming the **sympathetic ganglion chain.**

The axons that leave the spinal cord through the ventral root belong to the **preganglionic neurons.** Sympathetic preganglionic axons enter the ganglia of the sympathetic chain. Most of the axons form synapses there, but others

Figure 3.29 The Autonomic Nervous System

The schematic figure shows the target organs and functions served by the sympathetic and parasympathetic branches of the autonomic nervous system.

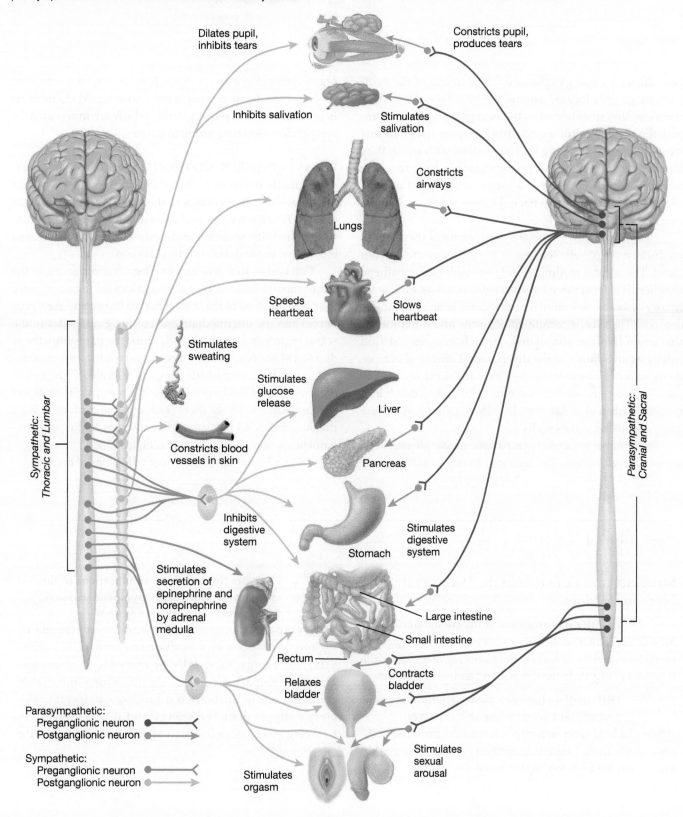

Table 3.2 The Major Divisions of the Peripheral Nervous System

Somatic Nervous System	Autonomic Nervous System (ANS)
Spinal Nerves	**Sympathetic Branch**
Afferents from sense organs	Spinal nerves (from thoracic and lumbar regions)
Efferents to muscles	Sympathetic ganglia
Cranial Nerves	**Parasympathetic Branch**
Afferents from sense organs	Cranial nerves (3rd, 7th, 9th, and 10th)
Efferents to muscles	Spinal nerves (from sacral region)
	Parasympathetic ganglia (adjacent to target organs)

pass through these ganglia and travel to one of the sympathetic ganglia located among the internal organs. With one exception (mentioned in the next paragraph), all sympathetic preganglionic axons form synapses with neurons located in one of the ganglia. The neurons with which they form synapses are called **postganglionic neurons.** The postganglionic neurons send axons to the target organs, such as the intestines, stomach, kidneys, or sweat glands. (See Figure 3.29.)

The sympathetic nervous system controls the **adrenal medulla,** a set of cells located in the center of the adrenal gland. The adrenal medulla closely resembles a sympathetic ganglion. It is innervated by preganglionic axons, and its secretory cells are very similar to postganglionic sympathetic neurons. These cells secrete epinephrine and norepinephrine when they are stimulated. These hormones function chiefly as an adjunct to the direct neural effects of sympathetic activity; for example, they increase blood flow to the muscles and cause stored nutrients to be broken down into glucose within skeletal muscle cells, thus increasing the energy available to these cells.

The terminal buttons of sympathetic preganglionic axons secrete acetylcholine. The terminal buttons on the target organs, belonging to the postganglionic axons, secrete another neurotransmitter: norepinephrine. (An exception to this rule is provided by the sweat glands, which are innervated by acetylcholine-secreting terminal buttons.)

PARASYMPATHETIC DIVISION OF THE ANS The **parasympathetic division** of the ANS supports activities that are involved with increases in the body's supply of stored energy. These activities include salivation, gastric and intestinal motility, secretion of digestive juices, and increased blood flow to the gastrointestinal system.

Cell bodies that give rise to preganglionic axons in the parasympathetic nervous system are located in two regions: the nuclei of some of the cranial nerves (especially the vagus nerve) and the intermediate horn of the gray matter in the sacral region of the spinal cord. Thus, the parasympathetic division of the ANS has often been referred to as the *craniosacral system.* Parasympathetic ganglia are located in the immediate vicinity of the target organs; the postganglionic fibers are therefore relatively short. The terminal buttons of both preganglionic and postganglionic neurons in the parasympathetic nervous system secrete acetylcholine.

Table 3.2 summarizes the major divisions of the PNS.

Section Review

Structure and Function of the Peripheral Nervous System

LO 3.11 **Identify the functions of the cranial nerves.**
Most of the cranial nerves serve sensory and motor functions of the head and neck region. The vagus nerve regulates the functions of organs in the thoracic and abdominal cavities.

LO 3.12 **Differentiate between the functions of afferent and efferent axons of the spinal nerves.**
Afferent axons carry sensory information from the body toward the CNS. Efferent axons carry motor information away from the CNS toward the body.

LO 3.13 **Compare the functions and locations of the sympathetic and parasympathetic divisions of the autonomic nervous system.**
The sympathetic nervous system innervates many regions of the body and functions to coordinate expenditure of energy, especially in response to stressors. The parasympathetic nervous system also innervates many regions of the body but functions to increase the body's supply of stored energy and return systems to a resting state following activation by the sympathetic nervous system.

Thought Question

When Maya experienced a pain attack, her mouth went dry, her heart rate and breathing became very fast, and she was terrified that she was having a heart attack. After the attack, she experienced anxiety and became constantly fearful of having another attack. She began working with a psychologist to practice progressive relaxation techniques to slow her breathing and heart rate and reduce her anxiety. Describe which branches of the ANS were responsible for the changes she experienced during the panic attack and during the progressive relaxation session. Where did these behavioral changes originate in the PNS? (Hint: To learn more about panic attacks, refer to Chapter 17.)

Chapter Review Questions

1. Explain the terms used to indicate directions and planes of sections of the nervous system.

2. Describe the flow of cerebrospinal fluid in the brain and explain the pathophysiology of an obstructive hydrocephalus.

3. Outline the development of the central nervous system and the evolution of the human brain.

4. Describe the telencephalon, one of the two major structures of the forebrain.

5. Explain the physiological significance and list the anatomical components of the limbic system.

6. "The thalamus is the sensory relay center." Justify this statement with two examples of sensory projection pathways.

7. A caudal block is sometimes used in pelvic surgery. What anatomical characteristic allows an anaesthesiologist to perform this kind of procedure?

Chapter 4
Psychopharmacology

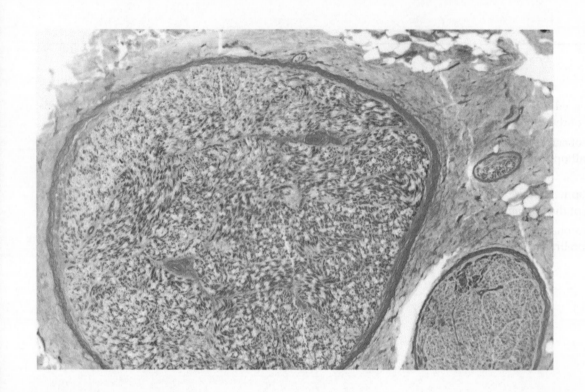

Chapter Outline

Learning Objectives

LO 4.1 Differentiate between the terms *drug, drug effect,* and *site of action.*

LO 4.2 Describe how the four steps of pharmacokinetics are related.

LO 4.3 Identify how drug effectiveness can be measured and list two reasons why drugs vary in their effectiveness.

LO 4.4 Differentiate between tolerance, sensitization, and withdrawal effects following repeated use of a drug.

LO 4.5 Describe a placebo and the placebo effect.

LO 4.6 Summarize how drug molecules can increase or decrease neurotransmitter synthesis.

LO 4.7 Distinguish between the effects of agonists and antagonists on storage and release of neurotransmitters.

LO 4.8 Contrast the effects of agonists and antagonists at the receptor.

LO 4.9 Describe the effects of agonists on neurotransmitter reuptake and degradation.

LO 4.10 Compare the features of the amino acid neurotransmitter systems.

LO 4.11 Summarize the features of the acetylcholine system.

LO 4.12 Summarize the key features of the monoamine systems.

LO 4.13 Contrast the features of peptide neurotransmitters with classical neurotransmitters.

LO 4.14 Summarize the features of the lipid neurotransmitter systems.

One Saturday night in 2011, a physician received a confusing text message from a patient named Lucas. Attached to the text was a photograph taken at night from a front porch showing a view of empty darkness. Lucas did not identify himself in the text, and the physician ignored the message thinking it was sent to him in error. The following morning, the physician received from the same phone number another text message that aroused concern. The physician subsequently called Lucas and had an hour-long phone conversation about the recent messages.

Lucas told his doctor that he began using bath salts purchased from a local store three weeks ago. He purchased the bath salts and began snorting them, as one might cocaine, and he described the effect and smell as similar to that of cocaine.

Bath salts typically contain several types of drugs that are similar to a stimulant called khat, which comes from the khat plant, Catha edulis. *Bath salts produce effects that are similar to other stimulants people abuse, like cocaine and methamphetamine, by increasing the activity of several neurotransmitters at the synapse, including dopamine and serotonin.*

Lucas continued using bath salts daily for three weeks. He was irritable, lost weight, and had frequent arguments with his family members. He described his mind as racing and suffered from insomnia. He also reported hallucinations that included people walking around his yard and house. The photograph taken from the porch was an attempt to document these people.

After his conversation with the physician, Lucas was taken to a local emergency department. Because of concerns about his hallucinations and other symptoms, Lucas was then admitted to the hospital and monitored overnight. Approximately thirty hours after he stopped using bath salts, Lucas' symptoms and mental status, including thought content, had returned to normal and he was discharged (Gunderson et al., 2013).

*****

This case study includes examples of several fundamental concepts in psychopharmacology that we will explore in this chapter: drug effects, sites of action, and route of administration. This case study also describes the effects of increasing the activity of monoamine neurotransmitter systems. The area of behavioral neuroscience described in this chapter is dedicated to understanding how drugs interact with the nervous system to affect not only behavior, but our physical, emotional, and psychological health.

As you read this chapter, keep in mind the number of individuals impacted by the therapeutic and recreational drugs described in this chapter. The chapter begins with the basic principles of psychopharmacology. Then the second section examines the sites of action. The last part of the chapter summarizes the particular neurotransmitters and neuromodulators. The figure on the next page presents several regions of the brain that we will be paying particular attention to in this chapter.

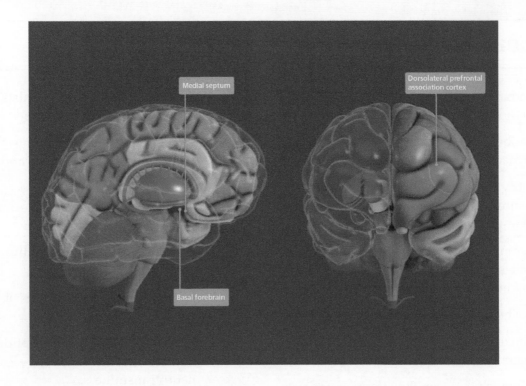

Principles of Psychopharmacology

Chapter 2 introduced you to the cells of the nervous system, and Chapter 3 described its basic structure. Now it is time to build on this information by introducing the field of psychopharmacology. **Psychopharmacology** is the study of the effects of drugs on the nervous system and behavior. This section will include an overview of the field of psychopharmacology and descriptions of pharmacokinetics, drug effectiveness, placebos, and the effects of repeatedly taking a drug.

An Overview of Psychopharmacology

LO 4.1 **Differentiate between the terms** *drug, drug effect,* **and** *site of action.*

What *is* a drug? Like many words, this one has several different meanings. In one context it refers to a medication that we would obtain from a pharmacist—a chemical that has a therapeutic effect on a disease or its symptoms. In another context the word refers to a chemical that people are likely to abuse, such as heroin or cocaine. (See Figure 4.1.)

The definition of a drug that will be used in this book (and the one generally accepted by pharmacologists) is "an exogenous chemical not necessary for normal cellular functioning that significantly alters the functions of certain cells of the body when taken in relatively low doses." Because the topic of this chapter is *psycho*pharmacology, we will concern ourselves here only with chemicals that alter the functions of cells within the nervous system.

The word *exogenous* is key to our understanding of drugs here. In this context, *exogenous* means produced from outside the body, so it rules out chemical messengers produced by the body, such as neurotransmitters, neuromodulators, or hormones. Chemical messengers produced by the body are not drugs. This definition of a drug also rules out essential nutrients, such as proteins, fats, carbohydrates, minerals, and vitamins that are necessary constituents of a healthy diet. Finally, it states that drugs are effective in low doses. This qualification is important, because large quantities of almost any substance—even common ones such as table salt—will alter the functions of cells.

As we will see in this chapter, drugs have *effects* and *sites of action*. **Drug effects** are the changes we can observe in an individual's physiological processes and behavior. For example, the effects of codeine, morphine, and other opiates include decreased sensitivity to pain, slowing of the digestive system, sedation, muscular relaxation, constriction of the pupils, and at high doses, euphoria. The **sites of action** of drugs are the points at which molecules of drugs interact with molecules located on or in cells of the body, thus affecting some biochemical processes of these cells. For example, the sites of action of the opiates are specialized receptors situated in the membrane of some neurons. When molecules of opiates attach to and activate these receptors, the drugs alter the activity of these neurons and produce their effects. This chapter considers both the effects of drugs and their sites of action.

Psychopharmacology is an important field of neuroscience. It has been responsible for the development of psychotherapeutic drugs, which are used to treat psychological and

Figure 4.1 Psychopharmacology: The Study of Drug Effects on the Nervous System and Behavior

Psychopharmacology is a sub discipline in the field of pharmacology. Psychopharmacologists study drugs that affect the nervous system and behavior in two broad classes: therapeutic drugs and drugs of abuse.

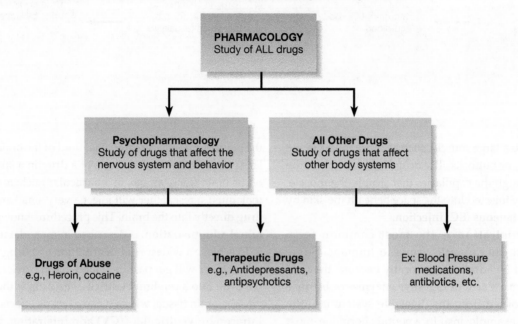

behavioral disorders. It has also provided tools that have enabled other investigators to study the functions of cells of the nervous system and the behaviors controlled by particular neural circuits.

This chapter does not contain all this book has to say about the subject of psychopharmacology. Throughout the book you will learn about the use of drugs to investigate the nature of neural circuits involved in the control of perception, memory, and behavior. In addition, Chapters 16 and 17 discuss the use of drugs to study and treat disorders such as schizophrenia, depression, and the anxiety disorders, and Chapter 18 discusses the physiology of substance abuse.

This chapter begins with a description of the basic principles of psychopharmacology: the routes of administration of drugs and their fate in the body. The second section discusses the sites of drug actions. The final section discusses specific neurotransmitters and neuromodulators and the physiological and behavioral effects of specific drugs that interact with them.

Pharmacokinetics

LO 4.2 Describe how the four steps of pharmacokinetics are related.

Pharmacokinetics includes the steps by which drugs are (1) absorbed, (2) distributed within the body, (3) metabolized, and (4) excreted. You can think of these steps as describing the life cycle of a drug molecule in the body. First, drug molecules are absorbed into the body based on how they are administered. For example, if a drug is taken orally, it is absorbed through the lining of the digestive system. You will learn more about the different ways that drugs can be administered in the following paragraphs. After being absorbed, drug molecules are distributed throughout the body by blood in the circulatory system, including to the CNS where many sites of action are located. At the same time, drug molecules are being metabolized, or changed into an inactive form, by enzymes. Most drug metabolizing enzymes are located in the liver. Finally, drug molecules are excreted and removed from the body, typically by the kidneys. (See Figure 4.2.)

ABSORPTION: ROUTES OF ADMINISTRATION First, let's consider some of the routes by which drugs can be administered. For laboratory animals the most common route is injection. The drug is dissolved or suspended in a liquid and injected through a hypodermic needle. The fastest route is **intravenous (IV) injection**—injection into a vein. The drug is absorbed and distributed immediately, reaching the brain within a few seconds. The disadvantages of IV injections are the increased care and skill they require in comparison to most other forms of injection and the fact that the entire dose reaches the bloodstream at once. If an individual is especially sensitive to the drug, there may be little time to administer another drug to counteract its effects.

An **intraperitoneal (IP) injection** is rapid but not as rapid as an IV injection. The drug is injected through the abdominal wall into the *peritoneal cavity*—the space that surrounds the stomach, intestines, liver, and other abdominal organs. IP injection is commonly used to administer drugs to small laboratory animals. An **intramuscular (IM) injection** is

Figure 4.2 The Four Components of Pharmacokinetics

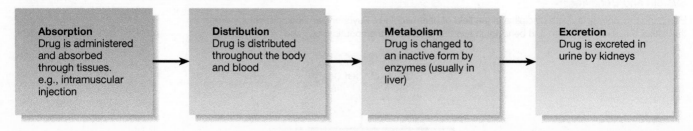

Absorption Drug is administered and absorbed through tissues. e.g., intramuscular injection	**Distribution** Drug is distributed throughout the body and blood	**Metabolism** Drug is changed to an inactive form by enzymes (usually in liver)	**Excretion** Drug is excreted in urine by kidneys

made directly into a large muscle, such as those found in the upper arm, thigh, or buttocks. The drug is absorbed into the bloodstream through the capillaries that supply the muscle. A drug can also be injected into the space beneath the skin by means of a **subcutaneous (SC) injection.**

Oral administration is the most common form of administering therapeutic drugs to humans. Some chemicals cannot be administered orally because they are destroyed by stomach acid or digestive enzymes or because they are not absorbed from the digestive system into the bloodstream. For example, insulin, a peptide hormone, must be injected. **Sublingual administration** of certain drugs can be accomplished by placing them beneath the tongue. The drug is absorbed into the bloodstream by the capillaries that supply the mucous membrane that lines the mouth. Some drugs used to treat migraine headaches are administered this way, resulting in faster onset of therapeutic effects and less risk of irritating the stomach.

The lungs provide another route for drug administration: **inhalation.** Nicotine, freebase cocaine, and marijuana are inhaled through smoking. In addition, many general anesthetics are gases that are administered through inhalation. The route from the lungs to the brain is very short, and drugs administered this way have very rapid effects.

Some drugs can be absorbed directly through the skin, so they can be given by means of **topical administration.** Natural or artificial steroid hormones can be administered in this way, as can nicotine (as a treatment to make it easier for a person to stop smoking). The mucous membrane lining the nasal passages also provides a route for topical administration. Commonly abused drugs such as cocaine and bath salts are often sniffed so that they come into contact with the nasal mucosa. This route delivers the drug to the brain very rapidly. The technical, but rarely used name for this route is **insufflation.** Note that sniffing or "snorting" is not the same as inhalation; when powdered drugs are sniffed, they enter circulation through the mucous membrane of the nasal passages, not the lungs.

Finally, drugs can be administered directly into the brain. As we saw in Chapter 2, the blood–brain barrier prevents certain chemicals from leaving capillaries and entering the brain. Some drugs cannot cross the blood–brain barrier. If these drugs are to reach the brain, they must be injected directly into

the brain or into the cerebrospinal fluid of the brain's ventricular system. To study the effects of a drug in a specific region of the brain (for example, in a particular nucleus of the hypothalamus), a researcher will inject a very small amount of the drug directly into the brain. This procedure, known as **intracerebral administration,** is described in more detail in Chapter 5. To achieve a widespread distribution of a drug in the brain, a researcher will get past the blood–brain barrier by injecting the drug into a cerebral ventricle. The drug is then absorbed into the brain tissue, where it can exert its effects. This route, **intracerebroventricular (ICV) administration,** is used very rarely in humans—primarily to deliver antibiotics directly to the brain to treat certain types of infections.

Figure 4.3 shows the time course of blood levels of a commonly abused drug, cocaine, after intravenous injection, inhalation, oral administration, and sniffing. The amounts received were not identical, but the graph illustrates the relative rapidity with which the drug reaches the blood.

DISTRIBUTION: ENTRY OF DRUGS INTO THE BRAIN
Drugs exert their effects only when they reach their sites

Figure 4.3 Cocaine in Blood Plasma

The graph shows the concentration of cocaine in blood plasma after intravenous injection, inhalation, oral administration, and sniffing.

(Adapted from Feldman, R. S., Meyer, J. S., and Quenzer, L. F., *Principles of Neuropsychopharmacology,* Sunderland, MA: Sinauer Associates, 1997; after Jones, R. T., *NIDA Research Monographs,* 1990, *99,* 30–41.)

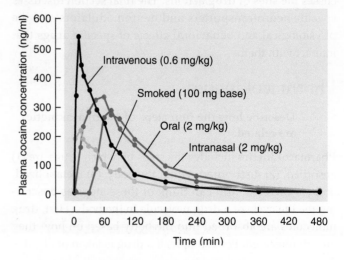

of action. In the case of drugs that affect behavior, most of these sites are located on or in cells in the CNS. The previous section described the routes by which drugs can be introduced into the body. With the exception of intracerebral or intracerebroventricular administration, the routes of drug administration vary only in the rate at which a drug enters the circulatory system. But what happens next? Drug molecules must next reach sites of action in the nervous system to produce changes in behavior and mental processes.

The most important factor that determines the rate at which a drug reaches sites of action within the brain is **lipid solubility,** or the ability of fat-based molecules to pass through cell membranes (see Chapter 2). The blood–brain barrier is a barrier only for water-soluble molecules. Molecules that are soluble in lipids pass through the cells that line the capillaries in the CNS, and they rapidly distribute themselves throughout the brain. For example, heroin (diacetylmorphine) is a more lipid soluble drug than morphine. Thus, an intravenous injection of heroin produces more rapid effects than does one of morphine. Even though the molecules of the two drugs are equally effective when they reach their sites of action in the brain, the fact that heroin molecules get there faster means that they produce a more intense "rush," and this explains why the abuse potential of heroin is greater than that of morphine.

METABOLISM AND EXCRETION Drugs do not remain in the body indefinitely. Many are metabolized and deactivated by enzymes, and all are eventually excreted, primarily by the kidneys. The liver plays an especially active role in enzymatic deactivation of drugs, but some deactivating enzymes are also found in the blood. The brain also contains enzymes that destroy some drugs. In some cases, enzymes transform molecules of a drug into other forms that themselves are biologically active. Occasionally, the transformed molecule is *even more* active than the one that is administered. In such cases the effects of a drug can have a very long duration. For example, chlordiazepoxide (Librium) is used to treat symptoms of anxiety. The effects of one dose of this drug can last more than 24 hours, in part because some of the metabolized molecules are active in the body for even longer than the original drug molecule (Greenblatt et al., 1981).

Drug Effectiveness

LO 4.3 Identify how drug effectiveness can be measured and list two reasons why drugs vary in their effectiveness.

Drugs vary widely in their effectiveness. The effects of a small dose of a relatively effective drug can equal or exceed the effects of larger amounts of a relatively ineffective drug. The best way to measure the effectiveness of a drug is to plot a **dose-response curve.** To do this, individuals are given various doses of a drug, usually defined as milligrams of drug per kilogram of an individual's body weight, and the

effects of the drug are plotted. Because the molecules of most drugs distribute themselves throughout the blood and then throughout the rest of the body, a heavier individual (human or laboratory animal) will require a larger quantity of a drug to achieve the same concentration as a smaller quantity will produce in a smaller individual. Increasingly higher doses of a drug cause increasingly larger effects until the point of maximum effect is reached. At this point, increasing the dose of the drug does not produce any more effect. (See Figure 4.4.)

Most drugs have more than one effect. Opiates such as morphine, codeine, or oxycodone produce analgesia (reduced sensitivity to pain), but they also depress the activity of neurons in the medulla that control heart rate and respiration. A physician who prescribes an opiate to relieve a patient's pain wants to administer a dose that is large enough to produce analgesia but not large enough to depress heart rate and respiration—effects that could be fatal. Figure 4.5 shows two dose-response curves, one for the analgesic effects of morphine and one for the drug's depressant effects on respiration. The difference between these curves indicates the drug's margin of safety. The most desirable drugs have a large margin of safety.

One measure of a drug's margin of safety is its **therapeutic index.** This measure is obtained by administering varying doses of the drug to a group of laboratory animals or human volunteers. Two numbers are obtained: the dose that produces the desired effects in 50 percent of the individuals and the dose that produces toxic effects in 50 percent of the individuals. The therapeutic index is the ratio of these two numbers. For example, if the toxic dose is five times higher than the effective dose, then the therapeutic index is 5.0. The lower the therapeutic index, the more care must be taken in prescribing the drug. For example, barbiturates are older drugs used to treat anxiety and have relatively low therapeutic indexes—as

---

Figure 4.4 A Dose-Response Curve

Increasingly stronger doses of the drug produce increasingly larger effects until the maximum effect is reached. After that point, increments in the dose do not produce any increments in the drug's effect. However, the risk of adverse side effects increases.

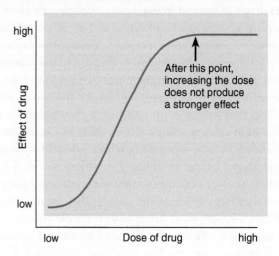

After this point, increasing the dose does not produce a stronger effect

Figure 4.5 Dose-Response Curves for Morphine

The dose-response curve on the left shows the analgesic effect of morphine, and the curve on the right shows one of the drug's adverse side effects: its depressant effect on respiration. A drug's margin of safety is reflected by the difference between the dose-response curve for its therapeutic effects and that for its adverse side effects.

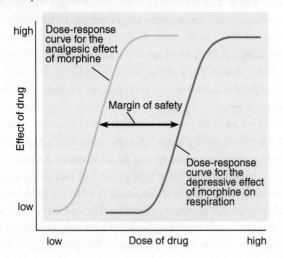

low as 2 or 3. In contrast, benzodiazepines such as diazepam (Valium) are considered more safe and have therapeutic indexes of well over 100. As a consequence, an accidental overdose of a barbiturate is much more likely to have tragic effects than a similar overdose of a benzodiazepine.

Why do drugs vary in their effectiveness? There are two reasons: sites of action and the affinity of a drug with its site of action.

First, different drugs—even those that produce the same behavioral effects—may have different sites of action. For example, both oxycodone (OxyContin) and aspirin have analgesic effects, but oxycodone suppresses the activity of neurons in the spinal cord and brain that are involved in pain perception, whereas aspirin reduces the production of a chemical involved in transmitting information from damaged tissue to pain-sensitive neurons. Because the drugs act very differently, a given dose of oxycodone produces much more pain reduction than the same dose of aspirin does.

The second reason that drugs vary in their effectiveness has to do with the affinity of the drug with its site of action. Most drugs of interest to psychopharmacologists exert their effects by binding at sites of action in the CNS—such as presynaptic or postsynaptic receptors, transporter molecules, or by interacting with enzymes involved in the production or deactivation of neurotransmitters. Drugs vary widely in their **affinity**—the readiness with which the two molecules join together—for the sites to which they attach. A drug with a high affinity will produce effects at a relatively low concentration, whereas a drug with a low affinity must be administered in higher doses. Thus, even two drugs with identical sites of action can vary widely in their effectiveness if they have different affinities for their binding sites. In addition, because most drugs have multiple effects, a drug can have high affinities for some of its sites of action and low affinities for others. The most desirable drug has a high

affinity for sites of action that produce therapeutic effects and a low affinity for sites of action that produce toxic side effects. One of the goals of research by drug companies is to find chemicals with just this pattern of effects.

Effects of Repeated Administration

LO 4.4 **Differentiate between tolerance, sensitization, and withdrawal effects following repeated use of a drug.**

Often, when a drug is administered repeatedly, its effects do not remain constant. In most cases its effects will diminish—a phenomenon known as **tolerance.** In other cases a drug becomes more and more effective—a phenomenon known as **sensitization.**

Let's consider tolerance first. Tolerance is seen in many drugs that are commonly abused. For example, a person who regularly uses heroin must take larger and larger amounts of the drug for it to be effective. And once a person has taken heroin regularly enough to develop tolerance, that individual will likely experience **withdrawal symptoms** if he or she suddenly stops taking the drug. Withdrawal symptoms are primarily the opposite of the effects of the drug itself. For example, heroin produces euphoria; withdrawal from it produces *dysphoria*—a feeling of anxious misery. Heroin also produces relaxation; withdrawal from it produces agitation.

Withdrawal symptoms are caused by the same mechanisms that are responsible for tolerance. Tolerance is the result of the body's attempt to compensate for the effects of the drug. That is, most systems of the body, including those controlled by the brain, are regulated so that they stay at an optimal value or set point. When the effects of a drug alter these systems for a prolonged time, compensatory mechanisms begin to produce the opposite reaction, at least partially compensating for the disturbance from the optimal value. These mechanisms account for the fact that more and more of the drug must be taken to achieve a given level of effects. Then, when the person stops taking the drug, the compensatory mechanisms make themselves felt as withdrawal symptoms, unopposed by the action of the drug. When a person has repeatedly used a drug enough to produce withdrawal symptoms when they stop using it, they are said to have **physical dependence** on the drug. Physical dependence is one aspect that contributes to substance abuse, which will be explored in greater detail in Chapter 18.

Research suggests that there are several types of compensatory mechanisms that accompany repeated use of a drug. As we will see, many drugs that affect the brain do so by binding with receptors and activating them. The first compensatory mechanism involves a decrease in the effectiveness of such binding. Either the receptors become less sensitive to the drug and their affinity for the drug decreases, or the receptors decrease in number. The second compensatory mechanism involves the process that couples the receptors to ion channels in the membrane or to the production of second messengers. After prolonged stimulation of the receptors, one or more steps in the coupling process become less effective. (Of course, *both* effects can occur.) The details of these compensatory mechanisms are described in Chapter 18, which discusses the causes and effects of substance abuse.

Many drugs have several different sites of action and thus produce several different effects. This means that some of the effects of a drug may show tolerance but others may not. For example, barbiturates cause sedation and also depress neurons that control respiration. The sedative effects show tolerance, but the respiratory depression does not. This means that if larger and larger doses of a barbiturate are taken to achieve the same level of sedation, the person begins to run the risk of taking a dangerously large dose of the drug that may cause respiratory failure.

Sensitization is the opposite of tolerance: Repeated doses of a drug produce greater and greater effects. Sensitization is less common than tolerance, and sensitization may develop for some of the effects of a drug while tolerance develops for others. For example, repeated injections of cocaine become more and more likely to produce movement disorders and seizures, whereas the euphoric effects of the drug do not show sensitization—and may even show tolerance. (See Figure 4.6.)

Placebo Effects

LO 4.5 **Describe a placebo and the placebo effect.**

A **placebo** is an inactive substance. But although placebos contain no active drug molecules, it is incorrect to say that they have *no* effect. If a person expects that a placebo can have a physiological or psychological effect, then administration of the placebo may actually produce that effect. Placebo responses can be the result of changes in motivation, expectation, or forms of learning such as classical conditioning (Price et al., 2008).

Many factors can be related to the experience of a placebo effect. External factors, such as viewing an injection of a placebo can result in postoperative pain relief (Price et al., 2008). Informing individuals that a placebo is a stimulant results in increases in heart rate and blood pressure.

Informing people that the same placebo is a depressant results in decreased physiological response (Blackwell et al., 1972; Kirsch, 1997). Taking two placebo capsules results in a greater response than taking one, and varying the color of capsules produces changes in response to the same placebo capsule (Blackwell et al., 1972).

Research has demonstrated that some placebo pain effects may operate via the opioid system (an endogenous pain-relieving system in the CNS). For example, administering a pain-relieving placebo increases activity in the opioid system and administering an opioid-blocking drug blocks the pain-relieving effects of a placebo (Price et al., 2008).

When experimenters want to investigate the behavioral effects of drugs in humans, they must use control groups whose members receive placebos, or they cannot be sure that the behavioral effects they observe were caused by specific effects of the drug. Studies with laboratory animals must also use placebos, even though we need not worry about the animals' "beliefs" about the effects of the drugs we give them. Consider the steps involved in administering a drug to an animal. If you have ever needed to give medications to a sick cat, dog, or other pet, you may be familiar with the unique challenges this involves! The animal is typically very frightened, so even if the substance you administer to an animal is harmless, the experience of receiving the drug could activate the animal's autonomic nervous system, cause the secretion of stress hormones, and have other physiological effects. If we want to know what the behavioral effects of a drug are, we must compare the behavior of drug-treated individuals (people or animals) with other individuals who receive a placebo, administered in exactly the same way as the drug. Only then can a researcher determine if a drug has significant behavioral effects, above and beyond the effects of administering and receiving any inactive substance. Drug researchers typically report the effects of a drug relative to a similar group that received a placebo. In fact, placebo control data is so important in determining drug effects that the Federal Drug Administration (FDA) typically requires multiple studies with placebo control groups before approving new drugs for sale in the United States.

Figure 4.6 Effects of Repeated Administration Identify Which of These Scenarios Represent Tolerance, Withdrawal, or Sensitization.

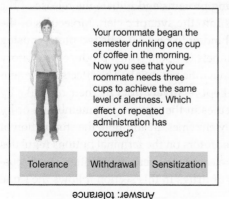

Your roommate began the semester drinking one cup of coffee in the morning. Now you see that your roommate needs three cups to achieve the same level of alertness. Which effect of repeated administration has occurred?

| Tolerance | Withdrawal | Sensitization |

Answer: tolerance

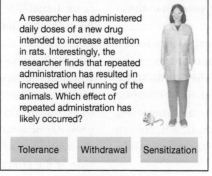

A researcher has administered daily doses of a new drug intended to increase attention in rats. Interestingly, the researcher finds that repeated administration has resulted in increased wheel running of the animals. Which effect of repeated administration has likely occurred?

| Tolerance | Withdrawal | Sensitization |

Answer: sensitization

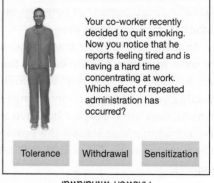

Your co-worker recently decided to quit smoking. Now you notice that he reports feeling tired and is having a hard time concentrating at work. Which effect of repeated administration has occurred?

| Tolerance | Withdrawal | Sensitization |

Answer: withdrawal

Section Review

Principles of Psychopharmacology

LO 4.1 Differentiate between the terms *drug*, *drug effect*, and *site of action*.

A drug is an exogenous chemical not necessary for normal cellular functioning that significantly alters the functions of certain cells of the body when taken in relatively low doses. Drug effects are the changes we can observe in an individual's physiological processes and behavior. The sites of action of drugs are the points at which molecules of drugs interact with molecules located on or in cells of the body, thus affecting some biochemical processes of these cells.

LO 4.2 Describe how the four steps of pharmacokinetics are related.

First, a drug molecule is absorbed. Varying the route of administration changes how quickly a drug is absorbed. Faster absorption produces a larger drug effect, with a faster onset. Then, a drug molecule is distributed. Distribution in the body is affected by several factors, such as lipid solubility. Next, the drug is metabolized. Metabolism is affected by the availability of enzymes. Finally, the drug is excreted. Excretion can be affected by kidney function.

LO 4.3 Identify how drug effectiveness can be measured and list two reasons why drugs vary in their effectiveness.

Drug effectiveness can be measured on a dose-response curve by plotting effects of the drug on the vertical axis and dose of the drug on the horizontal axis. Two reasons that drugs vary in their effectiveness are that different drugs have different sites of action and vary in their affinity for their binding sites.

LO 4.4 Differentiate between tolerance, sensitization, and withdrawal effects following repeated use of a drug.

With repeated use, drugs can produce tolerance (diminishing effects of a given dose), sensitization (increasing effects of a given dose), and withdrawal (the opposite effects of the drug itself; indicative of physical dependence).

LO 4.5 Describe a placebo and the placebo effect.

A placebo is an inactive substance that can produce physiological or psychological effects. The placebo effect occurs when an individual expects that a placebo can have a physiological or psychological effect, and the placebo subsequently produces an effect.

Thought Question

Recently, the head of Amsterdam's health services declared that sugar was a drug and urged people to stop using it excessively. Based on the widely accepted definition of "drug" and your emerging understanding of the principles of pharmacology, draft an e-mail to a friend explaining whether sugar should be considered a drug.

Sites of Drug Action

Throughout the history of our species, people have discovered that plants—and some animals and fungi—produce chemicals that act on the nervous system. Some of these chemicals have been used for their pleasurable effects; others have been used to treat illness, reduce pain, or poison other animals (or enemies). More recently, scientists have learned to produce completely artificial drugs, known as synthetic drugs, some with potencies far greater than those of the naturally occurring drugs.

In addition to their traditional uses, drugs today are used in research to investigate the operations of the nervous system. Most drugs that affect behavior do so by affecting synaptic transmission. Drugs that affect synaptic transmission are classified into two general categories. Those that block or inhibit the postsynaptic effects are called **antagonists.** Those that facilitate them are called **agonists.**

This section will describe the basic effects of drugs on synaptic activity. Recall from Chapter 2 that the sequence of synaptic activity goes like this: Neurotransmitters are synthesized and stored in synaptic vesicles. The synaptic vesicles travel to the presynaptic terminal membrane, where they become docked. When an axon fires, voltage-dependent calcium channels in the presynaptic membrane open, permitting the entry of calcium ions. The calcium ions interact with the docking proteins and initiate the release of the neurotransmitters into the synaptic cleft. Molecules of the neurotransmitter bind with postsynaptic receptors, causing particular ion channels to open, which produces excitatory or inhibitory postsynaptic potentials. The effects of the neurotransmitter are kept relatively brief by their reuptake by transporter molecules in the presynaptic membrane or by their destruction by enzymes. In addition, the stimulation of presynaptic autoreceptors on the terminal buttons regulates the synthesis and release of the neurotransmitter. The discussion of the effects of drugs in this section follows the same

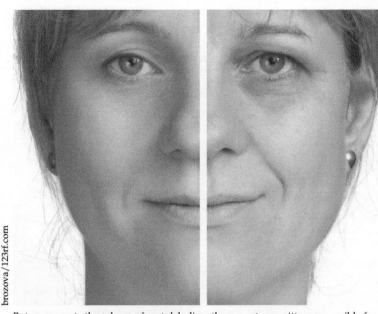

Botox prevents the release of acetylcholine, the neurotransmitter responsible for signaling muscle contractions in the PNS.

basic sequence. The effects we will describe are summarized in Figure 4.7, with additional details shown in subsequent figures. We should warn you that some of the effects are complex, so the discussion that follows bears careful reading.

Effects on Production of Neurotransmitters

LO 4.6 **Summarize how drug molecules can increase or decrease neurotransmitter synthesis.**

Before they are released into the synapse, neurotransmitters are produced (or, synthesized) by presynaptic neurons. Some psychoactive drugs produce their effects by altering the production of neurotransmitters. For example, most neurotransmitters are produced from molecules called precursors. Some drugs produce their effects by acting as precursors to increase the amount of neurotransmitter a cell can synthesize and release into the synapse (see step 1 in Figure 4.7). Precursor drugs are considered agonists because administering them increases activity of the neurotransmitter system. For example, symptoms of Parkinson's disease are due to death of dopamine-releasing cells in the substantia nigra. One treatment for this disease involves administering L-DOPA. L-DOPA is a precursor for dopamine. The remaining cells use the L-DOPA to synthesize additional dopamine, thus replacing some of the lost neurotransmission and reducing symptoms of the disease. Look for more information on this treatment strategy in Chapter 15.

It's also important to remember that neurotransmitter synthesis is controlled by enzymes. Therefore, if a drug deactivates one of these enzymes, it will prevent the neurotransmitter from being produced. Such a drug serves as an antagonist (see step 2 in Figure 4.7). For example, *p*-chlorophenylalanine (PCPA) inhibits an enzyme necessary for the synthesis of serotonin (Dringenberg et al., 1995). PCPA is typically used as a research drug in studies to better understand functions of the serotonin system.

Effects on Storage and Release of Neurotransmitters

LO 4.7 **Distinguish between the effects of agonists and antagonists on storage and release of neurotransmitters.**

After production or recycling, neurotransmitters are stored in synaptic vesicles until they are transported to the presynaptic membrane and release their contents following an action potential.

Vesicles are filled with neurotransmitter by vesicle transporter molecules located in the membrane of synaptic vesicles. **Vesicle transporters** pump molecules of the neurotransmitter across the vesicle membrane, filling the vesicles. It's important to notice that the *vesicle* transporters are different from the transporters found on the terminal membrane. Although they both move neurotransmitter molecules, the terminal membrane transporters move the molecules from the synapse into the cytoplasm of the presynaptic cell. The *vesicle* transporters then move the molecules into the vesicles.

Some drugs can block vesicle transporters by binding with a particular site on the transporter and inactivating it. These drugs serve as antagonists (see step 3 in Figure 4.7). Because the synaptic vesicles remain empty, nothing is released when the vesicles eventually release their contents into the synapse. Reserpine is an example of a drug that blocks vesicle transporters for monoamine neurotransmitter systems. Due to adverse side effects, this drug is typically only used in research; however, it is sometime used to reduce blood pressure. You will read more about reserpine in the monoamine section of this chapter.

Some drugs act as antagonists by preventing the release of neurotransmitters from the terminal button. They do so by deactivating the proteins that cause docked synaptic vesicles to fuse with the presynaptic membrane and expel their contents into the synaptic cleft (see step 5 in Figure 4.7). An example of a drug with this action is botulinum toxin (Botox). Botox prevents the release of acetylcholine, the neurotransmitter responsible for signaling muscle contractions in the PNS. Other drugs have the opposite effect: They act as agonists by binding with these proteins and directly triggering release of the neurotransmitter (see step 4 in Figure 4.7).

Figure 4.7 Drug Effects on Synaptic Transmission

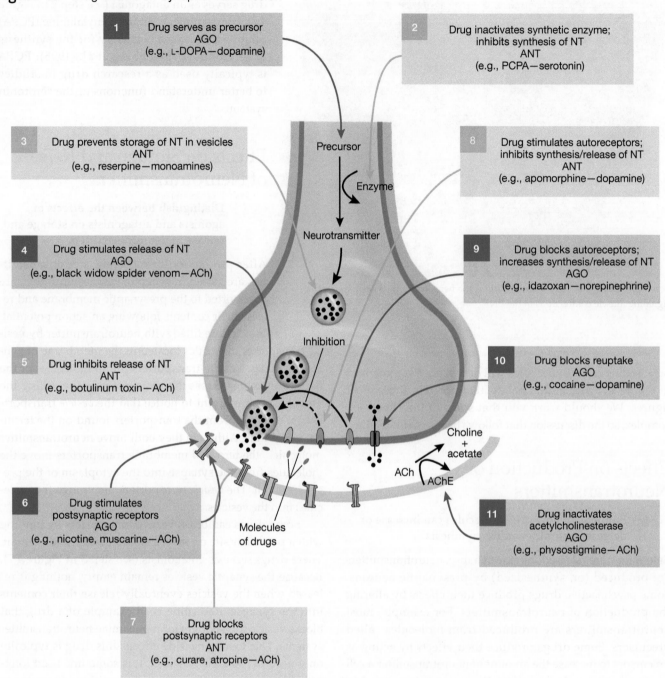

1 Drug serves as precursor AGO (e.g., L-DOPA—dopamine)

2 Drug inactivates synthetic enzyme; inhibits synthesis of NT ANT (e.g., PCPA—serotonin)

3 Drug prevents storage of NT in vesicles ANT (e.g., reserpine—monoamines)

8 Drug stimulates autoreceptors; inhibits synthesis/release of NT ANT (e.g., apomorphine—dopamine)

4 Drug stimulates release of NT AGO (e.g., black widow spider venom—ACh)

9 Drug blocks autoreceptors; increases synthesis/release of NT AGO (e.g., idazoxan—norepinephrine)

5 Drug inhibits release of NT ANT (e.g., botulinum toxin—ACh)

10 Drug blocks reuptake AGO (e.g., cocaine—dopamine)

6 Drug stimulates postsynaptic receptors AGO (e.g., nicotine, muscarine—ACh)

11 Drug inactivates acetylcholinesterase AGO (e.g., physostigmine—ACh)

7 Drug blocks postsynaptic receptors ANT (e.g., curare, atropine—ACh)

Precursor • Enzyme • Neurotransmitter • Inhibition • Molecules of drugs • Choline + acetate • ACh • AChE

Effects on Receptors

LO 4.8 Contrast the effects of agonists and antagonists at the receptor.

The effects of a particular drug that binds with a particular type of receptor can be very complex. The effects depend on where the receptor is located, what its normal effects are, and whether the drug activates the receptor or blocks its actions.

The most important—and most complex—site of action of drugs in the nervous system is on receptors, both presynaptic and postsynaptic. Let's consider postsynaptic receptors first. (Here is where the careful reading should begin.) Once a neurotransmitter is released, it must stimulate the postsynaptic receptors. Some drugs bind with these receptors, just as the neurotransmitter does. Once a drug has bound with the receptor, it can serve as either an agonist or an antagonist (see steps 6 and 7 in Figure 4.7).

A drug that mimics the effects of a neurotransmitter acts as a **direct agonist.** Molecules of the drug attach to the binding site to which the neurotransmitter normally attaches. This binding causes the receptor to respond in the same way as when the neurotransmitter is present. For example, nicotine binds to the nicotinic acetylcholine receptor, mimicking the effects of the acetylcholine and contributing to the stimulant effects of the drug.

Drugs that bind with postsynaptic receptors can also serve as antagonists. Molecules of such drugs bind with the receptors but *block* them from being activated. Because they occupy the receptor's binding site, they prevent the neurotransmitter from activating the receptor. These drugs are called **receptor blockers** or **direct antagonists.** These types of drugs can have therapeutic effects, such as the dopamine antagonist chlorpromazine, which reduces some of the symptoms of schizophrenia.

Some receptors have multiple binding sites, to which different ligands can attach. Molecules of the neurotransmitter bind with one site, and other substances (such as neuromodulators and various drugs) bind with the others. Binding of a molecule with one of these alternative sites is referred to as **noncompetitive binding**, because the molecule does not compete with molecules of the neurotransmitter for the same binding site. If a drug attaches to one of these alternative sites and prevents the ion channel from opening, the drug is said to be an **indirect antagonist.** (See Figure 4.8.) Two examples of drugs that work in this way are PCP and ketamine. These drugs bind to noncompetitive sites as antagonists of the NMDA glutamate receptor. The ultimate *effect* of an indirect antagonist is similar to that of a direct antagonist, but its site of action is different. If a drug attaches to one of the alternative sites and *facilitates* the opening of the ion channel, it is said to be an **indirect agonist.** Diazepam (Valium) is used to treat the symptoms of anxiety. Diazepam is an indirect agonist and requires concurrent binding of GABA to produce its antianxiety effects.

As we saw in Chapter 2, the presynaptic membranes of some neurons contain autoreceptors that regulate the amount of neurotransmitter that is released. Because stimulation of these receptors causes less neurotransmitter to be released, drugs that selectively activate presynaptic receptors act as antagonists. Drugs that *block* presynaptic autoreceptors have the opposite effect: They *increase* the release of the neurotransmitter, acting as agonists (see steps 8 and 9 in Figure 4.7).

Effects on Reuptake or Destruction of Neurotransmitters

LO 4.9 **Describe the effects of agonists on neurotransmitter reuptake and degradation.**

Shortly after being released from a presynaptic cell, the neurotransmitter is removed from the synapse, clearing the way for a new chemical message to follow. As you read in Chapter 2, two processes accomplish the task of removing the neurotransmitter from the synapse: Molecules of the neurotransmitter are taken back into the terminal button of the presynaptic cell through the process of reuptake or they are deactivated by an enzyme. Remember, terminal membrane transporters are different from the vesicle transporters. Drugs can interfere with either of these processes.

Figure 4.8 Drug Actions at Binding Sites

(a) Competitive binding: Direct agonists and antagonists act directly on the neurotransmitter binding site.
(b) Noncompetitive binding: Indirect agonists and antagonists act on an alternative binding site and modify the effects of the neurotransmitter on opening of the ion channel.

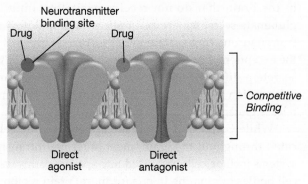

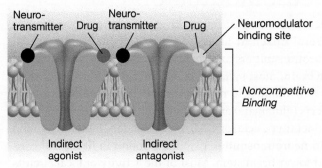

(a) (b)

Some drug molecules, such as cocaine, attach to the terminal membrane transporter molecules responsible for reuptake and inactivate them, thus blocking reuptake. Other drug molecules can bind with enzymes that normally destroy the neurotransmitter and prevent the enzymes from

working. Because both types of drugs prolong the presence of molecules of the neurotransmitter in the synaptic cleft (and hence in a location where these molecules can stimulate postsynaptic receptors), they serve as *agonists* (see steps 10 and 11 in Figure 4.7).

Section Review

Sites of Drug Action

LO 4.6 **Summarize how drug molecules can increase or decrease neurotransmitter synthesis.**

Some agonist drugs produce their effects by acting as precursors to increase the amount of neurotransmitter a cell can synthesize and release into the synapse. Other drugs are antagonists that inactivate neurotransmitter-synthesizing enzymes to prevent neurotransmitters from being produced.

LO 4.7 **Distinguish between the effects of agonists and antagonists on storage and release of neurotransmitters.**

Agonists can directly stimulate the release of neurotransmitters from a vesicle. Antagonists can block vesicle transporters or deactivate the cellular machinery responsible for vesicle docking and release to reduce the amount of neurotransmitters available in the synapse.

LO 4.8 **Contrast the effects of agonists and antagonists at the receptor.**

Agonists activate the receptor by binding directly to the neurotransmitter site (direct agonist) or to another site on

the receptor (indirect agonist). Antagonists block the receptor by binding either directly or indirectly to the receptor site.

LO 4.9 **Describe the effects of agonists on neurotransmitter reuptake and degradation.**

Agonists block neurotransmitter reuptake or deactivation to retain more of the neurotransmitter in the synapse available to bind to receptors.

Thought Question

Some grocery and health food stores sell the supplement 5-HTP, which is a precursor for the neurotransmitter serotonin. Draft an e-mail to a curious store manager and explain how a precursor supplement such as 5-HTP can function as a drug. While it is unclear how much of the supplement crosses the blood—brain barrier, explain to the manager how the precursor is intended to work to change neurotransmitter activity.

Neurotransmitters and Neuromodulators

There are many different kinds of neurotransmitters— several dozen at least (see Table 4.1 for a selection of neurotransmitters and their nervous system functions). In the brain, most synaptic communication is accomplished by two amino acid neurotransmitters: one with excitatory effects (glutamate) and one with inhibitory effects (gamma-aminobutyric acid, or GABA). A secondary inhibitory amino acid neurotransmitter, glycine, is found in the spinal cord and lower brain stem. Most of the activity of local circuits of neurons involves balances between the excitatory and inhibitory effects of these chemicals, which are responsible

for most of the information transmitted from place to place within the brain. In fact, there are probably no neurons in the brain that do not receive excitatory input from glutamate-secreting terminal buttons and inhibitory input from neurons that secrete either GABA or glycine. With the exception of neurons that detect painful stimuli, which secrete a different peptide, all sensory organs transmit information to the brain through axons whose terminals release glutamate.

While GABA and glutamate are released by cells located throughout the brain, most other neurotransmitter systems include cells organized into specific pathways with cell bodies originating in one (or more) brain regions projecting to one (or more) other brain regions. Look for this

Table 4.1 Neurotransmitter Systems

Neurotransmitter	Examples of CNS Functions	Examples of PNS Functions
Glutamate	Excitatory; interacts with other neurotransmitter systems	N/A
GABA	Inhibitory, interacts with other neurotransmitter systems	N/A
Acetylcholine (ACh)	Learning, memory, REM sleep	Muscle contraction
Dopamine	Voluntary movement, attention, learning, reinforcement, planning, problem solving	N/A
Norepinephrine/Epinephrine	Vigilance	Autonomic nervous system regulation (regulate heart rate, blood pressure, etc.)
Serotonin	Mood regulation, eating, sleep, dreaming, arousal, impulse control	Involved in the enteric nervous system (digestive tract)
Histamine	Wakefulness	Immune response
Opioids	Reinforcement, pain modulation	Pain modulation
Endocannabinoids	Appetite regulation	Immune response

pattern of pathways among the neurotransmitters presented throughout this chapter.

What do all the other neurotransmitters do? In general, they have modulating effects rather than information-transmitting effects. That is, the release of neurotransmitters other than glutamate, GABA, and glycine tends to activate or inhibit entire circuits of neurons that are involved in particular brain functions related to behavior and mental processes. Because particular drugs can selectively affect neurons that secrete particular neurotransmitters, they can have specific effects on behavior.

This section introduces some of the most important neurotransmitters, discusses some of their behavioral functions, and describes drugs that interact with them. As we saw in the previous section of this chapter, drugs have many different sites of action. Fortunately for your information-processing capacity (and perhaps your sanity), not all types of neurons are affected by all types of drugs. As you will see, that still leaves a good number of drugs to be mentioned by name and some are more important than others. Those whose effects we describe in some detail are more important than those we mention in passing.

Amino Acids

LO 4.10 **Compare the features of the amino acid neurotransmitter systems.**

Some neurons secrete simple amino acids as neurotransmitters. Because amino acids are used for protein synthesis by all cells of the brain, it is a challenge to prove that a particular amino acid is a neurotransmitter. However, investigators suspect that at least eight amino acids may serve as neurotransmitters in the mammalian CNS. Two specific amino acids are especially important because they are the most common neurotransmitters in the CNS: glutamate and GABA.

GLUTAMATE

Neurotransmitter Production, Storage, and Release   As you read in the introduction to this section, **glutamate** is the main excitatory neurotransmitter in the brain and spinal cord. Glutamate is synthesized from a precursor (*glutamine*) by an enzyme (*glutaminase*) in one step. After being synthesized, glutamate is stored in vesicles. **Vesicle glutamate transporters** package glutamate into vesicles. Glutamate is released from the presynaptic neuron following an action potential.

Receptors   Investigators have discovered four major types of glutamate receptors. Three of these receptors are ionotropic: the **NMDA receptor,** the **AMPA receptor,** and the **kainate receptor.** The other glutamate receptor—the **metabotropic glutamate receptor**—is (obviously!) metabotropic. Among other functions, some metabotropic glutamate receptors serve as presynaptic autoreceptors.

Most drugs that affect glutamate transmission do so by interacting with the glutamate receptors. Chemicals called NMDA, AMPA, and kainate serve as direct agonists at the receptors named after them. In addition, one of the most common drugs—alcohol—serves as an antagonist of NMDA receptors. As we will see in Chapter 18, this effect is responsible for the seizures that can be provoked by sudden withdrawal from heavy long-term alcohol intake.

Focusing for a moment on the ionotropic glutamate receptors, the AMPA receptor is the most common glutamate receptor. It controls a sodium channel, so when glutamate attaches to the binding site, it produces EPSPs. The kainate receptor has similar effects. The NMDA receptor has some special—and very important—characteristics. It contains at least six different binding sites: four located on the exterior of the receptor and two located deep within the ion channel. When it is open, the ion channel controlled by the NMDA receptor permits both sodium and calcium ions to enter the cell. The influx of both of these ions causes a depolarization, of course, but the entry of calcium (Ca^{2+}) is especially important. Calcium serves as a second messenger, binding with—and activating—various enzymes within the cell. These enzymes have profound effects on the biochemical and structural properties of the cell. As we shall see, one important result is alteration in the characteristics of the synapse that provide one of the building blocks of a newly formed memory. These effects of NMDA receptors will be discussed in much more detail in Chapter 13, where you will read about their role in memory formation.

Figure 4.9 presents an NMDA receptor and its binding sites. Obviously, glutamate binds with one of these sites, or we would not call it a glutamate receptor. However, glutamate by itself cannot open the calcium channel. For that to happen, a molecule of glycine must be attached to the glycine binding site, located on the outside of the receptor. (We do not yet understand why glycine—which also serves as an inhibitory neurotransmitter in some parts of the CNS—is required for this ion channel to open.) The drug **AP5 (2-amino-5-phosphonopentanoate)** blocks the glutamate binding site on the NMDA receptor and impairs synaptic plasticity and certain forms of learning.

An additional requirement for the opening of the calcium channel is that a magnesium ion *not* be attached to the magnesium binding site, located deep within the channel. Under normal conditions, when the postsynaptic membrane is at the resting potential, a magnesium ion (Mg^{2+}) is attracted to the magnesium binding site and blocks the calcium channel. If a molecule of glutamate attaches to its binding site, the channel widens, but the magnesium ion still blocks it, so no calcium can enter the postsynaptic neuron. However, if the postsynaptic membrane is partially depolarized, the magnesium ion is repelled from its binding site. Thus, the NMDA receptor opens only if glutamate is present *and* the postsynaptic membrane is depolarized. The NMDA receptor, then, is a voltage- and neurotransmitter-dependent ion channel.

The PCP site, located deep within the ion channel near the magnesium binding site, binds with a hallucinogenic drug, **PCP** (phencyclidine). PCP serves as an indirect antagonist; when it attaches to its binding site, calcium ions cannot pass through the ion channel. Another drug has similar effects and is thought to bind to this site too: **ketamine.** Ketamine and PCP were originally developed as anesthetics, however their hallucinatory effects made them largely unacceptable for human use. In addition to its recreational use, ketamine is still used as an anesthetic for veterinary practice and recent clinical trials have suggested a new use as a therapeutic drug in treatment-resistant depression.

Reuptake and Destruction   Glutamate is removed from the synapse by **excitatory amino acid transporters** and broken down into its building block precursor (glutamine) by the enzyme **glutamine synthase.** A failure to remove glutamate from the synapse can have negative consequences. Too much glutamate stimulation in the synapse can produce **glutamate excitotoxicity** and damage neurons by prolonged over excitation. As you will read in Chapter 15, glutamate excitotoxicity is believed to be involved in damage to the brain in stroke and amyotrophic lateral sclerosis (ALS; Lou Gehrig's disease). Although drugs that enhance reuptake or destruction of excess glutamate remain to be developed, riluzole (Rilutek) is used in ALS treatment and likely reduces glutamate signaling by reducing glutamate vesicle docking with the presynaptic terminal membrane. If you were a researcher trying to develop a new drug to prevent or reduce glutamate excitotoxicity, what would you look for in a new drug? How could you target reuptake and destruction of the neurotransmitter to reduce neuronal damage due to glutamate over excitation? What side effects might this drug produce by reducing glutamate signaling?

GABA

Neurotransmitter Production, Storage, and Release   **GABA** (gamma-aminobutyric acid) is an inhibitory neurotransmitter, and it appears to have a widespread distribution throughout the brain and spinal cord. GABA is produced from a precursor (*glutamic acid*) by the action of an enzyme (*glutamic acid decarboxylase*, or *GAD*). The drug **allylglycine** inactivates GAD and thus prevents the synthesis of GABA (step 2 of Figure 4.7). Allylglycine is typically used as a research drug to understand the GABA system. It has little therapeutic use because the reduction in GABA contributes to the likelihood of seizures. GABA is packaged into vesicles by the **vesicle GABA transporter,** where it is stored until being released following an action potential.

As you know, neurons in the brain are greatly interconnected. Without the activity of inhibitory synapses these

Figure 4.9 NMDA Receptor

This schematic illustration of an NMDA receptor shows its binding sites.

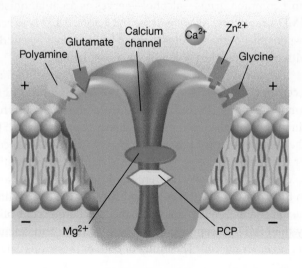

interconnections would make the brain unstable. That is, through excitatory synapses neurons would excite their neighbors, which would then excite *their* neighbors, which would then excite the originally active neurons, and so on, until most of the neurons in the brain would be firing uncontrollably. In fact, this event does sometimes occur, and we refer to it as a *seizure*. Normally, an inhibitory influence is supplied by GABA-secreting neurons, which are present in large numbers in the brain. Some investigators believe that one of the causes of seizure disorders is an abnormality in the biochemistry of GABA-secreting neurons or in GABA receptors.

Receptors　Several GABA receptors have been identified. More specifically, many drugs interact with the GABA$_A$ receptor and we will focus the discussion of drug effects on the GABA system here. GABA$_A$ receptors are ionotropic and control chloride channels.

　Like NMDA receptors, GABA$_A$ receptors are complex; they contain at least five different binding sites. The primary binding site is for GABA. The drug **muscimol** serves as a direct agonist for this site. Another drug, **bicuculline**, blocks this GABA binding site, serving as a direct antagonist. A second site on the GABA$_A$ receptor binds with a class of drugs called the **benzodiazepines**. These drugs include **diazepam** (Valium) and **alprazolam** (Xanax), which are used to reduce symptoms of anxiety, reduce seizure activity, and produce muscle relaxation. The third site binds with barbiturates, an older class of sedative and antianxiety drugs. Alcohol binds with an as-yet-unknown site on the GABA$_A$ receptor. Another site binds with various steroids, including some steroids used to produce general anesthesia. The GABA$_A$ receptor includes several other binding sites; however, they are beyond the scope of discussion here. (See Figure 4.10.)

　Benzodiazepines and barbiturates promote the activity of the GABA$_A$ receptor; thus, these drugs serve as indirect agonists. Benzodiazepines are very effective **anxiolytics**, or "anxiety-dissolving" drugs. They are used to treat the symptoms of anxiety disorders. Barbiturates are older drugs that have similar effects, however they are not considered a first-line therapeutic treatment option due to their potentially dangerous sedative effects. Drugs that are related to the benzodiazepines, such as **zolpidem** (Ambien) and **eszopiclone** (Lunesta), are effective sleep medications. Picrotoxin has effects opposite to those of benzodiazepines and barbiturates: It *inhibits* the activity of the GABA$_A$ receptor, thus serving as an indirect antagonist. In high enough doses, this drug causes seizures.

　Various steroid hormones are normally produced in the body, and some hormones related to progesterone (the principal pregnancy hormone) act on the steroid-binding site of the GABA$_A$ receptor, producing a relaxing, anxiolytic sedative effect. However, the brain does not produce Valium,

Figure 4.10 GABA Receptor

This schematic illustration of a GABA$_A$ receptor shows its binding sites.

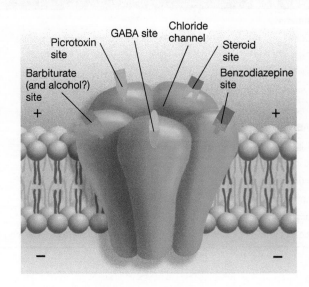

barbiturates, or picrotoxin. The natural ligands for these binding sites have not yet been discovered.

Reuptake and Destruction　GABA is removed from the synapse by **GABA transporters. Tiagabine** (Gabitril) is a GABA transporter antagonist used to increase availability of GABA and reduce the likelihood of seizures. GABA is broken down by the enzyme, *GABA aminotransferase*. **Vigabatrin** (Sabril) blocks the activity of GABA aminotransferase to increase the amount of GABA available in the synapse. Vigabatrin is also used as a therapeutic treatment for seizures and epilepsy. For a summary of some important drugs that act on the glutamate and GABA systems, see Table 4.2.

Acetylcholine

LO 4.11　Summarize the features of the acetylcholine system.

The next several examples of neurotransmitter systems are organized slightly differently from the amino acid neurotransmitter systems the brain. To help you understand the different neurotransmitter systems, think about their similarities and differences as you read the following section.

PATHWAYS　Unlike the neurons that release the amino acid neurotransmitters and are located throughout the brain, most acetylcholine-releasing neurons are found in specific locations and pathways in the CNS. Three pathways have received the most attention from neuroscientists: those originating in the dorsolateral pons, the basal forebrain (or nucleus basalis), and the medial septum. The effects of acetylcholine (ACh) release in the brain are generally

Table 4.2 Drugs that Act on the Glutamate and GABA Systems

Drug	Mechanism	Effect
Glutamate		
PCP	Indirect NMDA receptor antagonist	Impairs learning
AP5	NMDA receptor antagonist	Impairs learning
NMDA	NMDA receptor agonist	Used in research to study this receptor
AMPA	AMPA receptor agonist	Used in research to study this receptor
Kainate	Kainate receptor agonist	Used in research to study this receptor
GABA		
Allylglycine	Inhibits GABA synthesis	Seizures
Muscimol	GABA receptor agonist	Sedation
Bicuculine	GABA receptor antagonist	Seizures
Benzodiazepines	Indirect GABA receptor agonists	Anxiolytic, sedation, memory impairment, muscle relaxation
Barbiturates	Indirect GABA receptor agonists	Sedation, memory impairment, muscle relaxation
Alcohol	Indirect GABA receptor agonist (among other mechanisms)	Sedation, memory impairment, muscle relaxation

facilitatory. The acetylcholinergic neurons located in the dorsolateral pons play a role in REM sleep (the phase of sleep during which dreaming occurs). Those located in the basal forebrain are involved in activating the cerebral cortex and facilitating learning, especially perceptual learning. Those located in the medial septum control the electrical rhythms of the hippocampus and modulate its functions, which include the formation of particular kinds of memories. (See Figure 4.11.)

ACh is unique as an important neurotransmitter because of its functions in both the central and peripheral nervous systems. It is the primary neurotransmitter secreted by axons of the PNS that terminate at muscle cells to control muscle contraction. Because ACh is found outside the CNS

Figure 4.11 Acetylcholinergic Pathways in a Rat Brain

This schematic figure shows the locations of the most important groups of acetylcholinergic neurons and the distribution of their axons and terminal buttons.

(Adapted from Woolf, N. J., Cholinergic systems in mammalian brain and spinal cord, *Progress in Neurobiology,* 1991, *37*, 475–524.)

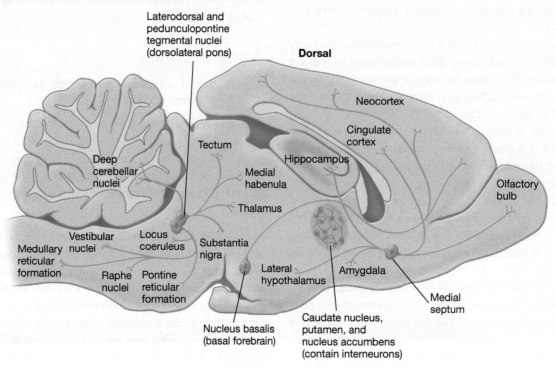

in locations that are easy to study, this neurotransmitter was the first to be discovered.

NEUROTRANSMITTER PRODUCTION, STORAGE, AND RELEASE   Acetylcholine is composed of two precursors: *choline* and *acetyl coenzyme A*. The enzyme **choline acetyltransferase (ChAT),** is required to produce ACh from the precursors. (See Figure 4.12.) To date, there has not been significant development of drugs that can interact with ChAT to increase or decrease ACh production. Why do you think a researcher might want to develop a ChAT antagonist (or agonist)?

ACh is loaded into vesicles by the **vesicle ACh transporter,** where it is stored until being released from the presynaptic cell. Two drugs, botulinum toxin and the venom of the black widow spider, affect the release of ACh. **Botulinum toxin (Botox)** is produced by *Clostridium botulinum,* a bacterium that can grow in improperly canned food. This drug prevents the release of ACh. Botulinum toxin is an extremely potent poison because the paralysis it can cause leads to suffocation. When used locally as an injection into a muscle (rather than being ingested and distributed to the entire body), botulinum toxin can have desired effects. Botox treatments involve injections of very dilute solution of botulinum toxin into facial muscles to stop muscular contractions that are causing wrinkles in the skin. Although much of the interest in Botox is for cosmetic reasons, Botox has also been used therapeutically to treat migraine headaches and severe muscle contraction. Due to compensatory actions by the presynaptic neuron, these injections are temporary and the effects eventually subside.

In contrast, **black widow spider venom** has the opposite effect: It stimulates the release of ACh. Although the effects of black widow spider venom can also be fatal, the venom is much less toxic than botulinum toxin. In fact, most healthy adults would have to receive several bites, but infants or those with health complications would be more susceptible.

RECEPTORS   There are two types of ACh receptors: one ionotropic and one metabotropic. The ionotropic ACh receptor is stimulated by **nicotine,** a drug found in tobacco leaves.

The metabotropic ACh receptor is stimulated by **muscarine,** a drug found in the poison mushroom *Amanita muscaria.* Consequently, these two ACh receptors are referred to as **nicotinic receptors** and **muscarinic receptors,** respectively.

Because muscle fibers in the PNS must be able to contract quickly, they contain the rapid-acting, ionotropic nicotinic receptors. Because muscarinic receptors are metabotropic in nature and thus control ion channels through the production of second messengers, their actions are slower and more prolonged than those of nicotinic receptors. The CNS contains both kinds of ACh receptors, but muscarinic receptors predominate. Some nicotinic receptors are found at axoaxonic synapses in the brain, where they produce presynaptic facilitation. Activation of these receptors is partially responsible for the reinforcing effects of nicotine.

Just as two different drugs stimulate the two classes of ACh receptors, two different drugs *block* them. The first drug, **atropine,** blocks muscarinic receptors. One of the effects of atropine administration is to reduce saliva production. This drug is sometimes used in surgery to reduce saliva that could obstruct a patient's airway while unconscious. Another drug, **curare,** blocks nicotinic receptors. Because these receptors are the ones found on muscles, curare, like botulinum toxin, causes paralysis. However, the effects of curare are much faster.

REUPTAKE AND DESTRUCTION   You will recall from Chapter 2 that after being released by the terminal button, ACh is deactivated by the enzyme *acetylcholinesterase (AChE),* which is present in the postsynaptic membrane. (See Figure 4.13.) AChE breaks down one molecule of ACh into its two precursors. Drugs that deactivate AChE are used for several purposes. AChE inhibitors are used to treat symptoms of a hereditary disorder called *myasthenia gravis.* Myasthenia gravis is caused by a person's immune system attacking ACh receptors located on skeletal muscles. The person becomes weaker and weaker as the muscles become less responsive to the neurotransmitter. If the person is given an AChE inhibitor such as **neostigmine,** the person

Figure 4.12 Synthesis of Acetylcholine

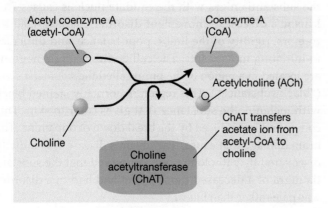

Figure 4.13 Destruction of Acetylcholine by Acetylcholinesterase

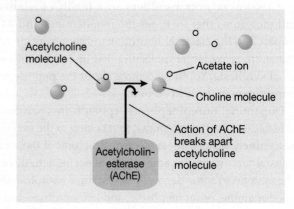

Table 4.3 Drugs that Act on the Acetylcholine System

Drug	Mechanism	Effect
Botulinum toxin	Prevents release of ACh in PNS	Prevents muscle contraction
Black widow spider venom	Stimulates release of ACh in PNS	Stimulates muscle contraction
Neostigmine	Inhibits AChE	Increases effect of ACh at receptors; used to treat symptoms of myasthenia gravis
Nicotine	Agonist at ionotropic receptors	Increases attention, reinforcing effects
Muscarine	Agonist at metabotropic receptors	Toxic, hallucinogenic effects
Curare	Antagonist at ionotropic receptors	Prevents muscle contraction
Atropine	Antagonist at metabotropic receptors	Blocks pupil constriction, saliva production

will regain some strength because the ACh that is released has a more prolonged effect on the remaining receptors.

After being broken down into its constituent parts, only choline is recycled by cholinergic cells. Presynaptic neurons in cholinergic synapses possess choline transporters for reuptake of this ACh precursor. **Hemicholinium-3** is a research drug that blocks the choline transporter. The effect of this drug is to reduce the rate of ACh production. For a summary of some important drugs that act on the ACh system, see Table 4.3.

The Monoamines

LO 4.12 Summarize the key features of the monoamine systems.

The monoamine neurotransmitters are produced by several systems of neurons in the brain. Most of these systems consist of a relatively small number of cell bodies located in the brain stem, whose axons branch repeatedly and give rise to an enormous number of terminal buttons distributed throughout many regions of the brain. Monoaminergic neurons thus serve to modulate the function of widespread regions of the brain, increasing or decreasing the activities of particular brain functions.

Monoamines are considered "classical" neurotransmitters. Classical neurotransmitters are a family of relatively small molecules that includes the monoamines and ACh. Compared to the classical neurotransmitters, peptide neurotransmitters are larger molecules that undergo a different type of synthesis. You'll read more about the peptide neurotransmitters in the next section.

Dopamine, norepinephrine, epinephrine, serotonin, and histamine are five chemicals that belong to the family of **monoamines.** Because the molecular structures of these neurotransmitters are similar, some drugs affect the activity of all of the systems to some degree. The first three neurotransmitters—dopamine, norepinephrine, and epinephrine—belong

Table 4.4 Classification of the Monoamine Neurotransmitters

Catecholamines	Indolamine	Ethylamine
Dopamine	Serotonin	Histamine
Norepinephrine		
Epinephrine		

to a subclass of monoamines called **catecholamines.** It is worthwhile learning the terms in Table 4.4, because they will be used throughout the rest of this book.

DOPAMINE The first catecholamine in Table 4.4, **dopamine (DA),** produces both excitatory and inhibitory postsynaptic potentials, depending on the postsynaptic receptor. Dopamine has been implicated in several important functions, including movement, attention, learning, and the reinforcing effects of drugs that people tend to abuse. It is discussed in Chapters 8, 9, 13, 16, and 18.

Pathways The brain contains several systems of dopaminergic neurons arranged in pathways, similar to the organization you read about for ACh neurons. The three most important dopamine pathways originate in midbrain structures: the substantia nigra and ventral tegmental area. The cell bodies of neurons of the **nigrostriatal system** are located in the substantia nigra and project their axons to the neostriatum: the caudate nucleus and the putamen. The neostriatum is an important part of the basal ganglia, which is involved in the control of movement. The cell bodies of neurons of the **mesolimbic system** are located in the ventral tegmental area and project their axons to several parts of the limbic system, including the nucleus accumbens, amygdala, and hippocampus. The nucleus accumbens plays an important role in the reinforcing (rewarding) effects of certain categories of stimuli, including those of drugs that people abuse. The cell bodies of neurons of the **mesocortical system** are also located in the ventral tegmental area. Their axons project to the prefrontal cortex. These neurons have an excitatory effect on the frontal cortex and affect such functions as formation of short-term memories, planning, and strategy preparation for problem solving. (See Figure 4.14.)

Degeneration of dopaminergic neurons that connect the substantia nigra with the caudate nucleus causes **Parkinson's disease,** a movement disorder characterized by tremors, rigidity of the limbs, poor balance, and difficulty in initiating movements. The cell bodies of these neurons are located in a region of the brain called the *substantia nigra* ("black substance"). This region is normally stained black with melanin, the substance that gives color to skin. This compound is produced by the breakdown of dopamine. The brain damage that causes Parkinson's disease was initially discovered by pathologists who observed that the substantia nigra of a deceased person who had had this disorder was pale rather than black.

Figure 4.14 Dopaminergic Pathways in a Rat Brain

This schematic figure shows the locations of the most important groups of dopaminergic neurons and the distribution of their axons and terminal buttons.

(Adapted from Fuxe, K., Agnati, L. F., Kalia, M., et al., Dopaminergic systems in the brain and pituitary, in *Basic and Clinical Aspects of Neuroscience: The Dopaminergic System,* edited by E. Fluckinger, E. E. Muller, and M. O. Thomas, Berlin: Springer–Verlag, 1985.)

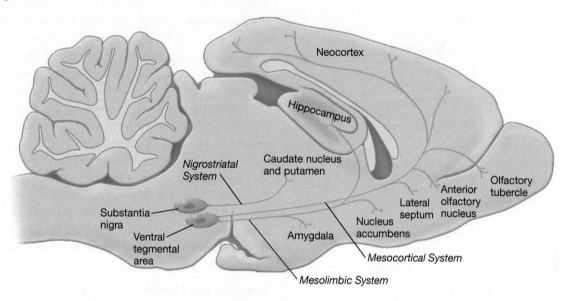

Neurotransmitter Production, Storage, and Release
Catecholamine synthesis is somewhat complicated, but each step is a simple one. The precursor molecule is modified slightly, step by step, until it achieves its final shape. Each step is controlled by a different enzyme, which causes a small part to be added or taken off. The precursor for the two major catecholamine neurotransmitters (dopamine and norepinephrine) is *tyrosine,* an essential amino acid that we must obtain from our diet. Tyrosine is modified by the enzyme *tyrosine hydroxylase* and becomes L-**DOPA** (L-3,4-dihydroxyphenylalanine). L-DOPA is then modified through the activity of the enzyme *DOPA decarboxylase* and becomes dopamine. Finally, the enzyme *dopamine β-hydroxylase* converts dopamine to norepinephrine. Only neurons that release norepinephrine contain dopamine β-hydroxylase; however, both dopamine- and norepinephrine-releasing neurons contain *tyrosine hydroxylase.* These reactions are shown in Figure 4.15.

The drug **AMPT** (or α-methyl-*p*-tyrosine), inactivates tyrosine hydroxylase, the enzyme that converts tyrosine to L-DOPA. Because this drug interferes with the synthesis of dopamine (and of norepinephrine as well), it serves as a catecholamine antagonist. The drug is not normally used medically, but it has been used as a research tool in laboratory animals.

People with Parkinson's disease are given the drug L-DOPA. Although dopamine cannot cross the blood–brain barrier, L-DOPA can. Once L-DOPA reaches the brain, it is taken up by dopaminergic neurons and is converted to dopamine. The increased synthesis of dopamine causes more dopamine to be released by the surviving dopaminergic neurons in

The drug l-DOPA causes dopamine to be released by surviving dopaminergic neurons in patients with Parkinson's disease, thus alleviating their symptoms.

patients with Parkinson's disease. As a consequence, the patients' symptoms are alleviated. (For additional information about Parkinson's disease, see Chapter 15.)

The drug **reserpine** prevents the storage of monoamines in synaptic vesicles by blocking the **vesicle monoamine transporters.** Because the synaptic vesicles remain

Figure 4.15 Synthesis of the Catecholamines

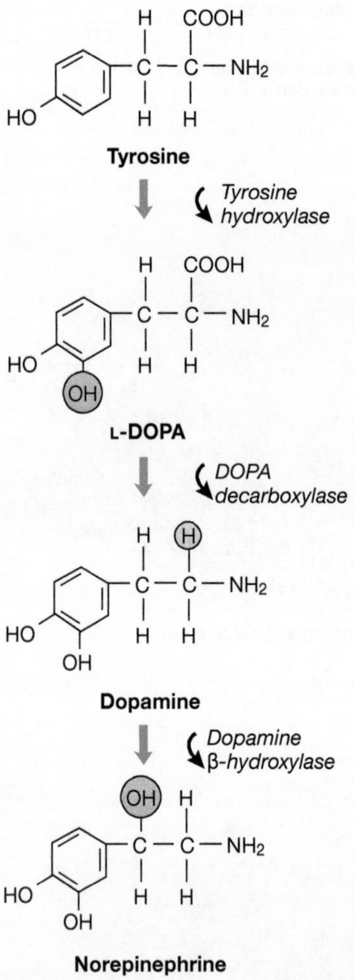

empty, no neurotransmitter is released when an action potential reaches the terminal button. Reserpine, then, is a monoamine antagonist. Reserpine was previously used to treat high blood pressure but produced depressive and sedative side effects. It has now been replaced by drugs with fewer side effects.

Receptors Several drugs stimulate or block specific types of dopamine receptors. Five metabotropic types of dopamine receptors have been identified and named the D_1, D_2, D_3, D_4, and D_5. receptors. D_1 and D_2 receptors are the most common. Stimulation of D_1 and D_5 receptors increases the production of the second messenger cyclic AMP, whereas stimulation of D_2, D_3, and D_4 receptors decreases production of cyclic AMP.

Dopamine has been implicated as one neurotransmitter that might be involved in schizophrenia, a serious mental disorder whose symptoms include hallucinations, delusions, and disruption of thought processes. Drugs such as **chlorpromazine,** which block D_2 receptors, alleviate some symptoms, such as hallucinations. Hence, investigators have speculated that these symptoms of schizophrenia

(the so-called *positive symptoms*) are produced by overactivity of dopaminergic neurons. More recently discovered drugs—the *atypical antipsychotics*—have more complicated actions, which are discussed in Chapter 16.

Autoreceptors are found in the dendrites, soma, and terminal buttons of dopaminergic neurons. Activation of the autoreceptors in the dendritic and somatic membrane decreases neural firing by producing hyperpolarizations. The presynaptic autoreceptors located in the terminal buttons suppress the activity of the enzyme tyrosine hydroxylase and thus decrease the production of dopamine—and ultimately its release. Dopamine autoreceptors resemble D_2 receptors, but there seem to be some differences. For example, the drug **apomorphine** is a D_2 agonist, but it seems to have a greater affinity for presynaptic D_2 receptors than for postsynaptic D_2 receptors. A low dose of apomorphine acts as an antagonist, because it stimulates the presynaptic receptors and inhibits the production and release of dopamine. Higher doses begin to stimulate postsynaptic D_2 receptors, and the drug begins to act as a direct agonist. (See Figure 4.16.)

Reuptake and Destruction **Dopamine transporters** are responsible for removing dopamine from the synapse. Several drugs inhibit the reuptake of dopamine, thus serving as potent dopamine agonists. The best known of these drugs are amphetamine, methamphetamine, cocaine, and methylphenidate (Ritalin). **Amphetamine** and **methamphetamine** have an interesting effect: They result in the release of both dopamine and norepinephrine by causing the transporters for these neurotransmitters to run in reverse, propelling dopamine and norepinephrine into the synaptic cleft. Of course, this action also blocks reuptake of these neurotransmitters. **Cocaine** and **methylphenidate** simply block dopamine reuptake. Because cocaine also blocks voltage-dependent sodium channels, it is sometimes used as a topical anesthetic, especially in the form of eye drops for eye surgery. Methylphenidate is used to enhance attention and impulse control in attention-deficit/hyperactivity disorder (ADHD).

The destruction of catecholamines is regulated by an enzyme called **monoamine oxidase (MAO).** This enzyme is found within monoaminergic terminal buttons, where it destroys excess neurotransmitter. A drug called **deprenyl** inhibits the particular form of monoamine oxidase (MAO-B) that is found in dopaminergic terminal buttons. Because deprenyl prevents the destruction of dopamine, more dopamine is available in the terminal buttons. Thus, deprenyl serves as a dopamine agonist and can be used to treat the symptoms of Parkinson's disease. (See Figure 4.17.)

NOREPINEPHRINE

Pathways Like ACh, **norepinephrine (NE)** is found in both the CNS and PNS. As you begin to read this section,

Figure 4.16 Effects of Low and High Doses of Apomorphine

At low doses, apomorphine serves as a dopamine antagonist; at high doses, it serves as an agonist.

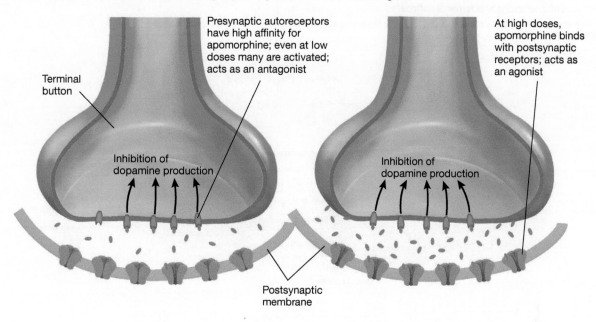

please note that the terms adrenaline and **epinephrine** are synonymous, as are noradrenaline and norepinephrine.

Almost every region of the brain receives input from noradrenergic neurons. The cell bodies of most of these neurons are located in seven regions of the pons and medulla and one region of the thalamus. The cell bodies of the most important noradrenergic system begin in the **locus coeruleus,** a nucleus located in the dorsal pons. The axons of these neurons project to the regions shown in Figure 4.18. As we will see later, the primary effect of activation of these neurons is an increase in vigilance—attentiveness to events in the environment.

Neurotransmitter Production, Storage, and Release As you already saw in the synthesis pathway for norepinephrine in Figure 4.15, norepinephrine is synthesized from dopamine by the enzyme dopamine β-hydroxylase. Blocking any portion of the synthesis pathway of dopamine or norepinephrine reduces the amount of norepinephrine that is produced by a neuron. The drug AMPT, which prevents the conversion of tyrosine to L-DOPA, blocks the production of norepinephrine as well as dopamine.

Most classical neurotransmitters are synthesized in the cytoplasm of the terminal button and then stored in newly

Figure 4.17 Role of Monoamine Oxidase

This schematic shows the role of monoamine oxidase in dopaminergic terminal buttons and the action of deprenyl.

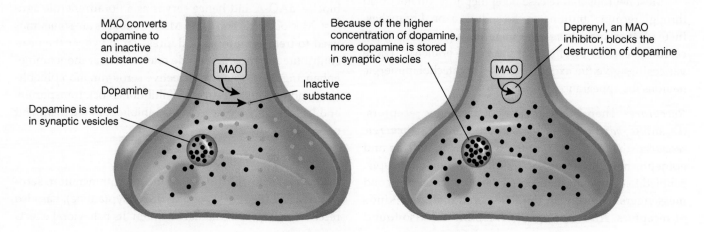

Figure 4.18 Noradrenergic Pathways in a Rat Brain

This schematic figure shows the locations of the most important groups of noradrenergic neurons and the distribution of their axons and terminal buttons.

(Adapted from Cotman, C. W. and McGaugh, J. L., *Behavioral Neuroscience: An Introduction*, New York: Academic Press, 1980.)

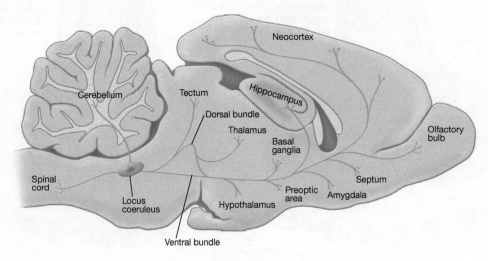

formed synaptic vesicles. However, for norepinephrine the final step of synthesis occurs inside the vesicles themselves. The vesicles are first filled with dopamine. Then the dopamine is converted to norepinephrine through the action of the enzyme dopamine β-hydroxylase located within the vesicles. The drug **fusaric acid** inhibits the activity of dopamine β-hydroxylase and thus blocks the production of norepinephrine without affecting the production of dopamine. Fusaric acid is sometimes used by researchers who want to investigate the norepinephrine system while leaving the dopamine system unaffected.

Norepinephrine is either synthesized within the vesicle, or when being recycled, loaded into the vesicle by the vesicle monoamine transporter. You have already encountered the vesicle monoamine transporter in the dopamine section of this chapter—the same vesicle transporter is used to fill vesicles in all of the monoamine systems. Remember that reserpine is a drug used to block the vesicle monoamine transporters.

Most neurons that release norepinephrine do not do so through terminal buttons on the ends of axonal branches. Instead, they usually release them through **axonal varicosities,** beadlike swellings of the axonal branches. These varicosities give the axonal branches of catecholaminergic neurons the appearance of beaded chains.

Receptors There are four types of *adrenergic* receptors, α_1- and α_2-*adrenergic receptors* and β_1- and β_2-*adrenergic receptors*, that are sensitive to both norepinephrine and epinephrine. All adrenergic receptors are metabotropic, coupled to G proteins that control the production of second messengers. Neurons in the CNS contain all four kinds of receptors. All four kinds of receptors are also found

in various organs of the body and are responsible for the effects of epinephrine and norepinephrine when they act as hormones in the PNS. The research drug **idazoxan** blocks α_2 autoreceptors and hence acts as an agonist. This drug is used to study the actions of the norepinephrine system.

Earlier in this chapter, you encountered two drugs that act on adrenergic receptors. Yohimbine blocks the adrenergic autoreceptor, resulting in symptoms of anxiety and increased heart rate and blood pressure. In contrast, clonidine (Catapres) acts as an agonist at the norepinephrine autoreceptor, decreasing the activity of this system and reducing heart rate and blood pressure. In the brain, all adrenergic autoreceptors appear to be of the α_2 type.

Reuptake and Destruction The **norepinephrine transporter** is responsible for removing excess norepinephrine from the synapse. Monoamine oxidase A (MAO-A) deactivates norepinephrine. The drug **moclobemide** specifically blocks MAO-A and hence serves as a noradrenergic agonist. Moclobemide and other MAO inhibitors are sometimes used to treat symptoms of depression, however they can contribute to problematic side effects. Newer monoamine-enhancing drugs, such as selective serotonin, norepinephrine, and dopamine reuptake inhibitors block transporters and have largely replaced MAO inhibitors in the treatment of depression.

SEROTONIN

Pathways The third monoamine neurotransmitter, **serotonin** (also called **5-HT,** or 5-hydroxytryptamine), has also received much experimental attention. Its behavioral effects

Figure 4.19 Serotonergic Pathways in a Rat Brain

This schematic figure shows the locations of the most important groups of serotonergic neurons and the distribution of their axons and terminal buttons.

(Adapted from Consolazione, A. and Cuello, A. C., CNS serotonin pathways, pp. 29–61, in *Biology of Serotonergic Transmission,* edited by N. N. Osborne, Chichester: England: Wiley & Sons, 1982.)

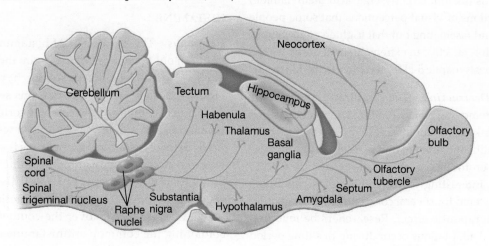

are complex. Serotonin plays a role in the regulation of mood; in the control of eating, sleep, and arousal; and in the regulation of pain. Serotonergic neurons are also involved in the control of dreaming.

The cell bodies of serotonergic neurons are found in nine clusters, most of which are located in the raphe nuclei of the midbrain, pons, and medulla. Like norepinephrine, 5-HT is released from varicosities rather than terminal buttons. The two most important clusters of serotonergic cell bodies are found in the dorsal and medial raphe nuclei, and we will restrict our discussion to these clusters. The word *raphe* means "seam" or "crease" and refers to the fact that most of the raphe nuclei are found at or near the midline "seam" of the brain stem. Both the dorsal and median raphe nuclei project axons to the cerebral cortex. In addition, neurons in the dorsal raphe innervate the basal ganglia, and those in the median raphe innervate the dentate gyrus, a part of the hippocampal formation. (See Figure 4.19.)

Neurotransmitter Production, Storage, and Release The precursor for serotonin is the amino acid *tryptophan.* The enzyme *tryptophan hydroxylase* acts on tryptophan, producing *5-HTP* (5-hydroxytryptophan). The enzyme *5-HTP decarboxylase* converts 5-HTP to 5-HT (serotonin). (See Figure 4.20.) The drug **PCPA** (*p*-chlorophenylalanine) blocks the activity of tryptophan hydroxylase and thus serves as a serotonergic antagonist. Similar to the other monoamines described in this chapter, 5-HT is loaded into vesicles using the vesicle monoamine transporter and released following an action potential.

Receptors Investigators have identified at least nine different types of serotonin receptors: 5-HT$_{1A-1B}$, 5-HT$_{1D-1F}$, 5-HT$_{2A-2C}$, and 5-HT$_3$. Of these the 5-HT$_{1B}$ and 5-HT$_{1D}$ receptors serve

as presynaptic autoreceptors. In the dorsal and median raphe nuclei, 5-HT$_{1A}$ receptors serve as autoreceptors in the membrane of dendrites and soma. All 5-HT receptors are metabotropic except for the 5-HT$_3$ receptor, which is ionotropic. The 5-HT$_3$ receptor controls a chloride channel, which means that it produces inhibitory postsynaptic potentials. These receptors appear to play a role in nausea and vomiting, because 5-HT$_3$ antagonists, such as **ondansetron,** are useful in reducing the side effects of chemotherapy and radiation for the treatment of cancer.

Figure 4.20 Synthesis of Serotonin

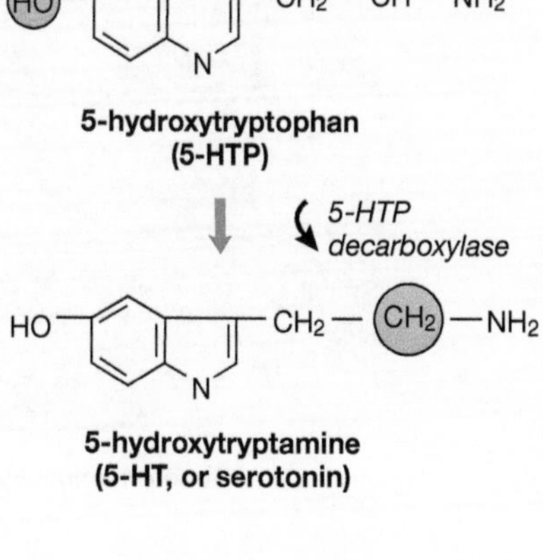

COOH
|
CH$_2$ — CH — NH$_2$

Tryptophan

Tyrosine hydroxylase

COOH
|
CH$_2$ — CH — NH$_2$

HO

5-hydroxytryptophan (5-HTP)

5-HTP decarboxylase

HO — CH$_2$ — CH$_2$ — NH$_2$

5-hydroxytryptamine (5-HT, or serotonin)

Some drugs selectively bind to other 5-HT receptors. For example, the 5-HT$_{1A}$ partial agonist **buspirone (BuSpar)** is used to treat symptoms of anxiety and depression. Several hallucinogenic drugs produce their effects by interacting with serotonergic transmission. **LSD** (lysergic acid diethylamide) produces distortions of visual perceptions that some people find awesome and fascinating but that frighten other people. This drug, which is effective in extremely small doses, is a direct agonist for postsynaptic 5-HT$_{2A}$ receptors in the forebrain.

Reuptake and Destruction The **serotonin transporter** is responsible for removing 5-HT from the synapse. Drugs that inhibit the reuptake of serotonin have found a very important place in the treatment of mental illness. These drugs increase the amount of serotonin available at the synapse to bind to 5-HT receptors. Interestingly, serotonin reuptake inhibitors must be administered for several consecutive weeks in order to achieve a therapeutic effect. Researchers believe that important neural adaptations occur during this time period to affect the activity of the 5-HT system. The best known of these drugs, **fluoxetine** (Prozac), is used to treat depression, some forms of anxiety disorders, and obsessive-compulsive disorder. These disorders and their treatment are discussed in Chapters 16 and 17. Another drug, **fenfluramine,** which causes the release of serotonin as well as inhibits its reuptake, was formerly used as an appetite suppressant in the treatment of obesity. Chapter 12 discusses the topic of obesity and its treatment by means of drugs.

MDMA (methylenedioxymethamphetamine or ecstasy) binds with norepinephrine and 5-HT transporters and causes them to run backward, releasing these neurotransmitters and inhibiting their reuptake, resulting in excitatory and hallucinogenic effects. Research indicates that MDMA can selectively damage serotonergic neurons and cause cognitive deficits.

Similar to the other monoamines, 5-HT is subject to being broken down by monoamine oxidase. As you have already read, monoamine oxidase inhibitors have antidepressant effects.

HISTAMINE

Pathways The cell bodies of histaminergic neurons are found in only one place in the brain: the *tuberomammillary nucleus,* located in the posterior hypothalamus. (See Figure 4.21.) Histaminergic neurons send their axons to widespread regions of the cerebral cortex and brain stem. **Histamine** plays an important role in wakefulness. In fact, the activity of histaminergic neurons is strongly correlated with the states of sleep and wakefulness, and drugs that block histamine receptors (also called *antihistamines)* cause drowsiness. You may have experienced this effect if you have ever taken an over-the-counter sleep medication containing the common antihistamine diphenhydramine to treat symptoms of allergies or insomnia.

Neurotransmitter Production, Storage, and Release Histamine is produced from the amino acid precursor *histidine* by the action of the enzyme *histidine decarboxylase.* Like the other monoamines, it is stored in vesicles and released following an action potential.

Receptors The CNS contains H$_1$, H$_2$, H$_3$ and H$_4$ receptors. Newer antihistamines that are used to treat the symptoms of allergies do not cross the blood–brain barrier, so they have no direct effects on the brain. In contrast, many over-the-counter sleep aids contain **diphenhydramine** with the goal of crossing the blood–brain barrier to produce drowsiness. You will read more about the histamine system and its role in sleep in Chapter 9. For a summary of some important drugs that act on monoamine systems, see Table 4.5.

Figure 4.21 Histaminergic Pathways in a Rat Brain
This schematic shows the locations of the most important group of histaminergic neurons and the distribution of their axons and terminal buttons.

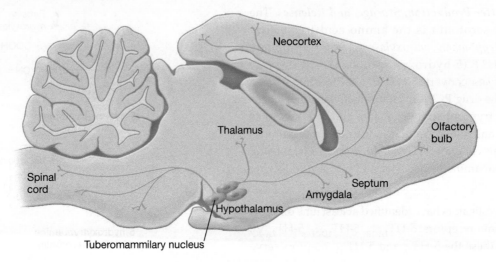

Table 4.5 Drugs that Act on Monoamine Systems

Drug	Mechanism	Effect
Dopamine		
L-Dopa	DA precursor	Enhances DA effects; treats Parkinson's disease symptoms
AMPT	Blocks tyrosine hydroxylase	Used in research
Apomorphine	D_2 antagonist	Used in research
Methylphenidate	Blocks DA reuptake	Stimulant; used to treat symptoms of ADHD
Cocaine	Blocks DA reuptake	Stimulant and reinforcing effects
Chlorpromazine	D_2 receptor antagonist	Used to treat positive symptoms of schizophrenia
Norepinephrine		
Idazoxan	α_2 autoreceptor antagonist	Used in research, may have antidepressant effects
Serotonin		
PCPA	Blocks tryptophan hydroxylase	Used in research
Fluoxetine	Blocks 5-HT reuptake	Used to treat symptoms of depression
Fenfluramine	Blocks 5-HT reuptake, causes 5-HT release	Appetite suppressant, no longer prescribed
MDMA	Blocks 5-HT reuptake, causes 5-HT release	Drug of abuse
Histamine		
Diphenhydramine	Blocks histamine receptors	Sedation
Multiple Systems		
Reserpine	Blocks monoamine storage in vesicles	Sedation, depression
AMPT	Blocks tyrosine hydroxylase	Used in research
Moclobemide	MAO inhibitor	Used to treat symptoms of depression
Deprenyl	MAO inhibitor	Used to treat Parkinson's disease

Peptides

LO 4.13 **Contrast the features of peptide neurotransmitters with classical neurotransmitters.**

In addition to amino acids and classical neurotransmitters, neurons of the CNS release a large variety of peptides. In contrast to the classical neurotransmitters, peptides consist of two or more amino acids linked together by peptide bonds.

NEUROTRANSMITTER PRODUCTION, STORAGE, AND RELEASE All the peptides that have been studied so far are produced from precursor molecules. These precursors are large polypeptides that are broken into smaller neurotransmitter molecules by special enzymes. Neurons manufacture both the polypeptides and the enzymes needed to break them apart in the right places. The appropriate sections of the polypeptides are retained, and the rest are destroyed. Because the synthesis of peptides takes place in the soma, vesicles containing these chemicals must be delivered to the terminal buttons by axoplasmic transport.

As we saw in Chapter 2, many terminal buttons contain two different types of synaptic vesicles, each filled with a different substance. These terminal buttons release peptides in conjunction with a classical neurotransmitter. One reason for the co-release of peptides is their ability to regulate the sensitivity of presynaptic or postsynaptic receptors to the neurotransmitter. Many peptides produced in the brain have interesting behavioral effects, which will be discussed in subsequent chapters.

Peptides are released from all parts of the terminal button, not just from the active zone; thus, only a portion of the molecules is released into the synaptic cleft. The rest presumably act on receptors belonging to other cells in the vicinity. Once released, peptides are destroyed by enzymes. In contrast to the other neurotransmitters presented so far, there is no mechanism for reuptake and recycling of peptides.

Several different peptides are released by neurons. Although most peptides appear to serve as neuromodulators, some act as neurotransmitters. One of the best known families of peptides are the **endogenous opioids.** Research has revealed that opiates (drugs such as **opium, morphine, heroin,** and **oxycodone**) reduce pain because they have direct effects on the brain.

RECEPTORS Although opiate drugs like opium have been used for centuries, receptors for opiate drugs were not discovered until the 1970s. At that time, no one knew about the endogenous opioids. Soon after the discovery of the opiate receptor, other neuroscientists discovered the natural ligands for these receptors, which were called **enkephalins.** We now know that the enkephalins are only two members of a family of endogenous opioids, all of which are synthesized from one of three large peptides that serve as precursors. In addition, we know that there are at least three different types of opiate receptors: μ (mu), δ (delta), and K (kappa).

Several different neural systems are activated when opiate receptors are stimulated. One type produces analgesia, another inhibits species-typical defensive responses such as fleeing and hiding, and another stimulates a system of neurons involved in reinforcement ("reward"). The last effect explains why opiates are often abused. The situations that cause neurons to secrete endogenous opioids are discussed in Chapter 7, and the brain mechanisms of opiate addiction are discussed in Chapter 18.

So far, pharmacologists have developed only two types of drugs that affect neural communication by means of opioids: direct agonists and antagonists. Many synthetic opiates, including heroin, **methadone,** and oxycodone, have been developed, and some are used clinically as analgesics. Several opiate receptor antagonists have also been developed. One of them, **naloxone** (Narcan), is used clinically to reverse opiate intoxication or overdose. This drug has saved the lives of many people who would otherwise have died from an opiate overdose.

Lipids

LO 4.14 **Summarize the features of the lipid neurotransmitter systems.**

Various substances derived from lipids can serve to transmit messages within or between cells. The best known, and probably the most important, are the **endocannabinoids**—natural ligands for the receptors that are responsible for the physiological effects of the active ingredient in marijuana. Matsuda et al. (1990) discovered that **THC** (tetrahydrocannabinol, the active ingredient of marijuana) stimulates cannabinoid receptors located in specific regions of the brain.

THC produces analgesia and sedation, stimulates appetite, reduces nausea caused by drugs used to treat cancer, relieves asthma attacks, decreases pressure within the eyes in patients with glaucoma, and reduces the symptoms of certain motor disorders. On the other hand, THC interferes with concentration and memory, alters visual and auditory perception, and distorts perceptions of the passage of time. THC can occur naturally (produced by the marijuana plant) or it can be manufactured synthetically (in drugs such as "Spice" or "K2" as a street drug, or **dronabinol** as a prescription drug).

Devane et al. (1992) discovered the first natural ligand for the THC receptor: a lipidlike substance that they named **anandamide,** from the Sanskrit word *ananda,* or "bliss." A few years after the discovery of anandamide, Mechoulam et al., (1995) discovered another endocannabinoid, 2-arachidonyl glycerol (2-AG).

NEUROTRANSMITTER PRODUCTION, STORAGE, AND RELEASE Lipid neurotransmitters, such as anandamide, appear to be synthesized on demand; that is, they are produced and released as needed and are not stored in synaptic vesicles. Can you think of any reason why it might be difficult to contain lipid neurotransmitters within the lipid-based membranes of a vesicle?

RECEPTORS Two types of cannabinoid receptors, CB_1 and CB_2, both metabotropic, have since been discovered. Besides THC, several drugs have been discovered that affect the actions of the endocannabinoids. For example, CB_1 receptors are blocked by the drug **rimonabant.**

CB_1 receptors are found on terminal buttons of glutamatergic, GABAergic, acetylcholinergic, noradrenergic, dopaminergic, and serotonergic neurons, where they serve as presynaptic heteroreceptors, regulating neurotransmitter release (Iversen, 2003). When activated, the receptors open potassium channels in the terminal buttons, shortening the duration of action potentials there and decreasing the amount of neurotransmitter that is released. When neurons release cannabinoids, the chemicals diffuse a distance of approximately 20 μm in all directions, and their effects persist for several tens of seconds. The short-term memory impairment that accompanies marijuana use appears to be caused by the action of THC on CB_1 receptors in the hippocampus. Endocannabinoids also appear to play an essential role in the reinforcing effects of opiates: A targeted mutation that prevents the production of CB_1 receptors abolishes the reinforcing effects of morphine but not of cocaine, amphetamine, or nicotine (Cossu et al., 2001). These effects of cannabinoids are discussed further in Chapter 18.

Agarwal et al. (2007) found that THC exerts its analgesic effects by stimulating CB_1 receptors in the PNS. In addition, a commonly used over-the-counter analgesic, *acetaminophen* (known as *paracetamol* in many countries), also acts on these receptors. Once it enters the blood, acetaminophen is converted into another compound that then joins with arachidonic acid, the precursor of anandamide. This compound binds with peripheral CB_1 receptors and activates them, reducing pain sensation. Because the compound does not cross the blood–brain barrier, it does not produce effects like those of THC. Administration of a CB_1 antagonist completely blocks the analgesic effect of acetaminophen (Bertolini et al., 2006).

REUPTAKE AND DESTRUCTION Anandamide is deactivated by the enzyme FAAH (fatty acid amide hydrolase), which is present in anandamide-secreting neurons. Because the enzyme is found there, molecules of anandamide must be transported back into these neurons, which is accomplished by anandamide transporters. Another drug, MAFP, inhibits FAAH acting as a cannabinoid agonist. In addition, cannabinoid reuptake is inhibited by the drug AM1172.

In conclusion, we have reviewed only some of many neurotransmitter systems that have so far been discovered. These systems are the most relevant to many of the behavioral examples you will encounter in the remainder of this book. In addition to the systems reviewed here, there are also nucleosides, such as adenosine, that serve as neuromodulators. You will read more about adenosine in Chapter 9. Recently, investigators have discovered that neurons use at least two simple, soluble gases—nitric oxide and carbon monoxide—to communicate with one another. As you will see in Chapter 13, nitric oxide may play a role in the establishment of neural changes that are produced by learning. For a summary of some important drugs that act on the peptide and lipid neurotransmitter systems, see Table 4.6.

Table 4.6 Drugs that Act on Peptide and Lipid Neurotransmitter Systems

Drug	Mechanism	Effect
Peptides		
Opiates	Opioid receptor agonists	Analgesia, sedation, reinforcing
Naloxone	Opioid antagonist	Reverses opioid overdose
Lipids		
THC	Cannabinoid receptor agonist	Increases appetite produces analgesia, cognitive effects
Rimonabant	Cannabinoid receptor antagonist	Suppresses appetite, used in smoking cessation
MAFP	Inhibits FAAH	Used in research. Increases cannabinoid system activity
AM1172	Blocks cannabinoid reuptake	Used in research. Increases cannabinoid system activity

Section Review

Neurotransmitters and Neuromodulators

LO 4.10 **Compare the features of the amino acid neurotransmitter systems.**

Glutamate is packaged into vesicles by the vesicle glutamate transporter; binds to AMPA, NMDA, kainate, and metabotropic glutamate receptors; is metabolized by the enzyme glutamine synthase; and is transported into the presynaptic cell by excitatory amino acid transporters. GABA is packaged into vesicles by the vesicle GABA transporter; binds to a variety of GABA receptors, including the $GABA_A$ receptor; is metabolized by the enzyme GABA aminotransferase; and is transported into the presynaptic cell by GABA transporters.

LO 4.11 **Summarize the features of the acetylcholine system.**

Acetylcholine neurons are organized into three pathways in the brain. Acetylcholine is synthesized by the enzyme choline acetyltransferase. It is packaged into vesicles by the vesicle ACh transporter, binds to nicotinic and muscarinic receptors, is metabolized by acetylcholinesterase, and its precursor is transported into the presynaptic cell by choline transporters.

LO 4.12 **Summarize the key features of the monoamine systems.**

The monoamines are classical neurotransmitters and include dopamine, norepinephrine, epinephrine, serotonin, and histamine. The neurons of each system are organized into pathways in the CNS. The monoamines are synthesized from amino acid precursors, loaded into vesicles by vesicle monoamine transporters, and released following an action potential. The monoamines bind to a variety of ionotropic and metabotropic receptors. Monoamines are metabolized by enzymes such as monoamine oxidase. Reuptake transporters, such as the dopamine transporter, norepinephrine transporter, and serotonin transporter, remove monoamines from the synapse.

LO 4.13 **Contrast the features of peptide neurotransmitters with classical neurotransmitters.**

Whereas the classical neurotransmitters are synthesized from relatively small amino acid precursors, peptide neurotransmitters are synthesized from large polypeptides. Both peptides and classical neurotransmitters are stored in vesicles, and can be co-released following an action potential. Peptide neurotransmitters can function as either neurotransmitters or neuromodulators to regulate the sensitivity of receptors to classical co-released neurotransmitters.

LO 4.14 **Summarize the features of the lipid neurotransmitter systems.**

Lipid neurotransmitters are synthesized on demand and are not stored in vesicles. Endocannabinoids bind to CB_1 and CB_2 receptors. Anandamide is deactivated by the enzyme FAAH within the presynaptic neuron, and the anandamide transporter is responsible for reuptake of anandamide to the presynaptic cell.

Thought Question

The placebo effect and its reward mechanisms rely heavily on intrinsic opioids and opioid receptors in the brain. What is the potential of using extrinsic opioid agonists such as morphine and opioid antagonists such as naloxone in behavioral training in humans and animals?

Chapter Review Questions

1. Describe the routes of administration and the distribution of drugs within the body.

2. Describe drug effectiveness, the effects of repeated administration, and the placebo effect.

3. Describe the effects of drugs on neurotransmitters and presynaptic and postsynaptic receptors.

4. Review the general role of neurotransmitters and neuromodulators.

5. Describe the nature and role of neurotransmitters in synaptic transmission at a cholinergic neuron, and explain the pathophysiology of myasthenia gravis.

6. Describe the structure of a GABAA receptor, and list various drugs that can bind and modulate the channel properties of this receptor.

7. Describe the action of botulinum toxin in muscles, and explain one of its medical uses.

8. List various types of receptors mediating the effects of norepinephrine, and identify the agonist and antagonist acting on these receptors.

9. Describe the location and physiological functions of serotoninergic pathways in the brain.

Chapter 5
Methods and Strategies of Research

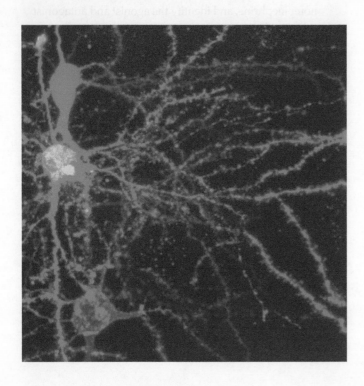

Chapter Outline

Learning Objectives

LO 5.1 Explain what researchers can learn from studies that involve lesioning.

LO 5.2 Compare various methods of producing brain lesions.

LO 5.3 Describe the process of stereotaxic surgery.

LO 5.4 Summarize the general steps of histological methods.

LO 5.5 Differentiate between techniques for tracing efferent and afferent axons.

LO 5.6 Contrast the methods used to study the structure of the living human brain.

LO 5.7 Compare recording neural activity using microelectrodes, macroelectrodes, and magnetoencephalography.

LO 5.8 Compare the types of metabolic and synaptic activity that can be revealed by autoradiography, staining for immediate early genes, positron emission tomography, and functional magnetic resonance imaging.

LO 5.9 Compare electrical and chemical neural stimulation, optogenetic methods, and transcranial magnetic stimulation.

LO 5.10 Describe how a researcher could identify a neuron that produces a particular neurochemical.

LO 5.11 Compare autoradiography and immunocytochemistry for localizing particular receptors.

LO 5.12 Review the steps involved in measuring brain chemicals using microdialysis.

LO 5.13 Describe how concordance rates in twins can be used to assess the genetic contribution to a behavior.

LO 5.14 Evaluate the role of adoption studies in investigating genetic contributions to a behavior.

LO 5.15 Identify examples of techniques that utilize knowledge of the human genome to understand behavior.

LO 5.16 Summarize how targeted mutations can be used to reveal genetic contributions to a behavior.

LO 5.17 Describe how antisense oligonucleotides function to change behavior.

In a now classic case documented in books and documentaries, several young people began showing up at neurology clinics in northern California during the summer of 1982 displaying dramatic symptoms (Langston et al., 1983). The most severely affected patients were almost totally paralyzed. They were unable to speak intelligibly, they salivated constantly, and their eyes were open with a fixed stare. Others, less severely affected, walked with a slow, shuffling gait and moved slowly and with great difficulty. The symptoms looked like those of Parkinson's disease, but that disorder has a very gradual onset. In addition, it rarely strikes people before late middle age, and the patients were all in their twenties or early thirties.

The common factor linking these patients was intravenous drug use; all of them had used a synthetic opiate. Some detective work revealed that the illicit drug was contaminated with MPTP, a toxic chemical that damaged dopaminergic neurons and caused the patients' neurological symptoms. Because the symptoms looked like those of Parkinson's disease, the patients were given L-DOPA, the dopamine precursor drug used to treat this disease, and they all showed significant improvement in their symptoms. Unfortunately, the improvement was temporary; the drug lost its effectiveness.

Two individuals affected by the MPTP traveled to Sweden to receive fetal tissue transplants containing dopamine-secreting neurons. This tissue was transplanted into the caudate and putamen with the hope that the new neurons from the tissue would survive and begin to produce dopamine, diminishing the Parkinson's disease–like symptoms that the patients were experiencing.

Before the transplant took place, one of the patients was given an injection of radioactive L-DOPA. Then, one hour later, he was wheeled into a small room that housed a PET scanner. His head was positioned in the scanner, and for the next several minutes the machine gathered data from subatomic particles that were emitted as the radioactive L-DOPA in his brain broke down. This data revealed the extent and location of damage to the dopamine system.

A few weeks later, the patient was admitted to the hospital for his surgery. Technicians removed dopaminergic neurons from the substantia nigra of several fetal brains and prepared them for implantation into the patient's brain. The patient was anesthetized, and the surgeon made cuts in his scalp to expose parts of his skull. The surgeon attached the frame of a stereotaxic apparatus

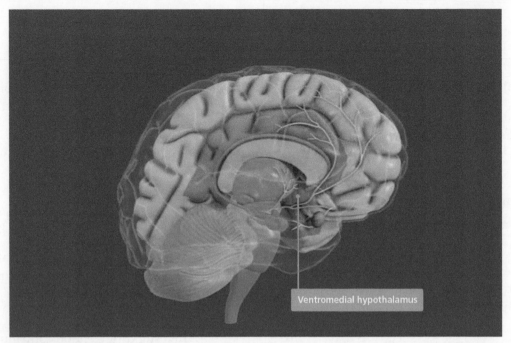

The figure here presents the ventromedial hypothalamus. Using many of the techniques described in this chapter, researchers have revealed important afferent and efferent connections to the structure that are essential for behavior.

to the patient's skull, made some measurements, and then drilled several holes. He used the stereotaxic apparatus to guide the injections of the fetal neurons into the patient's caudate nucleus and putamen. Once the injections were complete, the surgeon removed the stereotaxic frame and sutured the incisions he had made in the scalp.

The operation was quite successful; the patient recovered much of his motor control. A little more than a year later, he was given another injection of radioactive L-DOPA, and again his head was placed in the PET scanner. The results of the second scan showed what his recovery implied: The transplanted cells had survived and were secreting dopamine. You can view the results of his PET scans in Figure 5.27 in this chapter.

*****

Despite the devastating effects of accidental administration in this group of patients, MPTP is now considered an important research tool in Parkinson's disease research. Its neurotoxic effects make MPTP an ideal candidate for creating selective chemical lesions of the dopamine system and producing the symptoms of Parkinson's disease. Researchers now rely on the MPTP model in laboratory animals to test the effectiveness of new treatments for the disease.

This case highlights several important methodological concepts explored in this chapter. Chemical lesioning, PET scan imaging, and stereotaxic surgery are all important methodological tools used by researchers as they try to better understand the structure and function of the nervous system and develop effective treatments for disease.

Behavioral neuroscience research involves the efforts of scientists in many disciplines, including physiology, neuroanatomy, biochemistry, psychology, endocrinology, and histology. Pursuing a research project in behavioral neuroscience requires competence in many experimental techniques. Because different procedures can produce contradictory results, investigators must be familiar with the advantages and limitations of the methods that are used. Researchers often receive a puzzling answer, only to realize later that they were not asking the question they thought they were. As we will see, the best conclusions about behavioral neuroscience are made not by any single experiment but by a program of research that enables us to compare the results of studies using different methods.

An enormous—and potentially confusing—array of research methods is available to researchers in behavioral neuroscience. A reader could get lost—or lose interest—if these methods were presented in a long list. Instead, we will present some of the most important and commonly used procedures, arranged by commonalities. This way, it should be easier to see the types of information provided by various research methods and to understand their advantages and disadvantages. It will also permit us to describe the strategies that researchers employ as they follow up the results of one experiment by designing and executing another one.

The first section begins with various methods of experimental ablation. The second looks at how researchers stimulate and record neural activity. Then the third and fourth sections examine neurochemical and genetic methods, respectively.

Experimental Ablation

An important research method used to investigate brain functions involves destroying part of the brain and evaluating an animal's subsequent behavior. This method is called **experimental ablation.** In most cases, experimental ablation does not involve the removal of brain tissue; instead, the researcher damages some tissue to disrupt its functioning and leaves it in place. Experimental ablation is the oldest method used in neuroscience.

Evaluating the Behavioral Effects of Brain Damage

LO 5.1 **Explain what researchers can learn from studies that involve lesioning.**

A *lesion* is a wound or injury, and a researcher who destroys part of the brain usually refers to the damage as a *brain lesion.* Experiments in which part of the brain is damaged and the individual's behavior is subsequently observed are called **lesion studies.** Intentional brain lesioning is performed in animal models; however, the behavioral results of naturally occurring lesions, such as those that result from accidental injuries or strokes, can also be studied in human research participants. The rationale for lesion studies is that the function of an area of the brain can be inferred from the behaviors that the individual can no longer perform after the area has been damaged. For example, if, after part of the brain has been destroyed, an animal can no longer perform tasks that require vision, we can conclude that the animal is blind—and that the damaged area plays some role in vision.

Just what can we learn from lesion studies? The goal is to discover what functions are performed by different regions of the brain and then to understand how these functions are combined to accomplish particular behaviors. The distinction between *brain function* and *behavior* is an important one. Circuits within the brain perform functions, not behaviors. No one brain region or neural circuit is solely responsible for a behavior; each region performs a function (or set of functions) that contributes to performance of the behavior. For example, the act of reading involves functions required for controlling eye movements, focusing the lens of the eye, perceiving and recognizing words and letters, comprehending the meaning of the words, and so on. Some of these functions also participate in other behaviors; for example, controlling eye movement and focusing are required for any task that involves looking, and brain mechanisms used for comprehending the meanings of words also participate in comprehending speech. The researcher's task is to understand the functions that are required for performing a particular behavior and to determine what circuits of neurons in the brain are responsible for each of these functions.

The interpretation of lesion studies is complicated by the fact that all regions of the brain are interconnected. Suppose that we have a good understanding of the functions required for performance of a particular behavior. We find that damage to one specific brain structure impairs a particular behavior. Can we necessarily conclude that a function essential to this behavior is performed by circuits of neurons located in this one specific structure? Unfortunately, we cannot. The functions we are interested in may actually be performed by neural circuits located elsewhere in the brain. Damage to one structure may simply interfere with the normal operation of the neural circuits in a different structure.

Producing Brain Lesions

LO 5.2 **Compare various methods of producing brain lesions.**

How are brain lesions produced experimentally? Usually, a researcher wants to inactivate regions that are hidden away in the depths of the brain. Brain lesions of subcortical regions (regions located beneath the cortex) are usually produced by passing electrical current through a stainless steel wire that is covered with an insulating coating except for the very tip. The wire is then guided to its destination using exact coordinates to a precise location within the brain. The researcher then activates a lesion-making device, which produces a radio frequency (RF) current—an alternating current of a very high frequency. The passage of the current through the brain tissue produces heat that kills cells in the region surrounding the tip of the electrode.

Lesions produced by these means destroy everything in the vicinity of the electrode tip, including neural cell bodies and the axons of neurons that pass through the region. A more selective method of producing brain lesions employs an excitatory amino acid, such as *kainic acid*, which kills neurons by stimulating them to death. Lesions produced in this way are referred to as **excitotoxic lesions.** When an excitatory amino acid is injected through a *cannula* (a small metal tube) into a region of the brain, the chemical destroys neural cell bodies in the vicinity but spares axons that belong to different neurons that happen to pass nearby. (See Figure 5.1.) This selectivity permits the investigator to determine whether the behavioral effects of destroying a particular brain structure are caused by the death of neurons located there or by the destruction of axons that pass nearby. For example, some researchers discovered that RF lesions of a particular region in the brain stem abolished REM sleep; therefore, they believed that this region was involved in the production of this stage of sleep. (REM sleep is the stage of sleep during which dreaming occurs. You will learn more about this topic in Chapter 9.) But later studies showed that when kainic acid was used to destroy the neurons located there, the animals' sleep was *not* affected. Therefore, the RF

Figure 5.1 Excitotoxic Lesion

(a) Section through an intact hippocampus of a rat brain. (b) A lesion produced by infusion of an excitatory amino acid in a region of the hippocampus. Arrowheads mark the ends of the region in which neurons have been destroyed.

(Courtesy of Benno Roozendaal, University of California, Irvine.)

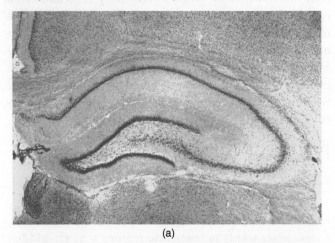

(a)

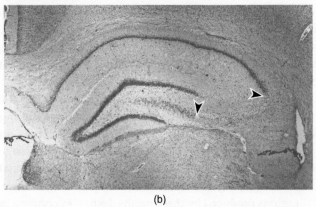

(b)

lesions must have altered sleep by destroying the axons that pass through the area.

Even more specific methods of targeting and killing particular types of neurons are available. For example, molecular biologists have devised ways to *conjugate* (attach together) *saporin,* a toxic protein, and antibodies that will bind with particular proteins found only on certain types of neurons in the brain. The antibodies target these proteins, and the saporin kills the cells to which the proteins are attached.

Note that, when subcortical lesions are produced by passing RF current through an electrode or infusing a chemical through a cannula, there is always additional damage caused to the brain. When an electrode or a cannula is passed through the brain to get to a target, it inevitably causes a small amount of damage even before turning on the lesion maker or starting the infusion. Thus, we cannot simply compare the behavior of brain-lesioned animals with that of unoperated control animals; the incidental damage to the brain regions above the lesion may actually be responsible for some of the behavioral deficits we see.

To control for this, researchers typically include an additional group of animals in a **lesion study** and produce **sham lesions.** To do so, researchers anesthetize each animal, insert the electrode or cannula, and lower it to the proper depth. In other words, they do everything they would do to produce the lesion except turn on the lesion maker or start the infusion. This group of animals serves as a control group; if the behavior of the animals with brain lesions is different from that of the sham-operated control animals, we can conclude that the lesions caused the behavioral deficits. (A sham lesion serves the same purpose as a placebo does in a pharmacology study.)

Most of the time, investigators produce permanent brain lesions, but sometimes it is advantageous to disrupt the activity of a particular region of the brain temporarily. The easiest way to do so is to inject a local anesthetic or a drug called *muscimol* into the appropriate part of the brain. The anesthetic blocks action potentials in axons entering or leaving that region, thus effectively producing a temporary lesion (usually called a *reversible* brain lesion). Muscimol, a drug that stimulates GABA receptors, inactivates a region of the brain by inhibiting the neurons located there. (You will recall that GABA is an important inhibitory neurotransmitter in the brain.) Another technique, optogenetics, can also be used to temporarily inhibit, or in some cases stimulate, brain regions. You will read more about this topic later in the chapter.

Stereotaxic Surgery

LO 5.3 Describe the process of stereotaxic surgery.

How do researchers get an electrode or cannula to a precise location in the depths of an animal's brain? The answer is **stereotaxic surgery.** *Stereotaxis* refers to the ability to locate objects in space. A *stereotaxic apparatus* contains a holder that keeps the animal's head in a standard position and an arm that moves an electrode or a cannula through measured distances in all three axes of space. However, to perform stereotaxic surgery, one must first study a *stereotaxic atlas.*

THE STEREOTAXIC ATLAS A **stereotaxic atlas** is a book, website, or software that contains images that correspond to frontal sections of the brain taken at various distances rostral and caudal to bregma. The skull is composed of several bones that grow together and form *sutures* (seams). The heads of babies contain a soft spot at the junction of the coronal and sagittal sutures called the *fontanelle.* Once this gap closes, the junction is called **bregma,** from the Greek word meaning "front of head." No two brains of animals of a given species are completely identical, but there is enough similarity among individuals to predict the location of particular brain structures relative to external features of the head. We can find bregma on a rat's skull, too, and it serves as a convenient reference point. For example, the page shown in

Figure 5.2 Stereotaxic Atlas

This sample page from a stereotaxic atlas of the rat brain shows the target (the fornix) in red. Labels have been removed for the sake of clarity.

(Adapted from Swanson, L. W., *Brain Maps: Structure of the Rat Brain*, New York: Elsevier, 1992.)

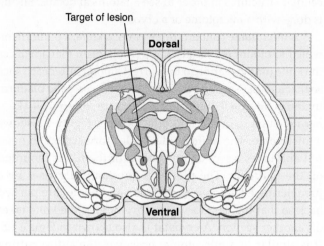

Target of lesion

Dorsal

Ventral

Figure 5.3 Stereotaxic Apparatus

This apparatus is used for performing brain surgery on rats.

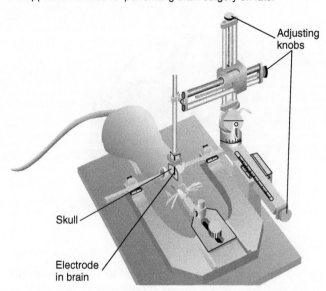

Adjusting knobs

Skull

Electrode in brain

Figure 5.2 is a drawing of a slice of the brain that contains a brain structure (shown in red) that we are interested in. If we wanted to place the tip of a wire in this structure (a bundle of axons called the fornix), we would have to drill a hole through the skull immediately above it. Each image of the stereotaxic atlas is labeled according to the distance of the section anterior or posterior to bregma. The grid on each image indicates distances of brain structures ventral to the top of the skull and lateral to the midline. To place the tip of a wire in the fornix, a researcher would drill a hole above the target and then lower the electrode through the hole until the tip was at the correct depth, relative to the skull height at bregma. Thus, by finding a neural structure (which cannot be seen from the outside of the skull) on one of the images of a stereotaxic atlas, the researcher can determine the structure's location relative to bregma (which can be seen from the outside of the skull). Note that, because of variations in different strains and ages of animals, the atlas gives only an approximate location. Researchers may need to try out a new set of coordinates, verifying the lesion placement using histological methods, correcting the numbers if necessary, and trying again. (Histological methods involve slicing and staining tissue and are described later.)

THE STEREOTAXIC APPARATUS A **stereotaxic apparatus** is a device that includes a head holder, which maintains the animal's skull in the proper orientation, a holder for an electrode or cannula, and a calibrated mechanism that moves the electrode/cannula holder in measured distances along the three axes: anterior–posterior, dorsal–ventral, and lateral–medial. Figure 5.3 illustrates a stereotaxic apparatus designed for small animals. The size of the stereotaxic apparatus can be scaled up or down to be used for different species.

Once a researcher obtains the coordinates from a stereotaxic atlas, he or she anesthetizes the animal, places it in the apparatus, and cuts the scalp open. The researcher will locate bregma, dial in the appropriate numbers on the stereotaxic apparatus, drill a hole through the skull, and lower the device into the brain by the correct amount. Now the tip of the cannula or electrode is where the researcher wants it to be, and he or she is ready to produce the lesion.

Stereotaxic surgery may be used for purposes other than lesion production. Wires placed in the brain can be used to stimulate neurons as well as to destroy them, and drugs can be injected that stimulate neurons or block specific receptors. A researcher can attach cannulas or wires permanently by following a procedure that will be described later in this chapter. In all cases, once surgery is complete, the scalp incision is sewn together, and the animal is taken out of the stereotaxic apparatus and allowed to recover from the anesthetic.

Stereotaxic apparatuses are also made for humans, by the way. Sometimes a neurosurgeon produces subcortical lesions—for example, to reduce the symptoms of Parkinson's disease, a treatment you'll encounter in Chapter 15. Usually, the surgeon uses multiple landmarks and verifies the location of the wire (or other device) inserted into the brain by taking brain scans or recording the activity of the neurons in that region before producing a brain lesion. **Deep brain stimulation** is another procedure that requires the use of a stereotaxic apparatus. Deep brain stimulation is used to treat chronic pain, movement disorders (including Parkinson's disease), epilepsy, depression, and obsessive-compulsive disorder. Deep brain stimulation utilizes a stereotaxic apparatus to implant a permanent electrode into the brain of patients. Rather than produce a lesion, electrical current

Figure 5.4 Stereotaxic apparatus on a Human Patient

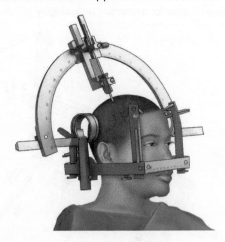

passed through the electrode is used to stimulate brain regions and reduce symptoms (Holtzheimer and Mayberg, 2011a; Sarem-Aslani and Mullett, 2011). (See Figure 5.4.)

Histological Methods

LO 5.4 **Summarize the general steps of histological methods.**

After producing a brain lesion and observing its effects on an animal's behavior, researchers must slice and stain the brain so that they can observe it under the microscope and see the location of the lesion. Brain lesions can miss the mark, so researchers have to verify the precise location of the brain damage after testing the animal behaviorally. To do so, histologists (specialists in these techniques) must fix, slice, stain, and examine the brain. Together, these procedures are referred to as *histological methods*. (The prefix *histo-* refers to body tissue.)

FIXATION AND SECTIONING To study brain tissue, it must be preserved from autolytic enzymes (*autolytic* means "self-dissolving"), which will otherwise break down the tissue, making it impossible to study. The tissue must also be preserved to prevent its decomposition by bacteria or molds. To achieve both of these objectives, neural tissue is placed in a **fixative**. The most commonly used fixative is **formalin,** an aqueous solution of formaldehyde, a gas. Formalin cross links protein to strengthen the very soft and fragile brain tissue, and kills any microorganisms that might destroy it.

Before the brain is fixed (that is, put into a fixative solution), it is usually perfused. **Perfusion** of tissue entails removal of the blood and its replacement with another fluid. The animal's brain is perfused because better histological results are obtained when no blood is present in the tissue. The animal whose brain is to be studied is humanely euthanized with an overdose of a general anesthetic. Blood is removed

from the vessels and replaced with a dilute salt solution. Finally a dilute fixative solution is pumped through the tissue, and the brain is removed from the skull and placed in a container filled with the fixative. Once the brain has been fixed, it must be sliced into thin sections and stained for various cellular structures in order to see anatomical details. Slicing is done with a microtome or a cryostat.

A **microtome** contains three parts: a knife, a platform on which to mount the tissue, and a mechanism that advances the knife (or the platform) the correct amount after each slice so that another section can be cut. In most cases the platform includes an attachment that freezes the brain to make it hard enough to be cut into thin sections. Figure 5.5 shows a microtome. The knife holder slides forward on an oiled rail and takes a section off the top of the tissue mounted on the platform. The platform automatically rises by a predetermined amount as the knife and holder are pushed back so that the next forward movement of the knife takes off another section. A **cryostat** is also shown in Figure 5.5. It is similar to a microtome; however, the entire cutting process occurs within a freezer, allowing sections to be cut at very cold temperatures. In some cases, a researcher may need to work quickly with unfixed tissue; in that situation a cryostat may be the tool of choice.

After the tissue is cut, the slices are attached to glass microscope slides. A researcher can then stain the tissue by putting the entire slide into various chemical solutions. Finally, the stained sections are covered with a small amount of a transparent liquid known as a *mounting medium* and a very thin glass coverslip is placed over the sections. The mounting medium keeps the coverslip in position.

STAINING If you looked at an unstained section of brain tissue under a light microscope, you would be able to see the outlines of some large cellular masses and the more prominent fiber bundles. However, no fine details would be revealed. For this reason the study of microscopic neuroanatomy requires special histological stains. Researchers have developed many different stains to identify specific substances within and outside of cells. For verifying the location of a brain lesion, many researchers use one of the simplest stains: a cell-body stain.

Methylene blue and *cresyl violet* are two examples of dyes that stain the cell bodies of brain tissue. The material that takes up the dye within the cell, known as the *Nissl substance*, consists of RNA, DNA, and associated proteins located in the nucleus and scattered, in the form of granules, in the cytoplasm. Figure 5.6 shows a frontal section of a brain stained with cresyl violet. Note that you can observe fiber bundles by their lighter appearance; they do not take up the stain. The stain is not selective for *neural* cell bodies; all cells are stained, neurons and glia alike. It is up to the investigator to determine which cell type is which—by size, shape, and location.

Figure 5.5 Microtome and Cryostat

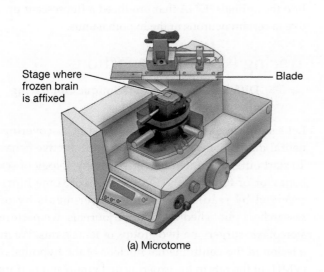

Stage where frozen brain is affixed

Blade

(a) Microtome

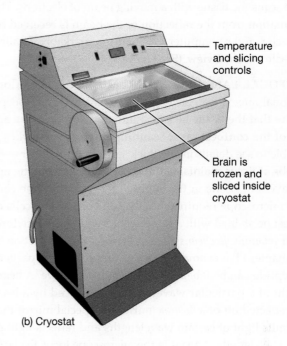

Temperature and slicing controls

Brain is frozen and sliced inside cryostat

(b) Cryostat

Figure 5.6 Frontal Section Stained with Cresyl Violet

The section is stained with cresyl violet, a cell-body stain. The arrowheads point to nuclei, or groups of cell bodies.

(Histological material courtesy of Mary Carlson.)

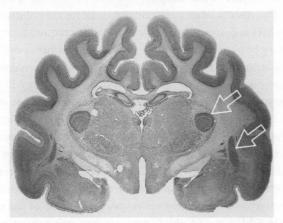

Figure 5.7 Electron Photomicrograph

This electron photomicrograph shows a section through an axodendritic synapse. Two synaptic regions are indicated by arrows, and a circle indicates a region of pinocytosis in an adjacent terminal button, presumably representing recycling of vesicular membrane. T = terminal button; f = microfilaments; M = mitochondrion.

(From Rockel, A. J., and Jones, E. G., Observations on the fine structure of the central nucleus of the inferior colliculus of the cat, *Journal of Comparative Neurology*, 1973, *147*, 61–92. Reprinted with permission.)

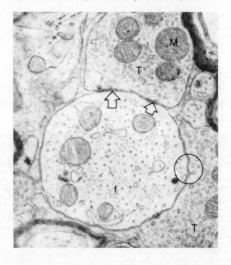

ELECTRON MICROSCOPY   While many researchers use light microscopes to examine stained tissue, the light microscope is limited in its ability to reveal extremely small details. To see very small anatomical structures as synaptic vesicles and details of cell organelles, investigators must use a **transmission electron microscope.** A beam of electrons is passed through a thin slice of the tissue to be examined. The beam of electrons casts a shadow of the tissue on a fluorescent screen, which can be photographed or scanned into a computer. Electron photomicrographs produced in this way can provide information about structural details on the order of a few tens of nanometers. (See Figure 5.7.)

A **scanning electron microscope** provides less magnification than a standard transmission electron microscope, which transmits the electron beam through the tissue.

However, it shows objects in three dimensions. The microscope scans the tissue with a moving beam of electrons. The information from the reflection of the beam is received by a detector, and a computer produces a remarkably detailed three-dimensional view. (See Figure 5.8.)

CONFOCAL LASER SCANNING MICROSCOPY Conventional microscopy or transmission electron microscopy require that the tissue be sliced into thin sections. The advent of the **confocal laser scanning microscope** makes it possible to see details inside thick sections of tissue or even in slabs of tissue maintained in tissue cultures or in the upper layers of tissue in the exposed living brain. The confocal microscope requires that the cells or parts of cells of interest be stained with a fluorescent dye. (This procedure, called *immunocytochemistry*, is described in next section of this chapter.) For example, neurons that produce a particular peptide can be labeled with a fluorescent dye. A beam of light of a particular wavelength is produced by a laser and reflected off of a *dichroic* mirror—a special mirror that transmits light of certain wavelengths and reflects light of other wavelengths. Lenses in the microscope focus the laser light at a particular depth in the tissue. This light triggers fluorescence in the tissue, which passes through the lenses and is transmitted through the dichroic mirror to a pinhole aperture. This aperture blocks extraneous light. The light that passes through the aperture is measured by a detector. Two moving mirrors cause the laser light to scan the tissue, which provides the computer with the information it needs to form an image of a slice of tissue located at a particular depth within the sample. If multiple scans are made while the location of the aperture is moved, a stack of images of slices through the tissue—remember, this can be living tissue—can be obtained.

Figure 5.8 Image from a Scanning Electron Microscope

This is an image of neurons and glia from a scanning electron microscope.

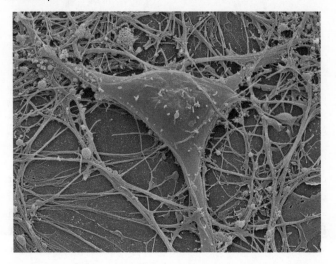

Figure 5.9 illustrates the use of confocal microscopy to examine two populations of cells in the rat hypothalamus. Molecular genetic methods had been used to insert a gene into the animals' DNA that produced a fluorescent protein dye in certain neurons in the hypothalamus.

Tracing Neural Connections

LO 5.5 **Differentiate between techniques for tracing efferent and afferent axons.**

Let's suppose that we were interested in discovering the neural mechanisms responsible for reproductive behavior. To start out, we wanted to study the physiology of sexual behavior of female rats. On the basis of some hints we received by reading reports of experiments by other researchers published in scientific journals, we performed stereotaxic surgery on two groups of female rats. We made a lesion in the ventromedial nucleus of the hypothalamus (VMH) of the rats in the experimental group and performed sham surgery on the rats in the control group. After a few days' recovery, and a receptive day of the estrus cycle, we placed the individual animals with male rats. The females in the control group engaged in courting behavior with the males followed by copulation. However, the females with the VMH lesions rejected the males' attention and refused to copulate with them. We confirmed with histology that the VMH was indeed destroyed in the brains of the experimental animals. By the way, the VMH was shown in the first figure of this chapter.

The results of our experiment indicate that neurons in the VMH appear to play a role in functions required for copulatory behavior in females. (By the way, it turns out that these lesions do not affect copulatory behavior in males.) So where do we go from here? What is the next step? In fact, there are many questions that we could pursue. One question concerns the system of brain structures that participate in female copulatory behavior. Certainly, the VMH does not function alone; it receives inputs from other structures and sends outputs to still others. Copulation requires integration of visual, tactile, and olfactory perceptions and organization of patterns of movements in response to those of the partner. In addition, the entire network requires activation by the appropriate sex hormones. What is the precise role of the VMH in this complicated system?

Before we can hope to answer this question, we must know more about the connections of the VMH with the rest of the brain. What structures send their axons to the VMH, and to what structures does the VMH, in turn, send its axons? Once we know what the connections are, we can investigate the role of these structures and the nature of their interactions. (See Figure 5.10.)

How do we investigate the connections of the VMH? The question cannot be answered by means of histological procedures that stain all neurons, such as cell-body stains. If we

Figure 5.9 Confocal Microscope and Image

(a) A laser scanning confocal microscope is shown in this simplified schematic diagram. (b) Confocal microscopic image of terminal buttons stained for the neurotransmitter GABA (red) and cell bodies stained for the neurotransmitter oxytocin (green) in rat hypothalamus.

(Courtesy of Dr. William E. Armstrong.)

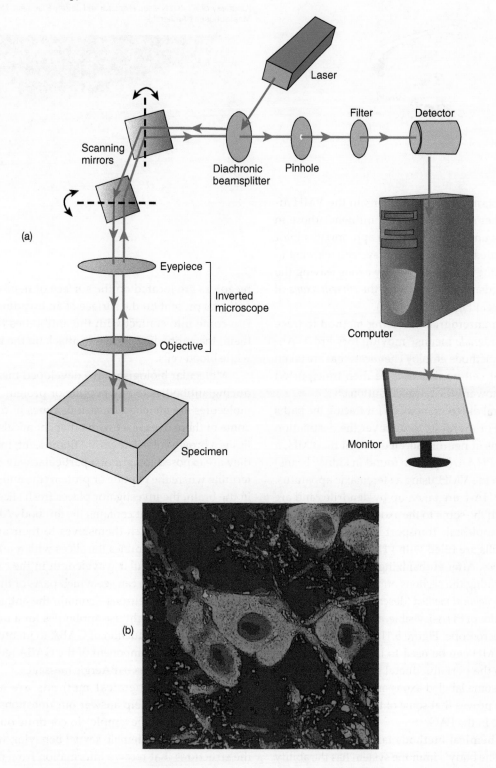

look closely at a brain that has been prepared by these means, we see a large set of all neurons in the region. But in recent years, researchers have developed very precise methods that make specific neurons stand out from all of the others.

TRACING EFFERENT AXONS Eventually, the VMH must affect behavior. That is, neurons in the VMH must send axons to parts of the brain that contain neurons that are responsible for muscular movements. The pathway is

Figure 5.10 Tracing Neural Circuits

Once we know that a particular brain region is involved in a particular function, we may ask what structures provide inputs to the region and what structures receive outputs from it.

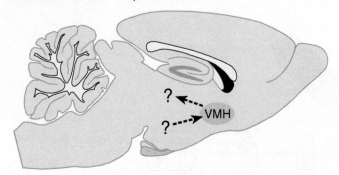

Figure 5.11 Anterograde Tracing Method

PHA-L was injected into the ventromedial nucleus of the hypothalamus, where it was taken up by dendrites and carried through the cells' axons to their terminal buttons. The section shows labeled axons and terminal buttons in the periaqueductal gray matter.

(Courtesy of Kirsten Nielsen Ricciardi and Jeffrey Blaustein, University of Massachusetts Amherst.)

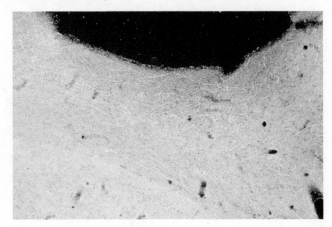

probably not direct; more likely, neurons in the VMH affect neurons in other structures, which influence those in yet other structures until, eventually, the appropriate motor neurons are stimulated. To discover this system, we want to be able to identify the paths followed by axons leaving the VMH. In other words, we want to trace the *efferent axons* of this structure. (Look at Figure 5.10 again).

We will use an **anterograde labeling method** to trace these axons. (*Anterograde* means "moving forward.") Anterograde labeling methods employ chemicals that are taken up by dendrites or cell bodies and are then transported through the axons toward the terminal buttons.

There are several different methods for tracing the paths of efferent axons. For example, to discover the destination of the efferent axons of neurons located within the VMH, a minute quantity of **PHA-L** (a protein found in kidney beans) can be injected into the VMH using a stereotaxic apparatus. The molecules of PHA-L are taken up by dendrites and are transported through the soma to the axon, where they travel by means of fast axoplasmic transport to the terminal buttons. Eventually cells are filled with PHA-L. Figure 5.14 illustrates this process. After euthanizing the animal, slicing the brain, and mounting the sections on microscope slides, a special *immunocytochemical method* (described below) is used to make the molecules of PHA-L visible, and the slides are examined under a microscope. Figure 5.11 shows how PHA-L injected into the VMH can be used to identify efferent axons that project to the periaqueductal gray matter (PAG). The PAG contains some labeled axons and terminal buttons (gold color), which proves that some of the efferent axons of the VMH terminate in the PAG.

Immunocytochemical methods take advantage of an immune reaction. The body's immune system has the ability to produce antibodies in response to antigens. *Antigens* are proteins (or peptides), such as those found on the surface of bacteria or viruses. *Antibodies,* which are also proteins, are produced by white blood cells to destroy invading microorganisms. Antibodies are either secreted by white blood cells or are located on their surface, in the way neurotransmitter

receptors are located on the surface of neurons. When the antigens present on the surface of an invading microorganism come into contact with the antibodies that recognize them, the antibodies trigger an attack on the invader by the white blood cells.

Molecular biologists have developed methods for producing antibodies to any peptide or protein. The antibody molecules are attached to various types of dye molecules. Some of these dyes react with other chemicals and stain the tissue a brown color. Others are fluorescent; they glow when they are exposed to light of a particular wavelength. To determine where the peptide or protein (the antigen) is located in the brain, the investigator places fresh slices of brain tissue in a solution that contains the antibody/dye molecules. The antibodies attach themselves to their antigen. When the investigator examines the slices with a microscope (under light of a particular wavelength in the case of fluorescent dyes), he or she can see which parts of the brain—even which individual neurons—contain the antigen. For example, a researcher might use antibodies for a protein enzyme involved in the production of GABA to identify GABAergic cells, or a protein component of the GABA receptor to identify cells that receive GABAergic messages.

Immunocytochemical methods are an important technique used to help answer our questions about neural circuits in the VMH example. To continue our study of the role of the VMH in female sexual behavior, we would find the structures that receive information from neurons in the VMH (such as the PAG) and see what happens when each of them is lesioned. Let's suppose that damage to some of these structures also impairs female sexual behavior. We could then inject these structures with PHA-L and see where *their* axons go. Eventually, we will discover the relevant pathways from the VMH to the motor neurons whose activity is necessary for copulatory behavior. (In fact, researchers have done so, and some of their results are presented in Chapter 10.)

TRACING AFFERENT AXONS   Tracing efferent axons from the VMH will tell us only part of the story about the neural circuitry involved in female sexual behavior: the part between the VMH and the motor neurons. What about the circuits *before* the VMH? Is the VMH somehow involved in the analysis of sensory information (such as the sight, odor, or touch of the male)? Or perhaps the VMH processes the activating effect of a female's sex hormones on her behavior through neurons whose axons form synapses there? To discover the parts of the brain that are involved in the "upstream" components of the neural circuitry, we need to find the inputs of the VMH—its afferent connections. To do so, we will employ a **retrograde labeling method.**

Retrograde means "moving backward." Retrograde labeling methods employ chemicals that are taken up by terminal buttons and carried *backward* through the axons toward the cell bodies. The method for identifying the afferent inputs to a particular region of the brain is similar to the method used for identifying its efferent outputs. First, we inject a small quantity of one example of a retrograde chemical called **fluorogold** into the VMH. The chemical is taken up by terminal buttons and is transported backward toward the cell bodies by means of retrograde axoplasmic transport to fill the afferent neurons. Similar to process for investigating efferent axons, after euthanizing the animal, slicing the brain, mounting the sections on microscope slides, and using immunocytochemical methods, the brain tissue is examined under light of the appropriate wavelength. The molecules of fluorogold fluoresce under this light. Through this process we discover that the medial amygdala is one of the regions that provides input to the VMH. (See Figure 5.12.)

Together, anterograde and retrograde labeling methods enable us to discover circuits of interconnected neurons. Thus, these methods help to provide us with a "wiring diagram" of the brain. (See Figure 5.13.) Armed with other research methods (including some to be described later in this chapter), we can try to discover the functions of each component of this circuit.

The anterograde and retrograde labeling methods that we have described identify a single link in a chain of neurons—neurons whose axons enter or leave a particular brain region. *Transneuronal* tracing methods identify a series of two, three, or more neurons that form serial synaptic connections with each other. The most effective retrograde transneuronal tracing method uses a **pseudorabies virus**—a weakened form of a pig herpes virus that was originally developed as a vaccine. For anterograde transneuronal tracing, a variety of the **herpes simplex virus,** similar to the one that causes cold sores, is used. The virus is injected directly into a brain region, is taken up by neurons there, and infects them. The virus spreads throughout the infected neurons and is eventually released by the terminal buttons, passing the infection to other neurons that form synaptic connections with them.

After the animal is euthanized and the brain is sliced, immunocytochemical methods are used to localize a protein produced by the virus. For example, Daniels et al., (1999) injected pseudorabies virus in the muscles responsible for female rats' mating posture. After a few days, the rats were euthanized, and their brains were examined for evidence of viral infection. The study indicated that the virus found its

Figure 5.12 Retrograde Tracing Method

Fluorogold was injected in the VMH, where it was taken up by terminal buttons and transported back through the axons to their cell bodies. The photograph shows these cell bodies, located in the medial amygdala.

(Courtesy of Yvon Delville, University of Massachusetts Medical School.)

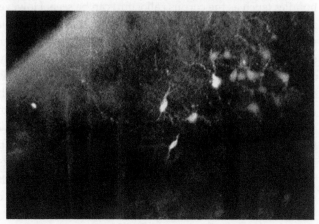

Figure 5.13 Results of Tracing Methods

The figure shows one of the inputs to the VMH and one of the outputs, as revealed by anterograde and retrograde labeling methods.

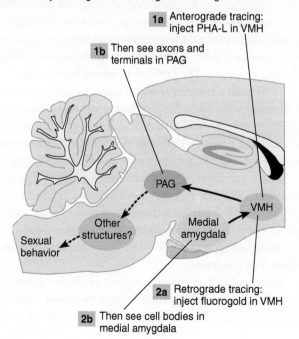

1a Anterograde tracing: inject PHA-L in VMH

1b Then see axons and terminals in PAG

PAG

Other structures?

Sexual behavior

Medial amygdala

VMH

2a Retrograde tracing: inject fluorogold in VMH

2b Then see cell bodies in medial amygdala

Figure 5.14 Labeling Efferent Axons

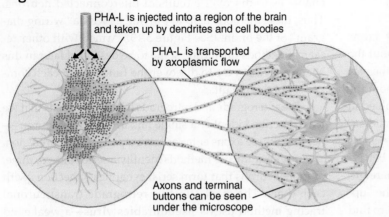

PHA-L is injected into a region of the brain and taken up by dendrites and cell bodies

PHA-L is transported by axoplasmic flow

Axons and terminal buttons can be seen under the microscope

way up the motor nerves to the motor neurons in the spinal cord, then to the reticular formation of the medulla, then to the periaqueductal gray matter, and finally to the VMH. These results confirm the results of the anterograde and retrograde labeling methods that were just described.

Studying the Structure of the Living Human Brain

LO 5.6 Contrast the methods used to study the structure of the living human brain.

There are many good reasons to investigate the functions of brains of animals other than humans. For example, we can compare the results of studies made with different species in order to make some inferences about the evolution of various neural systems. Even if our primary interest is in the functions of the human brain, we cannot ethically ask people to submit to brain surgery for the purposes of research. But diseases and accidents do occasionally damage the human brain, and if we know where the damage occurs, we can study the people's behavior and try to make the same sorts of inferences we make with deliberately produced brain lesions in laboratory animals. The problem is, where is the lesion?

In the past a researcher might have studied the behavior of a person with brain damage and never found out exactly where the lesion was located. The only way to be sure was to obtain the patient's brain when he or she died and examine slices of it under a microscope. But it was often impossible to do this. Sometimes the patient outlived the researcher. Sometimes the patient moved out of town. Sometimes (often, perhaps) the family refused permission for an autopsy. Because of these practical problems, study of the behavioral effects of damage to specific parts of the human brain made rather slow progress.

Advances in X-ray techniques and computers have led to the development of several noninvasive methods for studying the anatomy of the living brain. These advances permit

researchers to study the location and extent of brain damage while the patient is still living. The first method that was developed is called **computerized tomography (CT)**. This procedure, usually referred to as a *CT scan*, works as follows: The patient's head is placed in a large doughnut-shaped ring. The ring contains an X-ray tube and, directly opposite it (on the other side of the patient's head), an X-ray detector. The X-ray beam passes through the patient's head, and the detector measures the amount of radioactivity that gets through it. The beam scans the head from all angles, and a computer translates the information it receives from the detector into pictures of the skull and its contents. (See Figure 5.15.)

Figure 5.16 shows a series of these CT scans taken through the head of a patient who sustained a stroke. The stroke damaged a part of the brain involved in bodily awareness and perception of space. The patient lost her awareness of the left side of her body and of items located on her left. You can see the damage as a white spot in the lower left corner of scan 5.

An even more detailed, high-resolution picture of what is inside a person's head is provided by a process called **magnetic resonance imaging (MRI)**. The MRI scanner resembles a CT scanner, but it does not use X-rays. Instead, it passes an extremely strong magnetic field through the patient's head. When a person's head is placed in this strong magnetic field, the nuclei of spinning hydrogen atoms align themselves to the magnetic field. When a pulse of a radio frequency wave is then passed through the brain, these nuclei flip at an angle to the magnetic field and then flip back to their original position at the end of the radio pulse. As they do so, they release energy that they absorbed from the radio pulse. The released energy is sensed by a coil of wire that serves as a detector. Because different tissues contain different amounts of water (and hence different concentrations of hydrogen atoms) they emit different amounts of energy. The computer associated with the MRI scanner analyzes the signal and prepares pictures of slices of the brain. (See Figure 5.17.)

As you can see in Figure 5.17, MRI scans distinguish between regions of gray matter and white matter, so major fiber bundles (such as the corpus callosum) can be seen. However, small fiber bundles are not visible on these scans. A special modification of the MRI scanner permits the visualization of even small bundles of fibers and the tracing of fiber tracts. Above absolute zero, all molecules move in random directions because of thermal agitation: The higher the temperature, the faster the random movement. **Diffusion tensor imaging (DTI)** takes advantage of the fact that the movement of water molecules in bundles of white matter will not be random but will tend to be in a direction parallel to the axons that make up the bundles. The MRI scanner uses information about the movement of the water molecules to determine the location and orientation of

Figure 5.15 Computerized Tomography

Within a CT scanner, a beam of X-rays is used to image progressive "slices" through tissues of the body, including the brain and skull. Differences in structure or tissue type, such as tumors or bleeding, can be seen in CT scans.

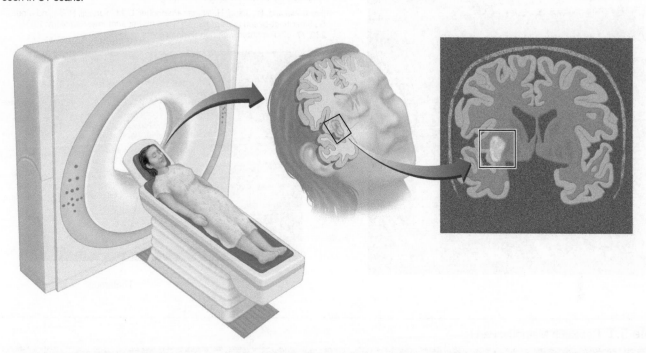

bundles of axons in white matter. Figure 5.18 shows a sagittal view of some of the axons that project from the thalamus to the cerebral cortex in the human brain, as revealed by DTI. The computer adds colors to distinguish different bundles of axons. The research methods described in this section are summarized in Table 5.1.

Figure 5.16 CT Brain Scans

The patient has a lesion in the right occipital-parietal area (scan 5). The lesion appears white because it was accompanied by bleeding; blood absorbs more radiation than the surrounding brain tissue. Rostral is up, caudal is down; left and right are reversed. Scan 1 shows a section through the eyes and the base of the brain.

(Courtesy of J. McA. Jones, Good Samaritan Hospital, Portland, Oregon.)

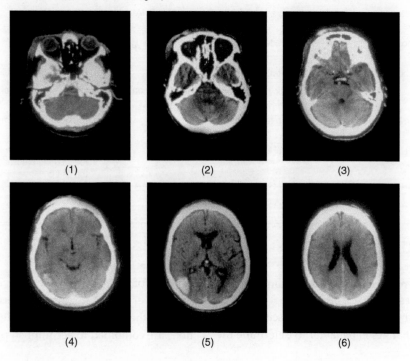

Figure 5.17 MRI Scans of Human Brain

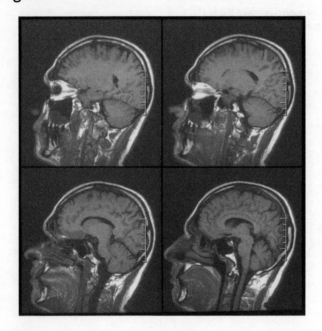

Figure 5.18 Diffusion Tensor Imaging

This image shows a sagittal view of some of the axons that project from the thalamus to the cerebral cortex in the human brain, as revealed by diffusion tensor imaging.

(From Wakana, S., Jiang, H., Nagae-Poetscher, L. M., van Zijl, P. C., and Mori, S., Fiber tract-based atlas of human white matter anatomy, *Radiology*, 2004, *230*, 77–87. Reprinted with permission.)

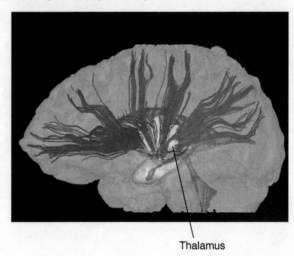

Thalamus

Table 5.1 Research Methods: Part I

Goal of Method	Method	Remarks
Destroy or inactivate specific brain region	Radio frequency lesion	Destroys all brain tissue near tip of electrode
	Excitotoxic lesion; uses excitatory amino acid such as kainic acid	Destroys only cell bodies near tip of cannula; spares axons passing through the region
	Infusion of local anesthetic or drug that produces local neural inhibition	Temporarily inactivates specific brain region; animal can serve as its own control
	Infusion of saporin conjugated with an antibody	Destroys neurons that contain the antibody; produces very precise brain lesions
Place electrode or cannula in specific region within brain	Stereotaxic surgery	Consult stereotaxic atlas for coordinates
Find location of lesion	Perfuse brain; fix brain; slice brain; stain sections	
Identify axons leaving a particular region and the terminal buttons of these axons	Anterograde tracing method, such as PHA-L	
Identify location of neurons whose axons terminate in a particular region	Retrograde tracing method, such as fluorogold	
Find location of lesion in living human brain	Computerized tomography (CT scanner)	Shows "slice" of brain; uses X-rays
	Magnetic resonance imaging (MRI scanner)	Shows "slice" of brain; better detail than CT scan; uses a magnetic field and radio waves
Find location of fiber bundles in living human brain	Diffusion tensor imaging (DTI)	Shows bundles of myelinated axons; uses an MRI scanner
Visualize details of cells in thick sections of tissue	Confocal laser scanning microscopy	Can be used to see "slices" of tissue in living brain; requires the presence of fluorescent molecules in the tissue

Section Review

LO 5.1 Explain what researchers can learn from studies that involve lesioning.

By lesioning a part of the nervous system, a researcher can observe the resulting changes in behavior to determine the function of that portion of the nervous system. The goal is to discover what functions are performed by different regions of the brain and then to understand how these functions are combined to accomplish particular behaviors. No one brain region or neural circuit is solely responsible for a behavior; each region performs a function (or set of functions) that contributes to performance of the behavior.

LO 5.2 Compare various methods of producing brain lesions.

Brain lesions can be produced by passing electrical current through a wire, or by injecting an excitatory amino acid, selective antibody, or local anesthetic into a specific brain region. Using an electrical current, an excitatory amino acid, or a selective antibody produces a permanent lesion. Using a local anesthetic produces a temporary lesion. Using an electrical current produces a nonselective lesion. The other methods produce lesions based on the type of neuron the lesioning agent selectively binds to.

LO 5.3 Describe the process of stereotaxic surgery.

Stereotaxic surgery involves using a stereotaxic atlas to identify a specific location in the brain. Once the location has been identified, the researcher places the head in a stereotaxic apparatus and positions a cannula over the correct location on the head. The researcher makes an incision in the scalp of the anesthetized animal (or human), drills a hole in the skull, and lowers the cannula into place. The researcher makes the lesion (or in some cases implants an electrode or transplants tissue), removes the cannula, and the animal (or human) recovers from the anesthetic.

LO 5.4 Summarize the general steps of histological methods.

Brain tissue is perfused and removed from the skull. Then, the tissue to be examined is placed in a fixative. Once the brain is fixed, it is sliced into thin sections on a cryostat or microtome. The slices are placed on a microscope slide and coverslipped. Brain tissue must be stained to reveal cellular and intracellular structures. Cells can be stained for cell bodies, nuclei, or specific proteins using dyes or specially labeled antibodies. Depending on the characteristics of the cell or intracellular structures of interest, light microscopes, transmission electron microscopes, scanning electron microscopes, or confocal laser scanning microscopes may be used to study the tissue samples.

LO 5.5 Differentiate between techniques for tracing efferent and afferent axons.

Tracing efferent axons allows researchers to learn about the target locations of sets of neurons. Using an anterograde labeling methods, a chemical is injected into the region containing cell bodies, taken up with the cells, and transported to the terminals. Immunocytochemical methods use antibodies to identify the structures that receive input from the cell bodies. Tracing afferent axons allows researchers to learn about neurons that provide input to a region of interest. Using a retrograde labeling method, a chemical is injected into the target region and taken up by the terminal buttons. The chemical then travels to the cell body of the neuron. Immunocytochemical methods use antibodies to identify the structures that send input to the target region of interest.

LO 5.6 Contrast the methods used to study the structure of the living human brain.

Computerized tomography (CT) uses X-rays to image the structure of the living human brain. Magnetic resonance imaging (MRI) uses a magnetic field to image the living brain and differentiates among different tissue types. Diffusion tensor imaging (DTI) uses information about the movement of water molecules to visualize small fiber bundles not visible in MRI scans.

Thought Question

Henry Molaison (H. M.) became a well-known figure in psychology and neuroscience after undergoing ablation of tissue in his temporal lobes to reduce seizures. The surgery was performed in 1957. H. M.'s brain and behavior were documented by physicians and researchers until his death in 2008. After his death, researchers at the University of California San Diego (UCSD) carefully preserved, sectioned, and stained his brain to learn more about it. Describe the techniques these researchers would need to use to examine H. M.'s brain after his death.

Recording and Stimulating Neural Activity

The first section of this chapter dealt with the anatomy of the brain and the effects of damage to particular regions. This section considers a different approach: studying the brain by recording or stimulating the activity of particular regions. Brain functions involve activity of circuits of neurons; thus, different perceptions and behavioral responses involve different patterns of activity in the brain. Researchers have devised methods to record these patterns of activity or artificially produce them.

Recording Neural Activity

LO 5.7 Compare recording neural activity using microelectrodes, macroelectrodes, and magnetoencephalography.

Axons produce action potentials, and terminal buttons elicit postsynaptic potentials in the membrane of the cells with which they form synapses. These electrical events can be recorded (as we saw in Chapter 2), and changes in the electrical activity of a particular region can be used to determine whether that region plays a role in various behaviors. For example, recordings can be made during stimulus presentations, decision making, or motor activities.

Recordings can be made *chronically*, over an extended period of time after the animal recovers from surgery, or *acutely*, for a relatively short period of time during which the animal is kept anesthetized. Acute recordings, made while the animal is anesthetized, are usually restricted to studies of sensory pathways. Acute recordings seldom involve behavioral observations, since the behavioral capacity of an anesthetized animal is limited.

RECORDINGS WITH MICROELECTRODES   Drugs that affect serotonergic and noradrenergic neurons also affect REM sleep. Suppose that, knowing this fact, we wondered whether the activity of serotonergic and noradrenergic neurons would vary during different stages of sleep. To find out, we would record the activity of these neurons with microelectrodes. **Microelectrodes,** usually made of thin wires, have a very fine tip, small enough to record the electrical activity of individual neurons. This technique is usually called **single-unit recording** (a unit refers to an individual neuron).

Because we want to record the activity of single neurons over a long period of time in unanesthetized animals, we want more durable electrodes. We can purchase arrays of very fine wires, gathered together in a bundle, which can simultaneously record the activity of many different neurons. The wires are insulated so that only their tips are bare.

We implant the electrodes in the brains of animals through stereotaxic surgery and bond them to the animals' skull, using plastics that were originally developed for the dental profession. Then, after recovery from surgery, the recording system can be activated. We can then observe both the animal's behavior during REM sleep and the corresponding activity of the serotonergic and noradrenergic neurons recorded by the implanted microelectrodes. (See Figure 5.19.)

The electrical signals detected by microelectrodes are quite small and must be amplified. Amplifiers used for this purpose work just like the amplifiers in a stereo system, converting the weak signals recorded in the brain into stronger ones. These signals can be displayed and saved on a computer.

What about the results of our recordings from serotonergic and noradrenergic neurons? As you will learn in Chapter 9, if we record the activity of these neurons during various stages of sleep, we will find that their firing rates fall almost to zero during REM sleep. This observation suggests that these neurons have an *inhibitory* effect on REM sleep. That is, REM sleep does not occur until these neurons stop firing.

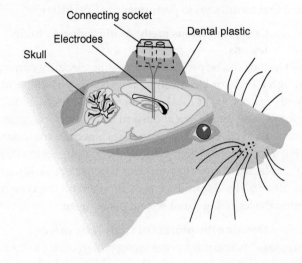

Figure 5.19 Implantation of Electrodes
The drawing shows a set of electrodes in a rat brain.

RECORDINGS WITH MACROELECTRODES   Sometimes, we want to record the activity of a region of the brain as a whole, not the activity of individual neurons. To do this, we would use macroelectrodes. **Macroelectrodes** do not detect the activity of individual neurons; rather, the records that are obtained with these devices represent the postsynaptic potentials of many thousands—or millions—of cells in the area of the electrode. These electrodes are sometimes implanted into the brain or onto the surface of the brain, but many are temporarily attached to the human scalp with a special paste that conducts electricity. Recordings taken from the scalp, especially, represent the activity of an enormous number of neurons, whose electrical signals pass through the meninges, skull, and scalp before reaching the electrodes.

The electrical activity of a human brain recorded through macroelectrodes is displayed on a *polygraph*. A polygraph plots the changes in voltage detected by the electrodes along a timeline during recording. The polygraph is displayed on a computer screen. Figure 5.20 illustrates electrical activity recorded from macroelectrodes attached to various locations on a person's scalp. Such records are called **electroencephalograms (EEGs),** or "writings of electricity from the head." They can be used to diagnose epilepsy or study the stages of sleep and wakefulness, which are associated with characteristic patterns of electrical activity.

In addition to their use in research, clinicians use macroelectrodes to help treat patients. Occasionally, neurosurgeons implant macroelectrodes directly into the human brain. The reason for doing so is to detect the source of abnormal electrical activity that is giving rise to frequent seizures. Once the source has been determined, the surgeon can remove the source of the seizures—usually scar tissue caused by brain damage that occurred earlier in life. Similarly, another clinical use of EEG is to monitor the condition

Figure 5.20 Recording Brain Activity with Macroelectrodes

Macroelectrodes record the summed electrical activity of many neurons. In this example, an electroencephalogram is created to visually represent the changes in summed postsynaptic potentials recorded by scalp electrodes.

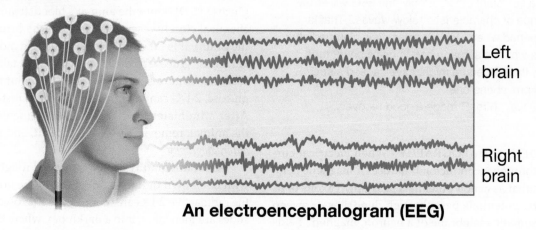

Left brain

Right brain

An electroencephalogram (EEG)

of the brain during procedures that could potentially damage it. One of the authors of this book (N. C.) witnessed just such a procedure several years ago. The procedure is described in the following case.

Mrs. F. had sustained one mild heart attack, and subsequent tests indicated a considerable amount of atherosclerosis, commonly referred to as "hardening of the arteries." Many of her arteries were narrowed by cholesterol-rich atherosclerotic plaque. A clot formed in a particularly narrow portion of one of her coronary arteries, which caused her heart attack. As the months passed after her heart attack, Mrs. F. had several *transient ischemic attacks,* brief episodes of neurological symptoms that appear to be caused by blood clots forming and then dissolving in cerebral blood vessels. In her case, they caused numbness in her right arm and difficulty in talking. Her physician referred her to a neurologist, who ordered an angiogram (a recording of heart activity). This procedure revealed that her left carotid artery was almost totally blocked. The neurologist referred Mrs. F. to a neurosurgeon, who urged her to have an operation that would remove the plaque from part of her left carotid artery and increase the blood flow to the left side of her brain.

The procedure is called a *carotid endarterectomy.* I was chatting with Mrs. F.'s neurosurgeon after a conference, and he happened to mention that he would be performing the operation later that morning. I asked whether I could watch, and he agreed. When I entered the operating room, scrubbed and gowned, I found Mrs. F. already anesthetized, and the surgical nurse had prepared the left side of her neck for the incision.

In addition, several EEG electrodes had been attached to her scalp, and I saw that Dr. L., a neurologist who specializes in clinical neurophysiology, was seated at his EEG machine.

The surgeon made an incision in Mrs. F.'s neck and exposed the carotid artery, at the point where the common carotid, coming from the heart, branched into the external and internal carotid arteries. He placed a plastic band around the common carotid artery and clamped it shut, stopping the flow of blood. "How does it look,?" he asked Dr. L. "No good—I see some slowing. You'd better shunt."

The surgeon quickly removed the constricting band and asked the nurse for a shunt, a short length of plastic tubing a little thinner than the artery. He made two small incisions in the artery well above and well below the region that contained the plaque, and inserted the shunt. Now he could work on the artery without stopping the flow of blood to the brain. He made a longitudinal cut in the artery, exposing a yellowish mass that he dissected away and removed. He sewed up the incision, removed the shunt, and sutured the small cuts he had made to accommodate it. "Everything still okay?" he asked Dr. L. "Yes, her EEG is fine."

Most neurosurgeons prefer to do an endarterectomy by temporarily clamping the artery shut while they work on it. The work goes faster, and complications are less likely. Because the blood supply to the two hemispheres of the brain are interconnected (with special *communicating arteries*), it is often possible to shut down one of the carotid arteries for a few minutes without causing any damage. However, sometimes the blood flow from one side of the brain to the other is insufficient to keep the other side nourished with blood and oxygen. The only way the surgeon can know is to have the patient's EEG monitored. If the brain is not receiving a sufficient blood supply, the EEG will show the presence of characteristic "slow waves." That is what happened when Mrs. F.'s artery was clamped shut, and that is why the surgeon had to use a shunt tube. Without it, the procedure might have caused a stroke instead of preventing one.

By the way, Mrs. F. made a good recovery.

MAGNETOENCEPHALOGRAPHY When electrical current flows through a conductor, it induces a magnetic field. This means that as action potentials pass down axons or as postsynaptic potentials pass through dendrites or sweep across the somatic membrane of a neuron, magnetic fields are also produced. These fields are very small, but engineers have developed superconducting detectors (called SQUIDs, or "superconducting quantum interference devices") that can detect minute magnetic fields.

Magnetoencephalography is performed with *neuromagnetometers*, devices that contain an array of several SQUIDs, oriented so that a computer can examine their output and calculate the source of particular signals in the brain. These devices can be used clinically—for example, to find the sources of seizures so that they can be removed surgically. They can also be used in experiments to measure regional brain activity that accompanies the perception of various stimuli or the performance of various behaviors or cognitive tasks.

An important advantage of magnetoencephalography is its temporal resolution. Another technique that you'll read about in this chapter, functional MRI (fMRI) provides excellent spatial resolution of regional activity in the brain, but the process is slow and provides relatively poor temporal resolution. That is, the image can accurately measure differences in activity of closely spaced regions of the brain, but the acquisition of an fMRI image takes a relatively long time compared with the rapid flow of information in the brain. The image produced by means of magnetoencephalography is not as detailed as an fMRI image, but it can be acquired much more rapidly and can consequently reveal fast-moving events.

Recording the Brain's Metabolic and Synaptic Activity

LO 5.8 **Compare the types of metabolic and synaptic activity that can be revealed by autoradiography, staining for immediate early genes, positron emission tomography, and functional magnetic resonance imaging.**

Electrical and magnetic signals are not the only signs of neural activity. If the neural activity of a particular region of the brain increases, the metabolic rate of this region increases,

too, largely due to increased operation of ion transporters in the membrane of the cells, which requires an increased use of cellular energy. This increased metabolic rate can be measured. The experimenter injects radioactive **2-deoxy-glucose (2-DG)** into the animal's bloodstream. Because this chemical closely resembles glucose (the principal food for the brain), it is taken into cells. Thus, the most active cells, which use glucose at the highest rate, will take up the highest concentrations of radioactive 2-DG. But unlike normal glucose, 2-DG cannot be metabolized, so it stays in the cell. After administering 2-DG, the experimenter euthanizes the animal, removes the brain, slices it, and prepares it for *autoradiography*.

Autoradiography can be translated roughly as "writing with one's own radiation." Sections of the brain containing the radioactive 2-DG are mounted on microscope slides. The slides are then taken into a darkroom, where they are coated with a photographic emulsion (the substance found on photographic film). Several weeks later, the slides, with their coatings of emulsion, are developed, just like photographic film. The molecules of radioactive 2-DG show themselves as spots of silver grains in the developed emulsion because the radioactivity exposes the emulsion, just as X-rays or light will do. The most active regions of the brain contain the most radioactivity, showing this radioactivity in the form of dark spots in the developed emulsion.

Another method of identifying active regions of the brain capitalizes on the fact that when neurons are activated (for example, by the terminal buttons that form synapses with them), particular genes in the nucleus called *immediate early genes* are turned on, and particular proteins are produced. These proteins then bind with the chromosomes in the nucleus. The presence of these nuclear proteins indicates that the neuron has just been activated.

One of the nuclear proteins produced during neural activation is called **Fos.** You will remember that earlier in this chapter we began an imaginary research project on the neural circuitry involved in the sexual behavior of female rats. Suppose we want to use the Fos method in this project to see what neurons are activated during a female rat's sexual activity. We place female rats with males and permit the animals to copulate. After euthanizing the animals, we remove the rats' brains, slice them, and follow a procedure that stains Fos protein. Figure 5.21 shows the results: Neurons in the medial amygdala of a female rat that has just mated show the presence of dark spots, indicating the presence of Fos protein. Thus, these neurons appear to be activated by copulatory activity—perhaps by the physical stimulation of the genitals that occurs then. As you will recall, when we injected a retrograde tracer (fluorogold) into the VMH, we found that this region receives input from the medial amygdala.

The metabolic activity of specific brain regions can be measured noninvasively in a living animal, by means of

Figure 5.21 Localization of Fos Protein

The photomicrograph shows a frontal section of the brain of a female rat, taken through the medial amygdala. The dark spots indicate the presence of Fos protein, localized by means of immunocytochemistry. The synthesis of Fos protein was stimulated by permitting the animal to engage in copulatory behavior.

(Courtesy of Marc Tetel, Skidmore College.)

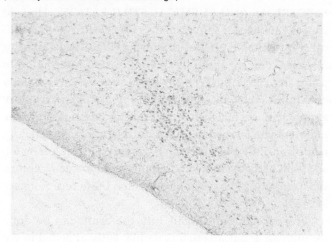

Figure 5.22 PET Scans

The top row shows three horizontal scans from a person at rest. The bottom row shows three scans from the same person while he was clenching and unclenching his right fist. The scans show increased uptake of radioactive 2-DG in regions of the brain that are devoted to the control of movement, which indicates increased metabolic rate in these areas. Different computer-generated colors indicate different rates of uptake of 2-DG, as shown in the scale at the bottom.

(Courtesy of the Brookhaven National Laboratory and the State University of New York, Stony Brook.)

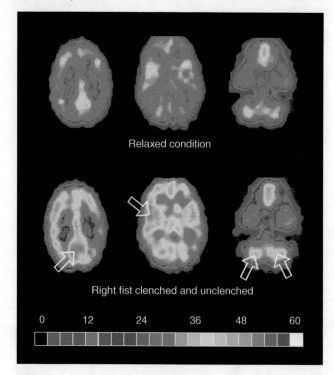

functional imaging—a computerized method of detecting metabolic or chemical changes within the brain. The first functional imaging method to be developed was **positron emission tomography (PET)**. First, a person (or other animal) receives an injection of radioactive 2-DG. (The chemical soon breaks down and leaves the cells. The dose given is harmless, and over time gradually leaves the cells.) The person's head is placed in a machine similar to a CT scanner. When the radioactive molecules of 2-DG decay, they emit subatomic particles called positrons, which meet nearby electrons. The particles annihilate each other and emit two photons, which travel in directly opposite paths. Sensors arrayed around the person's head detect these photons, and the scanner plots the locations from which these photons are being emitted. From this information, the computer produces a picture of a slice of the brain, showing the activity level of various regions in that slice. (See Figure 5.22.)

One of the disadvantages of PET scanners is their operating cost. For reasons of safety, the radioactive chemicals that are administered have very short half-lives; that is, they decay and lose their radioactivity very quickly. For example, the half-life of radioactive 2-DG is 110 minutes; the half-life of radioactive water (also used for PET scans) is only 2 minutes. Because these chemicals decay so quickly, they must be produced on site, in an atomic particle accelerator called a *cyclotron*. Therefore, to the cost of the PET scanner must be added the cost of the cyclotron and the salaries of the personnel who operate it.

Another disadvantage of PET scans is the relatively poor spatial resolution (the blurriness) of the images. The temporal resolution is also relatively poor. The positrons being emitted from the brain must be sampled for a fairly long time, which means that rapid, short-lived events within the brain are likely to be missed. These disadvantages are not seen in functional MRI, described in the next paragraph. However, PET scanners can do something that functional MRI scanners cannot do: measure the concentration of particular chemicals in various parts of the brain. We will describe this procedure later in this chapter.

Currently, the brain-imaging method with the best spatial resolution is **functional MRI (fMRI)**. Engineers have devised modifications to existing MRI scanners and their software that permit the devices to acquire images that indicate regional metabolism. Brain activity is measured indirectly, by detecting levels of oxygen in the brain's blood vessels. Increased activity of a brain region stimulates blood flow to that region, which increases the local blood oxygen level. The formal name of this type of imaging is *BOLD*: blood oxygen level–dependent signal. Functional MRI scans have a higher resolution than PET scans do. Thus, they reveal more detailed information about the activity of particular brain regions. You will read about many functional imaging studies that employ fMRI scans in subsequent chapters of this book.

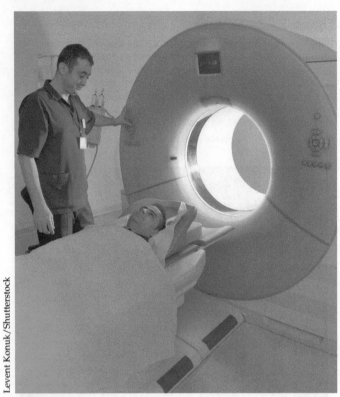

Levent Konuk/Shutterstock

Functional MRI scans reveal more detailed information about the activity of particular brain regions.

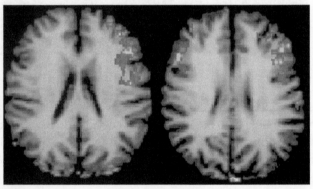

FUNCTIONAL MRI SCANS These scans of human brains show localized average increases in neural activity of males (left) and females (right) while they were judging whether pairs of written words rhymed. (From Shaywitz, B. A., et al., Sex differences in the functional organization of the brain for language, *Nature*, 1995, *373*, 607–609. Reprinted with permission.)

Stimulating Neural Activity

LO 5.9 **Compare electrical and chemical neural stimulation, optogenetic methods, and transcranial magnetic stimulation.**

So far, this section has been concerned with research methods that measure the activity of specific regions of the brain. But sometimes we may want to artificially change the activity of these regions to see what effects these changes have on behavior. For example, female rats will copulate with males only if certain female sex

hormones are present. If we remove the rats' ovaries, the loss of these hormones will abolish the rats' sexual behavior. We found in our earlier studies that VMH lesions disrupt this behavior. Perhaps if we *activate* the VMH, we will make up for the lack of female sex hormones and the rats will copulate again.

ELECTRICAL AND CHEMICAL STIMULATION How do we activate neurons? We can do so by electrical or chemical stimulation. Electrical stimulation involves passing an electrical current through a wire inserted into the brain using stereotaxic surgery. Chemical stimulation is usually accomplished by injecting a small amount of an excitatory amino acid, such as kainic acid or glutamic acid, into the brain. As you learned in Chapter 4, the principal excitatory neurotransmitter in the brain is glutamic acid (glutamate), and both of these substances stimulate glutamate receptors, thus activating the neurons on which these receptors are located.

Injections of chemicals into the brain can be done through an apparatus that is permanently attached to the skull so that the animal's behavior can be observed several times. A researcher can place a metal cannula (a guide cannula) in an animal's brain using stereotaxic surgery and cement its top to the skull. A smaller cannula of measured length can be placed inside the guide cannula and used to inject a chemical into the brain. Because the animal is free to move about, it is possible to observe the effects of the injection on its behavior. (See Figure 5.23.)

Figure 5.23 An Intracranial Cannula

(a) A guide cannula is permanently attached to the skull. (b) At a later time a thinner cannula can be inserted through the guide cannula into the brain. Chemicals can be infused into the brain through this device.

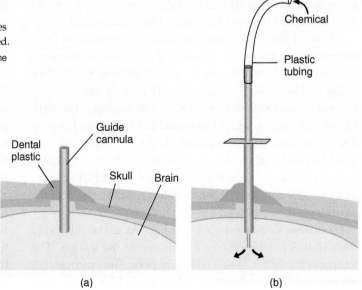

The principal disadvantage of chemical stimulation is that it is slightly more complicated than electrical stimulation; chemical stimulation requires cannulas, tubes, special pumps or syringes, and sterile solutions of excitatory amino acids. However, it has a distinct advantage over electrical stimulation: It activates cell bodies but not axons. Because only cell bodies (and their dendrites) contain glutamate receptors, we can be assured that an injection of an excitatory amino acid into a particular region of the brain excites the cells there but not the axons of other neurons that happen to pass through the region. Thus, the effects of chemical stimulation are more localized than are the effects of electrical stimulation.

You might have noticed that we just said that kainic acid, which we described earlier as a neurotoxin, can be used to stimulate neurons. These two uses are not really contradictory. Kainic acid produces excitotoxic lesions by stimulating neurons to death. Whereas large doses of a concentrated solution kill neurons, small doses of a dilute solution simply stimulate them.

When chemicals are injected into the brain through cannulas, molecules of the chemicals diffuse over a region that includes many different types of neurons: excitatory neurons, inhibitory neurons, interneurons that participate in local circuits, projection neurons that communicate with different regions of the brain, and neurons that release or respond to a wide variety of neurotransmitters and neuromodulators. Stimulating a particular brain region with electricity or an excitatory chemical affects all of these neurons, and the result is unlikely to resemble normal brain activity, which involves coordinated activation and inhibition of many different neurons. Ideally, we would like to be able to stimulate or inhibit selected populations of neurons in a given brain region.

What about the results of our hypothetical experiment? In fact (as we shall see in Chapter 10), VMH stimulation *does* substitute for female sex hormones. Perhaps, then, the female sex hormones exert their effects in this nucleus. We will see how to test this hypothesis in the final section of this chapter.

TRANSCRANIAL MAGNETIC STIMULATION As we saw earlier in this chapter, neural activity induces magnetic fields that can be detected by means of magnetoencephalography. Similarly, magnetic fields can be used to stimulate neurons by inducing electrical currents in brain tissue. **Transcranial magnetic stimulation (TMS)** uses a coil of wires, usually arranged in the shape of the numeral 8, to noninvasively stimulate neurons in the cerebral cortex. The stimulating coil is placed on top of the skull so that the crossing point in the middle of the 8 is located immediately above the region to be stimulated. Pulses of electricity send magnetic fields that activate neurons in the cortex. Figure 5.24 shows an electromagnetic coil used in transcranial magnetic stimulation and its placement on a person's head.

Figure 5.24 Transcranial Magnetic Stimulation

Pulses of electricity through the coil produce a magnetic field that stimulates a region of the cerebral cortex under the crossing point in the middle of the figure 8.

(Photograph courtesy of the Kastner Lab, Princeton University, Princeton, New Jersey.)

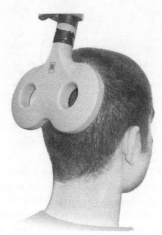

The effects of TMS are very similar to those of direct stimulation of the exposed brain. For example, as we shall see in Chapter 6, stimulation of a particular region of the visual association cortex will disrupt a person's ability to detect movements in visual stimuli. In addition, as we will see in Chapters 15 and 16, TMS has been used to treat the symptoms of neurological and mental disorders. Depending on the strength and pattern of stimulation, TMS can either excite the region of the brain over which the coil is positioned or interfere with its functions.

OPTOGENETIC METHODS Recent developments are providing the means to not only observe, but also control the activation of individual neurons: **Optogenetic methods** can be used to stimulate or inhibit particular types of neurons in specific brain regions (Boyden et al., 2005; F. Zhang et al., 2007; Baker, 2011). Photosensitive proteins have evolved in many organisms—even single-celled organisms such as algae and bacteria. Researchers have discovered that one of these proteins, *Channelrhodopsin-2 (ChR2)*, found in green algae, controls ion channels that, when open, permit the flow of sodium, potassium, and calcium ions. When blue light strikes a ChR2-ion channel, the channel opens, and the rush of positively charged sodium and calcium ions depolarizes the membrane, causing excitation. A second photosensitive protein, *Natronomonas pharaonis halorhodopsin (NpHR)*, is found in a bacterium. This protein controls a transporter that moves chloride into the cell when activated by yellow light. This influx of negatively charged ions hyperpolarizes the membrane, causing inhibition. The action of both of these photosensitive proteins begins and ends very rapidly when light of the appropriate wavelength (blue or yellow) is turned on and off.

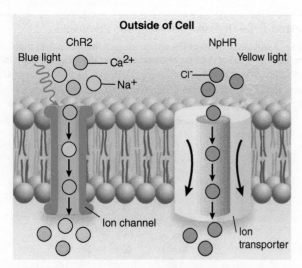

Outside of Cell

ChR2

Blue light

Ca²⁺

Na⁺

NpHR

Yellow light

Cl⁻

Ion channel

Ion transporter

OPTOGENETIC METHODS Photosensitive proteins can be inserted into neural membranes by means of genetically modified viruses. Blue light causes ChR2-ion channels to depolarize the membrane, and yellow light causes NpHR-ion transporters to hyperpolarize it.

(Adapted from Hausser, M., and Smith, S. L. *Nature*, 2007, 446, 617–619.)

ChR2 and NpHR can be introduced into neurons by attaching the genes that code for them into the genetic material of harmless viruses. The viruses are then injected into the brain, where they infect neurons and begin expressing the proteins, which are inserted into the cell membrane. The genes can be modified so that the proteins will be expressed only in particular types of neurons. In this way, researchers can observe the effects of turning on or off particular types of neurons in a specific region of the brain.

Because ChR2 and NpHR are activated by light, researchers must be able to introduce light into the brain. If the neurons that express these photosensitive proteins are located in the cerebral cortex, a small hole can be drilled in the skull, and light-emitting diodes (LEDs) can be attached directly above the hole. To activate photosensitive proteins in the membranes of neurons deep within the brain, optical fibers

can be implanted by means of stereotaxic surgery, just like electrodes or cannulas, and light can be transmitted through these fibers. For example, Tsai et al. (2009) used optogenetic methods to insert ChR2-ion channels into the membranes of dopaminergic neurons in the ventral tegmental area of rats. (Other research has shown that these neurons play an essential role in behavioral reinforcement.) The investigators found that if these neurons were stimulated when the rats were in one of two chambers in a testing apparatus, the animals preferred to spend time in that chamber.

The development of optogenetic procedures has caused much excitement among neuroscientists because they suggest ways to study the functions of particular neural circuits in the brain. Some investigators are also exploring possible clinical uses of photosensitive proteins. For example, retinitis pigmentosa is a genetic disease that causes blindness in humans. People with this disease are born with normal vision, but they gradually become blind as the photoreceptor cells in their retinas degenerate. The retina contains two major categories of photoreceptors: *rods,* which are responsible for night vision, and *cones,* which are responsible for daytime vision. The rods of people with retinitis pigmentosa die, but although the cones lose their sensitivity to light, their cell bodies survive. Busskamp et al. (2010) used an optogenetic method to try to reestablish vision in mice with a genetic modification that causes them to develop retinitis pigmentosa. The investigators targeted the animals' cones with NpHR. (Because the membranes of photoreceptors are normally hyperpolarized by light, they chose to use this protein.) Electrical recording and behavioral studies found that the treatment at least partially reestablished the animals' vision. Furthermore, the same treatment reestablished light sensitivity in retinal tissue removed from deceased people who had suffered from retinitis pigmentosa. These findings provide hope that further research may develop a treatment for this form of blindness.

Table 5.2 summarizes the research methods presented in this section.

Table 5.2 Research Methods: Part II

Goal of Method	Method	Remarks
Record electrical activity of single neurons	Microelectrodes	Microelectrodes can be implanted permanently to record neural activity as animal moves
Record electrical activity of regions of brain	Macroelectrodes	In humans, usually attached to the scalp with a special paste
Record magnetic fields induced by neural activity	Magnetoencephalography; uses a neuromagnetometer, which contains an array of SQUIDs	Can determine the location of a group of neurons firing synchronously
Record metabolic activity of regions of brain	2-DG autoradiography Measurement of Fos protein 2-DG PET scan Functional magnetic resonance imaging (fMRI) scan	Measures local glucose utilization Identifies neurons that have recently been stimulated Measures regional metabolic activity of human brain Measures regional metabolic activity of living, unanesthetized brain

(continued)

Goal of Method	Method	Remarks
Measure neurochemicals in the living human brain	PET scan	Can localize any radioactive substance taken up in the human brain
Stimulate neural activity	Electrical stimulation	Stimulates neurons near the tip of the electrode and axons passing through region
	Chemical stimulation with excitatory amino acid	Stimulates only neurons near the tip of the cannula, not axons passing through region
	Transcranial magnetic stimulation	Stimulates neurons in the human cerebral cortex with an electromagnet placed on the head

Section Review

Recording and Stimulating Neural Activity

LO 5.7 Compare recording neural activity using microelectrodes, macroelectrodes, and magnetoencephalography.

Microelectrodes can be used to record the electrical activity of individual neurons and must be placed into a single neuron. Macroelectrodes are used to record the summed electrical activity of many neurons in the vicinity of the electrode. Macroelectrodes can be placed in the brain or on the surface of the skull or scalp. Magnetoencephalography measures changes in magnetic fields of neurons and is used to detect groups of synchronously activated neurons.

LO 5.8 Compare the types of metabolic and synaptic activity that can be revealed by autoradiography, staining for immediate early genes, positron emission tomography, and functional magnetic resonance imaging.

Autoradiography is a postmortem technique that involves measuring the radioactivity from cells that have taken up radioactive 2-DG while they are metabolically active prior to tissue collection. Staining for immediate early genes reveals the neurons that were recently activated prior to tissue collection. Positron emission tomography (PET) visualizes activity of brain regions that are metabolically active in a living brain (it also uses radioactive 2-DG). Functional MRI (fMRI) visualizes brain regions that have increased blood flow and local blood oxygen levels in a living brain.

LO 5.9 Compare electrical and chemical neural stimulation, optogenetic methods, and transcranial magnetic stimulation.

Electrical and chemical stimulation of neurons are accomplished by passing an electrical current or injecting a chemical into a specific brain region through a cannula. Optogenetic methods are used to stimulate or inhibit particular types of neurons in specific brain regions. These neurons are genetically modified to express a protein that is wavelength-sensitive. Researchers implant LEDs into the brain that can emit the corresponding wavelengths of light. Turning the light on and off allows the researcher to control the activity of the neurons that are light sensitive. Transcranial magnetic stimulation (TMS) uses a magnetic signal to stimulate or inhibit neurons beneath the TMS device. Unlike other methods of stimulating neural activity, TMS is noninvasive.

Thought Question

Have you heard about brain-training programs or apps that claim to activate your brain? Have you wondered if these claims are accurate or how they could be tested? Write an e-mail to a friend who is curious about the research behind measuring brain activation using brain-training programs. In your message, describe what technique you predict the researchers used to measure brain activation in the participants of the study. Explain why this technique would be appropriate.

Neurochemical Methods

Sometimes we are interested not in the general metabolic activity of particular regions of the brain, but in the location of neurons that possess particular types of receptors or produce particular types of neurotransmitters or neuromodulators. We might also want to measure the amount of these chemicals secreted by neurons in particular brain regions during particular circumstances.

Finding Neurons That Produce Particular Neurochemicals

LO 5.10 Describe how a researcher could identify a neuron that produces a particular neurochemical.

Suppose we learn that a particular drug affects behavior. How would we go about discovering the neural circuits that are responsible for the drug's effects? To answer this question, let's take a specific example. Physicians discovered several years ago that farm workers who had been exposed to certain types of insecticides (the organophosphates) had particularly intense and bizarre dreams and even reported having hallucinations while awake. A plausible explanation for these symptoms is that the drug stimulates the neural circuits involved in control of REM sleep—the phase of sleep during which dreaming occurs. (After all, dreams are hallucinations that we have while sleeping.)

The first question to ask relates to how the organophosphate insecticides work. Pharmacologists have the answer: These drugs are acetylcholinesterase inhibitors. As you learned in Chapter 4, acetylcholinesterase inhibitors are potent acetylcholine agonists. By inhibiting AChE, the drugs prevent the rapid destruction of ACh after it is released by terminal buttons and thus prolong the postsynaptic potentials at acetylcholinergic synapses.

Now that we understand the action of the insecticides, we know that these drugs act at acetylcholinergic synapses. What neurochemical methods should we use to discover the sites of action of the drugs in the brain? First, let's consider

methods by which we can localize particular neurochemicals, such as neurotransmitters and neuromodulators. (In our case we are interested in acetylcholine.) There are at least two basic ways of localizing neurochemicals in the brain: localizing the chemicals themselves or localizing the enzymes that produce them.

Chemicals that are peptides (or proteins) can be localized directly by means of immunocytochemical methods, which were described earlier in this chapter. Slices of brain tissue are exposed to an antibody for the peptide and linked to a dye (usually, a fluorescent dye). The slices are then examined under a microscope using light of a particular wavelength. For example, Figure 5.25a shows the location of axons in the forebrain that contain vasopressin, a peptide neurotransmitter. Two sets of axons are shown. One set, which forms a cluster around the third ventricle at the base of the brain, shows up as a rusty color. The other set, scattered through the lateral septum, looks like strands of gold fibers. (As you can see, a properly stained brain section can be beautiful.)

Figure 5.25 Localization of a Peptide and an Enzyme

(a) The peptide is revealed by means of immunocytochemistry. The photomicrograph shows a portion of a frontal section through the rat forebrain. The gold- and rust-colored fibers are axons and terminal buttons that contain vasopressin, a peptide neurotransmitter.

(Courtesy of Geert DeVries, University of Massachusetts Amherst.)

(b) An enzyme responsible for the synthesis of a neurotransmitter is revealed by immunocytochemistry. The photomicrograph shows a section through the pons. The orange neurons contain choline acetyltransferase, which implies that they produce (and thus secrete) acetylcholine.

(Courtesy of David A. Morilak and Roland Ciaranello, Nancy Pritzker Laboratory of Developmental and Molecular Neurobiology, Department of Psychiatry and Behavioral Sciences, Stanford University School of Medicine.)

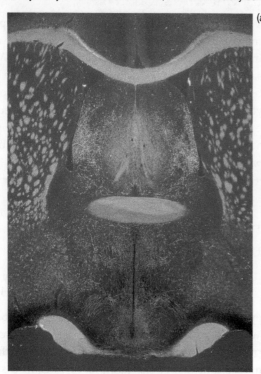

(a)

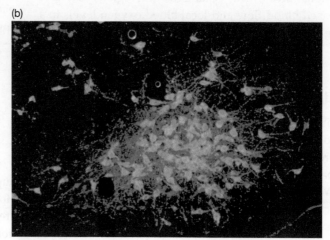

(b)

How can a researcher localize chemicals that are *not* peptides? In our example, we are interested in studying acetylcholine, which is not a peptide. Therefore, we cannot use immunocytochemical methods to find this neurotransmitter directly. However, we can use these methods to localize the enzyme that produces it. Enzymes are peptides, and we can use immunocytochemical methods to localize them. Acetylcholine is synthesized by the enzyme choline acetyltransferase (ChAT). Thus, neurons that contain this enzyme almost certainly secrete ACh. Figure 5.25b shows acetylcholinergic neurons in the pons that have been identified by means of immunocytochemistry; the brain tissue was exposed to an antibody to ChAT attached to a fluorescent dye. In fact, research using many of the methods described in this chapter indicates that these neurons play a role in controlling REM sleep.

Returning to our example of hallucinations following pesticide exposure, if we were to conduct an experiment to confirm the effects of continuous organophosphate exposure on the ACh system, we might consider comparing the brain changes in a group of rats exposed to organophosphates with a control group that was not exposed. We could then examine the brains of animals in these two conditions to evaluate the effects of organophosphate exposure on the ACh system. Using immunocytochemical techniques to investigate ChAT might reveal that organophosphate exposure resulted in reduced ChAT in the neurons, supporting our hypothesis that the pesticides had an effect on the ACh system. To confirm a behavioral effect, we could have also observed the animals in the REM sleep stage using another technique in this chapter—EEG.

Localizing Particular Receptors

LO 5.11 **Compare autoradiography and immunocytochemistry for localizing particular receptors.**

As we saw in Chapter 2, neurotransmitters, neuromodulators, and hormones convey their messages to their target cells by binding with receptors on or in these cells. The location of these receptors can be determined by two different procedures.

The first procedure to determine the location of receptors uses autoradiography. The basic steps involved in autoradiography to determine the location of cells that were metabolically active (by consuming radioactive 2-DG) were presented earlier in the chapter. In a similar procedure, autoradiography to determine the locations of *receptors* requires us to expose slices of brain tissue to a solution containing a radioactive ligand for a particular receptor, instead of radioactive 2-DG that can be used to identify any metabolically active cell. Next, we rinse the slices so that the only radioactivity remaining in them is derived from molecules of the radioactive ligand bound to their receptors. Finally, the slides are taken into a darkroom

and coated with a photographic emulsion and developed to localize the radioactive ligand—and thus the receptors.

Let's apply this method for localizing receptors to the first line of investigation we considered in this chapter: the role of the ventromedial hypothalamus (VMH) in the sexual behavior of female rats. So far, we have discovered that lesions of the VMH abolish this behavior. We also saw that the behavior does not occur if the rat's ovaries are removed but that the behavior can be activated by stimulation of the VMH with electricity or an excitatory amino acid. These results suggest that the sex hormones produced by the ovaries act on neurons in the VMH. We could next use autoradiography to look for the receptors for the sex hormone. We would expose slices of rat brain to the radioactive hormone, rinse them, and perform autoradiography. If we did so, we would indeed find radioactivity in the VMH. (And if we compared slices from the brains of female and male rats, we would find evidence of more hormone receptors in the females' brains.)

The second procedure for localizing receptors in the brain uses another technique you have already encountered in this chapter: immunocytochemistry. Receptors are proteins; therefore, we can produce antibodies against them. We expose slices of brain tissue to the appropriate antibody (labeled with a fluorescent dye) and look at the slices with a microscope under light of a particular wavelength.

We could use this technique to learn more about the role of sex hormones in the VMH and their involvement in female sexual behavior. Instead of using autoradiography to identify the locations of the sex hormone receptors, we could instead use antibodies for the receptors. This would allow us to use immunocytochemistry, attach a dye molecule to the antibodies, and view the labeled receptors under a microscope. Although this approach will yield the same results as using autoradiography to localize particular receptors, the advantages include not needing to obtain a radioactive ligand and being able to view individually labeled cells under a microscope.

Measuring Chemicals Secreted in the Brain

LO 5.12 **Review the steps involved in measuring brain chemicals using microdialysis.**

While we can use autoradiography and immunocytochemistry to measure particular receptors involved in female sexual behavior in the rat, this information only tells us about structures located on the *post*synaptic cells. Suppose we are also interested in learning about what chemicals are secreted by *pre*synaptic cells in the VMH. To measure the amount of neurotransmitter released in particular regions of the brain, we use a procedure called **microdialysis.**

Dialysis is a process in which substances are separated by means of an artificial membrane that is permeable to some

Figure 5.26 Microdialysis

A dilute salt solution is slowly infused into the microdialysis tube, where it picks up molecules that diffuse in from the extracellular fluid. The contents of the fluid are then analyzed.

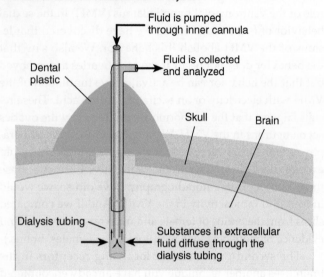

Figure 5.27 PET Scans of a Patient with Parkinson's Disease–like Symptoms

The scans show uptake of radioactive L-DOPA in the basal ganglia of a patient with Parkinson's disease–like symptoms induced by a toxic chemical before and after receiving a transplant of fetal dopaminergic neurons. (a) Preoperative scan. (b) Scan taken 13 months postoperatively. The increased uptake of L-DOPA indicates that the fetal transplant was secreting dopamine.

(Adapted from Widner, H., Tetrud, J., Rehncrona, S., et al., Bilateral fetal mesencephalic grafting in two patients with Parkinsonism induced by 1-methyl-4-phenyl-L,2,3,6-tetrahydropyridine (MPTP), *New England Journal of Medicine*, 1992, *327*, 1556–1563. Scans reprinted with permission.)

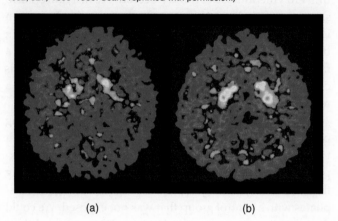

(a)   (b)

molecules but not others. A microdialysis probe consists of a small metal tube that introduces a solution into a section of dialysis tubing—a piece of artificial membrane shaped in the form of a cylinder, sealed at the bottom. Another small metal tube leads the solution away after it has circulated through the pouch. A drawing of such a probe is shown in Figure 5.26.

We can use stereotaxic surgery to place a microdialysis probe in a rat's brain so that the tip of the probe is located in the region we are interested in (the VMH). We pump a small amount of a solution similar to extracellular fluid through one of the small metal tubes into the dialysis tubing. The fluid circulates through the dialysis tubing and passes through the second metal tube, from which it is taken for analysis. As the fluid passes through the dialysis tubing, it collects molecules from the extracellular fluid of the brain, which are pushed across the membrane by the force of diffusion.

We analyze the contents of the fluid that has passed through the dialysis tubing by an extremely sensitive analytical method. This method is so sensitive that it can detect neurotransmitters (and their breakdown products) that have been released by the terminal buttons and have escaped from the synaptic cleft into the rest of the extracellular fluid. We find that the cells of the VMH release a number of different neurotransmitters, including norepinephrine. Microdialysis reveals that norepinephrine release is increased when females administered sex hormones subsequently displayed sexual behavior, but was not increased when the behavior was absent (Vathy & Etgen, 1989).

In a few special cases (for example, in monitoring brain chemicals of people with intracranial hemorrhages or head trauma) the microdialysis procedure has been applied to study of the human brain, but ethical reasons prevent doing so for research purposes. Fortunately, there is a noninvasive way to measure neurochemicals in the human brain. Although PET scanners are expensive machines, they are also versatile. They can be used to localize *any* radioactive substance that emits positrons.

Figure 5.27 shows PET scans of the brain of one of the patients who developed Parkinson's disease–like symptoms after using a synthetic opiate in the case that opened this chapter. A stereotaxic apparatus was used to transplant fetal dopamine-secreting neurons into his basal ganglia. As you read, PET scans were taken of his brain before his surgery and a little more than a year afterward. He was given an injection of radioactive L-DOPA one hour before each scan was made. As you learned in Chapter 4, L-DOPA is taken up by the terminals of dopaminergic neurons, where it is converted to dopamine; thus, the radioactivity shown in the scans indicates the presence of dopamine-secreting terminals in the basal ganglia. The scans show the amount of radioactivity before (part a) and after (part b) he received the transplant. As you can see, the basal ganglia contained substantially more dopamine after the surgery.

We wish we could say that the fetal transplantation procedure has cured people stricken with Parkinson's disease and those whose brains were damaged with the contaminated drug. Unfortunately, as we will see in Chapter 15, the therapeutic effects of the transplant are often temporary, and with time, serious side effects often emerge.

Table 5.3 summarizes the research methods presented in this section.

Table 5.3 Research Methods: Part III

Goal of Method	Method	Remarks
Measure neurotransmitters and neuromodulators released by neurons	Microdialysis	A wide variety of substances can be analyzed
Identify neurons producing a particular neurotransmitter or neuromodulator	Immunocytochemical localization of peptide or protein	Requires a specific antibody
	Immunocytochemical localization of enzyme responsible for synthesis of substance	Useful if substance is not a peptide or protein
Identify neurons that contain a particular type of receptor	Autoradiographic localization of radioactive ligand Immunocytochemical localization of receptor	Requires a specific antibody

Section Review

Neurochemical Methods

LO 5.10 **Describe how a researcher could identify a neuron that produces a particular neurochemical.**

Using immunocytochemical methods, a researcher could localize the chemicals themselves or localize the enzymes that produce the neurochemicals of interest, within specific neurons.

LO 5.11 **Compare autoradiography and immunocytochemistry for localizing particular receptors.**

Autoradiography to identify specific receptors involves immersing brain tissue in a solution containing a radioactive ligand for the receptor of interest. Slides of the tissue are then developed to expose the locations of the receptors for the ligand. Immunocytochemistry for specific receptors involves exposing brain tissue to antibodies that are selective for a protein on the receptor of interest.

LO 5.12 **Review the steps involved in measuring brain chemicals using microdialysis.**

First, a microdialysis probe is placed into the brain region of interest using stereotaxic surgery. A small amount of a solution similar to extracellular fluid is pumped into the brain through one of the small metal tubes into the dialysis tubing. The fluid circulates through the dialysis tubing and passes through the second metal tube, from which it is taken for analysis. As the fluid passes through the dialysis tubing, it collects molecules from the extracellular fluid of the brain, which are pushed across the membrane by the force of diffusion. A researcher can then analyze the brain chemical contents of the fluid that has passed through the dialysis tubing by an extremely sensitive analytical method.

Thought Question

With the development of non-invasive recording and imaging techniques, many neuroscientists are expecting a paradigm shift from animal-based models to human-based ones. Write an essay comparing the earlier invasive methods and their newer non-invasive counterparts, and explain how they constitute an advancement in behavioral neuroscience research.

Genetic Methods

All behavior is determined by interactions between an individual's brain and his or her environment. Many behavioral characteristics—such as talents, personality variables, and mental disorders—seem to run in families. This fact suggests that genetic factors may play a role in the development of physiological differences that are ultimately responsible for these characteristics. In some cases, the genetic link is very clear: A defective gene interferes with brain development, and a neurological abnormality causes behavioral deficits. In other cases, the links between heredity and behavior are much more subtle, and special genetic methods must be used to reveal them.

Twin Studies

LO 5.13 **Describe how concordance rates in twins can be used to assess the genetic contribution to a behavior.**

A powerful method for estimating the influence of heredity on a particular trait is to compare the *concordance rate* for this trait in pairs of monozygotic and dizygotic twins. Monozygotic twins (identical twins) have identical genotypes—that is, their chromosomes, and the genes they contain, are identical. In contrast, the genetic similarity between dizygotic twins (fraternal twins) is, on the average, 50 percent. Investigators study records to identify pairs of twins in which at least one member has the trait—for example, a diagnosis of a particular mental disorder. If both twins have been diagnosed with this disorder, they are said to be *concordant*. If only one has received this diagnosis, the twins are said to be *discordant*. Thus, if a disorder has a strong genetic basis, the percentage of monozygotic twins who are concordant for the diagnosis will be higher than that for dizygotic twins. For example, as we will see in Chapter 16, the concordance rate for schizophrenia in twins is at least four times higher for monozygotic twins than for dizygotic twins, a finding that provides strong evidence for a genetic component in the development of schizophrenia. Twin studies have found that many individual characteristics, including personality traits, prevalence of obesity, incidence of alcohol abuse, and a wide variety of mental disorders, are influenced by genetic factors.

Adoption Studies

LO 5.14 **Evaluate the role of adoption studies in investigating genetic contributions to a behavior.**

Another method for estimating the heritability of a particular behavioral trait is to compare people who were adopted early in life with their biological and adoptive family members. All behavioral traits are affected to some degree by hereditary factors, environmental factors, and an interaction between these factors. Environmental factors are physical, social, and biological in nature. For example, the mother's health, nutrition, and drug-taking behavior during pregnancy are prenatal environmental factors, and the child's diet, medical care, and social environment (both inside and outside the home) are postnatal environmental factors. If a child is adopted soon after birth, the genetic factors will be associated with the biological parents, the prenatal environmental factors will be associated with the biological mother, and most of the postnatal environmental factors will be associated with the adoptive parents.

Adoption studies require that the investigator knows the identity of the parents of the people being studied and is able to measure the behavioral trait in the biological and adoptive parents. If the people being studied strongly resemble their biological parents, we conclude that the trait is probably influenced by genetic factors. To be certain, researchers need to rule out possible differences in the prenatal environment of the adopted children. If, instead, the people resemble their adoptive parents, we conclude that the trait is influenced by environmental factors. (It would take further study to determine just what these environmental factors might be.) Remember that both hereditary and environmental factors are involved in the expression of a given behavior and the people being studied will resemble both their biological and adoptive parents to some degree.

Genomic Studies

LO 5.15 **Identify examples of techniques that utilize knowledge of the human genome to understand behavior.**

The human **genome** consists of the DNA that encodes our genetic information. Because of the accumulation of mutations over past generations of our species, no two people, with the exception of monozygotic twins, have identical genetic information. The particular form of an individual gene is called an **allele.** For example, different alleles of the gene responsible for the production of iris pigment in the eye produce pigments with different colors. Genomic studies attempt to determine the location in the genome of genes responsible for various physical and behavioral traits.

Linkage studies identify families whose members vary with respect to a particular trait—for example, the presence or absence of a particular hereditary disease. A variety of *markers*, sequences of DNA whose locations are already known, are compared with the nature of an individual person's trait. For example, the gene responsible for *Huntington's disease*, a neurological disorder discussed in Chapter 15, was found to be located near a known marker on chromosome 4. Researchers studied people in an extended family in Venezuela that contained many members with Huntington's disease and found that the presence or absence of the disease correlated with the presence or absence of the marker.

Similarly, *genomewide association studies* have been made possible by the development of methods to obtain the DNA sequence of the entire human genome. These studies permit researchers to compare all or portions of the genomes of different individuals to determine whether differences in the people's genomes correlate with the presence or absence of diseases (or other traits). As we will see in Chapter 16, these studies are beginning to reveal the location of genes that control characteristics that contribute to the development of various mental disorders.

Targeted Mutations

LO 5.16 **Summarize how targeted mutations can be used to reveal genetic contributions to a behavior.**

A genetic method developed by molecular biologists has put a powerful tool in the hands of neuroscientists. **Targeted**

mutations are mutated genes produced in the laboratory and inserted into the chromosomes of mice. In some cases, the genes (also called knockout genes) are defective: These genes fail to produce a functional protein. In many cases the target of the mutation is an enzyme that controls a particular chemical reaction. In other cases, the genes (also called knock-in genes) produce a new functional protein to replace a missing protein, or make increased amounts of a protein. For example, we will see in Chapter 13 that lack of a particular enzyme interferes with learning. This result suggests that the enzyme is partly responsible for changes in the structure of synapses required for learning to occur. In other cases the target of the mutation is a protein that itself serves useful functions in the cell. For example, we will see in Chapter 18 that a particular type of cannabinoid receptor is involved in the reinforcing and analgesic effects of opiates. Researchers can even produce *conditional knockouts* that cause the animal's genes to stop expressing a particular gene when the animal is given a particular drug. This permits the targeted gene to express itself normally during the animal's development and then be knocked out (inactivated) at a later time. Investigators can also use methods of genetic engineering to insert new genes into the DNA of mice. These genes can cause increased production of proteins normally found in the host species, or they can produce entirely new proteins.

Antisense Oligonucleotides

LO 5.17 Describe how antisense oligonucleotides function to change behavior.

Another genetic method involves molecules that block the production of proteins encoded by particular genes by injecting **antisense oligonucleotides.** The most common types of antisense oligonucleotides are modified strands of RNA or DNA that will bind with specific molecules of messenger RNA and prevent them from producing their protein. Once the molecules of mRNA are trapped in this way, they are destroyed by enzymes present in the cell. (See Figure 5.28.) The term *antisense* refers to the fact that the synthetic oligonucleotides contain a sequence of bases complementary to those contained by a particular gene or molecule of mRNA.

What role does this method have in helping us to understand behavior? Destroying proteins in this way can produce changes in behavior, highlighting the importance of intracellular proteins in behavior. For example, injecting antisense oligonucleotides that destroy receptors for sex hormones in the VMH of female rats inhibited female sexual behavior (Pollio et al., 1993; Mani et al., 1994). This method can be used to confirm the importance of sex hormones in the VMH in contributing to female sexual behavior in rats. The results obtained using this technique complement the results of using other methods highlighted throughout this chapter.

Table 5.4 summarizes the research techniques described in this section.

Figure 5.28 Antisense Oligonucleotides

Antisense oligonucleotides block the production of proteins encoded by particular genes.

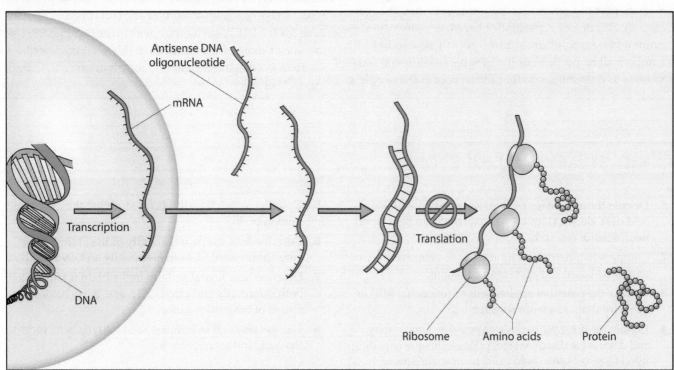

Table 5.4 Research Methods: Part IV

Goal of Method	Method	Remarks
Genetic methods	Twin studies	Comparison of concordance rates of monozygotic and dizygotic twins estimates heritability of trait
	Adoption studies	Similarity of offspring and adoptive and biological parents estimates heritability of trait
	Targeted mutations	Inactivation, insertion, or increased expression of a gene
	Antisense oligonucleotides	Bind with messenger RNA; prevent synthesis of protein

Section Review

Genetic Methods

LO 5.13 Describe how concordance rates in twins can be used to assess the genetic contribution to a behavior.

Concordance rates help researchers understand the contributions of genetic differences to variations in behavior. For example, if a disorder has a strong genetic basis, the percentage of monozygotic twins who are concordant for the diagnosis will be higher than that for dizygotic twins.

LO 5.14 Evaluate the role of adoption studies in investigating genetic contributions to a behavior.

Adoption studies help researchers understand the genetic and environmental contributions to a behavior.

LO 5.15 Identify examples of techniques that utilize knowledge of the human genome to understand behavior.

Linkage studies identify families whose members vary with respect to a particular trait—for example, the presence or absence of a particular hereditary disease. Genomewide association studies permit researchers to compare all or portions of the genomes of different individuals to determine whether differences in the people's genomes correlate with the presence or absence of diseases (or other traits).

LO 5.16 Summarize how targeted mutations can be used to reveal genetic contributions to a behavior.

Targeted mutations are used to change the production of a specific protein. The resulting change in behavior can be associated with the mutated protein.

LO 5.17 Describe how antisense oligonucleotides function to change behavior.

Antisense oligonucleotides can be used to block the production of a specific protein, revealing its role in a behavior.

Thought Question

Humans have a variety of behavioral responses to tasting the chemical phenylthiocarbamide (PTC). The majority (about 75 percent) of people perceive this harmless chemical as bitter-tasting and respond to it with avoidance and negative facial reactions. A minority of people perceive PTC as tasteless and show no behavioral response. The gene for the PTC taste receptor was identified in 2003. Using one or more of the methods in this section, describe a study to investigate the genetic contribution to PTC tasting and behavior.

Chapter Review Questions

1. Discuss the advantage of chemical ablation with kainic acid over electrical lesion with electrodes in behavioral neuroscience research.

2. Compare the merits and limitations of neuronal tracing with MRI-based diffusion tensor imaging.

3. Discuss the potential applications of functional MRI in behavioral neuroscience research.

4. Explain the principle of positron emission tomography, and discuss the disadvantages of this technique regarding its widespread use in behavioral neuroscience research.

5. Describe research methods for studying the living human brain.

6. Describe how the neural activity of the brain is measured and recorded, both electrically and chemically.

7. Describe how neural activity in the brain is stimulated, both chemically and electrically, and the behavioral effects of brain stimulation.

8. Discuss research techniques to identify genetic factors that may influence behavior.

Chapter 6
Vision

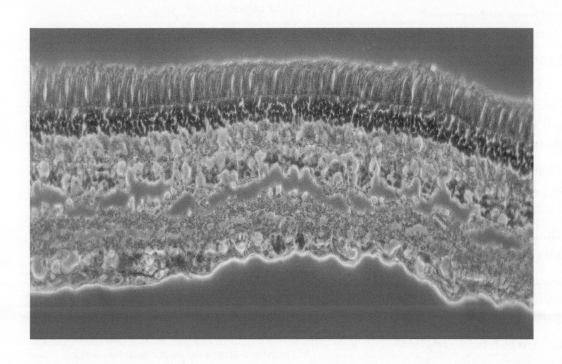

Chapter Outline

Learning Objectives

LO 6.1 Differentiate between sensation and perception.

LO 6.2 Describe visible light, hue, saturation, and brightness in the perception of light.

LO 6.3 Identify the structures of the eye and describe their function in visual processing.

LO 6.4 Contrast the location and function of rods and cones.

LO 6.5 Describe the process of transduction of visual stimuli including the role of photopigments and bipolar cells.

LO 6.6 Compare the characteristics of central and peripheral vision, including receptive fields and eye movements.

LO 6.7 Explain how stimuli are conveyed to the brain through the optic nerves.

LO 6.8 Describe processing of information in the visual pathway, including the roles of the striate and extrastriate cortex.

LO 6.9 Describe the pattern of retinal ganglion cell input and the layers of the LGN.

LO 6.10 Identify the role of the striate cortex in visual processing, including functions of visual field mapping, CO blobs, and modular organization.

LO 6.11 Identify the role of the extrastriate cortex in visual processing, including the dorsal and ventral streams.

LO 6.12 Compare the activity of ON, OFF, and ON/OFF retinal ganglion cells in response to light.

LO 6.13 Differentiate between the trichromatic and opponent-color system theories.

LO 6.14 List the contributions of the parvocellular and koniocellular systems to perception of color in the striate cortex.

LO 6.15 Using examples from human and animal research, describe the role of the extrastriate cortex in color perception and achromatopsia.

LO 6.16 Examine the benefit of neural circuits that analyze spatial frequency in the striate cortex.

LO 6.17 Use examples from the research literature to support the roles of the ventral stream and fusiform face area in perception of form.

LO 6.18 Identify the retina's contributions to perception of spatial location.

LO 6.19 Describe the contributions of retinal disparity, and the dorsal and ventral streams to visual perception of spatial location.

LO 6.20 Discuss examples from the research literature that support the role of the extrastriate cortex in perception of spatial location.

LO 6.21 Explain how cells in the striate cortex identify orientation and function as movement detectors.

LO 6.22 Describe the roles of region V5, MSTd, and the extrastriate body in the perception of movement.

Mrs. R. experienced a stroke that had not impaired her ability to talk or to move, but had affected her vision. She described her visual experience by saying, "I just don't seem to be able to recognize things. When I'm working in my kitchen, I know what everything is as long as no one moves anything. A few times my husband tried to help me by putting things away, and I couldn't see them anymore." She laughed. "Well, I could see them, but I just couldn't say what they were."

A neuropsychologist conducting an examination took some objects out of a paper bag and placed them on the table in front of

Mrs. R. The doctor asked Mrs. R to identify the objects without touching them.

Mrs. R. stared intently at the objects.

The doctor pointed to one of them, a wristwatch. "Tell me what you see here," she said.

"I see something round, and it has two things attached to it, one on the top and one on the bottom. There are some things inside the circle, I think, but I can't make out what they are."

After the doctor asked her to pick the object up, Mrs. R. said, "Oh. It's a wristwatch." At the doctor's request, she picked up the rest of the objects, one by one, and identified each of them correctly.

Mrs. R then described her difficulty recognizing people.

"While I was still in the hospital, my husband and my son both came in to see me, and I couldn't tell who was who until my husband said something—then I could tell which direction his voice was coming from. Now I've trained myself to recognize my husband. I can usually see his glasses and his bald head, but I have to work at it. And I've been fooled a few times." She laughed again. "One of our neighbors is bald and wears glasses, too, and one day when he and his wife were visiting us, I thought he was my husband, so I called him 'honey.' It was a little embarrassing at first, but everyone understood."

"What does a face look like to you?" asked the doctor.

"Well, I know that it's a face, because I can usually see the eyes, and it's on top of a body. I can see a body pretty well, by how it moves. Sometimes I can recognize a person by how he moves. You know, you can often recognize friends by the way they walk, even when they're far away. I can still do that. That's funny, isn't it? I can't see people's faces very well, but I can recognize the way they walk."

The doctor made some movements with his hands. "Can you tell what I'm pretending to do?" she asked.

"Yes, you're mixing something—like some cake batter."

She mimed the gestures of turning a key, writing, and dealing out playing cards, and Mrs. R. recognized them without any difficulty.

"Do you have any trouble reading?" she asked.

"Well, a little, but I don't do too badly."

The doctor handed Mrs. R a magazine, and she began to read the article aloud—somewhat hesitantly but accurately. "Why is it," she asked, "that I can see the words all right but have so much trouble with things and with people's faces?"

Mrs. R was diagnosed with visual agnosia. Agnosia ("failure to know") refers to any inability to perceive or identify a stimulus, even though its details can be detected and the person retains relatively typical intellectual capacity. In this case, the agnosia was specific to Mrs. R's sense of vision. She also suffered from prosopagnosia, an agnosia for specific faces. Her agnosia was caused by damage to the visual cortex following her stroke.

*****

This case study illustrates several important ideas from this chapter, including the roles the eyes and various brain regions play in vision and types of blindness such as object agnosia and prosopagnosia. As we saw in Chapter 3, the brain performs two major functions: It controls the movements of the muscles, producing useful behaviors, and it regulates the body's internal environment. To perform both these tasks, the brain must be informed about what is happening both in the external environment and within the body. Such information is received by the sensory systems.

The next chapter considers the sensory modalities of audition, the vestibular senses, the somatosenses, gustation (taste), and olfaction (smell). This chapter, however, is exclusively dedicated to vision, the sensory modality that receives a great deal of attention from neuroscientists, psychologists, anatomists, and physiologists. One reason for

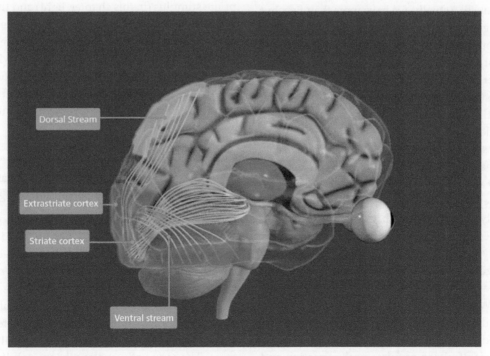

This figure shows brain regions crucial to vision: the striate cortex, the extrastriate cortex, and the dorsal and ventral streams.

this attention derives from the fascinating complexity of the sensory organs of vision and the relatively large proportion of the human brain that is devoted to the analysis of visual information. A large portion of the human cerebral cortex plays a direct role in the analysis of visual information (Wandell et al., 2007).

The first section of this chapter is dedicated to the structure and functions of the eye itself. The second section examines the brain regions involved in vision. The remaining sections focus on the perception of color, form, spatial location, and movement.

The Eye

In this section, we will explore the role of the eye in vision. The section begins with an introduction to sensation and perception, which is relevant to both this chapter and the following chapter. Next, this section includes a discussion of the stimulus detected by the eye: light. Then, we will explore the anatomy of the eye and the role of the photoreceptors in the process of transduction as well as central and peripheral vision. Finally, this section concludes with a description of the role of the optic nerves and provides a general overview of the visual pathway that will be examined in greater depth through the rest of the chapter.

Introduction to Sensation and Perception

LO 6.1 **Differentiate between sensation and perception.**

People often say that we have five senses: sight, hearing, smell, taste, and touch. Actually, we have more than five, but even experts disagree about how the lines between the various categories should be drawn. We could add the vestibular senses that control movement and balance in space to the list of senses; the inner ear, in addition to providing us with auditory information, supplies information about head orientation and movement. Also, the sense of touch (or, more accurately, *somatosensation*) detects changes in pressure, warmth, cold, vibration, limb position, and several different kinds of events that damage tissue (that is, produce pain). Everyone agrees that we can detect all of these stimuli; the issue is whether we should say that they are detected by separate senses.

Look carefully at Figure 6.1. What do you see? Do you see an image in color? Does it look the same in dim and bright light? Do you see shapes in the image? Do you see parts of the image in three dimensions? Can you identify what is in the image and where it is in space? Is the image still or moving? What parts of your nervous system allow you to understand the picture in terms of these elements of color, shape, and dimension?

The experience of vision requires both sensation and perception. **Sensation** involves the cells of the nervous

Figure 6.1 An Example of a Visual Illusion
What do you see in this figure?

system that are specialized to detect stimuli from the environment. These stimuli occur in specific forms of energy (such as light, sound, or heat), and the neurons that detect this energy transform it into action potentials that get sent through the nervous system. **Perception** is the conscious experience and interpretation of information from the senses and involves neurons in the central nervous system.

This chapter and the next will include specific examples of sensation and perception. To make it easier to see similarities among the different senses (and their perception), these chapters will follow very similar organizational structures. For each sense, we will begin with a discussion of the appropriate stimulus (in this chapter, light) and the physical organ that detects it (in this chapter, the eye). This is followed with information about the brain regions that are involved in processing sensory information. Finally, we will conclude with a discussion of how the nervous system perceives sensory information (for example, light and dark, color, form, spatial location, orientation, and movement of visual stimuli).

The Stimulus: Light

LO 6.2 **Describe visible light, hue, saturation, and brightness in the perception of light.**

Photoreceptors in the eye detect the presence of light stimuli. For humans, visible light is a narrow band of the spectrum of electromagnetic radiation. Electromagnetic radiation with a wavelength of between 380 and 760 nm (a nanometer, nm, is one-billionth of a meter) is visible to us. (See Figure 6.2.) Other animals can detect different ranges of electromagnetic radiation. For example, honeybees can detect differences in ultraviolet radiation reflected by flowers that appear white to us. The range of wavelengths we call *light* is simply the part of the continuum that we humans can detect.

Figure 6.2 The Electromagnetic Spectrum

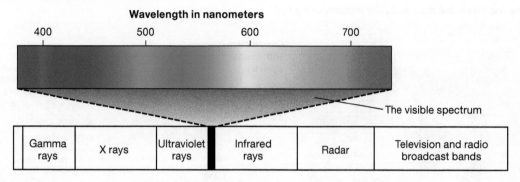

The visible spectrum

| Gamma rays | X rays | Ultraviolet rays | Infrared rays | Radar | Television and radio broadcast bands |

Three dimensions determine the perceived color of light: *hue, saturation,* and *brightness.* Light travels at a constant speed of approximately 300,000 kilometers (186,000 miles) per second. Thus, if the frequency of oscillation of the wave varies, the distance between the peaks of the waves will vary similarly but in inverse fashion. Slower oscillations lead to longer wavelengths, and faster ones lead to shorter wavelengths. Wavelength determines the first of the three perceptual dimensions of light: **hue.** The visible spectrum displays the range of hues that our eyes can detect.

Light can also vary in intensity, which corresponds to the second perceptual dimension of light: **brightness.** If the intensity of the electromagnetic radiation is increased, the apparent brightness increases, too. The third dimension, **saturation,** refers to the relative purity of the light that is being perceived. If all the radiation is of one wavelength, the perceived color is pure, or fully saturated. Conversely, if the radiation contains all visible wavelengths, it produces no sensation of hue—it appears white. Colors with intermediate amounts of saturation consist of different mixtures of wavelengths.

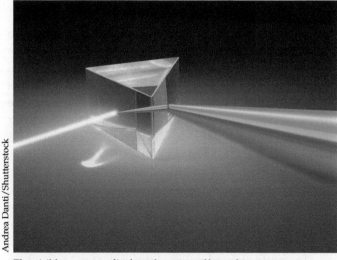

The visible spectrum displays the range of hues that our eyes can detect.

Anatomy of the Eye

LO 6.3 **Identify the structures of the eye and describe their function in visual processing.**

We receive information about the environment from **sensory receptors**—specialized neurons that detect a variety of physical events. Do not confuse *sensory receptors* with receptors for neurotransmitters, neuromodulators, and hormones. Sensory receptors are specialized *neurons,* and the other types of receptors are specialized *proteins* that bind with certain molecules. Stimuli are detected by sensory receptors that alter, through various processes, the membrane potentials of the cells. This process is known as **sensory transduction** because sensory events are *transduced* ("transferred") into changes in the cells' membrane potential. These electrical changes are called **receptor potentials.** Unlike many other types of neurons, most sensory receptors lack axons; a portion of their somatic membrane forms synapses with the dendrites of other neurons. Receptor potentials affect the release of neurotransmitters and can modify the pattern of firing in neurons with which these cells form synapses.

For an individual to see, an image must be focused on the **retina,** the inner lining of the eye. This image causes changes in the electrical activity of millions of sensory receptors in the retina, which results in messages being sent through the optic nerves to the rest of the brain. The retina is part of the brain; it and the optic nerve are in the central—not peripheral—nervous system.

The bones and muscles surrounding the eye aid in focusing an image on the retina. Knowledge of the bones, muscles, and physical structure of the eye is important to understanding how stimuli are received and transduced into neural signals. The eyes are suspended in the *orbits,* bony pockets in the front of the skull. The eyes are held in place and moved by six extraocular muscles attached to the tough, white outer coat of the eye called the *sclera.* Normally, we cannot look behind our eyeballs and see these muscles because the conjunctiva hides their attachments to the eyes. These mucous membranes line the eyelid and fold back to attach to the eye (thus preventing a contact lens that

Figure 6.3 The Eye

(a) The extraocular muscles move the eye. (b) The anatomy of the eye.

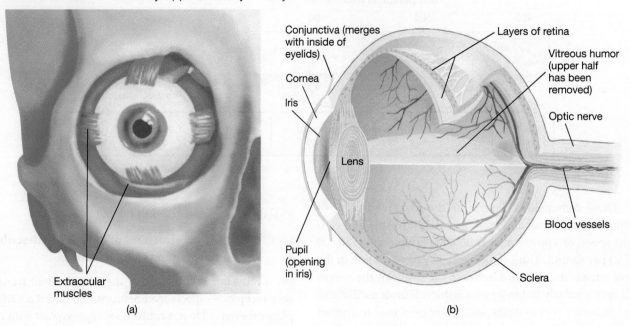

(a)

(b)

has slipped off the cornea from "falling behind the eye"). Figure 6.3 illustrates the anatomy of the eye.

The white outer layer of most of the eye, the sclera, is opaque and does not permit entry of light into the eye. However, the cornea, the outer layer at the front of the eye, is transparent. The amount of light that enters is regulated by the size of the pupil, which is an opening in the iris, the pigmented ring of muscles behind the cornea. The lens, situated immediately behind the iris, consists of a series of transparent, onionlike layers. The shape of the lens can be altered by contraction of the *ciliary muscles*. These changes in shape permit the eye to focus images of near or distant objects on the retina—a process called **accommodation.**

After passing through the lens, light traverses the main part of the eye, which is filled with *vitreous humor,* a clear, gelatinous substance. After passing through the vitreous humor, light falls on the retina. Receptor cells called **rods** and **cones** (named for their shapes), collectively known as **photoreceptors,** are located in the retina.

The human retina contains three main cellular layers: the photoreceptive layer, the bipolar cell layer, and the ganglion cell layer. Note that the photoreceptors are at the *back* of the retina and light must pass through the overlying layers to get to them. Fortunately, these layers are transparent. The roles of cells in the bipolar and ganglion cell layers will be described later in this section. (See Figure 6.4.)

Photoreceptors

LO 6.4 Contrast the location and function of rods and cones.

The human retina contains approximately 120 million rods and 6 million cones. Although they are greatly outnumbered

Figure 6.4 Layers of the Retina

The human retina contains layers of ganglion, bipolar, and photoreceptor cells.

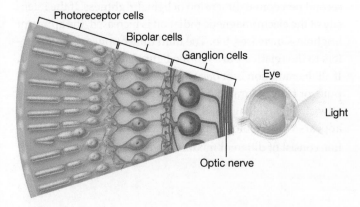

by rods, cones provide us with most of the visual information about our environment. In particular, they are responsible for our daytime vision. They provide us with information about small features in the environment and thus are the source of vision of the highest sharpness, or *acuity*. The **fovea,** or central region of the retina, which mediates our most acute vision, contains only cones. Cones are also responsible for color vision—our ability to discriminate light of different wavelengths. Although rods do not detect different colors and provide vision of poor acuity, they are more sensitive to light. In a very dimly lighted environment we use our rod vision; therefore, in very dim light we are color-blind and lack foveal vision. (See Table 6.1.)

The **optic disk** is located at the back of the eye, where the axons conveying visual information gather together and

Table 6.1 Locations and Response Characteristics of Photoreceptors

Cones	Rods
Most prevalent in the central retina; found in the fovea	Most prevalent in the peripheral retina; not found in the fovea
Sensitive to moderate to high levels of light	Sensitive to low levels of light
Provide information about hue	Provide only monochromatic information
Provide excellent acuity	Provide poor acuity

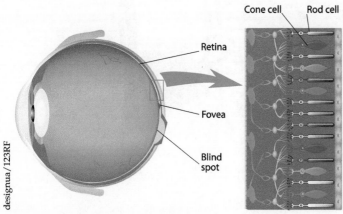

Photoreceptor cells in the retina of the eye.

leave the eye through the optic nerve. The optic disk produces a *blind spot* because no receptors are located there. We do not normally perceive our blind spots, but their presence can be demonstrated. If you have not found yours, you may want to try the exercise described in Figure 6.5.

The photoreceptors form synapses with **bipolar cells,** neurons whose two arms connect the shallowest and deepest layers of the retina. In turn, bipolar cells form synapses with the **ganglion cells,** neurons whose axons travel through the optic nerves (the second cranial nerves) and carry visual information into the rest of the brain. In addition, the retina contains **horizontal cells** and **amacrine cells,** both of which transmit information in a direction parallel to the surface of the retina and thus combine messages from adjacent photoreceptors. (See Figure 6.6.)

Transduction

LO 6.5 Describe the process of transduction of visual stimuli, including the role of photopigments and bipolar cells.

The first step in the chain of events that eventually leads to visual perception involves a special chemical called a photopigment. **Photopigments** are embedded in the **lamellae;** thin plates of membrane that make up the outer segment of photoreceptors. Each photoreceptor consists of an outer segment connected by a cilium to the inner segment, which contains the cell nucleus.

A single human rod contains approximately 10 million photopigment molecules. The molecules consist of two parts: an **opsin** (a protein) and **retinal** (a lipid). There are several forms of opsin; for example, the photopigment of human rods, **rhodopsin,** consists of *rod opsin* plus retinal. Retinal is synthesized from vitamin A, which explains why carrots, which are rich in this vitamin, are said to be good for your eyesight.

Figure 6.5 A Test for the Blind Spot

With your left eye closed, look at the plus sign with your right eye and move the page nearer to and farther from you. When the page is about 20 centimeters from your face, the green circle disappears because its image falls on the blind spot of your right eye.

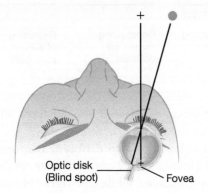

Optic disk
(Blind spot)   Fovea

Figure 6.6 Details of Retinal Circuitry

(Adapted from Dowling, J. E., and Boycott, B. B., Organization of the primate retina: Electron microscopy, *Proceedings of the Royal Society of London, B*, 1966, *166*, 80–111.)

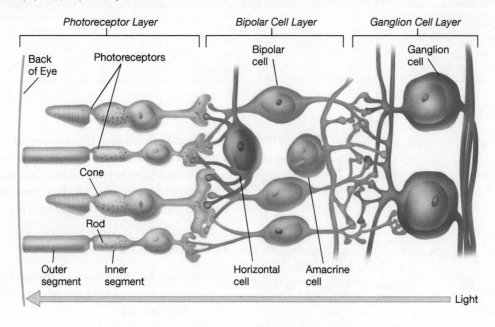

Transduction is the name of the process by which energy from the environment (for example, light) is converted to a change in membrane potential in a neuron. It is a process that converts an external stimulus (such as light, sound, or heat) to an internal stimulus (the action potential generated by light-, sound-, or heat-detecting neurons). Remember that changes in membrane potential can be excitatory (depolarizing) or inhibitory (hyperpolarizing). Photopigments are responsible for transduction of light energy into changes in membrane potential. When a molecule of rhodopsin is exposed to light, it breaks into its two constituents: rod opsin and retinal. In vertebrates, splitting the photopigment triggers a cascade of intracellular events that hyperpolarize the photoreceptor membrane.

Most other types of sensory receptors (such as hair cells in the ear for audition) become *depolarized* by stimuli. Another way to understand transduction in the visual system is to think about the photoreceptors as "darkness detectors." When the receptors experience *darkness* they respond by depolarizing. When they experience light, they respond by hyperpolarizing. For a review of hyperpolarization and depolarization, see Chapter 2.

In the vertebrate retina, photoreceptors provide input to both bipolar cells and horizontal cells in a circuit. Photoreceptors and bipolar cells do not produce action potentials. Instead, their release of neurotransmitter (glutamate) is regulated by their membrane potential; depolarizations increase the release of neurotransmitter, and hyperpolarizations decrease it. In the dark, photoreceptors are depolarized and constantly release glutamate into synapses with bipolar cells. In the light, photoreceptors are hyperpolarized

Figure 6.7 Neural Circuitry in the Retina

Light striking a photoreceptor produces a hyperpolarization, so the photoreceptor releases less neurotransmitter. Because the neurotransmitter normally hyperpolarizes the membrane of the bipolar cell, the reduction causes a depolarization. This depolarization causes the bipolar cell to release more neurotransmitter, which excites the ganglion cell.

(Adapted from Dowling, J. E., in The Neurosciences: Fourth Study Program, edited by F. O. Schmitt and F. G. Worden. Cambridge, Mass.: MIT Press, 1979.)

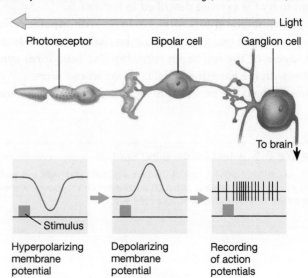

and less glutamate is released into synapses with bipolar cells. (See Figure 6.7.)

Bipolar cells have two different responses to the presence of glutamate. ON center bipolar cells are hyperpolarized by glutamate, while OFF center bipolar cells are

Figure 6.8 Foveal vs. Peripheral Acuity

Ganglion cells in the fovea receive input from a smaller number of photoreceptors than those in the periphery and hence provide more acute visual information.

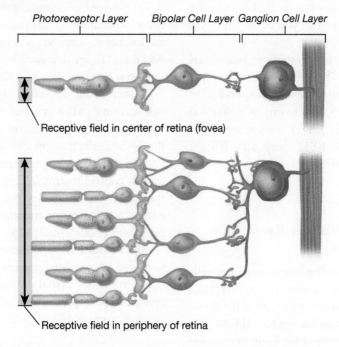

Photoreceptor Layer   *Bipolar Cell Layer*   *Ganglion Cell Layer*

Receptive field in center of retina (fovea)

Receptive field in periphery of retina

depolarized. The ON and OFF center bipolar cells then synapse with ganglion cells and influence *their* rate of firing. Thus, light shining on the photoreceptor can produce a variety of responses from bipolar and ganglion cells as the transduced message begins to make its way out of the retina and to the brain for additional visual processing. The two types of pathways from ON and OFF center bipolar cells play an important role in perceiving light and dark, which will be discussed in more detail later in the chapter.

Central and Peripheral Vision

LO 6.6 **Compare the characteristics of central and peripheral vision, including receptive fields and eye movements.**

The **receptive field** of a neuron in the visual system is the part of the visual field that an individual neuron "sees"— that is, the place in which a visual stimulus must be located to produce a response in that neuron. The location of the receptive field of a particular neuron depends on the location of the photoreceptors that provide it with visual information. If a neuron receives information from photoreceptors located in the fovea, its receptive field will be at the fixation point—the point at which the eye is looking. If the neuron receives information from photoreceptors located in the periphery of the retina, its receptive field will be located off to one side.

FOVEA AND PERIPHERY At the periphery of the retina many individual receptors converge on a single ganglion cell, bringing information from a relatively large area of the retina—and hence a relatively large area of the visual field. However, the fovea contains approximately equal numbers of ganglion cells and cones. These receptor-to-axon relationships explain the fact that our foveal (central) vision is very acute but our peripheral vision is much less precise. (See Figure 6.8.)

TYPES OF EYE MOVEMENTS To keep stimuli from the environment projecting to the retina, particularly the fovea, the eyes make three types of movements: vergence movements, saccadic movements, and pursuit movements. **Vergence movements** are cooperative movements that keep both eyes fixed on the same target—or, more precisely, that keep the image of the target object on corresponding parts of the two retinas. If you hold up a finger in front of your face, look at it, and then bring your finger closer to your face, your eyes will make vergence movements toward your nose. If you then look at an object on the other side of the room, your eyes will rotate outward, and you will see two separate blurry images of your finger.

When you scan the scene in front of you, your gaze does not roam slowly and steadily across its features. Instead, your eyes make jerky **saccadic movements**—you shift your gaze abruptly from one point to another. When you read a line in this book, your eyes stop several times, moving very quickly between each stop. You cannot consciously control the speed of movement between stops; during each *saccade* the eyes move as fast as they can. Only by performing a **pursuit movement**—say, by looking at your finger while you move it around—can you make your eyes move more slowly.

In Chapter 9, you'll read about *rapid eye movements* that occur during REM sleep. These movements are saccades that occur during dreaming and correspond with self-reports of visual imagery in the dreams of awakened sleepers (Roffwarg et al., 1962). Other researchers have suggested that the saccades in REM sleep may trigger dream images (Ogawa et al., 2005).

The Optic Nerves

LO 6.7 **Explain how stimuli are conveyed to the brain through the optic nerves.**

At the back of each eye, axons of the retinal ganglion cells bundle together to form the **optic nerve.** The optic nerves convey information from the retina to a portion of the thalamus called the **dorsal lateral geniculate nucleus (LGN).** The optic nerves join together at the base of the brain to form the X-shaped **optic chiasm.** There, axons from ganglion cells serving the inner halves of the retina (the nasal sides) cross through the chiasm and ascend to the LGN on the opposite side of the brain. The axons from the outer halves of the retina (the temporal sides) remain on the same side of the brain. The lens inverts the image of the world projected on the retina (and similarly reverses left and right). Therefore, because the

axons from the nasal halves of the retinas cross to the other side of the brain, each hemisphere receives information from the contralateral half (opposite side) of the visual scene. That is, if a person looks straight ahead, the right hemisphere receives information from the left half of the visual field, and the left hemisphere receives information from the right. It is *not* correct to say that each hemisphere receives visual information solely from the contralateral eye. (See Figure 6.9.)

Fibers from the retina also take several other nonimage forming pathways. For example, one pathway to the hypothalamus synchronizes an animal's activity cycles to the 24-hour rhythms of day and night. (We will study this system in Chapter 9.) Other pathways coordinate eye movements, control the muscles of the iris (and thus the size of the pupil) and the ciliary muscles (which control the lens), and help to direct our attention to sudden movements in the periphery of our visual field.

Blindsight is a phenomenon in which cortical regions involved in conscious perception of visual stimuli are damaged, but other visual pathways that are not involved in conscious perception are intact. The case of Mr. J. illustrates the symptoms of blindsight.

Natalie J. had brought her grandfather to see Dr. M., a neuropsychologist. Mr. J.'s stroke had left him almost completely blind; all he could see was a tiny spot in the middle of his visual field. Dr. M. had learned about Mr. J.'s condition from his neurologist and had asked Mr. J. to come to his laboratory so that he could do some tests for his research project.

Figure 6.9 The Visual Field

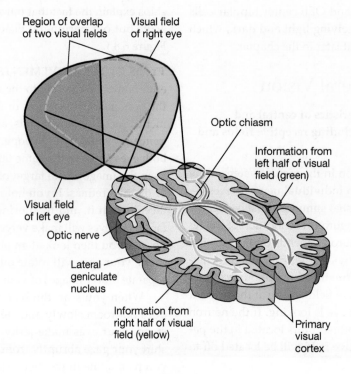

Region of overlap of two visual fields

Visual field of right eye

Optic chiasm

Information from left half of visual field (green)

Visual field of left eye

Optic nerve

Lateral geniculate nucleus

Information from right half of visual field (yellow)

Primary visual cortex

Dr. M. helped Mr. J. find a chair and sit down. Mr. J., who walked with the aid of a cane, gave it to his granddaughter to hold for him. "May I borrow that?" asked Dr. M.

Natalie nodded and handed the cane to Dr. M.

"The phenomenon I'm studying is called blindsight," he said. "Let me see if I can show you what it is. Mr. J., please look straight ahead. Keep looking that way, and don't move your eyes or turn your head. I know that you can see a little bit straight ahead of you, and I don't want you to use that piece of vision for what I'm going to ask you to do. Fine. Now, I'd like you to reach out with your right hand and point to what I'm holding."

"But I don't see anything—I'm blind!" said Mr. J., obviously exasperated.

"I know, but please try, anyway."

Mr. J. shrugged his shoulders and pointed. He looked startled when his finger encountered the end of the cane, which Dr. M. was holding toward him.

"Gramps, how did you do that?" asked Natalie, amazed. "I thought you were blind."

"I am!" he said, emphatically. "It was just luck."

"Let's try it just a couple more times, Mr. J.," said Dr. M. "Keep looking straight ahead." He reversed the cane, so that the handle was pointing toward Mr. J. "Now I'd like you to grab hold of the cane."

Mr. J. reached out with an open hand and grabbed hold of the cane.

"Good. Now put your hand down, please." Dr. M then rotated the cane 90 degrees, so that the handle was oriented vertically. "Now reach for it again."

Mr. J. did so. As his arm came up, he turned his wrist so that his hand matched the orientation of the handle, which he grabbed hold of again.

"Good. Thank you, you can put your hand down." Dr. M. turned to Natalie. "I'd like to test your grandfather now, but I'll be glad to talk with you later."

As Dr. M. explained to Natalie afterward, the human brain contains not one but several mechanisms involved in vision. The system of cortical structures for conscious perception of vision is responsible for our ability to perceive the world around us. At least one, separate nonimage forming pathway is devoted mainly to controlling eye movements and bringing our attention to sudden movements that occur off to the side of our field of vision.

Mr. J.'s stroke had damaged the cortical visual system. Cases like his show that after this system is damaged, people can use the nonimage forming pathways to guide hand movements toward an object even though they cannot see what they are reaching for.

Overview of the Visual Pathway

LO 6.8 **Describe processing of information in the visual pathway, including the roles of the striate and extrastriate cortex.**

From the eye, visual information is sent to the brain for additional processing. The journey of information from light detection in the retina to the experience of complex visual scenes occurs along the **visual pathway.** (Look at Figure 6.9 again.)

As you have just read, the visual pathway begins in the photoreceptors of the retina, which synapse with bipolar and retinal ganglion cells. The axons of the retinal ganglion cells then send visual information to the rest of the brain by ascending through the optic nerves to the LGN in the thalamus. The neurons in the LGN send their axons through *optic radiations* to the **primary visual cortex,** or **V1** (the first cortical area devoted to vision), in the occipital lobe. The primary visual cortex is also called the **striate cortex** because it contains a dark-staining layer (*striation*) of cells.

From the primary visual cortex, visual information is sent to a number of areas in the **visual association cortex** or **V2.** V2 (the second cortical area for vision processing) is also known as the **extrastriate cortex** because this region surrounds the striate cortex. Information about more complex aspects of visual processing may also travel on to additional cortical areas, such as V4 or V5. This general pathway, from eyes to thalamus to cortex, provides the framework for the rest of the information in the chapter. (See Figure 6.10.)

Figure 6.10 The Visual Pathway

The visual pathway begins with photoreceptors in the retina, which send information to the LGN through the optic nerves. From the LGN, visual information is conveyed to the visual cortex.

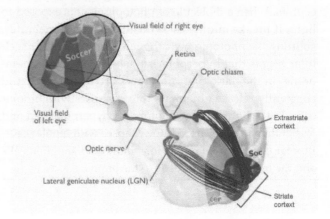

Section Review

The Eye

LO 6.1 Differentiate between sensation and perception.

Sensation involves the cells of the nervous system that are specialized to detect stimuli from the environment. Perception is the conscious experience and interpretation of information from the senses and involves neurons in the central nervous system.

LO 6.2 Describe visible light, hue, saturation, and brightness in the perception of light.

Visible light includes the portion of the spectrum that is detected by the photoreceptors of an organism. Hue is determined by wavelength of light. Brightness is determined by intensity of light. Saturation is determined by the relative purity of light being perceived (containing one or more different wavelengths).

LO 6.3 Identify the structures of the eye and describe their function in visual processing.

The bones and muscles surrounding the eye aid in focusing an image on the retina. The pupil regulates the amount of light entering the eye. The lens is responsible for accommodation. The retina of the eye contains the photoreceptors (rods and cones), which detect light and transduce it into receptor potentials.

LO 6.4 Contrast the location and function of rods and cones.

Rods are located throughout the retina, except in the fovea. They are sensitive to low intensity light but do not contribute to color or high acuity vision. Cones are prevalent in the central retina, including the fovea, and are responsible for color vision and acuity. There are more rods than cones in the human retina.

LO 6.5 Describe the process of transduction of visual stimuli, including the role of photopigments and bipolar cells.

Transduction converts light into a change in membrane potential that occurs in the photopigments of photoreceptors. When a molecule of photopigment is exposed to light, it breaks into its two constituents. In vertebrates, splitting the photopigment triggers a cascade of intracellular events that hyperpolarize the photoreceptor membrane. In the dark, photoreceptors are depolarized and constantly release glutamate into synapses with bipolar cells. In the light, photoreceptors are hyperpolarized and less glutamate is released into synapses with bipolar cells. Bipolar cells then relay this information to ganglion cells and the information proceeds to the brain.

LO 6.6 Compare the characteristics of central and peripheral vision, including receptive fields and eye movements.

The receptive field of a neuron in the visual system is the part of the visual field that an individual neuron "sees." At the periphery of the retina many individual receptors converge on a single ganglion cell, bringing information from a relatively large area of the retina and visual field. The fovea contains approximately equal numbers of ganglion cells and cones. These receptor-to-axon relationships explain the fact that our foveal (central) vision is very acute but our peripheral vision is much less precise. To keep stimuli from the environment projecting to the retina, particularly the fovea, the eyes make three types of movements: vergence movements, saccadic movements, and pursuit movements.

LO 6.7 Explain how stimuli are conveyed to the brain through the optic nerves.

Bundled together to form the optic nerves from each eye, axons from ganglion cells serving the inner halves of the retina (the nasal sides) cross through the optic chiasm ascending to the lateral geniculate nucleus (LGN) on the opposite side of the brain, and then on to striate cortex. Information about stimuli to the outer halves of the retina (the temporal sides) passes through the optic nerves and the LGN to the striate cortex to remain on the same side of the brain.

LO 6.8 Describe processing of information in the visual pathway, including the roles of the striate and extrastriate cortex.

The visual pathway begins in the photoreceptors of the retina, which synapse with bipolar and retinal ganglion cells. The axons of the retinal ganglion cells then send visual information to the rest of the brain by ascending through the optic nerves to the LGN in the thalamus. The neurons in the LGN send their axons through optic radiations to the striate cortex. From the striate cortex, visual information is sent to the extrastriate cortex.

Thought Question

People who try to see faint, distant lights or stars at night are often advised to look just to the side of the location where they expect to see the lights. Is this good advice? Explain the rationale for why this advice is helpful (or not helpful).

Brain Regions Involved in Visual Processing

After leaving the eye, visual information is sequentially processed by several brain regions, beginning in the LGN of thalamus, followed by the striate cortex, and finally by the extrastriate cortex. The following section will describe the structures and functions of the LGN, striate cortex, and extrastriate cortex in more detail.

Lateral Geniculate Nucleus

LO 6.9 **Describe the pattern of retinal ganglion cell input and the layers of the LGN.**

The LGN contains six layers of neurons. Each layer receives information from the retinal ganglion cells in the optic nerve of only one eye in a semialternating fashion. Layers 1, 4, and 6 receive input from the contralateral (or opposite) eye, and layers 2, 3, and 5 receive input from the ipsilateral eye. (See Figure 6.11.)

The neurons in the two inner layers of the LGN contain cell bodies that are larger than those in the outer four layers. The inner two layers are called the **magnocellular layers**, and the outer four layers containing smaller cell bodies are called the **parvocellular layers.** A third set of neurons in the **koniocellular sublayers** are found below each of the magnocellular and parvocellular layers. As we will see later, these three sets of layers belong to different systems, which are responsible for the analysis of different types of visual information.

Striate Cortex

LO 6.10 **Identify the role of the striate cortex in visual processing, including functions of visual field mapping, CO blobs, and modular organization.**

The pioneering studies of Nobel Prize winners David Hubel and Torsten Wiesel at Harvard University during the 1960s began a revolution in the study of the physiology of visual perception (see Hubel and Wiesel, 1977, 1979). Hubel and Wiesel discovered that neurons in the visual cortex did not simply respond to spots of light; they selectively responded to specific *features* (or *contours*) of the visual world. That is, the neural circuitry within the visual cortex combines information from several sources (for example, from axons carrying information received from several different ganglion cells via the LGN) in such a way as to detect features that are larger than the receptive field of a single ganglion cell or a single cell in the LGN. The striate cortex (V1), receives input from the LGN and is the first cortical region involved in combining visual information from several sources.

The retinal ganglion cells encode information about the relative amounts of light falling on the center and surround regions of their receptive fields and, in many cases, about the wavelength of that light. The striate cortex performs additional processing of this information, which it then transmits to the extrastriate cortex.

If we consider the striate cortex of one hemisphere as a whole—that is, if we imagine that we remove it and spread it out on a flat surface—we find that it contains a map of the contralateral (or opposite) half of the visual field. (Remember that each side of the brain sees the opposite side of the visual field.) The map is disproportionate, however; a large portion (approximately 25 percent) of the striate cortex is devoted to the analysis of information from the fovea, which corresponds to only a very small part of the visual field. (The area of the visual field seen by the fovea is approximately the size of a large grape held at arm's length.)

Figure 6.11 Lateral Geniculate Nucleus
The LGN is composed of six layers of cells.

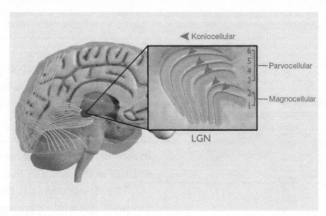

The striate cortex is a highly organized structure. It contains neurons arranged in layers, groups called cytochrome oxidase blobs, and modules. These organizational divisions will be described in the following paragraphs.

LAYERS Similar to the LGN, the striate cortex consists of six layers arranged in bands parallel to the surface. The fourth layer is further subdivided into sublayers 4A, 4B, 4Cα, and 4Cβ. These layers contain the nuclei of cell bodies and dendritic trees that show up as bands of light or dark in sections of tissue that have been dyed with a cell-body stain. (See Figure 6.12.)

CYTOCHROME OXIDASE (CO) BLOBS In the striate cortex, information from color-sensitive ganglion cells is transmitted, through the parvocellular and koniocellular layers of the LGN, to special cells grouped together in **cytochrome oxidase (CO) blobs.** CO blobs are found in layers 2 and 3 and (more faintly) layers 5 and 6 of striate cortex (Horton and Hubel, 1980; Humphrey and Hendrickson, 1980).

Figure 6.13 shows a photomicrograph of a slice through the striate cortex and an adjacent area of extrastriate cortex of a macaque monkey. You can see the CO blobs within the striate cortex (V1). CO blobs are also found in the extrastriate cortex. The distribution of CO-rich neurons in the extrastriate cortex consists of three kinds of stripes: *thick stripes, thin stripes,* and *pale stripes.*

Neurons in CO blobs of the striate cortex project to thin stripes, and neurons outside the blobs (in interblob areas) project to thick stripes and pale stripes of the extrastriate cortex (Sincich et al., 2010). Neurons in the thin stripes receive information concerning color, and those in the thick stripes and pale stripes receive information about orientation, spatial frequency, movement, and retinal disparity.

Figure 6.12 Layers of the Striate Cortex

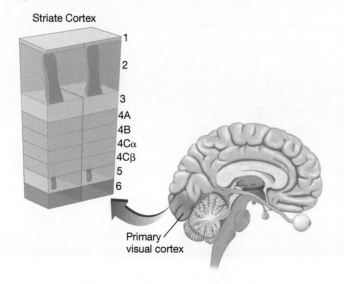

Striate Cortex

Primary visual cortex

Figure 6.13 Blobs and Connections in V1 and V2

(a) A photomicrograph (actually, a montage of several different tissue sections) showing a slice through the striate cortex (area V1) and a region of visual association cortex (V2) of a macaque monkey, stained for cytochrome oxidase. Area V1 shows spots ("blobs"), and area V2 shows three types of stripes: thick, thin (both dark), and pale. (b) Neurons located in CO blobs of V1 project to thin stripes in V2. Neurons in the interblob regions of V1 project to pale and thick stripes of V2.

(From Sincich, L. C., and Horton, J. C., The circuitry of V1 and V2: Integration of color, form, and motion, *Annual Review of Neuroscience,* Volume 28 © 2005, 303–326, by Annual Reviews www.annualreviews.org)

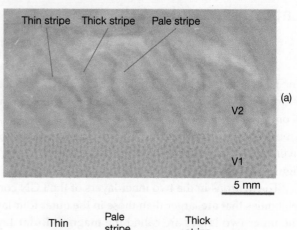

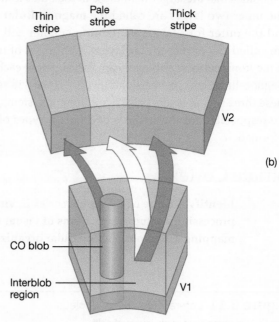

MODULES Most investigators believe that the cortex is organized in modules, which probably range in size from a hundred thousand to a few million neurons. Each module receives information from other modules, performs some calculations, and then passes the results to other modules. In recent years, investigators have been learning the characteristics of the modules that are found in the visual cortex.

The striate cortex is divided into approximately 2,500 modules containing approximately 150,000 neurons. The neurons in each module are devoted to the analysis of various features contained in one very small portion of the visual field. Collectively, these modules receive information from the entire visual field, the individual modules serving like the tiles in a mosaic mural. Input from the parvocellular, koniocellular, and magnocellular layers of the LGN is received by different sublayers of the striate cortex: The koniocellular input is received by sublayers 2 and 3 in the striate cortex, magnocellular input is received by sublayer 4Cα, and parvocellular input is received by sublayer 4Cβ (Nassi and Callaway, 2009).

The modules actually consist of two segments, each surrounding a CO blob. Neurons located within the blobs have a special function: Most of them are sensitive to color. In addition, their receptive fields are monocular—they receive visual information from only one eye (Kaas and Collins, 2001; Landisman and Ts'o, 2002).

Outside the CO blob, in the *interblob regions*, neurons show sensitivity to orientation, movement, and binocular disparity, but most do not respond to color (Born and Tootell, 1991; Edwards et al., 1995; Livingstone and Hubel, 1984). Each half of the module receives input from only one eye, but the circuitry within the module combines the information from both eyes, which means that most of the neurons are binocular. (See Figure 6.14.)

Extrastriate Cortex

LO 6.11 **Identify the role of the extrastriate cortex in visual processing, including the dorsal and ventral streams.**

The striate cortex is necessary for visual perception, but the perception of objects and of entire visual scenes does not

Figure 6.14 One Module of the Primary Visual Cortex

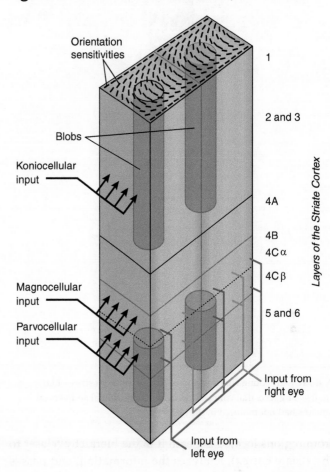

Research has identified over two dozen distinct regions and subregions of the visual cortex of the rhesus monkey.

take place there. Each of the thousands of modules of the striate cortex sees only what is happening in one tiny part of the visual field. Thus, for us to perceive objects and entire visual scenes, the information from these individual modules must be combined. That combination takes place in the extrastriate cortex.

STRUCTURES OF THE EXTRASTRIATE CORTEX Visual information received from the striate cortex is further analyzed in the extrastriate cortex, the region of the visual association cortex that surrounds the striate cortex. The primate extrastriate cortex consists of several additional regions (named V2–V5), each of which contains one or more independent maps of the visual field. Each region is specialized, containing neurons that respond to particular features of visual information, such as orientation, movement, spatial frequency, retinal disparity, or color. So far, investigators have identified over two dozen distinct regions and subregions of the visual cortex of the rhesus monkey. These regions are arranged hierarchically, beginning with the striate cortex (Grill-Spector and Malach, 2004; Wandell et al., 2007). Most of the information passes up the hierarchy; each region receives information

123rf.com

A study with young children and objects of different sizes—like chairs—suggests that connections between the dorsal and ventral streams had not matured in the children.

from regions located beneath it in the hierarchy (closer to the striate cortex), analyzes the information, and passes the results on to "higher" regions (farther from the striate cortex) for further analysis. Some information is also transmitted in the opposite direction, but axons that descend the hierarchy are much less numerous than those that ascend it.

PATHWAYS OF THE EXTRASTRIATE CORTEX Visual processing in the extrastriate cortex divides into two pathways: the **dorsal stream** and the **ventral stream.** The streams begin to diverge after area V2. The *ventral stream* begins with the neurons in the pale and thin stripes of area V2, continues forward to area V4, and then projects to a variety of

subareas of the **inferior temporal cortex.** The *dorsal stream* begins with the neurons in the thick stripes of area V2 and ascends into regions of the **posterior parietal cortex.** Some axons conveying information received from the magnocellular system bypass area V2: They project from area V1 directly to area V5 (also called area MT for medial temporal), a region of the dorsal stream devoted to the analysis of movement. (See Figure 6.15.)

The dorsal and ventral streams of the visual association cortex play distinctly different roles in visual processing. The primary behavioral function of the dorsal stream is to provide visual information that guides navigation and skilled movements directed toward objects, and that of the ventral stream is to provide visual information about the size, shape, color, and texture of objects (including, as we shall see, other people). The ventral stream recognizes *what* an object is and what colors it has, and the dorsal stream recognizes *where* the object is located and, if it is moving, its speed and direction of movement.

A fascinating study with young children demonstrates the importance of communication between the dorsal and ventral streams of the visual system in perception of form (DeLoache et al., 2004). The experimenters let children play with large toys: an indoor slide that they could climb and slide down, a chair that they could sit on, and a toy car that they could enter. After the children played in and on the large toys, the children were taken out of the room, the large toys were replaced with identical miniature versions, and the children were then brought back into the room. When the children played with the miniature toys, they acted as if they were the large versions: They tried to climb onto the slide, climb into the car, and sit on the chair. One child said "In!" several times and turning to his mother, apparently asked her to help him. The authors suggest that this child's behavior reflects incomplete maturation of connections between the dorsal and ventral streams. The ventral stream recognizes the identity of the objects, and the dorsal stream recognizes their size, but in the developing brain the information is not adequately shared between these two systems.

Figure 6.15 Structures and Pathways of the Extrastriate Cortex
The dorsal stream terminates in the posterior parietal lobe and conveys "where" information. The ventral stream terminates in the inferior temporal lab and conveys "what" information.

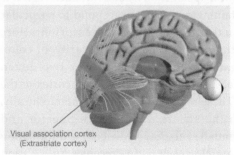

Visual association cortex
(Extrastriate cortex)

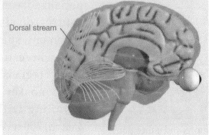

Dorsal stream

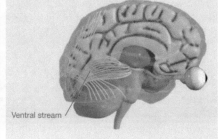

Ventral stream

Section Review

Brain Regions Involved in Visual Processing

LO 6.9 **Describe the pattern of retinal ganglion cell input and the layers of the LGN.**

Of the six cell layers in the LGN, layers 1, 4, and 6 receive input from the retinal ganglion cells of the contralateral eye, and layers 2, 3, and 5 receive input from the ipsilateral eye. The two inner layers of the LGN are the magnocellular layers, and the four outer layers are the parvocellular layers. The koniocellular sublayers are found beneath each of the six layers.

LO 6.10 **Identify the role of the striate cortex in visual processing, including functions of visual field mapping, CO blobs, and modular organization.**

The striate cortex is the first cortical region involved in combining visual information from several sources. It receives visual input from the LGN and performs additional processing of this information, which it then transmits to the extrastriate cortex. The striate cortex contains six layers. Layer four contains four sublayers (4A, 4B, 4Cα and 4Cβ). CO blobs are groups of cells that receive information about color from the parvocellular and koniocellular layers of the LGN. Neurons in CO blobs of the striate cortex project to thin stripes, and neurons outside the blobs (in interblob areas) project to thick stripes and pale stripes of the extrastriate cortex. Neurons in the thin stripes receive information concerning color, and those in the thick stripes and pale stripes receive information about orientation, spatial frequency, movement, and retinal disparity. The striate cortex is divided into many modules, each containing thousands of neurons devoted to analysis of specific features of a portion of the visual field.

LO 6.11 **Identify the role of the extrastriate cortex in visual processing, including the dorsal and ventral streams.**

The extrastriate cortex is responsible for combining information from individual modules of the striate cortex to allow an individual to perceive objects and entire visual scenes. Each region of extrastriate cortex is specialized, containing neurons that respond to particular features of visual information, such as orientation, movement, spatial frequency, retinal disparity, or color. The ventral stream terminates in the inferior temporal cortex and is responsible for processing what an object is and what colors it has. The dorsal stream terminates in the posterior parietal cortex and is responsible for processing where the object is located and, if it is moving, its speed and direction of movement.

Thought Question

Take a moment to look at the scene in front of you right now, and imagine how its features are encoded by neurons in your striate cortex. Describe one object or aspect of your current visual scene and summarize where this information is processed in the extrastriate cortex.

Perception of Color

With a basic understanding of the structures of the visual system, we will now turn our attention to understanding the roles these structures play in more specific visual functions. Not all components of the visual system have the same amount of involvement in different visual functions. For example, the retina is highly involved in basic functions such as distinguishing between light and dark, while both retinal and cortical processing are required for more complex aspects of vision, such as recognizing faces. We will first explore the role of the retina in perception of light and color. Subsequent sections will explore the contributions of the retina, LGN, striate, and extrastriate cortex to perception of color, form, spatial location, orientation, and movement.

Role of the Retinal Ganglion Cells in Light/Dark Perception

LO 6.12 **Compare the activity of ON, OFF, and ON/OFF retinal ganglion cells in response to light.**

Objects in our environment selectively absorb some wavelengths of light and reflect others, which, to our eyes, give them different colors. The retinas of humans and many species of nonhuman primates contain three different types of cones, which provide them (and us) with color vision (Hunt et al., 1998; Jacobs, 1996).

Over 70 years ago, Hartline (1938) discovered that the frog retina contained three types of ganglion cells. ON cells responded with an excitatory burst of action potentials when the retina was illuminated, OFF cells responded when the light was turned off, and ON/OFF cells responded briefly when the light went on and again when it went off. Kuffler (1952, 1953), recording from ganglion cells in the retina of the cat, discovered that their receptive field consists of a roughly circular center, surrounded by a ring. Stimulation of the center or surrounding fields had contrary effects: ON cells were excited by light falling in the central field (*center*) and were inhibited by light falling in the surrounding field (*surround*), whereas OFF cells responded in the opposite manner. ON/OFF ganglion cells were briefly excited when light was turned on or off. In primates most of these ON/OFF cells project mainly to the superior colliculus, which is primarily involved in visual reflexes in response to moving or suddenly-appearing stimuli (Schiller and Malpeli, 1977); thus, these cells do not appear to play a direct role in form perception. (See Figure 6.16.)

Figure 6.16 also illustrates a rebound effect that occurs when the light is turned off again. Neurons whose firing is inhibited while the light is on will show a brief burst of excitation when it is turned off. In contrast, neurons whose firing is increased will show a brief period of inhibition when the light is turned off.

The two major categories of ganglion cells (ON and OFF) and the organization of their receptive fields into opposing center and surround activation provide useful information to the rest of the visual system. Let us consider these two types of ganglion cells first. Ganglion cells normally produce action potentials at a relatively low rate. Then, when the level of illumination in the center of their receptive field increases or decreases (for example, when an object moves or the eye makes a saccade), the ganglion cells signal the change in illumination. ON cells signal increases in illumination and OFF cells signal decreases, but both convey changes in illumination through an increased rate of firing action potentials.

Several studies have confirmed that ON cells and OFF cells signal different kinds of information about light and dark. When monkeys received a drug that selectively blocked synaptic transmission in ON bipolar cells, the animals had difficulty detecting spots that were brighter than the background but had no difficulty detecting spots that were slightly darker than the background (Schiller et al., 1986). Administering this drug completely blocked vision in very dim light, which is normally mediated by rods (Dolan and Schiller, 1989). Thus, rod bipolar cells must all be of the ON type. (If you think about it, that arrangement makes sense; in very dim light we are more likely to see brighter objects against a dark background than dark objects against a light background.)

The center-surround organization of retinal ganglion cell receptive fields enhances our ability to detect the outlines of objects even when the contrast between the object and the background is low. Figure 6.17 illustrates this phenomenon. This figure shows six uniformly gray squares arranged in order of brightness. Even though each square is of uniform darkness, the right edge of each square looks lighter, and the left edge looks darker, making the borders between the squares stand out. Our visual systems perceive them to be lighter because of the center-surround organization of the receptive fields of the retinal ganglion cells.

Figure 6.16 ON and OFF Ganglion Cells

This figure shows responses of ON and OFF ganglion cells to stimuli presented in the center or the surround of the receptive field.

(Adapted from Kuffler, S. W., Neurons in the retina: Organization, inhibition and excitation problems, *Cold Spring Harbor Symposium for Quantitative Biology*, 1952, *17*, 281–292.)

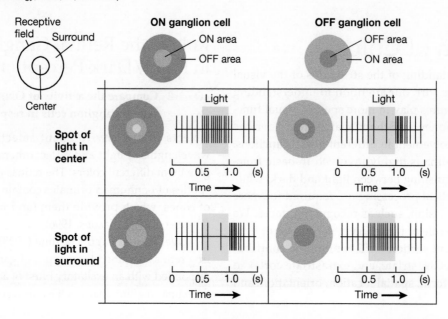

Figure 6.17 Enhancement of Contrast

(a) Although each gray square is of uniform darkness, the right edge of each square looks somewhat lighter, and the left edge looks somewhat darker. This effect appears to be caused by the opponent center-surround arrangement of the receptive fields of the retinal ganglion cells. (b) This figure shows a schematic explanation of the phenomenon shown in panel a. Only ON cells are shown; OFF cells are responsible for the darker appearance of the left side of the darker square. We see the centers and surrounds of the receptive fields of several ganglion cells. (In reality these receptive fields would be overlapping, but the simplified arrangement is easier to understand. This example also includes only ON cells—again, for the sake of simplicity.) The image of the transition between lighter and darker regions falls across some of these receptive fields. The cells whose centers are located in the brighter region but whose surrounds are located at least partially in the darker region will have the highest rate of firing.

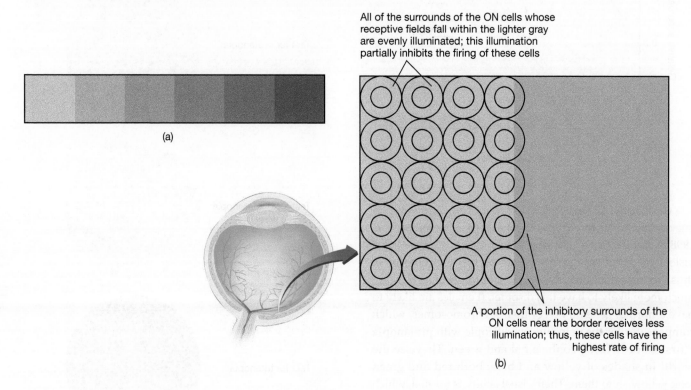

All of the surrounds of the ON cells whose receptive fields fall within the lighter gray are evenly illuminated; this illumination partially inhibits the firing of these cells

(a)

A portion of the inhibitory surrounds of the ON cells near the border receives less illumination; thus, these cells have the highest rate of firing

(b)

Role of the Retina in Color Perception

LO 6.13 **Differentiate between the trichromatic and opponent-color system theories.**

Various theories of color vision have been proposed for many years—long before it was possible to disprove or validate them by physiological means. The *trichromatic (three-color) theory* was proposed in 1802 and suggested that the eye detected different colors because it contained three types of receptors, each sensitive to a single hue. An alternative explanation, the *opponent-color system theory,* suggested that color might be represented in the visual system as opponent colors: red versus green and yellow versus blue.

Many people consider yellow, blue, red, and green as primary colors—colors that seem unique and do not appear to be blends of other colors. (Black and white are primary, too, but we perceive them as colorless.) All other colors can be described as mixtures of these primary colors. The trichromatic system cannot explain why *yellow* is included in this group—why it is perceived as a pure color. In addition, some colors appear to blend, whereas others do not.

For example, one can speak of a bluish green or a yellowish green, and orange appears to have both red and yellow qualities. Purple resembles both red and blue. But try to imagine a reddish green or a bluish yellow. It is impossible; these colors seem to be opposite to each other. Again, these facts are not explained by the trichromatic theory. As we shall see in the following sections, the visual system uses both trichromatic and opponent-color systems to encode information related to color.

PHOTORECEPTORS: TRICHROMATIC CODING Physiological investigations of retinal photoreceptors in higher primates support the trichromatic theory: Three different types of photoreceptors (three different types of cones) are responsible for color vision. Figure 6.18 demonstrates light absorbance by blue, green, and red light sensitive cones. Investigators have studied the absorption characteristics of individual photoreceptors, determining the amount of light of different wavelengths that is absorbed by the photopigments. These characteristics are controlled by the particular opsin a photoreceptor contains; different opsins absorb particular wavelengths more readily.

Figure 6.18 Absorbance of Light by Rods and Cones

The graph shows the relative absorbance of light of various wavelengths by rods and the three types of cones in the human retina.

(Based on data from Dartnall et al., 1983.)

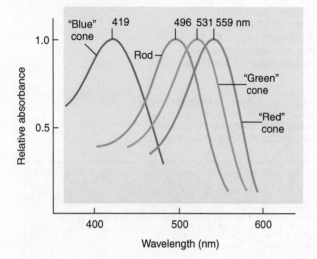

Figure 6.19 Testing for Color Vision

Special images are used to assess protanopia, deuteranopia, and tritanopia. The tester shows the individual the images and asks them to identify the number in the circle. In protanopia, people have difficulty seeing the color red because their "red" cones are filled with "green" cone opsin. In deuteranopia, people have difficulty seeing green because their "green" cones appear to be filled with "red" cone opsin. In tritanopia, people have difficulty seeing blue because their retinas lack "blue" cones.

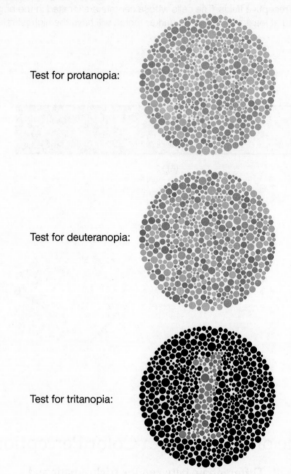

Test for protanopia:

Test for deuteranopia:

Test for tritanopia:

Genetic defects in color vision result from anomalies in one or more of the three types of cone (Wissinger and Sharpe, 1998; Nathans, 1999). The first two kinds of defective color vision described here involve genes on the X chromosome; thus, because males have only one X chromosome, they are much more likely to have this disorder. (Females are likely to have a normal gene on one of their X chromosomes, which compensates for the defective one.) People with **protanopia** ("first-color defect") confuse red and green. They see the world in shades of yellow and blue; both red and green look yellowish to them. Their visual acuity is normal, which suggests that their retinas do not lack "red" or "green" cones. This fact and their sensitivity to lights of different wavelengths suggest that their "red" cones are filled with "green" cone opsin. People with **deuteranopia** ("second-color defect") also confuse red and green and also have normal visual acuity. Their "green" cones appear to be filled with "red" cone opsin. (In other words, their vision is dichromatic, or "two color," like that of our ancestors and most present-day mammals.)

Mancuso et al., (2009) attempted to perform gene therapy on adult squirrel monkeys whose retinas lacked the gene for "red" cone pigment. Although most female squirrel monkeys have trichromatic color vision, males have only dichromatic vision and cannot distinguish red from green. Mancuso and her colleagues used a genetically modified virus to insert a human gene for the pigment of that "red" cone into the retinas of male monkeys. Color vision tests before and after surgery confirmed that the gene insertion converted the monkeys from dichromats into trichromats: They could now distinguish between red and green.

Tritanopia ("third-color defect") is rare, affecting fewer than 1 in 10,000 people. This disorder involves a faulty gene that is not located on an X chromosome; thus, it is equally prevalent in males and females. People with tritanopia have difficulty with hues of short wavelengths and see the world in greens and reds. To them a clear blue sky is a bright green, and yellow looks pink. Their retinas lack "blue" cones. Because the retina contains so few of these cones, their absence does not noticeably affect visual acuity.

Finally, some people possess a very rare genetic condition in which the retina completely lacks cones. These individuals have monochromatic vision and see the visual world in black and white and shades of grey. For an example of the stimuli used to asses color blindness, see Figure 6.19.

RETINAL GANGLION CELLS: OPPONENT-PROCESS CODING Unlike cones, retinal ganglion cells use an opponent-color system. These neurons respond specifically to pairs of primary colors, with red opposing green and blue opposing yellow (Daw, 1968; Gouras, 1968). Thus, the retina contains two kinds of color-sensitive ganglion cells: *red-green* and

Figure 6.20 Receptive Fields of Color-Sensitive Ganglion Cells

When a portion of the receptive field is illuminated with the color shown, the cell's rate of firing increases. When a portion is illuminated with the complementary color, the cell's rate of firing decreases.

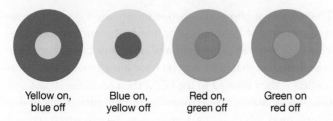

Yellow on, blue off   Blue on, yellow off   Red on, green off   Green on red off

yellow-blue. Some color-sensitive ganglion cells respond in a center-surround fashion. For example, a cell might be excited by red and inhibited by green in the center of their receptive field while showing the opposite response in the surrounding ring. (See Figure 6.20.) Other ganglion cells that receive input from cones do not respond differentially to different wavelengths but simply encode relative brightness in the center and surround. These cells serve as "black-and-white detectors."

The response characteristics of retinal ganglion cells to light of different wavelengths are determined by the particular circuits that connect the three types of cones with the two types of ganglion cells.

Figure 6.21 helps to explain how hues are detected by "red," "green," and "blue" cones and translated into excitation or inhibition of the red-green and yellow-blue ganglion cells. The diagram does not show the actual neural circuitry, which includes the retinal neurons that connect the cones with the ganglion cells. The arrows in Figure 6.21 refer to the *effects* of the light falling on the retina.

Detection and coding of pure red, green, or blue light is the easiest to understand. For example, red light excites "red" cones, which causes the excitation of red-green ganglion cells. (See Figure 6.21a.) Green light excites "green" cones, which causes the *inhibition* of red-green cells. (See Figure 6.21b.) But consider the effect of yellow light. Because the wavelength that produces the sensation of yellow is intermediate between the wavelengths that produce red and green, it will stimulate both "red" and "green" cones about equally. Yellow-blue ganglion cells are excited by both "red"

Figure 6.21 Color Coding in the Retina

(a) Red light stimulating a "red" cone, which causes excitation of a red-green ganglion cell. (b) Green light stimulating a "green" cone, which causes inhibition of a red-green ganglion cell. (c) Yellow light stimulating "red" and "green" cones equally but not affecting "blue" cones. The stimulation of "red" and "green" cones causes excitation of a yellow-blue ganglion cell. (d) Blue light stimulating a "blue" cone, which causes inhibition of a yellow-blue ganglion cell. The arrows labeled E and I represent neural circuitry within the retina that translates excitation of a cone into excitation or inhibition of a ganglion cell. For clarity, only some of the circuits are shown.

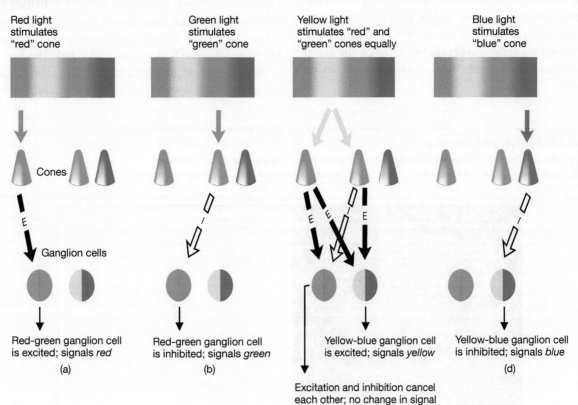

Red light stimulates "red" cone   Green light stimulates "green" cone   Yellow light stimulates "red" and "green" cones equally   Blue light stimulates "blue" cone

Cones

Ganglion cells

Red-green ganglion cell is excited; signals *red*
(a)

Red-green ganglion cell is inhibited; signals *green*
(b)

Yellow-blue ganglion cell is excited; signals *yellow*

Yellow-blue ganglion cell is inhibited; signals *blue*
(d)

Excitation and inhibition cancel each other; no change in signal
(c)

and "green" cones, so their rate of firing increases. However, red-green ganglion cells are excited by red and inhibited by green, so their firing rate does not change. The brain detects an increased firing rate from the axons of yellow-blue ganglion cells, which it interprets as yellow. (See Figure 6.21c.) Blue light inhibits the activity of yellow-blue ganglion cells. (See Figure 6.21d.)

The opponent-color system employed by the ganglion cells explains why we cannot perceive a reddish green or a bluish yellow: An axon that signals red or green (or yellow or blue) can either increase or decrease its rate of firing; it cannot do both at the same time. A reddish green would have to be signaled by a ganglion cell firing slowly and rapidly at the same time, which is impossible.

Figure 6.22 demonstrates an interesting property of the visual system: the formation of a **negative afterimage**. Stare at the cross in the center of the image on the left for approximately 30 seconds. Then quickly look at the cross in the center of the white rectangle to the right. You will have a fleeting experience of seeing the red and green colors of an apple—colors that are complementary, or opposite, to the ones on the left. Complementary items go together to make up a whole. In this context **complementary colors** are those that make white (or shades of gray) when added together.

The most important cause of negative afterimages is adaptation in the rate of firing of retinal ganglion cells. When ganglion cells are excited or inhibited for a prolonged period of time, they later show a *rebound effect*, firing faster or slower than normal. For example, the green of the apple in Figure 6.22 inhibits some red-green ganglion cells. When this region of the retina is then stimulated with the neutral-colored light reflected off the white rectangle, the red-green ganglion cells—no longer inhibited by the green light—fire faster than normal. Thus, we see a red afterimage of the apple.

Role of the Striate Cortex

LO 6.14   **List the contributions of the parvocellular and koniocellular systems to perception of color in the striate cortex.**

The retinal ganglion cells encode information about the relative amounts of light falling on the center and surround regions of their receptive field and, in many cases, about the wavelength of that light. As you have already read, this information is then relayed to the LGN, then on to the striate cortex. The striate cortex performs additional processing of this information, which it then transmits to the extrastriate cortex.

Researchers previously believed that the parvocellular system transmitted all information pertaining to color to the striate cortex. However, we now know that the parvocellular system receives information only from "red" and "green" cones; additional information from "blue" cones is transmitted through the koniocellular system (Chatterjee and Callaway, 2003; Hendry and Yoshioka, 1994).

Role of the Extrastriate Cortex

LO 6.15   **Using examples from human and animal research, describe the role of the extrastriate cortex in color perception and achromatopsia.**

As we saw, the parvocellular, koniocellular, and magnocellular systems provide different kinds of information. Only the cells in the parvocellular and koniocellular systems receive information about wavelength from cones; thus, these systems provide information concerning color. Cells in the parvocellular system also show high spatial resolution and low temporal resolution; that is, they are able to detect very fine details, but their response is slow and prolonged. The koniocellular system, which receives information only from "blue" cones, which are much less numerous than "red" and "green" cones,

---

Figure 6.22 A Negative Afterimage

Stare for approximately 30 seconds at the plus sign in the center of the left figure; then quickly transfer your gaze to the plus sign in the center of the right figure. You will see colors that are complementary to the originals.

Table 6.2 Properties of the Magnocellular, Parvocellular, and Koniocellular Divisions of the Visual System

Property	Magnocellular Division	Parvocellular Division	Koniocellular Division
Color	No	Yes (from "red" and "green" cones)	Yes (from "blue" cones)
Sensitivity to contrast	High	Low	Low
Spatial resolution (ability to detect fine details)	Low	High	Low
Temporal resolution	Fast (transient response)	Slow (sustained response)	Slow (sustained response)

does not provide information about fine details. In contrast, neurons in the magnocellular system are color-blind. They are not able to detect fine details, but they can detect smaller contrasts between light and dark. They are also especially sensitive to movement. (See Table 6.2.) The dorsal stream receives mostly magnocellular input, but the ventral stream receives approximately equal input from the magnocellular and the parvocellular/koniocellular systems. (See Figure 6.23.)

Neurons within the CO blobs in the striate cortex respond differentially to colors. Like the ganglion cells in the retina (and the parvocellular and koniocellular neurons in the dorsal lateral geniculate nucleus), these neurons respond in opponent fashion. This information is analyzed by the regions of the extrastriate cortex that are a part of the ventral stream (refer to Figure 6.15 to review the dorsal and ventral streams).

The appearance of the colors of objects remains much the same whether we observe them under artificial light, under an overcast sky, or at noon on a cloudless day. This phenomenon is known as **color constancy.** Our visual system does not simply respond according to the wavelength of the light reflected by objects in each part of the visual field; instead, it compensates for the source of the light. This compensation appears to be made by simultaneously comparing the color composition of each point in the visual field with the average color of the entire scene. If the scene contains a particularly high level of long-wavelength light (as it would if an object were illuminated by the light of a setting sun), then some long-wavelength light is "subtracted out" of the perception of each point in the scene. This compensation helps us to see what is actually out there.

STUDIES WITH LABORATORY ANIMALS In the monkey brain, color-sensitive neurons in the CO blobs of the striate cortex send color-related information to the thin stripes in area V2. Neurons in V2 send information to an adjacent region of the extrastriate cortex, called V4. Zeki (1980) found that neurons in this region respond selectively to colors, but their response characteristics are much more complex than those of neurons in V1 or V2. Unlike the neurons we have encountered so far, these neurons respond to a variety of wavelengths, not just the wavelengths that correspond to red, green, yellow, and blue.

Figure 6.23 Color Processing via Parvocellular and Koniocellular Systems

The dorsal stream receives mostly magnocellular input (light/dark contrast and movement).

The ventral stream receives approximately equal input from the magnocellular, parvocellular ("red" and "green" cones) and koniocellular ("blue" cones) systems.

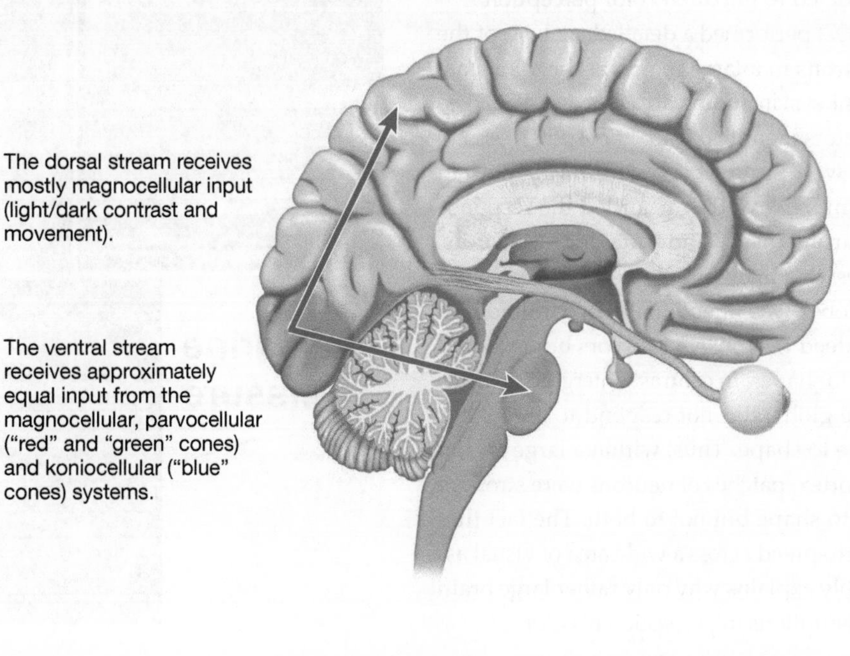

Schein and Desimone (1990) performed a careful study of the response characteristics of neurons in area V4 of the monkey extrastriate cortex, which receives input from the pale and thin stripes of area V2. They found that these neurons responded to specific colors. Some also responded to colored bars of specific orientation; thus, area V4 seems to be involved in the analysis of form as well as color. The color-sensitive neurons had a rather unusual secondary receptive field: a large region surrounding the primary field. When stimuli were presented in the secondary receptive field, the neuron did not respond. However, stimuli presented there could suppress the neuron's response to a stimulus presented in the primary field. For example, if a cell would fire when a red spot was presented in the primary field, it would fire at a slower rate (or not at all) when an additional red stimulus was presented in the surrounding secondary field. In other words, these cells responded to particular wavelengths of light but subtracted out the amount of that wavelength that was present in the background. As Schein and Desimone point out, this subtraction could serve as the basis for color constancy.

Walsh et al., (1993) confirmed this prediction; damage to area V4 does disrupt color constancy. The investigators found that, although monkeys could still discriminate between different colors after area V4 had been damaged, their performance was impaired when the color of the overall illumination was changed. But the fact that the monkeys could still perform a color discrimination task under constant illumination means that some region besides area V4 must be involved in color vision.

A study by Heywood et al., (1995) suggested that a portion of the inferior temporal cortex just anterior to area V4—a region of the monkey brain that is usually referred to as area TEO—plays a critical role in visual discrimination. The investigators destroyed area TEO, leaving area V4 intact, and observed severe impairment in color discrimination. The monkeys had no difficulty in discriminating shades of gray, so the deficit was restricted to impaired color perception.

Conway et al., (2007) performed a detailed analysis of the responsiveness of neurons in a large region of the visual association cortex in monkeys, including areas V4 and TEO. Using fMRI, the investigators identified color "hot spots"—small scattered regions that were strongly activated by changes in the color of visual stimuli. Next, they recorded the response characteristics of neurons inside and outside these spots, which they called *globs*. (It's likely the similarity between the terms "blobs" and "globs" was intentional.) They found that glob neurons were indeed responsive to colors but also had some weak sensitivity to shapes. In contrast, interglob neurons (those located outside globs) did not respond to colors but were strongly selective to shape. Thus, within a large region of visual association cortex, patches of neurons were strongly sensitive to colors or to shape but not to both. The fact that color-sensitive globs are spread across a wide area of visual association cortex probably explains why only rather large brain lesions cause severe disruptions in perception of color.

STUDIES WITH HUMANS   Lesions of a restricted region of the human extrastriate cortex can cause loss of color vision without disruption of visual acuity. Some patients describe their vision as resembling a black-and-white film. In addition, they may not be able to imagine colors or remember the colors of objects they saw before their brain damage occurred (Damasio et al., 1980; Heywood and Kentridge, 2003). The condition is known as **cerebral achromatopsia.** If the brain damage is unilateral, people will lose color vision in only half of the visual field. The case of Mrs. D. illustrates a unique example of cerebral achromatopsia.

> Mrs. D. was a 74-year old woman who loved oil painting as a hobby. She suffered two strokes that affected her occipital cortex, one in each hemisphere. After the strokes, testing revealed that she had a full visual field; however, Mrs. D. reported seeing the world in shades of grey. Several months later, she described seeing the world in reddish-brownish shades, and occasionally perceived bright, saturated colors (Bartolomeo et al., 1997).

As we just saw, Heywood et al., (1995) found a region of the inferior temporal cortex of the monkey brain whose damage disrupted the ability to make color discriminations. The analogous region in humans appears to play a critical

Figure 6.24 Case of Damage to the Extrastriate Cortex that Resulted in Loss of Form, but Not Color, Perception
Patient P. B. experienced damage to the extrastriate cortex. Structural and functional MRI data from the patient P. B. show activation in area V1 (white areas on the MRI scans) when correctly identifying colors, though he could not perceive the form or shape of the stimulus.
Source: (Zeki et al., 1999)

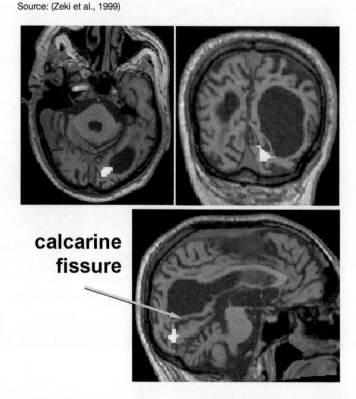

calcarine fissure

role in color perception as well. An fMRI study by Hadjikhani et al., (1998) found a color-sensitive region that included the lingual and fusiform gyri, in a location corresponding to area TEO in the monkey's cortex, which they called area V8. An analysis of 92 cases of achromatopsia by Bouvier and Engel (2006) confirmed that damage to this region (which is adjacent to and partly overlaps the *fusiform face area*, discussed later in this chapter) disrupts color vision.

The function of our ability to perceive different colors is to help us perceive different objects in our environment. Thus, to perceive and understand what is in front of us, we must have information about color combined with other forms of information. Some people with brain damage lose the ability to perceive shapes but can still perceive colors. For example, Zeki et al., (1999) described a patient who could identify colors but was otherwise blind. Patient P. B. received an electrical shock that caused both cardiac and respiratory arrest. He was revived, but the period of anoxia caused extensive damage to his extrastriate cortex. As a result, he lost all form perception. However, even though he could not recognize objects presented on a video monitor, he could still identify their colors. (See Figure 6.24.)

Section Review

Perception of Color

LO 6.12 Compare the activity of ON, OFF, and ON/OFF retinal ganglion cells in response to light.

ON, OFF, and ON/OFF retinal ganglion cells contain a center and surround portion of their receptive fields. In ON cells, light stimulating the center (but not the surround) portion of the receptive field results in a burst of action potentials. In OFF cells, light stimulating the surround (but not the center) portion of the receptive field results in a burst of action potentials. ON/OFF cells respond when the light goes on and again when it goes off. These cells project mainly to the superior colliculus, which is involved in visual reflexes in response to moving or suddenly appearing stimuli.

LO 6.13 Differentiate between the trichromatic and opponent-color system theories.

The trichromatic theory explains that the eye detects different colors because it contains three types of receptors, each sensitive to a single hue (blue, green, or red). The opponent-color system theory explains that color is represented in the visual system as opponent colors: red versus green and yellow versus blue. Research has revealed that cones are sensitive to blue, green, and red light, in support of the trichromatic theory and that retinal ganglion cells respond specifically to pairs of colors, with red opposing green and blue opposing yellow, in support of the opponent-color system theory.

LO 6.14 List the contributions of the parvocellular and koniocellular systems to perception of color in the striate cortex.

The parvocellular system receives information only from "red" and "green" cones; additional information from "blue" cones is transmitted through the koniocellular system.

LO 6.15 Using examples from human and animal research, describe the role of the extrastriate cortex in color perception and achromatopsia.

Neurons in monkey extrastriate cortex region V4 are sensitive to a variety of wavelengths, orientations, and color constancy, adding complexity to the color processing begun in the striate cortex and suggesting that area V4 is involved in the analysis of form as well as color. Other research has revealed that area TEO in primate extrastriate cortex is responsible for additional color and shape perception. Research with human volunteers revealed a region for color perception, V8, that is analogous to TEO. Damage to this region results in achromatopsia.

Thought Question

Imagine that you have been asked to create a figure that would produce a negative afterimage. Describe how you would construct the image to produce a negative afterimage and what directions you would give to viewers to help them experience the negative afterimage. For review, refer to Figure 6.22.

Perception of Form

The analysis of visual information that leads to the perception of form begins with neurons in the striate cortex that are sensitive to spatial frequency. These neurons send information to area V2 and then on to the ventral stream of the extrastriate cortex. Let's look at this process in closer detail.

Role of the Striate Cortex

LO 6.16 Examine the benefit of neural circuits that analyze spatial frequency in the striate cortex.

Early studies by Hubel and Wiesel suggested that neurons in the primary visual cortex detected lines and edges, and subsequent research found that cells in the striate cortex actually responded strongest to sine-wave gratings (De Valois

Figure 6.25 Spatial Frequency

This figure compares two kinds of gratings: (a) Square-wave grating, and (b) sine-wave grating. (c) Angles are drawn between the sine waves, with the apex at the viewer's eye. The *visual angle* between adjacent sine waves is smaller when the waves are closer together.

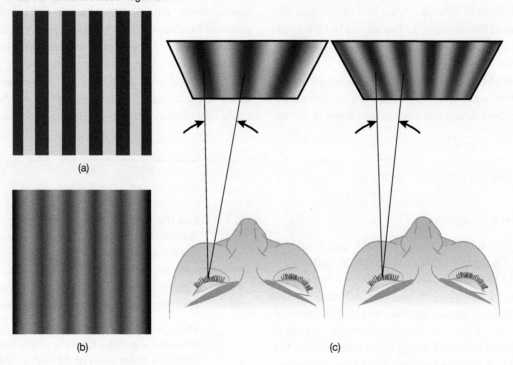

(a)

(b)

(c)

et al., 1978). Figure 6.25 compares a sine-wave grating with a square-wave grating. A square-wave grating consists of a simple set of rectangular bars that vary in brightness; the brightness along the length of a line perpendicular to them would vary in a stepwise (square-wave) fashion. (See Figure 6.25a.) A **sine-wave grating** looks like a series of fuzzy, unfocused parallel bars. Along any line perpendicular to the long axis of the grating, the brightness varies according to a sine-wave function. (See Figure 6.25b.)

A sine-wave grating is designated by its spatial frequency. Frequencies (for example, of sound waves or radio waves) are often expressed in terms of time or distance (such as cycles per second or wavelength in cycles per meter). But because the image of a stimulus on the retina varies in size according to how close it is to the eye, the visual angle is generally used instead of the physical distance between adjacent cycles. Thus, the **spatial frequency** of a sine-wave grating is its variation in brightness measured in cycles per degree of visual angle.

Most neurons in the striate cortex respond best when a sine-wave grating of a particular spatial frequency is placed in the appropriate part of the visual field. Different neurons detect different spatial frequencies.

What is the point of having neural circuits that analyze spatial frequency? Consider the types of information provided by high and low spatial frequencies. Small objects, details within a large object, and large objects with sharp edges provide a signal rich in high frequencies, whereas

large areas of light and dark are represented by low frequencies. An image that is deficient in high-frequency information looks fuzzy and out of focus, like the image seen by a nearsighted person who is not wearing corrective lenses. This image still provides much information about forms and objects in the environment; thus, the most important visual information is that contained in *low spatial frequencies*. When low-frequency information is removed, the shapes of images are very difficult to perceive. (The evolutionary older magnocellular system provides low-frequency information.)

Many experiments have confirmed that the concept of spatial frequency analysis plays a central role in visual perception, and mathematical models have shown that the information present in a scene can be represented very efficiently if it is first encoded in terms of spatial frequency. Thus, the brain probably represents the information in a similar way. Here we will describe an example to help show the validity of the concept. Look at the two pictures in Figure 6.26. You can see that the picture on the right looks much more like the face of Abraham Lincoln than the one on the left does. Yet the two pictures contain the same information. The creators of the pictures, Harmon and Julesz (1973), constructed the figure on the left, which consists of a series of squares, each representing the average brightness of a portion of a picture of Lincoln. The one on the right is simply a transformation of the first one in which high frequencies have been removed. Sharp edges contain high spatial frequencies, so the transformation eliminates them. In the case of the picture on the left,

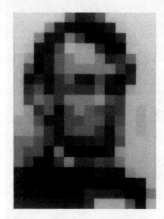

Figure 6.26 Spatial Filtering

The two pictures contain the same amount of low-frequency information, but extraneous high-frequency information has been filtered from the picture on the right. If you look at the pictures from across the room, they look identical.

(From Harmon, L. D., and Julesz, B., Masking in visual recognition: Effects of two-dimensional filtered noise, *Science*, 1973, *180*, 1191–1197. Copyright 1973 by the American Association for the Advancement of Science. Reprinted with permission.)

these frequencies have nothing to do with the information contained in the original picture; thus, they can be seen as visual "noise." The filtration process removes this noise—and makes the image much clearer to the human visual system. Presumably, the high frequencies produced by the edges of the squares in the left figure stimulate neurons in the striate cortex that are tuned to high spatial frequencies. When the visual association cortex receives this noisy information, it has difficulty perceiving the underlying form.

If you want to watch the effect of filtering the extraneous high-frequency noise, try the following demonstration. Look at the pictures in Figure 6.26 from across the room. The distance "erases" the high frequencies, because they exceed the resolving power of the eye, and the two pictures look identical. Now walk toward the pictures, focusing on the left figure. As you get closer, the higher frequencies reappear, and this picture looks less and less like the face of Lincoln.

Role of the Extrastriate Cortex

LO 6.17 **Discuss examples from the research literature that support the roles of the ventral stream and fusiform face area in perception of form.**

Much of our understanding about the role of the extrastriate cortex in form perception has come from research in humans and other animals. The following sections describe research supporting the role of the extrastriate cortex in recognizing objects, patterns, and categories.

STUDIES WITH LABORATORY ANIMALS In primates the recognition of visual patterns and identification of particular objects take place in the inferior temporal cortex,

located in the ventral part of the temporal lobe. This region of visual association cortex is located at the end of the ventral stream. It is here that analyses of form and color are put together, and perceptions of three-dimensional objects and backgrounds are achieved. The inferior temporal cortex consists of two major regions: a posterior area (TEO) and an anterior area (TE). Damage to these regions causes severe deficits in visual discrimination (Dean, 1976; Gross, 1973; Mishkin, 1966). (Refer to Figure 6.15 to review the dorsal and ventral streams).

As we saw earlier, the analysis of visual information is hierarchical: Area V1 is concerned with the analysis of elementary aspects of information in very small regions of the visual field, and successive regions (V2 etc.) analyze more complex characteristics. The size of the receptive fields also grows as the hierarchy is ascended. The receptive fields of neurons in area TEO are larger than those in area V4, and the receptive fields of neurons in area TE are the largest of all, often encompassing the entire contralateral half of the visual field (Boussaoud et al., 1991). In general, these neurons respond best to three-dimensional objects (or photographs of them). They respond poorly to simple stimuli such as spots, lines, or sine-wave gratings. Most of them continue to respond even when complex stimuli are moved to different locations, are changed in size, are placed against a different background, or are partially occluded by other objects (Kovács et al., 1995; Rolls and Baylis, 1986). Thus, they appear to participate in the recognition of objects rather than the analysis of specific features.

The fact that neurons in the primate inferior temporal cortex respond to very specific complex shapes suggests that the development of the circuits responsible for detecting them must involve learning. Indeed, that seems to be the case. For example, several studies have found neurons in the inferior temporal cortex that respond specifically to objects that the monkeys have already seen many times but not to unfamiliar objects (Baker et al., 2002; Kobatake et al., 1992; Logothetis et al., 1995). The role of the inferior temporal cortex in learning will be discussed in more detail in Chapter 13.

STUDIES WITH HUMANS Study of people who have sustained brain damage to the extrastriate cortex has told us much about the organization of the human visual system. In recent years our knowledge has been greatly expanded by functional-imaging studies.

Visual Agnosia Damage to the human extrastriate cortex can cause a category of deficits known as **visual agnosia.** Mrs. R., whose case was described in the opening of this chapter, had visual agnosia caused by damage to the ventral stream of her extrastriate cortex. As we saw, she could not identify common objects by sight, even though she had relatively normal visual acuity. However, she could still read, even small print, which indicates that reading involves different brain regions than object perception does.

(Chapter 14 discusses research that has identified brain regions involved in visual recognition of letters and words.) When she was permitted to hold an object that she could not recognize visually, she could immediately recognize it by touch and say what it is, which proves that she had not lost her memory for the object or simply forgotten how to say its name.

Recognizing Categories Visual agnosia is caused by damage to the parts of the extrastriate cortex that contribute to the ventral stream. This is vividly illustrated by a case report of patient J.S. by Karnath et al., (2009).

> Patient J. S. sustained a stroke in which the ventral stream was seriously damaged, but the dorsal stream was intact. He was unable to recognize objects or faces and could no longer read. He could not recognize shapes or orientations of visual stimuli (ventral stream functions). However, his ability to reach for and pick up objects was preserved, and if he knew in advance what they were, he could handle them appropriately (dorsal stream functions). For example, if he knew where his clothes were, he could pick them up and get dressed. He could shake hands when someone else extended his hand to him. He could walk around his neighborhood, enter a store, and give a written list to the clerk.

With the advent of functional imaging, investigators have studied the responses of the typical human brain and have discovered several regions of the ventral stream that are activated by the sight of particular categories of visual stimuli. For example, researchers have identified regions of the inferior temporal and lateral occipital cortex that are specifically activated by categories such as animals, tools, cars, flowers, letters and letter strings, faces, bodies, and scenes. (See Grill-Spector and Malach, 2004, and Tootell et al., 2003 for a review.) However, not all of these findings have been replicated, and general-purpose regions contain circuits that can learn to recognize shapes that do not fall into these categories. A relatively large region of the ventral stream of the visual association cortex, the **lateral occipital complex (LOC)**, appears to respond to a wide variety of objects and shapes.

A functional-imaging study by Downing et al., (2006) suggests that there are few regions of the extrastriate cortex devoted to the analysis of specific categories of stimuli. The investigators presented images of objects from 19 different categories to a control group and found only three regions that showed the greatest activation to the sight of specific categories: faces, bodies, and scenes. Bell et al., (2009) found that in both the human and the monkey brain, regions that responded to faces and body parts were adjacent to each other, as were those that responded to objects and scenes of places. (See Figure 6.27.)

Figure 6.27 Category-Selective Regions in Monkeys and Humans

Views of the temporal lobes of monkeys *E* and *J* as well as the grouped human dataset showing category-selective regions throughout the brain. Voxels are colored according to their preference for one of the four categories tested.

(Bell et al., 2009.)

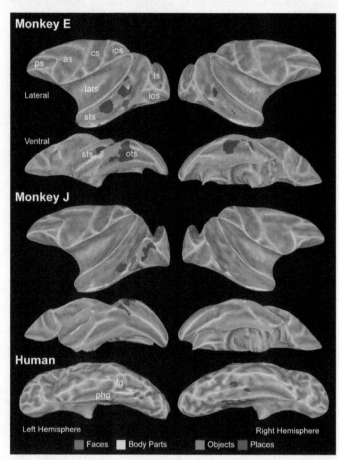

Recognizing Faces A common symptom of visual agnosia is **prosopagnosia,** inability to recognize particular faces (*prosopon* is Greek for "face"). That is, patients with this disorder can recognize that they are looking at a face, but they cannot say whose face it is—even if it belongs to a relative or close friend. They see eyes, ears, a nose, and a mouth, but they cannot recognize the particular configuration of these features that identifies an individual face. They still remember who these people are and will usually recognize them when they hear the person's voice. As one patient said, "I have trouble recognizing people from just faces alone. I look at their hair color, listen to their voices . . . I use clothing, voice, and hair. I try to associate something with a person one way or another . . . what they wear, how their hair is worn" (Buxbaum et al., 1999, p. 43).

Studies with people who have experienced brain damage and functional-imaging studies suggest that these special face-recognizing circuits are found in the **fusiform face** area (FFA), located in the fusiform gyrus on the base of the temporal lobe. For example, Grill-Spector et al., (2004) obtained fMRI scans of the brains of people who looked at pictures of faces and several other categories of objects and found that regions of the fusiform cortex were selectively activated by viewing faces.

Perhaps the most unusual piece of evidence for a special face-recognition region comes from a report by Moscovitch et al., (1997), who studied a man with a visual agnosia for objects but not for faces. For example, he recognized the face shown in Figure 6.28 but not the flowers, fruits, and vegetables that compose it. Presumably, some regions of his visual association cortex were damaged, but the fusiform face region was not.

Some people suffer from congenital prosopagnosia—the inability to recognize faces without having obvious damage to the FFA. Such people often report that their inability to

recognize people they have met several times is perceived by the other people as an insult. Behrman et al., (2007) found that the anterior fusiform gyrus is smaller in people with congenital prosopagnosia, and a diffusion tensor imaging study by Thomas et al., (2009) found evidence that people with congenital prosopagnosia show decreased connectivity within the occipito-temporal cortex.

Another interesting region of the ventral stream is the **extrastriate body area (EBA),** which is just posterior to the FFA and partly overlaps it. Downing et al., (2001) found that this region was specifically activated by photographs, silhouettes, or stick drawings of human bodies or body parts and not by control stimuli such as photographs or drawings of tools, scrambled silhouettes, or scrambled stick drawings of human bodies. Figure 6.29 shows the magnitude of the fMRI response in the nonoverlapping

Figure 6.28 Visual Object Agnosia Without Prosopagnosia
A patient could recognize the face in this painting but not the flowers, fruits, and vegetables that compose it.

(Giuseppe Arcimboldo. 1527–1593. *Vertumnus.* Erich Lessing/Art Resource, New York.)

Figure 6.29 Perception of Faces and Bodies
The fusiform face area (FFA) and extrastriate body area (EBA) were activated by images of faces, headless bodies, body parts, and assorted objects.

(Adapted from Schwarzlose, R. F., Baker, C. I., and Kanwisher, N., Separate face and body selectivity on the fusiform gyrus, *Journal of Neuroscience*, 2005, 23, 11055–11059.)

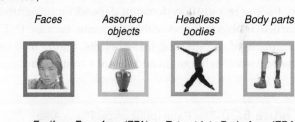
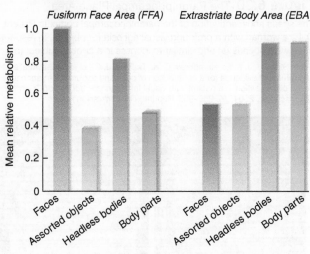

regions of the FFA and EBA to several categories of stimuli (Schwarzlose et al., 2005). As you can see, the FFA responded to faces more than any of the other categories, and the EBA showed the greatest response to headless bodies and body parts.

Urgesi et al., (2004) used transcranial magnetic stimulation (TMS) to temporarily disrupt the normal neural activity of the EBA. (As we saw in Chapter 5, the TMS procedure applies a strong localized magnetic field to the brain by passing an electrical current through a coil of wire placed on the scalp.) The investigators found that the disruption temporarily impaired people's ability to recognize photographs of body parts, but not parts of faces or motorcycles.

As we will see in Chapter 13, the hippocampus and nearby regions of the medial temporal cortex are involved in spatial perception and memory. Several studies have identified a **parahippocampal place area (PPA),** located in a region of limbic cortex bordering the ventromedial temporal lobe, that is activated by the sight of scenes and backgrounds. For example, Steeves et al., (2004) studied Patient D. F., a 47-year-old woman who had sustained brain damage caused by accidental carbon monoxide poisoning 14 years earlier. Bilateral damage to her lateral occipital cortex (an important part of the ventral stream) caused a profound visual agnosia for objects. However, she was able to recognize both natural and human-made scenes (beaches, forests, deserts, cities, markets, and rooms). Functional imaging showed activation of her intact PPA. These results suggest that scene recognition does not depend on recognition of particular objects found within the scene, because D. F. was incapable of recognizing these objects. Figure 6.30 shows the activation in her brain and that of a control participant.

Figure 6.30 The Parahippocampal Place Area

The scans show activation of the parahippocampal cortex in Patient D. F., a woman with a profound visual agnosia for objects, in response to viewing scenes (a) and similar responses in a control subject (b).

(From Steeves, J. K. E., Humphrey, G. K., Culham, J. C., et al., Behavioral and neuroimaging evidence for a contribution of color and texture information to scene classification in a patient with visual form agnosia, *Journal of Cognitive Neuroscience*, 2004, *16*, 955–965. Reprinted by permission.)

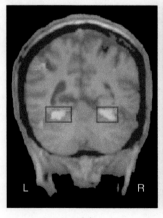 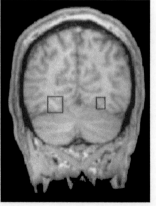

(a)　　　　　(b)

Expert Recognition As we just saw, the ability to recognize faces by sight depends on a specific region of the fusiform gyrus. But must we conclude that the development of this region is a result of natural selection and that the FFA comes prewired with circuits devoted to the analysis of faces? Several kinds of evidence suggest that the answer is no—that the face-recognition circuits develop as a result of the experience we have of seeing people's faces. Because of the extensive experience we have of looking at faces, we can become expert at recognizing them.

It appears that recognition of specific complex stimuli by experts, too, is disrupted by lesions that cause prosopagnosia: inability of a farmer to recognize his cows, inability of a bird expert to recognize different species of birds, and inability of a driver to recognize his own car except by reading its license plate (Bornstein et al., 1969; Damasio et al., 1982). Two functional-imaging studies (Gauthier et al., 2000; Xu, 2005) found that when bird or car experts (but not nonexperts) viewed pictures of birds or cars, the fusiform face area was activated. Another study (Gauthier et al., 1999) found that when people had spent a long time becoming familiar with computer-generated objects they called "greebles," viewing the greebles activated the fusiform face area. Tarr and Gauthier (2000) suggested we should relabel the FFA as the *flexible* fusiform area.

A functional-imaging study (Golby et al., 2001) found higher activation of the fusiform face area when people viewed pictures of faces of members of their own race (African Americans or European Americans). Participants in this study recognized faces of people of their own race more accurately than faces of people of another race. Presumably, this difference reflected the fact that the people in the study had more experience seeing members of their own race, which indicates that expertise does appear to play a role in face recognition.

There is no doubt that a region of the fusiform gyrus plays an essential role in the analysis of particular faces. In fact, a face-responsive area exists in a similar location in the monkey brain, and this area contains neurons that respond to the faces of both monkeys and humans (Tsao et al., 2006). Two issues are still disputed by investigators interested in the FFA. First, is analysis of faces the sole function of this region, or is it really a "flexible fusiform area" involved in visual analysis of categories of very similar stimuli that can be discriminated only by experts? The activation of the FFA by greebles in the brains of greeble experts suggests that the FFA is an expertise area rather than an exclusively face area. However, perhaps a more important issue is the relative roles of genetic programming and experience in development of a brain region critically involved in face perception.

Developmental Aspects of Recognition A functional-imaging study indicates that although the relative size of the LOC, which responds to objects other than faces and

Figure 6.31 Fusiform Gyrus Responses to Faces

This "inflated" ventral view of the brain of an 8-year-old child and an adult from the study by Golarai et al., (2007) shows the regions of the fusiform gyrus that responded to the sight of faces. The FFA is much larger in adults.

(Courtesy of Golijeh Golarai, Department of Psychology, Stanford University.)

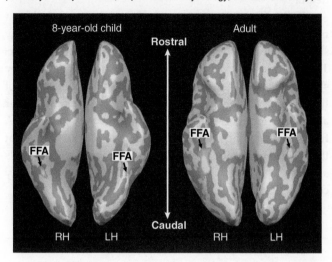

Figure 6.32 Preference of Newborn Babies for Viewing Stimuli that Resemble Faces

An asterisk above a stimulus indicates that the babies spent more time looking at it than the other member of the pair. If neither stimulus is marked with an asterisk, the baby indicated no preference.

(Adapted from Farroni, T., Johnson, M. H., Menon, E., Zulian, L., Faraguna, D., and Csibra, G., Newborns' preference for face-relevant stimuli: effects of contrast polarity, *Proceedings of the National Academy of Sciences, USA*, 2005, *102*, 17245–17250.)

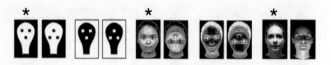

bodies, is the same in children and adults, the left FFA does not reach its eventual size until adulthood, and the ability to recognize faces is directly related to the expansion of the FFA (Golarai et al., 2007). These findings are consistent with the suggestion that the ability to recognize faces is a learned skill that grows with experience. Figure 6.31 shows the regions on the left and right fusiform cortex of an 8-year-old child and an adult. You can see the age-related size difference and also the difference between the size of this region in the left and right hemispheres.

Evidence indicates that newborn babies prefer to look at stimuli that resemble faces, which suggests the presence of prewired circuits in the human brain that dispose babies to look at faces and hence learn to recognize them. Farroni et al., (2005) presented newborn babies (between 13 and 168 hours old) with pairs of stimuli and found that they preferred to look at the ones that bore the closest resemblance to faces viewed in their normal, upright orientation, with the lighting coming from above, as it normally does. Figure 6.32 illustrates the stimuli that Farroni and her colleagues used. An asterisk above a stimulus indicates that the babies spent more time looking at it than at the other member of the pair. If neither stimulus is marked with an asterisk, that means that the baby indicated no preference—and as you can see, these pairs of stimuli bore the least resemblance to a face illuminated from above.

A review of the literature by Johnson (2005) suggests that a baby's preference for faces is controlled by a fast, low-spatial-frequency, subcortical pathway that is present in newborn infants. This circuit survives in many adults with prosopagnosia caused by cortical damage, who can realize that they are looking at a face even though they cannot recognize it and can even recognize facial expressions such as

happiness, fear, or anger. (This phenomenon is discussed in more detail in Chapter 11, which deals with emotion.) The subcortical pathway guarantees that babies will look at faces, which increases social bonding with other humans as well as facilitating the development of face-sensitive circuits in the cerebral cortex.

A study by Le Grand et al., (2001) discovered that the experience of seeing faces very early in life plays a critical role in the development of the skills necessary for recognizing them later in life. The investigators tested the ability of people (aged 9–21 years) who had been born with congenital cataracts to recognize subtle differences between pairs of faces. These people had been unable to see more than light and dark until they received eye surgery at 62–187 days of age that made normal vision possible. The early visual deprivation resulted in a severe deficit, compared with the performance of control participants, in recognizing the facial differences.

A follow-up study by Le Grand et al., (2003) tested people who were born with cataracts in only one eye. Because of the immaturity of the newborn brain, visual information received by one eye is transmitted only to the contralateral visual cortex. (You may recall that we said earlier in this chapter that it is not correct to say that each hemisphere receives visual information solely from the contralateral eye. However, our admonition does not apply to newborn babies.) This means that the right hemisphere of a person born with a cataract in the left eye does not receive patterned visual information until the cataract is removed. Le Grand and his colleagues predicted that because the right fusiform gyrus is critical for facial recognition, people born with cataracts in their left eye would show a deficit in recognizing faces but that people born with cataracts in the right eye would show normal discrimination—and that is exactly what they found.

As we will see in Chapter 17, people with autism spectrum disorder have difficulty developing typical social relations with other people. Grelotti et al., (2002) found that people with this disorder showed a deficit in the ability to recognize faces and that looking at faces failed to activate the fusiform gyrus. (See Figure 6.33.) The authors speculate

Figure 6.33 fMRI of the Brain During Facial Recognition

fMRI maps of the brain during face perception. Activation of the fusiform gyrus to faces is shown in red/yellow and identified by arrows in a typically developing young adult (a). Note the clear focus of face-related activation bilaterally in the fusiform gyrus. In contrast, a young adult with autism shows a lack of activation (b).

(Grelotti, D. J., Gauthier, I., & Schultz, R. T., Social interest and the development of cortical face specialization: What autism teaches us about face processing, *Developmental Psychobiology*, 2002, *40*(3), 213–225.)

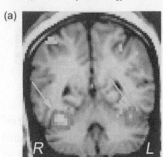
(a)

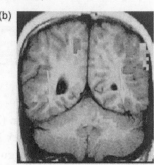
(b)

that the lack of interest in other people, caused by the brain abnormalities responsible for autism spectrum disorder, resulted in a lack of motivation that normally promotes the acquisition of expertise in recognizing faces as a child grows up. Chapter 17 discusses autism spectrum disorder in more detail.

Williams syndrome is a genetic condition caused by a mutation on chromosome 7. People with this disorder usually show intellectual deficits and an intense interest in music. They are generally very sociable, charming, and kind. They show great interest in other people and spend a great deal of time looking closely at their faces. They are generally better at recognizing faces than people without the syndrome. A functional-imaging study by Golarai et al., (2010) found that the fusiform face area was enlarged in people with William's syndrome and that the size of the FFA was positively correlated with a person's ability to recognize faces.

Section Review

Perception of Form

LO 6.16 Examine the benefit of neural circuits that analyze spatial frequency in the striate cortex.

Small objects, details within a large object, and large objects with sharp edges provide a signal rich in high frequencies, whereas large areas of light and dark are represented by low frequencies. Possessing neural circuits that can differentiate between these types of stimuli is beneficial in filtering noise from a visual stimulus, making the image more clear in the human visual system, and allowing an individual to perceive the underlying form.

LO 6.17 Use examples from the research literature to support the roles of the ventral stream and fusiform face area in perception of form.

Recognition of visual patterns and identification of particular objects takes place in the inferior temporal cortex (part of the ventral stream) in primates. It is here that analyses of form and color are put together, and perceptions of three-dimensional objects and backgrounds are achieved. For example, studies have found neurons in the inferior temporal cortex that respond specifically to objects that have been seen many times but not to unfamiliar objects. Damage to the human extrastriate cortex can cause a category of deficits known as visual agnosia, a failure to recognize familiar objects or categories of objects, including faces. The fusiform face area is specifically devoted to facial recognition. Development of this region may be a result of extensive experience looking at faces; expertise with other complex stimuli such as artificial creatures (greebles) causes the development of circuits devoted to the perception of these stimuli as well. Development of the fusiform face area is altered in people with autism spectrum disorder, possibly because of insufficient motivation to become expert in recognizing other people's faces.

Thought Question

A classmate is having trouble remembering the locations and functions of the dorsal and ventral visual processing streams. To help your peer, devise a strategy for remembering these important pathways, the brain regions they involve, and their functions.

Perception of Spatial Location

Perception of spatial location requires contributions from the retina, striate, and extrastriate cortex. Together, these structures contribute to depth perception, perceiving and remembering the locations of objects, and controlling movements of the eyes and the limbs.

Role of the Retina

LO 6.18 Identify the retina's contributions to perception of spatial location.

We perceive depth by many means, most of which involve cues that can be detected monocularly, that is, by one eye alone. For example, perspective, relative retinal size, loss of detail through the effects of atmospheric haze, and relative

Binocular cues help us to perceive depth.

Veronica Lara/Shutterstock

apparent movement of retinal images as we move our heads all contribute to depth perception and do not require binocular vision. However, binocular vision provides a vivid perception of depth through the process of stereoscopic vision, or *stereopsis*. If you have seen a three-dimensional movie, you know what we mean. Stereopsis is particularly important in the visual guidance of fine movements of the hands and fingers.

Role of the Striate Cortex

LO 6.19 Describe the contributions of retinal disparity and the dorsal and ventral streams to visual perception of spatial location.

Most neurons in the striate cortex are *binocular*—that is, they respond to visual stimulation of either eye. Many of these binocular cells, especially those found in a layer that receives information from the magnocellular system, have response patterns that appear to contribute to the perception of depth (Poggio and Poggio, 1984). In most cases the cells respond most vigorously (by firing action potentials) when each eye sees a stimulus in a slightly *different* location. That is, the neurons respond to **retinal disparity,** a stimulus that produces images on slightly different parts of the retina of each eye. This is exactly the information that is needed for stereopsis: Each eye sees a three dimensional scene slightly differently, and the presence of retinal disparity indicates differences in the distance of objects from the observer.

Many neurons throughout almost all regions of the visual cortex are responsive to binocular disparity, which, as we saw earlier, serves as the basis for stereoscopic depth perception (Parker, 2007; Roe et al., 2007). The disparity-sensitive neurons found in the dorsal stream, which is

involved in spatial perception, respond to large, extended visual surfaces, whereas those found in the ventral stream, which is involved in object perception, respond to the contours of three-dimensional objects.

Role of the Extrastriate Cortex

LO 6.20 Discuss examples from research literature that support the role of the extrastriate cortex in perception of spatial location.

The parietal lobe is involved in spatial and somatosensory perception, and it receives visual, auditory, somatosensory, and vestibular information to perform these tasks. Damage to the parietal lobes disrupts performance on a variety of tasks that require perceiving and remembering the locations of objects and controlling movements of the eyes and the limbs. The dorsal stream of the visual association cortex terminates in the posterior parietal cortex.

The anatomy of the posterior parietal cortex is shown in Figure 6.34. We see an "inflated" dorsal view of the left hemisphere of a human brain. Five regions within the

Figure 6.34 The Posterior Parietal Cortex

An "inflated" dorsal view of the left hemisphere of a human brain shows the anatomy of the posterior parietal cortex.

(Adapted from Astafiev, S. V., Shulman, G. L., Stanley, C. M., et al., Functional organization of human intraparietal and frontal cortex for attending, looking, and pointing, *Journal of Neuroscience*, 2003, *23*, 4689–4699.)

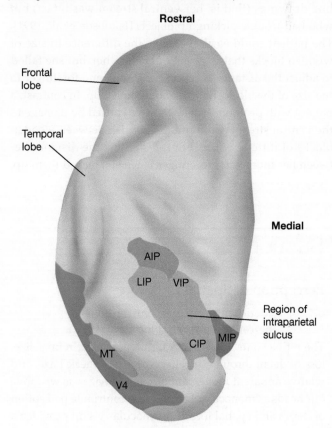

intraparietal sulcus (IPS) are of particular interest: AIP, LIP, VIP, CIP, and MIP (anterior, lateral, ventral, caudal, and medial IPS) are indicated.

Single-unit studies with monkeys and functional-imaging studies with humans indicate that neurons in the IPS are involved in visual attention and control of saccadic eye movements (LIP and VIP), visual control of reaching and pointing (VIP and MIP), visual control of grasping and manipulating hand movements (AIP), and perception of depth from stereopsis (CIP) (Astafiev et al., 2003; Culham and Kanwisher, 2001; Frey et al., 2005; Snyder et al., 2000; Tsao et al., 2003).

Goodale and his colleagues (Goodale and Milner, 1992; Goodale and Westwood, 2004; Goodale et al., 1994) suggest that the primary function of the dorsal stream of the visual cortex is to guide actions rather than simply to perceive spatial locations. As Ungerleider and Mishkin (1982) originally put it, the ventral and dorsal streams tell us "what" and "where." Goodale and his colleagues suggested that the better terms are "what" and "*how.*" First, they noted that the visual cortex of the posterior parietal lobe is extensively connected to regions of the frontal lobe involved in controlling eye movements, reaching movements of the limbs, and grasping movements of the hands and fingers. Second, they noted that damage to the dorsal stream can produce deficits in visually guided movements. (Chapter 8 discusses in more detail the role of the posterior parietal cortex in control of movements.) They cited the case of a woman with damage to the dorsal stream who had no difficulty recognizing line drawings (that is, her ventral stream was intact) but who had trouble picking up objects (Jakobson et al., 1991). The patient could easily perceive the difference in size of wooden blocks that were set out before her, but she failed to adjust the distance between her thumb and forefinger to the size of the block she was about to pick up. In contrast, a patient with profound visual agnosia caused by damage to the ventral stream could not distinguish between wooden blocks of different sizes but *could* adjust the distance between her thumb and forefinger when she picked them up.

She made this adjustment by means of vision, before she actually touched them (Goodale et al., 1994; Milner et al., 1991). A functional-imaging study of this patient (James et al., 2003) showed normal activity in the dorsal stream while she was picking up objects—especially in the anterior intraparietal sulcus (AIP), which is involved in manipulating and grasping.

The suggestion by Goodale and his colleagues seems a reasonable one. Certainly, the dorsal stream is involved in perception of the location of object's space—but then, if its primary role is to direct movements, it *must* be involved in location of these objects, or else how could it direct movements toward them? In addition, it must contain information about the size and shape of objects, or else how could it control the distance between thumb and forefinger?

Two functional-imaging studies provide further evidence that the dorsal stream is involved in visual control of movement. Valyear et al., (2006) presented photographs of pairs of elongated stimuli, one after the other, and noted which regions of the brain responded to the difference between the two stimuli. They found that a region of the ventral stream responded differentially to pairs of stimuli that differed in their form (for example, a fork versus a clarinet) but did not distinguish between the same object shown in different orientations (for example, one tipped 45 degrees to the right of vertical and the other tipped 45 degrees to the left). In contrast, a region of the dorsal stream distinguished between different orientations but ignored changes in the identity of the two objects. A follow-up study published the next year (Rice et al., 2007) showed volunteers photographs of two different types of objects: graspable ones, such as forks and hammers, and nongraspable ones, such as tractors and pieces of furniture. The investigators found that, as before, the region of the dorsal stream ignored changes in the identity of the objects but distinguished between orientations. However, the region distinguished between the orientations only of stimuli that a person could grasp. This region did *not* distinguish between the orientations of photos of stimuli that could not be picked up, such as tractors and pieces of furniture.

Section Review

Perception of Spatial Location

LO 6.18 Identify the retina's contributions to perception of spatial location.

The retina contributes to perspective, relative retinal size, loss of detail through the effects of atmospheric haze, and relative apparent movement of retinal images as we move our heads as monocular features that contribute perception of depth and spatial location. Binocular vision provides a

vivid perception of depth through the process of stereopsis involving information from both retinas.

LO 6.19 Describe the contributions of retinal disparity and the dorsal and ventral streams to visual perception of spatial location.

Most neurons in the striate cortex are binocular and contribute to depth perception via retinal disparity. The disparity-sensitive neurons found in the dorsal stream, which is involved in spatial perception, respond to large, extended visual surfaces, whereas those found in the ventral stream, which is involved in object perception, respond to the contours of three-dimensional objects.

LO 6.20 Discuss examples from research literature that support the role of the extrastriate cortex in perception of spatial location.

The dorsal stream of the extrastriate cortex terminates in the parietal cortex. The parietal lobe is involved in spatial and somatosensory perception, and it receives visual, auditory, somatosensory, and vestibular information to perform these tasks. Single-unit studies with monkeys and functional-imaging studies with humans indicate that neurons in the intraparietal sulcus (IPS) are involved in visual attention and control of saccadic eye movements (LIP and VIP), visual control of reaching and pointing (VIP and MIP), visual control of grasping and manipulating hand movements (AIP), and perception of depth from stereopsis (CIP).

Thought Question

As a well-known vision researcher in the future, you are asked to consult on a case study of an individual with an unusual agnosia. The female patient has been diagnosed with Turner syndrome, a genetic disorder in which females have only one functional copy of the X chromosome. Like many other women with Turner syndrome, the patient has form blindness (cannot perceive geometric shapes) and deficits in spatial perception but has otherwise normal vision. Suggest areas of the brain that may be involved in these visual agnosias.

Perception of Orientation and Movement

We need to know not only what things are, but also where they are located and where they are going. Without the ability to perceive the direction and velocity of movement of objects, we would have no way to predict where they will be. We would be unable to catch the objects (or avoid letting them catch us). This section examines the perception of movement.

Role of the Striate Cortex

LO 6.21 Explain how cells in the striate cortex identify orientation and function as movement detectors.

Most neurons in the striate cortex are sensitive to orientation. That is, if a line or an edge (the border of a light and a dark region) is positioned in the cell's receptive field and rotated around its center, the cell will respond only when the line is in a particular position—a particular orientation. Some neurons respond best to a vertical line, some to a horizontal line, and some to a line oriented somewhere in between. Figure 6.35 shows the responses of a neuron in the striate cortex when lines were presented at various orientations. As you can see, this neuron responded best when a vertical line was presented in its receptive field.

Role of the Extrastriate Cortex

LO 6.22 Describe the roles of region V5, MSTd, and the extrastriate body in the perception of movement.

Research with humans and other animals has helped to reveal the role of the extrastriate cortex in visual perception

Figure 6.35 Orientation Sensitivity

An orientation-sensitive neuron in the striate cortex will become active only when a line of a particular orientation appears within its receptive field. For example, the neuron depicted in this figure responds best to a bar that is vertically oriented.

(Adapted from Hubel, D. H., and Wiesel, T. N., Receptive fields of single neurones in the cat's striate cortex, *Journal of Physiology [London]*, 1959, *148*, 574–591.)

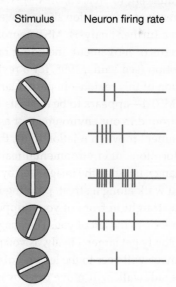

of orientation and movement. We will look at both fields of study in this section.

STUDIES WITH LABORATORY ANIMALS Area V5 of the extrastriate cortex—also known as area MT, for *medial temporal*—contains neurons that respond to movement. Damage to this region severely disrupts a monkey's ability to perceive moving stimuli (Siegel and Andersen, 1986). Area V5 receives input directly from the striate cortex and from several other regions of the extrastriate cortex. It also receives input from the superior colliculus, which is involved in visual reflexes, including reflexive control of eye movements.

Accurately determining the velocity and direction of movement of an object is an important ability. That moving object could be a prey animal trying to run away, a predator trying to catch you, or a projectile you are trying to catch (or keep from hitting you). If we are to accurately track moving objects, the information received by V5 must be up to date. In fact, the axons that transmit information from the magnocellular system are thick and heavily myelinated, which increases the rate at which they conduct action potentials. Petersen et al. (1988) recorded the responses of neurons in areas V4 and V5 and found that visual information reached the V5 neurons sooner than it reached those in area V4, whose neurons are involved in the analysis of form and color.

The input from the superior colliculus contributes in some way to the movement sensitivity of neurons in area V5. Rodman et al., (1989, 1990) found that destruction of the striate cortex or the superior colliculus alone does not eliminate the movement sensitivity of V5 neurons, but destruction of both areas does. The roles played by these two sources of input are not yet known. Clearly, both inputs provide useful information; Seagraves et al., (1987) found that monkeys still could detect movement after lesions of the striate cortex but had difficulty estimating its rate.

A region adjacent to area V5, area MST, or *medial superior temporal*, receives information about movement from V5 and performs a further analysis. MST neurons respond to complex patterns of movement, including radial, circular, and spiral motion (see Vaina, 1998, for a review). One important function of this region—in particular, the dorsolateral MST, or MSTd—appears to be analysis of **optic flow.** As we move around in our environment or as objects in our environment move in relation to us, the sizes, shapes, and locations of environmental features on our retinas change. Imagine the image seen by a video camera as you walk along a street, pointing the lens of the camera straight in front of you. Suppose you will pass a mailbox to the left of you. The image of the mailbox will slowly get larger. Finally, as you pass the mailbox, its image will veer to the left and disappear. Points on the sidewalk will move downward, and branches of trees that you pass under will move upward. Analysis of the relative movement of the visual elements of your environment—the optic flow—will tell you where you are heading, how fast you are approaching different items in front of you, and whether you will pass to the left or right (or under or over) these items. The point toward which we are moving does not move, but all other points in the visual scene move away from it. Therefore, this point is called the *center of expansion.* If we keep moving in the same direction, we will eventually bump into an object that lies at the center of expansion. We can also use optic flow to determine whether an object approaching us will hit us or pass us by.

Bradley et al., (1996) recorded from single units in MSTd of monkeys and found that particular neurons responded selectively to the center of expansion located in particular regions of the visual field. These neurons compensated for eye movements, which means that their activity identified the location in the environment toward which an animal was moving. Britten and van Wezel (1998) found that electrical stimulation of MSTd disrupted monkeys' ability to perceive the apparent direction in which they were heading; thus, these neurons do indeed seem to play an essential role in heading estimation derived from optic flow.

STUDIES WITH HUMANS   Research with human participants has been essential in improving understanding of the functions of extrastriate cortex in the perception of motion, optic flow, form from motion, biological motion, and the compensation of eye movements in motion.

Perception of Motion   Functional-imaging studies suggest that motion-sensitive area V5 is found within the inferior temporal sulcus of the human brain (Dukelow et al., 2001). However, a more recent study suggests that this region is located in the lateral occipital cortex, between the lateral and inferior occipital sulci (Annese et al., 2005). Annese and his colleagues examined sections of the brains of deceased individuals that had been stained for the presence of myelin. As we just saw, area V5 receives a dense projection of thick, heavily myelinated axons, and the location of this region was revealed by the myelin stain. (See Figure 6.36.)

Figure 6.36 The Location of Visual Area V5

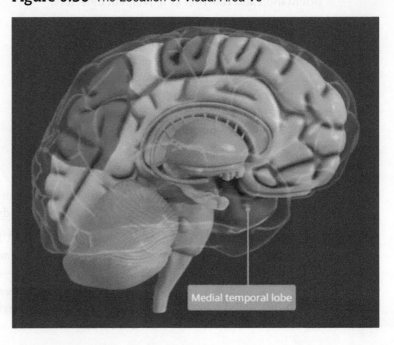

Medial temporal lobe

Bilateral damage to the human brain that includes area V5 produces an inability to perceive movement—**akinetopsia.** Instead of a smooth progression of movement in their environment, individuals with akinetopsia experience a series of still images that appear to refresh periodically. For example, Zihl et al., (1991) reported the case of a woman (L. M.) with bilateral lesions of the lateral occipital cortex and area V5.

Patient L. M. had an almost total loss of movement perception. She was unable to cross a street without traffic lights because she could not judge the speed at which cars were moving. Although she could perceive movements, she found moving objects very unpleasant to look at. For example, while talking with another person, she avoided looking at the person's mouth because she found its movements very disturbing. When the investigators asked her to try to detect movements of a visual target in the laboratory, she said, "First the target is completely at rest. Then it suddenly jumps upwards and downwards" (Zihl et al., 1991, p. 22–44). She was able to see that the target was constantly changing its position, but she was unaware of any sensation of movement.

Walsh et al., (1998) used TMS to temporarily inactivate area V5 in a control group of volunteers. The investigators found that during the TMS procedure people were unable to detect which of several objects displayed on a computer screen was moving. When the current was off, the volunteers had no trouble detecting the motion. The current had no effect on the volunteers' ability to detect stimuli that varied in their form.

Optic Flow   As we saw in the previous subsection, neurons in area MSTd of the monkey brain respond to optic flow, an important source of information about the direction in which the animal is heading. A functional-imaging study by Peuskens et al. (2001) found that area V5 became active when people judged their heading while viewing a display showing optic flow. Vaina and her colleagues (Jornales et al., 1997; Vaina, 1998) found that people with lesions that included this region were able to perceive motion but could not perceive heading from optic flow.

Form from Motion   Perception of movement can even help us to perceive three-dimensional forms—a phenomenon known as *form from motion.* Johansson (1973) demonstrated just how much information we derive from movement. He dressed actors in black and attached small lights to several points on their bodies, such as their wrists, elbows, shoulders, hips, knees, and feet. He made movies of the actors in a darkened room while they were performing various behaviors, such as walking, running, jumping, limping, doing push-ups, and dancing with a partner who was also equipped with lights. Even though observers who watched the films could see only a pattern of moving lights against a dark background, they could readily perceive the pattern as belonging to a moving human and could identify the behavior the actor was performing. Subsequent studies (Barclay et al., 1978; Kozlowski and Cutting, 1977) showed that people could even tell, with reasonable accuracy, the sex of the actor wearing the lights. The cues appeared to be supplied by the relative amounts of movement of the shoulders and hips as the person walked.

McCleod et al., (1996) suggest that the ability to perceive form from motion does not involve area V5. They reported that patient L. M. (studied by Zihl et al., 1991) could recognize people depicted solely by moving points of light *even though she could not perceive the movements themselves.* Vaina and her colleagues (reported by Vaina, 1998) described a patient with a lesion in the medial right occipital lobe who showed just the opposite deficits: Patient R. A. could perceive movement—even complex radial and circular optic flow—but could not perceive form from motion. Thus, perception of motion and perception of form from motion involve different regions of the visual association cortex.

A functional-imaging study by Grossman et al., (2000) found that when people viewed a video that showed form from motion, a small region on the ventral bank of the posterior end of the superior temporal sulcus became active. More activity was seen in the right hemisphere, whether the images were presented to the left or right visual field. Grossman and Blake (2001) found that this region became active even when people *imagined* that they were watching points of light representing form from motion. (See Figure 6.37.) Grossman et al., (2005) found that inactivation of this area with TMS disrupted perception of form from motion.

Perception of form from motion might not seem like a phenomenon that has any importance outside the laboratory. However, this phenomenon does occur under natural

Figure 6.37 Responses to Viewing Form from Motion
This figure shows horizontal and lateral views of neural activity that occurred while the subject was viewing videos of biological motion. Maximum activity is seen in a small region on the ventral bank of the posterior end of the superior temporal sulcus, primarily in the right hemisphere.

(Based on Grossman, E. D., and Blake, R., Brain activity evoked by inverted and imagined biological motion, *Vision Research*, 2001, *41*, 1475–1482.)

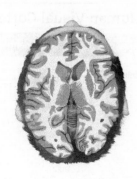
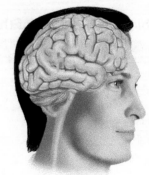

circumstances, and it appears to involve brain mechanisms different from those involved in normal object perception. For example, as we saw in the prologue to this chapter, people with visual agnosia can often still perceive *actions* (such as someone pretending to stir something in a bowl as described in the opening case study of this chapter) even though they cannot recognize objects by sight. They may be able to recognize friends by the way they walk, even though they cannot recognize the friends' faces.

Lê et al., (2002) reported the case of patient S. B., a 30-year-old man whose ventral stream was damaged extensively bilaterally by an infection when he was 3 years old. As a result, he was unable to recognize objects, faces, textures, or colors. However, he could perceive movement and could even catch a ball that was thrown to him. Furthermore, he could recognize other people's arm and hand movements that mimed common activities such as cutting something with a knife or brushing one's teeth, and he could recognize people he knew by their gait.

Biological Motion   As we saw earlier in this chapter, neurons in the extrastriate body area (EBA) are activated by the sight of human body parts. A functional-imaging study by Pelphrey et al., (2005) showed participants a computer-generated image of a person who made hand, eye, and mouth movements. (Note that the participants were perceiving motion made by a human being, not form from the motion of individual points of light as described in the previous subsection.) The investigators found that movements of different body parts activated different locations just anterior to the EBA.

Compensation for Eye Movements   So far, this discussion has been confined to movement of objects in the visual field. But if a person moves his or her eyes, head, or whole body, the image on the retina will move even if everything within the person's visual field remains stable. Often, of course, *both* kinds of movements will occur at the same time. The problem for the visual system is to determine which of these images are produced by movements of objects in the environment and which are produced by the person's own eye, head, and body movements.

To illustrate this problem, think about how a paragraph of text looks as you read it. If we could make a recording of one of your retinas, we would see that the image of the text projected there is in constant movement as your eyes make several saccades along a line and then snap back to the beginning of the next line. Yet the text seems perfectly still to you. On the other hand, if you look at a single point (say, a period at the end of a sentence) and then move the image around while following the period with your eyes, you perceive the text as moving, even though the image on your retina remains relatively stable. (Try it.) Then think about the images on your retina while you are driving in busy traffic, constantly moving your eyes around to keep track of your own location and that of other cars moving in different directions at different speeds. You are perceiving not only the simple movement of objects, but optic flow as well, which helps you keep track of the trajectories of the objects relative to each other and to yourself.

Haarmeier et al., (1997) reported the case of a patient with bilateral damage to the extrastriate cortex who could not compensate for image movement caused by head and eye movements. When the patient moved his eyes, it looked to him as if the world was moving in the opposite direction. Without the ability to compensate for head and eye movements, any movement of a retinal image was perceived as movement of the environment. On the basis of evidence from EEG and MEG (magnetoencephalography) studies in human participants and single-unit recordings in monkeys, Thier et al., (2001) suggest that this compensation involves extrastriate cortex located at the junction of the temporal and parietal lobes near a region involved in the analysis of signals from the vestibular system. Indeed, the investigators note that when patients with damage to this region move their eyes, the lack of compensation for these movements makes them feel very dizzy.

The previous sections explored the structures and functions of the visual system related to perception of color, form, spatial location, orientation, and movement. Although these sections included a lot of information, you may have noticed themes. For example, each type of perception involved areas of the striate cortex, extrastriate cortex, and the dorsal and ventral processing streams. Much of this information has been summarized in Table 6.3. Review this table to ensure you understand the roles of these structures in the various aspects of visual processing.

Table 6.3   Regions of the Human Visual Cortex and Their Functions

Region of Human Visual Cortex	Name of Region (If Different)	Function
V1	Striate cortex	Small modules that analyze orientation, movement, spatial frequency, retinal disparity, and color
V2		Further analysis of information from V1
Ventral Stream		
V3+VP		Further analysis of information from V2
V3A		Processing of visual information across entire visual field of contralateral eye

Region of Human Visual Cortex	Name of Region (If Different)	Function
V4d/V4v	V4 dorsal/ventral	Analysis of form; processing of color constancy; V4d = lower visual field, V4v = upper visual field
V8		Color perception
LO	Lateral occipital complex	Object recognition
FFA	Fusiform face area	Face recognition, object recognition by experts ("flexible fusiform area")
PPA	Parahippocampal place area	Recognition of particular places
EBA	Extrastriate body area	Perception of body parts other than face
Dorsal Stream		
V7		Visual attention; control of eye movements
MT/MST	Medial temporal/medial superior temporal (named for locations in monkey brain)	Perception of motion; perception of biological motion and optic flow in specific subregions
LIP	Lateral intraparietal area	Visual attention; control of saccadic eye movements
VIP	Ventral intraparietal area	Control of visual attention to particular locations; control of eye movements; visual control of pointing
AIP	Anterior intraparietal area	Visual control of hand movements: grasping, manipulation
MIP	Middle intraparietal area; parietal reach region (monkeys)	Visual control of reaching
CIP	Caudal intraparietal area; caudal parietal disparity region	Perception of depth from stereopsis

Section Review

Perception of Orientation and Movement

LO 6.21 **Explain how cells in the striate cortex identify orientation and function as movement detectors.**

Most neurons in the striate cortex are sensitive to orientation and respond by increasing their rate of firing action potentials when a line is in a particular position in their receptive field.

LO 6.22 **Describe the roles of region V5, MSTd, and the extrastriate body in the perception of movement.**

Area V5 of the extrastriate cortex (area MT) contains neurons that respond to movement. Bilateral damage to the human brain that includes area V5 produces akinetopsia.

MST neurons receive information from V5 and respond to complex patterns of movement, including radial, circular, and spiral motion. More specifically, MSTd neurons analyze optic flow. Movements of different body parts activate cells in the extrastriate body.

Thought Question

Two patients are in the neurology department. In one patient, the dorsal pathway is disrupted due to an infarct in the parietal lobe, and in another patient the ventral pathway is disrupted due to an infarct in the lower temporal region. Which patient is more likely to adapt to daily routine activities, and why?

Chapter Review Questions

1. Discuss the anatomical structures of the eye and their functions.

2. Describe the structure and function of different photoreceptors, and explain the mechanism of transduction of visual stimuli in photoreceptors.

3. Describe the arrangement of various cell types in the retina and explain how this arrangement leads to coding of visual information to be carried by the optic nerves.

4. Illustrate the visual pathway from the retina to the primary visual cortex.

5. Describe the trichromatic theory and the color opponent theory of color vision, and discuss the genetic basis of color blindness.

6. Describe the layers of the striate cortex and discuss how this arrangement helps in the detection of orientation.

7. Discuss the role of the dorsal and ventral pathways of the extrastriate cortex in various aspects of visual perception.

8. Describe the role of the striate cortex in perception of form, spatial location, and movement.

Chapter 7
Audition, the Body Senses, and the Chemical Senses

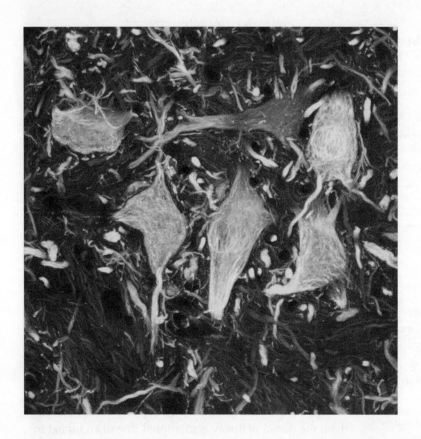

Chapter Outline

Learning Objectives

LO 7.1 Describe the characteristics of sound that are perceived by humans.

LO 7.2 Identify the structures of the outer, middle, and inner ear.

LO 7.3 Compare the structure, function, and location of hair cells as they contribute to transduction of auditory information.

LO 7.4 Describe the structure and function of the cochlear nerve, subcortical structures, and cortex in the auditory pathway.

LO 7.5 Contrast place and rate coding in perception of pitch.

LO 7.6 Contrast how loudness in high- and low-frequency sounds is represented in the auditory system using action potentials.

LO 7.7 Identify the aspects of timbre that must be distinguished by auditory processing.

LO 7.8 Compare the roles of arrival time, phase difference, intensity difference, and timbre in perception of spatial location.

LO 7.9 Describe the roles of the two processing streams of the auditory cortex in the perception of complex sounds.

LO 7.10 Summarize the biological basis for perception of music.

LO 7.11 Identify the structures and functions of the vestibular apparatus.

LO 7.12 Outline the vestibular pathway.

LO 7.13 Provide examples of stimuli that activate receptors for the somatosenses.

LO 7.14 Describe the anatomy and somatosensory receptors of the skin.

LO 7.15 Describe receptors involved in the perception of touch, temperature, pain, and itch.

LO 7.16 Describe the pathway for somatosensory processing from nerves to subcortical and cortical structures.

LO 7.17 Describe why pain is experienced, the perceptual and behavior effects of pain, and how pain perception can be modified.

LO 7.18 List the six qualities of taste stimuli.

LO 7.19 Identify the location and structure of taste buds and taste receptor cells.

LO 7.20 Outline the process of transduction for perception of salt, sour, bitter, sweet, and umami.

LO 7.21 Describe the path of gustatory processing from nerves to subcortical and cortical structures.

LO 7.22 Identify the stimulus and describe the structure and function of the olfactory apparatus.

LO 7.23 Summarize the process of transducing the signal from an odorant molecule for olfactory perception.

LO 7.24 Explain how a relatively small number of receptors can detect a wide variety of odors.

Thirteen-year-old Ashlyn was in the kitchen, stirring ramen noodles, when the spoon slipped from her hand and dropped into the pot of boiling water. Without thinking, she reached her right hand in to retrieve the spoon, then took her hand out of the water and stood looking at it, emotionless. She walked to the sink and ran cold water over her hands and the many faded white scars from previous accidents. She then called to her mother who rushed to her daughter's side with ice and pressed it against her daughter's hand, relieved that the burn wasn't worse.

Throughout her childhood, Ashlyn was asked lots of questions by her schoolmates and friends. Was she Superman? Could she feel pain from a punch to the face? Could she walk across burning coals as if she were walking on grass? Would it hurt if she were stabbed in the arm? The answers are no, no, yes, no. She can feel pressure and texture. She can feel a hug and a handshake. She cannot feel pain (Heckert, 2012).

*****

Ashlyn has a congenital insensitivity to pain. Due to a gene mutation, her nervous system developed without functional nociceptors; specialized neurons activated by painful stimuli. You'll read more about pain receptors and pathways in the somatosenses section of this chapter. Ashlyn's case study introduces several important concepts from this chapter including the role of specialized somatosensory receptors and the importance of senses in guiding our behavior.

This chapter contains five sections: audition, the vestibular system, the somatosenses, gustation, and olfaction. All are vital to how we perceive and navigate the world around us. The figure here presents the sensory association cortex, which both play important roles in the senses described in this chapter.

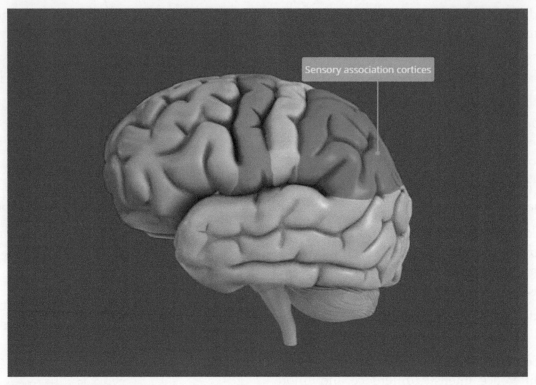

The sensory association cortex.

Audition

Hearing, or *audition*, has three primary functions: to detect sounds, to determine the location of their sources, and to recognize the identity of these sources—and thus their meaning and relevance to us (Heffner and Heffner, 1990; Yost, 1991). The auditory system does a phenomenal job of analyzing the vibrations that reach our ear. For example, we can understand speech, recognize a person's emotion from his or her voice, appreciate music, detect the approach of a vehicle or another person, or recognize an animal's call. We can recognize not only what the source of a sound is but also where it is located. This section describes the nature of the stimulus, the sensory receptors, the brain mechanisms devoted to audition, and some of the details of the physiology of auditory perception.

The Stimulus

LO 7.1 **Describe the characteristics of sound that are perceived by humans.**

We hear sounds, which are produced by objects that vibrate and set molecules of air into motion. When an object

vibrates, its movements cause molecules of air surrounding it to alternate between compressing and expanding, producing waves that travel away from the object at approximately 1,200 kilometers (km) per hour. If the vibration ranges between approximately 30 and 20,000 times per second, these waves will stimulate receptor cells in human ears and will be perceived as sounds. (See Figure 7.1.)

Figure 7.1 Sound Waves

Changes in air pressure from sound waves move the eardrum in and out. Air molecules are closer together in regions of higher pressure and farther apart in regions of lower pressure.

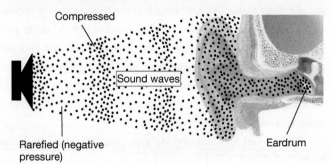

Compressed

Sound waves

Rarefied (negative pressure)

Eardrum

Figure 7.2 Physical and Perceptual Dimensions of Sound Waves

Sound has three perceptual dimensions: Pitch, loudness, and timbre.

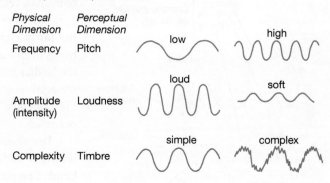

Physical Dimension	Perceptual Dimension		
Frequency	Pitch	low	high
Amplitude (intensity)	Loudness	loud	soft
Complexity	Timbre	simple	complex

In Chapter 6, we saw that light has three perceptual dimensions—hue, brightness, and saturation—that correspond to three physical dimensions. Similarly, sounds vary in their pitch, loudness, and timbre. The perceived **pitch** of an auditory stimulus is determined by the frequency of vibration, which is measured in **hertz (Hz),** or cycles per second. **Loudness** is a function of intensity—the degree to which the compressions and expansions of air differ from each other. More vigorous vibrations of an object produce more intense sound waves and hence louder ones. **Timbre** provides information about the nature of the particular sound—for example, the sound of an oboe or a train whistle. Most natural acoustic stimuli are complex, consisting of several different frequencies of vibration. The particular mixture determines the sound's timbre. (See Figure 7.2.)

Anatomy of the Ear

LO 7.2 **Identify the structures of the outer, middle, and inner ear.**

The anatomy of the ear helps to direct sound waves to the auditory receptors. Structures of the ear can be organized by their location in the *outer, middle,* and *inner* ear. Figure 7.3 shows the outer anatomy of the ear and auditory canal and illustrates many of the structures of the middle and inner ear.

OUTER EAR Sound is funneled via the *pinna* (external ear) through the ear canal to the **tympanic membrane** (eardrum), which vibrates with the sound. When the tympanic membrane is damaged by trauma, infection, or autoimmune attack, hearing is impaired, particularly for sounds with low frequencies (Mehta et al., 2006).

Demonstrating the role of the pinna in sound localization, researchers created inserts that altered the shape of the pinna and asked volunteers to wear the inserts in one ear for up to six weeks. The volunteers' ability to localize the source of various sounds was significantly disrupted at first. After several days, however, auditory adaptation occurred and the volunteers were able to accurately determine the location of sounds (Hofman et al., 1998).

MIDDLE EAR The *middle ear* consists of a small hollow region behind the tympanic membrane. It contains the bones of the middle ear, called the **ossicles,** which are set into vibration by the tympanic membrane. The **malleus** (hammer) connects with the tympanic membrane and transmits vibrations via the **incus** (anvil) and **stapes** (stirrup) to the **cochlea,** the structure that contains the receptors. The bottom of the stapes presses against the membrane behind the **oval window,** the opening in the bone surrounding the cochlea. (Look again at Figure 7.3.)

INNER EAR The cochlea is part of the *inner ear.* It is filled with fluid and sounds transmitted through the air must be transferred into its liquid medium. This process normally is very inefficient—99.9 percent of the energy of airborne sound would be reflected away if the air impinged directly against the oval window of the cochlea. The chain of ossicles, however, serves as an efficient means of energy transmission. The bones provide a mechanical advantage, with the baseplate of the stapes making smaller but more forceful excursions against the oval window than the tympanic membrane makes against the malleus.

The name *cochlea* comes from the Greek word *kokhlos,* or "land snail." It is indeed snail-shaped, consisting of two and three-quarters turns of a gradually tapering cylinder, 35 mm long. The cochlea is divided longitudinally into three sections, the *scala vestibuli* ("entrance stairway"), the *scala media* ("middle stairway"), and the *scala tympani* ("tympanic stairway"), as shown in Figure 7.4. The receptive organ, known as the **organ**

Figure 7.3 Anatomy of the Ear

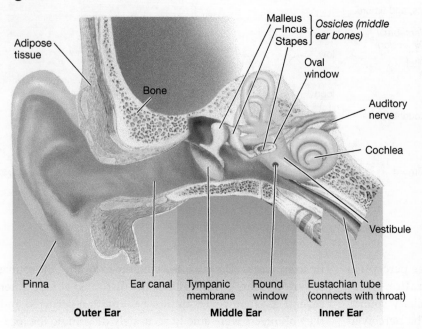

Adipose tissue

Bone

Malleus
Incus
Stapes

Ossicles (middle ear bones)

Oval window

Auditory nerve

Cochlea

Vestibule

Pinna

Ear canal

Tympanic membrane

Round window

Eustachian tube (connects with throat)

Outer Ear　　　　**Middle Ear**　　　　**Inner Ear**

cells, and they are anchored, via rodlike **Deiters's cells,** to the **basilar membrane.** The cilia of the hair cells pass through the *reticular membrane,* and the ends of some of them attach to the fairly rigid **tectorial membrane,** which hangs overhead like a shelf. Sound waves cause the basilar membrane to move relative to the tectorial membrane, which bends the cilia of the hair cells. This bending produces receptor potentials.

The vibratory energy exerted on the oval window causes the basilar membrane to bend. The portion of the basilar membrane that bends the most is determined by the frequency of the sound: High-frequency sounds cause the base of the membrane—the end nearest the oval window—to bend. A flexible membrane-covered opening, the **round window,** allows the fluid inside the cochlea to move back and forth. The base of the stapes vibrates against the membrane behind the oval window and introduces sound waves of high or low frequency into the cochlea. The vibrations cause part of the basilar membrane to flex

of Corti, consists of the *basilar membrane,* the *hair cells,* and the *tectorial membrane.* The auditory receptor cells are called **hair**

Figure 7.4 The Organ of Corti

This cross section through the cochlea shows the organ of Corti.

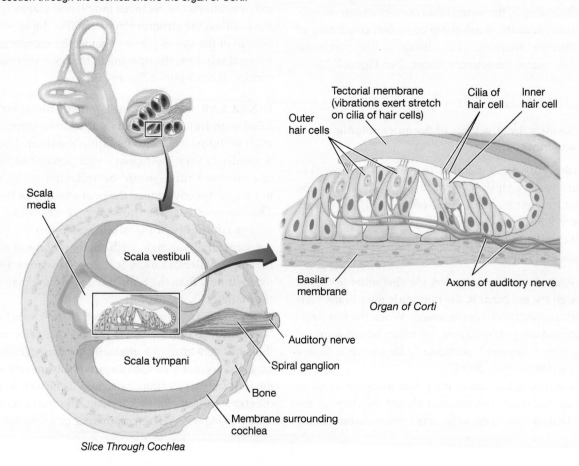

Scala media

Scala vestibuli

Basilar membrane

Scala tympani

Auditory nerve

Spiral ganglion

Bone

Membrane surrounding cochlea

Slice Through Cochlea

Tectorial membrane (vibrations exert stretch on cilia of hair cells)

Cilia of hair cell

Inner hair cell

Outer hair cells

Axons of auditory nerve

Organ of Corti

back and forth. Pressure changes in the fluid underneath the basilar membrane are transmitted to the membrane of the round window. When the base of the stapes pushes in, the membrane behind the round window bulges out. As we will see in a later subsection, different frequencies of sound vibrations cause different portions of the basilar membrane to flex. (See Figure 7.5.)

Auditory Hair Cells and the Transduction of Auditory Information

LO 7.3 **Compare the structure, function, and location of hair cells as they contribute to transduction of auditory information.**

Two types of auditory receptors, *inner* and *outer* auditory hair cells, are located on the basilar membrane. Hair cells contain **cilia,** fine hairlike projections, arranged in rows according to height. The human cochlea contains approximately 3,500 inner hair cells and 12,000 outer hair cells. The hair cells form synapses with dendrites of bipolar neurons whose axons bring auditory information to the brain.

The inner hair cells are necessary for normal hearing. In fact, mutant mice whose cochleas contain *only* outer hair cells apparently cannot hear at all (Deol and Gluecksohn-Waelsch, 1979). Subsequent research indicates that the outer hair cells are *effector* cells, involved in altering the mechanical characteristics of the basilar membrane and thus influencing the effects of sound vibrations on the inner hair cells. We will discuss the role of outer hair cells in the section on place coding of pitch.

The bases of the cilia are attached to the basilar membrane while the tips of the cilia of outer hair cells are attached to the tectorial membrane above. Sound waves cause both the basilar membrane and the tectorial membrane to flex up and down. These movements bend the cilia of the

hair cells in one direction or the other. The cilia of the inner hair cells do not touch the overlying tectorial membrane, but the relative movement of the two membranes causes the fluid within the cochlea to flow past them, making them bend back and forth, too.

Cilia contain a core of actin filaments surrounded by myosin filaments, and these proteins make the cilia rigid (Flock, 1977). Adjacent cilia are linked to each other by elastic filaments known as **tip links.** Each tip link is attached to the end of one cilium and to the side of an adjacent cilium. The points of attachment, known as **insertional plaques,** look dark under an electron microscope. Receptor potentials are triggered at the insertional plaques. Normally, tip links are slightly stretched, which means that they are under a small amount of tension. Thus, movement of the bundle of cilia in the direction of the tallest of them further stretches these linking fibers, whereas movement in the opposite direction relaxes them. The bending of the bundle of cilia causes receptor potentials (See Figure 7.6.)

Unlike the fluid that surrounds most neurons, the fluid that surrounds the auditory hair cells is rich in potassium. Each insertional plaque contains a single cation channel, identified as TRPA1, a member of the *transient receptor potential cation channel,* subfamily A, type 1 (Corey et al., 2004). (We mention the TRP family of receptors because this family includes receptors involved in perception of touch, temperature, and taste, and you will encounter them again later in the chapter.) When the bundle of cilia is straight, the probability of an individual ion channel being open is approximately 10 percent. This means that a small amount of the cations K^+ and Ca^{2+} diffuses into the cilium. When the bundle moves toward the tallest cilium, the increased tension on the tip links opens all the ion channels, the flow of cations into the cilia increases, and the membrane depolarizes. As a result, the

Figure 7.5 Responses to Sound Waves

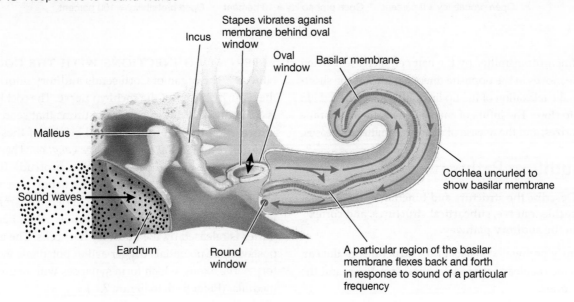

Incus

Stapes vibrates against membrane behind oval window

Oval window

Basilar membrane

Malleus

Sound waves

Eardrum

Round window

Cochlea uncurled to show basilar membrane

A particular region of the basilar membrane flexes back and forth in response to sound of a particular frequency

Figure 7.6 Transduction in Hair Cells of the Inner Ear

(a) The figure shows the appearance of the cilia of an auditory hair cell. (b) Movement of the bundle of cilia toward the tallest one increases the firing rate of the cochlear nerve axon attached to the hair cell, while movement away from the tallest one decreases it. (c) Movement toward the tallest cilium increase tension on the tip links, which opens the ion channels and increase the influx of K^+ and Ca^{2+} ions. Movement toward the shortest cilium removes tension from the tip links, which permits the ion channels to close, stopping the influx of cations.

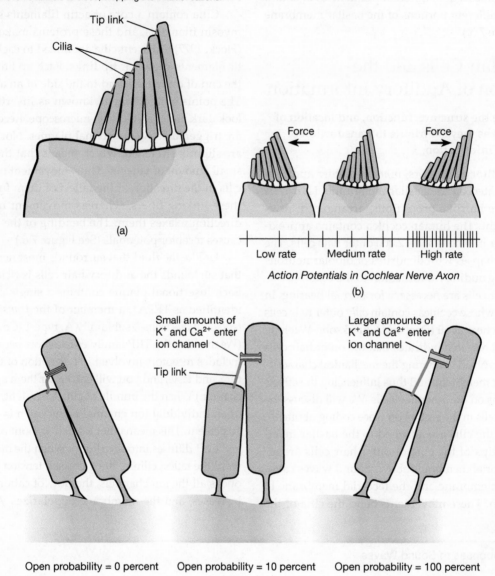

release of neurotransmitter by the hair cell increases. When the bundle moves in the opposite direction, toward the shortest cilium, the relaxation of the tip links allows the opened ion channels to close. The influx of cations ceases, the membrane hyperpolarizes, and the release of neurotransmitter decreases.

The Auditory Pathway

LO 7.4 **Describe the structure and function of the cochlear nerve, subcortical structures, and cortex in the auditory pathway.**

The auditory pathway consists of the structures of the ear, as well as the cochlear nerve, subcortical structures, and the auditory cortex.

AFFERENT CONNECTIONS WITH THE COCHLEAR NERVE The organ of Corti sends auditory information to the brain by means of the **cochlear nerve.** The cochlear nerve is a bundle of axons of bipolar neurons that send auditory information to the brain. The cell bodies of these bipolar neurons reside in the *cochlear nerve ganglion.* These unique neurons have axonal processes that protrude from both ends of the soma that can convey an action potential. One end of the axonal process acts like a dendrite, responding with excitatory postsynaptic potentials when neurotransmitter is released by the auditory hair cells. The excitatory postsynaptic potentials trigger action potentials in the auditory nerve axons, which form synapses with neurons in the medulla. (Refer back to Figure 7.4.)

EFFERENT CONNECTIONS WITH THE COCHLEAR NERVE The cochlear nerve contains efferent axons as well as afferent ones. The source of the efferent axons is the superior olivary complex, a group of nuclei in the medulla; thus, the efferent fibers constitute the **olivocochlear bundle.** The fibers form synapses directly on outer hair cells and on the dendrites that serve the inner hair cells. While the excitatory neurotransmitter at the afferent synapses is glutamate, the efferent terminal buttons secrete acetylcholine, which has an inhibitory effect on the hair cells. Why would neurons in the brain need to send messages to the cochlea? Several functions of this inhibitory pathway have been proposed, including a protective mechanism to prevent noise-induced damage to the cochlea (Ciuman, 2010).

SUBCORTICAL STRUCTURES The anatomy of the subcortical components of the auditory system is more complicated than that of the visual system. Rather than giving a detailed verbal description of the pathways here, we will refer you to Figure 7.7.

Note that axons enter the **cochlear nucleus** of the medulla and synapse there. Most of the neurons in the cochlear nucleus send axons to the **superior olivary complex,** also located in the medulla. Axons of neurons in these nuclei pass through a large fiber bundle called the **lateral lemniscus** to the inferior colliculus, located in the dorsal midbrain. Neurons there send their axons to the medial geniculate nucleus of the thalamus, which sends its axons to the auditory cortex of the temporal lobe. Each hemisphere of the brain receives information from both ears but primarily from the contralateral one. Some auditory information also makes its way to the cerebellum and reticular formation. Altogether, subcortical auditory processing requires many neurons and synapses in complicated networks that span multiple regions of the brain.

AUDITORY CORTEX Let's take a closer look at the final destination of the auditory pathway: the auditory cortex. The auditory cortex has a unique relationship with the basilar membrane in the cochlea. The frequency map of the basilar membrane is preserved through processing in the subcortical

Figure 7.7 Pathways of the Auditory System
The major pathways are indicated by heavy arrows.

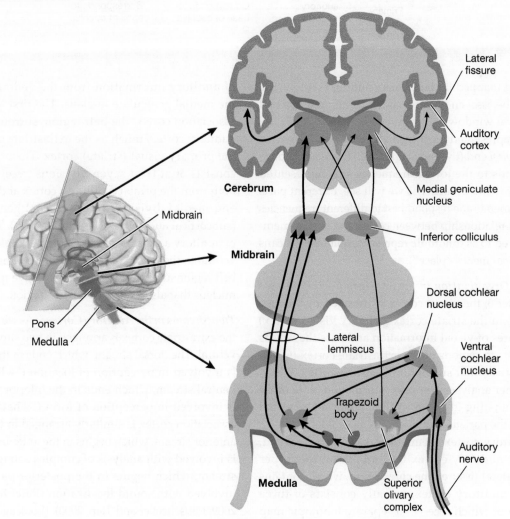

Figure 7.8 Tonotopic Mapping in the Cochlea and Auditory Cortex

The frequency map of the basilar membrane is preserved through processing in the subcortical structures and mapped in the primary auditory cortex.

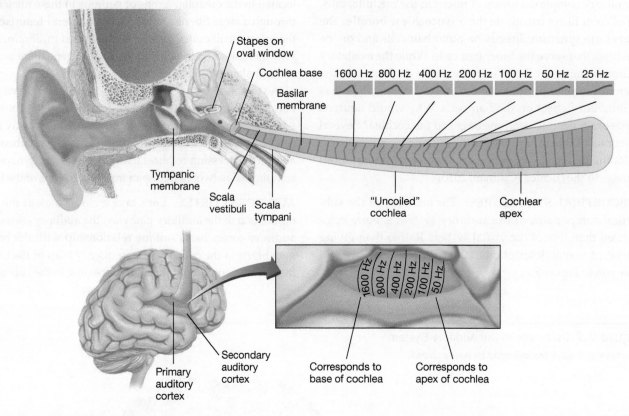

structures and mapped in the primary auditory cortex. (See Figure 7.8.) The *basal* end of the basilar membrane (the end toward the oval window, which responds to the highest frequencies) is represented most medially in the auditory cortex, and the *apical* end (the end farther from the oval window, which responds to the lowest frequencies) is represented most laterally there. Because, as we will see, different parts of the basilar membrane respond best to different frequencies of sound, this relationship between cortex and basilar membrane is referred to as **tonotopic representation** (*tonos* means "tone," and *topos* means "place").

Hierarchical Organization in the Auditory Cortex As we saw in Chapter 6, the visual cortex is arranged in a hierarchy. Modules in the striate cortex (primary visual cortex) analyze features of visual information and pass the results of this analysis to regions of the extrastriate cortex (visual association areas) that surround the striate cortex, which perform further analyses and pass information on to other regions, culminating in the most complex levels of visual processing in the parietal and inferior temporal lobes.

The auditory cortex seems to be similarly arranged. The primary auditory cortex lies hidden on the upper bank of the lateral fissure. The **core region,** which contains the primary auditory cortex, actually consists of three regions, each of which receives a separate tonotopic map

of auditory information from the ventral division from the medial geniculate nucleus. The first level of auditory association cortex, the **belt region,** surrounds the primary auditory cortex, much as the extrastriate cortex surrounds the primary visual (striate) cortex. The belt region, which consists of at least seven divisions, receives information both from the primary auditory cortex and from the dorsal and medial divisions of the medial geniculate nucleus (subcortical auditory processing regions). The highest level of auditory association cortex, the **parabelt region,** located ventral to the lateral parabelt, receives information from the belt region and from the divisions of the medial geniculate nucleus that also project to the belt region. (See Figure 7.9.)

Two Streams in the Auditory Cortex As we saw in Chapter 6, the extrastriate cortex is arranged in two streams—dorsal and ventral. The dorsal stream, which ends in the parietal cortex, is involved in perception of location ("where"), while the ventral stream, which ends in the inferior temporal cortex, is involved in perception of form ("what"). The auditory association cortex is similarly arranged in two streams. The anterior stream, which begins in the anterior parabelt region, is involved with analysis of complex sounds. The posterior stream, which begins in the posterior parabelt region, is involved with sound localization (Rauschecker and Scott, 2009; Rauschecker and Tian, 2000). (Look again at Figure 7.9.)

Figure 7.9 The Auditory Cortex

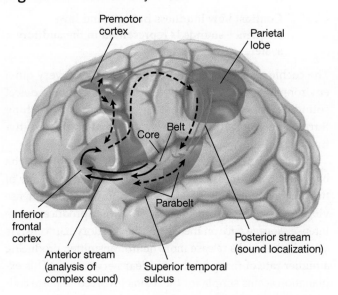

Premotor cortex

Parietal lobe

Core Belt

Parabelt

Inferior frontal cortex

Anterior stream (analysis of complex sound)

Superior temporal sulcus

Posterior stream (sound localization)

Perception of Pitch

LO 7.5 **Contrast place and rate coding in perception of pitch.**

As you saw in the previous section, the perceptual dimension of pitch corresponds to the physical dimension of frequency. The cochlea detects frequency by two means: moderate to high frequencies are detected by place coding and low frequencies are detected by rate coding. These two types of coding are described next.

PLACE CODING Due to the mechanical construction of the cochlea and basilar membrane, acoustic stimuli of different frequencies cause different parts of the basilar membrane to flex back and forth. This suggests that at least some frequencies of sound waves are detected by means of a **place code.** For example, if neurons at one end of the basilar membrane are excited by higher frequencies and those at the other end are excited by lower frequencies, we can say that the frequency of the sound is *coded* by the particular neurons that are active. In turn, the firing of particular axons in the cochlear nerve tells the brain about the presence of specific frequencies of sound.

Evidence for place coding of pitch comes from several sources. High doses of the antibiotic drugs produce degeneration of the auditory hair cells. The damage begins at the basal end of the cochlea and progresses toward the apical end. The progressive death of hair cells induced by an antibiotic closely parallels a progressive hearing loss: The highest frequencies are the first to be lost, and the lowest are the last. High-frequency hearing loss can also be caused by exposure to loud sounds.

Cochlear Implants Good evidence for place coding of pitch in the human cochlea comes from the effectiveness of cochlear implants. **Cochlear implants** are devices that are used to restore hearing in people with deafness caused by damage to the hair cells. The external part of a cochlear implant consists of a microphone and a miniaturized electronic signal processor. The internal part contains a very thin, flexible array of electrodes, which the surgeon carefully inserts into the cochlea in such a way that it follows the snail-like curl and ends up resting along the entire length of the basilar membrane. Each electrode in the array stimulates a different part of the basilar membrane. Information from the signal processor is passed to the electrodes by means of flat coils of wire, implanted under the skin. (See Figure 7.10.)

Figure 7.10 Cochlear Implant

A microphone and processor are worn over the ear, and the headpiece contains a coil that transmits signals to the implant.

Cochlear implants are most useful for two groups of people: individuals who became deaf in adulthood and very young children (Moore and Shannon, 2009). The primary purpose of a cochlear implant is to restore a person's ability to understand speech. Because most of the important acoustical information in speech is contained in frequencies that are too high to be accurately represented by a rate code, the multichannel electrode was developed in an attempt to duplicate the place coding of pitch on the basilar membrane (Copeland and Pillsbury, 2004). When different regions of the basilar membrane are stimulated, the person perceives sounds with different pitches. The signal processor in the external device analyzes the sounds detected by the microphone and sends separate signals to the appropriate portions of the basilar membrane.

Deaf Culture   Like other people who closely identify with their cultures, members of the Deaf community feel pride in a common heritage and language. Some deaf people say that if they were given the opportunity to hear, they would refuse it or would be relieved to have children who are deaf too because they would be a part of their own Deaf culture. Deaf individuals see themselves as different but not at all defective.

RATE CODING   The previous section described how the frequency of a sound can be detected by place coding. However, the lowest frequencies do not appear to be accounted for in this manner. Lower frequencies are detected by neurons that fire in synchrony with the movements of the apical end of the basilar membrane. Lower frequencies are detected by means of **rate coding.**

The most convincing evidence of rate coding of pitch also comes from studies of people with cochlear implants. Pijl and Schwarz (1995a, 1995b,) found that stimulation of a single electrode with pulses of electricity produced sensations of pitch that were proportional to the frequency of the stimulation. In fact, the participants could even recognize familiar tunes produced by modulating the pulse frequency. (The participants had become deaf later in life, after they had already learned to recognize the tunes.) As we would expect, the participants' perceptions were best when the tip of the basilar membrane was stimulated, and only low frequencies could be distinguished by this method.

Perception of Loudness

LO 7.6   Contrast how loudness in high- and low-frequency sounds is represented in the auditory system using action potentials.

The cochlea is an extremely sensitive organ. In very quiet environments, a healthy ear is limited in its ability to detect sounds in the air by the masking noise of blood rushing through the cranial blood vessels rather than by the sensitivity of the auditory system itself.

The axons of the cochlear nerve appear to inform the brain of the loudness of a stimulus by altering their rate of firing action potentials. Louder sounds produce more intense vibrations of the eardrum and ossicles, which produce a more intense *shearing force* on the cilia of the auditory hair cells. As a result, these cells release more neurotransmitter, producing a higher rate of firing by the cochlear nerve axons. This explanation seems simple for the axons involved in place coding of pitch; in this case, pitch is signaled by which neurons fire, and loudness is signaled by their rate of firing. However, the neurons in the apex of the basilar membrane that signal the lowest frequencies do so by their rate of firing. If they fire more frequently, they signal a higher pitch. Therefore, most investigators believe that the loudness of low-frequency sounds is signaled by the *number* of axons arising from these neurons that are active at a given time. (See Table 7.1.)

Perception of Timbre

LO 7.7   Identify the aspects of timbre that must be distinguished by auditory processing.

Although laboratory investigations of the auditory system often employ single-frequency sound stimuli, these sounds are seldom encountered outside the laboratory. Instead, we hear sounds with a rich mixture of frequencies—sounds of complex timbre. For example, consider the sound of a clarinet playing a particular note. If we hear it, we can identify it as a clarinet and not a flute or a violin. The reason we can do so is that these three instruments produce sounds of different timbre, which our auditory system can distinguish.

The clarinet note possesses a **fundamental frequency,** which corresponds to the perceived pitch of the note. The note also has many **overtones,** frequencies of complex tones

Table 7.1 Perception of Pitch and Loudness for High-, Moderate-, and Low-Frequency Sounds

This table summarizes how pitch and loudness are represented by the activity of hair cells in the cochlea.

	Perception of Pitch	Perception of Loudness
High-frequency sounds	Place coding; firing by hair cells at *location* of basilar membrane that is active	Determined by *rate* of action potentials from hair cells
Moderate-frequency sounds	Place coding; firing by hair cells at *location* of basilar membrane that is active	Determined by *rate* of action potentials from hair cells
Low-frequency sounds	Rate coding; hair cells at apical end of basilar membrane fire in synchrony with *frequency* of sound wave	Determined by *number* of active hair cells

that occur at multiples of the fundamental frequency. Different instruments produce overtones with different intensities. Electronic synthesizers simulate the sounds of real instruments by producing a series of overtones of the proper intensities, mixing them, and passing them through a speaker.

When the basilar membrane is stimulated by the sound of a clarinet, different portions respond to each of the overtones. This response produces a unique anatomically coded pattern of activity in the cochlear nerve, which is subsequently identified by circuits in the auditory association cortex.

Actually, the recognition of complex sounds is not quite that simple. The explanation above only applies to the analysis of a *sustained* sound of a clarinet. Most sounds are dynamic; that is, their beginning, middle, and end are different from each other. The beginning of a note played on a clarinet (the *attack*) contains frequencies that appear and disappear in a few milliseconds. At the end of the note (the *decay*), some frequencies disappear before others. If we are to recognize different sounds, the auditory cortex must analyze a complex sequence of multiple frequencies that appear, change in amplitude, and disappear. And when you consider the fact that we can listen to an orchestra and identify several instruments that are playing simultaneously, you can appreciate the complexity of the analysis performed by the auditory system.

Perception of Spatial Location

LO 7.8 **Compare the roles of arrival time, phase difference, intensity difference, and timbre in perception of spatial location.**

So far, we have discussed coding of pitch, loudness, and timbre only (the last of which is actually a complex frequency analysis). The auditory system also responds to other qualities of acoustic stimuli. For example, our ears are very good at determining whether the source of a sound is to the right or left of us. Three physiological mechanisms detect the location of sound sources: We use *phase differences* for low frequencies (less than approximately 3,000 Hz) and *intensity differences* for high frequencies; in addition, we use an *analysis of timbre* to determine the height of the source of a sound and recognize whether it is in front of us or behind us.

LOCALIZATION BY MEANS OF ARRIVAL TIME AND PHASE DIFFERENCES Even without visual information, we can still determine with rather good accuracy the location of a stimulus that emits a click. We are most accurate at judging the *azimuth*—that is, the horizontal (left or right) angle of the source of the sound relative to the midline of our body. Neurons in our auditory system respond selectively to different *arrival times* of the sound waves at the left and right ears. If the source of the click is to the right or left of the midline, the sound pressure wave will reach one ear sooner and initiate action potentials there first. Only if the stimulus is straight ahead will the ears be stimulated simultaneously. Many neurons in

the auditory system respond to sounds presented to either ear. Some of these neurons, especially those in the superior olivary complex of the medulla, respond according to the difference in arrival times of sound waves produced by clicks presented *binaurally* (that is, to both ears). Their response rates reflect differences as small as a fraction of a millisecond.

Of course, we can hear continuous sounds as well as clicks, and we can also perceive the location of their source. We detect the source of continuous low-pitched sounds by means of phase differences. **Phase differences** refer to the simultaneous arrival, at each ear, of different portions (phases) of the oscillating sound wave. For example, if we assume that sound travels at approximately 1,200 km per hour through the air, adjacent cycles of a 1,000-Hz tone are approximately 30 centimeters (cm) apart. Thus, if the source of the sound is located to one side of the head, one eardrum is pulled out while the other is pushed in. The movement of the eardrums will reverse, or be 180° *out of phase*. If the source were located directly in front of the head, the movements would be perfectly in phase (0° out of phase). (See Figure 7.11.) Because some auditory neurons respond only when the eardrums (and thus the bending of the basilar membrane) are at least somewhat out of phase, neurons in the superior olivary complex in the brain are able to use the information they provide to detect the source of a continuous sound.

Neurons receive information from two sets of axons coming from the two ears. Each neuron serves as a *coincidence detector*; it responds only if it received signals simultaneously from synapses belonging to both sets of axons. If a signal reaches the two ears simultaneously, neurons in the middle of the array will fire. However, if the signal reaches one ear before the other, then neurons farther away from the "early" ear will be stimulated (Jeffress, 1948). (See Figure 7.12.)

Coincidence detectors can be studied in the barn owl, a nocturnal bird that can detect very accurately the source of a sound (such as that made by an unfortunate mouse). (See Figure 7.13.) The branches of two axons, one from each ear, project to the nucleus laminaris, the barn owl analog of the mammalian medial superior olivary complex. Axons from the ipsilateral and contralateral ears enter the nucleus from opposite directions; therefore, dorsally located neurons within the nucleus are stimulated by sounds that first reach the contralateral ear. Carr and Konishi (1989, 1990) recorded from single units within the nucleus and found that the response characteristics of the neurons located there were consistent with the coincidence-detector model.

LOCALIZATION BY MEANS OF INTENSITY DIFFERENCES The auditory system cannot readily detect binaural phase differences of high-frequency stimuli; the differences in phases of such rapid sine waves are just too short to be measured by the neurons. However, high-frequency stimuli that occur to the right or left of the midline stimulate the ears unequally. The head absorbs high frequencies, producing a

Figure 7.11 Sound Localization

This method localizes the source of low-frequency and medium-frequency sounds through phase differences. (a) Source of a 1,000-Hz tone to the right. The pressure waves on each eardrum are out of phase; one eardrum is pushed in while the other is pushed out. (b) Source of a sound directly in front. The vibrations of the eardrums are synchronized (in phase).

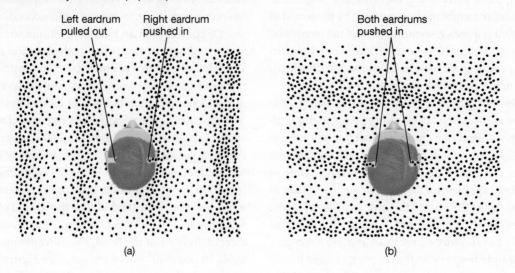

Left eardrum pulled out   Right eardrum pushed in

Both eardrums pushed in

(a)   (b)

"sonic shadow," so the ear closest to the source of the sound receives the most intense stimulation. Some neurons in the auditory system respond differentially to binaural stimuli of different intensity in each ear, which means that they provide information that can be used to detect the source of tones of high frequency.

The neurons that detect binaural differences in loudness are located in the superior olivary complex. But whereas neurons that detect binaural differences in phase or arrival time are located in the *medial* superior olivary complex, these neurons are located in the *lateral* superior olivary complex. Information from both sets of neurons is sent to other levels of the auditory system.

LOCALIZATION BY MEANS OF TIMBRE We just saw that left–right localization of the source of high- and low-frequency sounds is accomplished by two different mechanisms: differences in phase and intensity. But how can we determine the elevation of the source of a sound and perceive whether it is in front of us or behind us? One answer is that we can turn and tilt our heads, thus transforming the discrimination into a left–right decision. But we have

Figure 7.12 Model of a Coincidence Detector

This model detector can determine differences in arrival times at each ear of an auditory stimulus.

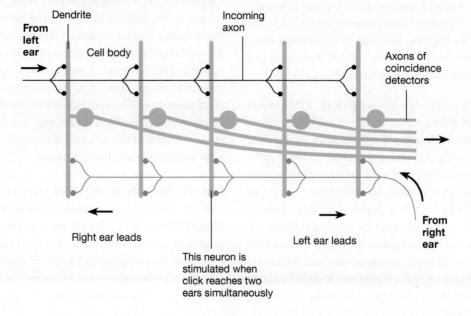

Dendrite   Incoming axon

From left ear   Cell body

Axons of coincidence detectors

Right ear leads   Left ear leads

From right ear

This neuron is stimulated when click reaches two ears simultaneously

Figure 7.13 Coincidence Detectors in the Barn Owl

Coincidence-detecting neurons in the owl's nucleus laminaris compare the arrival of sound in the right and left ears to determine the location of the mouse. Auditory stimuli reaching the left ear first indicate that the source of the sound is on the left side of the head.

(From Knudsen, E. I., Instructed learning in the auditory localization pathway of the barn owl. *Nature*, 2002, *417*(6886), 322–328.)

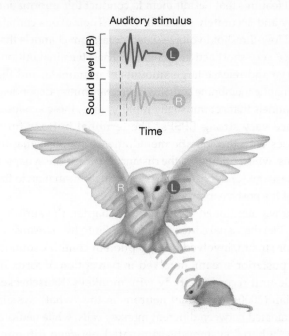

Figure 7.14 Changes in Timbre of Sounds with Changes in Elevation

The graphs are transfer functions, which compare the intensity of various frequencies of sound received by the ear to the intensity of these frequencies received by a microphone in open air. For ease of comparison, the 0° transfer function (green) is superimposed on the transfer functions obtained at 60° (red), 30° (orange), and –30° (blue). The differences in the transfer functions at various elevations provide cues that aid in perception of the location of a sound source.

(Adapted from Oertel, D., and Young, E. D., What's a cerebellar circuit doing in the auditory system?, *Trends in Neuroscience*, 2004, *27*, 104–110.)

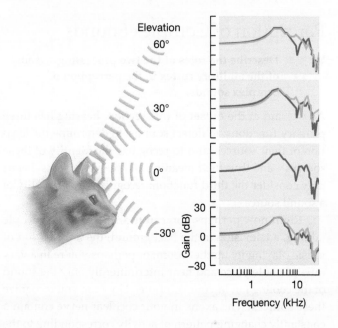

another means by which we can determine elevation and distinguish front from back: analysis of timbre.

This method involves a part of the auditory system that we have not said much about: the external ear (pinna). People's external ears contain several folds and ridges. Most of the sound waves that we hear bounce off the folds and ridges of the pinna before they enter the ear canal. Depending on the angle at which the sound waves strike these folds and ridges, different frequencies will be enhanced or attenuated. In other words, the pattern of reflections will change with the location of the source of the sound, which will alter the timbre of the sound that is perceived. Sounds coming from behind the head will sound different from those coming from above the head or in front of it, and sounds coming from above will sound different from those coming from the level of our ears. The timbre of sounds that reaches an ear changes along with elevation of the source of the sound. Figure 7.14 shows the effects of elevation on the intensity of sounds of various frequencies received at an ear (Oertel and Young, 2004). The experimenters placed a small microphone in a cat's ear and recorded the sound produced by an auditory stimulus presented at various elevations relative to the cat's head. They used a computer to plot the ear's transfer functions—a graph that compares the intensity of various frequencies of sound received by the ear to the intensity of these frequencies received by a microphone in open air. The important point in Figure 7.14 is that the transfer functions

varied with the elevation of the source of the sound. The timbre of sounds that reaches the cat's ear changed along with elevation of the source of the sound.

People's ears differ in shape; thus, the changes in the timbre of a sound coming from different locations will also differ from person to person. In addition, as children grow, the size of their ears changes. Thus, each individual must learn to recognize the subtle changes in the timbre of sounds that originate in locations in front of the head, behind it, above it, or below it. The neural circuits that accomplish this task are not genetically programmed; they must be acquired as a result of experience.

An experiment by Zwiers et al., (2001) found evidence for the role of experience in calibrating the sensitivity of the auditory system to changes in elevation. They found that individuals who were blind had more difficulty judging the elevation of sounds than people with sight did, especially if some noise was present. Presumably, the increased accuracy of sighted people reflected the fact that they had had the opportunity to calibrate the changes in timbre of sounds caused by changes in the height of their sources, which they could see. In contrast, the ability of individuals who were blind to perceive the horizontal location of the sources of sounds was equal to that of sighted people. Blind individuals have much experience navigating to and around the sources of sounds located at ground level (and objects that reflect sounds, such as that of a tapping cane). These perceptions can be calibrated by physical contact with these objects.

Kumpik et al., (2010) obtained further evidence for the role of learning in the ability to recognize the location of the source of sounds. They found that when one ear was partially plugged, people had difficulty localizing sounds. However, if they practiced several days for a period of time with the plug in, they learned to accurately localize sounds.

Perception of Complex Sounds

LO 7.9 **Describe the roles of the two processing streams of the auditory cortex in the perception of complex sounds.**

As we said at the outset of this section, hearing has three primary functions: to detect sounds, to determine the location of their sources, and to recognize the identity of these sources—and thus their meaning and relevance to us. Let us now consider the third function: recognizing the identity of a sound source.

Right now perhaps you can hear the sound of people talking, a television in the background, the muffled din of music playing in another room, or perhaps you're in a very quiet, remote place and hear intermittently only the sound of the cooling fan in your computer. How can you recognize these sources? The axons in your cochlear nerve contain a constantly changing pattern of activity corresponding to the constantly changing mixtures of frequencies that strike your eardrums. Somehow, the auditory system of your brain recognizes particular patterns that belong to particular sources, and you perceive each of them as an independent entity.

PERCEPTION OF ENVIRONMENTAL SOUNDS AND THEIR LOCATION The task of the auditory system in identifying sound sources is one of *pattern recognition*. The auditory system must recognize that particular patterns of constantly changing activity belong to different sound sources. And as we saw, few patterns are simple mixtures of fixed frequencies. For example, notes of different pitches produce different patterns of activity in our cochlear nerve, yet we recognize each of the notes as belonging to a clarinet. In addition, the notes played on a clarinet have a characteristic attack and decay. And consider the complexity of sounds that occur in the environment: cars honking, birds chirping, people coughing, doors slamming, and so on. (We will discuss speech recognition—an even more complicated task—in Chapter 14.) Perhaps unsurprisingly, we are far from understanding how pattern recognition of such complex sounds works.

Perception of complex sounds appears to be accomplished by circuits of neurons in the auditory cortex. However these sounds are recognized, it is clear that the circuits that perform the analysis must receive accurate information. Recognition of complex sounds requires that the timing of changes in the components of the sounds be preserved all the way to the auditory cortex. In fact, the neurons that convey information to the auditory cortex contain special features that permit them to conduct this information rapidly and accurately (Trussell, 1999). Their axons contain special low-threshold voltage-gated potassium channels that produce very short action potentials. Their terminal buttons are large and release large amounts of glutamate, and the postsynaptic membrane contains neurotransmitter-dependent ion channels that act unusually rapidly; thus, these synapses produce very strong EPSPs. The terminal buttons form synapses with the somatic membrane of the postsynaptic neurons, which minimizes the distance between the synapses and the axon—and the delay in conducting information to the axon of the postsynaptic neuron.

As we mentioned earlier in this chapter, the auditory cortex, like the visual cortex, is organized into two streams: an anterior stream, involved in perception of complex sounds; and a posterior stream, involved in perception of form. In a single-unit recording study with monkeys, Rauschecker and Tian (2000) found that neurons in the "what" system discriminated between different monkey calls, while neurons in the "where" system discriminated between different locations of loudspeakers presenting these calls.

Figure 7.15 compares the regions of the monkey brain that are devoted to the processing of visual and auditory information. As you can see, the visual and auditory "where" streams overlap in the parietal lobe. This overlap is undoubtedly related to the fact that monkeys (and humans, too) can use the convergence of sight and sound to recognize which of several objects in the environment is making a noise. In addition, we can learn the association

Figure 7.15 Processing Visual and Auditory Information

Regions of monkey brain devoted to processing visual and auditory information. vlPFC=ventrolateral prefrontal cortex, dlPFC=dorsolateral prefrontal cortex.

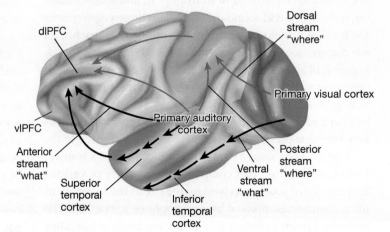

between the sight of an object and the sounds it makes. Information from both the visual and auditory systems is also projected to specific regions of the frontal lobes—again, with a region where both systems overlap. The role of the frontal lobes in learning and memory is discussed in Chapter 13.

DAMAGE TO THE AUDITORY CORTEX IMPAIRS PERCEPTION OF COMPLEX SOUNDS As we saw in Chapter 6, lesions of the visual association cortex can selectively impair various aspects of visual perception. Damage to the ventral stream can produce visual agnosias—the inability to recognize objects even though the visual acuity may be good ("what")—and lesions of the dorsal stream disrupt performance on a variety of tasks that require perceiving and remembering the locations of objects ("where"). Lesions of the auditory association cortex can produce deficits analogous to these—impairment of various aspects of auditory perception, even though the individuals are not deaf.

A review of 38 functional-imaging studies with human participants (Arnott et al., 2004) reported a consistent result: Perception of the identity of sounds activated the "what" stream of the auditory cortex and perception of the location of sounds activated the "where" stream. A functional MRI (fMRI) study by Alain et al., (2008) supports this conclusion. The investigators presented people with sounds of animals, humans, and musical instruments (for example, the bark of a dog, a cough, and the sound of a flute) in one of three locations: 90° to the left, straight ahead, or 90° to the right. On some blocks of trials the participants were asked to press a button when they heard two sounds of any kind from the same location. On other blocks of trials they were asked to indicate when they heard the same kind of sound twice in a row, regardless of its location. As Figure 7.16 shows, judgments of location activated dorsal regions ("where"), and judgments of the nature of a sound activated ventral regions ("what").

Inhibiting structures in these pathways results in specific deficits in perceiving "what" and "where" for auditory stimuli. Lomber and Malhotra (2008) implanted coiled tubes that circulated a chilled liquid in the cerebral cortex of cats. Circulating the liquid temporarily deactivated the cortical area under the coil. Deactivation of a region of the "what" pathway disrupted the cats' ability to recognize an auditory stimulus, and deactivation of a region of the "where" pathway disrupted their ability to recognize its location.

Although damage can impair perception of complex sounds, there is also plasticity in the auditory processing pathways. For example, the superior auditory abilities of blind individuals have long been recognized: Loss of vision appears to increase the sensitivity of the auditory system. A functional-imaging study by Klinge et al., (2010) found that input to the auditory cortex was identical in individuals who were blind and sighted, but that neural connections

Figure 7.16 "Where" vs. "What"

The figure shows regional brain activity in response to judgments of category (blue) and location (red) of sounds. IFG = inferior frontal gyrus, IPL = inferior parietal lobule, MFG = middle frontal gyrus, SFG = superior frontal gyrus, SPL = superior parietal lobule, STG = superior temporal gyrus.

(From Alain, C., He, Y., and Grady, C., The contribution of the inferior parietal lobe to auditory spatial working memory, *Journal of Cognitive Neuroscience,* 2008, *20*, 285–295. Reprinted with permission.)

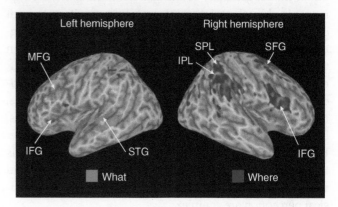

between the auditory cortex and the visual cortex were stronger in people who were blind. In addition, the visual cortex showed enhanced responsiveness to auditory stimuli. These findings suggest that the analysis of auditory stimuli can be extended to the visual cortex in people who are blind.

Clarke et al., (2000) reported the cases of three patients with brain damage that affected different portions of the auditory cortex. The investigators tested the patients' ability to recognize environmental sounds, to identify the locations from which the sounds were coming, and to detect when the source of a sound was moving. Patient F. D. had difficulty recognizing environmental sounds but could identify sound location or movement. Patient C. Z. could recognize environmental sounds but could not identify sound location or movement. Finally, although patient M. A. was not deaf, she showed deficits in all three tasks: recognition, localization, and perception of movement. Although the lesions in these patients were too large to determine the exact locations of the brain regions responsible for perception of environmental sounds and the location of their sources, we can certainly conclude that different regions of the auditory cortex are involved in perceiving *what* and *where*.

Perception of Music

LO 7.10 **Summarize the biological basis for perception of music.**

Perception of music is a special form of auditory perception. Music consists of sounds of various pitches and timbres played in a particular sequence with an underlying rhythm.

Particular combinations of musical notes played simultaneously are perceived as consonant or dissonant, pleasant or unpleasant. The intervals between notes of musical scales follow specific rules, which may vary in the music of different cultures. In Western music, melodies played using notes that follow one set of rules (the major mode) usually sound happy, while those played using another set of rules (the minor mode) generally sound sad. In addition, a melody is recognized by the relative intervals between its notes, not by their absolute value. A melody is perceived as unchanging even when it is played in different keys—that is, when the pitches of all the notes are raised or lowered without changing the relative intervals between them. Thus, musical perception requires recognition of sequences of notes, their adherence to rules that govern permissible pitches, harmonic combinations of notes, and rhythmical structure. Because the duration of musical pieces is several seconds to many minutes, musical perception involves a substantial memory capacity. The neural mechanisms required for musical perception are complex.

Studies with monkeys and humans have found that the primary auditory cortex responds to pure tones of different frequencies but that recognition of the pitch of complex sounds is accomplished only by the auditory association cortex (Bendor and Wang, 2006). Functional-imaging studies with humans indicate that pitch discrimination takes place in a region of the superior temporal gyrus rostral and lateral to the primary auditory cortex, in a region of the "what" stream. (See Figure 7.17.)

Different regions of the brain are involved in different aspects of musical perception (Peretz and Zatorre, 2005). For example, the inferior frontal cortex appears to be involved in recognition of harmony, the right auditory cortex appears to be involved in perception of the underlying beat in music, and the left auditory cortex appears to be involved in perception of rhythmic patterns that are superimposed on the rhythmic beat. (Think of a drummer indicating the regular, underlying beat by operating the foot pedal of the bass drum and superimposing a more complex pattern of beats on smaller drums with the drumsticks.) In addition, the cerebellum and basal ganglia are involved in timing of musical rhythms, as they are in the timing of movements.

Everyone learns a language, but only some people become musicians. Musical training obviously makes changes in the brain—changes in motor systems involved in singing or playing an instrument, and changes in the auditory system involved in recognizing subtle complexities of harmony, rhythm, and other characteristics of musical structure. Here, we will consider aspects of musical expertise related to audition.

Some of the effects of musical training can be seen in changes in the structure or activity of portions of the auditory system of the brain. For example, a study by Schneider et al., (2002) found that the volume of the primary auditory

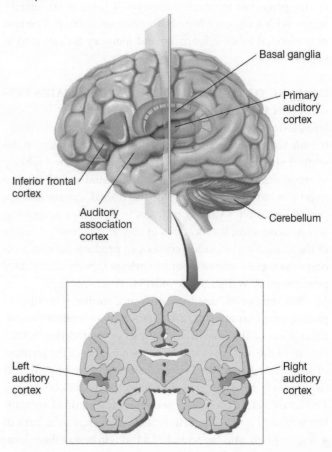

Figure 7.17 Regions of the Brain Involved in Musical Perception

cortex of musicians was 130 percent larger than that of nonmusicians, and the neural response in this area to musical tones was 102 percent greater in musicians. Moreover, both of these measures were positively related to a person's musical aptitude.

Evidence suggests that neural circuits used to process music are already present in newborn infants. A functional-imaging study by Perani et al., (2010) found that one- to three-day-old infants showed changes in brain activity (primarily in the right hemisphere) when music they were hearing changed key. (See Figure 7.18.) Brain activity also altered when babies heard dissonant music, which adults find unpleasant.

Patient I. R., a right-handed woman in her early forties, sustained bilateral damage during surgical treatment of aneurysms located on her middle cerebral arteries. Aneurysms (discussed in more detail in Chapter 15) are balloonlike swellings on blood vessels that can sometimes rupture, having fatal consequences. The surgery successfully clipped off the aneurysms but resulted in damage to most of the left superior temporal gyrus, and some of the inferior frontal and parietal lobes bordering

Figure 7.18 Consonance Versus Dissonance in Newborn Infants

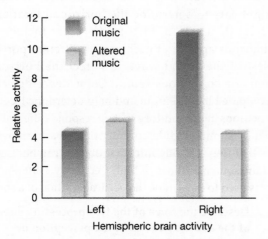

the lateral fissure. Damage to the right hemisphere was less severe but included the anterior third of the superior temporal gyrus and the right inferior and middle frontal gyri.

Ten years after the surgery I. R. had normal hearing, could understand speech and converse, and could recognize environmental sounds, but she showed a nearly complete **amusia**—loss of the ability to perceive or produce melodic or rhythmic aspects of music. She had been raised in a musical environment; both her grandmother and brother were professional musicians. After her surgery, she lost the ability to recognize melodies that she had been familiar with previously, including simple pieces such as "Happy Birthday." She was no longer able to sing (Peretz et al., 1998).

Remarkably, she insisted that she still enjoyed listening to music and I. R. was still able to recognize

emotional aspects of music. Although she could not recognize specific pieces of music, she recognized whether the music sounded happy or sad. She could also recognize happiness, sadness, fear, anger, surprise, and disgust in a person's tone of voice. The ability to recognize emotion in music contrasts with her inability to recognize dissonance in music—a quality that listeners typically find intensely unpleasant. Peretz and her colleagues (2001) discovered that I. R. was totally insensitive to changes in music that irritate normal listeners. Even four-month-old babies prefer consonant music to dissonant music, which shows that recognition of dissonance develops very early in life (Zentner and Kagan, 1998).

Approximately 4 percent of the population exhibits congenital amusia that becomes apparent early in life. People with amusia cannot recognize or differentiate between tunes, and they even try to avoid social situations that involve music.

Musical ability in general and congenital amusia in particular appear to have a genetic basis. Drayna et al., (2001) had pairs of twins listen to simple popular melodies and determine which ones contained some wrong—and discordant—notes. They found that the correlation between the scores of the twin pairs was .67 for monozygotic twins but only .44 for dizygotic twins. These results indicate a heritability index in this kind of musical ability of approximately .75 (on a scale of 0–1.0). Peretz et al., (2007) found that 39 percent of first-degree relatives (siblings, parents, or children) of people with amusia also had amusia, compared with an incidence of only 3 percent in the first-degree relatives of people in control families.

Section Review

Audition

LO 7.1 Describe the characteristics of sound that are perceived by humans.

The perceived pitch of an auditory stimulus is determined by the frequency of vibration, which is measured in hertz (Hz). Loudness is a function of intensity—the degree to which the compressions and expansions of air differ from each other. Timbre provides information about the nature of the particular sound—for example, the sound of an oboe or a train whistle.

LO 7.2 Identify the structures of the outer, middle, and inner ear.

The outer ear contains the pinna, ear canal, tympanic membrane. The middle ear contains the ossicles (malleus, incus, and stapes). The inner ear contains the cochlea, organ of Corti (including the basilar membrane, hair cells,

tectorial membrane, and reticular membrane) and the round window.

LO 7.3 Compare the structure, function, and location of hair cells as they contribute to transduction of auditory information.

Inner and outer auditory hair cells are located on the basilar membrane. Hair cells contain rows of cilia and synapse with dendrites of bipolar neurons whose axons bring auditory information to the brain. Movement of the basilar membrane causes the cilia to move, bending back and forth. Cilia are arranged in bundles and bending the bundle of cilia causes receptor potentials. The inner hair cells are necessary for normal hearing. The outer hair cells are involved in altering the mechanical characteristics of the basilar membrane and influencing the effects of sound vibrations on the inner hair cells.

LO 7.4 **Describe the structure and function of the cochlear nerve, subcortical structures, and cortex in the auditory pathway.**

The organ of Corti sends auditory information to the brain through the cochlear nerve. Auditory information travels from the cochlear nerve to the superior olivary nucleus, and on to the inferior colliculus, the medial geniculate nucleus, and finally to the auditory cortex. The auditory cortex has a tonotopic representation for auditory stimuli and is divided into primary and association areas. Processing in the auditory cortex progresses from the core region (primary cortex), to the belt region and then the parabelt region (association cortex). Cortical auditory processing consists of two streams. The anterior stream, which begins in the anterior parabelt region, is involved with analysis of complex sounds. The posterior stream, which begins in the posterior parabelt region, is involved with sound localization.

LO 7.5 **Contrast place and rate coding in perception of pitch.**

The cochlea detects frequency by two means: Moderate to high frequencies are detected by place coding, and low frequencies are detected by rate coding. Place coding occurs because acoustic stimuli of different frequencies cause different parts of the basilar membrane to flex back and forth, triggering the neurons in those locations to fire. Rate coding occurs because lower frequencies are detected by neurons that fire in synchrony with the movements of the apical end of the basilar membrane.

LO 7.6 **Contrast how loudness in high- and low-frequency sounds is represented in the auditory system using action potentials.**

Loudness in high-frequency sounds is represented by an increased rate of action potentials from the auditory hair cells. Loudness in low frequency cells is represented by the number of axons arising from the low-frequency-detecting neurons at the apical end of the basilar membrane that are active at a given time.

LO 7.7 **Identify the aspects of timbre that must be distinguished by auditory processing.**

Timbre includes identifying a fundamental frequency and overtones as well as identifying the beginning, middle, and end of a sound.

LO 7.8 **Compare arrival time, phase difference, intensity difference, and timbre in perception of spatial location.**

Neurons in our auditory system respond selectively to different arrival times of the sound waves at the left and right ears to determine the horizontal location of an intermittent sound. Phase differences include the simultaneous arrival, at each ear, of different portions (phases) of the sound wave to detect the horizontal location of a continuous sound. Coincidence-detecting cells compare binaural input and help determine location. Some neurons in the auditory system respond differentially to binaural stimuli of different intensity in each ear, which means that they provide information that can be used to detect the source of tones of high frequency. Difference in timbre is used to determine the vertical location of a sound.

LO 7.9 **Describe the roles of the two processing streams of the auditory cortex in the perception of complex sounds.**

The anterior stream is involved in perception of complex sounds ("what") and the posterior stream is involved in perception of location ("where"). Damage to these streams can lead to impairment of various aspects of auditory perception, even though the individuals are not deaf. Inhibiting structures in these pathways results in specific deficits in perceiving "what" and "where" for auditory stimuli.

LO 7.10 **Summarize the biological basis for perception of music.**

Different regions of the brain are involved in different aspects of musical perception. The primary auditory cortex responds to pure tones of different frequencies, and recognition of the pitch of complex sounds is accomplished by the auditory association cortex. The inferior frontal cortex is involved in recognition of harmony, the right auditory cortex is involved in perception of the underlying beat in music, and the left auditory cortex is involved in perception of rhythmic patterns that are superimposed on the rhythmic beat. Damage to the auditory cortex can result in amusia. Musical ability and the occurrence of congenital amusia appear to have a genetic basis.

Thought Question

As a student in a laboratory studying auditory processing you have been asked to propose a new line of research to enhance hearing. For your proposal, select one area of the auditory processing pathway and describe one possible intervention that could enhance auditory perception by targeting this area.

Vestibular System

The functions of the vestibular system include balance, maintenance of the head in an upright position, and adjustment of eye movement to compensate for head movements.

Vestibular stimulation does not produce any readily definable sensation; however certain low-frequency stimulation of the vestibular sacs can produce nausea, and stimulation of the semicircular canals can produce dizziness and rhythmic eye movements (*nystagmus*). Typically, we are not directly aware of the information received from these organs. This section describes the vestibular apparatus and the vestibular pathway in the brain.

Anatomy of the Vestibular Apparatus

LO 7.11 **Identify the structures of the vestibular apparatus.**

The vestibular system has two components: the vestibular sacs and the semicircular canals. They represent the second and third components of the *labyrinths* of the inner ear. (We just studied the first component, the cochlea.) The **vestibular sacs** respond to the force of gravity and inform the brain about the head's orientation. The **semicircular canals** respond to angular acceleration—changes in the rotation of the head—but not to steady rotation. They also respond (but rather weakly) to changes in position or to linear acceleration.

Figure 7.19 shows the labyrinths of the inner ear, which include the cochlea, the semicircular canals, and the two vestibular sacs: the **utricle** ("little pouch") and the **saccule** ("little sack"). The semicircular canals approximate the three major

planes of the head: sagittal, transverse, and horizontal. Receptors in each canal respond maximally to angular acceleration in one plane. The semicircular canal consists of a membranous canal floating within a bony one; the membranous canal contains a fluid called *endolymph*. An enlargement called the **ampulla** contains the organ in which the sensory receptors reside. The sensory receptors are hair cells similar to those found in the cochlea. Their cilia are embedded in a gelatinous mass called the **cupula,** which blocks part of the ampulla.

To explain the effects of angular acceleration on the semicircular canals, we will first describe an "experiment." If we place a glass of water on the exact center of a turntable and then start the turntable spinning, the water in the glass will, at first, remain stationary (the glass will move with respect to the water it contains). Eventually, however, the water will begin rotating with the container. If we then stop the turntable, the water will continue spinning for a while because of its inertia.

The semicircular canals operate on the same principle. The endolymph within these canals, like the water in the glass, resists movement when the head begins to rotate. This inertial

Figure 7.19 Receptive Organ of the Semicircular Canals

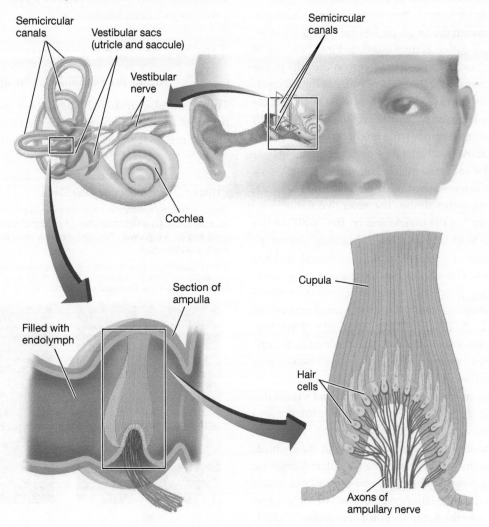

Figure 7.20 Receptive Tissue of the Vestibular Sacs: The Utricle and the Saccule

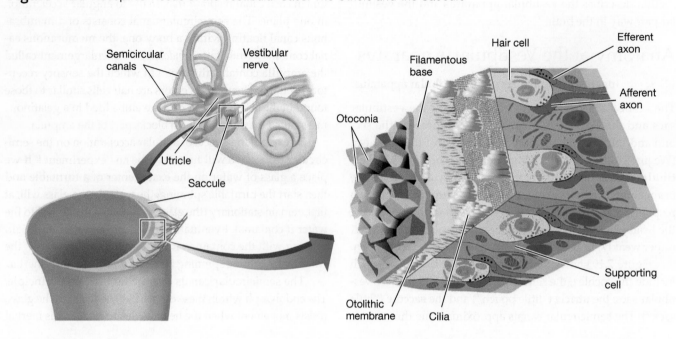

resistance pushes the endolymph against the cupula, causing it to bend, until the fluid begins to move at the same speed as the head. If the head rotation is then stopped, the endolymph, still circulating through the canal, pushes the cupula the other way. Angular acceleration is thus translated into bending of the cupula, which exerts a shearing force on the cilia of the hair cells. (Of course, unlike the glass of water in the example, we do not normally spin around in circles; the semicircular canals measure very slight and very brief rotations of the head.) With this explanation in mind, what might be responsible for the perception of movement after a person *stops* spinning?

The vestibular sacs (the utricle and saccule) work very differently. These organs are roughly circular, and each contains a patch of receptive tissue. The receptive tissue is located on the "floor" of the utricle and on the "wall" of the saccule when the head is in an upright position. The receptive tissue, like that of the semicircular canals and cochlea, contains hair cells. The cilia of these receptors are embedded in an overlying gelatinous mass, which contains something rather unusual: *otoconia,* which are small crystals of calcium carbonate. (See Figure 7.20.) The weight of the crystals causes the gelatinous mass to shift in position as the orientation of the head changes. Thus, movement produces a shearing force on the cilia of the receptive hair cells.

The hair cells of the semicircular canal and vestibular sacs are similar in appearance. Each hair cell contains several cilia, graduated in length from short to long. These hair cells resemble the auditory hair cells found in the cochlea, and their transduction mechanism is also similar: A shearing force of the cilia opens ion channels, and the entry of potassium ions depolarizes the ciliary membrane. All three forms of hair cells employ the same receptor molecules: TRPA1,

which we described earlier in this chapter. Figure 7.21 shows two views of a hair cell of a bullfrog saccule made by a scanning electron microscope.

The Vestibular Pathway

LO 7.12 Outline the vestibular pathway.

The vestibular and cochlear nerves constitute the two branches of the eighth cranial nerve (auditory nerve). The bipolar cell bodies that give rise to the afferent axons of the

---

Figure 7.21 Saccular Hair Cells

These scanning electron microscope views of hair cells of a bullfrog saccule show (a) an oblique view of a normal bundle of vestibular hair cells and (b) a top view of a bundle of hair cells from which the longest has been detached.

(From Hudspeth, A. J., and Jacobs, R., Stereocilia mediate transduction in vertebrate hair cells, *Proceedings of the National Academy of Sciences, USA,* 1979, *76,* 1506–1509. Reprinted with permission.)

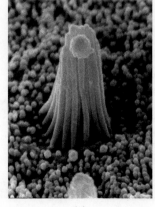

(a)   (b)

vestibular nerve (a branch of the eighth cranial nerve) are located in the **vestibular ganglion,** which appears as a nodule on the vestibular nerve.

Most of the axons of the vestibular nerve synapse within the vestibular nuclei in the medulla, but some axons travel directly to the cerebellum. Neurons of the vestibular nuclei send their axons to the cerebellum, spinal cord, medulla, and pons. There also appear to be vestibular projections to the temporal cortex, but the precise pathways have not been determined. Most investigators believe that the cortical projections are responsible for feelings of dizziness; the activity of projections to the lower brain stem can produce the nausea and vomiting that accompany motion sickness. Projections to brain stem nuclei controlling neck muscles are clearly involved in maintaining an upright position of the head.

Perhaps the most interesting connections are those to the cranial nerve nuclei (third, fourth, and sixth) that control the eye muscles. As we walk or (especially) run, the head is jarred. The vestibular system exerts direct control on eye movement to compensate for the sudden head movements. This process, called the *vestibulo-ocular reflex,* maintains a fairly steady retinal image. Test this reflex yourself: Look at a distant object and hit yourself (gently) on the side of the head. Note that your image of the world jumps a bit but not too much. People who have suffered vestibular damage and who lack the vestibulo-ocular reflex have difficulty seeing anything while walking or running. Everything becomes a blur of movement.

Section Review

Vestibular System

LO 7.11 Identify the structures and functions of the vestibular apparatus.

The vestibular apparatus contains the vestibular sacs (the utricle and saccule) and the semicircular canals of the ear. The vestibular sacs respond to the force of gravity and inform the brain about the head's orientation. The semicircular canals respond to angular acceleration and changes in position or linear acceleration.

LO 7.12 Outline the vestibular pathway.

From the hair cells, vestibular information is relayed to the brain via the vestibular and cochlear nerves. The vestibular nerve projects to the medulla, which sends information to cerebellum, spinal cord, pons, and to other regions of the medulla. The cranial nerve relays information to the eye muscles to compensate for sudden head movements. There also appear to be vestibular projections to the temporal cortex, but the precise pathways have not been determined.

Thought Question

Persistent dizziness has a lifetime prevalence of approximately 25 percent and represents a significant risk factor for falls among older adults. Select one structure involved in vestibular perception and explain how damage or dysfunction in this structure could contribute to the experience of dizziness (even if the exact cortical pathways are not yet known).

Somatosenses

This chapter began with the case of Ashlyn, who had a congenital lack of functional pain receptors. This case highlights the important role of somatosenses in influencing our behavior. The somatosenses provide information about what is happening on the surface of our body and inside it. The **cutaneous senses** (skin senses) are the most studied of the somatosenses and include several submodalities commonly referred to as *touch*. **Proprioception** and **kinesthesia** provide information about body position and movement. We will describe the contribution of sensory receptors in the skin to these perceptual systems in this section. The muscle receptors and their role in feedback from limb position and movement are discussed in this section and in Chapter 8. The **organic senses** arise from receptors in and around the internal organs. (See Table 7.2.)

Table 7.2 Somatosenses

Somatosense	Function
Cutaneous Senses	Provide information from the surface of the body.
Proprioception	Provide information about location of body in space.
Kinesthesia	Provide information about movement of body though space.
Organic Senses	Provide information from in and around internal organs.

The Stimuli

LO 7.13 Provide examples of stimuli that activate receptors for the somatosenses.

The cutaneous senses respond to several different types of stimuli: pressure, vibration, heating, cooling, and events that cause tissue damage (and hence pain). Feelings of pressure are caused by mechanical deformation of the skin. Vibration occurs when we move our fingers across a rough surface. Thus, we use vibration sensitivity to judge an object's roughness. Sensations of warmth and coolness are produced by objects that raise or lower skin temperature. Sensations of pain can be caused by many different types of stimuli, but it appears that most cause at least some tissue damage.

One source of kinesthesia is the stretch receptors found in skeletal muscles that report changes in muscle length to the central nervous system. Receptors within joints between adjacent bones respond to the magnitude and direction of limb movement. However, the most important source of kinesthetic feedback appears to come from receptors that respond to changes in the stretching of the skin during movements of the joints or of the muscles themselves, such as those in the face (Johansson and Flanagan, 2009). Muscle length detectors, located within the muscles, do not give rise to conscious sensations; their information is used to control movement. These receptors will be discussed separately in Chapter 8.

We are aware of some of the information received by means of the organic senses, which can provide us with unpleasant sensations such as stomachaches or gallbladder attacks, or pleasurable ones such as those provided by a warm drink on a cold winter day. We are unaware of some information, such as that provided from receptors in the digestive system, kidneys, liver, heart, and blood vessels that are sensitive to nutrients and minerals. This information, which plays a role in the control of metabolism and water and mineral balance, is described in Chapter 12.

Anatomy of the Skin and Its Receptive Organs

LO 7.14 Describe the anatomy and somatosensory receptors of the skin.

The skin is a complex and vital organ of the body—one that we often tend to take for granted. We cannot survive without it; extensive skin burns are fatal. Our cells, which must be bathed by a warm fluid, are protected from the hostile environment by the skin's outer layers. The skin participates in thermoregulation by producing sweat, thus cooling the body, or by restricting its circulation of blood, thus conserving heat. Its appearance varies widely across the body, from mucous membrane to hairy skin to the smooth, hairless skin of the palms and the soles of the feet, which is known as **glabrous skin.** Skin consists of subcutaneous tissue, dermis, and epidermis and contains various receptors scattered throughout these layers. Glabrous skin contains a dense, complex mixture of receptors, which reflects the fact that we use the palms of our hands and the inside surfaces of our fingers to actively explore the environment: We use our hands and fingers to hold and touch objects. In contrast, the rest of our body most often contacts the environment passively; that is, other things come into contact with it.

Figure 7.22 shows the appearance of free nerve endings and the four types of encapsulated somatosensory receptors (**Merkel's disks, Ruffini corpuscles, Meissner's corpuscles**, and **Pacinian corpuscles**). The locations and functions of these receptors are listed in Table 7.3.

Figure 7.22 Cutaneous Receptors

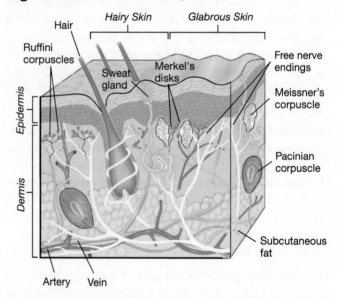

Table 7.3 Categories of Cutaneous Receptors

Size and Nature of Receptive Field	Identity of Receptor	Location of Receptor	Function of Receptor
Small, sharp borders	Merkel's disks	Hairy and glabrous skin	Detection of form and roughness, especially by fingertips
Large, diffuse borders	Ruffini corpuscles	Hairy and glabrous skin	Detection of static force against skin; skin stretching; proprioception
Small, sharp borders	Meissner's corpuscles	Glabrous skin	Detection of edge contours; Braille-like stimuli, especially by fingertips
Large, diffuse borders	Pacinian corpuscles	Hairy and glabrous skin	Detection of vibration; information from end of elongated object being held, such as tool
	Hair follicle ending	Base of hair follicle	Detection of movement of hair
	Free nerve ending	Hairy and glabrous skin	Detection of thermal stimuli (coolness or warmth), noxious stimuli (pain), tickle
	Free nerve ending	Hairy skin	Detection of pleasurable touch from gentle stroking with soft object

Perception of Cutaneous Stimulation

LO 7.15 **Describe receptors involved in the perception of touch, temperature, pain, and itch.**

The three most important qualities of cutaneous stimulation are touch, temperature, and pain. These qualities, along with itch, are described in the sections that follow.

TOUCH Stimuli that cause vibration in the skin or changes in pressure against it (*tactile* stimuli) are detected by **mechanoreceptors**—the encapsulated receptors shown in Figure 7.22 and some types of free nerve endings. Most investigators believe that the encapsulated nerve endings serve only to modify the physical stimulus transduced by the dendrites that reside within them. But what is the mechanism of transduction? How does movement of the dendrites of mechanoreceptors produce changes in membrane potentials? It appears that the movement causes ion channels to open, and the flow of ions into or out of the dendrite causes a change in the membrane potential. You will recall that TRPA1, a member of the TRP (transient receptor potential) family of receptor proteins, is responsible for transduction of mechanical information in auditory and vestibular hair cells.

Most information about tactile stimulation is precisely localized—that is, we can perceive the location on our skin where we are being touched. However, a case study by Olausson et al., (2002) discovered a new category of tactile sensation. Read the case study below to learn more about a unique case of cutaneous stimulation.

Patient G. L., a 54-year-old woman, experienced a permanent loss of afferent neurons involved in somatosensation. G. L. lost the ability to perceive tickle but retained the ability to perceive temperature, pain, and itch (Olausson et al., 2002, pp. 902–903).

When the hairy skin on her forearm or the back of her hand was stroked with a soft brush, she reported a faint, pleasant sensation. However, she could not determine the direction of the stroking or its precise location. An fMRI analysis showed that this stimulation activated the insular cortex, a region that is known to be associated with emotional responses and sensations from internal organs. The somatosensory cortex was not activated. When regions of hairy skin of control participants were stimulated this way, fMRI showed activation of the primary and secondary somatosensory cortex as well as the insular cortex because the stimulation activated both large and small axons. The glabrous skin on the palm of the hand is served only by large-diameter, myelinated axons. When this region was stroked with a brush, G. L. reported no sensation at all, presumably because of the absence of small, unmyelinated axons. The investigators concluded that, besides conveying information about noxious and thermal stimuli, small-diameter unmyelinated axons constitute a "system for limbic touch that may underlie emotional, hormonal and affiliative responses to caresslike, skin-to-skin contact between individuals" (Olausson et al., 2002, p. 900). And, as we saw, G. L. could no longer perceive tickle. Tickling sensations, which were previously believed to be transmitted by these small axons, are apparently transmitted by the large, myelinated axons that were destroyed in patient G. L.

Olausson and his colleagues (Löken et al., 2009) note that the sensory endings that detect pleasurable stroking are found only in hairy skin, and that stroking of glabrous skin does not provide these sensations. However, we can think of pleasurable tactile stimuli that can be experienced through the glabrous skin of the palms and fingers—for example, those provided by stroking a warm, furry animal or touching a loved one. When our hairy skin contacts the skin of another person, it is more likely that that person is touching us. In contrast, when our glabrous skin contacts the skin of another person, it is more likely that we are touching them. Thus, we might expect receptors in hairy skin to provide pleasurable sensations when someone caresses us but expect receptors in glabrous skin to provide pleasurable sensations when we caress someone else.

Our cutaneous senses are often used to analyze shapes and textures of stimulus objects that are moving with respect to the surface of the skin. Sometimes, the object itself moves, but more often, we do the moving ourselves. If an object is placed in your palm and you are asked to keep your hand still, you will have a great deal of difficulty recognizing the object by touch alone. If you are then allowed to move your hand, you will manipulate the object, letting its surface slide across your palm and the pads of your fingers. You will be able to describe the object's three-dimensional shape, hardness, texture, slipperiness, and so on. In order to describe it, your motor system must cooperate, and you need kinesthetic sensation from your muscles and joints, in addition to the cutaneous information. If you squeeze the object and feel a lot of well-localized pressure in return, it is hard. If you feel a less intense, more diffuse pressure in return, it is soft. If it produces vibrations as it moves over the ridges on your fingers, it is rough. If very little effort is needed to move the object while pressing it against your skin, it is slippery. If it does not produce vibrations as it moves across your skin, but moves in a jerky fashion, and if it takes effort to remove your fingers from its surface, it is sticky. Thus, our somatosenses work dynamically with the motor system to provide useful information about the nature of objects that come into contact with our skin.

Studies of people who make especially precise use of their fingertips show changes in the regions of somatosensory cortex that receive information from this part of the body. For example, violinists must make very precise movements of the four fingers of the left hand, which are used to play notes by pressing the strings against the fingerboard. Tactile feedback and proprioceptive feedback are very important in accurately moving and positioning these fingers so that sounds of the proper pitch are produced. In contrast, placement of the thumb, which slides along the bottom of the neck of the violin, is less critical. In a study of violin players, Elbert et al., (1995) found that the portions of their right somatosensory cortex that receive information from the four fingers of their left hand were enlarged relative to the corresponding parts of the left somatosensory cortex. The amount of somatosensory cortex that receives information from the thumb was not enlarged. (The right hand holds the bow, and the violinist makes precise movements with the arm and wrist, but tactile information from the fingers of this hand is much less important.)

TEMPERATURE   Feelings of warmth and coolness are relative, not absolute, except at the extremes. There is a temperature level that, for a particular region of skin, will produce a sensation of temperature neutrality—neither warmth nor coolness. This neutral point is not an absolute value but depends on the prior history of thermal stimulation of that area. If the temperature of a region of skin is raised by a few degrees, the initial feeling of warmth is replaced by one of neutrality. If the skin temperature is lowered to its initial value, it now feels cool. Thus, increases in temperature lower the sensitivity of warmth receptors and raise the sensitivity of cold receptors. The converse holds for decreases in skin temperature. This adaptation to temperature can be demonstrated easily by placing one hand in a bucket of warm water and the other in a bucket of cool water until some adaptation has taken place. If you then simultaneously immerse both hands in water at room temperature, it will feel warm to one hand and cool to the other.

There are two categories of free nerve-ending thermal receptors: those that respond to warmth and those that respond to coolness. Cold sensors in the skin are located just beneath the epidermis, and warmth sensors are located more deeply in the skin. We can detect thermal stimuli over a very wide range of temperatures, from less than 8° C (noxious cold) to over 52° C (noxious heat). Investigators have long believed that no single receptor could detect such a range of temperatures, and recent research indicates that this belief was correct. At present we know of six mammalian thermoreceptors—all members of the TRP family (Bandell et al., 2007; Romanovsky, 2007). The thermoreceptors are listed in Table 7.4.

Table 7.4 Categories of Mammalian Thermal Receptors

Name of Receptor	Type of Stimulus	Temperature Range
TRPV2	Noxious heat	Above 52° C
TRPV1, capsaicin	Heat	Above 43° C
TRPV3	Warmth	Above 31° C
TRPV4	Warmth	Above 25° C
TRPM8, menthol	Coolness	Below 28° C

Some of the thermal receptors respond to particular chemicals as well as to changes in temperature. For example, the *M* in TRPM8 stands for menthol, a compound found in the leaves of many members of the mint family. Peppermint tastes cool in the mouth, and menthol is added to some cigarettes to make the smoke feel cooler and perhaps less harsh and damaging to the lungs. Menthol provides a cooling sensation because it binds with and stimulates the TRPM8 receptor and produces neural activity that the brain interprets as coolness.

Chemicals can produce the sensation of heat also. Later in this chapter, you'll learn more about perception of "heat" from *capsaicin*, the chemical responsible for the burning sensation you experience when eating chile peppers. This experience of heat is due to activation of pain receptors.

PAIN   The story of pain is quite different from that of temperature and pressure; pain is a much more complicated sensation. Our awareness of pain and our emotional reaction to it are controlled by mechanisms within the brain. Stimuli that produce pain also tend to trigger species-typical escape and withdrawal responses. Subjectively, these stimuli *hurt*, and we try hard to avoid or escape from them. However, sometimes we are better off ignoring pain and getting on with important tasks. In fact, our brains possess mechanisms that can reduce pain, partly through the action of the endogenous opioids. These mechanisms are described in more detail in a later section of this chapter.

Pain perception, like thermoreception, is accomplished by the networks of free nerve endings in the skin. There appear to be at least three types of pain receptors (usually referred to as *nociceptors*, or "detectors of noxious stimuli"). High-threshold mechanoreceptors are free nerve endings that respond to intense pressure, which might be caused by something striking, stretching, or pinching the skin. A second type of free nerve ending appears to respond to extremes of heat, to acids, and to the presence of capsaicin, the active ingredient in chile peppers. (Note that we say that chile peppers make food taste "hot.") This type of fiber contains TRPV1 receptors (Kress and Zeilhofer, 1999). The *V* stands for *vanilloid*—a group of chemicals of which capsaicin is a member. Caterina et al., (2000) found that mice with a knockout of the gene for the TRPV1 receptor showed less sensitivity to painful high-temperature stimuli and would drink water to which capsaicin had been added. The mice responded normally to noxious mechanical stimuli. Presumably, the TRPV1 receptor is responsible for pain produced by burning of the skin and to changes in the acid/base balance within the skin. These receptors are responsible for the irritating effect of chemicals such as ammonia on the mucous membranes of the nose (Dhaka et al., 2009). TRPV1 receptors also appear to play a role in regulation of body temperature. In addition, Ghilardi et al., (2005) found that a drug that blocks TRPV1 receptors reduced pain in patients with bone cancer, which is apparently caused by the production of acid by the tumors.

Another type of nociceptive fiber contains TRPA1 receptors, which, as we saw earlier in this chapter, are found in the cilia of auditory and vestibular hair cells. TRPA1 receptors are sensitive to pungent irritants found in mustard oil, wintergreen oil, horseradish, and garlic and to a variety of environmental irritants, including those found in vehicle exhaust and tear gas (Bautista et al., 2006; Nilius et al., 2007). The primary function of this receptor appears to be to provide information about the presence of chemicals that produce inflammation.

ITCH   Another noxious sensation, itch (or, more formally, *pruritus*) is caused by skin irritation. Itch was defined by a seventeenth-century German physician as an "unpleasant sensation that elicits the desire or reflex to scratch" (Ikoma et al., 2006, p. 535). If an adult sees a child scratching at an insect bite or other form of skin irritation, the adult is likely to say, "Stop that—it will only make it worse!" The scratching may indeed make the irritation worse, but the immediate effect of scratching is to reduce the itching.

Davidson et al., (2009) found that scratching inhibited the activity of neurons in the spinothalamic tract of monkeys

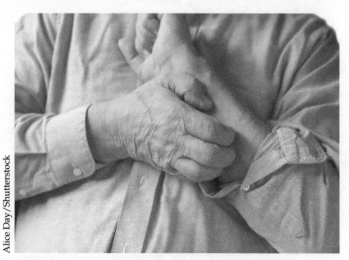

Little is known about the receptors that are responsible for the sensation of itch.

that transmit itch sensations to the brain. Presumably, the scratch response to stimuli that produce itching helps rid skin of irritating debris or parasites (Davidson and Giesler, 2010). Scratching reduces itching because pain suppresses itching (and, ironically, itching reduces pain). Histamine and other chemicals released by skin irritation and allergic reactions are important sources of itching. Experiments have shown that painful stimuli such as heat and electrical shock can reduce sensations of itch produced by an injection of histamine into the skin, even when the painful stimuli are applied up to 10 cm from the site of irritation (Nilsson et al., 1997; Ward et al., 1996). On the other hand, the administration of an opiate into the epidural space around the spinal cord diminishes pain but often produces itching as an unwelcome side effect (Chaney, 1995). Naloxone, a drug that blocks opiate receptors, has been used to reduce *cholestatic pruritus*, a condition of itching that sometimes accompanies pregnancy (Bergasa, 2005).

Little is known about the receptors that are responsible for the sensation of itch, but at least two different types of neurons transmit itch-related information to the CNS. Johanek et al. (2007) produced itch in volunteers with intradermal injections of histamine and applications of cowhage spicules—tiny, needlelike plant fibers that contain an enzyme that breaks down proteins in the skin. Both treatments produce intense itch, but only histamine produces an area of vasodilation. Pretreatment of a patch of skin with a topical antihistamine prevented histamine from producing an itch at that spot but had no effect on the itch produced by cowhage. In contrast, pretreatment of a patch of skin with capsaicin prevented cowhage-induced itch but not histamine-induced itch.

The Somatosensory Pathways

LO 7.16   **Describe the pathway for somatosensory processing from nerves to subcortical and cortical structures.**

The somatosensory pathways relay information about somatosensation from the receptors, through subcortical structures to the primary and secondary somatosensory cortex, enabling somatosensory perception.

NERVES AND SUBCORTICAL PROCESSING   Somatosensory axons from the skin, muscles, or internal organs enter the central nervous system via spinal nerves. Those located in the face and head primarily enter through the trigeminal nerve (fifth cranial nerve). The cell bodies of the unipolar neurons are located in the dorsal root ganglia and cranial nerve ganglia. Axons that convey precisely localized information, such as fine touch, ascend through the *dorsal columns* in the white matter of the spinal cord to nuclei in the lower medulla. From there, axons cross the brain and ascend through the *medial lemniscus* to the *ventral posterior nuclei of* *the thalamus,* the relay nuclei for somatosensation. Axons from the thalamus project to the primary somatosensory cortex, which in turn sends axons to the secondary somatosensory cortex. In contrast, axons that convey poorly localized information, such as pain or temperature, form synapses with other neurons as soon as they enter the spinal cord. The axons of these neurons cross to the other side of the spinal cord and ascend through the *spinothalamic tract* to the ventral posterior nuclei of the thalamus. (See Figure 7.23.)

THE SOMATOSENSORY CORTEX The primary and secondary regions of somatosensory cortex are arranged in columns and divided into multiple maps of the body surface.

Column Organization Recall from Chapter 6 that the primary visual cortex contains columns of cells, each of which responds to particular features, such as orientation, ocular dominance, or spatial frequency. Within these columns are blobs that contain cells that respond to particular colors. The somatosensory cortex also has a columnar arrangement; in fact, cortical columns were discovered in the somatosensory cortex before they were found in the visual and auditory cortex (Mountcastle, 1957). Within a column, neurons respond to a particular type of stimulus (for example, temperature or pressure) applied to a particular part of the body.

Map Organization Dykes (1983) has reviewed research indicating that the primary and secondary somatosensory cortical areas are divided into at least five (and perhaps as many as ten) different maps of the body surface. Within each map, cells respond to a particular submodality of somatosensory receptors. Separate areas have been identified

---

Figure 7.23 Somatosensory Pathways

The figure shows the somatosensory pathways from the spinal cord to the somatosensory cortex. Note that precisely localized information (such as fine touch) and imprecisely localized information (such as pain and temperature) are transmitted by different pathways.

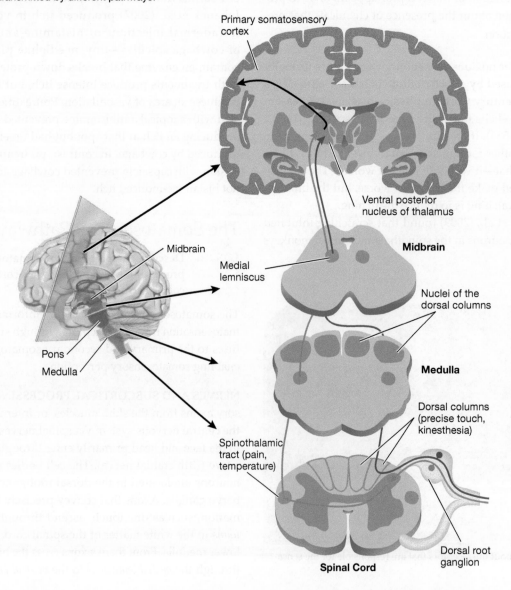

Primary somatosensory cortex

Ventral posterior nucleus of thalamus

Midbrain

Midbrain

Medial lemniscus

Nuclei of the dorsal columns

Pons

Medulla

Medulla

Dorsal columns (precise touch, kinesthesia)

Spinothalamic tract (pain, temperature)

Dorsal root ganglion

Spinal Cord

that respond to cutaneous receptors, receptors that detect changes in muscle length, receptors located in the joints, and Pacinian corpuscles.

As we saw in Chapter 6, damage to the visual association cortex can cause visual agnosia, and as we saw earlier in this chapter, damage to the auditory association cortex can cause auditory agnosia. You may not be surprised, then, to learn that damage to the somatosensory association cortex can cause tactile agnosia.

Patient E. C., a woman with left parietal lobe damage, was unable to recognize common objects by touch. For example, she identified a pine cone as a brush, a ribbon as a rubber band, and a snail shell as a bottle cap. The deficit was not due to a simple loss of tactile sensitivity; the patient was still sensitive to light touch and to warm and cold objects, and she could easily discriminate objects by their size, weight, and roughness (Reed et al., 1996).

Nakamura et al., (1998) described patient M. T., who had a different type of tactile agnosia. M. T. had bilateral lesions of the angular gyrus, a region of the parietal lobe surrounding the caudal end of the lateral fissure. This patient, like E. C., had normal tactile sensitivity, but he could not identify objects by touch. However, unlike E. C., he could *draw* objects that he touched even though he could not recognize what they were. (See Figure 7.24.) The fact that he could draw the objects means that his ability to perceive three-dimensional objects by touch must have been intact. However, the brain damage prevented the information analyzed by the somatosensory association cortex from being transmitted to parts of the brain responsible for control of language—and for consciousness.

Perception of Pain

LO 7.17 **Describe why pain is experienced, the perceptual and behavior effects of pain, and how pain perception can be modified.**

Pain is a curious phenomenon. It is more than a mere sensation; it can be defined only by some sort of withdrawal reaction or, in humans, by verbal report. Pain can be modified by opiates, by hypnosis, by the administration of placebos, by emotions, and even by other forms of stimulation, such as acupuncture. Recent research efforts have made remarkable progress in discovering the physiological bases of these phenomena.

WHY DO WE EXPERIENCE PAIN? We might reasonably ask *why* we experience pain. The answer is that in most cases pain serves a constructive role. For example, inflammation,

Figure 7.24 Tactile Agnosia

(a) Drawings of wrenches felt but not seen by M. T. Although the patient did not recognize the objects as wrenches, he was able to draw them accurately. (b) Drawings of objects felt but not seen by E. C. The patient could neither recognize the objects by touch nor draw them accurately.

(Based on Nakamura, J., Endo, K., Sumida, T., and Hasegawa, T., Bilateral tactile agnosia: A case report, *Cortex*, 1998, *34*, 375–388; and Reed, C. L., Caselli, R. J., and Farah, M. J., Tactile agnosia. Underlying impairment and implications for normal tactile object recognition, *Brain*, 1996, *119*, 875–888. Reprinted with permission.)

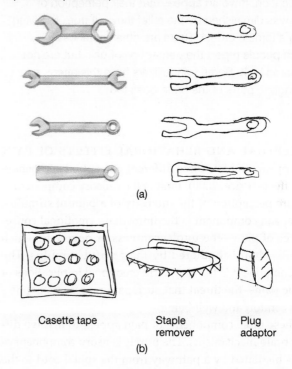

which often accompanies injuries to skin or muscle, greatly increases sensitivity of the inflamed region to painful stimuli. This effect motivates the individual to minimize movement of the injured part and avoid contact with other objects. The effect is to reduce the likelihood of further injury.

Cox et al., (2006) studied three families from northern Pakistan whose members included several people with a complete absence of pain and discovered the location of the gene responsible for this disorder. The gene, an autosomal recessive allele located on chromosome 2, encodes for a voltage-dependent sodium channel. The case that brought the families to the researchers' attention was a 10-year-old boy who performed a "street theater" during which he would thrust knives through his arms and walk on burning coals without feeling any pain. He died just before his fourteenth birthday after jumping off the roof of a house. All six of the affected people in the three families had injuries to their lips or tongues caused by self-inflicted bites. They all suffered from bruises and cuts, and many sustained bone fractures that they did not notice until the injuries impaired their mobility. Despite their total lack of pain from any type of noxious stimulus, they had normal sensations of touch, warmth, coolness, proprioception, tickle, and pressure.

Some environmental events diminish the perception of pain. For example, Beecher (1959) noted that many wounded American soldiers back from the battle at Anzio, Italy, during World War II reported that they felt no pain from their wounds. They did not even want medication. It would appear that their perception of pain was diminished by the relief they felt from surviving such a terrible ordeal. There are other instances in which people report the perception of pain but are not bothered by it. Some tranquilizers have this effect, and damage to parts of the brain does too.

PERCEPTUAL AND BEHAVIORAL EFFECTS OF PAIN

Pain appears to have three different perceptual and behavioral effects (Price, 2000). First is the sensory component—the pure perception of the intensity of a painful stimulus. The second component is the immediate emotional consequences of pain—the unpleasantness or degree to which the individual is bothered by the painful stimulus. The third component is the long-term emotional implications of chronic pain—the threat that such pain represents to one's future comfort and well-being.

These three components of pain appear to involve different brain mechanisms. The purely sensory component of pain is mediated by a pathway from the spinal cord to the ventral posterolateral thalamus to the primary and secondary somatosensory cortex. The immediate emotional component of pain appears to be mediated by pathways that reach the anterior cingulate cortex (ACC) and insular cortex. The long-term emotional component appears to be mediated by pathways that reach the prefrontal cortex. (See Figure 7.25.)

Let's look at some evidence for brain mechanisms involved in short-term and long-term emotional responses to pain. Several studies have found that painful stimuli activate the insular cortex and the ACC. In addition, Ostrowsky et al., (2002) found that electrical stimulation of the insular cortex caused reports of painful burning and stinging sensations. Damage to this region decreases people's emotional response to pain: They continue to feel the pain but do not seem to recognize that it is harmful (Berthier et al., 1988). They do not withdraw from pain or the threat of pain.

Rainville et al., (1997) produced pain sensations in participants by having them put their arms in ice water. Under one condition, the researchers used hypnosis to diminish the unpleasantness of the pain. The hypnosis worked; the participants said that the pain was less unpleasant, even though it was still as intense. Meanwhile, the investigators used a PET scanner to measure regional activation of the brain. They found that the painful stimulus increased the

Figure 7.25 The Three Components of Pain

A simplified, schematic diagram shows the brain mechanisms involved in the three components of pain: the sensory component, the immediate emotional component, and the long-term emotional component.

(Adapted from Price, D. B. Science, 2000, 288, 1769–1772.)

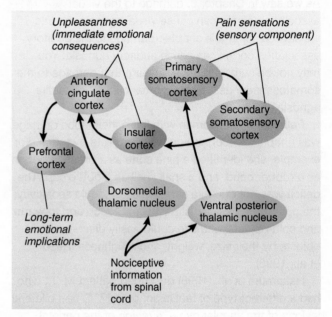

activity of both the primary somatosensory cortex and the ACC. When the participants were hypnotized and found the pain less unpleasant, the activity of the ACC decreased, but the activity of the primary somatosensory cortex remained high. Presumably, the primary somatosensory cortex is involved in the perception of pain, and the ACC is involved in its immediate emotional effects—its unpleasantness. (See Figure 7.26.)

In another study from the same laboratory, Hofbauer et al., (2001) produced the opposite effect. They presented participants with a painful stimulus and used hypnotic suggestion to reduce the perceived intensity of the pain. They found that the suggestion reduced participants' ratings of pain and also decreased the activation of the somatosensory cortex. Thus, changes in perceived *intensity* of pain are reflected in changes in activation of the somatosensory cortex, whereas changes in perceived *unpleasantness* of pain is reflected in changes in activation of the ACC.

Several functional-imaging studies have shown that under certain conditions, stimuli associated with pain can activate the ACC even when no actual painful stimulus is applied. Osaka et al., (2004) found that the ACC was activated when participants heard Japanese words that vividly denote various types of pain (for example, a throbbing pain, a splitting headache, or the pain caused by being stuck with thorns). In a test of romantically involved couples, Singer et al., (2004) found that when women received a painful electrical shock to the back of their hand, their ACC, anterior insular cortex, thalamus, and somatosensory cortex became

Figure 7.26 Sensory and Emotional Components of Pain

The PET scans show brain regions that respond to pain. *Top:* Dorsal views of the brain. Activation of the primary somatosensory cortex (circled in red) by a painful stimulus was not affected by a hypnotically suggested reduction in unpleasantness of a painful stimulus, indicating that this region responded to the sensory component of pain. *Bottom:* Midsagittal views of the brain. The anterior cingulate cortex (circled in red) showed much less activation when the unpleasantness of the painful stimulus was reduced by hypnotic suggestion.

(From Rainville, P., Duncan, G. H., Price, D. D., Carrier, B., and Bushnell, M. C., Pain affect encoded in human anterior cingulate but not somatosensory cortex, *Science*, 1997, *277*, 968–971. Copyright © American Association for the Advancement of Science. Reprinted with permission.)

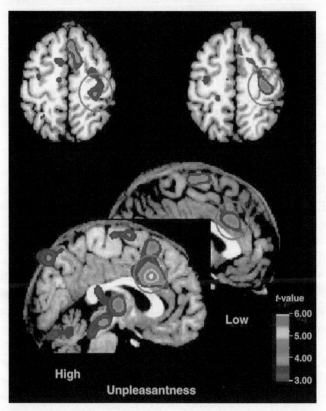

Table 7.5 Brain Regions Involved in Perceptual and Behavior Effects of Pain

Effects of pain	Brain Regions Involved
Sensory component	Pathway from spinal cord to thalamus to primary/secondary somatosensory cortex
Immediate emotional consequences	Insular cortex, ACC, primary somatosensory cortex
Long-term emotional consequences	Prefrontal cortex

A particularly interesting form of pain sensation occurs after a limb has been amputated. After the limb is gone, up to 70 percent of amputees report that they feel as though the missing limb still exists and that it often hurts. This phenomenon is referred to as the **phantom limb** (Melzak, 1992; Ramachandran and Hirstein, 1998). People with phantom limbs report that the limb feels very real, and they often say that if they try to reach out with it, it feels as though it were responding. Sometimes, they perceive it as sticking out, and they may feel compelled to avoid knocking it against the side of a doorframe or sleeping in a position that would make it come between them and the mattress. People have reported all sorts of sensations in phantom limbs, including pain, pressure, warmth, cold, wetness, itching, sweatiness, and prickliness.

The classic explanation for phantom limbs has been activity of the sensory axons belonging to the amputated limb. Presumably, the nervous system interprets this activity as coming from the missing limb. When nerves are cut and connections cannot be reestablished between the proximal and distal portions, the cut ends of the proximal portions form nodules known as *neuromas*. The treatment for phantom pain has been to cut the nerves above these neuromas, to cut the dorsal roots that bring the afferent information from these nerves into the spinal cord, or to make lesions in somatosensory pathways in the spinal cord, thalamus, or cerebral cortex. Sometimes these procedures work for a while, but often the pain returns.

Melzak (1992) suggested that the phantom limb sensation is inherent in the organization of the parietal cortex. The parietal cortex is involved in our awareness of our own bodies. Indeed, people with lesions of the parietal lobe (especially in the right hemisphere) have been known to push their own leg out of bed, believing that it belongs to someone else. Melzak reports that some people who were born with missing limbs nevertheless experience phantom limb sensations, which would suggest that our brains are genetically programmed to provide sensations for all four limbs.

A unique therapy can be helpful for some types of pain or discomfort experienced from phantom limbs. It is further thought that phantom limb pain can arise from a conflict between visual feedback and proprioceptive feedback from the phantom limb. Mirror box therapy requires the patient

active. When they saw their partners receive a painful shock but did not receive one themselves, the same regions (except for the somatosensory cortex) became active. Thus, the emotional component of pain—in this case, a vicarious experience of pain, provoked by empathy with the feelings of someone a person loved—caused responses in the brain similar to the ones caused by actual pain. Just as we saw in the study by Rainville et al., (1997), the somatosensory cortex is activated only by an actual noxious stimulus.

The final component of pain—the emotional consequences of chronic pain—appears to involve the prefrontal cortex. As we will see in Chapter 11, damage to the prefrontal cortex impairs people's ability to make plans for the future and to recognize the personal significance of situations in which they are involved. Along with the general lack of insight, people with prefrontal damage tend not to be concerned with the implications of chronic conditions—including chronic pain—for their future. (See Table 7.5.)

Figure 7.27 Mirror Box Therapy

Mirror box therapy for phantom limb pain requires the patient to substitute visual feedback for the missing limb by reflecting a mirror image of the intact limb.

to substitute visual feedback for the missing limb by reflecting a mirror image of the intact limb. Clinical trials of mirror box therapy support the utility of this intervention for reducing phantom limb pain when the mirror image is used to represent an image of moving and stretching the phantom limb (Chan et al., 2007). (See Figure 7.27.)

ENDOGENOUS MODIFICATION OF PAIN SENSITIVITY
For many years, investigators have known that perception of pain can be modified by environmental stimuli. Recent work, beginning in the 1970s, has revealed the existence of neural circuits whose activity can produce analgesia. A variety of environmental stimuli can activate these analgesia-producing circuits. Most of these stimuli cause the release of the endogenous opioids, which were described in Chapter 4.

Electrical stimulation of particular locations within the brain can cause analgesia, which can even be profound enough to serve as an anesthetic for surgery in rats (Reynolds, 1969). The most effective locations appear to be within the periaqueductal gray matter and in the rostroventral medulla. For example, electrical stimulation of the periaqueductal gray matter produced analgesia in rats equivalent to that produced by at least 10 milligrams (mg) of morphine per kilogram (kg) of body weight, which is a large dose (Mayer and Liebeskind, 1974). The technique has even found an application in reducing severe, chronic pain in humans: Fine wires are surgically implanted in parts of the central nervous system and attached to a radio-controlled device that permits the patient to administer electrical stimulation when necessary (Kumar et al., 1990).

Analgesic brain stimulation apparently triggers the neural mechanisms that reduce pain, primarily by causing endogenous opioids to be released. Basbaum and Fields (1978, 1984) proposed a neural circuit that mediates opiate-induced analgesia. Basically, they proposed the following: Endogenous opioids (released by environmental stimuli or administered as a drug) stimulate opiate receptors on neurons in the periaqueductal gray matter. Because the effect of opiates appears to be inhibitory (Nicoll et al., 1980), Basbaum and Fields proposed that the neurons that contain opiate receptors are themselves inhibitory interneurons. Thus, the administration of opiates activates the neurons on which these interneurons synapse.

Neurons in the periaqueductal gray matter send axons to the **nucleus raphe magnus,** located in the medulla. The neurons in this nucleus send axons to the dorsal horn of the spinal cord gray matter; destruction of these axons eliminates analgesia induced by an injection of morphine. The inhibitory effects of these neurons apparently involve one or two interneurons in the spinal cord.

Pain sensitivity can be regulated by direct neural connections, as well as by secretion of the endogenous opioids. The periaqueductal gray matter receives inputs from the frontal cortex, amygdala, and hypothalamus (Beitz, 1982; Mantyh, 1983). These inputs permit learning and emotional reactions to affect an animal's responsiveness to pain even without the secretion of opioids.

PLACEBO ANALGESIA Pain can be reduced, at least in some people, by administering a pharmacologically inert placebo. When some people take a medication that they believe will reduce pain, it triggers the release of endogenous opioids and actually does so. This effect is eliminated if the people are given an injection of naloxone, a drug that blocks opiate receptors (Eippert et al., 2009). Thus, for some people a placebo is not pharmacologically inert—it has a

The schematic shows the neural circuit that mediates opiate-induced analgesia, as hypothesized by Basbaum and Fields (1978).

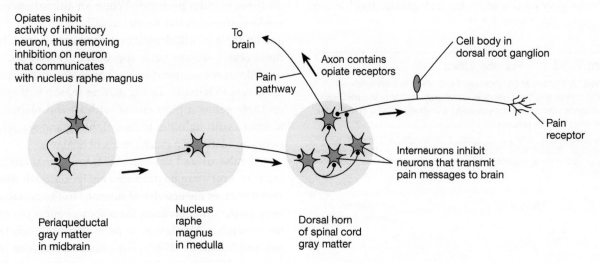

Opiates inhibit activity of inhibitory neuron, thus removing inhibition on neuron that communicates with nucleus raphe magnus

To brain

Pain pathway

Axon contains opiate receptors

Cell body in dorsal root ganglion

Pain receptor

Interneurons inhibit neurons that transmit pain messages to brain

Periaqueductal gray matter in midbrain

Nucleus raphe magnus in medulla

Dorsal horn of spinal cord gray matter

physiological effect. The placebo effect may be mediated through connections of the frontal cortex with the periaqueductal gray matter. A functional-imaging study by Zubieta et al., (2005) found that placebo-induced analgesia did indeed cause the release of endogenous opiates. They used a PET scanner to detect the presence of μ-opioid neurotransmission in the brains of people who responded to the effects of a placebo. As Figure 7.28 shows, several regions of the brain, including the anterior cingulate cortex and insular cortex, showed evidence of increased endogenous opioid activity.

An interesting study by Waber et al., (2008) found that the efficacy of a placebo was directly related to its perceived value. Volunteers were given a placebo pill that was alleged to reduce pain. Some people were told that the pills normally cost $2.50 each, and others were told that the price had been discounted to 10 cents each. Before and after taking the pill, the participants received electric shocks to their wrists and rated the intensity of the pain that the shocks produced. As Figure 7.29 shows, participants who believed that they had

Figure 7.29 Effect of Perceived Price of a Drug on Placebo Analgesia

The graph shows that participants reported less pain reduction from a placebo when they thought it was priced at a discount.

received an expensive pill showed a stronger reduction in pain perception than those who believed they had received an inexpensive one.

A functional-imaging study by Wager et al., (2004) supports the suggestion that the prefrontal cortex plays a role in placebo analgesia. They administered painful stimuli (heat or electrical shocks) to the skin with or without the application of an "analgesic" skin cream that was actually an unmedicated placebo. They observed a placebo effect—reports of less intense pain and decreased activity in the primary pain-reactive regions of the brain, including the thalamus, ACC, and insular cortex. They also observed *increased* activity in the prefrontal cortex and the periaqueductal gray matter of the midbrain. Presumably, the expectation of decreased

Figure 7.28 Brain Regions Involved in Response to Pain-Relieving Placebo

PET imaging demonstrates the endogenous opioids binding to μ opioid receptors following administration of a placebo in several brain regions.

Based on: Zubieta et al., 2005

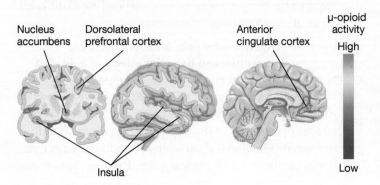

Nucleus accumbens

Dorsolateral prefrontal cortex

Anterior cingulate cortex

μ-opioid activity

High

Insula

Low

sensitivity to pain caused the increased activity of the prefrontal cortex, and connections of this region with the periaqueductal gray matter activated endogenous mechanisms of analgesia. (See Figure 7.30.)

Figure 7.30 The Placebo Effect

Functional MRI scans show increased activity in the dorsolateral prefrontal cortex and the periaqueductal gray matter of the midbrain of participants who showed decreased sensitivity to pain in response to administration of a placebo.

(Based on Wager, T. D., Rilling, J. K., Smith, E. E., Sokolik, A., Casey, K. L., Davidson, R. J., Kosslyn, S. M., Rose, R. M., and Cohen, J. D., Placebo-induced changes in fMRI in the anticipation and experience of pain, *Science*, 2004, *303*, 1162–1166.)

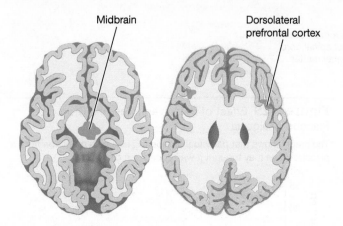

It appears that a considerable amount of neural circuitry is devoted to reducing the intensity of pain. What functions do these circuits perform? When an animal encounters a noxious stimulus, the animal usually stops what it is doing and engages in withdrawal or escape behaviors. Obviously, these responses are quite appropriate. However, they are sometimes counterproductive. For example, males fighting for access to females during mating season will fail to pass on their genes if pain elicits withdrawal responses that interfere with fighting. In fact, fighting and sexual activity both stimulate brain mechanisms of analgesia.

Komisaruk and Larsson (1971) found that tactile stimulation of a rat's vagina produced analgesia. Such stimulation also increases the activity of neurons in the periaqueductal gray matter and decreases the responsiveness of neurons in the ventrobasal thalamus to painful stimulation (Komisaruk and Steinman, 1987). The phenomenon also occurs in humans; Whipple and Komisaruk (1988) found that self-administered vaginal stimulation reduces sensitivity to painful stimuli but not to neutral tactile stimuli. Presumably, copulation triggers analgesic mechanisms. The adaptive significance of this phenomenon is clear: Painful stimuli encountered during the course of copulation are less likely to cause the behavior to be interrupted; thus, the chances of pregnancy are increased.

Section Review

Somatosenses

LO 7.13 Provide examples of stimuli that activate receptors for the somatosenses.

Mechanical deformation of the skin activates pressure receptors. Changes in temperature activate temperature receptors. Sensations of pain can be caused by many different types of stimuli, but most cause tissue damage and activate nociceptors. Skeletal muscle stretch and limb movement activate kinesthetic receptors.

LO 7.14 Describe the anatomy and somatosensory receptors of the skin.

Skin consists of subcutaneous tissue, dermis, and epidermis. Skin contains free nerve endings and encapsulated receptors.

LO 7.15 Describe receptors involved in the perception of touch, temperature, pain, and itch.

Mechanoreceptors are activated by vibration. Vibratory movement causes ion channels to open and change membrane potential to transduce the signal. Thermal receptors are free nerve endings that are activated by a relative change in temperature. Pain receptors are free nerve endings that are stimulated by intense pressure, heat, and

chemical irritants. Little is known about the receptors that are responsible for the sensation of itch.

LO 7.16 Describe the pathway for somatosensory processing from nerves to subcortical and cortical structures.

Somatosensory axons enter the central nervous system via spinal and cranial nerves. Information from the nerves passes through the medulla, the medial lemniscus of the midbrain, the ventral posterior nucleus of the thalamus, the primary somatosensory cortex, and finally the secondary (association) somatosensory cortex. Sensory cortex includes column organization by stimulus type and multiple maps of the body surface, each corresponding to different types of somatosensory information.

LO 7.17 Describe why pain is experienced, the perceptual and behavior effects of pain, and how pain perception can be modified.

Pain serves a constructive role: to reduce the likelihood of further injury. It consists of three perceptual and behavioral effects: perceptions of the intensity of a painful stimulus, immediate emotional consequences, and long-term emotional implications of chronic pain. Pain perception can be modified by activating analgesia circuits, through the release of endogenous opioids, or by administering exogenous opioids.

Thought Question

Do all placebos have the same effects on pain reduction? Design an experiment to test the effects of various characteristics of a placebo on pain relief. Consider what aspects of a placebo may make it more effective (for example, price was described in the previous section) and how it may be administered or for what kinds of pain it may be most effective.

Gustation

A 75-year-old woman experienced a sudden stroke while cooking in her kitchen. Six months following the stroke, the woman had recovered many of her impaired functions (which included weakness on her right side); however, she had lost 6.35 kg (approximately 14 lb.) and found her favorite foods unappealing. She reported that everything she ate tasted unappetizing to her and although she could distinguish among different tastes, she perceived foods to have unusual, non-food-like flavors This experience resulted in the patient eating less food, losing weight, and experiencing feelings of isolation because she did not enjoy sharing meals or eating in restaurants with friends or family. CT scans of the patient's brain immediately following the stroke revealed that the lesion was localized to the left insular cortex (Dutta et al., 2013).

The stimuli that we have encountered so far produce receptor potentials by imparting physical energy: thermal, photic (involving light), or kinetic. However, the stimuli received by the last two senses to be studied—gustation and olfaction—interact with their receptors chemically. This section discusses the first of them: gustation. As demonstrated in the case study above, gustation is important in maintaining both adequate nutrition and quality of life. Like the other senses, regions of the cortex are devoted to perception of taste and damage to these regions can result in loss of sensory perception.

The Stimuli

LO 7.18 **List the six qualities of taste stimuli.**

Gustation is clearly related to eating; this sense modality helps us to determine the nature of things we put in our mouths. For a substance to be tasted, molecules of it must dissolve in the saliva and stimulate the taste receptors on the tongue. Tastes of different substances vary, though much less than we generally realize. There are only six qualities of taste: *bitterness, sourness, sweetness, saltiness, umami,* and *fat*.

Flavor, as opposed to taste, is a composite of olfaction and gustation. Much of the flavor of food depends on its odor; people with *anosmia* (who lack the sense of smell) or people whose nostrils are blocked have difficulty distinguishing between different foods by taste alone.

Most vertebrates possess gustatory systems that respond to all six taste qualities. (An exception is the cat family; lions, tigers, leopards, and domestic cats do not detect sweetness.) Sweetness receptors are food detectors. Most sweet-tasting foods, such as fruits and some vegetables, are safe to eat (Ramirez, 1990). Saltiness receptors detect the presence of sodium chloride. In some environments, it is difficult to obtain adequate amounts of this mineral from the usual sources of food, so sodium chloride detectors help the animal to detect its presence. Injuries that cause bleeding deplete an organism of its supply of sodium rapidly, so the ability to find salt quickly can be critical. In recent years, researchers have recognized the existence of a fifth taste quality: *umami*. **Umami,** a Japanese word that means "good taste," refers to the taste of monosodium glutamate (MSG), a substance that is often used as a flavor enhancer in Asian cuisine (Kurihara, 1987; Scott and Plata-Salaman, 1991). The umami receptor detects the presence of glutamate, an amino acid found in proteins. Presumably, the umami receptor provides the ability to taste proteins, an important nutrient.

Most vertebrates possess gustatory systems that respond to all six taste qualities, but the cat family cannot detect sweetness.

WilleeCole/Shutterstock

Most species of animals will readily ingest substances that taste sweet or somewhat salty. Similarly, they are attracted to foods that are rich in amino acids, which explains the use of MSG as a flavor enhancer. However, they will tend to avoid substances that taste sour or bitter. Because of bacterial activity, many foods become acidic when they spoil. In addition, most unripe fruits are acidic. Acidity tastes sour and causes an avoidance reaction. (However, we have learned to make highly preferred mixtures of sweet and sour, such as lemonade.) Bitterness is almost universally avoided and cannot easily be improved by adding some sweetness. Many plants produce poisonous alkaloids, which protect them from being eaten by animals. Alkaloids taste bitter; thus, the bitterness receptor undoubtedly serves to warn animals away from these chemicals.

For many years, researchers have known that many species of animals (including our own) show a distinct preference for high-fat foods. Because there is not a distinct taste that is associated with the presence of fat, most investigators concluded that we detected fat by its odor and texture ("mouth feel"). However, Fukuwatari et al., (2003) found that rats whose olfactory sense was destroyed continued to show a preference for a liquid diet containing a long-chain fatty acid, one of the breakdown products of fat. When fats reach the tongue, some of these molecules are broken down into fatty acids by an enzyme called *lingual lipase,* which is found in the vicinity of taste buds. The activity of lingual lipase ensures that fatty acid detectors are stimulated when food containing fat enters the mouth. Cartoni et al., (2010) identified two G protein-coupled receptors that appear to be responsible for detecting the presence of fatty acids in the mouth. The investigators found that mice with a targeted mutation against the genes responsible for the production of these receptors showed a decreased preference for fatty acids, and that responses of the taste nerves to fatty acids were also diminished.

Anatomy of the Taste Buds and Gustatory Cells

LO 7.19   Identify the location and structure of taste buds and taste receptor cells.

The tongue, palate, pharynx, and larynx contain approximately 10,000 taste buds. Most of these receptive organs are arranged around *papillae,* small protuberances of the tongue. *Fungiform papillae,* located on the anterior two-thirds of the tongue, contain up to eight taste buds, along with receptors for pressure, touch, and temperature. *Foliate papillae* consist of up to eight parallel folds along each edge of the back of the tongue. Approximately 1,300 taste buds are located in these folds. *Circumvallate papillae,* arranged in an inverted V on the posterior third of the tongue, contain approximately 250 taste buds. They are shaped like little

plateaus surrounded by moatlike trenches. Taste buds consist of groups of 20 to 50 receptor cells, specialized neurons arranged somewhat like the segments of an orange. Cilia are located at the end of each cell and project through the opening of the taste bud (the pore) into the saliva that coats the tongue. Tight junctions between adjacent taste cells prevent substances in the saliva from diffusing freely into the taste bud itself. Figure 7.31 shows the appearance of a circumvallate papilla; a cross section through the surrounding trench contains a taste bud.

Taste receptor cells form synapses with dendrites of bipolar neurons whose axons convey gustatory information to the brain through the seventh, ninth, and tenth cranial nerves. The neurotransmitter released by the receptor cells is adenosine triphosphate (ATP), the molecule produced by mitochondria that stores energy within cells (Finger et al., 2005). The receptor cells have a life span of only 10 days. They quickly wear out, being directly exposed to a rather hostile environment. As they degenerate, they are replaced by newly developed cells; the dendrite of the bipolar neuron is passed on to the new cell (Beidler, 1970).

Perception of Gustatory Information

LO 7.20   Outline the process of transduction for perception of salt, sour, bitter, sweet, and umami.

Transduction of taste is similar to the chemical transmission that takes place at synapses: The tasted molecule binds with the receptor and produces changes in membrane permeability that cause receptor potentials. Different substances bind with different types of receptors, producing different taste sensations. In this section we will describe what we know about the nature of the molecules with particular tastes and the receptors that detect their presence.

SALT   To taste salty, a substance must ionize. Although the best stimulus for saltiness receptors is sodium chloride

Figure 7.31 The Tongue

(a) Papillae on the surface of the tongue. (b) Taste buds.

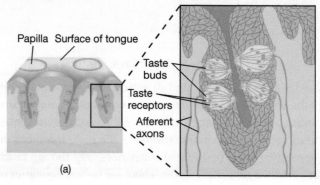

(NaCl), a variety of salts containing metallic cations (such as Na^+, K^+, and Li^+) with a small anion (such as Cl^-, Br^-, SO_4^{2-}, or NO_3^-) taste salty. The receptor for saltiness seems to be a simple sodium channel. When present in the saliva, sodium enters the taste cell and depolarizes it, triggering action potentials that cause the cell to release a neurotransmitter (Avenet and Lindemann, 1989; Kinnamon and Cummings, 1992). The best evidence that sodium channels are involved is the fact that amiloride, a drug that is known to block sodium channels, prevents sodium chloride from activating taste cells and decreases sensations of saltiness. However, the drug does not completely block these sensations in humans, so most investigators believe that more than one type of receptor is involved (Ossebaard et al., 1997; Schiffman et al., 1983).

SOUR Sourness receptors appear to respond to the hydrogen ions present in acidic solutions. However, because the sourness of a particular acid is not simply a function of the concentration of hydrogen ions, the anions must have an effect as well. The reason for this anion effect is not yet known.

BITTER, SWEET, AND UMAMI The stimulus for sourness—the presence of acids—is clear. However, bitter and sweet substances are more difficult to characterize. The typical stimulus for bitterness is a plant alkaloid such as quinine; for sweetness it is a sugar such as glucose or fructose. The fact that some molecules elicit both sensations suggested to early researchers that bitterness and sweetness receptors may be similar. For example, the Seville orange rind contains a glycoside (complex sugar) that tastes extremely bitter; the addition of a hydrogen ion to the molecule makes it taste intensely sweet (Horowitz and Gentili, 1974). Some amino acids taste sweet. Indeed, the commercial sweetener aspartame consists of just two amino acids: aspartate and phenylalanine.

Receptors sensitive to bitterness and sweetness are linked to a G protein known as *gustducin*, which is very similar in structure to *transducin*, the G protein involved in transduction of photic information in the retina. Receptors sensitive to umami are linked to both gustducin and transducin (He et al., 2004; McLaughlin et al., 1993; Wong et al., 1996). When a bitter molecule binds with the receptor, the G protein activates an enzyme that begins a cycle of chemical reactions that causes the release of ATP, the neurotransmitter of taste receptor cells.

Recent evidence has discovered two families of receptors responsible for detecting sweet, bitter, and umami tastes (see Scott, 2004, for a review). The first family, T1R, has three members: T1R1, T1R2, and T1R3, produced by three different genes. The sweet receptor consists of two components: T1R2 + T1R3. The umami receptor consists of T1R1 + T1R3. A gustatory receptor cell can be sensitive to sweet or umami but not both. Bitter compounds are detected by the second family of receptors, T2R, of which there are 30 members (Matsunami et al., 2000). A gustatory receptor cell sensitive

to bitterness contains one of the many different varieties of T2R, which indicates that each cell can detect the presence of many different bitter-tasting molecules. As we saw, many compounds found in nature that taste bitter are poisonous. Rather than entrusting detection of these compounds to a single receptor, the process of evolution has given us the ability to detect a wide variety of compounds with different molecular shapes. (See Figure 7.32.)

We mentioned earlier that cats are insensitive to sweet tastes. Li et al., (2005) discovered the reason for the absence of sweet sensitivity: Cat DNA lacks functional genes that produce T1R2 proteins, one of the components of sweet receptors. (Look again at Figure 7.32.) The investigators suggested that this mutation was probably an important event in the evolution of cats' carnivorous behavior.

Figure 7.32 Structure of Taste Receptors

This schematic drawing of the structure of receptors responsible for detection of sweet, umami, and bitter tastes.

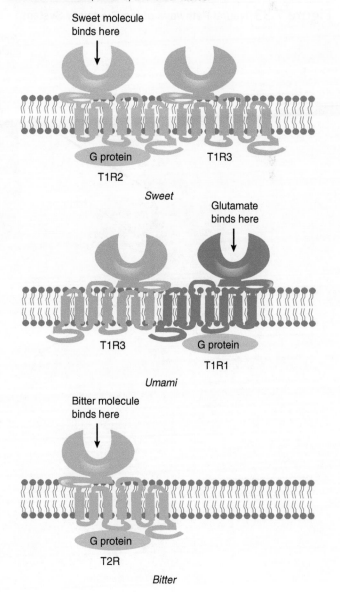

The Gustatory Pathway

LO 7.21 **Describe the path of gustatory processing from nerves to subcortical and cortical structures.**

Gustatory information is transmitted through cranial nerves 7, 9, and 10. Information from the anterior part of the tongue travels through the **chorda tympani,** a branch of the seventh cranial nerve (facial nerve). Taste receptors in the posterior part of the tongue send information through the lingual (tongue) branch of the ninth cranial nerve (glossopharyngeal nerve); the tenth cranial nerve (vagus nerve) carries information from receptors of the palate and epiglottis. The chorda tympani gets its name because it passes through the middle ear just beneath the tympanic membrane.

The first relay station for taste is the **nucleus of the solitary tract,** located in the medulla. In primates the taste-sensitive neurons of this nucleus send their axons to the ventral posteromedial thalamic nucleus, a nucleus that also receives somatosensory information received from the trigeminal nerve (Beckstead et al., 1980). Thalamic taste-sensitive neurons send their axons to the primary gustatory cortex, which is located in the base of the frontal cortex and in the insular cortex (Pritchard et al., 1986). Neurons in this region project to the secondary gustatory cortex, located in the caudolateral orbitofrontal cortex (Rolls et al., 1990). Unlike most other sense modalities, taste is ipsilaterally represented in the brain; that is, the right side of the tongue projects to the right side of the brain, and the left side projects to the left. (See Figure 7.33.)

Figure 7.33 Neural Pathways of the Gustatory System

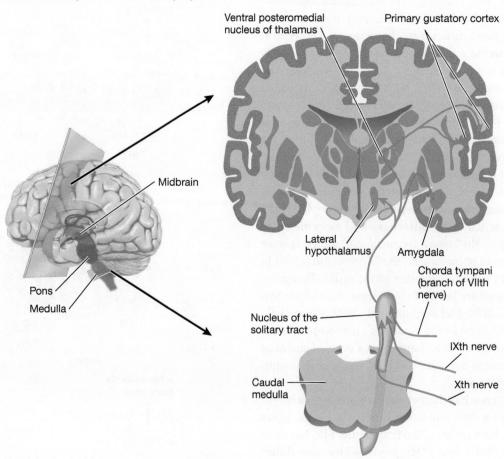

Besides receiving information from taste receptors, the gustatory cortex also receives thermal, mechanical, visceral, and nociceptive (painful) stimuli, which undoubtedly play a role in determining the palatability of food (Carleton et al., 2010). Gustatory information also reaches the amygdala and the hypothalamus and adjacent basal forebrain (Nauta, 1964; Russchen et al., 1986). Many investigators believe that the hypothalamic pathway plays a role in mediating the reinforcing effects of sweet, umami, and slightly salty tastes. In fact, some neurons in the hypothalamus respond to sweet stimuli only when the animal is hungry (Rolls et al., 1986).

MAP ORGANIZATION IN THE GUSTATORY CORTEX
In a functional-imaging study, Schoenfeld et al., (2004) had people sip water that was flavored with sweet, sour, bitter, and umami tastes. The investigators found that tasting each flavor activated different regions in the primary gustatory area of the insular cortex. Although the locations of the taste-responsive regions differed from person to person, the same pattern was seen when a given individual was tested on different occasions. Thus, the representation of tastes in the gustatory cortex is idiosyncratic but stable.

Section Review

Gustation

LO 7.18   List the six qualities of taste stimuli.
The six qualities of taste are bitterness, sourness, sweetness, saltiness, umami, and fat.

LO 7.19   Identify the location and structure of taste buds and taste receptor cells.
The tongue contains the taste buds. Most taste buds are arranged around papillae and contain groups of receptor cells.

LO 7.20   Outline the process of transduction for perception of salt, sour, bitter, sweet, and umami.
Molecules bind with receptor cells and produce changes in membrane permeability that cause receptor potentials. The receptor for saltiness seems to be a simple sodium channel, which allows sodium ions to enter the cell and depolarize it. The receptors for sour likely interact with hydrogen and anions. Receptors sensitive to bitterness, sweetness, and umami are linked to a G protein.

LO 7.21   Describe the path of gustatory processing from nerves to subcortical and cortical structures.
Taste receptors in the tongue send taste information to the brain via cranial nerves. Taste information first enters the nucleus of the solitary tract in the medulla, then to the thalamus, then the primary gustatory cortex, and finally the secondary gustatory cortex. Unlike most other sense modalities, taste is ipsilaterally represented in the brain. The primary gustatory cortex contains a taste map.

Thought Question

Review the case study that was presented at the beginning of this section. Imagine that any tool or technique is available to you as a clinician specializing in gustatory rehabilitation, now or in the future when new technologies or interventions have been developed. What approach might you take to assist the patient to regain their sense of taste and improve their quality of life?

Olfaction

Olfaction, another chemical sense, helps us to identify food and avoid food that has spoiled and is unfit to eat. It helps the members of many species to track prey or detect predators and to identify friends, foes, and receptive mates. Although many other mammals, such as dogs, have more sensitive olfactory systems than humans do, we should not underrate our own. The olfactory system is second only to the visual system in the number of sensory receptor cells, with an estimated 10 million cells. We can smell some substances at lower concentrations than the most sensitive laboratory instruments can detect.

Recent research is beginning to suggest that part of the greater olfactory sensitivity of other mammals compared to humans is that other mammals put their noses where odors are the strongest—just above the ground. For example, a dog following an odor trail sniffs along the ground, where the odors of a passing animal may have clung. A bloodhound's nose would not be as useful if it were located nearly two meters above the ground, as an average human's is. When people sniff the ground as dogs do, their olfactory system works much better. Porter et al., (2007) prepared a scent trail—using a string moistened with essential oil of chocolate and placed in a grassy field. The participants were blindfolded and wore earmuffs, kneepads, and gloves, which prevented them from using anything other than their noses to follow the scent trail. They did quite well, and they adopted the same zigzag strategy used by dogs.

The Stimulus and Anatomy of the Olfactory Apparatus

LO 7.22 **Identify the stimulus and describe the structure and function of the olfactory apparatus.**

The stimulus for odor (known formally as an *odorant*) consists of volatile substances having a molecular weight in the range of approximately 15–300. Almost all odorous compounds are lipid soluble and of organic origin. However, many substances that meet these criteria have no odor at all, so we still have much to learn about the nature of odorants.

Our 6 million olfactory receptor cells reside within two patches of mucous membrane (the **olfactory epithelium**), each having an area of about one square inch. The olfactory epithelium is located at the top of the nasal cavity, as shown in Figure 7.34. Less than 10 percent of the air that enters the nostrils reaches the olfactory epithelium; a sniff is needed to sweep air upward into the nasal cavity so that it reaches the olfactory receptors.

OLFACTORY RECEPTORS Figure 7.34 illustrates a group of olfactory receptor cells, along with their supporting cells. Olfactory receptor cells are bipolar neurons whose cell bodies lie within the olfactory mucosa that lines the *cribriform plate*, a bone at the base of the rostral part of the brain. There

is a constant production of new olfactory receptor cells, but their life is considerably longer than those of gustatory receptor cells. Supporting cells contain enzymes that destroy odorant molecules and thus help to prevent them from damaging the olfactory receptor cells.

Olfactory receptor cells send a process toward the surface of the mucosa, which divides into 10 to 20 cilia that penetrate the layer of mucus. Odorous molecules must dissolve in the mucus and stimulate receptor molecules on the olfactory cilia. Approximately 35 bundles of axons, ensheathed by glial cells, enter the skull through small holes in the cribriform plate. The olfactory mucosa also contains free nerve endings of trigeminal nerve axons; these nerve endings presumably mediate sensations of pain that can be produced by sniffing some irritating chemicals, such as ammonia.

OLFACTORY PROCESSING The **olfactory bulbs** lie at the base of the brain on the ends of the stalklike olfactory tracts. Each olfactory receptor cell sends a single axon into an olfactory bulb, where it forms synapses with dendrites of **mitral cells** (named for their resemblance to a bishop's miter, or ceremonial headgear). These synapses take place in the complex axonal and dendritic arborizations called **olfactory glomeruli**. There are approximately 10,000 glomeruli, each of which receives input from a bundle of approximately 2,000 axons.

Figure 7.34 The Olfactory System

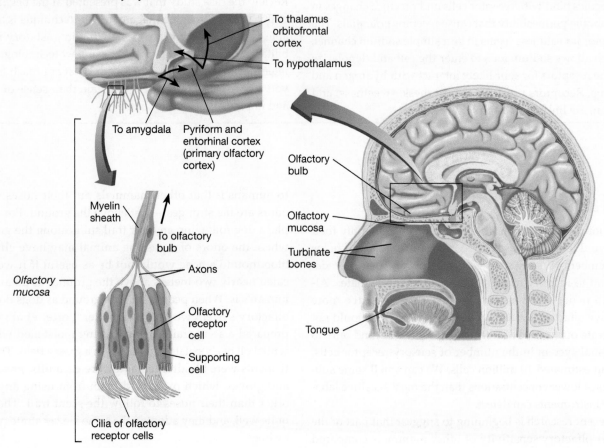

Figure 7.35 Olfactory Pathway

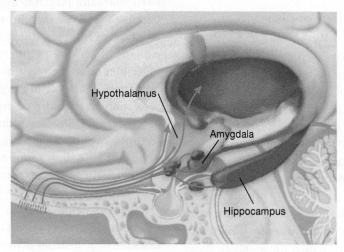

The axons of the mitral cells travel to the rest of the brain through the olfactory tracts. Some of these axons terminate in other regions of the ipsilateral forebrain; others cross the brain and terminate in the contralateral olfactory bulb.

Olfactory tract axons project directly to the amygdala and to two regions of the limbic cortex: the piriform cortex (the primary olfactory cortex) and the entorhinal cortex. (Look again at Figure 7.34.) The amygdala sends olfactory information to the hypothalamus, the entorhinal cortex sends it to the hippocampus, and the piriform cortex sends it to the hypothalamus and to the orbitofrontal cortex via the dorsomedial nucleus of the thalamus (Buck, 1996; Shipley and Ennis, 1996). As you may recall, the orbitofrontal cortex also receives gustatory information; thus, it may be involved in the combining of taste and olfaction into flavor. The hypothalamus also receives a considerable amount of olfactory information, which is probably important for the acceptance or rejection of food and for the olfactory control of reproductive processes seen in many species of mammals. (See Figure 7.35.)

MAPPING SPECIFIC ODORS Zou et al., (2001) investigated the specificity of olfactory information in the pathway from olfactory receptors to olfactory glomeruli to the olfactory cortex. The investigators found that, just as retinotopic information is maintained in the visual system and tonotopic information is maintained in the auditory system, "olfactotopic" information is maintained in the olfactory system. That is, the particular glomeruli that receive information from particular olfactory receptors send this information to specific regions of the olfactory cortex. These regions appeared to occur in identical locations in different mice.

Transduction of Olfactory Information

LO 7.23 **Summarize the process of transducing the signal from an odorant molecule for olfactory perception.**

For many years, researchers have recognized that olfactory cilia contain receptors that are stimulated by molecules of odorants, but the nature of the receptors was unknown. Jones and Reed (1989) identified a particular G protein, which they called G_{olf}. This protein is able to activate an enzyme that catalyzes the synthesis of cyclic AMP, which, in turn, can open sodium channels and depolarize the membrane of the olfactory cell (Firestein et al., 1991; Menco et al., 1992; Nakamura and Gold, 1987).

As we saw in Chapter 2, G proteins serve as the link between metabotropic receptors and ion channels: When a ligand binds with a metabotropic receptor, the G protein either opens ion channels directly or does so indirectly, by triggering the production of a second messenger. The discovery of G_{olf} suggested that olfactory cilia contained odorant receptors linked to this G protein. Indeed, Buck and Axel (1991) used molecular genetics techniques and discovered a family of genes that code for a family of olfactory receptor proteins (and in 2004 won a Nobel Prize for doing so). So far, olfactory receptor genes have been isolated in more than 12 species of vertebrates, including mammals, birds, and amphibians (Mombaerts, 1999). Humans have 339 different olfactory receptor genes, and mice have 913 (Godfrey et al., 2004; Malnic et al., 2004). Molecules of odorant bind with olfactory receptors, and the G proteins coupled to these receptors open sodium channels and produce depolarizing receptor potentials.

Perception of Specific Odors

LO 7.24 **Explain how a relatively small number of receptors can detect a wide variety of odors.**

For many years, recognition of specific odors has been an enigma. Humans can recognize up to 10,000 different odorants, and other animals can probably recognize even more (Shepherd, 1994). Even with 339 different olfactory receptors, that leaves many odors unaccounted for. And every year, chemists synthesize new chemicals, many with odors unlike those that anyone has previously detected. How can we use a relatively small number of receptors to detect so many different odorants?

Before we answer this question, we should look more closely at the relationship between receptors, olfactory neurons, and the glomeruli to which the axons of these neurons project. First, the cilia of each olfactory neuron contain only one type of receptor (Nef et al., 1992; Vassar et al., 1993). As we saw, each glomerulus receives information from approximately 2,000 olfactory receptor cells. Ressler et al., (1994) discovered that each of these 2,000 cells contains the same type of receptor molecule. Thus, there are as many types of glomeruli as there are types of receptor molecules. Furthermore, the location of particular types of glomeruli (defined by the type of receptor that sends information to them) appears to be the same in each of the olfactory bulbs in a given animal and may even be the same from one animal to another. (See Figure 7.36.)

Now let's go back to the question that was just posed: How can we use a relatively small number of receptors to detect so many different odorants? The answer is that a particular odorant binds to more than one receptor. Thus, because a given glomerulus receives information from only one type of receptor, different odorants produce different *patterns* of activity in different glomeruli. Recognizing a particular odor, then, is a matter of recognizing a particular pattern of activity in the glomeruli. The task of chemical recognition is transformed into a task of spatial recognition.

Figure 7.37 illustrates this process. The left side of the figure shows the shapes of eight hypothetical odorants. The right side shows four hypothetical odorant receptor molecules. If a portion of the odorant molecule fits the binding site of the receptor molecule, it will activate it and stimulate the olfactory neuron. As you can see, each odorant molecule fits the binding site of at least one of the receptors and in most cases fits more than one of them. Notice also that the *pattern* of receptors activated by each of the eight odorants is different, which means that if we know which pattern of receptors is activated, we know which odorant is present. Even though a particular odorant might bind with several different types of receptor molecules, it might not bind equally well with each of them. For example, it might bind very well with one receptor molecule, moderately well with another, weakly with another, and so on. The spatial pattern of "olfactotopic" information is maintained in the olfactory cortex.

Johnson and Leon (2007) presented a variety of odorants to rats and recorded the regions of activation on the surface of an exposed olfactory bulb. They found that

---

Figure 7.36 Connections of Olfactory Receptor Cells with Glomeruli

Each glomerulus of the olfactory bulb receives information from only one type of receptor cell. Olfactory receptor cells of different colors contain different types of receptor molecules.

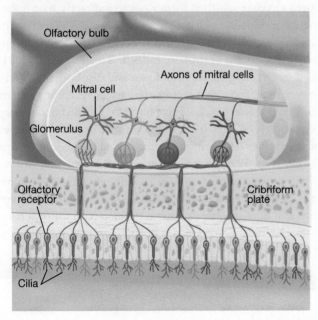

Figure 7.37 Coding of Olfactory Information

A hypothetical explanation of the coding suggests that different odorant molecules attach to different combinations of receptor molecules. (Activated receptor molecules are shown in blue.) Unique patterns of activation represent particular odorants.

(Adapted from Malnic, B., Hirono, J., Sato, T., and Buck, L. B., Combinatorial receptor codes for odors, *Cell*, 1999, *96*, 713–723.)

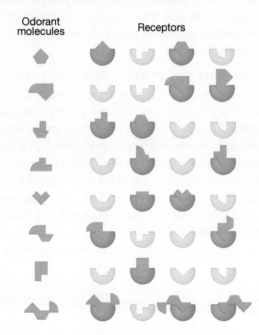

different categories of molecules activated different regions of the olfactory bulb. Figure 7.38 shows the patterns of activity. Characteristics of odorant molecules are represented by particular patterns of activity in the olfactory bulbs.

QUALITIES OF ODORANTS Although odorants are categorized according to their molecular characteristics within the olfactory bulb, the coding scheme changes at the level of the piriform cortex (the primary olfactory cortex). A functional-imaging study with humans by Gottfried et al., (2006) found that groups of neurons in the anterior region represent the chemical structures of odorants, just as

neurons in the olfactory bulb do, but groups of neurons in the posterior region represent the qualities of odorants. Another functional-imaging study (Howard et al., 2009) found that odorants normally associated with particular objects (in this case, odorants that people perceive as minty, woody, or citrusy) produced particular patterns of activity in the posterior piriform cortex, regardless of the chemical structure of the odorants. The investigators presented the participants with three different minty odorants, three different woody odorants, and three different citrusy odorants. Each of the three odorants in each of these categories had very different chemical structures. Nevertheless, the patterns of activity on the posterior piriform cortex were correlated with the odor category, not the molecular structure.

We do not yet know how maps of chemical structure in the olfactory bulb are combined to form maps of perceptual quality in the posterior piriform cortex. Presumably, learning plays some role in this process.

Figure 7.38 Clusters and Zones in the Olfactory Bulb

Specific regions of the olfactory bulb respond to specific features or properties of odorant molecules.

(Adapted from Johnson, B. A., and Leon, M., Chemotopic odorant coding in a mammalian olfactory system, *Journal of Comparative Neurology*, 2007, *503*, 1–34.)

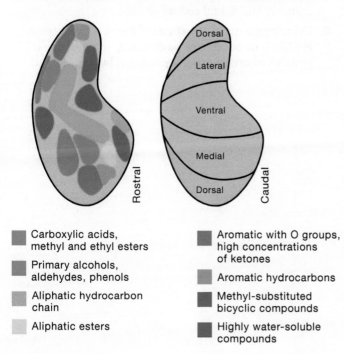

- Carboxylic acids, methyl and ethyl esters
- Primary alcohols, aldehydes, phenols
- Aliphatic hydrocarbon chain
- Aliphatic esters
- Aromatic with O groups, high concentrations of ketones
- Aromatic hydrocarbons
- Methyl-substituted bicyclic compounds
- Highly water-soluble compounds

ODORANT MASKING Several studies have found that interactions can take place between glomeruli within the olfactory bulb. For example, some odors have the ability to mask others. (The existence of the deodorant and air-freshener industries depends on this fact.) Cooks in various cultures have long known that as long as it is not too strong, the unpleasant, rancid off-flavor of spoiled food can be masked by the spices fennel and clove. Takahashi et al., (2004) found that evidence for this masking can be seen in the responses of olfactory glomeruli. Examination of the rat olfactory bulbs with a microscope showed local areas of increased blood flow when different odorants were presented, which indicated regions of increased neural activity. Takahashi and his colleagues mapped the regions of the olfactory bulb that responded to bad-smelling odorants and to the odors of fennel and clove. They found that responses to the bad odors were suppressed by the presence of the spice odors, indicating that the masking took place in the olfactory bulbs. Presumably, the glomeruli that responded to the spice odors inhibited those that responded to the rancid ones.

Section Review

Olfaction

LO 7.22 Identify the stimulus and describe the structure and function of the olfactory apparatus.

The stimuli for olfaction are chemical molecules that are typically lipid soluble and organic. Olfactory receptor cells are bipolar neurons whose cell bodies lie within the olfactory mucosa that lines the cribriform plate. These neurons send information to the olfactory bulb and through the brain via olfactory tracts. Some information proceeds to the

limbic system and integrates with gustatory information. Olfactory information is processed in the olfactory cortex. Regions of olfactory cortex contain olfactotopic maps.

LO 7.23 Summarize the process of transducing the signal from an odorant molecule for olfactory perception.

Molecules of odorant bind with olfactory receptors, and the G proteins coupled to these receptors open sodium channels and produce depolarizing receptor potentials.

LO 7.24   Explain how a relatively small number of receptors can detect a wide variety of odors.

A particular odorant binds to more than one receptor and different odorants produce different patterns of activity in different glomeruli. Recognizing a particular odor involves recognizing a particular pattern of activity in the glomeruli. The primary olfactory cortex contains an olfactory map that appears to be based on the chemical structure of odorant molecules.

Thought Question

Have you ever encountered an odor that you knew was somehow familiar, but you couldn't say exactly why? Can you think of any explanations? Might this phenomenon have something to do with the fact that the sense of olfaction developed very early in our evolutionary history?

Chapter Review Questions

1. Describe the parts of the ear and the auditory pathway.
2. Describe the detection of pitch, loudness, and timbre.
3. Discuss the perception of spatial location, the perception of complex sounds, and the perception of music.
4. Discuss the structure of vestibular sac with reference to its role in the maintenance of equilibrium, and describe the signal transduction mechanism in its receptor hair cells.
5. Describe the receptors involved in pain perception, the components and pathways of pain, and the intrinsic analgesic system.

6. Describe the somatosensory pathways and the perception of pain.
7. Describe the taste qualities, the anatomy of the taste buds and how they detect taste, and the gustatory pathway and neural coding of taste.
8. Describe the major structures of the olfactory system, explain how odors may be detected, and describe the patterns of neural activity produced by these stimuli.

Chapter 8
Control of Movement

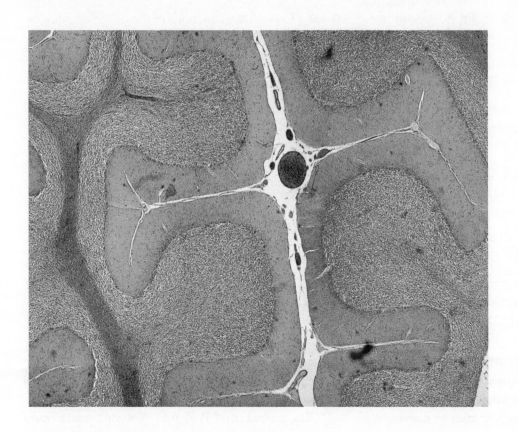

Chapter Outline

Learning Objectives

LO 8.1 Describe the structures of a skeletal muscle.

LO 8.2 List the steps involved in neurotransmission at the neuromuscular junction that result in a muscle fiber twitch.

LO 8.3 Contrast the types of information detected by afferent axons of muscle spindles and Golgi tendon organs.

LO 8.4 Explain the function of monosynaptic stretch reflexes.

LO 8.5 Explain the function of the gamma motor system and its role in regulating the length of muscles.

LO 8.6 Contrast the structures and function of polysynaptic reflexes with monosynaptic reflexes.

LO 8.7 Describe the pathways and functions of cortical regions involved in control of motor behavior.

LO 8.8 Describe the components and functions of the descending pathways.

LO 8.9 Explain the functions of the motor association cortex (including the supplementary motor area and the premotor cortex) in planning and initiating movement.

LO 8.10 Describe the functions of subcortical regions involved in control of motor behavior.

LO 8.11 Describe the location, components, and functions of the mirror neuron system.

LO 8.12 Summarize the contributions of the parietal cortex in reaching and grasping behavior.

LO 8.13 Describe how brain lesions can produce limb apraxia.

LO 8.14 Describe how brain lesions can produce constructional apraxia.

Although Mr. J., a 48-year-old photographer, had just had a severe stroke that damaged much of his left parietal lobe, he was still a pleasant and cheerful man, who waved hello when his neurologist, Dr. R., first introduced him to us.

"Mr. J., will you now please show us how people wave hello?" asked Dr. R.

The patient made a clumsy movement with his right hand and smiled apologetically. He clearly had difficulty displaying this gesture.

"Hold up your index finger, like this," said Dr. R., pointing toward the ceiling.

Mr. J. held up his hand, pursed his lips together, and, with a determined look on his face, clenched and unclenched his fist. He was trying as hard as he could to point with his index finger, but he just could not move it without also moving his other fingers.

Dr. R. addressed the rest of us. "You can see that Mr. J.'s apraxia is severe. But now watch this." He turned to Mr. J. "Will you please take off your glasses?"

Mr. J. reached up to his glasses, took hold of the earpieces, and smoothly removed them.

"Fine. Now put them back on."

He did so.

Dr. R. then asked, "Do you know what a hammer is?"

"Sure," answered Mr. J.

"Okay, will you show us how you would use a hammer if you had one in your hand?"

Mr. J. looked at his hand and then began slapping it hard and almost uncontrollably against his thigh.

"Okay, you can stop." With great effort Mr. J. finally ceased making the movements. "Now let's try this," said Dr. R. He placed a block of wood on the table in front of Mr. J. and handed him an actual hammer and nail. "Can you hammer this nail into the wood?"

Mr. J. held the nail upright with the fingers of his left hand, grasped the hammer with his right hand, and skillfully drove the nail into the wood.

After Mr. J. left, Dr. R. said, "Mr. J. can make skilled movements, but he cannot make these movements when we ask him to. He can manipulate his glasses and he can use a hammer, but he can't make even the simplest voluntary movements out of context, when he's not actually performing the act itself. Did you notice that he waved to you when I introduced him, even though he couldn't do so when I asked him to show us how to wave 'hello'? The movement was an automatic one he learned to make long ago, and it was triggered by the experience of meeting other people. The left parietal lobe is involved in the control of movements—especially sequences of movements—that are not dictated by the context. Because this region of his brain was damaged by the stroke, Mr. J. finds it almost impossible to follow verbal requests to make arbitrary movements."

*****

This case study illustrates the complexity of motor control by the nervous system. In this chapter you will learn more about the role of the brain and spinal cord in reflexive and voluntary motor behavior. So far, we have explored the nature of neural communication, the basic structure of the nervous system, and the physiology of sensation and perception. Now it is time to consider the ultimate function of the nervous system: control of behavior. The brain is the organ that moves the muscles and allows us to engage in motor behavior.

This chapter describes the principles of muscular contraction, some reflex circuitry within the spinal cord, and the means by which the brain initiates behaviors. The first section starts us off with a discussion of skeletal muscle. The second and third sections then focus on how the spinal cord and brain control our movement. The fourth section focuses on complex motor behavior, and the final section describes deficits in motor movements. The figure here provides an overview of the brain regions particularly vital to the control of movement.

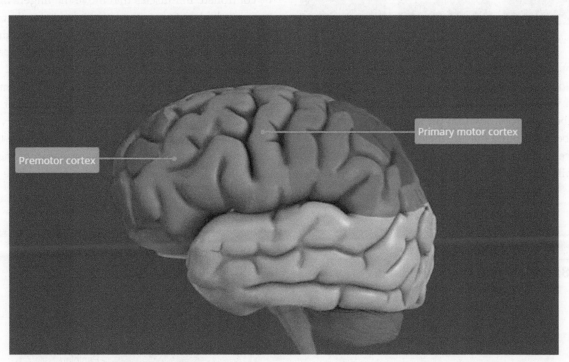

Brain regions vital to the control of movement.

Skeletal Muscle

Skeletal muscles are the ones that move us around and thus are responsible for our actions. Most of them are attached to bones at each end and move the bones when they contract. (Exceptions include eye muscles and some abdominal muscles, which are attached to bone at one end only.) Muscles are fastened to bones via *tendons,* strong bands of connective tissue. Several different classes of movement can be accomplished by the skeletal muscles, but we will refer principally to two of them: flexion and extension.

Contraction of a flexor muscle produces **flexion,** moving a limb toward the body. **Extension,** which is the opposite movement or moving a limb away from the body, is produced by contraction of extensor muscles. These are the so-called *antigravity muscles*—the ones we use to stand up.

Sometimes, people say that they "flex" their muscles. This is an incorrect use of the term. Muscles *contract;* limbs *flex.* Bodybuilders show off their arm muscles by simultaneously contracting the flexor and extensor muscles of that limb. (See Figure 8.1.)

Anatomy

LO 8.1 Describe the structures of a skeletal muscle.

The detailed structure of a skeletal muscle is shown in Figure 8.2. As you can see, it consists of two types of muscle fibers. The **extrafusal muscle fibers** are served by axons of the **alpha motor neurons.** Contraction of these fibers provides the muscle's motive force. The **intrafusal muscle fibers** are specialized sensory organs that are served by

Figure 8.1 Flexion and Extension

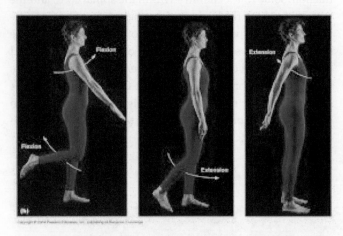

two axons, one sensory and one motor. These organs are also called *muscle spindles* because of their shape. In fact, the Latin word *fusus* means "spindle"; hence, *intrafusal* muscle fibers are found within the spindles, and *extrafusal* muscle fibers are found outside them.

The central region *(capsule)* of the intrafusal muscle fiber contains sensory endings that are sensitive to stretch applied to the muscle fiber. Actually, there are two types of intrafusal muscle fibers, but for simplicity's sake, only one kind is shown here. The efferent axon of the **gamma motor neuron** causes the intrafusal muscle fiber to contract; however, this contraction contributes an insubstantial amount of force. As we will see, the function of this contraction is to modify the sensitivity of the fiber's afferent ending to stretch.

A single myelinated axon of an alpha motor neuron serves several extrafusal muscle fibers. In primates the number of muscle fibers served by a single axon varies considerably, depending on the precision with which the muscle can be controlled. In muscles that move the fingers or eyes, the ratio can be less than one to ten; in muscles that move the leg, it can be one to several hundred. An alpha motor neuron, its axon, and associated extrafusal muscle fibers constitute a **motor unit.**

A single muscle fiber consists of a bundle of **myofibrils,** each of which consists of overlapping strands of **actin** and **myosin.** Note the small protrusions on the myosin filaments; these structures *(myosin cross bridges)* are the motile elements that interact with the actin filaments and produce muscular contractions. The regions in which the actin and

Figure 8.2 Anatomy of Skeletal Muscle

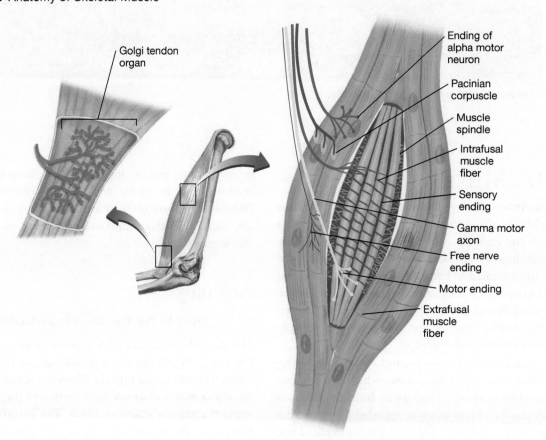

Golgi tendon organ

Ending of alpha motor neuron

Pacinian corpuscle

Muscle spindle

Intrafusal muscle fiber

Sensory ending

Gamma motor axon

Free nerve ending

Motor ending

Extrafusal muscle fiber

Figure 8.3 Muscle Cell Anatomy

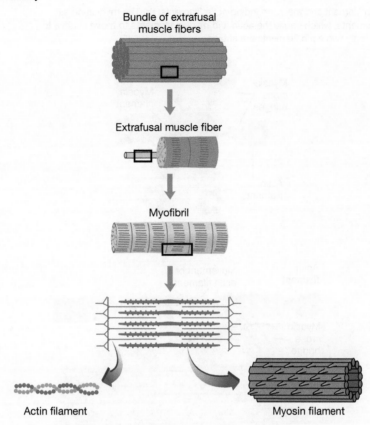

Bundle of extrafusal muscle fibers

Extrafusal muscle fiber

Myofibril

Actin filament

Myosin filament

myosin filaments overlap produce dark stripes, or *striations;* hence, skeletal muscle is often referred to as **striated muscle.** (See Figure 8.3.)

The Physical Basis of Muscular Contraction

LO 8.2 **List the steps involved in neurotransmission at the neuromuscular junction that result in a muscle fiber twitch.**

The synapse between the terminal button of an efferent neuron and the membrane of a muscle fiber is called a **neuromuscular junction.** The terminal buttons of the neurons synapse on **motor endplates,** located in grooves along the surface of the muscle fibers. When an axon fires, acetylcholine is liberated by the terminal buttons and produces a depolarization of the postsynaptic membrane—an **endplate potential.** The endplate potential is much larger than an excitatory postsynaptic potential in synapses between neurons; an endplate potential *always* causes the muscle fiber to fire, propagating the potential along its length. This action potential induces a contraction, or *twitch,* of the muscle fiber.

The depolarization of a muscle fiber opens the gates of voltage-dependent calcium channels, permitting calcium ions to enter the cytoplasm. This event triggers the contraction. Calcium acts as a cofactor that permits the myofibrils to extract energy from the adenosine triphosphate (ATP) that is present in the cytoplasm. The myosin cross bridges alternately attach to the actin strands, bend in one direction, detach themselves, bend back, reattach to the actin at a point farther down the strand, and so on. Thus, the cross bridges "row" along the actin filaments. Figure 8.4 illustrates this rowing sequence and shows how this sequence results in shortening the muscle fiber.

A single impulse of a motor neuron produces a single twitch of a muscle fiber. The physical effects of the twitch last considerably longer than will the action potential, because of the elasticity of the muscle and the time required to rid the cell of calcium. (Like sodium, calcium is actively removed from a cell by a pump in the membrane.)

As you know from your own experience, muscular contraction is not an all-or-nothing phenomenon, as are the twitches of the constituent muscle fibers. The strength of a muscular contraction is determined by the average rate of firing of the various motor units. If, at a given moment,

Figure 8.4 Mechanisms of Muscular Contraction

(a) Cross section through a myosin filament and the surrounding actin filaments. (b) The myosin cross bridges performing "rowing" movements, which cause the actin and myosin filaments to move relative to each other. For the sake of clarity, only two actin filaments are shown.

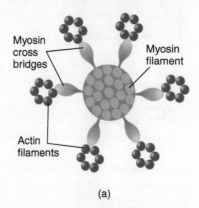

(a)

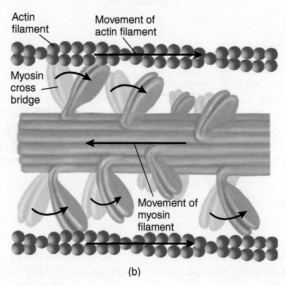

(b)

many units are firing, the contraction will be forceful. If few are firing, the contraction will be weak.

Sensory Feedback from Muscles

LO 8.3 Contrast the types of information detected by afferent axons of muscle spindles and Golgi tendon organs.

As we saw, the intrafusal muscle fibers contain sensory endings that are sensitive to stretch. The intrafusal muscle fibers are arranged in parallel with the extrafusal muscle fibers. Therefore, they are stretched when the muscle lengthens and are relaxed when it shortens. Thus, even though these afferent neurons are *stretch receptors*, they serve as *muscle length detectors*. This distinction is important. Stretch receptors are also located within the tendons, in the **Golgi tendon organ.** These receptors detect the total amount of stretch exerted by the muscle, through its tendons, on the bones to which the muscle is attached. The stretch receptors of the Golgi tendon organ encode the degree of stretch by the rate of firing. They respond not to a muscle's length but to how hard it is pulling. In contrast, the receptors on intrafusal muscle fibers detect muscle length, not tension.

Figure 8.5 shows the response of afferent axons of the muscle spindles and Golgi tendon organ to various types of movements. Figure 8.5a shows the effects of passive lengthening of muscles, the kind of movement that would be seen if your forearm, held in a completely relaxed fashion, were slowly lowered by someone who was supporting it. The rate of firing of one type of muscle spindle afferent neuron (MS_1) increases, while the activity of the afferent of the Golgi tendon organ remains unchanged. Figure 8.5b shows the results when the arm is dropped quickly; note that this time the second type of muscle spindle afferent neuron (MS_2) fires a rapid burst of impulses. This fiber, then, signals rapid changes in muscle length. Figure 8.5c shows what would happen if a weight were suddenly dropped into your hand while your forearm was held parallel to the ground. Neurons MS_1 and MS_2 (especially MS_2, which responds to rapid changes in muscle length) briefly fire, because your arm lowers briefly and then comes back to the original position. The Golgi tendon organ, monitoring the strength of contraction, fires in proportion to the stress on the muscle, so it increases its rate of firing as soon as the weight is added.

Figure 8.5 Responses of Muscle and Tendon Receptors

The figure shows effects of arm movements on the firing of muscle and tendon afferent axons: (a) slow, passive extension of the arm; (b) rapid extension of the arm; (c) addition of a weight to an arm held in a horizontal position. MS_1 and MS_2 are two types of muscle spindles; GTO is an afferent fiber from the Golgi tendon organ.

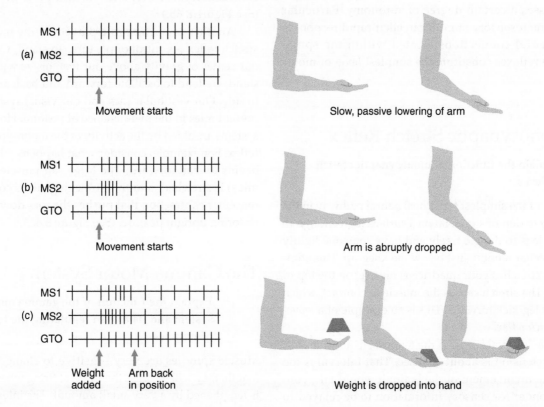

Section Review

Skeletal Muscle

LO 8.1   Describe the structures of a skeletal muscle.
Skeletal muscles contain extrafusal muscle fibers, which provide the force of contraction. The alpha motor neurons form synapses with the extrafusal muscle fibers and control their contraction. Skeletal muscles also contain intrafusal muscle fibers, which detect changes in muscle length. The length of the intrafusal muscle fiber, and hence its sensitivity to increases in muscle length, is controlled by the gamma motor neuron. Besides the intrafusal muscle fibers, the muscles contain stretch receptors in the Golgi tendon organs, located at the ends of the muscles.

LO 8.2   List the steps involved in neurotransmission at the neuromuscular junction that result in a muscle fiber twitch.
When a neuron synapses on a muscle fiber at the neuromuscular junction, the neuron releases acetylcholine (ACh) into the synapse. ACh binds to receptors on the muscle fiber to produce an endplate potential. The depolarization of a muscle fiber opens the gates of voltage-dependent calcium channels, permitting calcium ions to enter the cytoplasm. This event triggers the contraction. Calcium allows the muscle cell to use ATP to allow cross bridges to "row" along actin to produce the contraction.

LO 8.3   Contrast the types of information detected by afferent axons of muscle spindles and Golgi tendon organs.
Intrafusal muscle fibers contain sensory endings that are sensitive to stretch. Receptors on intrafusal muscle fibers detect muscle length. Golgi tendon organs contain stretch receptors for tendons.

Thought Question

Weight lifters can lift heavier weights if their Golgi tendon organs are deactivated with an injection of a local anesthetic. Considering the normal function of these organs, why might these injections be unwise?

Control of Movement by the Spinal Cord

Although behaviors are controlled by the brain, the spinal cord possesses a certain degree of autonomy. Particular kinds of somatosensory stimuli can elicit rapid responses through neural connections located within the spinal cord. These reflexes constitute the simplest level of motor integration.

The Monosynaptic Stretch Reflex

LO 8.4   Explain the function of monosynaptic stretch reflexes.

The activity of the simplest functional neural pathway in the body is easy to demonstrate. Sit on a surface high enough to allow your legs to dangle freely and have someone lightly tap your patellar tendon, just below the kneecap. This stimulus briefly stretches your quadriceps muscle, on the top of your thigh. The stretch causes the muscle to contract, which makes your leg kick forward. This is an example of a *monosynaptic stretch reflex*.

The time interval between the tendon tap and the start of the leg extension is about 50 msec. That interval is too short for the involvement of the brain; it would take considerably longer for sensory information to be relayed to the brain and for motor information to be relayed back. For example, suppose a person is asked to move his or her leg as quickly as possible after being *touched* on the knee. This response would not be reflexive but would involve sensory and motor mechanisms of the brain. In this case the interval between the stimulus and the start of the response would be several times greater than the time required for the patellar reflex.

The patellar reflex on its own is not very useful. There is no advantage to individuals that kick a limb when a tendon is tapped. However, if a more natural stimulus is applied, the utility of this mechanism becomes more clear. Figure 8.6b shows the effects of placing a weight in a person's hand. Figure 8.6a includes a piece of the spinal cord, with its roots, to show the neural circuit that composes the **monosynaptic stretch reflex**. First, follow the circuit: Starting at the muscle spindle, afferent impulses are conducted to terminal buttons in the gray matter of the spinal cord. These terminal buttons synapse on an alpha motor neuron that innervates the extrafusal muscle fibers of the same muscle. Only one synapse is encountered along the route from receptor to effector—hence the term *monosynaptic*. (See Figure 8.6a.)

Now consider a useful function this reflex performs. If the weight the person is holding is increased, the forearm begins to move downward. This movement lengthens the muscle and increases the firing rate of the muscle spindle afferent neurons, whose terminal buttons then stimulate the alpha motor neurons, increasing their rate of firing. Consequently, the strength of the muscular contraction increases, and the arm pulls the weight up. (See Figure 8.6b.)

Another important role played by the monosynaptic stretch reflex is control of posture. To stand, we must keep our center of gravity above our feet, or we will fall. As we stand, we tend to oscillate forward and back and from side to side. Our vestibular sacs and our visual system play important roles in the maintenance of posture. However, these systems are aided by the activity of the monosynaptic stretch reflex. For example, consider what happens when a person begins to lean forward. The large calf muscle (gastrocnemius) is stretched, and this stretching elicits compensatory muscular contraction that pushes the toes downward, thus restoring upright posture. (See Figure 8.6c.)

The Gamma Motor System

LO 8.5   Explain the function of the gamma motor system and its role in regulating the length of muscles.

Muscle spindles are very sensitive to changes in muscle length; they will increase their rate of firing when the muscle is lengthened by a very small amount. The interesting thing is that this detection mechanism is adjustable. Remember that the ends of the intrafusal muscle fibers can be contracted by activity of the associated efferent axons of the gamma motor neurons; their rate of firing determines the degree of contraction. When the muscle spindles are relaxed, they are relatively insensitive to stretch. However, when the gamma motor neurons are active, they become shorter and hence become much more sensitive to changes in muscle length. This property of adjustable sensitivity simplifies the role of the brain in controlling movement. The more control that can occur in the spinal cord, the fewer messages must be sent to and from the brain.

We have already seen that the afferent axons of the muscle spindle help to maintain limb position even when the load carried by the limb is altered. Efferent control of the muscle spindles permits these muscle length detectors to assist in changes in limb position as well. Consider a single muscle spindle. When its efferent axon is completely silent, the spindle is completely relaxed and extended. As the firing rate of the efferent axon increases, the spindle gets shorter and shorter. If, simultaneously, the rest of the entire muscle also gets shorter, there will be no stretch on the central region that contains the sensory endings, and the afferent axon will not respond. However, if the muscle spindle contracts faster than does the muscle as a whole, there will be a considerable amount of afferent activity.

Figure 8.6 Examples of Monosynaptic Stretch Reflexes

(a) Neural circuit. (b) A useful function. (c) The monosynaptic stretch reflex in postural control.

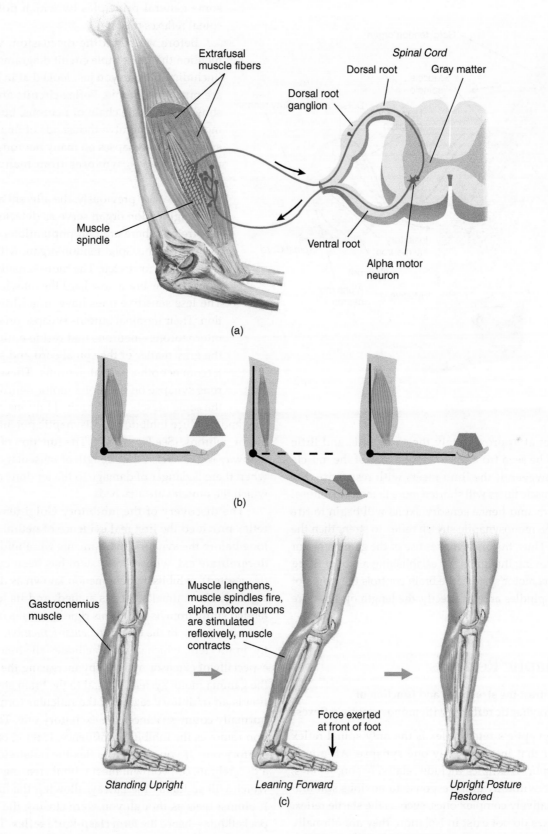

The motor system makes use of this phenomenon in the following way: When commands from the brain are issued to move a limb, both the alpha motor neurons and the gamma motor neurons are activated. The alpha motor neurons start the muscle contracting. If there is little resistance, both the extrafusal and intrafusal muscle fibers

Figure 8.7 Polysynaptic Inhibitory Reflex

Input from the Golgi tendon organ can cause inhibitory postsynaptic potentials to occur on the alpha motor neuron.

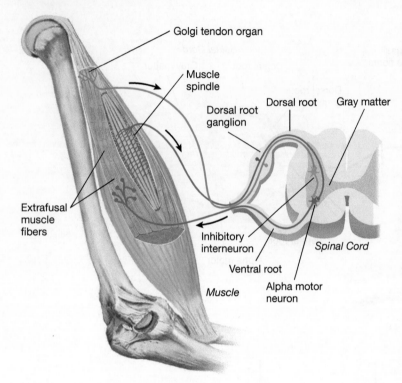

will contract at approximately the same rate, and little activity will be seen from the afferent axons of the muscle spindle. However, if the limb meets with resistance, the intrafusal muscle fibers will shorten more than the extrafusal muscle fibers, and hence sensory axons will begin to fire and cause the monosynaptic stretch reflex to strengthen the contraction. Thus, the brain makes use of the gamma motor system in moving the limbs. By establishing a rate of firing in the gamma motor system, the brain controls the length of the muscle spindles and, indirectly, the length of the entire muscle.

Polysynaptic Reflexes

LO 8.6 **Contrast the structures and function of polysynaptic reflexes with monosynaptic reflexes.**

The monosynaptic stretch reflex is the only spinal reflex we know of that involves only one synapse. All others are *polysynaptic*. Examples include relatively simple ones, such as limb withdrawal in response to noxious stimulation, and relatively complex ones, such as the startle reflex. Spinal reflexes do not exist in isolation; they are normally controlled by the brain. For example, Chapter 2 described how inhibition from the brain can prevent a person from

dropping a hot mug, even though the painful stimuli received by the fingers cause reflexive extension of the fingers. This section will describe some general principles by which polysynaptic spinal reflexes operate.

Before we begin the discussion, we should mention that the simple circuit diagrams used here (including the one you just looked at in Figure 8.6) are much too simple. Reflex circuits are typically shown as a single chain of neurons, but in reality most reflexes involve thousands of neurons. Each axon usually synapses on many neurons, and each neuron receives synapses from many different axons.

As we saw previously, the afferent axons from the Golgi tendon organ serve as detectors of muscle stretch. There are two populations of afferent axons from the Golgi tendon organ, with different sensitivities to stretch. The more sensitive afferent axons tell the brain how hard the muscle is pulling. The less sensitive ones have an additional function. Their terminal buttons synapse on spinal cord interneurons—neurons that reside entirely within the gray matter of the spinal cord and serve to interconnect other spinal neurons. These interneurons synapse on the alpha motor neurons serving the same muscle. The terminal buttons release glycine and produce inhibitory postsynaptic potentials on the motor neurons. (See Figure 8.7.) The function of this reflex pathway is to decrease the strength of muscular contraction when there is danger of damage to the tendons or bones to which the muscles are attached.

The discovery of the inhibitory Golgi tendon organ reflex provided the first real evidence of neural inhibition, long before the synaptic mechanisms were understood. A **decerebrate** cat, whose brain stem has been cut through (transected), exhibits a phenomenon known as **decerebrate rigidity.** The animal's back is arched, and its legs are extended stiffly from its body. This rigidity results from excitation originating in the caudal *reticular formation,* a region of the brain stem, which greatly facilitates all stretch reflexes, especially of extensor muscles, by increasing the activity of the gamma motor system. Rostral to the brain stem transection is an inhibitory region of the reticular formation that normally counterbalances the excitatory one. The transection removes the inhibitory influence, leaving only the excitatory one. If you attempt to flex the outstretched leg of a decerebrate cat, you will meet with increasing resistance, which will suddenly melt away, allowing the limb to flex. It almost feels as though you were closing the blade of a pocketknife—hence the term **clasp-knife reflex.** The sudden release is mediated by activation of the Golgi tendon organ reflex.

Control of Movement by the Brain

The brain and spinal cord include several different motor systems, each of which can simultaneously control particular kinds of movements. For example, a person can walk and talk with a friend simultaneously. While doing so, the person can gesture with the hands to emphasize a point, scratch an itch, brush away a fly, wipe sweat off his or her forehead, and so on. Walking, postural adjustments, talking, movement of the arms, and movements of the fingers all involve different specialized motor systems, which we will look at in more detail in this section.

Movements can be initiated by several means. For example, rapid stretch of a muscle triggers the monosynaptic stretch reflex, a stumble triggers righting reflexes, and the rapid approach of an object toward the face causes a startle response, a complex reflex consisting of movements of several muscle groups. Other stimuli initiate sequences of movements that we have previously learned. For example, the presence of food causes eating, and the sight of a loved one evokes a hug and a kiss. Because there is no single cause of behavior, we cannot find a single starting point in our search for the neural mechanisms that control movement.

In this section, we will explore the role of the brain in controlling movements, and we will do so by highlighting the roles of some specific motor regions of cortical and subcortical structures.

Cortical Structures

LO 8.7 **Describe the pathways and functions of cortical regions involved in control of motor behavior.**

Cortical structures involved in the control of movement include the primary motor cortex, supplementary motor area, and the premotor cortex. These regions and their contributions to motor control will be described in the following sections.

PRIMARY MOTOR CORTEX The primary motor cortex lies on the precentral gyrus, just rostral to the central sulcus. Stimulation studies (including those in awake humans) have shown that the activation of neurons located in particular parts of the primary motor cortex causes movements of particular parts of the body. In other words, the primary motor cortex shows **somatotopic organization** (from *soma*, "body," and *topos*, "place"). Figure 8.8 shows a *motor homunculus* based on the observations of Penfield and Rasmussen (1950). Note that a disproportionate amount of cortical area is devoted to movements of the fingers and the muscles used for speech, as represented by the disproportionately large mouth on the human figure in Figure 8.8.

It is important to recognize that the primary motor cortex is organized in terms of particular *movements* of particular parts of the body. Each movement may be accomplished by the contraction of several muscles. For example, when the arm is extended in a particular direction, many muscles in the shoulder, upper arm, and forearm must contract. This fact means that complex neural circuitry is located between

Figure 8.8 Motor Cortex and the Motor Homunculus

Stimulation of various regions of the primary motor cortex causes movement in muscles of various parts of the body.

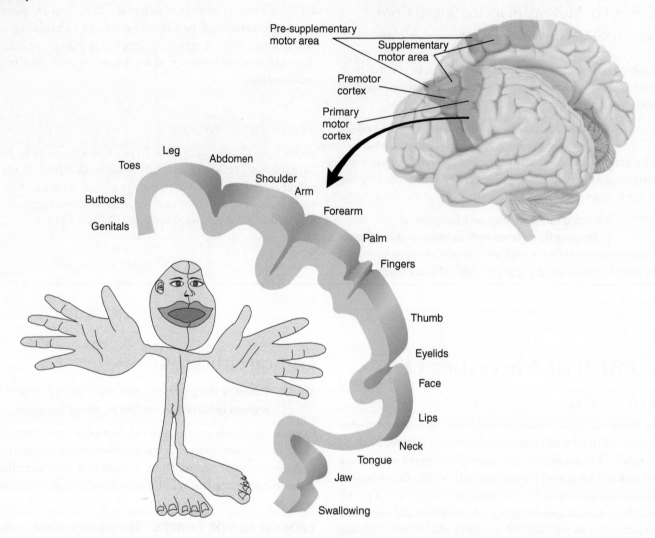

individual neurons in the primary motor cortex and the motor neurons in the spinal cord that cause motor units to contract. The commands for movement initiated in the motor cortex are assisted and modified—most notably, by the basal ganglia and the cerebellum.

A study by Graziano and Aflalo (2007) found that although brief stimulation of particular regions of the primary motor cortex of monkeys caused brief movements of various parts of the body, prolonged stimulation produced much more complex movements. For example, stimulation of one region caused the hand to close and then approach the mouth and the mouth then to open. Stimulation of another region caused the face to squint, the head to turn quickly to one side, and the arms to fling up, as if to protect the face from something that was going to hit it. Stimulation of different zones of the motor cortex caused different categories of actions. The map of

these categories was consistent from animal to animal. (See Figure 8.9.)

SUPPLEMENTARY MOTOR AREA AND PREMOTOR CORTEX Two regions immediately adjacent to the primary motor cortex—the *supplementary motor area* and the *premotor cortex*—are especially important in the control of movement. Both regions receive sensory information from the parietal and temporal lobes, and both send efferent axons to the primary motor cortex. The **supplementary motor area (SMA)** is located on the medial surface of the brain, just rostral to the primary motor cortex. The **premotor cortex** is located primarily on the lateral surface, also just rostral to the primary motor cortex. The locations of primary motor cortex, supplementary motor cortex and premotor cortex are shown in Figure 8.10. The roles that these regions play in the control of movement are discussed later in this chapter.

Figure 8.9 Stimulation of the Motor Cortex

Categories of movements elicited by prolonged stimulation of specific regions of the motor cortex of monkeys.

(Adapted from Graziano, M. S. A., and Aflalo, T. N., Mapping behavioral repertoire onto the cortex, *Neuron*, 2007, *56*, 239–251.)

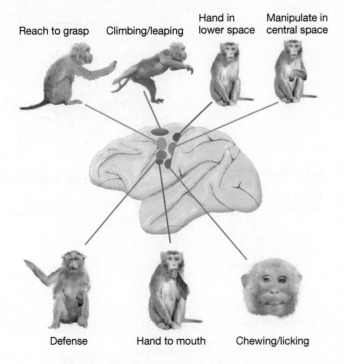

Reach to grasp   Climbing/leaping   Hand in lower space   Manipulate in central space

Defense   Hand to mouth   Chewing/licking

Cortical Control of Movement: Descending Pathways

LO 8.8 Describe the components and functions of the descending pathways.

Next, we will examine the pathways from the brain that are responsible for communicating information to the muscles of the body.

Neurons in the primary motor cortex control movements by two groups of descending tracts, the **lateral group** and the **ventromedial group,** named for their locations in the white matter of the spinal cord. The lateral group consists of the *corticospinal tract,* the *corticobulbar tract,* and the *rubrospinal tract.* This system is primarily involved in control of independent limb movements, particularly movements of the hands and fingers. *Independent* limb movements mean that the right and left limbs make different movements or one limb moves while the other remains still. These movements contrast with coordinated limb movements, such as those involved in locomotion. The ventromedial group consists of the *vestibulospinal tract,* the *tectospinal tract,* the *reticulospinal tract,* and the *ventral corticospinal tract.* These tracts control more automatic movements: gross movements of the muscles of the trunk and coordinated trunk and limb movements involved in posture and locomotion.

Figure 8.10 Organization of the Motor Cortex

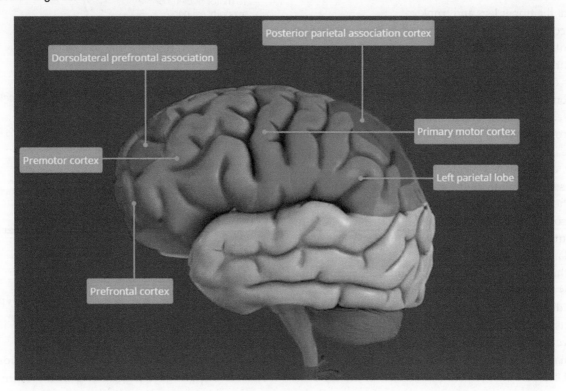

Dorsolateral prefrontal association

Posterior parietal association cortex

Premotor cortex

Primary motor cortex

Left parietal lobe

Prefrontal cortex

LATERAL GROUP Let's first consider the lateral group of descending tracts. The **corticospinal tract** consists of axons of cortical neurons that terminate in the gray matter of the spinal cord. The largest concentration of cell bodies responsible for these axons is located in the primary motor cortex, but neurons in the parietal and temporal lobes also send axons through the corticospinal tract. The axons leave the cortex and travel through subcortical white matter to the ventral midbrain, where they enter the cerebral peduncles. They leave the peduncles in the medulla and form the **pyramidal tracts,** so called because of their shape. At the level of the caudal medulla, most of the fibers decussate (cross over) and descend through the contralateral spinal cord, forming the **lateral corticospinal tract.** The rest of the fibers descend through the ipsilateral spinal cord, forming the **ventral corticospinal tract.** Because of its location and function, the ventral corticospinal tract is actually part of the ventromedial group. (See Figure 8.11.)

Most of the axons in the lateral corticospinal tract originate in the regions of the primary motor cortex and supplementary motor area that control the distal parts of the limbs: the arms, hands, and fingers and the lower legs, feet, and toes. They form synapses, directly or via interneurons, with motor neurons in the gray matter of the spinal cord—in the lateral part of the ventral horn. These motor neurons control muscles of the distal limbs, including those that move the arms, hands, and fingers.

The axons in the ventral corticospinal tract originate in the upper leg and trunk regions of the primary motor cortex. They descend to the appropriate region of the spinal cord and divide, sending terminal buttons into both sides of the gray matter. They control motor neurons that move the muscles of the upper legs and trunk.

The corticospinal pathway controls hand and finger movements and is indispensable for moving the fingers independently when reaching and manipulating. Postural adjustments of the trunk and use of the limbs for reaching and locomotion are controlled by other systems.

The second of the lateral group of descending pathways, the **corticobulbar tract,** projects to the medulla (sometimes called the *bulb*). This pathway is similar to the corticospinal pathway, except that it terminates in the motor nuclei of the fifth, seventh, ninth, tenth, eleventh, and twelfth cranial nerves (the trigeminal, facial, glossopharyngeal, vagus, spinal accessory, and hypoglossal nerves). These nerves control movements of the face, neck, and tongue and parts of the extraocular eye muscles.

The third member of the lateral group is the **rubrospinal tract.** This tract originates in the red nucleus (*nucleus ruber*) of the midbrain. The red nucleus receives its most important inputs from the motor cortex via the **corticorubral tract** and (as we shall see later) from the cerebellum. Axons of the rubrospinal tracts terminate on motor neurons in the spinal cord that control independent movements of the forearms

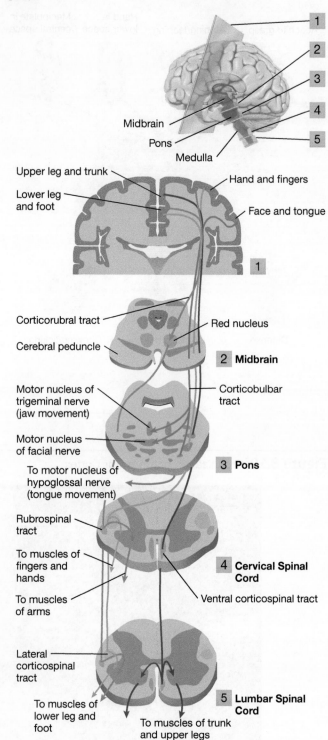

Figure 8.11 Lateral Group of Descending Motor Tracts
The figure shows the lateral corticospinal tract (light blue lines), corticobulbar tract (green lines), and rubrospinal tract (red lines). The ventral corticospinal tract (dark blue lines) is part of the ventromedial group.

and hands—that is, movements that are independent of trunk movements. (They do not control the muscles that move the fingers.)

VENTROMEDIAL GROUP Now let's consider the second set of pathways originating in the brain stem: the ventromedial group. This group includes the **vestibulospinal tracts,** the **tectospinal tracts,** and the **reticulospinal tracts,** as well as the ventral corticospinal tract (already described). These tracts control motor neurons in the ventromedial part of the spinal cord gray matter. Neurons of all these tracts receive input from the portions of the primary motor cortex that control movements of the trunk and proximal muscles (that is, the muscles located on the parts of the limbs close to the body). In addition, the reticular formation receives a considerable amount of input from the premotor cortex and from several subcortical regions, including the amygdala, hypothalamus, and basal ganglia.

The cell bodies of neurons of the vestibulospinal tracts are located in the vestibular nuclei. As you might expect, this system plays a role in the control of posture. The cell bodies of neurons in the tectospinal tracts are located in the superior colliculus and are involved in coordinating head and trunk movements with eye movements. The cell bodies of neurons of the reticulospinal tracts are located in many nuclei in the brain stem and midbrain reticular formation. These neurons control several automatic functions, such as muscle tonus, respiration, coughing, and sneezing; but they are also involved in behaviors that are under direct neocortical control, such as walking. (See Figure 8.12.)

Table 8.1 on page 260 summarizes the names of these pathways, their locations, and the muscle groups they control.

Planning and Initiating Movements: Role of the Motor Association Cortex

LO 8.9 **Explain the functions of the motor association cortex (including the supplementary motor area and the premotor cortex) in planning and initiating movement.**

The motor association cortex includes the supplementary motor area and premotor cortex. The supplementary motor area and the premotor cortex are involved in the planning of movements, and they execute these plans through their connections with the primary motor cortex. Functional-imaging studies show that when people execute sequences of movements—or even imagine them—these regions become activated (Roth et al., 1996). More recent evidence indicates that the motor association cortex is also involved in imitating the actions of other people (an ability that makes it possible to learn new behaviors from them) and even in understanding the functions of other people's behavior.

The supplementary motor area and the premotor cortex receive information from association areas of the parietal and temporal cortex. As we saw in Chapter 6, the visual association cortex is organized in two streams: dorsal and ventral. The ventral stream, which terminates in the inferior temporal cortex, is involved in perceiving and recognizing particular objects—the "what" of visual perception.

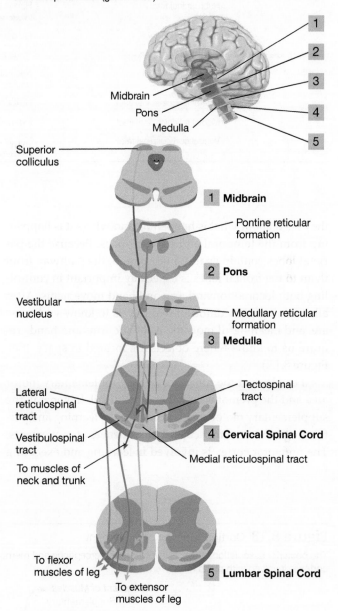

Figure 8.12 Ventromedial Group of Descending Motor Tracts

The figure shows the tectospinal tract (blue lines), lateral reticulospinal tract (purple lines), medial reticulospinal tract (orange lines), and vestibulospinal tract (green lines).

Midbrain
Pons
Medulla

Superior colliculus

1 **Midbrain**

Pontine reticular formation

2 **Pons**

Vestibular nucleus

Medullary reticular formation

3 **Medulla**

Lateral reticulospinal tract

Tectospinal tract

Vestibulospinal tract

4 **Cervical Spinal Cord**

Medial reticulospinal tract

To muscles of neck and trunk

To flexor muscles of leg

5 **Lumbar Spinal Cord**

To extensor muscles of leg

The dorsal stream, which terminates in the posterior parietal lobe, is involved in perception of location—the "where" of visual perception. In addition, the parietal lobes are involved in organizing visually guided movements that interact with objects in the environment—the "how" of visual perception.

Besides receiving information about space from the visual system, the parietal lobes receive information about spatial location from the somatosensory, vestibular, and auditory systems and integrate this information with visual information. Thus, the regions of the frontal cortex that are involved in planning movements receive the information

Table 8.1 Major Motor Pathways

Group	Tract	Muscle Group	Function
Lateral Group	Lateral corticospinal tract	Fingers, hands, and arms	Grasping and manipulating objects
	Rubrospinal tract	Hands (not fingers), lower arms, feet, and lower legs	Movement of forearms and hands independent from that of the trunk
	Corticobulbar tract	Face and tongue	Face and tongue movements
Ventromedial Group	Vestibulospinal tract	Trunk and legs	Posture
	Tectospinal tract	Neck and trunk	Coordination of eye movements with those of trunk and head
	Lateral reticulospinal tract	Flexor muscles of legs	Walking
	Medial reticulospinal tract	Extensor muscles of legs	Walking
	Ventral corticospinal tract	Hands (not fingers), lower arms, feet, and lower legs	Locomotion and posture

they need about what is happening and where it is happening from the temporal and parietal lobes. Because the parietal lobes contain spatial information, the pathway from them to the frontal lobes is especially important in controlling both locomotion and arm and hand movements. After all, meaningful locomotion requires us to know where we are, and meaningful movements of our arms and hands require us to know where objects are located in space. (See Figure 8.13.)

Let's look at the functions of the supplementary motor area and the premotor cortex in more detail. In general, the supplementary motor cortex is involved in learning and performing behaviors that consist of sequences of movements. The premotor cortex is involved in learning and executing responses that are signaled by the presence of arbitrary stimuli. As a component of the mirror neuron system, it is also involved in imitating responses of other people and in understanding and predicting these actions. You will read more about the mirror neuron system later in this chapter.

SUPPLEMENTARY MOTOR AREA The supplementary motor area (SMA) plays a critical role in behavioral sequences. Damage to this region disrupts the ability to execute well-learned sequences of responses in which the performance of one response serves as the signal that the next response must be made.

Research with Nonhuman Primates Chen et al., (1995) found that lesions of the SMA severely impaired monkeys'

Figure 8.13 Cortical Control of Movement

The posterior association cortex is involved with perceptions and memories, and the frontal association cortex is involved with plans for movement.

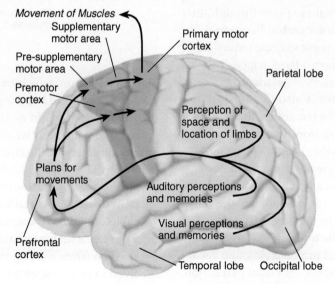

ability to perform a simple sequence of two responses: pushing a lever in and then turning it to the left, receiving a peanut after each response. Shima and Tanji (1998) temporarily inactivated the SMA in monkeys with injections of muscimol, a drug that stimulates GABA receptors and thus inhibits neural activity. They found that after inactivation of this region, monkeys could still reach for objects or make particular movements in response to visual cues but could no longer make a sequence of three movements they had previously learned.

A single-unit recording study came to similar conclusions. Mushiake et al., (1991) trained monkeys to perform a memorized series of responses, pressing each of three buttons in a specific sequence. While the monkeys were performing this task, more than half of the neurons in the SMA became activated. However, when the sequence was cued by visual stimuli—the monkeys simply had to press the button that was illuminated—these neurons showed little activity. In another study, Shima and Tanji (2000) taught monkeys sequences of three motor responses, such as push, then pull, then turn. They recorded from neurons in the SMA and found neurons whose activity appeared to encode elements of these sequences. For example, some neurons responded just before a particular sequence of three movements occurred; some neurons responded between two particular responses; and some neurons responded as the monkey was preparing the make the last response of the sequence. Presumably, these neurons were members of circuits that encoded the information necessary to perform the six sequences.

Research with Humans Studies with human participants have obtained results similar to those obtained with monkeys. For example, a functional-imaging study by Hikosaka et al., (1996) observed increased activity in the posterior SMA during performance of a learned sequence of button presses. Gerloff et al., (1997) taught people to make a sequence of sixteen finger presses on an electronic piano. When the experimenters disrupted the activity of the SMA with transcranial magnetic stimulation (TMS), the performance of the sequence was disrupted. However, the disruption was not immediate: The participants continued the sequence for approximately one second and then stopped, saying that they "did not know anymore which series of keys to press next." Apparently, the SMA is involved in planning the elements *yet to come* in sequences of movements. The actual execution of the movements appears to be controlled elsewhere—likely by the primary motor cortex.

Once we have learned a sequence of movements using one hand, we can easily perform the sequence with the other hand. Presumably, the learning has taken place in the hemisphere that controls the hand that first performed the sequence. Perez et al. (2008) trained people to perform a 12-item sequence of finger movements using four fingers of the right hand. While they were learning the task, the experimenters supplied TMS to the participants' left SMA with a sequence of pulses that temporarily disrupted the activity of this region. If the disrupting stimulation occurred just before each response was to be made, the participants learned the task with their right hand but performed poorly when they were later tested with their left hand. If the stimulation occurred during each finger movement, transfer to the left hand was normal. Perez and her colleagues noted that the left and right SMA have strong interconnections and suggest that during the learning of the sequence, information about the previous response was transmitted from the left SMA to the right SMA. The disrupting TMS interfered with this transfer.

A region just anterior to the supplementary motor area, the *pre-SMA*, appears to be involved in control of spontaneous movements—or at least in the perception of control. It has long been known that although electrical stimulation of the motor cortex causes movements, it does not produce the *desire* to move. The movement is perceived as automatic and involuntary. In contrast, electrical stimulation of the medial surface of the frontal lobes (including the SMA and pre-SMA) often provokes the urge to make a movement or at least the anticipation that a movement is about to occur (Fried et al., 1991).

A functional-imaging study by Lau et al. (2004) found that the pre-SMA appears to play a role in voluntary behavior. They found that this region became active just before people performed spontaneous movements. The experimenters asked the participants to make a finger movement from time to time, whenever they felt like doing so. The participants watched a red light that moved around a clock face at about 2.5 sec per revolution. They were asked to pay attention to the instant when they decided to make the movement and report the position of the red dot at that time. The decision appeared to occur approximately 0.2 sec before the movement began. However, fMRI showed that the activity of the pre-SMA actually began to increase approximately 2–3 sec earlier than that, which suggests that the neural activity responsible for the decision to move begins before a person is even aware of making that decision. The results suggest that although we feel that we consciously decide when to make a response, the decision is actually made by brain processes of which we are unaware. We do not become aware of the decision until later.

Evidence suggests that the decision to move is not made by neurons in the SMA. Sirigu et al. (2004) used a task similar to the one in the study by Lau et al., (2004) to investigate decision making in people with lesions of the posterior parietal cortex. They found that people with these lesions could accurately report when they started the movement, but they were not aware of an intention to move prior to making the movement. The investigators suggest that neural activity in the posterior parietal cortex "generates a predictive internal model of the upcoming movement" (p. 80).

What neural circuits are actually responsible for making a decision to move? Sirigu et al., (2004) note that lesions of the prefrontal cortex (even more anterior than the pre-SMA) disrupt people's plans for voluntary action. People with prefrontal lesions will *react* to events but show deficits in *initiating* behavior, so perhaps the prefrontal cortex is an important source of these decisions. The posterior parietal cortex may be involved in monitoring one's own plans and intentions rather than directly forming these intentions.

A functional-imaging study by Soon et al., (2008) found evidence that a region of the prefrontal cortex—the *frontopolar cortex,* located at the rostral tip of the cerebral hemispheres—may play a critical role in deciding to make a motor response. The investigators had participants perform a task similar to the one used by Lau et al. (2004). The participants were told to watch a screen that displayed a stream of letters and to press one of two buttons whenever they felt like it. The choice of button and the timing of the response was up to them. After each response, the participants reported the letter they had seen on the screen at the time they decided to press one of the buttons, which indicated the time between the awareness of this decision and their movement—which averaged about one second. Examination of the pattern of brain activation on each trial enabled the investigators to predict the decision to press the right or left button. Approximately 10 sec before the response, the decision about which button should be pressed could accurately be predicted by particular patterns of activity in the frontopolar cortex. The decision could be predicted shortly thereafter by the pattern of activity in the posterior parietal cortex, and then by the activity in the SMA. Finally, the primary motor cortex became activated, causing the finger to move. These results suggest that the prefrontal cortex plays a critical role in decision making of the kind the investigators studied. The posterior parietal cortex appears to be involved in storing the information about the decision and transmitting it to the SMA, where the process of executing the response begins. (See Table 8.2.)

PREMOTOR CORTEX The premotor cortex is involved in learning and executing complex movements that are guided by sensory information. The results of several studies suggest that the premotor cortex is involved in using arbitrary stimuli to indicate what movement should be made. For example, reaching for an object that we see in a particular location involves *nonarbitrary* spatial information; that is, the visual information provided by the location of the object specifies just where we should target our reaching movement.

But we also have the ability to learn to make movements based on *arbitrary* information—information that is not directly related to the movement that it signals. The case at the beginning of this chapter describes deficits in making movements based on arbitrary information (being asked to wave versus waving in response to seeing new people). For example, a person can point to a particular object when someone says its name, or a dancer can make a particular movement when asked to do so by a choreographer. Different languages use different sounds to indicate the names of objects, and different choreographers could invent different names for movements used in their dances. Or a person could be told to "wave your left hand when you hear the buzz and touch your nose when you hear the bell." The associations between these stimuli and the movements they designate are arbitrary and must be learned.

Research with Nonhuman Primates Kurata and Hoffman (1994) trained monkeys to move their hand toward the right or left in response to either a spatial or a nonspatial signal. The spatial signal required the animals to move in the direction indicated by signal lights located to the right and left of its hand. The nonspatial signal consisted of a pair of lights, one red and one green, located in the middle of the display. The red light signaled a movement to the left, and the green light signaled a movement to the right. The investigators temporarily inactivated the premotor cortex with injections of muscimol. When this region was inactivated, the monkeys could still move their hand toward a signal light located to the left or right (a nonarbitrary signal), but they could no longer make the

Table 8.2 Role of SMA and Associated Regions from Human Studies

Brain Region	Role	Research Results
Posterior SMA	Perform sequences of learned movements	Increased activity during series of button presses
SMA	Plan the elements yet to come in a series of movements	TMS disrupted performance of series of key presses
Left SMA	Transfer of learned movement sequence to right hemisphere of SMA	TMS disrupted transfer of learned sequence to other hand
Pre-SMA	Control of spontaneous movements	Stimulation provokes urge or anticipation of movement
Pre-SMA	Control of spontaneous movements	Region activated just before spontaneous movement
Posterior parietal cortex	Decision to move	Lesions disrupt awareness of intention to move
Frontopolar cortex	Decision to move	Region activated prior to decision to move

appropriate movements when the red or green signal lights were illuminated (an arbitrary signal).

Research with Humans Similar results are seen in people with damage to the premotor cortex. Halsband and Freund (1990) found that patients with these lesions could learn to make six different movements in response to spatial cues but not to arbitrary visual cues. That is, they could learn to point to one of six locations in which they had just seen a visual stimulus, but they could not learn to use a set of visual, auditory, and tactile cues to make particular movements.

Nowak et al., (2009) found further evidence that the premotor cortex plays a role in learning to control movements in response to arbitrary stimuli. The investigators trained participants to grasp and lift an object positioned between the thumb and forefinger of their right (dominant) hand. The participants watched a computer screen; when a blue dot appeared, they immediately gripped the object and lifted it. Sometimes the dot was pale blue, and sometimes it was dark blue. The light blue dot indicated that the object would weigh 350 g, and the dark blue dot indicated that it would weigh 550 g. Thus, the force needed to grip and lift the object was indicated by an arbitrary signal. The participants learned to grip the object more forcefully when the dark blue dot (heavy signal) appeared, indicating that the object would be heavy. Next, 20 sec of repetitive TMS was applied to the participants' left dorsal premotor cortex, which inhibits this brain region for approximately 30 minutes. When the participants were again tested on the task, they did not adjust the force of their grip; instead, they used a more forceful grip regardless of the brightness of the blue dot.

Subcortical Structures

LO 8.10 Describe the functions of subcortical regions involved in control of motor behavior.

In addition to the cortical regions and the spinal cord, control of motor behavior also involves several *subcortical structures,* including the reticular formation, cerebellum, and the basal ganglia. These structures contain sets of nuclei in the mid- and hindbrain that are involved in control of voluntary and involuntary motor behavior, posture, locomotion, and limb movements. They receive information from regions of the motor cortex and help convey it to the spinal cord and nerves. (See Figure 8.14.)

THE RETICULAR FORMATION The reticular formation consists of a large number of nuclei located in the core of the medulla, pons, and midbrain. The reticular formation controls the activity of the gamma motor system and hence regulates muscle tonus. In addition, the pons and medulla contain several nuclei with specific motor functions. For example, different locations in the medulla control automatic or semiautomatic responses such as respiration, sneezing, coughing, and vomiting. As we saw, pathways in the ventromedial group originate in the superior colliculi, vestibular nuclei, and reticular formation. Thus, the reticular formation plays a role in the control of posture.

The reticular formation also plays a role in locomotion. Stimulation of the **mesencephalic locomotor region,** located ventral to the inferior colliculus, causes a cat to make pacing movements (Shik and Orlovsky, 1976). The mesencephalic

Figure 8.14 Subcortical Structures Involved in Control of Movement

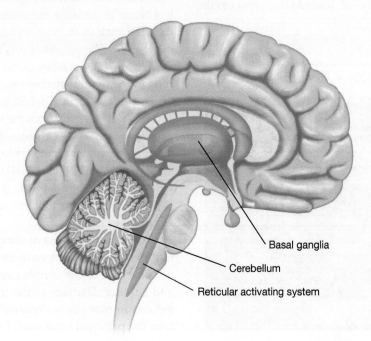

Basal ganglia

Cerebellum

Reticular activating system

locomotor region does not send fibers directly to the spinal cord but apparently controls the activity of reticulospinal tract neurons.

The reticular formation also appears to exert control over some very specific behaviors. For example, Siegel and McGinty (1977) recorded from 35 single neurons in the reticular formation of unanesthetized, freely moving cats. Thirty-two of these neurons responded during *specific* movements of the head, tongue, facial muscles, ears, forepaw, or shoulder. The specific nature of the relationships suggests that the neurons play some role in controlling the movements. For example, one neuron responded when the tongue moved out and to the left. The functions of these neurons and the range of movements they control are not yet known.

THE CEREBELLUM   A second subcortical structure, the cerebellum, is an important part of the motor system. It contains about 50 billion neurons, compared to the approximately 22 billion neurons in the cerebral cortex. Its outputs project to every major motor structure of the brain. When it is damaged, people's movements become jerky, erratic, and uncoordinated. The cerebellum consists of two hemispheres that contain several deep nuclei situated beneath the wrinkled and folded cerebellar cortex. Thus, the cerebellum resembles the cerebrum in miniature. The medial part of the cerebellum is evolutionarily older than the lateral part, and it participates in control of the ventromedial system. The **flocculonodular lobe,** located at the caudal end of the cerebellum, receives input from the vestibular system and projects axons to the vestibular nucleus. (See Figure 8.15.) You may not be surprised to learn that this system is involved in postural reflexes. (See the green lines in Figure 8.16.) The **vermis,** located on the midline, receives auditory and visual information from the tectum and cutaneous and kinesthetic information from the spinal cord. It sends its outputs to the

fastigial nucleus (one of the set of deep cerebellar nuclei). Neurons in the fastigial nucleus send axons to the vestibular nucleus and to motor nuclei in the reticular formation. Thus, these neurons influence behavior through the vestibulospinal and reticulospinal tracts, two of the three ventromedial pathways. (See the blue lines in Figure 8.16.)

The rest of the cerebellar cortex receives most of its input from the cerebral cortex, including the primary motor cortex and association cortex. This input is relayed to the cerebellar cortex through the pontine tegmental reticular nucleus. The intermediate zone of the cerebellar cortex projects to the **interposed nuclei,** which in turn project to the red nucleus. Thus, the intermediate zone influences the control of the rubrospinal system over movements of the arms and legs. The interposed nuclei also send outputs to the ventrolateral thalamic nucleus, which projects to the motor cortex. (See the red lines in Figure 8.16.)

The lateral zone of the cerebellum is involved in the control of independent limb movements, especially rapid, skilled movements. Such movements are initiated by neurons in the frontal association cortex, which control neurons in the primary motor cortex. But although the frontal cortex can plan and initiate movements, it does not contain the neural circuitry needed to calculate the complex, closely timed sequences of muscular contractions that are needed for rapid, skilled movements. That task falls to the lateral zone of the cerebellum.

Both the frontal association cortex and the primary motor cortex send information about intended movements to the lateral zone of the cerebellum via the **pontine nucleus.** The lateral zone also receives information from the somatosensory system, which informs it about the current position and rate of movement of the limbs—information that is necessary for computing the details of a movement. When the cerebellum receives information that the motor cortex has begun to initiate a movement, it computes the contribution that various muscles will have to make to perform that movement. The results of this computation are sent to the **dentate nucleus,** another of the deep cerebellar nuclei. Neurons in the dentate nucleus pass the information on to the ventrolateral thalamus, which projects to the primary motor cortex. The projection from the ventrolateral thalamus to the primary motor cortex enables the cerebellum to modify the ongoing movement that was initiated by the frontal cortex. The lateral zone of the cerebellum also sends efferents to the red nucleus (again, via the dentate nucleus); thus, it helps to control independent limb movements through this system as well. (See Figure 8.17.)

In humans, lesions of different regions of the cerebellum produce different symptoms. Damage to the flocculonodular lobe or the vermis causes disturbances in posture and balance. Damage to the intermediate zone produces deficits in movements controlled by the rubrospinal system; the principal symptom of this damage is limb rigidity.

Figure 8.15 Vermis and Lateral Zones

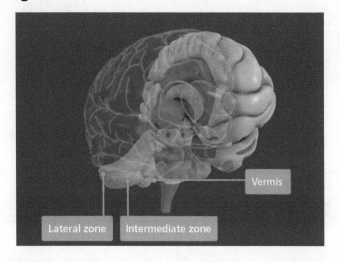

Vermis

Lateral zone   Intermediate zone

Figure 8.16 Inputs and Outputs of Cerebellum

The figure shows the inputs and outputs of three systems: flocculonodular lobe (green lines), the vermis (blue lines), and the intermediate zone of the cerebellar cortex (red lines).

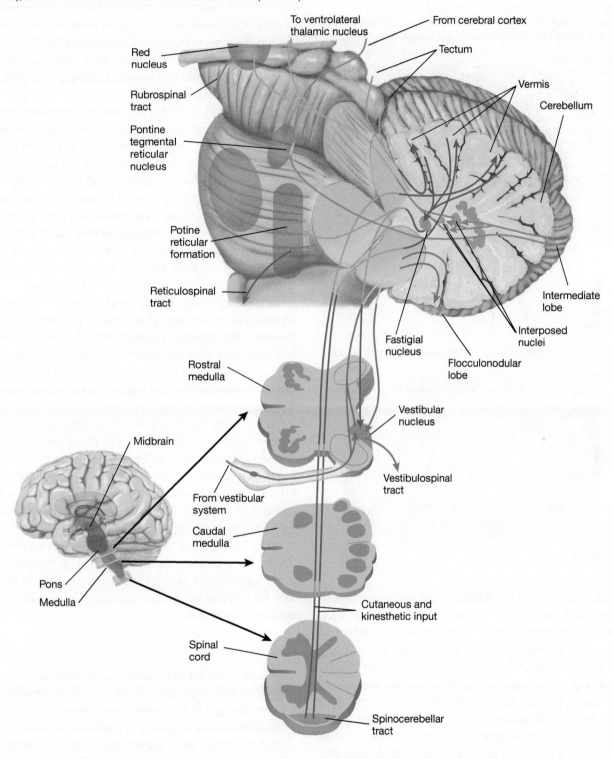

Damage to the lateral zone causes weakness and *decomposition of movement*. For example, a person with this kind of damage who is attempting to bring the hand to the mouth will make separate movements of the joints of the shoulder, elbow, and wrist instead of performing simultaneous smooth movements.

Lesions of the lateral zone of the cerebellar cortex also appear to impair the timing of rapid *ballistic* movements. Ballistic (literally, "throwing") movements occur too fast to be modified by feedback. The sequence of muscular movements must then be programmed in advance, and the individual muscles must be activated at the proper times.

Figure 8.17 Inputs and Outputs of the Lateral Zone of the Cerebellar Cortex

The lateral zone receives information about impending movements from the frontal lobes and helps to smooth and integrate the movements through its connections to the primary motor cortex and red nucleus through the dentate nucleus and ventral thalamus.

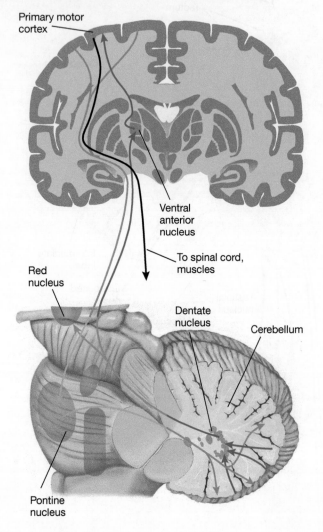

Primary motor cortex

Ventral anterior nucleus

To spinal cord, muscles

Red nucleus

Dentate nucleus

Cerebellum

Pontine nucleus

You might like to try this common neurological test: Have a friend place his or her finger in front of your face, about three-quarters of an arm's length away. While your friend slowly moves his or her finger around to serve as a moving target, alternately touch your nose and your friend's finger as rapidly as you can. If your cerebellum is functioning normally, you can successfully hit your nose and your friend's finger without too much trouble. People with lateral cerebellar damage have great difficulty; they tend to miss the examiner's hand and poke themselves in the eye. (We have often wondered why neurologists do not adopt a less dangerous test.)

When making rapid, aimed movements, we cannot rely on feedback to stop the movement when we reach the target. By the time we perceive that our finger has reached the proper place, it is too late to stop the movement, and we will overshoot the target if we try to stop it then. Instead of relying on feedback, the movement appears to be timed. We estimate the distance between our hand and the target, and our cerebellum calculates the amount of time that the muscles will have to be turned on. After the proper amount of time, the cerebellum briefly turns on antagonistic muscles to stop the movement. In fact, Kornhuber (1974) suggested that one of the primary functions of the cerebellum is timing the duration of rapid movements. Learning must play a role in controlling such movements.

Timmann et al., (1999) reported an interesting example of the role the cerebellum plays in timing sequences of muscular contractions. When tossing a ball at a target using an overarm throw, a person raises his or her hand above the shoulder, rotates the arm forward, and then releases the ball by extending the fingers—moving them apart. The timing of the release is critical: too soon and the ball goes too high, too late and it goes too low. The researchers found that healthy participants released the ball within an 11-msec window 95 percent of the time. Patients with cerebellar lesions did five times worse: Their window was 55 msec wide.

The cerebellum also appears to integrate successive *sequences* of movements that must be performed one after the other. For example, a patient with a lesion in the cerebellum described their movement by saying: "The movements of my left arm are done subconsciously, but I have to think out each movement of the right [affected] arm. I come to a dead stop in turning and have to think before I start again" (Holmes, 1939). Many neurons in the dentate nuclei (which receive inputs from the lateral zone of the cerebellar cortex) showed response patterns that predict the *next* movement in a sequence rather than the one that is currently taking place (Thach, 1978). Presumably, deliberately planning the movements was necessary due to the cerebellum damage that affected the patient's right arm.

The case of Mr. P. illustrates the unique role of the cerebellum in regulating movements. As you will read, other brain regions (and sensory feedback) can help to compensate for missing cerebellum control of movement, but are not nearly as efficient.

Dr. S., a professor of neurology at the medical school, stood on the stage of the auditorium as he presented a case to a group of physicians and students. He discussed the symptoms and possible causes of cerebellar–brain stem degeneration. "Now I'd like to present Mr. P.," he said, as a set of MRI scans appeared on the screen. "As you can see, Mr. P.'s cerebellum shows substantial degeneration, but we can't see evidence of any damage to the brain stem."

Dr. S. left the stage and returned, pushing Mr. P. onstage in a wheelchair.

"Mr. P., how are you feeling today?"

"I'm fine," he replied. "Of course, I'd feel better if I could have walked out here myself."

"Of course."

Dr. S. chatted with Mr. P. for a few minutes, getting him to talk enough so that we could see that his mental condition was lucid and that he had no obvious speech or memory problems.

"Okay, Mr. P., I'd like you to make some movements." He faced Mr. P. and said, "Please stretch your hands out and hold them like this." Dr. S. suddenly raised his arms from his sides and held them out straight in front of him, palms down, fingers pointing forward.

Mr. P. did not respond immediately. He looked as if he were considering what to do. Suddenly, his arms straightened out and lifted from the armrests of the wheelchair. Instead of stopping when they were pointed straight ahead of him, they continued upward. Mr. P. grunted, and his arms began flailing around—up, down, left, and right—until he finally managed to hold them outstretched in front of him. He was panting with the effort to hold them there.

"Thank you, Mr. P. Please put your arms down again. Now try this." Dr. S. very slowly raised his arms from his side until they were straight out in front of them. Mr. P. did the same, and this time there was no overshoot.

After a few more demonstrations, Dr. S. thanked Mr. P. and wheeled him offstage. When he returned, he reviewed what we had seen.

"When Mr. P. tried to quickly raise his arms in front of him, his primary motor cortex sent messages to the appropriate muscles, and his arms straightened out and began to rise. Normally, the cerebellum is informed about the movement and, through its connections back to the motor cortex, begins to contract the antagonistic muscles at the appropriate time, bringing the arms to rest in the intended position. Mr. P. could get the movement started just fine, but the damage to his cerebellum eliminated the help this structure gives to rapid movements, and he couldn't stop his arms in time. When he tried to move slowly, he could use visual and kinesthetic feedback from the position of his arms to control the movement."

THE BASAL GANGLIA Another set of subcortical nuclei, the basal ganglia, constitute an important component of the motor system. We know that they are important because their destruction by disease or injury causes severe motor deficits. The motor nuclei of the basal ganglia include the caudate nucleus, putamen, and globus pallidus. The basal ganglia receive most of their input from all regions of the cerebral cortex (but especially the primary motor cortex and primary somatosensory cortex) and the substantia nigra. The primary outputs of the basal ganglia are as follows: the primary motor cortex, supplementary motor area, premotor cortex (via the thalamus), and motor nuclei of the brain stem that contribute to the ventromedial pathways. Through these connections the basal ganglia influence movements under the control of the primary motor cortex and exert some direct control over the ventromedial system.

Figure 8.18 illustrates the components of the basal ganglia: the **caudate nucleus**, the **putamen**, and the **globus pallidus**. It also shows some nuclei associated with the basal ganglia: the **ventral anterior nucleus** and **ventrolateral nucleus** of the thalamus, the **subthalamic nucleus**, and the substantia nigra of the ventral midbrain.

Figure 8.18 shows some of the more important connections of the basal ganglia and helps to explain the role these structures play in the control of movement. For the sake of clarity, this figure leaves out many connections, including inputs to the substantia nigra from the basal ganglia and other structures. In the following sections, we will more closely examine (1) connections between basal ganglia and cortex, and (2) the effects of motor behavior when the basal ganglia are damaged by neurodegenerative disorders.

Connections with Cortex First, let's take a look at the connections between the basal ganglia and cortex. The frontal, parietal, and temporal cortex send axons to the caudate nucleus and the putamen, which then connect with the globus pallidus, forming a loop. The globus pallidus sends information back to the motor cortex via the ventral anterior and ventrolateral nuclei of the thalamus, completing the loop. Thus, the basal ganglia can monitor somatosensory information and are informed of movements being planned and executed by the motor cortex. Using this information (and other information they receive from other parts of the brain), they can then influence the movements controlled by the motor cortex. Throughout this circuit, information is represented somatotopically. That is, projections from neurons in the motor cortex that cause movements in particular parts of the body project to particular parts of the putamen, and this segregation is maintained all the way back to the motor cortex. (See Figure 8.18.)

Now let's consider some of the complexities of the cortical–basal ganglia loop. The links in the loop are made by both excitatory (glutamate-secreting) neurons and inhibitory (GABA-secreting) neurons. The caudate nucleus and putamen receive excitatory input from the cerebral cortex. They send inhibitory axons to the external and internal divisions of the globus pallidus (the GP_i and the GP_e, respectively). The subthalamic nucleus also receives excitatory input from the cerebral cortex, and it sends excitatory input to the GP_i. In Figure 8.18, the pathway shown in solid lines that includes the GP_i is known as the **direct pathway**. Neurons in GP_i send inhibitory axons to the ventral anterior and ventrolateral thalamus (VA/VL thalamus), which send excitatory projections to the motor cortex.

Figure 8.18 Basal Ganglia

The major connections of the basal ganglia and associated structures. Excitatory connections are shown as black lines; inhibitory connections are shown as red lines. The direct pathway is indicated by arrows with solid lines. The indirect pathway is indicated by arrows with broken lines. The hyperdirect pathway is indicated by arrows with dotted lines. Many connections, such as the inputs to the substantia nigra, are omitted for clarity.

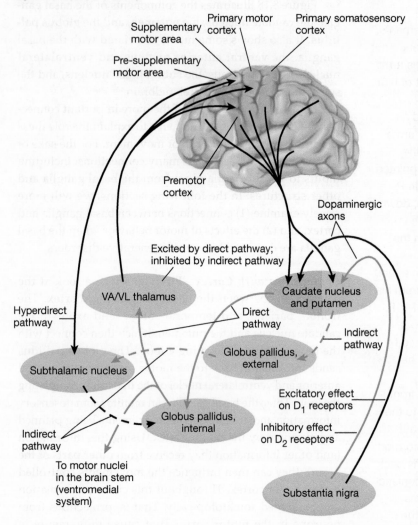

that the ultimate effect of this loop on the thalamus and frontal cortex is *inhibitory*. The globus pallidus also sends axons to various motor nuclei in the brain stem that contribute to the ventromedial system. The effect of this pathway is to inhibit the motor cortex. (Look once again at Figure 8.18.)

A third pathway shown in Figure 8.18 is known as the **hyperdirect pathway.** Neurons in the pre-SMA send excitatory input to the subthalamic nucleus, which sends excitatory input to the GP_i. As we just saw, the GP_i has an inhibitory effect on the motor cortex, so the hyperdirect pathway inhibits movements. The general functions of the direct and indirect pathways have long been understood. However, the hyperdirect pathway was recognized much more recently (Gerfen, 2000; Nambu et al., 2002). This pathway bypasses the caudate nucleus and putamen and is thus able to inhibit movement with a much shorter delay than the indirect pathway.

Most investigators believe that this pathway plays a role in preventing or quickly stopping movements that are being initiated by the direct pathway (Nachev et al., 2008; Nambu, 2008). For example, suppose that you are jogging down a city street. As you approach a cross street, you see that the stoplight is red, so you stop running. The indirect pathway plays a role in the inhibition of your jogging. (Perhaps not completely—perhaps you jog in place while you wait for the light to change.) The light turns green, and this go signal is reflected by increased activity of your direct pathway. You lean forward and raise a foot to begin jogging again. Suddenly, you hear the roar of a speeding car immediately to your left. You quickly stop, and before you can turn your head to look for the source of the noise, a car that has just run through the red light passes in front of you. Activity in your hyperdirect pathway has just saved your life.

Another important input to the basal ganglia comes from the substantia nigra of the midbrain. We saw in Chapter 4 that degeneration of the nigrostriatal bundle, the dopaminergic pathway from the substantia nigra to the caudate nucleus and putamen (the *neostriatum*), causes Parkinson's disease, which we will discuss in more detail in the next subsection. (Look again at Figure 8.18.)

Neurodegenerative Disorders of the Basal Ganglia Now that we have explored the connections between basal ganglia and motor cortex, we can begin to understand the symptoms and treatment of two important neurological disorders that affect these brain regions: Parkinson's disease and Huntington's disease. Each of these is a progressive,

The net effect of the loop is excitatory because it contains two inhibitory links. Each inhibitory link (red arrow) reverses the sign of the input to that link. Thus, excitatory input to the caudate nucleus and putamen causes these structures to *inhibit* neurons in the GP_i. This inhibition *removes* the inhibitory effect of the connections between the GP_i on the VA/VL thalamus; in other words, neurons in the VA/VL thalamus become more excited. This excitation is passed on to the motor cortex, where it facilitates movements. (Look again at Figure 8.18.)

The pathway shown in broken lines, which includes the GP_e, is known as the **indirect pathway.** Neurons in GP_e send inhibitory input to the subthalamic nucleus, which sends excitatory input to the GP_i. From there on, the circuit is identical to the one we just examined—except neurodegenerative disease characterized by motor deficits. These diseases are described in greater detail in Chapter 15.

In general, Parkinson's disease is characterized by an impairment in initiating movement, particularly actions that were previously automatic, such as regaining balance after being bumped or walking from point to point. The symptoms of Parkinson's disease are caused by degeneration of dopamine-secreting cells in the substantia nigra and subsequent disruption of the afferent pathways to the caudate and putamen. In contrast, Huntington's disease is characterized by uncontrollable movements and an impaired ability to cease motor movements. The symptoms of Huntington's disease are produced by degeneration of GABAergic and acetylcholinergic neurons in the caudate and putamen. The loss of inhibition provided by these GABA-secreting neurons increases the activity of the GP_e, which then inhibits the subthalamic nucleus. As a consequence, the activity level of the GP_i decreases, and excessive movements occur.

Section Review

Control of Movement by the Brain

LO 8.7 **Describe the pathways and functions of cortical regions involved in control of motor behavior.**

The supplementary motor area and the premotor cortex receive information from the parietal lobe and help to initiate movements through their connections with the primary motor cortex, which is responsible for causing movements of particular parts of the body.

LO 8.8 **Describe the components and functions of the descending pathways.**

The descending pathways relay motor information from the cortex to the muscles of the body through the lateral and ventromedial groups. The lateral group consists of the corticospinal tract, the corticobulbar tract, and the rubrospinal tract and is involved in control of independent limb movements, particularly movements of the hands and fingers. The ventromedial group consists of the vestibulospinal tract, the tectospinal tract, the reticulospinal tract, and the ventral corticospinal tract, which control automatic trunk and limb movements involved in posture and locomotion.

LO 8.9 **Explain the functions of the motor association cortex (including the supplementary motor area and the premotor cortex) in planning and initiating movement.**

The supplementary motor area is involved in well-learned behavioral sequences. Neurons there fire at particular points in behavioral sequences, and disruption or damage impairs the ability to perform these sequences. The pre-SMA is involved in awareness of our decisions to make spontaneous movements. The premotor cortex is involved in learning and executing complex movements that are guided by arbitrary sensory information, such as verbal instructions.

LO 8.10 **Describe the functions of subcortical regions involved in control of motor behavior.**

The reticular formation regulates muscle tone and is involved in some involuntary behaviors and movements of specific body parts. The cerebellum controls repetitive movements that require accurate aiming and timing, smoothly guides movements, stops movements at the correct time/position, and integrates sequences of movements. The basal ganglia receive input from the motor cortex regions and also direct their output to these regions and the ventromedial pathway. The basal ganglia also control inhibition of unwanted movements. Through these connections the basal ganglia influence movements under the control of the primary motor cortex and exert some direct control over the ventromedial system.

Thought Question

The primate brain includes many different brain structures devoted wholly or in part to motor control. Identify one or more of these regions and describe how motor control might be affected by a lesion to this area.

Complex Motor Behavior

Now that you are familiar with the basic central nervous system structures involved in motor control, we will turn our attention to examining how these structures interact to produce several examples of complex motor behavior. This section of the chapter will focus on planning and initiating movement, imitating and comprehending movements, and the control of reaching and grasping.

Imitating and Comprehending Movements: Role of the Mirror Neuron System

LO 8.11 **Describe the location, components, and functions of the mirror neuron system.**

Rizzolatti and his colleagues (Gallese et al., 1996; Rizzolatti et al., 2001; Rizzolatti and Sinigaglia, 2010) made some interesting observations that have changed the way we think about imitating and comprehending the behavior of others. The investigators found that neurons in an area of the rostral part of the ventral premotor cortex in the monkey brain (referred to as area F5) became active when monkeys saw people or other monkeys perform various grasping, holding, or manipulating movements with objects or when they performed these movements themselves. Thus, the neurons responded to either the sight or the execution of particular movements. The investigators named these cells **mirror neurons.** These neurons, located in the ventral premotor cortex, are reciprocally connected with neurons in the posterior parietal cortex, and further investigation found that this region also contains mirror neurons. Given the characteristics of mirror neurons, we might expect that they play a role in a monkey's ability to imitate the movements of other monkeys—and Rizzolatti and his colleagues found that this inference was correct.

Several functional-imaging studies have shown that the human brain also contains a circuit of mirror neurons in the rostral part of the inferior parietal lobule (a region of the posterior parietal cortex) and the ventral premotor area. For example, in a functional-imaging study, Buccino et al., (2004) had nonmusicians watch and then imitate video clips of an expert guitarist placing his fingers on the neck of a guitar to play a chord. Both watching and imitating the guitarist's movements activated the mirror neuron circuit. (See Figure 8.19.)

Several studies have found that the mirror neuron system is activated most strongly when one watches a behavior in which one is already competent. For example, Calvo-Merino et al., (2006) had professional ballet dancers watch videos of men or women perform ballet moves. Some moves are performed only by men, some only by women, and some by both men and women, but all of the moves have been *seen* many times by both male and female ballet dancers. The investigators found that when women watched women's moves or when men watched men's moves, the mirror neuron system was strongly activated. However, when women watched men's moves or when men watched women's moves, much less activity was seen in this circuit. Thus, the mirror neuron circuit develops sensitivity to the sight of movements that the person actually performs, not simply actions that the person has seen performed. Once this sensitivity develops, the circuit is activated by watching another person perform those movements.

Mirror neurons are activated not only by the performance of an action or the sight of someone else performing that action, but also by sounds that indicate the occurrence of a familiar action. For example, Kohler et al., (2002) found that mirror neurons in the ventral prefrontal cortex of monkeys became active when the animals heard sounds they recognized, such as a peanut breaking, a piece of paper being ripped, or a stick being dropped. Individual neurons—the researchers called them *audiovisual neurons*—responded to the sounds of particular actions and to the sight of those actions being performed. Presumably, activation of these neurons by these familiar sounds reminds the animals of the actions the sounds represent.

Haslinger et al., (2005) found that the interaction between audition and vision worked in the other direction as well. The investigators showed professional pianists silent videos of a hand playing the piano or making meaningless finger movements above a piano keyboard. Functional imaging showed that when the participants watched actual piano playing, the mirror neuron system and visual cortex were activated, as would be expected, but the auditory cortex was activated as well. Presumably, the musicians imagined what it was like to make the meaningful hand and finger movements, activating the mirror neuron system, but also imagined what the piano would sound like when the keys were pressed, activating the auditory cortex.

Rizzolatti et al., (2001) suggest that the mirror neuron circuit helps us to understand the actions of others:

> [A]n action is understood when its observation causes the motor system of the observer to "resonate." So, when we observe a hand grasping an apple, the same population of neurons that control the execution of grasping movements becomes active in the observer's motor areas. . . . In other words, we understand an action because the motor representation of that action is activated in our brain. (p. 661)

By "resonation," Rizzolatti et al., mean that the neural circuits responsible for performing a particular action are activated when we see someone else beginning to

Figure 8.19 Important Motor Regions of the Human Brain
In the human brain, the inferior parietal lobule and the ventral premotor cortex constitute the primary mirror neuron circuit. The parietal reach region plays a role in reaching, and the anterior intraparietal sulcus plays a role in grasping.

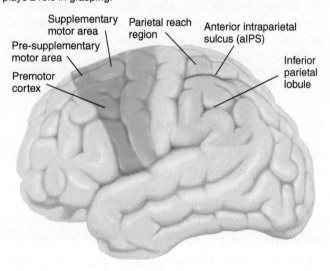

perform that action or even when we hear the characteristic sounds produced by that action. Feedback from the activation of these circuits gives rise to the recognition of the action.

The next time you intently watch someone executing a skilled action—say, pitching a baseball, kicking a soccer ball, performing a difficult dance move, or playing the violin—see whether you don't find yourself tensing the muscles that you would use if you were performing the action. Presumably, the activation of the mirror neuron circuit is responsible for this effect. As we will see in Chapter 11, we also tend to copy facial expressions of emotion that other people make, and feedback from doing so tends to evoke a similar emotional state in us.

A functional-imaging study by Iacoboni et al., (2005) suggests that the mirror neuron system helps us to understand other people's intentions. The researchers showed participants video clips of an arm and hand reaching for and grasping a mug. The actions were shown in isolation or in the context of objects set out for a snack (mug, teapot, milk pitcher, sugar bowl, sealed jam jar, plate of cookies, and the like) or the same objects after the snack had been eaten (mug, milk pitcher overturned, cookies missing from the plate, open jam jar, and the like). The first context suggests that the intent of the action is that of drinking, and the second suggests that the intent is that of cleaning up. The investigators found that watching the reaching action activated the mirror neuron system of the ventral premotor cortex, but there were differences in the activation when the action occurred in the two different contexts. (There were no differences in the activation caused by simply looking at the contexts.) The authors concluded that the mirror neuron system encodes not only an action but the intent of that action. (See Figure 8.20.)

Control of Reaching and Grasping: Role of the Parietal Cortex

LO 8.12 **Summarize the contributions of the parietal cortex in reaching and grasping behavior.**

Much of our behavior involves interacting with objects in our environment. Many of these interactions involve reaching for something and then doing something with it, such as picking it up, moving it, or otherwise manipulating it. Researchers investigating these interactions classify them into two major categories: reaching and grasping. It turns out that different brain mechanisms are involved in these two activities.

REACHING BEHAVIOR Most reaching behavior is controlled by vision. As we saw in Chapter 6, the dorsal stream of the visual system is involved in determining the location of objects and, if they are moving, the direction and speed of their movement. You may not be surprised to learn that connections between the parietal lobe (the endpoint of the dorsal stream of the visual association cortex) and the frontal lobe play a critical role in reaching.

As we saw in Chapter 6, several regions of the visual association cortex are named for particular types of objects that we perceive, for example, fusiform face area, extrastriate body area, and parahippocampal place area. One region of the medial posterior parietal cortex has been named the **parietal reach region.** Connolly et al., (2003) found that when people were about to make a pointing or reaching movement to a particular location, this region became active. Presumably, the parietal cortex determines the location of the target and supplies information about this location to motor mechanisms in the frontal cortex. (See Figure 8.21 and refer again to Figure 8.19.)

Figure 8.20 Understanding Intentions

The photographs show the actions and contexts presented to the participants in the experiment by Iacoboni et al. (2005).

(From Iacoboni, M., Molnar-Szakacs, I., Gallese, V., Buccino, G., Mazziotta, J. C., Rizzolatti, G., Grasping the intentions of others with one's own mirror neuron system, *PLoS Biology*, 2005, *3*, e79.)

Figure 8.21 Parietal Reach Region

An inflated left cerebral hemisphere shows fMRI activation of the parietal reach region (PRR) just as people were about to make a pointing or reaching movement. POS = parieto-occipital sulcus.

(From Connolly, J. D., Andersen, R. A., and Goodale, M. A., fMRI evidence for a parietal reach region in the human brain, *Experimental Brain Research*, 2003, *153*, 140–145. Reprinted with permission.)

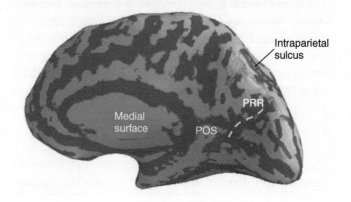

Figure 8.22 Activation of the Anterior Intraparietal Sulcus

The activation is produced by grasping movements made while reaching for objects with different shapes. Activity made by reaching for and simply touching the objects was subtracted from activity made by reaching and grasping, leaving only the grasping component of fMRI activation.

(Based on Frey, S. H., Vinton, D., Norlund, R., and Grafton, S. T. Cognitive Brain Research, 2005, 23, 397–405.)

GRASPING BEHAVIOR Another region of the posterior parietal cortex, the anterior part of the intraparietal sulcus (aIPS), is involved in controlling hand and finger movements involved in grasping the target object. A functional-imaging study by Frey et al. (2005) had people reach for objects of different shapes, which required them to make a variety of hand and finger movements to hold onto the objects. The brain activity directly related to grasping movements was determined by subtracting the activity produced by reaching for and simply touching the objects from the activity produced by reaching for and grasping the objects. The grasping activity activated the aIPS. (See Figure 8.22.)

An experiment by Tunik et al. (2005) confirmed the importance of the aIPS to grasping. The investigators had participants reach for and grasp a rectangular object that was oriented with its long side in a vertical or horizontal position. On some trials ("perturbed trials") the object suddenly rotated during the participants' reaching movements, which required the participants to adjust the position of their hand or fingers before they reached the object. On some of these perturbed trials the investigators applied transcranial magnetic stimulation (TMS) that disrupted the activity of the aIPS. When the disruptive stimulation occurred shortly after the rotation of the object, the participants' ability to accurately change grip posture was disrupted. Stimulation of the hand area of the primary motor cortex or other parts of the parietal lobe had no effect.

The visual input to the aIPS is from the dorsal stream of the visual system. In a functional-imaging study by Shmuelof and Zohary (2005), participants watched brief videos of a hand reaching out to grasp a variety of objects. Sometimes the hand appeared in the left visual field and the object appeared in the right visual field; sometimes the locations for the hand and the object were reversed. (The participants focused their gaze on a fixation point located between the hand and the object.) This procedure means that, for a particular trial, visual information about an object was transmitted to one side of the brain, and visual information about a hand shaped to grasp the object was transmitted to the other side of the brain. Analysis of the brain activation showed that information about the nature of the object activated the ventral stream ("what") of the visual system and information about the shape of the hand activated the aIPS, which is part of the dorsal stream ("where"). The results suggest that the aIPS is involved in recognition of grasping movements as well as their execution.

Section Review

Complex Motor Behavior

LO 8.11 Describe the location, components, and functions of the mirror neuron system.

The mirror neuron system is located in the ventral premotor cortex. The neurons of the mirror neuron system are active when an individual engages in a behavior as well as when the individual observes (or hears) the behavior. Another circuit of mirror neurons is located in the posterior parietal lobe. The proposed function of the mirror neuron system is to help an individual understand the actions of others.

LO 8.12 Summarize the contributions of the parietal cortex in reaching and grasping behavior.

The dorsal stream of the visual association cortex contributes spatial information to the parietal reaching region, which calculates the reaching movement that must be made and transmits this information to the motor association cortex. During the reaching movement the cortex located in the anterior intraparietal sulcus sends information to the motor association cortex that moves the hand and fingers to be ready to grasp an object.

Thought Question

The discovery of mirror neurons has helped us in explaining how humans can imitate others' actions and feel empathy, which provide several advantages and seem to have played a significant role in the evolution of the human race and culture. Write an essay with examples on the contribution of mirror neurons in shaping human civilization.

Deficits of Skilled Movements: The Apraxias

Damage to the frontal or parietal cortex on the left side of the brain can produce a category of movement deficits called **apraxia.** Literally, the term means "without action," but apraxia differs from paralysis or weakness that occurs when motor structures such as the precentral gyrus, basal ganglia, brain stem, or spinal cord are damaged. *Apraxia* refers to the inability to imitate movements or produce them in response to verbal instructions or inability to demonstrate the movements that would be made in using a familiar tool or utensil (Leiguarda and Marsden, 2000). Neuropsychological studies of the apraxias have provided information about the way skilled behaviors are organized and initiated.

There are four major types of apraxia, two of which we will discuss in this chapter. *Limb apraxia* refers to problems with movements of the arms, hands, and fingers. *Constructional apraxia* refers to difficulty in drawing or constructing objects. *Oral apraxia* refers to problems with movements of the muscles used in speech. *Apraxic agraphia* refers to a particular type of writing deficit. Because of their relation to language, we will describe oral apraxia and the various forms of agraphia in Chapter 14.

Limb Apraxia

LO 8.13   Describe how brain lesions can produce limb apraxia.

Limb apraxia is characterized by movement of the wrong part of the limb, incorrect movement of the correct part, or correct movements but in the incorrect sequence. It is assessed by asking patients to perform movements—for example, imitating hand gestures made by the examiner. The most difficult movements involve pantomiming particular acts without the presence of the objects that are normally acted upon. For example, the examiner might say to the patient, "Pretend you have a key in your hand and open a door with it." In response, a patient with limb apraxia might wave his wrist back and forth rather than rotating it or might rotate his wrist first and then pretend to insert the key. Or if asked to pretend that she is brushing her teeth, a patient might use her finger as though it were a toothbrush rather than pretending to hold a toothbrush in her hand.

To perform behaviors on verbal command without having a real object to manipulate, a person must comprehend the command and be able to imagine the missing article as well as to make the proper movements; therefore, these requests are the most difficult to carry out. Somewhat easier are tasks that involve imitating behaviors performed by the experimenter. Sometimes, a patient who cannot mime the use of a key can copy the examiner's hand movements. The easiest tasks involve the actual use of objects. For example, the examiner might give the patient a door key and ask him or her to demonstrate its use. If the brain lesion makes it impossible for the patient to understand speech, then the examiner cannot assess the ability to perform behaviors on verbal command. In this case the examiner can only measure the patient's ability to imitate movements or use actual objects. (See Heilman, Rothi, et al., 1983, for a review.)

Why does damage to the left parietal hemisphere, but usually not the right, cause an apraxia of both hands? The answer seems to be that the right hemisphere is involved with extrapersonal space and the left hemisphere is involved with one's own body. A functional-imaging study by Chaminade et al., (2005) supports this explanation. The investigators asked participants to watch another person perform hand and arm gestures and then either imitate the gestures or make different ones with the same arm or the other arm. On the basis of the activity seen by fMRI scans, the authors concluded that posterior regions of the right hemisphere tracked the movements of the model in space, while the left parietal lobe organized the movements that would be made in response.

Although the frontal and parietal lobes are both involved in imitating hand gestures made by other people, the frontal cortex appears to play a more important role in recognizing the meaning of these gestures. Pazzaglia et al., (2008) tested patients with limb apraxia caused by damage to the left frontal or parietal lobes. They tested the patients' recognition of hand gestures by having them watch video clips in which a person performed the gestures correctly or incorrectly. For example, incorrect gestures included playing a broom as if it were a guitar or pretending to hitchhike by extending the little finger instead of the thumb. Patients with apraxia who have damage to the inferior frontal gyrus, but not to the parietal cortex, showed deficits in comprehension of the gestures.

Constructional Apraxia

LO 8.14   Describe how brain lesions can produce constructional apraxia.

Constructional apraxia is caused by lesions of the right hemisphere, particularly the right parietal lobe. People with this disorder do not have difficulty making most types of skilled movements with their arms and hands. They have no trouble using objects properly, imitating their use, or pretending to use them. However, they have trouble drawing pictures or assembling objects from elements such as toy building blocks.

The primary deficit in constructional apraxia appears to involve the ability to perceive and imagine geometrical relations. For example, because of this deficit, a person cannot draw a picture of a cube, because he or she cannot imagine

Figure 8.23 Constructional Apraxia

An attempt to copy a cube by a patient with constructional apraxia caused by a lesion of the right parietal lobe.

(Based on *Fundamentals of Human Neuropsychology*, by B. Kolb and I. Q. Whishaw. W. H. Freeman and Company. Copyright (C) 1980.)

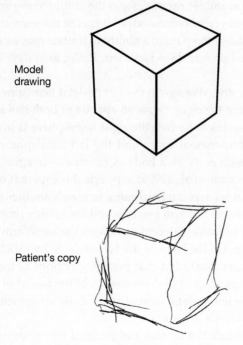

Model drawing

Patient's copy

what the lines and angles of a cube look like, not because of difficulty controlling the movements of his or her arm and hand. (See Figures 8.23 and 8.24.) Besides being unable to draw accurately, a person with constructional apraxia invariably has trouble with other tasks involving spatial perception, such as following a map.

Figure 8.24 Parietal Lobes and Apraxia

Damage to the frontal or parietal lobes can cause apraxia. This figure demonstrates parietal lobe locations involved in limb and constructional apraxias.

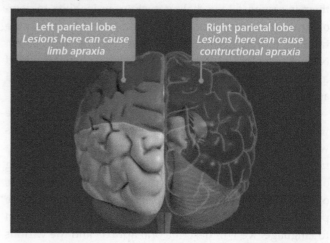

Left parietal lobe
Lesions here can cause limb apraxia

Right parietal lobe
Lesions here can cause constructional apraxia

Section Review

Deficits of Skilled Movements: The Apraxias

LO 8.13 Describe how brain lesions can produce limb apraxia.

Most cases of limb apraxia are produced by lesions of the left frontal or parietal cortex. The left parietal cortex directly controls movement of the right limb by activating neurons in the left primary motor cortex and indirectly controls movement of the left limb by sending information to the right frontal association cortex.

LO 8.14 Describe how brain lesions can produce constructional apraxia.

Constructional apraxia is caused by lesions of the right hemisphere, particularly the right parietal lobe. People with this disorder have trouble drawing pictures or assembling objects from elements such as toy building blocks.

Thought Question

Patients with apraxia may experience a reduction in their quality of life due to their symptoms. Suggest one or more ways that patients might adapt their behavior to compensate for motor deficits due to limb or constructional apraxia.

Chapter Review Questions

1. Explain the role of the muscle spindle and gamma motor system in regulating the length of muscles during the relaxed state and the contracted state.

2. Describe the organization of motor cortex and the role of motor cortex regions in initiating, imitating, and comprehending movements.

3. Differentiate between the role of ventromedial and lateral descending tracts in the control of particular movements.

4. Discuss the role of the cerebellum and the reticular formation in the control of movement.

5. Discuss the anatomy and function of the basal ganglia and its role in Parkinson's disease and Huntington's disease.

6. Describe the symptoms and causes of limb apraxia and constructional apraxia.

Chapter 9
Sleep and Biological Rhythms

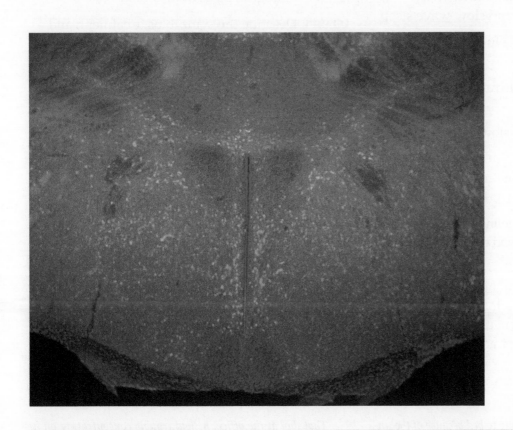

Chapter Outline

Learning Objectives

LO 9.1 Describe the progression, behaviors, and EEG characteristics of the stages of sleep.

LO 9.2 Explain the patterns of brain activity present during REM and slow-wave sleep.

LO 9.3 Suggest some possible functions of slow-wave sleep.

LO 9.4 Identify some possible functions of REM sleep.

LO 9.5 Compare the roles of slow-wave and REM sleep in learning.

LO 9.6 Explain how adenosine contributes to regulating sleep.

LO 9.7 Describe how acetylcholine, norepinephrine, serotonin, histamine, and orexin contribute to regulating arousal.

LO 9.8 Summarize the roles of homeostatic/allostatic/circadian factors, brain regions, flip-flop circuits, and neurotransmitter systems in regulating transitions between sleep and wake.

LO 9.9 Describe the role of flip-flop circuits in neural control of transition to REM.

LO 9.10 Describe the symptoms, treatment, and biological basis of insomnia.

LO 9.11 Describe the symptoms, treatment, and biological basis of narcolepsy.

LO 9.12 Describe the symptoms, treatment, and biological basis of REM sleep behavior disorder.

LO 9.13 Describe the symptoms, treatment, and biological basis of bedwetting, sleepwalking, and night terrors.

LO 9.14 List examples of circadian rhythms and zeitgebers.

LO 9.15 Identify the role of the suprachiasmatic nucleus in regulating circadian rhythms, and explain how the clock mechanism functions.

LO 9.16 Describe the relationship between the pineal gland and melatonin.

LO 9.17 Suggest why shift work and jet lag result in changes in circadian rhythms.

Lately, Miguel felt anxious about going to bed because of the unpleasant experiences he had been having. Several times in the past few months he felt as if he were paralyzed as he lay in bed, waiting for sleep to come. It was a strange feeling; was he really paralyzed, or was he just not trying hard enough to move? He always fell asleep before he was able to decide. A couple of times he woke up just before it was time for his alarm to go off and felt unable to move. Then the alarm would ring, and he would quickly shut it off. That meant that he really wasn't paralyzed, didn't it?

His dreams had become more intense in a disturbing way. One night brought the worst experience of all. As Miguel was falling asleep, he felt again as if he were paralyzed. Then he saw his former roommate enter his bedroom. But that wasn't possible! Since the time he graduated from college he had lived alone, and he always locked the door. He tried to say something, but he couldn't. His roommate was holding a hammer. He walked up to the bed, stood over Miguel, and suddenly raised the hammer, as if to smash in his forehead. When Miguel awoke in the morning, he shuddered with the remembrance. It had seemed so real! It must have been a dream, but he didn't think he was asleep.

That day at the office, he had trouble concentrating on his work. He forced himself to review his notes, because he had to present the details of a new project to the board of directors. This was his big chance; if the project were accepted, he would certainly be chosen to lead it, and that would mean a promotion and a substantial raise. Naturally, with so much at stake, he felt nervous when he entered the boardroom. His boss introduced Miguel and asked him to begin. Miguel glanced at his notes and opened his mouth to talk. Suddenly, he felt his knees buckle. All his strength seemed to slip away. He fell heavily to the floor. He could hear people running over and asking what had happened. He couldn't move anything except his eyes. His boss asked, "Miguel, are you all right?" Miguel looked at his boss and tried to answer, but he couldn't say a thing. A few seconds later, he felt his strength coming back. He opened his mouth and said, "I'm okay." He struggled to his knees and then sat in a chair, feeling weak and frightened.

"You have a condition known as narcolepsy," said the doctor whom Miguel visited after his experience in the boardroom. "It's a problem that concerns the way your brain controls sleep. I'll have you spend a night in the sleep clinic and get some recordings done

to confirm this diagnosis. You told me that lately you've been taking short naps during the day. What were these naps like? Were you suddenly struck by an urge to sleep?" Miguel nodded. "I just had to put my head on the desk, even though I was afraid that my boss might see me. But I don't think I slept more than five minutes or so." "Did you still feel sleepy when you woke?" "No," he replied, "I felt fine again." The doctor nodded. "All the symptoms you describe—the sleep attacks, the paralysis you experienced before sleeping and after waking up, the spell you had today—they all fit together. Fortunately, we can usually control narcolepsy with medication. In fact, we have a new one that does an excellent job. There is no reason why you can't continue with your job. If you'd like, I can talk with your boss and reassure her, too."

*****

Miguel's story illustrates several aspects of sleep that will be explored in more depth throughout the following chapter. Sleep is a complex behavior that involves many regions of the brain. The regulation of sleep and wake cycles is an intricate balance between activity in neural circuits, the actions of hormones, and environmental factors. As you read this chapter, consider the different aspects of sleep represented in Miguel's case, from an intense motivation to sleep, to visual hallucination, to muscle paralysis. In fact, Miguel's experience prompts a very basic question: Why do we sleep? Why do we spend at least one-third of our lives doing something that provides most of us with only a few fleeting memories?

We will attempt to answer this question in several ways. In the first two sections of this chapter we will describe what is known about the phenomenon of sleep and why we do it. In the third section we will describe the search for the chemicals and the neural circuits that control sleep and wakefulness. In the fourth section we examine sleep disorders, including insomnia, narcolepsy, sleepwalking, and others. In the final section of the chapter we will discuss the brain's biological clock—the mechanism that controls daily rhythms of sleep and wakefulness. The figure here presents the suprachiasmatic nucleus and pineal gland, two regions to which we will be paying particular attention in our examination of sleep and biological rhythms.

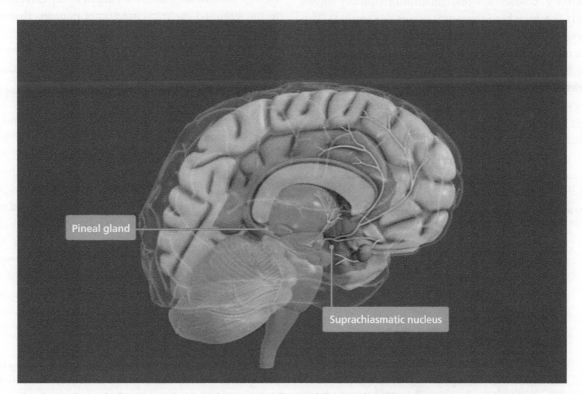

This figure shows the location of the suprachiasmatic nucleus and the pineal gland.

What Is Sleep?

Sleep is a behavior. That statement might seem peculiar, because we usually think of behaviors as activities that involve movements, such as walking or talking. Except for the rapid eye movements that accompany a particular stage, sleep is not distinguished by movement. What characterizes sleep is that the insistent urge of sleepiness (a motivation) forces us to seek out a quiet, warm, comfortable place; lie down; and remain there for several hours (a behavior). Because we remember very little about what happens while we sleep, we tend to think of sleep more as a change in consciousness than as a behavior. The change in consciousness is undeniable, but it should not prevent us from noticing the behavioral changes.

Stages of Sleep

LO 9.1 **Describe the progression, behaviors, and EEG characteristics of the stages of sleep.**

The best research on human sleep is conducted in a sleep laboratory. A sleep laboratory, usually located at a university or medical center, consists of one or several small bedrooms adjacent to an observation room, where the experimenter spends the night (trying to stay awake). The experimenter prepares the sleeper for electrophysiological measurements by attaching electrodes to the scalp to monitor the brain's activity with an *electroencephalogram* (EEG), and to the face to monitor muscle activity, recorded as the **electromyogram (EMG)**. Electrodes attached around the eyes monitor eye movements, recorded as the **electro-oculogram (EOG)**. In addition, other electrodes and transducing devices can be used to monitor autonomic measures such as heart rate, respiration, and changes in the ability of the skin to conduct electricity. (See Figure 9.1.)

During wakefulness the EEG of a normal person shows two basic patterns of activity: *alpha activity* and *beta activity*. **Alpha activity** consists of regular, medium-frequency waves of 8–12 Hz (hertz, which measures cycles per second). The brain produces this activity when a person is resting quietly, not particularly aroused or excited and not engaged in strenuous mental activity (such as problem solving). Although alpha waves sometimes occur when a person's eyes are open, they are much more prevalent when they are closed. The other type of waking EEG pattern, **beta activity**, consists of irregular, mostly low-amplitude waves of 13–30 Hz.

Figure 9.1 Participant in a Sleep Study

Electrodes allow researchers to measure electrophysiological activity from the brain and muscles in the face and around the eyes.

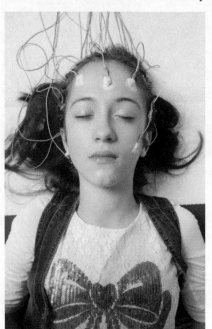

Beta activity shows *desynchrony;* it reflects the fact that many different neural circuits in the brain are actively processing information. Desynchronized activity occurs when a person is alert and attentive to events in the environment or is thinking actively.

EEG electrodes record from many neurons all at once, reporting on the sum of their electrical activity. If the cells are active at about the same time, their electrical messages are synchronized and appear as a large, clear wave in the EEG data. If they are active at random, their electrical messages are desynchronized and appear as small, chaotic waveforms without a clear pattern in the EEG data. Imagine that all of the neurons in a particular cortical region are swimmers in a pool. These swimmers are all making waves by pushing the water with their hands. When the swimmers are *synchronized* and all push together to make their individual waves, their waves combine to make one big wave moving across the pool. When the swimmers are *desynchronized,* each individual makes their own waves at random. Some of the small waves crash into each other and cancel out the progress of other waves. The pool is full of many small, chaotic individual waves moving in every direction, similar to the summed electrical activity of neurons that are active when beta activity is recorded. (See Figure 9.2.)

Researchers and physicians have carefully examined the EEG record of sleepers and identified particular patterns of waveform activity that correspond with different periods, or *stages,* of sleep. The first physiological description of sleep stages was published in 1957, and by 1968 Rechtschaffen and Kales had published a manual for a standardized sleep stage scoring method known as the R & K method (Dement and Kleitman, 1957; Rechtschaffen and Kales, 1968). In additional to wakefulness, the original scoring guidelines included four stages of *non-REM sleep* (stages 1–4) and one stage of *REM sleep,* composed of EEG waveforms of different frequencies and amplitudes. Since the early 2000s, a revised scoring system has been proposed by the American Academy of Sleep Medicine (AASM method). The new system identifies stages of wakefulness (stage W), three stages of non-REM sleep (NREM 1, 2, and 3) and one REM sleep stage (stage R) (Berry et al., 2012; Silber et al., 2007). (See Table 9.1.)

Let's look at a typical night's sleep of a female college student in a sleep laboratory, using the new sleep stage scoring guidelines. (An experimenter would obtain similar results from a male, with one exception, which is noted later.) The experimenter attaches the electrodes, turns the lights off, and closes the door. Our volunteer becomes drowsy and soon enters stage 1 sleep, marked by the presence of some **theta activity** (3.5–7.5 Hz), which indicates that the firing of neurons in the neocortex is becoming more synchronized. This stage is actually a transition between sleep and wakefulness; if we watch our volunteer's eyelids, we will see that from time

Figure 9.2 Synchronous and Desynchronous EEG activity

(a) If the cells are active at about the same time, their electrical messages are synchronized and appear as a large, clear wave in the EEG data. This is an example of synchronous delta activity.
(b) If neurons are active at random, their electrical messages are desynchronized and appear as small, chaotic waveforms without a clear pattern in the EEG data. This is an example of desynchronous beta wave activity.

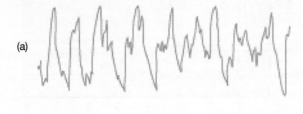

(a)

(b)

to time they slowly open and close and that her eyes roll upward and downward. (Look again at Table 9.1.) During this time, the sleeper may experience *hypnic jerks*,

muscle contractions followed by relaxation. Many people experience these along with a falling sensation. About 10 minutes later she enters stage 2 sleep. The EEG during this stage is generally irregular but contains periods of theta activity, *sleep spindles,* and *K complexes.* Sleep spindles are short bursts of waves of 12–14 Hz that occur between two and five times a minute during stages 1–3 of sleep. They appear to play a role in consolidation of memories, and increased numbers of sleep spindles are correlated with increased scores on tests of intelligence (Fogel and Smith, 2011). (The role of sleep in memory is discussed later in this chapter.) K complexes are sudden, sharp waveforms, which, unlike sleep spindles, are usually found only during stage 2 sleep. They spontaneously occur at the rate of approximately one per minute but often can be triggered by noises—especially unexpected noises. Cash et al., (2009) recorded the activity of single neurons in the human cerebral cortex during sleep and found that K complexes consisted of isolated periods of neural inhibition. (The recordings were made from the brains of patients who were being evaluated for neurosurgery.) K complexes appear to be the forerunner of delta waves, which appear in the deepest levels of sleep.

Table 9.1 Sleep Stages

Sleep Stages	Description	EEG Data
Waking	Alpha (8–12Hz) and beta (13–30Hz) activity	Alpha activity Beta activity
Stage 1	NREM sleep, consists of theta activity (3.5–7.5Hz).	Theta activity
Stage 2	NREM sleep, contains sleep spindles and K complexes	Sleep spindle K complex
Stage 3	Slow wave sleep, consists of delta activity (<3.5Hz)	Delta activity
REM	REM sleep, consists of theta and beta activity	Theta activity Beta activity

Based on: Silber et al., 2007 and Horne, *J. A. Why we sleep: The functions of sleep in humans and other mammals.* Oxford, England: Oxford University Press, 1988. REM=rapid eye movement; NREM=Non REM sleep

The person is sleeping soundly now; but if awakened, she might report that she has not been asleep. This phenomenon often is reported by nurses who awaken loudly snoring hospital patients early in the night and find that the patients insist that they were lying there awake all the time. About 15 minutes later the volunteer enters *slow-wave sleep,* signaled by the occurrence of high-amplitude **delta activity** (less than 3.5 Hz) in stage 3 sleep. (Look again at Table 9.1.)

About 90 minutes after the beginning of sleep, we notice an abrupt change in a number of physiological measures recorded from our volunteer. The EEG suddenly becomes mostly desynchronized, with occasional occurrences of theta waves, very similar to the record obtained during stage 1 sleep. (Refer back to Table 9.1.) We also note that her eyes are rapidly moving back and forth beneath her closed eyelids. We can see this activity in the EOG, recorded from electrodes attached to the skin around her eyes, or we can observe the eye movements directly—the cornea produces a bulge in the closed eyelids that can be seen to move about. We also see that the EMG becomes silent; there is a profound loss of muscle tone. In fact, physiological studies have shown that, aside from occasional twitching, a person actually becomes paralyzed during REM sleep. This peculiar stage of sleep is quite distinct from the quiet sleep we saw earlier. It is usually referred to as **REM sleep** (named for the **r**apid **e**ye **m**ovements that characterize it).

By most criteria, stage 3 is the deepest stage of sleep; only loud noises will cause a person to awaken, and when awakened, the person acts groggy and confused. In contrast, during REM sleep a person might not react to most noises, but he or she is easily aroused by meaningful stimuli, such as the sound of his or her name. Also, when awakened from REM sleep, a person appears alert and attentive.

If we wake our volunteer during REM sleep and ask her what was going on, she will almost certainly report that she had been dreaming. The dreams of REM sleep tend to be narrative in form, with a storylike progression of events. On the other hand, if we wake her during slow-wave sleep and ask, "Were you dreaming?" she will most likely say, "No." However, if we question her more carefully, she might report the presence of a thought, an image, or some emotion.

During the rest of the night our volunteer's sleep alternates between periods of REM and non-REM sleep. Each cycle is approximately 90 minutes long, containing a 20- to 30-minute bout of REM sleep. Thus, an 8-hour sleep will contain four or five periods of REM sleep. Figure 9.3 shows a graph of a typical night's sleep. The vertical axis indicates the EEG activity that is being recorded; thus, REM sleep and stage 1 sleep are placed on the same line because similar patterns of EEG activity occur at these times. Note that most slow-wave sleep occurs during the first half of night. Subsequent bouts of non-REM sleep contain more and more stage

Figure 9.3 A Typical Pattern of Sleep Stages During a Single Night

The dark blue shading in this figure indicates REM sleep.

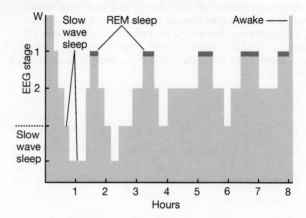

2 sleep, and bouts of REM sleep (indicated by the horizontal bars) become more prolonged.

As we saw, during REM sleep we become paralyzed; most of our spinal and cranial motor neurons are strongly inhibited. (The ones that control respiration and eye movements are not inhibited.) At the same time the brain is very active. Cerebral blood flow and oxygen consumption are accelerated. In addition, during most periods of REM sleep a male's penis and a female's clitoris will become at least partially erect, and a female's vaginal secretions will increase (Schmidt and Schmidt, 2004). However, Fisher et al., (1965) found that, in males, genital changes do not signify that the person is experiencing a dream with sexual content. (People can have dreams with sexual content. In males some dreams culminate in ejaculation—the so-called nocturnal emissions, or "wet dreams." Females, too, experience orgasm during sleep.)

The fact that penile erections occur during REM sleep, independent of sexual arousal, has been used clinically to assess the causes of impotence (Karacan et al., 1978; Singer and Weiner, 1996). A participant sleeps in the laboratory with a device attached to his penis that measures its circumference. If penile enlargement occurs during REM sleep, then his failure to obtain an erection during attempts at intercourse is not caused by physiological problems such as nerve damage or a circulatory disorder.

The important differences between REM sleep and slow-wave sleep are listed in Table 9.2.

Brain Activity During Sleep

LO 9.2 Explain the patterns of brain activity present during REM and slow-wave sleep.

Although we do not respond very much to the environment while we are asleep, we are not unconsciousness. In

Table 9.2 Principal Characteristics of REM and Slow-Wave Sleep

REM Sleep	Slow-Wave Sleep
EEG desynchrony (rapid, irregular waves)	EEG synchrony (slow waves)
Lack of muscle tonus	Moderate muscle tonus
Rapid eye movements	Slow or absent eye movements
Penile erection or vaginal secretion	Lack of genital activity
Dreams	

the morning we usually forget what we experienced while asleep, so in retrospect we conclude that we were unconscious. However, when experimenters wake sleeping volunteers, the reports that the volunteers give make it clear that they were conscious. In fact, the brain is very active in sleep. Next, we will explore this topic with a focus on what is known about brain activity in REM and slow-wave sleep.

BRAIN ACTIVITY IN REM AND DREAMING Researchers have found that the rate of cerebral blood flow in the human brain during REM sleep is high in the extrastriate cortex (visual association cortex) but low in the striate (primary) visual cortex and the prefrontal cortex (Braun et al., 1998; Madsen et al., 1991). The lack of activity in the striate cortex reflects the fact that the eyes are not receiving visual input; the high level of activity in the extrastriate cortex likely reflects the visual hallucinations that occur during dreams. As we shall see in Chapter 13, the prefrontal cortex is involved in making plans, keeping track of the organization of events in time, and distinguishing illusion from reality. As some researchers have noted, dreams are characterized by good visual images but are poorly organized with respect to time; for example, past, present, and future are often interchanged (Hobson, 1988). And as Melges (1982) put it, "The dreamer often has no feeling of striving for long-term goals but rather is carried along by the flow of time by circumstances that crop up in an unpredictable way." This quote could just as well be describing the daily life of a person whose prefrontal cortex has been damaged. (See Figure 9.4.)

Some people experience *lucid dreaming*, or an awareness that they are dreaming and are not awake. Some researchers have hypothesized that activation of the normally inactive prefrontal cortex during REM could be involved in the experience of lucid dreaming. Lucid dreaming may also occur in non-REM sleep.

Stumbrys et al., (2013) designed an interesting experiment to test the role of prefrontal cortex activity in lucid dreaming. The researchers recruited volunteers to spend three nights in a sleep research lab. On the first night,

participants acclimated to the lab. On the second and third nights, a technique called transcranial direct current stimulation (tDCS) was used to apply a weak current to the scalp of participants to activate the dorsolateral prefrontal cortex on one night. On the other night participants received a sham activation. Participants were awakened after each REM episode and asked to report their dreams. Participants reported more lucid dreams in response to tDCS versus sham stimulation. Although very preliminary, this study hints at the role of at least one brain region involved in REM lucid dreaming.

Several investigators have suggested that the eye movements made during REM sleep are related to the visual imagery that occurs while we dream. Roffwarg et al., (1962) recorded the eye movements of participants during REM sleep and then awakened the participants and asked them to describe what had been happening in their dreams. They found that the eye movements were similar to what would have been expected if the participants had actually been watching these events. In addition, evidence indicates that the particular brain mechanisms that become active during a dream are those that would become active if the events in the dream were actually occurring. For example, cortical and subcortical motor mechanisms become active during a dream that contains movement, as if the person were actually moving (McCarley and Hobson, 1979). In addition, if a dream involves talking and

Figure 9.4 Striate, Extrastriate, and Prefrontal Cortex Activity in REM Sleep

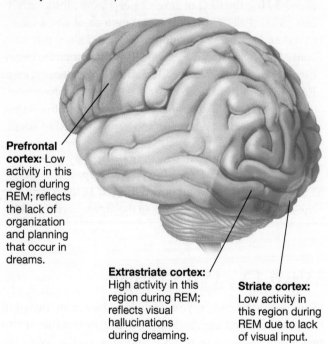

Prefrontal cortex: Low activity in this region during REM; reflects the lack of organization and planning that occur in dreams.

Extrastriate cortex: High activity in this region during REM; reflects visual hallucinations during dreaming.

Striate cortex: Low activity in this region during REM due to lack of visual input.

It has been theorized that the eye movements made during REM sleep are related to the visual imagery that occurs while we dream.

listening, regions of the dreamer's brain that are involved in speaking and listening become especially active (Hong et al., 1996). (Brain mechanisms of verbal communication are discussed in Chapter 14.)

BRAIN ACTIVITY IN SLOW-WAVE SLEEP Although narrative, storylike dreaming and the associated brain activity most often occur during REM sleep, changes in brain activity can also accompany dreamlike imagery experienced during slow-wave sleep. Regional cerebral blood flow during slow-wave sleep is generally decreased throughout the brain compared to waking. However, some researchers have found localized increases in the visual and auditory cortexes, which are hypothesized to be the neural basis for the dreamlike imagery experienced during slow-wave sleep. Blood flow to the thalamus and cerebellum is decreased in slow-wave sleep (Hofle et al., 1997).

Section Review

What Is Sleep?

LO 9.1 Describe the progression, behaviors, and EEG characteristics of the stages of sleep.

The stages of non-REM sleep, stages 1–3, are defined by EEG activity. Slow-wave sleep in stage 3 is the deepest stage of sleep. Alertness consists of desynchronized beta activity (13–30 Hz); relaxation and drowsiness consist of alpha activity (8–12 Hz); stage 1 sleep consists of alternating periods of alpha activity, irregular fast activity, and theta activity (3.5–7.5 Hz); the EEG of stage 2 sleep lacks alpha activity but contains sleep spindles (short periods of 12–14 Hz activity) and occasional K complexes; stage 3 sleep primarily consists of delta activity. About 90 minutes after the beginning of sleep, people enter REM sleep. Thereafter, cycles of REM and non-REM sleep occur in periods of approximately 90 minutes. Muscle tone decreases throughout the stages, resulting in deepest relaxation and paralysis in REM sleep.

LO 9.2 Explain the patterns of brain activity present during REM and slow-wave sleep.

The rate of cerebral blood flow during REM sleep is high in the extrastriate cortex but low in the striate cortex and the prefrontal cortex. This activity reflects a lack of visual input in REM (little or no activation in the striate cortex), but the presence of active visual hallucinations during dreaming (activation in the extrastriate cortex). Lack of prefrontal cortex activity likely reflects the lack of organization and planning that occur in dreams. Regional cerebral blood flow during slow-wave sleep is generally decreased throughout the brain compared to waking. However, some researchers have found localized increases in the visual and auditory cortexes, which are hypothesized to be the neural basis for the dreamlike imagery experienced during slow-wave sleep. Blood flow to the thalamus and cerebellum is decreased in slow-wave sleep.

Thought Question

Some people report that they are "in control" of some of their dreams—that they feel as if they determine what comes next and are not simply swept along passively. Have you ever had this experience? Have you ever had a "lucid dream," in which you were aware of the fact that you were dreaming? Describe evidence for changes in brain activity associated with lucid dreaming.

Why Do We Sleep?

From past experience, you probably know how insistent the urge to sleep can be and how uncomfortable it can feel when we have to resist it and stay awake. With the exception of the effects of severe pain and the need to breathe, sleepiness is probably the most insistent drive that we can experience. People can commit suicide by refusing to eat or drink, but even the most stoical person cannot indefinitely defy the urge to sleep. Sleep will come, sooner or later, no matter how hard a person tries to stay awake.

Earlier in the chapter, we posed the question "Why do we sleep?" Researchers have attempted to answer this question in a variety of ways. Although the issue is not yet settled, most researchers believe that the primary function of slow-wave sleep is to permit the brain to rest. In addition, slow-wave sleep and REM sleep promote different types of learning, and REM sleep appears to promote brain development.

Functions of Slow-Wave Sleep

LO 9.3 **Suggest some possible functions of slow-wave sleep.**

Sleep is a universal phenomenon among vertebrates. As far as we know, all mammals and birds sleep (Durie, 1981). Reptiles also sleep, and fish, amphibians, and even insects enter periods of quiescence that resemble sleep. However, only warm-blooded vertebrates (mammals and birds) exhibit clear REM sleep, with muscular paralysis, EEG signs of desynchrony, and rapid eye movements. Birds such as flamingos, which sleep while perched on one leg, do not lose tone in the muscles they use to remain standing. Also, animals such as moles, which move their eyes very little while awake, show few signs of eye movement while asleep. The functions of REM sleep will be discussed separately, in a later section.

Sleep appears to be essential to survival. Evidence for this statement comes from the fact that sleep is found in some species of mammals that would seem to be better off without it. For example, some species of marine mammals have developed an extraordinary pattern of sleep: The cerebral hemispheres take turns sleeping, presumably because that strategy always permits at least one hemisphere to be alert and keep the animal from drowning. In addition, the eye contralateral to the active hemisphere remains open. Some birds (for example, mallard ducks) can also sleep with only one hemisphere, keeping the opposite eye open to watch for predators (Rattenborg et al., 1999). The bottlenose dolphin (*Tursiops truncatus*) and the porpoise (*Phocoena phocoena*) both sleep with one hemisphere at a time (Mukhametov, 1984). Figure 9.5 shows the EEG recordings from the two hemispheres in a dolphin; note that slow-wave sleep occurs independently in the left and right hemispheres.

EFFECTS OF SLEEP DEPRIVATION When we are forced to miss a night's sleep, we become very sleepy. The fact that sleepiness is so motivating suggests that sleep is a necessity of life. If so, it should be possible to deprive people or laboratory animals of sleep and see what functions are disrupted. We should then be able to infer the role that sleep plays. However, the results of sleep deprivation studies have not revealed as much as investigators had originally hoped. The following sections examine the results of sleep deprivation research in humans and laboratory animals.

Figure 9.5 Sleep in Dolphins

The two hemispheres sleep independently, presumably so that the animal remains behaviorally alert.

(Adapted from Mukhametov, L. M., Sleep in marine mammals, in *Sleep Mechanisms*, edited by A. A. Borbély and J. L. Valatx. Munich: Springer-Verlag, 1984.)

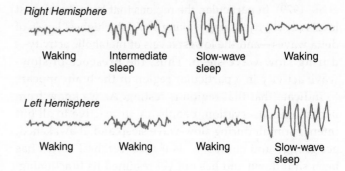

Right Hemisphere

Waking   Intermediate sleep   Slow-wave sleep   Waking

Left Hemisphere

Waking   Waking   Waking   Slow-wave sleep

Studies with Humans Sleep deprivation studies with human participants have not obtained persuasive evidence that sleep is needed to keep the body functioning normally. Horne (1978) reviewed over fifty experiments in which people had been deprived of sleep. He reported that most of them found that sleep deprivation did not interfere with people's ability to perform physical exercise. In addition, the studies found no evidence of a physiological stress response to sleep deprivation. Thus, the primary role of sleep does not seem to be rest and recuperation of the *body*. However, people's cognitive abilities were affected; some people reported perceptual distortions or even hallucinations and had trouble concentrating on mental tasks. Even with only one night of sleep deprivation, people's ability to recognize emotional facial expressions is impaired (van der Helm et al., 2010). Perhaps sleep provides the opportunity for the *brain* to rest.

What happens to sleep-deprived individuals after they are permitted to sleep again? Most of them sleep longer the next night or two, but they never regain all of the sleep they lost. In one remarkable case a 17-year-old boy stayed awake for 264 hours so that he could obtain a place in the *Guinness Book of World Records* (Gulevich et al., 1966). After his ordeal the boy slept for a little less than 15 hours and awoke feeling fine. He slept slightly more than 10 hours the second night and just under 9 hours the third. Almost 67 hours of missing sleep were never made up. However, percentages of recovery were not equal for all stages of sleep. Only 7 percent of stages 1 and 2 were made up, but 68 percent of slow-wave sleep and 53 percent of REM sleep were made up. Other studies have found similar results, suggesting that slow-wave sleep and REM sleep are more important than the other stages (Kales et al., 1970).

What do we know about the possible functions of slow-wave sleep? What happens in slow-wave sleep that is so important? Although the human brain contains only

2 percent of the total body weight, it expends 20 percent of the body's energy during quiet wakefulness. Both cerebral metabolic rate and cerebral blood flow decline during slow-wave sleep, falling to about 75 percent of the waking level (Buchsbaum et al., 1989; Maquet, 1995; Sakai et al., 1979). In particular, the regions that have the highest levels of activity during waking show the highest levels of delta waves—and the lowest levels of metabolic activity—during slow-wave sleep. Thus, the presence of slow-wave activity in a particular region of the brain appears to indicate that that region is resting. As we know from behavioral observation, people are unreactive to all but intense stimuli during slow-wave sleep and, if awakened, act groggy and confused, as if their cerebral cortex has been shut down and has not yet resumed its functioning. These observations suggest that during slow-wave sleep the brain is indeed resting.

The available evidence suggests that the brain needs to rest periodically to recover from adverse side effects of its waking activity. But what is the nature of these adverse effects? Siegel (2005) suggests that among the waste products produced by the high metabolic rate associated with waking activity of the brain are free radicals, chemicals that contain at least one unpaired electron. Free radicals are highly reactive oxidizing agents; they can bind with electrons from other molecules and damage the cells in which they are found, a process known as *oxidative stress*. Prolonged sleep deprivation caused an increase in free radicals in the brains of rats and resulted in oxidative stress (Ramanathan et al., 2002). During slow-wave sleep the lowered rate of metabolism permits restorative mechanisms in the cells to destroy the free radicals and prevent their damaging effects.

An inherited neurological disorder called **fatal familial insomnia** results in damage to portions of the thalamus (Gallassi et al., 1996; Montagna et al., 2003; Sforza et al., 1995). The symptoms of this disease, which is related to Creuzfeldt-Jacob disease and bovine spongiform encephalopathy ("mad cow disease"; see Chapter 15), include deficits in attention and memory, followed by a dreamlike, confused state; loss of control of the autonomic nervous system and the endocrine system; increased body temperature; and insomnia. The first signs of sleep disturbances are reductions in sleep spindles and K complexes. As the disease progresses, slow-wave sleep completely disappears, and only brief episodes of REM sleep (without the accompanying paralysis) remain. As the name indicates, the disease is fatal. Whether the insomnia, caused by the brain damage, contributes to the other symptoms and to the patient's death is not known.

Schenkein and Montagna (2006a, 2006b) describe the case of a man diagnosed with a form of fatal familial insomnia that usually causes death within 12 months. Because several relatives had died of this disorder, the man knew what to expect, and he enlisted the aid of several physicians to administer drugs and treatments designed to help him sleep. For several months the treatments did help him to sleep, and the man survived about a year longer than would have been expected, with a higher quality of life during the course of his illness. Further studies will be needed to determine whether his increased survival time was a direct result of the increased sleep.

Studies with Laboratory Animals Rechtschaffen and his colleagues (Rechtschaffen and Bergmann, 1995, 2002; Rechtschaffen et al., 1983, 1989) devised a procedure to keep rats from sleeping without forcing them to exercise continuously. (A group of control animals exercised just as much as the experimental participants but were able to engage in normal amounts of sleep.)

Sleep deprivation had serious effects. The control animals remained in perfect health. However, the experimental animals looked sick and stopped grooming their fur. They became weak and uncoordinated and lost their ability to regulate their body temperature. Although they began eating much more food than normal, their metabolic rates became so high that they continued to lose weight. Eventually, the rats died. The cause of death is still not understood. The rats' brains appeared to be normal, and there were no obvious signs of inflammation or damage to other internal organs. The animals' levels of stress hormones were not unusually high, so the deaths could not be attributed to simple stress. If they were given a high-calorie diet to compensate for their increased metabolic rate, the rats lived longer, but eventually they succumbed (Everson and Wehr, 1993). As we will see later in this chapter, damage to parts of the basal forebrain causes insomnia, and if the animals do not recover from their sleeplessness, they die.

As we just saw, the symptoms of the neurodegenerative disorder called fatal familial insomnia resemble the effects of forced sleep deprivation in rats. Budka et al., (1998) reported another similarity. The investigators studied five people with fatal familial insomnia who, along with insomnia, memory loss, and autonomic dysfunction, exhibited prominent weight loss.

EFFECTS OF PHYSICAL ACTIVITY ON SLOW-WAVE SLEEP Sleep deprivation studies with humans suggest that the brain may need slow-wave sleep to recover from the day's physical activities. Another way to determine whether sleep is needed for restoration of physiological functioning is to look at the effects of daytime activity on nighttime sleep. If the function of sleep is to repair the effects on the body of physical activity during waking hours, then we should expect that sleep and exercise are related. We should sleep more after a day of vigorous exercise than after a day spent quietly at a desk or watching TV.

Perhaps surprisingly, the relationship between sleep and exercise does not appear to be very strong. In fact, there were *no* changes in slow-wave or REM sleep of healthy participants who spent six weeks resting in bed (Ryback and Lewis, 1971). If sleep repairs wear and tear, we would expect these people to sleep less. Studying the sleep of individuals with severe paralysis due to spinal cord injury revealed only a small decrease in slow-wave sleep as compared with uninjured people (Adey et al., 1968). Thus, although sleep certainly provides the body with rest, its primary function appears to be something else.

EFFECTS OF COGNITIVE ACTIVITY ON SLOW-WAVE SLEEP If the primary function of slow-wave sleep is to permit the brain to rest and recover from its daily activity, then we might expect that a person would spend more time in slow-wave sleep after a day of intense cerebral activity. Tasks that demand alertness and mental activity *do* increase glucose metabolism in the brain (Roland, 1984). The most significant increases are seen in the frontal lobes, where slow-wave activity is most intense during non-REM sleep. In an experiment that supports this interpretation, Huber et al., (2004) had people perform a motor learning task just before going to sleep. The task required participants to make hand movements whose directions were indicated by a visual display. During sleep the participants showed increased slow-wave activity in the region of the neocortex that became active while they were performing the task. Presumably, the increased activity of these cortical neurons called for more rest during the following night's sleep. A follow-up study by Huber et al., (2006) found that immobilizing one arm for 12 hours produced the opposite result: During sleep the people showed *less* slow-wave activity in the regions of the neocortex that received somatosensory information from that arm and controlled its movements.

In an ingenious study, Horne and Minard (1985) found a way to increase mental activity without affecting physical activity and without causing stress. The investigators told participants to show up for an experiment in which they were supposed to take some tests designed to measure reading skills. When the participants arrived, however, they were told that the plans had been changed. They were invited for a day out, at the expense of the experimenters. (Not surprisingly, the participants willingly accepted.) They spent the day visiting an art exhibition, a shopping center, a museum, an amusement park, a zoo, and an interesting mansion. After a scenic drive through the countryside, they watched a movie in a local theater. They were driven from place to place and did not become overheated or tired by physical exercise. After the movie, they returned to the sleep laboratory. They said they were tired, and they readily fell asleep. Their sleep duration was normal, and they awoke feeling refreshed. However, their slow-wave sleep was increased. After all that mental exercise, the brain appears to have needed more rest than usual.

Functions of REM Sleep

LO 9.4 **Identify some possible functions of REM sleep.**

REM sleep is a time of intense physiological activity. The eyes dart about rapidly, the heart rate shows sudden accelerations and decelerations, breathing becomes irregular, and the brain becomes more active. It would be unreasonable to expect that REM sleep has the same functions as slow-wave sleep. An early report on the effects of REM sleep deprivation (Dement, 1960) observed that as the deprivation progressed, participants had to be awakened from REM sleep more frequently; the "pressure" to enter REM sleep built up. Furthermore, after several days of REM sleep deprivation, participants would show a **rebound phenomenon** when permitted to sleep normally; they spent a much greater-than-normal percentage of the recovery night in REM sleep. This rebound suggests that there is a need for a certain amount of REM sleep—that REM sleep is controlled by a regulatory mechanism. If selective deprivation causes a deficiency in REM sleep, the deficiency is made up later, when uninterrupted sleep is permitted.

Researchers have long been struck by the fact that the highest proportion of REM sleep is seen during the most active phase of brain development. Perhaps, then, REM sleep plays a role in this process (Siegel, 2005). Species in which young are born with immature brains, such as ferrets or humans, spend much more time in REM sleep than species with young born with well-developed brains, such as guinea pigs or cattle (Jouvet-Mounier et al., 1970; Roffwarg et al., 1966). But if the function of REM sleep is to promote brain development, why do adults have REM sleep? One possibility is that REM sleep facilitates the massive changes in the brain that occur during development but also some of the more modest changes responsible for learning that occur throughout the lifespan. As we will see in the next subsection, evidence does suggest that REM sleep facilitates learning—but so does slow-wave sleep.

Sleep and Learning

LO 9.5 **Compare the roles of slow-wave and REM sleep in learning.**

Research with both humans and laboratory animals indicates that sleep does more than allow the brain to rest: It also aids in the consolidation of long-term memories (Marshall and Born, 2007). Slow-wave sleep and REM sleep play different roles in memory consolidation.

As we will see in Chapter 13, there are two major categories of long-term memory: *declarative memory* (also called *explicit memory*) and *nondeclarative memory* (also called *implicit memory*). Declarative memories include those that people can talk about, such as memories of past episodes in their lives. They also include memories of the relationships between stimuli or events, such as the spatial relationships between landmarks that permit us to navigate around our environment. Nondeclarative memories include those gained through experience and practice that do not necessarily involve an attempt to "memorize" information, such as learning to drive a car, throwing and catching a ball, or recognizing a person's face. Research has found that slow-wave sleep and REM sleep play different roles in the consolidation of declarative and nondeclarative memories.

Let's explore evidence from two studies that looked at the effects of a nap on memory consolidation. Mednick et al., (2003) had participants learn a nondeclarative visual discrimination task at 9:00 A.M. The participants' ability to perform the task was tested 10 hours later, at 7:00 P.M. Some, but not all, of the participants took a 90-minute nap during the day between training and testing. The investigators recorded the EEGs of the sleeping participants to determine which of them engaged in REM sleep and which of them did not. (All of them engaged in slow-wave sleep, because this stage of sleep always comes first in healthy people.) The investigators found that the performance of participants who did not take a nap was worse when they were tested at 7:00 P.M. than it had been at the end of training. The participants who engaged only in slow-wave sleep did about the same during testing as they had done at the end of training. However, the participants who engaged in REM sleep performed significantly better. Thus, REM sleep strongly facilitated the consolidation of a nondeclarative memory. (See Figure 9.6.)

In the second study, Tucker et al., (2006) trained participants on two tasks: a declarative task (learning a list of paired words) and a nondeclarative task (learning

to trace a pencil-and-paper design while looking at the paper in a mirror). Afterward, some of participants were permitted to take a nap lasting for about 1 hour. Their EEGs were recorded, and they were awakened before they could engage in REM sleep. The participants' performance on the two tasks was then tested 6 hours after the original training. The investigators found that, compared with participants who stayed awake, a nap consisting of just slow-wave sleep increased the participants' performance on the declarative task but had no effect on performance of the nondeclarative task. (See Figure 9.7.) So these two experiments (and many others we have not described) indicate that REM sleep facilitates consolidation of nondeclarative memories and that slow-wave sleep facilitates consolidation of declarative memories.

Peigneux et al., (2004) had participants learn their way around a computerized virtual-reality town. This task is very similar to what people do when they learn their way around a real town. They must learn the relative locations of landmarks and streets that connect them so that they can find particular locations when the experimenter "placed" them at various starting points. As we will see in Chapter 13, the hippocampus plays an essential role in learning of this kind. Peigneux and his colleagues used functional brain imaging to measure regional brain activity and found that the same regions of the hippocampus were activated during route learning and during slow-wave sleep the following night. These patterns were *not* seen during REM sleep.

Using a similar virtual reality navigation task, Wamsley et al., (2010) awakened participants from slow-wave sleep during an afternoon nap that followed training and asked them to report everything that they were thinking about.

Figure 9.6 REM Sleep and Learning

Only after a 90-minute nap that included both slow-wave sleep and REM sleep was an improvement seen in the participants' performance on a nondeclarative visual discrimination task.

(Based on data from Mednick et al., 2003.)

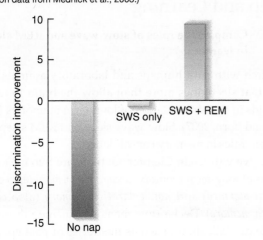

Figure 9.7 Slow-Wave Sleep and Learning

Participants learned a declarative learning task (list of paired words) and a nondeclarative learning task (mirror tracing). After a nap that included just slow-wave sleep, only participants who learned the declarative learning task showed improved performance, compared with participants who stayed awake.

(Based on data from Mednick et al., 2003.)

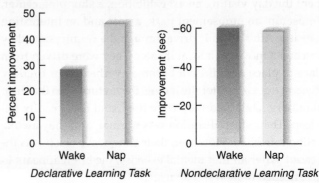

They found that participants whose thoughts were related to the task performed much better during a subsequent session on the navigation task than those who did not report such thoughts. Thus, although people who are awakened during slow-wave sleep seldom report narrative dreams, the sleeping brain rehearses information that was acquired during the previous period of wakefulness. (See Figure 9.8.)

Many studies with laboratory animals have directly recorded the activity of individual neurons in the animals' brains. These studies, too, indicate that the brain appears to rehearse newly learned information during slow-wave sleep (O'Neill et al., 2010). Chapter 13 reviews this evidence and describes research on the relevant brain mechanisms.

Figure 9.8 Thinking About Past Experiences While Asleep

The graph shows superior performance of participants who, when awakened, reported having thoughts about a virtual reality navigation task they had been learning the previous day.

(Based on data from Wamsley et al., 2010.)

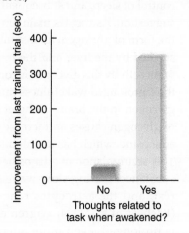

Section Review

Why Do We Sleep?

LO 9.3 Suggest some possible functions of slow-wave sleep.

One important function of slow-wave sleep seems to be to lower the brain's metabolism and permit it to rest. In support of this hypothesis, research has shown that slow-wave sleep reduces the brain's metabolic rate and that increased mental activity (the surprise fun-day-out experiment) can cause an increase in slow-wave sleep the next night.

LO 9.4 Identify some possible functions of REM sleep

The functions of REM sleep are less understood than those of slow-wave sleep. REM sleep may promote brain development and facilitate changes responsible for learning that occur throughout the lifespan.

LO 9.5 Compare the roles of slow-wave and REM sleep in learning.

Both REM sleep and slow-wave sleep promote learning: REM sleep facilitates nondeclarative learning, and slow-wave sleep facilitates declarative learning.

Thought Question

In this section, you read about the roles of slow-wave sleep and REM sleep in performance on declarative and nondeclarative memory tasks. List some tasks from your own life that require you to use your declarative and nondeclarative memory. Imagine that you have just taught someone else how to perform these tasks. Using information from this section, recommend how your "student" could use a nap to their advantage in performing the task you have taught them. How long should they sleep? When should they wake up? What kind of sleep stages should they try to achieve to excel on the task?

Physiological Mechanisms of Sleep and Waking

So far, we have discussed the nature of sleep and its functions. Now it is time to examine what researchers have discovered about the physiological mechanisms that are responsible for the behavior of sleep and for its counterpart, alert wakefulness.

Neural Control of Sleep

LO 9.6 **Explain how adenosine contributes to regulating sleep.**

As we have seen, sleep is *regulated;* that is, an organism deprived of slow-wave sleep or REM sleep will make up at least part of the missed sleep when permitted to do so. In addition, the amount of slow-wave sleep that a person obtains during a daytime nap is deducted from the amount of slow-wave sleep he or she obtains the next night (Karacan et al., 1970). These facts suggest that some physiological mechanism monitors the amount of sleep that an organism needs—in other words, keeps track of the sleep debt we incur during hours of wakefulness. What might this mechanism be?

One possible explanation is that the body produces a sleep-promoting substance that accumulates during wakefulness and is destroyed during sleep. The longer someone is awake, the longer he or she has to sleep to deactivate this substance. And because REM sleep deprivation produces an independent REM sleep debt, there might have to be two substances, one for each stage of sleep.

Where might such substances be produced? They do not appear to be found in the general circulation of the body. As we saw earlier, the cerebral hemispheres of the bottlenose dolphin sleep at different times (Mukhametov, 1984). If sleep were controlled by chemicals in the blood, the hemispheres should sleep at the same time. This observation suggests that if sleep is controlled by chemicals, these chemicals are produced within the brain and act there. In support of this suggestion, Oleksenko et al., (1992) obtained evidence that indicates that each hemisphere of the brain incurs its own sleep debt. The researchers deprived a bottlenose dolphin of sleep in only one hemisphere. When they allowed the animal to sleep normally, they saw a rebound of slow-wave sleep only in the deprived hemisphere.

Benington et al., (1995) suggested that **adenosine,** a nucleoside neuromodulator, might play a primary role in the control of sleep, and subsequent studies have supported this suggestion. Astrocytes maintain a small stock of nutrients in the form of glycogen, an insoluble carbohydrate that is also stocked by the liver and the muscles. In times of increased brain activity this glycogen is converted into fuel for neurons; thus, prolonged wakefulness causes a decrease in the level of glycogen in the brain (Kong et al., 2002). A fall in the level of glycogen causes an increase in the level of extracellular adenosine, which has an inhibitory effect on neural activity. This accumulation of adenosine serves as a sleep-promoting substance. During slow-wave sleep, neurons in the brain rest, and the astrocytes renew their stock of glycogen (Basheer et al., 2004; Wigren et al., 2007). If wakefulness is prolonged, even more adenosine accumulates, which inhibits neural activity and produces the cognitive and emotional effects that are seen during sleep deprivation. (As we saw in Chapter 4, caffeine blocks adenosine receptors to reduce sleepiness.) Halassa et al., (2009) prepared a targeted mutation in the brains of mice that interfered with the release of adenosine by astrocytes. As a result, the animals spent less time than normal in slow-wave sleep. (See Figure 9.9.)

Figure 9.9 Adenosine Across Sleep/Wake Cycle

Adenosine accumulates during wakefulness and is reduced during slow-wave sleep. Caffeine blocks the adenosine receptors, preventing the inhibitory effect on neural activity and reducing the effects of sleep deprivation.

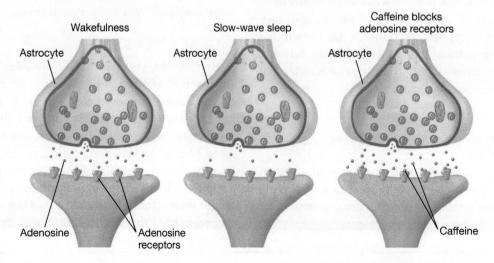

As we all know, people differ in their sleep need. Evidence suggests that genetic factors affect the typical duration of a person's slow-wave sleep. Rétey et al., (2005) discovered one of these factors—variability in the gene that encodes for an enzyme, adenosine deaminase, which is involved in the breakdown of adenosine. The investigators found that people with the G/A allele for this gene, which encodes for a form of the enzyme that breaks down adenosine more slowly, spent approximately 30 minutes more time in slow-wave sleep than did people with the more common G/G allele. Levels of adenosine in people with the G/A allele decreased more slowly during slow-wave sleep, and as a consequence the slow-wave sleep of these people was prolonged.

The role of adenosine as a sleep-promoting factor is discussed in more detail later in this chapter, in a section devoted to the regulation of sleep/wake transitions.

Neural Control of Arousal

LO 9.7 Describe how acetylcholine, norepinephrine, serotonin, histamine, and orexin contribute to regulating arousal.

As we have seen, sleep is not a unitary condition but consists of several different stages with very different characteristics. The waking state, too, is nonuniform; sometimes we are alert and attentive, and sometimes we fail to notice much about what is happening around us. Sleepiness has an effect on wakefulness; if we are fighting to stay awake, the struggle might impair our ability to concentrate on other things. But everyday observations suggest that even when we are not sleepy, our alertness can vary. For example, when we observe something very interesting (or frightening or simply surprising), we become more alert and aware of our surroundings.

Circuits of neurons that secrete at least five different neurotransmitters play a role in some aspect of an animal's level of alertness and wakefulness—what is commonly called *arousal*: acetylcholine, norepinephrine, serotonin, histamine, and orexin.

ACETYLCHOLINE One of the most important neurotransmitters involved in arousal—especially of the cerebral cortex—is acetylcholine (ACh). Two groups of acetylcholinergic neurons, one in the pons and one located in the basal forebrain, produce activation and cortical desynchrony when they are stimulated (Jones, 1990; Steriade, 1996). A third group of acetylcholinergic neurons, located in the medial septum, controls the activity of the hippocampus. (See Figure 9.11)

Researchers have long known that acetylcholinergic agonists increase EEG signs of cortical arousal and that acetylcholinergic antagonists decrease them (Vanderwolf, 1992). Marrosu et al., (1995) used microdialysis probes to measure the release of acetylcholine in the hippocampus and neocortex, two regions whose activity is closely related to an animal's alertness and behavioral arousal. They found that

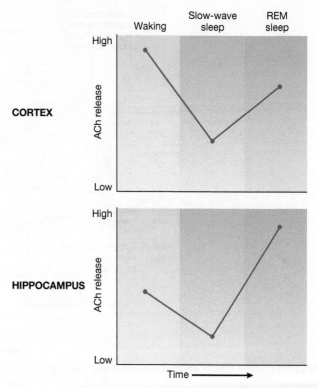

Figure 9.10 Release of Acetylcholine During the Sleep/Waking Cycle

Acetylcholine is released from the cortex and hippocampus..

(Based on data from Marrosu et al., 1995.)

the levels of ACh in these regions were high during both waking and REM sleep—periods during which the EEG displayed desynchronized activity—but low during slow-wave sleep. (See Figure 9.10.)

Rasmusson et al., (1994) electrically stimulated a region of the dorsal pons and found that the stimulation activated the cerebral cortex and increased the release of ACh there by 350 percent (as measured by microdialysis probes). A group of acetylcholinergic neurons located in the basal forebrain forms an essential part of the pathway that is responsible for this effect. If these neurons were deactivated by infusing a local anesthetic or drugs that blocked synaptic transmission, the activating effects of the pontine stimulation were abolished. In contrast, Cape and Jones (2000) found that drugs that activated these neurons caused wakefulness. Lee et al., (2004) found that most neurons in the basal forebrain showed a high rate of firing during both waking and REM sleep and a low rate of firing during slow-wave sleep. (See the pattern of acetylcholine release during waking and REM in the cortex and hippocampus in Figure 9.10.)

NOREPINEPHRINE Investigators have long known that catecholamine agonists such as amphetamine produce arousal and sleeplessness. These effects appear to be mediated primarily by the noradrenergic system of the **locus coeruleus (LC)**, located in the dorsal pons. Neurons of the locus coeruleus give rise to axons that branch widely, releasing

Figure 9.11 Acetylcholine Pathways in a Rat Brain

This schematic shows the locations of the most important groups of acetylcholinergic neurons and the distribution of their axons and terminal buttons.

(Adapted from Woolf, N. J. Progress in Neurobiology, 1991, 37, 475–524.)

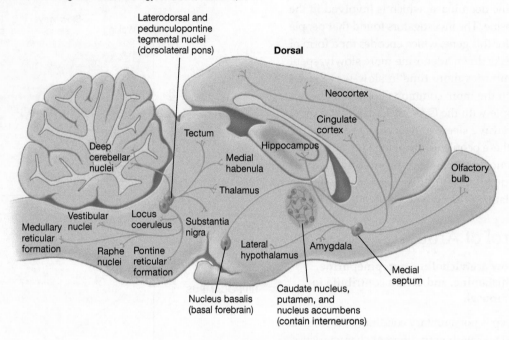

norepinephrine (from axonal varicosities) throughout the neocortex, hippocampus, thalamus, cerebellar cortex, pons, and medulla; thus, they potentially affect widespread and important regions of the brain. (See Figure 9.13)

Aston-Jones and Bloom (1981) recorded the activity of noradrenergic neurons of the LC across the sleep/wake cycle in unrestrained rats. They found that this activity was closely related to behavioral arousal: The firing rate of these neurons was high during wakefulness, low during slow-wave sleep, and almost zero during REM sleep. Within a few seconds of awakening, the rate of firing increased dramatically. (See Figure 9.12.)

Carter et al., (2010) used a viral vector to insert genes for two photosensitive proteins, ChR2 and NpHR, into noradrenergic cells of the locus coeruleus. As we saw in the section on optogenetics in Chapter 5, exposure of ChR2 to blue light activates the neurons, and exposure of NpHR to yellow light inhibits them. Previous experiments, which used electrical or chemical stimulation, activated many neurons in and around the locus coeruleus and thus produced effects that were not specific to noradrenergic neurons. Carter and his colleagues found that stimulation of the neurons caused immediate waking, and that inhibition decreased wakefulness and increased slow-wave sleep.

Most investigators believe that activity of noradrenergic LC neurons increases an animal's vigilance—its ability to pay attention to stimuli in the environment. For example, Aston-Jones et al., (1994) recorded the electrical activity of noradrenergic LC neurons in monkeys performing a task that required them to watch for a particular stimulus that would appear on

Figure 9.12 Norepinephrine and the Sleep/Waking Cycle

This graph shows the activity of noradrenergic neurons in the locus coeruleus of freely moving rats during various stages of sleep and waking.

(From Aston-Jones, G., and Bloom, F. E., Activity of norepinephrine-containing locus coeruleus neurons in behaving rats anticipates fluctuations in the sleep-waking cycle, The Journal of Neuroscience, 1981, 1, 876–886. Copyright 1981, The Society for Neuroscience.)

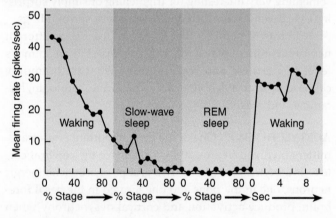

a video display. The investigators observed that the monkeys performed best when the rate of firing of the LC neurons was high. After the monkeys worked for a long time at the task, the neurons' rate of firing decreased, and so did the monkeys' performance. These results support the conclusion that the activation of LC neurons (and their release of norepinephrine) increases vigilance.

SEROTONIN A third neurotransmitter, serotonin (5-HT), also appears to play a role in activating behavior. Almost all

Figure 9.13 Noradrenergic Pathways in a Rat Brain

This schematic shows the locations of the most important groups of noradrenergic neurons and the distribution of their axons and terminal buttons.

(Adapted from Cotman, C. W. and McGaugh, J. L. Behavioral Neuroscience: An Introduction. New York Academic.)

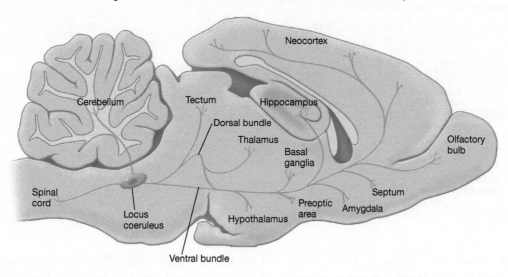

of the brain's serotonergic neurons are found in the **raphe nuclei,** which are located in the medullary and pontine regions of the reticular formation. The axons of these neurons project to many parts of the brain, including the thalamus, hypothalamus, basal ganglia, hippocampus, and neocortex. Stimulation of the raphe nuclei causes locomotion and cortical arousal (as measured by the EEG), whereas PCPA, a drug that prevents the synthesis of serotonin, reduces cortical arousal (Peck and Vanderwolf, 1991). (See Figure 9.15.)

Jacobs and Fornal (1999) suggested that one specific contribution of serotonergic neurons to activation is facilitation of continuous, automatic movements, such as pacing, chewing, and grooming. On the other hand, when animals engage in orienting responses to novel stimuli, the activity of serotonergic neurons decreases. Perhaps serotonergic neurons are involved in facilitating ongoing activities and suppressing the processing of sensory information, preventing reactions that might disrupt the ongoing activities.

Figure 9.14 shows the activity of serotonergic neurons, recorded by Trulson and Jacobs (1979). As you can see, these neurons, like the noradrenergic neurons studied by Aston-Jones and Bloom (1981), were most active during waking. Their firing rate declined during slow-wave sleep and became virtually zero during REM sleep. However, once the period of REM sleep ended, the neurons temporarily became very active again.

HISTAMINE The fourth neurotransmitter implicated in the control of wakefulness and arousal is **histamine,** a compound synthesized from histidine, an amino acid. You may already be aware that antihistamines, which are used to treat allergies, can cause drowsiness. They do so by blocking histamine H_2 receptors in the brain. More modern antihistamines cannot cross the blood–brain barrier, so they do not cause drowsiness.

The cell bodies of histaminergic neurons are located in the **tuberomammillary nucleus (TMN)** of the hypothalamus, located at the base of the brain just rostral to the mammillary bodies. The axons of these neurons project primarily to the cerebral cortex, thalamus, basal ganglia, basal forebrain, and other regions of the hypothalamus. The projections to the cerebral cortex directly increase cortical activation and arousal, and projections to acetylcholinergic neurons of the basal forebrain and dorsal pons do so indirectly, by increasing the release of acetylcholine in the cerebral cortex (Brown et al., 2001; Khateb et al., 1995). The activity of histaminergic neurons is high during waking but low during slow-wave sleep and REM sleep (Steininger et al., 1996). In addition, injections of drugs that prevent the synthesis of histamine or block histamine H_1 receptors

Figure 9.14 Serotonin and the Sleep/Waking Cycle

This graph shows the activity of serotonergic (5-HT secreting) neurons in the dorsal raphe nuclei of freely moving cats during various stages of sleep and waking

(Adapted from Trulson, M. E., and Jacobs, B. L. Brain Research, 1979, 163, 135–150.

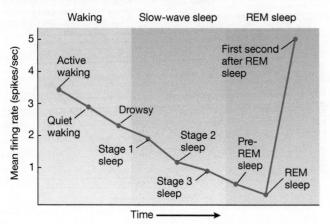

Figure 9.15 Serotonergic Pathways in a Rat Brain

This schematic shows the locations of the most important groups of serotonergic neurons and the distribution of their axons and terminal buttons.

(Adapted from Consolazione, A. and Cuello, A. C. CNS serotonin pathways. In Biology of Serotonergic Transmission, edited by N. N. Osborne. Chichester: England Wiley & Sons, 1982.)

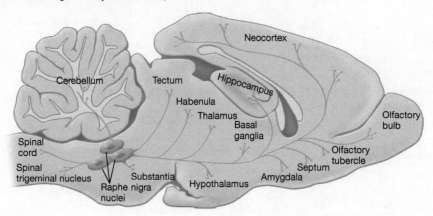

decrease waking and increase sleep (Lin et al., 1998). Also, infusion of histamine into the basal forebrain region of rats causes an increase in waking and a decrease in non-REM sleep (Ramesh et al., 2004).

Although histamine clearly plays an important role in wakefulness and arousal, evidence suggests that control of wakefulness is shared with the other neurotransmitters discussed in this section. For example, Parmentier et al., (2002) found that mice with a targeted mutation that blocks the synthesis of histamine showed normal amounts of spontaneous wakefulness. However, the animals showed less arousal in response to environmental stimuli. For example, normal mice placed in a novel environment remain awake for 2–3 hours, but the histamine-deprived mice fell asleep within a few minutes. Similarly, Takahashi et al., (2006) found that histaminergic neurons did not respond to environmental stimuli unless the stimuli elicited a state of overt attention. Gerashchenko et al., (2004) suggested that the brain's arousal systems promote wakefulness at different times or in different situations and that no one of these systems plays a critical role under all conditions.

OREXIN This section will describe the importance of the peptide neurotransmitter orexin in the neural control of arousal. This neurotransmitter has an interesting history. It is called *hypocretin* by some researchers and *orexin* by others. The name "hypocretin" comes from the fact that the lateral *hypo*thalamus contains the cell bodies of all of the neurons that se*cret*e this peptide. The name "orexin" comes from the role this peptide plays in the control of eating and metabolism, discussed in more detail in Chapter 12. Orexin also plays a crucial role in the physiological and behavioral effects of some drugs, discussed in Chapter 18. Two laboratories independently discovered the peptide; hence it has two names.

The cause of narcolepsy is degeneration of orexinergic neurons in humans and a hereditary absence of one type

of orexin receptors in dogs. The cell bodies of neurons that secrete orexin are located in the lateral hypothalamus. Although there are only about 7,000 orexinergic neurons in the human brain, the axons of these neurons project to almost every part of the brain, including the cerebral cortex and all of the regions involved in arousal and wakefulness, including the locus coeruleus, raphe nuclei, tuberomammillary nucleus, and acetylcholinergic neurons in the dorsal pons and basal forebrain (Sakurai, 2007). Orexin has an excitatory effect in all of these regions.

Mileykovskiy et al., (2005) recorded the activity of single orexinergic neurons in unanesthetized rats and found that the neurons fired at a high rate during alert or active waking and at a low rate during quiet waking, slow-wave sleep, and REM sleep. The highest rate of firing was seen when the rats were engaged in exploratory activity. (See Figure 9.16.)

Figure 9.16 Orexin and the Sleep/Waking Cycle

This graph shows the activity of single orexinergic neurons during various stages of sleep and waking.

(Based on Mileykovskiy, B. Y., Kiyashchenko, L. I., and Siegel, J. M. Neuron, 2005, *46*, 787–798.)

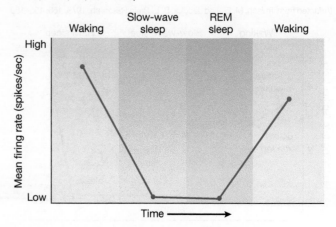

Table 9.3 Summary of Neurochemical Levels Involved in Regulation of the Sleep/Waking Cycle

Chemical	Brain Region Containing Cell Bodies	Waking Levels	SWS Levels	REM Levels
Adenosine	–	Increase with longer periods of wake	Decreasing	–
Acetylcholine	Pons, basal forebrain, medial septum	High	Low	High
Norepinephrine	Locus coeruleus	High	Low	Low
Serotonin	Raphe nuclei	High	Decreasing	Low
Histamine	Tuberomammillary nucleus	High	Low	Low
Orexin	Lateral hypothalamus	High	Low	Low

Adamantidis et al., (2010) used genetic transfer to insert ChR2 protein into orexinergic neurons of the lateral hypothalamus of mice. They found that optogenetic activation of these neurons with blue light awakened the animals from either REM or non-REM sleep.

Narcolepsy is most often treated with modafinil, a drug that suppresses the drowsiness associated with this disorder. Ishizuka et al., (2010) found that the alerting effects of modafinil are exerted by stimulating the release of orexin in the TMN, which activates the histaminergic neurons located there (see Table 9.3).

Neural Control of Sleep/Wake Transitions

LO 9.8 **Summarize the roles of homeostatic/allostatic/ circadian factors, brain regions, flip-flop circuits, and neurotransmitter systems in regulating transitions between sleep and wake.**

The following sections will explore homeostatic, allostatic, and circadian factors, as well as the roles of the preoptic area, adenosine, and orexin in controlling sleep/wake transitions.

HOMEOSTATIC, ALLOSTATIC, AND CIRCADIAN FACTORS If we go without sleep for a long time, we will eventually become sleepy, and once we sleep, we will be likely to sleep longer than usual and make up at least some of our sleep debt. This control of sleep is *homeostatic* in nature, and follows the principles that regulate our eating and drinking, which are described in Chapter 12. But under some conditions, it is important for us to stay awake—for example, when we are being threatened by a dangerous situation or when we are dehydrated and are looking for some water to drink. This control of sleep is *allostatic* in nature, a term that refers to reactions to stressful events in the environment (danger, lack of water, and so on) that serve to override homeostatic control. Finally, *circadian* factors, or time of day factors, tend to restrict our period of sleep to a particular portion of the day/night cycle. (Circadian control of sleep cycles is described in the last section of this chapter.)

As we saw earlier in this chapter, the primary homeostatic factor that controls sleep is the presence or absence of adenosine, a chemical that accumulates in the brain during wakefulness and is destroyed during slow-wave sleep.

Allostatic control is mediated primarily by hormonal and neural responses to stressful situations (described in Chapter 11) and by neuropeptides (such as orexin) that are involved in hunger and thirst.

This subsection describes the neural circuitry that controls the transition between sleep and wake and the means by which adenosine exerts its homeostatic effect. When we are awake and alert, most of the neurons in our brain—especially those of the forebrain—are active, which enables us to pay attention to sensory information and process this information, to think about what we are perceiving, to retrieve and think about our memories, and to engage in a variety of behaviors that we are called on to perform during the day. The level of brain activity is largely controlled by the five sets of arousal neurons described in the previous section. A high level of activity of these neurons keeps us awake, and a low level puts us to sleep.

THE PREOPTIC AREA But what controls the activity of the arousal neurons? What causes this activity to fall, thus putting us to sleep? The first hint at an answer to this question was suggested in the early twentieth century by careful observations of a Viennese neurologist, Constantin von Economo, who noticed that patients afflicted by a new type of encephalitis in Europe and North America showed severe disturbance in sleep and waking (Triarhou, 2006). Most patients slept excessively, waking only to eat and drink. (We would now say that they were wakened by allostatic factors.) According to von Economo, these patients had brain damage at the junction of the brain stem and forebrain, at a location that would destroy the axons of the arousal neurons entering the forebrain. Some patients, however, showed just the opposite symptoms: They slept only a few hours each day. Although they were tired, they had difficulty falling asleep and usually awakened shortly thereafter. Von Economo reported that patients who displayed insomnia had damage to the region of the anterior hypothalamus. We now know that this region, usually referred to as the *preoptic area,* is the one most involved in control of sleep. The preoptic area contains neurons whose axons form inhibitory synaptic connections with the brain's arousal neurons. When our preoptic neurons (let's call them *sleep neurons*) become active, they suppress the activity of our arousal neurons, and we fall asleep (Saper et al., 2005).

Nauta (1946) found that destruction of the preoptic area produced total insomnia in rats. The animals subsequently fell into a coma and died; the average survival time was only three days. The effects of electrical stimulation of the preoptic area are just the opposite: It causes drowsiness and sleep (Sterman and Clemente, 1962a, 1962b).

The majority of the sleep neurons are located in the **ventrolateral preoptic area (vlPOA).** In addition, some are located in the nearby *median preoptic nucleus (MnPN).* Damage to vlPOA neurons suppresses sleep (Lu et al., 2000), and the activity of these neurons, measured by their levels of Fos protein, increases during sleep. Experiments have shown that the sleep neurons secrete the inhibitory neurotransmitter GABA and that they send their axons to the five brain regions involved in arousal described in the previous section (Gvilia et al., 2006; Sherin et al., 1998; Suntsova et al., 2007). As we saw, activity of neurons in these five regions causes cortical activation and behavioral arousal. Inhibition of these regions, then, is a necessary condition for sleep.

Flip-Flop Circuits for Sleep/Wake Transitions The sleep neurons in the preoptic area receive inhibitory inputs from some of the same regions they inhibit, including the tuberomammillary nucleus, raphe nuclei, and locus coeruleus (Chou et al., 2002); thus, they are inhibited by histamine, serotonin, and norepinephrine. As Saper and his colleagues (Saper et al., 2001; Saper et al., 2010) suggest, this mutual inhibition may provide the basis for establishing periods of sleep and waking. They note that reciprocal inhibition also characterizes an electronic circuit known as a *flip-flop.* A flip-flop can assume one of two states, usually referred to as on or off—or 0 or 1 in computer applications. Thus, either the sleep neurons are active and inhibit the wakefulness neurons, or the wakefulness neurons are

active and inhibit the sleep neurons. Because these regions are mutually inhibitory, it is impossible for neurons in both sets of regions to be active at the same time. In fact, sleep neurons in the vlPOA are silent until an animal shows a transition from waking to sleep (Takahashi et al., 2009). (See Figure 9.17.)

Stability in Flip-Flop Circuits A flip-flop has an important advantage: When it switches from one state to another, it does so quickly. Clearly, it is most advantageous to be either asleep or awake; a state that has some of the characteristics of both sleep and wakefulness would be maladaptive. However, there is one problem with flip-flops: They can be unstable. In fact, people with narcolepsy and animals with damage to the orexinergic system of neurons exhibit just this characteristic. They have great difficulty remaining awake when nothing interesting is happening, and they have trouble remaining asleep for an extended amount of time. (They also show intrusions of the characteristics of REM sleep at inappropriate times. We will discuss this phenomenon in the next section.)

Saper et al., (2001, 2010) suggest that an important function of orexinergic neurons is to help stabilize the sleep/waking flip-flop through their excitatory connections to the wakefulness neurons. Activity of this system of neurons tips the activity of the flip-flop toward the waking state, thus promoting wakefulness and inhibiting sleep. Perhaps your success at staying awake in a boring lecture depends on maintaining a high rate of firing of your orexinergic neurons, which would keep the flip-flop in the waking state. (See Figure 9.18.) A mathematical model of the sleep/waking flip-flop constructed by Rempe et al., (2010) confirmed the role of orexigenic neurons in stabilizing the circuit.

Figure 9.17 The Sleep/Waking Flip-Flop

According to Saper et al., (2001), the major sleep-promoting region (the vlPOA) and the major wakefulness-promoting regions (the basal forebrain and pontine regions that contain acetylcholinergic neurons; the locus coeruleus, which contains noradrenergic neurons; the raphe nuclei, which contain serotonergic neurons; and the tuberomammillary nucleus of the hypothalamus, which contains histaminergic neurons) are reciprocally connected by inhibitory GABAergic neurons. (a) When the flip-flop is in the "wake" state, the arousal systems are active and the vlPOA is inhibited, and the animal is awake. (b) When the flip-flop is in the "sleep" state, the vlPOA is active and the arousal systems are inhibited, and the animal is asleep.

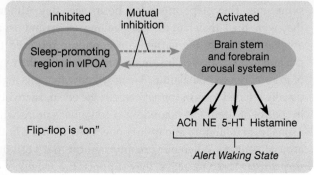

(a)

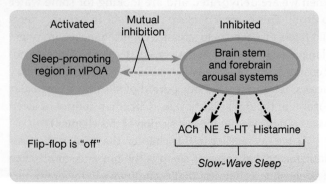

(b)

Figure 9.18 Role of Orexinergic Neurons in Sleep

The schematic diagram shows the effect of activation of the orexinergic system of neurons of the lateral hypothalamus on the sleep/waking flip-flop. Motivation to remain awake or events that disturb sleep activate the orexinergic neurons.

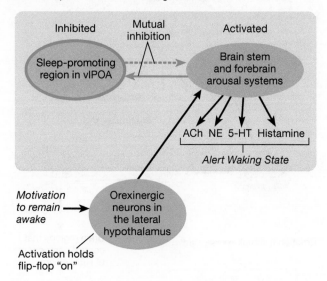

Figure 9.19 Adenosine and Sleep

Extracellular adenosine in the cat basal forebrain region is shown during 6 hours of prolonged waking and 3 hours of recovery sleep, as measured by microdialysis.

(From Porkka-Heiskanen, T., Strecker, R. E., Thakkar, M., et al., Adenosine: a mediator of the sleep-inducing effects of prolonged wakefulness, *Science*, 1997, *276*, 1265–1268. Copyright 1997 by the American Association for the Advancement of Science.)

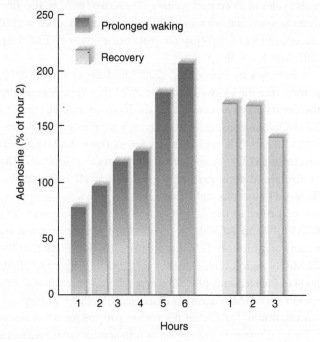

Mochizuki et al., (2004) found that mice with a targeted mutation against the orexin gene showed normal amounts of sleep and waking, but their bouts of wakefulness and slow-wave sleep were very brief, showing many more transitions between sleep and waking. These results provide further support for the hypothesis that orexinergic neurons help stabilize the sleep/waking flip-flop.

ROLE OF ADENOSINE IN SLEEP/WAKE TRANSITIONS As we saw earlier in this chapter, adenosine is released by astrocytes when neurons are metabolically active, and the accumulation of adenosine produces drowsiness and sleep. Porkka-Heiskanen et al., (2000) used microdialysis to measure adenosine levels in several regions of the brain. They found that the level of adenosine increased during wakefulness and slowly decreased during sleep, especially in the basal forebrain. (See Figure 9.19.)

Scammell et al., (2001) found that infusion of an adenosine agonist into the vlPOA activated neurons there, decreased the activity of histaminergic neurons of the tuberomammillary nucleus, and increased slow-wave sleep. However, adenosine receptors are found on neurons in many regions of the brain, including the orexinergic neurons of the lateral hypothalamus (Thakkar et al., 2002). Thus, it is unlikely that all of the sleep-promoting effects of adenosine involve the neurons of the vlPOA.

ROLE OF OREXIN IN SLEEP/WAKE TRANSITIONS Seeing that orexinergic neurons help to hold the sleep/waking flip-flop in the waking state, an important question to ask is, what factors control the activity of orexinergic neurons? During the waking part of the day/

night cycle, orexinergic neurons receive an excitatory signal from the biological clock that controls rhythms of sleep and waking. These neurons also receive signals from brain mechanisms that monitor the animal's nutritional state: Hunger-related signals activate orexinergic neurons, and satiety-related signals inhibit them. Thus, orexinergic neurons maintain arousal during the times when an animal should search for food. In fact, if normal mice (but not mice with a targeted mutation against orexin receptors) are given less food than they would normally eat, they stay awake longer each day (Yamanaka et al., 2003; Sakurai, 2007). Finally, orexinergic neurons receive inhibitory input from the vlPOA, which means that sleep signals that arise from the accumulation of adenosine can eventually overcome excitatory input to orexinergic neurons, and sleep can occur. Thus, orexinergic neurons are involved in all three factors that control sleep and wakefulness: homeostatic, allostatic, and circadian.

Neural Control of Transition to REM

LO 9.9 Describe the role of flip-flop circuits in neural control of transition to REM.

As we saw earlier in this chapter, REM sleep consists of desynchronized EEG activity, muscular paralysis, rapid eye movements, and increased genital activity. The rate of cerebral metabolism during REM sleep is as high as it is during waking (Maquet et al., 1990), and if the skeletal muscles of the body were not paralyzed, the level of *physical* activity would also be high.

FLIP-FLOP CIRCUITS FOR TRANSITION TO REM REM sleep is controlled by a flip-flop similar to the one that controls cycles of sleep and waking. The sleep/waking flip-flop determines when we wake and when we sleep; once we fall asleep, the REM flip-flop controls our cycles of REM sleep and slow-wave sleep.

Reviews by Fort et al., (2009) and Saper et al., (2010) summarize the evidence for the REM flip-flop. A region of the dorsal pons, just ventral to the locus coeruleus, contains REM-ON neurons, cells that fire at a high rate only during REM. In rats this region is known as the **sublaterodorsal nucleus (SLD).** A region of the dorsal midbrain, the **ventrolateral periaqueductal gray matter (vlPAG),** contains REM-OFF neurons, cells that suppress REM. For simplicity we will refer to the *REM-ON* and *REM-OFF* regions. The REM-ON and REM-OFF regions are interconnected by means of inhibitory GABAergic neurons. Stimulation of the REM-ON region with infusions of glutamate agonists elicits most of the elements of REM sleep, whereas inhibition of this region with GABA agonists disrupts REM sleep. In contrast, stimulation of the REM-OFF region suppresses REM sleep, whereas damage to this region or infusions of GABA agonists dramatically increases REM sleep. (See Figure 9.20.)

The mutual inhibition of these two regions means that they function like a flip-flop: Only one region can be active at any given time. During waking, the REM-OFF region receives excitatory input from the orexinergic neurons of the lateral hypothalamus, and this activation tips the REM flip-flop into the off state. (Additional excitatory input to the REM-OFF region is received from two sets of wakefulness neurons: the noradrenergic neurons of the locus coeruleus and the serotonergic neurons of the raphe nuclei.) When the sleep/waking flip-flop switches into the sleep phase, slow-wave sleep begins. The activity of the excitatory orexinergic, noradrenergic, and serotonergic inputs to the REM-OFF

region begins to decrease. Eventually, the REM sleep flip-flop switches to the on state, and REM sleep begins. Figure 9.21 shows the control of the REM sleep flip-flop by the sleep/waking flip-flop.

Once sleep begins, the activity of orexinergic neurons ceases, which removes one source of the excitatory input to the REM-OFF region. As we saw in Figures 9.12 and 9.14, as sleep progresses, the activity of noradrenergic and serotonergic neurons gradually decreases. As a consequence, more of the excitatory input to the REM-OFF region is removed. The REM flip-flop tips to the on state, and REM sleep begins.

Flip-Flop Circuit Impairment in Narcolepsy We can see now why degeneration of orexinergic neurons causes narcolepsy. The daytime sleepiness and the fragmented sleep occur because without the influence of orexin, the sleep/waking flip-flop becomes unstable. The release of orexin in the REM-OFF region normally keeps the REM flip-flop in the off state. With the loss of orexinergic neurons, emotional episodes such as laughter or anger, which activate the amygdala, tip the REM flip-flop into the on state—even during waking—and the result is an attack of cataplexy. (Look again at Figure 9.21.) In fact, a functional-imaging study by Schwartz et al., (2008) found that when people with cataplexy watched humorous sequences of photographs, the hypothalamus was activated less, and the amygdala was activated more, than the same structures in control participants. The investigators suggest that the loss of orexinergic neurons removed an inhibitory influence of the hypothalamus on the amygdala. The increased

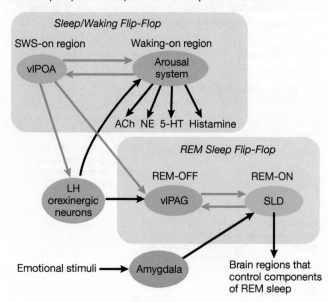

Figure 9.21 Integrating Flip-Flop Circuits

This figure integrates the flip-flop circuit responsible for REM regulation with the flip-flop circuit responsible for sleep-wake transitions.

Figure 9.20 The REM Sleep Flip-Flop

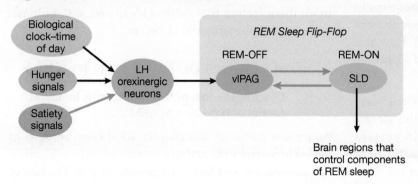

Figure 9.22 Humor and Narcolepsy

The figure shows the activation of the hypothalamus and amygdala in healthy participants and patients with narcolepsy watching neutral and humorous sequences of photos.

(From Schwartz, S., Ponz, A., Poryazova, R., et al., Abnormal activity in hypothalamus and amygdala during humour processing in human narcolepsy with cataplexy, *Brain*, 2008, *131*, 514–522. Reprinted by permission.)

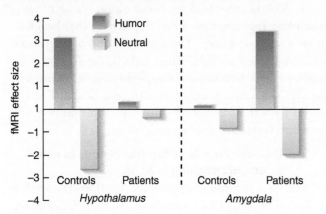

Figure 9.23 Control of Components of REM Sleep by the REM-ON Region

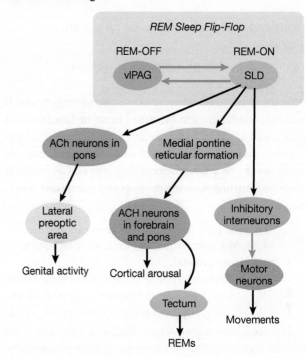

amygdala activity could account at least in part for the increased activity of REM-ON neurons that occurs even during waking in people with cataplexy. (See Figure 9.22.)

Flip-Flop Circuits Control REM Muscle Paralysis As we saw earlier, REM sleep has several behavioral components, including rapid eye movements, genital activity, and muscular paralysis. The last of these phenomena, muscular paralysis, is particularly interesting. As you will read in the next section, patients with REM sleep behavior disorder fail to become paralyzed during REM sleep and therefore act out their dreams. The same thing happens to cats when a lesion is made in a particular region of the midbrain responsible for the muscular paralysis that occurs during REM sleep (Jouvet, 1972). While asleep, the cats made movements and appeared to play with invisible mice. The lesioned neurons are located just ventral to the area we now know to be part of the REM-ON region (Lai et al., 2010). Some of the axons that leave this region travel to the spinal cord, where they excite inhibitory interneurons whose axons form synapses with motor neurons. This means that when the REM flip-flop tips to the on state, motor neurons in the spinal cord become inhibited and cannot respond to the signals arising from the motor cortex in the course of a dream. Damage to the REM-ON region removes this inhibition, and the person (or one of Jouvet's cats) acts out his or her dreams. (See Figure 9.23.)

The fact that our brains contain an elaborate mechanism whose sole function is to keep us paralyzed while we dream—that is, to prevent us from acting out our dreams—suggests that the motor components of dreams are as important as the sensory components. Perhaps the practice our motor system gets during REM sleep helps us to improve our performance of behaviors we have learned that day. The inhibition of the

motor neurons in the spinal cord prevents the movements being practiced from actually occurring, with the exception of a few harmless twitches of the hands and feet.

Flip-Flop Circuits in Cortical Arousal, Rapid Eye Movements, and Genital Activity in REM Neurons in the REM-ON region also send axons to regions of the thalamus that are involved in the control of cortical arousal, which may at least partly account for the EEG activation that is seen during REM sleep. In addition, they send axons to glutamatergic neurons in the medial pontine reticular formation, which, in turn, send axons to the acetylcholinergic neurons of the basal forebrain. Activation of these forebrain neurons produces arousal and cortical desynchrony. The control of rapid eye movements appears to be achieved by projections from acetylcholinergic neurons in the dorsal pons to the tectum (Webster and Jones, 1988).

Little is known about the function of genital activity that occurs during REM sleep or about the neural mechanisms responsible for them. A study by Schmidt et al., (2000) found that lesions of the lateral preoptic area in rats suppressed penile erections during REM sleep but had no effect on erections during waking. Salas et al., (2007) found that penile erections could be triggered by electrical stimulation of acetylcholinergic neurons in the pons that become active during REM sleep. The investigators note that evidence suggests that these pontine neurons may be directly connected with neurons in the lateral preoptic area and thus may be responsible for the erections. (Look again at Figure 9.23.)

Section Review

Physiological Mechanisms of Sleep and Waking

LO 9.6 Explain how adenosine contributes to regulating sleep.

Adenosine is released when neurons use glycogen, and it serves as the link between increased brain metabolism and the necessity of sleep. When neurons are active, glycogen is depleted and adenosine accumulates. Accumulating adenosine serves as a sleep-promoting signal. Glycogen is replenished during slow-wave sleep and adenosine levels decrease.

LO 9.7 Describe how acetylcholine, norepinephrine, serotonin, histamine, and orexin contribute to regulating arousal.

Five systems of neurons appear to be important for alert, active wakefulness. The acetylcholinergic system of the pons and the basal forebrain is involved in cortical activation. The noradrenergic system of the locus coeruleus is involved in vigilance. The serotonergic system of the raphe nuclei is involved in activation of automatic behaviors such as locomotion and grooming. The histaminergic neurons of the tuberomammillary nucleus are involved in maintaining wakefulness. The orexinergic system of the lateral hypothalamus is involved in maintaining wakefulness.

LO 9.8 Summarize the roles of homeostatic/allostatic/circadian factors, brain regions, flip-flop circuits, and neurotransmitter systems in regulating transitions between sleep and wake.

Homeostatic control of sleep maintains the balance of sleep/wake at an optimal level. Sleep can also be regulated by allostatic control, which responds to environmental stressors to override homeostatic control when needed. Circadian factors entrain periods of sleep to particular portions of the light/dark cycle. Slow-wave sleep occurs when neurons in the ventrolateral preoptic area (vlPOA) become active. These neurons inhibit the systems of neurons that promote wakefulness. In turn, the vlPOA is inhibited by these same wakefulness-promoting regions, thus a flip-flop circuit that keeps us either awake or asleep. The accumulation of adenosine promotes sleep by inhibiting wakefulness-promoting regions and activating the sleep-promoting neurons of the vlPOA. Activity of the orexinergic neurons of the lateral hypothalamus keeps the flip-flop that controls sleep and waking in the "waking" state.

LO 9.9 Describe the role of flip-flop circuits in neural control of transition to REM.

REM sleep is controlled by another flip-flop. The sublaterodorsal nucleus (SLD) serves as the REM-ON region, and the ventrolateral periaqueductal gray region (vlPAG) serves as the REM-OFF region. This flip-flop is controlled by the sleep/waking flip-flop; only when the sleep/waking flip-flop is in the "sleeping" state can the REM flip-flop switch to the "REM" state. The muscular paralysis that prevents us from acting out our dreams is produced by connections between neurons in the SLD that excite inhibitory interneurons in the spinal cord.

Thought Question

Have you ever been lying in bed, almost asleep, when you suddenly thought of something important you had forgotten to do? Did you then suddenly become fully awake and alert? If so, neurons in your brain's arousal systems likely became active, which aroused your cerebral cortex. What do you think the source of this activation was? What activated the arousal systems? How would you go about answering this question? What research methods described in Chapter 5 would be helpful?

Disorders of Sleep

Because we spend about one-third of our lives sleeping, sleep disorders can have a significant impact on our quality of life. They can also affect the way we feel while we are awake.

Insomnia

LO 9.10 Describe the symptoms, treatment, and biological basis of insomnia.

Insomnia is a problem that is said to affect approximately 25 percent of the population occasionally and 9 percent regularly (Ancoli-Israel and Roth, 1999). *Primary insomnia* is characterized as difficulty falling asleep after going to bed or after awakening during the night. *Secondary insomnia* is an inability to sleep due to another mental or physical condition, such as pain, substance use, or a psychological or neurological condition.

A significant problem in identifying insomnia is the unreliability of self-reports. Most patients who receive a prescription for a sleeping medication are given one on the basis of their own description of their symptoms. That is, they tell their physician that they sleep very little at night, and the drug is prescribed on the basis of this testimony.

Very few patients are observed during a night's sleep in a sleep laboratory; thus, insomnia is one of the few medical problems that physicians treat without having direct clinical evidence for its existence. But studies on the sleep of people who complain of insomnia show that most of them underestimate the amount of time they actually sleep. In fact, Rosa and Bonnet (2000) evaluated in a sleep laboratory the sleep of people who complained of insomnia and people who did not and found no differences between the two groups in time spent sleeping. They *did*, however, find personality differences, which could account for the complaints.

Many people spend much of their time in a sleep-deprived state not because they suffer from insomnia but because the demands of their daily schedules lead them to stay up late or get up early (or both), thus receiving less than the optimal amount of sleep. Chronic sleep deprivation can lead to serious health problems, including increased risk of obesity, diabetes, and cardiovascular disease (Orzel-Gryglewska, 2010).

TREATMENT Pharmacological and nonpharmacological interventions can be effective for treating insomnia. Nonpharmacological interventions include cognitive behavior therapy (CBT), progressive relaxation techniques, and changes in sleep hygiene. Sleep hygiene recommendations include maintaining a consistent sleep schedule (e.g., waking up and going to sleep at the same time each day), and keeping bedrooms dark, quiet, and cool. Pharmacological interventions include a class of drugs called the *hypnotics*. These drugs include zolpidem (Ambien) and zaleplon (Sonata) which are agonists at the $GABA_A$ receptor. Benzodiazepines and over-the-counter antihistamines such as diphenhydramine are also used to treat insomnia (Benca, 2014). These drugs can produce side effects such as sleepiness or difficulty concentrating the following day. Chronic use of sleep-promoting drugs can lead to tolerance and *rebound insomnia* (a return and increase in insomnia) when their use is ended.

SLEEP APNEA A particular form of insomnia is caused by an inability to sleep and breathe at the same time. Patients with this disorder, called **sleep apnea,** fall asleep and then cease to breathe. Nearly all people, especially people who snore, have occasional episodes of sleep apnea, but not to the extent that it interferes with sleep. During a period of sleep apnea the level of carbon dioxide in the blood stimulates chemoreceptors (neurons that detect the presence of certain chemicals), and the person wakes up, gasping for air. The oxygen level of the blood returns to normal, the person falls asleep, and the whole cycle begins again. Because sleep is disrupted, people with this disorder typically feel sleepy and groggy during the day. Fortunately, many cases of sleep apnea are caused by an obstruction of the airway that can be corrected surgically or relieved by

Studies on the sleep of people who complain of insomnia show that most of them underestimate the amount of time they actually sleep.

a device that attaches to the sleeper's face and provides pressurized air that keeps the airway open (Piccirillo et al., 2000; Sher, 1990).

Narcolepsy

LO 9.11 **Describe the symptoms, treatment, and biological basis of narcolepsy.**

Narcolepsy is a neurological disorder characterized by sleep (or some of its components) at inappropriate times (Nishino, 2007). The symptoms can be described in terms of what we know about the phenomena of sleep.

SLEEP ATTACKS The primary symptom of narcolepsy is the **sleep attack.** In narcolepsy, a sleep attack is an overwhelming urge to sleep that can happen at any time but occurs most often under monotonous, boring conditions. Sleep (which appears to be entirely normal) generally lasts for 2–5 minutes. The person usually wakes up feeling refreshed.

CATAPLEXY Another symptom of narcolepsy—perhaps the most striking one—is **cataplexy.** During a cataplectic attack, a person will sustain varying amounts of muscle weakness. In some cases the person will become completely paralyzed and slump down to the floor. The person will lie there, *fully conscious,* for a few seconds to several minutes. What apparently happens is that one of the phenomena of REM sleep—muscular paralysis—occurs at an inappropriate time. This loss of muscle tone is caused by massive inhibition of motor neurons in the spinal cord. When this happens during waking, the person loses control of his or her muscles. As in REM sleep, the person continues to breathe and is able to control eye movements.

Cataplexy is quite different from a narcoleptic sleep attack; cataplexy is usually precipitated by strong emotional reactions or by sudden physical effort, especially if the patient is caught unawares. Laughter, anger, or an effort to catch a suddenly thrown object can trigger a cataplectic attack. In fact, as Guilleminault et al., (1974) noted, even people who do not have cataplexy sometimes lose muscle strength after a bout of intense laughter. Miguel, the man described in the opener to this chapter, had his first cataplectic attack when he was addressing the board of directors of the company he worked for. Wise (2004) notes that patients with narcolepsy often try to avoid thoughts and situations that are likely to evoke strong emotions because they know that these emotions are likely to trigger cataplectic attacks.

SLEEP PARALYSIS REM sleep paralysis sometimes intrudes into waking at a time that does not present any physical danger—just before or just after normal sleep, when a person is already lying down. This symptom of narcolepsy is referred to as **sleep paralysis,** an inability to move just before the onset of sleep or on waking in the morning. A person can be snapped out of sleep paralysis by being touched or by hearing someone call his or her name. Sometimes, the mental components of REM sleep intrude into sleep paralysis; that is, the person dreams while lying awake, paralyzed. These episodes, called **hypnagogic hallucinations,** are often alarming or even terrifying. In the case study at the beginning of the chapter, Miguel experienced a hypnagogic hallucination and thought that his former roommate was trying to attack him with a hammer.

PHYSIOLOGICAL BASIS OF NARCOLEPSY Fortunately, human narcolepsy is relatively rare, with an incidence of approximately one in 2,000 people. This hereditary disorder

The primary symptom of narcolepsy is the sleep attack.

appears to involve a gene found on chromosome 6, but it is strongly influenced by unknown environmental factors (Mahowald and Schenck, 2005; Mignot, 1998; Nishino, 2007). Years ago, researchers began a program to maintain breeds of dogs that are afflicted with narcolepsy, with the hopes that discovery of the causes of canine narcolepsy would further our understanding of the causes of human narcolepsy. Eventually, this research paid off. Lin et al., (1999) discovered that a mutation of a specific gene is responsible for canine narcolepsy. The product of this gene is a receptor for orexin. There are two orexin receptors, A and B. Lin and his colleagues discovered that the mutation responsible for canine narcolepsy involves the orexin-B receptor.

Chemelli et al., (1999) prepared a targeted mutation in mice against the orexin gene and found that the animals showed symptoms of narcolepsy. Like human patients with narcolepsy, they went directly into REM sleep from waking and showed periods of cataplexy while they were awake. Gerashchenko et al., (2001, 2003) prepared a toxin that attacked only orexinergic neurons and administered it to rats. The destruction of the orexin system produced the symptoms of narcolepsy.

Loss of orexinergic neurons is the cause of most cases of narcolepsy in humans as well. Nishino et al., (2000) performed an analysis of the cerebrospinal fluid of healthy participants and patients with narcolepsy. They found a complete absence of orexin in seven of the nine patients with narcolepsy. They hypothesized that the cause of narcolepsy in these seven patients was a hereditary disorder that caused the immune system to attack and destroy orexin-secreting neurons. Most patients with narcolepsy are born with orexinergic neurons, but during adolescence the immune system attacks these neurons, and the symptoms of narcolepsy begin (Fontana et al., 2010). The narcolepsy seen in the two patients with high levels of orexin may have been caused by a mutation of a gene responsible for production of the orexin-B receptor—the same mutation that causes canine narcolepsy. Peyron et al., (2002) reported the case of one patient with early onset narcolepsy (before age 2) with a different genetic defect: mutation of the gene responsible for the production of orexin.

The symptoms of narcolepsy can be treated with drugs. Sleep attacks can be diminished by stimulants such a methylphenidate (Ritalin), a catecholamine agonist (Vgontzas and Kales, 1999). The REM sleep phenomena (cataplexy, sleep paralysis, and hypnagogic hallucinations) can be alleviated by antidepressant drugs, which facilitate both serotonergic and noradrenergic activity (Hublin, 1996; Mivtler, 1994). As we will see in Chapter 16, abnormalities in patterns of REM sleep are seen in people suffering from depression. The fact that drugs that reduce depression also suppress the phenomena of REM sleep is probably not coincidental.

rSnapshotPhotos/Shutterstock

At the present time, modafinil, a stimulant drug whose precise site of action is still unknown, is widely used to treat narcolepsy (Fry, 1998; Nishino, 2007). (Miguel, the man discussed in the opener to this chapter, takes this drug.) Scammell et al. (2000) found that administration of modafinil increased the expression of Fos protein in orexinergic neurons, which indicates that the neurons had been activated. However, the drug must act on other targets, because the drug treats the symptoms of people with narcolepsy, whose brains lack these neurons. The connections of orexinergic neurons with other regions of the brain involved in sleep and wakefulness are discussed later in this chapter.

REM Sleep Behavior Disorder

LO 9.12 Describe the symptoms, treatment, and biological basis of REM sleep behavior disorder.

As you now know, REM sleep is typically accompanied by muscle paralysis. Although neurons in the motor cortex and subcortical motor systems are extremely active during REM sleep (McCarley and Hobson, 1979), people are unable to move at this time. (The occasional twitches that are seen during REM sleep are apparently signs of intense activity of motor neurons that are not completely suppressed.) The fact that people are paralyzed while they dream suggests the possibility that, if not for the paralysis, they would act out their dreams. In **REM sleep behavior disorder,** the behavior of people with this disorder corresponds with the contents of their dreams in REM. Consider the following case:

> I was a halfback playing football, and after the quarterback received the ball from the center he lateraled it sideways to me and I'm supposed to go around end and cut back over tackle and—this is very vivid—as I cut back over tackle there is this big 280-pound tackle waiting, so I, according to football rules, was to give him my shoulder and bounce him out of the way . . . when I came to I was standing in front of our dresser and I had [gotten up out of bed and run and] knocked lamps, mirrors and everything off the dresser, hit my head against the wall and my knee against the dresser. (Schenck et al., 1986, p. 294)

Like narcolepsy, REM sleep behavior disorder appears to be a neurodegenerative disorder with at least some genetic component (Schenck et al., 1993). It is often associated with neurodegenerative disorders such as Parkinson's disease (Boeve et al., 2007). These disorders are called α-*synucleinopathies* because they involve the inclusion of α-synuclein protein in degenerating neurons. In addition, REM sleep behavior disorder can be caused by brain damage—in some cases to the neural circuits in

the brain stem that control the phenomena of REM sleep (Culebras and Moore, 1989). The symptoms of REM sleep behavior disorder are the opposite of those of cataplexy. Instead of exhibiting paralysis outside REM sleep, patients with REM sleep behavior disorder *fail* to exhibit paralysis *during* REM sleep. As you might expect, drugs are used to treat the symptoms of cataplexy will worsen the symptoms of REM sleep behavior disorder (Schenck and Mahowald, 1992). REM sleep behavior disorder is usually treated by clonazepam, a benzodiazepine (Aurora et al., 2010; Frenette, 2010).

Problems Associated with Slow-Wave Sleep

LO 9.13 Describe the symptoms, treatment, and biological basis of bedwetting, sleepwalking, and night terrors.

Some maladaptive behaviors occur during slow-wave sleep. These behaviors include bedwetting (*nocturnal enuresis*), sleepwalking (*somnambulism*), and night terrors (*pavor nocturnus*). All three events occur most frequently in children. Often bedwetting can be cured by training methods, such as having a special electronic circuit ring a bell when the first few drops of urine are detected in the bed sheet (a few drops usually precede the ensuing flood). Night terrors consist of anguished screams, trembling, a rapid pulse, and usually no memory of what caused the terror. Night terrors and somnambulism usually cure themselves as the child gets older. Neither of these phenomena is related to REM sleep; a sleepwalking person is *not* acting out a dream. Especially when it occurs in adulthood, sleepwalking appears to have a genetic component (Hublin et al., 1997).

Sometimes, people can engage in complex behaviors while sleepwalking. Consider the following cases:

> One evening Ed Weber got up from a nap on the sofa, polished off a half-gallon of chocolate chip ice cream, then dozed off again. He woke up an hour later and went looking for the ice cream, summoning his wife to the kitchen and insisting, to her astonishment, that someone else must have eaten it.
>
> [T]elevision talk show host Montel Williams . . . told viewers he had removed raw foods from his refrigerator because "I wake up in the morning and there's a pack of chicken and there's a bite missing out of it. . . . I can take a whole pound of ham or bologna . . . and then wake up in the morning and not realize that I had [eaten] it and ask, 'Who ate my lunch meat?'" (Boodman, 2004, p. HE01)

Schenck et al., (1991) reported 19 cases of people with histories of eating during the night while they were asleep, which they labeled **sleep-related eating disorder.** Almost half of the patients had become overweight from night eating. Once patients realize that they are eating in their sleep, they often employ stratagems such as keeping their food under lock and key or setting alarms that will awaken them when they try to open their refrigerator.

Sleep-related eating disorder usually responds well to dopaminergic agonists or topiramate, an antiseizure medication, and may be provoked by zolpidem, a benzodiazepine agonist that has been used to treat insomnia (Howell and Schenck, 2009). An increased incidence of nocturnal eating in family members of people with this disorder suggests that heredity may play a role (De Ocampo et al., 2002).

Sleep walking has been used as a defense in several homicide cases in which the defendant claimed to have committed acts of violence while sleep walking in slow-wave sleep. For an interesting account of one case study, see Cartwright, 2004.

Sleepwalking is one of the maladaptive behaviors that occur during slow-wave sleep.

Helder Almeida/Shutterstock

Section Review

Disorders of Sleep

LO 9.10 Describe the symptoms, treatment, and biological basis of insomnia.

Primary insomnia is characterized as difficulty falling asleep after going to bed or after awakening during the night. Secondary insomnia is an inability to sleep due to another mental or physical condition, such as pain, substance use, or a psychological or neurological condition. Insomnia treatments include cognitive behavior therapy (CBT), progressive relaxation techniques, changes in sleep hygiene, as well as hypnotic, benzodiazepine, and antihistamine drugs. Research has found no difference in time spent sleeping in people with and without insomnia. Insomnia can be caused by sleep apnea, and can be treated with surgery or a medical device to keep the airway open.

LO 9.11 Describe the symptoms, treatment, and biological basis of narcolepsy.

Narcolepsy is characterized by sleep (or some of its components) at inappropriate times. The symptoms of narcolepsy include sleep attacks, cataplexy, sleep paralysis, and hypnogogic hallucinations. Narcolepsy is associated with mutations of a gene in chromosome 6 for the orexin receptor or a lack of orexin. Some patients develop narcolepsy after an autoimmune attack of orexin neurons. Narcolepsy is treated with stimulants, antidepressants, or modafinil.

LO 9.12 Describe the symptoms, treatment, and biological basis of REM sleep behavior disorder.

REM sleep behavior disorder is caused by a neurodegenerative disease that damages brain mechanisms that produce paralysis during REM sleep. As a result, the patient acts out his or her dreams. REM behavior disorder can be treated with a benzodiazepine.

LO 9.13 Describe the symptoms, treatment, and biological basis of bedwetting, sleepwalking, and night terrors.

During slow-wave sleep some people experience bedwetting (nocturnal enuresis), sleepwalking (somnambulism), or night terrors (pavor nocturnus). These problems are most common in children, who usually outgrow them. People with sleep-related eating disorder seek and consume food while sleepwalking. Treatments include training for bed wetting, dopamine agonists, or topiramate for sleep eating. Many children eventually outgrow night terrors.

Thought Question

Suppose you were spending the night at a friend's house and, hearing a strange noise during the night, got out of bed and found your friend walking around, still asleep. How would you tell whether your friend was sleepwalking or had REM sleep behavior disorder?

Biological Clocks

Much of our behavior follows regular rhythms. For example, we saw that the stages of sleep are organized around a 90-minute cycle of REM and slow-wave sleep. Our daily pattern of sleep and waking follows a 24-hour cycle. Finally, many animals display seasonal rhythms in which reproductive behaviors and hormone levels show yearly fluctuations. In recent years investigators have learned much about the neural mechanisms that are responsible for these rhythms.

Circadian Rhythms and Zeitgebers

LO 9.14   List examples of circadian rhythms and zeitgebers.

Daily rhythms in behavior and physiological processes are found throughout the plant and animal world. These cycles are generally called **circadian rhythms.** (*Circa* means "about," and *dies* means "day"; therefore, a circadian rhythm is one with a cycle of approximately 24 hours.) Some of these rhythms are passive responses to changes in illumination. However, other rhythms are controlled by mechanisms within the organism—by "internal clocks." For example, Figure 9.24 shows the activity of a rat during various conditions of illumination. Each horizontal line represents 24 hours. Black lines indicate the time the rat spends in wakefulness. Remember, rats are nocturnal animals, active at night. Actual records from a rat would show more variability and some short periods of waking during the day and perhaps some catnaps (ratnaps?) during the night. The upper portion of the figure shows the activity of the rat during a normal day/night cycle, with alternating 12-hour periods of light and dark.

Next, the light/dark cycle was shifted; the dark portion of the cycle now began 4 hours earlier. The animal's activity cycle quickly followed the change. (See the middle portion of Figure 9.24.) Finally, dim lights were left on continuously. The cyclical pattern in the rat's activity remained. Because there were no cycles of light and dark in the rat's environment, the source of rhythmicity must be located within the animal; that is, the animal must possess an internal, biological clock. You can see that the rat's clock was not set precisely to 24 hours; when the illumination was held constant, the clock ran a bit slow. The animal began its bout of activity approximately 1 hour later each day. (See the bottom portion of Figure 9.24.)

The phenomenon illustrated in Figure 9.24 is typical of the circadian rhythms shown by many species. A free-running clock, with a cycle of approximately 25 hours, controls some biological functions—in this case, sleep and wakefulness. Regular daily variation in the level of illumination (that is, sunlight and darkness) normally keeps the clock adjusted to 24 hours. Light serves as a **zeitgeber** (German for "time giver"); it synchronizes the endogenous rhythm. Studies with many species of animals have shown that if

Figure 9.24 Wheel-Running Activity of a Rat

Top: The animal's activity occurs at "night" (that is, during the 12 hours the light is off). Middle: The period of waking follows the new dark period when the light cycle is changed. Bottom: When the animal is maintained in constant dim illumination, it displays a free-running activity cycle of approximately 25 hours, which means that its period of waking begins about 1 hour later each day. The horizontal bars represent the portion of the light/dark cycle that the animal is active.

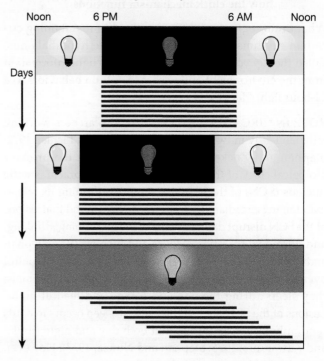

they are maintained in constant darkness (or constant dim light), a brief period of bright light will reset their internal clock, advancing or slowing it depending on when the light flash occurs (Aschoff, 1979). For example, if an animal is exposed to bright light soon after dusk, the biological clock is set back to an earlier time—as if dusk had not yet arrived. On the other hand, if the light occurs late at night, the biological clock is set ahead to a later time—as if dawn had already come. Using zeitgebers such as clocks or other time cues, individuals who are blind or live in polar regions with extended periods of light or dark easily adapt to a 24-hour environment.

Like other animals, humans exhibit circadian rhythms. Our normal period of inactivity begins several hours after the start of the dark portion of the day/night cycle and persists for a variable amount of time into the light portion. Without the benefits of modern civilization we would probably go to sleep earlier and get up earlier than we do; we use artificial lights to delay our bedtime and window shades to extend our time for sleep. Under constant illumination our biological clocks will run free, gaining or losing time like a watch that runs too slow or too fast. Different people have different cycle lengths, but most people in that situation will begin to live a "day" that is approximately 25 hours long.

This works out quite well, because the morning light, acting as a zeitgeber, simply resets the clock.

The Suprachiasmatic Nucleus

LO 9.15 **Identify the role of the suprachiasmatic nucleus in regulating circadian rhythms, and explain how the clock mechanism functions.**

What brain regions might be involved in maintaining circadian rhythms? A specific region of the hypothalamus, called the *suprachiasmatic nucleus,* receives light information from the environment and uses it to entrain behaviors to a 24-hour light/dark cycle.

ROLE IN CIRCADIAN RHYTHMS   Researchers working independently in two laboratories (Moore and Eichler, 1972; Stephan and Zucker, 1972) discovered that the primary biological clock of the rat is located in the **suprachiasmatic nucleus (SCN)** of the hypothalamus. Confirming its role in maintaining circadian rhythms, researchers found that lesions of the SCN disrupt daily patterns of wheel running, drinking, and hormonal secretion (Moore and Eichler, 1972; Stephan and Zucker, 1972). The SCN also provides the primary control over the timing of sleep cycles. Rats are nocturnal animals; they sleep during the day and forage and feed at night. Lesions of the SCN abolish this pattern; sleep occurs in bouts randomly dispersed throughout both day and night (Ibuka and Kawamura, 1975; Stephan and Nuñez, 1977). However, rats with SCN lesions still obtain the same amount of sleep that normal animals do. The lesions disrupt the circadian control of sleep but do not affect its homeostatic control.

Figure 9.25 shows the suprachiasmatic nuclei in a cross section through the hypothalamus of a mouse; they appear as two clusters of dark-staining neurons at the base of the brain, just above the optic chiasm. The suprachiasmatic nuclei of the rat consist of approximately 8,600 small neurons, tightly packed into a volume of 0.036 mm³ (Moore et al., 2002).

Figure 9.25 The SCN

The location and appearance of the suprachiasmatic nuclei in a rat are shown here. Cresyl violet stain was used to color the nuclei in this cross section of a rat brain.

(Courtesy of Geert DeVries, University of Massachusetts)

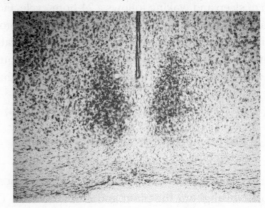

Because light is the primary zeitgeber for most mammals' activity cycles, we would expect that the SCN receives input from the visual system. Indeed, anatomical studies have revealed a direct projection from the retina to the SCN: the *retinohypothalamic pathway* (Aronson et al., 1993; Hendrickson et al., 1972). (See Figure 9.26.)

The photoreceptors in the retina that provide photic information to the SCN are neither rods nor cones—the cells that provide us with the information used for visual perception. Freedman et al., (1999) found that targeted mutations against genes necessary for production of both rods and cones did not disrupt the synchronizing effects of light. However, when they removed the mice's eyes, these effects *were* disrupted. These results suggested that there is a special photoreceptor that provides information about the ambient level of light that synchronizes circadian rhythms. Provencio et al., (2000) found the photochemical responsible for this effect, which they named **melanopsin.**

Figure 9.26 The Retinohypothalamic Pathway

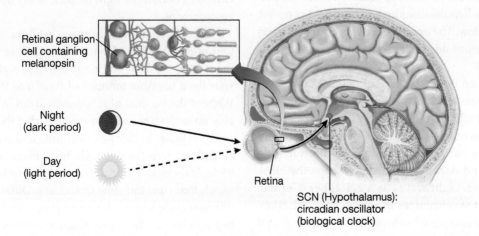

Retinal ganglion cell containing melanopsin

Night (dark period)

Day (light period)

Retina

SCN (Hypothalamus): circadian oscillator (biological clock)

Unlike the other retinal photopigments, which are found in rods and cones, melanopsin is present in ganglion cells—the neurons whose axons transmit information from the eyes to the rest of the brain. Melanopsin-containing ganglion cells are sensitive to light, and their axons terminate in the SCN. They also terminate in the region of the midbrain that controls the response of the pupils to changes in the level of illumination (Berson et al., 2002; Gooley et al., 2003; Hattar et al., 2002). Apparently, melanopsin-containing ganglion cells, and not rods and cones, are involved in the pupillary response to light.

Because the synchronizing effects of light on the SCN are mediated by specialized ganglion cells and not by rods and cones, people who have become blind because of loss of these photoreceptors can still show normal circadian rhythms. Although they cannot see, the melanopsin-containing ganglion cells in their retinas can still detect changes in light levels and synchronize the activity of their SCN.

SUPRACHIASMATIC NUCLEUS CONTROL OF SLEEP AND WAKE   How does the SCN control cycles of sleep and waking? Efferent axons of the SCN responsible for organizing cycles of sleep and waking terminate in the *subparaventricular zone (SPZ)*, a region just dorsal to the SCN (Deurveilher and Semba, 2005). Lu et al., (2001) found that excitotoxic lesions of the ventral part of the SPZ disrupted circadian rhythms of sleep and waking. The ventral SPZ projects to the *dorsomedial nucleus of the hypothalamus (DMH)*, which in turn projects to several brain regions, including two that play critical roles in the control of sleep and waking: the vlPOA and the orexinergic neurons of the lateral hypothalamus. The projections to the vlPOA are inhibitory and thus inhibit sleep, whereas the projections to the orexinergic neurons are excitatory and thus promote wakefulness (Saper et al., 2005). The activity of these connections varies across the day/night cycle. In diurnal animals (such as ourselves) the activity of these connections is high during the day and low during the night. (See Figure 9.27.)

Although connections of SCN neurons with the SPZ play a critical role in circadian control of sleep and waking, several experiments suggest that the SCN can also control these rhythms by secretion of chemicals that diffuse through the brain's extracellular fluid. Lehman et al., (1987) destroyed the SCN and then transplanted in its place a new set of suprachiasmatic nuclei obtained from donor animals. The grafts succeeded in reestablishing circadian rhythms, even though very few synaptic connections were observed between the graft and the recipient's brain.

The most convincing evidence for chemical communication between the SCN and other parts of the brain comes from a transplantation study by Silver et al., (1996). Silver and her colleagues first destroyed the SCN in a group of hamsters, abolishing their circadian rhythms. Then, a few weeks later, they removed SCN tissue from donor animals and placed it in tiny semipermeable capsules, which they then implanted in the animals' third ventricles. Nutrients and other chemicals could pass through the walls of the capsules, keeping the SCN tissue alive, but the neurons inside the capsules were not able to establish synaptic connections with the surrounding tissue. Nevertheless, the transplants reestablished circadian rhythms in the recipient animals. Evidence suggests that the chemical signal may be a *prokineticin 2 (PK2)*, a protein contained in a subset of SCN neurons (Zhang et al., 2009). Presumably, the chemicals secreted by cells in the SCN affect rhythms of sleep and waking by diffusing into the SPZ and binding with receptors on neurons located there. In fact, Hu et al., (2007) found that mice with a targeted mutation against the PK2 gene showed disrupted circadian rhythms.

THE NATURE OF THE CLOCK   All clocks must have a time base. Mechanical clocks use flywheels or pendulums; electronic clocks use quartz crystals. The SCN, too, must contain a physiological mechanism that parses time into units. After years of research, investigators are finally beginning to discover the nature of the biological clock in the SCN.

Figure 9.27 Control of Circadian Rhythms in Sleep and Waking by the SCN

During the day cycle, the DMH inhibits the vlPOA and excites the brain stem and forebrain arousal systems, thus stimulating wakefulness.

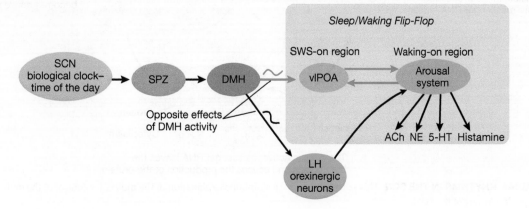

Several studies have demonstrated daily activity rhythms in the SCN, which indicates that the circadian clock is indeed located there. A study by Schwartz and Gainer (1977) nicely demonstrated day/night fluctuations in the activity of the SCN. The investigators injected some rats with radioactive 2-DG during the day and injected others at night. The animals were then euthanized, and autoradiographs of cross sections through the brain were prepared. (2-DG autoradiography was described in Chapter 5.) The autoradiographs revealed radioactivity (and hence a high metabolic rate) in the SCN when 2-DG was administered during the day, but not during the night.

The "ticking" of the biological clock within the SCN is due to activity within individual neurons themselves. Several studies have succeeded in keeping individual SCN neurons alive in a culture medium. Welsh et al., (1995) removed tissue from the rat SCN and dissolved the connections between the cells with papain, an enzyme that is sometimes used as a meat tenderizer. The cells were placed on top of an array of microelectrodes so that their electrical activity could be measured. Unlike neurons in the intact SCN, whose rhythms are synchronized, the cultured neurons displayed individual, independent, circadian rhythms in activity.

GENE PRODUCTS What causes intracellular ticking? Circadian rhythms in the SCN are produced as protein production rises to a certain level in the cell. When this maximal level is reached, the high concentration of protein in the cell turns off its own production through a negative feedback loop (see Chapter 12 for a review of *negative feedback* and *homeostasis*). As a result, the levels of the protein begin to decline, removing the inhibition, starting the production cycle again.

This mechanism was first discovered in *Drosophila melanogaster,* the common fruit fly. Subsequent research with mammals revealed a similar system. (See Golombek and Rosenstein, 2010, for a review.) The system involves at least seven genes and their proteins and two interlocking feedback loops. When one of the proteins produced by the first loop reaches a sufficient level, it starts the second loop, which eventually inhibits the production of proteins in the first loop, and the cycle begins again. Thus, the intracellular ticking is regulated by the time it takes to produce and degrade a set of proteins.

Yan and Silver (2004) found that if animals that are kept in the dark are exposed to a brief period of bright light, the levels of these proteins change. Furthermore, pulses of light presented during different phases of the animal's circadian rhythm produce different effects on the production of these proteins. As we saw earlier, exposure to light at different times of day had different effects on the animals' behavior, setting their biological clocks either forward or backward (Aschoff, 1979).

Genetic studies have found evidence for similarities between the human SCN and that of laboratory animals. Toh et al., (2001) found that a mutation on chromosome 2 of a gene for one of the proteins involved in the feedback loops we mentioned earlier in this subsection (*per2*) is responsible for the **advanced sleep phase syndrome.** This syndrome causes a 4-hour advance in rhythms of sleep and temperature cycles. People with this syndrome fall asleep around 7:30 P.M. and awaken around 4:30 A.M. The mutation appears to change the relationship between the zeitgeber of morning light and the phase of the circadian clock that operates in the cells of the SCN. Ebisawa et al., (2001) found evidence that the opposite disorder, the **delayed sleep phase syndrome,** may be caused by mutations of another gene, the *per3* gene, found on chromosome 1. This syndrome consists of a 4-hour delay in sleep/waking rhythms. People with this disorder are typically unable to fall asleep before 2:00 A.M. and have great difficulty waking before midmorning. Allebrandt

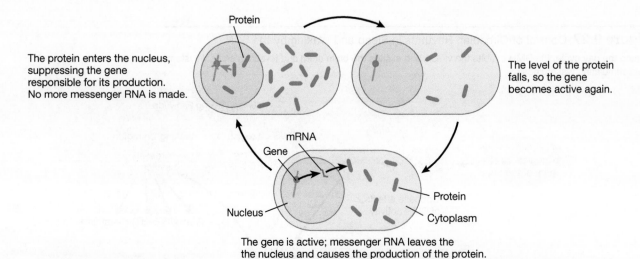

The protein enters the nucleus, suppressing the gene responsible for its production. No more messenger RNA is made.

The level of the protein falls, so the gene becomes active again.

Protein

mRNA

Gene

Nucleus

Protein

Cytoplasm

The gene is active; messenger RNA leaves the the nucleus and causes the production of the protein.

CIRCADIAN RHYTHMS IN THE SCN This schematic shows a simplified explanation of the molecular control of the daily "ticking" of neurons of the SCN.

et al., (2010) found yet another set of gene variants (in the *clock* gene) that affect people's sleep duration.

Control of Seasonal Rhythms: The Pineal Gland and Melatonin

LO 9.16 **Describe the relationship between the pineal gland and melatonin.**

Although the SCN has an intrinsic rhythm of approximately 24 hours, it also plays a role in much longer rhythms. (We could say that it is involved in a biological calendar as well as a biological clock.)

THE PINEAL GLAND The control of seasonal rhythms involves another part of the brain: the **pineal gland** (Bartness et al., 1993). This structure sits on top of the midbrain, just in front of the cerebellum. (See Figure 9.28.) The pineal gland secretes a hormone called **melatonin,** so named because it has the ability in certain animals (primarily fish, reptiles, and amphibians) to turn the skin temporarily dark. (The dark color is produced by a chemical known as *melanin*.) In mammals, melatonin controls seasonal rhythms. Neurons in the SCN make indirect connections with neurons in the *paraventricular nucleus of the hypothalamus* (the PVN). The axons of these neurons travel all the way to the spinal cord, where they form synapses with preganglionic neurons of the sympathetic nervous system. The postganglionic neurons innervate the pineal gland and control the secretion of melatonin.

MELATONIN In response to input from the SCN, the pineal gland secretes melatonin during the night. This melatonin acts back on various structures in the brain (including the SCN, whose cells contain melatonin receptors) and controls hormones, physiological processes,

Figure 9.28 Pineal Gland

(Adapted from Paxinos, G., and Watson, C., *The Rat Brain in Stereotaxic Coordinates,* Sydney: Academic Press, 1982. Redrawn with permission.)

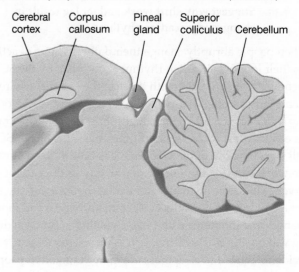

and behaviors that show seasonal variations. During long nights a large amount of melatonin is secreted, and the animals go into the winter phase of their annual cycle. Lesions of the SCN, the PVN, or the pineal gland disrupt seasonal rhythms that are controlled by day length—and so do knife cuts that interrupt the neural connection between the SCN and the PVN, which indicates that this is one function of the SCN that is mediated through its neural connections with another structure. Furthermore, although transplants of fetal suprachiasmatic nuclei will restore circadian rhythms in animals with SCN lesions, they will not restore seasonal rhythms, because the transplanted tissue does not establish neural connections with the PVN (Ralph and Lehman, 1991). (See Figure 9.29.)

Figure 9.29 The SCN and Pineal Gland

Melatonin is released by the pineal gland during the dark period. Light information, relayed from the retina to the SCN and PVN, suppresses the release of melatonin by the pineal gland. Disrupting this pathway interferes with seasonal rhythms that are controlled by day length.

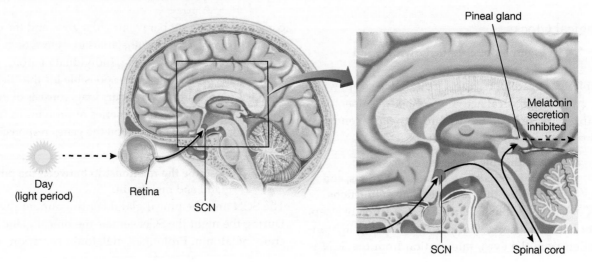

Changes in Circadian Rhythms: Shift Work and Jet Lag

LO 9.17   Suggest why shift work and jet lag result in changes in circadian rhythms.

When people abruptly change their daily rhythms of activity, their internal circadian rhythms, controlled by the SCN, become desynchronized with those in the external environment. For example, if a person who normally works on a day shift begins working on a night shift or if someone travels east or west across several time zones, his or her SCN will signal the rest of the brain that it is time to sleep during the work shift (or the middle of the day in the case of jet travel). This disparity between internal rhythms and the external environment results in sleep disturbances and mood changes and interferes with people's ability to function during waking hours. Problems such as ulcers, depression, and accidents related to sleepiness are more common in people whose work schedules shift frequently (Drake et al., 2004).

Jet lag is a temporary phenomenon; after several days, people who have crossed several time zones find it easier to fall asleep at the appropriate time, and their daytime alertness improves. Shift work can present a more enduring problem when people are required to change shifts often. The solution to jet lag and to the problems caused by shift work is to get the internal clock synchronized with the external environment as quickly as possible. One way to start is to try to provide strong zeitgebers at the appropriate time. If a person is exposed to bright light before the low point in the daily rhythm of body temperature (which occurs an hour or two before the person usually awakens), the person's circadian rhythm is delayed. If the exposure to bright light occurs after the low point, the circadian rhythm is advanced (Dijk et al., 1995). In fact, several studies have shown that exposure to bright lights at the appropriate time helps to ease the transition to a new circadian pattern (Boulos et al., 1995). Similarly, people adapt to shift work more rapidly if artificial light is kept at a brighter level in the workplace and if their bedroom is kept as dark as possible (Horowitz et al., 2001).

As we saw in the previous subsection, the role of melatonin in seasonal rhythms is well established. Studies in recent years suggest that melatonin may also be involved in circadian rhythms. As we saw, melatonin is secreted during the night, which, for diurnal mammals such as ourselves, is the period during which we sleep. But although our species lacks strong seasonal rhythms, the daily rhythm of melatonin secretion persists. Thus, melatonin must have some functions besides regulation of seasonal rhythms.

Studies have found that melatonin, acting on receptors in the SCN, can affect the sensitivity of SCN neurons to zeitgebers and can itself alter circadian rhythms (Gillette and McArthur, 1995; Starkey et al., 1995). Researchers do not yet understand exactly what role melatonin plays in the control of circadian rhythms, but they have already discovered practical applications. Melatonin secretion normally reaches its highest levels early in the night, at around bedtime. Investigators have found that the administration of melatonin at the appropriate time (in most cases, just before going to bed) significantly reduces the adverse effects of both jet lag and shifts in work schedules (Arendt et al., 1995; Deacon and Arendt, 1996). Blind people who have lost their eyes or sustained retinal damage that includes their melanopsin-containing retinal ganglion cells as well as their rods and cones will show unsynchronized, free-running circadian rhythms. In such cases, bedtime melatonin has been used to synchronize their circadian rhythms and has improved their cycles of sleep (Skene et al., 1999).

Section Review

Biological Clocks

LO 9.14   List examples of circadian rhythms and zeitgebers.

Examples of circadian rhythms include the sleep/wake cycle, cycles of physical activity and body temperature. Examples of zeitgebers include the presence of illumination, clocks, or other time cues.

LO 9.15   Identify the role of the suprachiasmatic nucleus in regulating circadian rhythms, and explain how the clock mechanism functions.

The SCN is responsible for circadian regulation of sleep, but not homeostatic regulation. After receiving light information from the eyes, information from the SCN is conveyed via the subparaventricular zone and the dorsomedial nucleus of the hypothalamus to regions of the brain involved in sleep and waking. Individual neurons, rather than circuits of neurons, are responsible for the "ticking." Each tick, approximately 24 hours long, consists of the production and breakdown of a series of proteins in two interlocking loops that act back on the genes responsible for their own production.

LO 9.16   Describe the relationship between the pineal gland and melatonin.

The SCN and the pineal gland control annual rhythms. During the night the SCN signals the pineal gland to secrete melatonin. Prolonged melatonin secretion, which occurs during winter, causes animals to enter the winter phase of their annual cycle. Melatonin also appears to be involved in synchronizing circadian rhythms: The hormone can help people to adjust to the effects of shift work or jet lag and even synchronize the daily rhythms of blind people for whom light cannot serve as a zeitgeber.

LO 9.17 Suggest why shift work and jet lag result in changes in circadian rhythms.

Shift work and jet lag result in changes in circadian rhythms because of desynchronization between the SCN and zeitgebers in the external environment.

Thought Question

Until recently (in terms of the evolution of our species), our ancestors tended to go to sleep when the sun set and wake up when it rose. Once our ancestors learned how to control fire, they undoubtedly stayed up somewhat later, sitting in front of a fire. But it was only with the development of cheap, effective lighting that many members of our species adopted the habit of staying up late and waking several hours after sunrise. Considering that our biological clock and the neural mechanisms it controls evolved long ago, do you think the changes in our daily rhythms impair any of our physical and intellectual abilities?

Chapter Review Questions

1. Describe the contributions of the acetylcholinergic, norepineprinergic, serotininergic, histaminergic and orexinergic neural circuits in arousal and the maintenance of wakeful state.

2. Describe the role of the preoptic area in regulation of sleep.

3. Explain how the orexinergic system acts as the flip-flop circuit in regulating the sleep/wake cycle.

4. Explain the physiological mechanisms and role of SCN in the regulation of the sleep/wake cycle.

5. Describe the role of suprachiasmatic nucleus in the control of seasonal rhythms.

6. Discuss the neural control of slow-wave and REM sleep.

7. Describe circadian rhythms, and discuss research on the role of the suprachiasmatic nucleus in the control of these rhythms.

8. Discuss the time base of the circadian clock, control of seasonal rhythms, and changes in circadian rhythms caused by work schedules and travel.

Chapter 10
Reproductive Behavior

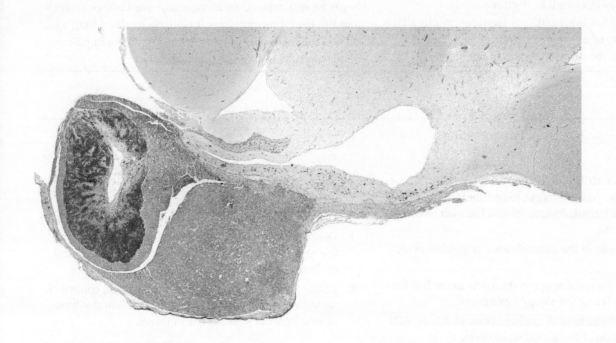

Chapter Outline

Learning Objectives

LO 10.1 Describe the processes of gamete production and fertilization.

LO 10.2 Explain how gonads, internal sex organs, and external genitalia develop.

LO 10.3 Compare the organizational effects of hormones on primary sex characteristics and the activational effects on secondary sex characteristics.

LO 10.4 Summarize the roles of hormones in phases of the menstrual cycle.

LO 10.5 Compare the roles of hormones in sexual behavior of male and female rodents.

LO 10.6 Contrast behavioral masculinization and defeminization in rodents.

LO 10.7 Compare the activational effects of hormones on sexual behavior of human males and females.

LO 10.8 Describe the roles of pheromones in reproductive behavior of humans and other animals.

LO 10.9 Identify the role of spinal and brain mechanisms in male sexual behavior.

LO 10.10 Identify the role of brain mechanisms in female sexual behavior.

LO 10.11 Compare the roles of oxytocin and vasopressin in pair bonding.

LO 10.12 Compare the roles of activational and organizational hormone effects in sexual orientation.

LO 10.13 Explain what can be learned about the role of prenatal androgen exposure in sexual orientation from congenital adrenal hyperplasia and androgen insensitivity.

LO 10.14 Explain what can be learned about the role of biological factors in sexual orientation from cloacal exstrophy.

LO 10.15 Compare sexually dimorphic features of a male and female brain, and explain what can be learned about the brain basis of sexual orientation from these dimorphisms.

LO 10.16 Summarize the relationships between prenatal environmental factors and sexual orientation.

LO 10.17 Summarize what is currently known of the role of heredity in sexual orientation.

LO 10.18 Describe examples of rodent maternal behavior.

LO 10.19 Explain the role of hormones in examples of maternal behavior.

LO 10.20 Identify brain regions and neural pathways involved in maternal behavior.

LO 10.21 Identify brain regions and neural pathways involved in paternal behavior.

At first a tragic surgical accident appeared to suggest that people's gender identity and sexual orientation were not under the strong control of biological factors and that these characteristics could be shaped by the way a child was raised (Money and Ehrhardt, 1972). Identical twin boys were raised similarly until seven months of age, at which time the penis of one of the boys was accidentally removed during circumcision. The cautery (a device that cuts tissue by means of electric current) was adjusted too high, and instead of removing just the foreskin, the current burned off the entire penis. After a period of agonized indecision, the parents decided to raise the child as a girl. John became Joan.

Joan's parents started dressing her in girl's clothing and treating her like a little girl. Surgeons performed a sex-change

operation, removing the testes and creating a vagina. At first, psychologists who studied Joan reported that she was a typically-developing, happy girl and concluded that it was a child's upbringing that determined his or her gender identity. Many people saw this case as a triumph of socialization over biology.

Unfortunately, this conclusion was premature (Diamond and Sigmundson, 1997). It turned out that although Joan did not know that her biological sex at birth was male, she was unhappy with a female gender identity. She felt that her gender was that of a boy and even tried to stand to urinate. When, as an unhappy adolescent, she threatened to commit suicide, her family and physicians agreed to a sex change. The estrogen treatment she had been receiving was terminated, she started taking androgens, she had a mastectomy, and surgeons began creating a phallus. Joan became John again. His father finally told him that he was born a boy, a revelation that John received with great relief. John later married and adopted his wife's children.

We now know this person's real names: Bruce became Brenda, who then chose the name David after resuming a male gender again. A book has told David's story (Colapinto, 2000), and a 2002 television documentary (NOVA's Sex: Unknown) presented interviews with David, his mother, the psychologist who worked with the family, and others involved in this unfortunate case. Sadly, David subsequently lost his job, he and his wife separated, and in May 2004, at the age of 38, he committed suicide.

*****

Reproductive behaviors constitute an important category of social behaviors, because without them, most species would not survive. These behaviors—which include courting, mating, parental behavior, and most forms of aggressive behaviors—are the most striking categories of **sexually dimorphic behaviors,** that is, behaviors that differ in males and females. As you will see, hormones that are present both before and after birth play a very special role in the development and control of sexually dimorphic behaviors as well as sexual orientation.

This chapter begins with a discussion of male and female sexual development. We then examine the hormonal and neural influences on sexual behavior and orientation, as well as gender identity. In the final section, we focus in on how hormonal and neural controls influence parenting behavior. The figure here presents the pituitary gland and the hypothalamus, two regions of the brain involved in reproductive behavior that we will be paying particular attention to in this chapter.

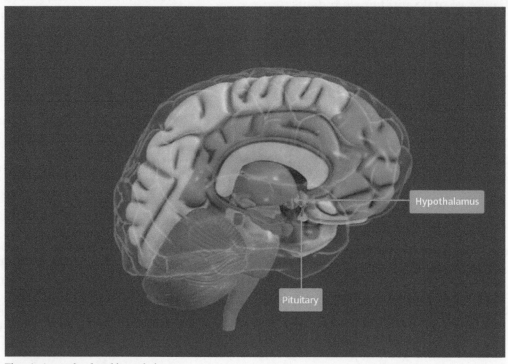

Hypothalamus

Pituitary

The pituitary gland and hypothalamus.

Sexual Development

A person's chromosomal sex is determined at the time of fertilization. However, this event is only the first in a series of steps that culminate in the development of the biological sex and gender identity of males, females, and intersex individuals. The term "sex" typically refers to the genetic or physiological characteristics of males and females, while the term "gender" typically refers to the socially-influenced identity, role, and/or behavior of an individual. The term "intersex" is a broad term used to describe a variety of combinations of biologically male and female characteristics, such as an individual born with external female genitalia and internal male sex organs. This section considers the major features of sexual development, from production of gametes, to development of internal sex organs and external genitalia.

Production of Gametes and Fertilization

LO 10.1 **Describe the processes of gamete production and fertilization.**

All cells of the human body (other than sperms or ova) contain 23 pairs of chromosomes. The genetic information

Figure 10.1 Determination of Genetic Sex

The genetic sex of an offspring depends on whether the sperm cell that fertilizes the ovum carries an X or a Y chromosome.

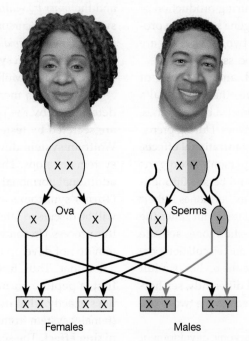

that programs the development of a human is contained in the DNA that constitutes these chromosomes. We pride ourselves on our ability to miniaturize computer circuits on silicon chips, but that accomplishment looks primitive when we consider that the blueprint for a human being is too small to be seen by the naked eye.

The production of **gametes** (ova and sperms) entails a special form of cell division called *meiosis*. This process produces cells that contain one set of each of the pairs of chromosomes. The development of a human begins at the time of fertilization, when a single sperm and ovum join, sharing their 23 single chromosomes to reconstitute the 23 pairs.

A person's **genetic sex** is determined at the time of fertilization of the ovum by the father's sperm. Twenty-two of the 23 pairs of chromosomes determine the organism's physical development independent of its sex. The last pair consists of two **sex chromosomes,** which contain genes that determine whether the offspring will be genetically male or female.

There are two types of sex chromosomes: X chromosomes and Y chromosomes. Genetic females have two X chromosomes (XX); thus, all the ova that a woman produces will contain an X chromosome. Genetic males have an X and a Y chromosome (XY). When a man's sex chromosomes divide, half the sperms contain an X chromosome, and the other half contain a Y chromosome. A Y-bearing sperm produces an XY-fertilized ovum and therefore a genetic male. An X-bearing sperm produces an XX-fertilized ovum and therefore a genetic female. (See Figure 10.1.)

Development of the Sex Organs

LO 10.2 Explain how gonads, internal sex organs, and external genitalia develop.

Males and females differ in many ways: Their bodies are different, parts of their brains are different, and their reproductive behaviors are different. Are all these differences directly encoded on the tiny Y chromosome, the sole piece of genetic material that distinguishes genetic males from females? The answer is no. The X chromosome and the 22 nonsex chromosomes found in the cells of both males and females contain all the information needed to develop the bodies of either sex. Exposure to sex hormones, both before and after birth, is responsible for our sexual dimorphism. What the Y chromosome does control is the development of the glands that produce the male sex hormones.

GONADS There are three general categories of sex organs: the gonads, the internal sex organs, and the external genitalia. The **gonads**—testes or ovaries—are the first to develop. Gonads have a dual function: They produce ova or sperms, and they secrete hormones. Through the sixth week of prenatal development, male and female fetuses are identical. Both sexes have a pair of identical undifferentiated gonads, which have the potential of developing into either testes or ovaries. The factor that controls their development appears to be a single gene on the Y chromosome called **SRY** (sex-determining region Y). This gene produces a protein that binds to the DNA of cells in the undifferentiated gonads and causes them to become testes. If the SRY gene is not present, the undifferentiated gonads become ovaries. Some instances of XX males have been reported. This can occur when the SRY gene becomes translocated from the Y chromosome to the X chromosome during production of the father's sperms. Although the SRY gene begins the process of gonadal differentiation, at least two other genes are also necessary for completion of this process.

Once the gonads have developed, another series of events is set into action that determines the individual's sexual development. These events are directed by hormones, which affect sexual development in two ways. During prenatal development these hormones have **organizational effects,** which influence the development of a person's sex organs and brain. These effects are permanent and persist throughout the person's life. The second role of sex hormones is their **activational effects.** These effects occur later in life, after the sex organs have developed. For example, hormones activate the production of sperms, make erection and ejaculation possible, and also induce ovulation. Because the bodies of adult males and females have been organized differently, sex hormones will have different activational effects in the two sexes.

INTERNAL SEX ORGANS   Early in embryonic development the internal sex organs are *bisexual;* that is, all embryos contain the precursors for both female and male sex organs. However, during the third month of gestation, only one of these precursors develops. The precursor of the internal female sex organs, which develops into the *fimbriae* and *fallopian tubes,* the *uterus,* and the *inner two-thirds of the vagina,* is called the **Müllerian system.** The precursor of the internal male sex organs, which develops into the *epididymis, vas deferens,* and *seminal vesicles,* is called the **Wolffian system.** (These systems were named after their discoverers, Müller and Wolff. See Figure 10.2.)

The development of internal sex organs of a fetus is determined by the presence or absence of hormones that are secreted by testes. If these hormones are present, the Wolffian system develops. If they are not, the Müllerian system develops. The Müllerian (female) system needs no additional hormonal stimulus from the gonads to develop. (Turner syndrome, a disorder of sexual development that will be discussed later in this chapter, provides evidence for this process.) In contrast, the cells of the Wolffian (male) system do not develop unless they are stimulated to do so by a hormone. Thus, testes secrete two types of hormones. The first, a peptide hormone called **anti-Müllerian hormone,** does exactly what its name says: It prevents the Müllerian (female) system from developing. It therefore has a **defeminizing effect.** The second, a set of steroid hormones called **androgens,** stimulates the development of the Wolffian system. Androgens have a **masculinizing effect.**

Figure 10.2 Development of the Internal Sex Organs

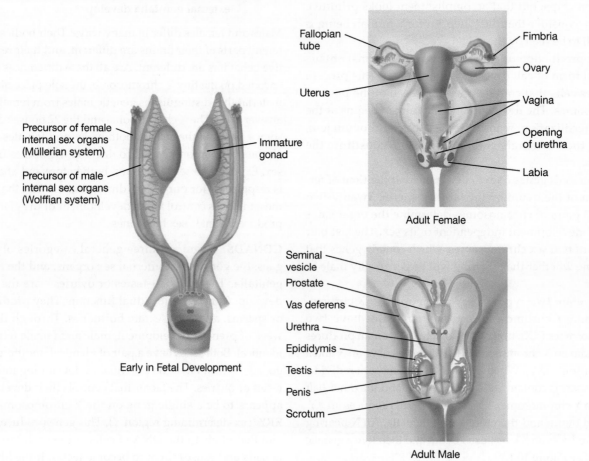

Precursor of female internal sex organs (Müllerian system)

Precursor of male internal sex organs (Wolffian system)

Immature gonad

Early in Fetal Development

Fallopian tube

Uterus

Fimbria

Ovary

Vagina

Opening of urethra

Labia

Adult Female

Seminal vesicle

Prostate

Vas deferens

Urethra

Epididymis

Testis

Penis

Scrotum

Adult Male

Two different androgens are responsible for masculinization. The first, **testosterone,** is secreted by the testes and gets its name from these glands. An enzyme called 5α *reductase* converts some of the testosterone into another androgen, known as **dihydrotestosterone.**

In Chapter 2, you read that hormones exert their effects on target cells by stimulating the appropriate hormone receptor. Thus, the precursor of the male internal sex organs—the Wolffian system—contains androgen receptors that are coupled to cellular mechanisms that promote growth and division. When molecules of androgens bind with these receptors, the epididymis, vas deferens, and seminal vesicles develop and grow. In contrast, the cells of the Müllerian system contain receptors for anti-Müllerian hormone that *prevent* growth and division. Thus, the presence of anti-Müllerian hormone prevents the development of the female internal sex organs.

The fact that the internal sex organs of the human embryo are bisexual and could potentially develop as either male or female is dramatically illustrated by two genetic disorders: *androgen insensitivity syndrome* and *persistent Müllerian duct syndrome.* Some people are insensitive to androgens; they have **androgen insensitivity syndrome** (MacLean et al., 1995; Money and Ehrhardt, 1972). The cause of androgen insensitivity syndrome is a genetic mutation that prevents the formation of functioning androgen receptors. (The gene for the androgen receptor is located on the X chromosome.) The primitive gonads of a genetic male fetus with androgen insensitivity syndrome become testes and secrete both anti-Müllerian hormone and androgens. The lack of androgen receptors prevents the androgens from having a masculinizing effect; thus, the epididymis, vas deferens, seminal vesicles, and prostate do not develop. However, the anti-Müllerian hormone still has its defeminizing effect, preventing the female internal sex organs from developing. The uterus, fimbriae, and Fallopian tubes do not develop either, and the vagina is shallow. The external genitalia are female, and at puberty the person develops a woman's body. Without a uterus and ovaries, the person cannot have children.

The second genetic disorder, **persistent Müllerian duct syndrome,** has two causes: either a failure to produce anti-Müllerian hormone or the absence of receptors for this hormone (Warne and Zajac, 1998). When this syndrome occurs in genetic males, androgens have their masculinizing effect, but defeminization does not occur. Thus, the person is born with *both* sets of internal sex organs, male and female. The presence of the additional female sex organs usually interferes with functioning of the male sex organs.

The development of a test based on a molecular probe for SRY was intended to ensure that potential competitors for the women's Summer Olympic events in Atlanta in 1996 had no SRY gene and therefore were not men attempting to compete as women. However, this controversial test could erroneously identify XY women with androgen insensitivity syndrome as

men. Given that androgens cannot stimulate muscle development in people whose cells are insensitive to these hormones, the presence of the SRY gene did not indicate that individuals were men trying to compete as women. Women with androgen insensitivity syndrome have women's bodies, with muscular strength typical of women. However, science and common sense prevailed, and this form of testing was eliminated by the time of the 2000 Summer Olympics.

So far, you have read about only male sex hormones. What about prenatal sexual development in females? The hormones produced by female sex organs are not needed for development of the Müllerian system. People with **Turner syndrome** have only one sex chromosome: an X chromosome. (Thus, instead of having XX cells, they have X0 cells—0 [zero] indicating a missing sex chromosome.) In most cases the existing X chromosome comes from the mother, which means that the cause of the disorder lies with a defective sperm (Knebelmann et al., 1991). Because a Y chromosome is not present, testes do not develop. In addition, because two X chromosomes are needed to produce ovaries, these glands are not produced either. But even though people with Turner syndrome have no gonads at all, their biological development is female, with typical female internal sex organs and external genitalia—which proves that fetuses do not require ovaries or the hormones they produce to develop as females. Individuals with Turner syndrome take supplemental estrogen to induce puberty and sexual maturation, but without ovaries they cannot produce ova.

EXTERNAL GENITALIA The external genitalia are the visible sex organs, including the penis and scrotum in males and the labia, clitoris, and outer part of the vagina in females. (See Figure 10.3.) As we just saw, the external genitalia do not need to be stimulated by female sex hormones to become female. In the presence of dihydrotestosterone, the external genitalia will become male. Thus, the development of a person's external genitalia is determined by the presence or absence of an androgen, which explains why people with Turner syndrome have female external genitalia even though they lack ovaries. People with androgen insensitivity syndrome have female external genitalia too, because without androgen receptors, their cells cannot respond to the androgens produced by their testes.

Figure 10.4 summarizes the factors that control the development of the gonads, internal sex organs, and genitalia.

Sexual Maturation

LO 10.3 Compare the organizational effects of hormones on primary sex characteristics and the activational effects on secondary sex characteristics.

The *primary* sex characteristics are influenced by organizational effects of hormones and include the gonads, internal sex organs, and external genitalia. These structures are present at birth. The *secondary* sex characteristics, such as

Figure 10.3 Development of the External Genitalia

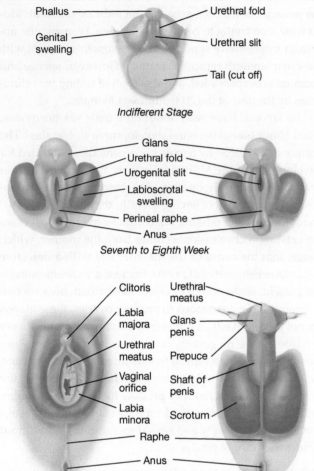

Indifferent Stage

Seventh to Eighth Week

Twelfth Week

(Adapted from Spaulding, M. H., The development of the external genitalia in the human embryo, in G. L. Streeter (ed.), *Contributions to Embryology*, Vol. 13, p. 67–88. Washington, DC: Carnegie Institute of Washington, 1921.)

enlarged breasts and widened hips or a beard and deep voice, are influenced by the activational effects of hormones and do not appear until puberty. At puberty the gonads are stimulated to produce their hormones, and these hormones

cause the person to mature sexually. The onset of puberty occurs when cells in the hypothalamus secrete **gonadotropin-releasing hormones (GnRH),** which stimulate the production and release of two **gonadotropic hormones** by the anterior pituitary gland. The gonadotropic hormones stimulate the gonads to produce *their* hormones, which are ultimately responsible for sexual maturation. (See Figure 10.5.)

The two gonadotropic hormones are **follicle stimulating hormone (FSH)** and **luteinizing hormone (LH),** named for the effects they produce in a female (production of a *follicle* and its subsequent *luteinization,* to be described in the next section of this chapter). However, the same hormones are produced in males, where they stimulate the testes to produce sperms and to secrete testosterone. If male and female pituitary glands are exchanged in rats, the ovaries and testes respond perfectly to the hormones secreted by the new glands (Harris and Jacobsohn, 1951–1952).

The secretion of GnRH, which directs the production of the gonadotropic hormones, which in turn stimulate puberty and production of the sex hormones secreted by the gonads, is under the control of another peptide: **kisspeptin.** (The unusual name of this peptide refers to Hershey, Pennsylvania, the location of the laboratory where the gene that encodes for the peptide was discovered. This city is also the home of the company that makes Hershey's Kisses, a chocolate candy.) Kisspeptin, produced by neurons in the arcuate nucleus of the hypothalamus, is essential for the initiation of puberty and the maintenance of male and female reproductive ability (Millar et al., 2010).

For over a century the age at which children (particularly girls) reach puberty has been diminishing in developed countries, presumably because of improved nutrition (Foster and Nagatani, 1999). Girls who remain unusually thin through exercise and diet tend to reach puberty later, while girls who are obese tend to reach puberty earlier (Frisch, 1990). As we will see in Chapter 12, *leptin,* a peptide hormone secreted by well-nourished fat cells, provides an important signal to the brain concerning the amount of fat tissue in the

Figure 10.4 Hormonal Control of Development of the Internal Sex Organs

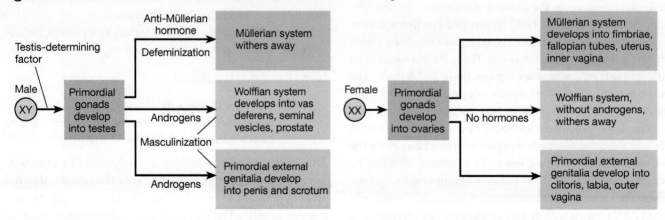

Figure 10.5 Sexual Maturation

Puberty is initiated when the hypothalamus secretes gonadotropin-releasing hormones, which activate the secretion of gonadotropic hormones by the anterior pituitary gland.

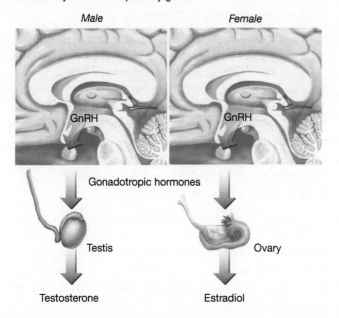

hormones known as **estrogens.** The testes produce testosterone, an androgen. Both types of glands also produce a small amount of the primary hormones of the other sex. The gonadal steroids affect many parts of the body. Both estradiol and androgens initiate closure of the growing portions of the bones and thus halt skeletal growth. In females, estradiol also causes breast development, growth of the lining of the uterus, changes in the deposition of body fat, and maturation of the female genitalia. In males, androgens stimulate growth of facial, axillary (underarm), and pubic hair; lower the voice; alter the hairline on the head (often causing baldness later in life); stimulate muscular development; and cause genital growth. This description leaves out two of the female secondary characteristics: axillary and pubic hair. These characteristics are produced not by estradiol but rather by androgens secreted by the cortex of the adrenal glands. Even a male who is castrated before puberty (whose testes are removed) will grow axillary and pubic hair, stimulated by his own adrenal androgens. A list of the principal sex hormones and examples of their effects are presented in Table 10.1. Note that some of these effects are discussed later in this chapter.

The bipotentiality of some of the secondary sex characteristics remains throughout life. If a man is treated with an estrogen (for example, to control an androgen dependent tumor), he will grow breasts, and his facial hair will become finer and softer. However, his voice will remain low, because the enlargement of the larynx is permanent. Conversely, a woman who receives high levels of an androgen (usually from a tumor that secretes androgens) will grow a beard, and her voice will become lower.

body. If body fat increases, the level of leptin in the blood increases and signals the brain to suppress appetite. This hormone also plays a role in determining the onset of puberty in females: It acts on leptin receptors found on kisspeptin-secreting neurons in the arcuate nucleus (Smith et al., 2006).

In response to the gonadotropic hormones (usually called *gonadotropins*) the gonads secrete steroid sex hormones. The ovaries produce **estradiol,** one of a class of

Table 10.1 Classification of Sex Hormones

Class	Principal Hormone in Humans (Where Produced)	Examples of Effects
Androgens	Testosterone (testes)	Development of Wolffian system; production of sperms; growth of facial, pubic, and axillary hair; muscular development; enlargement of larynx; inhibition of bone growth; sex drive in men (and women?)
	Dihydrotestosterone (produced from testosterone by action of 5α reductase)	Maturation of male external genitalia
	Androstenedione (adrenal glands)	In women, growth of pubic and axillary hair; less important than testosterone and dihydrotestosterone in men
Estrogens	Estradiol (ovaries)	Maturation of female genitalia; growth of breasts; alterations in fat deposits; growth of uterine lining; inhibition of bone growth; sex drive in women (?)
Gestagens	Progesterone (ovaries)	Maintenance of uterine lining
Hypothalamic hormones	Gonadotropin-releasing hormone (hypothalamus)	Secretion of gonadotropins
Gonadotropins	Follicle-stimulating hormone (anterior pituitary)	Development of ovarian follicle
	Luteinizing hormone (anterior pituitary)	Ovulation; development of corpus luteum
Other hormones	Prolactin (anterior pituitary)	Milk production; male refractory period (?)
	Oxytocin (posterior pituitary)	Milk ejection; orgasm; pair bonding (especially females); bonding with infants
	Vasopressin (posterior pituitary)	Pair bonding (especially males)

Section Review

Sexual Development

LO 10.1 Describe the processes of gamete production and fertilization.

Gametes are produced via meiosis, a cell division process that results in cells that contain one member of each pair of chromosomes. The development of a human begins at the time of fertilization, when a single sperm and ovum join, sharing their 23 single chromosomes to reconstitute the 23 pairs.

LO 10.2 Explain how gonads, internal sex organs, and external genitalia develop.

The SRY gene controls the development of testes from undifferentiated gonads. Without this gene, ovaries develop. Organizational effects of hormones control the development of internal sex organs. The Y chromosome controls the development of glands that produce male sex hormones, which cause the development of the Wolffian system. Without exposure to these hormones, the Müllerian system develops. In the presence of dihydrotestosterone, male external genitalia develop. Without exposure to this hormone, female genitalia develop.

LO 10.3 Compare the organizational effects of hormones on primary sex characteristics and the activational effects on secondary sex characteristics.

Masculinization and defeminization are referred to as *organizational* effects of hormones; *activational* effects occur after development is complete. Organizational effects impact the initial development of sex organs and genitalia (primary sex characteristics that are present at birth). Activational effects occur at puberty as a result of mature gonads that produce sex hormones.

Thought Question

Suppose that people could determine the biological sex of their child, say, by having one of the would-be parents take a drug before conceiving the baby. What would the consequences be?

Hormonal Control of Sexual Behavior

Hormones are responsible for sexual dimorphism in the structure of the body and its organs. Hormones have organizational and activational effects on the internal sex organs, genitals, and secondary sex characteristics. All of these effects influence a person's behavior. But hormones do more than just give us masculine or feminine bodies; they also affect behavior by interacting directly with the nervous system. Androgens that are present during prenatal development affect the development of the nervous system. In addition, both male and female sex hormones have activational effects on the adult nervous system that influence both physiological processes and behavior. This section considers how some of these hormones affect female reproductive cycles, sexual behavior of laboratory animals, organizational effects of androgens, and human sexual behavior. This section also includes a discussion of a closely related topic—pheromones.

Hormonal Control of Female Reproductive Cycles

LO 10.4 Summarize the roles of hormones in phases of the menstrual cycle.

The reproductive cycle of female primates is called a **menstrual cycle.** Females of other species of mammals also have reproductive cycles, called **estrous cycles.** The primary feature that distinguishes menstrual cycles from estrous cycles is the monthly growth and loss of the lining of the uterus. The other features are approximately the same, except that the estrous cycle of other mammals can be shorter. For example, the estrous cycle of rats takes four days. Also, the sexual behavior of other female mammals with estrous cycles is linked to ovulation, whereas most female primates can mate at any time during their menstrual cycle.

Menstrual cycles and estrous cycles consist of a sequence of events that are controlled by hormonal secretions of the pituitary gland and ovaries. These glands interact, the secretions of one affecting those of the other. A cycle begins with the secretion of gonadotropins by the anterior pituitary gland. These hormones (especially FSH) stimulate the growth of **ovarian follicles,** small spheres of epithelial cells surrounding each ovum. Women normally produce one ovarian follicle each month; if two are produced and fertilized, dizygotic (fraternal) twins will develop. Monozygotic (identical) twins develop from the same ovum and follicle. As ovarian follicles mature, they secrete estradiol, which causes growth of the lining of the uterus in preparation for implantation of the ovum, should it be fertilized by a sperm. Feedback from the increasing level of estradiol eventually triggers the release of a surge of LH by the anterior pituitary gland. Figure 10.6 shows how the uterine changes correspond with hormone changes.

The LH surge causes *ovulation*: The ovarian follicle ruptures, releasing the ovum. Under the continued influence of LH, the ruptured ovarian follicle becomes a **corpus luteum** which produces estradiol and **progesterone.** (Look again at Figure 10.6.) The latter hormone promotes pregnancy

Figure 10.6 Neuroendocrine Control of the Menstrual Cycle

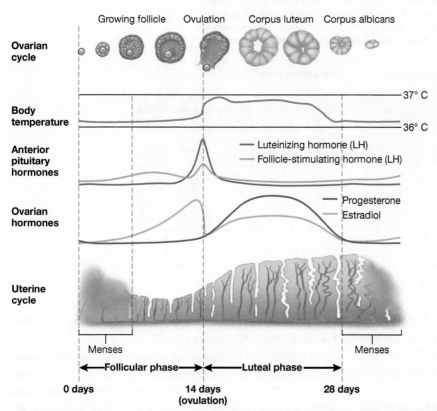

Growing follicle   Ovulation   Corpus luteum   Corpus albicans

Ovarian cycle

Body temperature — 37° C / — 36° C

Anterior pituitary hormones
— Luteinizing hormone (LH)
— Follicle-stimulating hormone (LH)

Ovarian hormones
— Progesterone
— Estradiol

Uterine cycle

Menses   Menses
◄—Follicular phase—►◄—Luteal phase—►
0 days   14 days   28 days
              (ovulation)

(*gestation*). It maintains the lining of the uterus, and it inhibits the ovaries from producing another follicle. Meanwhile, the ovum enters one of the fallopian tubes and begins its progress toward the uterus. If it meets sperm cells during its travel down the fallopian tube and becomes fertilized, it begins to divide, and several days later it will implant itself into the uterine wall.

If the ovum is not fertilized or if it is fertilized too late to develop sufficiently by the time it gets to the uterus, the corpus luteum will stop producing estradiol and progesterone, and then the lining of the walls of the uterus will slough off. At this point, menstruation will commence.

Hormonal Control of Sexual Behavior of Laboratory Animals

LO 10.5 **Compare the roles of hormones in sexual behavior of male and female rodents.**

The interactions between sex hormones and the human brain can be difficult to study. Often, we must turn to two sources of information: experiments with animals and various developmental disorders in humans. We will first consider the evidence gathered from research with laboratory animals.

MALES Male sexual behavior is varied, although the essential features of *intromission* (entry of the penis into the female's vagina), *pelvic thrusting* (rhythmic movement of the hindquarters, causing genital friction), and *ejaculation* (discharge of semen) are characteristic of all male mammals, including rats and mice.

The sexual behavior of rats has been studied more than that of any other laboratory animal (Hull and Dominguez, 2007). Male rats reach sexual maturity between 45 and 75 days of age. When an adult male rat encounters a receptive female, he will spend some time nuzzling her and sniffing her face and genitals, mount her, and engage in several rapid, shallow pelvic thrusts. If he detects her vagina, he will make a deeper thrust, achieve intromission, and then dismount. He will mount her several times, achieving intromission on most of the mountings. After eight to fifteen intromissions approximately 1 minute apart (each lasting only about one-quarter of a second), the male will ejaculate.

After ejaculating, the male refrains from sexual activity for a period of time (minutes, in the rat). Most mammals will return to copulate several times, finally showing a longer pause, called a **refractory period.** In some mammals, if a male is presented with a novel female during a refractory period, he begins to respond quickly—often as fast as he did in his initial contact with the first female. Successive introductions of new females can maintain this behavior. This phenomenon is important in species in which a single male inseminates all the females in a group. Species with approximately equal numbers of reproductively active males and females are less likely to engage in this behavior. This effect of introducing novel females is called the **Coolidge effect.**

Sexual behavior of male rodents depends on testosterone, a fact that has long been recognized (Bermant and Davidson, 1974). If a male rat is castrated (that is, if his testes are removed), his sexual activity eventually ceases. However, the behavior can be reinstated by injections of testosterone. The neural basis of this activational effect will be described later in this chapter.

Other hormones play a role in male sexual behavior. **Oxytocin** is a hormone produced by the posterior pituitary gland that contracts the milk ducts and thus causes milk ejection in lactating females. It is also produced in males, where it plays no role in lactation. Oxytocin is released at the time of orgasm in both males and females and appears to contribute to the contractions of the smooth muscle in the male ejaculatory system and of the vagina and uterus (Carmichael et al., 1987; Carter, 1992). The effects of this hormonal release can be seen in lactating women, who may release some milk at the time of orgasm. Oxytocin plays an important role in establishment of pair bonding, a phenomenon that will be discussed later in this chapter.

Figure 10.7 Comparison of Menstrual Cycle of Humans and Estrous Cycle of Rats

(a) The human menstrual cycle consists of two phases (follicular and luteal) which are each approximately 14 days long. Ovulation occurs at the midpoint of the cycle. (b) The rat estrous cycle consists of four phases (metestrus, diestrus, proestrus and estrus) which are each approximately one day long. Ovulation occurs during the estrus phase. Notice that the estrus phase is shown twice in the figure to demonstrate the cyclic pattern of the phases.

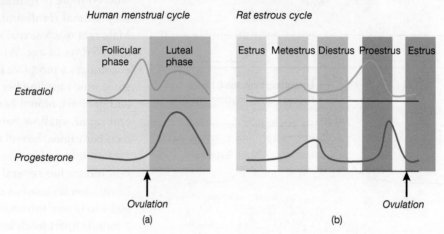

FEMALES Like males, female mammals also display a variety of sexual behaviors. In some rodent species, such as hamsters, females adopt a posture that exposes her genitals to the male during a receptive period in the estrous cycle, called **estrus**. This behavior is called the **lordosis** response. The female will also move her tail away (if she has one) and stand rigidly enough to support the weight of the male. The behavior of a female rodent in *initiating* copulation is very active. If a male attempts to copulate with a nonreceptive rodent, the female will either actively flee or rebuff him. When the female is in a receptive state, she will often approach the male, nuzzle him, sniff his genitals, and show behaviors characteristic of her species. For example, a receptive female rat will exhibit quick, short, hopping movements and rapid ear wiggling, which most male rats find irresistible (McClintock and Adler, 1978).

Sexual behavior of female rodents depends on the gonadal hormones present during estrus: estradiol and progesterone. In rats, estradiol increases about 40 hours before the female becomes receptive; just before receptivity occurs, the corpus luteum begins secreting large quantities of progesterone (Feder, 1981). Ovariectomized rats (rats whose ovaries have been removed) are not sexually receptive. Although sexual receptivity can be produced in ovariectomized rodents by administering large doses of estradiol alone, the most effective treatment duplicates the normal sequence of hormones: a small amount of estradiol, followed by progesterone. Progesterone alone is ineffective; thus, the estradiol "primes" its effectiveness. Priming with estradiol takes about 16–24 hours, after which an injection of progesterone produces receptive behaviors within an hour (Takahashi, 1990). The neural mechanisms that are responsible for these effects will be described later in this chapter. The four phases of the rat estrous cycle (estrus, metestrus, diestrus

and proestrus), along with their corresponding hormone levels, are presented in Figure 10.7.

Studies with targeted mutations confirm the importance of estradiol and progesterone on sexual behavior in female rodents. Rissman et al., (1997) found that female mice without estrogen receptors were unreceptive to males even after treatment with estradiol and progesterone, and Lydon et al. (1995) observed similar effects in female mice without progesterone receptors.

The sequence of estradiol followed by progesterone has three effects on female rats: It increases their receptivity, their proceptivity, and their attractiveness. *Receptivity* refers to a female's ability and willingness to copulate by displaying lordosis when a male attempts to mount her. *Proceptivity* refers to a female's interest in copulation, as shown by seeking out a male and engaging in behaviors that tend to increase his sexual interest. *Attractiveness* refers to physiological and behavioral changes in the female that affect the male. The male rat (along with many other male mammals) is most responsive to females who are in the estrus phase of the estrous cycle ("in heat"). Males will ignore a female whose ovaries have been removed, but injections of estradiol and progesterone will restore her attractiveness (and also change her behavior toward the male). The stimuli that increase a male rat's sexual interest include her odor and her behavior. In some species, visible changes, such as swollen skin in the genital region of a female monkey, also affect sex appeal.

Women do not show obvious physical changes during the fertile period of their menstrual cycle, but some subtle changes do occur. Roberts et al., (2004) took photos of women's faces during fertile and nonfertile periods of their menstrual cycle and found that both men and women judged the photos taken during the fertile period to be more attractive than those taken during a nonfertile period. (The

Figure 10.8 Female Faces When Fertile and Not Fertile

This graph shows the mean preferences for fertile phase over luteal phase images of faces of the same woman. In this sample, fertile images were preferred more than expected by chance by both male and female raters.

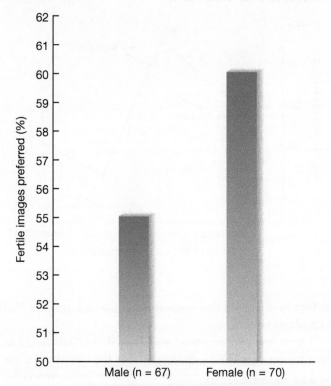

(Roberts, S. C., Havlicek, J., Flegr, J., Hruskova, M., Little, A. C., Jones, B. C., and Petrie, M. Female facial attractiveness increases during the fertile phase of the menstrual cycle. *Proceedings of the Royal Society of London B: Biological Sciences*, 2004, *271*(Suppl 5), S270–S272.)

women whose pictures were taken were not told the object of the study until afterward, to prevent them from unknowingly changing their facial expressions in a way that might bias the results.) (See Figure 10.8.)

Organizational Effects of Androgens on Behavior: Masculinization and Defeminization

LO 10.6 **Contrast behavioral masculinization and defeminization in rodents.**

If a rodent's brain is *not* exposed to androgens during a critical period of development, the animal will engage in female sexual behavior as an adult (if the animal is then given estradiol and progesterone). This critical time comes shortly after birth for rats and for several other species of rodents that are born in a rather immature condition. Thus, if a male rat is castrated immediately after birth, permitted to grow to adulthood, and then given injections of estradiol and progesterone, it will respond to the presence of another

male by displaying female-like behavior and lordosis (Blaustein and Olster, 1989).

In contrast, if a rodent brain is exposed to androgens during development, two phenomena occur: behavioral defeminization and behavioral masculinization. *Behavioral defeminization* refers to the organizational effect of androgens that prevents the animal from displaying female sexual behavior in adulthood. As we shall see later, this effect is accomplished by suppressing the development of neural circuits controlling female sexual behavior. For example, if a female rodent is ovariectomized and given an injection of testosterone immediately after birth, she will *not* respond to a male rat when, as an adult, she is given injections of estradiol and progesterone. *Behavioral masculinization* refers to the organizational effect of androgens that enables animals to engage in male sexual behavior in adulthood. This effect is accomplished by stimulating the development of neural circuits controlling male sexual behavior. For example, if the female rodent in the previous example is given testosterone in adulthood rather than estradiol and progesterone, she will mount and attempt to copulate with a receptive female. (See Breedlove, 1992, and Carter, 1992, for references to specific studies.) (See Figure 10.9.)

Human Sexual Behavior

LO 10.7 **Compare the activational effects of hormones on sexual behavior of human males and females.**

Human sexual behavior, like that of other mammals, is influenced by activational effects of gonadal hormones and, almost certainly, by organizational effects as well.

Figure 10.9 Organizational Effects of Testosterone

Around the time of birth, testosterone masculinizes and defeminizes rodents' sexual behavior.

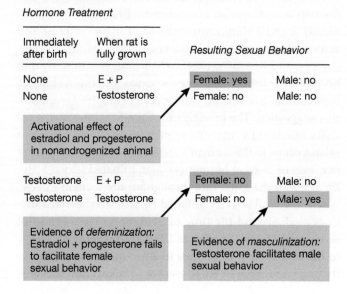

If hormones have organizational effects on human sexual behavior, they must exert these effects by altering the development of the brain. Although there is good evidence that prenatal exposure to androgens affects development of the human brain, the consequences of this exposure are not yet fully understood. The evidence pertaining to these issues is discussed later, in a section on sexual orientation.

ACTIVATIONAL EFFECTS OF SEX HORMONES IN WOMEN As we saw, the sexual behavior of most female mammals other than higher primates is controlled by the ovarian hormones estradiol and progesterone. (In some species, such as cats and rabbits, only estradiol is necessary.) As Wallen (1990) points out, the ovarian hormones control not only the interest of an estrous female in mating but also her ability to mate. A male rat cannot copulate with a female rat that is not in estrus. The female's lordosis response would not occur, and the male would be unable to achieve intromission. Thus, the evolutionary process in rats seems to have selected animals that mate only at a time when the female is able to become pregnant. In higher primates (including our own species) the ability to mate is not controlled by ovarian hormones. There are no physical barriers to sexual intercourse during any part of the menstrual cycle.

Although ovarian hormones do not *control* women's sexual activity, they may still have an influence on women's sexual interest. Early studies reported that fluctuations in the level of ovarian hormones had only a minor effect on women's sexual interest (Adams et al., 1978; Morris et al., 1987). However, the early studies almost all involved married women living with their husbands in relationships in which sexual activity could be initiated by either partner (Wallen, 1990). Even if the women were not interested in sexual activity on a given day, they may have engaged in this behavior for other reasons, such as their affection for their partners. Thus, changes in sexual interest and arousability might not always be reflected in changes in sexual behavior.

A study of lesbian couples (whose menstrual cycles and fluctuations in ovarian hormones are likely to be synchronized) found a significant increase in sexual interest and activity during the middle portions of the women's cycles (Matteo and Rissman, 1984), which suggests that ovarian hormones *do* influence women's sexual interest. A study of heterosexual partners by Van Goozen et al., (1997) supports this suggestion. The investigators found that the sexual activity initiated by men and women showed very different relationships to the woman's menstrual cycle (and hence to her level of ovarian hormones). Men initiated sexual activity at about the same rate throughout the woman's cycle, whereas sexual activity initiated by women showed a distinct peak around the time of ovulation, when estradiol levels are highest. (See Figure 10.10.) Bullivant et al., (2004) found that women were more likely to initiate sexual activity and were more likely to engage in sexual fantasies just

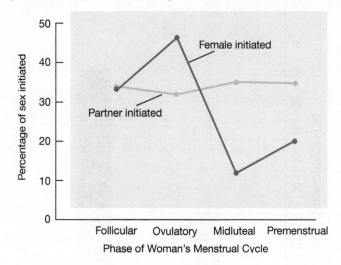

Figure 10.10 Sexual Activity of Heterosexual Couples
This graph shows the distribution of sexual activity initiated by the man and by the woman during the phases of the woman's menstrual cycle.
(Based on data from Wallen, 2001.)

before and during the surge in luteinizing hormone that stimulates ovulation.

A review by Gangestad and Thornhill (2008) suggests that women's sexuality changes across the menstrual cycle in a particular way. Women do not become indiscriminately more interested in sexual contact during their fertile period, which occurs around the time of ovulation. Instead, because they are more likely to become pregnant if they engage in unprotected sex at that time, they become more selective in mate choice. In particular, they become more attracted to male characteristics that might indicate high genetic quality (or did so in the evolution of our species). For example, Gangestad and Thornhill note that studies have shown that at midcycle, women's preference increases for the sight of facial and bodily masculinity, for masculine behavioral displays, for masculine vocal qualities, for androgen-related scents, and for body symmetry, which correlates with genetic fitness. (Of course, these changes are irrelevant for women in monogamous relationships—after all, they have already chosen their partners—or for women using hormone-based contraceptives such as birth-control pills, which stabilize levels of circulating hormones.)

The tendency is even more strongly expressed in female chimpanzees (Stumpf and Boesch, 2005). During their infertile periods, female chimpanzees initiate sexual activity with many males in their group. However, during their period of peak fertility, they become much more selective and tend to mate with the same few males—presumably, those that showed the most promise of being able to supply good genes for their offspring.

Wallen (2001) points out that although ovarian hormones may affect a woman's sexual interest, her behavior can be influenced by other factors as well. For example, if a woman does not want to become pregnant and does not have absolute confidence in her method of birth control, she may avoid sexual intercourse at midcycle, around the time of ovulation—even if her potential sexual interest is at a peak. In fact, Harvey (1987) found that women were more likely to engage in autosexual activity at this time. On the other hand, women who *want* to become pregnant are more likely to initiate sexual intercourse during the time when they are most likely to conceive.

Several studies suggest that women's sexual interest can be stimulated by androgens. There are two primary sources of androgens in the female body: the ovaries and the adrenal glands. The primary ovarian sex steroids are estradiol and progesterone, but these glands also produce testosterone. The adrenal glands produce another androgen, androstenedione, along with other adrenocortical steroids. However, the available evidence indicates that androgens by themselves (in the absence of estradiol) do not directly stimulate women's sexual interest but appear to amplify the effects of estradiol. For example, Shifren et al., (2000) studied ovariectomized women aged 31–56 who were receiving estrogen-replacement therapy. The women were given, in addition to the estrogen, either a placebo or testosterone, delivered through transdermal patches. Although the estrogen+placebo produced a positive effect, the addition of testosterone produced an even greater increase in sexual activity and rate of orgasm: The percentage of women who had sex fantasies, masturbated, and had intercourse increased two to three times over baseline levels, and these women reported higher levels of well-being.

ACTIVATIONAL EFFECTS OF SEX HORMONES IN MEN Although women and mammals with estrous cycles differ in their behavioral responsiveness to sex hormones, men resemble other mammals in their behavioral responsiveness to testosterone. Without testosterone, sperm production and sexual interest ceases. In a double-blind study, Bagatell et al., (1994) gave a placebo or a gonadotropin-releasing hormone (GnRH) antagonist to young male volunteers to suppress secretion of testicular androgens. Within two weeks, the participants who received the GnRH antagonist reported a decrease in sexual interest, sexual fantasy, and intercourse. Men who received replacement doses of testosterone along with the antagonist did not show these changes.

The decline of sexual activity after castration is variable. As reported by Money and Ehrhardt (1972), some men decrease sexual activity immediately, whereas others show a slow, gradual decline over several years. Wallen and his colleagues (Wallen et al., 1991; Wallen, 2001) injected a GnRH antagonist in seven adult male rhesus monkeys that were part of a larger group. The injection suppressed testosterone secretion, and sexual behavior declined after one week. However, the decline was related to the animal's social rank and sexual experience: More sexually experienced, high-ranking males continued to copulate. In fact, the highest-ranking male continued to copulate and ejaculate at the same rate as before, even though his testosterone secretion was suppressed for almost eight weeks. The mounting behavior of the lowest ranking monkey completely ceased and did not resume until testosterone secretion recovered from the anti-GnRH treatment.

Testosterone not only affects sexual activity but also is affected by it—or even by thinking about it. A scientist stationed on a remote island (Anonymous, 1970) removed his beard with an electric shaver each day and weighed the clippings. Just before he left for visits to the mainland (and to the company of a female companion), his beard began growing faster. Because rate of beard growth is related to androgen levels, the effect indicates that his anticipation of sexual activity stimulated testosterone production.

Women show similar changes in testosterone level in anticipation of sexual activity. Hamilton and Meston (2010) studied women in long-distance relationships who saw their romantic partners only intermittently. The investigators found that the women's testosterone levels in saliva increased the day before they rejoined their partners—presumably in anticipation of their reunion. These findings support the conclusions from the previous subsection that testosterone, as well as estradiol, plays a role in women's sexual interest and activity. In another study, Goldey and van Anders (2011) found that imagining a positive sexual encounter with an attractive person increased testosterone levels among women, but only those not taking hormone contraceptives. (See Figure 10.11.)

Effects of Pheromones

LO 10.8 Describe the roles of pheromones in reproductive behavior of humans and other animals.

Hormones transmit messages from one part of the body (the secreting gland) to another (the target tissue). Another class of chemicals, called **pheromones,** carries messages from one *animal* to another. Some of these chemicals, like hormones, affect reproductive behavior. Pheromones are released by one animal and directly affect the physiology or behavior of another. In mammalian species most pheromones are detected by means of specialized receptors that detect the presence of pheromone molecules, similar to olfaction.

As you learned in Chapter 7, detection of odors is accomplished by the olfactory bulbs, which constitute the primary olfactory system. However, many of the effects that pheromones have on reproductive cycles are mediated by another sensory organ—the **vomeronasal organ (VNO)**—which consists of a small group of sensory receptors arranged around a pouch connected by a duct to the nasal passage. The VNO, which is present in all orders of mammals except for cetaceans (whales and dolphins), projects to

Figure 10.11 Long-Distance Relationships and Testosterone Levels in Women

Testosterone levels increased in women anticipating sexual activity with a partner.

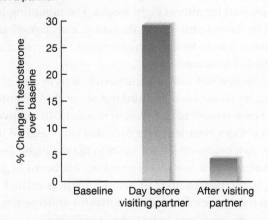

(Data from Hamilton, L. D., & Meston, C. M. The effects of partner togetherness on salivary testosterone in women in long distance relationships. *Hormones and Behavior*, 2010, *57*(2), 198–202.)

the **accessory olfactory bulb,** located immediately behind the olfactory bulb (Wysocki, 1979). (See Figure 10.12.) The VNO contains over 200 G-protein-linked receptor molecules that detect many of the chemicals that serve as pheromones (Dulac and Axel, 1995; Ryba and Tirindelli, 1997; Stowers and Marton, 2005). These receptor molecules are only distantly related to the ones present in the olfactory epithelium.

The accessory olfactory bulb sends axons to the **medial nucleus of the amygdala,** which in turn projects to the preoptic area and anterior hypothalamus and to the ventromedial nucleus of the hypothalamus. (As you learned in Chapter 7, so does the main olfactory bulb.) Thus, the neural circuit responsible for the effects of pheromones appears to involve these regions. As we shall see, the preoptic area, the medial amygdala, the ventromedial nucleus of the

Figure 10.12 The Rodent Accessory Olfactory

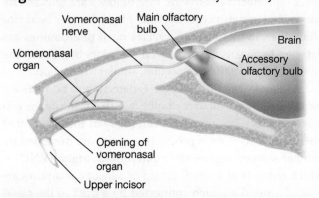

(Adapted from Wysocki, C. J., Neurobehavioral evidence for the involvement of the vomeronasal system in mammalian reproduction, *Neuroscience & Biobehavioral Reviews*, 1979, *3*, 301–341.)

Figure 10.13 The Amygdala of a Rat

This schematic of a cross section through a rat brain shows the location of the amygdala.

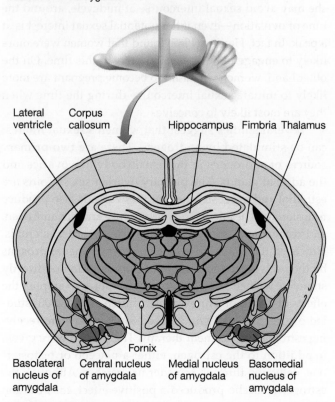

(Adapted from Swanson, L. W. *Brain Maps: Structure of the Rat Brain.* New York: Elsevier, 1992.)

hypothalamus, and the medial preoptic area all play important roles in reproductive behavior. (See Figure 10.13.)

Although the VNO can respond to some airborne molecules, it is primarily sensitive to nonvolatile compounds found in urine or other substances (Brennan and Keverne, 2004). Luo et al., (2003) found that neurons of the vomeronasal system responded only when the mice were actively investigating the other animal's face or anogenital region. In addition, the neurons selectively responded to different strains of mice and between male and female mice.

ANIMAL EXAMPLES He et al., (2008) investigated cells of the mouse VNO and reported that although many neurons were activated by mouse urine, only two or three responded uniquely to male urine, and approximately eight responded uniquely to female urine. It seems, then, that a small number of receptors are tuned specifically to chemicals secreted by males or females. Urine from different *individuals* produced different patterns of activity of large numbers of neurons, undoubtedly reflecting the existence of different concentrations of large numbers of chemicals in the animals' urine.

The VNO is essential for the ability of a rodent to identify the sex of another individual. If transduction of chemical information in the VNO is prevented by a knockout of a gene required for this process (TRPC2), mice can no longer distinguish between males and females (Stowers et al., 2002). Normally, when a male mouse smells another mouse, he approaches and sniffs the other mouse's face and anogenital region. In mammals, pheromones are found in urine, vaginal secretions, saliva, and tears. This investigatory behavior permits the animal to detect nonvolatile chemicals secreted by the other animal. If the other animal is a female in estrus, the male courts and mates with her. If it is an unfamiliar male, he attacks it. If it is a familiar male (say, one of its littermates), he will usually tolerate its presence. So the main olfactory system stimulates investigatory behavior when the presence of another mouse is detected, and information provided by the vomeronasal system determines the gender, estrous condition, and identity of the other animal. Without the information from the VNO, the animal indiscriminately displays sexual behavior. In contrast, if a male mouse is made anosmic (incapable of detecting odors) by removal of the olfactory bulbs, by a genetic knockout that prevents transduction of olfactory information in the main olfactory epithelium, or by application of a chemical that damages olfactory receptors, he will not approach and sniff another mouse and, consequently, will not attack or attempt to mate with it (Mandiyan et al., 2005; Wang et al., 2006).

The males of some species produce sex-attractant pheromones that affect the behavior of females. For example, a pheromone present in the saliva of boars (male pigs) elicits sexual behavior in sows. This response persists even after the sow's VNO is destroyed, which indicates that the main olfactory system can detect the pheromone and elicit the behavior (Dorries et al., 1997). Other male pheromones that attract females are also detected by the main olfactory system. For example, Mak et al., (2007) found that the odor of soiled bedding taken from the cage of a male mouse activated neurons in the main olfactory system and hippocampus of female mice. The odor even stimulated neurogenesis (production of new neurons); Mak et al. found new neurons in the olfactory bulb and hippocampus. Moreover, bedding from cages of dominant males stimulated neurogenesis more effectively than did bedding from subordinate males.

Pheromones can affect reproductive physiology or behavior. First, let us consider the effects on reproductive physiology. When groups of female mice are housed together, their estrous cycles slow down and eventually stop. This phenomenon is known as the **Lee-Boot effect** (van der Lee and Boot, 1955). If groups of females are exposed to the pheromones of a male (or of his urine), they begin cycling again, and their cycles tend to be synchronized. This phenomenon is known as the **Whitten effect** (Whitten, 1959). The **Vandenbergh effect** (Vandenbergh et al., 1975) is the acceleration of the onset of puberty in a female rodent caused by the pheromone of a male. Both the Whitten effect and the Vandenbergh effect are caused by a group of compounds that are present only in the urine of intact adult males (Ma et al., 1999; Novotny et al., 1999); the urine of a juvenile or castrated male has no effect. Thus, the production of the pheromone by a male requires the presence of testosterone.

The **Bruce effect** (Bruce, 1960a) occurs when a recently impregnated female mouse encounters a male mouse other than the one with which she mated, and the pregnancy is aborted. This effect, too, is caused by a substance secreted in the urine of intact males—but not of males that have been castrated. Thus, a male mouse that encounters a pregnant female is able to prevent the birth of offspring carrying another male's genes and subsequently impregnate the female himself. This phenomenon may be advantageous from the female's (and new male's) point of view. The fact that the new male has managed to take over the old male's territory indicates that he is likely to be healthier; therefore, his genes will contribute to offspring that are more likely to survive. (See Table 10.2.)

HUMAN EXAMPLES It appears that at least some pheromone-related phenomena occur in humans. McClintock (1971) studied the menstrual cycles of women attending an all-female college. She found that women who spent a large amount of time together tended to have synchronized cycles: Their menstrual periods began within a day or two of one another. In addition, women who regularly spent some time in the presence of men tended to have shorter cycles than those who rarely spent time with (smelled?) men.

Russell et al., (1980) obtained direct evidence that pheromones can synchronize women's menstrual cycles. The investigators collected daily samples of a woman's underarm sweat. They dissolved the samples in alcohol and swabbed them on the upper lips of a group of women three times each week, in the order in which they were originally taken. The cycles of the women who received the extract (but not those of control participants whose lips were swabbed with pure alcohol) began to synchronize with the cycle of the odor donor. These results were confirmed by a similar study

Table 10.2 Pheromones and Behavior

Effect of Pheromone	Description
Lee-Boot Effect	Estrous cycles stop in groups of female rodents living together
Whitten Effect	Groups of female rodents who are not cycling are exposed to male urine and begin cycling synchronously
Vandenbergh Effect	Acceleration of onset of puberty in female rodent exposed to odor of male
Bruce Effect	Exposure to urine of novel male results in failure of pregnancy in newly-pregnant female

by Stern and McClintock (1998), who found that compounds from the armpits of women that were taken around the time of ovulation lengthened other women's menstrual cycles, and compounds taken late in the cycle shortened them. Preti et al., (2003) performed a similar experiment but exposed women to extracts of sweat collected from men. They found that the extract (but not a placebo) advanced the onset of the next pulse of the women's LH secretion, reduced tension, and increased relaxation.

Several studies have found that compounds present in human sweat have different effects in men and women. Singh and Bronstad (2001) had men smell T-shirts that had been worn by women for several days. The men reported that shirts worn by women during the fertile phase of their menstrual cycle smelled more pleasant and more sexy than those worn during the nonfertile phase.

Jacob and McClintock (2000) found that the androgenic chemical *androstadienone (AND),* found in men's sweat, increases alertness and positive mood in women but decreases positive mood in men. Wyart et al., (2007) found that women who smelled AND showed higher levels of cortisol (an adrenal hormone involved in a variety of emotional behaviors) and reported a more positive mood and an increase in sexual arousal. Saxton et al., (2008) applied a solution containing AND or a placebo to women's upper lips and then had them participate in a "speed-dating" event organized by a private agency at a local bar. During the event, the women met and talked with several men, one at a time, for three minutes each. Afterward, the women were asked to rate the men's attractiveness. Most of the women exposed to AND found the men they met to be more attractive.

Men show a brain response to a chemical found in women's urine. A functional-imaging study by Savic et al., (2001) found that the estrogenic chemical *estratetraene (EST)* activated the paraventricular nucleus and dorsomedial hypothalamus in men but not in women.

What sensory organ detects the presence of human pheromones? Although humans have a small VNO located along the nasal septum (bridge of tissue between the nostrils) approximately 2 cm from the opening of the nostril (Garcia-Velasco and Mondragon, 1991), the human VNO is thought to be a vestigial, nonfunctional, organ. The density of neurons in the VNO is very sparse, and investigators have not found any neural connections from this organ to the brain (Doty, 2001). Evidence clearly shows that human reproductive physiology is affected by pheromones, but it appears that these chemical signals are detected by the "standard" olfactory system—the receptor cells in the olfactory epithelium—and not by cells in the VNO. In support of this conclusion, Savic et al., (2009) found that the odor EST activated the brains of men with intact olfactory systems, but not in men whose olfactory epithelium had been destroyed by nasal polyps but whose VNOs were intact.

Whether or not pheromones play an important role in sexual attraction in humans, the familiar odor of a sex partner probably has a positive effect on sexual arousal—just like the sight of a sex partner or the sound of his or her voice. We are not generally conscious of the fact, but we can identify other people on the basis of olfactory cues. For example, a study by Russell (1976) found that people were able to distinguish by odor between T-shirts that they had worn and those previously worn by other people. They could also tell whether the unknown owner of a T-shirt was male or female. Thus, it is likely that men and women can learn to be attracted by their partners' characteristic odors, just as they can learn to be attracted by the sound of their voice. In an instance like this, the odors are serving simply as sensory cues, not as pheromones.

Section Review

Hormonal Control of Sexual Behavior

LO 10.4 **Summarize the roles of hormones in phases of the menstrual cycle.**

The menstrual cycle begins with the maturation of one or more ovarian follicles, which occurs in response to the secretion of FSH by the anterior pituitary gland. As the ovarian follicle matures, it secretes estradiol, which causes the lining of the uterus to develop. When estradiol reaches a critical level, it causes the pituitary gland to secrete a surge of LH, triggering ovulation. The empty ovarian follicle becomes a corpus luteum, under the continued influence of LH, and secretes estradiol and progesterone. If pregnancy does not occur, the corpus luteum dies and stops producing hormones, and menstruation begins.

LO 10.5 **Compare the roles of hormones in sexual behavior of male and female rodents.**

Sexual behavior of male rodents depends on testosterone. Sexual behavior of female rodents depends on estradiol and progesterone. In rats, after being primed with estradiol, progesterone levels increase just before the onset of the receptive period. Both estradiol and progesterone are low in the estrus phase, and then increase moderately in the metestrus phase before decreasing again in diestrus. Both of these hormones increase more in the proestrus phase, which ends with ovulation. Levels of both hormones decline after ovulation and return to estrus levels. Oxytocin is released at the time of orgasm in both males and females and appears to contribute to the contractions of the smooth muscle in the male ejaculatory system and of the vagina and uterus.

LO 10.6 Contrast behavioral masculinization and defeminization in rodents.

In response to prenatal androgen exposure, behavioral defeminization occurs to prevent displaying female sexual behavior in adulthood and behavioral masculinization occurs to enable individuals to engage in male sexual behavior in adulthood.

LO 10.7 Compare the activational effects of hormones on sexual behavior of human males and females.

Testosterone has an activational effect on the sexual behavior of men. Women do not require estradiol or progesterone to experience sexual interest or to engage in sexual behavior. Some research suggests proceptivity may be related to ovarian hormones, even in higher primates. Studies with women suggest that variations in levels of ovarian hormones across the menstrual cycle affect sexual interest but that other factors (such as initiation of sexual activity by partners or a desire to avoid or attain pregnancy) can also affect sexual behavior. The presence of androgens may facilitate the effect of estradiol on women's sexual interest.

LO 10.8 Describe the roles of pheromones in reproductive behavior of humans and other animals.

Pheromones can affect sexual physiology and behavior. Odorants present in the urine of female mice affect their estrous cycles, lengthening and eventually stopping them (the Lee-Boot effect). Odorants present in the urine of male mice abolish these effects and cause the females' cycles to become synchronized (the Whitten effect). (Phenomena similar to the Lee-Boot effect and the Whitten effect also occur in women.) Odorants can also accelerate the onset of puberty in females (the Vandenbergh effect). In addition, the odor of the urine from a male other than the one that impregnated a female mouse will cause her to abort (the Bruce effect). Connections between the olfactory system and the amygdala appear to be important in stimulating male sexual behavior. The main olfactory system detects volatile chemicals that signal the presence of another animal, and the VNO determines the other animal's sex, estrous condition, and identity.

Pheromones present in the underarm sweat of both men and women affect women's menstrual cycles, and substances present in male sweat improve women's mood. Because the human VNO does not appear to have sensory functions, these effects must be mediated by the main olfactory bulb. The search for sex attractant pheromones in humans has not produced definitive results, but the odors of AND (produced by males) and EST (produced by females) have effects on brain activity and changes in ratings of people's attractiveness. Research also indicates that we may recognize our sex partners by their odors.

Thought Question

Imagine that you have accepted a research position working in a lab that studies human pheromones. What research questions would you be most interested in studying and why?

Neural Control of Sexual Behavior

The control of sexual behavior—at least in laboratory animals—involves different neural mechanisms in males and females. This section describes these mechanisms.

Males

LO 10.9 Identify the role of spinal and brain mechanisms in male sexual behavior.

Both spinal and brain mechanisms are important in the neural control of male sexual behavior. These mechanisms coordinate to control male sexual posturing, erection, and ejaculation.

SPINAL MECHANISMS Some sexual responses are controlled by neural circuits contained within the spinal cord. Men with injuries that totally transect the spinal cord have become fathers when their wives have been artificially inseminated with semen obtained by mechanical stimulation (Hart, 1978). Brackett et al., (1998) found that vibratory stimulation of the penis successfully elicited ejaculation in most men with complete spinal cord transection above the tenth thoracic segment, which suggests that the circuits in the spinal cord that control the ejaculatory response are located below this region. Because the spinal damage prevents sensory information from reaching the brain, these men are unable to feel the stimulation and do not experience an orgasm.

Ejaculation occurs after sufficient amount of tactile stimulation of an erect penis causes activation of the *spinal ejaculation generator.* Coolen and her colleagues (Coolen, 2005; Coolen et al., 2004) have identified a group of neurons in the lumbar region of the rat spinal cord that appear to constitute a critical part of the spinal ejaculation generator. These neurons project to adjacent neurons in the spinal cord that control the sympathetic and parasympathetic mechanisms that result in emission and ejaculation of semen. They also project to a nucleus in a specific part of the posterior intralaminar thalamus, so the investigators refer to them as *lumbar spinothalamic (LSt) cells.* This projection presumably provides input to the brain that constitutes part of the pleasurable orgasmic sensation. In rats, ejaculation, but not mounts or intromissions without ejaculation, activates these neurons. Specific destruction of these neurons with a toxin completely abolishes ejaculation but does not impair the animal's ability to produce an erection, mount an estrous female, and achieve intromission.

BRAIN MECHANISMS As we just saw, erection and ejaculation are controlled by circuits of neurons that reside in the spinal cord. However, brain mechanisms have both excitatory and inhibitory control of these circuits. Although tactile stimulation of a man's genitals can stimulate erection and ejaculation, these responses can be inhibited by the context. For example, the outcomes of tactile stimulation of a man's penis will have different outcomes when his physician is carrying out physical examination or when his partner touches him while they are lying in bed. In addition, a man's penis can become erect when he sees his partner or has erotic thoughts—even when his penis is not being touched. Thus, there must be brain mechanisms that can activate or suppress the spinal mechanisms that control genital reflexes.

The **medial preoptic area (MPA)**, located just rostral to the hypothalamus, is the forebrain region most critical for male sexual behavior. (As we will see later in this chapter, it is also critical for other sexually dimorphic behavior, including maternal behavior.) Electrical stimulation of this region elicits male copulatory behavior (Malsbury, 1971), and sexual activity increases the firing rate of single neurons in the MPA (Shimura et al., 1994; Mas, 1995). In addition, the act of copulation activates neurons in the MPA (Oaknin et al., 1989; Robertson et al., 1991; Wood and Newman, 1993). Dominguez et al., (2006) found that mating increased the release of glutamate in the MPA and that infusion of glutamate into the MPA increased the frequency of ejaculation. Finally, destruction of the MPA abolishes male sexual behavior (Heimer and Larsson, 1966/1967).

The organizational effects of androgens are responsible for sexual dimorphisms in brain structure. Gorski et al., (1978) discovered a nucleus within the MPA of the rat that is three to seven times larger in males than in females. This area is called (appropriately enough) the **sexually dimorphic nucleus (SDN)** of the preoptic area. (This brain region, which is called the uncinate nucleus in humans, is sexually dimorphic in our species as well and involved in gender identity.) The size of this nucleus is controlled by the amount of androgens present during fetal development. According to Rhees et al., (1990a, 1990b), the critical period for masculinization of the SDN appears to start on the eighteenth day of gestation and end once the animals are five days old. (Normally, rats are born on the twenty-second day of gestation.) De Jonge et al., (1989) found that lesions of the SDN decrease masculine sexual behavior. (See Figure 10.14.)

Androgens also exert their activational effects on neurons in the MPA and associated brain regions. If a male rodent is castrated in adulthood, its sexual behavior will cease. However, the behavior can be reinstated by implanting a small amount of testosterone directly into the MPA or in two regions whose axons project to the MPA: the central tegmental field and the medial amygdala (Coolen and Wood, 1999; Sipos and Nyby, 1996). Both of these regions contain a high concentration of androgen receptors in the male rat brain (Cottingham and Pfaff, 1986).

As we saw earlier in this chapter, the primary and accessory olfactory systems play important roles in reproductive behavior. Both of these systems send axons to the medial nucleus of the amygdala, which in turn sends axons to the MPA. Several studies (for example, Heeb and Yahr, 2000; Lehman and Winans, 1982) have found that lesions of the medial amygdala abolished the sexual behavior of male rodents, presumably because the lesions disrupted the activating effects of pheromones on the MPA. The medial amygdala, like the MPA, is sexually dimorphic: One region within this structure (which contains an especially high concentration of androgen receptors) is 85 percent larger in male rats than in female rats (Hines et al., 1992). The MPA also receives somatosensory information from the genitals through connections with the central tegmental field of the midbrain and the medial amygdala. The act of copulation activates neurons in both of these regions (Gréco et al., 1998).

As we saw in the previous subsection, the lumbar region of the spinal cord contains a group of neurons that play a critical role in ejaculation (Coolen et al., 2004). Anatomical tracing studies suggest that the most important connections between the MPA and the spinal ejaculation generator are accomplished through the **periaqueductal gray matter (PAG)** of the midbrain and the **nucleus paragigantocellularis (nPGi)** of the medulla (Marson and McKenna, 1996; Normandin and Murphy, 2008). The nPGi normally inhibits spinal cord sexual reflexes, so one of the tasks of the pathway originating in the MPA is to suppress this inhibition. The MPA suppresses the nPGi directly through an inhibitory

Figure 10.14 Preoptic Area of the Rat Brain

This figure shows the preoptic area of a rat brain in (a) a typical male, (b) a typical female, and (c) an androgenized female, given an injection of testosterone shortly after birth. SDN-POA = sexually dimorphic nucleus of the preoptic area; OC = optic chiasm; V = third ventricle; SCN = suprachiasmatic nucleus; AC = anterior commissure.

(Based on Gorski, R. A., in Neuroendocrine Perspectives, Vol. 2, edited by E. E. Müller and R. M. MacLeod. Amsterdam: Elsevier-North Holland, 1983.)

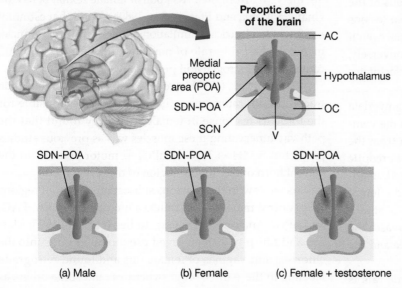

pathway and does so indirectly by inhibiting the activity of the PAG, which normally excites the nPGi.

The inhibitory connections between neurons of the nPGi and those of the spinal ejaculation generator are serotonergic. As Marson and McKenna (1992) showed, application of serotonin (5-HT) to the spinal cord suppresses ejaculation.

This connection may explain a well-known side effect of specific serotonin reuptake inhibitors (SSRIs). Men who take SSRIs as a treatment for depression often report that they have no trouble attaining an erection but have difficulty achieving an ejaculation. Presumably, the action of the drug as an agonist at the serotonergic synapses in the spinal cord increases the inhibitory influence of nPGi on the spinal ejaculation generator.

Figure 10.15 summarizes the evidence for brain regions involved in neural control of male sexual behavior presented so far in this section.

A functional-imaging study by Holstege et al., (2003b) examined the pattern of brain activation during ejaculation in men that was elicited by the men's female partners by means of manual stimulation. Ejaculation was accompanied by neural activity in many brain regions, including the junction between the midbrain and the diencephalon, which includes the ventral tegmental area (probably involved in the pleasurable, reinforcing effects of orgasm), other midbrain regions, several thalamic nuclei, the lateral putamen (part of the basal ganglia), and the cerebellum. *Decreased* activity was seen in the amygdala and the nearby entorhinal cortex. As we will see in Chapter 11, the amygdala is involved in defensive behavior and in negative emotions such as fear and anxiety—and these emotions certainly interfere with erection and ejaculation. Decreased activation is also seen in this structure when people who are deeply in love see pictures of their loved one (Bartels and Zeki, 2000, 2004).

Figure 10.15 Male Sexual Behavior

This schematic shows a possible explanation of the interacting excitatory effects of pheromones, genital stimulation, and testosterone on male sexual behavior. Black arrows represent excitatory pathways. Red arrows represent inhibitory pathways.

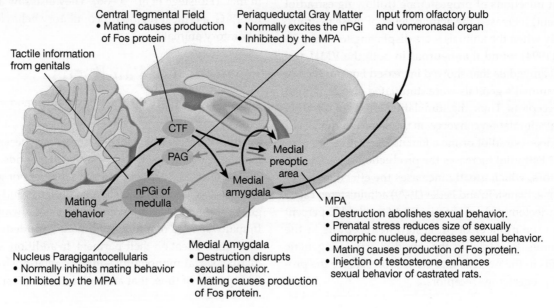

Females

LO 10.10 Identify the role of brain mechanisms in female sexual behavior.

Just as the MPA plays an essential role in male sex behavior, another region in the ventral forebrain plays a similar role in female sexual behavior: the **ventromedial nucleus of the hypothalamus (VMH)**. A female rat with bilateral lesions of the ventromedial nuclei will not display lordosis, even if she is treated with estradiol and progesterone. Conversely, electrical stimulation of the ventromedial nucleus facilitates female sexual behavior (Pfaff and Sakuma, 1979).

As we saw in the previous section, the medial amygdala of males receives chemosensory information from the vomeronasal system and somatosensory information from the genitals, and it sends efferent axons to the medial preoptic area. These connections are found in females as well. In addition, neurons in the medial amygdala also send efferent axons to the VMH. In fact, copulation or mechanical stimulation of the genitals or flanks of a female rat increases the activation of neurons in both the medial amygdala and the VMH (Pfaus et al., 1993; Tetel et al., 1993).

As we saw earlier, sexual behavior of female rats is activated by a priming dose of estradiol, followed by progesterone. The estrogen sets the stage, so to speak, and the progesterone stimulates the sexual behavior. Injections of these hormones directly into the VMH will stimulate sexual behavior even in females whose ovaries have been removed (Pleim and Barfield, 1988; Rubin and Barfield, 1980). If a chemical that blocks the production of progesterone receptors is injected into the VMH, the animal's sexual behavior is disrupted (Ogawa et al., 1994). Thus, estradiol and progesterone exert their effects on female sexual behavior by activating neurons in this nucleus.

Rose (1990) recorded from single neurons in the ventromedial hypothalamus of freely moving female hamsters and found that injections of progesterone (following estradiol pretreatment) increased the activity level of these neurons, particularly when the animals were displaying lordosis. Tetel et al., (1994) found that neurons in both the VMH and the medial amygdala that showed increased Fos production when the animal's genitals were stimulated also contained estrogen receptors. Thus, the stimulating effects of estradiol and genital stimulation converge on the same neurons.

How does estradiol prime a female's sensitivity to progesterone? Estradiol increases the production of progesterone receptors, which greatly increases the effectiveness of progesterone. Blaustein and Feder (1979) administered estradiol to ovariectomized guinea pigs and found a 150 percent increase in the number of progesterone receptors in the hypothalamus. Presumably, the estradiol activates genetic mechanisms in the nucleus that are responsible for the production of progesterone receptors.

The neurons of the ventromedial nucleus send axons to the periaqueductal gray matter. This region, too, has been implicated in female sexual behavior; Sakuma and Pfaff (1979a, 1979b) found that electrical stimulation of the PAG facilitates lordosis in female rats and that lesions there disrupt it. In addition, Hennessey et al., (1990) found that lesions disconnecting the VMH from the PAG abolish female sexual behavior. Finally, Sakuma and Pfaff (1980a, 1980b) found that estradiol treatment or electrical stimulation of the ventromedial nuclei increases the firing rate of neurons in the PAG. (The PAG contains both estrogen and progesterone receptors.)

Daniels et al., (1999) injected a transneuronal retrograde tracer, pseudorabies virus, in the muscles responsible for the lordosis response in female rats. They found that the pathway innervating these muscles was as previous studies predicted: VMH → PAG → nPGi → motor neurons in the ventral horn of the lumbar region of the spinal cord.

As we saw in the previous subsection, the brain regions that control male genital reflexes include the MPA, PAG, and nPGi. Anatomical tracing studies (Marson, 1995; Marson and Murphy, 2006) injected pseudorabies virus into the clitorises and vaginas of female rats and found retrograde labeling in these three brain structures (and some others as well). Thus, it seems likely that erections of the penis and clitoris are controlled by similar brain mechanisms. This finding is not surprising, because these organs derive from the same embryonic tissue.

Figure 10.16 summarizes the evidence for brain regions involved in neural control of female sexual behavior presented so far in this section.

A functional-imaging study by Holstege et al., (2003a) investigated the neural activation that accompanies orgasm in women, elicited by manual clitoral stimulation supplied by the women's male partners. They observed activation in the junction between the midbrain and diencephalon, the lateral putamen, and the cerebellum, just as was observed in men (Holstege et al., 2003b). They also saw activation in the PAG, a critical region for copulatory behavior in female laboratory animals.

Formation of Pair Bonds

LO 10.11 Compare the roles of oxytocin and vasopressin in pair bonding.

In approximately 5 percent of mammalian species, males and females form monogamous, long-lasting bonds. In humans, such bonds are formed between members of gay, lesbian, and bisexual couples as well. As naturalists and anthropologists have pointed out, monogamy is not always exclusive: In many species of animals, humans included, individuals sometimes cheat on their partners. In addition, some people display serial monogamy—intense relationships that last for a period of time, that are replaced with similarly intense

Figure 10.16 Female Sexual Behavior

This schematic shows a possible explanation of the interacting excitatory effects of pheromones, genital stimulation, and estradiol and progesterone on female sexual behavior. All pathways are excitatory.

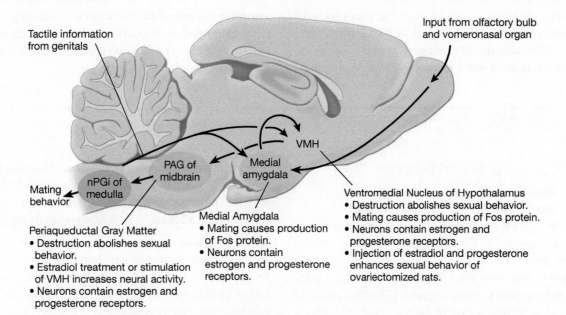

relationships with new partners. Members of some cultures engage in polygamy. But there is no doubt that pair bonding occurs in some species, including our own.

Several laboratories have investigated pair bonding in some closely related species of voles (small rodents that are often mistaken for mice). The different species appear to be almost identical; however, they display very different patterns of behavior. Prairie voles *(Microtus ochrogaster)* are monogamous; males and females form pair bonds after mating, and the fathers help to care for the pups. In the wild, most prairie voles whose mates die never take another partner (Getz and Carter, 1996). Meadow voles *(Microtus pennsylvanicus)* are promiscuous; after mating, the male leaves, and the mother cares for the pups by herself.

Several studies have revealed a relationship between monogamy and the levels of two peptides in the brain: vasopressin and oxytocin. These compounds are both released as hormones by the posterior pituitary gland and as neurotransmitters by neurons in the brain. In males, vasopressin appears to play the more important role. Monogamous voles have a higher level of V1a vasopressin receptors in the ventral forebrain than do polygamous voles (Insel et al., 1994). This difference appears to be responsible for the presence or absence of monogamy. Lim and Young (2004) found that mating induced the production of Fos protein in the ventral forebrain of male prairie voles and that an injection into this region of a drug that blocks V1a receptors disrupted the formation of pair bonds. Lim et al., (2004) performed an even more convincing experiment. They injected a genetically

modified virus that contained the gene for the V1a receptor into the ventral forebrain of normally polygamous male meadow voles. This manipulation increased the synthesis of the V1a receptor in this brain region and transformed the animals from polygamy to monogamy. Unlike prairie voles, which spend much time in physical contact with their partners after mating, meadow voles normally spend little time with them. Lim et al. found that male meadow voles with artificially increased levels of V1a receptors spent much more time huddling side by side with their mates.

In female voles, oxytocin appears to play a major role in pair bonding. Mating stimulates the release of oxytocin, and peripheral injection of oxytocin or injection into the cerebral ventricles facilitates pair bonding in female prairie voles (Williams et al., 1994). In contrast, a drug that blocks oxytocin receptor disrupts formation of pair bonds (Cho et al., 1999).

Many investigators believe that oxytocin and vasopressin may play a role in the formation of pair bonding in humans. For example, after intercourse, at a time when blood levels of oxytocin are increased, people report feelings of calmness and well-being, which are certainly compatible with the formation of bonds with one's partner. However, it is difficult to envision ways to perform definitive research on this topic. Experimenters can study the effects of these hormones or their antagonists on pair bonding in laboratory animals, but cannot do so with humans. However, Heinrichs et al., (2003) found that injections of oxytocin caused relaxation and a reduction of anxiety in human participants. In addition, Kosfeld et al., (2005) found that oxytocin increased trust. The investigators had participants play a "trust" game, in which they were given money, some or all of which they could give to another player (the trustee) to invest. If the trustee made money with his investment (all participants were male), he could share the winnings with the first player—or he could be selfish and keep everything for himself. Fifty minutes before the start of the game, the participants received a nasal spray containing oxytocin or a placebo. The oxytocin appeared to increase people's trust in other people: The participants who received the oxytocin gave 18 percent more money to the trustees, and they were twice as likely to give them all of their money to invest. A second study found that oxytocin did not simply make the participants feel more confident. They were no more likely to risk their money in an investment game that did not involve other people.

Section Review

Neural Control of Sexual Behavior

LO 10.9 Identify the role of spinal and brain mechanisms in male sexual behavior.
Sexual reflexes such as sexual posturing, erection, and ejaculation are organized in the spinal cord. Vibratory stimulation of the penis can elicit ejaculation in men with complete transection of the spinal cord, as long as the damage is located above the tenth thoracic segment. LSt cells, a group of neurons in the lumbar region of the rat spinal cord, play a critical role in triggering an ejaculation. Brain mechanisms have excitatory and inhibitory control of the circuits responsible for erection and ejaculation. Stimulating the MPA produces copulatory behavior; destroying it permanently abolishes the behavior. Destruction of the SDN (part of the MPA) in laboratory animals impairs mating behavior. Ejaculation in men is accompanied by increased behavior in the brain's reinforcement mechanisms, several thalamic nuclei, the lateral putamen, and the cerebellum.

LO 10.10 Identify the role of brain mechanisms in female sexual behavior.
The most important forebrain region for female sexual behavior is the ventromedial nucleus of the hypothalamus (VMH). Its destruction abolishes copulatory behavior, and its stimulation facilitates this behavior. Both estradiol and progesterone exert their facilitating effects on female sexual behavior in this region, and studies have confirmed the existence of progesterone and estrogen receptors there. The priming effect of estradiol is caused by an increase in progesterone receptors in the VMH. The steroid sensitive neurons of the VMH send axons to the periaqueductal gray matter (PAG) of the midbrain; these neurons, through their connections with the medullary reticular formation, control the particular responses that constitute female sexual behavior. Orgasm in women is accompanied by increased activity in regions similar to those activated during ejaculation in men and, in addition, in the periaqueductal gray matter.

LO 10.11 Compare the roles of oxytocin and vasopressin in pair bonding.
Vasopressin and oxytocin, peptides that serve as hormones and as neurotransmitters in the brain, appear to facilitate pair bonding. The insertion of the gene for vasopressin receptors in the basal forebrain of polygamous male voles induces monogamous behavior. Vasopressin plays the most important role in males, and oxytocin plays the most important role in females. In humans, oxytocin appears to increase trust in other people.

Thought Question

Imagine that you have been approached by an organization that is working on a breeding program for an endangered species of rodent. The organization is interested in your suggestions to increase the reproductive behavior of the animals. The brain structures and endocrine functions of the endangered rodent are very similar to those of laboratory rats that have been studied. (Figures 10.15 and 10.16 summarize the results of much of the research on brain regions involved in reproductive behaviors in laboratory rats). Using information from this chapter, make several recommendations to the organization about interventions or strategies that could be used to increase reproductive behavior in males and females. Imagine that experts working with the organization have access to any feasible intervention (such as brain stimulation, hormone exposure, or pheromone exposure).

Sexual Orientation

What controls a person's sexual orientation? Researchers once believed that sexual orientation was determined by childhood experiences, especially through interactions between parent and child. A large-scale study, conducted by Bell et al., (1981) concluded that there was no evidence to support such claims. Instead, their findings were consistent with biological contributions to sexual orientation. The accumulation of research over the 30 years since this study continues to support a biological basis for sexual orientation.

The following sections will describe research in support of biological contributions to sexual orientation using examples from individuals with congenital adrenal hyperplasia, androgen insensitivity, and cloacal exstrophy. Other research identifies the development of specific brain structures, fraternal birth order, and maternal immune sensitivity as factors involved in the determination of sexual orientation. Further support for a biological basis of sexual orientation is provided by the results of heritability and twin studies. Much of the biological evidence points toward a role for organization hormone effects, and, as you will read in this section, most research suggests that sexual orientation is determined before birth (see also Bogaert and Skorska, 2011; Burri et al., 2011; Hines, 2011; Rahman, 2005).

Activational and Organizational Effects of Hormones

LO 10.12 **Compare the roles of activational and organizational hormone effects in sexual orientation.**

What role might sex hormones play in influencing sexual orientation? Could prenatal, organizational effects or later, activational effects of sex hormones contribute to sexual orientation? It appears that sexual orientation is *not* strongly related to variations in the levels of sex hormones during adulthood, ruling out a role for activational effects of sex hormone exposure. Many studies have examined the levels of testosterone in gay and heterosexual men and found no differences between these groups. Similarly, most studies have found no difference in sex hormones between groups of women who are heterosexual and those who are not. A few studies suggest that some lesbian women have elevated levels of testosterone (but still lower than those found in men, Meyer-Bahlburg, 1984, Hines, 2011). Men who experience reduced testosterone in adulthood do not change their sexual orientation, and men and women who are treated with sex hormones for medical reasons do not change their sexual orientation, further suggesting that exposure to hormones in adulthood is not a factor in the development of sexual orientation (Hines, 2011).

A more likely biological factor involved in differences in sexual orientation is a subtle difference in brain structure caused by differences in prenatal exposure to androgens. Prenatal exposure to sex hormones produces permanent, organizational effects (see the *Development of Sex Organs* section for review). The following sections describe evidence from research concerning congenital adrenal hyperplasia, androgen insensitivity, cloacal exstrophy, heritability, and

prenatal factors that suggest prenatal sex hormone exposure permanently influences brain development and structure, resulting in later behavior related to sexual orientation.

Role of Androgens

LO 10.13 **Explain what can be learned about the role of prenatal androgen exposure in sexual orientation from congenital adrenal hyperplasia and androgen insensitivity.**

Evidence suggests that prenatal androgens can affect human social behavior and sexual orientation, as well as anatomy. In a disorder known as **congenital adrenal hyperplasia (CAH)**, the adrenal glands secrete abnormal amounts of androgens. The secretion of androgens begins prenatally; thus, the syndrome causes prenatal masculinization. Boys born with CAH develop typically; the extra androgen does not seem to have significant effects. However, a girl with CAH will be born with an enlarged clitoris, and her labia may be partly fused together. (The scrotum and labia develop from the same tissue in the fetus.) If masculinization of the genitals is pronounced, surgery is sometimes performed to correct them. Once the syndrome has been identified, the person will be given a synthetic hormone that suppresses the excessive secretion of androgens. As a group, approximately one third of females with CAH describe themselves as bisexual or homosexual (Cohen-Bendahan et al., 2005b).

A plausible explanation for the increased incidence of lesbian or bisexual sexual orientation of women with CAH is that the androgens affect development of the brain. Androgens also affect the genitals; perhaps changes in genitals played a role in shaping the development of the girls' sexual orientation. However, Meyer-Bahlberg et al., (2008) studied women with a much milder form of the disorder called *non-classical CAH (NCAH)*. Girls born with NCAH show typical female genitalia at birth and do not show signs of increased androgen levels until late childhood or adolescence. At that

It appears that sexual orientation is not strongly related to variations in the levels of sex hormones during adulthood.

time, the girls receive medical treatment to suppress androgen secretion. Meyer-Bahlberg et al. found women with NCAH, like those with CAH, are more likely to identify as lesbian or bisexual. The investigators suggest that the presence of NCAH caused a mild increase in androgen secretion during early prenatal development that changed brain development but did not masculinize the girls' genitals.

In another example of the contributions of androgens to sexual orientation, genetic males with androgen insensitivity syndrome develop female external genitalia, but internally retain the testes and do not develop a uterus or fallopian tubes. If an individual with this syndrome is raised as a girl, the testes are typically removed because they often become cancerous; but if they are not removed, the body will mature into that of a woman at the time of puberty through the effects of the small amounts of estradiol produced by the testes. (If the testes are removed, the person may be given estradiol and achieve same result.) At adulthood the individual will function sexually as a woman, although surgical lengthening of the vagina may be necessary. Individuals with this syndrome report average sex drives, including normal frequency of orgasm in intercourse and are often, though not always, attracted to male partners (Wisniewski et al., 2000).

Cloacal Exstrophy

LO 10.14 Explain what can be learned about the role of biological factors in sexual orientation from cloacal exstrophy.

The case presented in the opener to this chapter (Bruce/Brenda/David) suggests that people's sexual identity and sexual orientation are strongly influenced by biological factors and cannot easily be changed by the way a child is raised (environmental factors). Presumably, the exposure of Bruce's brain to androgens prenatally and during the first few months of life affected his neural development, contributing to male sexual identity and an attraction toward women as romantic and sexual partners. Fortunately, cases of penile ablation are rare.

A developmental abnormality known as *cloacal exstrophy* results in the birth of an intersex individual who is genetically male with fully developed testes but urogenital abnormalities, often including the lack of a penis. In the past, many genetically male individuals born with this condition were raised as females, primarily because it is relatively easy to surgically construct a vagina that can function in intercourse but very difficult to construct a functioning penis. However, studies have shown that approximately 50 percent of intersex individuals with cloacal exstrophy later expressed dissatisfaction with their surgical gender assignment and began living as men, often undergoing gender-change procedures (Gooren, 2006; Meyer-Bahlberg, 2005; Reiner, 2005). Individuals with cloacal exstrophy are often sexually attracted to females. If we consider the social pressure against someone who has been raised as a girl subsequently adopting a male sex role, 50 percent is a large number. Meyer-Bahlberg (2005) reports the case of an exstrophy patient raised as a female who underwent a gender change at the age of 52, after both parents had died. Presumably, fear of parental disapproval had prevented this person from making the change earlier.

The Sexually Dimorphic Brain

LO 10.15 Compare sexually dimorphic features of a male and female brain, and explain what can be learned about the brain basis of sexual orientation from these dimorphisms.

The human brain is a sexually dimorphic organ. This fact was long suspected, even before confirmation was received from anatomical and functional imaging studies. For example, neurologists discovered that the two hemispheres of a woman's brain appear to share functions more than those of a man's brain do. If a man sustains a stroke that damages the left side of the brain, he is more likely to show impairments in language than will a woman with similar damage. Presumably, the woman's right hemisphere shares language functions with the left, so damage to one hemisphere is less devastating in women than it is in men. Also, men's brains are, on average, somewhat larger—apparently because men's bodies are generally larger than those of women. In addition, the sizes of some specific regions of the telencephalon and diencephalon are different in males and females, and the shape of the corpus callosum may also be sexually dimorphic. (For specific references, see Breedlove, 1994; Goldstein et al., 2001; and Swaab et al., 1995.)

Most investigators believe that the sexual dimorphism of the human brain is a result of differential exposure to androgens prenatally and during early postnatal life. Additional changes could occur at the time of puberty, when another surge in androgens occurs. Sexual dimorphism in the human brain could also be a result of differences in the social environments of males and females. We cannot manipulate the hormone levels of humans before and after birth as we can with laboratory animals, so it might be a long time before enough evidence is gathered to permit us to make definite conclusions.

Several postmortem studies have examined the brains of gay and heterosexual men and women. So far, these studies have found differences in the size of three different subregions of the brain: the suprachiasmatic nucleus (SCN), a sexually dimorphic nucleus of the hypothalamus, and the anterior commissure (Allen and Gorski, 1992; Bao and Swaab, 2011; LeVay, 1991; Swaab and Hofman, 1990). You are already familiar, from Chapter 9, with the SCN. The anterior commissure is a fiber bundle that interconnects parts of the left and right temporal lobes. However, from what we know about brain functions, there is no reason to

Figure 10.17 Dimorphic Regions of the Brain

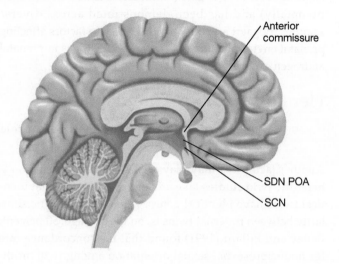

Figure 10.18 Sexual Orientation and SDN

Sexual dimorphism and role of sexual orientation in the volume and number of neurons in the SDN in sheep.

(Based on data from Roselli et al., 2004.)

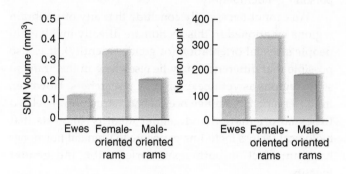

expect that differences in the SCN or the corpus callosum would play a role in sexual orientation. Also, a follow-up study confirmed the existence of a sexually dimorphic nucleus in the hypothalamus but failed to find a relationship between its size and sexual orientation in men (Byne et al., 2001). (See Figure 10.17.)

Approximately 8 percent of domestic rams (male sheep) show a sexual orientation for other males. These animals do not show female-typical behavior; they show typical male mounting behavior but direct this behavior toward other males rather than females (Price et al., 1988). A study by Roselli et al., (2004) discovered a sexually dimorphic nucleus in the medial preoptic/anterior hypothalamic area that was significantly larger in males than in females. They also found that this nucleus was twice as large in female-oriented male rams as in male-oriented rams. (See Figure 10.18.)

Functional-imaging studies have found that the brains of gay men and women reacted differently to the odors of AND and EST, two chemicals that may serve as human pheromones. Savic et al., (2005) found that the response of brain regions of gay men to AND and EST was similar to that of the heterosexual women. Berglund et al., (2006) found that the response of brain regions of lesbian women to these substances was similar to those of heterosexual men. These studies suggest that a person's sexual orientation affects (or is affected by) his or her response pattern to these potential sexual pheromones.

Although this section has been considering sexual orientation—the sex of those to whom an individual is sexually and romantically attracted—another sexual characteristic is related to structural differences in the brain. In a study of postmortem brains, Zhou et al., (1995) found that the size of a particular region of the forebrain, the central subdivision of the *bed nucleus of the stria terminalis (BNST)*, is larger in

males than in females. They also found that in transgender females the size of this nucleus is consistent with genetically female individuals who identify as female. The size of this nucleus was the same in males, regardless of their sexual orientation. Thus, its size was related to gender identity, not to sexual orientation. Kruijver et al., (2000) replicated these results and found that the size of this region in transgender males was within the range of sizes seen in all males. (See Figure 10.19.)

Garcia-Falgueras and Swaab (2008) found another sexually dimorphic region of the human brain: the *uncinate nucleus* of the hypothalamus. They found that this nucleus, which is the human version of the *medial preoptic nucleus* in rodents, is approximately twice as large in males as in females. The size of this nucleus in transgender females is consistent with that of all females. The investigators also

Figure 10.19 The Human BNST

These photomicrographs of slices of the human brain contain the central subdivision of the bed nucleus of the stria terminalis (BNST).

(From Zhou, J.-N., Hofman, M. A., Gooren, L. J. G., and Swaab, D. F., A sex difference in the human brain and its relation to transsexuality, *Nature*, 1995, *378*, 68–70. Reprinted with permission.)

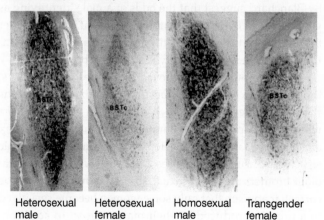

Heterosexual male   Heterosexual female   Homosexual male   Transgender female

provide evidence that the neurons in the uncinate nucleus send axons to the BNST, the size of which was previously shown to be related to gender identity. They suggest that these two structures are part of a neural circuit that affects a person's gender identity.

We cannot necessarily conclude that any of the brain regions mentioned in this section are directly involved in people's sexual orientation (or gender identity). It is also possible that differences may lie elsewhere in the brain, in some regions as yet unexplored by researchers. However, the observation that differences in brain structure are related to sexual orientation and gender identity suggests that biological factors including exposure to prenatal hormones have an effect on both sexual orientation and gender identity.

Role of Prenatal Environment in Sexual Orientation

LO 10.16 **Summarize the relationships between prenatal environmental factors and sexual orientation.**

If sexual orientation is, indeed, affected by differences in exposure of the developing brain to androgens, what prenatal environmental factors might cause this exposure to vary? Presumably, something must decrease the prenatal androgen levels among gay men and increase the levels among lesbian women. As we saw, congenital adrenal hyperplasia exposes the developing fetus to increased levels of androgens, but most lesbian women do not have CAH. So far, no other plausible sources of high levels of prenatal androgens have been proposed.

Studies by Blanchard (2001) and by Bogaert (2006) found that gay men tend to have more older brothers—but not more older sisters or younger brothers or sisters. In contrast, the numbers of brothers or sisters (younger or older) of women of any sexual orientation did not differ, nor did the age of the mother or father or the interval between births. The presence of older brothers and sisters had no effect on women's sexual orientation. The data obtained by Blanchard suggest that the odds of a male identifying as gay increased by approximately 3.3 percent for each older brother. Thus, the odds are still strongly against a boy identifying as gay even in a family with several boys.

When mothers are exposed to several male fetuses, their immune system may become sensitized to proteins that only males possess (such as Y-linked proteins). As a result, the response of the mother's immune system may affect the prenatal brain development of sexually dimorphic structures of later male fetuses. Most men who have several older brothers are heterosexual, so even if this hypothesis is correct, it appears that only some women become sensitized to a protein produced by their male fetuses. In addition, this relationship appears to hold true primarily among right-handed individuals (handedness is also determined prenatally) and has been demonstrated across diverse samples (Bogaert and Skorska, 2011). These factors affecting prenatal environment may be related to changes in prenatal androgen exposure.

Heredity and Sexual Orientation

LO 10.17 **Summarize what is currently known of the role of heredity in sexual orientation.**

Another factor that may play a role in sexual orientation is heredity. Twin studies take advantage of the fact that identical twins have identical genes, whereas the genetic similarity between fraternal twins is, on the average, 50 percent. Bailey and Pillard (1991) found that the concordance rate for nonheterosexual sexual orientation among twin brothers was 52 percent for identical twins and only 22 percent for fraternal twins—a difference of 30 percent. Other studies have shown differences of up to 60 percent (Gooren, 2006), suggesting that a genetic component plays a role in sexual orientation in males.

Genetic factors also appear to affect female sexual orientation. Bailey et al., (1993) found that the concordance of female monozygotic twins for nonheterosexual sexual orientation was 48 percent, while that of dizygotic twins was 16 percent. Another study, by Pattatucci and Hamer (1995), found an increased prevalence of homosexual and bisexual sexual orientation in sisters, daughters, nieces, and female cousins (through a paternal uncle) of lesbian women.

For several years, investigators have been puzzled by an apparent paradox. On average, men with homosexual sexual orientation have approximately 80 percent fewer children than males with heterosexual sexual orientation (Bell and Weinberg, 1978). This reduced fecundity should exert strong selective pressure against any genes involved in homosexual sexual orientation. Some investigators have suggested that men with homosexual sexual orientation may play an important supportive role in their families, thus increasing the fecundity of their relatives, who share some of their genes (Wilson, 1975). However, more recent studies (Bobrow and Bailey, 2001; Rahman and Hull, 2005) have found that gay men do not provide more financial or emotional support to their siblings. A study by Camperio-Ciani et al., (2004) suggests a possible explanation. They found that the female maternal relatives (for example, maternal aunts and grandmothers) of men with homosexual sexual orientation had higher fecundity rates. No differences were found in the female paternal relatives. Because men are likely to share an X chromosome with female maternal relatives but not with female paternal relatives, the investigators suggested that a gene or genes on the X chromosome that are involved in men's homosexual sexual orientation also increase a female's fecundity.

To summarize, evidence suggests that two important biological factors—prenatal hormonal exposure and heredity—may affect a person's sexual orientation (see also Table 10.3). We can hope that research on the biological origins of sexual orientation will reduce prejudice and misunderstanding and help people to better understand the variety of sexual orientations and gender identities that exist.

Table 10.3 Summary of Factors Possibly Contributing to Sexual Orientation

Factor	Description
Genetics/Heredity	Twin studies suggest that heredity may play a role in sexual orientation in both men and women.
Hormone Exposure	
Organizational Effects	Evidence from prenatally androgenized girls, androgen insensitivity, and cloacal exstrophy suggest a role for prenatal androgen exposure in sexual orientation.
Activational Effects	There is little or no evidence to suggest a role for activational effects of hormones in sexual orientation.
Environment	
Prenatal Environment	Boys with more older brothers have a higher likelihood of identifying as gay. It has been hypothesized that exposure to multiple male fetuses changes a mother's immune system, affecting the prenatal environment of subsequent male offspring.
Postnatal environment	There is little or no evidence to suggest a role for the postnatal environment in sexual orientation.

Section Review

Sexual Orientation

LO 10.12 Compare the roles of activational and organizational hormone effects in sexual orientation.

There is little support for a role of activational effects of hormones in sexual orientation. There is stronger evidence for a role of organizational effects of hormones in sexual orientation.

LO 10.13 Explain what can be learned about the role of prenatal androgen exposure in sexual orientation from congenital adrenal hyperplasia and androgen insensitivity

Studies of prenatally androgenized girls suggest that organizational effects of androgens influence the development of sexual orientation; androgenization appears to enhance the likelihood of a sexual orientation toward women. If androgens cannot act (as they cannot in cases of androgen insensitivity syndrome), the person's anatomy and behavior are feminized.

LO 10.14 Explain what can be learned about the role of biological factors in sexual orientation from cloacal exstrophy.

Studies of genetic males with cloacal exstrophy, who are born without a penis, support the conclusion that prenatal exposure to androgens promotes a male gender identity and a sexual orientation toward females.

LO 10.15 Compare sexually dimorphic features of a male and female brain, and explain what can be learned about the brain basis of sexual orientation from these dimorphisms.

The sizes of some specific regions of the telencephalon and diencephalon are different in males and females, and the shape of the corpus callosum may also be sexually dimorphic. Several postmortem studies have examined the brains of gay and heterosexual men and women. So far, these studies have found differences in the size of three different subregions of the brain: the suprachiasmatic nucleus (SCN), a sexually dimorphic nucleus of the hypothalamus, and the anterior commissure.

LO 10.16 Summarize the relationships between prenatal environmental factors and sexual orientation.

Gay men tend to have more older brothers. When mothers are exposed to several male fetuses, their immune system may become sensitized to proteins that only males possess, which may result in changes to the prenatal environment to subsequent male children.

LO 10.17 Summarize what is currently known of the role of heredity in sexual orientation.

Twin studies suggest that heredity may play a role in sexual orientation in both men and women.

Thought Question

Whatever the relative roles played by biological and environmental factors may be, most investigators agree that a person's sexual orientation is not a matter of choice. What brain or endocrine-based evidence supports this assertion?

Parental Behavior

In most mammalian species, reproductive behavior takes place at the time of conception, as well as after offspring are born. This section examines the role of hormones in the initiation and maintenance of parental behavior, and the role of the neural circuits that are responsible for their expression. Most of the research has involved rodents; less is known about the neural and endocrine bases of parental behavior in primates.

Although most research on the physiology of parental behavior has focused on maternal behavior, some researchers study paternal behavior shown by the males of some species of rodents. Parental behavior of human fathers is very important for the offspring of our species, but the physiological basis of this behavior is not yet well understood.

Maternal Behavior of Rodents

LO 10.18 Describe examples of rodent maternal behavior.

The final test of the fitness of an animal's genes is the number of offspring that survive to a reproductive age. Just as the process of natural selection favors reproductively competent animals, it favors those that care adequately for their young, if their young in fact require care. Rat and mouse pups certainly do; they cannot survive without a mother to attend to their needs.

At birth, rats and mice resemble fetuses. The infants are blind (their eyes are still shut), and they can only wriggle helplessly. They are poikilothermous ("cold-blooded"); their brain is not yet developed enough to regulate body temperature. They even lack the ability to release their own urine and feces spontaneously and must be helped to do so by their mother. As we will see shortly, this phenomenon actually serves a useful function.

Nest-building provides one important example of maternal behavior. During gestation, female rats and mice build nests. The form this structure takes depends on the material available for its construction. In the laboratory the animals are usually given strips of paper or lengths of rope or twine. A good *brood nest*, as it is called, is shown in Figure 10.20. This nest is made of hemp rope; a piece of the rope is shown below the nest. The mouse laboriously shredded the rope and then wove an enclosed nest, with a small hole for access to the interior.

At the time of **parturition** (birth of offspring) the female begins to groom and lick the area around her vagina. As a pup begins to emerge, she assists the uterine contractions by pulling the pup out with her teeth. She then eats the placenta and umbilical cord and cleans off the fetal membranes—a quite delicate operation. (A newborn pup looks as though it is sealed in very thin plastic wrap.) After all the pups have been born and cleaned up, the mother will probably nurse them. Milk is usually present in the mammary glands very near the time of birth.

Figure 10.20 A Mouse's Brood Nest

Beside the nest is a length of the kind of rope the mouse used to construct it.

Periodically, the mother licks the pups' anogenital region, stimulating reflexive urination and defecation. Friedman and Bruno (1976) have shown the utility of this mechanism. They noted that a lactating female rat produces approximately 48 grams (g) of milk on the tenth day of lactation. This milk contains approximately 35 milliliters (ml) of water. The experimenters injected some of the pups with tritiated (radioactive) water and later found radioactivity in the mother and in the littermates. They calculated that a lactating rat normally consumes 21 ml of water in the urine of her young, thus recycling approximately two-thirds of the water she gives to the pups in the form of milk. The water, traded back and forth between mother and young, serves as a vehicle for the nutrients—fats, protein, and sugar—contained in milk. Because each day the milk production of a lactating rat is approximately 14 percent of her body weight (for a human weighing 120 pounds, that would be around 2 gallons), the recycling is extremely useful, especially when the availability of water is a problem.

Besides cleaning, nursing, and helping her offspring urinate and defecate, a female rodent will retrieve pups if they leave or are removed from the nest. The mother will even construct another nest in a new location and move her litter there, should the conditions at the old site become unfavorable (for example, when an inconsiderate experimenter puts a heat lamp over it). The way a female rodent picks up her pup is quite consistent: She gingerly grasps the animal, managing not to injure it with her very sharp teeth. (We can personally attest to the sharpness of a

Figure 10.21 A Female Mouse Carrying a Pup

mouse's teeth and the strength of its jaw muscles.) She then carries the pup with a characteristic prancing walk, her head held high. (See Figure 10.21.) The pup is brought back to the nest and is left there. The female then leaves the nest again to search for another pup. She continues to retrieve pups until she finds no more; she does not count her pups and then stop retrieving when she has them all. A mouse or rat will usually accept all the pups she is offered, if they are young enough. We once observed two lactating female mice with nests in corners of the same cage, diagonally opposite each other. Disturbing their nests triggered a long bout of retrieving, during which each mother stole youngsters from the other's nest. The mothers kept up their exchange for a long time, passing each other in the middle of the cage.

Under normal conditions, one of the stimuli that induce a female rat to begin taking care of pups is the act of parturition. Female rodents normally begin taking care of their pups as soon as they are born. Some of this effect is caused by prenatal hormones, but the passage of the pups through the birth canal also stimulates maternal behavior: Artificially distending the birth canal in nonpregnant females stimulates maternal behavior, whereas cutting the sensory nerves that innervate the birth canal slows the appearance of maternal behavior (Graber and Kristal, 1977; Yeo and Keverne, 1986).

Hormonal Control of Maternal Behavior

LO 10.19 **Explain the role of hormones in examples of maternal behavior.**

As we saw earlier in this chapter, most sexually dimorphic behaviors are controlled by the organizational and activational effects of sex hormones. Maternal behavior is somewhat different in this respect. First, there is no evidence that organizational effects of hormones play a role in parental behavior. Under the correct conditions, males will take care of infants. Second, although maternal behavior is affected by hormones, it is not *controlled* by them. Most virgin female rats will begin to retrieve and care for young pups after having infants placed with them for several days (Wiesner and Sheard, 1933). And once the rats are sensitized, they will thereafter take care of pups as soon as they encounter them; sensitization lasts for a lifetime.

Although hormones are not *essential* for the activation of maternal behavior, many aspects of maternal behavior are facilitated by hormones. Nest-building behavior is facilitated by progesterone, the principal hormone of pregnancy (Lisk et al., 1969). After parturition, mothers continue to maintain their nests, and they construct new nests if necessary, even though their blood level of progesterone is very low then.

Although pregnant female rats will not immediately care for foster pups that are given to them during pregnancy, they will do so as soon as their own pups are born. The hormones that influence a female rodent's responsiveness to her offspring are the ones that are present shortly before parturition. Figure 10.22 shows the levels of the three hormones that have been implicated in maternal behavior: progesterone, estradiol, and **prolactin.** Note that just before parturition the level of estradiol begins rising, then the level of progesterone falls dramatically, followed by a sharp increase in prolactin, the hormone produced by the anterior pituitary gland that is responsible for milk production. If ovariectomized virgin female rats are given progesterone, estradiol, and prolactin in a pattern that duplicates this sequence, the time it takes to sensitize their maternal behavior is drastically reduced (Bridges et al., 1985).

As we saw in the previous section, pair bonding involves vasopressin and oxytocin. In at least some species, oxytocin also appears to be involved in formation of a bond between mother and offspring. In rats the administration of oxytocin facilitates the establishment of maternal behavior (Insel, 1997). Van Leengoed et al., (1987) injected an oxytocin antagonist into the cerebral ventricles of rats as soon as they began giving birth. The experimenters removed the pups from the cage as soon as they were born. When the pups were given back to the mothers 40 minutes later, their mothers ignored them. Control rats that were given a placebo began caring for their pups as soon as the pups were returned to them. (See Table 10.4.)

Neural Control of Maternal Behavior

LO 10.20 **Identify brain regions and neural pathways involved in maternal behavior.**

The medial preoptic area, the region of the forebrain that plays the most critical role in male sexual behavior, appears

Figure 10.22 Hormones in Pregnant Rats

The graph shows blood levels of progesterone, estradiol, and prolactin in pregnant rats.

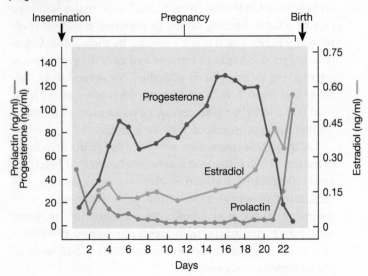

(From Rosenblatt, J. S., Siegel, H. I., and Mayer, A. D., Progress in the study of maternal behavior in the rat: hormonal, nonhormonal, sensory, and developmental aspects, *Advances in the Study of Behavior*, 1979, *10*, 225–310. *Reprinted with permission.*)

to play a similarly important role in maternal behavior. Numan (1974) found that lesions of the MPA disrupted both nest building and pup care in rodents. The mothers ignored their offspring. However, female sexual behavior was unaffected by these lesions. Del Cerro et al., (1995) found that the metabolic activity of the MPA, measured by 2-DG autoradiography, increased immediately after parturition. They also found that virgin female rodents whose maternal behavior had been sensitized by exposure to pups showed increased activity in the MPA. Thus, stimuli that facilitate pup care activate the MPA.

Prolactin appears to exert its stimulating effect on maternal behavior by acting on receptors in the medial preoptic area. Bridges et al., (1997, 2001) found that an infusion of prolactin into the MPA of virgin female rats that have been primed with estradiol and progesterone stimulated maternal behavior, and an infusion of a prolactin antagonist into the MPA delayed the onset of maternal behavior.

Table 10.4 Hormonal Control of Maternal Behavior

Hormone	Effect on Maternal Behavior
Progesterone	Facilitates nest building
Progesterone + estradiol + prolactin (sequence that occurs during pregnancy)	Maternal care of pups
Oxytocin	Facilitates bonding between mother and offspring; onset of maternal behavior

Olfaction plays an important role in sensitization of maternal behavior in the rat. A virgin female rat does not normally approach a rat pup; in fact, when she encounters one, she retreats from the pup. Fleming and Rosenblatt (1974) confirmed that the avoidance is based on smell. They rinsed the olfactory mucosa of virgin female rats with zinc sulfate, which temporarily eliminates olfactory sensitivity. The treatment abolished the animals' aversion to the pups, and they started taking care of the pups sooner than control rats did. Thus, sensitization involves overcoming a natural aversion to the odor of pups.

But sensitization of maternal behavior involves more than overcoming an aversion to pups—it involves a physiological process in the female that makes pups and their odors attractive to her. On the last day of pregnancy a female rat carrying her first litter spends more time around bedding that has been in contact with rat pups (Kinsley and Bridges, 1990). Lee et al., (2000) also found that postpartum female rats, but not pregnant rats, would learn to press a lever to receive access to pups.

Numan (2007) has reviewed research from his laboratory that has traced the neural pathways responsible for the two forms of sensitization to pups: inhibition of circuits responsible for the aversion to the odor of pups and activation of circuits responsible for caring for pups. It turns out that the MPA is involved in both forms of sensitization. First, let's consider the aversive response that virgin females make toward the odor of pups. As we saw earlier in this chapter, the olfactory system provides input to the medial amygdala, which plays an important role in sexual behavior. Lesions of the medial amygdala abolish the aversion of virgin females to pups just as treatment with zinc sulfate does, which indicates that the medial amygdala plays a role in mediating the aversive effects of pup odors. Some neurons in the medial amygdala send axons to the anterior hypothalamus (AH), which in turn projects to the periaqueductal gray matter (PAG). Because studies have shown that connections between the AH and the PAG play a role in defensive behavior and avoidance responses, Numan (2007) suggests that the role of the MPA in habituation to the odor of pups may be to inhibit the activity of the AH → PAG circuit. (See Figure 10.23.)

The neural circuitry of the system responsible for caring for pups is somewhat more complex. As you learned earlier, in the discussion of the neural basis of male sexual behavior, the MPA sends axons to the midbrain and lower brain stem. Numan and Numan (1997) found that neurons of the MPA that were activated by the performance of maternal behavior sent their axons to the ventral tegmental area (VTA). In turn, dopaminergic neurons in the VTA send axons to the nucleus accumbens (NAC). As we will see in Chapters 13 and 18, the VTA → NAC system is critically involved in motivation and reinforcement. For example, this system is activated when

Figure 10.23 Hormonal and Neural Pathways

(a) This schematic shows the pathways for habituation to the aversive effect of the odor of pups. According to Numan (2007), the hormonal state of a lactating female or prolonged exposure of a virgin female to pups activates the medial preoptic area, which inhibits the anterior hypothalamus (AH) and periaqueductal gray matter (PAG). (b) This schematic shows the neural circuits involved in the maternal behavior of lactating females or virgin females sensitized to pups, according to Numan (2007). DA = dopamine. Black arrows represent excitatory pathways. Red arrows represent inhibitory pathways.

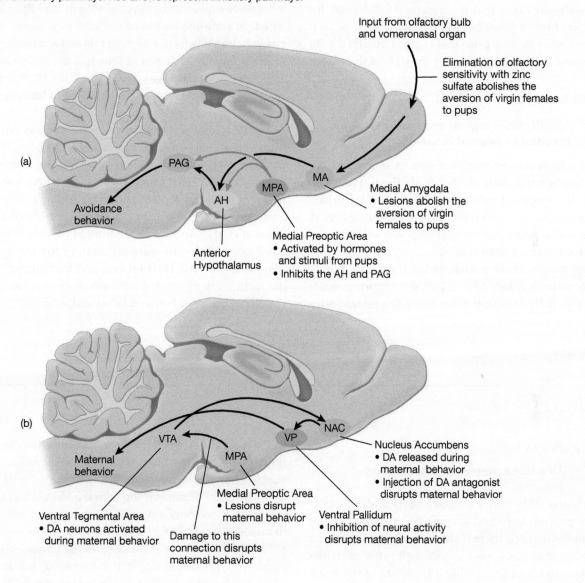

a hungry animal receives food, a thirsty animal receives water, an animal gets the opportunity to engage in sexual activity—or a sensitized or lactating female encounters pups. In fact, an fMRI study with rats (yes, their tiny little heads really were put in a special fMRI scanner) found that regions of the brain that are involved in reinforcement are activated when the mothers are presented with their pups (Ferris et al., 2005). The same regions are activated by artificial reinforcers such as cocaine. However, cocaine activates these regions only in virgin females; lactating females actually showed a *reduction* of activation there when they received injections of the drug. To a lactating female

the presence of pups becomes extremely reinforcing, and the potency of other stimuli, which might distract her from providing maternal care, appears to become weaker.

Numan and his colleagues have shown that dopamine is released in the NAC during maternal behavior, and that lesions of the NAC or injection of a dopamine antagonist into the NAC disrupt maternal behavior (Numan, 2007). Finally, axons from the NAC project to the ventral pallidum, a region of the basal ganglia involved in control of motivated behaviors, and injection of muscimol into the ventral pallidum suppressed maternal behavior. (Muscimol, a GABA agonist, inhibits neural activity.)

An fMRI study—this time with humans—found that when mothers looked at pictures of their infants, brain regions involved in reinforcement and those that contain receptors for oxytocin and vasopressin showed increased activity. Regions involved with negative emotions, such as the amygdala, showed decreased activity (Bartels and Zeki, 2004). We already know that mothers (and fathers too, for that matter) form intense bonds with their infants, so it should not come as a surprise that regions involved with reinforcement should be activated by the sight of their faces.

Neural Control of Paternal Behavior

LO 10.21 Identify brain regions and neural pathways involved in paternal behavior.

Newborn infants of most species of mammals are cared for by their mother and their mother feeds them. However, males of a few species of rodents share the task of infant care with the mothers, and the brains of these nurturing fathers show some interesting differences compared with those of nonpaternal fathers of other species.

Monogamous male prairie voles form pair bonds with their mates and help to care for their offspring, while polygamous male meadow voles leave the female after mating. The release of vasopressin, elicited by mating, facilitates this process. The size of the MPA, which plays an essential role in maternal behavior, shows less sexual dimorphism in monogamous voles than in promiscuous voles (Shapiro et al., 1991).

Kirkpatrick et al., (1994) found that when male prairie voles were exposed to a pup, neurons in the MPA were activated. In addition, lesions of the MPA produce severe deficits in paternal behavior of male rats and another species of monogamous voles (Lee and Brown, 2007; Rosenblatt et al., 1996; Sturgis and Bridges, 1997). Thus, the MPA appears to play a similar role in parental behavior of both males and females.

Little is known about the brain mechanisms involved in human paternal behavior, but evidence suggests that both prolactin and oxytocin facilitate a father's role in infant care. Fleming et al., (2002) found that fathers with higher blood levels of prolactin reported stronger feelings of sympathy and activation when they heard the cries of infants. Gordon et al., (2010) found that higher levels of prolactin were associated with more exploratory toy-manipulating play behavior with their infants, and that higher levels of oxytocin were associated with synchronous, coordinated emotional behavior between father and infant.

Section Review

Parental Behavior

LO 10.18 Describe examples of rodent maternal behavior.

Rodent maternal behavior includes nest building, delivery of pups, cleaning pups, keeping them warm, nursing them, and retrieving them if they are moved out of the nest. The mothers must even induce their pups' urination and defecation, and the mother's ingestion of the urine recycles water, which is often a scarce commodity.

LO 10.19 Explain the role of hormones in examples of maternal behavior.

Nest-building behavior is facilitated by progesterone, the principal hormone of pregnancy. Injections of progesterone, estradiol, and prolactin that duplicate the sequence that occurs during pregnancy facilitate maternal behavior. Oxytocin facilitates the onset of maternal behavior.

LO 10.20 Identify brain regions and neural pathways involved in maternal behavior.

Injections of progesterone, estradiol, and prolactin that duplicate the sequence that occurs during pregnancy facilitate maternal behavior. The hormones appear to act in the medial preoptic area (MPA). Connections between the MPA and the medial amygdala are responsible for the suppression of the aversive effects of the odor of pups, and a different circuit starting with the MPA is involved in establishing the reinforcing effect of pups and enhancing motivation to care for them: MPA → VTA → NAC → ventral pallidum. Oxytocin, which facilitates the formation of pair bonds in female rodents, is also involved in formation of a bond between mother and her pups. An fMRI study with rats showed activation of brain mechanisms of reinforcement when the mothers were presented with their pups. Women who look at pictures of their infants show increased activity in similar brain regions.

LO 10.21 Identify brain regions and neural pathways involved in paternal behavior.

Paternal behavior is relatively rare in mammalian species, but research indicates that sexual dimorphism of the MPA is less pronounced in male voles of monogamous, but not promiscuous, species. Lesions of the MPA abolish paternal behavior of male rats. Some aspects of parental care may be related to blood levels of prolactin and oxytocin in human fathers.

Thought Question

As you saw, both male sexual behavior and maternal behavior are disrupted by lesions of the medial preoptic area; thus, the MPA performs some functions necessary for both behaviors. Do you think that the functions are common to the two categories of behavior, or do you think that different functions are involved? If you think the former possibility is true, what might these functions be? Can you think of any common features of male sexual behavior and maternal behavior?

Chapter Review Questions

1. Describe mammalian sexual development, and explain the factors that control it.

2. Describe the hormonal control of the female reproductive cycle and of male and female sexual behavior.

3. Describe the role of pheromones in reproductive and sexual behavior.

4. Discuss the activational effects of gonadal hormones on the sexual behavior of women and men.

5. Discuss the physiological variables that affect sexual orientation and gender identity in men and women.

6. Describe the neural basis and control of male and female sexual behaviors in animal models.

7. Describe the hormonal and neural basis of maternal behavior in rodents.

8. Describe the neural mechanisms involved in regulation of paternal behavior in monogamous rodents.

Chapter 11
Emotion

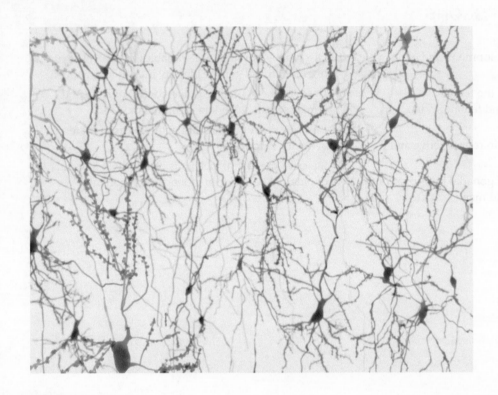

Chapter Outline

Learning Objectives

LO 11.1 Describe the three components of an emotional response.

LO 11.2 Explain what has been learned about the role of the amygdala and ventromedial prefrontal cortex in fear, fear conditioning, and extinction based on results of research with laboratory animals.

LO 11.3 Describe the role of the amygdala and ventromedial prefrontal cortex in emotional conditioning, extinction, and emotional memory in humans.

LO 11.4 Describe what is known from research with laboratory animals about serotonin and the neural circuitry of aggression and predation.

LO 11.5 Evaluate the roles of heredity and serotonin in human aggression.

LO 11.6 Summarize the role of hormonal control of aggression, citing evidence from studies involving humans and other animals.

LO 11.7 Cite examples supporting the role of the ventromedial prefrontal cortex in impulse control.

LO 11.8 Provide evidence for a developmental factor in impulse control.

LO 11.9 Compare brain differences involved in impulse control between those convicted of a crime or diagnosed with antisocial personality disorder and typically-developing adults.

LO 11.10 Explain the role of serotonin in impulse control regulation.

LO 11.11 Describe the brain regions involved in emotional aspects of moral decision making and cite evidence from the research literature.

LO 11.12 Describe evidence in support of emotional expressions as innate responses.

LO 11.13 Summarize the brain structures involved in emotional recognition, by addressing laterality, direction of gaze, imitation, and disgust.

LO 11.14 Review the brain structures involved in emotional expression, by addressing laterality, laughter, and humor.

LO 11.15 Summarize the evidence for and against the James-Lange theory of emotion.

LO 11.16 Explain the role of feedback from emotional expressions in mood and activity of the autonomic nervous system.

Samantha has a rare neurological condition, Urbach-Wiethe disease, which resulted in loss of neural tissue. The disease has affected her temporal lobes, causing bilateral amygdala destruction. Samantha demonstrates typical measures of attention, cognition, memory, visual ability, language, and executive function such as planning and decision making. She is a single mother of three boys, and has been described by interviewers as "pleasant and friendly, and reflective and thoughtful" (Tranel et al., 2006, p. 224). She exhibits empathy for others, and has experienced considerable adversity in her life, including difficult childhood experiences, the loss of a parent at a young age, and limited financial and social resources.

The effects of her amygdala damage are not immediately apparent. The functions related to this structure are restricted to negative emotions. Samantha experiences a reduced sense of danger and distrust in others. She both experiences and exhibits a lack of fear and anger in most contexts, and cannot recognize these emotions in others. For example, she did not report experiencing fear when watching movie clips from films such as The Shining *and* Silence of the Lambs.

*****

From this case study, we can begin to understand the role of brain regions for specific emotions. The word *emotion* refers to positive or negative reactions to particular situations. There is no such thing as a neutral emotion. For example, being treated unfairly makes us angry, seeing someone suffer makes us sad, and being close to a loved one makes us feel happy. Emotions consist of patterns of physiological changes and accompanying behaviors—or at least urges to perform these behaviors. These responses are accompanied by feelings. In fact, most of us use the word *emotion* to refer to the feelings, not to the behaviors. But it is behavior, not private experience, that has consequences for survival and reproduction. Therefore, the useful purposes served by emotional behaviors are what guided the evolution of our brain.

The first two sections in this chapter consider the patterns of behavioral and physiological responses that constitute the negative emotions of fear and anger. The third section describes the role of emotions in impulse control, moral judgments and social behavior. The fourth section describes the communication of emotions—their expression and recognition. The final section examines the nature of the feelings that accompany emotions. The figure here displays the amygdala, hypothalamus, and ventromedial prefrontal cortex, which are all involved in our processing of emotion.

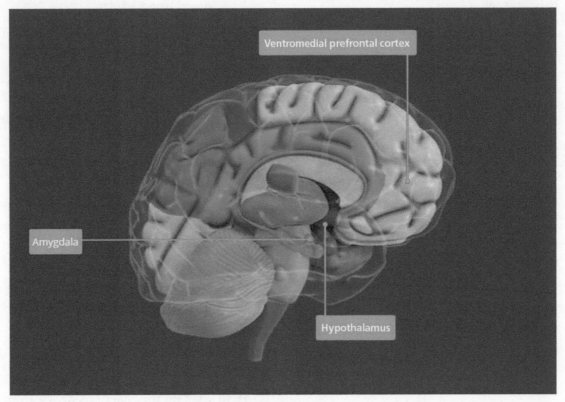

The amygdala, hypothalamus, and ventromedial prefrontal cortex.

Fear

Fear is an adaptive emotional response that is coordinated in the brain by the nuclei of the amygdala. An extensive body of research exists investigating the neurological basis for fear in laboratory animals and human volunteers.

Components of Emotional Response

LO 11.1 Describe the three components of an emotional response.

An emotional response consists of three types of components: behavioral, autonomic, and hormonal. The *behavioral* component consists of muscular movements that are appropriate to the situation that elicits them. For example, a dog defending its territory against an intruder first adopts an aggressive posture, growls, and shows its teeth. If the intruder does not leave, the defender runs toward it and attacks.

Autonomic responses facilitate the behaviors and provide quick mobilization of energy for vigorous movement. In this example the activity of the sympathetic branch increases while that of the parasympathetic branch decreases. As a consequence the dog's heart rate increases, and changes in the size of blood vessels shunt the circulation of blood away from the digestive organs toward the muscles. *Hormonal* responses reinforce the autonomic responses. The hormones secreted by the adrenal medulla—epinephrine and norepinephrine—further increase blood flow to the muscles and cause nutrients stored in the muscles to be converted into glucose. In addition, the adrenal cortex secretes steroid hormones, which also help to make glucose available to the muscles. (See Figure 11.1.)

This section discusses research on the control of overt emotional behaviors and the autonomic and hormonal responses that accompany them. Special behaviors that serve to communicate emotional states to other animals, such as

Figure 11.1 Components of an Emotional Response

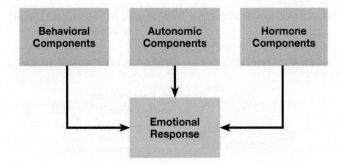

the threat gestures that precede an actual attack and the smiles and frowns used by humans, are discussed in the second section of the chapter. As you will see, negative emotions receive much more attention than positive ones do. Most of the research on the physiology of emotions has been confined to fear and anger—emotions associated with situations in which we may defend ourselves or our loved ones. The physiology of behaviors associated with positive emotions—such as those associated with lovemaking, caring for one's offspring, or enjoying a good meal or a cool drink of water (or an alcoholic beverage)—is described in other chapters but not in the specific context of emotions. Chapter 18 discusses the consequences of situations that evoke negative emotions: stress.

As we saw, emotional responses involve behavioral, autonomic, and hormonal components. These components are controlled by separate neural systems. The *integration* of the components of fear appears to be controlled by the amygdala.

Research with Laboratory Animals

LO 11.2 **Explain what has been learned about the role of the amygdala and ventromedial prefrontal cortex in fear, fear conditioning, and extinction based on results of research with laboratory animals.**

The amygdala plays a special role in physiological and behavioral reactions to objects and situations that have biological significance, such as those that warn of pain or other unpleasant consequences or signify the presence of food, water, salt, potential mates or rivals, or infants in need of care. Researchers in several different laboratories have shown that single neurons in various nuclei of the amygdala become active when emotionally relevant stimuli are presented. For example, these neurons are excited by such stimuli as the sight of a device that has been used to squirt either a bad-tasting solution or a sweet solution into the animal's mouth, the sound of another animal's vocalization, the sound of the opening of the laboratory door, the smell of smoke, or the sight of another animal's face (Jacobs and McGinty, 1972; Leonard et al., 1985; O'Keefe and Bouma,

1969; Rolls, 1982). And as we saw in Chapter 10, the amygdala is involved in the effects of olfactory stimuli on reproductive physiology and behavior. This section describes research on the role of the amygdala in organizing emotional responses produced by aversive stimuli.

The amygdala (or, more precisely, the *amygdaloid complex*) is located within the temporal lobes. It consists of several groups of nuclei, each with different inputs and outputs—and with different functions (Amaral et al., 1992; Pitkänen et al., 1997; Stefanacci and Amaral, 2000). The amygdala has been subdivided into approximately twelve regions, each containing several subregions. However, we will focus on just three major regions: the *lateral nucleus,* the *basal nucleus,* and the *central nucleus.*

The **lateral nucleus** receives information from all regions of the neocortex, including the ventromedial prefrontal cortex, the thalamus, and the hippocampal formation. The lateral nucleus sends information to the **basal nucleus** and to other parts of the brain, including the ventral striatum (a brain region involved in the effects of reinforcing stimuli on learning) and the dorsomedial nucleus of the thalamus, whose projection region is the prefrontal cortex. The lateral and basal nuclei send information to the ventromedial prefrontal cortex and the **central nucleus,** which projects to regions of the hypothalamus, midbrain, pons, and medulla that are responsible for the expression of the various components of emotional responses. As we will see, activation of the central nucleus elicits a variety of emotional responses: behavioral, autonomic, and hormonal. (See Figure 11.2.)

The central nucleus of the amygdala is the single most important part of the brain for the expression of emotional responses provoked by aversive stimuli. When threatening stimuli are perceived, neurons in the central nucleus become activated (Campeau et al., 1991; Pascoe and Kapp, 1985). Damage to the central nucleus (or to the nuclei that provide it with sensory information) reduces or abolishes a wide range of emotional behaviors and physiological responses. After the central nucleus has been destroyed, animals no longer show signs of fear when confronted with stimuli that have been paired with aversive events. They also act more tamely when handled by humans, their blood levels of stress hormones are lower, and they are less likely to develop ulcers or other forms of stress-induced illnesses (Coover et al., 1992; Davis, 1992; LeDoux, 1992). Monkeys typically show signs of fear when they see a snake, but those with amygdala lesions do not (Amaral, 2003). In contrast, when the central amygdala is stimulated by means of electricity or by an injection of an excitatory amino acid, the animal shows physiological and behavioral signs of fear and agitation (Davis, 1992), and long-term stimulation of the central nucleus produces stress-induced illnesses such as gastric ulcers (Henke, 1982). These observations suggest that the autonomic and endocrine responses controlled by the central nucleus are among those responsible for the harmful effects

Figure 11.2 Amygdala Projections

This figure shows a much-simplified diagram of the major divisions and connections of the amygdala that play a role in emotions.

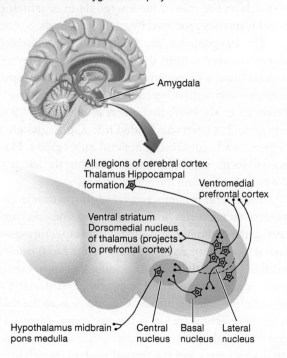

Figure 11.3 The Outputs of the Central Nucleus of the Amygdala

Shown here are some important brain regions that receive input from the central nucleus of the amygdala and the emotional responses controlled by these regions.

(Adapted from Davis, M., Trends in Pharmacological Sciences, 1992, 13, 35–41.)

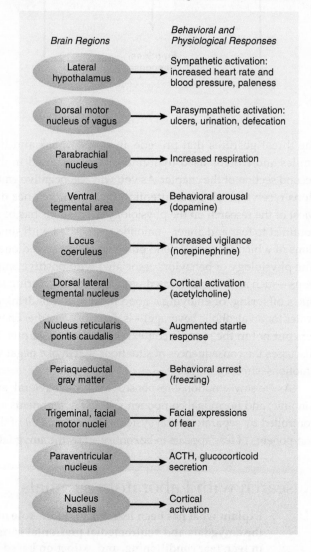

of long-term stress, which are discussed in Chapter 18. Figure 11.3 summarizes the regions receiving information from the amygdala and the responses they control.

EMOTIONAL CONDITIONING A few stimuli automatically activate the central nucleus of the amygdala and produce fear reactions—for example, loud unexpected noises, the approach of large animals, heights, or (for some species) specific sounds or odors. Even more important, however, is the ability to *learn* that a particular stimulus or situation is dangerous or threatening. Once the learning has taken place, that stimulus or situation will evoke fear: heart rate and blood pressure will increase, the muscles will become more tense, the adrenal glands will secrete epinephrine, and the animal will proceed cautiously, alert and ready to respond.

The most basic form of emotional learning is a **conditioned emotional response,** which is produced by a neutral stimulus that has been paired with an emotion-producing stimulus. The word *conditioned* refers to the process of *classical conditioning,* which is described in more detail in Chapter 13. Briefly, classical conditioning occurs when a neutral stimulus is regularly followed by a stimulus that automatically evokes a response. For example, if a dog regularly hears a bell ring just before it receives some food that makes it salivate, it will begin salivating as soon as it hears the sound of the bell.

Several laboratories have investigated the role of the amygdala in the development of classically conditioned emotional responses. For example, these responses can be produced in rats by presenting an auditory stimulus such as a tone, followed by a brief electrical shock delivered to the feet through the floor on which the animals are standing. (See Figure 11.4.) By itself the shock produces an *unconditioned* emotional response: The animal jumps, its heart rate and blood pressure increase, its breathing becomes more rapid, and its adrenal glands secrete catecholamines and steroid stress hormones. After several pairings of the tone and the shock, classical conditioning is normally established.

The next day, if the tone is presented alone—not followed by a shock—physiological monitoring will show the same physiological responses the animals produced when they were shocked during training. In addition, they will show a species-typical defensive response called *freezing.* In other words, the animals act as if they were expecting to receive a shock. The tone becomes a *conditioned stimulus (CS)* that elicits freezing: a *conditioned response (CR).*

Figure 11.4 Context Conditioning: An Example of a Conditioned Emotional Response

In this example, a rat experiences a shock in an enclosure with a blue floor. In the signaled condition, the shock is paired with the sound of a bell. The animal will now experience fear in the enclosure with the blue floor, demonstrated by freezing behavior. The animal is then placed in an enclosure with a purple floor. In the unsignaled condition, the rat does not experience fear, as demonstrated by standing up and engaging in exploratory behavior. In the signaled condition, the rat will experience fear and freeze when it hears the sound of the bell, even in this new purple-floor environment. The bell has become a conditioned stimulus, even in this new environment.

Context conditioning

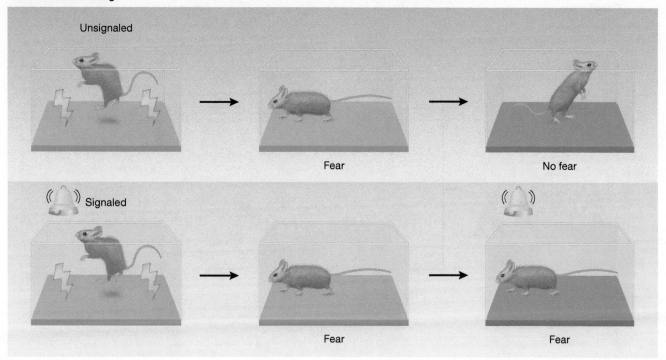

Research indicates that the physical changes responsible for the classical conditioning of a conditioned emotional response take place in the lateral nucleus of the amygdala (Paré et al., 2004). Neurons in the lateral nucleus communicate with neurons in the central nucleus, which in turn communicate with regions in the hypothalamus, midbrain, pons, and medulla that are responsible for the behavioral, autonomic, and hormonal components of a conditioned emotional response. More recent studies indicate that the neural circuitry responsible for the process of classical conditioning is actually more complex than that (Ciocchi et al., 2010; Duvarci et al., 2011; Haubensak et al., 2010), but the details of this process will be postponed until Chapter 13, which discusses the physiology of learning and memory.

EXTINCTION The neural mechanisms responsible for classically conditioned emotional responses evolved because they play a role in an animal's survival and increase the likelihood that an animal can avoid dangerous situations, such as places where it encountered aversive events. In the laboratory, if the CS (tone) is presented repeatedly by itself, the previously established CR (emotional response) eventually disappears—it becomes *extinguished*. After all, the value of a conditioned emotional response is that it prepares an animal to confront (or, better yet, avoid) an aversive stimulus. If the CS occurs repeatedly but the aversive stimulus does not follow, then it is better for the emotional

Figure 11.5 Extinction

In this example, rats experience fear conditioning, pairing the sound of a bell with a shock. One half of the rats experience extinction (repeatedly hearing the bell without the shock) in new enclosures with either purple or green floors, as demonstrated by standing up and engaging in exploratory behavior. When the groups of animals are tested after extinction, the animals demonstrate extinction in the same enclosure where they learned not the respond to the bell (extinction). Extinction learning is context dependent. In this example, when extinction occurs in one environment, or context (green floor), it does not generalize to a new environment (purple floor) where the rat continues to experience fear and engage in freezing behavior.

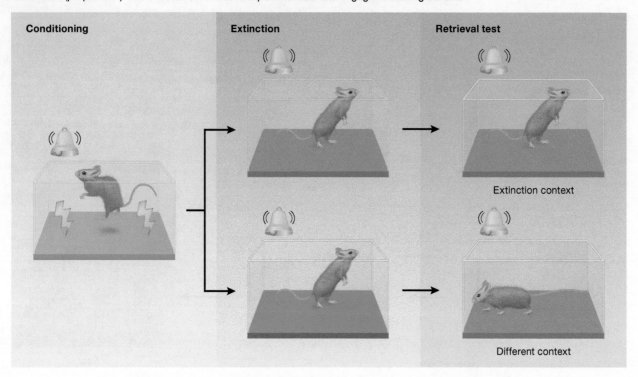

response—which itself is disruptive and unpleasant—to disappear. And that is exactly what happens.

Behavioral studies have shown that extinction is not the same as forgetting. Instead, the animal learns that the CS is no longer followed by an aversive stimulus, and, as a result of this learning, the expression of the CR is inhibited; the memory for the association between the CS and the aversive stimulus is not erased. (See Figure 11.5.) This inhibition is supplied by the **ventromedial prefrontal cortex (vmPFC;** Amano et al., 2010; Sotres-Bayon and Quirk, 2010). For example, lesions of the vmPFC impair extinction, stimulation of this region inhibits conditioned emotional responses, and extinction training activates neurons there. Besides playing an essential role in extinction of conditioned emotional responses, the vmPFC can modulate the expression of fear in different circumstances. Depending on the situation, one subregion of the prefrontal cortex can become active and suppress a conditioned fear response, and another subregion can become active and enhance the response.

The vmPFC is located just where its name suggests, at the bottom front of the cerebral hemispheres. (See Figure 11.6.) The vmPFC receives direct inputs from the dorsomedial thalamus, temporal cortex, ventral tegmental area, olfactory system, and amygdala. Its outputs go to several brain regions, including the cingulate cortex, hippocampal formation, temporal cortex, lateral hypothalamus, and amygdala. Finally, it communicates with other regions of the prefrontal cortex. Thus, its inputs provide it with information about what is happening in the environment and what plans are being made by the rest of the frontal lobes, and its outputs permit it to affect a variety of behaviors and physiological responses, including emotional responses organized by the amygdala. (See Table 11.1.)

Table 11.1 Brain Regions Involved in Fear Response

Nucleus	Function
Central Nucleus of the Amygdala	Activation produces fear-related behaviors; lesioning prevents production of fear-related behaviors
Lateral Nucleus of the Amygdala	Involved in producing conditioned emotional response
Ventromedial Prefrontal Cortex (vmPFC)	Involved in extinction of conditioned emotional response

Figure 11.6 The Ventromedial Prefrontal Cortex

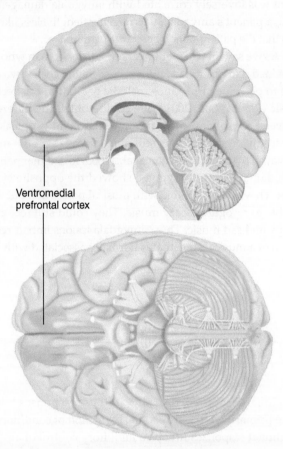

Ventromedial
prefrontal cortex

Research with Humans

LO 11.3 **Describe the role of the amygdala and ventromedial prefrontal cortex in fear, fear conditioning, extinction, and emotional memory in humans.**

We humans also acquire conditioned emotional responses. Let's use an example to illustrate this. Suppose you are studying with a friend and decide to have a snack. You put some food in the microwave to heat it up. The microwave makes an unusual noise and you open it to check on your food. Opening the door gives you a painful electrical shock. Your first response would be a defensive reflex: You would let go of the door, which would end the shock. This response is *specific*; it is aimed at terminating the painful stimulus. In addition, the painful stimulus would elicit *nonspecific* responses controlled by your autonomic nervous system: For example, your eyes would dilate, your heart rate and blood pressure would increase, and you would breathe faster. The painful stimulus would also trigger the secretion of some stress-related hormones, another nonspecific response.

Suppose that a while later you visit your friend again and make popcorn in the microwave. Your friend tells

you that the microwave is perfectly safe. It has been fixed. Just seeing the microwave and thinking of using it again makes you a little nervous, but you accept your friend's assurance, open the door, and place the popcorn inside. Just then, it makes the same unusual noise that it did when it shocked you. What would your response be? Almost certainly, you would let go of the door again, even if it did not give you a shock. Your pupils would dilate, your heart rate and blood pressure would increase, and your endocrine glands would secrete some stress-related hormones. The unusual sound would trigger a conditioned emotional response.

EMOTIONAL CONDITIONING Evidence indicates that the amygdala is involved in emotional responses in humans. One of the earliest studies observed the reactions of people who were being evaluated for surgical removal of parts of the brain to treat severe seizure disorders. These studies found that stimulation of parts of the brain (for example, the hypothalamus) produced autonomic responses that are often associated with fear and anxiety but that only when the amygdala was stimulated did people also report that they actually *felt* afraid (Gloor et al., 1982; Halgren et al., 1978; White, 1940).

Many studies have shown that lesions of the amygdala decrease people's emotional responses. For example, Bechara et al., (1995) and LaBar et al., (1995) found that people with lesions of the amygdala showed impaired acquisition of a conditioned emotional response, just as rats do.

Most human fears are probably acquired socially, not through firsthand experience with painful stimuli (Olsson et al., 2007). For example, a child does not have to be attacked by a dog to develop a fear of dogs: He or she can develop this fear by watching another person being attacked or (more often) by seeing another person display signs of fear when encountering a dog. People can also acquire a conditioned fear response through instruction. For example, suppose that someone is told (and believes) that if a warning light goes on, he or she should leave the room immediately because the light is connected to a sensor that detects dangerous levels of carbon monoxide gas. If the light does go on, the person will leave the room and is also likely to experience a fear response while doing so.

EXTINCTION We saw that studies with laboratory animals indicate that the vmPFC plays a critical role in extinction of a conditioned emotional response. The same is true for humans. Phelps et al. (2004) directly established a conditioned emotional response in volunteers by pairing the appearance of a square visual stimulus with electric shocks to the wrist and then extinguished the response by presenting the squares alone, without any shocks. Increased activity of the medial prefrontal cortex correlated with extinction of the conditioned response.

EMOTIONAL MEMORY   Damage to the amygdala interferes with the effects of emotions on memory. Normally, when people encounter events that produce a strong emotional response, they are more likely to remember these events. Cahill et al., (1995) studied a patient with bilateral degeneration of the amygdala. The investigators narrated a story about a young boy walking with his mother on his way to visit his father at work. To accompany the story, they showed a series of slides. During one part of the story, the boy was injured in a traffic accident, and gruesome slides illustrated his injuries. When this slide show is presented to healthy volunteers, they remember more details from the emotion-laden part of the story. However, a patient with amygdala damage showed no such increase in memory. In another study (Mori et al., 1999), researchers questioned patients with Alzheimer's disease who had witnessed the devastating earthquake that struck Kobe, Japan, in 1995. They found that memory of this frightening event was inversely correlated with amygdala damage: The more a patient's amygdala was degenerated, the less likely it was that the patient remembered the earthquake.

As we saw in Chapter 7, Patient I. R., a woman who had sustained damage to the auditory association cortex, was unable to perceive or produce melodic or rhythmic aspects of music (Peretz et al., 2001). She could not tell the difference between consonant (pleasant) and dissonant (unpleasant) music. However, she was still able to recognize the mood conveyed by music. Gosselin et al., (2005) found that patients with damage to the amygdala showed the opposite symptoms: They had no trouble with musical perception but were unable to recognize scary music. They could still recognize happy and sad music. Thus, amygdala lesions impair recognition of a musical style that is normally associated with fear.

Section Review

Fear

LO 11.1 Describe the three components of an emotional response.

The behavioral component consists of muscular movements that are appropriate to the situation that elicits them. Autonomic responses facilitate the behaviors and provide quick mobilization of energy for vigorous movement. Hormonal responses reinforce the autonomic responses.

LO 11.2 Explain what has been learned about the role of the amygdala and ventromedial prefrontal cortex in fear, fear conditioning, and extinction based on results of research with laboratory animals.

The amygdala organizes behavioral, autonomic, and hormonal responses to a variety of situations, including those that produce fear, anger, or disgust. In addition, it is involved in the effects of odors and pheromones on sexual and maternal behavior. It receives inputs from the olfactory system, the association cortex of the temporal lobe, the frontal cortex, and the rest of the limbic system. Its outputs go to the frontal cortex, hypothalamus, hippocampal formation, and brain stem nuclei that control autonomic functions and some species-typical behaviors. Electrical recordings of single neurons in the amygdala indicate that some of them respond when the animal perceives particular stimuli with emotional significance. Stimulation of the amygdala leads to emotional responses, and its destruction disrupts them. Pairing of neutral stimuli with those that elicit emotional responses results in classically conditioned emotional responses. Learning of these responses takes place primarily in the amygdala. Extinction of conditioned emotional responses involves inhibitory control of amygdala activity by the vmPFC.

LO 11.3 Describe the role of the amygdala and ventromedial prefrontal cortex in emotional conditioning, extinction, and emotional memory in humans.

Studies of people with amygdala lesions and functional-imaging studies with humans indicate that the amygdala is involved in emotional reactions in our species, too. However, many of our conditioned emotional responses are acquired by observing the responses of other people or even through verbal instruction. Study of people with amygdala lesions and functional-imaging studies indicate that the amygdala is involved in the effects of emotions on learning and emotional memory. The vmPFC plays an important role in the extinction of a conditioned emotional response.

Thought Question

Phobias can be seen as dramatic examples of conditioned emotional responses. These responses can even be contagious; we can acquire them without direct experience with an aversive stimulus. For example, a child who sees a parent show signs of fear in the presence of a dog may also develop a fear reaction to the dog. Do you think that some biases or prejudices might be learned in this way, too?

Aggression

Almost all species of animals engage in aggressive behaviors, which involve threatening gestures or actual attack directed toward another animal. Aggressive behaviors are species typical; that is, the patterns of movements (for example, posturing, biting, striking, or hissing) are organized by neural circuits whose development is largely programmed by an animal's genes. Many aggressive behaviors are related to reproduction. For example, aggressive behaviors that gain access to mates, defend territory needed to attract mates or to provide a site for building a nest, or defend offspring against intruders can all be regarded as reproductive behaviors. Other aggressive behaviors are related to self-defense, such as that of an animal threatened by a predator or an intruder of the same species.

Aggressive behavior can consist of actual attacks, or they may simply involve **threat behaviors,** which consist of postures or gestures that warn the adversary to leave or it will become the target of an attack. The threatened animal might show **defensive behaviors**—threat behaviors or an actual attack against the animal that is threatening it—or it might show **submissive behaviors**—behaviors that indicate that it accepts defeat and will not challenge the other animal. In the natural environment most animals display far more threats than actual attacks. Threat behaviors are useful in reinforcing social hierarchies in organized groups of animals or in warning intruders away from an animal's territory. They have the advantage of not involving actual fighting, which can harm one or both of the combatants.

Predation involves a member of one species attacking a member of another species, usually for food. While engaged in attacking a member of the *same* species or defending itself against the attack, an animal appears to be extremely aroused and excited, and the activity of the sympathetic branch of its autonomic nervous system is high. In contrast, a predatory attack *lacks* a high level of sympathetic activation. A predator is not angry with its prey; attacking the prey is simply a means to an end.

Research with Laboratory Animals

LO 11.4 **Describe what is known from research with laboratory animals about serotonin and the neural circuitry of aggression and predation.**

The motor behaviors that an animal displays during aggression are programmed by neural circuits in the brain stem. Whether an animal attacks depends on many factors, including the nature of the eliciting stimuli in the environment and the animal's previous experience. The activity of the brain stem circuits appears to be controlled by the hypothalamus and the amygdala, which also influence many other species-typical behaviors. And, the activity of the limbic system is controlled by perceptual systems that detect the status of the environment, including the presence of other animals.

NEURAL CIRCUITRY A series of studies by Shaikh, Siegel, and their colleagues (reviewed by Gregg and Siegel, 2001) investigated the neural circuitry involved in aggressive attack and predation by recording from the brains of cats. They found that aggressive attack and predation can be elicited by stimulation of different parts of the periaqueductal gray matter (PAG). In addition, the hypothalamus and amygdala influence attack and predation behaviors through excitatory and inhibitory connections with the PAG. Three principal regions of the amygdala and two regions of the hypothalamus affect defensive rage and predation, both of which appear to be organized by the PAG. A possible connection between the lateral hypothalamus and the ventral PAG has not yet been verified. Figure 11.7 summarizes some of the neural connections involved in predation and defensive behavior.

ROLE OF SEROTONIN The cumulative results of many studies suggest that the activity of serotonergic synapses

---

Figure 11.7 Neural Circuitry in Defensive Behavior and Predation

The diagram shows interconnections of parts of the amygdala, hypothalamus, and periaqueductal gray matter (PAG) and their effects on defensive behaviors and predation in cats, based on the studies by Shaikh, Siegel, and their colleagues. Black arrows indicate excitation; red arrows indicate inhibition.

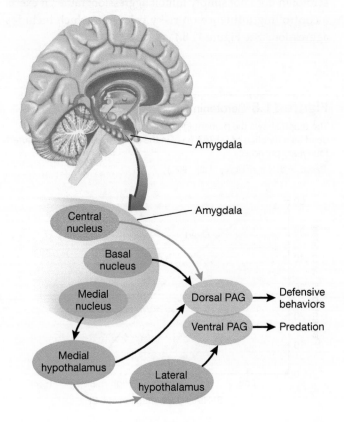

inhibits aggression (e.g., Audero et al., 2013). In contrast, destruction of serotonergic axons in the forebrain (Vergnes et al., 1988) or targeted mutation to reduce serotonin synthesis (Mosienko et al., 2012) facilitates aggressive attack, presumably by removing an inhibitory effect.

A group of researchers has studied the relationship between serotonergic activity and aggressiveness in a free-ranging colony of rhesus monkeys (reviewed by Howell et al., 2007). They assessed serotonergic activity by capturing the monkeys, removing a sample of cerebrospinal fluid (CSF), and analyzing it for 5-HIAA, a metabolite of serotonin (5-HT). When 5-HT is released, most of the neurotransmitter is taken back into the terminal buttons by means of reuptake, but some escapes and is broken down to 5-HIAA, which finds its way into the CSF. High levels of 5-HIAA in the CSF indicate increased serotonergic activity. The investigators found that young male monkeys with the lowest levels of 5-HIAA showed a pattern of risk-taking behavior, including high levels of aggression directed toward animals that were older and much larger than themselves. The young monkeys were much more likely to take dangerous leaps from tree to tree at a height of more than 7 m (27.6 ft.). They were also more likely to pick fights that they could not possibly win. Of 49 preadolescent male monkeys that the investigators followed for four years, 46 percent of those with the lowest 5-HIAA levels died, while none of the monkeys with the highest levels died. Most of the monkeys that died were killed by other monkeys. In fact, the first monkey to be killed had the lowest level of 5-HIAA and was seen attacking two mature males the night before his death. It appears that serotonin does not simply inhibit aggression; rather, it exerts a controlling influence on risky behavior, which includes aggression. (See Figure 11.8.)

Figure 11.8 Serotonin and Risk-Taking Behavior

The graph shows the percentage of young male monkeys alive or dead as a function of 5-HIAA level in the cerebrospinal fluid, measured four years previously.

(Based on data from Higley et al., 1996.)

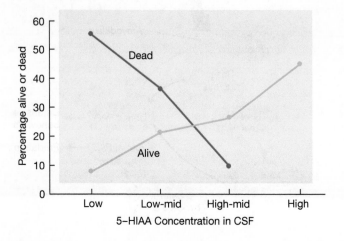

Genetic studies with other species confirm the conclusion that serotonin has an inhibitory role in aggression. For example, selective breeding of rats and silver foxes has yielded animals that display tameness and friendly responses to human contact. These animals showed increased brain levels of serotonin and 5-HIAA (Popova, 2006).

Research with Humans

LO 11.5 **Evaluate the roles of heredity and serotonin in human aggression.**

Human violence and aggression are serious social problems. Consider the following case histories:

> Steve was hyperactive, irritable, and disobedient as a toddler. . . . After dropping out of school at age 14, Steve spent his teen years fighting, stealing, taking drugs, and beating up girlfriends. . . . School counseling, a probation officer, and meetings with child protective service failed to forestall disaster: At 19, several weeks after his last interview with researchers, Steve visited a girlfriend who had recently dumped him, found her with another man, and shot him to death. The same day he tried to kill himself. Now he's serving a life sentence without parole. (Holden, 2000, p. 580)

> By the time Joshua had reached the age of 2, . . . he would bolt out of the house and into traffic. He kicked and head-butted relatives and friends. He poked the family hamster with a pencil and tried to strangle it. He threw regular temper tantrums and would stage toy-throwing frenzies. "At one point he was hurting himself—banging his head against a wall, pinching himself", not to mention leaping off the refrigerator [said his mother]. . . . Showering Joshua with love . . . made little difference: By age 3, his behavior got him kicked out of his preschool. (Holden, 2000, p. 581)

The cases of Steve and Joshua illustrate the emergence of aggressive behaviors early in life. These cases also demonstrate a pervasive pattern of aggressive behavior among some individuals. Neuroscience research has begun to reveal the importance of heredity and activity in the serotonin system in aggressive behavior in humans.

ROLE OF HEREDITY Early experiences can certainly impact the development of aggressive behavior, but studies have shown that heredity plays a significant role. For example, Viding et al., (2005, 2008) studied a group of same-sex twins at the ages of 7 years and 9 years and found a higher correlation between monozygotic twins than dizygotic twins on measures of antisocial behavior and levels of callous, unemotional behavior, which indicates a genetic component in development of these traits. No evidence was found that a shared environment played a role.

ROLE OF SEROTONIN Some, but not all, studies have found that serotonergic neurons play an inhibitory role in human aggression (Duke et al., 2013). Reduced serotonin release (indicated by low levels of 5-HIAA in the CSF) is associated with aggression and other forms of antisocial behavior, including assault, arson, murder, and child abuse (Lidberg et al., 1984, 1985; Virkkunen et al., 1989). Among men with a history of aggression, those with the lowest serotonergic activity were most likely to have close relatives with a history of similar behavior problems (Coccaro et al., 1994). On the other hand, more recent studies have reported a very weak inverse relationship between serotonin and aggression, suggesting that more research is needed (Duke et al., 2013).

If low levels of serotonin release contribute to aggression, drugs that act as serotonin agonists might help to reduce aggressive behavior. Coccaro and Kavoussi (1997) found that fluoxetine (Prozac), a serotonin agonist, decreased irritability and aggressiveness, as measured by a psychological test. Joshua, the little boy described in the introduction to this subsection, came under the care of a psychiatrist who prescribed monoaminergic agonists and began a course of behavior therapy that reduced Joshua's violent outbursts and risk-taking behaviors. (See Figure 11.9.)

Hormonal Control of Aggressive Behavior

LO 11.6 **Summarize the role of hormonal control of aggression, citing evidence from studies involving humans and other animals.**

Many instances of aggressive behavior are related to reproduction. For example, males of some species establish territories that attract females during the breeding season. To do so, they must defend the territories against the intrusion of other males. Even in species in which breeding does not depend on establishing a territory, males may compete for access to females, competition that also involves aggressive behavior. Females, too, often compete with other females for space in which to build nests or dens in which to rear their offspring, and they will defend their offspring against the intrusion of other animals. As you learned in Chapter 10, most reproductive behaviors are controlled by the organizational and activational effects of hormones; therefore, it makes sense that many forms of aggressive behavior are, like mating, affected by hormones.

AGGRESSION IN FEMALES Two adult female rodents that meet in a neutral territory are less likely than males to fight. But aggression between females, like aggression between males, appears to be facilitated by testosterone. Van de Poll et al., (1988) ovariectomized female rats and then gave them daily injections of testosterone, estradiol, or a placebo for 14 days. The animals were then placed in a test cage, and an unfamiliar female was introduced. As Figure 11.10 shows, testosterone increased aggressiveness, whereas estradiol had no effect.

Androgens have an organizational effect on the aggressiveness of females, and a certain amount of prenatal androgenization appears to occur naturally. Most rodent fetuses share their mother's uterus with brothers and sisters, arranged in a row like peas in a pod. A female mouse may have zero, one, or two brothers adjacent to her. Researchers refer to these females as 0M, 1M, or 2M, respectively. (See Figure 11.11.) Being next to a male fetus has an effect on a female's blood levels of androgens prenatally. Vom Saal and Bronson (1980) found that females located between two males had significantly higher levels of testosterone in their blood than did females located between two females (or between a female and the end of the uterus). When they are tested as adults, 2M females are more likely to exhibit interfemale aggressiveness.

Females of some primate species (for example, rhesus monkeys and baboons) are more likely to engage in fights around the time of ovulation (Carpenter, 1942; Saayman, 1971). This phenomenon is probably caused by their increased sexual interest and consequent proximity to males. Another period of fighting occurs just before menstruation (Mallow, 1979; Sassenrath et al., 1973). During this time, females tend to attack other females. In humans, progesterone levels in the luteal phase (before menstruation) appear to be related to aggression in women. Low concentrations of progesterone in the luteal phase were associated with high levels of self-reported aggression and irritability (Ziomkiewicz et al., 2012).

AGGRESSION IN MALES Adult males of many species fight for territory or access to females. In laboratory rodents, androgen secretion occurs prenatally, decreases, and then increases again at the time of puberty. Intermale aggressiveness also begins around the time of puberty, which suggests that the behavior is controlled by neural circuits that are stimulated by androgens. It has long been known that castration reduces aggressiveness and injections of testosterone reinstate it (Beeman, 1947).

In Chapter 10 we saw that early androgenization has an *organizational effect*. The secretion of androgens early in development modifies the developing brain, making neural circuits that control male sexual behavior become more responsive to testosterone. Similarly, early androgenization has an organizational effect that stimulates the development of testosterone-sensitive neural circuits that facilitate intermale aggression after *activational* hormone exposure at puberty.

The organizational effect of androgens on intermale aggression (aggressive displays or actual fights between two males of the same species) is important, but it is not an all-or-none phenomenon. Prolonged administration of testosterone will eventually induce intermale aggression even in

Figure 11.9 Serotonin Activity and Aggression

(a) Some studies have found that serotonergic neurons play an inhibitory role in human aggression.
(b) Selective serotonin reuptake inhibitors (SSRIs) block the serotonin transporter (shown in green on the presynaptic cell), preventing serotonin reuptake by the presynaptic cell. Use of SSRIs results in increased serotonin available in the synapse to bind to receptors and is associated with reduced aggressive behavior.

Activity in serotonin synapse in brain

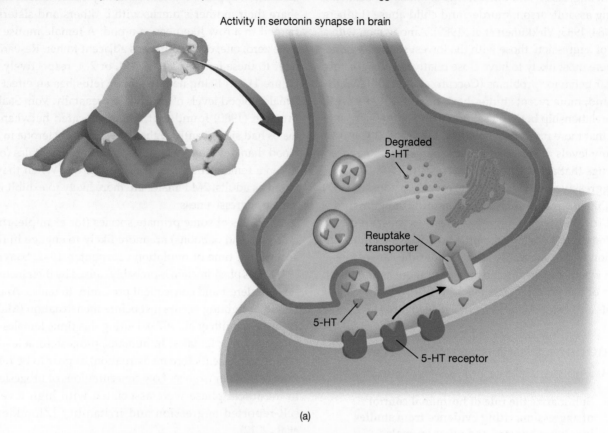

(a)

Increased activity in serotonin synapse in brain

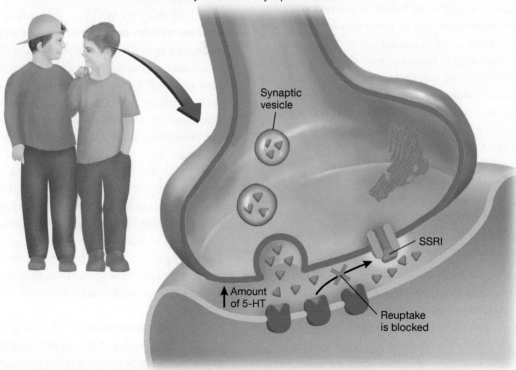

(b)

Figure 11.10 Effects of 14 Days of Estradiol and Testosterone Administration on Interfemale Aggression in Rats

(Based on data from van de Poll et al., 1988.)

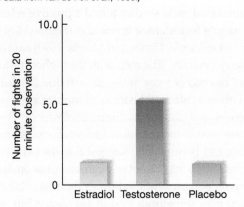

Figure 11.12 Organizational and Activational Effects of Testosterone on Social Aggression

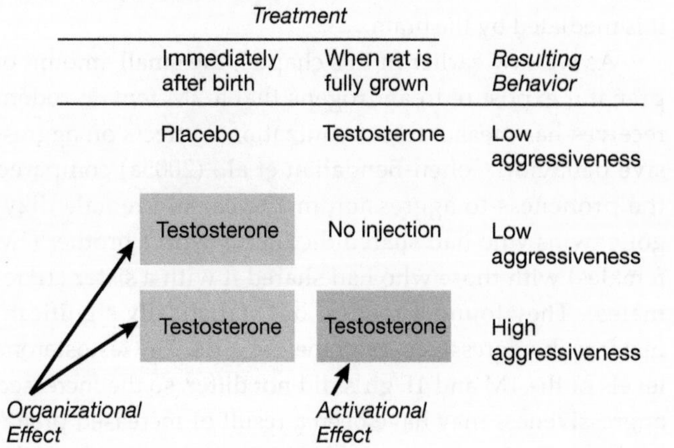

	Treatment	
Immediately after birth	When rat is fully grown	*Resulting Behavior*
Placebo	Testosterone	Low aggressiveness
Testosterone	No injection	Low aggressiveness
Testosterone	Testosterone	High aggressiveness

Organizational Effect   *Activational Effect*

rodents that were castrated immediately after birth. Exposure to androgens early in life decreases the amount of exposure that is necessary to activate aggressive behavior later in life (vom Saal, 1983). Thus, early androgenization *sensitizes* the neural circuits: The earlier the androgenization, the more effective is the sensitization. (See Figure 11.12.)

In Chapter 10 we also saw that androgens stimulate male sexual behavior by interacting with androgen receptors in neurons located in the medial preoptic area (MPA). This region appears to be important in mediating the effects of androgens on intermale aggression as well. Implanting testosterone in the MPA reinstated intermale aggression in castrated male rats (Bean and Conner, 1978). Presumably, the testosterone directly activated the behavior by stimulating

Figure 11.11 0M, 1M, and 2M Female Mouse Fetuses

(Adapted from vom Saal, F. S., in *Hormones and Aggressive Behavior*, edited by B. B. Svare. New York: Plenum Press, 1983.)

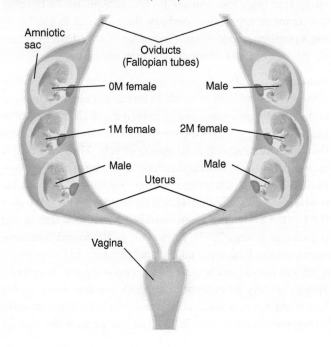

the androgen-sensitive neurons located there. The MPA appears to be involved in several behaviors related to reproduction: male sexual behavior, maternal behavior, and intermale aggression.

Males of most species more readily attack other males but usually do not attack females. Their ability to discriminate the sex of the intruder appears to be based on the presence of particular pheromones. Intermale aggression was abolished in mice by cutting the vomeronasal nerve, which deprives the brain of input from the vomeronasal organ (Bean, 1982). And if the urine of female mice is painted on a male mouse, he will not be attacked if he is introduced into another male's cage (Dixon, 1973; Dixon and Mackintosh, 1971). A targeted mutation against proteins that are essential for the detection of pheromones by the vomeronasal organ abolishes a male mouse's ability to discriminate between males and females. Because male intruders were not recognized as rival males, they were not attacked. In fact, the mice with the targeted mutation attempted to copulate with the intruders (Prince et al., 2013; Stowers et al., 2002).

EFFECTS OF ANDROGENS ON HUMAN AGGRESSIVE BEHAVIOR Boys are generally more aggressive than girls. Many societies tolerate assertiveness and aggressive behavior from boys more than they do from girls. Socialization of boys and girls plays an important role in sex differences in aggressiveness in our species. The question is not whether socialization has an effect (it does) but whether biological influences, such as exposure to androgens, have an effect too.

Organizational Effects Prenatal androgenization increases aggressive behavior in all species that have been studied, including primates. Therefore, if androgens did not affect aggressive behavior in humans, our species would be exceptional. After puberty, androgens also begin to have activational effects. Boys' testosterone levels begin to increase during the early teens, at which time aggressive behavior and intermale fighting also increase (Mazur, 1983). Boys' social status changes during puberty, and testosterone affects their muscles as well as their brains, so we cannot be certain that the effect is hormonally produced or, if it is, that it is mediated by the brain.

As we saw earlier in this chapter, the small amount of prenatal exposure to androgens that a 2M female rodent receives has measurable organizational effects on aggressive behavior. Cohen-Bendahan et al., (2005a) compared the proneness to aggression in 13-year-old female dizygotic twins who had shared the uterus with a brother (1M females) with those who had shared it with a sister (1F females). They found a modest but statistically significant increase in aggressiveness in the 1M girls. The testosterone levels of the 1M and 1F girls did not differ, so the increased aggressiveness may have been a result of increased prenatal exposure to androgens. It is impossible to rule out the possibility that being raised with a same-aged brother might have an effect on a girl's proneness to aggression too.

As we saw in Chapter 10, girls with congenital adrenal hyperplasia (CAH) are exposed to abnormally high levels of androgens—produced by their own adrenal glands—during prenatal development. The effects of this exposure include a preference for boys as playmates, interest in toys and games that boys typically prefer, and, in adulthood, an increased prevalence of sexual attraction to other women. Parental socialization and biological differences contribute to sex-typical toy play, but not other characteristics such as spatial ability (Wong et al., 2012). Berenbaum and Resnick (1997) found that women and adolescent girls with CAH displayed higher levels of aggression, as measured by parents' ratings and paper-and-pencil tests.

Activational Effects   Scientifically rigorous evidence concerning the activational effects of androgens on aggression in adulthood is difficult to obtain in humans. In the past, authorities attempted to suppress sex-related aggression by castrating convicted male sex offenders. Investigators reported that aggressive attacks disappeared, along with the offender's sex drive (Hawke, 1951; Laschet, 1973; Sturup, 1961). However, the studies typically lack appropriate control groups and usually do not measure aggressive behavior directly.

Some cases of aggressiveness, especially sexual assault, have been treated with synthetic steroids that inhibit the production of androgens by the testes. Treatment with drugs is preferable to castration, because the effects of drugs are reversible. However, the efficacy of treatment with antiandrogens has yet to be established conclusively. According to Walker and Meyer (1981), these drugs decrease sex-related aggression but have no effect on other forms of aggression. In fact, Zumpe et al., (1991) found that one of these drugs decreased sexual activity and aggression toward females when administered to male monkeys but actually *increased* intermale aggression.

Another way to determine whether androgens affect aggressiveness in humans is to examine the testosterone levels of people who exhibit varying levels of aggressive behavior. However, even though this approach poses fewer ethical problems, it presents methodological ones. First, let's review some evidence. In a review of the literature, Archer (1994) found that most studies found a positive relationship between men's testosterone levels and their level of aggressiveness. For example, Dabbs and Morris (1990) studied 4,462 U.S. military veterans. The men with the highest testosterone levels had records of more antisocial activities, including assaults on other adults and histories of more trouble with parents, teachers, and classmates during adolescence. The largest effects were seen in men of lower socioeconomic status.

Mazur and Booth (1998) suggest that the primary social effect of androgens may be not on aggression, but on *dominance*. If androgens enhance motivation to dominate others, that motivation may sometimes lead to aggression but not in all situations. For example, a person might strive to defeat others symbolically (through athletic competition or acquisition of symbols of status) rather than through direct aggression.

Role of Environment   In any event we must remember that *correlation* does not necessarily indicate *causation*. A person's environment can affect his or her testosterone level. For example, losing a competition causes a fall in blood levels of testosterone (Elias, 1981; Mazur and Lamb, 1980). Even winning or losing a game of chance carried out in a psychology laboratory can affect participants' testosterone levels: Winners feel better afterward and have a higher level of testosterone (McCaul et al., 1992). Bernhardt et al., (1998) found that basketball and soccer fans showed an increase in testosterone levels if their team won and a decrease if it lost. People adopting open, expressive postures (called "power poses") experience an increase in testosterone levels and feelings of power, but not necessarily aggression (Carney et al., 2010). Thus, we cannot be sure in any correlational study that high testosterone levels *cause* people to become dominant or aggressive; perhaps their success in establishing a position of dominance increases their testosterone levels relative to those of the people they dominate.

Anabolic Steroids   As news reports have publicized, some athletes take anabolic steroids to increase their muscle mass and strength and, supposedly, to increase their competitiveness. Anabolic steroids include natural androgens and synthetic hormones with androgenic effects. Thus, we might expect that these hormones would increase aggressiveness, a response sometimes called "roid rage" in popular media. Use of anabolic steroids in Sweden, Australia, and the United States is approximately 1 percent or less of the population (Dunn, 2015). Yates et al., (1992) found that male weight lifters who were taking anabolic steroids were more aggressive and hostile than those who were not. However, approximately 40 percent of anabolic steroid users report increased aggression, but that means that approximately 60 percent do *not* (Dunn, 2015). The role of anabolic steroid use in aggression is not yet clear, and we cannot be certain that steroid use is responsible for the increased aggressiveness; it could be that the men who were already more competitive and aggressive are more likely to choose to take steroids (Dunn, 2015; Yates et al., 1992).

Alcohol   An interesting set of experiments with another species of primates might have some relevance to human aggression. Evidence suggests that the effects of alcohol may interact with those of androgens. Winslow and Miczek (1985, 1988) found that alcohol increases intermale aggression in dominant male squirrel monkeys, but only during the mating season, when their blood level of testosterone is two to three times higher than that during the nonmating season. These studies suggest that the effects of alcohol interact both with social status and with testosterone. (See Figure 11.13.) This suggestion was confirmed by Winslow et al., (1988), who tested monkeys during the nonmating season. They found that alcohol increased the aggressive behavior of dominant monkeys if the monkeys were also given injections of testosterone. However, these treatments were ineffective in subordinate monkeys, which presumably had learned not to be aggressive. The next step will be to find the neural mechanisms that are responsible for these interactions.

Figure 11.13 Alcohol, Mating, and Aggressive Behavior in Monkeys

The graph shows the effect of alcohol intake on frequency of aggressive behavior of dominant and subordinate male squirrel monkeys during the mating season and the nonmating season.

(Based on data from Winslow and Miczek, 1988.)

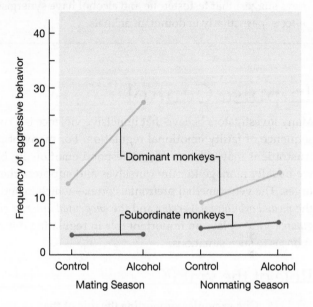

Section Review

Aggression

LO 11.4 Describe what is known from research with laboratory animals about serotonin and the neural circuitry of aggression and predation.

Aggressive behaviors are species-typical and serve useful functions most of the time. The periaqueductal gray matter appears to be involved in defensive behavior and predation. These mechanisms are modulated by the hypothalamus and amygdala. The activity of serotonergic neurons appears to inhibit risk-taking behaviors, including aggression. Destruction of serotonergic axons in the forebrain enhances aggression, and administration of drugs that facilitate serotonergic transmission reduces it. Low CSF levels of 5-HIAA (a metabolite of serotonin) are correlated with increased risk-taking and aggressive behavior in monkeys. High levels of brain serotonin and 5-HIAA in rats and silver foxes are associated with reduced aggression.

LO 11.5 Evaluate the roles of heredity and serotonin in human aggression.

Low CSF levels of 5-HIAA are correlated with increased risk-taking and aggressive behavior in humans. Genetic factors play a role in people's level of aggression and antisocial behavior.

LO 11.6 Summarize the role of hormonal control of aggression, citing evidence from studies involving humans and other animals.

Because many aggressive behaviors are related to reproduction, these behaviors are influenced by hormones, especially sex steroid hormones. Androgens primarily affect offensive attack; they are not necessary for defensive behaviors, which are shown by females as well as males. In males, androgens have organizational and activational effects on offensive attack, just as they have on male sexual behavior. The effects of androgens on intermale aggression appear to be mediated by the medial preoptic area. Female rodents will fight when they meet in neutral territory but less often than males. Female rodents that have been slightly androgenized (2M females) are more likely to attack other females. Female primates are most likely to fight around the time of ovulation, perhaps because their increased sexual interest brings them closer to males. Androgens apparently promote aggressive behavior in humans, but this topic is more difficult to study in our species than in laboratory animals. Evidence from girls with congenital adrenal hyperplasia and female dizygotic twins who shared the uterus with a brother suggests that prenatal androgens promote aggressive behavior later in life. Research suggests that the primary effect of androgens may be to increase motivation to achieve dominance and that increased aggression may be secondary to this effect. It is not clear whether higher androgen levels promote dominance or whether successful dominance increases androgen levels. Studies with monkeys suggest that testosterone and alcohol have synergistic effects, particularly in dominant animals.

Thought Question

From the point of view of evolution, aggressive behavior and a tendency to establish dominance have useful functions. In particular, they increase the likelihood that only the healthiest and most vigorous animals will reproduce. Can you think of examples of beneficial and detrimental effects of these tendencies among members of our own species?

Impulse Control

Many investigators believe that impulsive violence is a consequence of faulty emotional regulation. For many of us, frustrations may elicit an urge to respond emotionally, but we usually manage to calm ourselves and suppress these urges. The ventromedial prefrontal cortex—which includes the *medial orbitofrontal cortex* and the *subgenual anterior cingulate cortex*—plays an important role in regulating our responses to such situations.

Role of the vmPFC

LO 11.7 Cite examples supporting the role of the ventromedial prefrontal cortex in impulse control.

The importance of the vmPFC in control of emotional behavior is demonstrated by the effects of damage to this region. One famous case comes from the mid-1800s. Phineas Gage, the foreman of a railway construction crew, was using a steel rod to ram a charge of blasting powder into a hole that had been drilled in solid rock. Suddenly, the charge exploded and sent the rod into his cheek, through his brain, and out the top of his head. (See Figure 11.14.) He survived, but by many accounts he was a different man. Before his injury Gage was described as serious, industrious, and energetic. Afterward, he was described as childish, irresponsible, thoughtless of others, unable to make or carry out plans, and his actions appeared to be capricious and whimsical. It was initially believed that his accident largely destroyed the vmPFC bilaterally (Damasio et al., 1994); however, some researchers have suggested that the damage was limited to the left vmPFC only (Ratiu and Ion-Florin, 2004). In addition, a reexamination of the historical evidence suggests that Gage may have made substantial

Figure 11.14 Phineas Gage's Accident.

The steel rod entered his left cheek and exited through the top of his head.

(From: Everett Collection Historical / Alamy)

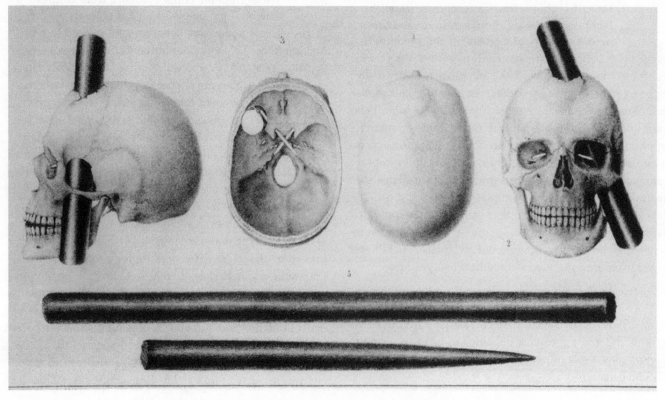

recovery following the accident, with less impairment to his emotional and impulse control than initially believed, consistent with damage to only one half of the vmPFC (Macmillan and Lena, 2010).

People whose vmPFC has been damaged by disease or accident are still able to accurately assess the significance of particular situations but only in a *theoretical* sense. For example, patient E. R. experienced bilateral damage of the vmPFC produced by a benign tumor, which was successfully removed (Eslinger and Damasio, 1985). E. R. displayed excellent social judgment and when he was given hypothetical situations involving moral, ethical, or practical dilemmas and asked what the people involved should do, he always gave sensible answers and justified them with carefully reasoned logic. However, his own life was a different matter. He spent his life's savings, lost one job after another, was unable to distinguish between trivial decisions and important ones, and his wife left and sued for divorce. Although E. R. "had learned and used normal patterns of social behavior before his brain lesion, and . . . could recall such patterns . . . , *real-life situations failed to evoke them*" (p. 1737).

Evidence suggests that the vmPFC serves as an interface between brain mechanisms involved in automatic emotional responses (both learned and unlearned) and those involved in the control of complex behaviors. This role includes using our emotional reactions to guide our behavior and in controlling the occurrence of emotional reactions in various social situations.

Damage to the vmPFC causes serious and often debilitating impairments of behavioral control and decision making. These impairments appear to be a consequence of emotional dysregulation. Anderson et al., (2006) obtained ratings of emotional behaviors of patients with lesions of the vmPFC, such as frustration tolerance, emotional instability, anxiety, and irritability, from the patients' relatives. They also obtained ratings of the patients' real-world competencies, such as judgment, planning, social inappropriateness, and financial and occupational status, from both relatives and clinicians. They found a significant correlation between emotional dysfunction and impairments in real-world competencies. There was no relationship between cognitive abilities and real-world competencies, which strongly suggests that emotional problems lie at the base of the real-world difficulties exhibited by people with vmPFC damage.

An interesting functional-imaging study by Nili et al., (2010) suggests that the vmPFC plays a role in brain mechanisms of courage. Nili and his colleagues scanned the brains of people who were or were not afraid of snakes. While the people were in the scanner, they could press buttons that controlled the action of a conveyer belt that brought a live snake toward or away from them. People who were not afraid of snakes brought the snake near them and showed no signs of fear. However, people who were afraid of snakes did show signs of fear as the snake approached. Some of the fearful people pressed the button that moved the snake away from them, but others brought the snake near to them, even though they were plainly afraid. In other words, they showed courage—they overcame their fear. A display of courage was accompanied by activation of a region of the vmPFC, the subgenual anterior cingulate cortex. Participants who succumbed to their fear—that is, those who moved the snake away—did not show activation of the subgenual anterior cingulate cortex. (See Figure 11.15.)

Brain Development and Impulse Control

LO 11.8 Provide evidence for a developmental factor in impulse control.

Many investigators believe that impulsive violence is a consequence of faulty emotional regulation. The amygdala plays an important role in provoking anger and violent

---

Figure 11.15 Role of the vmPFC

The participants' task was to reach maximal proximity to either a live snake or a toy bear, by repeatedly choosing whether to bring the object closer or move it away, while undergoing fMRI brain scanning.
A display of courage was accompanied by activation of a region of the vmPFC, the subgenual anterior cingulate cortex.

(Nili, U., Goldberg, H., Weizman, A., and Dudai, Y., Fear thou not: Activity of frontal and temporal circuits in moments of real-life courage, *Neuron*, 2010, *66*(6), 949–962.)

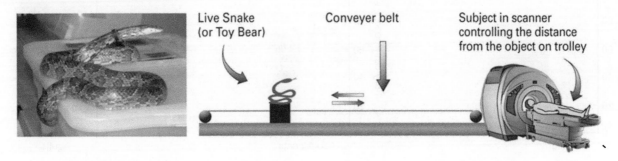

emotional reactions, and the prefrontal cortex plays an important role in suppressing such behavior by making us see its negative consequences. The amygdala matures early in development, but the prefrontal cortex matures much later, during late childhood and early adulthood. (See Figure 11.16.) As the prefrontal cortex matures, adolescents show increases in speed of cognitive processing, abstract reasoning ability, ability to shift attention from one topic to another, and ability to inhibit inappropriate responses (Yurgelun-Todd, 2007). In fact, a structural imaging study by Whittle et al., (2008) found that aggressive behavior during parent–child interactions during adolescence was positively related to the volume of the amygdala and negatively related to the relative volume of the right medial prefrontal cortex.

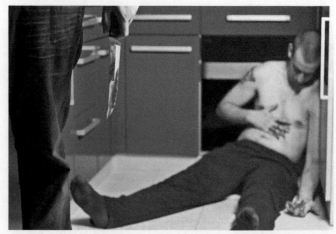

According to research, people with antisocial personality disorder showed an 11 percent reduction in volume of the gray matter of the prefrontal cortex.

Crime and Impulse Control

LO 11.9 Compare brain differences involved in impulse control between those convicted of a crime or diagnosed with antisocial personality disorder and typically-developing adults.

Raine et al., (1998) found evidence of decreased prefrontal activity and increased subcortical activity (including the amygdala) in the brains of convicted murderers. These changes were primarily seen in impulsive, emotional murderers. Cold-blooded, calculating, predatory murderers—whose crimes were not accompanied by anger and rage—showed more typical patterns of brain activity. Presumably, increased activation of the amygdala reflected an increased tendency for display of negative emotions, and the decreased activation of the prefrontal cortex reflected a decreased ability to inhibit the activity of the amygdala and thus control the people's emotions. Raine et al., (2002) found that people with antisocial personality disorder showed an 11 percent reduction in volume of the gray matter of the prefrontal cortex.

Serotonin and Impulse Control

LO 11.10 Explain the role of serotonin in impulse control regulation.

Earlier in this chapter we saw that decreased activity of serotonergic neurons is associated with aggression, violence, and risk taking. As we saw in that subsection, decreased activity of the prefrontal cortex is also associated with antisocial behavior. These two facts appear to be linked. The prefrontal cortex receives a major projection of serotonergic axons. Research indicates that serotonergic input to the prefrontal cortex activates this region. For example, a functional-imaging study by Mann et al., (1996) showed that fenfluramine, a drug that stimulates the release of 5-HT, increases the activity of the prefrontal cortex, which presumably inhibits the activity of the amygdala and suppresses aggressive behavior. Crockett et al., (2010) found that a single high dose of a 5-HT agonist decreased the likelihood of

---

Figure 11.16 Development of Amygdala Over Lifespan

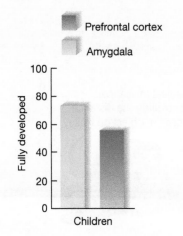

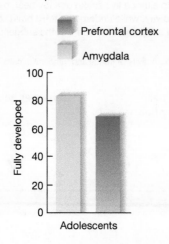

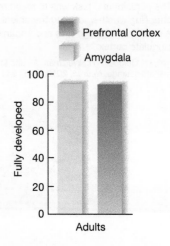

participants making a decision to cause harm in scenarios that presented moral dilemmas. It seems likely, therefore, that an abnormally *low* level of serotonin release can result in decreased activity of the prefrontal cortex and increased likelihood of utilitarian judgments (the next section includes more information about utilitarian judgments) or, in the extreme, antisocial behavior.

Several studies have found evidence for deficits in serotonergic innervation of the PFC associated with impulsive behavior. New et al., (2002) found that a serotonin-releasing drug increased the activity of the orbitofrontal cortex in healthy, nonviolent participants but failed to do so in participants with a history of impulsive aggression. A functional-imaging study found evidence for lower levels of serotonin transporters in the medial prefrontal cortex of people with impulsive aggression (Frankle et al., 2005). Because serotonin transporters are found in the membrane of serotonergic terminal buttons, this study suggests that the medial prefrontal cortex of these people contains decreased serotonergic input.

As we saw earlier, impulsive aggression has been successfully treated with specific serotonin reuptake inhibitors such as fluoxetine. A functional-imaging study by New et al., (2004) measured regional brain activity of people with histories of impulsive aggression before and after 12 weeks of treatment with fluoxetine. They found that the drug increased the activity of the prefrontal cortex and reduced aggressiveness.

Moral Decision Making

LO 11.11 **Describe the brain regions involved in emotional aspects of moral decision making, and cite evidence from the research literature.**

Evidence suggests that emotional reactions guide moral judgments as well as decisions involving personal risks and rewards and that the prefrontal cortex plays a role in these judgments as well. In previous years, moral judgments were believed to be a product of conscious, rational decision making. However, recent research on the role of neural mechanisms of emotion suggest that emotions play an important role—perhaps the *most* important role—in the formation of moral judgments.

Consider the following moral dilemma (Thomson, 1986): You see a runaway trolley hurtling down a track leading to a cliff. There are five people on the track. Without your intervention these people will soon die. However, you are standing near a switch that will shunt the trolley off to another track, where the vehicle will stop safely. But there is another person on that track, and he will be killed if you throw the switch to save the five people on the other track. Should you stand by and watch the trolley kill the five people, or should you save them—and kill the man on the other track?

Most people conclude that the better choice would be to throw the switch; saving five people justifies the sacrifice

of one man. This decision is based on conscious, logical application of a rule that it is better to kill one person than five people. But consider a variation of this dilemma. As before, the trolley is hurtling toward doom, but there is no switch at hand to shunt it to another track. Instead, you are standing on a bridge over the track. A very large man is standing there too, and if you give him a push, his body will fall onto the track and stop the trolley. (In this scenario, you are too small to stop the trolley, so you cannot save the five people by sacrificing yourself.) What should you do? (See Figure 11.17.)

Most people feel repugnance at the thought of pushing the man off the bridge and balk at the idea of doing so, even though the result would be the same as the first dilemma: one person lost, five people saved. Whether we kill someone by sending a trolley his way or by pushing him off a bridge into the path of an oncoming trolley, he dies when the trolley strikes him. But somehow, imagining yourself pushing a person's body and causing his death seems more emotionally wrenching than throwing a switch that changes the course of a runaway trolley. Thus, moral judgments appear to be guided by emotional reactions and are not simply the products of a rational, logical decision-making processes.

In a functional-imaging study, Greene et al., (2001) presented people with moral dilemmas such as the one we just described and found that thinking about them activated several brain regions involved in emotional reactions, including the vmPFC. Making innocuous decisions, such as whether to take a bus or train to some destination, did not activate these regions. Perhaps, then, our reluctance to push someone to his death is guided by the unpleasant emotional reaction we feel when we contemplate this action.

Let's reconsider the contrast between the decision to throw a switch to save four lives and the decision to shove someone onto the tracks to accomplish the same goal. Consideration of the first dilemma raises a much smaller emotional reaction than consideration of the second dilemma does, and consideration of only the second dilemma strongly activates the vmPFC. We might expect that people with vmPFC damage, who show impairments of emotional reaction, might choose to push the man onto the track in the second dilemma. In fact, that is exactly what they do. Koenigs et al., (2007) presented nonmoral, impersonal moral, and personal moral scenarios to patients with vmPFC lesions, patients with brain damage not including this region, and healthy controls. The table lists examples of the scenarios that the investigators of the study presented to their participants. (See Table 11.2.)

Koenigs and his colleagues predicted that patients with vmPFC lesions should make the same decisions as participants in the other two groups on the nonmoral and impersonal moral judgments, because these decisions are normally solved rationally, without a strong emotional component. Only the outcome, or *utility*, of the choice need be considered. However, the emotional deficits of

Figure 11.17 Moral Decision-Making Scenario: The Case of the Trolley

In scenario (a) a person must decide to throw a switch to save five people or one person. In scenario (b) a person must decide to push a man off a bridge to save five people.

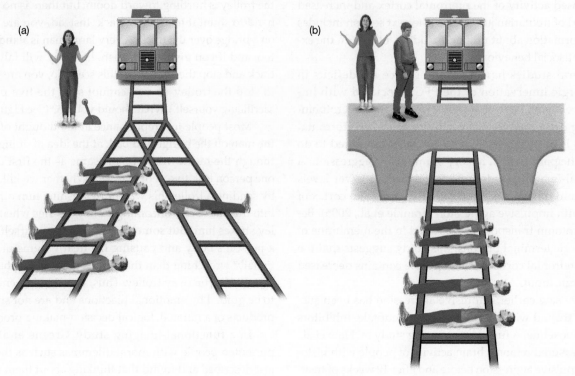

patients with prefrontal damage would be expected to lead to utilitarian judgments even in the case of personal moral judgments—and that is precisely what was seen. The patients with vmPFC lesions were much more likely to say "yes" to the question posed at the end of the scenarios.

Reluctance to push someone to his death even though that action would save the lives of others might be caused by the unpleasant thought of what it would feel like to commit that action and see the man fall to his death. If this is true, then perhaps people with vmPFC lesions say that they are willing to push the man off the bridge because thinking about doing so does not evoke an unpleasant emotional reaction. In fact, Moretto et al., (2009) found that people without brain damage showed physiological signs of an unpleasant emotional reaction when they contemplated pushing the man off the bridge—and said that they would not push him. People with vmPFC lesions did not show signs of this emotional reaction—and said that they *would* push him.

Table 11.2 Examples of Scenarios Involving Nonmoral, Impersonal Moral, and Personal Moral Judgments from the Study by Koenigs et al. (2007)

Brownies (Nonmoral scenario)

You have decided to make a batch of brownies for yourself. You open your recipe book and find a recipe for brownies. The recipe calls for a cup of chopped walnuts. You don't like walnuts, but you do like macadamia nuts. As it happens, you have both kinds of nuts available to you.

Would you substitute macadamia nuts for walnuts in order to avoid eating walnuts?

Speedboat (Impersonal moral scenario)

While on vacation on a remote island, you are fishing from a seaside dock. You observe a group of tourists board a small boat and set sail for a nearby island. Soon after their departure you hear over the radio that there is a violent storm brewing, a storm that is sure to intercept them. The only way that you can ensure their safety is to warn them by borrowing a nearby speedboat. The speedboat belongs to a miserly tycoon who would not take kindly to your borrowing his property.

Would you borrow the speedboat in order to warn the tourists about the storm?

Lifeboat (Personal moral scenario)

You are on a cruise ship when there is a fire on board, and the ship has to be abandoned. The lifeboats are carrying many more people than they were designed to carry. The lifeboat you're in is sitting dangerously low in the water—a few inches lower, and it will sink. The seas start to get rough, and the boat begins to fill with water. If nothing is done it will sink before the rescue boats arrive, and everyone on board will die. However, there is an injured person who will not survive in any case. If you throw that person overboard the boat will stay afloat and the remaining passengers will be saved.

Would you throw this person overboard in order to save the lives of the remaining passengers?

Section Review

Impulse Control

LO 11.7 **Cite examples supporting the role of the ventromedial prefrontal cortex in impulse control.**

The vmPFC plays an important role in emotional reactions. This region communicates with the dorsomedial thalamus, temporal cortex, ventral tegmental area, olfactory system, amygdala, cingulate cortex, lateral hypothalamus, and other regions of the frontal cortex, including the dorsolateral prefrontal cortex. People with vmPFC lesions show impulsive behavior and often display outbursts of inappropriate anger. They are able to explain the implications of complex social situations but often respond inappropriately when they find themselves in these situations. The activity of the vmPFC increases when people show courageous behavior (impulse control)—letting a snake approach them even though they fear snakes.

LO 11.8 **Provide evidence for a developmental factor in impulse control.**

The amygdala is responsible for anger and violence and matures before the prefrontal cortex, which suppresses violent behavior. Research found that aggressive behavior during adolescence was positively related to the volume of the amygdala and negatively related to the relative volume of the right medial prefrontal cortex.

LO 11.9 **Compare brain differences involved in impulse control between those convicted of a crime or diagnosed with antisocial personality disorder and typically-developing adults.**

Decreased prefrontal activity and increased subcortical activity are associated with impulsive, violent behavior. People with antisocial personality disorder have reduced gray matter volume in the prefrontal cortex.

LO 11.10 **Explain the role of serotonin in impulse control regulation.**

Serotonergic input to the prefrontal cortex inhibits the amygdala and suppresses aggressive and impulsive behavior. Increasing serotonergic activity reduces impulsive behavior. The vmPFC of people with impulsive aggression contains less dense serotonergic input.

LO 11.11 **Describe the brain regions involved in emotional aspects of moral decision making, and cite evidence from the research literature.**

The vmPFC is involved in making moral judgments. When people make judgments that involve conflicts between utilitarian judgments and personal moral judgments, the vmPFC is activated. People with damage to the vmPFC display utilitarian moral judgments.

Thought Question

Is there value in understanding the neural basis of moral behavior and decision making? How might this information be used by clinicians, police, judges, jury members, or educators?

Communication of Emotions

As described earlier in this chapter, emotions are organized responses (consisting of behavioral, autonomic, and hormonal components) that prepare an animal to deal with existing situations in the environment, such as events that pose a threat to the organism. For our earliest premammalian ancestors, that is likely all there was to emotions. But over time, other responses, with new functions, evolved. Many species of animals (including our own) communicate their emotions to others by means of postural changes, facial expressions, and nonverbal sounds (such as sighs, moans, and growls). These expressions serve useful social functions: They tell other individuals how we feel and—more to the point—what we are likely to do. For example, they warn a rival that we are angry or tell friends that we are sad and would like some comfort and reassurance. They can also indicate that a danger might be present or that something interesting seems to be happening. This section examines such expression and communication of emotions.

Facial Expression of Emotions: Innate Responses

LO 11.12 **Describe evidence in support of emotional expressions as innate responses.**

Charles Darwin (1872/1965) suggested that human expressions of emotion have evolved from similar expressions in other animals. He said that emotional expressions are innate, unlearned responses consisting of a complex set of movements, principally of the facial muscles. Thus, a person's sneer and a wolf's snarl are biologically determined response patterns, both controlled by innate brain mechanisms, just as coughing and sneezing are. Some of these movements resemble the behaviors themselves and may have evolved from them. For example, a snarl shows one's teeth and can be seen as an anticipation of biting.

Darwin obtained evidence for his conclusion that emotional expressions were innate by observing his own children and by corresponding with people living in various isolated cultures around the world. He reasoned that if people all over the world, no matter how isolated, show the same facial expressions of emotion, then these expressions must be inherited instead of learned. The logical argument goes like this: When groups of people are isolated for many years, they develop different languages. Thus, we can say that the words people use are arbitrary; there is no biological basis for using particular words to represent particular concepts. However, if facial expressions are inherited, then they should take approximately the same form in people from all cultures, despite their isolation from one another. Darwin did, indeed, find that people in different cultures used the same patterns of movement of facial muscles to express a particular emotional state.

Classic research by Ekman and his colleagues (Ekman and Friesen, 1971; Ekman, 1980) tends to confirm Darwin's hypothesis that facial expression of emotion uses an innate, species-typical repertoire of movements of facial muscles (Darwin, 1872/1965). For example, Ekman and Friesen (1971) studied the ability of members of an isolated tribe in New Guinea to recognize facial expressions of emotion produced by Westerners. They had no trouble doing so and they produced facial expressions that Westerners readily recognized. Figure 11.18 shows four photographs taken from videotapes of a man from this tribe reacting to stories designed to evoke facial expressions of happiness, sadness, anger, and disgust.

Because the same facial expressions were used by people who had not previously been exposed to each other, Ekman and Friesen concluded that the expressions were unlearned behavior patterns. In contrast, different cultures use different words to express particular concepts; production of these words does not involve innate responses but must be learned.

Other researchers have compared the facial expressions of blind and sighted people. They reasoned that if the facial expressions of the two groups are similar, then the expressions are innate for our species and do not require learning by imitation. In fact, the facial expressions of young blind and sighted children are very similar (Izard, 1971; Woodworth and Schlosberg, 1954). In addition, a study of the emotional expressions of people competing (and winning or losing) in athletic events in the Paralympic Games found no differences between the expressions of congenitally blind, noncongenitally blind, and sighted athletes (Matsumoto

Figure 11.18 Facial Expressions in a New Guinea Tribesman

The tribesman made these expressions when he heard the following stories: (a) "Your friend has come and you are happy." (b) "Your child had died." (c) "You are angry and about to fight." (d) "You see a dead pig that has been lying there a long time."

(From Ekman, P., *The Face of Man: Expressions of Universal Emotions in a New Guinea Village*, New York: Garland STPM Press, 1980. Reprinted with permission.)

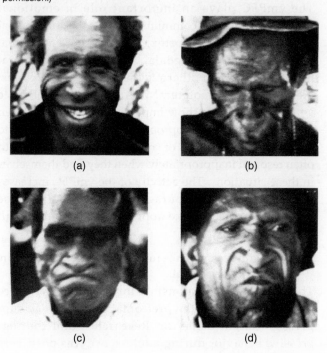

(a)   (b)

(c)   (d)

and Willingham, 2009). Thus, both the cross-cultural studies and the investigations of people who are blind confirm the innate quality of these facial expressions of emotions.

A study by Sauter et al., (2010) reached similar conclusions. The investigators carried out a vocal version of the study by Ekman and Friesen. They presented European English-speakers and natives of isolated northern Namibian villages with recordings of sounds of nonverbal vocalizations to situations that would be expected to produce the emotions of anger, disgust, fear, sadness, surprise, or amusement. The participants were told a story and then heard two different vocalizations (sighs, groans, laughs, and so on), one of which would be appropriate for the emotion produced by the story. Members of both cultures had no difficulty choosing the correct vocalizations of members of their culture and the other culture.

Neural Basis of the Communication of Emotions: Recognition

LO 11.13 Summarize the brain structures involved in emotional recognition, by addressing laterality, direction of gaze, imitation, and disgust.

Effective communication is a two-way process. That is, the ability to display one's emotional state by changes in expression is useful only if other people are able to recognize them. Kraut and Johnston (1979) unobtrusively observed people in circumstances that would be likely to make them happy. They found that happy situations (such as making a strike while bowling, seeing the home team score, or experiencing a beautiful day) produced only small signs of happiness when the people were alone. However, when the people were interacting socially with other people, they were much more likely to smile. For example, bowlers who made a strike usually did not smile when the ball hit the pins, but when they turned around to face their companions, they often smiled. Jones et al., (1991) found that even 10-month-old children showed this tendency to display emotion when an audience was present.

Recognition of another person's facial expression of emotions is generally automatic, rapid, and accurate. Tracy and Robbins (2008) found that observers quickly recognized brief expressions of a variety of emotions. If they were given more time to think about the expression they had seen, the participants showed very little improvement. Rapid assessments are sometimes called "thin slice" judgments by researchers. Thin slice assessments of situations and behaviors with emotional content (such as deception or communication) have been found to be as accurate when exposure to content is less than 30 seconds, as when it is 300 seconds. Additional time to assess emotional content does not lead to greater accuracy in these examples either (Ambady and

William Perugini/Shutterstock

Research shows that observers quickly recognize brief expressions of a variety of emotions.

Rosenthal, 1992). Similar research in music reported accurate assessment of emotional content in songs after only 300–400 ms of exposure (Krumhansl, 2010).

LATERALITY OF EMOTIONAL RECOGNITION We recognize other people's feelings by means of vision and audition—seeing their facial expressions and hearing their tone of voice and choice of words. Many studies have found that the right hemisphere plays a more important role than the left hemisphere in comprehension of emotion. For example, Bowers et al., (1991) found that patients with right hemisphere damage had difficulty producing or describing mental images of facial expressions of emotions.

Several functional-imaging studies have confirmed these results. For example, George et al., (1996) had participants listen to some sentences and identify their emotional content. In one condition the participants listened to the meaning of the words and said whether they described a situation in which someone would be happy, sad, angry, or neutral. In another condition the participants judged the emotional state from the tone of the voice. The investigators found that comprehension of emotion from word meaning increased the activity of the prefrontal cortex bilaterally, the left hemisphere more than the right. Comprehension of emotion from tone of voice increased the activity of only the right prefrontal cortex. (See Figure 11.19.)

Heilman et al., (1983) recorded a particularly interesting case of a man with a disorder called *pure word deafness,* caused by damage to the left temporal cortex. (This syndrome is described in Chapter 14.) The man could not comprehend the meaning of speech but had no difficulty identifying the emotion being expressed by its intonation. This case, like the functional-imaging study by George et al., (1996), indicates that comprehension of words and recognition of tone of voice are independent functions.

ROLE OF THE AMYGDALA AND PREFRONTAL CORTEX As we saw in the previous sections, the amygdala plays a special role in emotional responses. It plays a role in emotional recognition as well. For example, several studies have found that lesions of the amygdala (the result of degenerative diseases or surgery for severe seizure disorders) impair a person's ability to recognize facial expressions of emotion, especially expressions of fear (Adolphs et al., 1994, 1995, 1999; Calder et al., 1996; Young et al., 1995). In addition, functional-imaging studies (Morris et al., 1996; Whalen et al., 1998) have found large increases in the activity of the amygdala when people view photographs of faces expressing fear but only small increases (or even decreases) when they look at photographs of happy faces. Although amygdala lesions impair visual recognition of facial expressions of emotion, several studies have found that they do not appear to affect people's ability to recognize emotions in tone of voice (Adolphs and Tranel, 1999; Anderson and Phelps, 1998).

Figure 11.19 Perception of Emotions

The PET scans indicate brain regions activated by listening to emotions expressed by meanings of words (red) or tone of voice (green).

(Tracings of brain activity from George et al., 1996.)

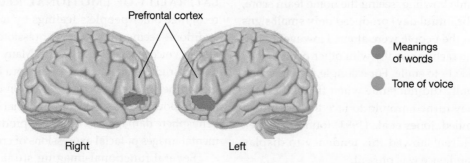

Prefrontal cortex

Right   Left

● Meanings of words
● Tone of voice

Several studies suggest that the amygdala receives visual information that we use to recognize facial expressions of emotion directly from the thalamus and not from the visual association cortex. Adolphs (2002) notes that the amygdala receives visual input from two sources: subcortical and cortical. The subcortical input (from the superior colliculus and the *pulvinar*, a large nucleus in the posterior thalamus) appears to provide the most important information for this task. In fact, some people with blindness caused by damage to the visual cortex can recognize facial expressions of emotion *even though they have no conscious awareness of looking at a person's face,* a phenomenon known as **affective blindsight** (Anders et al., 2004; de Gelder et al., 1999). Tamietto et al. (2009) confirmed that "emotional contagion" can take place even without conscious awareness. They presented photographs of faces expressing happiness or fearfulness to the sighted and blind fields of people with unilateral visual cortex lesions. Although the people did not report seeing an emotional expression (or even a face) in their blind fields, they automatically made facial expressions of their own that matched those of the faces in the photographs. Figure 11.20 shows the contraction of a "smile muscle" and a "frown muscle" under these conditions. Note that the appropriate muscles contracted when the happy or fearful face was presented to either the sighted field ("seen stimuli") or the blind field ("unseen stimuli").

People can express emotions through their body language, as well as through muscular movements of their face (de Gelder, 2006). For example, a clenched fist might accompany an angry facial expression, and a fearful person might run away. The sight of photographs of bodies posed in gestures of fear activates the amygdala, just as the sight of fearful faces does (Hadjikhani and de Gelder, 2003). Meeren et al., (2005) prepared computer-modified photographs of people showing facial expressions of emotions that were either congruent with the person's body posture (for example, a facial expression of fear and a body posture of fear) or incongruent (for example, a facial expression of anger and a body posture of fear). The investigators asked people

Figure 11.20 Unconscious Imitation of Facial Expressions of Emotions

When patients with unilateral damage to the visual cortex saw photographs of happy or fearful faces, they smiled or frowned when the photographs were presented to their sighted or blind field, which indicates that visual information concerning emotional expressions can take place without conscious awareness.

(Based on data from Tamietto et al., 2009.)

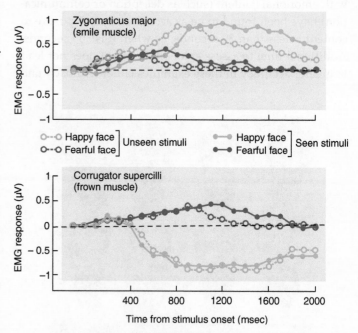

Zygomaticus major (smile muscle)

○--○ Happy face ┐ Unseen stimuli   ● Happy face ┐ Seen stimuli
○--○ Fearful face ┘   ● Fearful face ┘

Corrugator supercilli (frown muscle)

Time from stimulus onset (msec)

to identify the facial expressions shown in the photos and found that the ratings were faster and more accurate when the facial and body expressions were congruent. In other words, when we look at other people's faces, our perception of their emotion is affected by their body posture as well as their facial expression.

As we saw in Chapter 6, the visual cortex receives information from two systems of neurons. The *magnocellular system* provides information about movement, depth, and very subtle differences in brightness in the scene before our eyes. This system appeared early in evolution of the mammalian brain and provides most mammals (dogs and cats, for example) with a monochromatic, somewhat fuzzy image of the world. The *parvocellular system* is found only in some primates, including humans. This system provides us with color vision and detection of fine details. The part of the visual association cortex responsible for recognition of faces, the *fusiform face area,* receives information primarily from the parvocellular system. The information that the amygdala receives from the superior colliculus and the pulvinar has its origin in the more primitive magnocellular system. (See Figure 11.21.)

An ingenious functional-imaging study by Vuilleumier et al., (2003) presented people with pictures of faces showing neutral or fearful expressions. Some of the pictures were normal, some had been filtered with a computer program so that they showed only high spatial frequencies, and some had been filtered to show only low spatial frequencies. (Chapter 6 described the concept of spatial frequencies.) As Figure 11.22 shows, high spatial frequencies show fine details of transitions between light and dark, and low spatial frequencies show fuzzy images. These photos primarily stimulate the parvocellular and magnocellular systems, respectively.

Vuilleumier and his colleagues found that the fusiform face area was better at recognizing individual faces and primarily used high spatial frequency (parvocellular) information to do so. In contrast, the amygdala (and the superior colliculus and pulvinar, which provide it with visual information) was able to recognize an expression of fear based on low spatial frequency (magnocellular) information but not on high spatial frequency information.

Krolak-Salmon et al. (2004) recorded electrical potentials from the amygdala and visual association cortex through electrodes that had been implanted in people who were being evaluated for neurosurgery to alleviate a seizure disorder. They presented the people with photographs of faces showing neutral expressions or expressions of fear, happiness, or disgust. They found that fearful faces produced the largest response and that the amygdala showed activity before the

Figure 11.22 Involvement of Magnocellular and Parvocellular Systems in Emotional Perception

The figure shows the stimuli used by Vuilleumier et al., (2003). The more primitive magnocellular system is sensitive to low spatial frequencies (SF), and the more recently evolved parvocellular system is sensitive to high spatial frequencies.

(From Vuilleumier, P., Armony, J. L., Driver, J., and Dolan, R. J., Distinct spatial frequency sensitivities for processing faces and emotional expressions, *Nature Neuroscience,* 2003, *6,* 624–631.)

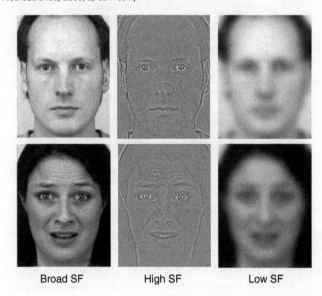

Broad SF   High SF   Low SF

visual cortex did. The rapid response supports the conclusion that the amygdala receives visual information from the magnocellular system (which conducts information very rapidly) that permits it to recognize facial expressions of fear.

So far, the evidence suggests that the amygdala plays an indispensable role in recognition of facial expressions of fear. However, a study by Adolphs et al., (2005) suggests that, under the appropriate conditions, other regions of the brain can perform this task. Adolphs et al. discovered that S. M., a woman with bilateral amygdala damage, failed to look at the eyes when she examined photographs of faces.

Figure 11.21 Brain Pathway Showing Input from the Two Visual Pathways to the Amygdala

The magnocellular pathway conveys monochromatic information about depth and motion. It projects to the amygdala and uses low spatial frequency information to quickly identify emotional information. The parvocellular pathway conveys information about color and fine details. It projects to the fusiform face area and uses high spatial frequency information.

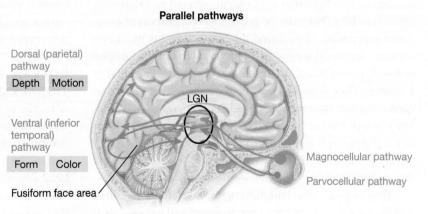

Parallel pathways

Dorsal (parietal) pathway

Depth Motion

Ventral (inferior temporal) pathway

Form Color

Fusiform face area

LGN

Magnocellular pathway

Parvocellular pathway

Figure 11.23 Eye Fixations After Amygdala Damage
The figure shows the numbers of fixations on a person's face made by a patient with bilateral amygdala damage compared to a control participant. Warmer colors indicate increasing numbers of fixations. Note that the patient does not look at the other person's eyes.

(Based on Spezio, M. L., Huang, P.-Y. S., Castelli, F., and Adolphs, R. Journal of Neuroscience, 2007, 27, 3994–3997. Copyright 2007, The Society for Neuroscience.)

Patient S. M.   Participant without amygdala lesion

Figure 11.24 Role of the White of Eyes in Emotional Response
The stimuli used in the study by Whalen et al. (2004) show that the whites of the eyes alone can convey the impression of a fearful expression.

(Based on Whalen, P. J., Kagan, J., Cook, R. G., Davis, F. C., Kim, H,, Polis, S., . . . and Johnstone, T., Human amygdala responsivity to masked fearful eye whites, Science, 2004, 306, 2061. Copyright 2004 American Association for the Advancement of Science.)

Fear   Happiness

Spezio et al., (2007) conducted a similar study, but this one measured S. M.'s eye movements while she was actually conversing with another person. Like the study by Adolphs et al., this one found that S. M. failed to direct her gaze to the other person's eyes. In contrast, she spent a large amount of time looking at the other person's mouth. (See Figure 11.23.)

By themselves, eyes are able to convey a fearful expression. A functional-imaging study by Whalen et al., (2004) found that viewing the fearful eyes shown in Figure 11.24 activated the ventral amygdala, the region that receives the majority of the cortical and subcortical inputs to the amygdala. So the fact that S. M. did not look at eyes suggests a cause for her failure to detect only this emotion. In fact, when Adolphs et al., (2005) instructed S. M. to look at the eyes of the face she was examining, she was able to recognize an expression of fear. However, unless she was reminded to do so, she soon stopped looking at eyes, and her ability to recognize a fearful expression disappeared again.

PERCEPTION OF DIRECTION OF GAZE Perrett and his colleagues (see Perrett et al., 1992) discovered an interesting brain function that may be related to recognition of emotional expression. They found that neurons in the monkey's superior temporal sulcus (STS) are involved in recognition of the direction of another monkey's gaze—or even that of a human. They found that some neurons in this region responded when the monkey looked at photographs of a monkey's face or a human face but only when the gaze of the face in the photograph was oriented in a particular direction. For example, Figure 11.25 shows the activity level of a neuron that responded when a human face was looking upward.

Why is gaze important in recognition of emotions? First, it is important to know whether an emotional expression is

directed toward you or toward someone else. For example, an angry expression directed toward you means something very different from a similar expression directed toward someone else. And if someone else shows signs of fear, the expression can serve as a useful warning, but only if you can figure out what the person is looking at. In fact, Adams and Kleck (2005) found that people more readily recognized anger if the eyes of another person were directed toward the observer and fear if they were directed somewhere else. As Blair (2008) notes, an angry expression directed toward the observer means that the other person wants the observer to stop what he or she is doing.

The neocortex that lines the STS seems to provide such information. Lesions there disrupt monkeys' ability to discriminate the direction of another animal's gaze, but they do not impair the monkeys' ability to recognize other animals' faces (Campbell et al., 1990; Heywood and Cowey, 1992). As we saw in Chapter 6, the posterior parietal cortex—the endpoint of the dorsal stream of visual analysis—is concerned with perceiving the location of objects in space. A functional-imaging study by Pelphrey et al., (2003) had people watch an animated cartoon of a face. When the direction of gaze changed, increased activity was seen in the right STS and posterior parietal cortex. Presumably, the connections between neurons in the STS and the parietal cortex enable the orientation of another person's gaze to direct one's attention to a particular location in space.

ROLE OF IMITATION IN RECOGNITION OF EMOTIONAL EXPRESSIONS: THE MIRROR NEURON SYSTEM
Adolphs et al., (2000) discovered a possible link between somatosensation and emotional recognition. They compiled computerized information about the locations of brain damage in 108 patients with localized brain lesions and correlated this information with the patients' ability to recognize and identify facial expressions of emotions. They found that the most severe damage to this ability was caused by

Figure 11.25 A Gaze Direction Cell

The graph shows the responses of a single neuron in the cortex lining in the superior temporal sulcus of a monkey's brain. The cell fired most vigorously when the monkey was presented a photograph of a face looking upward.

(Based on Perrett, D. I., Harries, M. H., Mistlin, A. J., et al. *International Journal of Comparative Psychology*, 1992, *4*, 25–55.)

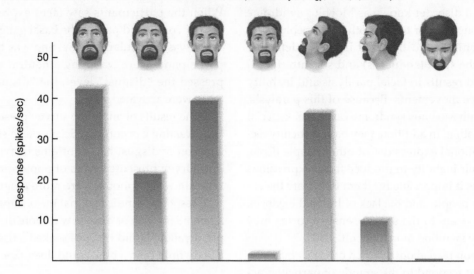

damage to the somatosensory cortex of the right hemisphere. (See Figure 11.26.) They suggest that, when we see a facial expression of an emotion, we unconsciously imagine ourselves making that expression. Often, we do more than imagine making the expressions—we actually imitate what we see. Adolphs et al. suggest that the somatosensory representation of what it feels like to make the perceived expression provides cues that we use to recognize the emotion being expressed in the face we are viewing. In support of this hypothesis, Adolphs et al. report that the ability of patients with right hemisphere lesions to recognize facial expressions of emotions is correlated with their ability to perceive somatosensory stimuli. That is, patients with somatosensory impairments (caused by right hemisphere lesions) also had impairments in recognition of emotions.

Figure 11.26 Brain Damage and Recognition of Facial Expressions of Emotion

This computer-generated image shows performance of participants with localized brain damage on recognition of facial expressions of emotion. The colored areas outline the site of the lesions. Lesions that resulted in good performance are shown in shades of blue; those that resulted in poor performance are shown in red and yellow.

(From Adolphs, R., Damasio, H., Tranel, D., Cooper, G., and Damasio, A. R. The *Journal of Neuroscience*, 2000, 20, 2683–2690.)

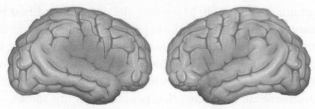

Right hemisphere   Left hemisphere

Hussey and Safford (2009) review a considerable amount of evidence that supports this hypothesis (the so-called *simulationist* hypothesis). For example, neuroimaging studies have shown that brain regions that are activated when particular emotional expressions are observed are also activated when these expressions are imitated. In addition, a study by Pitcher et al., (2008) used transcranial magnetic stimulation to disrupt the normal activity of brain regions involved in visual perception of faces or perception of somatosensory feedback from one's own face. They found that disruption of *either* region impaired people's ability to recognize facial expressions of emotion. Finally, a study by Oberman et al., (2007) had people hold a pen between their teeth in a way that interfered with smiling. When they did so, they had difficulty recognizing facial expressions of happiness, but not expressions of disgust, fear, and sadness, which involve the upper part of the face more than smiling does.

We are beginning to understand the neural circuit that provides this form of feedback. In Chapter 8 you read about the role of *mirror neurons* in the control of movement. Mirror neurons are activated when an animal performs a particular behavior or when it sees another animal performing that behavior. Presumably, these neurons are involved in learning to imitate the actions of others. These neurons, which are located in the ventral premotor area of the frontal lobe, receive input from the superior temporal sulcus and the posterior parietal cortex. As we saw in Chapter 8, this circuit is activated when we see another person perform a goal-directed action, and feedback from this activity helps us to understand what the person is trying to accomplish. Carr et al., (2003) suggest that the mirror neuron system, which is activated when we observe facial movements of other people, provides feedback that helps us to understand how other people feel. In other words, the mirror neuron system may be involved in our ability to empathize with the emotions of other people.

A neurological disorder known as Moebius syndrome provides further support for this hypothesis. Moebius syndrome is a congenital condition that involves defective development of the sixth (abducens) and seventh (facial) cranial nerves and results in facial paralysis and inability to make lateral eye movements. Because of this paralysis, people affected with Moebius syndrome cannot make facial expressions of emotion. In addition, they have difficulty recognizing the emotional expressions of other people (Cole, 2001). Perhaps their inability to produce facial expressions of emotions makes it impossible for them to imitate the expressions of other people, and the lack of internal feedback from the motor system to the somatosensory cortex may make the task of recognition more difficult.

In Chapter 8 you read about research on *audiovisual neurons*—neurons that respond to the sounds of particular actions and to the sight of those actions. Warren et al., (2006) obtained evidence that audiovisual neurons play a role in communication of emotions, too. The investigators asked volunteers to make emotional sounds in response to written scenarios that presented situations expected to evoke triumph, amusement, fear, and disgust. The volunteers were asked not to make verbal responses such as "yuck" or "yippee" but to restrict themselves to nonverbal vocal responses. These sounds were presented to participants while they underwent fMRI scanning. The scans showed that hearing the emotional vocalizations activated the same regions of the brain that were activated by facial expressions of these emotions. When we hear other people make nonverbal emotional sounds, our mirror neuron system is activated, and the feedback from this activation may contribute to our recognition of the emotions being expressed by these sounds.

PERCEIVING DISGUST   Several studies have found that damage to the insular cortex and basal ganglia impair people's ability to recognize facial expressions of a very specific emotion: disgust (Calder et al., 2000; Sprengelmeyer et al., 1996, 1997). In addition, a functional-imaging study by Wicker et al., (2003) found that both smelling a disgusting odor and seeing a face of a person showing an expression of disgust activate the insular cortex. Disgust is an emotion provoked by something that tastes or smells bad—or by an action that we consider to be in bad taste. Disgust produces a very characteristic facial expression. As we saw in Chapter 7, the insula contains the primary gustatory cortex, so perhaps it is not a coincidence that this region is also involved in recognition of "bad taste."

A functional-imaging study by Thielscher and Pessoa (2007) asked participants to press one of two levers to indicate whether the facial expression they saw was one of disgust or fear. The expressions varied in intensity, and one of them was actually neutral, indicating neither disgust nor fear. Nevertheless, the participants were asked to press one of the levers on every trial, indicating disgust or fear. When the participants saw faces expressing disgust, the insular cortex and part of the basal ganglia were activated. What was particularly interesting was that even when the participants were watching a neutral expression, if they pressed the "disgust" lever, the "disgust" regions of the brain were activated.

The results of an online survey presented on the British Broadcasting Corporation Science web site suggest that the emotion of disgust has its origins in avoidance of disease. The survey presented pairs of photos and asked people to indicate which photos were more disgusting. The people who responded indicated that the one that appeared to hold a potential threat of disease was more disgusting. For example, a yellow liquid that has soaked a tissue looks more like a body fluid than a blue liquid does. (See Figure 11.27.)

Neural Basis of the Communication of Emotions: Expression

LO 11.14   **Review the brain structures involved in emotional expression, by addressing laterality, laughter, and humor.**

We saw in the previous section that the amygdala is involved in the recognition of facial expression of emotions. Research indicates that it is not involved in emotional *expression*. Anderson and Phelps (2000) reported the case of S. P., a 54-year-old woman whose right amygdala was removed to treat a serious seizure disorder. Because of a pre-existing lesion of the left amygdala, the surgery resulted in a bilateral amygdalectomy. After the surgery, S. P. lost the ability to recognize facial expressions of fear, but she had no difficulty recognizing individual faces, and she could easily identify male and female faces and accurately judge their ages. What is particularly interesting is that the amygdala lesions did not impair S. P.'s ability to produce her own facial expressions of fear. She had no difficulty accurately expressing fear, anger, happiness, sadness, disgust, and surprise. However, when she saw a photograph of herself showing fear, she could not tell what emotion her face had been expressing.

Facial expressions of emotion are automatic and involuntary (although, as we saw, they can be modified by display rules). It is not easy to produce a realistic facial expression of emotion when we do not really feel that way. In fact, Ekman and Davidson confirmed an early observation by a nineteenth-century neurologist, Guillaume-Benjamin Duchenne de Boulogne, that genuinely happy smiles, as opposed to false smiles or social smiles people make when

Figure 11.27 Disease and Disgust

The figure shows pairs of photographs with high and low relation to the threat of disease used in the online survey presented on the BBC Science web site. The numbers in red or green indicate the mean ratings (range = 1–5) made by people who completed the survey.

(From Curtis, V., Aunger, R., and Rabie, T., Evidence that disgust evolved to protect from risk of disease, *Biology Letters*, 2004, *271*, S131–S133.)

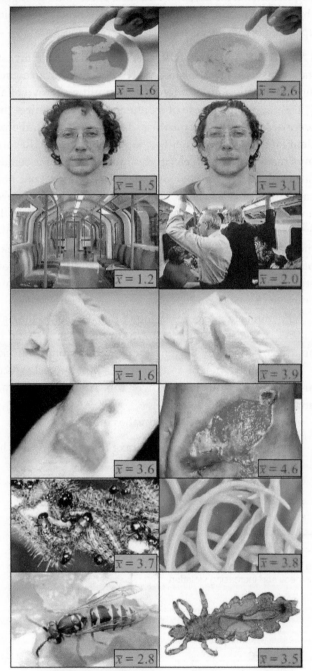

Disease irrelevant   Disease relevant

Figure 11.28 An Artificial Smile

The photograph shows Dr. Duchenne electrically stimulating muscles in the face of a volunteer, causing contraction of muscles around the mouth that become active during a smile. As Duchenne discovered, however, a true smile also involves muscles around the eyes.

(From: Curtis, V., Aunger, R., and Rabie, T., Biology Letters, 2004, 271, S131–S133; Royal Society of London. Permission by Copyright Clearance Center.)

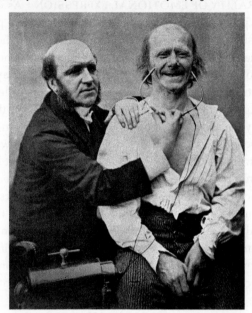

the soul; the . . . fake joy, the deceitful laugh, cannot provoke the contraction of this latter muscle" (Duchenne, 1862/1990, p. 72). (See Figure 11.28.) The difficulty actors have in voluntarily producing a convincing facial expression of emotion is one of the reasons that led Constantin Stanislavsky to develop his system of *method acting,* in which actors attempt to imagine themselves in a situation that would lead to the desired emotion. Once the emotion is evoked, the facial expressions follow naturally (Stanislavsky, 1936).

The observation that emotion is followed by facial expression is confirmed by two neurological disorders with complementary symptoms (Hopf et al., 1992; Michel et al., 2008; Topper et al., 1995; Urban et al., 1998). The first, **volitional facial paresis,** is caused by damage to the face region of the primary motor cortex or to the fibers connecting this region with the motor nucleus of the facial nerve, which controls the muscles responsible for movement of the facial muscles. The interesting thing about volitional facial paresis is that a patient cannot voluntarily move the facial muscles but will express a genuine emotion with those muscles. For example, a patient will not be able to make a smile when told to do so on command, but will spontaneously smile when they perceive something as humorous. In contrast, **emotional facial paresis** is caused by damage to the insular region of the prefrontal cortex, to the white matter of the frontal lobe, or to parts of the thalamus. This system joins the system responsible for voluntary movements of the facial muscles in the medulla or caudal pons. People with this disorder can move their face

they greet someone else, involve contraction of a muscle near the eyes, the lateral part of the orbicularis oculi—now sometimes referred to as Duchenne's muscle (Ekman, 1992; Ekman and Davidson, 1993). As Duchenne put it, "The first [zygomatic major muscle] obeys the will but the second [orbicularis oculi] is only put in play by the sweet emotions of muscles voluntarily but do not express emotions on the affected side of the face. These two syndromes clearly indicate that different brain mechanisms are responsible for voluntary movements of the facial muscles and automatic, involuntary expression of emotions involving the same muscles.

LATERALITY OF EMOTIONAL EXPRESSION As we saw in the previous subsection, the right hemisphere plays a more significant role in recognizing emotions in the voice or facial expressions of other people—especially negative emotions. The same hemispheric specialization appears to be true for expressing emotions. When people show emotions with their facial muscles, the left side of the face usually makes a more intense expression. For example, researchers have taken photographs of people who were expressing emotions, divided them into right and left halves, prepared mirror images of each of them, and pasted them together, producing so-called *chimerical faces* (Indersmitten and Gur, 2003; Sackeim and Gur, 1978). They found that the left halves were more expressive than the right ones and that participants rated the expressions as more significantly more intense than faces of right halves. Because motor control is contralateral, the results suggest that the right hemisphere is more expressive than the left.

Moscovitch and Olds (1982) made more natural observations of people in restaurants and parks and found that the left side of their faces appeared to make stronger expressions of emotions. They confirmed these results in the laboratory by analyzing videotapes of people telling sad or humorous stories. A review of the literature by Borod et al., (1998) found 48 other studies that obtained similar results.

Left hemisphere lesions do not usually impair vocal expressions of emotion. For example, people with Wernicke's aphasia (described in Chapter 14) usually modulate their voice according to mood, even though the words they say make no sense. In contrast, right hemisphere lesions do impair expression of emotion, both facially and by tone of voice.

Using the chimerical faces technique, Hauser (1993) found that rhesus monkeys, like humans, express emotions more strongly in the left sides of their faces. Analysis of videotapes further showed that emotional expressions also begin sooner in the left side of the face. These findings suggest that hemispherical specialization for emotional expression appeared before the emergence of our own species.

LAUGHTER AND HUMOR Several studies have investigated the brain mechanisms involved in laughter, an expression of emotion more intense than smiling. Arroyo et al., (1993) reported the case of a patient who had seizures that were accompanied by mirthless laughter—that is, the patient laughed but was neither happy nor amused. Recordings made with depth electrodes indicated that the seizure began in the left anterior cingulate gyrus. Removal of a noncancerous tumor located nearby ended both the seizures and the mirthless laughter. The authors suggest that the anterior cingulate cortex may be involved in the muscular movements that produce laughter. In contrast, stimulation of subthalamic nuclei in patients undergoing deep brain stimulation to treat Parkinson's disease resulted in mirthful laughter (Krack et al., 2001).

Shammi and Stuss (1999) found that damage to the right vmPFC impaired people's ability to understand—and be amused by—jokes. For example, consider the following joke:

Mr. Smith's neighbor approaches him and asks, "Say, are you using your lawnmower this afternoon?" "Yes, I am," replies Mr. Smith.

Which alternative below finishes the joke?

a. "Oops!" as he steps on a rake that barely misses his face.

b. "Fine, then you won't be wanting your golf clubs— I'll just borrow them."

Figure 11.29 Humor and Volition of Social Norms

The graph shows the activation of the right ventromedial prefrontal cortex and the left orbitofrontal cortex, as measured by fMRI, by exposure to humorous cartoons with increasing funniness and increasing violation of social norms.

(Based on data from Goel and Dolan, 2007.)

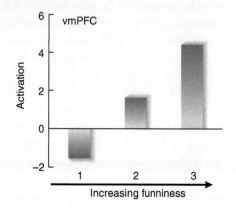
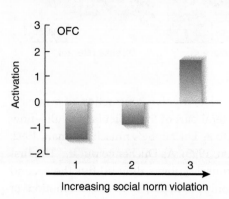

c. "Oh well, can I borrow it when you're done, then?"

d. "The birds are always eating my grass seed."

The funny alternative in this example is (b). But people with ventromedial prefrontal damage usually chose (a), presumably because its slapstick aspect reminded them of humor that they had seen in the past.

A functional-imaging study by Goel and Dolan (2001) found that different types of jokes activated different regions of the brain, but all of them activated one region: the right vmPFC. Another functional-imaging study by the same authors (Goel and Dolan, 2007) presented participants with socially appropriate and socially inappropriate cartoon jokes. The investigators found that increasingly funny jokes produced increasing activation of several regions, including the nucleus accumbens (a region involved in reinforcement and reward) and the right vmPFC, while jokes with increasing violation of social norms produced increasing activation of several regions, including the right amygdala and the left orbital frontal cortex. (See Figure 11.29.)

Section Review

Communication of Emotions

LO 11.12 Describe evidence in support of emotional expressions as innate responses.

Darwin believed that such expressions of emotion were innate—that these muscular movements were inherited behavioral patterns. Ekman and his colleagues performed cross-cultural studies with members of an isolated tribe in New Guinea. Their results supported Darwin's hypothesis. The facial expressions of young blind and sighted children are very similar.

LO 11.13 Summarize the brain structures involved in emotional recognition, by addressing laterality, direction of gaze, imitation, and disgust.

Recognition of other people's emotional expressions involves the right hemisphere more than the left. Studies show that recognition of particular faces involves neural circuits different from those needed to recognize facial expressions of emotions. The amygdala plays a role in recognition of emotional expression; lesions of the amygdala disrupt the ability to recognize facial expressions of fearfulness. One of the reasons that bilateral amygdala damage impairs recognition of fearful facial expressions appears to be failure to look at people's eyes. Neurons in the superior temporal sulcus are sensitive to direction of gaze and transmit this information to other parts of the brain, including the amygdala. Mirror neurons in the ventral premotor cortex receive visual information concerning the facial expression of other people that activate the neural circuits responsible for these expressions. Feedback from this activity, which may be transmitted to the somatosensory cortex, helps us to comprehend the emotional intentions of other people. Damage to the basal ganglia and insular cortex disrupts recognition of facial expressions of disgust, and functional-imaging studies show increased activity in the insular cortex (which contains the primary gustatory cortex) when people smell disgusting odors or see faces displaying disgust. Damage to the right somatosensory cortex results in impaired facial emotion recognition and is thought to be due to impaired ability to imitate the emotion.

LO 11.14 Review the brain structures involved in emotional expression, by addressing laterality, laughter, and humor.

The anterior cingulate gyrus appears to play a role in the motor aspects of laughter, while the appreciation of humor appears to involve the right vmPFC. Genuine expressions of emotion are controlled by special neural circuits. The best evidence for this assertion comes from the complementary syndromes of emotional and volitional facial paresis. People with emotional facial paresis can move their facial muscles voluntarily but not in response to an emotion, whereas people with volitional facial paresis show the opposite symptoms. In addition, the left halves of people's faces—and the faces of monkeys—tend to be more expressive than the right halves.

Thought Question

Do you think it is important to be able to recognize other people's emotions? Why? Suppose that you could no longer recognize people's facial expressions of emotions. What consequences would that loss have for you?

Feelings of Emotions

So far, we have examined the organization of patterns of responses that deal with the situation that provokes the emotion and the communication of emotional states with other members of the species. The final aspect of emotion to be examined in this chapter is feelings of emotion. In this section you will encounter explanations for how situations evoke feelings of emotions and how feedback from feeling an emotion alters activity in the nervous system.

The James-Lange Theory

LO 11.15 **Summarize the evidence for and against the James-Lange theory of emotion.**

William James (1842–1910), an American psychologist, and Carl Lange (1834–1900), a Danish physiologist, independently suggested similar explanations for emotion, which most people refer to collectively as the **James-Lange theory** (James, 1884; Lange, 1887). Basically, the theory states that emotion-producing situations elicit an appropriate set of physiological responses, such as trembling, sweating, and increased heart rate. The situations also elicit behaviors, such as clenching fists or fighting. The brain receives sensory feedback from the muscles and from the organs that produce these responses, and it is this feedback that constitutes our feeling of emotion.

James said that our own emotional feelings are based on what we find ourselves doing and on the sensory feedback we receive from the activity of our muscles and internal organs. For example, when we find ourselves trembling and feel queasy, we experience fear. Where feelings of emotions are concerned, we are self-observers. Thus, the two aspects of emotions reported in the first two sections of this chapter (patterns of emotional responses and expressions of emotions) give rise to the third: feelings. (See Figure 11.30.)

James' description of the process of emotion might strike you as being at odds with your own experience. Many people think that they experience emotions directly, internally. They consider the outward manifestations of emotions to be secondary events. But have you ever found yourself in an unpleasant confrontation with someone else and discovered that you were trembling, even though you did not think that you were so bothered by the encounter? Or did you ever find yourself blushing in response to some public remark that was made about you? Or did you ever find tears coming to your eyes while you watched a film that you did not think was affecting you? What would you conclude about your emotional states in situations like these? Would you ignore the evidence from your own physiological reactions?

A well-known physiologist, Walter Cannon, criticized James's theory. He said that the internal organs were relatively insensitive and that they could not respond very quickly, so feedback from them could not account for our feelings of emotions. In addition, he observed that cutting the nerves that provide feedback from the internal organs to the brain did not alter emotional behavior (Cannon, 1927). However, subsequent research indicated that Cannon's criticisms are not relevant. For example, although the viscera are not sensitive to some kinds of stimuli, such as cutting and burning, they provide much better feedback than Cannon suspected. Moreover, many changes in the viscera can occur rapidly enough that they could be the causes of feelings of emotion.

Cannon cited the fact that cutting the sensory nerves between the internal organs and the central nervous system does not abolish emotional behavior in laboratory animals. However, this observation misses the point. It does not prove that feelings of emotion survive this surgical disruption—only that emotional *behaviors* do. We do not know how the animals feel; we know only that they will snarl and attempt to bite if threatened. In any case, James did not attribute all feelings of emotion to the internal organs; he also said that feedback from muscles was important. The threat might make the animal snarl and bite, and the feedback from the facial and neck muscles might constitute a "feeling" of anger, even if feedback from the internal organs was cut off. But we have no way to ask the animal how it felt.

James's theory is difficult to verify experimentally because it attempts to explain *feelings* of emotion, not the causes of emotional responses, and feelings are private events. Some anecdotal evidence supports the theory. For example, Sweet (1966) reported the case of a man in whom some sympathetic nerves were severed on one side of the body to treat a cardiovascular disorder. The man—a music lover—reported that the shivering sensation he felt while listening to music now occurred only on the unoperated side of his body. He still enjoyed listening to music, but the surgery had altered his emotional reaction.

In one of the few tests of James's theory, Hohman (1966) collected data from people with spinal cord damage. He asked these people about the intensity of their emotional feelings. If feedback is important, one would expect that emotional feelings would be less intense if the injury were

---

Figure 11.30 The James-Lange Theory of Emotion

An event in the environment triggers behavioral, autonomic, and endocrine responses. Feedback from these responses produces feelings of emotions.

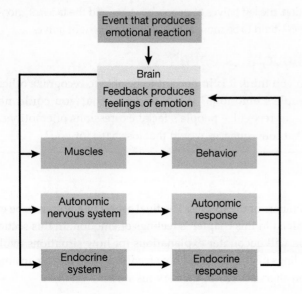

high (that is, close to the brain) than if it were low, because a high spinal cord injury would make the person become insensitive to a larger part of the body. In fact, this result is precisely what Hohman found: The higher the injury, the less intense the feeling was. As one of Hohman's participants said:

> I sit around and build things up in my mind, and I worry a lot, but it's not much but the power of thought. I was at home alone in bed one day and dropped a cigarette where I couldn't reach it. I finally managed to scrounge around and put it out. I could have burned up right there, but the funny thing is, I didn't get all shook up about it. I just didn't feel afraid at all, like you would suppose. (Hohman, 1966, p. 150)

Another participant showed that angry behavior (an emotional response) does not appear to depend on *feelings* of emotion. Instead, the behavior is evoked by the situation (and by the person's evaluation of it) even if the spinal cord damage has reduced the intensity of the person's emotional feelings:

> Now, I don't get a feeling of physical animation, it's sort of cold anger. Sometimes I act angry when I see some injustice. I yell and cuss and raise hell, because if you don't do it sometimes, I've learned people will take advantage of you, but it doesn't have the heat to it that it used to. It's a mental kind of anger. (Hohman, 1966, p. 151)

Feedback from Emotional Expressions

LO 11.16 **Explain the role of feedback from emotional expressions in mood and activity of the autonomic nervous system.**

James stressed the importance of two aspects of emotional responses: emotional behaviors and autonomic responses. As we saw earlier in this chapter, a particular set of muscles—those of the face—helps us to communicate our emotional state to other people. Several experiments suggest that feedback from the contraction of facial muscles can affect people's moods and even alter the activity of the autonomic nervous system.

As you read previously, people can be directed to move particular facial muscles to simulate the emotional expressions of fear, anger, surprise, disgust, sadness, and happiness. Ekman, Levensen, and their colleagues (Ekman et al., 1983; Levenson et al., 1990) asked participants to follow a set of directions to make facial expressions. While the participants made the expressions, the investigators monitored several physiological responses controlled by the autonomic nervous system.

The simulated expressions *did* alter the activity of the autonomic nervous system. In fact, different facial expressions produced somewhat different patterns of activity. For example, anger increased heart rate and skin temperature, fear increased heart rate but decreased skin temperature,

and happiness decreased heart rate without affecting skin temperature.

Why should a particular pattern of movements of the facial muscles cause changes in mood or in the activity of the autonomic nervous system? Perhaps the connection is a result of experience; in other words, perhaps the occurrence of particular facial movements along with changes in the autonomic nervous system leads to classical conditioning, so that feedback from the facial movements becomes capable of eliciting the autonomic response—and a change in perceived emotion. Or perhaps the connection is innate. As we saw earlier, the adaptive value of emotional expressions is that they communicate feelings and intentions to others. The research presented earlier in this chapter on the role of mirror neurons and the somatosensory cortex suggests that one of the ways we communicate feelings is through unconscious imitation.

A study by Lewis and Bowler (2009) found that interfering with muscular movement associated with a particular emotion decreased people's ability to experience that emotion. Injections of a very dilute solution of botulinum toxin (Botox) into facial muscles can reduce wrinkling of the skin caused by chronic contraction of facial muscles. Lewis and Bowler studied people who had been treated with injections of Botox into the corrugator muscle, whose contraction is responsible for a large part of the facial expression of frowning, which is associated with negative emotions. They found that these people showed significantly less negative mood, compared with people who had received other forms of cosmetic treatment. These results, like those described earlier in this subsection, suggest that feedback from a person's facial expressions can affect his or her mood.

A functional-imaging study by Damasio et al., (2000) asked people to recall and try to reexperience past episodes from their lives that evoked feelings of sadness, happiness, anger, and fear. The investigators found that recalling these emotions activated the participants' somatosensory cortex and upper brain stem nuclei involved in control of internal organs and detection of sensations received from them. These responses are certainly compatible with James's theory. As Damasio et al., put it,

> Emotions are part of a neural mechanism based on structures that regulate the organism's current state by executing specific actions via the musculoskeletal system, ranging from facial and postural expressions to complex behaviors, and by producing chemical and neural responses aimed at the internal milieu, viscera and telencephalic neural circuits. The consequences of such responses are represented in both subcortical regulatory structures . . . and in cerebral cortex . . . , and those representations constitute a critical aspect of the neural basis of feelings. (p. 1049)

The tendency to imitate the expressions of other people appears to be innate. Field et al., (1982) had adults make

Figure 11.31 Imitation in Infants

The photographs show happy, sad, and surprised faces posed by an adult and the responses made by an infant.

facial expressions in front of infants. The infants' own facial expressions were videotaped and were subsequently rated by people who did not know what expressions the adults were displaying. Field and her colleagues found that even newborn babies (with an average age of 36 hours) tended to imitate the expressions they saw. The effect occurs too early in life to be a result of learning. Figure 11.31 shows photographs of adult expressions and the expressions they elicited in a baby.

Perhaps imitation provides one of the channels by which organisms communicate their emotions—and evoke feelings of empathy. For example, if we see someone looking sad, we tend to assume a sad expression ourselves. The feedback from our own expression helps to put us in the other person's place and makes us more likely to respond with solace or assistance. And perhaps one of the reasons we derive pleasure from making someone else smile is that their smile makes *us* smile and feel happy. In fact, a functional-imaging study by Pfeifer et al., (2008) found that when 10-year-old children watched and imitated emotional expressions, increased activity was seen in the frontal mirror neuron system. In addition, the level of neural activation was positively correlated with measures of the children's empathetic behavior and their interpersonal skills.

Section Review

Feelings of Emotions

LO 11.15 Summarize the evidence for and against the James-Lange theory of emotion.

From the earliest times, people recognized that emotions were accompanied by feelings that seemed to come from inside the body, which probably provided the impetus for developing physiological theories of emotion. James and Lange suggested that emotions were primarily responses to situations. Feedback from the physiological and behavioral reactions to emotion-producing situations gave rise to the feelings of emotion; thus, feelings are the *results*, not the *causes*, of emotional reactions. Hohman's study of people with spinal cord damage supported the James-Lange theory; people who could no longer feel the reactions from most of their body reported that they no longer experienced intense emotional states. Cannon proposed that the body could not respond quickly enough to account for feedback and feelings of emotion, however this was not supported by subsequent research.

LO 11.16 Explain the role of feedback from emotional expressions in mood and activity of the autonomic nervous system.

Ekman and his colleagues have shown that even simulating an emotional expression causes changes in the activity of the autonomic nervous system. Perhaps feedback from these changes explains why an emotion can be "contagious": We see someone smile with pleasure, we ourselves imitate the smile, and the internal feedback makes us feel at least somewhat happier. The tendency to mimic the facial expression of others appears to be a consequence of activity in the brain's system of mirror neurons.

Thought Question

What is the evolutionary advantage of the fact that human infants can mimic the facial emotional expressions of adults?

Chapter Review Questions

1. Discuss the behavioral, autonomic, and hormonal components of an emotional response and the role of the amygdala in controlling them.

2. Discuss the nature, functions, and neural control of aggressive behavior.

3. Discuss the role of the prefrontal cortex in the analysis of social situations and the effects of damage to this region.

4. Explain the role of the amygdala in fear conditioning and describe the neural mechanism responsible for the extinction of a conditioned emotional response.

5. Explain the role of serotonin, citing evidence from research literature, in regulation of human aggression and impulse control.

6. Explain the evolutionary significance of aggressive behavior and how hormones control this behavior in males.

7. Describe the neural control of the recognition of emotional expression in healthy individuals and individuals with brain damage.

8. Discuss the neural control of emotional expression in healthy individuals and those with brain damage.

9. Discuss the James-Lange theory of feelings of emotion and evaluate relevant research.

Chapter 12
Ingestive Behavior

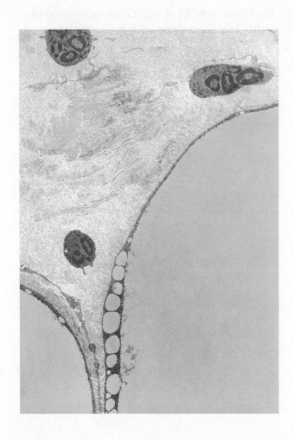

Chapter Outline

Learning Objectives

LO 12.1 Explain the characteristics of a physiological regulatory mechanism.

LO 12.2 Compare osmometric and volumetric thirst.

LO 12.3 Identify the roles of the subfornical organ and median preoptic nucleus in regulating thirst.

LO 12.4 Describe the function, location, and contents of the short-term reservoir.

LO 12.5 Describe the function, location, and contents of the long-term reservoir.

LO 12.6 Compare the pathways for the use of glucose, fat, and amino acids by the brain and body in the fasting phase.

LO 12.7 Compare the pathways for the use of glucose, fat, and amino acids by the brain and body in the absorptive phase.

LO 12.8 Describe ghrelin's function as a hunger signal including its origin and relationship to obesity, fasting, and absorptive phases.

LO 12.9 Describe how metabolic signals can play a role in starting a meal.

LO 12.10 Describe the general function of short-term satiety signals.

LO 12.11 Identify examples of environmental factors that contribute to satiety.

LO 12.12 Identify sensory factors that contribute to satiety.

LO 12.13 Explain how the stomach can provide satiety signals.

LO 12.14 Describe how the intestines can provide satiety signals.

LO 12.15 Explain how the liver provides late-stage satiety signals.

LO 12.16 Describe how insulin can function as a satiety signal.

LO 12.17 Contrast the function of satiety signals from adipose tissue with short-term satiety signals.

LO 12.18 Identify the functions of the brain stem involved in eating regulation.

LO 12.19 Describe the role of nuclei and neurochemical systems of the hypothalamus in hunger and satiety.

LO 12.20 Discuss the contributions of environment, physical activity, and genetics to the development of obesity.

LO 12.21 Evaluate the roles of reinforcement, stress, surgery, pharmacology, and behavioral interventions in treating obesity.

LO 12.22 Discuss the roles of brain changes, starvation, excessive exercise, and genetic factors in eating disorders.

LO 12.23 List strategies used in eating disorder interventions.

Gianna was a frail baby with weak muscle tone and poor reflexes. She ate very little, apparently because she was so weak. For several years she was underweight. Her motor development and cognitive development were much slower than that of her peers, she often seemed to have trouble breathing, and her hands and feet were especially small. Finally, her appetite seemed to improve. She began gaining weight and soon surpassed other children of her age. Previously, she had been passive and reserved, but now she began to display tantrums. She also showed compulsive behavior—picking at her skin, collecting and lining up objects, and protesting violently when her parents tried to put things away.

The biggest change, though, was her appetite. She ate everything she could and never seemed satisfied. At first her parents were so pleased to see Gianna finally gaining weight that they gave her food whenever she asked for it. But after a while it was clear that she was becoming obese. A specialist diagnosed her condition, told her parents that they would have to strictly limit Gianna's food intake, and prescribed appetite-suppressing medications. Because of her weak muscles and low metabolic rate, she needed only 1,200 calories per day to maintain a normal weight. But Gianna was constantly looking for food. She would take food out of the refrigerator until her parents installed a lock on it and on the cabinets where they put food. They had to be careful of how they disposed of leftover food, because Gianna would take it out of the garbage and eat it.

When Gianna went to school, she began gaining weight once more. She would quickly eat everything on her lunch tray and would then eat everything her classmates did not finish. If anyone dropped food on the floor near her, she would pick that up and eat it too. Because of Gianna's special needs, the school appointed an assistant to monitor her food intake to be sure that she ate only the low-calorie meal that she was served.

*****

Gianna has Prader-Willi syndrome, caused by deletion of several genes in a segment of chromosome 15. This region appears to be involved in production of proteins that are critical to normal functioning of the hypothalamus, which helps integrate signals of hunger and satiety. Most cases of Prader-Willi syndrome appear to be caused by random accidents that occur during the production of the father's sperm cells. The prevalence of Prader-Willi syndrome is estimated at 1/10,000–3/10,000 individuals (Cassidy et al., 2011). As

you will learn in this chapter, much progress has been made in our understanding of the neural and hormonal mechanisms that control appetite and regulate body weight. Undoubtedly, we will soon learn which of these mechanisms are disrupted in Prader-Willi syndrome.

To help us regulate our food and water needs, the digestive, respiratory, circulatory, and excretory systems have evolved. We also have the behaviors necessary for finding and ingesting food and water. Regulation of the fluid that bathes our cells is part of a process called **homeostasis** ("similar standing"). This chapter discusses the means by which we mammals achieve homeostatic control of the vital characteristics of our extracellular fluid through our **ingestive behavior:** intake of food, water, and minerals such as sodium. First, we will examine the general nature of regulatory mechanisms; then we will consider drinking and eating and the neural mechanisms that are responsible for these behaviors. Finally, we will explore some research on eating disorders. The figure here displays the lateral and ventromedial hypothalamus, regions of the brain involved in ingestive behavior that we will be paying particular attention to in this chapter.

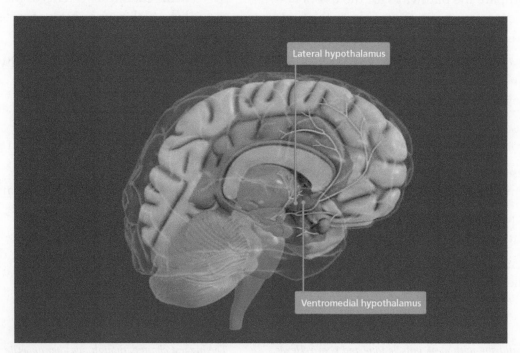

The lateral and ventromedial hypothalamus.

Drinking

To understand any ingestive behavior, such as drinking and eating, we must understand the general physiological regulatory mechanisms that maintain the constancy of some internal characteristics of the organism in the face of external variability—for example, keeping body temperature constant despite changes in the ambient temperature.

Physiological Regulatory Mechanisms

LO 12.1 Explain the characteristics of a physiological regulatory mechanism.

A regulatory mechanism contains four essential features: the **system variable** (the characteristic to be regulated), a **set point** (the optimal value of the system variable), a **detector**

Figure 12.1 Example of a Regulatory System

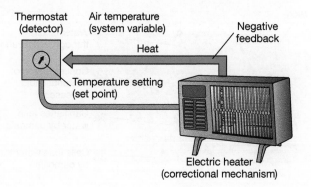

that monitors the value of the system variable, and a **correctional mechanism** that restores the system variable to the set point. The activity of the system is regulated by **negative feedback,** a process whereby the effect produced by an action serves to diminish or terminate the action.

An example of a regulatory system is a room whose temperature is regulated by a thermostatically controlled heater. (See Figure 12.1.) The system variable is the air temperature of the room, and the detector for this variable is a thermostat. This device can be adjusted so that contacts of a switch will be closed when the temperature falls below a preset value (the set point). Closure of the contacts turns on the correctional mechanism—the coils of the heater. If the room cools below the set point of the thermostat, the thermostat turns the heater on, and the heater warms the room. The rise in room temperature causes the thermostat to turn the heater off. Because the activity of the correctional mechanism (heat production) feeds back to the thermostat and causes it to turn the heater off, this process is called negative feedback. Negative feedback is an essential characteristic of all regulatory systems.

This chapter considers regulatory systems that involve ingestive behaviors: drinking and eating. These behaviors are correctional mechanisms that replenish the body's depleted stores of water or nutrients. Because of the delay between ingestion and replenishment of the depleted stores, ingestive behaviors are controlled by **satiety mechanisms** as well as by detectors that monitor the system variables. Satiety mechanisms are brain-based mechanisms that reduce hunger or thirst related to behaviors that result in adequate intake of nutrients or water. Satiety mechanisms are required because of the physiology of our digestive system. For example, suppose you spend some time in a hot, dry environment and lose body water. The loss of water causes internal detectors to initiate the correctional mechanism: drinking. You quickly drink a glass or two of water and then stop. What stops your ingestive behavior? The water is still in your digestive system, and has not yet moved into the fluid surrounding your cells, where it is needed. Therefore, although drinking was initiated by detectors that measure your body's need for water, *it was stopped by other means.* There must be a satiety mechanism that says, in effect, "Stop—this water, when absorbed by the digestive system into the blood, will eventually replenish the body's need." Satiety mechanisms monitor the activity of the correctional mechanism (in this case, drinking), not the system variables themselves. When a sufficient amount of drinking occurs, the satiety mechanisms stop further drinking *in anticipation* of the replenishment that will occur later. (See Figure 12.2.)

To maintain our internal milieu at its optimal state, we have to drink water. The rest of this section examines the control of this form of ingestive behavior.

Two Types of Thirst

LO 12.2 Compare osmometric and volumetric thirst.

Approximately two-thirds of the body's water is contained in the **intracellular fluid,** the fluid portion of the cytoplasm of cells. The rest is **extracellular fluid,** which includes the **intravascular fluid** (the blood plasma), the cerebrospinal fluid, and the **interstitial fluid** (fluid that bathes our cells). The volume of two of the fluid compartments of the body must be kept within precise limits: the intracellular fluid and the intravascular fluid. A loss of intracellular water deprives cells of the ability to perform many chemical reactions, and a gain of water can cause their membranes to rupture. The volume of intravascular fluid must be closely regulated because of the mechanics of the operation of the heart. If the

Figure 12.2 Outline of the System That Controls Drinking

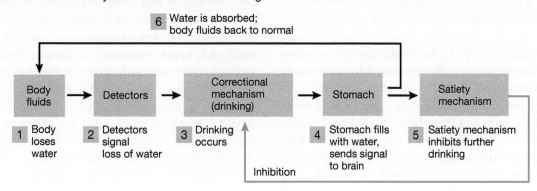

blood volume falls too low, the heart can no longer pump the blood effectively; if the volume is not restored, heart failure will result. This condition is called **hypovolemia.** The vascular system of the body can make some adjustments for loss of blood volume by contracting the muscles in smaller veins and arteries, thereby presenting a smaller space for the blood to fill, but this correctional mechanism has definite limits.

Therefore, for our bodies to function properly, the volume of two fluid compartments—intracellular and intravascular—must be regulated. Intracellular and intravascular fluids are monitored by two different sets of receptors. A single set of receptors would not work because it is possible for one of these fluid compartments to be changed without affecting the other. For example, a loss of blood reduces the volume of the intravascular fluid, but it has no effect on the volume of the intracellular fluid. On the other hand, a salty meal dehydrates cells and reduces the volume of intracellular fluid, but it will not cause hypovolemia. Thus, the body needs two sets of receptors, one measuring blood volume and another measuring cell volume. Most of the time, we ingest more water than we need, and the kidneys excrete the excess. However, if the levels of water fall too low, correctional mechanisms—drinking water—are activated.

Because loss of water from either the intracellular or intravascular fluid compartments stimulates drinking, researchers have adopted the terms *osmometric thirst* and *volumetric thirst* to describe them. The term *volumetric* refers to the metering (measuring) of the volume of the blood plasma. The term *osmometric* will be explained in greater detail in the next section, but in general it refers to an increase in *osmotic pressure* on intracellular fluid that occurs when a cell is dehydrated. The term *thirst* generally refers to a sensation that people say they have when they are dehydrated, but because we do not know how other animals feel, *thirst* simply means a tendency to seek water and to ingest it.

Our bodies lose water continuously, primarily through evaporation. Each breath exposes the moist inner surfaces of the respiratory system to the air; thus, each breath causes the loss of a small amount of water. In addition, our skin is not completely waterproof; some water finds its way through the layers of the skin and evaporates from the surface. The moisture that is lost through evaporation is pure water. (See Figure 12.3.) The body loses water through sweating, too; but because it loses salt along with the water, sweating produces a need for sodium as well as for water.

OSMOMETRIC THIRST **Osmometric thirst** occurs when the solute concentration of the interstitial fluid increases. *Solutes* are substances, such as salts, dissolved in a solution. An increase in interstitial solute concentration draws water out of the cells, and they shrink in volume. The term *osmometric* refers to the fact that the detector cells are actually responding to (metering) changes in the concentration of the interstitial fluid that surrounds them. *Osmosis* is the

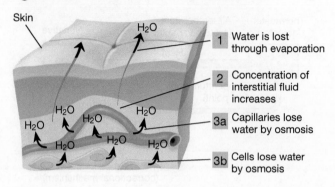

Figure 12.3 Water Loss Through Evaporation

Skin

H_2O

1 Water is lost through evaporation

H_2O H_2O H_2O

H_2O H_2O H_2O H_2O

2 Concentration of interstitial fluid increases

3a Capillaries lose water by osmosis

3b Cells lose water by osmosis

movement of water through a semipermeable membrane from a region of low solute concentration to one of high solute concentration.

The existence of neurons that respond to changes in the solute concentration of the interstitial fluid was first hypothesized by Verney (1947). Verney suggested that these detectors, which he called **osmoreceptors** are neurons whose firing rate is affected by their level of hydration. That is, if the interstitial fluid surrounding them became more concentrated, they lose water through osmosis. The shrinkage causes them to alter their firing rate, which sends signals to other parts of the brain. Zhang et al., (2007) found that osmoreceptors are a special kind of mechanoreceptor that transduce changes in the volume of the cell into changes in membrane potential, and hence in neural firing rate. (See Figure 12.4).

When we eat a salty meal, we incur a pure osmometric thirst. The salt is absorbed from the digestive system into the blood plasma. The salt concentration of the blood draws water from the interstitial fluid, which in turn causes water to leave the cells. The osmoreceptors responsible for osmometric thirst are located in a brain region known as the *lamina terminalis*. The lamina terminalis contains two specialized *circumventricular organs:* the *OVLT* and the *SFO*. (See figure 12.6.)

The **organum vasculosum of the lamina terminalis (OVLT)** and the **subfornical organ (SFO)** are located outside the blood–brain barrier. That means that substances dissolved in the blood pass easily into the interstitial fluid within these organs. Evidence suggests that most of the osmoreceptors responsible for osmometric thirst are located in the OVLT, but some are also located in the SFO (McKinley et al., 2004).

In a functional-imaging study by Egan et al., (2003), the investigators administered intravenous injections of a salty solution to human volunteers while their brains were being scanned. The researchers observed strong activation of several brain regions, including the lamina terminalis and the **anterior cingulate cortex.** When the participants were permitted to drink water, they did so and almost immediately reported that their thirst had been satisfied. Simultaneously, the activity in the anterior cingulate cortex returned to baseline values. However, the activity in the lamina terminalis

Figure 12.4 Osmoreceptors

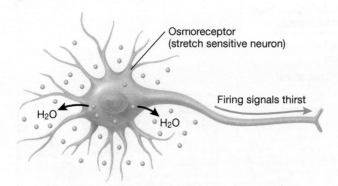

As solute concentration of the interstitial fluid increases, water leaves the cell and the cell decreases in volume. The reduction in cell volume triggers a change in firing rate, which signals thirst.

As solute concentration of the interstitial fluid decreases, water enters the cell and the cell increases in volume. The increase in cell volume triggers a change in firing rate, which signals satiety.

remained high. These results suggest that the activity of the anterior cingulate cortex reflected the participants' thirst, which was immediately relieved by a drink of water. (As we saw in Chapter 7, activity of this region is correlated with people's perception of the unpleasantness of painful stimuli.) In contrast, the continued activity in the lamina terminalis reflected the fact that the blood plasma still contained a high concentration of solutes. After all, it takes around 20 minutes for a drink of water to be absorbed into the general circulation. As we saw in the discussion of Figure 12.2, satiety is an anticipatory mechanism, triggered by the act of drinking. The fall in the activity of the anterior cingulate cortex appears to reflect the activation of this satiety mechanism. (See Figure 12.5.)

Two other functional-imaging studies (Farrell et al., 2006; Xiao et al., 2006) confirm that thirst activates the anterior cingulate cortex. An anatomical tracing study by Hollis et al., (2008) found that in rats, osmoreceptive neurons in the OVLT were connected to the cingulate cortex via the dorsal midline nuclei of the thalamus. This pathway between the osmoreceptors in the OVLT and the cingulate cortex is probably responsible for the activation seen in the functional-imaging studies.

VOLUMETRIC THIRST Volumetric thirst occurs when the volume of the blood plasma—the intravascular volume—decreases. As we saw earlier, when we lose water through evaporation, we lose it from all three fluid compartments: intracellular, interstitial, and intravascular. Thus, evaporation produces both volumetric thirst and osmometric thirst. In addition, loss of blood, vomiting, and diarrhea all cause loss of blood volume (hypovolemia) without depleting the intracellular fluid.

Loss of blood is the most obvious cause of pure volumetric thirst. From the earliest recorded history, reports of battles note that the wounded survivors called out for water. In addition, because hypovolemia involves a loss of

Figure 12.5 Osmometric Thirst in Humans

Functional MRI scans show brain activation produced by osmometric thirst. (a) Activation in the anterior cingulate cortex and hypothalamus, corresponding to a sensation of thirst. (b) Activation in the lamina terminalis, the location of the brain's osmoreceptors.

(From Egan, G., Silk, T., Zamarripa, F., et al., Neural correlates of the emergence of consciousness of thirst, *Proceedings of the National Academy of Science, USA*, 2003, *100*, 15241–15246.)

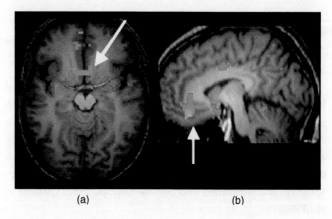

(a)   (b)

sodium as well as water (that is, the sodium that was contained in the fluid that was lost), volumetric thirst leads to a salt appetite.

Detector cells in the heart and kidneys contribute to monitoring blood volume and inducing volumetric thirst when intravascular fluid is low. Cells in the kidneys detect decreases in blood flow. In response to low blood volume, the kidneys are responsible for the presence of the hormone *angiotensin* following a cascade of biochemical events. Angiotensin initiates drinking and a salt appetite, causes the kidneys to conserve water and salt, and increases blood pressure. Therefore, reduced blood flow to the kidneys causes water and salt to be retained, encourages the animal to find and ingest water and salt and allows the organism to compensate for reduced blood volume until fluid balance can be restored.

Figure 12.6 The Circumventricular Organs

This sagittal section of the rat brain shows the location of the circumventricular organs. *Inset:* A hypothetical circuit connecting the subfornical organ with the median preoptic nucleus.

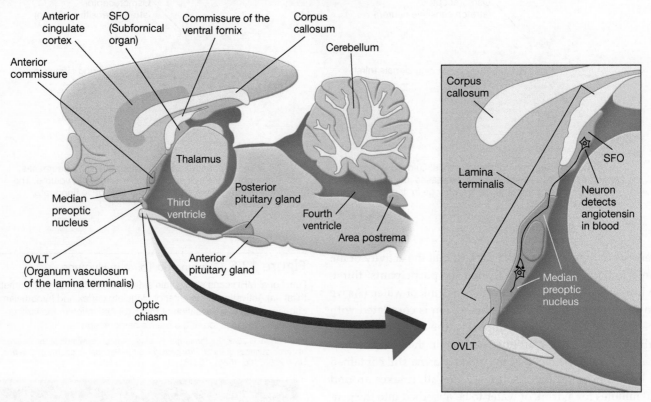

A second set of receptors for volumetric thirst is located in the atria of the heart. These baroreceptor cells are stretch sensitive and detect when blood volume in the heart falls. A reduction in blood flow to the heart increases drinking and severing the nerves to the atrial baroreceptors decreases drinking, demonstrating the important role of these receptor cells (Fitzsimmons and Moore-Gillon, 1980; Quillen et al., 1990).

Neural Mechanisms of Thirst

LO 12.3 **Identify the roles of the subfornical organ and median preoptic nucleus in regulating thirst.**

As you have already learned, the osmoreceptors that initiate drinking are located in the OVLT and SFO of the lamina terminalis. The lamina terminalis seems to be the part of the brain where osmometric and volumetric signals are integrated to control drinking. The signal for volumetric thirst is provided by angiotensin. Because this peptide does not cross the blood–brain barrier, it cannot directly affect neurons in the brain except for those located outside the blood–brain barrier, such as the OVLT and SFO. In fact, research indicates that the SFO is the site at which blood angiotensin acts to produce thirst. (Refer again to Figure 12.6)

SUBFORNICAL ORGAN (SFO) Simpson et al., (1978) found that very low doses of angiotensin injected directly into the SFO caused drinking and that destruction of the SFO or injection of a drug that blocks angiotensin receptors abolished the drinking that normally occurs when angiotensin is injected into the blood. In addition, Phillips and Felix (1976) found that injections of minute quantities of angiotensin into the SFO increased the firing rate of single neurons located there; evidently, these neurons contain angiotensin receptors.

MEDIAN PREOPTIC NUCLEUS Neurons in the SFO send their axons to another part of the lamina terminalis: the **median preoptic nucleus** (not to be confused with the *medial* preoptic nucleus), a small nucleus wrapped around the front of the anterior commissure, a fiber bundle that connects the amygdala and anterior temporal lobe. (Refer to the inset in Figure 12.6.)

On the basis of these findings, Thrasher and his colleagues (see Thrasher, 1989) suggested that the median preoptic nucleus acts as an integrating system for most or all of the stimuli for osmometric and volumetric thirst. As you just read, the median preoptic nucleus receives information from angiotensin-sensitive neurons in the SFO. In addition, this nucleus receives information from the OVLT (which

Figure 12.7 Neural Circuitry Concerned with the Control of Drinking

Not all connections are shown, and some connections may be indirect. Although most of the osmoreceptors are located in the OVLT (organum vasculosum of the lamina terminalis), some are also located in the subfornical organ.

(Adapted from Thrasher, T. N. Acta Physiologica Scandinavica, 1989, 136, 141–150.)

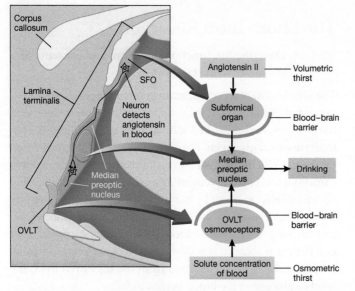

contains osmoreceptors) and from the nucleus of the solitary tract (which receives information from the atrial baroreceptors). Excitotoxic lesions of the median preoptic nucleus, which destroy cell bodies but spare axons passing through the structure, cause severe deficits in osmometric thirst (Cunningham et al., 1992). According to Thrasher and his colleagues, the median preoptic nucleus integrates the information it receives and, through its efferent connections with other parts of the brain, controls drinking. (See Figure 12.7.)

This region of the lamina terminalis seems to play a critical role in fluid regulation in humans as well. As we saw earlier, functional imaging indicates that osmometric thirst increases the activity of this region. In addition, McIver et al., (1991) reported that brain damage that includes this region can cause *adipsia*—lack of drinking. The patients report no sensation of thirst even after they are given an injection of hypertonic saline. To survive, they must deliberately drink water at regular intervals each day, even though they feel no need to do so.

Section Review

Drinking

LO 12.1 Explain the characteristics of a physiological regulatory mechanism.

A regulatory system contains four features: a system variable (the variable that is regulated), a set point (the optimal value of the system variable), a detector to measure the system variable, and a correctional mechanism to change it. Physiological regulatory systems, such as control of body fluids and nutrients, require a satiety mechanism to anticipate the effects of the correctional mechanism, because the changes brought about by eating and drinking occur only after a considerable period of time.

LO 12.2 Compare osmometric and volumetric thirst.

Osmometric thirst occurs when the interstitial fluid draws water out of cells. This event, which can be caused by evaporation of water from the body or by ingestion of a salty meal, is detected by osmoreceptors in the OVLT, a circumventricular organ located in the lamina terminalis. Activation of these osmoreceptors stimulates drinking. The sensation of thirst in humans appears to involve the anterior cingulate cortex.

Volumetric thirst occurs along with osmometric thirst when the body loses fluid through evaporation. Pure volumetric thirst is caused by blood loss, vomiting, and diarrhea. The primary stimulus for volumetric thirst is provided by a fall in blood flow to the kidneys and heart. This event triggers formation of angiotensin, which acts on neurons in

the SFO and stimulates thirst. The hormone also increases blood pressure and stimulates the secretion of pituitary and adrenal hormones that inhibit the secretion of water and sodium by the kidneys and induce a sodium appetite. (Sodium is needed to help restore the plasma volume.)

LO 12.3 Identify the roles of the subfornical organ and median preoptic nucleus in regulating thirst.

A nucleus in the lamina terminalis, the median preoptic nucleus, receives and integrates osmometric and volumetric information. Information about hypovolemia conveyed by angiotensin reaches the median preoptic nucleus directly from the SFO. Osmotic information reaches this nucleus from osmoreceptors in both the OVLT and the SFO. Neurons in the median preoptic nucleus stimulate drinking through their connections with other parts of the brain. The anterior cingulate cortex also receives information from the OVLT via the dorsal midline nucleus of the thalamus, and this region may be involved in sensations of thirst.

Thought Question

While many people would agree that consuming too little water can lead to health problems, can you predict what happens when an individual consumes too much water? Write a memo to your campus health promotions office suggesting ideas for a campaign in gyms or in recreation or athletics facilities on a college campus to inform users of the importance of maintaining fluid balance in a healthy range and how the brain is involved.

Eating: What Is Metabolism?

Eating is one of the most important things we do, and it can also be one of the most pleasurable. Much of what an animal learns to do is motivated by the constant struggle to obtain food; therefore, the need to eat undoubtedly shaped the evolutionary development of our own species. Control of eating is even more complicated than the control of drinking. We can achieve water balance by the intake of two ingredients: water and sodium chloride. When we eat, we must obtain adequate amounts of carbohydrates, fats, amino acids, vitamins, and minerals other than sodium. Thus, our food-ingestive behaviors are more complex, as are the physiological mechanisms that control them.

The rest of this chapter describes research on the control of eating: metabolism, regulation of body weight, the environmental and physiological factors that begin and stop a meal, and the neural mechanisms that monitor the nutritional state of our bodies and control our ingestive behavior. It also describes several serious eating disorders. Despite all the effort that has gone into understanding the physiology of ingestive behavior, these disorders are still difficult to treat. Our best hope of finding effective treatments is to achieve a better understanding of the physiology of metabolism and ingestive behavior.

As you saw in the discussion of the physiology of drinking, you must know something about the fluid compartments of the body and the functions of the kidney to understand the physiology of drinking. Therefore, you will not be surprised that this part of the chapter begins with a discussion of metabolism. Your first inclination might be to skip over this section, but if you do so, you will find that you will not understand experiments that are described later. For example, the system variables that cause an animal to seek food and eat it are related to the animal's metabolism. This section will discuss only as much about this subject as you will need to understand these experiments.

When we eat, molecules that were once part of other living organisms are incorporated into our own bodies. We ingest these molecules for two reasons: to construct and maintain our own organs and to obtain energy for muscular movements and for keeping our bodies warm. In other words, we need both building blocks and fuel. Although food used for building blocks is essential, we will discuss only the food used for fuel, because most of the molecules we eat get "burned" to provide energy for movement and heating.

To stay alive, our cells must be supplied with fuel and oxygen. Fuel comes from the digestive tract, and its presence there is a result of eating. But the digestive tract is sometimes empty; in fact, most of us wake up in the morning in that condition. So there has to be a reservoir that stores nutrients to keep the cells of the body nourished when the gut is empty. Indeed, there are two reservoirs: one short-term and the other long-term. The short-term reservoir stores carbohydrates, and the long-term reservoir stores fats. When the digestive tract is empty, we are in the *fasting phase.* When the digestive tract is full, we are in the *absorptive phase.* These phases will be described in greater detail in upcoming sections. Table 12.1 provides an example of how the reservoirs and phases might be used by the nervous system in a typical day's activities.

The Short-Term Reservoir

LO 12.4 Describe the function, location, and contents of the short-term reservoir.

The short-term reservoir sustains our fuel needs for several hours between meals. It is located in the cells of the liver and the muscles, and it is filled with a complex, insoluble carbohydrate called **glycogen.** For simplicity we will focus only on the liver. Cells in the liver convert glucose (a simple, soluble carbohydrate) into glycogen and store the glycogen. They are stimulated to do so by the presence of **insulin,** a peptide hormone produced by the pancreas. Thus, when glucose and insulin are present in the blood, some of the glucose is used as a fuel, and some of it is stored as glycogen. Later, when all of the food has been absorbed from the digestive tract, the level of glucose in the blood begins to fall.

The fall in glucose is detected by cells in the pancreas and in the brain. The pancreas responds by stopping its secretion of insulin and starting to secrete a different peptide hormone: **glucagon.** The effect of glucagon is opposite that of insulin: It stimulates the conversion of glycogen (stored in the liver) into glucose. (Unfortunately, the terms *glucose, glycogen,* and *glucagon* are similar enough that it is easy to confuse them. Even worse, you will soon encounter another one: *glycerol.*) (See Figure 12.8.) The liver soaks up excess glucose and stores it as glycogen when plenty of glucose is available, and it releases glucose from its reservoir when the digestive tract becomes empty and the level of glucose in the blood begins to fall.

The carbohydrate reservoir in the liver is reserved primarily for the central nervous system (CNS). When you wake in the morning, your brain is being fed by your liver, which is in the process of converting glycogen to glucose

Table 12.1 Use of Reservoirs by the Nervous System

Time	Activity	Phase	Reservoir Used by the Nervous System
0:00 — Day 1	Sleeping	Fasting	Short-term
6:00	Eating breakfast	Absorptive	None
10:00	Working	Fasting	Short-term
12:00	Eating lunch	Absorptive	None
18:00	Exercising	Fasting	Short-term
20:00	Missed dinner	Fasting	Short-term
0:00 — Day 2	Sleeping	Fasting	**Long-term** *(Long-term reservoirs are used when short-term reservoirs are depleted during prolonged fasting)*
6:00	Eating breakfast	Absorptive	None

Figure 12.8 Effects of Insulin and Glucagon on Glucose and Glycogen

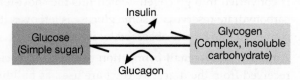

and releasing it into the blood. The glucose reaches the CNS, where it is absorbed and metabolized by the neurons and the glia. This process can continue for a few hours, until all of the carbohydrate reservoir in the liver is used up. (The average liver holds approximately 300 calories of carbohydrate.) Usually, we eat some food before this reservoir gets depleted, which permits us to refill it. But if we do not eat, the CNS (and the rest of the body) must start living on the products of the long-term reservoir.

The Long-Term Reservoir

LO 12.5 **Describe the function, location, and contents of the long-term reservoir.**

Our long-term reservoir consists of adipose tissue (fat tissue). This reservoir is filled with fats or, more precisely, with **triglycerides.** Triglycerides are complex molecules that contain **glycerol** (a soluble carbohydrate, also called *glycerine*) combined with three **fatty acids** (stearic acid, oleic acid, and palmitic acid). Adipose tissue is found beneath the skin and in various locations in the abdominal cavity. It consists of cells that are capable of absorbing nutrients from the blood, converting them to triglycerides, and storing them. These cells can expand enormously in size; in fact, the primary physical difference between a person who is obese and a person who is not is the size of their fat cells. The size of the fat cells is determined by the amount of triglycerides that these cells contain.

The long-term fat reservoir is what keeps us alive when we are fasting. As we begin to use the contents of our short-term carbohydrate reservoir, fat cells start converting triglycerides into fuels that the cells can use and releasing these fuels into the bloodstream. As we just saw, when we wake in the morning with an empty digestive tract, our brain (in fact, all of the CNS) is living on glucose released by the liver. But what about the other cells of the body? They are living on fatty acids, reserving the glucose for the brain. As you will recall from Chapter 3, the sympathetic nervous system is primarily involved in the breakdown and utilization of stored nutrients. When the digestive system is empty, there is an increase in the activity of the sympathetic axons that innervate adipose tissue, the pancreas, and the adrenal medulla. All three effects (direct neural stimulation, secretion of glucagon, and secretion of catecholamines) cause triglycerides in the long-term fat reservoir to be broken down into glycerol and fatty acids. The fatty acids can be directly metabolized by cells in all of the body *except the brain*, which needs glucose.

That leaves glycerol. The liver takes up glycerol and converts it to glucose. That glucose, too, is available to the brain.

You may be asking why the cells of the rest of the body treat the brain so kindly, letting it consume almost all the glucose that the liver releases from its carbohydrate reservoir and constructs from glycerol. The answer is that insulin has several other functions besides causing glucose to be converted to glycogen. One of these functions is controlling the entry of glucose into cells. Glucose easily dissolves in water, but it will not dissolve in fats. Cell membranes are made of lipids (fatlike substances); thus, glucose cannot directly pass through them. To be taken into a cell, glucose must be transported there by *glucose transporters*—protein molecules that are situated in the membrane and are similar to those responsible for the reuptake of transmitter substances. Glucose transporters contain insulin receptors, which control their activity; only when insulin binds with these receptors can glucose be transported into the cell. But the cells of the nervous system are an exception to this rule. Their glucose transporters do not contain insulin receptors, and these cells can absorb glucose *even when insulin is not present.*

Fasting Phase

LO 12.6 **Compare the pathways for the use of glucose, fat, and amino acids by the brain and body in the fasting phase.**

Figure 12.9 reviews what we have said so far about the metabolism that takes place while the digestive tract is empty, which physiologists refer to as the **fasting phase** of metabolism. A fall in blood glucose level causes the pancreas to stop secreting insulin and to start secreting glucagon. The absence of insulin means that most of the cells of the body can no longer use glucose; thus, all the glucose present in the blood is reserved for the CNS. The presence of glucagon and the absence of insulin instruct the liver to start drawing on the short-term carbohydrate reservoir—to start converting its glycogen into glucose. The presence of glucagon and the absence of insulin, along with increased activity of the sympathetic nervous system, also instruct fat cells to start drawing on the long-term fat reservoir—to start breaking down triglycerides into fatty acids and glycerol. Most of the body lives on the fatty acids, and the glycerol, which is converted into glucose by the liver, gets used by the brain. If fasting is prolonged, proteins (especially protein found in muscle) will be broken down to amino acids, which can be metabolized by all of the body except the CNS.

Absorptive Phase

LO 12.7 **Compare the pathways for the use of glucose, fat, and amino acids by the brain and body in the absorptive phase.**

The phase of metabolism that occurs when food is present in the digestive tract is called the **absorptive phase.** Now that you understand the fasting phase, this one is simple. Suppose that we eat a balanced meal of carbohydrates, proteins, and fats. The carbohydrates are broken down into glucose, and the proteins are broken down into amino acids. The fats basically remain as fats. Let us consider each of these three nutrients:

1. Glucose: As we start absorbing the nutrients, the level of glucose in the blood rises. This rise is detected by cells in the brain, which causes the activity of the sympathetic nervous system to decrease and the activity of the parasympathetic nervous system to increase. This change tells the pancreas to stop secreting glucagon and

to begin secreting insulin. The insulin permits all the cells of the body to use glucose as a fuel. Extra glucose is converted into glycogen, which fills the short-term carbohydrate reservoir. If some glucose is left over, it is converted into fat and absorbed by fat cells.

2. Amino acids: A small proportion of the amino acids received from the digestive tract are used as building blocks to construct proteins and peptides; the rest are converted to fats and stored in adipose tissue.

3. Fat: Fat is not used as a fuel at this time; it is simply stored in adipose tissue. (Look again at Figure 12.9.)

Figure 12.9 Metabolic Pathways During the Fasting Phase and Absorptive Phase of Metabolism

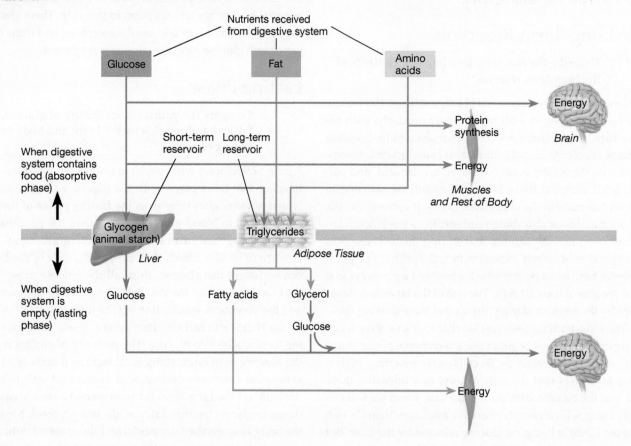

Section Review

Eating: What Is Metabolism?

LO 12.4 Describe the function, location, and contents of the short-term reservoir.

The short-term reservoir supplies nutrients to the brain during brief periods of fasting (between meals). It is located in the liver, where energy is stored in glycogen molecules until needed.

LO12.5 Describe the function, location, and contents of the long-term reservoir.

The long-term reservoir supplies nutrients to the brain and body during prolonged periods of fasting. It is located in the adipose tissue, where energy is stored in triglyceride molecules until needed.

LO 12.6 Compare the pathways for the use of glucose, fat, and amino acids by the brain and body in the fasting phase.

Unused glucose, fat, and amino acids are stored in the liver and adipose tissues for later use during the fasting phase. During the fasting phase the activity of the parasympathetic nervous system falls, and the activity of the sympathetic nervous system increases. In response, the level of insulin falls, and the levels of glucagon and the adrenal catecholamines rise. These events cause liver glycogen to be converted to glucose and triglycerides to be broken down into glycerol and fatty acids. In the absence of insulin, only the central nervous system can use the glucose that is available in the blood; the rest of the body lives on fatty acids. Glycerol is converted to glucose by the liver, and the brain metabolizes the glucose.

LO 12.7 Compare the pathways for the use of glucose, fat, and amino acids by the brain and body in the absorptive phase.

During the absorptive phase we receive glucose, amino acids, and fats from the intestines. The blood level of insulin is high, which permits all cells to metabolize glucose. In addition, the liver and the muscles convert glucose to glycogen, which replenishes the short-term reservoir. Excess carbohydrates and amino acids are converted to fats, and fats are placed into the long-term reservoir in the adipose tissue.

Thought Question

In your opinion, what features of the environment of the distant ancestors of our species favored the evolution of two nutrient reservoirs and the ability to convert one type of nutrient to another? What does this suggest about the diets of our distant ancestors?

Eating: Signals to Start a Meal

If you were faced with the kind of meal presented in Figure 12.10, what factors might be involved in your decisions about what to eat, how much to eat, and when to begin eating? Many different factors are involved in our eating behavior. The environment, for example, plays an important role in when we eat, how much we eat, and when we start eating. So do internal processes. This section will focus on the internal mechanisms that compel us to eat, looking first at signals from the digestive system and then metabolic responses to the need for food.

Signals from the Digestive System

LO 12.8 Describe ghrelin's function as a hunger signal, including its origin and relationship to obesity, fasting, and absorptive phases.

An empty stomach and upper intestine provide an important endocrine signal to the brain that it is time to start thinking about finding something to eat. A peptide hormone called **ghrelin** is released from the gastrointestinal system

Figure 12.10 Starting a Meal

Which foods would you select? How much would you eat? What factors might influence your behavior in this situation?

(especially the stomach) when individuals are in the fasting phase and the digestive system is empty (Kojima et al., 1999). Ghrelin then binds to receptors in the hypothalamus to help stimulate eating behavior. (See Figure 12.11.)

Figure 12.11 Ghrelin Signals

Ghrelin relays signals from the stomach and digestive tract to the hypothalamus.

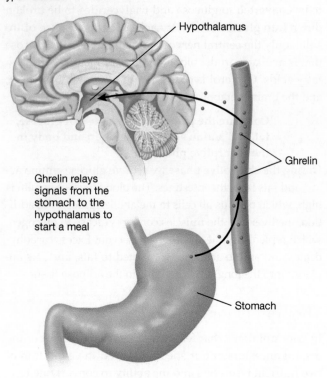

Ghrelin relays signals from the stomach to the hypothalamus to start a meal

Figure 12.12 Level of Ghrelin in Human Blood Plasma

A rise in the level of this peptide precedes each meal.

(Based on data from Cummings et al., 2001.)

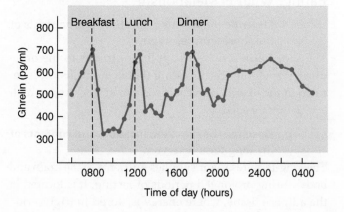

Blood levels of ghrelin increase with fasting and are reduced after a meal. Blocking the ghrelin signal inhibits eating and increasing ghrelin can cause weight gain by increasing food intake and decreasing the metabolism of fats. Blood levels of ghrelin increase shortly before each meal, which suggests that this peptide is involved in the initiation of a meal (Cummings, 2006). Figure 12.12 shows the relationship between blood levels of ghrelin and food intake during the course of a day.

Ghrelin is a potent stimulator of food intake.

Ghrelin is a potent stimulator of food intake, and it even stimulates thoughts about food. Schmid et al., (2005) found that a single intravenous injection of ghrelin not only enhanced appetite in typical participants; it also elicited vivid images of foods that the participants liked to eat. As we saw in the case at the beginning of this chapter, one of the symptoms of Prader-Willi syndrome is obesity caused by almost continuous eating. A possible cause of the overeating is chronic elevation in the blood level of ghrelin—a level that remains high even after a meal (DelParigi et al., 2002). You will read more about obesity interventions that reduce ghrelin levels later in this chapter.

Although ghrelin is an important short-term hunger signal, it clearly cannot be the only one. For example, people who have undergone successful gastric bypass surgery have very low levels of ghrelin in the blood. Although they eat less and lose weight, they do not stop eating. In addition, mice with a targeted mutation against the ghrelin gene or the ghrelin receptor have normal food intake and body weight (Sun et al., 2003; Sun et al., 2004). However, Zigman et al., (2005) found that this mutation protected mice from overeating and gaining weight when they were fed a tasty, high-fat diet that induces obesity in normal mice. Thus, alternative mechanisms can stimulate feeding, which, given the vital importance of food, is not surprising. In fact, one of the factors that complicates research on ingestive behavior is the presence of redundant systems. (But we are undoubtedly better off with these complicating factors.)

Metabolic Signals

LO 12.9 Describe how metabolic signals can play a role in starting a meal.

Most of the time, we begin a meal a few hours after the previous one, so our nutrient reservoirs are seldom in serious need of replenishment. But if we skip several meals, we get hungrier and hungrier, presumably because of physiological signals indicating that we have been withdrawing nutrients from our long-term reservoir. What happens to the level of nutrients in our body as time passes after a meal? As you learned earlier in this chapter, during the absorptive phase of metabolism we live on food that is being absorbed from the digestive tract. After that we start drawing on our nutrient reservoirs: The brain lives on glucose, and the rest of the body lives on fatty acids. Although the metabolic needs of the cells of the body are being met, we are taking fuel out of our long-term reservoir—making withdrawals rather than deposits. This is the time to start thinking about our next meal.

GLUCOSE AND LIPIDS A fall in blood glucose level (a condition known as *hypoglycemia*) is a potent stimulus for hunger. Hypoglycemia can be produced experimentally by giving an animal a large injection of insulin, which causes cells in the liver, muscles, and adipose tissue to take up glucose and store it away. We can also deprive cells of glucose by injecting an animal with 2-deoxyglucose (2-DG). You are already familiar with this chemical, because it was described in several experiments from previous chapters that used radioactive 2-DG in conjunction with PET scanners or autoradiography to study the metabolic rate of different parts of the brain. When (nonradioactive) 2-DG is given in large doses, it interferes with glucose metabolism by competing with glucose for access to the mechanism that transports glucose through the cell membrane and for access to the enzymes that metabolize glucose. Both hypoglycemia and 2-DG cause **glucoprivation;** that is, they deprive cells of glucose. And glucoprivation, whatever its cause, stimulates eating.

Hunger can also be produced by causing **lipoprivation**—depriving cells of lipids. More precisely, they are deprived of the ability to metabolize fatty acids through injection of a drug such as *mercaptoacetate*.

DETECTORS What is the nature of the detectors that monitor the level of metabolic fuels, and where are they located? The evidence that has been gathered so far indicates that there are two sets of detectors: one set located in the brain and another set located in the liver. The detectors in the brain monitor the nutrients that are available on their side of the blood–brain barrier, and the detectors in the liver monitor the nutrients that are available to the rest of the body. Because the brain can use only glucose, its detectors are sensitive to glucoprivation, and because the rest of the body can use both glucose and fatty acids, the detectors in the liver are sensitive to both glucoprivation and lipoprivation.

Liver Detectors Let's review the evidence for glucose and lipid detectors in the liver. A study by Novin et al., (1973) suggested that receptors in the liver can stimulate glucoprivic hunger. The investigators infused 2-DG into a vein to the liver. The infusions of 2-DG caused immediate eating. When researchers cut the vagus nerve, which connects the liver with the brain, the infusions no longer stimulated eating. Thus, the brain receives the glucoprivic hunger signal from the liver through the vagus nerve.

Lipoprivic hunger appears to be stimulated by receptors in the liver as well. Ritter and Taylor (1990) induced lipoprivic hunger and found that cutting the vagus nerve abolished this hunger. Thus, the liver appears to contain receptors that detect low availability of glucose or fatty acids (glucoprivation or lipoprivation) and send this information to the brain through the vagus nerve (Friedman et al., 2005). (See Figure 12.13.)

Figure 12.13 Nutrient Receptors for Glucose and Lipids in the Liver

Receptors for glucose and lipids are located in the liver, and convey signals about gluco- and lipoprivation to the brain through the vagus nerve. These receptors are located outside the blood–brain barrier. Receptors for glucose are also located in the brain, inside the blood–brain barrier.

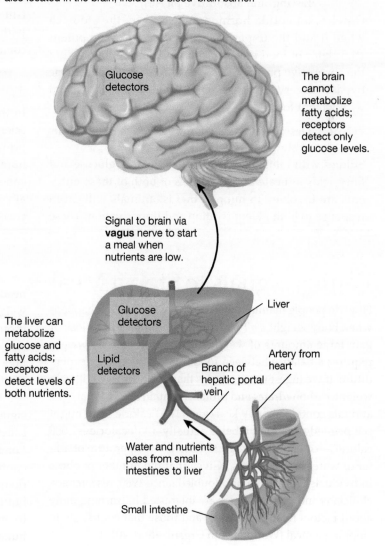

Glucose detectors

The brain cannot metabolize fatty acids; receptors detect only glucose levels.

Signal to brain via **vagus** nerve to start a meal when nutrients are low.

The liver can metabolize glucose and fatty acids; receptors detect levels of both nutrients.

Glucose detectors

Lipid detectors

Liver

Artery from heart

Branch of hepatic portal vein

Water and nutrients pass from small intestines to liver

Small intestine

Brain Detectors   Now let's look at some of the evidence that indicates that the brain has its own nutrient detectors. Because the brain can use only glucose, it would make sense that these detectors respond to glucoprivation—and, indeed, they do. Ritter et al., (2000) found that injections of a drug that produces glucoprivation into two regions of the hindbrain—the dorsomedial and ventrolateral medulla—induced eating. The role of these regions in control of food intake and metabolism is discussed later in this chapter.

To summarize: The brain contains detectors that monitor the availability of glucose (its only fuel) inside the blood–brain barrier, and the liver contains detectors the monitor the availability of nutrients (glucose and fatty acids) outside the blood–brain barrier.

It is important to remember that no single set of receptors is solely responsible for the information the brain uses to control eating. For example, mice with a knockout of the ghrelin gene eat almost normally. In addition, Tordoff et al., (1982) found that cutting the hepatic branch of the vagus nerve, which prevents hunger signals originating in the liver from reaching the brain, had little effect on an animal's day-to-day eating. Finally, lesions of the medulla that abolish both glucoprivic and lipoprivic signals do not lead to long-term disturbances in the control of feeding (Ritter et al., 1992). Apparently, the control of metabolism and ingestive behavior is just too important to entrust to one mechanism.

Section Review

Eating: Signals to Start a Meal

LO 12.8 **Describe ghrelin's function as a hunger signal, including its origin and relationship to obesity, fasting, and absorptive phases.**

Ghrelin, a peptide hormone released by the stomach when it and the upper intestine are empty, is a potent stimulator of food intake. Ghrelin levels are low during the absorptive phase, and increase before a meal. Gastric bypass surgery reduces ghrelin levels and is associated with weight loss.

LO 12.9 **Describe how metabolic signals can play a role in starting a meal.**

Studies with inhibitors of the metabolism of glucose and fatty acids indicate that low levels of both of these nutrients are involved in hunger; that is, animals will eat in response to both glucoprivation and lipoprivation. These signals are normally present only after more than one meal has been missed. Receptors in the liver detect both glucoprivation and lipoprivation and transmit this information to the brain through sensory axons of the vagus nerve. Glucoprivic eating can also be stimulated by interfering with glucose metabolism in the medulla; thus, the brain contains its own glucose-sensitive detectors.

Thought Question

In the future (when you've become a successful neuroscientist), zoologists approach you about an endangered primate species with a nervous system very similar to the human's. These animals won't eat, and the zoologists are concerned. Imagine that you have any neuroscience tool at your disposal. What would you recommend to help increase eating behavior for these animals?

Eating: Signals to Stop a Meal

How do people maintain their body weights? What happens when body weight *isn't* maintained and individuals lose or gain large amounts of weight? Regulation of body weight requires a balance between food intake and energy expenditure. If we ingest more calories than we burn, we will gain weight; carbohydrates and proteins contain about 4 kcal/gm, and fats contain about 9 kcal/gm. (The "calorie" you might see printed on a food label is actually a kilocalorie—1,000 calories—or enough energy to raise the temperature of a liter of water by 1° Celsius.) Given that the number of obese individuals worldwide has doubled since 1980, researchers, clinicians and policy makers are interested in learning more about factors related to satiety and those that contribute to stopping a meal (World Health Organization, 2015).

Assuming that our energy expenditure is constant, we need two mechanisms to maintain a relatively constant body weight. One mechanism must increase our motivation to eat if our long-term nutrient reservoir is becoming depleted, and another must restrain our food intake if we begin to take in more calories than we need. Unfortunately, the first mechanism is more effective than the second one.

In general, there are two primary sources of satiety signals—the signals that stop a meal: short- and long-term satiety signals. Short-term satiety signals stop a single meal. Long-term satiety signals arise in the adipose tissue, which contains the long-term nutrient reservoir. These signals do not control the beginning and end of a particular meal, but they do, in the long run, control the intake of calories by modulating the sensitivity of brain mechanisms to the hunger and satiety signals that they receive. The following section will investigate the influence of a variety of short-term and long-term satiety signals. (See Figure 12.14.)

Short-Term Satiety

LO 12.10 **Describe the general function of short-term satiety signals.**

In addition to factors arising from the body's fuel needs, consider the following case study description and reflect on what additional factor may be involved in short-term satiety:

Patient B. R. was a 59-year-old male who experienced an acute episode of encephalitis that resulted in bilateral damage to his medial temporal lobes, including the hippocampus and amygdala. As a result, he experienced profound short-term memory impairment, no awareness of a memory problem, and no familiarity with the hospital environment and room that he had lived in for most of a year. To evaluate the role of explicit memory in ending a meal, researchers presented a midday meal to B. R. each day for three days. Researchers removed B. R.'s plate when he finished the meal. After a 10- to 30-minute break, a second meal was presented. A third meal was presented following another 10- to 30-minute break. B. R. completed every first and second meal that was offered. On one day, he began eating a third meal as well.

The researchers concluded "that memory of recent eating plays an important, but previously unappreciated, role in the onset and termination of meals by humans" (Rozin et al., 1998, p. 394). In addition to signals to be discussed in the following section, memory of our most recent meals may also play an important role in stopping a meal.

Short-term satiety signals come from the immediate effects of eating a particular meal, which begin long before the food is digested. To search for these signals, we will follow the pathway traveled by ingested food: the eyes, nose, and

Figure 12.14 Satiety Signals

Short-term signals are presented in blue; long-term signals in red.

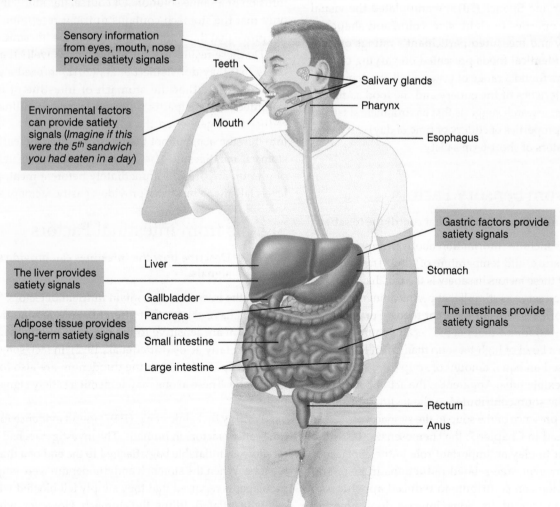

Sensory information from eyes, mouth, nose provide satiety signals

Environmental factors can provide satiety signals (*Imagine if this were the 5th sandwich you had eaten in a day*)

Teeth

Mouth

Salivary glands

Pharynx

Esophagus

Gastric factors provide satiety signals

The liver provides satiety signals

Liver

Stomach

Gallbladder

Pancreas

Adipose tissue provides long-term satiety signals

Small intestine

Large intestine

The intestines provide satiety signals

Rectum

Anus

mouth; the stomach; the small intestine; and the liver. Each of these locations can potentially provide a signal to the brain that indicates that food has been ingested and is progressing on the way toward absorption. We will first start with the broader context and impact of environmental factors.

Signals from Environmental Factors

LO 12.11 **Identify examples of environmental factors that contribute to satiety.**

Because the consequences of starvation are much more serious than the consequences of overeating, the process of natural selection has given us strong mechanisms to start eating and weaker ones to stop eating. The relatively weak inhibitory control of eating is shown by the fact that many environmental factors can increase meal size. If there were strong constraints on food intake, then it should be difficult to get a person to eat more than a normal amount. de Castro and his colleagues (reviewed by de Castro, 2004) found that people ate a larger meal if the food was especially tasty, if it was eaten in the company of other people, if the portions were larger, and if the meal began later than usual in the day.

Demonstrating the effect of environmental factors on eating, Harrar and Spence (2013) manipulated the visual and tactile properties (weight, size, color, and shape) of plastic cutlery and measured participant's ratings of taste and liking of identical foods presented on varying cutlery. The researchers found a range of taste and liking depending on the characteristics of the cutlery and the food sampled. Taken together, research suggests that environmental factors (for example, properties of cutlery or time of day) can be important regulators of short-term satiety.

Signals from Sensory Factors

LO 12.12 **Identify sensory factors that contribute to satiety.**

Sensory factors include information about the appearance, odor, taste, texture, and temperature of food. The most important role of these factors in satiety is the fact that taste and odor of food can serve as stimuli that permit animals to learn about the caloric contents of different foods. For example, Cecil et al., (1998) found that people became more satiated when they ate a bowl of high-fat soup than when the experimenters infused an equal amount of soup into their stomachs with a flexible tube. Apparently, the act of tasting and swallowing the soup contributed to the feeling of fullness caused by the presence of the soup in the stomach.

As you read in Chapter 7, the chemosenses (taste and smell) interact to play an important role in the experience of eating. However, age-related reductions in taste and smell perception can contribute to reduced appetite and weight loss in older adults. Some interventions aimed to maintaining body weight and nutritional status in this population involve enhancing the taste and smell of foods to make them more palatable (Schiffman, 2000).

Signals from Gastric Factors

LO 12.13 **Explain how the stomach can provide satiety signals.**

The stomach apparently contains receptors that can detect the presence of nutrients. Davis and Campbell (1973) allowed rats to eat their fill; shortly thereafter, they removed food from the rats' stomachs through an implanted tube. When the rats were permitted to eat again, they ate almost exactly the same amount of food that had been taken out. This finding suggests that animals are able to monitor the amount of food in their stomachs.

Deutsch and Gonzalez (1980) confirmed and extended these findings. They found that when they removed food from the stomach of a rat that had just eaten all it wanted, the animal would immediately eat just enough food to replace what had been removed—even if the experimenters replaced the food with a nonnutritive saline solution. It appears that the rats did not simply measure the volume of the food in their stomachs, because they were not fooled by the infusion of a saline solution. Of course, this study indicates only that the stomach contains nutrient receptors; it does not prove that there are not detectors in the intestines too.

Do these results extend to humans as well? It appears likely that they do. Steinert et al., (2012) infused a glucose solution into either the stomach or intestine of healthy volunteers. Participants reported increased fullness and reduced hunger when the glucose solution was infused into the stomach, but not the intestine. As stated earlier, the stomach and digestive tract release ghrelin. While high levels of ghrelin are present immediately before a meal, ghrelin levels fall after a meal and provide a gastric factor of satiety.

Signals from Intestinal Factors

LO 12.14 **Describe how the intestines can provide satiety signals.**

Indeed, the intestines do contain nutrient detectors. Studies with rats have shown that afferent axons arising from the duodenum are sensitive to the presence of glucose, amino acids, and fatty acids (Ritter et al., 1992). In fact, some of the chemoreceptors found in the duodenum are also found in the tongue. These axons may transmit a satiety signal to the brain.

A study by Feinle et al., (1997) found evidence for intestinal satiety factors in humans. The investigators had people swallow an inflatable bag attached to the end of a thin, flexible tube. When the stomach and duodenum were empty, the participants reported that they simply felt bloated when the bag was inflated, filling the stomach. However, when fats or carbohydrates were infused into the duodenum while the bag was being inflated, the people reported sensations of fullness like those experienced after eating a meal. Thus, stomach and intestinal satiety factors can interact. That's not surprising, given the fact that, by the time we finish a normal meal, our stomachs are full and a small quantity of nutrients has been received by the duodenum.

After food reaches the stomach, it is mixed with hydrochloric acid and pepsin, an enzyme that breaks proteins into their constituent amino acids. As digestion proceeds, food is gradually introduced from the stomach into the duodenum. There, the food is mixed with bile and pancreatic enzymes, which continue the digestive process. The duodenum controls the rate of stomach emptying by secreting a peptide hormone called **cholecystokinin (CCK)**. This hormone receives its name from the fact that it causes the gallbladder (cholecyst) to contract, injecting bile into the duodenum. (Bile breaks fats down into small particles so that they can be absorbed from the intestines.) CCK is secreted in response to the presence of fats, which are detected by receptors in the walls of the duodenum. In addition to stimulating contraction of the gallbladder, CCK causes the pylorus to constrict and inhibits gastric contractions, thus keeping the stomach from giving the duodenum more food.

The blood level of CCK must be related to the amount of nutrients (particularly fats) that the duodenum receives from the stomach. Thus, this hormone could potentially provide a satiety signal to the brain, telling it that the duodenum was receiving food from the stomach. Many studies have indeed found that injections of CCK suppress eating (Moran, 2009). However, mice with a targeted mutation against the gene responsible for the production of CCK ate normal amounts of food and did not become obese. Presumably, compensatory mechanisms prevented the animals from overeating. CCK does not act directly on the brain; instead, it acts on receptors located in the junction between the stomach and the duodenum (Moran et al., 1989). South and Ritter (1988) found that the appetite-suppressing effect of CCK was abolished by the application of *capsaicin* to the vagus nerve. Capsaicin, a drug extracted from chile peppers, destroys sensory axons in the vagus nerve. This finding indicates that signals from CCK receptors are transmitted to the brain via the vagus nerve.

As we saw earlier in this chapter, secretion of ghrelin by the stomach provides a signal that increases hunger. Once a meal begins and food starts to enter the duodenum, the secretion of ghrelin is suppressed. The suppression of a hunger signal could be another factor that brings a meal to its end.

Investigators have discovered a chemical produced by cells in the gastrointestinal tract that appears to serve as an additional satiety signal. This chemical, **peptide YY$_{3-36}$** (let's just call it **PYY**), is released by the small intestine after a meal in amounts proportional to the calories that were just ingested (Pedersen-Bjergaard et al., 1996). Only nutrients caused PYY to be secreted; a large drink of water had no effect. Injections of PYY significantly decrease the size of meals eaten by members of several species, including rats and both lean and obese humans (Batterham et al., 2007; Schloegl et al., 2011). In addition, Stoeckel et al. (2008) found that the amount of PYY released after a meal correlates positively with people's ratings of satiety. (See Figure 12.15.)

Signals from Liver Factors

LO 12.15 **Explain how the liver provides late-stage satiety signals.**

Satiety produced by gastric factors and duodenal factors is anticipatory; that is, these factors predict that the food in the digestive system will, when absorbed, eventually restore the system variables that cause hunger. Not until nutrients are absorbed from the intestines can they be used to nourish the cells of the body and replenish the body's nutrient reservoirs. The last stage of satiety signaling appears to originate in the liver, which is the first organ to learn that food is finally being received from the intestines.

Evidence that nutrient detectors in the liver play a role in satiety comes from several sources. For example, Tordoff and Friedman (1988) infused small amounts of two nutrients, glucose and fructose, into the hepatic portal vein. The amounts they used were similar to those that are produced when a meal is being digested. Both of the infusions "fooled" the liver; both nutrients reduced the amount of food that the rats ate. Fructose cannot cross the blood–brain barrier and is metabolized very poorly by cells in the rest of the body, but it can readily be metabolized by the liver. Therefore, the signal

---

Figure 12.15 Effects of PYY on Hunger

The graph shows the amount of food (in kilocalories) eaten at a buffet meal 30 minutes after people received a 90-minute intravenous infusion of saline or PYY. Data points from each person are connected by straight lines.

(Data from Batterham, R. L., ffytche, D. H., Rosenthal, J. M., et al., PYY modulation of cortical and hypothalamic brain areas predicts feeding behaviour in humans, *Nature*, 2007, *450*, 106–109.)

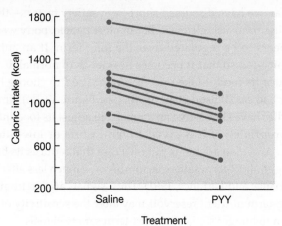

from this nutrient must have originated in the liver. These results strongly suggest that when the liver receives nutrients from the intestines, it sends a signal to the brain that produces satiety. More accurately, the signal *continues* the satiety that was already started by signals arising from the stomach and upper intestine.

Signals from Insulin

LO 12.16 Describe how insulin can function as a satiety signal.

As you read earlier, the absorptive phase of metabolism is accompanied by an increased level of insulin in the blood. Insulin permits organs other than the brain to metabolize glucose, and it promotes the entry of nutrients into fat cells, where they are converted into triglycerides. Remember that cells in the brain do not need insulin to metabolize glucose. Nevertheless, the brain contains insulin receptors (Unger et al., 1989). What purpose do these insulin receptors serve? They appear to detect insulin present in the blood, which tells the brain that the body is probably in the absorptive phase of metabolism. Thus, in addition to its other roles, insulin may serve as a satiety signal (Woods et al., 2006).

Insulin is a peptide and would not normally be admitted to the brain. However, a transport mechanism delivers it through the blood–brain barrier, and it reaches neurons in the hypothalamus that are involved in regulation of hunger and satiety. Infusion of insulin into the third ventricle inhibits eating and causes a loss of body weight (Woods et al., 1979). In addition, Brüning et al., (2000) prepared a targeted mutation in mice that prevented the production of insulin receptors in the brain without affecting their production elsewhere in the body. The mice became obese, especially when they were fed a tasty, high-fat diet, which would be expected if one of the satiety factors was absent.

Long-Term Satiety: Signals from Adipose Tissue

LO 12.17 Contrast the function of satiety signals from adipose tissue with short-term satiety signals.

So far, we have discussed short-term satiety factors—those arising from a single meal. But in most people, body weight appears to be regulated over the long term. If an animal is force-fed so that it becomes heavier than normal, it will reduce its food intake once it is permitted to choose how much to eat (Wilson et al., 1990). (See Figure 12.16.) Similar studies have shown that an animal will adjust its food intake appropriately if it is given a high-calorie or low-calorie diet. And if an animal is put on a diet that reduces its body weight, short-term satiety factors become much less effective (Cabanac and Lafrance, 1991). Thus, signals arising from the long-term nutrient reservoir may alter the sensitivity of the brain to hunger signals or short-term satiety signals.

Figure 12.16 Effects of Force Feeding

After rats were fed an excess of their normal food intake, their subsequent food intake fell and recovered only when their body weight returned to normal.

(Based on data from Wilson et al., 1990.)

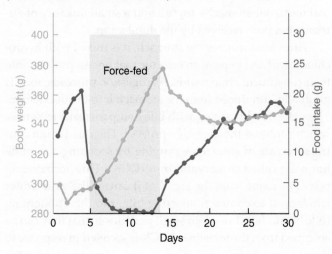

What exactly is the system variable that permits the body weight of most organisms to remain relatively stable? It is likely that some variable related to body fat is regulated. The basic difference between people who are obese and those who are not is the amount of fat stored in their adipose tissue. Perhaps fat tissue provides a signal to the brain that indicates how much of it there is. If so, the signal is almost certainly some sort of chemical, because cutting the nerves that serve the fat tissue in an animal's body does not affect its total body fat.

The discovery of a long-term satiety signal from fat tissue came after years of study with a strain of genetically obese mice. The **ob mouse** (as this strain is called) has a low metabolism, overeats, and becomes overweight. It also develops diabetes in adulthood, just as many people who are obese do. (See Figure 12.17.) Researchers in

Figure 12.17 Effects of Leptin on Obesity in Mice of the Ob Strain

The ob mouse on the left is untreated; the one on the right received daily injections of leptin.

(Photo courtesy of Dr. J. Sholtis, The Rockefeller University. Copyright © 1995 Amgen, Inc.)

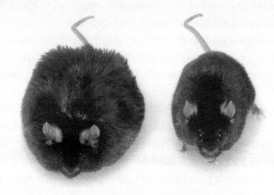

several laboratories reported the discovery of the cause of the obesity (Campfield et al., 1995; Halaas et al., 1995; Pelleymounter et al., 1995). A particular gene, called OB, normally produces a peptide hormone that has been given the name **leptin.** Leptin is normally secreted by well-nourished fat cells. Because of a genetic mutation, the fat cells of ob mice are unable to produce leptin.

Leptin has profound effects on metabolism and eating, acting as an antiobesity hormone. If ob mice are given daily injections of leptin, their metabolic rate increases, their body temperature rises, they become more active, and they eat less. As a result, their weight returns to an average amount.

The discovery of leptin has stimulated much interest among researchers who are seeking ways to treat human obesity. Because it is a natural hormone, it appeared to provide a way to help people to lose weight without the use of drugs that have potentially harmful effects. Unfortunately, as we shall see later in this chapter, leptin is not a useful treatment for obesity for most people.

Section Review

Eating: Signals to Stop a Meal

LO 12.10 Describe the general function of short-term satiety signals.

Short-term satiety signals control the size of a meal. Short-term satiety signals come from the immediate effects of eating a particular meal, which begin long before the food is digested.

LO 12.11 Identify examples of environmental factors that contribute to satiety.

People eat a larger meal if the food is especially tasty, if it is eaten in the company of other people, if the portions are larger, and if the meal begins later than usual in the day.

LO 12.12 Identify sensory factors that contribute to satiety.

Sensory factors include information about the appearance, odor, taste, texture, and temperature of food. Sensory factors related to satiety include feedback from the nose and mouth about the nutritive value of the food eaten.

LO 12.13 Explain how the stomach can provide satiety signals.

Gastric satiety factors are activated by the entry of food into the stomach. The stomach possesses nutrient detectors that convey satiety signals. As presented earlier in this chapter, the stomach and intestines also secrete ghrelin and a fall in ghrelin provides a satiety signal to the brain.

LO 12.14 Describe how the intestines can provide satiety signals.

Intestinal satiety factors are activated by the passage of food from the stomach into the duodenum. The intestines possess nutrient detectors that convey satiety signals. Another satiety signal from the intestine is provided by CCK, which is secreted by the duodenum when it receives fat-rich food from the stomach. Information about the secretion of CCK is transmitted to the brain through the afferent axons of the vagus nerve. PYY, a peptide secreted after a meal by the intestines, also acts as a satiety signal. As presented earlier in this chapter, the stomach and intestines also secrete ghrelin and a fall in ghrelin provides a satiety signal to the brain.

LO 12.15 Explain how the liver provides late-stage satiety signals.

A satiety signal comes from the liver, which detects nutrients being received from the intestines through the hepatic portal vein.

LO 12.16 Describe how insulin can function as a satiety signal.

Although a high level of insulin in the blood causes glucoprivic eating by reducing blood levels of glucose, moderately high levels, associated with the absorptive phase of metabolism, provide a satiety signal to the brain.

LO 12.17 Contrast the function of satiety signals from adipose tissue with short-term satiety signals.

Unlike short-term satiety signals that regulate the size of meal, signals arising from fat tissue affect food intake on a long-term basis, apparently by modulating the effectiveness of short-term hunger and satiety signals. Force-feeding facilitates satiety, and starvation inhibits it. Studies of the ob mouse led to the discovery of leptin, a peptide hormone secreted by well-nourished adipose tissue that increases an animal's metabolic rate and decreases food intake.

Thought Question

How are hormones involved in eating regulation? Make a table organizing information about the role of hormones in short-term and long-term satiety. First, make a list of all of the hormone signals in this section. For each hormone, decide if it is likely to be present or absent when a typical person is in the absorptive or fasting phase. Make a column for "absorptive phase" and another column for "fasting phase." For each hormone, indicate if it is present (+) or absent (–) in each phase. After making your table, do you think more hormone signals are involved in starting or stopping a meal? Why might that be?

Brain Mechanisms

Although many hunger and satiety signals originate in the digestive system and in the body's nutrient reservoirs, the target of these signals is the brain. This section explores some of the research on the brain mechanisms that control food intake and metabolism.

Brain Stem

LO 12.18 Identify the functions of the brain stem involved in eating regulation.

Ingestive behaviors are phylogenetically ancient. All our ancestors ate and drank or died prematurely of dehydration or starvation. Therefore, we should expect that the basic ingestive behaviors of chewing and swallowing are programmed by phylogenetically ancient brain circuits. Indeed, studies have shown that these behaviors can be performed by decerebrate rats, whose brains were transected between the diencephalon and the midbrain (Flynn and Grill, 1983; Grill and Kaplan, 1990; Norgren and Grill, 1982). **Decerebration** disconnects the motor neurons of the brain stem and spinal cord from the neural circuits of the cerebral hemispheres (such as the cerebral cortex and basal ganglia) that normally control them. The only behaviors that decerebrate animals can display are those that are directly controlled by neural circuits located within the brain stem. (See Figure 12.18.)

Decerebrate rats cannot approach and eat food; the experimenters must place food, in liquid form, into their mouths. Decerebrate rats can distinguish between different tastes; they drink and swallow sweet or slightly salty liquids and spit out bitter ones. They even respond to hunger and satiety signals.

They drink more sucrose after having been deprived of food for 24 hours, and they drink less of it if some sucrose is first injected directly into their stomachs. They also eat in response to glucoprivation. These studies indicate that the brain stem contains neural circuits that can detect hunger and satiety signals and control at least some aspects of food intake.

The region of the dorsal medulla that includes the area postrema and the nucleus of the solitary tract (henceforth referred to as the AP/NST) receives taste information from the tongue and a variety of sensory information from the internal organs, including signals from detectors in the stomach, duodenum, and liver. In addition, we saw that this region contains a set of detectors that are sensitive to the brain's own fuel: glucose. All this information is transmitted to regions of the forebrain that are more directly involved in control of eating and metabolism. Evidence indicates that events that produce hunger increase the activity of neurons in the AP/NST. In addition, lesions of this region abolish both glucoprivic and lipoprivic feeding (Ritter et al., 1994; Ritter and Taylor, 1990).

Hypothalamus

LO 12.19 Describe the role of nuclei and neurochemical systems of the hypothalamus in hunger and satiety.

Discoveries made in the 1940s and 1950s focused the attention of researchers interested in ingestive behavior on two regions of the hypothalamus: the lateral area and the ventromedial area. For many years, investigators believed that these two regions controlled hunger and satiety, respectively; one was the accelerator, and the other was the brake. The basic findings were these: After the lateral

---

Figure 12.18 Decerebration

The operation disconnects the forebrain from the hindbrain so that the muscles involved in ingestive behavior are controlled solely by hindbrain mechanisms.

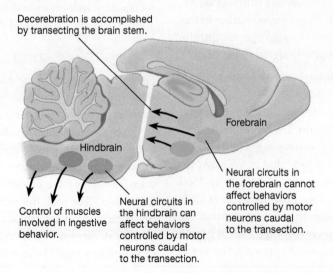

Decerebration is accomplished by transecting the brain stem.

Forebrain

Hindbrain

Control of muscles involved in ingestive behavior.

Neural circuits in the hindbrain can affect behaviors controlled by motor neurons caudal to the transection.

Neural circuits in the forebrain cannot affect behaviors controlled by motor neurons caudal to the transection.

hypothalamus was destroyed, animals stopped eating or drinking (Anand and Brobeck, 1951; Teitelbaum and Stellar, 1954). Electrical stimulation of the same region would produce eating, drinking, or both behaviors. Conversely, lesions of the ventromedial hypothalamus produced overeating that led to obesity, whereas electrical stimulation suppressed eating (Hetherington and Ranson, 1942). (See Figure 12.19.)

ROLE IN HUNGER   Several peptides produced by neurons in the hypothalamus play a special role in the control of feeding and metabolism (Arora and Anubhuti, 2006).

MCH and Orexin   Two of these peptides, **melanin-concentrating hormone (MCH)** and *orexin* produced by neurons in the lateral hypothalamus, stimulate hunger and decrease metabolic rate, thus increasing and preserving the body's energy stores.

Researchers refer to MCH and orexin (also known as *hypocretin*) as *orexigens*, "appetite-inducing chemicals." Injections of either of these peptides into the lateral ventricles or various regions of the brain induce eating. If rats are deprived of food, production of MCH and orexin in the lateral hypothalamus increases (Dube et al., 1999; Qu et al., 1996; Sakurai et al., 1998). Mice with a targeted mutation against the MCH gene or those that receive injections of an MCH receptor antagonist eat less than normal mice and are consequently

underweight (Ito et al., 2010; Shimada et al., 1998). In addition, genetically engineered mice with increased production of MCH in the hypothalamus overeat and gain weight (Ludwig et al., 2001).

Besides playing a role in the regulation of sleep cycles (as we saw in Chapter 9), orexin may also play a role in the relationship between eating and sleep. Mieda et al., (2004) studied mice with a targeted mutation against the orexin gene. Healthy mice that are fed one meal at the same time each day show increased locomotor activity shortly before mealtime. They also show increased activation of orexin-secreting neurons at this time. Presumably, in the wild this anticipatory activity would manifest itself in a hunger-induced search for food. Mieda and his colleagues found that mice with the orexin knockout adjusted their intake so that they received a sufficient amount of food during the single meal, but they did not show increased wakefulness or anticipatory activity just before mealtime. Yamanaka et al., (2003) suggest that the decreased activity seen in orexin-secreting neurons after feeding may contribute to the sleepiness that is often felt after a meal.

The axons of MCH and orexin neurons travel to a variety of brain structures that are known to be involved in motivation and movement, including the neocortex, periaqueductal gray matter, reticular formation, thalamus,

---

Figure 12.19 Role of the Hypothalamus
The lateral hypothalamus regulates hunger, while the ventromedial hypothalamus regulates satiety.

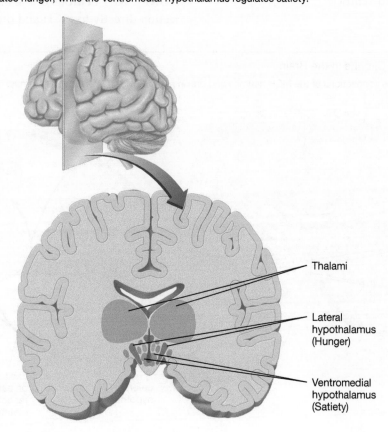

Thalami

Lateral
hypothalamus
(Hunger)

Ventromedial
hypothalamus
(Satiety)

and locus coeruleus. These neurons also have connections with neurons in the spinal cord that control the autonomic nervous system, which explains how they can affect the body's metabolic rate (Nambu et al., 1999; Sawchenko, 1998). These connections are shown in Figure 12.20.

Neuropeptide Y   As we saw earlier, hunger signals caused by an empty stomach or by glucoprivation or lipoprivation arise from detectors in the abdominal cavity and brain stem. How do these signals activate the MCH and orexin neurons of the lateral hypothalamus? Part of the pathway involves a system of neurons that secrete a neurotransmitter called **neuropeptide Y (NPY),** an extremely potent stimulator of food intake (Clark et al., 1984). Infusion of NPY into the hypothalamus produces ravenous, almost frantic eating. Rats that receive an infusion of this peptide into the brain will work very hard, pressing a lever many times for each morsel of food; they will eat food made bitter with quinine; and they will continue to drink milk even when doing so means that they receive an electric shock to their tongue (Flood and Morley, 1991; Jewett et al., 1992).

Yang et al., (2009) found that a genetic manipulation that increased the production of NPY in the hypothalamus increased food intake in rats. In contrast, a manipulation that decreased its production reduced eating, obesity, and diabetes in members of a strain of rats that had been selectively bred to overeat and become obese.

The cell bodies of most of the neurons that secrete NPY are found in the **arcuate nucleus,** located in the hypothalamus at the base of the third ventricle.

Neurons that secrete NPY are affected by hunger and satiety signals; Sahu et al., (1988) found that hypothalamic levels of NPY are increased by food deprivation and reduced by eating. In addition, Myers et al., (1995) found that hypothalamic injections of a drug that blocks neuropeptide Y receptors suppress eating caused by food deprivation. Li and Ritter (2004) found that glucoprivation increased the production of NPY in some neurons.

As we saw earlier, ghrelin, released by the stomach, provides a potent hunger signal to the brain. Shuto et al., (2002) found that rats with a targeted mutation that prevents ghrelin receptors from being produced in the hypothalamus ate less and gained weight more slowly than normal rats did. Evidence indicates that ghrelin exerts its effects on appetite and metabolism by stimulating receptors located on NPY neurons (Nakazato et al., 2001; Van den Top et al., 2004; Willesen et al., 1999). Thus, two important hunger signals—glucoprivation and ghrelin—activate the orexigenic NPY neurons.

Dopamine   A study by Abizaid et al., (2006) found that ghrelin also activates neurons in the mesolimbic motivation and reinforcement system. Dopaminergic (DA) neurons in the ventral tegmental area (VTA) contain ghrelin receptors, and the investigators found that intraperitoneal injections of ghrelin or infusion of ghrelin directly into the VTA elicited eating in rats and mice. The administration of ghrelin also increased the activity of DA neurons and triggered the release of activity in the nucleus accumbens, the major target of VTA dopaminergic neurons.

AGRP   NPY neurons of the arcuate nucleus send a projection directly to MCH and orexin neurons in the lateral

---

Figure 12.20 Feeding Circuits in the Brain

This schematic diagram shows connections of the MCH neurons and orexin neurons of the lateral hypothalamus.

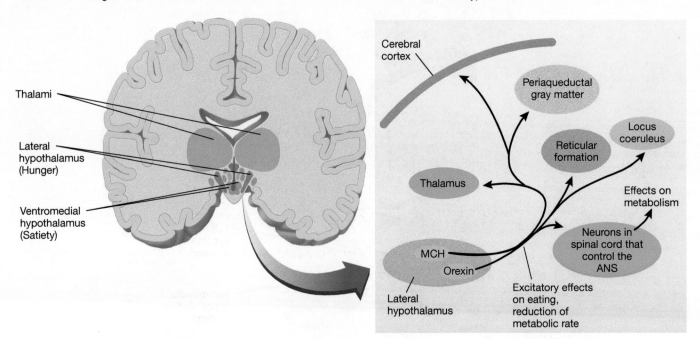

One of the effects of the THC contained in marijuana is an increase in appetite.

hypothalamus (Broberger et al., 1998; Elias et al., 1998b). These connections appear to be primarily responsible for the feeding elicited by activation of NPY neurons. In addition, NPY neurons send a projection of axons to the **paraventricular nucleus (PVN),** a region of the hypothalamus where infusions of NPY affect metabolic functions, including the secretion of insulin (Bai et al., 1985).

The terminals of hypothalamic NPY neurons release another orexigenic peptide in addition to neuropeptide Y: **agouti-related protein,** otherwise known as **AGRP** (Hahn et al., 1998). The two hormones appear to act together. AGRP, like NPY, is a potent and extremely long-lasting orexigen. Infusion of a very small amount of this peptide into the third ventricle of rats produces an increase in food intake that can last for six days (Lu et al., 2001).

Endocannabinoids   The endocannabinoids are another class of orexogenic compounds. (See Di Marzo and Matias, 2005, and Bellocchio, 2010, for reviews). One of the effects of the THC contained in marijuana is an increase in appetite—especially for highly palatable foods. THC is an agonist for endocannabinoid receptors. The endocannabinoids, whose actions are mimicked by THC, stimulate eating, apparently by increasing the release of MCH and orexin. (Recall from Chapter 4, cannabinoid receptors are found on terminal buttons, where they regulate the release of other neurotransmitters.) Levels of endocannabinoids are highest during fasting and lowest during feeding. A genetic mutation that disrupts the production of FAAH, the enzyme that destroys the endocannabinoids after they have been released, causes

overweight and obesity. Cannabinoid agonists have been used to increase the appetite of cancer patients, and until adverse side effects were discovered, cannabinoid antagonists were used as an aid to weight reduction. (You will read more about this use later in this chapter, in the section on obesity.)

In summary, activity of MCH and orexin neurons of the lateral hypothalamus increases food intake and decreases metabolic rate. These neurons are activated by NPY/AGRP-secreting neurons of the arcuate nucleus, which are sensitive to ghrelin and which receive excitatory input from NPY neurons in the medulla that are sensitive to glucoprivation. The NPY/AGRP neurons of the arcuate nucleus also project to the paraventricular nucleus, which plays a role in control of insulin secretion and metabolism. The endocannabinoids stimulate appetite by increasing the release of MCH and orexin. (See Figure 12.21.)

ROLE IN SATIETY   The ventromedial hypothalamus is an important satiety regulator. Here, satiety signals converge to inhibit eating behavior. Several hormones, the *anorexigens* or appetite-suppressing peptides, function as signals for satiety with effects in the ventromedial hypothalamus.

Leptin   As we saw earlier in this chapter, leptin, a hormone secreted by adipose tissue, suppresses eating and raises the animal's metabolic rate. The interactions of this long-term satiety signal with neural circuits involved in hunger are now being discovered. Leptin produces its behavioral and metabolic effects by binding with receptors in the brain—in particular, on neurons that secrete the orexigenic peptides NPY and AGRP.

Activation of leptin receptors on NPY/AGRP-secreting neurons in the arcuate nucleus has an inhibitory effect on neurons secreting NPY and AGRP (Glaum et al., 1996; Jobst et al., 2004). Because NPY/AGRP neurons normally activate orexin and MCH neurons, the presence of leptin in the arcuate nucleus decreases the release of these orexigens. Leptin appears to suppress animals' sensitivity to both olfactory and gustatory stimuli associated with food. Getchell et al., (2006) found that ob mice, who lack the leptin gene, found buried food much faster than normal mice did. An injection of leptin into the mutant mice increased their time to find food. Kawai et al., (2000) found that leptin decreased the sensitivity of gustatory sweet receptors to the taste of sucrose and saccharine.

CART   The arcuate nucleus contains another system of neurons that secrete two peptide anorexigens. Douglass et al., (1995) discovered the first of these peptides, which is now called **CART** (for *cocaine- and amphetamine-regulated transcript*). When cocaine or amphetamine is administered to an animal, levels of this peptide increase, which may have something to do with the fact that these drugs suppress appetite. CART neurons appear to play an important role

Figure 12.21 Action of Hunger Signals on Feeding Circuits in the Brain
The diagram shows connections of the NPY neurons of the arcuate nucleus.

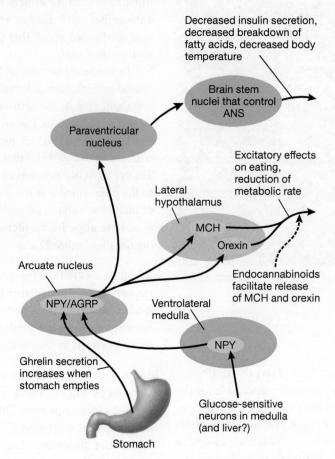

in satiety. If animals are deprived of food, levels of CART decrease. Injection of CART into the cerebral ventricles inhibits feeding, including the feeding stimulated by NPY. Infusion of a CART antibody, which destroys molecules of CART, increases feeding (Kristensen et al., 1998).

Activity of CART neurons appears to suppress eating by inhibiting MCH and orexin neurons and to increase metabolic rate through connections of these neurons with neurons in the paraventricular nucleus. CART neurons contain leptin receptors that have an *excitatory* effect; thus, activation of CART-secreting neurons appears to be at least partly responsible for the satiating effect of leptin (Elias et al., 1998a).

α-MSH A second anorexigen, **α-melanocyte-stimulating hormone (α-MSH),** is also released by CART neurons. This peptide is an agonist of the **melanocortin 4 receptor (MC4R);** it binds with the receptor and inhibits feeding. You will recall that NPY neurons also release AGRP, which stimulates eating. Both α-MSH and AGRP bind with the MC4R. However, whereas AGRP binds with MC4 receptors and causes feeding (as we saw in the previous subsection), α-MSH binds with MC4 receptors and *inhibits* eating.

In summary, leptin appears to exert at least some of its satiating effects by binding with leptin receptors on neurons in the arcuate nucleus. Leptin inhibits NPY/AGRP neurons, which suppresses the feeding that these peptides stimulate and prevents the decrease in metabolic rate that they provoke. Leptin activates CART/α-MSH neurons, which then inhibit MCH and orexin neurons in the lateral hypothalamus and prevent their stimulatory effect on appetite. PYY, released by the gastrointestinal tract just after a meal, inhibits orexigenic NPY/AGRP neurons. (See Figure 12.22.)

Appetite for food is controlled by a balance between orexigenic and anorexigenic factors. We saw that ghrelin activates NPY/AGRP neurons, which directly increases appetite. Ghrelin also inhibits CART/α-MSH neurons, which decreases the anorexic effect of these two peptides (Cowley et al., 2003). Another appetite-stimulating peptide, orexin, also inhibits CART/α-MSH neurons (Ma et al., 2007). Thus, two important orexigenic peptides inhibit the activity of anorexigenic peptides.

Figure 12.22 Action of Satiety Signals on Hypothalamic Neurons Involved in Control of Hunger and Satiety

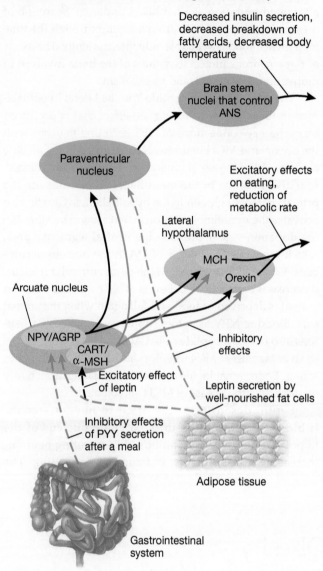

Section Review

Brain Mechanisms

LO 12.18 Identify the functions of the brain stem involved in eating regulation.

The brain stem contains neural circuits that are able to control acceptance or rejection of sweet or bitter foods and can even be modulated by satiation or physiological hunger signals, such as a decrease in glucose metabolism or the presence of food in the digestive system. The area postrema and nucleus of the solitary tract (AP/NST) receive signals from the tongue, stomach, small intestine, and liver and send the information on to many regions of the forebrain. These signals interact and help to control food intake. Lesions of the AP/NST disrupt both glucoprivic and lipoprivic eating.

LO 12.19 Describe the role of nuclei and neurochemical systems of the hypothalamus in hunger and satiety.

The lateral hypothalamus is involved in initiating eating and the ventromedial hypothalamus is involved in regulating satiety. The lateral hypothalamus contains two sets of neurons whose activity increases eating and decreases metabolic rate. These neurons secrete the peptides orexin and MCH (melanin-concentrating hormone). Food deprivation increases the level of these peptides, and mice with a targeted mutation against MCH undereat. Secretion of orexin also keeps animals from sleeping through the time for a meal if food is available only intermittently. The axons of these neurons project to regions of the brain involved in motivation, movement, and metabolism.

The release of neuropeptide Y in the lateral hypothalamus induces ravenous eating, an effect that is produced by excitatory connections of NPY-secreting neurons with the orexin and MCH neurons. NPY neurons in the arcuate nucleus of the hypothalamus receive input from glucose-sensitive neurons in the medulla. NPY neurons are the primary target of ghrelin in the hypothalamus. Ghrelin also activates the mesolimbic reinforcement system by stimulating dopaminergic neurons in the ventral tegmental area, which increases the release of DA in the nucleus accumbens. When NPY is infused in the paraventricular nucleus, it decreases metabolic rate. Levels of NPY increase when an animal is deprived of food and fall again when the animal eats. Blocking NPY receptors suppresses eating. NPY neurons also release a peptide called AGRP. This peptide serves as an antagonist at MC4 receptors and, like NPY, stimulates eating. Endocannabinoids also stimulate eating, apparently by increasing the release of MCH and orexin.

Leptin desensitizes the brain to hunger signals. It binds with receptors in the arcuate nucleus of the hypothalamus, where it inhibits NPY-secreting neurons, increasing metabolic rate and suppressing eating. The arcuate nucleus also contains neurons that secrete CART, a peptide that suppresses eating. These neurons, which are *activated* by leptin, have inhibitory connections with MCH and orexin neurons in the lateral hypothalamus. CART neurons also secrete a peptide called α-MSH, which serves as an agonist at MC4 receptors and inhibits eating. Ghrelin, which activates NPY/AGRP neurons and stimulates hunger, also inhibits CART/α-MSH neurons and suppresses the satiating effect of the peptides secreted by these neurons. The anorexigenic peptide, PYY, which is released by the gastrointestinal system, suppresses the release of NPY and AGRP.

Thought Question

A local dog breeder approaches you with concerns about some of their dogs that eat too much. These dogs are gaining weight rapidly and the breeder fears they may experience negative health outcomes such as diabetes and cardiovascular disease. The breeder wants to know what neuroscience can do to help. Recommend two possible treatments or interventions (currently available to humans that could be adapted or to be developed in the future) that may help reduce how much the dogs are eating. The breeder is interested in the brain or endocrine basis for your recommendations, so don't forget to provide an explanation of how the intervention will affect the nervous system. You may also assume that any plausible intervention is possible, even if a technology, brain-based method, or drug is not yet available.

Obesity

Obesity is increasing in both developed and developing countries as household incomes rise. For example, over a 10-year period, the incidence of obesity in young urban children in China increased by a factor of eight (Ogden et al., 2003; Zorrilla et al., 2006). The known health risks of obesity include cardiovascular disease, diabetes, stroke, arthritis, and some forms of cancer. Until recently type II diabetes was almost never seen in people before the age of 40. However, because of the increased incidence of obesity in children, this disorder is becoming more common, even among children. One way of assessing body weight and health risks associated with being under or overweight is to calculate a body mass index (BMI) score. The formula to calculate a BMI score is: weight (kg) / [height (m)]^2 or weight (lb.) / [height (in.)]$^2 \times 703$. BMI scores are categorized in four basic categories, listed in Table 12.2.

The following case of A. J. presents one approach to weight loss in obesity.

A. J. was a 17-year-old female with a BMI score of 53. She had been involved in an intensive weight-loss program for several years; she received nutritional information, regular physical exercise, and support from a counselor. This intervention, however, proved to be ineffective. As an alternative, A. J. decided to pursue gastric surgery to reduce her body weight and improve her health. A. J. underwent a sleeve gastrectomy. This procedure removes the majority of the stomach pouch, leaving a "sleeve" that is much smaller than the original stomach. Six months after the surgery, she had lost 36.5 kg (approximately 80 lb.). Twelve months after surgery she lost an additional 3.7 kg (8 lb.), and after 24 months, an additional 11.4 kg (25 lb.). Altogether her BMI was reduced to 35, along with a dramatic reduction in the volume of visceral and subcutaneous adipose tissue (see Figure 12.23; Blüher et al., 2013). This weight loss had important health implications for A. J. Following surgery, previously elevated measures of liver enzymes

Table 12.2 BMI Categories

Category	BMI Scores (kg/m^2)
Underweight	< 18.5
Normal range	18.5–25
Overweight	> 25
Obese	> 30

(indicative of poor liver function) and insulin resistance (a predictor of developing type II diabetes) returned to within normal ranges.

The case study of A. J. highlights the current challenges we face in overcoming obesity. Effectively treating obesity is difficult, despite the availability of many different interventions. For some individuals, strict regulation of diet and a rigorous exercise program is effective, but often it is not. For other individuals, gastric surgery (such as A. J.'s sleeve gastrectomy, or the Roux-en-Y gastric bypass that you will read about later in the chapter) is an effective treatment, but these surgeries are not guaranteed to work either.

The challenges presented by obesity are complex, and we will look more closely at the factors that lead to obesity and that also might prove effective in combating it. Gastric surgical procedures, for example, don't just change the amount of food consumed, they also impact hunger and satiety signals in the hypothalamus. Patients in one study reported reduced feelings of hunger and fewer food cravings following sleeve gastrectomy (Rieber et al., 2013) and experienced reduced ghrelin and leptin levels (Yousseif et al., 2014).

Possible Causes

LO 12.20 Discuss the contributions of environment, physical activity, and genetics to the development of obesity.

What causes obesity? Genetic differences—and their effects on development of the endocrine system and brain mechanisms that control food intake and metabolism—appear to be responsible for the majority of cases of extreme obesity. But, as we just saw, the problem of obesity has been growing over recent years. Rapid changes in the gene pool are unlikely to account for the majority of this increase; instead, environmental causes that have produced changes in people's behavior are a significant contributing factor.

ENVIRONMENTAL FACTORS Body weight is the result of the difference between two factors: calories consumed and energy expended. If we consume more calories than we expend as heat and work, we gain weight. If we expend more than we consume, we lose weight. In modern industrialized societies, inexpensive, convenient, good-tasting, high-calorie food is readily available, which promotes an increase in intake. In most places, fast-food restaurants are close at hand, parking is convenient (or unnecessary at restaurants with drive-up windows), and the size of the portions served has increased in recent years. People eat out more often than they used to, and most often they do so at inexpensive fast-food restaurants.

Of course, fast-food restaurants are not the only environmental factor responsible for the increased incidence of obesity. Snack foods that are readily available in convenience stores, vending machines, and cafeterias make high-calorie, high-fat foods and sweetened beverages available, often in unlimited, all-you-can-eat quantities.

Figure 12.23 Reduction in Adipose Tissue 24 Months After Gastric Surgery

This cross section of A. J.'s waist shows the reduction in adipose tissue surrounding her organs (in red) and in subcutaneous adipose tissue (blue) before gastric surgery (Pre-OP) and during 6-, 12-, and 24-month follow up.

(Based on Blüher, S., Raschpichler, M., Hirsch, W., and Till, H., A case report and review of the literature of laparoscopic sleeve gastrectomy in morbidly obese adolescents: Beyond metabolic surgery and visceral fat reduction, *Metabolism*, 2013, *62*[6], 761–767.)

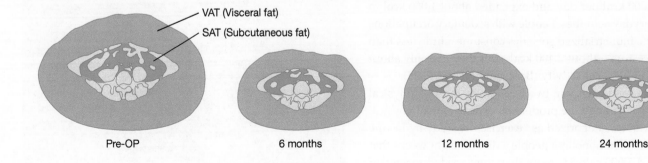

VAT (Visceral fat)
SAT (Subcutaneous fat)

Pre-OP   6 months   12 months   24 months

As Bray et al., (2004) point out, consuming high-fructose corn syrup, found in many prepared foods, including soft drinks, fruit drinks, processed foods, and baked goods, may contribute to obesity. Fructose, unlike glucose, does not stimulate insulin secretion or enhance leptin production, so this form of sugar is less likely to activate the brain's satiety mechanisms (Teff et al., 2004).

The transition to college life is often associated with changes in eating and physical activity patterns. Many students are familiar with the idea of the "freshman five (or fifteen)"—gaining five pounds (or often more) during the first year of college. This phenomenon was partially confirmed in a sample of Canadian college students. Seventy percent of the students in the study gained weight during their four years in college, averaging gains of 5.3 ± 4.7 kg (11.7 ± 9.1 lb.). While this weight gain was consistent with expected growth for males and females from 18 to 20 years of age, it is important to note that BMI and percentage body fat also increased in this group. Furthermore, the percent of obese individuals in the sample increased from 18 percent at the beginning of the four-year study to 31 percent at the end (Gropper et al., 2012). A similar study in a sample of American college students revealed that female students gained 1.8 ± 2.9 kg (4.0 ± 6.3 lb) while male students gained 1.6 ± 3.9 kg (3.5 ± 8.5 lb). Both groups experienced significantly increased BMI. The significant weight gains in this study all occurred within the first four months of college (Holm-Denoma et al., 2008).

In a longitudinal study of college students across seven semesters, Small et al., (2012) found that students reduced their intake of fruits and vegetables and the number of days that they engaged in vigorous physical activity from their first to their fourth year of college. Students living off campus were the least likely to consume fruits and vegetables and engage in vigorous exercise. In contrast, students consumed fewer sugar-sweetened beverages over time.

PHYSICAL ACTIVITY FACTORS   Another modern trend contributing to the obesity epidemic involves changes in people's expenditure of energy. The proportion of people employed in jobs that require a high level of physical activity has decreased considerably, which means that on the average we need less food than previous generations did. Our hunter-gatherer ancestors probably consumed about 3,000 kcal per day and expended about 1,000 kcal in their everyday activities. People with sedentary occupations in today's industrialized societies consume a little less than their ancestors—about 2,400 kcal—but they use only about 300 kcal in physical activity (Booth and Neufer, 2005).

We expend energy in two basic ways: through physical activity and through the production of heat. Not all physical activity can be categorized as "exercise." A study by Levine et al., (1999) fed nonobese people a diet for eight weeks that contained 1,000 calories more than they needed to sustain their weight. Approximately 39 percent of the calories were converted into fat tissue, and approximately 26 percent went into lean tissue, increased resting metabolic rate, and the energy required to digest the extra food. The rest, approximately 33 percent, went into an increase in involuntary activity: muscle tone, postural changes, and fidgeting. Levine and his colleagues referred to this phenomenon as "nonexercise activity thermogenesis," or NEAT. The amount of fat tissue that a person gained was inversely related to his or her level of NEAT. Levine et al., (2005) measured NEAT levels in a group of people with sedentary lifestyles that included both lean and moderately obese individuals. The investigators found that the people who were overweight remained seated 2.5 hours per day more than the lean people.

Recently, some researchers have suggested that work stations and environments can be redesigned to increase NEAT by facilitating standing or walking on a treadmill rather than sitting at a desk. In fact, a one-year trial in an office that replaced its traditional chair-based desks with treadmill desks revealed that employees engaged in more NEAT, lost weight, and reduced their waist circumference (Keopp et al., 2013). (See Figure 12.24.)

GENETIC FACTORS   Differences in body weight—perhaps reflecting physiological differences in metabolism, activity levels (including NEAT), or appetite—have a strong hereditary basis. Twin studies suggest that between 40 percent and 70 percent of the variability in body fat is due to genetic differences. Twin studies have also found strong genetic effects on the amount of weight that people gain or lose when they are placed on high- or low-calorie diets (Bouchard et al., 1990; Hainer et al., 2001). Thus, heredity appears to affect people's metabolic efficiency. However, until recently, variations in only two genes were found to cause obesity in humans: the gene for the MC4 receptor and the FTO gene (fat mass and obesity related gene), which codes for an enzyme that acts in hypothalamic regions related to energy balance, such as the PVN, and the arcuate

Figure 12.24 Treadmill Desk

nucleus (Olszewski et al., 2009; Willer et al., 2009). A massive study with 145 authors (Willer et al., 2009) discovered six new genetic loci that are associated with body mass index (BMI). However, these genes are very rare, so none of them can account for the prevalence of obesity in the general population. The high level of heritability of obesity must be explained, then, as the additive effects of a large number of genes, each of which has a small effect on BMI.

Just as cars differ in their fuel efficiency, so do living organisms, and hereditary factors can affect the level of efficiency. People differ in this form of efficiency. Those with an efficient metabolism have calories left over to deposit in the long-term nutrient reservoir, and these calories accumulate in the form of increased adipose tissue. Researchers have referred to this condition as a "thrifty phenotype." In contrast, people with an inefficient metabolism (a "spendthrift phenotype") can eat large meals without getting fat. A fuel-efficient automobile is desirable, but a fuel-efficient body runs the risk of becoming obese—at least in an environment where food is cheap and plentiful.

Why are there genetic differences in metabolic efficiency? As we saw earlier in this chapter, natural selection for mechanisms that helped our ancestors to avoid starvation was much stronger than natural selection for mechanisms that helped them to avoid becoming obese. Perhaps individual differences in metabolic efficiency reflect the nature of the environment experienced by their ancestors. Perhaps people whose ancestors lived in regions where food was scarce or subject to periods of famine are more likely to have inherited efficient metabolisms.

This hypothesis has received support from epidemiological studies. Ravussin et al., (1994) studied two populations of Indigenous Americans: the Pima. Pima live in two different geographic locations; one group lives in the southwestern United States and the other in northwestern Mexico. Members of the two groups share the same genetic background, speak the same language, and have common historical traditions. The two groups separated 700–1,000 years ago and now live under very different environmental conditions. Pima in the southwestern United States eat a high-fat American diet and weigh an average of 90 kg (198 lb.), men and women combined. In contrast, the lifestyle of the Mexican Pima has remained largely unchanged for many generations. These individuals engage in subsistence farming and eat a low-fat diet—and weigh an average of 64 kg (141 lb.). The average cholesterol level among American Pima is much higher than that of Mexican Pima, and the American Pimas' rate of diabetes is more than five times higher. These findings demonstrate that genes that promote an efficient metabolism are beneficial in environments in which people expend many calories in daily life and consume foods that are not calorie-dense but that these same genes can pose a liability when people live in an environment where the physical demands are low and high-calorie food is easily accessible.

Leptin   As we saw earlier, study of the ob mouse led to the discovery of leptin, the hormone secreted by well-nourished adipose tissue. So far, researchers have found several cases of familial obesity caused by the absence of leptin produced by mutations of genes responsible for production of leptin or the leptin receptor (Farooqi and O'Rahilly, 2005). Treatment of people who are leptin-deficient with injections of leptin has dramatic effects on body weight. (See Figure 12.25.) Unfortunately, leptin has no effect on people who lack leptin receptors. In any case, mutations of the genes for leptin or leptin receptors are very rare, so they do not explain the vast majority of cases of obesity.

When leptin was discovered, researchers hoped that this naturally occurring peptide could be widely used to treat obesity. In fact, a drug company paid a large sum of money for the rights to develop this compound. However, it turns out that most people that are obese already have a high blood level of leptin, and increasing this level with injections of the peptide has little or no effect on their food intake.

Several investigators have suggested that a *fall* in blood levels of leptin should be regarded as a hunger signal. Starvation decreases the blood level of leptin, which removes an inhibitory influence on NPY/AGRP neurons and an excitatory influence on CART/α-MSH neurons. That is, a low level of leptin increases the release of orexigenic peptides and decreases the release of anorexigenic peptides. And as Flier (1998) suggests, people with a thrifty metabolism should show resistance to a high level of leptin, which would permit weight gain in times of plenty. People with a spendthrift metabolism should not show leptin resistance and should eat less as their level of leptin rises.

Treatment

LO 12.21   **Evaluate the roles of reinforcement, stress, surgery, pharmacology, and behavioral interventions in treating obesity.**

As we've discussed, obesity is extremely difficult to treat; the enormous financial success of diet books and weight reduction programs attests to the trouble people have in losing weight. More precisely, many programs help people to lose weight initially, but then the weight is quickly regained. Kramer et al., (1989) reported that four to five years after participating in a 15-week behavioral weight-loss program, fewer than 3 percent of the participants maintained the weight loss they had achieved during the program. Some experts have suggested that, given the extremely low long-term success rate, perhaps we should stop treating people for obesity until our treatments are more successful. Perhaps the fact that there are so many different weight treatments offered to the public simply shows that we really do not know how to help people to lose weight over the long term. To better understand the challenges involved in weight loss, the following sections will explore the roles

Figure 12.25 Hereditary Leptin Deficiency

The photographs show three patients with hereditary leptin deficiency before (a) and after (b) treatment with leptin for 18 months. The faces of the patients are obscured for privacy.

(From Licinio, J., Caglayan, S., Ozata, M., et al., Phenotypic effects of leptin replacement on morbid obesity, diabetes mellitus, hypogonadism, and behavior in leptin-deficient adults, *Proceedings of the National Academy of Science, USA*, 2004, *101*, 4531–4536.)

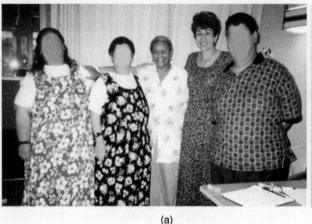

(a)

(b)

of reinforcement, stress, surgery, pharmacology, and behavioral intervention in the treatment of obesity.

ROLE OF REINFORCEMENT AND STRESS Evidence suggests that the physiological mechanisms that make it difficult for people to reduce their caloric intake are related to the mechanisms that make it difficult for people to stop taking drugs of abuse. Overeating shares many attributes with addiction. For example, although some overweight people who participate in treatment programs succeed in eating less and losing weight, many return to the former behaviors and regain the weight they lost. Similarly, people who succeed in stopping their use of a drug often return to their former behavior and being using the drug again. In both cases, stress and anxiety can cause reinstatement of the eating or drug taking, apparently by means of similar brain mechanisms (Nair et al., 2009). Both dopamine, which plays an important role in reinforcement, and corticotrophin-releasing hormone (CRH), which plays an important role in stress, are involved in relapse in both food seeking and drug seeking behavior. Cottone et al., (2009) found that rats that had become accustomed to a tasty, high-calorie diet, showed signs of withdrawal symptoms, accompanied by increased CRH secretion and increased activation of the central nucleus of the amygdala when their access to the diet was curtailed. In fact, in some ways, changing behaviors associated with a "food addiction" is more difficult than changing behaviors associated with a drug addiction. It is possible to stop taking a drug altogether and stay away from people and places associated with obtaining and abusing the drug, but it is not possible to completely stop eating.

The extraordinary difficulty in reducing caloric intake for a sustained period of time (often a lifetime) has led to the development of many interventions. The next sections will describe some surgical, pharmacological, and behavioral

methods that have been devised to reduce eating behavior to lose weight.

SURGICAL INTERVENTIONS Surgeons have become involved in trying to help people who are obese lose weight. The procedures they have developed (called *bariatric surgery*) are designed to reduce the amount of food that can be eaten during a meal or interfere with absorption of calories from the intestines. Bariatric surgery has been aimed at the stomach, the small intestine, or both.

One form of bariatric surgery is a special form of gastric bypass called the *Roux-en-Y gastric bypass*, or *RYGB*. Similar to sleeve gastronectomy (described in the case that opened this chapter), this procedure produces a small pouch in the upper end of the stomach. However, in this procedure, the stomach pouch is attached to a lower portion of the intestine. The effect is to produce a small stomach whose contents enter the jejunum (second portion of the small intestine), bypassing the duodenum (first portion of the small intestine). Digestive enzymes that are secreted into the duodenum pass through the upper intestine and meet up with the meal that has just been received from the stomach pouch. (See Figure 12.26.)

The RYGB procedure works well, although it often causes an iron and vitamin B_{12} deficiency, which may be controlled by increased intake of these substances. In the United States alone, approximately 200,000 bariatric surgeries are performed each year. Brolin (2002) reported that the average postsurgical loss of excessive weight of obese patients was about 35 percent of their initial weight. Even patients who sustained smaller weight losses showed improved health, including reductions in hypertension and diabetes. A meta-analysis of 147 studies by Maggard et al., (2005) reported an average weight loss of 43.5 kg (approximately 95 lb.) one year after RYGB surgery and 41.5 kg after three

Figure 12.26 Roux-en-Y Gastric Bypass (RYGB)

This procedure almost totally suppresses the secretion of ghrelin. (a) The stomach and small intestine before surgery. (b) The small pouch made from the stomach and the connection to the roux limb of the small intestine (the second part of the small intestine, downstream of the duodenum). This procedure reduces the size of the stomach and bypasses the duodenum.

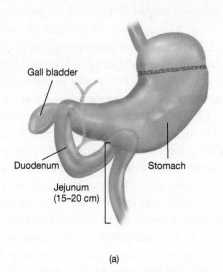

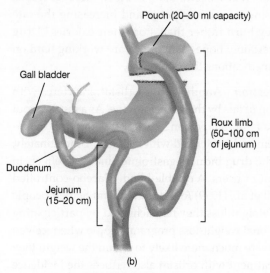

(a)   (b)

years. And although the biological response to starvation is very strong—and is seen in people that are obese and who are successfully losing weight—RYGB surgery does *not* induce these changes. Instead, much like the case study of A. J. at the beginning of this section, after surgery people report that they feel less hungry and their level of exercise increases (Berthoud et al., 2011). However, like other forms of major surgery, adverse outcomes (including death) occasionally occur; the rate of complications is lowest for surgeons with the most experience performing the procedures (Smith et al., 2010).

Similar to the sleeve gastronectomy described in the case study of A. J., one important reason for the success of the RYGB procedure appears to be that it disrupts the secretion of ghrelin. The procedure also increases blood levels of PYY (Chan et al., 2006; Reinehr et al., 2007). Both of these changes would be expected to decrease food intake: A decrease in ghrelin should reduce hunger, and an increase in PYY should increase satiety. A plausible explanation for the decreased secretion of ghrelin could be disruption of communication between the upper intestine and the stomach; as you will recall, although ghrelin is secreted by the stomach, the upper intestine controls this secretion. Presumably, because the surgery decreases the speed at which food moves through the small intestine, more PYY is secreted.

PHARMCOLOGICAL INTERVENTION   Another type of therapy for obesity—drug treatment—is the subject of active research programs by the pharmaceutical industry. Possible ways in which drugs could help people lose weight are to suppress appetite and reduce the amount of food they eat, or prevent some of the food they eat from being digested.

Suppress Appetite   Some serotonergic agonists suppress eating. However, a drug used for this purpose, fenfluramine, was found to have dangerous side effects, including

pulmonary hypertension and damage to the valves of the heart, so the drug was withdrawn from the market in the United States (Blundell and Halford, 1998). Fenfluramine acts by stimulating the release of 5-HT. Another drug, sibutramine, has similar effects on eating, but a study of people who were taking the drug found increased incidence of heart attacks and strokes, so this drug, too, was withdrawn from the market (Li and Cheung, 2011).

As we mentioned earlier, the fact that marijuana often elicits a craving for highly palatable foods led to the discovery that the endocannabinoids have an orexigenic effect. The drug rimonabant, which blocks CB1 cannabinoid receptors, was found to suppress appetite, produce a significant weight loss, lower blood levels of triglycerides and insulin, and increase blood levels of HDL ("good" cholesterol), with apparently minimal adverse side effects (Di Marzo and Matias, 2005). However, use of rimonabant was subsequently found to be associated with depressive mood disorders, anxiety, and increased suicide risk, so it is no longer on the market as an antiobesity treatment (Christensen et al., 2007). As we will see in Chapter 18, rimonabant has also been shown to help people stop smoking. Although the drug is not approved for this purpose either, its efficacy suggests that the craving for nicotine, like the craving for food, involves the activity of endocannabinoids in the brain.

As we have seen, appetite can be stimulated by activation of NPY, MCH, orexin, and ghrelin receptors, and it can be suppressed by the activation of leptin, CCK, CART, and MC4 receptors. Appetite can also be suppressed by activation of inhibitory presynaptic Y2 autoreceptors by PYY. Most of these orexigenic and anorexigenic chemicals also affect metabolism: Orexigenic chemicals tend to decrease metabolic rate, and anorexigenic chemicals tend to increase it. In addition, uncoupling protein causes nutrients to be "burned"—converted into heat instead of adipose tissue. Do these discoveries hold any promise for the treatment of obesity? Is there any possibility that researchers will find drugs that will stimulate or block these receptors, thus decreasing people's appetite and increasing the rate at which they burn rather than store their calories? Drug companies certainly hope so, and they are working hard on developing medications that will do so.

Prevent Digestion Another drug, orlistat, interferes with the absorption of fats by the small intestine. As a result, about a third of the fat in the person's diet passes through the digestive system and is excreted with the feces. Unfortunately, as a result, the drug induces gastrointestinal side effects in 15–30 percent of users. A double-blind, placebo-controlled study by Hill et al., (1999) found that orlistat helped people to maintain weight loss they had achieved by participating in a conventional weight-loss program. People who received the placebo were much more likely to regain the weight they had lost. Treatment with orlistat also reduces the incidence of type II diabetes, and has beneficial effects on blood pressure, lipid, and fasting glucose levels among patients with diabetes (Padwal and Majumdar, 2007).

BEHAVIORAL INTERVENTIONS Another form of therapy for obesity—exercise—has significant benefits. As we mentioned earlier, decreased physical activity is an important contributor to weight gain. Exercise consumes calories, of course, but it also appears to have beneficial effects on metabolic rate. Bunyard et al., (1998) found that when middle-aged men participated in an aerobic exercise program for six months, their body fat decreased and their daily energy requirement increased—by 5 percent for obese men and by 8 percent for lean men. Gutin et al., (1999) found that an exercise program helped children who were obese to lose fat and had the additional benefit of increasing bone density. Hill et al., (2003) calculated that an increased energy expenditure through exercise of only 100 kcal per day could prevent weight gain in most people. The effort would require a relatively small change in behavior for most people—about 14 minutes of walking each day. Other behavioral interventions for weight loss include in-person or online health-coaching programs, cognitive behavioral therapies, and incentive programs.

The variety of methods—surgical, pharmacological, and behavioral —that therapists and surgeons have developed to treat obesity attests to the tenacity of the problem. The basic difficulty, beyond that caused by having an efficient metabolism, is that eating is pleasurable and satiety signals are easy to ignore or override. By learning more about the physiology of hunger signals, satiety signals, and the reinforcement provided by eating, many hope that researchers and clinicians will be able to develop safe and effective interventions that attenuate the signals that encourage us to eat and strengthen those that encourage us to stop eating.

This section and the previous one introduced several neuropeptides and peripheral peptides that play a role in control of eating and metabolism. Table 12.3 summarizes information about these compounds.

Table 12.3 Neuropeptides and Peripheral Peptides Involved in Control of Food Intake and Metabolism

Neuropeptides				
Name	**Location of Cell Bodies**	**Location of Terminals**	**Interaction with Other Peptides**	**Physiological or Behavioral Effects**
Melanin-concentrating hormone (MCH)	Lateral hypothalamus	Neocortex, periaqueductal gray matter, reticular formation, thalamus, locus coeruleus, neurons in spinal cord that control the sympathetic nervous system	Activated by NPY/AGRP; inhibited by leptin and CART/α-MSH	Eating, decreased metabolic rate
Orexin	Lateral hypothalamus	Similar to those of MCH neurons	Activated by NPY/AGRP; inhibited by leptin and CART/α-MSH	Eating, decreased metabolic rate
Neuropeptide Y (NPY)	Arcuate nucleus of hypothalamus	Paraventricular nucleus, MCH and orexin neurons of the lateral hypothalamus	Activated by ghrelin; inhibited by leptin	Eating, decreased metabolic rate
Agouti-related protein (AGRP)	Arcuate nucleus of hypothalamus (colocalized with NPY)	Same regions as NPY neurons	Inhibited by leptin	Eating, decreased metabolic rate; acts as antagonist at MC4 receptors
Cocaine- and amphetamine-regulated transcript (CART)	Arcuate nucleus of hypothalamus	Paraventricular nucleus, lateral hypothalamus, periaqueductal gray matter, neurons in spinal cord that control the sympathetic nervous system	Activated by leptin	Suppression of eating, increased metabolic rate
α-melanocyte stimulating hormone (α-MSH)	Arcuate nucleus of hypothalamus (colocalized with CART)	Same regions as CART neurons	Activated by leptin	Suppression of eating, increased metabolic rate; acts as agonist at MC4 receptors

(continued)

Peripheral Peptides			
Name	**Where Produced**	**Site of Actions**	**Physiological or Behavioral Effects**
Leptin	Fat tissue	Inhibits NPY/AGRP neurons; excites CART/α-MSH neurons	Suppression of eating, increased metabolic rate
Insulin	Pancreas	Similar to leptin	Similar to leptin
Ghrelin	Gastrointestinal system	Activates NPY/AGRP neurons	Eating
Cholecystokinin (CCK)	Duodenum	Neurons in pylorus	Suppression of eating
Peptide YY_{3-36} (PYY)	Gastrointestinal system	Inhibits NPY/AGRP neurons	Suppression of eating

Section Review

Obesity

LO 12.20 **Discuss the contributions of environment, physical activity, and genetics to the development of obesity.**

Environmental factors can affect how many calories are expended through physical exercise and ingested in calorie-dense foods. In places, inexpensive, convenient, good-tasting, high-calorie food is readily available, which promotes an increase in intake. Reduced physical activity contributes to obesity, along with less "nonexercise activity thermogenesis," or NEAT.

Interactions between genetic and environmental factors are illustrated by the example of Pima living in the United States and Mexico. A high percentage of Pima who live in the United States and consume a high-fat diet become obese and, as a consequence, develop diabetes. In contrast, Pima living in Mexico, who engage in subsistence farming and eat a low-fat diet, remain thin and have a low incidence of obesity.

Obesity is strongly affected by heredity. Some people have inherited a thrifty metabolism, which makes it difficult for them to lose weight. One of the manifestations of a thrifty metabolism is a low level of nonexercise activity thermogenesis, or NEAT. Obesity in humans is related to a hereditary absence of leptin or leptin receptors only in a few families. In general, people who are obese have very high levels of leptin in their blood. However, they show resistance to the effects of this peptide, apparently because the transport of leptin through the blood–brain barrier is reduced. The most significant simple genetic cause of severe obesity is mutation of the gene for the MC4 receptor and the FTO gene. The MC4 receptor responds to the orexigen AGRP and the anorexigen α-MSH, and the FTO gene codes for an enzyme that acts in hypothalamic regions involved in energy balance. In addition, mutations that inactivate the genes responsible for the production of leptin or leptin receptors result in obesity.

LO 12.21 **Evaluate the roles of reinforcement, stress, surgery, pharmacology, and behavioral interventions in treating obesity.**

Stress and anxiety can cause reinstatement of eating or drug taking, apparently by means of similar brain mechanisms. Both dopamine, which plays an important role in reinforcement, and corticotrophin releasing hormone (CRH), which plays an important role in stress, are involved in relapse in food seeking and drug seeking. Researchers have evaluated many behavioral, surgical, and pharmacological treatments for obesity, but no universally successful program has yet been found. The RYGB procedure, a special form of gastric bypass operation, is one successful form of bariatric surgery. The effectiveness of this operation is probably due primarily to its suppression of ghrelin secretion and stimulation of PYY secretion. Two drugs initially appeared to show some promise in the treatment of obesity. Fenfluramine, a serotonin agonist, and rimonabant, a cannabinoid antagonist, suppress appetite, but adverse side effects have prevented their use. At present many pharmaceutical companies are trying to apply the results of the discoveries of orexigens and anorexigens described in this chapter to the development of antiobesity drugs. Another drug, orlistat, prevents the absorption of calories from fat.

Thought Question

One of the last prejudices that people admit to publicly is a dislike of people who are obese. Is this fair, given that genetic differences in metabolism are such an important cause of obesity?

Eating Disorders

Eating disorders include anorexia nervosa, bulimia nervosa, and binge eating disorder. Each of these disorders include extreme changes in eating behavior. Individuals with eating disorders are at an increased risk of mortality, particularly those diagnosed with anorexia nervosa (Arcelus et al., 2011). As you read the case of N. B. below, consider the changes to eating behavior that are described, and any possible biological correlates.

N. B. is a 17-year old female who spent much of her time thinking about food, controlling her weight through dieting, and comparing nutritional labels. She maintained a low calorie diet and reported feeling hungry most of the time. She occasionally binged and stole food. At age 14, she began to diet in response to a period of weight gain. She adopted rigid eating patterns and sought treatment from a mental health professional. At that time, she began lying about food, engaging in compulsive physical exercise, and placing weights in her bra to conceal her true weight by making it appear that she had been gaining weight, though she continued to engage in restricted eating behavior and excessive exercise. At age 16 she was hospitalized due to extremely low body weight. After being discharged, N. B. lost weight by restricting her food intake again. She then began stealing food from classmates and binging and purging. She was prescribed a drug that was an antagonist at serotonin and norepinephrine receptors; however, this treatment was ended due to lack of effect. Finally, N. B. began a cognitive behavioral therapy intervention that reduced the frequency of her binging and restricted eating, and she began to gain weight (Martín-Murcia et al., 2011).

The case study of N. B. highlights several important aspects of eating disorders that will be explored in the following section. As you will read, the prevalence of some eating disorders is higher among females and several eating disorders include many of the symptoms that N. B. displayed: restricted eating, excessive exercise, eating large amounts of food in a short period of time (binging), and engaging in compulsive exercise or other behaviors such as vomiting to reduce the number of calories consumed (purging). Eating disorders are challenging to treat, and many individuals undergo repeated interventions in an effort to reduce their symptoms. Many eating disorder interventions have a low success rate. While the exact causes of eating disorders are unknown, it is likely that a variety of environmental and genetic elements are contributing factors.

The *Diagnostic and Statistical Manual of Mental Disorders* of the American Psychiatric Association (fifth edition; DSM) groups several related diagnoses together in the category "Feeding and Eating Disorders." These disorders are characterized by several distinct criteria, including a persistent pattern of eating behavior that impairs physical health or psychosocial functioning. The DSM does *not* consider obesity a mental illness at this time due to research implicating genetic, physiological, behavioral, and environmental contributing factors.

Most people, if they have an eating problem, tend to overeat. However, some people, especially among adolescent women, have the opposite problem: They eat too little, even to the point of starvation. This disorder is called **anorexia nervosa.** Another eating disorder, **bulimia nervosa,** is characterized by a loss of control of food intake. People with bulimia nervosa periodically gorge themselves with food, especially dessert or snack food and especially in the afternoon or evening. These binges are usually followed by self-induced vomiting or the use of laxatives, along with feelings of depression and guilt. With this combination of binging and purging, the net nutrient intake (and consequently, the body weight) of people with bulimia can vary, though a large proportion eat an overall normal amount of food and maintain a normal body weight (Kaye et al., 2000; Weltzin et al., 1991). Episodes of bulimia are seen in some patients with anorexia nervosa. A third disorder, **binge-eating** disorder, is characterized by eating a large quantity of food in a relatively short period of time (binging) and a loss of control over eating behavior. Unlike bulimia nervosa, binge-eating disorder is not associated with compensatory purging behavior. A lifetime history of binge-eating disorder is associated with obesity. The criteria for diagnosis of three important eating disorders are included in Table 12.4. These criteria are summarized from the Diagnostic and Statistical Manual of Mental Disorders (DSM).

The incidence of anorexia nervosa is estimated at 0.5–2 percent; that of bulimia nervosa at 1–3 percent; and that of binge-eating disorder at 2–7 percent. Women are 10 to 20 times more likely than men to develop anorexia nervosa and approximately 10 times more likely to develop bulimia nervosa (see Klein and Walsh, 2004). Lifetime prevalence of binge-eating disorder does not appear to vary between men and women (Hudson et al., 2007). Tragically, the suicide rate in patients with anorexia is higher than that of the rest of the population (Pompili et al., 2004).

Eating disorders are challenging to treat, and many individuals undergo repeated interventions in an effort to reduce their symptoms.

Table 12.4 Criteria for Eating Disorders

Anorexia Nervosa	Bulimia Nervosa	Binge-Eating Disorder
Restricted eating that leads to low body weight	Episodes of binge-eating	Episodes of binge-eating
Fear of gaining weight	Compensatory behaviors to prevent gaining weight that follow binge eating	Distress related to binge-eating
Persistent behavior to prevent weight gain	Critical evaluation of body weight or shape	No use of compensatory behaviors
Disturbance in self-perception or failure to perceive seriousness of low body weight		

Source: Based on American Psychiatric Association, 2013

Possible Causes

LO 12.22   Discuss the roles of brain changes, starvation, excessive exercise, and genetic factors in eating disorders.

The literal meaning of the word *anorexia* suggests a loss of appetite, but people with this disorder are usually interested in—even preoccupied with—food. They may enjoy preparing meals for others to consume, collect recipes, and even hoard food that they do not eat. Although people with anorexia are very interested in food, they express an intense fear of becoming obese, which continues even if they become dangerously thin. Many exercise by cycling, running, or almost constant walking and pacing.

BRAIN CHANGES   Anorexia is a serious disorder. Five to 17 percent of people with anorexia die of complications of the disease or of suicide (Bergh et al., 2013). Many people with anorexia suffer from osteoporosis, and bone fractures are common. When the weight loss becomes severe enough, women with anorexia cease menstruating. An example of brain changes associated with anorexia is illustrated in Figure 12.27. Some reports (Artmann et al., 1985; Golden et al., 1996; Herholz, 1996; Katzman et al., 2001; Kingston et al., 1996) indicate the presence of enlarged ventricles and widened sulci in the brains of patients with anorexia, which indicate shrinkage of brain tissue. Some research suggests that this tissue loss can be reversed with successful treatment of the eating disorder (Golden et al., 1996).

STARVATION   Many researchers and clinicians have concluded that anorexia nervosa and bulimia nervosa are symptoms of an underlying mental disorder. However, evidence suggests just the opposite: that the symptoms of eating disorders are actually symptoms of starvation. A famous study carried out at the University of Minnesota by Ancel Keys and his colleagues (Keys et al., 1950) recruited 36 physically and psychologically healthy young men to observe the effects of semistarvation. For six months, the men ate approximately 50 percent of what they had been eating previously and, as a result, lost approximately 25 percent of their original body weight. As the volunteers lost weight, they began displaying disturbing symptoms, including preoccupation with food and eating, ritualistic eating, erratic mood, impaired cognitive performance, and physiological changes such as decreased body temperature. They began hoarding food and nonfood objects and were unable to explain (even to themselves) why they bothered to accumulate objects for which they had no use. At first, they were gregarious, but as time went on, they became withdrawn and isolated.

These men were not diagnosed with eating disorders, yet, once they began to experience starvation, they displayed many of the symptoms that are commonly associated with eating disorders. This has been interpreted as support for the claim that the symptoms of eating disorders arise from starvation rather than an underlying mental disorder. The obsessions with food and weight loss and the compulsive rituals that people with anorexia nervosa develop suggest a possible linkage with obsessive-compulsive disorder (described in more detail in Chapter 17). However, the fact that these obsessions and compulsions were seen in the men of the Minnesota study—none of whom showed these symptoms previously—suggests that they are effects rather than causes of the eating disorder. Both anorexia and semistarvation include symptoms such as mood swings, depression, and insomnia. Even hair loss is seen in both conditions. Although binge eating is a symptom of anorexia, eating very slowly is, too. Patients with anorexia tend to dawdle over a meal, and so did the volunteers in the Minnesota study. "Toward the end of starvation some of the men would dawdle for almost two hours over a meal which previously they would have consumed in a matter of minutes" (Keys et al., 1950, p. 833).

EXCESSIVE EXERCISE   As we saw, excessive exercising is a prominent symptom of anorexia (Zandian et al., 2007). In fact, Manley et al., (2008) reported that many fitness instructors recognize that some of their clients may have an eating disorder and have expressed concern about ethical or liability issues in permitting such clients to participate in their classes or facilities.

Studies with animals suggest that the increased activity may actually be a result of the fasting. When rats are allowed access to food for one hour each day, they will spend more

Figure 12.27 Brain Comparison of Individuals with Anorexia

(a) Patient with anorexia nervosa, showing enlarged sulci (yellow circle), third ventricle (red circle), and lateral ventricle (green circle). (b) Healthy control patient shows typical anatomy in same regions.

(Based on Golden, N. H., Ashtari, M., Kohn, M. R., Patel, M., Jacobson, M. S., Fletcher, A., and Shenker, I. R., Reversibility of cerebral ventricular enlargement in anorexia nervosa, demonstrated by quantitative magnetic resonance imaging, *Journal of Pediatrics*, 1996, *128*[2], 296–301.)

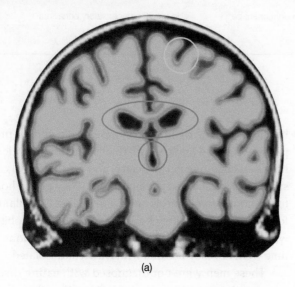 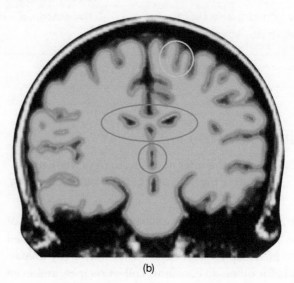

(a) (b)

and more time running in a wheel if one is available and will lose weight and eventually die of emaciation (Smith, 1989). One explanation for the increased activity of rats on a semistarvation diet is that it reflects an innate tendency to seek food when it becomes scarce. Normally, hungry rats would extend their activity by exploring the environment and searching for food, but because of their confinement the tendency to explore is expressed through wheel running. The fact that starving rats increase their activity suggests that the excessive activity of patients with anorexia may be a symptom of starvation, not a weight-loss strategy.

Blood levels of NPY are elevated in patients with anorexia. Nergårdh et al., (2007) found that infusion of NPY into the cerebral ventricles further increased the time spent running in rats on a restricted feeding schedule. Normally, NPY stimulates eating (as it does in rats with unlimited access to food), but under conditions of starvation it stimulates wheel-running activity instead. The likely explanation for this phenomenon is that, if food is not present, NPY increases the animals' activity level, which would normally increase the likelihood that they would find food. Increased levels of NPY may also play a role in the obsession with food that is often seen in patients with anorexia.

GENETIC FACTORS By now, you may be wondering why anorexia develops in the first place. Even if the symptoms of anorexia are largely those of starvation, what initiates the behavior that leads to starvation? The simple answer is that we still do not know. One possibility is a genetic predisposition for this behavior. There is good evidence,

primarily from twin studies, that hereditary factors play an important role in the development of anorexia nervosa (Kortegaard et al., 2001; Russell and Treasure, 1989; Walters and Kendler, 1995). In fact, between 58 and 76 percent of the variability in the occurrence of anorexia nervosa appears to be under control of genetic factors (Klein and Walsh, 2004). In addition, the incidence of anorexia nervosa is higher in girls who were born prematurely or who sustained birth trauma during complicated deliveries (Cnattingius et al., 1999), which suggests that biological factors independent of heredity may play a role. Perhaps some young women (and a small number of young men) go on a diet to bring their body weight closer to what they perceive as ideal. Once they get set on this course and begin losing weight, physiological and endocrinological changes bring about the symptoms of starvation previously outlined, and the vicious cycle begins. In fact, at the end of the Minnesota semistarvation study when the volunteers were permitted to eat normally again, Keys and his colleagues found that a few volunteers displayed symptoms of anorexia, engaging in dieting behavior and complaining about the fat in their abdomens and thighs (Keys et al., 1950). This phenomenon suggests that strongly restricted access to food may contribute to inducing anorexia in people (men, in this case) with a predisposition to this disorder.

The fact that anorexia nervosa is seen primarily in young women has prompted both biological and social explanations. Most psychologists favor the latter, concluding that the emphasis that most modern industrialized societies places on slimness—especially in women—is responsible for this disorder. Another possible cause could be the changes in hormones that accompany puberty. Whatever the cause, young men and women differ in their response to even a short period of fasting. Södersten et al. (2006) had high school students visit their laboratory at noon one day, where they were given all the food they wanted to eat for lunch. Seven days later, they returned to the laboratory again. This time, they had been fasting since lunch on the previous day. The men ate more food than they had the first time. However, the women actually ate *less* than they had before. (See Figure 12.28.) Apparently, at least under some circumstances, women may not compensate for a period of food deprivation by eating more food.

Treatment

LO 12.23 List strategies used in eating disorder interventions.

Eating disorders are very difficult to treat successfully. As illustrated in the case of N. B., many patients undergo repeated rounds of treatment, including hospitalization. Eating disorder treatment strategies include a variety of cognitive behavioral therapies, pharmacological therapies, and some novel alternative therapies.

COGNITIVE BEHAVIORAL THERAPY Cognitive behavior therapy, considered by many clinicians to be the most effective approach, has a success rate of less than 50 percent and a relapse rate of 22 percent during a one-year treatment period (Pike et al., 2003). Unfortunately, a meta-analysis by Steinhausen (2002) indicates that the success rate in treating anorexia has not improved in the last 50 years.

PHARMACOLOGY Researchers have tried to treat anorexia nervosa with many drugs that increase appetite in laboratory animals or in people without eating disorders—for example,

antipsychotic medications, drugs that stimulate adrenergic α_2 receptors, L-DOPA, and THC (the active ingredient in marijuana). Unfortunately, none of these drugs has been shown to be helpful (Mitchell, 1989). In any event, the fact that people with anorexia are usually obsessed with food (and show high levels of neuropeptide Y and ghrelin) suggests that the disorder is not caused by the absence of hunger. Researchers have had more success treating bulimia nervosa; several studies suggest that serotonin agonists such as fluoxetine (an antidepressant drug that is best known as Prozac) may aid in the treatment of this disorder (Advokat and Kutlesic, 1995; Kaye et al., 2001). However, fluoxetine does not help patients with anorexia (Attia et al., 1998).

ALTERNATIVE THERAPIES Bergh, Södersten, and their colleagues (Court et al., 2008; Zandian et al., 2007) have devised a novel and apparently effective treatment protocol for anorexia. The patients are taught to eat faster by placing a plate of food on an electronic scale attached to a computer that displays the time course of their actual and ideal intake. After the meal the patients are kept in a warm room, which reduces their anxiety and their activity level. Remarkably, this treatment strategy has resulted in a 75 percent success rate, with a 10 percent relapse rate after treatment and 0 percent mortality. The remaining 15 percent of patients did not complete the treatment for various reasons (e.g., lack of insurance coverage; Bergh et al., 2013). Future research investigating this strategy and replicating these results could provide strong evidence for this approach to treating eating disorders.

Eating disorders are serious conditions; understanding their causes is more than an academic matter. We can hope that research on the biological and social control of eating and metabolism and the causes of compulsive behaviors will help us to understand these puzzling and dangerous disorders.

Figure 12.28 Reactions of Young Men and Women to Fasting

The graph shows food intake and eating rate during a buffet lunch after a 24-hour period of fasting or after a period during which they ate meals at their normal times.

(Data from Södersten, P., Bergh, C., and Zandian, M., Understanding eating disorders, *Hormones and Behavior*, 2006, 50, 572–578.)

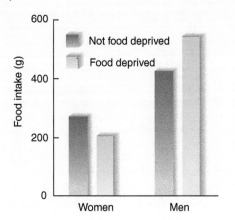 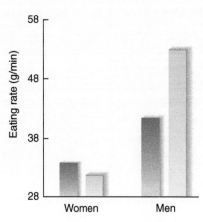

Section Review

Eating Disorders

LO 12.22 **Discuss the roles of brain changes, starvation, excessive exercise, and genetic factors in eating disorders.**
Eating disorders are associated with enlarged ventricles and reduced brain volume. Some research suggests that preoccupation with food and eating, ritualistic eating, erratic mood, excessive exercising, impaired cognitive performance, and physiological changes such as decreased body temperature are symptoms of starvation and not the underlying causes of anorexia. Birth complications are associated with eating disorders. Twin studies support a role for heredity in eating disorders.

LO 12.23 **List strategies used in eating disorder interventions.**
Interventions for eating disorders include cognitive behavioral therapy, pharmacological treatments, and alternative therapies. The success rates for most eating disorder treatments are low, however some alternative therapies have shown higher success rate.

Thought Question

Anorexia has both environmental and physiological contributing factors. After reading the last section of this chapter, what do you think is the cause of the sex difference in the incidence of this disorder (that is, the fact that almost all people with anorexia are female)? Is it caused entirely by social factors (such as the emphasis on thinness in societies), biological factors, or does the combination play a significant role?

Chapter Review Questions

1. Explain the characteristics of a regulatory mechanism.
2. Describe the fluid compartments of the body and explain the control of osmometric and volumetric thirst.
3. Discuss the neural control of thirst.
4. Describe the characteristics of the short- and long-term reservoirs and the absorptive and fasting phases of metabolism.
5. Discuss social and environmental factors and hunger signals that are responsible for starting a meal.
6. Discuss the factors responsible for stopping a meal.
7. Discuss the role of the lateral and ventromedial areas of the hypothalamus in regulation of eating behavior.
8. Describe the role of leptin and neuropeptide Y in the regulation of eating behavior.
9. Discuss the factors that may contribute to obesity.
10. Discuss some surgical, pharmacological, and behavioral treatments of obesity.
11. Discuss the physiological factors that may contribute to eating disorders.

Chapter 13
Learning and Memory

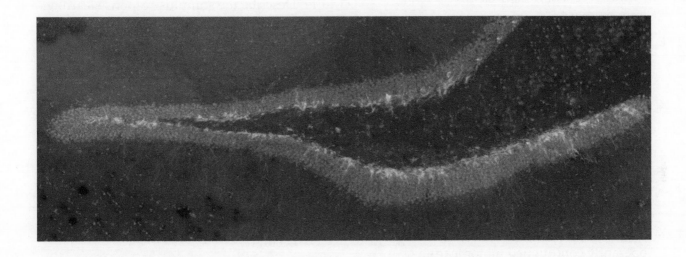

Chapter Outline

Learning Objectives

LO 13.1 Compare characteristics of four types of learning: stimulus-response, motor, perceptual, and relational learning.

LO 13.2 Contrast characteristics of three types of memory: sensory, short-term, and long-term memory.

LO 13.3 Describe the role of the amygdala and AMPA and NMDA receptors in classical conditioning.

LO 13.4 Explain the roles of the basal ganglia, mesolimic and mesocortical pathways, and the prefrontal cortex in reinforcement related to operant conditioning.

LO 13.5 List the contributions of various cortical regions to motor learning.

LO 13.6 Explain the role of the basal ganglia in operantly conditioned motor learning.

LO 13.7 Explain the roles of cortical regions in learning to recognize and remembering stimuli.

LO 13.8 Contrast the roles of extrastriate and prefrontal cortex in retaining perceptual information in short-term memory.

LO 13.9 Describe the role of the hippocampus in consolidation, reconsolidation, and neurogenesis related to relational learning and episodic memories.

LO 13.10 Describe the role of the cortex in semantic memory.

LO 13.11 Compare the role of the hippocampus in consolidation and retrieval of memories.

LO 13.12 Describe the stimulus-response learning ability of patients with hippocampal damage.

LO 13.13 Describe the motor learning ability of patients with hippocampal damage.

LO 13.14 Describe the perceptual learning ability of patients with hippocampal damage.

LO 13.15 Describe the role of the hippocampus in relational learning ability citing research from human and animal models.

LO 13.16 Identify the events required for LTP to occur.

LO 13.17 Compare the relationship between NMDA and AMPA receptors in LTP.

LO 13.18 Describe how AMPA receptors contribute to LTP.

LO 13.19 List the changes in presynaptic neurons, postsynaptic neurons, and protein synthesis that accompany LTP.

Patient H. M. appeared to have surprisingly few symptoms following surgery to remove part of his temporal lobes in an effort to control severe seizures. His intellectual ability and his immediate verbal memory were apparently normal. He could repeat seven numbers forward and five numbers backward, and he could carry on conversations, rephrase sentences, and perform mental arithmetic. He was unable to remember events that occurred during several years preceding his brain surgery, but he could recall older memories very well. He showed no personality change after the operation, and he was generally polite and good-natured.

However, after his surgery, H. M. was unable to learn anything new. He did not know the names of people he had met since the operation (performed in 1953, when he was twenty-seven

years old). His family moved to a new house after his operation, and he never learned how to get around in the new neighborhood. He was aware of his disorder and often said something like this:

> *Every day is alone in itself, whatever enjoyment I've had, and whatever sorrow I've had. . . . Right now, I'm wondering. Have I done or said anything amiss? You see, at this moment everything looks clear to me, but what happened just before? That's what worries me. It's like waking from a dream; I just don't remember. (Milner, 1970, p. 37)*

H. M. was capable of remembering a small amount of verbal information as long as he was not distracted; constant rehearsal

could keep information in his immediate memory for a long time. However, rehearsal did not appear to have any long-term effects; if he was distracted for a moment, he would completely forget whatever he had been rehearsing. He could complete repetitive tasks very well. Because he so quickly forgot what previously happened, he did not easily become bored. He could endlessly reread the same magazine or laugh at the same jokes, finding them fresh and new each time. His time was typically spent solving crossword puzzles and watching television.

On December 2, 2008, H. M., whom we now know as Henry Molaison, died at the age of 82. Researchers had the privilege of studying H. M. throughout his life. What they learned from his experience has been instrumental in enhancing our understanding of how memories are formed, the types of memory, and the brain regions that underlie them. H. M.'s contributions to the study of learning and memory continue today. You'll read more about H. M.'s ongoing contributions to our understanding of learning and memory later in the chapter.

*****

Experiences change us; encounters with our environment alter our behavior by modifying our nervous system. As many investigators have said, an understanding of the physiology of learning and memory is the ultimate challenge to neuroscience research. The brain is complex, and so are learning and remembering. However, despite the difficulties, the long years of research finally seem to be paying off. New approaches and new methods have evolved from old ones, and real progress has been made in understanding the anatomy and physiology of learning and remembering.

In this chapter, we will explore how we learn and how we remember. The first section begins with an overview of learning and memory processes. The four sections that follow will each focus on one of four types of learning: stimulus-response, motor, perceptual, and relational. Then we will consider impairments to learning and memory before concluding with a look at the role of long-term potentiation. The figure here shows two regions of the brain that are vital to learning and memory processes: the amygdala and hippocampus.

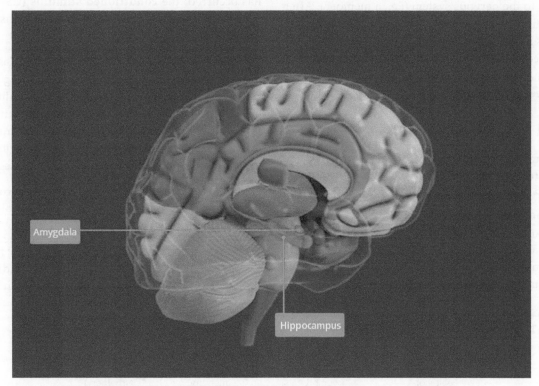

The amygdala and hippocampus, two regions of the brain that are vital to learning and memory.

Overview of Learning and Memory

Learning allows us to acquire new information and refers to the process by which experiences change our nervous system and our behavior. Long-term changes in the nervous system following learning are referred to as *memories*. Memories persist over time and are formed when something is learned. Experiences are not "stored" in the brain as memories; rather, they change the way we perceive, perform, think, plan and behave. Learning something new and creating a memory physically changes the structure of the nervous system, altering neural circuits that participate in perceiving, performing, thinking, planning, and behaving.

Learning, memory, and their effects on behavior are only possible through plasticity. As you will read in this chapter, the nervous system demonstrates synaptic plasticity among existing neurons in learning and forming memories. Exciting new research is also revealing the role of the creation of new neurons (neurogenesis) in learning and memory. You'll learn more about synaptic plasticity in the final section of the chapter.

The information-processing model of memory provides an overall summary of the basic steps linking learning to memory. In this model, learning produces changes in the nervous system by *encoding* the new information to be learned. The encoding process includes *consolidation*, which strengthens changes associated with the initial information that is learned, helping to make a more permanent change to the nervous system (i.e., a memory). After being consolidated, the memory is *stored* via these persistent changes in the nervous system. Finally, *retrieval* is the process of accessing and using the information stored in the neural changes that make up a memory to engage in a behavior. (See Figure 13.1.)

Types of Learning

LO 13.1 **Compare characteristics of four types of learning: stimulus-response, motor, perceptual, and relational learning.**

Learning can take at least four basic forms: stimulus-response learning, motor learning, perceptual learning, and relational learning. We will introduce each of these four types of learning in this section, and return to each of them in greater detail in subsequent sections of the chapter.

STIMULUS-RESPONSE LEARNING **Stimulus-response learning** is the ability to learn to perform a particular behavior when a particular stimulus is present. Thus, it involves the establishment of connections between circuits involved in perception and those involved in movement. The behavior could be an automatic response such as a defensive reflex, or it could be a complicated sequence of movements, such as performing a piece of music. Stimulus-response learning includes two major categories of learning that psychologists have studied extensively: *classical conditioning* and *operant conditioning*. *Conditioning* is a term that is often used to refer to learning that may require several exposures to stimuli to produce a lasting change in behavior.

Classical Conditioning **Classical conditioning** is a form of learning in which an unimportant stimulus acquires the properties of an important one. It involves an *association between two stimuli*. A stimulus that previously had little effect on behavior becomes able to evoke a reflexive, species-typical behavior. For example, an eyeblink response can be conditioned to a tone. If we direct a brief puff of air toward an eye, the eye will automatically blink. The response is called an **unconditioned response (UR)** because it occurs without any special training. The stimulus that produces it (the puff of air) is called an **unconditioned stimulus (US)**. Now we begin the training. We present a series of brief tones (auditory stimuli), each followed very quickly (500 msec later) by a puff of air. After several trials the eye begins to close in response to the tone, even before the puff of air occurs. We can measure the eyeblink response using EMG electrodes connected to a computer. Classical conditioning has occurred; the **conditioned stimulus (CS—the 1,000-Hz tone)** now elicits the **conditioned response (CR—the eyeblink)**. (See Figure 13.2.)

Operant Conditioning The second major class of stimulus-response learning is **operant conditioning** (also called *instrumental conditioning*). Operant conditioning is a form of learning in which a reinforcing or punishing outcome follows a specific behavior in a specific situation. The reinforcer increases the likelihood of the behavior occurring again in the future, while the punisher decreases it.

Differences between classical and operant conditioning
Operant conditioning and classical conditioning differ in several important ways.

1. Classical conditioning involves automatic reflexes that do not have to be learned. Operant conditioning involves brand new behaviors that have been learned.

Figure 13.1 The Steps of Learning and Memory

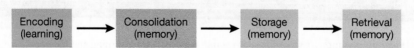

Figure 13.2 Classical Conditioning

In eye-blink conditioning, a puff of air (US) causes the eye to blink (UR). The puff of air is paired with a tone (CS) for several trials. After pairing, the tone alone elicits a blink (CR).

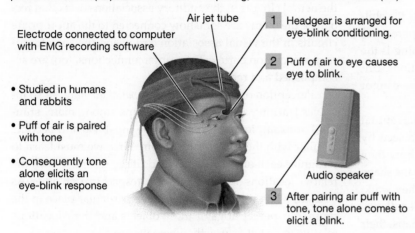

Electrode connected to computer with EMG recording software

Air jet tube

1 Headgear is arranged for eye-blink conditioning.

2 Puff of air to eye causes eye to blink.

- Studied in humans and rabbits
- Puff of air is paired with tone
- Consequently tone alone elicits an eye-blink response

Audio speaker

3 After pairing air puff with tone, tone alone comes to elicit a blink.

2. Classical conditioning involves an association between two stimuli (for example, a tone and a puff of air). Operant conditioning involves an *association between a stimulus and a response* (such as a tone and lever-pressing behavior). One easy way to remember this difference is that operant conditioning involves *operating* something in the environment, such as pressing a lever. There is nothing to "operate" in classical conditioning; the organism simply engages in a reflexive behavior.

3. Operant conditioning permits an organism to change its behavior according to the consequences of that behavior. For example, when a behavior is followed by favorable consequences (a **reinforcing stimulus**), the behavior tends to occur more frequently; when it is followed by unfavorable consequences (a **punishing stimulus**), it tends to occur less frequently. For example, a response that enables a hungry organism to find food will be reinforced, and a response that causes pain will be punished. (Psychologists often refer to these terms as *reinforcers* and *punishers*.)

Reinforcement Let's consider the process of reinforcement. Briefly stated, reinforcement causes changes in an animal's nervous system that increase the likelihood that a specific stimulus will elicit a particular response behavior. For example, when a hungry rat is first put in an operant chamber, it is not very likely to press the lever mounted on a wall. However, if it does press the lever and if it receives a piece of food immediately afterward, the likelihood of its pressing the lever increases. Put another way, reinforcement causes the sight of the lever to serve as the stimulus that elicits the lever-pressing response. It is not accurate to say simply that a particular behavior becomes more frequent. If no lever is present, a rat that has learned to press one will not wave its paw around in the air. The *sight of a lever* is needed to produce the response. Thus, the process of reinforcement strengthens a connection between neural circuits involved in perception (the sight of the lever) and those involved in movement (the act of lever pressing). As we will see later in this chapter, the brain contains reinforcement mechanisms that control this process. (See Figure 13.3.)

MOTOR LEARNING The second major category of learning, **motor learning,** is actually a component of stimulus-response learning. Motor learning is the establishment of changes (responses) within motor systems following a stimulus. Motor learning cannot occur without sensory stimulus from the environment. For example, most skilled movements involve interactions with objects: such as bicycles, video game controllers, tennis racquets, knitting needles, and keyboards. Motor learning differs from other forms of learning

Figure 13.3 A Simple Neural Model of Operant Conditioning

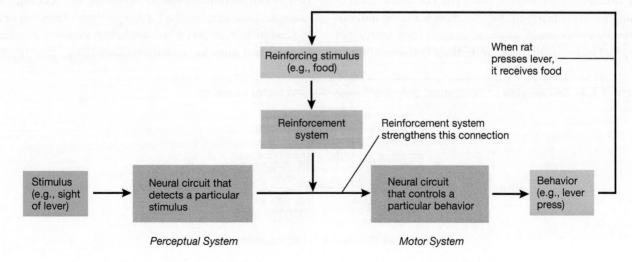

Reinforcing stimulus (e.g., food)

When rat presses lever, it receives food

Reinforcement system

Reinforcement system strengthens this connection

Stimulus (e.g., sight of lever)

Neural circuit that detects a particular stimulus

Neural circuit that controls a particular behavior

Behavior (e.g., lever press)

Perceptual System

Motor System

primarily in the degree to which new forms of behavior are learned; the more novel the behavior, the more the neural circuits in the motor systems of the brain must be modified.

PERCEPTUAL LEARNING **Perceptual learning** is the ability to learn to recognize stimuli that have been perceived before. The primary function of this type of learning is the ability to identify and categorize objects and situations. Unless we have learned to recognize something, we cannot learn how we should behave with respect to it.

Each of our sensory systems is capable of perceptual learning. For example, we can learn to recognize objects by their visual appearance, the sounds they make, how they feel, or how they smell. We can recognize people by the shape of their faces, the movements they make when they walk, or the sound of their voices. When we hear people talk, we can recognize the words they are saying and, perhaps, their emotional state. As we shall see, perceptual learning appears to be accomplished primarily by changes in the sensory association cortex. That is, learning to recognize complex visual stimuli involves changes in the visual association cortex, learning to recognize complex auditory stimuli involves changes in the auditory association cortex, and so on.

A particular learning situation can involve varying amounts of all three types of learning that we have described so far: perceptual, stimulus-response, and motor. For example, if we teach an animal to make a new response whenever we present a stimulus it has never seen before, the animal must learn to recognize the stimulus (perceptual learning) and make the response (motor learning), and a connection must be established between these two new memories (stimulus-response learning). If we teach the animal to make a response that it has already learned whenever we present a new stimulus, only perceptual learning and stimulus-response learning will take place.

RELATIONAL LEARNING The three forms of learning we have described so far consist primarily of changes in one sensory system, between one sensory system and the motor system, or in the motor system (See Figure 13.4). But learning is usually more complex than that. The fourth form of learning involves learning the *relationships* among individual stimuli. For example, a somewhat more complex form of perceptual learning involves connections between different

areas of the association cortex. When we hear the sound of a cat meowing in the dark, we can imagine what a cat looks like and what it would feel like if we touched its fur. Thus, the neural circuits in the auditory association cortex that recognize the meow are somehow connected to the appropriate circuits in the visual association cortex and the somatosensory association cortex. These interconnections, too, are accomplished as a result of learning.

Perception of spatial location—*spatial learning*—also involves learning about the relationships among many stimuli. For example, consider what we must learn to become familiar with the contents of a room. First, we must learn to recognize each of the objects. In addition, we must learn the relative locations of the objects with respect to each other. As a result, when we find ourselves in a particular place in the room, our perceptions of these objects and their locations relative to us tell us exactly where we are.

As we will see in a later section of this chapter, a special system that involves the hippocampus and associated structures appears to perform coordinating functions required for many types of learning that go beyond simple perceptual, stimulus-response, or motor learning.

Types of Memory

LO 13.2 **Contrast characteristics of three types of memory: sensory, short-term, and long-term memory.**

Researchers describe the process of forming memories as occurring in three general stages: the sensory, short-term, and long-term stages of memory (See Figure 13.5).

SENSORY MEMORY Information is first processed by *sensory memory*. Sensory memory is a brief period of time (ranging from fractions of a second to a few seconds) that the initial sensation of environmental stimuli is initially remembered. Sensory memory occurs in each of the senses and allows an individual to retain the experience of the sensation slightly longer than the original stimulus. Sensory memory is often experienced as a brief period in which sensory experiences can be remembered as repeating or "echoing." For example, have you ever had the experience of reading or being completely involved in a task when someone interrupts you to ask a question or tell you something? Immediately

Figure 13.4 An Overview of Perceptual, Stimulus-Response, and Motor Learning

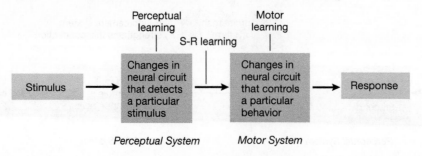

Figure 13.5 The Learning Process

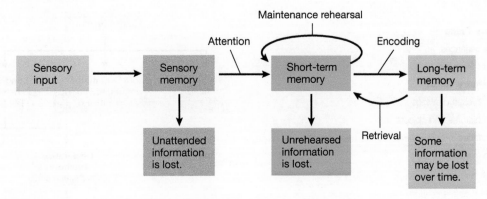

Nondeclarative memories, like riding a bicycle or driving a car, do not require that we be aware of all the movements we make while we are performing them.

you say "What?" because you were so involved in your task that you didn't hear them. Almost as soon as you say the word "What," you experience an echo of their voice and know the answer to your own question. This is an example of *echoic memory* for auditory sensory memory.

SHORT-TERM MEMORY   Only a small fraction of information passes from sensory memory to the second stage of memory formation. The second stage is *short-term* or *working memory*. If information is meaningful or salient enough to be passed on from sensory memory, it will move to the short-term memory stage. This stage is longer than sensory memory, but still limited to seconds or minutes. The memory capacity of short-term memory is limited to a few items, such as the digits in a phone number or the letters in a name. The length of short-term memory can be extended through *rehearsal*. For example, you might be able to remember the phone number longer if you repeat it to yourself until you enter it in a phone. The capacity of short-term memory can be expanded through techniques such as *chunking* (grouping

pieces of information together, like the sections of a social security number or phone number).

LONG-TERM MEMORY   The third and final stage of memory is *long-term memory*. This stage is relatively permanent and can last for minutes, hours, days, or decades. Information that will be retained from short-term memory is *consolidated* into long-term memory. Again, not all information from short-term memory makes it to long-term memory. Long-term memories can be retrieved throughout a lifetime and strengthened with increased retrieval.

Nondeclarative Memory   There are two major categories of long-term memory: nondeclarative and declarative memory. *Nondeclarative memory*, or implicit memory, includes memories that we are not necessarily conscious of. Nondeclarative memories appear to operate automatically. They do not seem to require memorization or include facts or experiences; instead, they control behaviors. For example, think about when you learned a new skill like riding a bicycle or driving a car. You did so consciously and developed declarative memories about your attempts: who helped you learn, where you were, and how you felt. But you also formed nondeclarative memories; you learned to ride or drive. You learned to make automatic adjustments with your hands and body.

The acquisition of specific motoric behaviors and skills is probably the most important form of nondeclarative memory. Driving a car, turning the pages of a book, playing a musical instrument, dancing, throwing and catching a ball, sliding a chair backward as we stand up—all of these skills involve coordination of movements with sensory information received from the environment and from our own moving body parts. We do not need to be able to describe these activities in order to perform them. We may not even be aware of all the movements we make while we are performing them.

Declarative Memory   The other category of memory, *declarative memory*, or explicit memory, is memory of events and

Table 13.1 Examples of Declarative and Nondeclarative Memory Tasks

Declarative Memory Tasks
Remembering past experiences
Finding way in new environment
Nondeclarative Memory Tasks
Learning to recognize broken drawings
Learning to recognize pictures and objects
Learning to recognize faces
Learning to recognize melodies
Classical conditioning
Operant conditioning
Learning sequence of button presses

Figure 13.6 Types of Memory

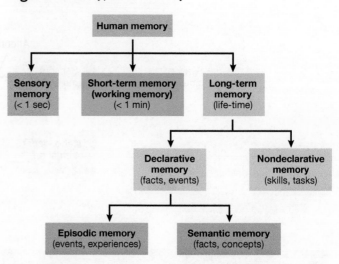

facts that we can think and talk about (Squire et al., 1989). Declarative memories are not simply verbal memories. For example, think about some event in your life, such as your last birthday. Think about where you were, when the event occurred, what other people were present, what happened, and so on. Although you could describe ("declare") this episode in words, the memory itself would not be verbal. In fact, it would probably be more like a video clip running in your head, one whose starting and stopping points—and fast forwards and rewinds—you could control. (See Table 13.1.)

Evidence suggests that declarative memory includes distinct forms of episodic and semantic memories. **Episodic memories** involve context; they include information about when and under what conditions a particular episode occurred and the order in which the events in the episode took place. Episodic memories are specific to a particular time and place because a given episode—by definition—occurs only once. **Semantic memories** involve facts, but they do not include information about the context in which the facts were learned. In other words, semantic memories are less specific than episodic memories. For example, knowing that the sun is a star involves a less specific memory than being able to remember when, where, and from whom you learned this fact. Semantic memories can be acquired gradually, over time. Episodic memories must be learned all at once. (See Figure 13.6.)

Section Review

Overview of Learning and Memory

LO 13.1 Compare characteristics of four types of learning: stimulus-response, motor, perceptual, and relational learning.

Stimulus-response learning, including classical and operant conditions, consists of connections between perceptual and motor systems. Classical conditioning occurs when a neutral stimulus is followed by an unconditioned stimulus (US) that naturally elicits an unconditioned response (UR). After this pairing, the neutral stimulus becomes a conditioned stimulus (CS); it now elicits the response by itself, which we refer to as the conditioned response (CR). Operant conditioning occurs when a response is followed by a reinforcing stimulus, such as a drink of water for a thirsty animal. The reinforcing stimulus increases the likelihood that the other stimuli that were present when the response was made will evoke the response. Motor learning, although it may primarily involve changes within neural circuits that control movement, is guided by sensory stimuli; thus, it is actually a form of stimulus-response learning. Perceptual learning consists primarily of changes in perceptual systems that make it possible for us to recognize stimuli so that we can respond to them appropriately. Relational learning, the most complex form of learning, includes the ability to recognize objects through more than one sensory modality, to recognize the relative location of objects in the environment, and to remember the sequence in which events occurred during particular episodes.

LO 13.2 Contrast characteristics of three types of memory: sensory, short-term, and long-term memory.

Sensory memory is very brief and involves remembering an initial sensation. A small fraction of information from sensory memory passes on to short-term memory, which lasts seconds or minutes and is limited to a few items.

Short-term memory capacity can be extended with rehearsal or chunking. Long-term memory is relatively permanent and memories can be retrieved throughout a lifetime and strengthened with increased retrieval. Long-term memory includes declarative and nondeclarative memory.

Thought Question

Describe specific examples of each of the categories of learning described in this section. Then describe an example that involves more than one category of learning.

Stimulus-Response Learning

The first section of this chapter introduced four basic types of learning: stimulus-response, motor, perceptual, and relational learning. The following sections of the chapter will explore each of these types of learning in greater detail, including what is known of their neural basis. Within each of these sections, learning produces memories as the information to be learned proceeds through sensory, short-term and finally long-term memory stages. We will begin by exploring the neural structures and systems that underlie classical and operant conditioning.

Classical Conditioning

LO 13.3 Describe the role of the amygdala and AMPA and NMDA receptors in classical conditioning.

Neuroscientists have studied the anatomy and physiology of classical conditioning using many models, such as the gill withdrawal reflex in *Aplysia* (a marine invertebrate) and the eyeblink reflex in the rabbit (Carew, 1989; Lavond et al., 1993). Here, we will describe a rodent model of classical conditioning—the conditioned emotional response—to illustrate the underlying neural activity responsible for conditioning emotional responses.

ROLE OF AMYGDALA The amygdala is important in classically conditioned emotional responses. An aversive stimulus such as a painful foot shock produces a variety of behavioral, autonomic, and hormonal responses: freezing, increased blood pressure, secretion of adrenal stress hormones, and so on. A classically conditioned emotional response is established by pairing a neutral stimulus (such as a tone) with an aversive stimulus (such as a brief foot shock). As we saw in Chapter 11, after these stimuli are paired, the tone becomes a CS; when it is presented by itself, it elicits the same type of responses as the unconditioned stimulus does.

After being processed by the auditory cortex, information about the CS (the tone) reaches the lateral nucleus of the amygdala. This nucleus also receives information about the US (the foot shock) from the somatosensory system. Thus, these two sources of information converge in the lateral nucleus, which means that synaptic changes responsible for learning could take place in this location.

A hypothetical neural circuit is shown in Figure 13.7. The lateral nucleus of the amygdala contains neurons whose axons project to the central nucleus. Terminal buttons from neurons that transmit auditory and somatosensory information to the lateral nucleus form synapses with dendritic spines on these neurons. When a rodent encounters a painful stimulus, somatosensory input activates strong synapses in the lateral nucleus. As a result, the neurons in this nucleus begin firing, which activates neurons in the central nucleus, evoking an unlearned (unconditioned) emotional response. If a tone is paired with the painful stimulus, the weak synapses in the lateral amygdala are strengthened. The synaptic changes responsible for this type of learning take place within this circuit.

ROLE OF GLUTAMATE The evidence from many studies indicates that the changes in the lateral amygdala responsible

---

Figure 13.7 Conditioned Emotional Responses

The figure shows the probable location of the changes in synaptic strength produced by the classically conditioned emotional response that results from pairing a tone with a foot shock.

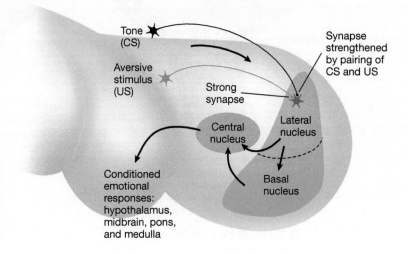

for acquisition of a conditioned emotional response involve a series of synaptic changes called *long-term potentiation (LTP)*. Long-term potentiation is described in detail in the final section of this chapter. LTP involves NMDA receptors and their relationship to increasing the number of AMPA glutamate receptors at the synapse. NMDA and AMPA ionotropic glutamate receptors are described in Chapter 4.

Briefly for now, LTP is accomplished through the activation of NMDA receptors and the insertion of additional AMPA receptors into the postsynaptic membrane. These synaptic changes in the glutamate system serve to increase the EPSP to the postsynaptic cell. For example, Rumpel et al., (2005) paired a tone with a shock and established a conditioned emotional response. They found that the learning experience caused additional AMPA receptors to be inserted and increased EPSPs to dendritic spines of synapses between lateral amygdala neurons and axons that provide auditory input. They also found that a procedure that prevented the insertion of AMPA receptors into the dendritic spines also prevented the establishment of fear conditioning. In addition, Migues et al., (2010) found that blocking steps involved in LTP in the lateral amygdala impaired the establishment of a conditioned emotional response. In fact, the magnitude of the deficit was directly related to the decrease in postsynaptic AMPA receptors, and presumably the decrease in EPSPs. The results of these studies support the conclusion that LTP among glutamate synapses in the lateral amygdala plays a critical role in the establishment of conditioned emotional responses. (See Figure 13.8.) Additional details about synaptic changes associated with LTP will be discussed later in this chapter. For greater detail on the process of inserting AMPA receptors, look ahead to Figure 13.34.

Figure 13.8 Overview of NMDA and AMPA Receptors in LTP Associated with Classical Conditioning

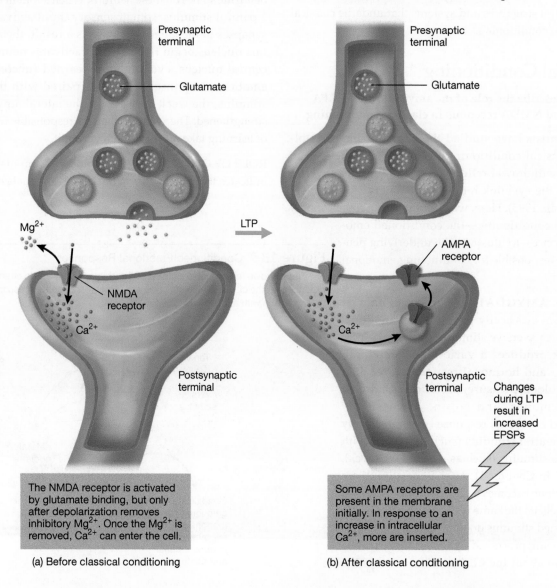

The NMDA receptor is activated by glutamate binding, but only after depolarization removes inhibitory Mg^{2+}. Once the Mg^{2+} is removed, Ca^{2+} can enter the cell.

(a) Before classical conditioning

Some AMPA receptors are present in the membrane initially. In response to an increase in intracellular Ca^{2+}, more are inserted.

Changes during LTP result in increased EPSPs

(b) After classical conditioning

Operant Conditioning

LO 13.4 **Explain the roles of the basal ganglia, mesolimic and mesocortical pathways, and the prefrontal cortex in reinforcement related to operant conditioning.**

Operant conditioning is one of the means by which we (and other animals) learn from interacting with our environment. If, in a particular situation, we make a response that has favorable outcomes, we will tend to make the response again. This section first describes the neural pathways involved in operant conditioning and then discusses the neural basis of reinforcement.

ROLE OF BASAL GANGLIA As we saw in the first section of this chapter, operant conditioning entails the strengthening of connections between neural circuits that detect a particular stimulus and neural circuits that produce a particular response. The circuits that are responsible for operant conditioning begin in various regions of the sensory association cortex, where perception takes place, and end in the motor association cortex of the frontal lobe, which controls movements. But what pathways are responsible for these connections, and where do the synaptic changes responsible for the learning take place?

There are two major pathways between the sensory association cortex and the motor association cortex: direct transcortical connections (connections from one area of the cerebral cortex to another) and connections via the basal ganglia and thalamus. (A third pathway, involving the cerebellum and thalamus, also exists, but the role of this pathway in operant conditioning has until very recently received little attention from neuroscientists.) These two pathways appear to be involved in operant conditioning, but they play different roles. (See Figure 13.9.)

Transcortical Pathways In conjunction with the hippocampal formation, the transcortical connections are involved in the acquisition of declarative, episodic memories—complex perceptual memories of sequences of events that we experience or that are described to us. The transcortical connections are also involved in the acquisition of complex behaviors that involve deliberation or instruction. For example, a person learning to drive a car with a manual transmission might say, "Let's see, push in the clutch, move the shift lever to the left and then away from me—there, it's in gear—now let the clutch come up—oh! It died—I should have given it more gas. Let's see, clutch down, turn the key. . . ." A memorized set of rules (or an instructor sitting next to us) provides a script for us to follow. Of course, this process does not have to be audible or even involve actual movements of the speech muscles; a person can think in words with neural activity that does not result in overt behavior.

At first, performing a behavior through observation or by following a set of rules is slow and awkward. And because so much of the brain's resources are involved in recalling the rules and applying them to our behavior, we cannot respond to other stimuli in the environment—we must ignore events that might distract us. But then, with practice, the behavior becomes much more fluid. Eventually, we perform it without thinking and can easily do other things at the same time, such as having a conversation with passengers as we drive our car.

Figure 13.9 Stimulus and Response Pathways

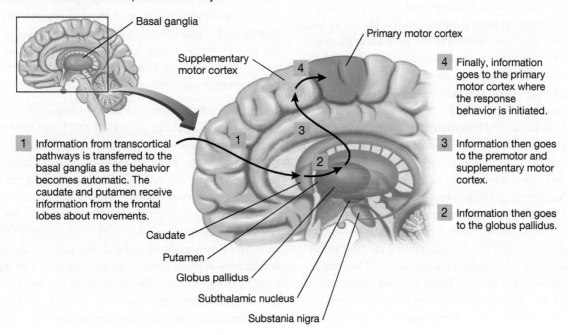

Basal ganglia

Primary motor cortex

Supplementary motor cortex

4 Finally, information goes to the primary motor cortex where the response behavior is initiated.

1 Information from transcortical pathways is transferred to the basal ganglia as the behavior becomes automatic. The caudate and putamen receive information from the frontal lobes about movements.

3 Information then goes to the premotor and supplementary motor cortex.

2 Information then goes to the globus pallidus.

Caudate

Putamen

Globus pallidus

Subthalamic nucleus

Substania nigra

Basal Ganglia Pathways Evidence suggests that as learned behaviors become automatic and routine, they are "transferred" to the basal ganglia. The process seems to work like this: As we deliberately perform a complex behavior, the basal ganglia receive information about the stimuli that are present and the responses we are making. At first the basal ganglia are passive "observers" of the situation, but as the behaviors are repeated again and again, the basal ganglia begin to learn what to do. Eventually, they take over most of the details of the process, leaving the transcortical circuits free to do something else. We need no longer think about what we are doing. Returning to the example of driving a car with a manual transmission, as the driver practices, processing is transferred to the basal ganglia, and the driver no longer needs to deliberately think through each step. Instead, the driver fluidly and automatically starts the engine, shifts gears, and drives the car.

The caudate nucleus and the putamen (two parts of the basal ganglia) receive sensory information from all regions of the cerebral cortex. They also receive information from the frontal lobes about movements that are planned or are actually in progress. (This means that the basal ganglia have all the information they need to monitor the progress of someone learning to drive a car.) The outputs of the caudate nucleus and the putamen are sent to another part of the basal ganglia: the globus pallidus (a third part of the basal ganglia). The outputs of this structure are sent to the frontal cortex: to the premotor and supplementary motor cortex, where plans for movements are made, and to the primary motor cortex, where they are executed. (See Figure 13.10.)

The transfer of memories from brain systems involved in acquisition of behavior sequences to those involved in storage of automatic procedures can be observed in the basal ganglia. For example, research with animal models has revealed that the area of the rat brain that corresponds to the caudate nucleus in humans and other primates is reciprocally connected with the prefrontal cortex. The area of the rat brain that corresponds to the primate putamen is reciprocally connected to sensory and motor regions of the cortex. Yin et al., (2009) and Thorn et al., (2010) found that the rat caudate analogue was involved in early learning of new skills, but that as practice continued and the behavior became more habitual and automatic, the putamen analogue began to take over control of the animal's behavior.

Lesions of the basal ganglia disrupt operant conditioning but do not affect other forms of learning. For example, Fernandez-Ruiz et al., (2001) lesioned portions of the caudate nucleus and putamen that receive visual information from the ventral stream in monkeys. They found that the lesions impaired the monkeys' ability to learn to make a visually guided operant response, but did not affect other forms of learning.

Williams and Eskandar (2006) trained monkeys to move a joystick in a particular direction (left, right, forward, or backward) when they saw a particular visual stimulus.

Figure 13.10 Diagram of the Basal Ganglia and Their Connections

Black arrows represent excitatory connections. Red arrows represent inhibitory connections.

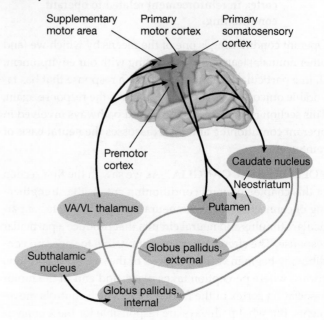

Correct responses were reinforced with a sip of fruit juice. As the monkeys learned the task, the firing rate of neurons in the caudate nucleus increased. The activity of caudate neurons was correlated with the animals' rate of learning. When the investigators further activated the caudate neurons through electrical stimulation during the reinforcement period, the monkeys learned a stimulus-response association more quickly. These results provide further evidence for the role of the basal ganglia in operant conditioning.

REINFORCEMENT Learning provides a means for us to profit from experience—to make responses that provide favorable outcomes. When good things happen (that is, when reinforcing stimuli occur), reinforcement mechanisms in the brain become active, and the establishment of synaptic changes is facilitated. The discovery of the existence of such reinforcement mechanisms occurred by accident.

Neural Circuits Involved in Reinforcement In 1954, James Olds, a young assistant professor, and Peter Milner, a graduate student, attempted to determine whether electrical stimulation of the reticular formation would facilitate maze learning in rats. The reticular formation is a large structure between the brainstem and midbrain that contains many different nuclei and pathways (see Chapter 3 for review). Olds and Milner planned to turn on the stimulator briefly each time an animal reached a choice point in the maze. The researchers applied a brief electrical current into that region around the reticular formation when the animals entered one corner of their enclosure. The animals quickly returned to the location following the stimulation. They returned to the original corner more and more quickly after each successive stimulation was applied (Olds, 1973).

Realizing that they were on to something big, Olds and Milner decided to stop their original experiment and study the phenomenon they had discovered. Subsequent research discovered that although there are several different reinforcement mechanisms, the activity of dopaminergic neurons plays a particularly important role in reinforcement. As we saw in Chapter 4, the *mesolimbic system* of dopaminergic neurons begins in the **ventral tegmental area (VTA)** of the midbrain and projects rostrally to several forebrain regions, including the amygdala, hippocampus, and **nucleus accumbens (NAC).** (See Figure 13.11.) Neurons in the NAC project to the ventral part of the basal ganglia, which, as we just saw, are involved in learning. The *mesocortical system* also plays a role in reinforcement. This system also begins in the ventral tegmental area but projects to the prefrontal cortex, the limbic cortex, and the hippocampus. Because the stimulation of several regions of the brain is reinforcing, the mesolimbic system is only one of several reinforcement pathways. In their study, Olds and Milner had inadvertently activated these pathways when they stimulated the reticular pathway, causing the animal's behavior during the stimulation (being in the corner of the enclosure) to be reinforced, and thus more likely to occur in the future.

Role of Dopamine in Reinforcement   Chapter 5 described a research technique called *microdialysis*, which enables an investigator to analyze the contents of the interstitial fluid within a specific region of the brain. Researchers using this method have shown that reinforcing electrical stimulation of the **medial forebrain bundle** or the ventral tegmental area or the administration of cocaine or amphetamine causes the release of dopamine in the nucleus accumbens (Moghaddam and Bunney, 1989; Nakahara et al., 1989; Phillips et al., 1992). The medial forebrain bundle connects the ventral tegmental area with the nucleus accumbens. (See Figure 13.12.) Microdialysis studies have also found that the presence of natural reinforcers, such as water, food, or a sex partner, stimulates the release of dopamine in the nucleus accumbens. Thus, the effects of reinforcing brain stimulation seem to be similar in many ways to those of naturally-occurring reinforcers.

Functional-imaging studies have shown that reinforcing events also activate the human nucleus accumbens. For example, Knutson et al., (2001) found that the nucleus accumbens became more active (and, presumably, dopamine was being released there) when people were presented with stimuli that indicated that they would be receiving money.

Like classical conditioning, operant conditioning involves strengthening synapses among neurons that have just been active. However, operant conditioning involves three elements: a discriminative stimulus, a response, and a reinforcing stimulus. How are the neural manifestations of these three elements combined, and what role does dopamine play?

Figure 13.11 The Ventral Tegmental Area and the Nucleus Accumbens
Diagrams of sections through a rat brain show the location of these regions.
(Adapted from Swanson, L. W., *Brain maps: Structure of the rat brain,* New York: Elsevier, 1992.)

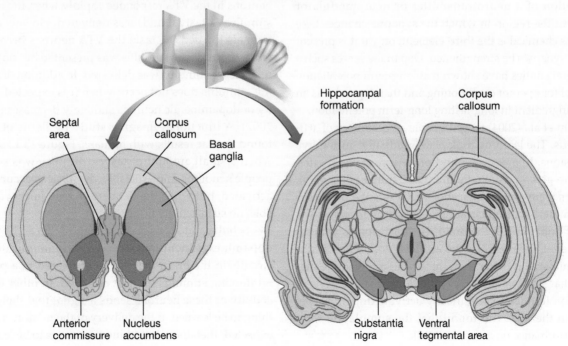

Figure 13.12 Dopamine and Reinforcement

Release of dopamine in the nucleus accumbens, measured by microdialysis, was produced when a rat pressed a lever that delivered electrical stimulation to the ventral tegmental area.

(Based on data from Phillips et al., 1992.)

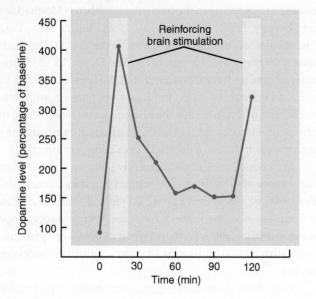

Let's consider a hungry rat learning to press a lever and obtain food. As in classical conditioning, one element (the discriminative stimulus—in this case the sight of the lever) activates only weak synapses on motor neurons responsible for a movement that causes a lever press. The second element—the particular circumstance that happened to induce the animal to press the lever—activates strong synapses, making the neurons fire. The third element comes into play only if the response is followed by a reinforcing stimulus. If it is, the reinforcement mechanism triggers the secretion of a neurotransmitter or neuromodulator throughout the region in which the synaptic changes take place. This chemical is the third element; only if it is present can weak synapses be strengthened. Dopamine serves such a role. Several studies have shown that long-term potentiation is essential for operant conditioning and that dopamine is an essential ingredient in long-lasting long-term potentiation.

Knecht et al., (2004) taught people a vocabulary of artificial words. The learning took place gradually, during five daily sessions. In a double-blind procedure, some participants were given L-DOPA 90 minutes before each session, and others were given a placebo. L-DOPA is the precursor for dopamine, so administration of this drug increases the release of dopamine in the brain. The participants who received the L-DOPA learned the artificial vocabulary faster and remembered it better than those who received the placebo. In that same vein, Tsai et al., (2009) used optogenetic stimulation in mice to specifically activate dopaminergic neurons in the VTA and found that the stimulation reinforced performance on an operant task.

Functions of the Reinforcement System A reinforcement system must perform two functions: detect the presence of a reinforcing stimulus (that is, recognize that something good has just happened) and strengthen the connections between the neurons that detect the discriminative stimulus (such as the sight of a lever) and the neurons that produce the operant response (a lever press). (Refer back to Figure 13.3.)

Assuming that this proposed mechanism is correct, several questions remain: What activates the dopaminergic neurons in the midbrain, causing their terminal buttons to release dopamine? What role does the release of dopamine play in strengthening synaptic connections? Where do these synaptic changes take place? Research that suggests some preliminary answers to these questions is discussed in the rest of this section.

Detecting Reinforcing Stimuli Reinforcement occurs when neural circuits detect a reinforcing stimulus and cause the activation of dopaminergic neurons in the ventral tegmental area. Detection of a reinforcing stimulus is not a simple matter; a stimulus that serves as a reinforcer in one situation may not in another. For example, the presence of food will reinforce the behavior of a hungry animal but not that of an animal that has just eaten. Thus, the reinforcement system is not automatically activated when particular stimuli are present; its activation also depends on the state of the animal or the environment the stimuli occur in.

Studies by Schultz and his colleagues, recording the activity of dopaminergic neurons in the nucleus accumbens, have discovered that the reinforcement system appears to be activated by *unexpected* reinforcing stimuli. For example, Mirenowicz and Schultz (1994, 1996) taught monkeys an operant task that required them to make a response when they heard an auditory stimulus. During training, dopaminergic neurons in the VTA responded rapidly when the reinforcing stimulus (a tasty liquid) was delivered. However, once the animals learned the task, the VTA neurons became active when the auditory stimulus was presented but not when the reinforcing stimulus was delivered. In addition, if a reinforcing stimulus does not occur when it is expected, the activity of dopaminergic neurons suddenly decreases (Day et al., 2007). A functional-imaging study by Berns et al. (2001) found similar results with humans. Figure 13.13 shows that when a small amount of tasty fruit juice was squirted in people's mouths unpredictably, the nucleus accumbens was activated, but when the delivery of fruit juice was predictable, no such activity occurred.

Schultz and his colleagues suggest that activation of the dopaminergic neurons of the VTA communicate to other circuits in the brain that an event related to a potentially reinforcing stimulus has just occurred. In other words, the activity of these neurons sends a signal that there is something to be learned. If the delivery of the reinforcer is already expected, then there is nothing that needs to be learned.

Figure 13.13 Expected and Unexpected Reinforcers

The functional MRI scans show the effects of expected and unexpected reinforcers (sips of fruit juice) on activity of the nucleus accumbens (arrows) in humans.

(Based on Berns, G. S., McClure, S. M., Pagnoni, G., and Montague, P. R. Journal of Neuroscience, 2001, 21, 2793–2798.)

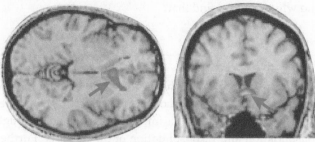

Unexpected reward

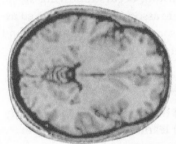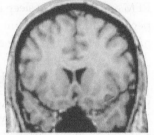

Expected reward

A functional-imaging study by Knutson and Adcock (2005) found that anticipation of a reinforcing stimulus (the opportunity to win some money) increased the activation of the ventral tegmentum and some of its projection regions (including the nucleus accumbens) in humans. The investigators found that the participants were more likely to remember pictures that they had seen while they were anticipating the chance to win some money. (See Table 13.2.)

Role of the Prefrontal Cortex As we have seen, the prefrontal cortex provides an important input to the ventral tegmental area. The terminal buttons of the axons connecting these two areas secrete glutamate, an excitatory neurotransmitter, and the activity of these synapses makes dopaminergic neurons in the ventral tegmental area fire in a bursting pattern, which greatly increases the amount of dopamine they secrete in the nucleus accumbens (Gariano and Groves, 1988). The prefrontal cortex is generally involved in devising strategies, making plans, evaluating progress made toward goals, and judging the appropriateness of one's own behavior. Perhaps the prefrontal cortex turns on the reinforcement mechanism when it determines that the ongoing behavior is bringing the organism nearer to its goals and that the present strategy is working.

Table 13.2 Activity of VTA Neurons in Response to Reinforcers

Event	Expected or Unexpected Reinforcement?	VTA Neurons Active or Inactive?
Walking by a vending machine you accidentally bump into it. A candy bar falls out.	Unexpected	Active
You type your password into an e-mail program and your e-mail account opens.	Expected	Inactive

Section Review

Stimulus-Response Learning

LO 13.3 Describe the role of the amygdala and AMPA and NMDA receptors in classical conditioning.

When an auditory stimulus (CS) is paired with a foot shock (US), the two types of information converge in the lateral nucleus of the amygdala. This nucleus is connected, directly and via the basal nucleus and accessory basal nucleus, with the central nucleus of the amygdala, which is connected with brain regions that control various components of the emotional response. Lesions anywhere in this circuit disrupt the response.

Recordings of single neurons in the lateral nucleus of the amygdala indicate that classical conditioning changes the response of neurons to the CS. The mechanism of synaptic plasticity in this system appears to be NMDA-mediated long-term potentiation. LTP is accomplished through the activation of NMDA receptors and the insertion of additional AMPA receptors into the postsynaptic membrane. Infusion of drugs that block LTP into the lateral nucleus blocks establishment of conditioned emotional responses, and blocking aspects of LTP in the lateral amygdala prevents the establishment of a conditioned emotional response.

LO 13.4 Explain the roles of the basal ganglia, mesolimic and mesocortical pathways, and the prefrontal cortex in reinforcement related to operant conditioning.

Operant conditioning involves strengthening connections between neural circuits that detect stimuli and neural circuits that produce responses. One of the locations of these changes appears to be the basal ganglia, especially the changes responsible for learning of automated and routine behaviors. The basal ganglia receive sensory information and information about plans for movement from the neocortex. Damage to the basal ganglia or infusion of a drug that blocks NMDA receptors there disrupts operant conditioning. The mesolimbic and mesocortical pathways are responsible for reinforcement in operant conditioning. The prefrontal cortex may be involved in activating the mesolimbic pathway to achieve goals.

Thought Question

Have you ever been working hard on a problem and suddenly thought of a possible solution? Did the thought make you feel excited and happy? What might we find if we had a microdialysis probe in your nucleus accumbens and why might we find that?

Motor Learning

Motor learning typically involves learning a novel sequence of motor behaviors over repeated trials. The cerebellum, thalamus, basal ganglia, and motor cortex are involved in motor learning across many different tasks (Hardwick et al., 2013). Chapter 8 describes the brain regions involved in the control of voluntary movement in greater detail, and the following section provides an introduction to the role of two key areas involved in motor learning: the cortex and basal ganglia.

Role of the Cortex

LO 13.5 List the contributions of various cortical regions to motor learning.

The primary motor cortex is responsible for controlling the movements of the body and is organized somatotopically. As you read in Chapter 8, several adjacent areas of cortex are critical in organizing complex, learned movements. For example, the supplementary motor area is involved in performing previously learned, automatic series of behaviors. The premotor cortex is involved in motor learning and memory that is guided by sensory information. The ventral premotor cortex is home to mirror neurons that facilitate motor learning when observing another individual.

Motor learning typically involves a period of fast learning when the motor movements to be learned show rapid improvement during initial trials. The memory of this motor behavior is improved in the period of time following the initial trials when no additional practice occurs, called between-session learning. This improvement is made through consolidation and reconsolidation of the memory. Further improvement in motor learning occurs following sleep. REM and slow-wave sleep are associated with enhanced aspects of motor learning in some motor learning tasks and may promote LTP (Censor et al., 2012).

Role of the Basal Ganglia

LO 13.6 Explain the role of the basal ganglia in operantly conditioned motor learning.

What brain regions are responsible for the acquisition of nondeclarative motor memories? As we saw earlier in this chapter, perceptual memories involve the sensory regions of the cerebral cortex. The basal ganglia appear to play an essential role in stimulus-response and motor learning. Several experiments have shown that people with diseases of the basal ganglia have deficits that can be attributed to difficulty in learning automatic responses. For example, Owen et al., (1992) found that patients with Parkinson's disease were impaired on learning a visually cued operant conditioning task, and Willingham and Koroshetz (1993) found that patients with Huntington's disease failed to learn a sequence of button presses. Parkinson's disease and Huntington's disease both involve degeneration of the basal ganglia and are described in detail in Chapter 15.

Section Review

Motor Learning

LO 13.5 List the contributions of various cortical regions to motor learning.
The primary motor cortex is responsible for executing motor behaviors, and input from the premotor area and supplementary motor area help to refine motor learning.

LO 13.6 Explain the role of the basal ganglia in motor learning.
The basal ganglia are responsible for learning automatic motor behaviors, such as in stimulus-response paradigms.

Thought Question

How can motor learning improve, even when an individual is *not* actively engaged in practicing the motor behavior? Explain the roles of between-session learning and sleep in motor learning and motor memory.

Perceptual Learning

Learning enables us to adapt to our environment and to respond to changes in it. In particular, it provides us with the ability to perform an appropriate behavior in an appropriate situation. Situations can be as simple as responding to the sound of a doorbell or as complex as the social interactions of a group of people.

Perceptual learning involves learning to *recognize* things. Perceptual learning can involve learning to recognize entirely new stimuli, or it can involve learning to recognize changes or variations in familiar stimuli. For example, if a friend gets a new hairstyle or replaces glasses with contact lenses, our visual memory of that person changes. We also learn that particular stimuli are found in particular locations or contexts or in the presence of other stimuli. We can even learn and remember particular *episodes*: sequences of events taking place at a particular time and place. The more complex forms of perceptual learning will be discussed in a later section of this chapter, which is devoted to relational learning. The following section will describe the roles of the cortex in learning to recognize stimuli and how the memories of those stimuli are formed.

Role of the Cortex

LO 13.7 **Explain the roles of cortical regions in learning to recognize and remembering stimuli.**

We will first describe the role of the cortex in learning to recognize stimuli, then provide evidence of cortical activity in later remembering stimuli. Finally, the role of the cortex will be discussed in the context of retaining perceptual information in short-term memory.

LEARNING In mammals with large and complex brains, objects are recognized visually by circuits of neurons in the extrastriate cortex. Visual learning can take place very rapidly, and the number of items that can be remembered is enormous. In fact, Standing (1973) showed people 10,000 color slides and found that they could recognize most of the slides weeks later. Other primates are capable of remembering items that they have seen for just a few seconds, and the experience changes the responses of neurons in their extrastriate cortex (Rolls, 1995).

As we saw in Chapter 6, the striate cortex receives information from the lateral geniculate nucleus of the thalamus. After the first level of analysis in the striate cortex, the information is sent to the extrastriate cortex. After analyzing particular attributes of the visual scene, such as form, color, and movement, subregions of the extrastriate cortex send the results of their analysis to the next level of the visual association cortex, which is divided into two "streams." The *ventral stream*, which is involved with object recognition, continues ventrally into the inferior temporal cortex. The *dorsal stream*, which is involved with perception of the location of objects, continues dorsally into the posterior parietal cortex. Most investigators agree that the ventral stream is involved with the *what* of visual perception, and the dorsal stream is involved with the *where*. (See Figure 6.15.)

Many studies have shown that lesions that damage the inferior temporal cortex—the end of the ventral stream—disrupt the ability to discriminate among visual stimuli. These lesions impair the ability to perceive (and thus to learn to recognize) particular kinds of visual information. As we saw in Chapter 6 , people with damage to the inferior temporal cortex may have excellent vision but be unable to recognize familiar, everyday objects such as scissors, cell phones, or light bulbs—and faces of friends and relatives.

MEMORY Perceptual learning involves changes in synaptic connections in the extrastriate cortex that establish new neural circuits. At a later time, when the same stimulus is seen again and the same pattern of activity is transmitted to the cortex, these circuits become active again. This activity constitutes the recognition of the stimulus—the readout, or replay, of the visual memory. For example, Yang and Maunsell (2004) trained monkeys to detect small differences in visual stimuli whose images were projected onto a specific region of the retina. After the training was complete, the monkeys were able to detect differences much smaller than those they could detect when the training first started. However, they were unable to detect these differences when the patterns were projected onto other regions of the retina. Recordings of single neurons in the extrastriate cortex showed that the response properties of neurons that received information from the "trained" region of the retina—but not from other regions—had become sensitive to small differences in the stimuli. Neural circuits in that region alone had been modified by the training. (See Figure 13.14.)

Let's look at some evidence from studies with humans that supports the conclusion that activation of neural circuits in the sensory association cortex constitutes the "replay" of a perceptual memory. Many years ago, Penfield and Perot (1963) discovered that when they stimulated the extrastriate and auditory association cortex as patients were undergoing seizure surgery, the patients reported memories of images or sounds—for example, images of a familiar street or the sound of the patient's mother's voice. (You will recall from the opening case in Chapter 3 that seizure surgery is performed under a local anesthetic so that the surgeons can test the effects of brain stimulation on the patients' cognitive functions.)

Damage to regions of the brain involved in visual perception not only impairs the ability to recognize visual stimuli but also disrupts people's *memory* of the visual properties of familiar stimuli. For example, Vandenbulcke et al., (2006) found that Patient J. A., who had sustained

Figure 13.14 Role of the Extrastriate Cortex in Perceptual Learning

Activation of neural circuits in the sensory association cortex constitutes the "readout" of perceptual memory. Seeing a specific visual stimulus results in a unique pattern of neural activity in the extrastriate cortex. The same visual stimulus, if seen again later, will stimulate the same neural activity in the extrastriate cortex.

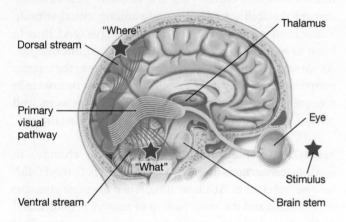

Figure 13.15 Evidence of Retrieval of Visual Memories of Movement

The bars represent the level of activation, measured by fMRI, of MT/MST, a region of the visual association cortex that responds to movement. Participants looked at photographs of static scenes or scenes that implied motion similar to the ones shown here.

(Based on data from Kourtzi and Kanwisher, 2000.)

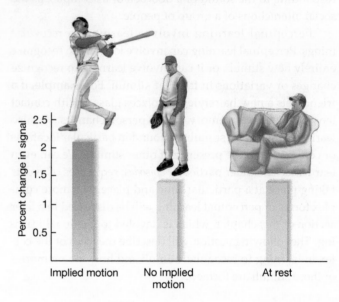

damage to the right fusiform gyrus, performed poorly on tasks that required her to draw or describe visual features of various animals, fruits, vegetables, tools, vehicles, or pieces of furniture. Her other cognitive abilities, including the ability to describe nonvisual attributes of objects, were intact. In addition, an fMRI study found that when healthy individuals were asked to perform the visual tasks that she performed poorly, activation was seen in the region of their brains that corresponded to J. A.'s lesion (in the right fusiform gyrus).

Kourtzi and Kanwisher (2000) found that specific kinds of visual information can activate very specific regions of extrastriate cortex. As we saw in Chapter 6, a region of the extrastriate cortex, MT/MST, plays an essential role in perception of movement. The investigators presented participants with photographs that implied motion—for example, an athlete getting ready to throw a ball. They found that photographs like these, but not photographs of people remaining still, activated area MT/MST. Even though the photographs did not move, the participants' memories presumably contained information about movements they had previously seen. (See Figure 13.15.)

A functional-imaging study by Goldberg et al., (2006) asked people questions that involved visual, auditory, tactile, and gustatory information. The researchers found that answering the questions activated the regions of association cortex involved in perception of the relevant sensory information. For example, questions about flavor activated the gustatory cortex, questions about tactile information activated the somatosensory cortex, and questions about visual and auditory information activated the visual and auditory association cortex.

Retaining Perceptual Information in Short-Term Memory

LO 13.8 **Contrast the roles of extrastriate and prefrontal cortex in retaining perceptual information in short-term memory.**

So far, all the studies we have mentioned involved recognition of stimuli, either particular objects or their locations. Often, recognition is all that is necessary: We see a stimulus and immediately make the appropriate response. But sometimes the situation demands that we make the appropriate response after a delay, even after the stimulus is no longer visible. For example, suppose that we have driven into a large parking lot, and because we will have to carry a heavy package, we want to park as near as possible to the entrance of a store located just in front of us. We look to the left and see a space about 100 feet away. We then look to the right and see a space about 50 feet away. Mentally comparing the distances, we turn to the right. Because we could not look in both directions simultaneously, we had to compare the distance to the second space with our memory of the distance to first one. In other words, we had to compare a perception with a short-term memory of something else we had just perceived. As you read at the beginning of this chapter, short-term memory is the memory for a stimulus or an event that lasts for a short period of time—usually just a few seconds.

As we just saw, learning to recognize a stimulus involves synaptic changes in the appropriate regions of the sensory association cortex that establish new circuits of neurons. *Recognition* of a stimulus occurs when sensory input activates these established sets of neural circuits. Short-term memory of a stimulus involves activity of these circuits—or other circuits that are activated by them—that continues even after the stimulus disappears. For example, *learning* to recognize a friend's face produces changes in synaptic strengths in neural circuits in the fusiform face region of our visual association cortex, *recognizing* that she is present involves activation of the circuits that are established by these changes, and *remembering* that she is still in the room even when we look elsewhere involves continued activity of these circuits (or other circuits connected to them). The following sections will explore the contributions of the extrastriate and prefrontal cortex regions in retaining perceptual information in short-term memory.

ROLE OF EXTRASTRIATE CORTEX   Functional-imaging studies have shown that retention of specific types of short-term visual memories involves activity of specific regions of the extrastriate cortex that we encountered in Chapter 6. One region of the ventral stream, the *fusiform face area,* is involved in recognition of faces, and another region, the *parahippocampal place area* (part of the ventral stream), is involved in recognition of places. A functional-imaging study by Ranganath et al., (2004) found evidence that short-term memory for particular faces and places was associated with neural activity in two different regions of the ventral stream of the visual association cortex. The investigators trained people on a delayed matching-to-sample task that required them to remember particular faces or places for a short period of time. In a **delayed matching-to-sample task,** a participant is shown a stimulus (the sample), and then, after a delay during which the stimulus disappears, the participant must indicate which of several alternatives matches the sample. Ranganath and his colleagues found that short-term memories of faces activated the fusiform face area and

that short-term memories of places activated the parahippocampal place area.

As we saw in Chapter 6, transcranial magnetic stimulation (TMS) of the extrastriate cortex interferes with visual perception. TMS can be used to induce a weak electrical current in the brain that disrupts neural activity and thus interferes with the normal functions of the stimulated region. Oliveri et al., (2001) trained people on a delayed matching-to-sample task that required them to remember either abstract figures or the locations of a white square on a video screen. On some trials the investigators applied TMS to regions of either the ventral stream or the dorsal stream during the delay interval, after the sample stimuli had been turned off. They found that, as expected, stimulating the ventral stream interfered with short-term memory for visual patterns and stimulating the dorsal stream interfered with short-term memory for location.

ROLE OF PREFRONTAL CORTEX   Although the neural circuits responsible for learning to recognize particular stimuli appear to reside in the sensory association cortex, perceptual short-term memories involve other brain regions as well—especially the prefrontal cortex. Miyashita (2004) suggests that the role of the prefrontal cortex in short-term memory is to "manipulate and organize to-be-remembered information, devise strategies for retrieval, and also monitor the outcome" of these processes (p. 435).

Baier et al., (2010) note that successfully remembering recently presented information in short-term memory requires two processes: filtering out irrelevant information and maintaining relevant information. The investigators presented stroke patients with short-term memory tasks that either required them to ignore extraneous, irrelevant information or tested their ability to hold several pieces of information in mind. They found that patients with damage to the left basal ganglia had difficulty filtering out irrelevant information, and patients with damage to the right prefrontal cortex had difficulty retaining more than a few pieces of information in short-term memory.

Section Review

Perceptual Learning

LO 13.7   **Explain the roles of cortical regions in learning to recognize and remembering stimuli.**

Visual recognition occurs in circuits in the dorsal and ventral streams. Perceptual learning occurs as a result of changes in synaptic connections within the sensory association cortex. Damage to the inferior temporal cortex—the highest level of the ventral stream—disrupts visual perceptual learning. Functional-imaging studies with humans have shown that retrieval of memories of pictures, sounds, movements, or spatial locations activates the appropriate regions of the sensory association cortex.

LO 13.8 **Contrast the roles of extrastriate and prefrontal cortex in retaining perceptual information in short-term memory.**

Perceptual short-term memory involves sustained activity of neurons in the sensory association cortex. Functional-imaging studies have shown that retention of specific types of short-term visual memories involves activity of specific regions of the extrastriate cortex. Transcranial magnetic stimulation of various regions of the human extrastriate cortex disrupts short-term perceptual memories. The prefrontal cortex is also involved in short-term memory. This region encodes information pertaining to the stimulus that must be remembered and is involved in manipulating and organizing information in short-term memory.

Successful retention of information in short-term memory requires filtering out irrelevant information, which involves the left basal ganglia, and maintaining relevant information, which involves the right prefrontal cortex.

Thought Question

How many perceptual memories does your brain hold? How many images, sounds, and odors can you recognize, and how many objects and surfaces can you recognize by touch? Select specific perceptual memories from two different senses and describe the brain regions involved in learning and remembering these stimuli.

Relational Learning

So far, this chapter has discussed relatively simple forms of learning, which can be understood as changes in circuits of neurons that detect the presence of particular stimuli or as strengthened connections between neurons that analyze sensory information and those that produce responses. But most forms of learning are more complex; most memories of real objects and events are related to other memories. Seeing a photograph of an old friend may remind you of the sound of the person's name and of the movements you have to make to pronounce it. You may also be reminded of things you have done with your friend: places you have visited, conversations you have had, experiences you have shared. Each of these memories can contain a series of events, complete with sights and sounds, that you will be able to recall in the proper sequence. The neural circuits in the extrastriate cortex that recognize your friend's face are connected to circuits in many other parts of the brain, and these circuits are connected to many others. This section discusses research on the role of the hippocampus and cortex in relational learning, which includes the establishment and retrieval of memories of events, episodes, and places.

Role of the Hippocampus

LO 13.9 **Describe the role of the hippocampus in consolidation, reconsolidation, and neurogenesis related to relational learning and episodic memories.**

The hippocampal formation consists of the dentate gyrus, regions called the CA fields of the hippocampus, and the subiculum (and its subregions). (See panel a of Figure 13.29.)

The most important input to the hippocampal formation is the entorhinal cortex; neurons there have axons that terminate in the dentate gyrus, CA3, and CA1. The entorhinal cortex receives its inputs from the amygdala, various regions of the limbic cortex, and all association regions of the neocortex, either directly or via two adjacent regions of limbic cortex: the **perirhinal cortex** and the **parahippocampal cortex.** Collectively, these three regions constitute the *limbic cortex of the medial temporal lobe.* (See Figure 13.16.)

The outputs of the hippocampal system come primarily from field CA1 and the subiculum. Most of these outputs are relayed back through the entorhinal, perirhinal, and parahippocampal cortex to the same regions of association cortex that provide inputs.

The hippocampal formation also receives input from subcortical regions via the fornix. These inputs select and modulate the functions of the hippocampal formation. The fornix carries dopaminergic axons from the ventral tegmental area, noradrenergic axons from the locus coeruleus, serotonergic axons from the raphe nuclei, and acetylcholinergic axons from the medial septum. The fornix also connects the hippocampal formation with the mammillary bodies, located in the posterior hypothalamus. The most prominent brain damage seen in cases of Korsakoff's syndrome—and presumably the cause of the anterograde amnesia, or difficulty learning new information—is degeneration of the mammillary bodies. (See Figure 13.17.) The symptoms of Korsakoff's syndrome will be described in greater detail later in this chapter.

CONSOLIDATION OF MEMORIES The hippocampal formation plays a role in the process through which declarative memories are formed. Most researchers believe that the process works something like this: The hippocampus

Figure 13.16 Cortical Connections of the Hippocampal Formation

(a) A view of the base of a monkey's brain. (b) Connections with the cerebral cortex.

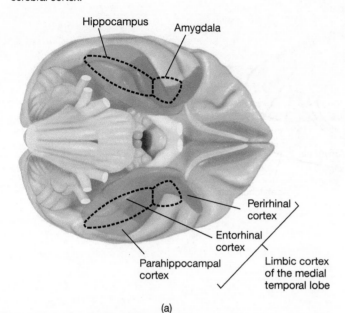

(a)

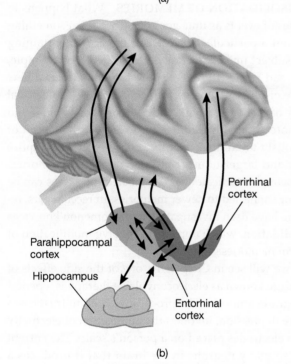

(b)

receives information about what is going on from the sensory and motor association cortexes and from some subcortical regions, such as the basal ganglia and amygdala. It processes this information and then, through its *efferent* connections with these regions, modifies the memories that are being consolidated there, linking them together in ways that will permit us to remember the relationships among the

elements of the memories—for example, the order in which events occurred, the context in which we perceived a particular item, and so on. Without the hippocampal formation, we would be left with individual, isolated memories without the linkage that makes it possible to remember—and think about—episodes and contexts.

Acquisition of both major categories of relational, declarative memories—episodic and semantic—appears to require the participation of the hippocampus. Manns et al., (2003) found that five patients with damage limited to the hippocampal formation showed an anterograde amnesia for semantic as well as episodic information.

As we saw earlier in this chapter, perceptual memories appear to be located in the sensory association cortex, the regions where the perceptions take place. Presumably, episodic memories, which consist of an integrated sequence of perceptual memories, are also located there. What about semantic memories—memories for factual information? Knowing that the sun is a star certainly involves memories different from knowing what the sun looks like. Thus, semantic memories are not simply perceptual memories. A degenerative neurological disorder known as **semantic dementia** suggests that the temporal cortex plays an important role in storing semantic information. Semantic dementia is caused by degeneration of the neocortex of the anterolateral temporal lobe (Lambon Ralph and Patterson, 2008). At least in the early stages of the degenerative process, the hippocampal formation and the rest of the medial temporal lobe are not affected. Murre et al., (2001) describe the case of patient A. M., born in 1930 and studied by the investigators between 1994 and 1997.

A. M. was an active, intelligent man who had received an undergraduate degree in engineering and a master's degree in science. He worked for an internationally renowned company, where he was responsible for managing over 450 employees. His neurological symptoms began with progressive difficulty in understanding the speech of others and finding appropriate words of his own. By the time Murre and his colleagues met A. M., his speech was fluent and grammatical but contained little meaning.

Examiner: Can you tell me about a time you were in hospital?
A. M.: Well one of the best places was in April last year here (ha ha) and then April, May, June, July, August, September, and then October, and then April today.
Examiner: Can you remember April last year?
A. M.: April last year, that was the first time, and eh, on the Monday, for example, they were checking

Figure 13.17 The Major Subcortical Connections of the Hippocampal Formation

A midsagittal view of a rat brain shows these connections. MMB = Mammillary bodies.

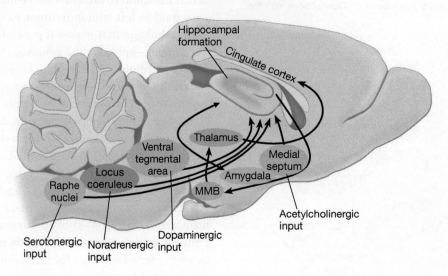

all my whatsit, and that was the first time, when my brain was, eh, shown, you know, you know that bar of the brain (indicates left), not the, the other one was okay, but that was lousy, so they did that and then doing everything like that, like this and probably a bit better than I am just now (indicates scanning by moving his hands over his head). (Murre et al., 2001, p. 651)

Patient A. M.'s loss of semantic information had a profound effect on his everyday activities. He seemed not to understand functions of commonplace objects. For example, he held a closed umbrella horizontally over his head during a rainstorm and brought his wife a lawnmower when she had asked for a stepladder. He put sugar into a glass of wine and put yogurt on a raw defrosting salmon steak and ate it. He nevertheless showed some surprisingly complex behaviors. Because he could not be trusted to drive a car, his wife surreptitiously removed the car keys from his key ring. He noticed their absence, and rather than complaining to her (presumably, he realized that would be fruitless), he surreptitiously removed the car keys from her key ring, went to a locksmith, and had a duplicate set made.

Although his semantic memory was severely damaged, his episodic memory was surprisingly good. The investigators reported that even when his dementia had progressed to the point at which he was scoring at chance levels on a test of semantic information, he answered a phone call that was meant for his wife, who was out of the house. When she returned later, he remembered to tell her about the call.

RECONSOLIDATION OF MEMORIES What happens to memories of events as time goes on? If we learn something new about a particular subject, our memories pertaining to that subject must somehow be modified. For example, as you read earlier in this chapter, if a friend gets a new hairstyle or replaces glasses with contact lenses, our visual memory of that person will change accordingly. And if you learn more about something—for example, the layout of a previously unfamiliar neighborhood—you will acquire a larger and larger number of interconnected memories. These examples indicate that established memories can be altered or connected to newer memories. In recent years, researchers have been investigating a phenomenon known as **reconsolidation,** which appears to involve modification of long-term memories.

As we will see in Chapter 16, one of the side effects of a procedure known as electroconvulsive therapy is a period of retrograde amnesia. The procedure, used to treat cases of severe depression, involves the application of electricity through electrodes placed on a person's scalp. The current excites so many neurons in the brain that it produces a seizure. Presumably, the seizure erases short-term memories present at the time and thus prevents consolidation of these memories.

Misanin et al., (1968) found that long-term memories, which are normally not affected by seizures, were vulnerable to disruption by electroconvulsive shock (ECS) if a reminder of the original learning experience was first presented. The investigators found that ECS given right after a learning experience prevented consolidation, but ECS given a day later did not. Apparently, the ECS given right after training disrupted the brain activity initiated by the training session and consequently interfered with consolidation. The ECS given the next day had no effect, because the memory had already been consolidated. However, if animals were given a "reminder" stimulus one day after training, which presumably reactivated the memory, an ECS treatment administered immediately afterward caused amnesia for the task when the animals were tested the following day. Reactivation of the memory made it susceptible to disruption.

These studies involved stimulus-response learning. More recent studies have found that long-term, well-consolidated relational memories are also susceptible to disruption. Presumably, the process of reconsolidation, which involves neural events similar to those responsible for the original consolidation, makes it possible for established memories to be altered or attached to new information (Nader, 2003). Events that interfere with consolidation also interfere with reconsolidation and can even erase memories or at least make them inaccessible. For example, Debiec et al., (2010) trained rats on two fear conditioning tasks. They paired two different tones (CSa and CSb) with shocks delivered to two different parts of the body (USa and USb). After training, they randomly presented only one of the shocks (USa or USb) to each animal followed by an infusion of anisomycin (which blocks protein production) or a placebo into the lateral amygdala. Protein production is an important step in long-term potentiation and memory formation. The next day, they tested the animals for retention of the conditioned responses. They found that the animals did *not* freeze when they presented the tone that had been paired with the US that had been presented just before the infusion of anisomycin on the previous day. In other words, presenting one of the shocks "reopened" the CS-US memory for possible reconsolidation, which made the memory link fragile. Blocking protein synthesis prevented the memory from going back to its original state.

ROLE OF HIPPOCAMPAL NEUROGENESIS IN CONSOLIDATION   As we saw in Chapter 3, new neurons can be produced in the hippocampus and the olfactory bulb of the adult brain. Stem cells located in the subgranular zone of the hippocampus divide and, in rats, give rise to 5,000–10,000 granule cells each day, which migrate into the dentate gyrus and extend axons along the mossy fiber tract. The new neurons form connections with other neurons in the dentate gyrus and with neurons in field CA3 (Kempermann et al., 2004; Shors, 2009). (See Figure 13.18.)

Morris et al., (1982) developed a task that other researchers have adopted as a standard test of rodents' spatial abilities. The task requires rats to find a particular location in space solely by means of visual cues external to the apparatus. The "maze" consists of a circular pool, 1.3 meters in diameter, filled with a mixture of water and something to increase the opacity of the water, such as powdered milk. The water mixture hides the location of a small platform, situated just beneath the surface of the liquid. Experimenters put the rats into the water and let

Figure 13.18 Adult Neurogenesis

Stem cells in the subgranular zone of the hippocampus divide and give rise to granule cells, which migrate into the dentate gyrus.

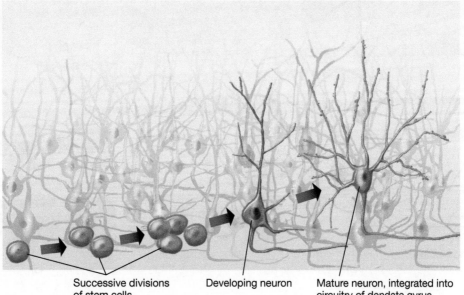

Successive divisions of stem cells

Developing neuron

Mature neuron, integrated into circuitry of dentate gyrus

them swim until they encountered the hidden platform and climbed onto it. They released the rats from a new position on each trial. After a few trials, the rats learned to swim directly to the hidden platform from wherever they were released.

The Morris water maze requires relational learning; to navigate around the maze, the animals use information from the relative locations of stimuli located outside the maze—furniture, windows, doors, and so on. But the maze can be used for nonrelational, stimulus-response learning, too. If the animals are always released at the same place, they learn to head in a particular direction—say, toward a particular landmark they can see above the wall of the maze (Eichenbaum et al., 1990).

If rats with hippocampal lesions are always released from the same place, they learn this nonrelational, stimulus-response task about as well as intact rats do. However,

if they are released from a new position on each trial, they swim in what appears to be an aimless fashion until they finally encounter the platform. (See Figure 13.19.)

Gould et al., (1999) trained rats on two versions of the Morris water maze: one requiring relational learning and one requiring only stimulus-response learning. Training on the relational task, which involves the hippocampus, doubled the number of newborn neurons in the dentate gyrus. Training on the stimulus-response task, which does not involve the hippocampus, had no effect on neurogenesis. Most newborn neurons die within a few weeks, but if the animal learns something new, many of the neurons survive.

Evidence suggests that new neurons in the dentate gyrus participate in learning. Tronel et al., (2010) found that maturation of dendritic trees of newborn neurons and their integration into neural circuits of the hippocampus

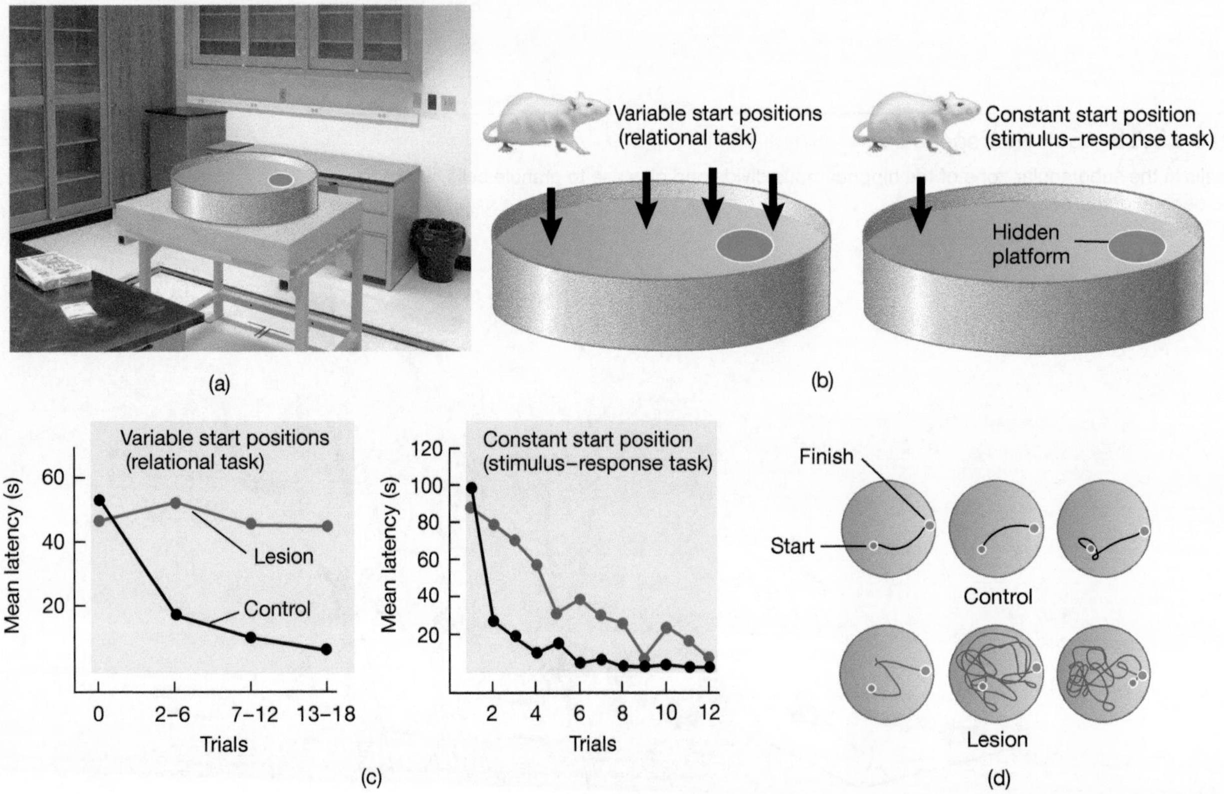

Figure 13.19 The Morris Water Maze

(a) Environmental cues present in the room provide information that permits the animals to orient themselves in space. (b) According to the task, start positions are variable or fixed. Normally, rats are released from a different position on each trial. If they are released from the same position every time, the rats can learn to find the hidden platform through stimulus-response learning. (c) The graphs show the performance of normal rats and rats with hippocampal lesions using variable or fixed start positions. Hippocampal lesions impair acquisition of the relational task. (d) Representative samples show the paths followed by normal rats and rats with hippocampal lesions on the relational task (variable start positions).

(Adapted from Eichenbaum, H., A cortical–hippocampal system for declarative memory, *Nature Reviews: Neuroscience*, 2000, *1*, 41–50. Data from Eichenbaum et al., 1990.)

were accelerated when animals were trained on a spatial learning task. They also found that infusion of a drug to block NMDA receptors (AP5) into the lateral ventricle did not affect the basal rate of neurogenesis, but it impaired learning and prevented the normal learning-induced changes in neurogenesis from taking place. These results suggest that long-term potentiation plays a role in the incorporation of newborn neurons into circuits that store new memories.

The rate of neurogenesis and the survival of new neurons are responsive to changes in the organism's environment. In rodents, access to a running wheel or exposure to an enriched cage environment with toys, tunnels, and other objects to explore increases the number of new neurons generated in the hippocampus and results in enhanced performance on the Morris water maze task. When animals have access to a running wheel (and use it), increased LTP is also found in the hippocampus. The number of new neurons produced in the hippocampus decreases with age, and these age-related decreases are reduced in rodents in an enriched environment (Clemenson et al., 2015). Antidepressant drugs increase hippocampal neurogenesis whereas stress hormones reduce it. Research using transgenic mice that display increased neurogenesis confirms that increased neurogenesis reduces anxiety- and depression-like behaviors in this model (Hill et al., 2015).

Although less research has been done on the role of neurogenesis in the olfactory bulb, some evidence suggests that neurogenesis in the olfactory bulb is also involved in learning. Nissant et al., (2009) found that LTP could be induced in newborn olfactory bulb neurons soon after they arrived in the olfactory bulb, but that this ability declined as the neurons grew older. Belnoue et al., (2011) found that newborn neurons in the olfactory bulb participated in olfactory learning.

We still do not know why neurogenesis takes place in only two parts of the brain. If it is useful there, why does it not occur elsewhere in the brain?

Role of the Cortex

LO 13.10 Describe the role of the cortex in semantic memory.

In semantic dementia, semantic information is lost, but episodic memory for recent events can be spared. The hippocampal formation and the limbic cortex of the medial temporal lobe appear to be involved in the consolidation and retrieval of declarative memories, both episodic and semantic, but the semantic memories themselves appear to be stored in the neocortex—in particular, the anterolateral temporal lobe. Pobric et al., (2007) found that TMS of the left anterior temporal lobe, which disrupts the normal neural activity of this region, produced the symptoms of semantic dementia. Volunteers who experienced TMS of the left anterior temporal lobe had difficulty naming pictures of objects and understanding the meanings of words, but they had no trouble performing other, nonsemantic tasks such as naming six-digit numbers and matching large numbers according to their approximate size.

Section Review

Relational Learning

LO 13.9 Describe the role of the hippocampus in consolidation, reconsolidation, and neurogenesis related to relational learning and episodic memories.

The hippocampus receives information about what is going on from sensory and motor association cortexes and from some subcortical regions, such as the basal ganglia and amygdala. It processes this information and then, through its efferent connections with these regions, modifies the memories that are being consolidated there, linking them together in ways that will permit us to remember the relationships among the elements of the memories—for example, the order in which events occurred, the context in which we perceived a particular item, and so on. Without the hippocampal formation, we would be left with individual, isolated memories without the linkage that makes it possible to remember—and think about—episodes and contexts.

Similarly, deactivation of the dorsal hippocampus prevents consolidation if it occurs one day after the animal learns a Morris water maze task but has no effect if it occurs 30 days later. In contrast, deactivation of regions of the cerebral cortex disrupts performance if it occurs 30 days after training but has no effect if it occurs one day after training, suggesting that these cortical regions are involved in storage of the memory of the task. The dentate gyrus is one of the two places in the brain where adult stem cells can divide and give rise to new neurons. These neurons establish connections with neurons in the hippocampus and appear to participate in learning.

Evidence indicates that these neurons play a role in the formation of new memories.

LO 13.10 **Describe the role of the cortex in semantic memory.**

Semantic memories appear to be stored in the anterolateral temporal lobe.

Thought Question

How could understanding of the processes of consolidation and reconsolidation of memories in the hippocampus be used in a therapeutic setting? Are there situations in which interfering with consolidation or later reconsolidation of memories could be beneficial?

Amnesia

One of the most dramatic and intriguing phenomena caused by human brain damage is *anterograde amnesia,* which, at first glance, appears to be the inability to learn new information. However, when we examine the phenomenon more carefully, we find that the basic abilities of perceptual learning, stimulus-response learning, and motor learning are intact but that complex relational learning is gone.

As we discussed earlier, the term **anterograde amnesia** refers to difficulty in learning new information. A person with pure anterograde amnesia can remember events that occurred in the past, from the time before the brain damage occurred, but cannot retain information encountered *after* the damage. In contrast, **retrograde amnesia** refers to the inability to remember events that happened *before* the brain damage occurred. (See Figure 13.20.) As we will see, pure anterograde amnesia is rare; usually, there is also a retrograde amnesia for events that occurred for a period of time before the brain damage occurred. In general, however, anterograde amnesia is relatively more common than retrograde amnesia.

In 1889, Sergei Korsakoff, a Russian physician, first described a severe memory impairment caused by brain damage, and the disorder was given his name. The most profound symptom of **Korsakoff's syndrome** is severe anterograde amnesia: The patients appear to be unable to form new memories, although they can still remember old ones. They can converse normally and can remember events that happened long before their brain damage occurred, but they cannot remember events that happened afterward. These patients experience degenerations of the mammillary bodies, which are connected to the hippocampus via the fornix.

As we will see in Chapter 15, the brain damage that causes Korsakoff's syndrome is usually (but not always) a result of chronic alcohol abuse. Chapter 15 also includes a description of another disease characterized by memory loss: Alzheimer's disease. Similar to Korsakoff's syndrome, Alzheimer's disease involves anterograde amnesia.

Anterograde amnesia can also be caused by damage to the temporal lobes, where the hippocampus is located. Scoville and Milner (1957) reported that bilateral removal of the medial temporal lobe produced a memory impairment in people that was apparently identical to that seen in Korsakoff's syndrome. H. M., the man described in the case that opened this chapter, received surgery in an attempt to treat his severe epilepsy, which could not be controlled even by high doses of anticonvulsant medication. The epilepsy appears to have been caused by a head injury he received when he was struck by a bicycle at age nine (Corkin et al., 1997).

The surgery successfully treated H. M.'s seizure disorder, but it became apparent that the operation had produced a serious memory impairment. Further investigation revealed that the critical site of damage was the hippocampus. Once it was known that bilateral medial temporal lobectomy (such as H. M.'s surgery) causes anterograde amnesia, neurosurgeons stopped performing this operation and are now careful to operate on only one temporal lobe. The remainder of this chapter will investigate the role of the hippocampus in amnesia as well as some aspects of memory that are *not* impaired in anterograde amnesia.

Role of the Hippocampus

LO 13.11 **Compare the role of the hippocampus in consolidation and retrieval of memories.**

H. M.'s history and memory deficits were described in the introduction to this chapter (Milner et al., 1968; Milner, 1970; Corkin et al., 1981). Because of his relatively pure amnesia, he was extensively studied. Milner and her colleagues based the following conclusions on his pattern of deficits:

1. *The hippocampus is not the location of long-term memories; nor is it necessary for the retrieval of long-term memories.* If it were, H. M. would not have been able to remember events from early in his life, and he would not have known how to talk.

Figure 13.20 Retrograde Amnesia and Anterograde Amnesia

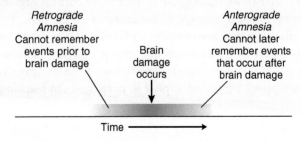

Retrograde Amnesia
Cannot remember events prior to brain damage

Brain damage occurs

Anterograde Amnesia
Cannot later remember events that occur after brain damage

Time ⟶

2. *The hippocampus is not the location of short-term memories.* If it were, H. M. would not be able to carry on a conversation, because he would not have remembered what the other person said long enough to think of a reply.

3. *The hippocampus* is *involved in converting short-term memories into long-term memories.* This conclusion is based on a particular hypothesis of memory function: that our short-term memory of an event is retained by neural activity and that long-term memories consist of relatively permanent biochemical or structural changes in neurons. The conclusion seems a reasonable explanation for the fact that, when presented with new information, H. M. seemed to understand it and remember it as long as he thought about it, but that a permanent record of the information was never made.

As we will see, these three conclusions are too simple. Subsequent research on patients with anterograde amnesia indicates that the facts are more complicated—and more interesting—than they first appeared to be. But to appreciate the significance of the findings of more recent research, we must understand these three conclusions and remember the facts that led to them. The following sections will explore these three conclusions further by investigating consolidation and retrieval in anterograde amnesia.

ANTEROGRADE AMNESIA: CONSOLIDATION Some of the clearest evidence that damage restricted to the hippocampal formation produces anterograde amnesia, including deficits in consolidation, came from a case studied by Zola-Morgan et al., (1986). Patient R. B., a 52-year-old man with a history of heart trouble, sustained a cardiac arrest. Although his heart was successfully restarted, the period of anoxia caused by the temporary halt in blood flow resulted in brain damage. The primary symptom of this brain damage was permanent anterograde amnesia, which Zola-Morgan et al., carefully documented. Five years after the onset of the amnesia, R. B. died of heart failure. His family gave permission for histological examination of his brain.

The investigators discovered that a region of the hippocampal formation called field CA1 was primarily affected and the neurons had completely degenerated. (See panel a in Figure 13.29). Subsequent studies reported other patients with anterograde amnesia caused by CA1 damage (Kartsounis et al., 1995; Rempel-Clower et al., 1996; Victor and Agamanolis, 1990).

Why is field CA1 of the hippocampus so sensitive to anoxia? The answer appears to lie in the fact that this region is especially rich in NMDA receptors. For some reason, metabolic disturbances of various kinds—including seizures, anoxia, or hypoglycemia—cause glutamatergic terminal buttons to release glutamate at abnormally high levels. The effect of this glutamate release is to stimulate NMDA receptors, which permit the entry of calcium. Within a few

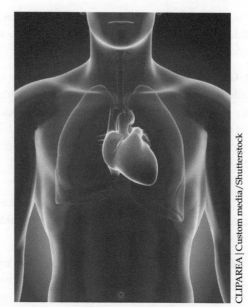

CLIPAREA | Custom media/Shutterstock

The period of anoxia caused by the temporary halt in blood flow resulted in damage to R.B.'s brain.

minutes, excessive amounts of intracellular calcium begin to destroy the neurons. If animals are pretreated with drugs that block NMDA receptors, a period of anoxia is much less likely to produce brain damage (Rothman and Olney, 1987). CA1 neurons contain many NMDA receptors, so long-term potentiation can quickly become established there. This flexibility undoubtedly contributes to our ability to learn as quickly as we do. But it also renders these neurons particularly susceptible to damage by metabolic disturbances.

In addition to information from case studies such as R. B.'s, evidence from functional-imaging studies indicates that the hippocampal formation plays a critical role in consolidation of relational memories and their transfer into the cerebral cortex. Studies with laboratory animals support this conclusion. For example, Maviel et al., (2004) trained mice in a Morris water maze and later tested their memory of the location of the platform. Just before testing the animal's performance, the investigators temporarily deactivated specific regions of the animals' brains with intracerebral infusions of lidocaine, a local anesthetic. If the hippocampus was deactivated one day after training, the mice showed no memory of the task. However, if the hippocampus was deactivated 30 days after training, their performance was normal. In contrast, inactivation of several regions of the cerebral cortex impaired memory retrieval 30 days after training, but not one day after training. These findings indicate that the hippocampus is required for newly learned spatial information but not for information learned 30 days previously. The findings also suggest that sometime during these 30 days the cerebral cortex takes on a role in retention of this information.

Returning again to the case of H. M., remember that his short-term memory was intact and if he could remember events from before his operation, then the problem must have been that consolidation did not take place.

Thus, the role of the hippocampal formation in memory is consolidation—converting short-term memories to long-term memories.

RETROGRADE AMNESIA: RETRIEVAL   As we saw, anterograde amnesia is usually accompanied by retrograde amnesia—the inability to remember events that occurred for a period of time before the brain damage occurred. The following example illustrates retrieval of early memories by a patient with a profound anterograde amnesia.

Patient E. P. made the following response when he was asked to describe an incident from the period before he attended school.

> When I was 5 years old, we moved from Oakland to the country. I was very excited and looked forward to the change. I remember the truck that dad rented. It was hardly full because we didn't have much furniture. When it was time to leave, mom got in the car and followed behind the truck. I rode in the truck with dad. (Reed and Squire, 1998, p. 3951)

Patient E. P. is also able to find his way around the neighborhood where he grew up but is completely lost in the neighborhood to which he moved after he became amnesic (Teng and Squire, 1999).

The fact that retrograde amnesia extends back for a limited period of time suggests that a gradual process controlled by the hippocampal formation transforms memories into permanent storage. Before this transformation is complete, the hippocampal formation is required for the retrieval of these memories. Later, retrieval of these memories can be accomplished even if the hippocampal formation has been damaged. Bayley et al., (2006) asked people with anterograde amnesia and healthy volunteers questions about news events that had occurred during the previous 30 years. They found a diminishing amount of retrograde amnesia in the patients with brain injuries for earlier and earlier events. In fact, recall of events more than 15 years old was about as good as that of control participants. However, memory of recent events was severely impaired. (See Figure 13.21.)

A functional-imaging study by Smith and Squire (2009) found evidence that supports the differential role of the hippocampal formation in recent memories and older ones. They used the test employed by Bayley et al., (2006) in order to evoke the retrieval of memories of various ages in a group of people with normal memories. Retrieval of the youngest memories caused the greatest activation of the hippocampus, and retrieval of the oldest ones caused the least activation. The opposite effect was seen in the frontal cortex. These results are consistent with the suggestion that memories initially stored in the hippocampus are gradually transferred to the frontal cortex.

Figure 13.21 Retrograde Amnesia in Patients with Hippocampal Damage

Hippocampal damage appears to disrupt the gradual storage of long-term memories. Memories older than approximately 15 years are relatively intact even in people with retrograde amnesia, which suggest that the storage process requires between 10 and 15 years to be completed.

(Data from Bayley et al., 2006.)

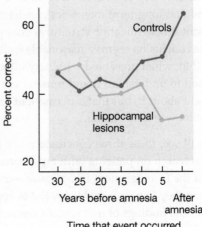

H. M.'s memory deficit is striking and dramatic. However, when he and other patients with anterograde amnesia were studied more carefully, it became apparent that the amnesia did not represent a total failure in learning ability. When patients are appropriately trained and tested, we find that they are capable of three of the four major types of learning described earlier in this chapter: perceptual learning, stimulus-response learning, and motor learning.

Stimulus-Response Learning

LO 13.12 Describe the stimulus-response learning ability of patients with hippocampal damage.

Investigators succeeded in demonstrating stimulus-response learning by H. M. and other individuals with amnesia. For example, Woodruff-Pak (1993) found that H. M. and another patient with anterograde amnesia could acquire a classically conditioned eyeblink response. H. M. even showed retention of the task two years later: He acquired the response again in one-tenth the number of trials that were needed previously. Sidman et al., (1968) successfully trained patient H. M. on an operant conditioning task—a visual discrimination task in which money was given for correct responses.

Motor Learning

LO 13.13 Describe the motor learning ability of patients with hippocampal damage.

Several studies have demonstrated motor learning in patients with anterograde amnesia. For example, Reber and Squire

(1998) found that participants with anterograde amnesia could learn a sequence of button presses in a serial reaction time task. They sat in front of a computer screen and watched an asterisk appear—apparently randomly—in one of four locations. Their task was to press the one of four buttons that corresponded to the location of the asterisk. As soon as they did so, the asterisk moved to a new location, and they pressed the corresponding button. (See Figure 13.22.)

Although experimenters did not say so, the sequence of button presses specified by the moving asterisk was not random. For example, it might be DBCACBDCBA, a ten-item sequence that is repeated continuously. With practice, participants become faster and faster at this task. Researchers know their rate increases because they have learned the sequence, because if the sequence is changed, their performance decreases. The individuals with amnesia learned this task just as well as healthy volunteers did.

A study by Cavaco et al., (2004) tested patients with amnesia on a variety of tasks modeled on real-world activities, such as weaving, tracing figures, operating a joystick that controlled a video display, and pouring water into small jars. Both patients with amnesia and healthy volunteers did poorly on these tasks at first, but their performance improved through practice. Thus, patients with anterograde amnesia are capable of a variety of tasks that require motor learning.

Perceptual Learning

LO 13.14 **Describe the perceptual learning ability of patients with hippocampal damage.**

How do researchers determine if patients with amnesia can retain perceptual learning abilities? Researchers use task such as the one in Figure 13.23, which shows two sample items from a test of the ability to recognize broken drawings; note how the drawings are successively more complete. Participants are first shown the least complete set (set I) of each

Figure 13.22 The Serial Reaction Time Test

In the procedure of the study by Reber and Squire (1998), participants pressed the button in a sequence indicated by movement of the asterisk on the computer screen.

DBCACBDCBA

Figure 13.23 Examples of Broken Drawings

(Reprinted with permission of author and publisher from Gollin, E. S., *Developmental studies of visual recognition of incomplete objects, Perceptual and Motor Skills*, 1960, *11*, 289–298.)

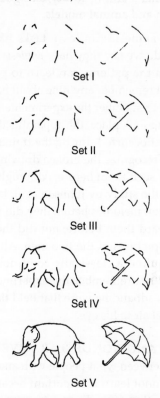

Set I

Set II

Set III

Set IV

Set V

of 20 different drawings. If they do not recognize a figure (and most people do not recognize set I), they are shown more complete sets until they identify it. One hour later, the participants are tested again for retention, starting with set I. When H. M. was given this test and was retested an hour later, he showed considerable improvement (Milner, 1970). When he was retested four months later, he *still* showed this improvement. His performance was not as good as that of healthy volunteers, but he showed unmistakable evidence of long-term retention.

Individuals with anterograde amnesia retained perceptual learning and memory in all of their senses. For example, Johnson et al., (1985) found that patients with anterograde amnesia could learn to recognize a variety of stimuli, including different faces. The researchers played unfamiliar melodies from Korean songs to amnesic patients and found that when they were tested later, the patients preferred these melodies to ones they had not heard before. The experimenters also presented photographs of two men along with stories of their lives: One man was said to be dishonest, mean, and vicious; the other was said to be nice enough to invite home to dinner. (Half of the patients heard that one of the men was the bad one, and the other half heard that the other man was.) Twenty days later, the patients with amnesia said they liked the picture of the "nice" man better than that of the "nasty" one.

Relational Learning

LO 13.15 Describe the role of the hippocampus in relational learning ability, citing research from human and animal models.

If patients with amnesia can learn tasks like these, you might ask, why do we say they have *amnesia*? The answer is this: Although the patients can learn to perform these tasks, they do not remember anything about having learned them. They do not remember the experimenters, the room in which the training took place, the apparatus that was used, or any events that occurred during the training. Although H. M. learned to recognize the broken drawings, he denied that he had ever seen them before. Although the patients with amnesia in the study by Johnson et al. learned to like some of the Korean melodies better, they did not recognize that they had heard them before; nor did they remember having seen the pictures of the two men. Although H. M. successfully acquired a classically conditioned eyeblink response, he did not remember the experimenter, the apparatus, or the headband he wore that held the device that delivered a puff of air to his eye.

DECLARATIVE AND NONDECLARATIVE MEMORIES

The distinction between what people with anterograde amnesia can and cannot learn is important because it reflects the basic organization of the learning process. There are at least two major categories of memories. As you read in the beginning of this chapter, people have conscious awareness of declarative memories that include details that can be spoken about or described. People cannot describe their nondeclarative memories, which can include some stimulus-response and motor memories.

In the experiment by Sidman et al., (1968), although H. M. learned to make the correct response (press a panel with a picture of a circle on it), he was unable to recall having done so. In fact, once H. M. had learned the task, the experimenters interrupted him, had him count (to distract him for a little while), and then asked him to say what he was supposed to do. He seemed puzzled by the question; he had absolutely no idea. But when they turned on the stimuli again, he immediately made the correct response. Although the patients with amnesia in Reber and Squire's study (1998) learned the sequence of button presses, they too had no declarative memory of the experience; in fact, they thought that the movement of the asterisk was random.

Patient E. P. (who you read about earlier in this chapter) developed anterograde amnesia when he was stricken with a case of viral encephalitis that destroyed much of his medial temporal lobe. Bayley et al., (2005) taught E. P. to point to a particular member of each of a series of eight pairs of objects. He eventually learned to do so, but he had no declarative memory of which objects were correct. When asked why he chose a particular object, he said, "It just seems that's the one. It's here (pointing to head) somehow or another and the hand goes for it. . . . I can't say memory. I just feel this is the one. . . . It's just jumping out at me. 'I'm the one. I'm the one' " (Bayley et al., 2005, p. 551). E. P. learned a nondeclarative stimulus-response task without at the same time acquiring any declarative memories about what he had learned.

SPATIAL MEMORY The discovery that hippocampal lesions produced deficits in spatial memory in humans stimulated interest in the exact role that this structure plays in the learning process. To pursue this interest, researchers have studied individuals with hippocampal damage and developed tasks that require relational learning. Laboratory animals with hippocampal lesions show memory deficits on such tasks, just as humans do.

Research with Humans You read that patient H. M. was unable to find his way around his environment after moving from his preamnesia home. Although spatial information need not be declared (we can demonstrate our topographical memories by successfully getting from place to place), people with anterograde amnesia are unable to consolidate information about the location of rooms, corridors, buildings, roads, and other important items in their environment. (See Figure 13.24.)

Bilateral medial temporal lobe lesions produce the most profound impairment in spatial memory, but significant deficits can be produced by damage that is limited to the right hemisphere. For example, Luzzi et al., (2000) reported the case of a man with a lesion of the right parahippocampal gyrus who lost his ability to find his way around a new environment. The only way he could find his room was by counting doorways from the end of the hall or by seeing a red napkin that was located on top of his bedside table.

Functional-imaging studies have shown that the right hippocampal formation becomes active when a person is remembering or performing a navigational task. For example, Maguire et al., (1997) had London taxi drivers describe the routes they would take in driving from one location to another. Functional imaging that was performed during their description of the route showed activation of the right hippocampal formation. London taxi drivers undergo extensive training to learn how to navigate efficiently in that city; in fact, this training takes about two years, and the drivers receive their license only after passing a rigorous set of tests. We would expect that this topographical learning would produce some changes in various parts of their brains, including their hippocampal formation. In fact, Maguire et al., (2000) found that the volume of the posterior hippocampus of London taxi drivers was larger than that of control participants. Furthermore, the longer an individual taxi driver had spent in this occupation, the larger was the volume of the right posterior hippocampus.

In a follow up study, Maguire et al., (2006) used a virtual-reality driving simulator to assess the navigational ability of

Figure 13.24 Bilateral Amygdala Damage in Patient H. M.

Note the lesions in H. M.'s temporal lobe and hippocampus that differ from a typical brain.

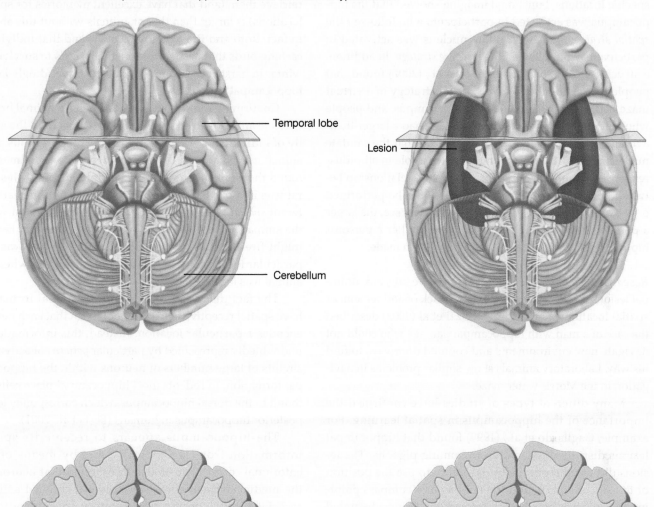

Temporal lobe

Lesion

Cerebellum

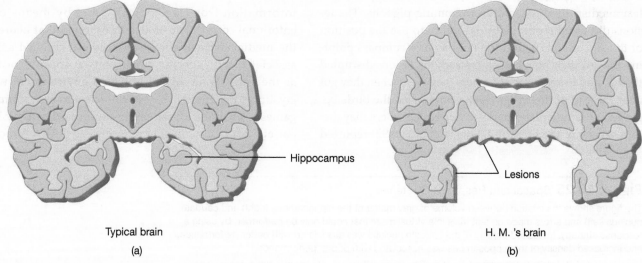

Hippocampus

Lesions

Typical brain

(a)

H. M. 's brain

(b)

patient T. T., who had sustained bilateral hippocampal damage due to encephalitis later in life. Prior to his illness, he had been a London cab driver for nearly 40 years. Despite hippocampal damage, T. T. was able to navigate main city streets using memory that had been consolidated decades before his hippocampal damage occurred. His ability to navigate side streets and non-main routes however was impaired. The researchers concluded that the hippocampus is required for more detailed levels of spatial navigation (Maguire et al., 2006).

As we will see later in this chapter, the dorsal hippocampus of rats (which corresponds to the posterior hippocampus of humans) contains *place cells*—neurons that are directly involved in navigation in space. You will read more about place cells in animal models later in this section.

Iaria et al., (2003) trained participants to navigate through a computerized virtual-reality maze that permitted them to learn the maze either through distant spatial cues or through a series of turns. About half of the participants spontaneously used spatial cues, and the other half spontaneously learned to make a sequence of specific turns at specific locations. Functional imaging showed that the hippocampus was activated in participants who followed the *spatial strategy* and the caudate nucleus was activated in participants who followed the *response strategy*. In addition, a structural MRI study by Bohbot et al., (2007) found that people who tended to follow a spatial strategy in a virtual maze had a larger-than-average hippocampus, and people who tended to follow a response strategy had a larger-than-average caudate nucleus. (You will recall that the caudate nucleus, part of the basal ganglia, plays a role in stimulus-response learning.) Figure 13.25 shows the relationship between performance on test trials that could be performed only by using a response strategy. As you can see, the larger a person's caudate nucleus is (and the smaller a person's hippocampus is), the fewer errors that person made.

Research with Laboratory Animals As we saw, hippocampal lesions disrupt the ability to keep track of and remember spatial locations. For example, Luzzi et al (2002) described the case of a man with hippocampal damage who could not navigate new environments and counted doorways to find his way. Laboratory animals show similar problems in navigation in the Morris water maze.

Many different types of studies have confirmed the importance of the hippocampus in spatial learning. For example, Gagliardo et al., (1999) found that hippocampal lesions disrupted navigation in homing pigeons. The lesions did not disrupt the birds' ability to use the position of the sun at a particular time of day as a compass pointing toward their home roost. Instead, the lesions disrupted their ability to keep track of where they were when they got near the end of their flight—at a time when the birds begin to use familiar landmarks to determine where they are. In a review of the literature, Sherry et al., (1992) reported

that the hippocampal formation of species of birds and rodents that normally store seeds in hidden caches and later retrieve them (and that have excellent memories for spatial locations) is larger than that of animals without this ability. In fact, Roth and Pravosudov (2009) found that individual caching birds that needed to store more seeds to survive the winter in harsher environments had correspondingly larger hippocampal regions.

Confirming the existence of place cells in animal brains, O'Keefe and Dostrovsky (1971), initially recorded the activity of individual pyramidal cells in the hippocampus as an animal moved around the environment. The experimenters found that some neurons fired at a high rate only when the rat was in a particular location. Different neurons had different *spatial receptive fields;* that is, they responded when the animals were in different locations. A particular neuron might fire 20 times per second when the animal was in a particular location but only a few times per hour when the animal was located elsewhere.

The fact that neurons in the hippocampal formation have spatial receptive fields does not mean that each neuron encodes a particular location. Instead, this information is undoubtedly represented by particular *patterns* of activity in circuits of large numbers of neurons within the hippocampal formation. In rodents most hippocampal place cells are found in the dorsal hippocampus, which corresponds to the posterior hippocampus in humans (Best et al., 2001).

The hippocampus appears to receive its spatial information from the parietal lobes by means of the entorhinal cortex. Sato et al., (2006) found that neurons in the medial parietal cortex of monkeys showed activity associated with specific movements at specific locations as the animals navigated a virtual environment with a joystick. (Yes, monkeys, too, can learn to play computer games.) When the investigators suppressed activity in the parietal cortex by infusing muscimol (a GABA A receptor

---

Figure 13.25 Spatial and Response Strategies

The figure shows the relation between volume of gray matter of the hippocampus (right) and caudate nucleus (left) and errors made on test trials in a virtual maze that could only be performed by using a response strategy. Increased density of the caudate nucleus was associated with better performance, and increased density of the hippocampus was associated with poorer performance.

(From Bohbot, V. D., Lerch, J., Thorndycraft, B., et al., Gray matter differences correlate with spontaneous strategies in a human virtual navigation task, *Journal of Neuroscience*, 2007, *27*, 10078–10083. Reprinted with permission.)

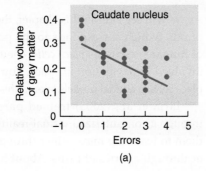

(a)

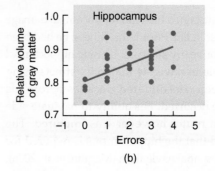

(b)

agonist), the animals became lost. Quirk et al., (1992) found that neurons in the entorhinal cortex have spatial receptive fields, although these fields are not nearly as clear-cut as those of hippocampal pyramidal cells. Damage to the entorhinal cortex disrupts the spatial receptive fields of place cells in the hippocampus and impairs the animals' ability to navigate in spatial tasks (Miller and Best, 1980).

Since the discovery of place cells, researchers have found that the hippocampal region also contains *grid cells,* *head direction cells,* and *border cells,* all found in the entorhinal cortex. Grid cells show an evenly spaced, crystal-like coverage of the entire environment in which the animal is located (Derdikman and Moser, 2010). Border cells fire when the animal is near one or more boundaries of the environment, such as the walls of box. Figure 13.26 shows the firing rate of a border cell in a square chamber and in the same chamber that was elongated in a horizontal or vertical direction (Solstad et al., 2008). As you can see, this cell continued to fire along the right-hand wall.

Head direction cells simply fire when the animal's head is facing a particular direction with respect to the distant cues in a particular environment. As the animal turns, different

Figure 13.26 Activity of a Hippocampal Border Cell

The firing rate of this cell is indicated by color; "hottest" colors represent the highest rate of firing. As you can see, the cell fired preferentially when the animal was located along the right border of the rectangular enclosure, regardless of the dimensions of the enclosure.

(From Solstad, T., Boccara, C. N., Kropff, E., et al., Representation of geometric borders in the entorhinal cortex, *Science*, 2008, *322*, 1865–1868. Reprinted with permission.)

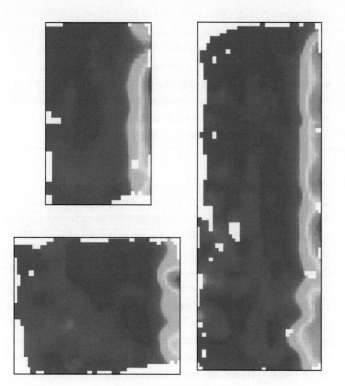

cells will fire according to the direction in which the animal is looking. These cells do not reflect the animal's location in the environment, only the direction of its head. The information provided by all of these cells reflects the animal's location and head direction, and this information is available to other regions of the brain. In fact, the information is available to investigators who implant multiarray microelectrodes in an animal's brain. Once a computer has correlated the activity of these cells with an animal's location as it explores an environment, it can use the activity of the neurons to draw a plot showing the animal's movements.

The activity of circuits of hippocampal place cells provides information about more than space. Wood et al., (2000) trained rats on a spatial alternation task in a T-maze. The task required the rats to enter the left and the right arms on alternate trials; when they did so, they received a piece of food in goal boxes located at the ends of the arms of the T. Corridors connecting the goal boxes led back to the stem of the T-maze, where the next trial began. (See Figure 13.27.)

Wood et al., recorded from neurons in CA1 of the hippocampus using multielectrode implants and, as expected, found that different cells fired when the rat was in different parts of the maze. However, two-thirds of the neurons fired differentially in the stem of the T on left-turn and right-turn trials. In other words, the cells not only encoded the rat's location in the maze but also signaled whether the rat was going to turn right or turn left after it got to the choice point. Thus, the activity of CA1 neurons encodes both the current location and the intended destination.

Figure 13.27 Apparatus Used by Wood et al.

The rats were trained to turn right and turn left at the end of the stem of the T-maze on alternate trials. The firing patterns of hippocampal place cells with spatial receptive fields in the stem of the maze were different on trials during which the animals turned left or right.

(Adapted from Wood, E. R., Dudchenko, P. A., Robitsek, R. J., and Eichenbaum, H., Hippocampal neurons encode information about different types of memory episodes occurring in the same location, *Neuron*, 2000, *27*, 623–633.)

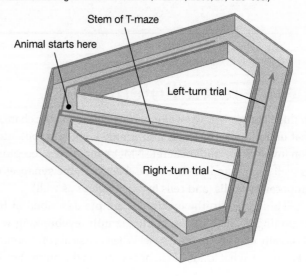

Section Review

Amnesia

LO 13.11 Compare the role of the hippocampus in consolidation and retrieval of memories.

The hippocampal formation receives information from other regions of the brain, processes this information, and then, through its efferent connections with these regions, modifies the memories that are being consolidated there, linking them together in ways that will permit us to remember the relationships among the elements of the memories. The hippocampal formation transfers memories into permanent storage in other areas of the brain. Before this transfer is complete, the hippocampal formation is required for the retrieval of these memories. Later, retrieval of these memories can be accomplished even if the hippocampal formation has been damaged.

LO13.12 Describe the stimulus-response learning ability of patients with hippocampal damage.

Patients with hippocampal damage display stimulus-response learning, but do not have an awareness that the learning has occurred. The hippocampus is not required for stimulus-response learning.

LO 13.13 Describe the motor learning ability of patients with hippocampal damage.

Patients with hippocampal damage display motor learning. They do not have awareness that learning has occurred. The hippocampus is not required for motor learning.

LO 13.14 Describe the perceptual learning ability of patients with hippocampal damage.

Patients with hippocampal damage display perceptual learning. They do not have awareness that learning has occurred. The hippocampus is not required for perceptual learning.

LO 13.15 Describe the role of the hippocampus in relational learning ability citing research from human and animal models.

The hippocampal formation—especially the right posterior hippocampus—is involved in spatial memory. Functional-imaging studies have shown that performance of spatial tasks increases activity in this region. Studies with laboratory animals indicate that damage to the hippocampal formation disrupts the ability to learn spatial relations. The hippocampal formation contains place cells—neurons that respond when the animal is in a particular location, which implies that the hippocampus contains neural networks that keep track of the relationships among stimuli in the environment that define the animal's location. Neurons in the hippocampal formation reflect where an animal "thinks" it is. Topographical information reaches field CA1 of hippocampus from the parietal lobe by means of the entorhinal cortex. Place cells encode more than space; they can include information about the response that the animal will perform next. Besides place cells, the hippocampal region also contains grid cells, head-direction cells, and border cells, which play a role in spatial perception and memory.

Thought Question

Imagine that you have been asked to evaluate the memory loss of a patient that has experienced a bilateral stroke that damaged both temporal lobes. Similar to H. M. and E. P., this patient is experiencing anterograde amnesia. To assess the forms of memory that are affected, you must design tasks that will reveal the extent of stimulus-response, motor, perceptual, and relational memory loss in this patient. First, describe the tasks you will use and explain what aspects of memory they will assess. Next, explain which brain regions are responsible for the type of memory you will assess. Finally, make predictions about how your patient will complete the tasks and if they will report recognizing the task or experimenter.

Long-Term Potentiation

In this final section, we will investigate the synaptic changes that underlie simple forms of learning. Long-term potentiation involves the glutamatergic NMDA and AMPA receptors, as well as pre- and postsynaptic changes in the synapses of hippocampal cells (and cells in other regions as well).

Think back to the eyeblink example described at the beginning of the chapter. In the example, eyeblinking was classically conditioned to a tone. When classical conditioning takes place, what kinds of changes occur in the brain? Before

conditioning, neurons that process auditory information are activated by the tone stimulus, but these neurons do not typically send strong EPSPs to neurons involved in eyeblink reflexes. The tone does not produce an eyeblink response. Neurons that process sensory information like puffs of air *do* send strong EPSPs to the neurons involved in the eyeblink response. Puffs of air activate the puff neurons that synapse onto the eyeblink neurons. This is a beneficial reflex and helps protect the eye in windy conditions or from moving objects.

After playing a tone and quickly following it with a puff of air several times, the tone neurons and the puff neurons become active at the same time. The **Hebb rule** says that if a synapse (in this case, involving the tone neurons) repeatedly becomes active at about the same time that the postsynaptic neurons fires (the eyeblink neurons), changes will take place in the structure or chemistry of the synapse that will strengthen the synapse and make the production of EPSPs more likely. Another way of re-stating the Hebb rule is "neurons that fire together, wire together." In this example, after several pairings of the tone and puff of air, activity in the tone neurons becomes strong enough to produce an EPSP on the eyeblink neurons and cause the eyeblink to occur, even without the help of the puff neurons. Learning has occurred.

How would the Hebb rule apply to our neural circuit? If the 1,000-Hz tone is presented first, then weak synapse T (for "tone") becomes active. If the puff is presented immediately afterward, then strong synapse P becomes active and makes the motor neuron fire. The act of firing then strengthens any synapse with the motor neuron *that has just been active*. This means that after several pairings of the two stimuli and after several increments of strengthening, synapse T becomes strong enough to cause the motor neuron to fire by itself. Learning has occurred. (Look at Figure 13.28.)

When Hebb formulated his rule, he was unable to determine whether it was true or false. Now, finally, enough progress has been made in laboratory techniques that the strength of individual synapses can be determined, and investigators are studying the physiological bases of learning.

On theoretical considerations alone, it would appear that learning must involve synaptic plasticity: changes in the structure or biochemistry of synapses that alter their effects on postsynaptic neurons. Recent years have seen an explosion of research on this topic, largely stimulated by the development of methods that permit researchers to observe structural and biochemical changes in microscopically small structures: the presynaptic and postsynaptic components of synapses.

Figure 13.28 A Simple Neural Model of Classical Conditioning

When the 1,000-Hz tone is presented just before the puff of air to the eye, synapse T is strengthened.

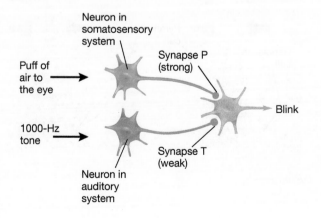

Induction of Long-Term Potentiation

LO 13.16 **Identify the events required for LTP to occur.**

Electrical stimulation of circuits within the hippocampal formation can lead to long-term synaptic changes that seem to be among those responsible for learning. Lømo (1966) discovered that intense electrical stimulation of axons leading from the entorhinal cortex to the dentate gyrus increased (or, strengthened) the magnitude of excitatory postsynaptic potentials in the postsynaptic neurons; this increase has come to be called **long-term potentiation (LTP)**. It is important to note that this increase in EPSPs is relatively long-term, lasting for months at a time (Bliss and Lømo, 1973).

The primary input to the hippocampal formation comes from the *entorhinal cortex*. The axons of neurons in the entorhinal cortex pass through the *perforant path* and form synapses with the granule cells of the *dentate gyrus*. To study this pathway experimentally, a stimulating electrode is placed in the perforant path, and a recording electrode is placed in the dentate gyrus, near the granule cells. (See Figure 13.29a.)

First, a single pulse of electrical stimulation is delivered to the perforant path, and then the resulting population EPSP is recorded in the dentate gyrus. The **population EPSP** is an extracellular measurement of the EPSPs produced by the synapses of the perforant path axons with the dentate granule cells. The size of the first population EPSP indicates the strength of the synaptic connections *before* long-term potentiation has taken place. Long-term potentiation can be induced by stimulating the axons in the perforant path with a burst of approximately 100 pulses of electrical stimulation, delivered within a few seconds. Evidence that long-term potentiation has occurred is obtained by periodically delivering single pulses to the perforant path and recording the response in the dentate gyrus. If the response is greater than it was before the burst of pulses was delivered, long-term potentiation has occurred. (See Figure 13.29b.)

A series of pulses delivered at a high rate all in one burst (i.e., 100-Hz stimulation) will produce LTP, but the same number of pulses given at a slow rate will not. A rapid rate of stimulation causes the EPSPs to summate, because each successive EPSP occurs before the previous one has dissipated. This means that rapid stimulation depolarizes the postsynaptic membrane much more than slow stimulation does. (See Figure 13.30.)

Role of NMDA Receptors

LO 13.17 **Compare the relationship between NMDA and AMPA receptors in LTP.**

Several experiments have shown that synaptic strengthening occurs when molecules of the neurotransmitter bind with postsynaptic receptors located in a dendritic spine that is already depolarized. Kelso et al., (1986) found that if they used

Figure 13.29 The Hippocampal Formation and Long-Term Potentiation

(a) This schematic diagram shows the connections of the components of the hippocampal formation and the procedure for producing long-term potentiation. (b) Population EPSPs were recorded from the dentate gyrus before and after electrical stimulation that led to long-term potentiation.

(From Berger, T. W., Long-term potentiation of hippocampal synaptic transmission affects rate of behavioral learning, *Science*, 1984, *224*, 627–630. Copyright 1984 by the American Association for the Advancement of Science. Reprinted with permission.)

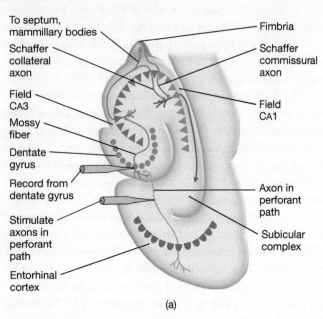

(a)

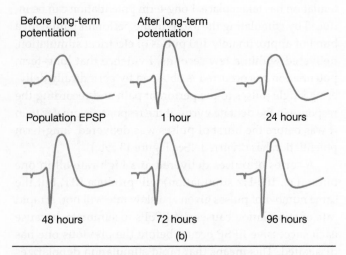

(b)

Figure 13.30 The Role of Summation in Long-Term Potentiation

If axons are stimulated rapidly, the EPSPs produced by the terminal buttons will summate, and the postsynaptic membrane will depolarize enough for long-term potentiation to occur. If axons are stimulated slowly, the EPSPs will not summate, and long-term potentiation will not occur.

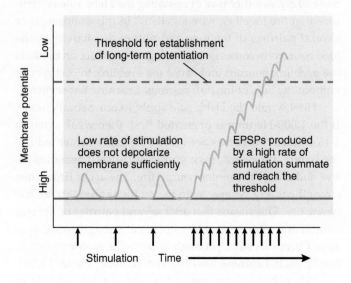

Figure 13.31 LTP Occurs When the Pre- and Postsynaptic Cells Are Depolarized at the Same Time

Synaptic strengthening occurs when synapses are active while the membrane of the postsynaptic cell is depolarized.

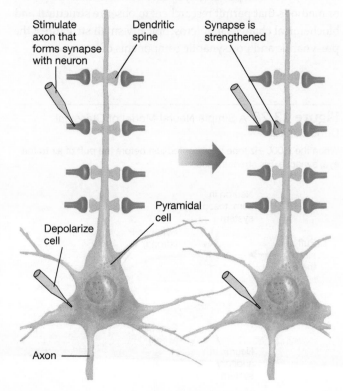

a microelectrode to artificially depolarize a neuron in field CA1 and then stimulated the axons that formed synapses with this neuron, the synapses became stronger. However, if the stimulation of the synapses and the depolarization of the neuron occurred at different times, no effect was seen; therefore, the two events had to occur together. (See Figure 13.31.)

Experiments such as the one described above indicate that LTP requires two events: activation of synapses and depolarization of the postsynaptic neuron. The explanation for this phenomenon, at least in many parts of the brain, lies in the characteristics of a very special type of glutamate receptor: the NMDA receptor. The **NMDA receptor** has some unusual properties. It is found in the hippocampal formation, especially in field CA1. It gets its name from a drug that specifically activates it: N-methyl-D-aspartate. The NMDA receptor controls a calcium ion channel. This channel is normally blocked by a magnesium ion (Mg^{2+}), which prevents calcium ions from entering the cell even when the receptor is stimulated by glutamate. But if the postsynaptic membrane is depolarized, the Mg^{2+} is ejected from the ion channel, and the channel is free to admit Ca^{2+} ions. Thus, calcium ions enter the cells through the channels controlled by NMDA receptors only when glutamate is present *and* when the postsynaptic membrane is depolarized. This means that the ion channel controlled by the NMDA receptor is a neurotransmitter- *and* voltage-dependent ion channel. (See Figure 13.32.)

Cell biologists have discovered that the calcium ion is used by many cells as a second messenger that activates various enzymes and triggers biochemical processes. The entry of calcium ions through the ion channels controlled by NMDA receptors is an essential step in long-term potentiation (Lynch et al., 1984). **AP5** (2-amino-5-phosphonopentanoate), a drug that blocks NMDA receptors, prevents calcium ions from entering the dendritic spines and thus blocks the establishment of LTP (Brown et al., 1989). These results indicate that the activation of NMDA receptors is necessary for the first step in the process of events that establishes LTP: the entry of calcium ions into dendritic spines.

In Chapter 2 you learned that only axons are capable of producing action potentials. Actually, they can also occur in dendrites of some types of pyramidal cells, including those

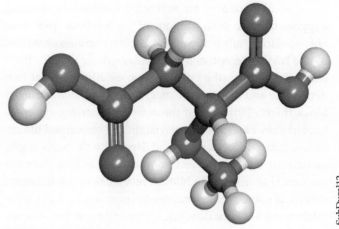

The structure of NMDA.

SubDural12

in field CA1 of the hippocampal formation. The threshold of excitation for **dendritic spikes** (as these action potentials are called) is rather high. As far as we know, they occur only when an action potential is triggered in the axon of the pyramidal cell. The backwash of depolarization across the cell body triggers a dendritic spike, which is propagated up the trunk of the dendrite. This means that whenever the axon of a pyramidal cell fires, all of its dendritic spines become depolarized for a brief time. If dendritic spikes are blocked by the administration of a toxin (tetrodotoxin), LTP does not occur (Magee and Johnston, 1997).

Figure 13.32 The NMDA Receptor

The NMDA receptor is a neurotransmitter- and voltage-dependent ion channel. (a) When the postsynaptic membrane is at the resting potential, Mg^{2+} blocks the ion channel, preventing Ca^{2+} from entering. (b) When the membrane is depolarized, the magnesium ion is evicted. Thus, the attachment of glutamate to the binding site causes the ion channel to open, allowing calcium ions to enter the dendritic spine.

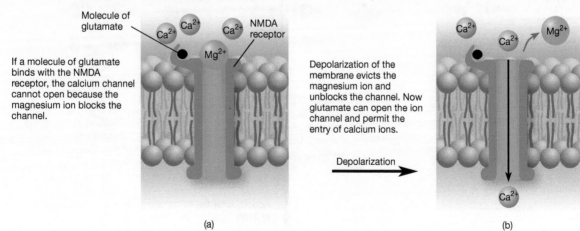

(a) (b)

If weak synapses are active by themselves, nothing happens because the membrane of the dendritic spine does not depolarize sufficiently for the calcium channels controlled by the NMDA receptors to open. (Remember that, for these channels to open, the postsynaptic membrane must first depolarize and displace the magnesium ions that normally block them.) However, if the activity of strong synapses located elsewhere on the postsynaptic cell has caused the cell to fire, then a dendritic spike will depolarize the postsynaptic membrane enough to eject the magnesium ions from the calcium channels of the NMDA receptors in the dendritic spines. If some weak synapses become active right then, calcium will enter the dendritic spines and cause the synapses to become strengthened. Thus, the special properties of NMDA receptors allow LTP to occur. (See Figure 13.33.)

Role of AMPA Receptors

LO 13.18 Describe how AMPA receptors contribute to LTP.

What is responsible for the increases in synaptic strength that occur during long-term potentiation? Dendritic spines on CA1 pyramidal cells contain two types of glutamate receptors: NMDA receptors and **AMPA receptors.** Research indicates that strengthening of an individual synapse is accomplished by insertion of additional AMPA receptors into the postsynaptic membrane of the dendritic spine (Shi et al., 1999). AMPA receptors control sodium channels; thus, when they are activated by glutamate, they produce EPSPs in the membrane of the dendritic spine. Therefore, with more AMPA receptors present, the release of glutamate by the presynaptic terminal button causes a larger excitatory postsynaptic potential. In other words, the synapse becomes stronger.

Where do these new AMPA receptors come from? Makino and Malinow (2009) used a two-photon laser scanning microscope to watch the movement of AMPA receptors in dendrites of CA1 pyramidal neurons in hippocampal slices. They found that the establishment of LTP first caused movement of AMPA receptors into the postsynaptic membranes of dendritic spines from adjacent nonsynaptic regions of the dendrites. Several minutes later, AMPA receptors were carried from the interior of the cell to the dendritic shaft, where they replaced the AMPA receptors that had been inserted in the postsynaptic membrane of the spines. (See Figure 13.34.)

How does the entry of calcium ions into the dendritic spine cause AMPA receptors to move into the postsynaptic membrane? This process appears to begin with the

---

Figure 13.33 Associative Long-Term Potentiation

If the activity of strong synapses is sufficient to trigger an action potential in the neuron, the dendritic spike will depolarize the membrane of dendritic spines, priming NMDA receptors so that any weak synapses active at that time will become strengthened.

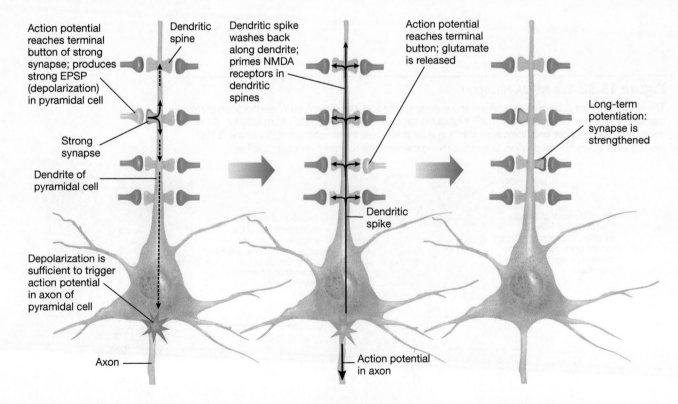

Figure 13.34 Synaptic Strengthening

(a) When the conditions for long-term potentiation are met, Ca²⁺ ions enter the dendritic spine through NMDA receptors. The calcium ions activate enzymes in the spine. (b) The activated enzymes cause AMPA receptors to move into the spine. (c) An increased number of AMPA receptors in the postsynaptic membrane strengthens the synapse.

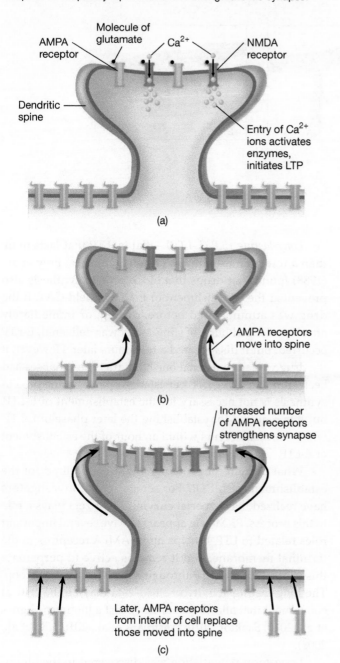

activation of several enzymes, including **CaM-KII** (type II calcium-calmodulin kinase), an enzyme found in dendritic spines. CaM-KII is a *calcium-dependent* enzyme, which is inactive until a calcium ion binds with it and activates it. Many studies have shown that CaM-KII plays a critical role in long-term potentiation. For example, Silva et al., (1992) found that LTP could not be established in mouse hippocampal tissue with a targeted mutation that prevented the production of CaM-KII. Shen and Meyer (1999) found that after LTP was established in hippocampal neurons, CaM-KII molecules accumulated in the postsynaptic densities of dendritic spines. Lledo et al., (1995) found that injection of activated CaM-KII directly into CA1 pyramidal cells strengthened synaptic transmission in those cells.

Role of Synaptic Changes

LO 13.19 List the changes in presynaptic neurons, postsynaptic neurons, and protein synthesis that accompany LTP.

Two other changes that accompany LTP are alteration of synaptic structure and production of new proteins.

POSTSYNAPTIC CHANGES Many studies have found that the establishment of LTP also includes changes in the size and shape of dendritic spines. For example, Bourne and Harris (2007) suggest that LTP causes the enlargement of thin spines into fatter, mushroom-shaped spines. Nägerl et al., (2007) found that the establishment of LTP even causes the growth of *new* dendritic spines. After about 15 to 19 hours, the new spines formed synaptic connections with terminals of nearby axons. (See Figure 13.35.)

PRESYNAPTIC CHANGES Researchers believe that LTP may also involve *presynaptic* changes in existing synapses, such as an increase in the amount of glutamate that is released by the terminal button. After all, alterations in synapses presumably require coordinated changes in both presynaptic and postsynaptic elements. But how could a process that begins postsynaptically, in the dendritic spines, cause presynaptic changes? A possible answer comes from the discovery that a gas neurotransmitter, nitric oxide, can

Figure 13.35 Growth of Dendritic Spines after LTP

Two-photon microscopic images show a segment of a dendrite of a CA1 pyramidal neuron before and after electrical stimulation that established long-term potentiation. Numbers in each box indicate the time before or after the stimulation.

(From Nägerl, U. V., Köstinger, G., Anderson, J. C., Martin, K. A. C., and Bonhoeffer, T., Protracted synaptogenesis after activity-dependent spinogenesis in hippocampal neurons, *Journal of Neuroscience*, 2007, 27, 8149–8156. Reprinted with permission.)

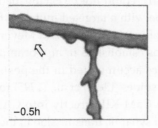

−0.5h

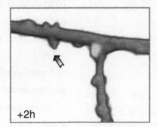

+2h

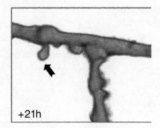

+21h

communicate retrograde messages from one cell to another. As we saw in Chapter 4, nitric oxide (NO) is a soluble gas produced from the amino acid arginine by the activity of an enzyme known as **nitric oxide synthase.** Once produced, NO lasts only a short time before it is destroyed. Thus, if it were produced in dendritic spines in the hippocampal formation, it could diffuse only as far as the nearby terminal buttons, where it might produce changes related to the induction of LTP.

Several experiments suggest that NO is important in the formation of LTP. Endoh et al., (1994) found that a calcium-activated NO synthase is found in several regions of the brain, including the dentate gyrus and fields CA1 and CA3 of the hippocampus. Although there is good evidence that NO is one of the signals the dendritic spine uses to communicate with the terminal button, most investigators believe that postsynaptic changes play a more important role in the establishment of LTP. There must be other signals as well.

PROTEIN SYNTHESIS For several years after its discovery, researchers believed that LTP involved a single process. Since then it has become clear that LTP consists of several stages. *Early LTP (E-LTP)* involves the process we have been describing so far:

1. Presynaptic membrane depolarization

2. Presynaptic release of glutamate

3. Postsynaptic activation of ligand- and voltage-gated NMDA receptors

4. Entry of calcium ions into the postsynaptic cell, and subsequent activation of enzymes such as CaM-KII

5. Movement of AMPA receptors into the postsynaptic membrane

6. Postsynaptic NO-synthase increases release of NO, which retrogradely travels to presynaptic terminal to increases release of glutamate

Long-lasting LTP (L-LTP)—that is, LTP that lasts more than a few hours—requires protein synthesis. Frey et al., (1988) found that drugs that block protein synthesis also prevented the establishment of L-LTP in field CA1. If the drug was administered before, during, or immediately after a prolonged burst of stimulation was delivered, E-LTP occurred, but it disappeared a few hours later. However, if the drug was administered one hour after the synapses had been stimulated, the LTP persisted. Apparently, the protein synthesis is not necessary for the establishment of E-LTP, but it is required for establishing the later phase of L-LTP, which normally occurs within an hour of the establishment of E-LTP.

What protein (or proteins) might be required for the establishment of L-LTP? For several years, investigators have realized that a special enzyme, PKM-zeta plays a role in this process. PKM-zeta appears to have several important roles related to LTP. It helps move AMPA receptors to the terminal membrane, and it remains active to perpetuate this contribution to LTP through a positive feedback loop. The long-lasting activity of PKM-zeta may be the critical component that allows memories to last a lifetime (Migues et al., 2010; Sacktor, 2010; Westmark et al., 2010; Yao et al., 2008).

Long-term potentiation was discovered in the hippocampal formation and has been studied more in this region than in others, but it also occurs in other regions of the brain as well. In addition to long-term potentiation, a phenomenon called *long-term depression* (LTD) has been documented. In contrast to LTP, LTD can be induced by *low*-frequency stimulation and results in *decreased* synaptic strength and *fewer* AMPA receptors in the postsynaptic membrane. Neural circuits involved in creating memories are established by strengthening some synapses through LTP and weakening others through LTD.

Section Review

Long-Term Potentiation

LO 13.16 Identify the events required for LTP to occur.
The perforant pathway must be depolarized either by exposure to stimuli in the environment or by delivery of a burst of pulses.

LO 13.17 Compare the relationship between NMDA and AMPA receptors in LTP.
NMDA and AMPA receptors are present on the postsynaptic membrane and are required to establish LTP. NMDA and AMPA receptors are both ionotropic receptors that respond to glutamate and are found in the hippocampus. NMDA receptors are blocked by an ion of magnesium at rest, and require depolarization to remove the Mg^{2+} ion. AMPA receptors contribute this local depolarization to facilitate removal of the Mg^{2+} ion. Once open, NMDA receptors allow Ca^{2+} ions to enter the cell, triggering intracellular events responsible for LTP and the recruitment of additional AMPA receptors to the terminal membrane.

LO 13.18 Describe how AMPA receptors contribute to LTP.
AMPA receptors are ionotropic receptors present on the postsynaptic membrane and help to depolarize the cell by controlling a sodium ion channel. AMPA receptors are also required for LTP. When glutamate binds to the AMPA receptor, the resulting depolarization removes the Mg^{2+} ion from the NMDA receptors, allowing Ca^{2+} to enter the cell. A result of calcium signaling is the insertion of additional AMPA receptors in the postsynaptic membrane, strengthening the depolarization of the membrane. This enhanced depolarization is responsible for strengthening the synapses involved in LTP.

LO 13.19 List the changes in presynaptic neurons, postsynaptic neurons, and protein synthesis that accompany LTP.
LTP may involve presynaptic changes in existing synapses, such as an increase in the amount of glutamate that is released by the terminal button. Presynaptic changes may be signaled from the postsynaptic cell via retrograde messengers. The establishment of LTP includes changes in the size and shape of postsynaptic dendritic spines into fatter, mushroom-shaped spines. Establishing LTP can cause the growth of new dendritic spines. Long-lasting LTP requires protein synthesis.

Thought Question

Have you heard of clicker training? It's a form of training that pairs a unique sound (a "click" from a small noise maker) with a treat or other positive reinforcer and is used to train animals. After several pairings with food (a primary reinforcer), eventually the "click" itself becomes reinforcing, and it can be used to reinforce the behavior that precedes the click. Explain what has happened in the hippocampus of the animal to induce LTP in the circuits associating the reinforcer with a behavior. Describe the steps of LTP and explain how the brain is changed in this form of learning.

Chapter Review Questions

1. Describe the four basic forms of learning: perceptual learning, stimulus-response learning, motor learning, and relational learning.

2. Discuss the role of the dopaminergic circuit in reinforcement of operant conditioning.

3. Identify the regions of the brain involved in recognition of visual stimuli and retention of perceptual information.

4. Discuss the physiology of the classically conditioned emotional response to aversive stimuli.

5. Describe the role of the basal ganglia in operant conditioning.

6. Discuss how the reinforcement system may detect reinforcing stimuli and strengthen synaptic connections.

7. Discuss the role of the hippocampal formation in episodic, semantic, and spatial memories and the role of the prefrontal cortex in evaluating the accuracy of memories.

8. Describe the neuro-chemical mechanism of long-term potentiation and its significance in synaptic transmission.

Chapter 14
Human Communication

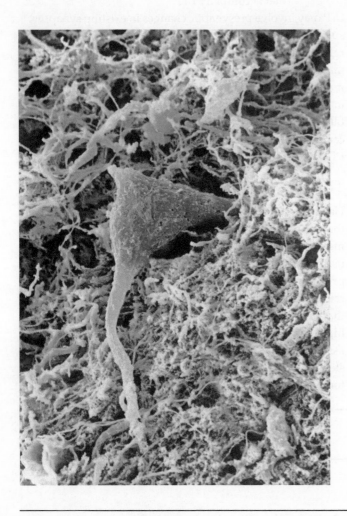

Chapter Outline

Learning Objectives

LO 14.1 Compare the language-related functions of the left and right hemispheres, and discuss the prevalence of these functions in the opposite hemisphere.

LO 14.2 List some of the factors involved in language production, and identify corresponding brain regions.

LO 14.3 Describe the factors involved in language comprehension, and identify corresponding brain regions.

LO 14.4 Describe evidence for common and language-specific brain regions for bilingual language processing.

LO 14.5 Identify brain structures and functions involved in prosody.

LO 14.6 Identify the brain regions involved in recognizing people's voices.

LO 14.7 Describe the symptoms and neural bases of Broca's aphasia, including agrammatism, anomia, and articulation.

LO 14.8 Describe the symptoms and neural bases of Wernicke's aphasia, including deficits in spoken word recognition, comprehension, and converting thoughts into words.

LO 14.9 Identify the symptoms of conduction aphasia, and describe their contribution to understanding about connections between Broca's and Wernicke's areas.

LO 14.10 Explain the brain processes involved in production and comprehension of American Sign Language.

LO 14.11 Describe the biological basis for stuttering and identify treatment strategies.

LO 14.12 Compare aphasias and disorders of reading and writing.

LO 14.13 Identify the symptoms of pure alexia, and describe the brain structures involved.

LO 14.14 Describe how research on acquired and developmental dyslexia helps us to understand the role of the brain in reading.

LO 14.15 Explain how research on audition, vision, memorization, and motor control helps us to understand the role of the brain in writing.

While driving her car to visit some friends, R. F., a 39-year-old woman, was hit by an intoxicated driver who ignored a stop sign. The left side of R. F.'s skull was fractured, and the bone fragments caused considerable damage to her brain. A neurosurgeon repaired the damage as best he could, but R. F. remained in a coma for several weeks. After considerable recovery, she had difficulty remembering the names of even the most common objects, and she could no longer read.

Although R. F. could not read, she could match words with pictures, which indicated that she could still perceive *words. This fact was made especially apparent one day when she was trying (without success) to read some words that I (N. C.) had typed. Suddenly, she said, "Hey! You spelled this one wrong." I looked at the word and realized that she was right; I had. But although she saw that the word was misspelled, she still could not say what it was, even when she tried very hard to sound it out. That evening I made up a list of 80 pairs of words, one spelled correctly and the other incorrectly. The next day I gave her a pencil and asked her to cross out the misspelled words. She was able to go through the list quickly and easily, correctly identifying 95 percent of the misspelled words. She was able to* read *only five of them.*

*****

The case of R. F. illustrates several intriguing aspects of language processing in the brain. Her ability to perceive words and their spelling, but not sound out words or recognize them as specific words, reveals that different pathways and brain structures are responsible for the various components of speech production and comprehension, including reading and writing.

Language and communication are important aspects of human social behavior. Our cultural evolution has been possible because we can communicate with others to share and record ideas. Language enables our discoveries to be cumulative; knowledge gained by one generation can be passed on to the next.

The basic function of language is seen in its effects on other people. When we communicate with someone, we almost always expect our message to induce the person to engage in some sort of behavior. Sometimes, the behavior is of advantage to us, as when we ask for an object or for help in performing a task. At other times we are asking for a social exchange: some attention and perhaps some conversation.

Although many people use speech as a form of language to communicate, keep in mind that language encompasses written, symbolic, and gestural forms of communication as well. While many examples in this chapter come from research on speech, research is expanding to help us better understand the brain's involvement in different forms of communication as well.

To begin to understand human communication, this chapter is organized with an introduction to the fundamental brain mechanisms of language production and comprehension, which will allow us to better understand the subsequent sections on disorders of language production and comprehension, and reading and writing. The figure below displays Broca's area, Wernicke's area, and the auditory cortex, three regions we will be paying particular attention to in this chapter.

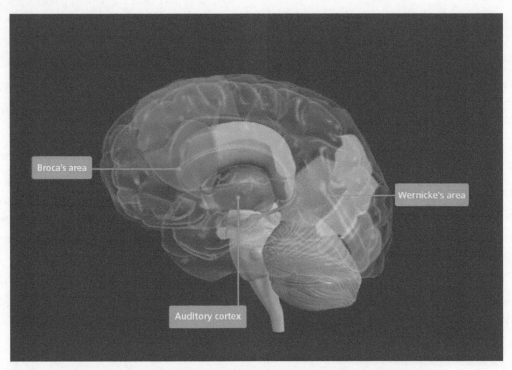

Broca's area, Wernicke's area, and the auditory cortex play vital roles in human communication.

Language Production and Comprehension: Brain Mechanisms

One source of information about the physiology of language has been obtained by observing the effects of brain lesions on people's verbal behavior. Although investigators have studied people who have undergone brain surgery or who have sustained head injuries, brain tumors, or infections, most of the observations have been made on people who have suffered strokes, or **cerebrovascular accidents.** The most common type of cerebrovascular accident is caused by obstruction of a blood vessel. The interruption in blood flow deprives a region of the brain of its blood supply, which causes cells in that region to die. Cerebrovascular accidents are discussed in greater detail in Chapter 15.

Another source of information about the physiology of language comes from studies using functional-imaging devices. Researchers have used these devices to gather information about language processes from healthy volunteers. In general, these studies have confirmed or complemented what we have learned by studying patients with brain damage.

One category of language disorders that has been studied extensively is **aphasia.** Aphasia is a disturbance in the comprehension or production of language, caused by brain damage. Not all language disturbances are aphasias; to receive a diagnosis of aphasia, a patient must have difficulty comprehending, repeating, or producing meaningful language, and this difficulty must not be caused by sensory or motor deficits or by lack of motivation. For example, inability to speak caused by deafness or paralysis of the speech muscles is not considered to be aphasia. In addition, the deficit must be relatively isolated; that is, the individual must appear to be aware of what is happening in his or her environment and to recognize that others are attempting to communicate.

Two examples of specific aphasias that are discussed in this chapter are Broca's and Wernicke's aphasias. Broca's aphasia is an expressive aphasia resulting from damage to Broca's area in the left frontal lobe. Individuals with Broca's aphasia have difficulty producing language, specifically speech. Damage to this area in individuals who communicate by primarily using American Sign Language (ASL) results in similar deficits in producing language through signs. Wernicke's aphasia is a receptive aphasia caused by damage to Wernicke's area in the left temporal gyrus. (See Figure 14.1.) This aphasia results in speech comprehension deficits. In individuals who primarily communicate using ASL, damage to this area results in deficits in comprehending signs (Campbell et al., 2007).

Lateralization

LO 14.1 **Compare the language-related functions of the left and right hemispheres, and discuss the prevalence of these functions in the opposite hemisphere.**

Much of our knowledge of the brain regions involved in language has been obtained from human volunteers. In the case of language, brain regions are distinguished based on function rather than on neuroanatomical differences. Language is largely a *lateralized* function; most language disturbances occur after damage to the left side of the brain, whether people are left-handed or right-handed. Using an imaging procedure to measure changes in cerebral blood flow while people performed a verbal task, Knecht et al. (2000) assessed the relationship between handedness and lateralization of speech mechanisms in people without any known brain damage. They found that right hemisphere speech dominance was seen in only 4 percent of right-handed people, in 15 percent of ambidextrous people, and in 27 percent of left-handed people. The left hemisphere of approximately 90 percent of the total population is dominant for speech and language functions.

Although the circuits that are *primarily* involved in language comprehension and production are located in one hemisphere (usually the left hemisphere), the opposite hemisphere also plays a role in speech and language. When we hear and understand words and when we talk about or think about our own perceptions or memories, we are using neural circuits besides those directly involved in speech. Thus, these circuits, too, play a role in communication. For example, damage to the right hemisphere makes it difficult for a person to read maps, perceive spatial relations, and recognize complex geometrical forms. People with such damage also have trouble talking about things like maps and complex geometrical forms or understanding what other people have to say about them. The right hemisphere also appears to be involved in organizing a narrative—selecting and assembling the elements of what we want to say (Gardner et al., 1983). As we saw in Chapter 11, the right hemisphere is involved in the expression and recognition of emotion in the tone of voice. And as we shall see in this

Figure 14.1 Language Areas

This figure shows the primary language areas of the brain.

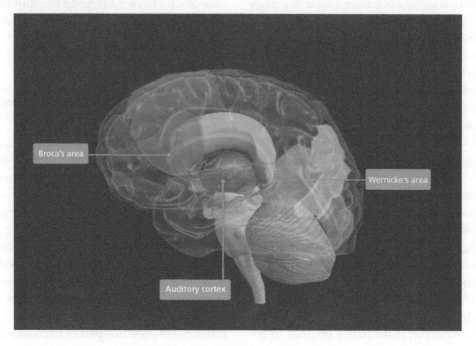

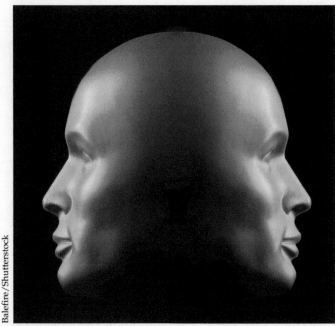

Something that patients may notice after a split-brain operation is that their left hand seems to have a "mind of its own."

chapter, it is also involved in control of *prosody*—the rhythm and stress found in speech. Therefore, both hemispheres of the brain contribute to our language abilities.

The importance of lateralization is also revealed through studies of patients who have undergone a surgical procedure known as the **split-brain operation.** This procedure involves surgically severing the corpus callosum, largely isolating each cerebral hemisphere. The split-brain surgical operation is sometimes used to treat very severe seizure disorders, when neurons in one side of the brain become uncontrollably overactive, and the overactivity is transmitted to the other side of the brain by the corpus callosum.

After the split-brain operation is performed, the two disconnected hemispheres operate independently; their sensory mechanisms, memories, and motor systems can no longer exchange information. Something that patients may notice after the operation is that their left hand seems to have a "mind of its own." For example, patients may find themselves putting down a book held in the left hand, even if they have been reading it with great interest. This conflict occurs because the right hemisphere, which controls the left hand, cannot read and therefore finds holding the book boring. At other times patients may surprise themselves by making gestures (with the left hand) when they had not intended to. A psychologist once reported that a man with a split brain attempted to hit his wife with one hand and protect her with the other.

You might think that disconnecting the brain hemispheres would be devastating, but the effects of the split-brain operation are not immediately obvious to the casual observer. This is because in many circumstances, stimuli are conveyed to both hemispheres simultaneously. For example, looking directly a picture of an apple using both eyes, the visual stimulus is conveyed through both the right and left visual fields and the left hemisphere is able to correctly answer "apple" when the person is asked to identify the picture. Only one hemisphere—as you just read, in most people, the left—controls language production and comprehension. If the information does not reach the left hemisphere, then the person cannot communicate about it. The right hemisphere of a person with a split brain appears able to understand instructions reasonably well, but it is incapable of producing language, therefore, any stimuli that reach the right hemisphere cannot be communicated, or at least not through language. For example, if the picture of an apple is shown only to the left visual field and conveyed only to the right hemisphere, without a language-processing center in the right hemisphere, the person cannot verbally identify the image (or use a non-verbal sign or gesture to identify it). In fact, the person will not even report being aware that the stimulus was seen. However, if the person is allowed to select a matching item from a list or draw a picture of the stimulus with their left hand, they will correctly identify an apple. If you then ask the person why they selected or drew the apple, they will not have a conscious reason for selecting it (consciousness in this sense requires the use of language).

The effects of cutting the corpus callosum reinforce the conclusion that we become conscious of something only if information about it is able to reach the parts of the brain responsible for language in the left hemisphere. If the information does not reach these parts of the brain, then that information does not reach consciousness. We still know very little about the physiology of consciousness, but studies of people who have undergone the split-brain operation are beginning to provide us with some useful insights.

Language Production

LO 14.2 List some of the factors involved in language production, and identify corresponding brain regions.

Being able to produce meaningful language requires several factors. First, the person must have something to communicate about. Let us consider what this means. To use speech as a form of communication, we can talk about something that is currently happening or something that happened in the past. When we talk about something that is happening, we are talking about our perceptions: things we are seeing, hearing, feeling, smelling, and so on. When we talk about something that happened in the past, we are talking about our memories. Both perceptions of current events and memories of events that occurred in the past involve brain mechanisms in the posterior part of the cerebral hemispheres (the

Balefire/Shutterstock

occipital, temporal, and parietal lobes). Thus, these regions are largely responsible for our having something to say.

We can also talk about something that *did not* happen. That is, we can use our imagination to make up a story (or to tell a lie). We know very little about the neural mechanisms that are responsible for imagination, but it seems likely that they involve the mechanisms responsible for perceptions and memories because when we make up a story, we usually base it on knowledge that we originally acquired through perception and have retained in our memory.

As we will see in the following sections, the conversion of perceptions, memories, and thoughts into language makes use of distinct brain regions. We will detail each of these in turn.

Language Comprehension

LO 14.3 Describe the factors involved in language comprehension, and identify corresponding brain regions.

In thinking about brain mechanisms involved in recognizing words and comprehending their meaning, the concept of a dictionary serves as a useful analogy. (See Figure 14.2.) Dictionaries contain entries (the words) and definitions (the meanings of the words). In the brain we have at least two types of entries: auditory and visual. That is, we can look up a word according to how it sounds or how it looks (in writing). Let us consider just one type of entry: the sound of a word. (Reading and writing will be discussed later in this chapter.) For example, we hear a familiar word and understand its meaning. How do we do so?

First, we must recognize the sequence of sounds that constitute the word: We find the auditory entry for the word in our "dictionary." These entries are stored in Wernicke's area in the auditory association cortex of the left temporal lobe. As you have already read, Wernicke's area is required for comprehension and production of *meaningful* language. It is possible to produce speech when Wernicke's area has been damaged, but the speech often does not make sense to the listener. Next, memories associated with the word are activated. Wernicke's area is connected through the posterior language area to neural circuits that contain these memories.

Language conveys more than simple words denoting objects or actions. It also conveys abstract concepts, some of them quite subtle. Studies of patients with brain damage (Brownell et al., 1983, 1990) suggest that comprehension of the more subtle, figurative aspects of language involves the right hemisphere in particular—for example, understanding the meaning behind metaphors, proverbs such as "People who live in glass houses shouldn't throw stones," or moral stories.

Functional-imaging studies confirm these observations. Nichelli et al. (1995) found that judging the moral of Aesop's fables (in contrast to judging more superficial aspects of the stories) also activated regions of the right hemisphere. Sotillo et al., (2005) found that a task that required comprehension of metaphors such as "green lung of the city" (that is, a park) activated the right superior temporal cortex. (See Figure 14.3.) Pobric et al. (2008) found that a temporary disruption of the right superior temporal cortex by means of TMS impaired people's ability to understand novel metaphors, such as a "conscience storm." The stimulation had no effect on the participants' ability to understand conventional metaphors, such as "sweet voice," that they had undoubtedly already heard, or literal expressions such as "snow storm."

Figure 14.2 The "Dictionary" in the Brain

Wernicke's area contains the auditory entries of words; the meanings are contained as memories in the sensory association areas. Black arrows represent comprehension of words—the activation of memories that correspond to a word's meaning. Red arrows represent translation of thoughts or perceptions into words.

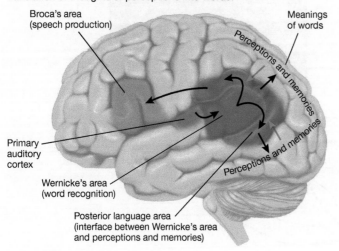

Figure 14.3 Evaluating Metaphors

These images of neural activity were produced by evaluating the meaning of metaphors.

(Based on Sotillo, M., Carretié, L., Hinojosa, J. A., Tapia, M., Mercado, F., López-Martín, S., and Albert, J. Neuroscience Letters, 2005, *373*, 5–9.)

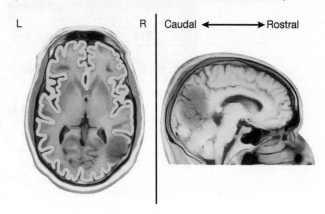

Bilingualism

LO 14.4 **Describe evidence for common and language-specific brain regions for bilingual language processing.**

The majority of people in the world are **bilingual** or multilingual. Are the brains of people who are bilingual different from those of people who are monolingual? What brain structures are involved in communicating in second (or third, or fourth, or fifth) languages? Some researchers have proposed that all languages used by an individual are processed in the same shared areas of the brain, while other researchers have proposed that each language is processed by different brain regions or circuits.

Observations of bilingual patients with lesions sometimes reveal aphasia symptoms in one language and not another, or specific deficits affecting (for example) speech in one language and writing in another. This led early researchers to conclude that different languages were processed by different brain structures. The development of imaging techniques such as fMRI and PET allowed researchers to more closely examine the brain regions involved in communication by bilingual (or multilingual) individuals. The accumulation of research from these studies revealed that communication in different languages involves some common regions and some language-specific regions in the brain.

Giussani et al., (2007) conducted a review of seven different electrostimulation studies of the cortex in bi- and multilingual patients. The patients in each of these studies were undergoing brain surgery, usually to remove lesions or tumors, and microelectrodes were used to stimulate brain regions to assess their language function prior to surgery. The patients were asked to complete tasks such as naming objects or reading in their primary and secondary languages while the stimulation occurred. If the patient's performance on the task was altered or interrupted during stimulation, then a function in that language was assigned to the brain area. This process allowed the neurosurgeon to map the language functions of the brain, avoiding damage to these regions as the lesion or tumor was removed. The electro-stimulation studies found *both* common and language-specific regions. Common and language-specific areas were found in the frontal and posterior temporal/parietal cortexes. In addition, language-specific areas were found in some subcortical structures. An example of language-specific and common language areas in a bilingual English-French speaking patient is included in Figure 14.4.

In other research investigating the neural basis of bilingualism, Mechelli et al. (2004) found that the structure of the cortex was changed by learning a second language. The researchers assessed the density of grey matter and found increased density in the left parietal cortex of bilingual compared to monolingual individuals. The change in density

---

Figure 14.4 Mapping Common and Language-Specific Areas of the Cortex

A 31-year-old bilingual English-French right-handed patient operated on for a small low-grade glioma located in the left parietal lobe. French was his native language. He started learning English after age 11. No language problem was detected preoperatively. Direct cortical electrostimulation revealed one French-specific naming interference site (single flag) whereas one site was common for English and French (overlapping flags).

(From Giussani et al., 2007.)

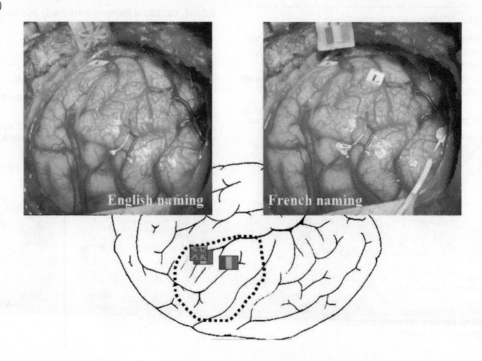

English naming   French naming

was greater among people that learned a second language early in life (before the age of five) and those who were most proficient in their second language.

Prosody

LO 14.5 Identify brain structures and functions involved in prosody.

When we speak, we do not merely utter words. Speech (and other forms of communication such as signing) has a regular rhythm and cadence. A speaker can give some words stress (for example, pronounce them louder), and vary the pitch of their voice to indicate phrasing and to distinguish between assertions and questions. In addition, a speaker imparts information about their emotional state through the rhythm, emphasis, and tone of their speech. These rhythmic, emphatic, and melodic aspects of speech are referred to as **prosody.** The importance of these aspects of communication is illustrated by our use of punctuation symbols to indicate some elements of prosody when we write. For example, a comma indicates a short pause; a period indicates a longer one with an accompanying fall in the pitch of the voice; a question mark indicates a pause and a rise in the pitch of the voice; and an exclamation mark indicates that the words are articulated with special emphasis.

The prosody of people with Wernicke's aphasias caused by lesions to posterior brain structures is normal. For example, their speech is rhythmical, with pauses after phrases and sentences, and has a melodic line. Even when the speech of a person with severe Wernicke's aphasia makes no sense, prosody is unaffected. In contrast, the anterior lesions that produce Broca's aphasia destroy grammar, and they also severely disrupt prosody. In patients with Broca's aphasia, articulation is labored and words are uttered slowly so that there is little opportunity for the patient to demonstrate any rhythmic elements. There is little variation in stress or pitch because prosodic variation usually goes along with the syntactic structure of a phrase or sentence, which is impaired in Broca's aphasia.

Although prosodic disruption can occur in aphasia, studies of healthy individuals and patients with right hemisphere brain lesions have also shown that the right hemisphere of the brain plays an important role in prosody. For example, Weintraub et al., (1981) presented participants with two written sentences and asked a question about them. They presented the following pair of sentences:

The man walked to the grocery store.
The woman rode to the shoe store.

The participants were instructed to answer questions by reading one of the sentences. Try this one yourself. Read the question below and then read aloud the sentence (above) that answers it.

A speaker imparts information about their emotional state through the rhythm, emphasis, and tone of their speech.

Who walked to the grocery store, the man or the woman?

The question asserts that someone walked to the grocery store but asks who that person was. When answering a question like this, people normally stress the requested item of information; in this case they say, "The *man* walked to the grocery store." However, Weintraub and her colleagues found that although patients with right hemisphere brain damage chose the correct sentence, they either failed to stress a word or stressed the wrong one. Thus, the right hemisphere plays a role in production of prosody.

In a functional-imaging study by Meyer et al., (2002), participants heard normal sentences or sentences that contained only the prosodic elements of speech with the meaningful sounds filtered out. As you can see in Figure 14.5, the meaningful components of speech primarily activated the left hemisphere (blue and green regions), whereas the prosodic components primarily activated the right hemisphere (orange and yellow regions).

Recognition of People's Voices

LO 14.6 Identify the brain regions involved in recognizing people's voices.

The words contained in spoken language convey information about events, ideas, and other forms of meaning—information that can be conveyed just as well in writing. Prosody can convey information about the speaker's emotional state or things the speaker wants to stress. Finally, speech can convey information completely independent of the meaning of the words: the identity of the speaker, his or her gender, and hints about his or her age.

Figure 14.5 Listening to Normal Speech or Its Prosodic Components

Functional MRI scans were made while participants listened to normal speech (blue and green regions) or the prosodic elements of speech with the meaningful components filtered out (orange and yellow regions).

(From Meyer, M., Alter, K., Friederici, A. D., Lohmann, G., and von Cramon, D. Y., FMRI reveals brain regions mediating slow prosodic modulations in spoken sentences, *Human Brain Mapping*, 2002, *17*, 73–88. Reprinted with permission.)

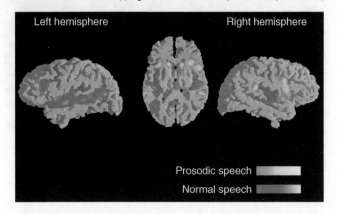

People learn at an early age to recognize the voices of particular individuals. Even newborn infants can recognize the voices of their parents, which they apparently learned while they were still in their mother's uterus (Ockleford et al., 1988). Some people with localized brain damage have great difficulty recognizing voices—a disorder known as *phonagnosia*.

Most cases of phonagnosia are caused by brain damage. Recognition of a particular voice is independent of the recognition of words and their meanings: Some people have lost the ability to understand words but can still recognize voices, while others display the opposite deficits (Belin et al., 2004). So far, all cases of acquired phonagnosia (phonagnosia caused by brain damage) show damage in the right hemisphere, usually in the parietal lobe or the anterior superior temporal cortex. Functional-imaging studies have implicated the right anterior superior temporal cortex in voice recognition. For example, von Kriegstein et al. (2003) found that this region was activated by a task that required participants to recognize particular voices but not particular words. The first recorded case of developmental phonagnosia (that is, phonagnosia not caused by brain damage) was reported by Garrido et al. (2009). The researchers studied the experiences of K. H.

K. H., a 60-year-old management consultant, has all her life had great difficulty recognizing people by their voices. K. H. read an article in a popular scientific magazine that described prosopagnosia, the difficulty—or even inability—to recognize people's faces. She realized that her disorder could be an auditory form of this disorder. Testing showed that her intelligence was above average and that she received normal or above normal scores on a variety of perceptual tasks, including face recognition, speech perception, recognition of environmental sounds, and perception of music. Structural MRI showed no evidence of brain abnormalities, but there certainly must be some subtle differences in brain organization to account for her disability.

Section Review

Language Production and Comprehension: Brain Mechanisms

LO 14.1 Compare the language-related functions of the left and right hemispheres, and discuss the prevalence of these functions in the opposite hemisphere.

Both hemispheres contribute to our language abilities. Speech and language functions are lateralized in the brain with circuits for comprehension and production located in the left hemisphere for the majority of people. The right hemisphere plays a role in processing emotional content, rhythm, and stress of speech and language.

LO 14.2 List some of the factors involved in language production, and identify corresponding brain regions.

To produce language, an individual must have something to communicate that is currently happening, happened in the past, or was imagined. The occipital, temporal, and parietal lobes are involved in perceptions of current events and memories. These regions are likely involved when communicating about an imaginary event. Broca's area, in the left frontal lobe just rostral to the region of the primary motor cortex that controls the muscles of speech, is involved with speech and language production.

LO 14.3 Describe the factors involved in language comprehension, and identify corresponding brain regions.

Language comprehension involves recognition of a word using Wernicke's area in the left hemisphere. Language comprehension also requires understanding the meanings of words. Comprehension of the figurative aspects of language involves the right hemisphere.

LO 14.4 Describe evidence for common and language-specific brain regions for bilingual language processing.

Bilingual individuals likely possess some brain regions devoted to specific languages as well as areas that are common to both languages used. These brain regions can be identified using imaging techniques such as PET and fMRI, or by direct electrostimulation. Research in bilingual patients revealed common and language-specific areas in the frontal and posterior temporal/parietal cortexes. In addition, language-specific areas were found in some subcortical structures.

LO 14.5 Identify brain structures and functions involved in prosody.

Prosody involves changes in intonation, rhythm, and stress that add meaning, especially emotional meaning, to language. Although Broca's aphasia (caused by left hemisphere damage) produces deficits in prosody, other neural mechanisms that control prosodic elements appear to be located in the right hemisphere.

LO 14.6 Identify the brain regions involved in recognizing people's voices.

Phonagnosia is a difficulty recognizing voices and is typically caused by damage to the right parietal or temporal cortex.

Thought Question

In a recent survey of 717 people, Seidman et al., (2013) found that when using a cell phone most right-handed people used their right ear to converse. Similarly, most left-handed people used their left ear. Although the survey only investigated correlational data, what are some plausible brain-based hypotheses that the researchers could test next? Propose possible explanations and research strategies to better address this topic.

Disorders of Language Production and Comprehension

Much of our understanding of the brain mechanisms of language has come from the study of disorders. Language disorders affect both production and comprehension, revealing different, but often overlapping, pathways, and structures.

Disorders of Language Production: Broca's Aphasia

LO 14.7 Describe the symptoms and neural bases of Broca's aphasia, including agrammatism, anomia, and articulation.

As you've already read, damage to the frontal lobe produces Broca's aphasia, a disorder characterized by slow, laborious, and nonfluent speech. Although they often mispronounce words, the words patients produce are usually meaningful. The posterior part of the cerebral hemispheres has something to communicate, but the damage to the frontal lobe makes it difficult for the patients to express these thoughts.

As you've already read, people with Broca's aphasia comprehend language better than they are able to produce it. People with Broca's aphasia find it easier to say some types of words than others. They have great difficulty saying small words with grammatical meaning, such as *a, the, some, in,* or *about.* These words are called **function words,** because they have important grammatical functions. People with Broca's aphasia use almost entirely **content words—** words that convey meaning, including nouns, verbs, adjectives, and adverbs, such as *apple, house, throw,* or *heavy.* Here is a sample of speech from a man with Broca's aphasia, who is trying to describe the scene shown in Figure 14.6. As you will see, his words are meaningful, but what he says is not grammatical. The dots indicate long pauses:

> kid. . . . kk . . . can . . . candy . . . cookie . . . candy . . . well I don't know but it's writ . . . easy does it . . . slam . . . early . . . fall . . . men . . . many no . . . girl. Dishes . . . soap . . . soap . . . water . . . water . . . falling pah that's all . . . dish . . . that's all. Cookies . . . can . . . candy . . . cookies cookies . . . he . . . down . . . That's all. Girl . . . slipping water . . . water . . . and it hurts . . . much to do . . . Her . . . clean up . . . Dishes . . . up there . . . I think that's doing it. (Obler and Gjerlow, 1999, p. 41)

Lesions that produce Broca's aphasia are certainly centered in the vicinity of Broca's area. However, damage that is restricted to only the cortex region of Broca's area does not

---

Figure 14.6 Assessment of Aphasia

The drawing of the kitchen story is part of the Boston Diagnostic Aphasia Test.

appear to produce Broca's aphasia; the damage must extend to surrounding regions of the frontal lobe and to the underlying subcortical white matter (Damasio, 1989; Naeser et al., 1989). In addition, there is evidence that lesions of the basal ganglia—especially the head of the caudate nucleus—can also produce a Broca's-like aphasia (Damasio et al., 1984). (See Figure 14.7.)

Watkins et al., (2002a, 2002b) studied three generations of a family, half of whose members are affected by a severe speech and language disorder caused by the mutation of a single gene found on chromosome 7. The primary deficit appears to involve the ability to perform the sequential movements necessary for speech, but the affected people also have difficulty repeating sounds they hear and forming the past tense of verbs. The mutation causes abnormal development of the caudate nucleus and the left inferior frontal cortex, including Broca's area.

What do the neural circuits in and around Broca's area do? Wernicke (1874) suggested that Broca's area contains motor memories—in particular, *memories of the sequences of muscular movements that are needed to articulate words.* Talking involves rapid movements of the tongue, lips, and jaw, and these movements must be coordinated with each other and with those of the vocal cords; thus, talking requires some very sophisticated motor control mechanisms. Circuits of neurons somewhere in the brain will, when properly activated, cause these sequences of movements to be executed. Because damage to the inferior caudal left frontal lobe (including Broca's area) disrupts the ability to articulate words, this region is a likely candidate for the location of these

"programs." The fact that this region is directly connected to the part of the primary motor cortex that controls the muscles used for speech certainly supports this conclusion.

But the speech functions of the left frontal lobe include more than just programming the movements used to speak. Broca's aphasia is much more than just a deficit in pronouncing words. In general, three major speech and language deficits are produced by lesions in and around Broca's area: *agrammatism, anomia,* and *articulation difficulties.* Although most patients with Broca's aphasia will have all of these deficits to some degree, their severity can vary considerably from person to person—presumably, because their brain lesions differ in size and location.

AGRAMMATISM **Agrammatism** refers to a patient's difficulty in using grammatical constructions. This disorder can appear all by itself, without any difficulty in pronouncing or retrieving words (Nadeau, 1988). As we saw, people with Broca's aphasia rarely use function words. In addition, they rarely use grammatical markers such as *-ed* or auxiliaries such as *have* (as in *I have gone*). For some reason they *do* often use *-ing,* perhaps because this ending converts a verb into a noun, or because *-ing* in English is the most common verb ending, and therefore might be a kind of "default" form of the verb. A study by Saffran et al. (1980) illustrates this difficulty. The following quotations are from people with agrammatism attempting to describe pictures:

> *Picture of a boy being hit in the head by a baseball*
> The boy is catch . . . the boy is hitch . . . the boy is hit the ball. (Saffran et al., 1980, p. 229)

Figure 14.7 Regions Involved in Broca's or Broca's-Like Aphasias

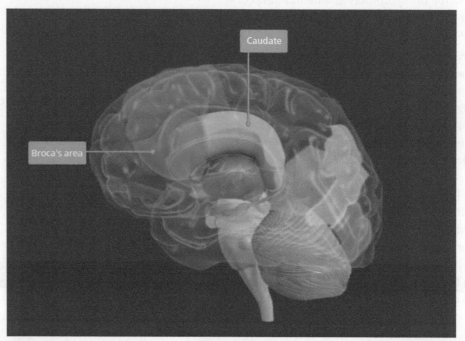

Picture of a girl giving flowers to her teacher
Girl . . . wants to . . . flowers . . . flowers and wants to . . . .
The woman . . . wants to . . . . The girl wants to . . . the flowers and the woman. (Saffran et al., 1980, p. 234)

So far, we have described Broca's aphasia as a disorder in language *production.* In ordinary conversation, people with Broca's aphasia seem to understand everything that is said to them. They are distressed by their inability to express their thoughts well, and they often make gestures to supplement their missing speech. The striking disparity between their speech and their comprehension often leads people to assume that their comprehension is normal. But it is not. Schwartz et al. (1980) showed people with Broca's aphasia pairs of pictures in which agents and objects of the action were reversed: a truck pulling a car and a car pulling a truck. As they showed each pair of pictures, they read the participant a sentence, for example, active sentences like *The truck pulls the car,* or passive sentences like *The car is pulled by the truck.* The patients' task was to point to the appropriate picture, indicating whether they understood the grammatical construction of the sentence. They performed very poorly on passive sentences like *The car is pulled by the truck,* where word order does not help with interpretation.

Functional-imaging studies by Opitz and Friederici (2003, 2007) have shown that Broca's area is activated when people are taught an artificial grammar, which supports the conclusion that this region is involved in learning grammatical rules. Sakai et al. (2002) had experimental participants read sentences that were correct, grammatically incorrect, or semantically incorrect (that is, did not make sense). While the participants were judging the grammatical or semantic correctness of the sentences, the investigators applied transcranial magnetic stimulation (TMS) to Broca's area. The parameters of stimulation were chosen to *activate* Broca's area, not disrupt its functioning. The investigators found that the stimulation facilitated grammatical judgments but not semantic judgments. This provides more evidence that Broca's area is crucially involved in processing grammatical aspects of language.

ANOMIA   The second major language deficit seen in Broca's aphasia is **anomia.** Anomia refers to a word-finding difficulty; because all people with aphasias omit words or use inappropriate ones, anomia is actually a primary symptom of *all* forms of aphasia. The facial expressions and frequent use of sounds such as "uh" make it clear that patients with Broca's aphasia are searching for the correct words.

ARTICULATION DIFFICULTIES   The third major characteristic of Broca's aphasia is *difficulty with articulation.* Patients mispronounce words, often altering the sequence of sounds. For example, *lipstick* might be pronounced "likstip." People with Broca's aphasia recognize that their pronunciation is erroneous, and they usually try to correct it.

These three deficits are seen in various combinations in different patients, depending on the exact location of the lesion and, to a certain extent, on their stage of recovery. We can think of these deficits as constituting a hierarchy. On the lowest, most elementary level is control of the sequence of movements of the muscles of speech; damage to this ability leads to articulation difficulties. The next higher level is selection of the particular "programs" for individual words; damage to this ability leads to anomia. Finally, the highest level is selection of grammatical structure, including word order, use of function words, and word endings; damage to this ability leads to agrammatism.

We might expect that the direct control of articulation would involve the face area of the primary motor cortex and portions of the basal ganglia, while the selection of words, word order, and grammatical markers would involve Broca's area and adjacent regions of the frontal association cortex. Some studies indicate that different categories of symptoms of Broca's aphasia do indeed involve different brain regions. Dronkers and her colleagues (Baldo et al., 2011; Dronkers, 1996) identified a critical location for control of speech articulation: the left precentral gyrus of the insula. The insular cortex is located on the lateral wall of the cerebral hemisphere behind the anterior temporal lobe. Normally, this region is hidden and can be seen only when the temporal lobe is dissected away. (See Figure 14.8a.) Dronkers discovered the apparent role of this region by plotting the lesions of patients with and without apraxia of speech who had strokes that damaged the same general area of the brain. (**Apraxia of speech** is an impairment in the ability to program movements of the tongue, lips, and throat that are required to produce the proper sequence of speech sounds.) Figure 14.8b shows the overlap of the lesions of 25 patients with apraxia of speech. As you can see, a region of 100 percent overlap, shown in yellow, falls on the left precentral gyrus of the insula. In contrast, *none* of the lesions of 19 patients who did not show apraxia of speech included damage to this region. (See Figure 14.8c.)

At least two functional-imaging studies support Dronkers's conclusion. Kuriki et al., (1999) and Wise et al. (1999) found that pronunciation of words caused activation of the left anterior insula. However, other studies suggest that Broca's area is also involved in articulation (Hillis et al., 2004; Nestor et al., 2003). Stewart et al. (2001) used TMS to interfere with the activity of neurons in Broca's area or the adjacent area of primary motor cortex, which controls the muscles used for speech. The participants reported that stimulation of the motor cortex made them feel as though they had lost control of their facial muscles. In contrast, stimulation of Broca's area made them feel as if they were unable to "get the word out."

Most of us have, at one time or other, had difficulty getting a word out even though the word was one that we knew well. This phenomenon has been called the "tip of the tongue phenomenon," or TOT. Shafto et al., (2007) found that people who often had difficulty thinking of the correct word to say but were sure that they knew it (that is, often

Figure 14.8 The Insular Cortex and Its Involvement in Speech

(a) The cortex is normally hidden behind the rostral temporal lobe. Evidence for involvement is shown by the percentage overlap in the lesions of 25 patients (b) with apraxia of speech and (c) without apraxia of speech. The only region common to all lesions that produced apraxia of speech was the precentral gyrus of the insular cortex.

((b) and (c) from Dronkers, N. F., A new brain region for coordinating speech articulation, *Nature*, 1996, *384*, 159–161. Reprinted with permission.)

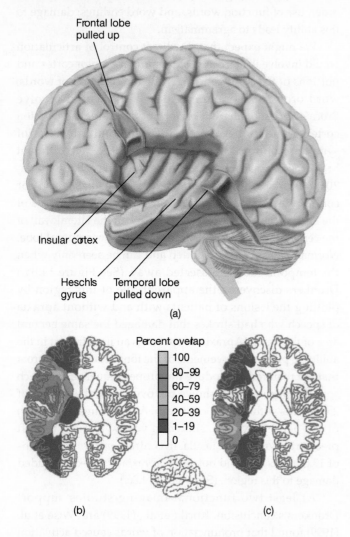

(a)

Percent overlap

100	
80–99	
60–79	
40–59	
20–39	
1–19	
0	

(b)   (c)

had a TOT experience) showed loss of gray matter in the left insular cortex. These findings, too, support the role of this region in articulation.

Disorders of Language Comprehension: Wernicke's Aphasia

LO 14.8 **Describe the symptoms and neural bases of Wernicke's aphasia, including deficits in spoken word recognition, comprehension, and converting thoughts into words.**

Comprehension of speech begins in the auditory system, which detects and analyzes sounds. But *recognizing* words is one thing; *comprehending* them—understanding their meaning—is another. Recognizing a spoken word is a complex

perceptual task that relies on memories of sequences of sounds. This task appears to be accomplished by neural circuits in the superior temporal gyrus of the left hemisphere, a region that has come to be known as Wernicke's area. (Refer back to Figure 14.1.)

As you have already read, the primary characteristics of Wernicke's aphasia are poor language comprehension and production of meaningless speech. Unlike Broca's aphasia, speech in Wernicke's aphasia is fluent and unlabored; the person does not strain to articulate words and does not appear to be searching for them. The patient maintains a melodic line, with the voice rising and falling normally. When you listen to the speech of a person with Wernicke's aphasia, it appears to be grammatical. That is, the person uses function words such as *the* and *but* and employs complex verb tenses and subordinate clauses. However, the person uses few content words, and the words that he or she strings together do not make sense, illustrated by the following quotation:

> *Examiner:* What kind of work did you do before you came into the hospital?
>
> *Patient:* Never, now mista oyge I wanna tell you this happened when happened when he rent. His—his kell come down here and is—he got ren something. It happened. In thesse ropiers were with him for hi—is friend—like was. And it just happened so I don't know, he did not bring around anything. And he did not pay it. And he roden all o these arranjen from the pedis on from iss pescid. In these floors now and so. He hadn't had em round here. (Kertesz, 1981, p. 73)

Because of the language deficits of people with Wernicke's aphasia, when assessing their ability to comprehend language, it is important to ask them to use nonverbal responses. We cannot assume that people with Wernicke's aphasia do not understand what other people communicate to them just because they do not give a correct verbal answer. For example, you could assess a person's ability to understand questions by pointing to objects on a table in front of them. A person might be asked to "Point to the one with ink." If the person points to an object other than the pen, they have not understood the request. When tested this way, people with severe Wernicke's aphasia do indeed show poor comprehension.

A remarkable fact about people with Wernicke's aphasia is that they often seem unaware of their deficit. These individuals do not appear to recognize that their language is impaired, nor do they recognize that they cannot understand the language of others. They do not look puzzled when someone tells them something, even though they cannot understand what they hear. It is possible that the comprehension deficit prevents them from realizing that what they say and hear makes no sense. People with Wernicke's aphasia still follow social conventions, taking turns in conversation with the examiner, even though they do not understand what the examiner says and what they say in return makes little sense. They remain sensitive to the other person's facial expression and tone of voice and begin talking when he or she asks a question and pauses for an answer. One patient with Wernicke's aphasia made the following responses when asked to name ten common objects:

toothbrush → "stoktery"

cigarette → "cigarette"

pen → "tankt"

knife → "nike"

fork → "fahk"

quarter → "minkt"

pen → "spentee"

matches → "senktr"

key → "seek"

comb → "sahk"

He acted confidently and gave no indication that he recognized that most of his responses were not actual words. The responses that he made were not new words that he had invented; he was asked several times to name the objects and gave different responses each time (except for *cigarette*, which he always named correctly).

Because the superior temporal gyrus is a region of auditory association cortex, and because a comprehension deficit is so prominent in Wernicke's aphasia, this disorder has been characterized as a *receptive* aphasia. Wernicke suggested that the region that now bears his name is the location of *memories of the sequences of sounds that constitute words*. This hypothesis is reasonable; it suggests that the auditory association cortex of the superior temporal gyrus recognizes the sounds of words, just as the visual association cortex of the inferior temporal gyrus recognizes the sight of objects.

But why should damage to an area that is responsible for the ability to recognize spoken words disrupt people's ability to speak? In fact, it does not; Wernicke's aphasia, like Broca's aphasia, actually appears to consist of several deficits. The abilities that are disrupted include *recognition of spoken words, comprehension of the meaning of words*, and the *ability to convert thoughts into words*. Let us consider each of these abilities in turn.

DEFICITS IN SPOKEN WORD RECOGNITION   As you read in the introduction to this section, *recognizing* a word is not the same as *comprehending* it. If you hear a new word several times, you will learn to recognize it; but unless someone tells you what it means, you will not comprehend it. Recognition is a perceptual task; comprehension involves retrieval of additional (linguistic) information from memory.

Damage to the left temporal lobe can produce a disorder of auditory word recognition. This syndrome is called **pure word deafness.** (See Figure 14.9.) People with pure word deafness are not deaf. They can perceive and recognize speech, but they cannot understand the words. As one patient put it, "I can hear you talking, I just can't understand what you're saying." Another said, "It's as if there were a bypass somewhere, and my ears were not connected to my voice" (Saffran et al., 1976, p. 211). These patients can recognize nonspeech sounds such as the barking of a dog, the sound of a doorbell, and the honking of a horn. Often, they can recognize the emotion expressed by the intonation of speech even though they cannot understand what is being said. More significantly, their own speech is unaffected. They can often understand what other people are saying by reading their lips. They can also read and write, and they sometimes ask people to communicate with them in writing. Pure word deafness is not an inability to comprehend the meaning of words; if it were, people with this disorder would not be able to read people's lips or read words written on paper. Their speech deficit is restricted only to the recognition of spoken words.

Even when specific spoken words are not recognized, individuals with pure word deafness correctly perceive the qualities of human speech and know that another person is speaking. Functional-imaging studies show that perception of speech sounds activates neurons in the auditory association cortex of the superior temporal gyrus. For example, Scott et al. (2000) identified a region of the left anterior superior temporal gyrus that was specifically activated by intelligible speech, indicating that activity in this region is specific to the perception of speech sounds, but not particular words. (See Figure 14.10.) Sharp et al. (2004) found that lesions of this same region produced deficits in language comprehension.

Figure 14.9 Pure Word Deafness

An MRI scan shows the damage to the superior temporal lobe of a patient with pure word deafness (arrow).

(From Stefanatos, G. A., Gershkoff, A., and Madigan, S., On pure word deafness, temporal processing, and the left hemisphere, *Journal of the International Neuropsychological Society*, 2005, *11*, 456–470. Reprinted with permission.)

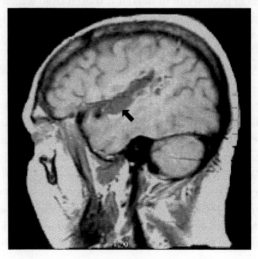

Figure 14.10 Responses to Speech Sounds

Results of PET scans indicate the regions of the superior temporal lobe that respond to speech sounds. *Red:* Regions that responded to phonetic information (normal speech sounds or a computerized transformation speech that preserved the complexity of the speech sounds but rendered it unintelligible). *Orange:* Region that responded to intelligible speech (normal speech sounds or a computerized transformation that removed most normal frequencies but preserved intelligibility).

(Based on data from Scott et al., 2000.)

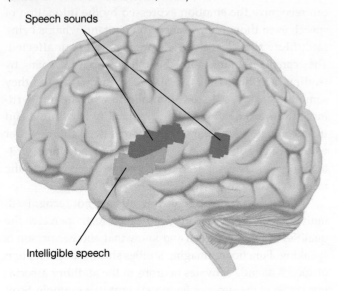

Speech sounds

Intelligible speech

What is involved in the analysis of speech sounds? Just what tasks does the auditory system have to accomplish? And what are the differences in the functions of the auditory association cortex of the left and right hemispheres? Most researchers believe that the left hemisphere is primarily involved in judging the timing of the components of rapidly changing complex sounds, whereas the right hemisphere is primarily involved in judging more slowly changing components, including melody. Evidence suggests that the most crucial aspect of speech sounds is timing, not pitch. People recognize words whether they are conveyed by the lower pitch of a man or the higher pitch of a woman or child. In fact, most people can understand speech from which almost all tonal information has been removed, leaving only some noise modulated by the rapid stops and starts that characterize human speech sounds.

Two types of brain injury can cause pure word deafness: disruption of auditory input to the superior temporal cortex or damage to the superior temporal cortex itself (Poeppel, 2001; Stefanatos et al., 2005). Either type of damage disturbs the analysis of the sounds of words and prevents people from recognizing other people's speech.

As we saw in Chapter 8, our brains contain circuits of *mirror neurons*—neurons activated when we either perform an action or see the action performed by someone else. Feedback from these neurons may help us to understand the intent of the actions of others. Although speech recognition is

an auditory event, research indicates that hearing words automatically engages brain mechanisms that control speech production, too. These brain circuits appear to contain mirror neurons that are activated by the sounds of words. For example, Fridricksson et al. (2008) found that when people watched (but did not hear) other people making speech movements, the temporal (auditory) and frontal (motor) cortical language areas were activated. These regions were *not* activated when the participants watched people making nonspeech movements with their mouths.

Several investigators have suggested that feedback from subvocal articulation (very slight movements of the muscles involved in speech that do not cause obvious movement) facilitate speech recognition (Pulvermüller and Fadiga, 2010). For example, a functional-imaging study by Pulvermüller et al., (2006) had participants articulate syllables that contained the consonants *p* or *t* (for example, *pa* and *ta)*, which involve movements of the lips or tongue. The participants said the syllables aloud, said them to themselves silently, and listened to the syllables spoken by someone else. As Figure 14.11 shows, in all three conditions, regions of the brain involved with lip movements (green) and tongue movements (red) were activated. Thus, speaking, watching other people speak, thinking about speaking, and listening to speech sounds all activate brain regions involved in language, which suggests that circuits of mirror neurons play a role in speech and language comprehension.

When we speak, or when we make subtle movements of the muscles involved in speaking, we receive somatosensory feedback from our tongue and the skin around our mouth. Ito et al. (2009) found that this feedback affects our perception of speech sounds. The investigators attached two arms of a mechanical device to the skin of participants, just past the corners of their mouths. The device could be made to pull the skin upward or downward by the computer

Figure 14.11 Mirror Neurons and Speech

Brain activation in the primary motor cortex that occurred when people said syllables aloud, said syllables to themselves silently, or heard someone else saying syllables. The two regions marked with yellow circles are involved in control of tongue movements (syllables that included the sound of *t*, shown in green) and lip movements (syllables that included the sound of *p*, shown in red).

(From Pulvermüller, F., Huss, M., Kherif, F., et al., Motor cortex maps articulatory features of speech sounds, *Proceedings of the National Academy of Sciences, USA*, 2006, *103*, 7865–7870. Reprinted with permission.)

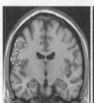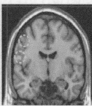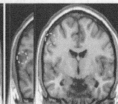

Said syllables aloud   Said syllables to themselves silently   Heard syllables said

controlling the experiment. The participants listened to computer-generated words that varied in ten steps between the sound of *head* to the sound of *had*. When the participants heard intermediate sounds that were neither *head* nor *had*, they were more likely to indicate that they heard *head* when their facial skin was stretched upward and *had* when their facial skin was stretched downward. (Say *head* and *had* to yourself while paying attention to the movements made by the corners of your mouth. You will feel that your mouth widens and the corners rise slightly when you say *head* and that your mouth opens slightly, pulling the corners down, when you say *had*.) So, as the results of these studies indicate, activity of mirror neurons as well as feedback from speech movements affects speech perception.

Experience with the patient described below suggests that monitoring of one's own speech plays an important role in producing accurate and fluent speech.

Dr. D. introduced Mr. S., a patient who had experienced a stroke that resulted in pure word deafness.

"Mr. S., will you tell us how you are feeling?" asked Dr. D.

The patient turned his head at the sound of his voice and said, "Sorry, I can't understand you."

"*How are you feeling?*" Dr. D. asked in a loud voice.

"Oh, I can hear you all right, I just can't understand you. Here," said Mr. S., handing Dr. D. a pencil and a small pad of paper.

Dr. D. took the pencil and paper and wrote something. He handed them back to Mr. S., who looked at it and said, "Fine. I'm just fine."

The conversation continued for several minutes as different people in the room asked Mr. S questions by writing them on paper with Mr. S answering them verbally.

After Mr. S. had left the room, someone observed that although Mr. S.'s speech was easy to understand, it seemed a bit strange. "Yes," said a speech therapist, "he almost sounds like a person who is deaf and has learned to talk but doesn't get the pronunciation of the words just right."

Dr. D. nodded and played a recording for us. "This recording was made a few months after his strokes, 10 years ago." We heard the same voice, but this time all of the words were pronounced accurately.

"Oh," said the speech therapist. "He has lost the ability to monitor his own speech, and over the years he has forgotten some of the details of how various words are pronounced."

"Exactly," said Dr. D. "The change has been a gradual one."

DEFICITS IN LANGUAGE COMPREHENSION   The other symptoms of Wernicke's aphasia—failure to comprehend the meaning of words and inability to express thoughts in meaningful speech—appear to be produced by damage that extends beyond Wernicke's area into the region that surrounds the posterior part of the lateral fissure, near the junction of the temporal, occipital, and parietal lobes. We will refer to this region as the *posterior language area*. (See Figure 14.12.) The posterior language area appears to serve as a place

Figure 14.12 Transcortical Sensory Aphasia and Wernicke's Aphasia

This schematic shows the location and interconnections of the posterior language area and an explanation of its role in transcortical sensory aphasia and Wernicke's aphasia.

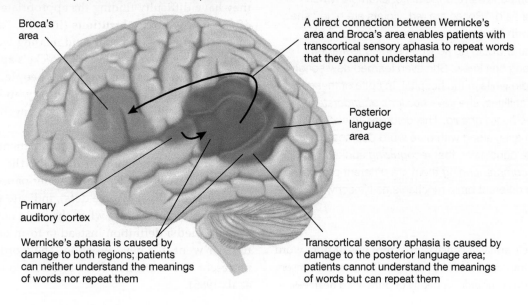

Broca's area

A direct connection between Wernicke's area and Broca's area enables patients with transcortical sensory aphasia to repeat words that they cannot understand

Posterior language area

Primary auditory cortex

Wernicke's aphasia is caused by damage to both regions; patients can neither understand the meanings of words nor repeat them

Transcortical sensory aphasia is caused by damage to the posterior language area; patients cannot understand the meanings of words but can repeat them for interchanging information between the auditory representation of words and the meanings of these words, stored as memories in the rest of the sensory association cortex.

Damage to the posterior language area alone, which isolates Wernicke's area from the rest of the posterior language area, produces a disorder known as **transcortical sensory aphasia.** (Look again at Figure 14.12) The difference between transcortical sensory aphasia and Wernicke's aphasia is that patients with transcortical sensory aphasia *can repeat what other people say to them;* therefore, they can recognize words. However, *they cannot comprehend the meaning of what they hear and repeat; nor can they produce meaningful speech of their own.* How can these individuals repeat what they hear without understanding it? Because their posterior language area is the area that is damaged, and repetition does not involve this part of the brain. There must be a direct connection between Wernicke's area and Broca's area that bypasses the posterior language area.

Consider the following case in which a woman's symptoms following brain injury reveal that circuits devoted to repetition are distinct from those devoted to comprehension:

A woman sustained extensive brain damage from carbon monoxide produced by a faulty water heater. She spent several years in the hospital before she died, without ever saying anything meaningful on her own. She did not follow verbal commands or otherwise give signs of understanding them. However, she often repeated what was said to her. For example, if an examiner said "Please raise your right hand," she would reply, "Please raise your right hand." Interestingly, she did not imitate accents different from her own, and if someone made a grammatical error while saying something to her, she sometimes repeated the sentence correctly, without the error. She could also recite poems if someone started them. For example, when an examiner said, "Roses are red, violets are blue," she continued with "Sugar is sweet and so are you." She could sing and would do so when someone started singing a song she knew. She even learned new songs from the radio while in the hospital. In spite of these impressive abilities, she gave *no signs of understanding anything she heard or said.* This disorder, transcortical sensory aphasia, along with pure word deafness, confirms the conclusion that *recognizing* spoken words and *comprehending* them are different processes and involve different brain mechanisms (Geschwind et al., 1968).

Wernicke's aphasia consists of symptoms of pure word deafness and transcortical sensory aphasia. Transcortical sensory aphasia can also occur independently of pure word deafness.

DEFICITS IN CONVERTING THOUGHTS INTO WORDS

As we have seen, Wernicke's area is involved in the analysis of speech sounds and thus in the recognition of words. Damage to the posterior language area does not disrupt people's ability to recognize words, but it does disrupt their ability to understand words or to produce meaningful speech of their own. But what, exactly, do we mean by the word *meaning?* And what types of brain mechanisms are involved?

The third ability that is disrupted in Wernicke's aphasia is the ability to convert thoughts and memories into words. Words refer to objects, actions, or relationships in the world. Thus, the meaning of a word is defined by particular memories associated with it. For example, knowing the meaning of the word *tree* means being able to imagine the physical characteristics of trees: what they look like, what the wind sounds like blowing through their leaves, what the bark feels like, and so on. It also means knowing facts about trees: about their roots, buds, flowers, nuts, and wood and the chlorophyll in their leaves. Action words such as *throw* involve memories of seeing someone throwing something and also involve imagining what it feels like to throw something yourself. These memories are stored not in the primary speech and language areas but in other parts of the brain, especially regions of the association cortex. Different categories of memories may be stored in particular regions of the brain, but they are somehow tied together, so hearing the word *tree* or *throw* activates all of them. (As we saw in Chapter 13, the hippocampal formation is involved in this process of tying related memories together.)

As you learned in the sections about Broca's aphasia, anomia, which is difficulty finding or remembering an appropriate word, is an important symptom of aphasia. One category of aphasia consists of almost pure anomia. Speech of patients with anomic aphasia is fluent and grammatical, and their comprehension is excellent, but they have difficulty finding the appropriate words. They often employ **circumlocutions** (literally, "speaking in a roundabout way") to get around missing words. Anomic aphasia alone *is different* from Wernicke's aphasia. Unlike patients with Wernicke's aphasia, people with anomic aphasia can understand what others say, and what people with anomic aphasia say makes sense, even if they often choose alternative ways to say it.

The following quotation is from a patient with anomic aphasia who was asked to describe the kitchen picture shown earlier, in Figure 14.6. Her pauses, which are marked with ellipses (three dots), indicate word-finding difficulties. In some cases, when she could not find a word, she supplied a definition instead (a form of circumlocution) or went in a new direction. The words in brackets represent words she may have intended to use (Margolin et al., 1985).

Examiner: Tell us about that picture.

Patient: It's a woman who has two children, a son and a daughter, and her son is to get into the . . . cupboard in the kitchen to get out [*take*] some . . . cookies out of the [*cookie jar*] . . . that she possibly had made, and consequently he's slipping [*falling*] . . . the wrong direction [*backward*] . . . on the . . . what he's standing on [*stool*], heading to the . . . the cupboard [*floor*] and if he falls backwards he could have some problems [*get hurt*], because that [*the stool*] is off balance.

Anomia has been described as a partial amnesia for words. It can be produced by lesions in either the anterior or the posterior regions of the brain, but only posterior lesions produce a *fluent* anomia. The most likely location of lesions that produce anomia without the other symptoms of aphasia, such as comprehension deficits, agrammatism, or difficulties in articulation, is the left temporal or parietal lobe, usually sparing Wernicke's area. In the case of the woman described above, the damage included the left middle and inferior temporal gyri, which includes an important region of the visual association cortex. Wernicke's area was not damaged.

The patient described above had more difficulty finding nouns than other types of words. Other researchers have reported similar patterns of deficits. For example, Semenza and Zettin (1989) and Manning and Campbell (1992) described patients who had difficulty naming objects but not actions. Several studies have found that anomia for verbs (more correctly called *averbia*) is caused by damage to the frontal cortex, in and around Broca's area (Bak et al., 2001; Damasio and Tranel, 1993; Daniele et al., 1994). The frontal lobes are devoted to planning, organizing, and executing actions, so they are involved in the task of remembering the names of actions.

Several functional-imaging studies have confirmed the importance of Broca's area and the region surrounding it in the production of verbs. For example, Hauk et al. (2004) had participants read verbs that related to movements of different parts of the body. For example, *bite, slap,* and *kick* involve movements of the face, arm, and leg, respectively. The investigators found that when the participants read a verb, they saw activation in the regions of the motor cortex that controlled the relevant part of the body. (See Figure 14.13.) A similar study by Buccino et al. (2005) found that hearing sentences that involved hand movements (for example, *He turned the key*) activated the hand region of the motor cortex and that hearing sentences that involved foot movements (for example, *He stepped on the grass*) activated the foot region. Presumably, thinking about particular actions activated regions that control these actions.

In conclusion, Wernicke's aphasia includes several types of symptoms, including deficits in spoken word recognition, comprehension, and converting thoughts into words.

Figure 14.13 Verbs and Movements

The figure shows the relative activation of regions of the motor cortex that control movements of the face, arm, and leg when people read verbs that described movements of these regions, such as *bite, slap,* and *kick.*

(Based on Hauk, O., Johnsrude, I., and Pulvermüller, F., Somatotopic representation of action words in human motor and premotor cortex, *Neuron,* 2004, *41,* 301–307.)

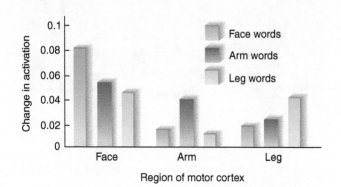

Conduction Aphasia

LO 14.9 Identify the symptoms of conduction aphasia, and describe their contribution to understanding about connections between Broca's and Wernicke's areas.

As we saw earlier in this section, the fact that people with transcortical sensory aphasia can repeat what they hear suggests that there is a direct connection between Wernicke's area and Broca's area—and there is: the **arcuate fasciculus.** This bundle of axons is found in the human brain but is absent or much smaller in the brains of nonhuman primates (Rilling et al., 2008). The arcuate fasciculus appears to convey information about the *sounds* of words but not their *meanings.* The best evidence for this conclusion comes from a syndrome known as conduction aphasia, which is produced by damage to the inferior parietal lobe that extends into the subcortical white matter and damages the arcuate fasciculus (Damasio and Damasio, 1980). (See Figure 14.14.)

Conduction aphasia is characterized by meaningful, fluent speech and relatively good comprehension but very poor repetition. For example, the spontaneous speech of patient L. B. (observed by Margolin and Walker, 1981) was excellent; he made very few errors and had no difficulty naming objects. The transcript of an interview, below, reveals that L. B.'s ability to repeat words was limited to *real* words. He was unable to repeat nonsense words or novel sounds.

Examiner: bicycle

Patient: bicycle

Examiner: hippopotamus

Patient: hippopotamus

Examiner: blaynge

Figure 14.14 Conduction Aphasia

MRI scans show the subcortical damage responsible for a case of conduction aphasia. This lesion damaged the arcuate fasciculus, a fiber bundle connecting Wernicke's area and Broca's area.

(Based on Arnett, P. A., Rao, S. M., Hussain, M., Swanson, S. J., and Hammeke, T. A. Neurology, 1996, *47*, 576–578.)

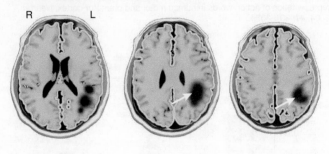

Patient: I didn't get it.

Examiner: Okay, some of these won't be real words, they'll just be sounds. Blaynge.

Patient: I'm not …

Examiner: blanch

Patient: blanch

Examiner: north

Patient: north

Examiner: rilld

Patient: Nope, I can't say.

You will notice that the patient can repeat individual words (all nouns, in this case) but cannot repeat nonwords. He can repeat a meaningful three-word phrase but not three unrelated words.

Sometimes, when a person with conduction aphasia is asked to repeat a word, he or she says a word with the same meaning or one that is related. For example, if the examiner says *house,* the patient may say *home.* If the examiner says *chair,* the patient may say *sit.* One patient made the following response when asked to repeat an entire sentence:

Examiner: The auto's leaking gas tank soiled the roadway.

Patient: The car's tank leaked and made a mess on the street.

The symptoms that are seen in transcortical sensory aphasia and conduction aphasia lead to the conclusion that there are pathways connecting the speech mechanisms of the temporal lobe with those of the frontal lobe. The direct pathway through the arcuate fasciculus simply conveys speech sounds from Wernicke's area to Broca's area. We use this pathway to repeat unfamiliar words—for example, when we are learning a new language or a new word in our own language or when we are trying to repeat a nonword such as *blaynge.* The second pathway, between the posterior language area and Broca's area, is indirect and is based on the *meaning* of words, not on the sounds they make. When patients with conduction aphasia hear a word or a sentence, the meaning of what they hear evokes some sort of image related to that meaning. (The patient in the second example presumably imagined the sight of a vehicle leaking fuel onto the pavement.) They are then able to describe that image, just as they would put their own thoughts into words. Of course, the words they choose might not be the same as the ones used by the person who spoke to them. (See Figure 14.15.)

A study by Catani et al., (2005) provides the first anatomical evidence for the existence of the two pathways between Wernicke's area and Broca's area, presented in Figure 14.15. The investigators used diffusion tensor imaging (DTI) to trace the branches of the arcuate fasciculus in the human brain. DTI-imaging techniques are described in detail in Chapter 5. The researchers found one deep pathway that directly connects these two regions and a shallower pathway that consists of two segments. The anterior segment connects Broca's area with the inferior parietal cortex, and the posterior segment connects Wernicke's area with the inferior parietal cortex. Damage to the direct pathway would be expected to produce conduction aphasia, whereas damage to the indirect pathway would be expected to spare the ability to repeat speech but would impair comprehension. (See Figure 14.16.)

The symptoms of conduction aphasia suggest that the connections between Wernicke's area and Broca's area play an important role in short-term memory of words and speech

Figure 14.15 Explanation of Conduction Aphasia

A lesion that damages the arcuate fasciculus disrupts the transmission of auditory information, but not information related to meaning, to the frontal lobe.

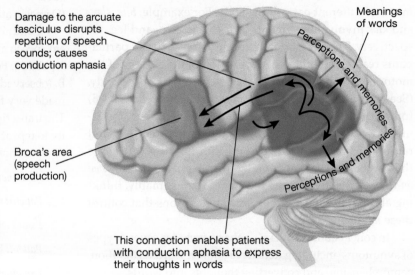

Damage to the arcuate fasciculus disrupts repetition of speech sounds; causes conduction aphasia

Meanings of words

Perceptions and memories

Broca's area (speech production)

Perceptions and memories

This connection enables patients with conduction aphasia to express their thoughts in words

Figure 14.16 Components of the Arcuate Fasciculus

A computer-generated reconstruction of the components of the arcuate fasciculus was obtained through diffusion tensor MRI.

(From Catani, M., Jones, D. K., and ffytche, D. H., Perisylvian language networks of the human brain, *Annals of Neurology*, 2005, *57*, 8–16. Reprinted with permission.)

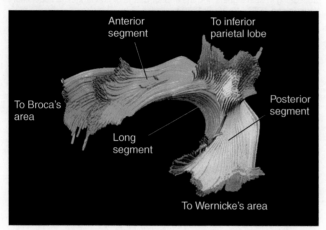

sounds that have just been heard. Presumably, rehearsal of such information can be accomplished by "talking to ourselves" inside our head without actually having to say anything aloud. Imagining ourselves saying the word activates the region of Broca's area, whereas imagining that we are hearing it activates the auditory association area of the temporal lobe. These two regions, connected by means of the arcuate fasciculus (which contains axons traveling in *both* directions), circulate information back and forth, keeping the short-term memory alive. Baddeley (1993) refers to this circuit as the *phonological loop.*

Aziz-Zadeh et al., (2005) obtained evidence that we do use Broca's area when we talk to ourselves. The investigators applied TMS to Broca's area while people were silently counting the number of syllables in words presented on a screen. The investigators used stimulation parameters that disrupted overt (actual) speech. They found that it disrupted covert speech as well; the participants took longer to count the syllables when the TMS was on.

The picture we have drawn so far suggests that comprehension of speech includes a flow of information from Wernicke's area to the posterior language area to various regions of the sensory and motor association cortexes, which contain memories that provide meanings to words. Production of spontaneous speech involves the flow of information concerning perceptions and memories from the sensory and motor association cortexes to the posterior language area to Broca's area. This model is an oversimplification, but it is a useful starting point in conceptualizing basic mental processes. For example, thinking in words probably involves two-way communication between the speech areas and surrounding association cortex (and regions such as the hippocampus and medial temporal lobe).

Aphasia in People Who Are Deaf

LO 14.10 **Explain the brain processes involved in production and comprehension of American Sign Language.**

So far, our discussion has been limited to brain mechanisms of spoken and written language. But communication among many people, including some members of the Deaf community involves another form: sign language. Sign language is expressed manually, by movements of the hands. Sign language is *not* English; nor is it French, Spanish, or Chinese. The most common sign language in North America is ASL—American Sign Language. ASL includes signs for nouns, verbs, adjectives, adverbs, and all the other parts of speech contained in oral languages. People can converse rapidly and efficiently by means of sign language, can tell jokes, and make puns based on the similarity between signs. People who communicate using ASL also use their language ability to think in words.

Some researchers believe that in the history of our species, sign language preceded spoken language—that our ancestors began using gestures to communicate before they switched to speech. As mentioned earlier in this chapter, mirror neurons become active when we see or perform particular grasping, holding, or manipulating movements. Some of these neurons are found in Broca's area. Presumably, these neurons play an important role in learning to mimic other people's hand movements. Indeed, they might have been involved in the development of hand gestures used for communication in our ancestors, and they undoubtedly are used by people when they communicate by sign language. A functional-imaging study by Iacoboni et al. (1999) found that Broca's area was activated when people observed and imitated finger movements. (See Figure 14.17.)

Several studies have found a linkage between speech and hand movements, which supports the suggestion that the spoken language of present-day humans evolved from hand gestures. For example, Gentilucci (2003) had participants speak the syllables *ba* or *ga* while they were watching him grasp objects of different sizes. When the experimenter grasped a large object, the participants opened their mouths more and said the syllable more loudly than when he grasped a small one. These results suggest that the region of the brain that controls grasping is also involved in controlling speech movements.

The grammar of ASL is based on its visual, spatial nature. For example, if a person makes the sign for *John* in one place and later makes the sign for *Mary* in another place, she can place her hand in the *John* location and move it toward the *Mary* location while making the sign for *love*. She is saying, "John loves Mary." Signers can also modify the meaning of signs through facial expressions or the speed and vigor with which they make a sign. Thus, many of the prepositions, adjectives, and adverbs found in spoken languages do not require specific words in ASL. The fact that signed languages

Figure 14.17 Mirror Neurons in Broca's Area

PET scans show a region of the inferior left frontal lobe that was activated when a person saw a finger movement or imitated it. (top) Horizontal section. (bottom) Lateral view of left hemisphere.

(From Iacoboni, M., Woods, R. P., Brass, M., Bekkering, H., Mazziotta, J. C., and Rizzolatti, G., Cortical mechanisms of human imitation, *Science*, 1999, *286*, 2526–2528. Copyright © 1999 by the American Association for the Advancement of Science. Reprinted with permission.)

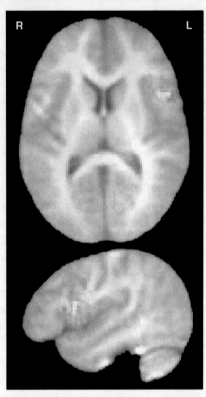

Figure 14.18 Brain Activation During a Rhyming Task

The same language-related regions of the brain are activated by deaf and hearing people when they decide whether two written words rhyme.

(Based on MacSweeney, M., Waters, D., Brammer, M.J., et al., Phonological processing in deaf signers and the impact of age of first language acquisition, *NeuroImage*, 2008, *40*, 1369–1379.)

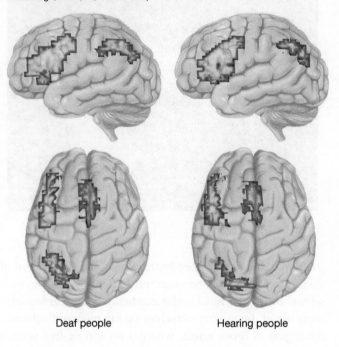

Deaf people   Hearing people

are based on three-dimensional hand and arm movements accompanied by facial expressions means that their grammars are very different from those of spoken languages. Therefore, a word-for-word translation from a spoken language to a signed language (or vice versa) is impossible.

The fact that the grammar of ASL is spatial suggests that aphasic disorders in people who use sign language exclusively, might be caused by lesions of the right hemisphere (which is primarily involved in spatial perception and memory). However, all the cases of people who are deaf with aphasia for signs that have been reported in the literature so far have involved lesions of the *left* hemisphere. Functional-imaging studies show that tasks that involve language activate the same regions of the left hemisphere in people who use spoken language and people who use ASL (MacSweeney et al., 2008a). When a hearing person is asked to look at a pair of drawings and say whether the names of the items they show rhyme, functional imaging shows increased activation in the region of Broca's area because the person "says" the two words subvocally. The same region is activated in people who are deaf and those who are not (MacSweeney et al., 2008b). (See Figure 14.18.)

As you read earlier in this chapter, the right hemisphere contributes to the more subtle, figurative aspects of spoken language. The same is true for signing. Hickok et al. (1999) described the case of two signers who were deaf and had damage to the right hemisphere. Both showed problems with discourse using sign language: One had trouble maintaining a coherent topic, and the other had difficulty with subtle uses of spatial features. A functional-imaging study by Newman et al. (2010) found that, when people who were deaf observed sign language that included the use of narrative devices such as facial expressions or movements of the head, eyes, and body, the inferior frontal cortex and superior temporal cortex of the right hemisphere were activated in addition to the expected language regions of the left hemisphere.

Stuttering

LO 14.11 Describe the biological basis for stuttering and identify treatment strategies.

Stuttering is a speech disorder characterized by frequent pauses, prolongations of sounds, or repetitions of sounds, syllables, or words that disrupt the normal flow of speech. Stuttering, which appears to be influenced by genetic factors, affects approximately 1 percent of the population and is three times more prevalent in men than in women (Brown et al., 2005; Fisher, 2010). Stuttering seldom occurs when a person says a single word or is asked to read a list of words;

Figure 14.19 Stuttering and the Brain

Computer-generated images show data from a meta-analysis of functional-imaging studies of fluent speakers (blue regions) and people who stutter (orange regions), taken while they were speaking.

(From Brown, S., Ingham, R. J., Ingham, J. C., Laird, A. R., and Fox, P. T., Stuttered and fluent speech production: An ALE meta-analysis of functional neuroimaging studies, *Human Brain Mapping*, 2005, *25*, 105–117. Reprinted with permission.)

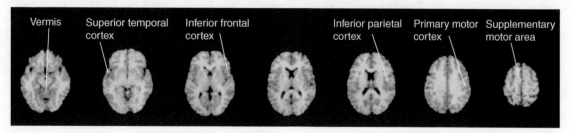

it most often occurs at the beginning of a sentence, especially if the planned sentence is long or grammatically complex. This fact suggests that stuttering is a disorder of "selection, initiation, and execution of motor sequences necessary for fluent speech production" (Watkins et al., 2008, p. 50).

Stuttering is not a result of abnormalities in the neural circuits that contain the motor programs for speech. For example, stuttering is reduced or eliminated when a person reads aloud with another speaker, sings, or reads in cadence with a rhythmic stimulus. The problem appears to lie more in the neural mechanisms that are involved in planning and initiation of speech. A meta-analysis of functional-imaging studies by Brown et al. (2005) found that people who stutter tend to show (relative to fluent speakers) excessive activation of Broca's area and the insula (regions involved in articulation), the supplementary motor area, and the vermis of the cerebellum and an absence of activation in auditory regions of the temporal lobe. Figure 14.19 compares regional brain activity of fluent speakers and people who stutter. Areas shaded in orange indicate regions that are more highly activated in the brains of people who stutter; areas shaded in blue indicate regions that are more highly activated in the brains of fluent speakers. (The only region in the latter category is in the temporal lobe.) The authors suggest that the problem may be caused by faulty auditory feedback from sounds of the person's own speech, shown by the lack of activity in the temporal lobe. They note that a magnetoencepholagraphic study by Salmelin et al. (2000) found disruptions in the normal timing of activation of brain regions involved in speech production.

Evidence in support of this suggestion includes the fact that delayed auditory feedback interferes with the speech of most fluent speakers but actually facilitates the speech of many people who stutter (Foundas et al., 2004). *Delayed auditory feedback* is a procedure in which a person wearing headphones tries to speak normally while hearing his or her own voice, which has been electronically delayed, usually by 50–200 msec. (Portable devices are commercially available that include a microphone, headphones, and an electronic apparatus that provides the delay.) If there were simply a problem with the control of articulation in people

who stutter, delayed auditory feedback would not be expected to have any effect on their fluency.

Watkins et al. (2008) used diffusion tensor imaging and found decreases in the white matter beneath the ventral premotor cortex of people who stuttered. They suggested that the axons in this white matter connect the ventral premotor cortex with regions of the superior temporal cortex and inferior parietal cortex that are involved in integrating the planning of speech with auditory feedback from one's own voice.

Neumann et al., (2005) provide further evidence that the apparently abnormal auditory feedback in people who stutter is reflected in decreased activation of their temporal cortex. The authors used functional MRI (fMRI) to measure the regional brain activation of people who stutter reading sentences aloud during two sessions, one before and one after a successful twelve-week course of fluency-shaping therapy. Figure 14.20 shows that, after the

Figure 14.20 Effects of Therapy for Stuttering

A functional MRI scan shows regions of the superior temporal lobe that showed increased activity one year after a successful course of therapy for stuttering.

(Based on Neumann, K., Preibisch, C., Euler, H. A., von Gudenberg, A. W., Lanfermann, H., Gall, V., and Giraud, A.-L., Cortical plasticity associated with stuttering therapy, *Journal of Fluency Disorders*, 2005, *30*, 23–39.)

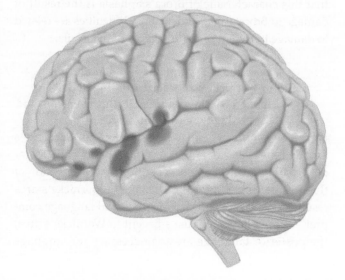

Table 14.1 Aphasic Syndromes Produced by Brain Damage

Disorder	Areas of Lesion	Spontaneous Speech	Comprehension	Repetition	Naming
Wernicke's aphasia	Posterior portion of superior temporal gyrus (Wernicke's area) and posterior language area	Fluent	Poor	Poor	Poor
Pure word deafness	Wernicke's area or its connection with primary auditory cortex	Fluent	Poor	Poor	Good
Broca's aphasia	Frontal cortex rostral to base of primary motor cortex (Broca's area)	Nonfluent	Good	Poor[a]	Poor
Conduction aphasia	White matter beneath parietal lobe superior to lateral fissure (arcuate fasciculus)	Fluent	Good	Poor	Good
Anomic aphasia	Various parts of parietal and temporal lobes	Fluent	Good	Good	Poor
Transcortical sensory aphasia	Posterior language area	Fluent	Poor	Good	Poor

[a]May be better than spontaneous speech.

therapy, the activation of the temporal lobe—a region that Brown et al. (2005) found to show decreased activation—was increased.

Because so many terms and symptoms were described in this section, the following table summarizes them. (See Table 14.1.)

Section Review

Disorders of Language Production and Comprehension

LO 14.7 Describe the symptoms and neural bases of Broca's aphasia, including agrammatism, anomia, and articulation.

Broca's aphasia is characterized by slow, laborious, and nonfluent speech due to damage to Broca's area in the frontal lobe. This aphasia is typically caused by brain damage that extends beyond Broca's region into subcortical white matter. Similar aphasia symptoms are produced by damage to the caudate nucleus. Broca's aphasia includes symptoms of agrammatism (difficulty using grammatical constructions), anomia (word-finding difficulty), and articulation difficulties. Research on agrammatism reveals that this characteristic of Broca's aphasia is the result of damage to Broca's area. Articulation difficulties are related to damage to the left precentral gyrus of the insula.

LO 14.8 Describe the symptoms and neural bases of Wernicke's aphasia, including deficits in spoken word recognition, comprehension, and converting thoughts into words.

Wernicke's aphasia, caused by damage to Wernicke's area and the posterior language area, consists of poor language comprehension, poor repetition, and production of fluent, meaningless speech. Damage to Wernicke's area results in deficits of speech perception and language comprehension. The region just adjacent to Wernicke's area, the posterior language area, is necessary for language comprehension and the translation of thoughts into words. Presumably, Wernicke's area contains memories of the sounds of words, each of which is connected through the posterior language area with circuits that contain memories about the properties of the things the words denote and with circuits that are responsible for pronouncing the words. Damage restricted to Wernicke's area causes pure word deafness—loss of the ability to understand speech but intact speech production, reading, and writing. The left hemisphere is involved in analysis of rapid changes in sounds, which is consistent with its role in the analysis of speech sounds, which are characterized by such changes. Transcortical sensory aphasia, caused by damage to the posterior speech area, consists of poor language comprehension and production, but the patients can repeat what they hear. Thus, the symptoms of Wernicke's aphasia consist of those of transcortical sensory aphasia plus those of pure word deafness. Feedback from mirror neurons that are activated when people hear the speech of other people may facilitate speech recognition.

LO 14.9 Identify the symptoms of conduction aphasia, and describe their contribution to understanding about connections between Broca's and Wernicke's areas.

Conduction aphasia is characterized by meaningful, fluent speech and relatively good comprehension but very poor repetition. The fact that people with transcortical sensory aphasia can repeat words that they cannot understand suggests that there is a direct connection between Wernicke's area and Broca's area. Indeed, there is: the arcuate fasciculus. Damage to the arcuate fasciculus produces conduction aphasia: disruption of the ability to repeat exactly what was heard without disruption of the ability to comprehend or produce meaningful speech and language. A parallel pathway, consisting of an anterior and a posterior bundle that connect in the inferior parietal cortex, may be responsible for the ability of people with pure conduction aphasia to understand and paraphrase what they hear.

LO 14.10   Explain the brain processes involved in production and comprehension of American Sign Language.

The left hemisphere plays the more important role in the language abilities of people who are deaf and use sign language, just as it does in people who communicate acoustically. Gestural language may have been a precursor to spoken language; mirror neurons in Broca's area are activated by hand movements.

LO 14.11   Describe the biological basis for stuttering and identify treatment strategies.

Stuttering appears to be caused by abnormalities in neural circuits that are involved in feedback and planning and initiating speech, not in the circuits that contain the motor programs for articulation. Functional imaging indicates deficient auditory feedback produced by the person's own voice. People who stutter show excessive activation of Broca's area and the insula, supplementary motor area, and vermis of the cerebellum and an absence of activation in auditory regions of the temporal lobe. Delayed auditory feedback, which impairs the speech of most fluent speakers, often facilitates the speech of stutterers.

Thought Question

Suppose that you were asked to determine the abilities and deficits of people with aphasia. What tasks would you include in your examination to test for the presence of particular deficits?

Disorders of Reading and Writing

Reading and writing are closely related to listening and talking; thus, oral and written language abilities have many brain mechanisms in common. This section discusses the neural bases of reading and writing disorders.

Relation to Aphasia

LO 14.12   Compare aphasias and disorders of reading and writing.

The reading and writing skills of people with aphasia almost always reflect their speaking and comprehending abilities. For example, patients with Wernicke's aphasia have as much difficulty reading and writing as they do speaking and understanding language. Patients with Broca's aphasia comprehend what they read about as well as they understand spoken language, but their reading aloud is poor. If a patient's speech is agrammatical, so is their writing; and if they fail to comprehend grammar when listening to speech, they also fail to do so when reading. Patients with conduction aphasia generally have some difficulty reading; when they read aloud, they often make semantic paraphasias (saying synonyms or related words for some of the words they read), just as they do when attempting to repeat what they hear. Depending on the location of the lesion, some patients with transcortical sensory aphasia may read aloud accurately but fail to comprehend what they read.

Pure Alexia

LO 14.13   Identify the symptoms of pure alexia, and describe the brain structures involved.

Dejerine (1892) described a remarkable syndrome, which we now call **pure alexia,** or sometimes *pure word blindness* or *alexia without agraphia.* His patient had a lesion in the visual cortex of the left occipital lobe and the posterior end of the corpus callosum. The patient could still write, although he had lost the ability to read. In fact, if he was shown some of his own writing, he could not read it. The case below illustrates the unique nature of pure alexia.

This case involves a man with pure alexia who discovered his ability to write in an interesting way. A few months after he sustained a head injury that caused his brain damage, he and his wife were watching a service person repair their washing machine. The patient wanted to say something privately to his wife, so he picked up a pad of paper and jotted a note. As he was handing it to her, they suddenly realized with amazement that although he could not read, he was able to write! His wife brought the note to their neurologist, who asked the patient to read it. Although he remembered the general content of the message, he could not read the words he had written.

Although patients with pure alexia cannot read, they can recognize words that are spelled aloud to them;

Figure 14.21 Pure Alexia

In this schematic, red arrows indicate the flow of information that has been interrupted by brain damage. (a) The route followed by information as a person with damage to the left primary visual cortex reads aloud. (b) Additional damage to the posterior corpus callosum interrupts the flow of information and produces pure alexia.

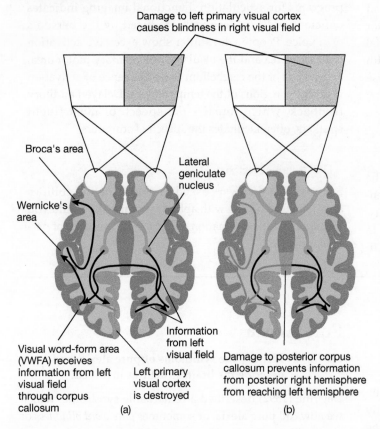

Damage to left primary visual cortex causes blindness in right visual field

Broca's area

Lateral geniculate nucleus

Wernicke's area

Visual word-form area (VWFA) receives information from left visual field through corpus callosum

Left primary visual cortex is destroyed

Information from left visual field

(a)

Damage to posterior corpus callosum prevents information from posterior right hemisphere from reaching left hemisphere

(b)

therefore, they have not lost their memories of the spellings of words. Pure alexia is a perceptual disorder; it is similar to pure word deafness, except that the patient has difficulty with visual input, not auditory input. The disorder is caused by lesions that prevent visual information from reaching the visual association cortex of the left hemisphere (Damasio and Damasio, 1983, 1986; Molko et al., 2002). Figure 14.21 explains why Dejerine's original patient could not read. The left side of the diagram shows the pathway that visual information would take if a person had damage *only to the left primary visual cortex*. In this case the person's right visual field would be blind; he or she would see nothing to the right of the fixation point. But people with this disorder can read. Their only problem is that they must look to the right of each word so that they can see all of it, which means that they read somewhat more slowly than someone with full vision. (See Figure 14.21a.)

Let's trace the flow of visual information for a person with this brain damage that enables that person to read words aloud. Information from the left side of the visual field is transmitted to the right striate cortex (primary visual cortex) and then to regions of right visual association cortex.

From there the information crosses the posterior corpus callosum and is transmitted to a region of the left visual association cortex known as the *visual word-form area (VWFA)*, where it is analyzed further. The information is then transmitted to speech mechanisms located in the left frontal lobe. Thus, the person can read the words aloud. (Look again at Figure 14.21a.)

The right side of the diagram shows Dejerine's patient. Notice how the additional lesion of the corpus callosum prevents visual information concerning written text from reaching the VWFA in the left hemisphere. Because this brain region is essential for the ability to recognize words, the patient cannot read. (See Figure 14.21b.)

Mao-Draayer and Panitch (2004) reported the case of a man with multiple sclerosis who displayed the symptoms of pure alexia after sustaining a lesion that damaged both the subcortical white matter of the left occipital lobe and the posterior corpus callosum. As you can see in Figure 14.22, the lesions are in the locations that Dejerine predicted would cause this syndrome, except that the white matter that serves the left primary visual cortex is damaged, not the cortex itself.

The diagrams shown in Figure 14.21 are as simple and schematic as possible. They illustrate only the pathway involved in seeing a word and pronouncing it, and they ignore neural structures that would be involved in understanding its meaning. As we will see later in this chapter, evidence from patients with brain lesions indicates that seeing and pronouncing words can take place independently of understanding them. Although the diagrams are simplified, they are not unreasonable, given what we know about the neural components of the reading process.

Figure 14.22 Pure Alexia in a Person with Multiple Sclerosis

The lesions correspond to those shown in Figure 14.21, except that the white matter that serves the left primary visual cortex is damaged, not the cortex itself.

(Based on Mao-Draayer, Y., and Panitch, H. Multiple Sclerosis, 2004, *10*, 705–707.)

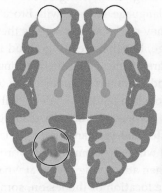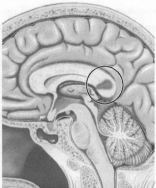

Damage to white matter that serves the left visual cortex

Damage to posterior corpus callosum

Writing is not the only form of visible language; people can also communicate by means of sign. Hickok et al., (1995) reported on a case of "sign blindness" caused by damage similar to that which causes pure alexia. The patient, a right-handed woman who was deaf, sustained a stroke that damaged her left occipital lobe and the posterior corpus callosum. The lesion did not impair her ability to sign in coherent sentences, but she could no longer understand other people's sign language, and she lost her ability to read. She had some ability to comprehend single signs (corresponding to single words), but she could not comprehend signed sentences.

Toward an Understanding of Reading

LO 14.14 **Describe how research on acquired and developmental dyslexia helps us to understand the role of the brain in reading.**

Reading involves at least two different processes: direct recognition of the word as a whole and sounding it out letter by letter. When we see a familiar word, we normally recognize it and pronounce it—a process known as **whole-word reading.** (With very long words we might instead perceive segments of several letters each.) The second method, which we use for unfamiliar words, requires recognition of individual letters and knowledge of the sounds they make. This process is known as **phonetic reading.**

Evidence for our ability to sound out words is easy to obtain. In fact, you can prove to yourself that phonetic reading exists by trying to read the following words:

glab trisk chint

These are not really words, but most readers are able to pronounce them. Readers don't *recognize* them, because they have probably never seen them before. Instead, readers use what they know about the sounds that are represented by particular letters (or small groups of letters, such as *ch*) to figure out how to pronounce the words.

The best evidence that people can read words without sounding them out, using the whole-word method, comes from studies of patients with acquired dyslexias. *Dyslexia* means "faulty reading." *Acquired* dyslexias are those caused by damage to the brains of people who already know how to read. In contrast, *developmental* dyslexias refer to reading difficulties that become apparent when children are learning to read. Developmental dyslexias, which appear to involve anomalies in brain circuitry, are discussed in a later section.

Figure 14.23 illustrates some elements of the reading processes. The diagram is an oversimplification of a very complex process, but it helps to organize some of the facts that investigators have obtained. It considers only reading and pronouncing single words, not understanding the meaning of text. When we see a familiar word, we normally recognize it as a whole and pronounce it. If we see an

Figure 14.23 Model of the Reading Process

In this simplified model, whole-word reading is used for most familiar words; phonetic reading is used for unfamiliar words and for nonwords such as *glab, trisk,* or *chint.*

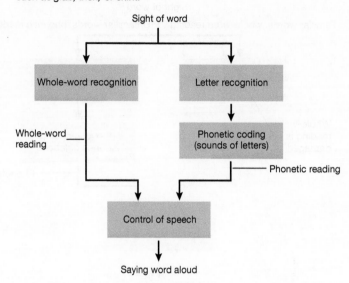

unfamiliar word or a pronounceable nonword, we must try to read it phonetically.

Investigators have reported several types of acquired dyslexias. Three of them will be described in this section: surface dyslexia, direct dyslexia, and phonological dyslexia.

SURFACE DYSLEXIA **Surface dyslexia** is a deficit in whole-word reading. The term *surface* reflects the fact that people with this disorder make errors related to the visual appearance of the words and to pronunciation rules, not to the meaning of the words, which is metaphorically "deeper" than the appearance.

Because patients with surface dyslexia have difficulty recognizing words as a whole, they must sound them out. They can easily read words with regular spelling, such as *hand, table,* or *chin.* However, they have difficulty reading words with irregular spelling, such as *sew, pint,* and *yacht.* In fact, they may read these words as *sue, pinnt,* and *yatchet.* They have no difficulty reading pronounceable nonwords, such as *glab, trisk,* and *chint.* Because people with surface dyslexia cannot recognize whole words by their appearance, they must, in effect, listen to their own pronunciation to understand what they are reading. If they read the word *pint* and pronounce it *pinnt,* they will say that it is not an English word (which it is not, pronounced that way). If the word is one member of a homophone, it will be impossible for them to understand it unless it is read in the context of a sentence. For example, if you hear the single word "pair" without additional information, you cannot know whether the speaker is referring to *pair, pear,* or *pare.* (See Figure 14.24.)

DIRECT DYSLEXIA As you read earlier in this chapter, recognizing a spoken word is different from understanding

Figure 14.24 Surface Dyslexia

In this hypothetical example, whole-word reading is damaged; only phonetic reading remains.

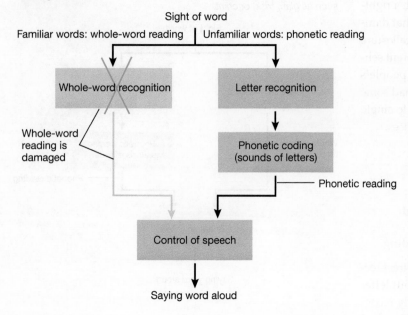

it. For example, patients with transcortical sensory aphasia can repeat what is said to them even though they show no signs of understanding what they hear or say. The same is true for reading. **Direct dyslexia** resembles transcortical sensory aphasia, except that the words in question are written, not spoken (Gerhand, 2001; Lytton and Brust, 1989; Schwartz et al., 1979). Patients with direct dyslexia are able to read aloud *even though they cannot understand the words they are saying.* After sustaining a stroke that damaged his left frontal and temporal lobes, Lytton and Brust's patient lost the ability to communicate verbally; his speech was meaningless, and he was unable to comprehend what other people said to him. However, he could read words with which he was already familiar. He could *not* read pronounceable nonwords; therefore, he had lost the ability to read phonetically. His comprehension deficit seemed complete; when the investigators presented him with a word and several pictures, one of which corresponded to the word, he read the word correctly but had no idea what picture went with it. Gerhand's patient showed a similar pattern of deficits except that she was able to read phonetically: She could sound out pronounceable nonwords. These findings indicate that the brain regions responsible for phonetic reading and whole-word reading are each directly connected with brain regions responsible for speech.

PHONOLOGICAL DYSLEXIA The symptoms of **phonological dyslexia** are opposite those of surface dyslexia: People with this disorder can read by the whole-word method but cannot sound words out. Thus, they can read words that they are already familiar with but have great difficulty figuring out how to read unfamiliar words or pronounceable nonwords (Beauvois and Dérouesné, 1979; Dérouesné and Beauvois, 1979). People with phonological dyslexia may be excellent readers if they had already acquired a good reading vocabulary before their brain damage occurred.

Phonological dyslexia provides further evidence that whole-word reading and phonological reading involve different brain mechanisms. Phonological reading, which is the only way we can read nonwords or words we have not yet learned, entails some sort of letter-to-sound decoding. Phonological reading of English requires more than decoding of the sounds produced by single letters, because, for example, some sounds are transcribed as two-letter sequences (such as *th* or *sh*) and the addition of the letter *e* to the end of a word lengthens an internal vowel (*can* becomes *cane*). (See Figure 14.25.)

The Japanese language provides a particularly interesting distinction between phonetic and whole-word reading. The Japanese language makes use of two kinds of written symbols. *Kanji* symbols are pictographs, adopted from the Chinese language (although they are pronounced as Japanese words). Kanji represent concepts by means of visual symbols but do not provide a guide to their pronunciation. Reading words expressed in kanji symbols is analogous, then, to whole-word reading. *Kana* symbols are phonetic

Figure 14.25 Phonological Dyslexia

In this hypothetical example, phonetic reading is damaged; only whole-word reading remains.

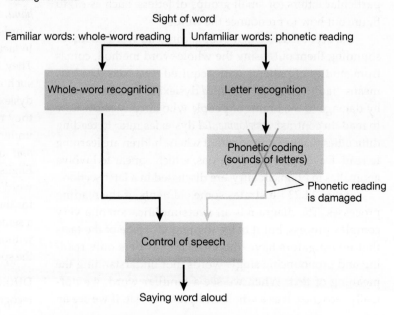

representations of syllables; thus, they encode acoustical information. These symbols are used primarily to represent foreign words or Japanese words that the average reader would be unlikely to recognize if they were represented by their kanji symbols. Reading words expressed in kana symbols is phonetic. (See Figure 14.26.)

Studies of people with localized brain damage that read both kana and kanji, have shown that reading kana and kanji symbols involves different brain mechanisms (Iwata, 1984; Sakurai et al., 2001). Difficulty reading kanji symbols is a form of surface dyslexia, whereas difficulty reading kana symbols is a form of phonological dyslexia. What regions are involved in these two kinds of reading?

Figure 14.26 Examples of Kanji and Kana

Evidence from lesion and functional-imaging studies with readers of English, Chinese, and Japanese suggest that the process of whole-word reading follows the ventral stream of the visual system to a region, the fusiform gyrus, located on the base of the temporal lobe. For example, functional-imaging studies by Liu et al., (2008) and Thuy et al., (2004) found that the reading of kanji words or Chinese characters (whole-word reading) activated the left fusiform gyrus, a region of the cerebral cortex located at the base of the temporal lobe. This region has come to be known as the **visual word-form area or VWFA** (Dehaene, 2009). As we saw in Chapter 6, part of the fusiform gyrus is also involved in the perception of faces and other shapes that require expertise to distinguish—and, recognizing whole words or kanji symbols requires expertise.

The location of the neural circuitry responsible for phonological reading is less certain. Many investigators believe that it involves the region of the cerebral cortex that surrounds the junction of the inferior parietal lobe and the superior temporal lobe (the temporoparietal cortex) and then follows a fiber bundle from this region to the inferior frontal cortex, which includes Broca's area (Jobard et al., 2003; Sakurai et al., 2000; Tan et al., 2005; Thuy et al., 2004). However, damage restricted to the cortex of the VWFA—without damage to underlying white matter—produces pure alexia (Beversdorf et al., 1997). Thus, although phonological reading may involve the temporoparietal cortex, the VWFA appears to play an essential role in both forms of reading. The fact that phonological reading involves Broca's area suggests that it may actually involve articulation—that we sound out words not so much by "hearing" them in our heads as by feeling ourselves pronounce them silently to ourselves. (As you read earlier in this chapter, feedback from the inferior frontal cortex plays a role in perception of spoken words.) Once words have been identified—by either means—their meaning must be accessed, which means that the two pathways converge on regions of the brain involved in recognition of word meaning, grammatical structure, and semantics. (See Figure 14.27 and Table 14.2.)

VISUAL WORD-FORM AREA The neural circuits involved in written and auditory information must also eventually converge, because both must have access to the same

Table 14.2 Comparing Phonological and Whole-Word Processing

Types of Reading	Applied to Reading Letters	Applied to Reading Symbols
Phonological	Sounding out unfamiliar words based on their letters	Sounding out unfamiliar words based on their kana
Whole-Word	Recognition of familiar whole word	Recognition of familiar whole kanji

Figure 14.27 Phonological and Whole-Word Reading
(a) Phonological reading. (b) Whole-word reading. VWFA = visual word-form area of the fusiform cortex.

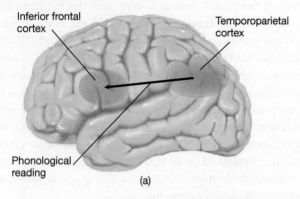

(a)

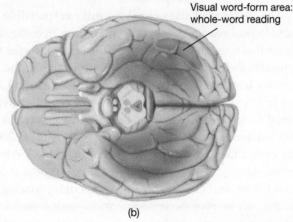

(b)

linguistic and semantic information that identify words and their meaning. An interesting study by Marinkovic et al., (2003) used magnetoencephalography to trace regional brain activation as people heard or read individual words. The study showed that neural activation responsible for the analysis of a spoken word began in the auditory cortex of the temporal lobe and spread to the auditory association cortex on the superior temporal lobe (including Wernicke's area) and then to the inferior frontal cortex (including Broca's area). The neural activation responsible for the analysis of a printed word began in the visual cortex and spread to the base of the temporal lobe (including the VWFA in the fusiform gyrus) and then to the inferior frontal cortex. The temporoparietal cortex received little activation, presumably because the participants were fluent readers who did not need to sound out the common words they were asked to read.

Let's consider the role of the VWFA. Some parts of the visual association cortex must be involved in perceiving written words. You will recall from Chapter 6 that visual agnosia is a perceptual deficit in which people with bilateral damage to the visual association cortex cannot recognize objects by sight. However, people with visual agnosia

can still read, which means that the perceptual analysis of objects and words involves at least some different brain mechanisms. This fact is both interesting and puzzling. Certainly, the ability to read cannot have shaped the evolution of the human brain, because the invention of writing is only a few thousand years old, and, until very recently, the vast majority of the world's population did not read or write. Thus, reading and object recognition use brain mechanisms that undoubtedly existed long before the invention of writing. However, just as experience seeing faces affects the development of the fusiform face area in the right hemisphere, experience learning to read words affects the development of the neural circuitry in the visual word-form area—which, probably not coincidentally, is found in the fusiform cortex of the left hemisphere. A functional-imaging study by Brem et al. (2010) scanned the brains of young children who had not yet learned to read. Initially, the sight of printed words activated the ventral posterior occipitotemporal region bilaterally. After 3–4 hours of teaching the associations of written letters and their sounds, the sight of words activated the left hemisphere. Learning to read affects the connections of the neural system involved in recognizing letters and words.

The fusiform face area has the ability to quickly recognize unique configurations of people's eyes, noses, lips, and other features of their faces even when the features of two people's faces are very similar. For example, relatives and close friends of identical twins can see at a glance which twin they are looking at. Similarly, our VWFA can recognize a word even if it closely resembles another one. (See Figure 14.28.) It can also quickly recognize words written in different *typestyles*, fonts, or CASES. This means that the VWFA can recognize whole words with different shapes; for example, chair and CHAIR do not look the same. It takes an experienced reader the same amount of time to read equally familiar three-letter words and six-letter words (Nazir et al., 1998), which means that the whole-word reading process does not have to identify the letters one at a time, just as the face-recognition process in the right fusiform cortex does not have to identify each feature of

Figure 14.28 Subtle Differences in Written Words
Unless you can read Arabic, Hindi, or Mandarin, you will probably have to examine these words carefully to find the small differences. However, as a reader of English, you will immediately recognize the words *cars* and *ears*.

(Adapted from Devlin, J. T., Jamison, H. L., Gonnerman, L. M., and Matthews, P. M., The role of the posterior fusiform gyrus in reading, *Journal of Cognitive Neuroscience*, 2006, *18*, 911–922.)

English	Arabic		Hindi		Mandarin	
cars ears	زمان	زمان	आज	आजा	夫	天
	pomegranate	time/era	today	come	man	sky

a face individually before the face is recognized. Instead, we recognize several letters and their locations relative to each other.

Many studies have found that damage to the VWFA produces surface dyslexia—that is, impairment of whole-word reading. A study by Gaillard et al., (2006) combined fMRI and lesion evidence from a single participant and suggested that the left fusiform cortex does, indeed, contain this region. A patient with a severe seizure disorder became a candidate for surgery to remove the seizure focus. Before the surgery was performed, the patient viewed printed words and pictures of faces, houses, and tools while his brain was being scanned. He knew that the seizure focus was located in a region that played a critical role in reading, but his symptoms were so severe that he elected to undergo the surgery. As expected, the surgery produced a deficit in whole-word reading. A combination of structural and functional imaging revealed that the lesion—a very small one—was located in the fusiform gyrus, the location of the VWFA.

PLASTICITY IN VISUAL WORD FORM AREA   What did the region of the visual association cortex that we now know as the VWFA do before people invented written language? What does it do in people who do not read or write? As Dehaene et al., (2010) note:

> Cultural inventions such as reading and mathematics are too recent to have influenced the human genome. Therefore, they must be acquired through the recycling of neuronal networks evolved for other purposes, but whose initial properties are sufficiently similar to the target function and which possess enough plasticity, particularly during childhood, for their functionality to be partially converted to this novel task. (p. 1837)

The ability to co-opt brain regions for new purposes allows humans across many different cultures, with many different languages and writing systems, to learn to read and write fluently. Fluency and literacy can develop very quickly in some cases, further supporting the idea that the relevant neural pathways are present prior to development of a new language. For example, consider that at least two written languages were invented by specific individuals. Hangul, the written form of the Korean language, was invented by King Sejong (and his scholars) in the fourteenth century. The characters of the Hangul alphabet are designed to look like the shapes the mouth makes when they are pronounced. In the early nineteenth century, Sequoyah, a Cherokee living in what is now the state of North Carolina, spent 12 years developing a written version of his language. He analyzed the sounds of his language and selected 85 symbols—from English and Greek letters and some additional symbols that he invented. He was not familiar with the sounds that English and Greek letters represented, so the sounds he assigned to them bore no relationship to those of the languages they came

from. Within a few months of the introduction of Sequoyah's alphabet, thousands of people learned to read and write the Cherokee language.

Changizi et al., (2006) analyzed the configurations of letters and symbols used in a large number of former and present writing systems from all over the world. They found that these characters seem to have been chosen by the cultures that invented them to match those found in objects in nature's scenes—and they all involve junctions of lines. Early forms of writing used actual pictures, but the pictures became simplified and eventually turned into simple lines or intersecting lines and curves. Even complex symbols such as Chinese characters consist of intersecting brush strokes. Figure 14.29 shows a few of the ways that different types of intersections of two line segments can be transformed into letters found in various writing systems. Presumably, the region of the brain that becomes the VWFA through the process of learning to read originally evolved to recognize objects by learning the configuration of lines (straight and curved) and their junctions. Our ancestors invented forms of writing that use symbols that are distinguished by these characteristics, and a portion of the fusiform gyrus became "recycled" (as Dehaene et al. phrased it) into the VWFA.

DEVELOPMENTAL DYSLEXIAS   Some children have great difficulty learning to read and never become fluent readers, even though they are intelligent. Specific language learning disorders, called **developmental dyslexias**, tend to occur in families, a finding that suggests a genetic (and hence biological) component. The concordance rate of developmental

Figure 14.29 Examples of Ways that Different Types of Intersections of Two Line Segments Can Be Transformed into Letters Found in Various Writing Systems

Segments can be transformed into letters found in various writing systems.

(Adapted from Changizi, M. A., Zhang, Q., Ye, H., and Shimojo, S., The structures of letters and symbols throughout human history are selected to match those found in objects in natural scenes, *American Naturalist*, 2006, 167, E117–E139.)

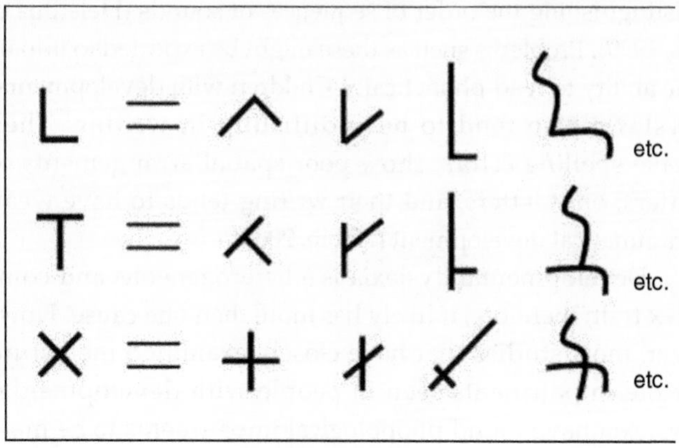

We should not expect that developmental dyslexia involves only deficits in reading.

dyslexia in monozygotic twins ranges from 84 percent to 100 percent and in dizygotic twins it ranges from 20 percent to 35 percent (Démonet et al., 2004). Linkage and association studies suggest that the chromosomes 3, 6, and 15 may contain genes responsible for different components of this disorder (Kang and Drayna, 2011).

As we saw earlier, the fact that written language is a recent invention means that natural selection is unlikely to have given us brain mechanisms whose only role is to interpret written language. Therefore, we should not expect that developmental dyslexia involves only deficits in reading. Indeed, researchers have found a variety of language deficits associated with dyslexia that do not directly involve reading. One common deficit is deficient phonological awareness. That is, people with developmental dyslexia have difficulty blending or rearranging the sounds of words that they hear (Eden and Zeffiro, 1998). For example, they have difficulty recognizing that if we remove the first sound from "cat," we are left with the word "at." They also have difficulty distinguishing the order of sequences of sounds (Helenius et al., 1999). Problems such as these might be expected to impair the ability to read phonetically. Children with developmental dyslexia also tend to have difficulty in writing: They make spelling errors, show poor spatial arrangements of letters, omit letters, and their writing tends to have weak grammatical development (Habib, 2000).

Developmental dyslexia is a heterogeneous and complex trait; therefore, it likely has more than one cause. However, most studies that have closely examined the nature of the impairments seen in people with developmental dyslexia have found phonological impairments to be most common. For example, a study of 16 people with developmental dyslexia by Ramus et al. (2003) found that all of the participants had phonological deficits. Ten of the people also had auditory deficits, four also had a motor deficit, and two also had a visual deficit. These deficits—especially auditory deficits—aggravated the people's difficulty in reading but did not appear to be primarily responsible for the difficulty. Five of the people had only phonological deficits, and these deficits were sufficient to interfere with their ability to read.

Some evidence has been obtained from functional-imaging studies that suggests that the brains of people with developmental dyslexia process written information differently than do the brains of proficient readers. For example, Shaywitz et al. (2002) had 70 children with dyslexia and 74 children without dyslexia read words and pronounceable nonwords. The researchers found significantly different patterns of brain activation in the two groups. A child's reading skill was positively correlated with activation of the left VWFA. Hoeft et al. (2007) found that people with dyslexia showed decreased activation in the left temporoparietal cortex (dorsal to the region identified by Shaywitz et al.) and in the VWFA. They also saw *hyper-activation* of the left inferior frontal cortex, including Broca's area. Presumably, the activation of Broca's area reflected an effort to decode the phonology of the incomplete information being received from the poorly functioning regions of the more posterior brain regions involved in reading.

Most languages—including English—contain many irregular words. For example, consider *cough, rough, bough,* and *through.* Because there is no phonetic rule that describes how these words are to be pronounced, readers of English are obliged to memorize them. In fact, the 40 sounds that distinguish English words can be spelled in up to 1,120 different ways. In contrast, Italian is much more regular; this language contains 25 different sounds that can be spelled in only 33 combinations of letters (Helmuth, 2001). Paulesu et al. (2001) found that developmental dyslexia is rare among people who speak Italian and is much more common among speakers of English and French (another language with many irregular words). Paulesu and his colleagues identified college students with a history of dyslexia from Italy, France, and Great Britain. The Italian students with dyslexia were much harder to find, and their disorders were much less severe than those of their English-speaking and French-speaking counterparts. However, functional imaging revealed that when all three groups were asked to read, their scans all showed the same pattern of activation: a decrease in the activity of the left occipitotemporal cortex—the same general region that Shaywitz et al. (2002) identified.

Paulesu et al., (2001) concluded that the brain anomalies that cause dyslexia are similar in the three countries they studied but that the regularity of Italian spelling made it much easier for people likely to develop dyslexia in Italy to learn to read. By the way, other "dyslexia-friendly" languages include Spanish, Finnish, Czech, and Japanese. One of the authors of this study, Chris D. Frith, cites the case of an Australian boy who lived in Japan. He learned to read Japanese but experienced dyslexia in English (Recer, 2001). If the spelling of words in the English language were regularized (for example, *frend* instead of *friend*, *frate* instead of *freight*, *koff* instead of *cough*), many children who develop dyslexia under the present system might develop into much better readers.

Toward an Understanding of Writing

LO 14.15 **Explain how research on audition, vision, memorization, and motor control helps us to understand the role of the brain in writing.**

Writing depends on knowledge of the words that are to be written, along with the proper grammatical structure of the sentences they are to form. Therefore, if a patient is unable to express himself or herself by speech, there is likely to be a writing disturbance *(dysgraphia)* as well. In addition, most cases of dyslexia are accompanied by dysgraphia.

One type of writing disorder involves difficulties in motor control—in directing the movements of a pen or pencil to form letters and words. Investigators have reported surprisingly specific types of writing disorders that fall into this category. For example, some patients can write numbers but not letters, some can write uppercase letters but not lowercase letters, some can write consonants but not vowels, some can write cursively but cannot print uppercase letters, and others can write letters normally but have difficulty placing them in an orderly fashion on the page (Alexander et al., 1992; Cubelli, 1991; Margolin and Goodman-Schulman, 1992; Silveri, 1996).

Many regions of the brain are involved in writing. For example, damage that produces various forms of aphasia will produce impairments in writing that are similar to those seen in speech. Organization of the motor aspects of writing involves the dorsal parietal lobe and the premotor cortex. These regions (and the primary motor cortex, of course) become activated when people engage in writing, and damage to these regions impairs writing (Katanoda et al., 2001; Menon and Desmond, 2001; Otsuki et al., 1999). A functional-imaging study by Rijntjes et al. (1999) had people sign their names with either their index finger or their big toe. In both cases, doing so activated the premotor cortex that controlled movements of the hand. This finding suggests that when we learn to make a complex series of movements, the relevant information is stored in regions of the motor association cortex that control the part of the body that is being used but that this information can be used to control similar movements in other parts of the body. Longcamp et al. (2005) found that simply looking at alphabetical characters activated the premotor cortex, on the left side

Figure 14.30 Writing and the Ventral Premotor Cortex
Volunteers viewing letters activated the ventral premotor cortex in the hemisphere used for writing: the left hemisphere in right-handed volunteers (yellow) and the right hemisphere in left-handed volunteers (red).

(Based on Longcamp, M., Anton, J.-L., Roth, M., and Velay, J.-L. Neuropsychologia, 2005, 43, 1801–1809.)

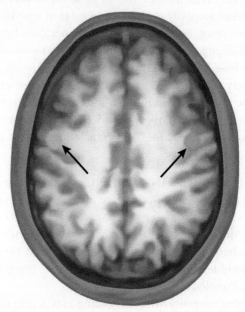

in right-handed people and on the right side in left-handed people. (See Figure 14.30.)

A more basic type of writing disorder involves problems in the ability to spell words, as opposed to problems with making accurate movements of the fingers. Like reading, which involves phonetic and whole-word processes, writing (or, more specifically, spelling) involves more than one method.

AUDITION IN WRITING The first method is related to audition. When children acquire language skills, they first learn to recognize the sounds of words, then learn to say them, then learn to read, and then learn to write. Reading and writing depend heavily on the skills that are learned earlier. For example, to write most words, we must be able to "sound them out in our heads," that is, to hear them and to articulate them subvocally. If you want to demonstrate this to yourself, try to write a long word such as *antidisestablishmentarianism* from memory and see whether you can do it without saying the word to yourself. If you recite a poem or sing a song to yourself (even subvocally) at the same time, you will see that the writing comes to a halt.

VISION IN WRITING A second method of writing involves transcribing an image of what a particular word looks like—copying a visual mental image. Have you ever looked off into the distance to picture a word so that you could remember how to spell it? Some people may not use phonological spelling and have to write some words down to see whether they look correct. This method involves *visual* memories, not acoustical ones.

MEMORIZATION IN WRITING A third method of writing involves memorization of letter sequences. We learn these sequences the way we learn poems or the lyrics to a song. For example, many Americans learned to spell *Mississippi* with a singsong chant that goes like this: **M**-i-s-**s**-i-s-**s**-i-**p**-p-**i**, emphasizing the boldfaced letters. (Similarly, many speakers of English say the alphabet with the rhythm of a children's song that is commonly used to teach it.) This method involves memorizing sequences of letter names, not translating sounds into the corresponding letters.

MOTOR MEMORY IN WRITING Finally, the fourth method of writing involves motor memories. We memorize motor sequences for very familiar words, such as our own names. Most of us need not sound out our names to ourselves when we write our signature, nor need we say the sequence of letters to ourselves, nor need we imagine what our signature looks like.

Writing normally involves holding a stylus (for example, a pen or pencil) and moving its point across a screen, piece of paper, or other surface. But we can also create visual records by typing with a keyboard. The first three methods of writing (sounding out the letters of a word, visualizing it, or reciting a memorized sequence of letters) apply as well to typing as they do to writing. However, the movements that we make with our hands and fingers are different when we write or type. Skilled typists learn automatic sequences of movements that produce frequently used words, but these are different from the movements we would make when we write these words. Otsuki et al., (2002) reported the case of a man who lost the ability to type after a stroke that damaged the ventral left frontal lobe. His ability to speak and understand speech, his ability to read, and his ability to write were not affected, and he showed no other obvious motor impairments besides his *dystypia*, as the investigators named it.

NEURAL BASIS OF WRITING Neurological evidence supports at least the first three of these methods of writing. Brain damage can impair the first of these methods: phonetic writing. This deficit is called **phonological dysgraphia** (Shallice, 1981). (*Dysgraphia* refers to a writing deficit, just as *dyslexia* refers to a reading deficit.) People with this disorder are unable to sound out words and write them phonetically. Thus, they cannot write unfamiliar words or pronounceable nonwords, such as the ones presented in the section on reading. They can, however, visually imagine familiar words and then write them.

Phonological dysgraphia appears to be caused by damage to regions of the brain involved in phonological processing and articulation. Damage to Broca's area, the ventral precentral gyrus, and the insula cause this disorder, and phonological spelling tasks activate these regions (Henry et al., 2007; Omura et al., 2004).

Orthographic dysgraphia is just the opposite of phonological dysgraphia: It is a disorder of visually based writing. People with orthographic dysgraphia can *only* sound words out; thus, they can spell regular words such as *care* or *tree*, and they can write pronounceable nonsense words. However, they have difficulty spelling irregular words such as *half* or *busy* (Beauvois and Dérouesné, 1981); they may write *haff* or *bizzy*. Orthographic dysgraphia (impaired phonological writing), like surface dyslexia, is caused by damage to the VWFA on the base of the temporal lobe (Henry et al., 2007).

Both lesion and functional-imaging studies implicate the posterior inferior temporal cortex in writing of irregularly spelled English words or kanji symbols (Nakamura et al., 2000; Rapcsak and Beeson, 2004). This region appears to be involved not in the motor aspects of writing but in knowledge of how irregular words are spelled or what strokes make up a kanji character.

The third method of spelling depends on a person's having memorized sequences of letters that spell particular words. Cipolotti and Warrington (1996) reported the case of a patient who lacked this ability. The patient sustained a left hemisphere stroke that severely disrupted his ability to spell words orally and impaired his ability to recognize words that the examiners would spell aloud. Presumably, his ability to spell written words depended on the first two methods of writing: auditory and visual. The examiners noted that when they spelled out words to him, he would make writing movements with his hand on top of his knee. When they asked him to clasp his hands together so that he could not make these writing movements, his ability to recognize four-letter words being spelled aloud dropped from 66 percent to 14 percent. It appears that he was using feedback from hand movements to recognize the words he was "writing" on his knee.

As we saw in the section on reading, some patients (those with direct dyslexia) can read aloud without being able to understand what they are reading. Similarly, some patients can write words that are dictated to them even though they cannot understand these words (Lesser, 1989; Roeltgen et al., 1986). They cannot communicate by means of writing, because they cannot translate their thoughts into words. Some of these patients can even spell pronounceable nonwords, which indicates that their ability to spell phonetically is intact. Roeltgen et al. (1986) referred to this disorder as *semantic agraphia*, but perhaps the term *direct dysgraphia* would be more appropriate because of the parallel with direct dyslexia. (See Table 14.3.)

Table 14.3 Brain Regions Involved in Disorders of Reading and Writing

Reading Disorder	Whole-Word Reading	Phonetic Reading	Region of Brain Damage	Remarks
Pure alexia	Poor	Poor	Left primary visual cortex and posterior corpus callosum	Can write
Surface dyslexia	Poor	Good	Visual word form area	
Phonological dyslexia	Good	Poor	VWFA. Others unknown; likely temporal-parietal cortex and inferior frontal cortex (including Broca's area).	
Direct dyslexia	Good	Good	Left frontal and temporal lobes	Cannot comprehend words
Writing Disorder	**Whole-Word Writing**	**Phonetic Writing**		
Phonological dysgraphia	Good	Poor	Broca's area, ventral precentral gyrus, insula	
Orthographic dysgraphia	Poor	Good	Posterior inferior temporal cortex	

Section Review

Disorders of Reading and Writing

LO 14.12 **Compare aphasias and disorders of reading and writing.**

As in aphasia, brain damage can produce reading and writing disorders. With few exceptions, aphasias are accompanied by writing deficits that parallel the language production deficits and by reading deficits that parallel the language comprehension deficits.

LO 14.13 **Identify the symptoms of pure alexia, and describe the brain structures involved.**

Pure alexia involves a deficit in reading that does not affect writing. Pure alexia is caused by lesions that produce blindness in the right visual field and that destroy fibers of the posterior corpus callosum, preventing visual information from reaching the visual association cortex.

LO 14.14 **Describe how research on acquired and developmental dyslexia helps us to understand the role of the brain in reading.**

Acquired dyslexias can fall into one of several categories (surface, direct, phonological), and the study of these disorders has provided information about brain mechanisms involved in reading. Analysis of written words begins in the left posterior inferior temporal cortex. Phonological information is then analyzed by the temporoparietal cortex and Broca's area, whereas word-form information is analyzed by the visual word-form area, located in the fusiform cortex. Surface dyslexia is a loss of whole-word reading ability. Phonological dyslexia is loss of the ability to read phonetically. Reading of kana (phonetic) and kanji (pictographic) symbols by Japanese people is equivalent to phonetic and whole-word reading, and damage to different parts of the brain interferes with these two forms of reading. Direct dyslexia is analogous to transcortical sensory aphasia; the patients can read words aloud but cannot understand what they are reading. Some can read both real words and pronounceable nonwords, so both phonetic and whole-word reading can be preserved.

Developmental dyslexia is a hereditary condition that may involve abnormal development of parts of the brain that play a role in language. Most people with developmental dyslexia have difficulty with phonological processing—of spoken words as well as written ones. Functional-imaging studies report decreased activation of a region of the left occipitotemporal and temporoparietal cortexes and hyperactivation of Broca's area may be involved in developmental dyslexia. Children who learn to read languages that have writing with regular correspondence between spelling and pronunciation (such as Italian) are much less likely to develop dyslexia than are those who learn to read languages with irregular spelling (such as English or French).

LO 14.15 Explain how research on audition, vision, memorization, and motor control helps us to understand the role of the brain in writing.

Brain damage can disrupt writing ability by impairing people's ability to form letters—or even specific types of letters, such as uppercase or lowercase letters or vowels. The dorsal parietal cortex appears to be the most critical region for knowledge of the movements that produce letters. Other deficits involve the ability to spell words. We normally use at least four different strategies to spell words: phonetic (sounding the word out), visual (remembering how it looks on paper), sequential (recalling memorized sequences of letters), and motor (recalling memorized hand movements in writing very familiar words). Two types of dysgraphia—phonological and orthographic—represent difficulties in implementing phonetic and visual strategies, respectively. The existence of these two disorders indicates that several different brain mechanisms are involved in the process of writing. One case of dystypia—a specific deficit in the ability to type without other reading or writing disorders—has been reported. In addition, some patients have a deficit parallel to direct dyslexia: They can write words they can no longer understand.

Thought Question

Think back to when you began learning how to read. Did you learn to read from a teacher or caregiver who used techniques in whole-word reading, phonetic reading, or both? Using examples from your own educational history, describe how your experience of learning to read likely activated whole-word and/or phonetic pathways in your brain. Using your understanding of how the brain processes reading, suggest what types of reading instruction would be most valuable in education today.

Chapter Review Questions

1. Discuss the statement "Language is a lateralized function." Describe the specific contributions of the right and left hemisphere in language.

2. Describe Broca's aphasia and the three major speech and language deficits that result from damage to Broca's area: agrammatism, anomia, and articulation difficulties.

3. Describe the symptoms of Wernicke's aphasia, pure word deafness, and transcortical sensory aphasia; explain how they are related; and describe the brain damage that causes these disorders.

4. Describe the symptoms of conduction aphasia and anomic aphasia, including aphasia in people who are deaf, and the brain damage that causes these disorders.

5. Describe research on the use of prosody in communication and the neural basis of stuttering.

6. Describe pure alexia, and explain why this disorder is caused by damage to two specific parts of the brain.

7. Describe whole-word and phonetic reading, and discuss the categories of acquired dyslexias.

8. Discuss research on the role of what we now call the VWFA before reading and writing were invented.

9. Describe research on the neurological basis of developmental dyslexias.

10. Describe the brain areas involved in sign language and how they differ from those involved in spoken language.

Chapter 15
Neurological Disorders

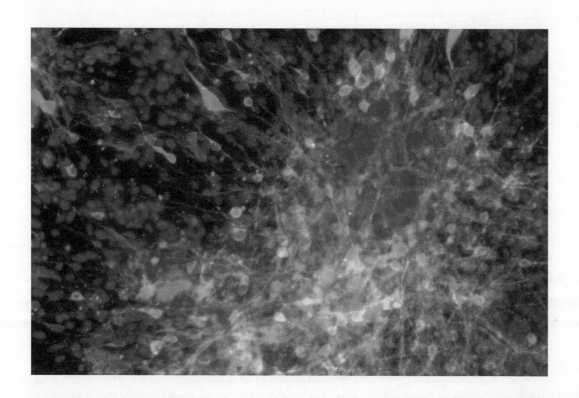

Chapter Outline

Learning Objectives

LO 15.1 Describe the primary symptoms, causes, and treatments for brain tumors.

LO 15.2 Describe the primary symptoms, causes, and treatments for seizures.

LO 15.3 Explain how cerebrovascular accidents can occur.

LO 15.4 Explain how treatments can be used to address the immediate and long-term symptoms of cerebrovascular accidents.

LO 15.5 Identify some causes of traumatic brain injury.

LO 15.6 Describe treatments for traumatic brain injuries.

LO 15.7 Describe the effects of alcohol on development of the nervous system.

LO 15.8 Contrast the symptoms, causes, and treatments of inherited metabolic disorders.

LO 15.9 Identify symptoms, cause, and interventions for Down syndrome.

LO 15.10 Describe how transmissible spongiform encephalopathies cause brain damage.

LO 15.11 Describe the symptoms, causes, and treatments for Parkinson's disease.

LO 15.12 Describe the symptoms, causes, and treatments for Huntington's disease.

LO 15.13 Describe the symptoms, causes, and treatments for amyotrophic lateral sclerosis.

LO 15.14 Describe the symptoms, causes, and treatments for multiple sclerosis.

LO 15.15 Describe the symptoms, causes, and treatments for Alzheimer's disease.

LO 15.16 Describe the symptoms and causes of Korsakoff's syndrome.

LO 15.17 Identify the symptoms, causes, and treatments for encephalitis.

LO 15.18 Identify the symptoms, causes, and treatments for meningitis.

Mrs. R., a divorced, 50-year-old elementary school teacher, was sitting in her car, waiting for a traffic light to change. Suddenly, her right foot began to shake. Afraid that she would inadvertently press the accelerator and move forward into the intersection, she quickly turned the car off. First her lower leg was shaking, then her upper leg as well. She felt her body, then her arm, begin to shake in rhythm with her leg. The shaking slowed and finally stopped. By this time the light had changed to green, and the cars behind her began honking. She missed that green light, but by the time the light changed again, she had recovered enough to drive home.

The next evening, some close friends visited her apartment for dinner. After dinner, her right foot began shaking again. This time she was standing up, and the shaking—much more violent than before—caused her to fall. Her friends heard the noise and came running to see what had happened. They saw Mrs. R. lying on the floor, her legs and arms held out stiffly before her, shaking uncontrollably. She was unconscious and did not respond to her friends as they tried to help her. The shaking stopped less than a minute later. Mrs. R. regained consciousness but seemed confused.

Mrs. R. was brought by ambulance to a hospital. After hearing a description of Mrs. R.'s symptoms, the emergency room physician immediately called a neurologist, who ordered a CT scan. The scan showed a small, circular white spot between the frontal lobes, above the corpus callosum. Two days later, a neurosurgeon removed a small benign tumor, and Mrs. R. fully recovered. She was relieved to learn that her type of brain tumor rarely produces brain damage if it is removed in time.

*****

The case of Mrs. R. highlights several important themes in this chapter. Mrs. R. experienced seizures as a result of a benign tumor. As you will read, there are different types of tumors and several different conditions that can produce seizures. Seizures can involve physical symptoms in restricted parts of the body or they can involve the entire body and include changes in consciousness. Amnesia and confusion following a seizure (as Mrs. R. experienced) are common, and most seizures end within a short period of time.

Although the brain is the most protected organ, many pathological processes can damage it or disrupt its functioning. Because much of what we have learned about the functions of the human brain has been gained by studying people with brain damage, you have already encountered many neurological disorders in this book: movement disorders, such as Parkinson's disease; perceptual disorders, such as visual agnosia and blindness caused by damage to the visual system; language disorders, such as aphasia, alexia, and agraphia; and memory disorders, such as Korsakoff's syndrome.

This chapter describes the major categories of the neuropathological conditions that the brain can sustain—tumors and seizures, cerebrovascular accidents, traumatic brain injury, disorders of development, degenerative disorders, and finally disorders caused by infectious diseases. Each section discusses the behavioral effects of these conditions and their treatments. The figure below shows the basal ganglia and substantia nigra, which we will be paying particular attention to in our examination of these conditions.

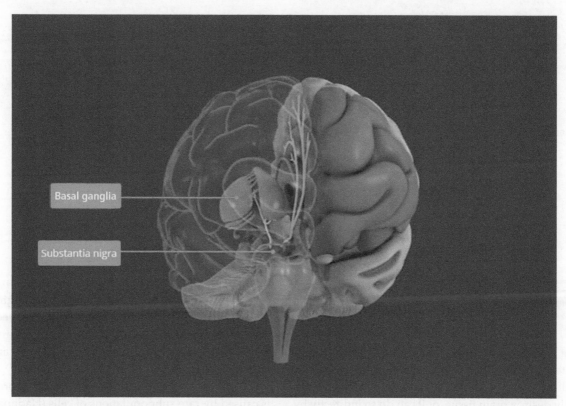

Basal ganglia and substantia nigra.

Tumors and Seizures

It is estimated that over 680,000 individuals are living with brain tumors in the United States alone (Porter et al., 2010), and that 3–5 percent of the global population will experience a seizure during their lifetime (Bell et al., 2014; Sander and Shorvon, 1996). These two conditions can occur separately, or, as in the case of Mrs. R., a tumor may cause a seizure. Approximately 2.5 million people in the United States have a seizure disorder. The following section will describe the biological basis and symptoms of tumors and seizures.

Tumors

LO 15.1 **Describe the primary symptoms, causes and treatments for brain tumors.**

A **tumor** is a mass of cells whose growth is uncontrolled and that serves no useful function. Some are **malignant,** or cancerous, but the majority of tumors are **benign** ("harmless") (Davis et al., 2001; Porter et al., 2010). The major distinction between malignancy and benignancy is whether the tumor is *encapsulated*: whether there is a distinct border between the mass of tumor cells and the surrounding tissue. If there is such a border, the tumor is benign; the surgeon can cut it out, and it will not regrow. However, if the tumor grows by *infiltrating* the surrounding tissue, there will be no clear-cut border between the tumor and healthy tissue. If the surgeon removes the tumor, some cells may be missed, and these cells will produce a new tumor. In addition, malignant tumors often give rise to **metastases.** A metastasizing tumor will shed cells, which then travel through the bloodstream, lodge in capillaries, and serve as seeds for the growth of new tumors in different locations in the body. (See Figure 15.1.)

Tumors damage brain tissue by two means: compression and infiltration. *Any* tumor growing in the brain,

Figure 15.1 Benign and Malignant Tumors

Benign tumors are encapsulated. Malignant tumors lack encapsulation and infiltrate surrounding tissue. Cells from a malignant tumor can travel to new places in the body and cause additional tumors to grow.

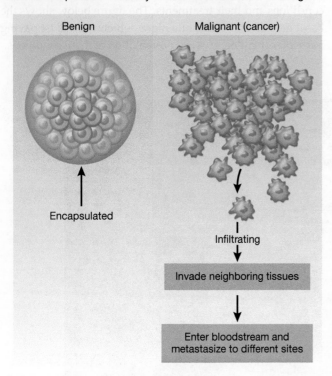

Figure 15.2 Compression in the Brain Due to a Benign Tumor

The photograph shows a slice of a human brain, showing how a large nonmalignant tumor (a meningioma) has displaced the right side of the brain toward the left. (The dashed line indicates the location of the midline.) The right lateral ventricle is almost completely occluded.

(Courtesy of A. D'Agostino, Good Samaritan Hospital, Portland, Oregon.)

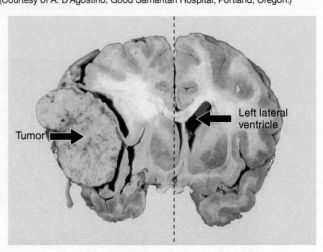

malignant or benign, can produce neurological symptoms and threaten the patient's life. Even a benign tumor occupies space and thus pushes against the brain. The compression can directly destroy brain tissue, or it can do so indirectly by blocking the flow of cerebrospinal fluid and causing hydrocephalus. Even worse are malignant tumors, which cause both compression and infiltration. As a malignant tumor grows, it invades the surrounding region and destroys cells in its path. Figure 15.2 illustrates the compressive effect of a large nonmalignant tumor. As you can see, the tumor has displaced the lateral and third ventricles.

CAUSES   Tumors do not arise from nerve cells, which are not capable of dividing. Instead, they arise from other cells found in the brain or from metastases originating elsewhere in the body. The most common types are listed in Table 15.1. The most serious types of tumors are metastases and the **gliomas** (derived from various types of glial cells), which are usually very malignant and fast growing. Figure 15.3a and Figure 15.3b show gliomas located in the basal ganglia and the pons, respectively. Figure 15.3c shows an ependymoma (a type of glioma) in the lateral ventricles.

The case at the beginning of this chapter described Mrs. R., whose sudden onset of seizures suggested the presence of a tumor near the top of the primary motor cortex. Indeed, she had a **meningioma,** an encapsulated, benign tumor

consisting of cells that typically make up the dura mater or arachnoid membrane. Such tumors tend to originate either in the part of the dura mater that is found between the two cerebral hemispheres or along the tentorium, the sheet of dura mater that lies between the occipital lobes and the cerebellum. (See Figure 15.3d.)

Evidence indicates that the malignancy of brain tumors is caused by rare subpopulations of cells (Hadjipanayis and Van Meir, 2009). Malignant gliomas contain **tumor initiating cells,** which originate from transformations of neural stem cells. These cells rapidly proliferate and give rise to a glioma.

TREATMENTS   Some tumors are sensitive to radiation and can be destroyed by a beam of radiation focused on them. Usually, a neurosurgeon first removes as much of the tumor as possible, and then the remaining cells are targeted by the radiation. Other tumors (such as the one Mrs. R. had) can be completely removed by surgery.

Some brain tumors respond to chemotherapy, with or without radiation or surgical interventions. Chemotherapy involves administration of a drug that causes rapidly dividing cells (such as cancer cells), to die, by interfering with their DNA replication. Chemotherapy drugs can be administered orally, intravenously, or by implantation directly in the region where the cancer cells are located. See Chapter 4 to review the routes of drug administration. When administered systemically, chemotherapy drugs target all dividing cells in the body (not just cancer cells), resulting in side effects such as hair loss due to the death of dividing cells in the hair follicles.

Table 15.1 Examples of Types of Brain Tumors

Type of Tumor	Tumors arise from these cells:
Gliomas	
Glioblastoma	Glial cells
Astrocytoma	Astrocytes
Ependymoma	Ependymal cells from the ventricles
Oligodendrocytoma	Oligodendrocytes
Meningioma	Cells of the meninges
Neurinoma	Schwann cells or cells of connective tissue covering cranial nerves
Angioma	Cells of blood vessels
Pinealoma	Cells of pineal gland

Figure 15.3 Types of Tumors

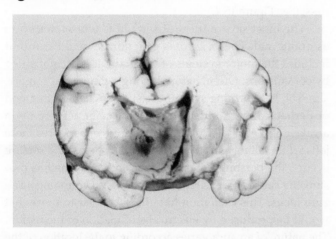

(a) The photograph shows a slice of a human brain, showing a large glioma located in the basal ganglia, which has invaded both the left and right lateral ventricles.

(Courtesy of A. D'Agostino, Good Samaritan Hospital, Portland, Oregon.)

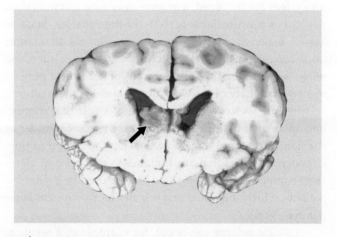

(c) The photograph shows a slice of a human brain, showing an ependymoma of the left lateral ventricle (arrowhead).

(Courtesy of A. D'Agostino, Good Samaritan Hospital, Portland, Oregon.)

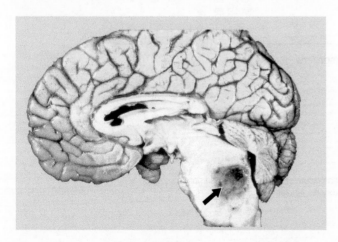

(b) The photograph shows a midsagittal view of a human brain, showing a glioma located in the dorsal pons (arrowhead).

(Courtesy of A. D'Agostino, Good Samaritan Hospital, Portland, Oregon.)

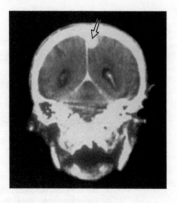

(d) The CT scan of a brain shows the presence of a meningioma (round white spot indicated by the arrow).

(Courtesy of J. McA. Jones, Good Samaritan Hospital, Portland, Oregon.)

Bevacizumab is a drug that inhibits angiogenesis, the growth of new blood vessels. Because a rapidly growing tumor requires an increased blood supply, its cells secrete vascular endothelial growth factor, a chemical that induces local angiogenesis (formation of new blood vessels). Bevacizumab binds with and deactivates the growth factor to slow the growth of a glioma. Unfortunately, the drug increases survival by only a few months, so more effective drugs—such as one that binds with proteins found specifically on tumor initiating cells—will be needed to completely destroy these tumors (Bredel, 2009; Chamberlain, 2011).

Seizures

LO 15.2 Describe the primary symptoms, causes, and treatments for seizures.

A *seizure* is a period of sudden, excessive activity of cerebral neurons. Sometimes, if neurons that make up the motor system are involved, a seizure can cause a **convulsion**, which is uncontrollable activity of the muscles, such as Mrs. R. experienced during her seizure. But not all seizures cause convulsions; in fact, most do not. In some cultures and religious traditions, seizures are considered to be a punishment from a deity or the work of demons. In other cultures, seizures are welcomed as evidence of a spiritual connection and signal that the individual may become a healer or shaman (Fadiman, 1997). In the Western medical tradition, Hippocrates noted that head injuries to soldiers and gladiators sometimes led to seizures like the ones he saw in his patients, which suggested that seizures had a physical cause (Hoppe, 2006).

A single seizure can occur, for example as a result of an injury or tumor, or a person may experience many seizures during a lifetime. Because of negative connotations, some physicians prefer not to use the term *epilepsy* to refer to a condition that involves seizures. Instead, they use the phrase **seizure disorder** to refer to a condition that has many causes.

Table 15.2 presents a summary of the basic categories of seizure disorders. Two distinctions are important: *partial* versus *generalized* seizures and *simple* versus *complex* ones. **Partial seizures** have a definite *focus*, or source of irritation: typically, either a scarred region caused by an old injury or a developmental abnormality such as a malformed blood vessel. The neurons that become involved in the seizure are restricted to a small part of the brain. **Generalized seizures** are widespread, involving most of the brain. In many cases they grow from a focus, but in some cases their origin is not discovered. Simple and complex seizures are two categories of partial seizures. **Simple partial seizures** often cause *changes* in consciousness but do not cause *loss* of consciousness. In contrast, because of their particular location and severity, **complex partial seizures** lead to loss of consciousness. (See Figure 15.4.)

The most severe form of seizure is often referred to as **grand mal**. This seizure is generalized, and because it includes the motor systems of the brain, it is accompanied by convulsions. Often, before having a grand mal seizure, a person has warning symptoms, such as changes in mood or perhaps a few sudden jerks of muscular activity upon awakening. (Almost everyone sometimes experiences these jolts while falling asleep.) A few seconds before the seizure occurs, the person may experience an **aura**, which is presumably caused by excitation of neurons surrounding a seizure focus. This excitation has effects similar to those that would be produced by electrical stimulation of the region. The nature of an aura varies according to the location of the focus. For example, because structures in the temporal lobe are involved in the control of emotional behaviors, seizures

Table 15.2 The Classification of Seizure Disorders

I. Generalized seizures (with no apparent local onset)
    A. Tonic-clonic (grand mal)
    B. Absence (petit mal)
    C. Atonic (loss of muscle tone; temporary paralysis)

II. Partial seizures (starting from a focus)
    A. Simple (no major change in consciousness)
        1. Localized motor seizure
        2. Motor seizure, with progression of movements as seizure spreads along the primary motor cortex
        3. Sensory (somatosensory, visual, auditory, olfactory, vestibular)
        4. Psychic (forced thinking, fear, anger, etc.)
        5. Autonomic (e. g., sweating, salivating, etc.)
    B. Complex (with altered consciousness)
        Includes 1–5, as above

III. Partial seizures (simple or complex) evolving to a generalized seizure: Starts as simple partial seizure or a complex partial seizure, then becomes a grand mal seizure

Figure 15.4 Comparing Partial and Generalized Seizures

(a) Partial seizures affect localized regions. For example, the yellow region in (a) represents seizure activity limited to the primary motor cortex. This region of the brain was likely involved in Mrs. R.'s first seizure while waiting at the traffic light, when only her foot, leg, arm and then body began shaking. (b) Generalized seizures affect the whole brain. For example, the yellow region in (b) represents seizure activity throughout the brain.

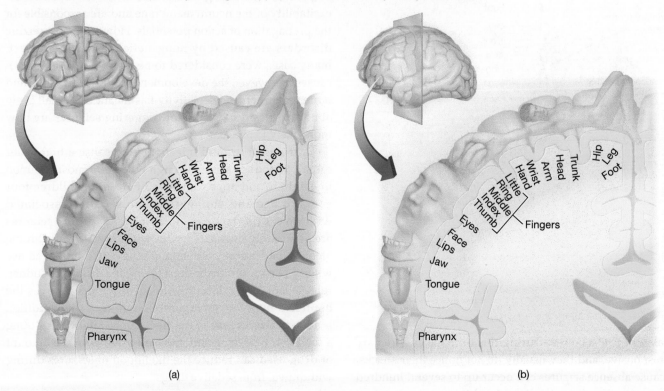

(a)　　　　　　　　　　　　　　(b)

that originate from a focus located there often begin with feelings of fear and dread or, occasionally, euphoria.

The beginning of a grand mal seizure is called the **tonic phase.** In this phase, all of a person's muscles contract forcefully. The arms are rigidly outstretched, and the person may make an involuntary cry as the tense muscles force air out of the lungs. (At this point the patient is unconscious.) The person holds a rigid posture for about fifteen seconds, and then the **clonic phase** begins. The muscles begin trembling, then start jerking convulsively—quickly at first, then more and more slowly. Meanwhile, the eyes roll, the person's facial muscles contract, and the tongue may be bitten. Intense activity of the autonomic nervous system manifests itself in sweating and salivation. After a short period of time, the person's muscles relax; only then does regular breathing begin again. The person may fall into an unresponsive sleep, which can last for several minutes. After that the person may awaken briefly but usually falls back into an exhausted sleep that may last for several hours.

Other types of seizures are far less dramatic. Partial seizures involve relatively small portions of the brain. The symptoms can include sensory changes, motor activity, or both. For example, a simple partial seizure that begins in or near the motor cortex can involve jerking movements that begin in one place and spread throughout the body

as the excitation spreads along the precentral gyrus. In the case described at the beginning of the chapter, Mrs. R. displayed such a progression, caused by a seizure triggered by a meningioma. The tumor was pressing against the "foot" region of the left primary motor cortex. When the seizure began, it involved the foot; and as it spread, it began involving the other parts of the body. (See Figure 15.5.) Mrs. R.'s first seizure was a simple partial seizure, but her second one would be classified as a complex partial seizure, because she lost consciousness. A seizure that begins in the occipital lobe may produce visual symptoms such as spots of color, flashes of light, or temporary blindness; one originating in the parietal lobe can evoke somatosensations, such as feelings of pain or heat and cold. Seizures in the temporal lobes may cause hallucinations that include old memories; presumably, neural circuits involved in these memories are activated by the spreading excitation. Depending on the location and extent of the seizure, the patient may or may not lose consciousness.

Children are especially susceptible to seizure disorders. Many children do not have grand mal episodes but instead have very brief seizures that are referred to as **absence seizures.** During an absence seizure, which is a *generalized* seizure, the child may stop what they are doing and stare off into the distance for a few seconds, often blinking their eyes repeatedly. These seizures are also sometimes referred

Figure 15.5 Primary Motor Cortex and Seizures

Mrs. R.'s seizure began in the foot region of the primary motor cortex, and as the seizure spread, more parts of her body became involved.

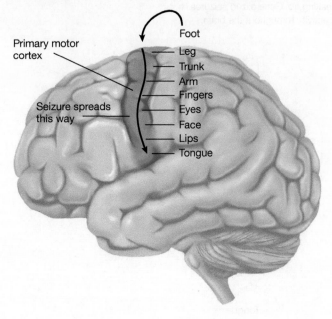

to as *petit mal* seizures. During this time the children are unresponsive, and they usually do not notice their attacks. Because absence seizures can occur up to several hundred times each day, they can disrupt a child's performance in school. Unfortunately, many of children experiencing absence seizures are considered inattentive and unmotivated unless a seizure disorder is diagnosed.

Seizures can have serious consequences: They can cause brain damage. Approximately 50 percent of patients with seizure disorders show evidence of damage to the hippocampus. The amount of damage is correlated with the number and severity of seizures the patient has had. Significant hippocampal damage can be caused by a single episode of **status epilepticus,** a relatively rare condition in which the patient undergoes a series of seizures without regaining consciousness. The damage appears to be caused by an excessive release of glutamate during the seizure, which can cause glutamate excitotoxicity (Thompson et al., 1996). Glutamate excitotoxicity will be further discussed in an upcoming section on cerebrovascular accidents and causes damage similar to excitotoxic lesions described in Chapter 5.

CAUSES Seizures have many causes. The most common cause is scarring, which may be produced by an injury, a stroke, a developmental abnormality, or the irritating effect of a growing tumor. Following a head injury the development of seizures may take a considerable amount of time. For example, often a person who receives a head injury from a vehicle accident will not have a seizure until several months later.

Genetic factors contribute to the incidence of seizure disorders (Berkovic et al., 2006). Nearly all of the genes that have been identified as playing a role in seizure disorders control the production of ion channels, which is not surprising, considering the fact that ion channels control the excitability of the neural membrane and are responsible for the propagation of action potentials. However, most seizure disorders are caused by nongenetic factors. In the past, many cases were considered to be *idiopathic* (of unknown causes). However, the development of MRIs with more and more resolution and sensitivity has meant that small brain abnormalities responsible for triggering seizures are now more likely to be seen.

Various drugs and infections that cause a high fever can also produce seizures. High fevers are most common in children, and approximately 3 percent of children four years of age and younger sustain seizures associated with fevers (Berkovic et al., 2006). In addition, seizures are commonly associated with withdrawal from chronic alcohol, barbiturate, and sometimes benzodiazepine use when a person suddenly stops taking the drug. The sudden release from the inhibiting effects of the drug leaves the brain in a hyperexcitable condition. In fact, this condition is a medical emergency because it can be fatal. Substituting a longer-acting drug and gradually reducing the amount of drug used can reduce the likelihood of seizures during withdrawal from sedative drugs.

TREATMENTS Seizure disorders are treated with anticonvulsant drugs, many of which work by increasing the effectiveness of inhibitory synapses, often by increasing inhibition via GABAergic synapses. Many people respond well to these medications and sustain a high quality of life. In a few instances, drugs provide little or no help. Sometimes, seizure foci remain so irritable that, despite drug treatment, brain surgery is required, as we saw in the opening case of Chapter 3. The surgeon removes the region of the brain surrounding the focus (usually located in the medial temporal lobe). Most patients recover well, with their seizures eliminated or greatly reduced in frequency. Mrs. R.'s treatment, described in the opening case of this chapter, was a different matter; in her case the removal of a tumor eliminated the source of the irritation and ended her seizures. No healthy brain tissue was removed.

Because seizure surgery often involves the removal of a substantial amount of brain tissue (usually from one of the temporal lobes), we might expect it to cause behavioral deficits. But in most cases the reverse is true; people's performance on tests of neuropsychological functioning usually *improves*. How can the removal of brain tissue improve a person's performance?

The answer is provided by looking at what happens in the brain not *during* seizures but *between* them. The seizure focus, usually a region of scar tissue, irritates the brain tissue surrounding it, causing increased neural activity that tends to spread to adjacent regions. Between seizures this increased excitatory activity is held in check by a compensatory increase in inhibitory activity. That is, inhibitory neurons in the region surrounding the seizure focus become more active. This phenomenon is known as *interictal inhibition*. A seizure occurs when the excitation overcomes the inhibition.

The problem is that the compensatory inhibition does more than hold the excitation in check; it also suppresses the normal functions of a rather large region of brain tissue surrounding the seizure focus. Thus, even though the focus may be small, its effects are experienced over a much larger area of the brain even between seizures. Removing the seizure focus and some surrounding brain tissue eliminates the source of the irritation and makes the compensatory inhibition unnecessary. Freed from interictal inhibition, the brain tissue located near the site of the former seizure focus can now function normally, and the patient's neuropsychological abilities will show an improvement.

Section Review

Tumors and Seizures

LO 15.1 **Describe the primary symptoms, causes, and treatments for brain tumors.**

Tumors produce brain damage by compression and, in the case of malignant tumors, infiltration. Brain tumors are caused by the uncontrolled growth of various types of cells other than neurons. Benign tumors are encapsulated and thus have a distinct border and may be successfully removed with surgery. Malignant tumors may be removed with surgery and the remaining cells may be treated with radiation or chemotherapy. Malignant gliomas contain tumor initiating cells, derived from neural stem cells, which are resistant to chemotherapy and radiation. Bevacizumab, a drug that inhibits the formation of blood vessels by malignant tumors, can help slow growth of these tumors.

LO 15.2 **Describe the primary symptoms, causes, and treatments for seizures.**

Seizures are periodic episodes of abnormal electrical activity of the brain. Partial seizures are localized, beginning with a focus—usually, some scar tissue caused by previous damage or a tumor. When they begin, they can produce an aura, consisting of particular sensations or changes in mood. Simple partial seizures do not produce profound changes in consciousness; complex partial seizures do. Generalized seizures may or may not originate at a single focus, but they involve most of the brain. Some seizures involve motor activity; including the grand mal convulsions that accompany generalized seizures. The convulsions are caused by involvement of the brain's motor systems; the patient first shows a tonic phase, consisting of a few seconds of rigidity, and then a clonic phase, consisting of rhythmic jerking. Absence seizures, also called petit mal seizures, are common in children. These generalized seizures are characterized by periods of inattention and temporary loss of awareness. Seizures produced by abstinence after chronic use of alcohol or other sedative drugs appear to be produced by a sudden release from inhibition. Seizures are treated with anticonvulsant drugs and, in the case of intractable seizure disorders caused by an abnormal focus, seizure surgery, which usually involves the medial temporal lobe.

Thought Question

As you read in the previous section, about 50 percent of people with seizure disorders show evidence of damage to the hippocampus, which is located in the temporal lobe. Many of the individuals with damage may have *temporal lobe epilepsy* in which seizure activity arises from a focus in the temporal lobe. Describe how a researcher could design a study to determine if the seizure activity caused the hippocampal damage, or whether the hippocampal damage caused the seizure activity.

Cerebrovascular Accidents

You have already learned about the effects of cerebrovascular accidents, or *strokes*, in earlier chapters. For example, you read that strokes can produce impairments in perception, emotional recognition and expression, memory, and language. This section will describe only the causes and treatments of strokes.

The incidence of strokes in the United States is approximately 750,000 per year. The likelihood of having a stroke is related to age; the probability doubles each decade after 45 years of age and reaches 1–2 percent per year by age 75.

Causes

LO 15.3 **Explain how cerebrovascular accidents can occur.**

The two major types of strokes are *hemorrhagic* and *ischemic*. **Hemorrhagic strokes** are caused by bleeding within the brain, usually from a malformed blood vessel or from one that has been weakened by high blood pressure. The blood that leaks out of the defective blood vessel accumulates within the brain, putting pressure on the surrounding brain tissue and damaging it. Loss of blood flow to a region is called *ischemia*. **Ischemic strokes**—those that block a blood vessel and obstruct the flow of blood—can be caused by thrombi or emboli. A **thrombus** is a blood clot that forms in blood vessels, especially in places where their walls are already damaged. Sometimes, thrombi become so large that blood cannot flow through the vessel, causing a stroke. People who are susceptible to the formation of thrombi are often advised to take a drug such as aspirin, which helps to prevent clot formation. An **embolus** is a piece of material that forms in one part of the vascular system, breaks off, and is carried through the bloodstream until it reaches an artery too small to pass through. It lodges there, damming the flow of blood through the rest of the vascular tree (the "branches" and "twigs" arising from the artery). Emboli can consist of a variety of materials, including bacterial debris from an infection in the lining of the heart or pieces broken off from a blood clot. (See Figure 15.6.)

What, exactly, causes the death of neurons when the blood supply to a region of the brain is interrupted? We might expect that the neurons simply starve to death because they lose their supply of glucose and of oxygen to metabolize it. However, research indicates that the immediate cause of neuron death is the presence of excessive amounts of glutamate. In other words, the damage produced by loss of blood flow to a region of the brain is actually an excitotoxic lesion, similar to those produced in a laboratory animal by the injection of an excitotoxic chemical described in Chapter 5. (See Koroshetz and Moskowitz, 1996, and Lo et al., 2003, for a review.)

When the blood supply to a region of the brain is interrupted, the oxygen and glucose in that region are quickly depleted. As a consequence, the sodium potassium transporters, which regulate the balance of ions inside and outside the cell, along with other cellular mechanism, stop functioning. Neural membranes become depolarized, which causes the release of glutamate. The activation of glutamate receptors further increases the inflow of sodium ions and causes cells to absorb excessive amounts of calcium through NMDA channels. The presence of excessive amounts of sodium and calcium within cells is toxic. The intracellular sodium causes the cells to absorb water and swell. The inflammation attracts microglia and activates them, causing them to become phagocytic. The phagocytic microglia begin destroying injured cells. Inflammation also attracts white blood cells, which can adhere to the walls of capillaries near the ischemic region and obstruct them. The presence of excessive amounts of calcium in the cells activates a variety of calcium dependent enzymes, many of which destroy molecules that are vital for normal cell functioning. Finally, damaged mitochondria produce **free radicals**—molecules with unpaired electrons that act as powerful oxidizing agents. Free radicals are extremely toxic; they destroy nucleic acids, proteins, and fatty acids.

Treatments

LO 15.4 **Explain how treatments can be used to address the immediate and long-term symptoms of cerebrovascular accidents.**

If a hemorrhagic stroke is caused by high blood pressure, medication is given to reduce the person's blood pressure. If a hemorrhagic stroke is caused by weak or malformed blood vessels, brain surgery may be used to seal off the faulty vessels to prevent another hemorrhage. If a thrombus was responsible for the stroke and if the patient reaches a stroke-treatment

---

Figure 15.6 Strokes

(a) Formation of thrombi and emboli. (b) An intracerebral hemorrhage.

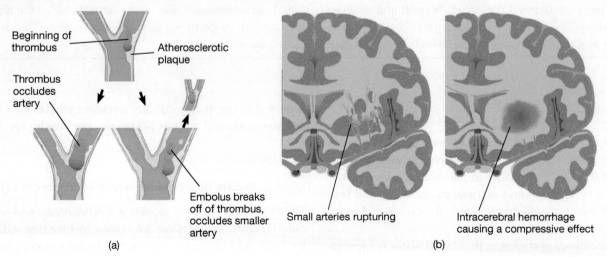

Beginning of thrombus

Atherosclerotic plaque

Thrombus occludes artery

Embolus breaks off of thrombus, occludes smaller artery

Small arteries rupturing

Intracerebral hemorrhage causing a compressive effect

(a)

(b)

center soon enough, attempts will be made to dissolve or physically remove the blood clot. Even if immediate treatment is not available, the patient will receive anticoagulant drugs to make the blood less likely to clot, reducing the likelihood of another stroke. If an embolus broke away from a bacterial infection, antibiotics will be given to suppress the infection.

Strokes produce permanent brain damage, but, depending on the size of the affected blood vessel, the amount of damage can vary from negligible to massive. Researchers have sought ways to minimize the amount of brain damage caused by strokes. One approach has been to administer drugs that dissolve blood clots in an attempt to reestablish circulation to an ischemic brain region. This approach has met with some success. Administration of a clot-dissolving drug called tPA (tissue plasminogen activator) after the onset of a stroke has clear benefits, but only if it is given within three hours (NINDS, 1995). tPA is an enzyme that causes the dissolution of *fibrin,* a protein involved in clot formation.

More recent research indicates that although tPA helps to dissolve blood clots and restore cerebral circulation, it also has toxic effects in the central nervous system. tPA is potentially neurotoxic if it is able to cross the blood–brain barrier and reach the interstitial fluid. Evidence suggests that in cases of severe stroke, in which the blood–brain barrier is damaged and tPA enters the interstitial fluid, tPA increases excitotoxicity, further damages the blood–brain barrier, and may even cause cerebral hemorrhage (Benchenane et al., 2004; Klaur et al., 2004; Medcalf, 2011). In cases in which

tPA quickly restores blood flow, the blood–brain barrier is less likely to be damaged, and the enzyme will remain in the vascular system, where it will do no harm. Another potential clot-reducing treatment is an anticoagulant enzyme called *desmoteplase,* isolated from the saliva of vampire bats. Research with laboratory animals indicates that unlike tPA, desmoteplase causes no excitotoxic injury when injected directly into the brain (Reddrop et al., 2005). A clinical trial of desmoteplase (Hacke et al., 2005) found that desmoteplase restored blood flow and reduced clinical symptoms in a majority of patients if given up to nine hours after the occurrence of a stroke. (See Figure 15.7.)

Occlusions of larger cerebral blood vessels can be removed by mechanical means (Frendl and Csiba, 2011). Two types of medical devices have been developed. Both types are inserted into a cerebral blood vessel and extended until they reach the obstruction. One type of device works like a corkscrew, grabbing the obstruction so that the surgeon can pull it out. The other type of device works by suction: Once the tip of the device touches the obstruction, a vacuum is applied, and the surgeon pulls out the clot. The disadvantage of these approaches is that some clots are difficult to reach, and attempts at mechanical removal can further damage the blood vessel. Trials of these procedures suggest that use of a suction device is more likely to produce clinical improvement and less likely to cause intracerebral bleeding.

How can strokes be prevented? Risk factors that can be reduced by medication or changes in lifestyle include high blood pressure, cigarette smoking, diabetes, and

Figure 15.7 Desmoteplase in the Treatment of Strokes

The graph shows the effects of desmoteplase and a placebo on restoration of cerebral blood flow to affected area *(reperfusion)* and favorable clinical outcome.

(Based on data from Hacke et al., 2005.)

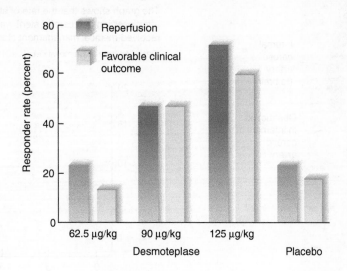

high blood levels of cholesterol. The actions we can take to reduce these risk factors are well known, so they will not be described in detail here. *Atherosclerosis*, a process in which the linings of arteries develop a layer of plaque, consisting of deposits of cholesterol, fats, calcium, and cellular waste products, is a precursor to heart attacks (myocardial infarction) and ischemic stroke, caused by clots that form around atherosclerotic plaques in cerebral and cardiac blood vessels.

Atherosclerotic plaques often form in the internal carotid artery—the artery that supplies most of the blood flow to the cerebral hemispheres. These plaques can cause severe narrowing of the interior of the artery, greatly increasing the risk of a massive stroke. This narrowing can be visualized in an angiogram, produced by injecting a radiopaque dye into the blood and examining the artery with a computerized X-ray machine. (See Figure 15.8.) If the narrowing is severe, a *carotid endarterectomy* can be performed. The surgeon makes an incision in the neck that exposes the carotid artery, inserts a shunt in the artery, cuts the artery open, removes the plaque, and sews the artery back again (and the neck too, of course). Endarterectomy has been shown to reduce the risk of stroke by 50 percent in people under 75 years of age.

Another surgical treatment option involves the placement of a stent in a narrowed carotid artery (Yadav et al., 2004). An arterial stent is an implantable device made of mesh that is used to expand and hold open a partially occluded artery. These devices were first developed for treatment of arteries that serve the heart and later modified for use in the carotid artery. Unfortunately the use of carotid stents is associated with an increased number of future strokes and the death rate following implantation is higher. (See Figure 15.9.)

Prior to research on the outcomes associated with stent placement, surgeons and hospitals were getting ready to make carotid stenting a standard procedure for narrowing of the carotid artery, at a cost of at least $20,000 and, as we now know, increased mortality. It is not clear what the future of stent development will bring, but new materials, including polymers that can release clot-breaking drugs, are being tested to evaluate the potential of stents once more.

What can be done after a stroke has occurred, assuming that intervention with clot dissolution or removal was unsuccessful or unavailable? The major strategies involve administration of drugs that block factors present in the brain that inhibit axonal growth, activating the brain's intrinsic neural growth factors, and reducing swelling and inflammation. For example, animal studies have shown that administration of antibodies against *NogoA*, a myelin protein that inhibits the branching and growth of axons, can increase recovery from brain damage, and administration of *inosine*, a naturally occurring chemical, activates a protein that also encourages axon growth (Benowitz and Carmichael, 2010). And depending on the location of the brain damage, people who have strokes will receive physical therapy and perhaps speech therapy

Figure 15.8 Atherosclerotic Plaque

An angiogram shows an obstruction in the internal carotid artery caused by an atherosclerotic plaque.

(From Stapf, C., and Mohr, J. P., Ischemic stroke therapy, *Annual Review of Medicine*, 2002, *53*, 453–475. Reprinted with permission.)

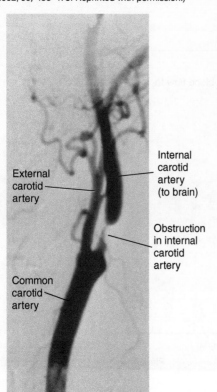

External carotid artery

Internal carotid artery (to brain)

Obstruction in internal carotid artery

Common carotid artery

Figure 15.9 Effects of Carotid Stents

The graph shows that the rate of strokes and deaths in the 15 months after insertion of a carotid stent was higher than that of patients who received medical management alone.

(Based on data of Chimowitz et al., 2011.)

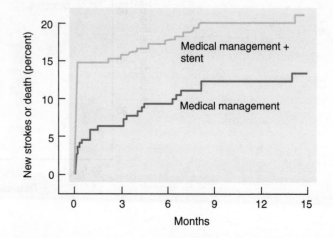

Figure 15.10 Constraint-Induced Movement Therapy

The graph shows the effects of constraint-induced (CI) therapy and placebo therapy on use of a limb whose movement was impaired by a stroke.

(Based on data from Taub et al., 2006.)

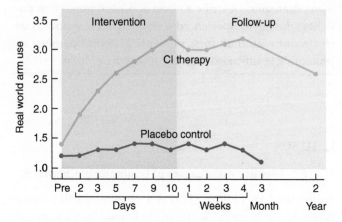

to help them recover lost function. Several studies have shown that exercise and sensory stimulation can facilitate recovery from the effects of brain damage (Cotman et al., 2007). For example, Taub et al., (2006) studied patients with strokes that impaired their ability to use one arm and hand. The researchers put the *unaffected* arm in a sling for 14 days and gave the patients training sessions during which the patients were forced to use the affected arm. A placebo group received cognitive, relaxation, and physical fitness exercises for the same amount of time. This procedure (which is called *constraint-induced movement therapy*) produced long-term improvement in the patients' ability to use the affected arm. (See Figure 15.10.)

A study by Liepert et al., (2000) found that constraint-induced movement therapy caused changes in the connections of the primary motor cortex. The investigators used transcranial magnetic stimulation to map the area of the contralateral motor cortex that was involved in control of the impaired arm before and after treatment. Aside from improving the patients' use of the impaired arm, the treatment caused an expansion of this region—apparently, into adjacent areas of the motor cortex—that was still present when the patients were tested six months later.

As you read in Chapter 8, mirror neurons in the parietal lobe and ventral premotor cortex become active when a person performs an action or sees someone else performing it. Ertelt et al., (2007) enrolled patients who had experienced a stroke in a course of therapy that combined repetitive practice of hand and arm movements used in daily life with the watching of videos of actors performing the same movements. The patients' motor functions showed long-term improvement relative to those of patients in a control group who performed the exercises but watched videos of sequences of geometric symbols. Moreover, functional-imaging showed increased activity in brain regions involved in movement, including the ventral premotor cortex and the supplementary motor area.

In some cases of brain or spinal cord damage, patients are unable to perform useful limb movements, even after intensive therapy. In such cases, investigators have attempted to devise brain–computer interfaces that permit the patient to control electronic and mechanical devices to perform useful actions. Developers of such interfaces have implanted arrays of microelectrodes directly into the patient's motor cortex and have applied surface electrodes to measure changes in EEG activity transmitted through the skull and scalp. These devices, while still experimental, permit patients to move prosthetic hands, perform actions with multijointed robotic arms, move the cursor of a computer display, and operate a computer (Wolpaw and McFarland, 2004; Hochberg et al., 2006).

Section Review

Cerebrovascular Accidents

LO 15.3 **Explain how cerebrovascular accidents can occur.**
Cerebrovascular accidents occur through rupture of a blood vessel or occlusion (obstruction) of a blood vessel by a thrombus or embolus. A thrombus is a blood clot that forms within a blood vessel. An embolus is a piece of debris that is carried through the bloodstream and lodges in an artery.

LO 15.4 **Explain how treatments can be used to address the immediate and long-term symptoms of cerebrovascular accidents.**
If a hemorrhagic stroke is caused by high blood pressure, medication is given to reduce the person's blood pressure. If a hemorrhagic stroke is caused by weak and malformed blood vessels, brain surgery may be used to seal off the faulty vessels to prevent another hemorrhage. If a thrombus was responsible for the stroke, attempts will be made to dissolve or physically remove the blood clot. Even if immediate treatment is not available, the patient will receive anticoagulant drugs to make the blood less likely to clot, reducing the likelihood of another stroke. If an embolus broke away from a bacterial infection, antibiotics will be given to suppress the infection. Drug treatments are being developed to reduce damage after a stroke has occurred, and to encourage regrowth of brain tissue. Physical therapy can facilitate recovery and

minimize a patient's deficits. Constraint-induced movement therapy has been shown to be especially useful in restoring movement of limbs following unilateral damage to the motor cortex. Movement therapy combined with watching the movements being performed has beneficial effects, perhaps because of stimulation of the mirror neuron system.

Thought Question

Many of the treatments currently available for cerebrovascular accidents have side effects or cannot be used by all patients. There is a great need for safer, more effective treatment strategies. Describe a novel approach to treating patients who have experienced a stroke. Describe how your treatment would address preventing neural damage or promoting brain-based recovery following a stroke.

Traumatic Brain Injury

A. P. was a 49-year old chemical dependency counselor. He had earned a college degree in social work and passed the licensing exams required to work as a professional counselor; however, he was having trouble finding and keeping a job in his chosen field. Throughout his life, A. P. sustained multiple traumatic brain injuries from fights and a serious car accident. A CT scan revealed damage to his right frontal lobe several years after the last injury. Following that injury, A. P. experienced significant executive function impairments and became easily distracted, irritable, impatient, disorganized, and had trouble controlling his anger in some situations.

To address two of his primary concerns about his employability, A. P. sought the help of a therapist to develop more effective strategies for organization and report-writing in his profession. After conducting several cognitive tests to assess A. P.'s strengths and weaknesses, the therapist designed report-writing software for social work interviews that would address A. P.'s executive and organizational deficits. Over the course of 10 weeks, the therapist worked with A. P. to refine and practice his report-writing skills. Following treatment, A. P. secured a position as a chemical-dependency counselor. He worked with his employer and therapist to further tailor his report-writing to the outpatient clinic he worked for. A. P. was successfully promoted to a more senior position in the clinic within a year (Turkstra and Flora, 2002).

The case of A. P. highlights several important themes in this section. A. P. experienced repeated traumatic brain injuries, the evidence of which was observable years later as a lesion in his frontal cortex. The injury resulted in cognitive and emotional impairments that had potentially serious consequences for his career and quality of life. An intervention to address these deficits allowed A. P. to pursue his professional development and meet his career goals (Turkstra and Flora, 2002).

Causes

LO 15.5 Identify some causes of traumatic brain injury.

Traumatic brain injury (TBI) is a serious health problem (Chen and D'Esposito, 2010). In the United States alone, approximately 1.4 million people are treated in an emergency department, 270,000 people are hospitalized, and 52,000 people die due to TBI. In particular, over 300,000 instances of TBI have been reported among U.S. military personnel since 2000 (Fischer, 2015). Traumatic brain injury can be caused by a projectile or a fall against a sharp object that fractures the skull, causing the brain to be wounded by the object or a piece of the broken skull. Closed-head injuries do not involve penetration of the brain, but these injuries can also cause severe injury or death. Among military personnel, a frequent cause of TBI has been injury by explosive devices. Undoubtedly, many other people receive brain injuries but not a diagnosis.

Penetrating brain injuries (also called open-head injuries) cause damage to the portion of the brain that is injured by the object or the bone. In addition, damage to blood vessels can deprive parts of the brain of their normal blood supply, and the accumulation of blood within the brain can cause further damage by exerting pressure within the brain. Closed-head injury—for example, caused by a blow with a blunt object against the right side of a person's forehead—will bruise the right frontal lobe as it comes into sudden impact with the inside of the skull. (This blow to the brain is known as the *coup*.) The brain will then recoil in the opposite direction and smash against the left posterior region of the skull. (This blow is known as the *contrecoup*.) In many cases, the contrecoup can produce more damage than the coup.

Closed-head injury can damage more than the cerebral cortex at the point of the coup and contrecoup. Bundles of axons can be torn and twisted, blood vessels can be ruptured, and cerebrospinal fluid can distort the walls of the ventricles. And as we saw in the section on seizure disorders, traumatic brain injury can be followed several months later by seizures.

Chronic traumatic encephalopathy (CTE), a form of TBI, results in neurodegeneration due to repeated head trauma.

Figure 15.11 Brain Changes in CTE

(a) This image shows a brain section from a patient with CTE (right) compared to a control section (left). The dark regions in the CTE section are areas where abnormal tau protein accumulated following brain injury. The white asterisk denotes dense accumulation of these proteins in the amygdala. (b) This image shows a diffusion tensor image scan of the corpus callosum from a control brain (in green, left) and the brain of a former professional boxer with CTE in (pink, right). The corpus callosum in the CTE patient's brain shows damage (shorter and less extensive white matter tracts) associated with the brain injury.

(From Baugh, C. M., et al., Chronic traumatic encephalopathy: Neurodegeneration following repetitive concussive and subconcussive brain trauma. *Brain Imaging and Behavior*, 2012, 6[2], 244–254.)

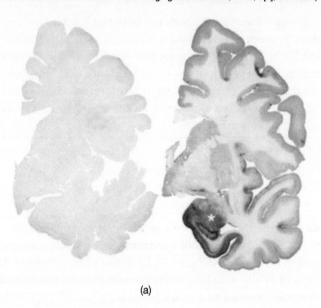

(a)

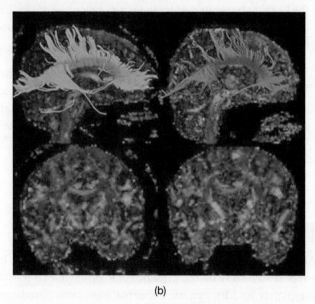

(b)

CTE has received attention for its prevalence in athletes who participate in contact sports and experience frequent and repeated head trauma. A diagnosis of CTE (like other neurodegenerative disorders you will read about later in this chapter) is confirmed by postmortem examination of brain tissue. CTE symptoms of mood and cognitive impairment appear years after the injury was sustained. Similar to the brains of individuals with Alzheimer's disease, abnormal tau protein accumulates in the cortex of CTE patients. Patients with CTE also display reduced brain volume and enlarged ventricles (Korngold et al., 2013). In particular, the corpus callosum, regions of the cortex, and the limbic system appear to be damaged, resulting in characteristic deficits in executive control and mood regulation that are associated with this disease (Baugh et al., 2012; Korngold et al., 2013). (See Figure 15.11)

Treatments

LO 15.6 **Describe treatments for traumatic brain injuries.**

Immediate, primary treatments for TBI typically include reducing swelling and intracranial pressure as well as ensuring adequate blood flow to the injured region (McConeghy et al., 2012).

Secondary to the immediate brain injury, TBI treatments address the symptoms that develop after the initial injury. Even mild cases of TBI can greatly increase a person's risk of sustaining symptoms that are not immediately obvious but that manifest themselves as the person ages. For example, the likelihood of Alzheimer's disease is much higher in a person who has received blows to the head earlier in life. Aside from causing physical trauma to the brain, TBI results in increased levels of adenosine and glutamate in the injured brain tissue. The increased glutamate converts the adenosine from its normal role as an anti-inflammatory agent to an agent that promotes inflammation, which causes further damage. Treatment with a drug that inhibits the release of glutamate can prevent this switch in the role of extracellular adenosine (Dai et al., 2010). Other pharmacological treatments have been tested in an attempt to reduce activity of intra- and extracellular processes related to neuron damage in TBI, but most results are negative or have not yet been tested in appropriate large, randomized clinical trials (McConeghy et al., 2012).

Treatment of the long-term behavioral and cognitive effects of TBI involves the same strategies as those employed in the treatment of brain damage caused by cerebrovascular accidents. The case of A. P. demonstrated one example of a behavioral intervention that addressed some of the long-term effects of TBI.

Section Review

Traumatic Brain Injury

LO 15.5 Identify some causes of traumatic brain injury.
Traumatic brain injury can be caused by a projectile or a fall against a sharp object that fractures the skull, causing the brain to be wounded by the object or a piece of the broken skull. Closed-head injuries can also produce traumatic brain injury.

LO 15.6 Describe treatments for traumatic brain injuries.
Treatments include interventions to immediately reduce swelling and intracranial pressure and provide adequate blood flow following injury. Drug treatment to reduce glutamate activity can also be used immediately following the injury. Behavioral interventions can be effective in addressing the long-term symptoms of TBI.

Thought Question

Although the exact relationship between head injury and development of CTE is not yet clear, it seems that reducing the severity and frequency of head trauma in contact sports is one way to reduce the incidence of CTE. Given what is known about CTE, what recommendations would you give to coaches to reduce CTE among the contact sport athletes they work with?

Disorders of Development

As you will read in this section, brain development can be affected adversely by the presence of toxic chemicals during pregnancy and by genetic abnormalities, both hereditary and nonhereditary. In some instances the result is severe impairment of cognitive development, or intellectual disability.

Toxic Chemicals

LO 15.7 Describe the effects of alcohol on development of the nervous system.

A common cause of intellectual disability is the presence of toxins that impair fetal development during pregnancy. A *teratogen* is any chemical or toxin that results in abnormal development of an embryo. For example, if a woman contracts rubella (German measles) early in pregnancy, the toxic chemicals released by the virus interfere with the chemical signals that control typical development of the brain. Most women with access to health care are immunized for rubella to prevent them from contracting it during pregnancy.

In addition to the toxins produced by viruses, various drugs can adversely affect fetal development. For example, intellectual disability can be caused by the ingestion of alcohol during pregnancy, especially during the third to fourth week (Sulik, 2005). Some investigators have suggested that damage to a developing nervous system can be caused by a single alcohol binge during a critical period of fetal development (Sokol et al., 2003). Babies born to women who chronically use alcohol during pregnancy are typically smaller than average and develop more slowly. Many of them exhibit *fetal alcohol spectrum disorder* an inclusive term for a range of neurodevelopmental changes characterized by abnormal facial development and impaired brain development related to prenatal alcohol exposure (Riley et al., 2011). **Fetal alcohol syndrome**, is a specific diagnosis within this category. Figure 15.12 shows photographs of the faces of a child with fetal alcohol syndrome, of a mouse fetus that was exposed to alcohol prenatally, and of a typically-developing mouse fetus. As you can see, alcohol produces similar abnormalities in the offspring of both species. The facial abnormalities are relatively unimportant. Much more serious are the corresponding abnormalities in the development of the brain.

Research suggests that alcohol disrupts typical brain development by interfering with a **neural adhesion protein**—a protein that helps to guide the growth of neurons in the developing brain (Abrevalo et al., 2008; Braun, 1996). Prenatal exposure to alcohol even appears to have direct effects on neural plasticity. Sutherland et al., (1997) found that the offspring of female rats that consumed moderate amounts of alcohol during pregnancy showed smaller amounts of long-term potentiation (described in Chapter 12). Finally, fetal alcohol exposure adversely alters the development of neuronal stem cells and progenitor cells (Vangipuram and Lyman, 2010).

Inherited Metabolic Disorders

LO 15.8 Contrast the symptoms, causes, and treatments of inherited metabolic disorders.

Several inherited "errors of metabolism" can cause brain damage or impair brain development. Normal functioning of cells requires intricate interactions among many biochemical systems. These systems depend on enzymes, which are responsible for constructing or breaking down particular chemical compounds. Enzymes are proteins and therefore are produced by mechanisms involving the chromosomes, which

Figure 15.12 Facial Malformation in Fetal Alcohol Syndrome

The photographs show a child with fetal alcohol syndrome, along with magnified views of mouse fetuses.
(a) Mouse fetus whose mother received alcohol during pregnancy. (b) Typically-developing mouse fetus.
(Photographs courtesy of Katherine K. Sulik.)

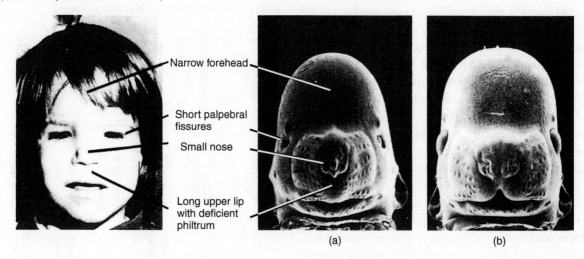

contain the recipes for their synthesis. "Errors of metabolism" refer to genetic abnormalities in which the recipe for a particular enzyme is in error, so the enzyme cannot be synthesized. If the enzyme is a critical one, the results can be very serious.

There are at least a hundred different inherited metabolic disorders that can affect the development of the brain. The most common is called **phenylketonuria (PKU)**. This disease is caused by an inherited lack of an enzyme that converts phenylalanine (an amino acid) into tyrosine (another amino acid). Excessive amounts of phenylalanine in the blood interfere with the myelinization of neurons in the central nervous system. Much of the myelinization of the cerebral hemispheres takes place after birth. Thus, when an infant born with PKU receives foods containing phenylalanine, the amino acid accumulates, and the brain fails to develop typically. The result is severe intellectual disability, with an average IQ of approximately 20 by six years of age. For comparison, the IQ scale is devised such that the average score in the general population is approximately 100.

Fortunately, PKU can be treated by putting the infant on a low-phenylalanine diet. The diet keeps the blood level of phenylalanine low, and myelinization of the central nervous system takes place normally. Once myelinization is complete, the dietary restraints can be relaxed somewhat, because a high level of phenylalanine no longer threatens brain development. During prenatal development a fetus is protected by its mother's metabolism, which removes the phenylalanine from its circulation. However, if the *mother* has PKU, she must follow a strict diet during pregnancy or the baby's brain will not develop correctly. If the mother eats a typical diet, rich in phenylalanine, the high blood level of

this compound will not damage her brain, but it will damage that of her fetus.

Diagnosing PKU immediately after birth is imperative so that the infant's brain is never exposed to high levels of phenylalanine. Consequently, many governments have passed laws that mandate a PKU test for all newborn babies. The test is inexpensive and accurate, and it has prevented many cases of intellectual disability.

Other genetic errors of metabolism can be treated in similar fashion. For example, untreated **pyridoxine dependency** results in damage to cerebral white matter, to the thalamus, and to the cerebellum. It is treated by large doses of vitamin B_6. Another error of metabolism, **galactosemia,** is an inability to metabolize galactose, a sugar found in milk. If it is not treated, it, too, causes damage to cerebral white matter and to the cerebellum. The treatment is use of a milk substitute that does not contain galactose. (Galactosemia should not be confused with *lactose intolerance,* which is caused by an insufficient production of lactase, the digestive enzyme that breaks down lactose. Lactose intolerance leads to digestive disturbance, not brain damage.)

Some other inherited metabolic disorders cannot yet be treated successfully. For example, **Tay-Sachs disease,** which occurs mainly in children of Eastern European Jewish descent, causes the brain to swell and damage itself against the inside of the skull and against the folds of the dura mater that encase it. The neurological symptoms begin by four months of age and include an exaggerated startle response to sounds, listlessness, irritability, spasticity, seizures, dementia, and finally death.

Tay-Sachs disease is one of several metabolic "storage" disorders. All cells contain sacs of material encased in membrane, called lysosomes. These sacs constitute the cell's waste-removal system; they contain enzymes that break down waste substances that cells produce in the course of their normal activities. The broken-down waste products are then recycled (used by the cells again) or excreted. Metabolic storage disorders are genetic errors of metabolism in which one or more vital enzymes are missing. Particular kinds of waste products cannot be destroyed, so they accumulate in the lysosomes. The lysosomes get larger and larger, the cells get larger and larger, and eventually the brain begins to swell and become damaged.

Researchers investigating hereditary errors of metabolism hope to prevent or treat these disorders in several ways. Some will be treated like PKU or galactosemia, by avoiding a constituent of the diet that cannot be tolerated. Others, such as pyridoxine dependency, will be treated by administering a substance that the body requires. Still others may be cured someday by the techniques of genetic engineering. Researchers hope to develop genetically modified viruses that will insert into infants' cells the genetic information needed to produce the enzymes that the cells lack, leaving the rest of the cells' functions intact.

Down Syndrome

LO 15.9 **Identify symptoms, cause, and interventions for Down syndrome.**

Down syndrome is a congenital disorder that results in abnormal development of the brain, producing intellectual disability in varying degrees. *Congenital* does not necessarily mean *hereditary*; it simply refers to a disorder that is present at birth. It is caused by the presence of an extra twenty-first chromosome. A small portion of the twenty-first chromosome, which includes approximately 300 genes, contains the critical region (Belichenko et al., 2010). The syndrome is associated with the mother's age; in the majority cases, an error in meiosis produces an ovum that has two (rather than one) twenty-first chromosomes (this same error can occur in sperm cells as well, but it is less common). The likelihood of this error increases in women over 35. When fertilization occurs, the addition of the father's twenty-first chromosome makes three, rather than two, twenty-first chromosomes. The extra chromosome presumably causes biochemical changes that impair normal brain development. The development of several relatively safe procedures for obtaining prenatal samples from the placenta, amniotic fluid, or umbilical cord has allowed physicians to identify cells with chromosomal abnormalities and thus to determine whether the fetus carries Down syndrome, using a karyotype to examine the chromosomes. (See Figure 15.13.)

Down syndrome, first described in 1866 by John Langdon Down, occurs in approximately 1 out of 700

Figure 15.13 Karyotype of Down Syndrome

A karyotype allows a physician to examine the number of chromosomes present in a sample of genetic material. In this example, notice that there are three copies of chromosome 21. (red arrow) This is the karyotype of a female with Down syndrome.

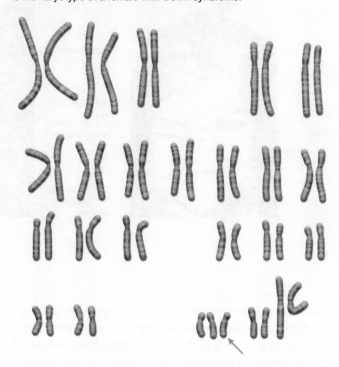

births in the United States. Individuals with this disorder often have short stature and changes in physical facial development. They may learn to speak later then their typically-developing peers, but most individuals with Down syndrome learn to speak by five years of age. The brain of a person with Down syndrome is approximately 10 percent lighter than that of a typically-developing peer, the convolutions (gyri and sulci) are smaller and less folded, the frontal lobes are smaller, and the superior temporal gyrus (the location of Wernicke's area) is thinner. After age 30, the brain of a person with Down syndrome develops abnormal microscopic structures and begins to degenerate. Because this degeneration resembles that of Alzheimer's disease, it will be discussed in the next section. If efforts to develop effective therapies for Alzheimer's disease are successful, they might also be useful in preventing the degeneration seen in the brains of people with Down syndrome.

The results of several studies suggest that some drug treatments may have beneficial effects on learning and memory impairment associated with Down syndrome. Mouse models of Down syndrome suggest that overactivity of the GABA system may impair hippocampal synaptic plasticity and associated learning and memory. Treatment

Table 15.3 Disorders of Development

Causes	Description	Symptoms
Exposure to Teratogens	Exposure to teratogens (such as alcohol) impairs brain development	Intellectual disability
Inherited Metabolic Disorders (PKU, pyridoxine dependency, galactosemia, Tay-Sachs disease)	Genetic abnormalities in the codes for specific enzymes. If untreated, leads to impaired brain development.	Intellectual disability; brain swelling in Tay-Sachs
Down syndrome	Three copies of the twenty first chromosome contribute to impaired brain development.	Intellectual disability; brain degeneration in adulthood.

with GABA antagonists enhanced long-term potentiation and improved performance on memory tasks that are dependent on the hippocampus in a mouse model of Down syndrome (Kleschevnikov et al., 2012).

While this research in animal models is promising, the therapeutic potential of GABA antagonist drugs is limited by their potential side effects. Drugs that reduce GABA activity can result in seizures, and individuals with Down syndrome are at increased risk for seizures compared to the general population (Martínez-Cué et al., 2014). Another potential drug treatment to improve learning and memory in a mouse model of Down syndrome is the selective serotonin reuptake inhibitor fluoxetine. Researchers found increased performance on memory tasks and long-term potentiation in the hippocampus of mice that possessed additional copies of chromosomes (as a model of Down syndrome) following fluoxetine administration. Fluoxetine treatment also resulted in reduced GABA concentrations in the brains of the mice, suggesting that this treatment might be beneficial in future clinical trials (Begenisic et al., 2014). For a review of the disorders of development discussed in this section, see Table 15.3.

Section Review

Disorders of Development

LO 15.7 **Describe the effects of alcohol on development of the nervous system.**

During pregnancy fetal brain development can be negatively impacted by exposure to alcohol, particularly during critical periods. Alcohol interferes with neural adhesion protein and neural plasticity, resulting in abnormal brain development.

LO 15.8 **Contrast the symptoms, causes, and treatments of inherited metabolic disorders.**

Several inherited metabolic disorders can impair brain development. For example, phenylketonuria is caused by the lack of an enzyme that converts phenylalanine into tyrosine. PKU interferes with myelin development, and if untreated, results in intellectual disability. This disorder can be treated with diet low in phenylalanine. Pyridoxine dependency causes damage to white matter, the thalamus, and the cerebellum and can be treated by vitamin B_6. Galactosemia can also damage white matter and the cerebellum, and can be treated with a diet that does not contain milk sugar. Storage disorders, such as Tay-Sachs disease, are caused by the inability of cells to destroy waste products within the lysosomes, which causes the cells to swell and eventually die. Treatment for Tay-Sachs is not currently available.

LO 15.9 **Identify symptoms, cause, and interventions for Down syndrome.**

Down syndrome is produced by the presence of an extra twenty-first chromosome. The brain development of people with Down syndrome is abnormal and results in cognitive impairment. After age 30 the brains of people with Down syndrome develop features similar to those of people with Alzheimer's disease. A study with an animal model of Down syndrome suggests that administration of GABA antagonists or selective serotonin reuptake inhibitors might be useful in facilitating learning and memory in mouse models of Down syndrome.

Thought Question

Suppose that you were in charge of a governmental or charitable agency that had a lot of money to spend on research on disorders of brain development. What kinds of approaches do you think would be the most effective in preventing or treating developmental disorders?

Degenerative Disorders

Many disease processes cause degeneration of the cells of the brain. Some of these conditions injure particular kinds of cells, a fact that provides the hope that research will uncover the causes of the damage and find a way to halt it and prevent it from occurring in other people. The following sections will discuss information about degenerative disorders that are caused by prion infection (transmissible spongiform encephalopathies), and affect motor behavior (Parkinson's disease, Huntington's disease, amyotrophic lateral sclerosis, multiple sclerosis) and cognition (Alzheimer's disease, Korsakoff's syndrome). For each disorder, information about causes and treatments will be presented.

Transmissible Spongiform Encephalopathies

LO 15.10 **Describe how transmissible spongiform encephalopathies cause brain damage.**

The outbreak of bovine spongiform encephalopathy (BSE, or "mad cow disease") in Great Britain in the late 1980s and early 1990s brought a peculiar form of brain disease to public attention. BSE is a **transmissible spongiform encephalopathy (TSE)**—a fatal contagious brain disease whose degenerative process gives the brain a spongelike (or Swiss cheese–like) appearance. Besides BSE, these diseases include Creutzfeldt-Jakob disease, fatal familial insomnia, and kuru, which affect humans, and scrapie, which primarily affects sheep. Although scrapie cannot be transmitted to humans, BSE can, and it produces a variant of Creutzfeldt-Jakob disease.

Unlike other transmissible diseases, TSEs are caused not by microorganisms but by simple proteins, which have been called **prions,** or "protein infectious agents" (Prusiner, 1982). Prion proteins are found primarily in the membrane of neurons, where they are believed to play a role in synaptic function and in preservation of the myelin sheath (Popko, 2010). Prion proteins are resistant to proteolytic enzymes—enzymes that are able to destroy proteins by breaking the peptide bonds that hold a protein's amino acids together. Prion proteins are also resistant to levels of heat that denature normal proteins, which explains why cooking meat from cattle with BSE does not destroy the infectious agent. The sequence of amino acids of normal prion protein (PrP^c) and infectious prion (PrP^{Sc}) are identical. How, then, can two proteins with the same amino acid sequences have such different effects? The answer is that the functions of proteins are determined largely by their three-dimensional shapes. The only difference between PrP^c and PrP^{Sc} is the way the protein is folded. (See Figure 15.14.) Once misfolded PrP^{Sc} is introduced into a cell, it causes normal PrP^c to become misfolded too, and the process of this transformation ultimately kills them. (See Miller, 2009, for a review.)

A familial form of Creutzfeldt-Jakob disease is transmitted as a dominant trait, caused by a mutation of the *PRNP* gene located on the short arm of chromosome 20, which codes for the human prion protein gene. Fatal familial insomnia, which you read about in Chapter 9, is also transmitted in families via an inherited mutation of the PRNP gene. However, most cases of TSEs are **sporadic.** That is, they occur in people without a family history of prion protein disease. Prion protein diseases are unique not only because they can be transmitted by means of a simple protein but also because they can be genetic or sporadic—and the genetic and sporadic forms can be transmitted to others. The most common form of transmission of Creutzfeldt-Jakob disease in humans is through transplantation of tissues such as dura mater or corneas, harvested from cadavers of people who were infected with a prion disease. One form of human prion protein disease, kuru, was transmitted through cannibalism: Out of respect for their recently departed relatives, members of indigenous groups in New Guinea ate their brains and sometimes thus contracted the disease. This practice has since been abandoned (Gajdusek, 1977). When the disease was initially described by Western physicians in the 1950s, they reported a higher incidence of kuru in women and children, who often consumed nervous system tissue, compared to adult men, who consumed other organs or muscle tissues. The word *kuru* means "to shiver" (or "to be afraid"). This term likely refers to the tremors or ataxia that result from degeneration of the cerebellum in this disorder (Collins et al., 2001).

Figure 15.14 Misfolded Proteins

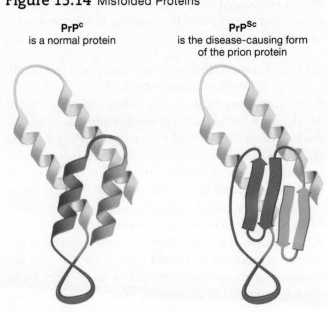

PrP^c
is a normal protein

PrP^{Sc}
is the disease-causing form of the prion protein

Whatever role normal PrP^c plays, it does not seem to be essential for the life of a cell. Bueler et al., (1993) found that the cells of mice with a targeted mutation of the prion protein gene produced absolutely no prion protein and did not develop mouse scrapie when they were inoculated with the misfolded prions that cause this disease. Normal mice inoculated with these prions died within six months.

A study by Steele et al., (2006) suggests that normal prion protein plays a role in neural development and differentiation in fetuses and neurogenesis in adults. The investigators produced a genetically engineered strain of mice that produced increased amounts of PrP^c and found increased numbers of proliferating cells in the subventricular zone and more neurons in the dentate gyrus, compared with normal mice.

Some investigators (for example, Bailey et al., 2004) have suggested that a prionlike mechanism could play a role in the establishment and maintenance of long-term memories. Long-term memories can last for decades, and prion proteins, which are resistant to the destructive effects of enzymes, might maintain synaptic changes for long periods of time. Criado et al., (2005) found that mice with a targeted mutation against the *PRNP* gene showed deficits in a spatial learning task and in establishment of long-term potentiation in the dentate gyrus. Papassotiropoulos et al., (2005) found that people with a particular allele of the prion protein gene remembered 17 percent more information 24 hours after a word list–learning task than did people with a different allele. (Both alleles are considered normal and are not associated with a prion protein disease.)

Mallucci et al., (2003) created a genetically modified mouse strain whose neurons produced an enzyme at 12 weeks of age that destroyed normal prion protein. When the animals were a few weeks of age, the experimenters infected them with misfolded mouse scrapie prions. Soon thereafter, the animals began to develop spongy holes in their brains, indicating that they were infected with mouse scrapie. Then, at 12 weeks, the enzyme became active and started destroying normal PrP^c. Although analysis showed that glial cells in the brain still contained misfolded PrP^Sc, the disease process stopped. Neurons stopped making normal PrP^c, which could no longer be converted into PrP^Sc, so the mice went on to live normal lives. The disease process continued to progress in mice without the special enzyme, and these animals soon died. The authors concluded that the process of conversion of PrP^c to PrP^Sc is what kills cells.

How might misfolded prion protein kill neurons? As we will see later in this chapter, the brains of people with several other degenerative diseases, including Parkinson's disease, Alzheimer's disease, frontotemporal dementia, amyotrophic lateral sclerosis, and Huntington's disease, also contain aggregations of misfolded proteins (Miller, 2009; Lee et al., 2010). We will also see that although these misfolded proteins are not prions, the disease process can be transmitted to the brains of other animals by inoculating them with the proteins. As we saw in Chapter 3, cells contain the means by which they can commit suicide—a process known as *apoptosis*. Apoptosis can be triggered either externally, by a chemical signal telling the cell that it is no longer needed (for example, during development), or internally, by evidence that biochemical processes in the cell have become disrupted so that the cell is no longer functioning properly. Perhaps the accumulation of misfolded, abnormal proteins provides such a signal. Apoptosis involves production of "killer enzymes" called **caspases**. Mallucci et al., (2003) suggest that inactivation of caspase-12, the enzyme that appears to be responsible for the death of neurons infected with PrP^Sc, may provide a treatment that could arrest the progress of transmissible spongiform encephalopathies. Let's hope they are right.

Parkinson's Disease

LO 15.11 **Describe the symptoms, causes, and treatments for Parkinson's disease.**

Parkinson's disease is caused by degeneration of the nigrostriatal system—the dopamine-secreting neurons of the substantia nigra that send axons to the basal ganglia. Parkinson's disease occurs in approximately 1 percent of people over 65 years of age. The primary symptoms of Parkinson's disease are muscular rigidity, slowness of movement, a resting tremor, and postural instability. For example, once a person with Parkinson's disease is seated, he or she finds it difficult to rise. Once the person begins walking, he or she has difficulty stopping. Reaching for an object can be accurate, but the movement usually begins only after a considerable delay. Writing is slow and labored, and as it progresses, the letters get smaller and smaller. Postural movements are impaired. A healthy person who is bumped while standing will quickly move to restore balance—for example, by taking a step in the direction of the impending fall or by reaching out with the arms to grasp onto a piece of furniture. However, a person with Parkinson's disease fails to do so and simply falls. A person with this disorder is even unlikely to put out his or her arms to break the fall. As we saw in Chapter 8, the motor deficits of patients with Parkinson's disease can be described as a deficiency of automatic, habitual responses caused by damage to the basal ganglia.

Parkinson's disease also produces a resting tremor—vibratory movements of the arms and hands that diminish somewhat when the individual makes purposeful movements. The tremor is accompanied by rigidity; the joints appear stiff. However, the tremor and rigidity are not the cause of the slow movements. In fact, some patients with Parkinson's disease show extreme slowness of movements but little or no tremor.

Examination of the brains of patients who had Parkinson's disease shows the near-disappearance of nigrostriatal dopaminergic neurons. Many surviving dopaminergic neurons show **Lewy bodies,** abnormal circular structures found within the cytoplasm. Lewy bodies have a dense protein core, surrounded by a halo of radiating fibers (Forno, 1996). (See Figure 15.15.)

What are the effects of the loss of dopaminergic neurons on normal brain functioning? Functional-imaging studies have shown that *akinesia* (difficulty in initiating movements) was associated with decreased activation of the supplementary motor area and that tremors are associated with abnormalities of a neural system involving the pons, midbrain, cerebellum, and thalamus (Buhmann et al., 2003; Grafton, 2004).

CAUSES Although most cases of Parkinson's disease do not appear to have genetic origins, researchers have discovered that the mutation of a particular gene located on chromosome 4 will produce this disorder (Polymeropoulos et al., 1996). This gene produces a protein known as α-**synuclein,** which is normally found in the presynaptic terminals and is thought to be involved in synaptic transmission in dopaminergic neurons (Moore et al., 2005). The mutation produces what is known as a **toxic gain of function** because it produces a protein that results in effects that are toxic to the cell. Mutations that cause toxic gain of function are normally dominant because the toxic substance is produced whether one or both members of the pair of chromosomes contains the mutated gene. Abnormal α-synuclein becomes misfolded and forms aggregations, especially in dopaminergic neurons (Goedert, 2001). The dense core of Lewy bodies consists primarily of these aggregations, along with neurofilaments and synaptic vesicle proteins.

Another hereditary form of Parkinson's disease is caused by mutation of a gene on chromosome 6 that produces a gene that has been named **parkin** (Kitada et al., 1998). This mutation causes a **loss of function,** which makes it a recessive disorder. If a person carries a mutated parkin gene on only one chromosome, the normal allele on the other chromosome can produce a sufficient amount of normal parkin for normal cellular functioning, and the person will not develop Parkinson's disease. Normal parkin plays a role in transferring defective or misfolded proteins to the **proteasomes**—organelles responsible for destroying these proteins (Moore et al., 2005). This mutation permits high levels of defective protein to accumulate in dopaminergic neurons and ultimately damage them. Figure 15.16 illustrates the role of parkin in the action of proteasomes. Parkin assists in the tagging of abnormal or misfolded proteins with numerous molecules of **ubiquitin,** a small, compact globular protein. Ubiquitination (as this process is called) targets the abnormal proteins for destruction by the proteasomes, which break them down into their constituent amino acids. Defective parkin fails to ubiquinate abnormal proteins, and they accumulate in the cell, eventually killing it. For some reason, dopaminergic neurons are especially sensitive to this accumulation.

Figure 15.15 Lewy Bodies

A photomicrograph of the substantia nigra of a patient with Parkinson's disease shows a Lewy body, indicated by the arrow.

(Photograph courtesy of Dr. Don Born, University of Washington.)

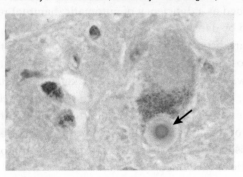

Figure 15.16 The Role of Parkin in Parkinson's Disease

Parkin is involved in the destruction of abnormal or misfolded proteins by the ubiquitin-proteasome system. If parkin is defective because of a mutation, abnormal or misfolded proteins cannot be destroyed, so they accumulate in the cell. If α-synuclein is defective because of a mutation, parkin is unable to tag it with ubiquitin, and it accumulates in the cell.

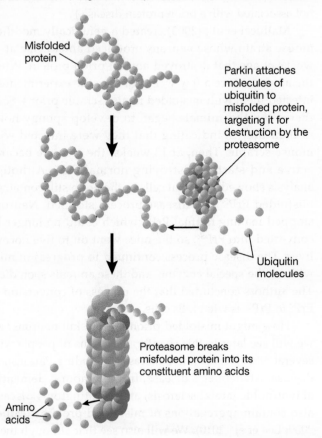

Misfolded protein

Parkin attaches molecules of ubiquitin to misfolded protein, targeting it for destruction by the proteasome

Ubiquitin molecules

Proteasome breaks misfolded protein into its constituent amino acids

Amino acids

The overwhelming majority of the cases of Parkinson's disease (approximately 95 percent) are sporadic. That is, they occur in people without a family history of Parkinson's disease. What, then, triggers the accumulation of α-synuclein and the destruction of dopaminergic neurons? Research suggests that Parkinson's disease may be caused by toxins present in the environment, by faulty metabolism, or by unrecognized infectious disorders. For example, the insecticides rotenone and paraquat can cause Parkinson's disease, and, presumably, so can other unidentified toxins. All of these chemicals inhibit mitochondrial function, which leads to the aggregation of misfolded α-synuclein, especially in dopaminergic neurons. These accumulated proteins eventually kill the cells (Dawson and Dawson, 2003).

The brain contains two major systems of dopaminergic neurons: the nigrostriatal system (whose damage causes Parkinson's disease), and the mesolimbic/mesocortical system, which consists of dopaminergic neurons in the ventral tegmental area that innervate the nucleus accumbens and the prefrontal cortex. Parkinson's disease damages only the nigrostriatal system, so there must be an important difference between the dopaminergic neurons in these two systems. Mosharov et al. (2009) suggest that the critical difference is that calcium channels are involved in regulating the spontaneous activity of DA cells in the nigrostriatal system and sodium channels are involved in regulating the activity of those in the mesolimbic/mesocortical system. Research with rodent models of Parkinson's disease suggests that the presence of α-synuclein, elevated intracellular calcium ions, and elevated levels of intracellular dopamine combine to kill these cells. Interference with any of these three factors prevents damage to these cells. Because DA neurons of the mesolimbic/mesocortical system do not contain elevated levels of calcium ions, they are spared.

TREATMENTS   Although there is no cure for Parkinson's disease, researchers and clinicians have developed several pharmacological and surgical interventions options to treat the symptoms of the disease.

Drug Treatments   As we saw in Chapter 4, the standard treatment for Parkinson's disease is L-DOPA, the precursor of dopamine. An increased level of L-DOPA in the brain causes a patient's remaining dopaminergic neurons to produce and secrete more dopamine and, for a time, alleviates the symptoms of the disease. But this compensation does not work indefinitely; eventually, the number of nigrostriatal dopaminergic neurons declines to such a low level that the symptoms become worse. Unfortunately, the L-DOPA also activates DA neurons in the mesolimbic/mesocortical system and produces side effects such as hallucinations and delusions.

Another drug, deprenyl, is often given to patients with Parkinson's disease, usually in conjunction with L-DOPA. As we saw in the beginning of Chapter 4, several people acquired the symptoms of Parkinson's disease after taking an illicit drug contaminated with MPTP. Subsequent studies with laboratory animals revealed that the toxic effects of this drug could be prevented by administration of deprenyl, a drug that inhibits the activity of the enzyme MAO-B. The original rationale for administering deprenyl to patients with Parkinson's disease was that it might prevent unknown toxins from producing further damage to dopaminergic neurons. Many studies (for example, Mizuno et al., 2010; Zhao et al., 2011) confirm that administration of deprenyl slows the progression of Parkinson's disease, especially if deprenyl therapy begins soon after the onset of the disease. However, the benefits of deprenyl and other inhibitors of MAO-B appear to be reduction in symptoms. The drugs do not appear to slow the degeneration of dopaminergic neurons (Williams, 2010). (See Figure 15.17.)

Neurosurgeons have been developing three stereotaxic procedures designed to alleviate the symptoms of Parkinson's disease that no longer respond to treatment with L-DOPA. The first one, transplantation of fetal tissue, attempts to reestablish the secretion of dopamine in the neostriatum. The tissue is obtained from the substantia nigra of aborted human fetuses and implanted into the caudate nucleus and putamen by means of stereotaxically guided needles. As we saw in Chapter 5, PET scans have shown that dopaminergic fetal cells are able to grow in their new host and secrete dopamine, reducing the patient's symptoms—at least, initially.

In a study of 32 patients with fetal tissue transplants, Freed (2002) found that those whose symptoms had previously responded to L-DOPA were most likely to benefit from the surgery. Presumably, these patients had a sufficient number of basal ganglia neurons with receptors that could be stimulated by the dopamine secreted by either the medication or the transplanted tissue. Unfortunately, many transplant patients later developed severe, persistent *dyskinesias*—troublesome and often painful involuntary movements. As a result, fetal transplants of dopaminergic fetal cells are no longer recommended (Olanow et al., 2003).

Further examination of the fate of fetal transplants has shown that although the transplanted cells can survive and form connections with neurons in the recipient's tissue, these cells eventually develop deposits of α-synuclein. Studies with animal models of Parkinson's disease show that misfolded α-synuclein is transferred from the recipient's own neurons to the grafted neurons (Kordower et al., 2011). As many investigators have noted, misfolded proteins responsible for several neurodegenerative diseases, including Parkinson's disease, can be transferred from cell to cell in the brain where they induce further protein misfolding, just like prion proteins (Lee et al., 2011). It appears that adding healthy cells to the basal ganglia of patients with Parkinson's disease will ultimately fail unless a way is found to stop the process that results in the deposition of misfolded α-synuclein.

Figure 15.17 Pharmacological Treatment Strategies for Parkinson's Disease

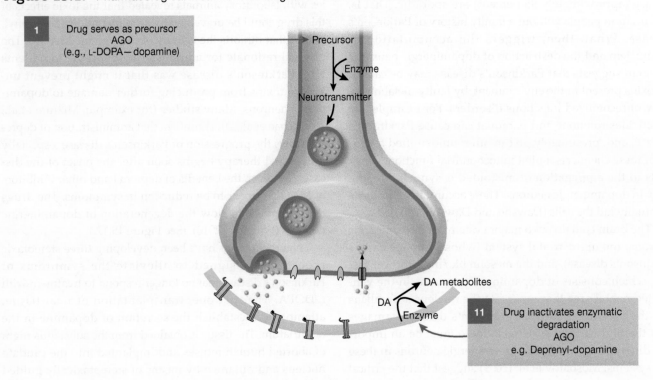

Surgical Procedures Another therapeutic procedure has a long history, but only recently have technological developments in imaging methods and electrophysiological techniques led to an increase in its popularity. The principal output of the basal ganglia comes from the **internal division of the globus pallidus (GP$_i$).** (The caudate nucleus, putamen, and globus pallidus are the three major components of the basal ganglia.) This output, which is directed through the subthalamic nucleus (STN) to the motor cortex, is inhibitory. Furthermore, a decrease in the activity of the dopaminergic input to the caudate nucleus and putamen causes an *increase* in the activity of the GP$_i$. Thus, damage to the GP$_i$ might be expected to relieve the symptoms of Parkinson's disease. (See Figure 15.18.)

In the 1950s, Leksell and his colleagues performed pallidotomies (surgical destruction of the internal division of the globus pallidus) in patients with severe Parkinson's disease (Laitinen et al., 1992; Svennilson et al., 1960). The surgery often reduced the rigidity and enhanced the patient's ability to move. Unfortunately, the surgery occasionally made the patient's symptoms worse and sometimes resulted in partial blindness. (The optic tract is located next to the GP$_i$.)

With the development of L-DOPA therapy in the late 1960s, pallidotomies were abandoned. However, it eventually became evident that L-DOPA worked for a limited time and that the symptoms of Parkinson's disease would eventually return. For that reason, in the 1990s, neurosurgeons again began experimenting with pallidotomies, first with laboratory animals and then with humans (Graybiel, 1996; Lai et al., 2000). This time, they used MRI scans to find the location of

the GP$_i$ and then inserted an electrode into the target region. The surgeon would then pass radiofrequency current to heat and destroy the brain tissue. The results of this procedure were so promising that several neurological teams began promoting its use in the treatment of relatively young patients whose symptoms no longer respond to L-DOPA.

Neurosurgeons have also targeted the STN in patients with advanced Parkinson's disease. As Figure 15.18 shows, the subthalamic nucleus has an excitatory effect on the GP$_i$; therefore, damage to the subthalamic nucleus decreases the activity of this region and removes some of the inhibition on motor output. This surgery brings depressed motor activity back to normal (Guridi and Obeso, 2001).

In Chapter 5 you read about optogenetic methods that enable a researcher to stimulate or inhibit specific types of neurons in specific locations of the brain. Kravitz et al., (2010) used a genetically engineered virus to insert into mice light-sensitive proteins in the neurons of the striatum that receive inputs from axons of dopaminergic neurons of the substantia nigra. They used two different procedures that enabled them to stimulate neurons that contained either dopamine D$_1$ receptors (part of the direct pathway of the cortical–basal ganglia loop) or dopamine D$_2$ receptors (part of the indirect pathway). As Figure 15.18 shows, activation of the direct pathway inhibits the GP$_i$ and activation of the indirect pathway excites the GP$_i$. They found that activation of the indirect pathway, which excites the GP$_i$, caused the mice to display the motor symptoms seen in Parkinson's disease. They also activated the direct pathway in mice with lesions of the nigrostriatal system, who displayed the symptoms of Parkinson's disease.

Figure 15.18 Connections of the Basal Ganglia

This schematic shows the major connections of the basal ganglia and associated structures. Excitatory connections are shown as black lines; inhibitory connections are shown as red lines. Many connections, such as the inputs to the substantia nigra, are omitted for clarity. Two regions that have been targets of stereotaxic surgery for Parkinson's disease—the internal division of the globus pallidus and the subthalamic nucleus—are outlined in blue. Damage to these regions reduces inhibitory input to the thalamus and facilitates movement. Deep brain stimulation of these regions produces similar effects.

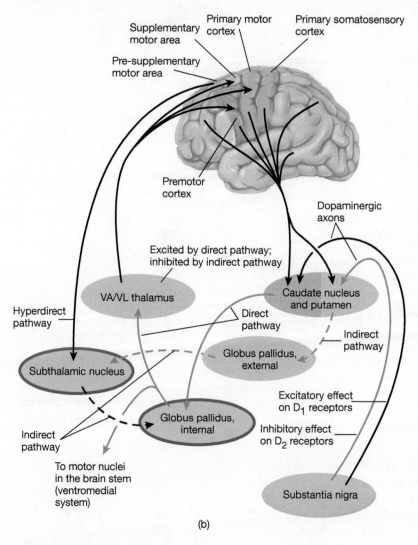

(b)

When they stimulated this pathway, which inhibits the GP$_i$, the parkinsonian symptoms disappeared. This experiment clearly and elegantly demonstrates that—at least in this mouse model—the motor symptoms of Parkinson's disease are produced by a shift of balance in favor of the indirect pathway. These findings explain why surgical lesions targeted at the GP$_i$ can reduce these symptoms.

The third stereotaxic procedure aimed at relieving the symptoms of Parkinson's disease involves implanting electrodes in the STN or the GP$_i$ and attaching a device that permits the patient to electrically stimulate the brain through the electrodes. (See Figure 15.19.) According to some studies, **deep brain stimulation (DBS)** of the subthalamic nucleus is as effective as brain lesions in suppressing tremors and has fewer adverse side effects (Esselink et al., 2009). In addition, a three-year follow-up study found no evidence of cognitive deterioration in patients who received implants for deep brain stimulation (Funkiewiez et al., 2004). DBS may also have effects on the affective and cognitive symptoms of Parkinson's disease such as depression and dementia, but the results of these studies are less clear (Castelli et al., 2006; Funkiewicz et al., 2004).

The fact that either lesions or stimulation alleviates tremors suggests that deep brain stimulation has an inhibitory effect on STN neurons, but an optogenetic study by Gradinaru et al. (2009) indicates that the effects of DBS are more complex than that. Gradinaru et al. produced unilateral motor symptoms of Parkinson's disease in mice by damaging the nigrostriatal dopamine system on the right side of the brain. They inserted inhibitory light-sensitive protein into the right subthalamic nucleus and found that inhibition of neurons in this nucleus had no effect on the motor symptoms, which suggests that DBS does not exert its beneficial effects by simply inhibiting neurons of the STN. Next, they inserted excitatory light-sensitive protein in the right STN and found that excitation of neurons in this nucleus did not affect motor symptoms, so DBS does not reduce parkinsonian motor symptoms through excitation of the STN, either. Next, the investigators inserted excitatory light-sensitive protein in the axons of neurons entering the STN. This time, excitation of these axons *did* suppress the parkinsonian motor symptoms. These results suggest that DBS exerts its therapeutic effects not through simple excitation or inhibition of neurons in the STN but by causing undoubtedly more complex changes in the firing of particular neurons in the STN by activating axons that enter this structure.

Researchers have been attempting to develop strategies of gene therapy to treat the symptoms of Parkinson's disease. Kaplitt et al. (2007) introduced a genetically modified virus into the subthalamic nucleus of patients with Parkinson's disease that delivered a gene for GAD, the enzyme responsible for the biosynthesis of the major inhibitory neurotransmitter, GABA. The production of GAD turned some of the excitatory, glutamate-producing neurons in the subthalamic nucleus into inhibitory, GABA-producing neurons. As a result, the activity of the GP$_i$ decreased, the activity of the supplementary motor area increased, and the symptoms of the patients improved. A larger double-blind clinical trial confirmed the efficacy and safety of this procedure (LeWitt et al., 2011).

Figure 15.19 Deep Brain Stimulation

Electrodes are implanted in the patient's brain, and wires are run under the skin to stimulation devices implanted near the collarbone.

(Based on Okun, M. S., Deep-brain stimulation for Parkinson's disease, *New England Journal of Medicine*, 2012, *367*[16], 1529–1538.)

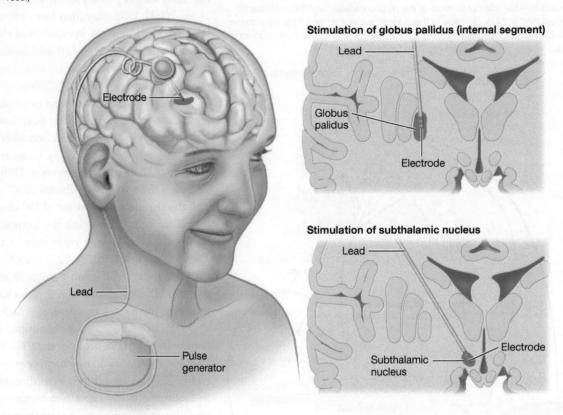

Huntington's Disease

LO 15.12 Describe the symptoms, causes, and treatments for Huntington's disease.

Another disease affecting the basal ganglia, **Huntington's disease,** is caused by degeneration of the caudate nucleus and putamen. Whereas Parkinson's disease causes a poverty of movements, Huntington's disease causes uncontrollable ones, especially jerky limb movements. The movements of Huntington's disease look like fragments of purposeful movements but occur involuntarily. This disease is progressive, includes cognitive and emotional changes, and eventually causes death, usually within 10–15 years after the symptoms begin. (See Figure 15.20.)

The symptoms of Huntington's disease usually begin in the person's thirties and forties but can sometimes begin in the early twenties. The first signs of neural degeneration occur in the putamen, in a specific group of inhibitory neurons: GABAergic medium spiny neurons. Damage to these neurons removes some inhibitory control exerted on the premotor and supplementary motor areas of the frontal cortex. Loss of this control leads to involuntary movements. As the disease progresses, neural degeneration is seen in many other regions of the brain, including the cerebral cortex.

Figure 15.20 Brain Tissue Loss in Huntington's Disease

Comparison of a normal brain (left) with that from a patient who died with Huntington's disease

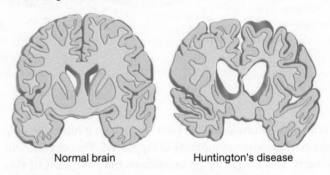

Normal brain   Huntington's disease

CAUSES Huntington's disease is a hereditary disorder, caused by a dominant gene on chromosome 4. In fact, the gene has been located, and its defect has been identified as a repeated sequence of bases (called CAG repeats) that code for the amino acid glutamine (Collaborative Research Group, 1993). This repeated sequence causes the gene product—a protein called **huntingtin (Htt)**—to contain an elongated stretch of glutamine. Abnormal Htt becomes

Figure 15.21 Elongated CAG Repeats in Huntington's Disease

In Huntington's disease, a sequence of bases (CAG) for the amino acid glutamine is repeated many times, contributing to the accumulation of abnormal huntingtin protein. The excess CAG repeats lead to an elongated stretch of glutamine.

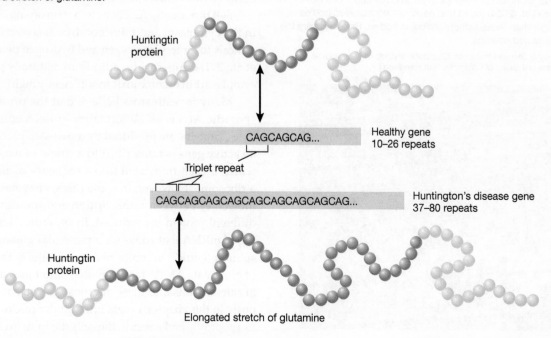

Huntingtin protein

CAGCAGCAG...

Healthy gene
10–26 repeats

Triplet repeat

CAGCAGCAGCAGCAGCAGCAGCAGCAG...

Huntington's disease gene
37–80 repeats

Huntingtin protein

Elongated stretch of glutamine

misfolded and forms aggregations that accumulate in the nucleus. Longer stretches of glutamine are associated with patients whose symptoms began at a younger age, a finding that indicates that this abnormal portion of the huntingtin molecule is responsible for the disease. (See Figure 15.21.) These facts suggest that the mutation causes the disease through a toxic gain of function—that abnormal Htt causes harm. In fact, the cause of death of neurons in Huntington's disease is apoptosis (cell "suicide"). Li et al. (2000) found that transgenic mice that are a model for Huntington's disease lived longer if they were given a caspase inhibitor, which suppresses apoptosis. Abnormal Htt may trigger apoptosis by impairing the function of the ubiquitin-protease system, which activates caspase, one of the enzymes involved in apoptosis (Hague et al., 2005).

Normal Htt is found in cells throughout the body, but it occurs in especially high levels in neurons and in cells of the testes. It is found in the cytoplasm, where it associates with microtubules, vesicular membrane, and synaptic proteins, which suggests that it plays a role in vesicular transport, release of neurotransmitter, and recycling of vesicular membrane (Levine et al., 2010). A targeted mutation against the Htt gene is fatal, causing death of the fetus early in development (Nasir et al., 1995), so the huntingtin protein plays an essential role in development.

Researchers have debated the role played by the accumulations of misfolded Htt in the nucleus (known as *inclusion bodies*) in development of the disease. These inclusions could cause neural degeneration, they could have a protective role, or they could play no role at all. Studies by Arrasate and her colleagues (Arrasate et al., 2004; Miller et al., 2010) strongly suggest that inclusion bodies actually protect neurons. The investigators prepared tissue cultures from rat striatal neurons that they infected with genes that expressed fragments of abnormal Htt. Some of the neurons that produced the mutant Htt formed inclusion bodies; others did not. The investigators used a robotic microscope to see what happened to the cells over a period of almost 10 days. They found that the inclusion bodies appeared to have a protective function. Neurons that contained inclusion bodies had lower levels of mutant Htt elsewhere in the cell, and these neurons lived longer than those without these accumulations. (See Figure 15.22.)

TREATMENTS At present there is no treatment for Huntington's disease. However, Southwell et al., (2009) prepared a special type of antibody that acts intracellularly (an *intrabody*) called Happ1. This antibody targets a portion of the huntingtin protein. Tests with five different experimental models of Huntington's disease in mice found that insertion of the Happ1 gene into the animals' brains suppressed production of mutant Htt and improved the animal's disease symptoms. Another approach by DiFiglia and her colleagues (DiFiglia et al., 2007; Pfister et al., 2009) involves injection of small interfering RNAs (siRNA) into the striatum that blocked the transcription of the Htt genes—and hence the production of mutant Htt protein—in this region. The treatment decreased the size of inclusion bodies in striatal neurons, prolonged the life of the striatal neurons, and reduced the animals' motor symptoms.

Figure 15.22 Infection with Abnormal Huntingtin

The photomicrograph shows two neurons that have been infected with genes that express fragments of abnormal huntingtin. The lower neuron shows an inclusion body (orange), and the upper one does not. Arrasate et al. (2004) found that neurons with inclusion bodies survived longer than those without inclusion bodies. Blue ovals are the nuclei of uninfected neurons.

(Photo courtesy of Steven Finkbeiner, Gladstone Institute of Neurological Disease and the University of California, San Francisco.)

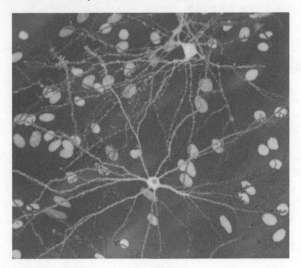

Amyotrophic Lateral Sclerosis

LO 15.13 **Describe the symptoms, causes, and treatments for amyotrophic lateral sclerosis.**

Amyotrophic lateral sclerosis (ALS) is a degenerative disorder that attacks spinal cord and cranial nerve motor neurons (Zinman and Cudkowicz, 2011). The incidence of this disease is approximately 5 in 100,000. The symptoms include spasticity (increased tension of muscles, causing stiff and awkward movements), exaggerated stretch reflexes, progressive weakness and muscular atrophy, and, finally, paralysis. The muscles that control eye movements are spared. Some cognitive abilities, such as executive function, working-memory, language and social cognition may also be affected (Goldstein and Abrahams, 2013). Death usually occurs 5–10 years after the onset of the disease as a result of failure of respiratory muscles.

CAUSES Ten percent of the cases of ALS are hereditary; the other 90 percent are sporadic. Of the hereditary cases, 10–20 percent are caused by a mutation in the gene that produces the enzyme *superoxide dismutase 1 (SOD1)*, found on chromosome 21. This mutation causes a toxic gain of function that leads to protein misfolding and aggregation, impaired axonal transport, and mitochondrial dysfunction. It also impairs glutamate reuptake into glial cells, which increases extracellular levels of glutamate and causes excitotoxicity in motor neurons (Bossy-Wetzel et al., 2004). And like the other degenerative brain disorders described that

involve misfolded proteins, mutant SOD1 can be transmitted from cell to cell, as prion proteins are. However, there is presently no evidence that the disease can be transmitted between individuals (Münch and Bertolotti, 2011).

SOD1 normally functions as a detoxifying enzyme found in the cytoplasm and mitochondria. It converts superoxide radicals to molecular oxygen and hydrogen peroxide (Milani et al., 2011). Superoxide radicals are naturally present in the cytoplasm but become toxic in sufficiently high concentrations.

Many investigators believe that the primary cause of sporadic ALS is an abnormality in RNA editing. In most cases, proteins are produced by a two-step process: a copy of an active gene is transcribed to a strand of messenger RNA, which is then translated into a sequence of amino acids at a ribosome. However, in some cases, enzymes alter mRNA molecules between transcription and translation so that a different protein is produced. In sporadic ALS, faulty editing of mRNA that codes for a particular glutamate receptor subunit (GluR2) in motor neurons results in the production of glutamate AMPA receptors that admit increased amounts of calcium ions into these neurons. As you have read previously in this chapter, excess intracellular calcium contributes to apoptosis, and a result, the cells die from excitoxicity.

Kawahara et al. (2004) examined the spinal cords and brains of five patients who had died of ALS and found evidence for deficient RNA editing in spinal cord motor neurons in all of them. All of the motor neurons from people without ALS showed normal RNA editing. Hideyama et al. (2010) prepared a targeted mutation against the gene for an enzyme involved in editing RNA responsible for the production of the GluR2 subunit and used a viral vector to insert this mutated gene into mouse motor neurons. The animals showed a decline in motor ability characteristic of ALS that was produced by slow death of motor neurons in the spinal cord and brain.

TREATMENTS The only current pharmacological treatment for ALS is riluzole, a drug that reduces glutamate-induced excitotoxicity, probably by decreasing the release of glutamate. Clinical trials found that patients treated with riluzole lived an average of approximately two months longer than those who received a placebo (Miller et al., 2003). Clearly, research to find more effective therapies is warranted.

Multiple Sclerosis

LO 15.14 **Describe the symptoms, causes, and treatments for multiple sclerosis.**

Multiple sclerosis (MS) is an autoimmune demyelinating disease. At scattered locations within the central nervous system, the person's immune system attacks myelin sheaths, leaving behind hard patches of debris called *sclerotic plaques*. (See Figure 15.23.) The normal transmission of neural messages through the demyelinated axons is interrupted.

Figure 15.23 Multiple Sclerosis

In this slice of the brain of a person who had multiple sclerosis, the arrowheads point to sclerotic plaques in the white matter.

(Courtesy of A. D'Agostino, Good Samaritan Hospital, Portland, Oregon.)

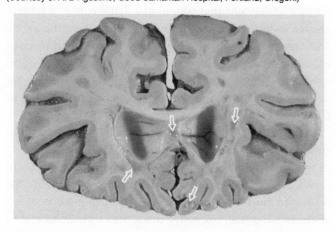

Because the damage occurs in white matter located throughout the brain and spinal cord, a wide variety of neurological symptoms are seen.

The symptoms of multiple sclerosis often appear, increase in intensity and then decrease, to be followed by another increase in symptoms after varying periods of time. In most cases, this pattern *(remitting-relapsing MS)* is followed by *progressive MS* later in the course of the disease. Progressive MS is characterized by a slow, continuous increase in the symptoms of the disease.

CAUSES Multiple sclerosis afflicts women somewhat more frequently than men, and the disorder usually occurs in people in their late twenties or thirties. People who spend their childhood in places far from the equator are more likely to be diagnosed with the disease than are those who live close to the equator. Hence, it is likely that some disease contracted during a childhood spent in a region in which the virus is prevalent causes the person's immune system to attack his or her own myelin. Perhaps a virus weakens the blood–brain barrier, allowing myelin protein into the general circulation and sensitizing the immune system to it, or perhaps the virus attaches itself to myelin. In addition, people born during the late winter and early spring are at higher risk, which suggests that infections contracted by a pregnant woman (for example, a viral disease contracted during the winter) may also increase susceptibility to this disease. Regardless of the origin, the process is a long-lived one, lasting for many decades.

TREATMENTS Only a few treatments for multiple sclerosis have shown promise (Aktas et al., 2009). The first is *interferon* β, a protein that modulates the responsiveness of the immune system. Administration of interferon β has been shown to reduce the frequency and severity of attacks and to slow the progression of neurological disabilities in some patients with multiple sclerosis (Arnason, 1999). However,

the treatment is only partially effective. Another partially effective treatment is *glatiramer acetate* (also known as copaxone or copolymer-1). Glatiramer acetate is a mixture of synthetic peptides composed from random sequences of the amino acids tyrosine, glutamate, alanine, and lysine. This compound was first produced in an attempt to *induce* the symptoms of multiple sclerosis in laboratory animals, but it turned out to actually reduce them. Interferon β and glatiramer acetate are effective only for the remitting-relapsing form of MS and not the progressive form.

An experimentally induced demyelinating disease known as *experimental allergic encephalitis (EAE)* can be produced in laboratory animals by injecting them with protein found in myelin. The immune system then becomes sensitized to myelin protein and attacks the animal's own myelin sheaths. Glatiramer acetate turned out to do just the opposite; rather than *causing* EAE, it prevented its occurrence, apparently by stimulating certain cells of the immune system to secrete anti-inflammatory chemicals such as *interleukin 4*, which suppress the activity of immune cells that would otherwise attack the patient's myelin (Farina et al., 2005). As you might expect, researchers tested glatiramer acetate in people with MS and found that the drug reduced the symptoms of patients who showed the relapsing-remitting form of the disease: periodic occurrences of neurological symptoms followed by partial remissions. The drug is now approved for treatment of this disorder. A structural MRI study by Sormani et al., (2005) found a reduction of 20–54 percent in white matter lesions in 95 percent of patients treated with glatiramer acetate.

Recent clinical trials have suggested that a new drug, BG-12, may be effective in reducing the number of brain lesions, the rate of relapse, and the rate of disability progression in relapsing MS (Fox et al., 2012; Gold et al., 2012; Kappos et al, 2014).

Although interferon β and glatiramer acetate provide some relief, neither treatment halts the progression of MS. One encouraging approach to treatment of MS is the transplantation of autologous hemopoietic stem cells—transplants of adult stem cells taken from a patient's own blood or bone marrow. A clinical trial with 21 MS patients reported significant improvements in neurological symptoms at the end of 37 months (Burt et al., 2009).

Because the symptoms of remitting-relapsing MS are episodic—new or worsening symptoms followed by partial recovery—patients and their families often attribute the changes in the symptoms to whatever has happened recently. For example, if the patient has taken a new medication or gone on a new diet and the symptoms get worse, the patient will blame the symptoms on the medication or diet. Conversely, if the patient gets better, he or she will credit the medication or diet. The best way to end exploitation of MS patients by people selling useless treatments is to develop genuinely effective therapies.

Symptoms of dementia affect individuals and their caregivers.

Lisa F. Young/Shutterstock

Dementia

LO 15.15 Describe the symptoms, causes, and treatments for Alzheimer's disease.

Several neurological disorders result in **dementia,** a deterioration of intellectual abilities resulting from an organic brain disorder. Lewy bodies were previously described in the context of Parkinson's disease; however, they are also frequently found to be associated with dementia. The presence of Lewy bodies is found in up to 20 percent of patients diagnosed with dementia (Breitve et al., 2014). The most common form of dementia is called **Alzheimer's disease,** which occurs in approximately 10 percent of the population above the age of 65 and almost 50 percent of people older than 85. It is characterized by progressive loss of memory and other cognitive functions. At first, people may have difficulty remembering appointments and sometimes fail to think of words or other people's names. As time passes, they show increasing confusion and difficulty with tasks such as managing their finances. The memory deficit most critically involves recent events, and thus it resembles the anterograde amnesia of Korsakoff's syndrome (described in the next section). If people with advanced Alzheimer's disease venture outside alone, they are likely to get lost. As this fatal disease progresses, symptoms become increasingly severe (Terry and Davies, 1980).

Alzheimer's disease produces severe degeneration of the hippocampus, entorhinal cortex, neocortex (especially the association cortex of the frontal and temporal lobes), nucleus basalis, locus coeruleus, and raphe nuclei. Figure 15.24 shows photographs of the brain of a patient with Alzheimer's disease and of a healthy control brain. You can see how much wider the sulci are in the patient's brain, especially in the frontal and temporal lobes, indicating substantial loss of cortical tissue.

Earlier, we mentioned that the brains of patients with Down syndrome usually develop abnormal structures that are also seen in patients with Alzheimer's disease: *amyloid plaques* and *neurofibrillary tangles.* **Amyloid plaques** are extracellular deposits that consist of a dense core of a protein known as β-amyloid, surrounded by degenerating axons and dendrites, along with activated microglia and reactive astrocytes, cells that are involved in destruction of damaged cells. Eventually, the phagocytic glial cells destroy the degenerating axons and dendrites, leaving only a core of β-amyloid (usually referred to as Aβ).

Neurofibrillary tangles consist of dying neurons that contain intracellular accumulations of twisted filaments of hyperphosphorylated **tau protein**. Normal tau protein serves as a component of microtubules, which provide the cells' transport mechanism. During the progression of Alzheimer's disease, excessive amounts of phosphate ions become attached to strands of tau protein, thus changing the molecular structure. Abnormal filaments are seen in the soma and proximal dendrites of pyramidal cells in the cerebral cortex, which disrupt transport of substances within the cell. Eventually the cell dies, leaving behind a tangle of protein filaments. (See Figure 15.25.)

Formation of amyloid plaques is caused by the production of a defective form of Aβ. The production of Aβ takes several steps. First, a gene encodes the production of the **β-amyloid precursor protein (APP),** a chain of approximately 700 amino acids. APP is then cut apart in two places by enzymes known as **secretases** to produce Aβ. The first, β-secretase, cuts the "tail" off of an APP molecule. The second, γ-secretase (gamma-secretase), cuts the "head" off. The result is a molecule of Aβ that contains either 40 or 42 amino acids. (See Figure 15.26.)

Figure 15.24 Alzheimer's Disease

(a) Dorsal view of the brain of a person with Alzheimer's disease. Note that the sulci are especially wide, indicating degeneration of the cortex. (b) Dorsal view of a normal brain.

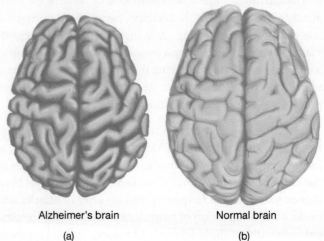

Alzheimer's brain

(a)

Normal brain

(b)

Figure 15.25 Microscopic Features of Alzheimer's Disease

The photomicrographs from deceased patients with Alzheimer's disease show (a) an amyloid plaque, filled with β-amyloid protein, and (b) neurofibrillary tangles.

(Photos courtesy of D. J. Selkoe, Brigham and Women's Hospital, Boston.)

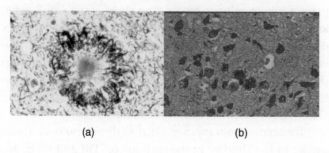

(a)   (b)

The location of the second cut of the APP molecule by γ-secretase determines which form is produced. In healthy brains, 90–95 percent of the Aβ molecules are of the short form; the other 5–10 percent are of the long form. In patients with Alzheimer's disease the proportion of long Aβ

Figure 15.26 β-Amyloid Protein

The schematic shows the production of β-amyloid protein (Aβ) from the amyloid precursor protein.

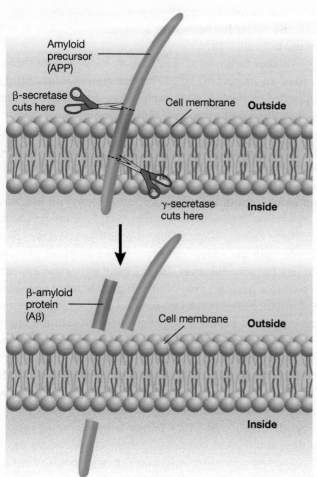

rises to as much as 40 percent of the total. High concentrations of the long form have a tendency to fold themselves improperly and form aggregations, which have toxic effects on the cell. (As we saw earlier in this chapter, abnormally folded prions and α-synuclein proteins form aggregations that result in brain degeneration.) Usually, small amounts of long Aβ can easily be cleared from the brain. The molecules are given an ubiquitin tag that marks them for destruction, and they are transported to the proteasomes, where they are rendered harmless. However, this system cannot keep up with abnormally high levels of production of long Aβ.

Acetylcholinergic neurons in the basal forebrain are among the first cells to be affected in Alzheimer's disease. Aβ serves as a ligand for the *p75 neurotrophic receptor*, a receptor that normally responds to stress signals and stimulates apoptosis (Sotthibundhu et al., 2008). Basal forebrain ACh neurons contain high levels of these receptors; thus, once the level of long-form Aβ reach a sufficiently high level, these neurons begin to die.

Figure 15.27 shows the abnormal accumulation of Aβ in the brain of a person with Alzheimer's disease. Klunk and his colleagues (Klunk et al., 2003; Mathis et al., 2005) developed *PiB*, a chemical that binds with Aβ and readily crosses the blood–brain barrier. They gave the patient and a healthy control subject an injection of a radioactive form of PiB and examined their brains with a PET scanner. You can see the accumulation of the protein in the patient's cerebral cortex. The ability to measure the levels of Aβ in the brains of Alzheimer's patients will enable researchers to evaluate the effectiveness of potential treatments for the disease. When such a treatment is devised, the ability to identify the accumulation of Aβ early in the development of the disease will make it possible to begin a patient's treatment before significant degeneration—and the accompanying decline in cognitive abilities—has occurred.

As we saw earlier, the brains of Alzheimer's patients contain abnormal forms of two types of proteins: Aβ and tau. It appears that excessive amounts of abnormal Aβ, but not tau protein, are responsible for the disease. Mutations in the Aβ precursor, APP, produce both forms of abnormal proteins and cause the development of both amyloid plaques and neurofibrillary tangles. However, mutations in the gene for tau protein (found on chromosome 17) produce only neurofibrillary tangles. The result of these mutations is a disorder known as **frontotemporal dementia** (also known as *Pick's disease*), which causes degeneration of the frontal and temporal cortex, resulting in emotional changes and loss of executive functions caused by damage to the prefrontal cortex and language disturbance caused by temporal lobe damage (Goate, 1998; Goedert and Spillantini, 2000).

It appears that the presence of excessive amounts of Aβ in the cytoplasm of cells, not the formation of extracellular

Figure 15.27 Detection of β-Amyloid Protein

The PET scans show the accumulation of β-amyloid protein (Aβ) in the brain of a patient with Alzheimer's disease and a healthy control volunteer. AD = Alzheimer's disease, MR = structural magnetic resonance image, [C-11]PIB PET = PET scan of brains after an injection of a radioactive ligand for Aβ.

(Courtesy of William Klunk, Western Psychiatric Institute and Clinic, Pittsburgh, PA.)

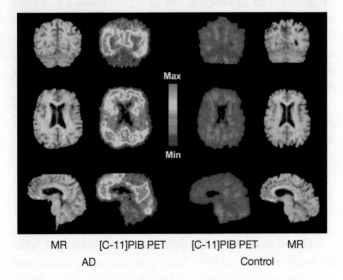

MR	[C-11]PIB PET	[C-11]PIB PET	MR
	AD		Control

amyloid plaques, is the cause of neural degeneration (Bossy-Wetzel et al., 2004). Intracellular *oligomers* of Aβ (aggregations of several Aβ molecules) activate microglia, causing an inflammatory response that triggers the release of toxic *cytokines*—chemicals produced by the immune system that normally destroy infected cells. Aβ oligomers also trigger an excessive release of glutamate by glial cells, which causes excitotoxicity because of excessive inflow of calcium ions through neural NMDA receptors. They also cause synaptic dysfunction and suppress the formation of long-term potentiation, perhaps because of interference with axonal and dendritic transport.

CAUSES Research has shown that at least some forms of Alzheimer's disease occur in families and thus appear to be hereditary. Because the brains of people with Down syndrome (caused by an extra twenty-first chromosome) also contain deposits of Aβ, some investigators hypothesized that the twenty-first chromosome may be involved in the production of this protein. In fact, St. George-Hyslop et al. (1987) found that chromosome 21 *does* contain the gene that produces APP.

Since the discovery of the APP gene, several studies have found specific mutations of this gene that produce familial Alzheimer's disease (Martinez et al., 1993; Farlow et al., 1994). In addition, other studies have found numerous mutations of two **presenilin** genes, found on chromosomes 1 and 14, that also produce Alzheimer's disease. Abnormal APP and presenilin genes all cause the defective long form of Aβ to be produced (Hardy, 1997). The two presenilin proteins, PS1 and PS2, are subunits of γ-secretase, which is not a simple enzyme but consists of a large multiprotein complex (De Strooper, 2003).

Yet another genetic cause of Alzheimer's disease is a mutation in the gene for **apolipoprotein E (ApoE),** a glycoprotein that transports cholesterol in the blood and also plays a role in cellular repair. One allele of the ApoE gene, known as E4, increases the risk of late-onset Alzheimer's disease, apparently by interfering with the removal of the long form of Aβ from the extracellular space in the brain (Roses, 1997; Bu, 2010). In contrast, the ApoE2 allele may actually protect people from developing Alzheimer's disease. (The most common form of ApoE is the E3 allele.)

Traumatic brain injuries, such as those you read about earlier in the chapter in the sections on TBI and CTE, are also a serious risk factor for Alzheimer's disease. For example, examination of the brains of people who have sustained closed head injuries reveals a widespread distribution of amyloid plaques. Risk of Alzheimer's disease following traumatic brain injury is especially high in people who possess the ApoE4 allele (Bu, 2010). Obesity, hypertension, high cholesterol levels, and diabetes are also risk factors, and these factors, too, are exacerbated by the presence of the ApoE4 allele (Martins et al., 2006). Although genetically triggered production of abnormal Aβ plays an important role in the development of Alzheimer's disease, the fact is that most forms of Alzheimer's disease are sporadic, not hereditary. So far, the strongest known nongenetic risk factor for Alzheimer's disease (other than age) is traumatic brain injury.

Another factor, level of education, has also been shown to play an important role. The Religious Orders Study, supported by the U.S. National Institute on Aging, measures the cognitive performance of older Catholic clergy (priests, nuns, and monks) and examines their brains when they die. A report by Bennett et al. (2003) found a positive relationship between increased number of years of formal education and cognitive performance, even in people whose brains contained significant concentrations of amyloid plaques. For example, people who had received some postgraduate education had significantly higher cognitive test scores than people with the same concentration of amyloid plaques but less formal education. Thus, formal education appears to enable a person to maintain a higher level of cognitive performance even in the face of brain degeneration. Ninety percent of the people who are participating in the study received some college education. It is possible that if people with much less formal education were studied, an even stronger relationship between education and resistance to dementia would be seen. Of course, it is possible that variables such as individual differences in cognitive ability affect the likelihood that a person will pursue advanced studies, and these differences, by themselves, could play an important role. In any case, engaging in vigorous intellectual activity and adopting a lifestyle that promotes good general health are probably the most important things a person can do to stave off the development of dementia.

Billings et al., (2007) performed an experiment with *AD mice,* a strain of genetically modified mice that contain a mutant human gene for APP that leads to the development of Alzheimer's disease. The investigators began training the mice early in life on the Morris water maze task, described in Chapter 13. The mice were trained at three-month intervals between the ages of 2 months and 18 months. The training delayed the accumulation of Aβ and led to a slower decline of the animals' performance. This study lends support to the conclusion that cognitive activity delays the appearance of Alzheimer's disease.

Like the transmissible spongiform encephalopathies caused by misfolded prion proteins, the misfolded Aβ responsible for Alzheimer's disease can also be propagated from cell to cell, and from animal to animal. Kane et al., (2000) prepared a dilute suspension of homogenized brain tissue taken from deceased patients with Alzheimer's disease and injected some of the liquid in the brains of mice. Three months later, they found profuse development of amyloid plaques and vascular deposits of Aβ. Even more unsettling, Eisele et al., (2009) coated stainless-steel wires with minute amounts of misfolded Aβ and implanted them in the brains of mice. This procedure, too, induced β-amyloidosis in the recipients—even when the wires had been boiled before they were implanted. As we saw, prion proteins retain their infective potency even after being heated to the boiling point. Apparently, misfolded Aβ also retains its ability to act as a seed that induces misfolding in a recipient brain. Fortunately, Eisele et al. found that more thorough sterilization of the wires blocked the ability of the Aβ to trigger the production of misfolded protein, so it is unlikely that Alzheimer's disease could be transmitted by means of surgical instruments.

TREATMENTS Currently, the only approved pharmacological treatments for Alzheimer's disease are acetylcholinesterase inhibitors (donepezil, rivastigmine, and galantamine) and an NMDA receptor antagonist (memantine). Because acetylcholinergic neurons are among the first to be damaged in Alzheimer's disease and because these neurons play a role in cortical activation and memory, drugs that inhibit the destruction of ACh and hence enhance its activity have been found to provide a modest increase in cognitive measures among patients with this disease. However, these drugs have no effect on the process of neural degeneration and do not prolong patients' survival. Memantine, a noncompetitive NMDA receptor blocker, appears to produce a slight improvement in symptoms of dementia by slowing excitotoxic destruction of acetylcholinergic neurons caused by the entry of excessive amounts of calcium (Rogawski and Wenk, 2003).

Perhaps the most promising approaches to the prevention of Alzheimer's disease come from immunological

research with AD mice. Schenk et al., (1999) and Bard et al., (2000) attempted to sensitize the immune system against Aβ. They injected AD mice with a vaccine that, they hoped, would stimulate the immune system to destroy Aβ. The treatment worked: The vaccine suppressed the development of amyloid plaques in the brains of mice that received the vaccine from an early age and halted or even reversed the development of plaques in mice that received the vaccine later in life.

A clinical trial with Alzheimer's patients attempted to destroy Aβ by sensitizing the patient's immune systems to the protein (Monsonego and Weiner, 2003). In a double-blind study, 30 patients with mild-to-moderate Alzheimer's disease were given injections of a portion of the Aβ protein. Twenty of these patients generated antibodies against Aβ, which slowed the course of the disease, presumably because their immune systems began destroying Aβ in their brain and reducing the neural destruction caused by the accumulation of this protein. Hock et al., (2003) compared the cognitive abilities of the patients who generated Aβ antibodies to those who did not. As Figure 15.28 shows, antibody production significantly reduced cognitive decline.

One of the patients whose immune system generated antibodies against Aβ died of a pulmonary embolism (a blood clot in a blood vessel serving the lungs). Nicoll et al., (2003) examined this patient's brain and found evidence that the immune system had removed Aβ from many regions of the cerebral cortex. Unfortunately, the injections of the Aβ antigen caused an inflammatory reaction in the brains of 5 percent of the patients, so the clinical trial was terminated. New approaches to treatment have included preliminary trials

Figure 15.28 Immunization Against Aβ

The graph shows the effect of immunization against Aβ on the cognitive decline of patients who generated Aβ antibodies (successfully immunized patients) and those who did not (controls). (Based on data from Hock et al., 2003.)

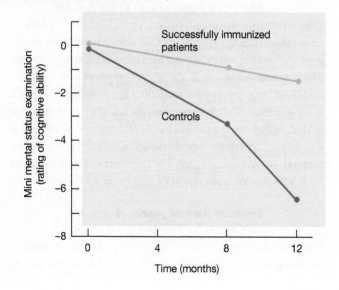

of *aducanumab*, a replica of a naturally-occurring protective antibody that recognizes Aβ oligomers. This research reflects a new approach to immunotherapy that will (we hope) avoid inflammatory reactions (Fu et al., 2010; Marciani, 2015).

Korsakoff's Syndrome

LO 15.16 **Describe the symptoms and causes of Korsakoff's syndrome.**

Another degenerative disorder characterized by symptoms of dementia, Korsakoff's syndrome, is neither hereditary nor contagious. It is caused by environmental factors—usually (but not always) involving chronic consumption of alcohol. The disorder actually results from a thiamine (vitamin B$_1$) deficiency that can be caused by alcohol abuse (Adams, 1969; Haas, 1988). Because people who abuse alcohol receive a substantial number of calories from the alcohol they ingest, they usually eat a poor diet, and their vitamin intake is consequently low. Furthermore, alcohol interferes with intestinal absorption of thiamine. The ensuing deficiency produces brain damage. Thiamine is essential for a step in metabolism: the carboxylation of pyruvate, an intermediate product in the breakdown of carbohydrates, fats, and amino acids. Korsakoff's syndrome sometimes occurs in people who have been severely malnourished and have then received intravenous infusions of glucose; the sudden availability of glucose to the cells of the brain without adequate thiamine with which to metabolize it damages the cells, probably because they

accumulate pyruvate. Hence, standard medical practice is to administer thiamine along with intravenous glucose to severely malnourished patients.

As we saw in Chapter 13, the brain damage incurred in Korsakoff's syndrome causes anterograde amnesia. Although degeneration is seen in many parts of the brain, the damage that characterizes this disorder occurs in the mammillary bodies, located at the base of the brain, in the posterior hypothalamus. (See Figure 15.29.)

Figure 15.29 Korsakoff's Syndrome

This brain slice shows the degeneration of the mammillary bodies in a patient with Korsakoff's syndrome.

(Courtesy of A. D'Agostino, Good Samaritan Hospital, Portland, Oregon.)

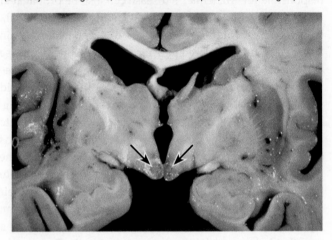

Section Review

Degenerative Disorders

LO 15.10 **Describe how transmissible spongiform encephalopathies cause brain damage.**

Transmissible spongiform encephalopathies such as Creutzfeldt-Jakob disease, scrapie, and bovine spongiform encephalopathy are produced by a simple protein molecule. The sequence of amino acids of normal prion protein (PrP^c) and infectious prion protein (PrP^{Sc}) are identical, but their three-dimensional shapes differ in the way that they are folded. Somehow, the presence of a misfolded prion protein in a neuron causes normal prion proteins to become misfolded, and a chain reaction ensues. The transformation of PrP^c into PrP^{Sc} kills the cell, apparently by triggering apoptosis.

LO 15.11 **Describe the symptoms, causes, and treatments for Parkinson's disease.**

Parkinson's disease is caused by degeneration of dopamine-secreting neurons of the substantia nigra that send axons to the basal ganglia and results in resting tremor and muscle rigidity, slowness of movement and postural instability. The death of these neurons is caused by the aggregation of misfolded protein, α-synuclein. Parkinson's disease is associated with two mutations. One mutation produces defective α-synuclein, and another produces defective parkin, a protein that assists in the tagging of abnormal proteins for destruction by the proteasomes. The accumulation of α-synuclein can also be triggered by some toxins, which suggests that nonhereditary forms of the disease may be caused by toxic substances present in the environment. Treatment of Parkinson's disease includes administration of L-DOPA, implantation of fetal dopaminergic neurons in the basal ganglia, stereotaxic destruction of a portion of the globus pallidus or subthalamic nucleus, and implantation of electrodes that enable the patient to electrically stimulate the subthalamic nucleus. Research using optogenetic methods reveals that the beneficial effects of DBS are produced by activation of axons that enter the subthalamic nucleus. Fetal transplants of dopaminergic neurons have been less successful than they had initially appeared to be, probably because the α-synuclein is transferred to the grafted neurons from the recipient's own neurons. A trial of gene therapy designed to reduce excitation in the subthalamic nucleus produced promising results.

LO 15.12 Describe the symptoms, causes, and treatments for Huntington's disease.

Huntington's disease, an autosomal dominant hereditary disorder, produces degeneration of the caudate nucleus and putamen. Symptoms include involuntary fragments of purposeful movement. Mutated huntingtin protein misfolds and forms aggregations that accumulate in the nucleus of GABAergic neurons in the putamen. Although the primary effect of mutated huntingtin is gain of toxic function, the disease also appears to involve a loss of function; a targeted mutation in mice against the Htt gene is fatal. Evidence also suggests that inclusion bodies have a protective function and that damage is done by mutated huntingtin dispersed throughout the cell. Animal studies that target intracellular antibodies against a portion of Htt and that transferred small interfering RNA targeted against the Htt gene have produced promising results. There are currently no treatments available, however research with intrabodies and siRNA show promising results.

LO 15.13 Describe the symptoms, causes, and treatments for amyotrophic lateral sclerosis.

Amyotrophic lateral sclerosis is a fatal degenerative disorder that attacks motor neurons and produces spasticity, exaggerated stretch reflexes, progressive weakness, muscular atrophy, and paralysis. Ten percent of the cases are hereditary, caused by a mutation of the gene for SOD1; the other 90 percent are sporadic. The primary cause of sporadic ALS appears to be an abnormality in RNA editing, which results in the production of AMPA receptor subunits that permit the entry of excessive amounts of calcium into the cells. The only pharmacological treatment is riluzole, a drug that reduces glutamate-induced excitotoxicity.

LO 15.14 Describe the symptoms, causes, and treatments for multiple sclerosis.

Multiple sclerosis (MS), a demyelinating disease, is characterized by periodic attacks of neurological symptoms, usually with partial remission between attacks (remitting-relapsing MS), followed by progressive MS later in life. Symptoms of MS include a variety of neurological symptoms. The damage appears to be caused by the body's immune system, which attacks the protein contained in myelin. Most investigators believe that a viral infection early in life somehow sensitizes the immune system to myelin protein. Effective treatments for remitting-relapsing MS include interferon β, and glatiramer acetate, a mixture of synthetic peptides that appears to stimulate certain immune cells to secrete anti-inflammatory chemicals.

LO 15.15 Describe the symptoms, causes, and treatments for Alzheimer's disease.

Alzheimer's disease, a neurodegenerative disease characterized by symptoms of dementia, involves much of the brain; the disease process eventually destroys most of the hippocampus and cortical gray matter. The brains of affected individuals contain many amyloid plaques, which contain a core of misfolded long-form Aβ protein surrounded by degenerating axons and dendrites, and neurofibrillary tangles, composed of dying neurons that contain intracellular accumulations of twisted filaments of tau protein. Hereditary forms of Alzheimer's disease involve defective genes for the amyloid precursor protein (APP), for the secretases that cut APP into smaller pieces, or for apolipoprotein E (ApoE), a glycoprotein involved in transport of cholesterol and the repair of cell membranes. A promising treatment is vaccination against Aβ, and administration of the antigen may provide a way to avoid triggering an inflammatory reaction. Temporary reduction of symptoms is seen in some patients who are treated with anticholinergic drugs or drugs that serve as NMDA antagonists. Exercise and intellectual stimulation appear to delay the onset of Alzheimer's disease, and obesity, high cholesterol levels, and diabetes are significant risk factors.

LO 15.16 Describe the symptoms and causes of Korsakoff's syndrome.

Korsakoff's syndrome produces anterograde amnesia and is often a result of alcohol abuse, but it can also be caused by malnutrition that results in a thiamine deficiency. The most obvious location of brain damage is the mammillary bodies, but damage also occurs in many other parts of the brain. Treatment includes preventative measures such as ensuring enough thiamine in the diet and administering thiamine along with glucose to severely malnourished patients.

Thought Question

You may have noticed several similarities among different degenerative disorders in this section. Identify two similarities among the disorders and explain why the disorders might share this element in common. You might consider common symptoms, genetic contributions, protein misfolding, or neurotransmitter alterations.

Disorders Caused by Infectious Diseases

Between 1991 and 1992, nine college students developed symptoms of headache, fever, neck stiffness, and altered mental status. The students all lived in the same community. The symptoms of three of the students were severe, and their illness was ultimately fatal.

Seeking to learn more about this unusual and alarming outbreak, epidemiologists tried to identify the cause of the students' symptoms and any possible connection among the cases. Researchers interviewed the surviving students and their friends about where they lived, what clubs and athletic or social activities they participated in, the classes they attended, their part-time jobs, and their contact with the other sick students. No direct link was found among the cases.

Upon further investigation, the researchers found that six of the students had visited the same local bar approximately one week prior to their illness. The researchers then surveyed community members about bars and restaurants in the area and respondents rated the bar as exceptionally crowded and smoky. Researchers hypothesized that a crowded and smoky environment facilitated the spread of the infectious organism. Follow up investigation revealed that the bar employees tested positive for *Neisseria meningitides,* the infectious agent responsible for the students' illness (Imrey et al., 1996).

The case study of the college students described above illustrates several characteristics of disorders caused by infectious diseases. Several neurological disorders can be caused by infectious disease, transmitted by bacteria, fungi or other parasites, or viruses. The most common are encephalitis and meningitis. **Encephalitis** is an infection that invades the entire brain. The symptoms of acute encephalitis include fever, irritability, and nausea, often followed by convulsions, delirium, and signs of brain damage, such as aphasia or paralysis. Unfortunately, there is no specific treatment aside from supportive care, and between 5 and 20 percent of the cases are fatal; 20 percent of the survivors show some residual neurological symptoms. (See Figure 15.30.)

Encephalitis

LO 15.16 **Identify the symptoms, causes, and treatments for encephalitis.**

Encephalitis can also be caused by the **herpes simplex virus,** which is the cause of cold sores (or "fever blisters") that most people develop in and around their mouth from time to time. Normally, the viruses live quietly in the *trigeminal nerve ganglia* nodules on the fifth cranial nerve that contain the cell bodies of somatosensory neurons that serve the face. The viruses proliferate periodically, traveling down to the ends of nerve fibers, where they cause sores to develop in mucous membrane. Unfortunately, they occasionally (but rarely) go the other way into the brain. Herpes encephalitis is a serious disease; the virus attacks the frontal and temporal lobes in particular and can severely damage them.

Two other forms of viral encephalitis may be familiar to you: polio and rabies. **Acute anterior poliomyelitis** ("polio") is fortunately very rare in developed countries since the development of vaccines that immunize people against the disease. The virus causes specific damage to motor neurons of the brain and spinal cord: neurons in the primary motor cortex; in the motor nuclei of the thalamus,

Figure 15.30 Meningitis and Encephalitis

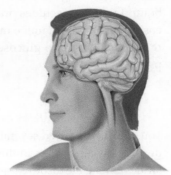

Meningitis
Inflammation or swelling of the meninges surrounding the brain and spinal cord.

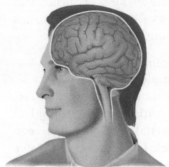

Encephalitis
Inflammation of the brain itself.

hypothalamus, and brain stem; in the cerebellum; and in the ventral horns of the gray matter of the spinal cord. Undoubtedly, these motor neurons contain some chemical substance that either attracts the virus or in some way makes the virus become lethal to them.

Rabies is caused by a virus that is passed from the saliva of an infected mammal directly into a person's flesh by means of a bite wound. The virus travels through peripheral nerves to the central nervous system and there causes severe damage. It also travels to peripheral organs, such as the salivary glands, which makes it possible for the virus to find its way to another host. The symptoms include a short period of fever and headache, followed by anxiety, excessive movement and talking, difficulty in swallowing, movement disorders, difficulty in speaking, seizures, confusion, and, finally, death within two to seven days of the onset of the symptoms. The virus has a special affinity for cells in the cerebellum and hippocampus, and damage to the hippocampus probably accounts for the emotional changes that are seen in the early symptoms.

Fortunately, the incubation period for rabies lasts up to several months while the virus climbs through the peripheral nerves. (If the bite is received in the face or neck, the incubation time will be much shorter because the virus has a smaller distance to travel before it reaches the brain.) During the incubation period a person can receive a vaccine that will confer immunity to the disease; the person's own immune system will destroy the virus before it reaches the brain.

Several infectious diseases cause brain damage even though they are not primarily diseases of the central nervous system. One such disease is caused by the human immunodeficiency virus (HIV), the cause of acquired immune deficiency syndrome (AIDS). Records of autopsies have revealed that at least 75 percent of people who died of AIDS show evidence of brain damage (Levy and Bredesen, 1989). Brain damage associated with an HIV infection can produce a range of syndromes, from mild neurocognitive disorder to HIV-associated dementia (also called *AIDS dementia complex,* or *ADC*). Neuropathology caused by HIV infection is characterized by damage to synapses and death of neurons in the hippocampus, cerebral cortex, and basal ganglia (Mattson et al., 2005; Valcour et al., 2011). Aggressive treatment with combination antiretroviral therapy, if started soon after the infection is discovered, can prevent or minimize damage to the brain. However, active viruses can persist in the brain even when they cannot be detected in the blood, so the patients' cognitive abilities and affective state should be carefully monitored. If the viral infection is not treated, the brain damage progresses and leads to a loss of cognitive and motor functions and is the leading cause of cognitive decline in people under 40 years of age. At first the patients may become forgetful, they may think and reason more slowly, and they may have word-finding difficulties (anomia). Eventually, they may become almost mute. Motor deficits may begin with tremor and difficulty in making complex movements but then may progress so much that the patient becomes bedridden (Maj, 1990).

For several years, researchers have been puzzled by the fact that although an HIV infection certainly causes neural damage, neurons are not themselves infected by the virus. Instead, the virus lives and replicates in the brain's astrocytes. The neuropathology appears to be caused by the glycoprotein *gp120* envelope that coats the RNA that is responsible for the AIDS infection. The gp120 binds with other proteins that trigger apoptosis (Alirezaei et al., 2007; Mattson et al., 2005).

Meningitis

LO 15.17 **Identify the symptoms, causes, and treatments for meningitis.**

Another category of infectious diseases of the brain actually involves inflammation of the meninges, the layers of connective tissue that surround the central nervous system. **Meningitis** can be caused by viruses or bacteria. The symptoms of all forms include headache, a stiff neck, and, depending on the severity of the disorder, convulsions, confusion or loss of consciousness, and sometimes death. The stiff neck is one of the most important symptoms. Neck movements cause the meninges to stretch; because they are inflamed, the stretch causes severe pain. Thus, the patient resists having his or her neck moved. The students in the case at the beginning of this section experienced meningitis. The outbreak in the community was reduced through vaccination of thousands of additional students.

The most common form of viral meningitis usually does not cause significant brain damage. However, various forms of bacterial meningitis do. The usual cause is spread of a middle-ear infection into the brain, introduction of an infection into the brain from a head injury, or the presence of emboli that have dislodged from a bacterial infection present in the chambers of the heart. Such an infection is often caused by unclean hypodermic needles; therefore, people who use intravenous drugs are at particular risk for meningitis (as well as many other diseases). The inflammation of the meninges can damage the brain by interfering with circulation of blood or by blocking the flow of cerebrospinal fluid through the subarachnoid space, causing hydrocephalus. In addition, the cranial nerves are susceptible to damage. Fortunately, bacterial meningitis can usually be treated effectively with antibiotics. Of course, early diagnosis and prompt treatment are essential, because neither antibiotics nor any other known treatment can repair a damaged brain.

Section Review

Disorders Caused by Infectious Diseases

LO 15.17 Identify the symptoms, causes, and treatments for encephalitis.

Encephalitis, usually caused by a virus, affects the entire brain and can cause symptoms of fever, irritability, nausea, seizures, and neurological symptoms. One form is caused by the herpes simplex virus, which infects the trigeminal nerve ganglia of most of the population. This virus tends to attack the frontal and temporal lobes. The polio virus attacks motor neurons in the brain and spinal cord, resulting in motor deficits or even paralysis. The rabies virus, acquired by an animal bite, travels through peripheral nerves and attacks the brain, particularly the cerebellum and hippocampus. An HIV infection also produces brain damage when the gp120 protein envelope of the HIV virus binds with other proteins that trigger apoptosis. Aggressive treatment with combination antiretroviral therapy can minimize brain damage.

LO 15.18 Identify the symptoms, causes, and treatments for meningitis.

Meningitis is an infection of the meninges, caused by viruses or bacteria that produce symptoms of headache, stiff neck, and, depending on the severity of the disorder, convulsions, confusion or loss of consciousness, and sometimes death. The bacterial form, which is usually more serious, is generally caused by an ear infection, a head injury, or an embolus from a heart infection.

Thought Question

Consider what precautions individuals living in close proximity to others should take to reduce their chances of contracting an infection that could result in encephalitis or meningitis. Imagine that you have been asked to design a pamphlet for incoming students at your school encouraging them to consider a meningitis vaccine before they move into a residence hall. What information would you share with them?

Chapter Review Questions

1. Discuss the causes, symptoms, and treatment of brain tumors, seizure disorders, cerebrovascular accidents, and traumatic brain injury.

2. Explain how prenatal exposure to alcohol may lead to fetal alcohol syndrome.

3. Describe how brain development is effected in children with phenylketonuria. What are the treatment strategies for it?

4. Describe the connections of basal ganglia, and explain the pathophysiological basis of the symptoms of Parkinson's disease and the mode of treatment.

5. Discuss the causes, symptoms, and potential treatments for the brain degeneration caused by Alzheimer's disease.

6. Discuss the causes, symptoms, and available treatments of the brain degeneration caused by amyotrophic lateral sclerosis (ALS), multiple sclerosis (MS), and Korsakoff's syndrome.

7. Discuss the causes, symptoms, and available treatments for encephalitis, HIV-associated dementia, and meningitis.

Chapter 16
Schizophrenia and the Affective Disorders

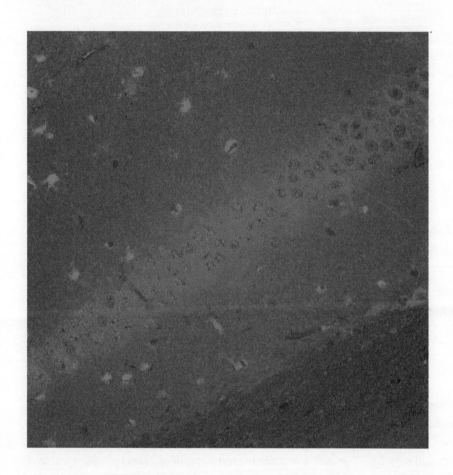

Chapter Outline

Learning Objectives

LO 16.1 Provide examples of positive, negative, and cognitive symptoms of schizophrenia.

LO 16.2 Describe evidence that supports a genetic contribution to the development of schizophrenia.

LO 16.3 Describe evidence that supports an environmental contribution to the development of schizophrenia.

LO 16.4 Describe the behavioral, physical, and brain anomalies associated with schizophrenia.

LO 16.5 Provide evidence of the role of the mesolimbic dopamine pathway in the positive symptoms of schizophrenia.

LO 16.6 Provide evidence of the role of the cortex in the negative and cognitive symptoms of schizophrenia.

LO 16.7 Contrast the symptoms of major depressive disorder and bipolar disorder.

LO 16.8 Describe evidence that supports a genetic contribution to the development of affective disorders.

LO 16.9 List the types of biological treatments for affective disorders.

LO 16.10 Describe the role of the frontal cortex in depression.

LO 16.11 Summarize the evidence in support of the monoamine theory of affective disorders.

LO 16.12 Critique the evidence for the role of allele polymorphism for the serotonin transporter in affective disorders.

LO 16.13 Explain the relationship between affective disorders, their treatment, and neurogenesis.

LO 16.14 Summarize the evidence for the role of changes in circadian rhythms in affective disorders.

Grant is a 22-year-old male who was taken to the emergency room by campus police from a local university. A roommate had called the campus police when Grant became very agitated, talking and yelling to himself and refusing to leave his residence hall room because of fears that he was under surveillance and being followed, although there was no evidence of either.

After doing well academically in high school, Grant struggled with his courses in college. He found it difficult to concentrate. He frequently found his mind racing, and he began hearing voices saying negative things repeatedly and telling him he would be a failure as a student. Eventually his grades did begin to suffer. People seemed surprised that Grant expressed no emotion in response to learning that he was failing all of his courses. Grant took a leave of absence from school after his first year.

After leaving school, Grant returned home to live with his parents. His parents became increasingly concerned about his auditory hallucinations, unusual beliefs about contaminated food, and the belief that people were following him or recording his thoughts. At his parent's insistence, Grant eventually made an appointment with a psychiatrist who diagnosed him with schizophrenia.

The doctor prescribed an atypical antipsychotic mediation. Despite gaining 15 pounds as a side effect of the medication, Grant responded well to the treatment and within several months made the decision to return to college. However, after a few weeks back, Grant became frustrated with the side effects of his medication and began to suspect that it was contaminated. He stopped taking it and avoided his follow up appointments with the psychiatrist. His symptoms returned, and within a few months he was on academic probation again. Once again, Grant left school and returned home.

This time, his symptoms were more severe and Grant was admitted to an in-patient clinic for treatment. With a different atypical antipsychotic medication, Grant's symptoms, including his unfounded beliefs about contamination and surveillance, began to subside again. He was released from the hospital and returned to school several months later. However, he once again began to display unusual behaviors, express fears about food contamination, and refuse to leave his room because of his belief that he was being followed, leading to the call to campus police and Grant's subsequent trip to the emergency room.

*****

Grant's case illustrates some of the important aspects of schizophrenia and its treatment. For many people, the symptoms of schizophrenia appear in late adolescence or early adulthood, and the disorder is more common in men than women. Individuals with schizophrenia can experience a wide range of symptoms, from auditory hallucinations, to delusions, to blunted affect, reduced social interaction, and problems with attention and focus. Treatments for schizophrenia include various types of therapeutic interventions, including cognitive behavioral therapies, family psycho-education, social skills training, supported employment, and antipsychotic medications (Mueser et al., 2013). Many people experience adverse side effects of these medications, however, and compliance with treatments can be challenging. While the symptoms of the disorder can be severe, with support, many individuals with schizophrenia can achieve a high quality of life and meet personal, professional, and academic goals.

Most of the discussion in this book has concentrated on the physiology of typical, adaptive behavior. The last three chapters summarize research on the nature and physiology of syndromes characterized by maladaptive behavior: mental disorders and substance abuse. The symptoms of mental disorders include deficient or inappropriate social behaviors; illogical, incoherent, or obsessional thoughts; inappropriate emotional responses, including depression, mania, or anxiety; and delusions and hallucinations. Research in recent years suggests that many of these symptoms are caused by abnormalities in the brain, both structural and biochemical.

Chapter 17 discusses anxiety disorders, autism, attention deficit disorder, and disorders associated with stress. Chapter 18 discusses substance abuse. This chapter discusses two groups of serious mental disorders: schizophrenia and mood disorders, including major depressive disorder and bipolar disorder. The figure of the brain below highlights the prefrontal cortex, an area that we will be discussing in this chapter.

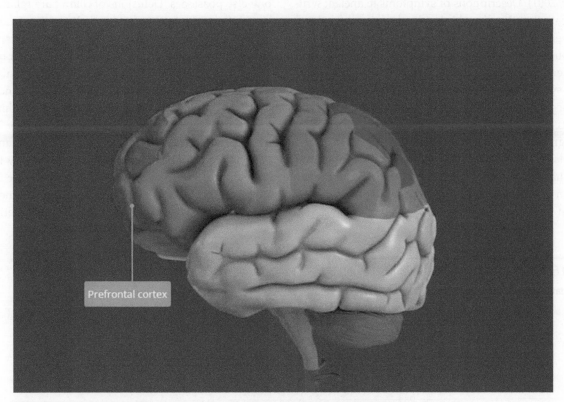

Shown here is the prefrontal cortex, an area implicated in symptoms of schizophrenia.

Schizophrenia

Description

LO 16.1 Provide examples of positive, negative, and cognitive symptoms of schizophrenia.

Schizophrenia may be one of the most misused psychological terms in existence. The word literally means "split mind,"

but it does *not* imply a split or multiple personality. The man who invented the term, Eugen Bleuler (1911/1950), intended "schizophrenia" to refer to a break with reality caused by disorganization of the various functions of the mind, such that thoughts and feelings no longer worked together in a typical fashion.

Schizophrenia is a serious mental disorder that afflicts approximately 1 percent of the world's population. Its

Schizophrenia is a serious mental disorder that afflicts approximately 1 percent of the world's population.

monetary cost to society is enormous; in the United States this figure exceeds that of the cost of all cancers (Thaker and Carpenter, 2001). Descriptions of symptoms in ancient writings indicate that the disorder has likely existed for thousands of years (Jeste et al., 1985).

Although studies have found that people who develop schizophrenia show some abnormalities even during childhood, the symptoms of schizophrenia typically begin in late adolescence or early adulthood. Figure 16.1 shows a graph of the ages of first signs of mental disorder in males and females diagnosed with schizophrenia.

The major symptoms of schizophrenia are universal, and clinicians have developed criteria for reliably diagnosing the disorder in people of a wide variety of cultures (Flaum and Andreasen, 1990).

POSITIVE SYMPTOMS   **Schizophrenia** is characterized by three categories of symptoms: positive, negative, and cognitive (Mueser and McGurk, 2004). **Positive symptoms** make themselves known by their presence. They include thought disorders, hallucinations, and delusions. A **thought disorder**—disorganized, irrational thinking—is an important symptom of schizophrenia. People with schizophrenia typically have difficulty arranging their thoughts logically and sorting out plausible conclusions from improbable ones. In conversation they may jump from one topic to another as new associations come up. Sometimes, they may use meaningless words or choose words for rhyme rather than for meaning. **Delusions** are beliefs that are contrary to fact and that are not held by a subgroup to which the person belongs (such as religious beliefs). Delusions of *persecution* are false beliefs that others are following, plotting, and conspiring against oneself. Delusions of *grandeur* are false beliefs in one's power and importance, such as a conviction that one has supernatural powers or has special knowledge that no one else possesses. Delusions of *control* are related to delusions of persecution; the person believes (for example) that he or she is being controlled by others through such means as radar or a tiny receiver implanted in his or her brain.

The third positive symptom of schizophrenia includes **hallucinations**, perceptions of stimuli that are not actually present. The most common hallucinations in schizophrenia are auditory, which are found in approximately 70 percent of individuals, followed by visual (25 percent), and hallucinations in any of the other senses (approximately 10 percent, Mueser et al., 1990). The typical schizophrenic hallucination consists of voices talking to the person. Sometimes, the voices order the person to do something; sometimes, they

Figure 16.1 Age at First Sign of Psychotic Symptoms in Patients with Schizophrenia
(Based on data from Häfner et al., 1993.)

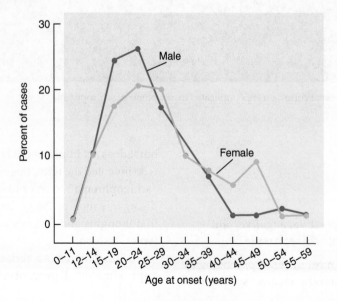

scold the person for his or her unworthiness; sometimes, they utter meaningless phrases. (See Table 16.1.)

NEGATIVE SYMPTOMS   In contrast to the positive symptoms, the **negative symptoms** of schizophrenia are known by the absence or diminution of typical behaviors: flattened emotional response, poverty of speech, lack of initiative and persistence, *anhedonia* (inability to experience pleasure), and social withdrawal.

COGNITIVE SYMPTOMS   The **cognitive symptoms** of schizophrenia may be produced by abnormalities in the brain regions that overlap with those involved in negative symptoms. These symptoms include difficulty sustaining attention, low *psychomotor speed* (for example, in movements that include a cognitive element, such as reaction time, connecting numbers or letters in sequence, or alternating numbers and letters), deficits in learning and memory, poor abstract thinking, and poor problem solving. (Look again at Table 16.1.)

Positive, negative, and cognitive symptoms are not specific to schizophrenia; they are seen in other disorders as well. Some of these other disorders also involve brain damage, especially to the frontal lobes. As we will see later in this chapter, positive symptoms appear to involve excessive activity in some neural circuits that include dopamine as a neurotransmitter, and negative symptoms and cognitive symptoms appear to be caused by developmental or degenerative processes that impair the typical functions of some regions of the brain. Along with positive, negative, and

cognitive symptoms, depression, anxiety, substance abuse, and smoking are very common in schizophrenia.

The symptoms of schizophrenia typically appear gradually, over a period of several years. Typically, the first clinical symptoms of schizophrenia tend to be symptoms of depression, which are followed by social withdrawal or impairment (negative symptoms) and cognitive difficulties (cognitive symptoms), and then positive symptoms (Häfner, 2000; Häfner and an der Heiden, 2003; Häfner et al., 1999; Häfner et al., 2003; Häfner et al., 2005). As we will see later, this progression of symptoms provides some hints about the nature of the brain abnormalities that are responsible for them.

Heritability

LO 16.2   **Describe evidence that supports a genetic contribution to the development of schizophrenia.**

Evidence from twin and adoption studies and research investigating mutations, paternal age, and epigenetics all support the hypothesis that schizophrenia is a biological disorder and that heritability plays a role in its development.

So far, researchers have not located a single "schizophrenia gene," although they have found many genes that appear to increase the likelihood of this disease. A review by Crow (2007) notes that evidence for linkage to susceptibility for schizophrenia has been reported for 21 of the 23 pairs of chromosomes, but many of the findings have not been replicated. Walsh et al. (2008) suggest that a large number of rare mutations in these genes play a role in the development of schizophrenia.

MUTATIONS   One rare mutation involves a gene known as *DISC1 (disrupted in schizophrenia 1)*. This gene is involved in regulation of embryonic and adult neurogenesis, neuronal migration during embryonic development, function of the postsynaptic density in excitatory neurons, and function of mitochondria (Brandon et al., 2009; Kim et al., 2009; Park et al., 2010; Wang et al., 2010). Mutations of this gene have been found in some families with a high incidence of schizophrenia (Chubb et al., 2008; Schumacher et al., 2009). Although the incidence of DISC1 mutation is very low, its presence appears to increase the likelihood of schizophrenia by a factor of 50 (Blackwood et al., 2001). This mutation also appears to increase the incidence of other mental disorders, including bipolar disorder, major depressive disorder, and autism (Kim et al., 2009). We will describe research on the role of DISC1 malfunction in an animal model later in this chapter.

TWIN AND ADOPTION STUDIES   Both adoption studies (Kety et al., 1968, 1994) and twin studies (Gottesman and Shields, 1982; Tsuang et al., 1991) indicate that schizophrenia is a heritable trait. If schizophrenia were a simple trait produced by a single gene, we would expect to see this disorder in at least 75 percent of the children of two parents with schizophrenia if the gene were dominant. If it were

Table 16.1 Symptoms of Schizophrenia

Symptom
Positive
Hallucinations
Thought disorders
Delusions
Persecution
Grandeur
Control
Negative
Flattened emotional response
Poverty of speech
Lack of initiative and persistence
Anhedonia
Social withdrawal
Cognitive
Difficulty in sustaining attention
Low psychomotor speed
Deficits in learning and memory
Poor abstract thinking
Poor problem solving

Both adoption studies and twin studies indicate that schizophrenia is a heritable trait.

recessive, *all* children of two parents with schizophrenia should develop the disorder. However, the actual incidence is less than 50 percent, which means either that several genes are involved or that having "schizophrenia genes" imparts a *susceptibility* to develop schizophrenia, the disease itself being triggered by other factors.

If the susceptibility hypothesis is true, then we would expect that some people carry "schizophrenia genes" but do not express them; that is, their environment is such that schizophrenia is never triggered. This hypothesis could be tested among monozygotic twins in which one twin was diagnosed with schizophrenia and the other was not. Gottesman and Bertelsen (1989) examined the children of both members of discordant pairs of monozygotic twins and found that the percentage of children with schizophrenia was nearly identical for both members of such pairs: 16.8 percent for the children of parents with schizophrenia and 17.4 percent for the children of parents without schizophrenia. For dizygotic twins the percentages were 17.4 percent and 2.1 percent, respectively. These results provide strong

evidence for the heritability of schizophrenia and also support the conclusion that carrying "schizophrenia genes" does not mean that a person will necessarily develop schizophrenia. (See Figure 16.2.)

In the past, most researchers assumed that discordance for schizophrenia in monozygotic twins must be caused by differential exposure to some environmental factors after birth. Not only are monozygotic twins genetically identical, but they also share the same intrauterine environment. Thus, because all prenatal factors should be identical, any differences must be a result of factors in the postnatal environment. However, some investigators have pointed out that the prenatal environment of monozygotic twins is *not* identical. In fact, there are two types of monozygotic twins: *monochorionic* and *dichorionic*. The formation of monozygotic twins occurs when the blastocyst (the developing organism) splits in two—when it clones itself. If twinning occurs before day 4, the two organisms develop independently, each forming its own placenta. (That is, the twins are *dichorionic*. The *chorion* is the outer layer of the blastocyst, which gives rise to the placenta.) If twinning occurs after day 4, the two organisms become *monochorionic*, sharing a single placenta. (See Figure 16.3.)

The placenta plays an extremely important role in prenatal development. It transports nutrients to the developing organism from the mother's circulation and transports waste products to her, which she metabolizes in her liver or excretes in her urine. It also constitutes the barrier through which toxins or infectious agents must pass if they are to affect fetal development. The prenatal environments of monochorionic twins, who share a single placenta, are more similar than those of dichorionic twins. Thus, we might expect that the concordance rates for schizophrenia of *monochorionic* monozygotic twins should be higher than those of *dichorionic* monozygotic twins, and as Davis et al. (1995) reported, they are. Davis and his colleagues examined sets of monozygotic twins who were concordant and discordant for schizophrenia. They used several indices to estimate whether a given pair was monochorionic or dichorionic. (For example, twins with mirror images of physical features

Figure 16.2 Heredity and Schizophrenia

The diagram outlines evidence that people can have an unexpressed "schizophrenia gene."

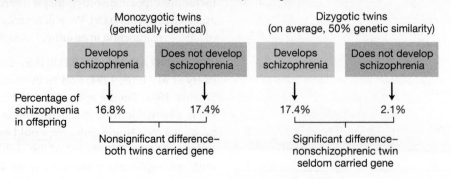

Figure 16.3 Monozygotic Twins

(a) Monochorionic twins, sharing a single placenta. (b) Dichorionic twins, each with its own placenta.

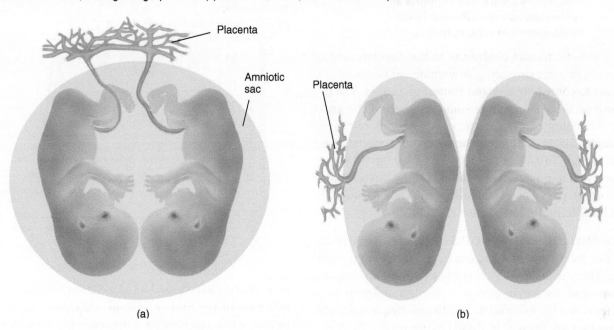

Placenta

Amniotic sac

Placenta

(a)

(b)

such as fingerprints, handedness, birthmarks, or hair swirls are more likely to be monochorionic.) The investigators estimated that the concordance rate for schizophrenia was 10.7 percent in the dichorionic twins and 60 percent in the monochorionic twins. These results provide strong evidence for an interaction between heredity and environment during prenatal development.

PATERNAL AGE   The effect of paternal age provides further evidence that genetic mutations may affect the incidence of schizophrenia (Brown et al., 2002; Sipos et al., 2004). Several studies have found that the children of older fathers are more likely to develop schizophrenia. Most investigators believe that the increased incidence of schizophrenia is caused by mutations in the spermatocytes, the cells that produce sperms. These cells divide every 16 days after puberty, which means that they have divided approximately 540 times by age 35. In contrast, women's oocytes divide 23 times before the time of birth and only once after that. The likelihood of a copying error in DNA replication when a cell divides increases with the number of cell divisions, and an increase in copying errors may cause an accumulation of mutations that are responsible for an increased incidence of schizophrenia.

EPIGENETICS   Several researchers (for example, Swerdlow, 2011; Tsankova et al., 2007) suggest that epigenetic mechanisms, as well as mutations, may contribute to the development of schizophrenia. *Epigenetic* mechanisms control the expression of genes. The long strands of DNA that constitute the chromosomes are wound around a series of

proteins known as *histones*. Groups of atoms can attach to the amino acids in the histone proteins and change their characteristics. For example, when methyl groups ($-CH_3$) attach to histone proteins, the regions of DNA wound around them draw in more tightly, which prevents these regions from being translated into messenger RNA. Thus, methylation of histone proteins prevents the expression of particular genes. (Other groups of atoms can also bind with histone proteins and either inhibit or promote gene expression.) Many epigenetic changes are initiated by environmental events such as exposure to toxins, and some epigenetic changes can be transmitted to offspring.

Several studies have found that the children of older fathers are more likely to develop schizophrenia.

cabania/Shutterstock

Environmental Factors

LO 16.3 **Describe evidence that supports an environmental contribution to the development of schizophrenia.**

While genetic factors contribute to the development of schizophrenia in many cases, environmental variables also interact to contribute risk and protective factors. The following sections summarize some research in the areas of epidemiology and obstetric complications related to schizophrenia. In addition to the factors discussed in these sections, individual risk factors such as immigrant status, poverty, and trauma such as childhood abuse can contribute to the development of schizophrenia (van Os & Kapur, 2009; van Os & McGuffin, 2003; Varese et al., 2012).

EPIDEMIOLOGICAL STUDIES **Epidemiology** is the study of the distribution and causes of diseases in populations. Thus, epidemiological studies examine the relative frequency of diseases in groups of people in different environments and try to correlate the disease frequencies with factors that are present in these environments. Evidence from these studies indicates that the incidence of schizophrenia is related to several environmental factors that occur independently or interact: season of birth, viral epidemics, vitamin D deficiency, population density, prenatal malnutrition, substance abuse, and complications of pregnancy and birth (Brown and Derkits, 2010; King et al., 2010). Let's examine each of these factors in turn.

Season of Birth Many studies have shown that people born during the late winter and early spring are more likely to develop schizophrenia—a phenomenon known as the **seasonality effect**. For example, Kendell and Adams (1991) studied the month of birth of over 13,000 patients with schizophrenia born in Scotland between 1914 and 1960. They found that disproportionately more patients were born in February, March, April, and May. (See Figure 16.4.) These results have been confirmed by studies in several parts of the Northern Hemisphere (Davies et al., 2003). In the Southern Hemisphere some studies have also reported a disproportionate number of people with schizophrenia born during late winter and early spring—during the months of August through December—while others have found no effect (McGrath and Welham, 1999).

Viral Epidemics What factors might be responsible for the seasonality effect? One possibility is that pregnant women may be more likely to contract a viral illness during a critical phase of their child's development if they are pregnant during the fall or winter. The brain development of the fetus may be adversely affected either by a toxin produced by the virus or—more likely—by the mother's antibodies against the virus, which cross the placenta barrier and attack cells of the developing fetus. As Selemon and Zecevic (2015)

Figure 16.4 The Seasonality Effect

The graph shows the number of individuals with schizophrenia per 10,000 live births.

(Based on data from Kendell and Adams, 1991.)

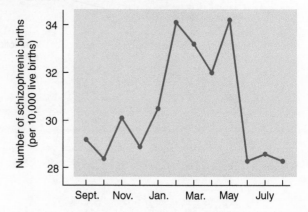

note, studies have found an association between maternal infection in the first or second trimester and increased incidence of schizophrenia in offspring. (As we will see later, evidence suggests that critical aspects of brain development occur during the second trimester.) In fact, Kendell and Adams (1991) found that the relative number of people who develop schizophrenia born in late winter and early spring was especially high if the temperature was lower than normal during the previous autumn—a condition that keeps people indoors and favors the transmission of viral illnesses.

If the viral hypothesis is true, then an increased incidence of schizophrenia should be seen in babies born a few months after an influenza epidemic, whatever the season. Several studies have observed just that (Mednick et al., 1990; Sham et al., 1992). A study by Brown et al. (2004) examined stored samples of blood serum that had been taken during pregnancy from mothers of children who later developed schizophrenia. They found elevated levels of interleukin-8, a protein secreted by cells of the immune system. The presence of this chemical indicates the presence of an infection or other inflammatory process, and supports the suggestion that maternal infections during the second trimester can increase the incidence of schizophrenia in the women's children. Brown (2006) notes that research has found that maternal infection with at least two other infectious diseases—rubella (German measles) and toxoplasmosis—is associated with an increased incidence of schizophrenia.

Vitamin D Deficiency Although cold weather and crowding may contribute to the seasonality effect by increasing the likelihood of contracting infectious illness, another variable may be a common factor: a vitamin D deficiency. Vitamin D is a fat-soluble chemical that is produced in the skin by the action of ultraviolet rays on a chemical derived from cholesterol. Harms et al (2011) summarized the results of a number of studies investigating vitamin D deficiency and its association with increased risk of schizophrenia. These studies reported a relationship between maternal vitamin D deficiency and schizophrenia in children in: more extreme latitudes (where the intensity and duration of sunlight exposure is reduced), urban areas (where lifestyle may reduce sunlight exposure), and among people with greater amounts of the pigment melanin in their skin, particularly at extreme latitudes where the risk of vitamin D deficiency is compounded by reduced sunlight exposure overall (melanin makes skin darker and reduces vitamin D synthesis; Harm et al., 2011). Interestingly, one study found that taking a vitamin D supplement during the first year of a child's life was associated with reduced incidence of schizophrenia among boys (McGrath et al., 2004). Because vitamin D plays an important role in brain development, deficiency may be a risk factor for schizophrenia. These considerations suggest that at least some of the increased incidence of schizophrenia in city dwellers and those who live in cold climates may be attributable to a vitamin D deficiency.

Population Density Several studies have found that the seasonality effect occurs primarily in cities but is rarely found in rural areas. In fact, the likelihood of developing schizophrenia is approximately three times higher in people who live in the middle of large cities than in those who live in rural areas (Eaton et al., 2000). Because viruses are more readily transmitted in regions with high population densities, this finding is consistent with the hypothesis that at least one of the causes of the seasonality effect is exposure of pregnant women to viral illnesses during the second trimester. However, Pedersen and Mortensen (2001) found that, up to the age of 15 years, the longer a person lives in a city, the more likely it becomes that the person develops schizophrenia. Thus, an urban environment may also affect people's susceptibility to schizophrenia postnatally as well as prenatally.

Prenatal Malnutrition Another prenatal effect was discovered by Susser and his colleagues (Susser and Lin, 1992; Susser et al., 1996), who found a twofold increase in the incidence of schizophrenia in the offspring of women who were pregnant during the Hunger Winter, a severe food shortage that occurred in the Netherlands when Germany blockaded the country during World War II. Davis and Bracha (1996) suggest that the specific cause of the famine-related schizophrenia may have been a thiamine deficiency—or, more precisely, an abrupt buildup of toxins in the brains of the developing fetuses when their mothers suddenly began eating a normal diet when the blockade ended in May 1945. As we saw in Chapter 14, sudden refeeding after a thiamine deficiency can cause brain damage. Other studies have shown that underweight women are more likely to give birth to babies who later develop schizophrenia and that low-birth-weight babies have a higher incidence of schizophrenia (Kunugi et al., 2001; Wahlbeck et al., 2001).

Substance Abuse A final environmental risk factor for development of schizophrenia is maternal substance abuse—particularly smoking. Zammit et al. (2009) studied the effects of maternal use of tobacco, cannabis, or alcohol during pregnancy and found that tobacco use was associated with increased risk. Even paternal tobacco use increased this risk, which suggests that secondhand smoke was sufficient to adversely affect fetal development. Excessive alcohol intake increased the risk of schizophrenia only if the mother drank more than 210 ml of pure alcohol per week. As we saw in Chapter 15, alcohol intake during pregnancy puts the fetus at risk for development of fetal alcohol syndrome.

Interactions and Protective Factors Many studies have found an interaction between hereditary factors and the environmental factors that we have just reviewed (Brown and Derkits, 2010; Freedman, 2010; Mittal et al., 2008). For example, a person born to a woman who had pyelonephritis during pregnancy is twice as likely to develop schizophrenia and four times more likely to do so if he or she has a family history of schizophrenia. (Pyelonephritis is an infectious disease introduced through the urinary tract that is often associated with pregnancy.) By itself, maternal depression does not increase the risk of developing schizophrenia in a woman's offspring, but the likelihood of schizophrenia increases by a factor of four in the case of familial genetic risk.

While a large body of research has focused on risk factors (genetic and environmental) involved in the development of schizophrenia, less research has been conducted to identify protective factors. Avoiding exposure to environmental toxins and infectious agents, nutritional stability during pregnancy, vitamin B and D supplementation when needed, avoidance of prenatal stressors, avoidance of early life stressors, avoidance of early life use of cannabis, and particularly supportive social and family environments may all be important protective factors among individuals at genetic risk for schizophrenia (Schlosser et al., 2012). Due to the correlational nature of many studies and the lack of specific focus on protective factors, understanding of these factors in schizophrenia is currently limited.

OBSTETRIC COMPLICATIONS Good evidence indicates that obstetric complications can also contribute to schizophrenia. In fact, several studies have found that if a person with schizophrenia does *not* have relatives with schizophrenia or a related disorder, that person is more likely to have had a history of complications at or around the time of childbirth, and the person is more likely to develop symptoms of schizophrenia at an earlier age. A meta-analysis of eight studies by M. Cannon et al. (2002) found that the most important factors are *complications of pregnancy*, including diabetes of the mother, Rh incompatibility between mother and fetus, bleeding, and preeclampsia (also known as *toxemia*, a condition characterized by high blood pressure, edema, and protein in the urine); *abnormal fetal development*, including low birth weight, congenital malformations, and reduced head circumference; and *complications of labor and delivery*, including emergency Caesarean section, uterine complications, and fetal oxygen deprivation. According to Boksa (2004), the most important characteristic of complications of labor and delivery is interruption of the blood flow or oxygen supply to the brain.

A study by Rehn et al. (2004) provided direct evidence that deprivation of an adequate blood supply to the uterus and placenta can have harmful effects on brain development. The investigators produced chronic placental insufficiency in pregnant guinea pigs by tying off one uterine artery at midgestation. When the offspring of these animals reached adolescence, they showed reduced brain weight and enlarged cerebral ventricles but no sign of gliosis in the brain. As we will see in the next subsection, these changes are also seen in the brains of people with schizophrenia.

As you read earlier, schizophrenia is a heritable disease, but its heritability is less than perfect. It is likely that what is inherited is a susceptibility to environmental factors that adversely affect brain development or cause brain damage later in life. According to this hypothesis, having some "schizophrenia genes" makes a person *more* likely to develop schizophrenia if he or she is exposed to these factors. However, genetic heritability is not necessarily required to develop the disorder; some cases of schizophrenia occur even in families with no history of schizophrenia or related mental illnesses. For a review of the environmental factors related to onset of schizophrenia, see Table 16.2.

Anomalies in Schizophrenia

LO 16.4 **Describe the behavioral, physical, and brain anomalies associated with schizophrenia.**

The development of schizophrenia is associated with changes in behavior, physical features, and brain structure and function. Some of these anomalies are present even before the onset of symptoms of schizophrenia, or are present in unaffected family members, supporting the biological basis for this disorder. The following sections will describe research in each of these areas.

BEHAVIORAL ANOMALIES Both behavioral and anatomical evidence indicates that abnormal development is associated with schizophrenia. Let's first consider behavioral evidence. Walker and her colleagues (Walker et al., 1996; Walker et al., 1994) obtained home movies from families with a child who was later diagnosed with schizophrenia. They had independent observers examine the behavior of the children. In comparison with their unaffected siblings, the children who were later diagnosed with schizophrenia displayed more negative affect in their facial expressions and were more likely to show abnormal

Table 16.2 Environmental Factors Related to Onset of Schizophrenia

Environmental Factor	Research Support for Role of Environmental Factor in Development of Schizophrenia
Season of birth	People born during the late winter and early spring are more likely to develop schizophrenia.
Viral epidemics	An increased incidence of schizophrenia is seen in people born a few months after an influenza epidemic.
Population density	The likelihood of developing schizophrenia is approximately three times higher in people who live in the middle of large cities than in those who live in rural areas.
Prenatal malnutrition	Low-birth-weight babies have a higher incidence of schizophrenia.
Substance abuse	Tobacco use during pregnancy is associated with increased risk of schizophrenia in offspring.
Interactions	A person born to a woman who had pyelonephritis during pregnancy is twice as likely to develop schizophrenia and four times more likely to do so if he or she has a family history of schizophrenia.
Obstetric complications	Emergency Caesarean section, uterine complications, and fetal oxygen deprivation at birth are associated with increased risk of schizophrenia.

movements. (The ratings were done blind; the observers did not know which children were later diagnosed with schizophrenia.) In a similar study, Schiffman et al. (2004) supported these results. In 1972, 265 Danish children, aged 11–13 years, were videotaped briefly while eating lunch. One-third of the group had one parent who was diagnosed with schizophrenia. In 1991, the investigators examined the medical records of these children and determined which of them had developed schizophrenia. Raters, who did not know the identities of the children, found that the children who later developed schizophrenia displayed less sociability. Among the boys, those who later developed schizophrenia also displayed somewhat deficient psychomotor functioning. The results of these studies are consistent with the hypothesis that although the symptoms of schizophrenia are not seen in childhood, the early brain development of children who later develop schizophrenia is altered.

PHYSICAL ANOMALIES Minor physical anomalies, such as a high-steepled palate or especially wide-set or narrow-set eyes, have also been shown to be associated with the incidence of schizophrenia (Schiffman et al., 2002). (See Table 16.3.) These differences were first reported in the late nineteenth century by Kraepelin, one of the pioneers in schizophrenia research. As Schiffman and his colleagues note, these anomalies provide evidence of factors that have adverse effects on development. They found that people who have relatives diagnosed with schizophrenia normally have an 11.9 percent likelihood of developing schizophrenia. This likelihood increases to 30.8 percent in people who also have minor physical anomalies; thus, the factors that produce minor physical anomalies are at least partly independent of

Table 16.3 Examples of Minor Physical Anomalies Associated with Schizophrenia

Location	Description
Head	Two or more hair whorls
	Head circumference outside normal range
Eyes	Skin fold at inner corner of eye
	Wide-set eyes
Ears	Low-seated ears
	Asymmetrical ears
Mouth	High-steepled palate
	Furrowed tongue
Hands	Curved fifth finger
	Single transverse crease in palm
Feet	Third toe longer than second toe
	Partial webbing of two middle toes

Source: Adapted from Schiffman et al., 2002.

Figure 16.5 Relative Ventricular Size in Patients with Schizophrenia and Control Participants

(Based on data from Weinberger and Wyatt, 1982.)

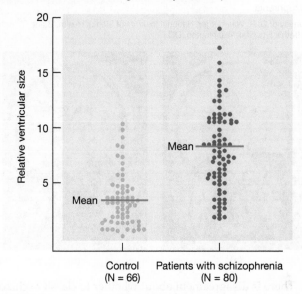

the genetic factors associated with schizophrenia. Many of the anomalies in Table 16.3 represent craniofacial changes of the head, eyes, ears and mouth. Anomalies in these physical features may be closely related to underlying brain development and may arise from common developmental processes (Weinberg et al., 2007).

BRAIN ANOMALIES Many studies have found evidence of loss of brain tissue in CT and MRI scans of people with schizophrenia. In one of the earliest studies, Weinberger and Wyatt (1982) obtained CT scans of 80 people with chronic symptoms of schizophrenia and 66 controls of the same mean age (29 years). Without knowledge of the patients' diagnoses they measured the area of the lateral ventricles in the scan that cut through them at their largest extent, and they expressed this area relative to the area of brain tissue in the same scan. The relative ventricle size of the schizophrenia group was more than twice as great as that of control group. (See Figure 16.5.)

The most likely cause of the enlarged ventricles is loss of brain tissue; thus, the scans provide evidence that schizophrenia is associated with brain abnormalities. In fact, Hulshoff-Pol et al. (2002) found that although everyone loses some cerebral gray matter as they age, the rate of tissue loss is greater in patients with schizophrenia. (See Figure 16.6.)

Gutiérrez-Galve et al. (2010) found that both patients with schizophrenia and their nondiagnosed relatives showed loss of gray matter in the frontal and temporal cortex, suggesting that genetic factors affected cortical development and increased susceptibility to factors that cause schizophrenia. Presumably, the healthy relatives did not encounter these factors.

As mentioned earlier, some monozygotic twins are discordant for schizophrenia; that is, one twin develops schizophrenia, and the other does not. Suddath et al. (1990)

obtained evidence that differences in the structure of the brain may reflect this discordance. The investigators examined MRI scans of monozygotic twins who were discordant for schizophrenia and found that in almost every case the twin with schizophrenia had larger lateral and third ventricles, their anterior hippocampus was smaller, and the total volume of the gray matter in the left temporal lobe was reduced. Figure 16.7 shows a set of MRI scans from a pair of twins; as you can see, the lateral ventricles are larger in the brain of the twin with schizophrenia.

Figure 16.6 Cerebral Gray Matter and Schizophrenia

The graph shows changes in volume of cerebral gray matter with age in healthy volunteers and people with schizophrenia.

(Based on data from Hulshoff-Pol et al., 2002.)

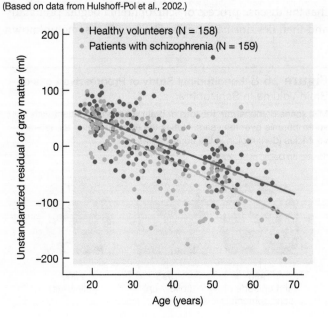

Figure 16.7 MRI Scans of the Brains of Twins Discordant for Schizophrenia

The arrows point to the lateral ventricles. (a) Healthy twin. (b) Twin with schizophrenia.

(Courtesy of D. R. Weinberger, National Institute of Mental Health, Saint Elizabeth's Hospital, Washington, DC.)

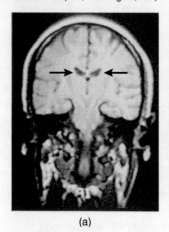 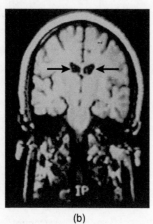

(a)   (b)

There is disagreement about whether to classify schizophrenia as a neurodegenerative disease. Similar to the other neurodegenerative diseases you read about in Chapter 15, schizophrenia symptoms are related to a loss in brain volume. Some researchers suggest that schizophrenia fits the definition of a neurodegenerative disease because it involves a chronic and progressive loss of brain tissue accompanied by neurological and behavioral symptoms. For example, DeLisi et al. (2006) demonstrated the progressive loss of brain volume (and enlarged ventricles) in an adult patient with chronic symptoms of schizophrenia over 10 years. (See Figure 16.8.) The authors further suggest that changes in brain structure are present prior to the onset of symptoms.

In contrast, Woods (1998) notes that MRI studies suggest that schizophrenia involves a sudden, rapid loss of brain volume, typically during young adulthood, with little evidence for continuing degeneration. Woods suggests that the disease process of schizophrenia begins prenatally and then lies dormant until puberty, when some unknown

Figure 16.8 Longitudinal Study of Progressive Loss of Brain Volume in Schizophrenia.

MRI scans demonstrate the loss of brain volume in a patient with schizophrenia over ten years. Notice the enlargement of the lateral ventricles (dark region in the center of the brain).

(Based on DeLisi et al., 2006.)

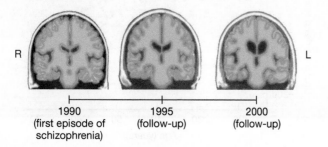

mechanism triggers degeneration of some population of neurons. The brain abnormalities that develop prenatally account for the deficits in social behavior and poor academic performance seen in people who later develop schizophrenia. Then, sometime after puberty, when many developmental changes occur in the brain, more serious degeneration occurs, and the symptoms of schizophrenia begin to appear.

A study by Thompson et al. (2001) found dramatic evidence for loss of cortical gray matter during adolescence in patients with early-onset schizophrenia. The investigators used structural MRI procedures to measure the volume of the gray matter of the cerebral cortex at two-year intervals in patients with schizophrenia and control participants. Adolescence is a time when "pruning" takes place in the brain, and the MRI scans showed an expected loss of cortical gray matter in control participants of about 0.5–1.0 percent. However, the loss of tissue was approximately twice as large in participants with schizophrenia. The degeneration started in the parietal lobes, and the wave of destruction continued rostrally, including the temporal lobes, somatosensory and motor cortexes, and dorsolateral prefrontal cortex (dlPFC). A subsequent study from the same laboratory (T. D. Cannon et al., 2002) compared the cortical gray matter of brains of members of identical twin pairs who were discordant for schizophrenia. Identical twins are genetically identical, so differences in their cortical gray matter are presumably related to the presence or absence of schizophrenia. The investigators found that volumes of several regions of the cerebral cortex—especially the dlPFC—were reduced in the twins that developed schizophrenia. (We'll say more about this part of the brain later in the chapter.)

The evidence we have cited so far suggests that the most important cause of schizophrenia is disturbance of prenatal brain development that, in most cases, ultimately manifests itself after puberty. Presumably, genetic factors make some fetuses more sensitive to events that can disturb development. In addition, damage caused by environmental

MRI studies suggest that schizophrenia involves a sudden, rapid loss of brain volume, typically during young adulthood.

obstetric complications can lead to development of schizophrenia even in the absence of hereditary factors. The effect of these factors is reflected in cortical development and, perhaps, in altered activity at dopaminergic synapses.

The Mesolimbic Dopamine Pathway: Positive Symptoms

LO 16.5 **Provide evidence of the role of the mesolimbic dopamine pathway in the positive symptoms of schizophrenia.**

Pharmacological evidence suggests that the positive symptoms of schizophrenia are caused by abnormalities in DA neurons. More specifically, a large body of evidence suggests that the positive symptoms of schizophrenia are the result of overactivity of DA synapses in the mesolimbic pathway. This hypothesis is supported by evidence from pharmacological interventions as well as biochemical abnormalities in the brains of people diagnosed with schizophrenia.

EFFECTS OF DOPAMINE AGONISTS AND ANTAGONISTS Around the middle of the twentieth century, a French drug company developed a compound called **chlorpromazine**, which seemed to reduce shock and anxiety following surgery (Snyder, 1974). Chlorpromazine was tried on patients with a variety of mental disorders: mania, depression, anxiety, neuroses, and schizophrenia (Delay and Deniker, 1952a, 1952b). The drug was not very effective in treating neuroses or affective psychoses, but it had dramatic effects on schizophrenia.

The discovery of the antipsychotic effects of chlorpromazine profoundly altered the way in which physicians treated patients with schizophrenia and made prolonged hospital stays unnecessary for many patients. The efficacy of antipsychotic drugs has been established in many double-blind studies (Baldessarini, 1977). Antipsychotic drugs eliminate, or at least diminish, positive symptoms of schizophrenia. The beneficial effects are not just a change in the patient's attitudes; the hallucinations and delusions go away or become less severe. Since the discovery of chlorpromazine, many other drugs have been developed that relieve the positive symptoms of schizophrenia. These drugs were found to have one property in common: They block D_2 and D_3 dopamine receptors (Creese et al., 1976; Strange, 2008).

Another category of drugs has the opposite effect. These drugs *produce* positive symptoms of schizophrenia. The drugs that can produce these symptoms have a pharmacological effect in common: They act as dopamine agonists. These drugs include amphetamine, cocaine, and methylphenidate (which block the reuptake of dopamine) and L-DOPA (which stimulates the synthesis of dopamine). The symptoms that these drugs produce can be alleviated with antipsychotic drugs, a result that further strengthens

the argument that the antipsychotic drugs exert their therapeutic effects by blocking dopamine receptors.

How might we explain the apparent link between overactivity of dopaminergic synapses and the positive symptoms of schizophrenia? As we saw in Chapters 4 and 13, the most important systems of dopaminergic neurons begin in two midbrain nuclei: the substantia nigra and the ventral tegmental area. Most researchers believe that the mesolimbic pathway, which begins in the ventral tegmental area and ends in the nucleus accumbens and amygdala, is more likely to be involved in the positive symptoms of schizophrenia. As we saw in Chapter 13, the activity of dopaminergic synapses in the mesolimbic system appears to be a vital link in the process of reinforcement. Drugs that act as agonists at these synapses (such as cocaine and amphetamine) strongly reinforce behavior; if taken in large doses, they also produce the positive symptoms of schizophrenia.

Perhaps the two effects of the drugs are related. If reinforcement mechanisms were activated at inappropriate times, then inappropriate behaviors—including delusional thoughts—might be reinforced. At one time or another, all of us have had some irrational thoughts, which we normally brush aside and forget. But if neural mechanisms of reinforcement became active while these thoughts were occurring, we would tend to take them more seriously. In time, delusions might develop. Fibiger (1991) suggests that paranoid delusions may be caused by increased activity of the dopaminergic input to the amygdala. Kapur (2003) further suggested that increased dopaminergic activity could enhance the salience and motivational aspects of stimuli (including stimuli such as hallucinations), prior to the full development of schizophrenia symptoms. As we saw in Chapter 11, the amygdala is involved with conditioned emotional responses elicited by aversive stimuli. The amygdala receives a strong projection from the mesolimbic dopaminergic system, so Fibiger's suggestion is certainly plausible. In support of this idea, Pinkham et al. (2011) reported that people with schizophrenia that experienced paranoia were more likely to misidentify a neutral facial expression as one showing anger. People with schizophrenia who were not currently exhibiting paranoid symptoms identified neutral facial expressions as did control participants.

ABNORMALITIES IN DOPAMINE TRANSMISSION What evidence suggests that dopaminergic activity in the brains of people with schizophrenia is abnormal? Studies have found evidence that dopaminergic neurons in the brain of a person diagnosed with schizophrenia may indeed release more dopamine (Breier et al., 1997; Laruelle et al., 1996). A functional-imaging study by Laruelle et al. measured the release of dopamine caused by an intravenous injection of amphetamine. As we saw in Chapter 4, amphetamine stimulates the release of dopamine, apparently by causing the dopamine transporters that are present in the terminal buttons to run backward, pumping dopamine out rather than retrieving it after it has been released. This effect inhibits the reuptake of dopamine as well. Laruelle et al. found that the amphetamine caused the release of more dopamine in the striatum of patients with schizophrenia than in control participants. They also found that patients with greater amounts of dopamine release showed greater increases in positive symptoms. (See Figure 16.9.)

Another possibility—that the brains of patients with schizophrenia contain a greater number of dopamine receptors—received much attention for several years. Because the earliest antipsychotic drugs appeared to work by blocking D_2 receptors, the earliest studies looked for increases in the numbers of these receptors in the brains of people with schizophrenia. Researchers have performed two types of analyses: postmortem measurements in the brains of people with schizophrenia and PET scans after treatment with radioactive ligands for dopamine receptors. Reviews of these studies (Kestler et al., 2001; Stone et al., 2007) concluded that there might be modest increases in the numbers of D_2 receptors in the brains of people with schizophrenia but that it seems unlikely that these increases are the primary cause of the disorder.

CONSEQUENCES OF LONG-TERM DRUG TREATMENT OF SCHIZOPHRENIA The discovery of drugs that reduce or eliminate the symptoms of schizophrenia has had a revolutionary effect on the treatment of this disorder. But for many years, all the drugs commonly used to treat schizophrenia caused serious side effects. Because these drugs reduce dopamine transmission, the side effects they produce are very similar to the symptoms of Parkinson's disease. Recall from Chapter 15 that symptoms of Parkinson's disease are due to the loss of dopaminergic neurons in the substantia nigra. By blocking dopamine transmission, the early antipsychotics all produced at least some symptoms resembling those of Parkinson's disease: slowness in movement, lack of facial expression, and general weakness. For most patients these symptoms were temporary. Unfortunately, a more serious side effect occurred in approximately one-third of all patients who took the "classic" antipsychotic drugs for an extended period.

As a result of taking an antipsychotic medication, many people developed a neurological disorder called **tardive dyskinesia.** Tardive dyskinesia appears to be the opposite of Parkinson's disease. Whereas patients with Parkinson's disease have difficulty moving, patients with tardive dyskinesia are unable to stop moving. Indeed, dyskinesia commonly occurs when patients with Parkinson's disease receive too much L-DOPA. The accepted explanation for tardive dyskinesia has been a phenomenon known as **supersensitivity**—a compensatory mechanism in which some types of receptors become more sensitive if they are inhibited for a period of time by a drug that blocks them. Presumably, when D_2 receptors in the caudate nucleus and putamen are chronically blocked by an antipsychotic drug, they become supersensitive, which in some cases overcompensates for the effects of the drug, causing the neurological symptoms to occur.

Figure 16.9 Increased Dopamine Activity Is Associated with Positive Symptoms of Schizophrenia

(a) Relative amount of dopamine released in response to amphetamine. (b) Relationship between dopamine release and changes in positive symptoms among patients with schizophrenia.

(Based on data from Laruelle et al., 1996.)

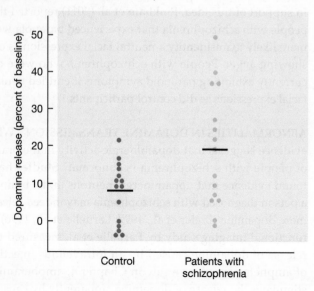

(a)

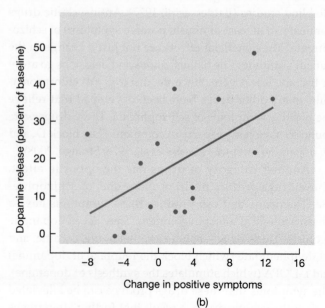

(b)

The Mesocortical Dopamine Pathway: Negative and Cognitive Symptoms

LO 16.6 **Provide evidence of the role of the cortex in the negative and cognitive symptoms of schizophrenia.**

Fortunately, researchers have discovered medications that treat the symptoms of schizophrenia without producing neurological side effects, and it appears that tardive dyskinesia can largely be avoided with newer drug treatments. At least one of these *atypical antipsychotics,* clozapine, seems to reduce the positive, negative, and cognitive symptoms. **Clozapine**, the first of the atypical antipsychotic medications, has been joined by several others, including risperidone, olanzapine, ziprasidone, and aripiprazole. These are the types of drugs that were prescribed to Grant in the case study at the beginning of this chapter. To understand how these drugs work, we first need to know more about the results of research on the neuropathology of schizophrenia, which brings us to the next section.

HYPOFRONTALITY So far, we have been discussing the physiology of the positive symptoms of schizophrenia—principally, hallucinations, delusions, and disordered thoughts. These symptoms could very well be related to one of the known functions of dopaminergic neurons: reinforcement. But the negative and cognitive symptoms of schizophrenia are different. Whereas the positive symptoms are unique to schizophrenia (and to amphetamine or cocaine psychosis), the negative and cognitive symptoms are similar to those produced by brain damage caused by several different means. Many pieces of evidence suggest that these symptoms of schizophrenia are indeed a result of brain abnormalities, especially in the prefrontal cortex, the target of the mesocortical pathway.

Weinberger (1988) first suggested that the negative symptoms of schizophrenia are caused primarily by **hypofrontality**, decreased activity of the frontal lobes—in particular, of the dlPFC. Many studies have shown that individuals with schizophrenia do poorly on neuropsychological tests that are sensitive to prefrontal damage.

Hypofrontality in the dlPFC that is responsible for negative symptoms may also be related to hyperactivity in the mesolimbic pathways that is responsible for positive symptoms. Typically, the dlPFC exerts inhibitory control over the mesolimbic pathways. In hypofrontality, control over the mesolimbic pathway is disinhibited, contributing to increased activity (and positive symptoms) arising from this region.

What might produce the hypofrontality that so many studies have observed? As we saw in the discussion of the role of dopamine in positive symptoms of schizophrenia, dopamine agonists such as cocaine and amphetamine can cause positive symptoms of schizophrenia. Two other drugs, PCP (phencyclidine, also known as "angel dust") and ketamine ("Special K"), can cause positive, negative,

and cognitive symptoms of schizophrenia (Adler et al., 1999; Avila et al., 2002; Lahti et al., 2001). Because PCP and ketamine elicit the full range of the symptoms of schizophrenia, many researchers believe that studying the physiological and behavioral effects of these drugs will help to solve the puzzle of schizophrenia.

The negative and cognitive symptoms produced by ketamine and PCP are apparently caused by a decrease in the metabolic activity of the frontal lobes. Jentsch et al. (1997) administered PCP to monkeys twice a day for two weeks. Then, one week later, they tested the animals on a task that involved reaching around a barrier for a piece of food, which is performed poorly by monkeys with lesions of the prefrontal cortex. Monkeys in the control group performed well, but those that had been treated with PCP showed a severe deficit. (See Figure 16.10.)

THE ROLE OF GLUTAMATE Impaired glutamate activity may be involved in the development of schizophrenia, particularly the negative and cognitive symptoms. Support for the *glutamate hypothesis* initially came from studies that reported reduced concentrations of glutamate in the CSF of patients with schizophrenia (Kim et al., 1980) and the observation that chronic, low doses of glutamate antagonist drugs, such as PCP and ketamine, produced negative and cognitive symptoms in healthy individuals (Coyle, 2006). These finding suggested that decreased glutamate activity may be involved in negative and cognitive symptoms in schizophrenia.

As you might recall from Chapter 4, PCP is an indirect antagonist of glutamate NMDA-receptors. (So is ketamine.) By inhibiting the activity of NMDA receptors, PCP suppresses the activity of several regions of the brain—most notably, the dlPFC. These drugs also decrease the level of dopamine utilization in this region (Elsworth et al.,

Figure 16.10 Chronic PCP Treatment

The graph shows the effects of two weeks of PCP treatment on the performance by monkeys on a task that requires reaching around a barrier. An increased number of reaches toward the barrier is an indication of perseveration of an incorrect response.

(Based on data from Jentsch et al., 1997.)

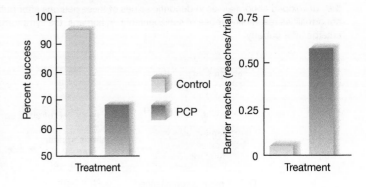

2008), possibly as a result of the inhibitory effect on NMDA receptors. The hypoactivity of NMDA and dopamine receptors appears to play an important role in the production of negative and cognitive symptoms: Suppression of these receptors causes hypofrontality, which appears to be the primary cause of these two categories of symptoms.

We saw that the atypical antipsychotic drug clozapine alleviates the positive, negative, and cognitive symptoms of schizophrenia. It also reduces the psychotic symptoms that are triggered in humans by ketamine (Malhotra et al., 1997). (Because PCP has toxic effects, it is not normally used in studies with humans.) In a study with monkeys, Youngren et al., (1999) found that injection of clozapine, which causes a *decrease* in the release of dopamine by the mesolimbic system, which apparently reduces the positive symptoms, also causes an *increase* in the release of dopamine in the prefrontal cortex, which apparently reduces the negative and cognitive symptoms.

There is one more interesting aspect of PCP and ketamine that might have some relevance to the causes of schizophrenia. As we saw, ketamine and PCP have similar effects. Ketamine is used as an anesthetic for children and animals. It is not often used as an anesthetic in adult humans because it produces episodes of psychosis when the person awakens after the surgery. Ketamine does not have this effect in prepubertal children, and administration of PCP does not damage the brains of rats until the animals reach puberty (Marshall and Longnecker, 1990; Stone et al., 2007). No one knows why ketamine (and probably PCP) produces psychotic behavior only in adults; perhaps the explanation is related to the fact that the symptoms of schizophrenia also emerge after puberty. (Whatever developmental changes occur after puberty that make the brain susceptible to the psychotic effects of NMDA antagonists may also be related to the emergence of symptoms of schizophrenia at this time.)

DEVELOPMENTAL CHANGES We mentioned earlier that a mutation of the DISC1 gene is a known genetic cause of schizophrenia. Niwa et al. (2010) infused a small interfering RNA (siRNA) that targeted the DISC1 gene into progenitor cells of the ventricular zone of fetal mice. (You will recall from Chapter 3 that these progenitor cells give rise to the brain's neurons.) The procedure suppressed DISC1 expression in pyramidal neurons of the prefrontal cortex during the last week of fetal development. At first, these neurons appeared normal, but at around the time of puberty, abnormalities were seen in the physiological characteristics of pyramidal neurons in the prefrontal cortex and in the structure of their dendritic spines. Abnormalities also began appearing in the mesocortical dopaminergic system that projects to the prefrontal cortex, which resulted in a lower level of dopamine in this region. While these changes were occurring, behavioral abnormalities resembling those of schizophrenia began to emerge. These findings suggest that abnormalities in the pyramidal neurons of the prefrontal cortex constitute the primary cause of the process that leads to schizophrenia. (See Figure 16.11.)

The findings of another study support a different hypothesis—that abnormalities in the striatal dopaminergic system may constitute the primary cause of the process that leads to schizophrenia. Lewis et al. (2005) reviewed evidence that the hypofrontality seen in people with schizophrenia appears to be a result of deficits in inhibitory GABAergic transmission in the dlPFC that disrupts normal electrical rhythms generated in this region. Li et al. (2011) used a genetically modified viral vector to insert genes in the striatum of mice (including both the dorsal striatum and the nucleus accumbens) that increased the production of D_2 dopamine receptors there. As in the study by Niwa et al., this procedure caused the development of behavioral deficits characteristic of schizophrenia, including abnormal activity of the dlPFC, caused by a deficit in inhibitory GABAergic transmission in this region. (See Figure 16.12.)

ATYPICAL ANTIPSYCHOTICS The research findings presented in this subsection explain why the "classic" antipsychotic drugs fail to reduce negative and cognitive symptoms: One of the causes of these symptoms is decreased

Figure 16.11 Role of DISC1 in the Development of Schizophrenia

Niwa et al. (2010) infused a siRNA that prevented the expression of DISC1 in progenitor cells in the ventricular zone of fetal mice. Although neurons in the prefrontal cortex appeared normal after birth, they developed abnormalities in dendritic spines of these neurons after puberty that led to behavioral abnormalities resembling those of schizophrenia. In humans, the symptoms of schizophrenia usually emerge after puberty.

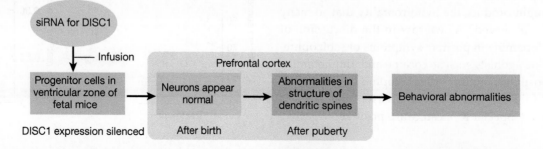

Figure 16.12 Role of Dopamine D$_2$ Receptors in the Development of Schizophrenia

Li et al. (2011) used a viral vector to increase expression of dopamine D$_2$ receptors in the striatum of mice. As a result, GABAergic transmission decreased in the dorsolateral prefrontal cortex, and the abnormal neural activity there led to behavioral deficits characteristic of schizophrenia.

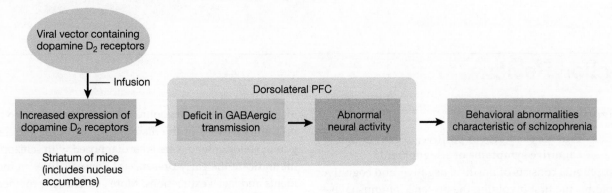

activation of dopamine receptors in the prefrontal cortex, and drugs that block dopamine receptors would, if anything, make these symptoms worse. What is different about the newer atypical antipsychotic drugs?

The atypical antipsychotic drugs seem to do the impossible: They increase dopaminergic activity in the prefrontal cortex and reduce it in the mesolimbic system. Let's examine the action of an atypical antipsychotic drug, *aripiprazole* (Lieberman, 2004; Winans, 2003). Aripiprazole acts as a *partial agonist* at dopamine receptors. A **partial agonist** is a drug that has a very high affinity for a particular receptor but activates that receptor less than the normal ligand does. This means that in a patient with schizophrenia, aripiprazole serves as an antagonist in the mesolimbic system, where too much dopamine is present, but serves as an agonist in regions such as the prefrontal cortex, where too little dopamine is present. Hence, this action appears to account for the ability of aripiprazole to reduce all three categories of schizophrenic symptoms. (See Figure 16.13.)

Figure 16.13 Effects of a Partial Agonist

The diagram explains the differential effects of a partial agonist in regions of high and low concentrations of the normal ligand. Numbers beneath each receptor indicate the degree of opening of the ion channel: 1.0 = fully open, 0.5 = partially open, 0.0 = fully closed. Partial agonists decrease the mean opening when the extracellular concentration of the neurotransmitter is high and increase it when the extracellular concentration of the neurotransmitter is low.

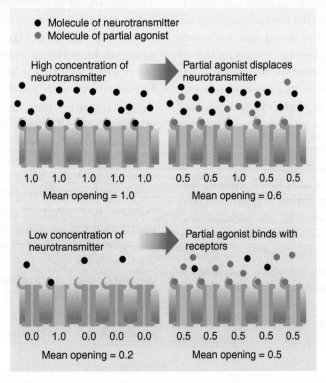

Schizophrenia is a complex and serious disorder, which has stimulated many hypotheses and much research. Some hypotheses have not been supported; others have not yet been adequately tested. Possibly, future research will find that all of the current hypotheses are incorrect or that new hypotheses will be correct.

Section Review

Schizophrenia

LO 16.1 Provide examples of positive, negative, and cognitive symptoms of schizophrenia.

Schizophrenia consists of positive, negative, and cognitive symptoms, the first involving the presence of unusual behavior (such as hallucinations, delusions, and disordered thoughts) and the latter two involving the absence or deficiency of normal behavior. Negative symptoms include flattened emotional response, poverty of speech, lack of initiative and persistence, anhedonia, and social withdrawal. Cognitive symptoms include difficulty sustaining attention, low psychomotor speed, and poor abstract thinking and problem solving.

LO 16.2 Describe evidence that supports a genetic contribution to the development of schizophrenia.

There is an increased incidence of schizophrenia among the children of parents with schizophrenia, although the disease does not appear to be a simple trait produced by a single gene. Among discordant dizygotic twins, there is an increased incidence of schizophrenia among the children of the twin with schizophrenia, compared to the children of the twin without schizophrenia. Evidence indicates that not all cases are caused by heredity, and many people who appear to carry "schizophrenia genes" do not develop the disorder. Recent evidence suggests that paternal age is a factor in schizophrenia, presumably because of the increased likelihood of mutations in the chromosomes of cells that produce sperms. A large variety of rare mutations or epigenetic factors may predispose people to schizophrenia.

LO 16.3 Describe evidence that supports an environmental contribution to the development of schizophrenia.

Studies of the epidemiology of schizophrenia indicate that season of birth, viral epidemics during pregnancy, a cold climate, increased population density, and prenatal malnutrition all contribute to the occurrence of schizophrenia. The most sensitive period appears to occur during the first or second trimester of pregnancy. A vitamin D deficiency, caused by insufficient exposure to sunlight or insufficient intake of the vitamin itself, may at least partly account for the effects of season of birth, population density, a cold climate, and maternal nutrition. Obstetric complications also increase the risk of schizophrenia, even in people who have no family history of the disorder. In addition, movies of young children who were later diagnosed with schizophrenia indicate the early presence of abnormalities in movements and facial expressions. More evidence is provided by the presence of an increased size of the third and lateral ventricles and a decreased size of the hippocampus in the non-affected member of monozygotic twins who are discordant for schizophrenia. The increased concordance rate of monochorionic monozygotic twins provides further evidence that hereditary and prenatal environmental factors may interact.

LO 16.4 Describe the behavioral, physical, and brain anomalies associated with schizophrenia.

Some behavioral symptoms, such as reduced sociality and abnormal motor movements, may precede a diagnosis of schizophrenia. Physical abnormalities associated with schizophrenia include minor physical anomalies. Brain anomalies associated with schizophrenia include enlarged ventricles and reduced brain volume.

LO 16.5 Provide evidence of the role of the mesolimbic dopamine pathway in the positive symptoms of schizophrenia.

The dopamine hypothesis, which was inspired by the findings that dopamine antagonists alleviate the positive symptoms of schizophrenia and that dopamine agonists increase or even produce them, states that the positive symptoms of schizophrenia are caused by hyperactivity of dopaminergic synapses in the mesolimbic system, which targets the nucleus accumbens and amygdala. The involvement of dopamine in reinforcement could plausibly explain the positive effects of schizophrenia; inappropriately reinforced thoughts could persist and become delusions. There is no evidence that an abnormally large amount of dopamine is released under resting conditions, but PET studies indicate that the administration of amphetamine causes a larger release of dopamine in the brains of people with schizophrenia. Evidence indicates that the brains of people with schizophrenia may contain slightly increased numbers of D_2 dopamine receptors, but this increase does not appear to play a primary role in the incidence of schizophrenia.

LO 16.6 **Provide evidence of the role of the cortex in the negative and cognitive symptoms of schizophrenia.**

The negative symptoms of schizophrenia appear to be a result of hypofrontality (decreased activity of the dorsolateral prefrontal cortex), which may be caused by a decreased release of dopamine in this region. People with schizophrenia do poorly on tasks that require activity of the prefrontal cortex, and functional-imaging studies indicate that the prefrontal cortex is hypoactive when the patients attempt to perform these tasks. Other research suggests abnormalities in the neurons of the prefrontal cortex constitute the primary cause of the process that leads to schizophrenia.

The drugs PCP and ketamine mimic both the positive and negative symptoms of schizophrenia. Long-term administration of PCP to monkeys disrupts their performance of a reaching task that requires the prefrontal cortex. Furthermore, the disruption is related to the decrease in prefrontal dopaminergic activity caused by the drug. Evidence suggests that hypofrontality causes an increase in the activity of dopaminergic neurons in the mesolimbic system, thus producing the positive symptoms of schizophrenia. Connections between the prefrontal cortex and the ventral tegmental area appear to be responsible for this phenomenon. Clozapine reduces hypofrontality, increases monkeys' performance on the reaching task, and decreases the release of dopamine in the ventral tegmental area—and decreases both the positive and negative symptoms of schizophrenia.

Thought Question

Suppose that a young woman with schizophrenia refuses to take antipsychotic medication or receive any other form of therapy for her diagnosis. She is homeless and undernourished and has extremely limited social support or contact with others. Her parents have tried to get her to seek help, but she believes that they are plotting against her. Suppose further that we can predict with 90 percent accuracy that she will die within a few years. She is not violent, and she has never talked about committing suicide, so we cannot prove that her behavior constitutes an immediate threat to herself or to others. Should her parents be able to force her to receive treatment, or does she have the right to refuse treatment and continue to lead her current lifestyle?

Affective Disorders

[A psychiatrist] asked me if I was suicidal, and I reluctantly told him yes. I did not particularize—since there seemed no need to—did not tell him that in truth many of the artifacts of my house had become potential devices for my own destruction: the attic rafters (and an outside maple or two) a means to hang myself, the garage a place to inhale carbon monoxide, the bathtub a vessel to receive the flow from my opened arteries. The kitchen knives in their drawers had but one purpose for me. Death by heart attack seemed particularly inviting, absolving me as it would of active responsibility, and I had toyed with the idea of self-induced pneumonia—a long frigid, shirt-sleeved hike through the rainy woods. Nor had I overlooked an ostensible accident . . . by walking in front of a truck on the highway nearby. . . . Such hideous fantasies, which cause well people to shudder, are to the deeply depressed mind what lascivious daydreams are to persons of robust sexuality. (Styron, 1990, pp. 66–67)

Affect, as a noun, refers to feelings or emotions. Just as the primary symptom of schizophrenia is disordered thoughts, the affective disorders (also called *mood disorders*) are characterized by disordered feelings. The description of life with major depressive disorder described by Styron (1990) captures many of the features of affective disorders, including the psychological symptoms of depression.

Description

LO 16.7 **Contrast the symptoms of major depressive disorder and bipolar disorder.**

Feelings and emotions are essential parts of human existence; they represent our evaluation of the events in our lives. In a very real sense, feelings and emotions are what human life is all about. The emotional state of most of us reflects what is happening to us: Our feelings are tied to events in the real world and are usually the result of reasonable assessments of the importance these events have for our lives. But for some people, affect becomes divorced from reality. These people have feelings of extreme elation (*mania*) or despair (*depression*) that are not justified by events in their lives. For example, depression that accompanies the loss of a loved one is normal, but depression that becomes a way of life—and will not respond to the sympathetic effort of friends and relatives or even to psychotherapy—is pathological. Depression has a prevalence of approximately 3 percent in men and 7 percent in women, which makes it the fourth leading cause of disability (Kessler et al., 2003).

There are two principal types of major affective disorders. The first type is characterized by alternating periods of mania and depression—a condition called **bipolar disorder**. This disorder afflicts men and women in approximately equal numbers. Episodes of mania can last from a few days to several months. Bipolar disorder is often severe, disabling, and treatment-resistant (Chen et al., 2010). The episodes of depression that follow generally last three times as long as the mania. The second type of affective disorder is **major depressive disorder (MDD)**, characterized by depression without mania. This depression may be continuous and unremitting or, more typically, may come in episodes. Mania without periods of depression sometimes occurs, but it is rare.

The affective disorders are dangerous; a person who suffers from a major affective disorder runs a considerable risk of death by suicide. According to Chen and Dilsaver (1996), 15.9 percent of people with MDD and 29.2 percent of people with bipolar disorder attempt to commit suicide. Schneider et al. (2001) found that the rate of death by unnatural causes (not all suicides are diagnosed as such) for people with affective disorders was 28.8 times higher than expected for people of the same age in the general population. In fact, individuals diagnosed with affective disorders and schizophrenia have similar increased risk of suicide (Inskip et al., 1998).

People who are depressed have very little energy, and they move and talk slowly, sometimes becoming almost torpid. At other times, they may pace around restlessly and aimlessly. They may cry a lot. They are unable to experience pleasure and lose their appetite for food and sex. Their sleep is disturbed; they usually have difficulty falling asleep and awaken early and find it difficult to get to sleep again. Even their body functions become depressed; they often become constipated, and secretion of saliva decreases. Severely depressed people usually feel extremely unworthy and have strong feelings of guilt.

Episodes of mania are characterized by a sense of euphoria that does not seem to be justified by circumstances.

A person who suffers from a major affective disorder runs a considerable risk of death by suicide.

The diagnosis of mania is partly a matter of degree; one would not call exuberance and a zest for life pathological. People with mania usually exhibit nonstop speech and motor activity, and grandiosity. They quickly change from topic to topic and often have delusions, but they lack the severe thought disorganization that is seen in schizophrenia. They are usually full of their own importance and often become irritable, angry, or defensive if they are contradicted. Frequently, they go for long periods without sleep, working furiously on projects that are often unrealistic, engaging in other increased goal-directed behaviors. Sometimes, their work is fruitful; George Frideric Handel wrote *Messiah*, one of the masterpieces of choral music, during one of his periods of mania.

Heritability

LO 16.8 **Describe evidence that supports a genetic contribution to the development of affective disorders.**

Evidence indicates that a tendency to develop an affective disorder is a heritable characteristic. (See Hamet and Tremblay, 2005, for a review.) For example, Rosenthal (1971) found that close relatives of people who suffer from affective disorders are 10 times more likely to develop these disorders than are people without afflicted relatives. Gershon et al. (1976) found that if one member of a set of monozygotic twins was afflicted with an affective disorder, the likelihood that the other twin was similarly afflicted was 69 percent. In contrast, the concordance rate for dizygotic twins was only 13 percent. The heritability of the affective disorders implies that they have a biological basis.

Genetic studies have found evidence that genes on several chromosomes may be implicated in the development of the affective disorders, but the findings of most of the earlier linkage studies have not been replicated (Hamet and Tremblay, 2005). A review of genomewide association studies (Terracciano et al., 2010) found that the *RORA gene*, involved in control of circadian rhythms, had the strongest association with the occurrence of major depressive disorder. Evidence suggested that another gene, *GRM8*, which codes for the production of a metabotropic glutamate receptor, may also be involved. McGrath et al. (2009) found that *RORB*, another circadian gene, was associated with rapid cycling bipolar disorder seen in children. As we will see later in this chapter, disturbances in sleep and circadian rhythms may play a role in the development of affective disorders.

Biological Treatments

LO 16.9 **List the types of biological treatments for affective disorders.**

There are several established and experimental biological treatments for major depressive disorder: monoamine

Chamille White/Shutterstock

oxidase (MAO) inhibitors, drugs that inhibit the reuptake of norepinephrine or serotonin or interfere with NMDA receptors, electroconvulsive therapy, transcranial magnetic stimulation, deep brain stimulation, vagus nerve stimulation, bright-light therapy (phototherapy), and sleep deprivation. (Phototherapy and sleep deprivation are discussed in a later section of this chapter.) Bipolar disorder can be treated by lithium and some anticonvulsant and antipsychotic drugs. The fact that these disorders often respond to biological treatment provides additional evidence that they have a physiological basis. Furthermore, the fact that lithium is effective in treating bipolar affective disorder but not major depressive disorder suggests that there is a fundamental difference between these two illnesses (Soares and Gershon, 1998).

PHARMACOLOGICAL TREATMENT Clinical trials suggest that approximately two-thirds of patients with symptoms of depression respond to antidepressant interventions, however approximately one-third also respond to placebo treatment. Approximately one-third of individuals with depression do not respond to standard antidepressant treatment at all (Stahl, 2008). This section will first discuss several antidepressant treatments, and then explore some additional pharmacological treatment strategies for affective disorders.

Before the 1950s there was no effective drug treatment for depression. In the late 1940s clinicians noticed that some drugs used for treating tuberculosis seemed to elevate the patient's mood. Researchers subsequently found that a derivative of these drugs, iproniazid, reduced symptoms of depression (Crane, 1957). Iproniazid inhibits the activity of MAO. As you read in Chapter 4, MAO destroys excess monoamine transmitter substances within terminal buttons. Thus, iproniazid increases the presence of dopamine, norepinephrine, and serotonin in the synapse. Other MAO inhibitors were soon discovered. Unfortunately, MAO inhibitors can have harmful side effects, so they must be used with caution.

Antidepressants Fortunately, another class of antidepressant drugs was soon discovered that did not have these side effects: the **tricyclic antidepressants**. These drugs were found to inhibit the reuptake of 5-HT and norepinephrine by terminal buttons. By reducing reuptake, the drugs keep the neurotransmitter in contact with the postsynaptic receptors, thus prolonging the postsynaptic potentials. Thus, both the MAO inhibitors and the tricyclic antidepressant drugs are monoaminergic agonists.

Since the discovery of the tricyclic antidepressants, other drugs have been discovered that have similar effects. The most important of these are the **selective serotonin reuptake inhibitors (SSRIs)**, whose action is described by their name. These drugs—for example, fluoxetine (Prozac),

citalopram (Celexa), and paroxetine (Paxil)—are widely prescribed for their antidepressant properties and for their ability to reduce the symptoms of obsessive-compulsive disorder and social phobia (described in Chapter 17). Another class of antidepressant drugs has been developed, the **serotonin and norepinephrine reuptake inhibitors (SNRIs)**, which also do what their name indicates. These include milnacipran, duloxetine, and venlafaxine, with relative effects on 5-HT and noradrenergic transporters of 1:1, 1:10, and 1:30, respectively (Stahl et al., 2005). These ratios refer to the selectivity of the drug molecule for blocking the serotonin:norepinephrine transporters to prevent reuptake of these neurotransmitters. SSRIs and SNRIs have fewer nonspecific actions, and therefore fewer side effects, than the tricyclic antidepressants and MAO inhibitors. (See Figure 16.14.)

The short-term effects of all antidepressant drugs are to increase the amount of monoamine neurotransmitter present in the synapse to bind to the postsynaptic and presynaptic receptors. This occurs as soon as the drug molecules reach the synapse, typically within minutes or hours of ingesting the drug. However, there is a **therapeutic lag** and it takes several weeks of taking the drug for a person to experience antidepressant effects. Why does it take so long for these drugs to be effective if they reach the synapse almost immediately?

One possible answer to this question is that in response to several weeks of elevated levels of neurotransmitter (particularly 5-HT), presynaptic autoreceptors *desensitize* and become less sensitive to the neurotransmitter. Recall from Chapter 4 that blocking (or in this case, desensitizing) autoreceptors results in an *increase* in release of neurotransmitter from the terminals. This further enhances the amount of neurotransmitter present in the synapse, amplifying the message to postsynaptic receptors. The time course for desensitization of presynaptic autoreceptors coincides with the onset of therapeutic effect of antidepressants and is thought to be responsible for some or all of the antidepressant action of these drugs. Unfortunately, stimulating the postsynaptic receptors not only produces therapeutic effects, it is also responsible for the side effects of these drugs (Stahl, 2008).

Ketamine Although most antidepressant drugs currently in use act as noradrenergic or serotonergic agonists by inhibiting the reuptake of these neurotransmitters, evidence shows that an NMDA antagonist, ketamine, may alleviate the symptoms of **treatment-resistant depression**. Research with laboratory animals found that injections of ketamine reduced behaviors similar to those seen in depressed humans, and imaging studies with humans indicate that depressed patients showed increased brain levels of glutamate, which suggests that interference with glutamatergic transmission might have therapeutic effects (Yilmaz et al., 2002; Sanacora et al., 2004). Zarate et al. (2006) administered injections of

Figure 16.14 Comparison of the Effects of Antidepressants

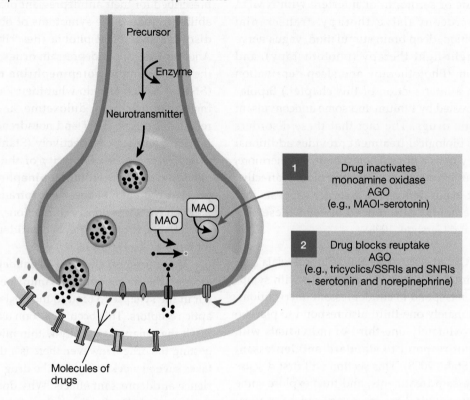

1 | Drug inactivates monoamine oxidase AGO (e.g., MAOI-serotonin)

2 | Drug blocks reuptake AGO (e.g., tricyclics/SSRIs and SNRIs – serotonin and norepinephrine)

Figure 16.15 Treatment of Depression with Ketamine

The graph shows the effects of ketamine on symptoms of depression.
(Based on data from Zarate et al., 2006.)

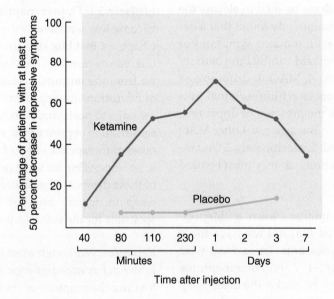

ketamine or placebo to patients with treatment-resistant depression. In less than two hours after the ketamine injections, 71 percent of the patients showed an improvement in their symptoms, and 29 percent showed a remission of their symptoms. This positive response persisted for at least one week. (See Figure 16.15.)

Ketamine is a very effective but short-term treatment for severe depression. The best use of ketamine may be to reduce the likelihood of suicide in severely depressed patients until another, slower-acting treatment can take effect. Unfortunately, by definition, people with treatment-resistant depression have not responded to other treatments. You will recall from the discussion of schizophrenia earlier in this chapter that chronic administration of ketamine or PCP, another NMDA antagonist, produces the symptoms of schizophrenia. Clearly, depression cannot be treated with long-term administration of large doses of ketamine, but in a test of safety of repeated doses of ketamine, ann het Rot et al. (2010) found that administration of six infusions of a moderate dose over a period of 12 days produced a strong antidepressant effect with only mild or transient side effects. The beneficial effects lasted an average of 19 days, with one patient free of symptoms for over three months. In another study of treatment-resistant patients with moderate to severe depression, a single infusion of ketamine was more effective than a control infusion in reducing depression symptoms. Approximately 40 percent of the ketamine group (and none of the control group) continued to experience improvement in depression symptoms for up to one month after the infusion (Murrough et al., 2013).

Lithium   The therapeutic effect of **lithium**, the drug used to treat bipolar affective disorders, occurs very rapidly. This drug, which is administered in the form of lithium carbonate, is most effective in treating the manic phase of a bipolar affective disorder; once the mania is eliminated, depression usually does not follow (Gerbino et al., 1978; Soares and Gershon, 1998). Lithium does not suppress normal feelings of emotions, but it leaves patients able to feel and express joy and sadness in response to events in their lives. Similarly, it does not impair intellectual processes; many patients have received the drug continuously for years without any apparent ill effects (Fieve, 1979). Between 70 and 80 percent of patients with bipolar disorder show a positive response to lithium within one to two weeks (Price and Heninger, 1994).

Lithium does have adverse side effects. As you read in Chapter 4, the therapeutic index is the difference between an effective dose and a toxic dose. Unfortunately, the therapeutic index for lithium is low. Side effects include hand tremors, weight gain, excessive urine production, and thirst. Toxic doses produce nausea, diarrhea, motor incoordination, confusion, and coma. Because of the low therapeutic index, patients' blood levels of lithium must be tested regularly to be certain that they do not receive an overdose. Unfortunately, some patients are not able to tolerate the side effects of lithium, and even more unfortunately, lithium is by far the most effective treatment for bipolar disorder.

Researchers have found that lithium has many physiological effects, but they have not yet discovered the specific pharmacological effects of lithium that are responsible for its ability to eliminate mania (Phiel and Klein, 2001). Some researchers suggest that the drug stabilizes the population of certain classes of neurotransmitter receptors in the brain (especially serotonin receptors), thus preventing wide shifts in neural sensitivity (Jope et al., 1996). Others have shown that lithium may increase the production of neuroprotective proteins that help to prevent cell death (Manji et al., 2001).

In fact, Moore et al. (2000) found that four weeks of lithium treatment for bipolar disorder increased the volume of cerebral gray matter in patients' brains, a finding that suggests that lithium facilitates neural or glial growth. We saw earlier in this chapter that schizophrenia can be caused by a mutation of the DISC1 gene, which is normally involved in neurogenesis, neuronal migration, function of the postsynaptic density in excitatory neurons, and mitochondrial function. Research indicates that lithium has an effect on the function of DISC1 in the postsynaptic density. Mutation of DISC1 increases the likelihood of bipolar disorder as well as schizophrenia, and lithium appears to compensate for the adverse effects of this mutation (Brandon et al., 2009; Flores et al., 2011).

ELECTROCONVULSIVE THERAPY   Another biological treatment for depression has an interesting history. Early in the twentieth century, a physician named von Meduna noted that patients with psychotic symptoms who were also subject to seizures showed improvement immediately after each attack. He reasoned that the storm of neural activity in the brain that constitutes a grand mal seizure somehow improved the patients' mental condition. He developed a way to produce seizures by administering a drug, but the procedure was dangerous to the patient. In 1937, Ugo Cerletti, an Italian psychiatrist, developed a less dangerous method for producing seizures (Cerletti and Bini, 1938). He decided to attempt to use electricity to induce a seizure more safely.

Cerletti tried the procedure on dogs and found that an electrical shock to the skull did produce a seizure and that the animals recovered with no apparent ill effects. He then used the procedure on humans and found it to be safer than the chemical treatment that was previously used. As a result of Cerletti's experiments, **electroconvulsive therapy (ECT)** became a common treatment for mental illness. Before a person receives ECT, he or she is anesthetized and is given a drug similar to curare, which paralyzes the muscles, preventing injuries that might be produced by a convulsion. The patient is attached to a respirator until the effects of this drug wear off. Electrodes are placed on the patient's scalp (most often to the non-speech-dominant hemisphere, to avoid damaging verbal memories), and electrical current is used to trigger a seizure. Usually, a patient receives 3 treatments per week until maximum improvement is seen, which usually involves 6 to 12 treatments. The effectiveness of ECT has been established by placebo studies, in which some patients are anesthetized but not given shocks (Weiner and Krystal, 1994). Although ECT was originally used for a variety of disorders, including schizophrenia, its use is now most typically limited to treatment of mania and depression.

Antidepressant drug treatment has some adverse side effects, including nausea, anxiety, sexual dysfunction, and weight gain. However, the major problem is that, in a substantial percentage of patients, the drug fails to relieve their depression. Between 20 and 40 percent of patients with major depressive disorder do not show a significant response to initial treatment with an antidepressant drug. When patients do not respond, physicians will try different drugs. Some of these patients do eventually respond, but others do not and exhibit treatment-resistant depression. The reason that the list of biological treatments presented in the first part of this section is so long is because no single treatment works for all patients—and for some patients, no treatment works at all. The existence of so many patients with treatment-resistant depression has motivated researchers to try to develop ways to alleviate the symptoms of patients who continue to suffer.

Even when depressed patients respond to treatment with antidepressant drugs, they do not do so immediately; improvement in symptoms is not usually seen before two to three weeks of drug treatment. In contrast, the effects of ECT are more rapid. A few seizures induced by ECT can effectively reduce symptoms of severe, treatment-resistant depression within a single treatment, or over the course of a few days. Remission of symptoms is greater than 50 percent, but relapse is a common problem (Holtzheimer and Mayberg, 2011b). Although prolonged and excessive use of ECT causes brain damage, resulting in long-lasting impairments in memory (Squire, 1974), the judicious use of ECT during the interim period before antidepressant drugs become effective has undoubtedly saved the lives of some suicidal patients. Since its initial development, improved ECT procedures have reduced the memory impairment associated with this treatment.

How does ECT exert its antidepressant effect? It has been known for a long time that seizures have an anticonvulsant effect: ECT decreases brain activity and raises the seizure threshold of the brain, making it less likely for another seizure to occur (Nobler et al., 2001; Sackeim et al., 1983). The changes associated with this effect may be responsible for reducing the symptoms of depression. However, evidence concerning the nature of the antidepressant effects of ECT is still inconclusive (Bolwig, 2011).

VAGUS NERVE STIMULATION Electrical stimulation of the vagus nerve is another experimental treatment that shows some promise of reducing the symptoms of depression (Groves and Brown, 2005). Vagus nerve stimulation provides an indirect form of brain stimulation. It is painless and does not elicit seizures—in fact, the procedure was originally developed as a treatment to *prevent* seizures in patients with seizure disorders. The stimulation is accomplished by means of an implanted device similar to the one used for deep brain stimulation, except that the stimulating electrodes are attached to the vagus nerve. Approximately 80 percent of the axons in the vagus nerve are afferent, so electrical stimulation of the vagus nerve activates several regions of the brain stem. (See Figure 16.16.) A review of the literature

by Daban et al. (2008) concluded that the procedure showed promise in treatment of patients with treatment-resistant depression but that further double-blind clinical trials are needed to confirm its efficacy.

TRANSCRANIAL MAGNETIC STIMULATION Researchers have investigated the ability of transcranial magnetic stimulation (TMS) to provide some of the benefits of ECT without introducing the risk of cognitive impairments or memory loss. Several studies suggested that TMS applied to the prefrontal cortex reduces the symptoms of depression without producing any apparent negative side effects (Fitzgerald, 2004; Kito et al., 2011; Padberg and Moller, 2003). Most studies show a response rate of less than 30 percent, and long-term relapse rates appear to be similar to those seen with ECT (Holtzheimer and Mayberg, 2011b).

DEEP BRAIN STIMULATION As we saw in Chapter 15, direct electrical stimulation of the brain of the subthalamic nucleus provides significant relief of the symptoms of Parkinson's disease. Preliminary research also suggests that deep brain stimulation (DBS) may also be a useful therapy for treatment-resistant depression (Mayberg et al., 2005; Lozano et al., 2008). Mayberg and her colleagues implanted electrodes just below the **subgenual anterior cingulate cortex (subgenual ACC)**, a region of the medial prefrontal cortex. If you look at a sagittal view of the corpus callosum, you will see that the front of this structure looks like a bent knee—*genu*, in Latin. The subgenual ACC is located below the "knee" at the front of the corpus callosum. Response to the stimulation began quickly, and it increased with time. One month after surgery, 35 percent

Figure 16.16 Vagus Nerve Stimulation

Electrical stimulation of the vagus nerve activate several regions of the brain. VNS=Vagus nerve stimulation

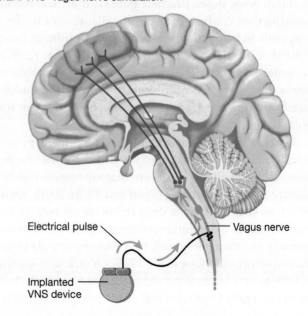

Electrical pulse

Vagus nerve

Implanted VNS device

of the patients showed an improvement in symptoms, and 10 percent showed a complete remission. Six months after surgery, 60 percent showed improvement, and 35 percent showed remission.

Deep brain stimulation has also been directed toward the nucleus accumbens. You will recall from Chapter 13 that the release of dopamine in this region plays a critical role in reinforcement and the response to pleasurable stimuli. In fact, animals will press a lever that causes stimulation of this region. Because depression is characterized by sadness, apathy, and loss of pleasure, this region appeared to be a logical target for DBS. Bewernick et al. (2010) found that DBS of the nucleus accumbens did indeed reduce the symptoms of depression in 50 percent of treatment-resistant patients who had previously shown no response to pharmacological treatment, psychotherapy, or ECT.

Role of the Frontal Cortex

LO 16.10 Describe the role of the frontal cortex in depression.

Mayberg and her colleagues (Holtzheimer and Mayberg, 2011b; Mayberg, 2009; Mayberg et al., 2005) suggest that the frontal cortex plays a critical role in development of depression. In particular, they hypothesize that the subgenual ACC serves as an important focal point in a network of brain regions that are involved in the regulation of mood and that

a decrease in the activity of this region is consistently seen after successful antidepressant treatment.

As we saw earlier, deep brain stimulation targeted at the subgenual ACC has been found to provide relief of depressive symptoms. In fact, a reliable finding in neuroimaging studies of depressed patients is hyperactivity of this region, along with decreased activity in other regions of the frontal cortex, including the dorsolateral PFC, the ventrolateral PFC, the ventromedial PFC, and the orbitofrontal cortex (Mayberg, 2009). Studies have shown that a variety of successful antidepressant treatments reliably decrease the activity of the subgenual ACC and, usually, increase the activity of other regions of the frontal cortex.

Figure 16.17 shows functional-imaging scans of patients with treatment-resistant depression taken before DBS of the subgenual ACC (a), after three months of DBS (b), and after six months of DBS (c). Increased activity is shown in red, and decreased activity is shown in blue. As you can see, the subgenual ACC initially was hyperactive, but after DBS successfully reduced symptoms of depression, this region decreased its activity. The responses are redrawn from the scans published in Mayberg et al. (2005) using a midsagittal view of the brain. Changes in activity that were seen in more lateral regions of the prefrontal cortex are not shown.

Figure 16.18 shows the results of functional-imaging scans of the medial frontal region of depressed patients who were successfully treated with a variety of treatments, including DBS,

---

Figure 16.17 Effects of Deep Brain Stimulation of the Subgenual ACC

Mayberg et al. (2005) implanted stimulating electrodes in the subgenual ACC of patients with treatment-resistant depression. The figure shows functional imaging scans of the patients (a) before DBS, (b) after three months of DBS, and (c) after six months of DBS. Increased activity is shown in red; decreased activity is shown in blue. The subgenual ACC initially showed increased activity, which decreased during the course of stimulation, and also reduced the symptoms of depression.

(From Mayberg, H. S., Lozano, A. M., Voon, V., et al., Deep brain stimulation for treatment-resistant depression, *Neuron*, 2005, *45*, 651–660. Reprinted with permission.)

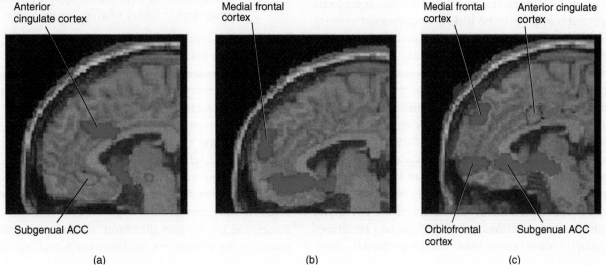

Figure 16.18 Decreased Activation of the Subgenual ACC After a Variety of Successful Treatments for Depression

The figure shows a standard drawing of an anterior midsagittal view of the human brain with tracings of regions of increased (red) or decreased (blue) activation seen in functional imaging studies of brain responses to successful treatment for the symptoms of depression. Treatment with (a) DBS, (b) TMS, (c) VNS, (d) SSRI, (e) SNRI, (f) placebo.

Tracings of brain activity from (a) Mayberg et al. (2005), (b) Kito et al. (2011), (c) Pardo et al. (2008), (d) Mayberg et al. (2002), (e) Kennedy et al. (2007), (f) Mayberg et al. (2002).

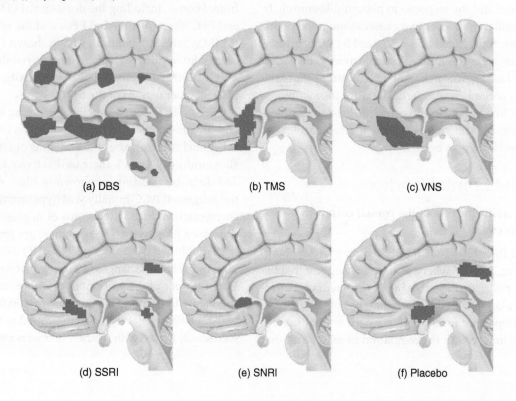

(a) DBS   (b) TMS   (c) VNS

(d) SSRI   (e) SNRI   (f) Placebo

TMS of the prefrontal cortex, ECT, vagus nerve stimulation (VNS), and administration of an SSRI, an SNRI, and a placebo. Successful treatment led to decreased activity in the subgenual ACC. As in Figure 16.17, increases in activity after successful treatment are shown in red; decreases are shown in blue.

Why does successful treatment of the symptoms of depression appear to be linked to decreased activity in the subgenual ACC and increased activity in regions of the prefrontal cortex? As we just saw, the subgenual ACC is reciprocally connected with several regions of the prefrontal cortex. It is also connected with the amygdala, hippocampus, and nucleus accumbens. As we saw in Chapter 11, the prefrontal cortex plays an important role in inhibition of the amygdala, which is involved in the acquisition and expression of negative emotional responses such as fear. Thus, successful treatment of the symptoms of depression, which decreases the activity of the subgenual ACC, may result in decreased activity of the amygdala through direct connections between these two structures and through indirect connections via the prefrontal cortex.

The precise role of the subgenual ACC will be elucidated only through further research.

The Monoamine Hypothesis

LO 16.11 Summarize the evidence in support of the monoamine theory of affective disorders.

The fact that depression can be treated with MAO inhibitors and drugs that inhibit the reuptake of monoamines suggested the **monoamine hypothesis:** Depression is caused by insufficient activity of monoaminergic neurons. Most investigators have focused their research efforts on two monoamines: norepinephrine and serotonin.

As we saw earlier in this chapter, the dopamine hypothesis of schizophrenia was suggested by the fact that dopamine agonists can produce the symptoms of schizophrenia and dopamine antagonists can reduce them. Similarly, the monoamine hypothesis of depression was suggested by the fact that monoamine antagonists can produce the symptoms of depression and monoamine

Patients who follow a low-tryptophan diet are liable to lapse into depression.

agonists can reduce them. As you will recall from Chapter 4, the drug *reserpine* blocks the activity of transporters that fill synaptic vesicles in monoaminergic terminals with the neurotransmitter. Reserpine was previously used to lower blood pressure by blocking the release of norepinephrine in muscles in the walls of blood vessels, which causes these muscles to relax. However, reserpine has a serious side effect: By interfering with the release of serotonin and norepinephrine in the brain, it can cause depression. In fact, in the early years of its use as a hypotensive agent, up to 15 percent of the people who received it became depressed (Sachar and Baron, 1979). As we can see, a monoamine antagonist produces the symptoms of depression, and monoamine agonists alleviate them.

Delgado et al. (1990) developed an ingenious approach to study of the role of serotonin in depression: the **tryptophan depletion procedure**. They studied depressed patients who were receiving antidepressant medication and were currently feeling well. For one day they had the patients follow a low-tryptophan diet (for example, salad, corn, cream cheese, and a gelatin dessert). Then the next day, the patients drank an amino acid "cocktail" that contained no tryptophan. The uptake of amino acids through the blood–brain barrier is accomplished by amino acid transporters. Because the patients' blood level of tryptophan was very low and that of the other amino acids was high, very little tryptophan found its way into the brain, and the level of tryptophan in the brain fell drastically. As you will recall, tryptophan is the precursor of 5-HT, or serotonin. Thus, the treatment lowered the level of serotonin in the brain.

Delgado and his colleagues found that the tryptophan depletion caused most of the patients to relapse back into depression. Then, when they began eating a normal diet again, they recovered. These results strongly suggest that the therapeutic effect of at least some antidepressant drugs depends on the availability of serotonin

in the brain. Subsequent studies have confirmed these results. These studies also indicate that tryptophan depletion has little or no effect on the mood of healthy people, but it does lower the mood of people with a personal or family history of affective disorders (Neumeister et al., 2004; Young and Leyton, 2002).

Most investigators believe that the simple monoamine hypothesis—that depression is caused by low levels of norepinephrine or serotonin—is just that: too simple. The effects of tryptophan depletion certainly suggest that serotonin plays a role in depression, but depletion causes depression only in people with a personal or family history of depression. An acute decrease in serotonergic activity in healthy people with no family history of depression has no effect on mood. Thus, there appear to be physiological differences in the brains of the vulnerable people. Also, although SSRIs and SNRIs increase the level of 5-HT or norepinephrine in the brain very rapidly, the drugs do not relieve the symptoms of depression until they have been taken for several weeks and monoaminergic neurons have adapted to the presence of increased neurotransmitter. This fact suggests that something other than a simple increase in monoaminergic activity is responsible for the normalization of mood. Many investigators believe that the increased extracellular levels of monoamines produced by administration of antidepressant drugs begin a chain of events that eventually produce changes in the brain that are ultimately responsible for antidepressant effect. The exact nature of this chain of events is still unknown.

Role of the 5-HT Transporter

LO 16.12 **Critique the evidence for the role of allele polymorphism for the serotonin transporter in affective disorders.**

Several studies have accumulated evidence that implicates the serotonin transporter in depression. A portion of the gene—the *promoter region*—for the 5-HT transporter (5-HTT) comes in two forms, short and long. A longitudinal study by Caspi et al. (2003) followed 847 people over a period of more than 20 years, starting at three years of age, and recorded the occurrence of stressful events in their lives, including abuse during childhood, romantic disasters, bereavements, illnesses, and job crises. The investigators found that the probability of major depression and suicidality increased with the number of stressful life events the people had experienced. Moreover, the increase was much greater for people with one or two copies of the short alleles for the 5-HTT promoter. This study showed evidence of an interaction between environment and genetics. (See Figure 16.19.)

The results of many other studies suggested that the 5-HTT promoter played an important role in the development of depression. For example, Rausch et al. (2002) found that depressed people with two long alleles for this

Figure 16.19 Stressful Life Events, 5-HTT, and Depression

The graph shows the probability of major depression and suicide ideation or attempts as a function of number of previous stressful life events of people with two long alleles (L/L), one short allele (S/L), or two short alleles (S/S) of the promoter region of the 5-HT transporter gene.

(Based on data from Caspi et al., 2003.)

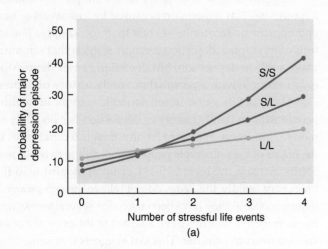

(a)

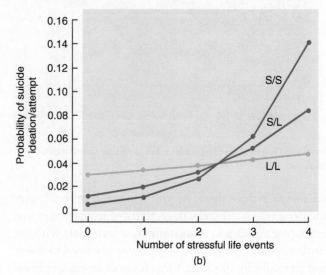

(b)

gene were more likely to respond to treatment with an antidepressant drug than were those with one or two short alleles. In fact, people with two long alleles were even more likely to respond to the placebo. A study by Lee et al. (2004) found that depressed people with two long alleles who were treated with antidepressant drugs had a much better long-term outcome (up to three years) than did people with one or two short alleles. Neumeister et al. (2002) found that tryptophan depletion was more likely to produce symptoms of depression in people with one or two short alleles.

Unfortunately, several meta-analyses of the studies investigating a possible role of the 5-HTT promoter in depression have concluded that, although some studies have found positive effects, when the results of all published studies are combined, no significant effects emerged (Risch et al., 2009; Taylor et al., 2010; Viviani et al., 2010). Until further research shows otherwise, it appears that a role of the 5-HTT promoter in depression is unproven.

Role of Neurogenesis

LO 16.13 Explain the relationship between affective disorders, their treatment, and neurogenesis.

As we saw in Chapter 3 and Chapter 13, neurogenesis can take place in the dentate gyrus—a region of the hippocampal formation—in the adult brain. Several studies with laboratory animals have shown that stressful experiences that produce the symptoms of depression suppress hippocampal neurogenesis, and the administration of antidepressant treatments, including

MAO inhibitors, tricyclic antidepressants, SSRIs, ECT, and lithium, increases neurogenesis. In addition, the delay in the action of antidepressant treatments is about the same length as the time it takes for newborn neurons to mature. Moreover, if neurogenesis is suppressed by a low-level dose of X-radiation, antidepressant drugs lose their effectiveness. (See Samuels and Hen, 2011, for a review.)

There is currently no way to measure the rate of neurogenesis in the human brain. So far, all the evidence about human neurogenesis has been by extrapolation from studies with laboratory animals. However, a study by Pereira et al. (2007) used an MRI procedure that permitted them to estimate the blood volume of particular regions of the hippocampal formation in both mice and humans. They found that exercise (running wheels for the mice, an aerobic exercise regimen for humans) increased the blood volume of the dentate gyrus—the region where neurogenesis takes place—in both species. Histological procedures verified that increased neurogenesis in the mouse brain correlated with the increased blood volume, which strongly supports the conclusion that the exercise induces neurogenesis in the human brain, as well. (See Figure 16.20.)

Role of Circadian Rhythms

LO 16.14 Summarize the evidence for the role of changes in circadian rhythms in affective disorders.

One of the most prominent symptoms of depression is disordered sleep. As you read in Chapter 9, sleep is composed

Persistent insomnia in a person with a history of depressive episodes increases the risk of relapsing into another one.

of several stages. The sleep of people with depression tends to be shallow; slow-wave sleep is reduced, and stage 1 is increased. Sleep is fragmented; people tend to awaken frequently, especially toward the morning. In addition, REM sleep occurs earlier, the first half of the night contains a higher proportion of REM periods, and REM sleep contains an increased number of rapid eye movements (Kupfer, 1976; Vogel et al., 1980). (See Figure 16.21.)

Evidence also suggests that up to 90 percent of people who experience an episode of depression report changes in

Figure 16.20 Exercise and Neurogenesis

The scans show the effect of a program of aerobic exercise on the blood volume of regions of the human hippocampal formation. This measure serves as an indirect measure of neurogenesis. (a) Subregions of the hippocampus. EC = entorhinal cortex, DG = dentate gyrus, SUB = subiculum. (b) Regional blood volume. "Hotter" colors indicate increased blood volume.

(From Pereira, A. C., Huddleston, D. E., Brickman, A. M., et al., An *in vivo* correlate of exercise- induced neurogenesis in the adult dentate gyrus, *Proceedings of the National Academy of Sciences, USA*, 2007, *104*, 5638–5643. Reprinted with permission.)

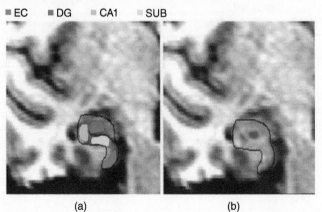

■ EC   ■ DG   ■ CA1   ■ SUB

(a)   (b)

Figure 16.21 Sleep and Depression

The diagram illustrates patterns of the stages of sleep of a healthy participant and of a patient with major depression. Note the reduced sleep latency, reduced REM latency, reduction in slow-wave sleep, and general fragmentation of sleep (arrows) in the patient with depression. The dark blue bars represent time spent in REM sleep.

(Based on Gillin, J. C., and Borbély, A. A., Sleep: A neurobiological window on affective disorders, *Trends in Neurosciences*, 1985, *8*, 537–542.)

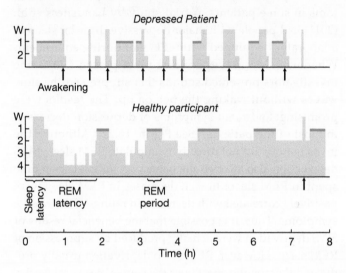

their patterns of sleep and usually have difficulty initiating and maintaining a good night's sleep (Wulff et al., 2010). In addition, persistent insomnia in a person with a history of depressive episodes increases the risk of relapsing into another one, and sleep disruption, experienced by new mothers, increases the risk of postpartum depression (Posmontier, 2008).

REM SLEEP DEPRIVATION One of the most effective antidepressant treatments is sleep deprivation, either total or selective. Selective deprivation of REM sleep, accomplished by monitoring people's EEG and awakening them whenever they show signs of REM sleep, alleviates depression (Vogel et al., 1990; Vogel et al., 1975). The therapeutic effect, like that of the antidepressant medications, occurs slowly, over the course of several weeks. Some patients show long-term improvement even after the deprivation is discontinued; thus, it is a practical as well as an effective treatment. In addition, regardless of their specific pharmacological effects, other treatments for depression suppress REM sleep, delaying its onset and decreasing its duration (Grunhaus et al., 1997; Scherschlicht et al., 1982; Thase, 2000; Vogel et al., 1990). These facts suggest that REM sleep and mood might somehow be causally related. These results suggest that an important effect of successful antidepressant treatment may be to suppress REM sleep, and the changes in mood may be a result of this suppression. However, at least one antidepressant drug has been shown in a double-blind, placebo-controlled study *not* to suppress REM sleep (Mayers and Baldwin, 2005). Thus, it is unlikely that suppression of REM sleep is the *only* way in which antidepressant drugs work.

SLOW-WAVE SLEEP DEPRIVATION Another form of selective sleep deprivation, slow-wave sleep deprivation (SWS deprivation) effectively reduces depressive symptoms in some patients. A trial study by Landsness et al. (2011) had people with major depressive disorder sleep in a laboratory equipped with EEG monitoring equipment. Whenever slow waves appeared in a person's EEG, the investigators presented sounds that suppressed the slow waves without waking the person up. The results were promising: Self-rated symptoms of depression decreased in most of the patients. (See Figure 16.22.) Although the investigators did not directly manipulate REM sleep, SWS deprivation also affected the percentage of total sleep time spent in REM sleep. In fact, decreases in REM sleep were positively correlated with decreases in ratings of depressive symptoms. Thus, it is possible that the beneficial results of SWS deprivation were actually produced by suppression of REM sleep. However, REM sleep deprivation usually produces a therapeutic effect over the course of several weeks, and the benefits in this study occurred after just one night of SWS deprivation. This promising approach appears to deserve further study.

TOTAL SLEEP DEPRIVATION Total sleep deprivation also has an antidepressant effect. Unlike specific deprivation of REM sleep, which takes several weeks to reduce depression, total sleep deprivation produces immediate effects (Wu and Bunney, 1990). Typically, the depression is lifted by the sleep deprivation but returns the next day, after a normal night's sleep. In fact, ketamine treatment and total sleep deprivation are the only treatments that produce an immediate (but transient) effect. Wu and Bunney suggest that, during sleep, the brain produces a chemical that has a *depressogenic* effect in susceptible people. During waking, this substance is gradually metabolized and hence inactivated. Some of the evidence for this hypothesis is presented in Figure 16.23. The data are taken from eight different studies (cited by Wu and Bunney, 1990) and show self-ratings of depression of people who did and did not respond to sleep deprivation. Total sleep deprivation improves the mood of patients with major depression approximately two-thirds of the time.

Why do only some people benefit from sleep deprivation? This question has not yet been answered, but several studies have shown that it is possible to predict who will respond and who will not (Haug, 1992; Riemann et al., 1991; Wirz-Justice and Van den Hoofdakker, 1999). In general, patients with depression whose mood remains stable will probably not benefit from sleep depression, whereas those whose mood fluctuates probably will. The patients who are most likely to respond are those who feel depressed in the morning but then gradually feel better as the day progresses. In these people, sleep deprivation appears to prevent the depressogenic effects of sleep from taking place and simply permits the trend to continue. If

Figure 16.22 Slow-Wave Sleep Deprivation

The diagram shows self-ratings of depressive symptoms of patients with major depressive disorder before and after a night's sleep during which EEG slow waves were suppressed with an acoustic stimulus. Each line indicates the ratings of a single patient. Arrows indicate group medians.

(Based on data from Landsness et al., 2011.)

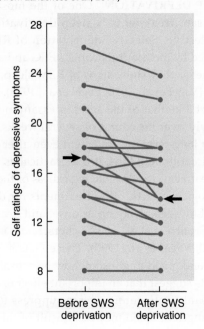

Figure 16.23 Antidepressant Effects of Sleep Deprivation

The graph shows the mean mood rating of responding and nonresponding patients deprived of one night's sleep as a function of the time of day.

(Based on data from Wu and Bunney, 1990.)

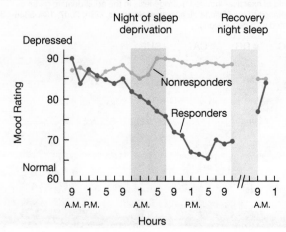

you examine Figure 16.23, you can see that the responders were already feeling better by the end of the day. This improvement continued through the sleepless night and during the following day. The next night they were permitted to sleep normally, and their depression was back the following morning. As Wu and Bunney note, these data are consistent with the hypothesis that sleep produces a substance with a depressogenic effect.

Although total sleep deprivation is not a practical method for treating depression (it is impossible to keep people awake indefinitely), several studies suggest that *partial* sleep deprivation can hasten the beneficial effects of antidepressant drugs. For example, Leibenluft et al. (1993) found that depriving treatment-resistant patients of sleep either early or late in the night facilitated treatment with antidepressant medication. Some investigators have found that *intermittent* total sleep deprivation (for example, twice a week for four weeks) can have beneficial results (Papadimitriou et al., 1993).

ROLE OF ZEITGEBERS Yet another phenomenon relates depression to sleep and waking—or, more specifically, to the mechanisms that are responsible for circadian rhythms. Some people become depressed during the winter season, when days are short and nights are long (Rosenthal et al., 1984). The symptoms of this form of depression, called **seasonal affective disorder (SAD)**, are somewhat different from those of major depression; both forms include lethargy and sleep disturbances, but seasonal depression includes a craving for carbohydrates and an accompanying weight gain. (As you will recall, many people with major depression tend to lose their appetite.)

SAD, like MDD and bipolar disorder, appears to have a genetic basis. In a study of 6,439 adult twins, Madden et al. (1996) found that SAD ran in families, and they estimated that at least 29 percent of the variance in seasonal mood disorders could be attributed to genetic factors. One of the genetic factors that contribute to susceptibility to SAD is a particular allele of the gene responsible for the production of melanopsin, the retinal photopigment that detects the presence of light and synchronizes circadian rhythms (Wulff et al., 2010).

González and Aston-Jones (2006; 2008) found that rats that spent six weeks in total darkness exhibited behavioral symptoms of depression in an animal model of this disorder. In addition, the investigators found increased apoptosis (programmed cell death) in noradrenergic neurons of the locus coeruleus, dopaminergic neurons of the ventral tegmental area, and serotonergic neurons of the raphe nuclei. In addition, they observed fewer NE, DA, and 5-HT terminals in the prefrontal cortex. (You will recall from Chapter 9 that these monoaminergic regions play an important role in sleep and waking.) Administration of desipramine, an antidepressant drug, decreased both the behavioral and anatomical signs of depression. Perhaps, the authors note, the anatomical changes they observed are responsible for the depressant effects of prolonged exposure to limited amounts of light. (See Figure 16.24.)

SAD can be treated by **phototherapy**: exposing people to bright light for several hours a day (Rosenthal et al., 1985; Stinson and Thompson, 1990). As you will recall, circadian rhythms of sleep and wakefulness are controlled by the activity of the suprachiasmatic nucleus of the hypothalamus. Light serves as a *zeitgeber*; that is, it synchronizes the activity of the biological clock to the day/night cycle. One possibility is that people with SAD require a stronger-than-normal zeitgeber to reset their biological clock. According to Lewy et al. (2006), SAD is caused by a mismatch between cycles of sleep and cycles of melatonin secretion. Normally, secretion of melatonin begins in the evening, before people go to sleep. In fact, the time between the onset of melatonin secretion and the midpoint of sleep (halfway between falling asleep and waking up in the morning) is approximately six hours. People with SAD most often show a *phase delay* between cycles of melatonin and sleep; that is, the time interval between the onset of melatonin secretion and the midpoint of sleep is more than six hours. Exposure to bright light in the morning or administration of melatonin late in the afternoon (or, preferably, both treatments) advances the circadian cycle controlled by the biological clock in the

Figure 16.24 Effects of Living in Total Darkness on Monoaminergic Systems

Rats that spent six weeks in total darkness showed apoptosis (cell death) in the NE neurons of the locus coeruleus, DA neurons of the ventral tegmental area, and 5-HT neurons of the raphe nuclei. The graph shows the number of terminal buttons in the prefrontal cortex from neurons in each of these areas after the six-week period.

(Based on data from Gonzalez and Aston-Jones, 2006, 2008.)

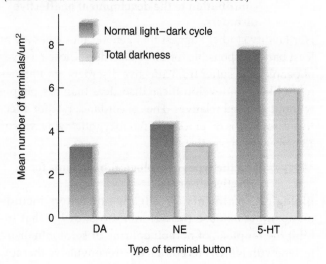

suprachiasmatic nucleus. (These cycles were discussed in Chapter 9.) Those people with SAD who show a *phase advance* in their cycles can best be treated with exposure to bright light in the evening and administration of melatonin in the morning. (See Figure 16.25.) By the way, phototherapy has been found to help patients with major depressive disorder, especially in conjunction with administration of antidepressant drugs (Terman, 2007).

Phototherapy is a safe and effective treatment for SAD. According to a study by Wirz-Justice et al. (1996), a special apparatus is not even needed. The authors found that a one-hour walk outside each morning reduced the symptoms of SAD. They noted that even on an overcast winter day, the early morning sky provides considerably more illumination than normal indoor artificial lighting, so a walk outside increases a person's exposure to light. The exercise helps, too. Many studies (for example, Dunn et al., 2005) have shown that a program of exercise improves the symptoms of depression.

Figure 16.25 Cycles of Sleep and Melatonin Secretion

Normally, melatonin secretion begins in the evening, approximately six hours before the midpoint of sleep. Most people with seasonal affective disorder begin secreting melatonin earlier, showing a phase delay between cycles of melatonin and sleep. A few people with this disorder show a phase advance, with melatonin secretion beginning at a later time.

(Based on data from Lewy et al., 2006.)

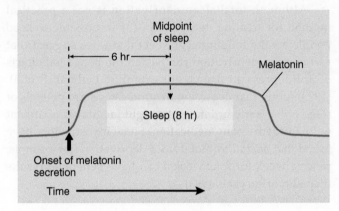

Section Review

Affective Disorders

LO 16.7 Contrast the symptoms of major depressive disorder and bipolar disorder.

The symptoms of major depressive disorder include chronic or episodic depression without mania. People with major depressive disorder feel sad, unworthy, and guilty and have an increased incidence of suicide. The symptoms of bipolar disorder include alternating periods of mania and depression. Symptoms of mania include feeling euphoric, exhibiting increased speech and motor activity, and grandiosity.

LO 16.8 Describe evidence that supports a genetic contribution to the development of affective disorders.

Heritability studies suggest that genetic anomalies are at least partly responsible for these disorders. Close relatives of people who suffer from affective disorders are 10 times more likely to develop these disorders than are people without afflicted relatives. The concordance rate for affective disorders is 69 percent in monozygotic twins, versus 13 percent in dizygotic twins.

LO 16.9 List the types of biological treatments for affective disorders.

Biological treatments for affective disorders include monoamine oxidase (MAO) inhibitors, drugs that inhibit the reuptake of norepinephrine or serotonin or interfere with NMDA receptors, electroconvulsive therapy,

transcranial magnetic stimulation, deep brain stimulation, vagus nerve stimulation, bright-light therapy (phototherapy), sleep deprivation, lithium, antipsychotics, and anticonvulsants.

LO 16.10 Describe the role of the frontal cortex in depression.

A reliable finding in neuroimaging studies of depressed patients is hyperactivity of subgenual ACC along with decreased activity in other regions of the frontal cortex, including the dorsolateral PFC, the ventrolateral PFC, the ventromedial PFC, and the orbitofrontal cortex. A variety of successful antidepressant treatments reliably decrease the activity of the subgenual ACC and, usually, increase the activity of other regions of the frontal cortex.

LO 16.11 Summarize the evidence in support of the monoamine theory of affective disorders.

The therapeutic effect of noradrenergic and serotonergic agonists and the depressant effect of reserpine, a monoaminergic antagonist, suggested the monoamine hypothesis of depression: That depression is caused by insufficient activity of monoaminergic neurons. Depletion of tryptophan (the precursor of 5-HT) in the brain causes a recurrence of depressive symptoms in depressed patients who are in remission, which lends further support to the conclusion that 5-HT plays a role in mood. However, although SSRIs have an immediate effect on serotonergic transmission in the brain, they do not relieve the symptoms of depression for several weeks, so the simple monoamine hypothesis appears not to be correct.

LO 16.12 Critique the evidence for the role of allele polymorphism for the serotonin transporter in affective disorders.

Stressful life experiences increase the likelihood of depression in people with one or two short alleles of the 5-HT transporter promoter gene, and a better response to antidepressant treatment is seen in depressed people with two long alleles. However, the results of existing meta-analyses do not support a significant role for the 5-HTT promoter in depression.

LO 16.13 Explain the relationship between affective disorders, their treatment, and neurogenesis.

Stress and depression are associated with reduced hippocampal neurogenesis. Antidepressant treatment increases hippocampal neurogenesis. The time period of onset of therapeutic effect coincides with the time period of increased neurogenesis.

LO 16.14 Summarize the evidence for the role of changes in circadian rhythms in affective disorders.

Sleep disturbances are characteristic of affective disorders. In fact, total sleep deprivation rapidly (but temporarily) reduces depression in many people, and selective deprivation of REM sleep does so slowly (but more lastingly). In addition, almost all effective antidepressant treatments suppress REM sleep. A specific form of depression, seasonal affective disorder, can be treated by exposure to bright light.

Thought Question

A television commentator, talking in particular about the suicide of a young pop star and in general about unhappy youth, asked with exasperation, "What would all these young people be doing if they had real problems like a Depression, World War II, or Vietnam?" If depression is caused by abnormal brain functioning, are these remarks justified? Explain why or why not.

Chapter Review Questions

1. Discuss the literal meaning of schizophrenia, and describe its different signs and symptoms.

2. Discuss the role of various genetic factors in the development of schizophrenia.

3. Discuss direct evidence that schizophrenia is associated with brain damage.

4. Why are drugs commonly used to treat schizophrenia likely to produce symptoms similar to Parkinson's disease?

5. Describe the two major affective disorders (major depressive disorder and bipolar disorder), the heritability of these diseases, and their physiological treatments.

6. Summarize the monoamine hypothesis of depression, changes in neurogenesis, evidence for brain abnormalities, and evidence concerning the role of the subgenual ACC in depression.

7. Explain the role of circadian and seasonal rhythms in affective disorders: the effects of REM sleep deprivation, slow-wave sleep deprivation, total sleep deprivation, and seasonal affective disorder.

Chapter 17
Stress, Anxiety, and Neurodevelopmental Disorders

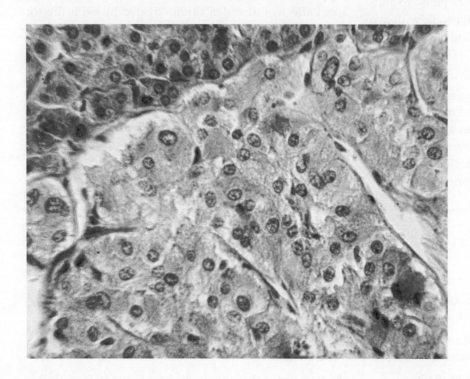

Chapter Outline

Learning Objectives

LO 17.1 Compare the SAM system and HPA axis in coordinating a stress response.

LO 17.2 Describe the negative health outcomes associated with chronic stress.

LO 17.3 Compare the effects of long-term glucocorticoid exposure and early nurturing experiences on the brain in response to stress.

LO 17.4 Summarize the relationship between the immune and nervous systems in response to stress.

LO 17.5 List the symptoms of PTSD.

LO 17.6 Describe the roles of genetic and environmental factors in the development of PTSD.

LO 17.7 Describe changes in the brain associated with PTSD.

LO 17.8 Summarize treatments for PTSD.

LO 17.9 List the symptoms of anxiety disorders.

LO 17.10 Describe the roles of genetic and environmental factors in the development of anxiety disorders.

LO 17.11 Describe changes in the brain associated with anxiety disorders.

LO 17.12 Summarize treatments for anxiety disorders.

LO 17.13 List the symptoms of OCD.

LO 17.14 Describe the roles of genetic and environmental factors in the development of OCD.

LO 17.15 Describe changes in the brain associated with OCD.

LO 17.16 Summarize treatments for OCD.

LO 17.17 List the symptoms of ASD.

LO 17.18 Describe the roles of genetic and environmental factors in the development of ASD.

LO 17.19 Describe changes in the brain associated with ASD.

LO 17.20 List the symptoms of ADHD.

LO 17.21 Describe the roles of genetic and environmental factors in the development of ADHD.

LO 17.22 Describe changes in the brain associated with ADHD.

Graciela is a busy college student, six weeks away from graduation. She is involved in intramural sports and works as an undergraduate researcher in a neuroscience lab on campus. Her hockey team is playing in the championship next week, and she is completing a study of serotonin cells that her advisor believes could be published in a prestigious journal. Graciela's week is filled with classes, time in the lab, hockey practices, and homework. She has also applied to six graduate programs and four full-time laboratory technician positions in hopes of beginning a career after graduation. She has three exams next week and has been staying up very late to study, but is having trouble remembering facts that used to come easily to her. On top of everything else, she has had a sinus infection for nearly a week, which is further draining her energy.

Hurrying across campus so she wouldn't be late to class one day, she suddenly felt herself filled with an intense fear. Her mind began racing. Did she complete all of her assignment? Had she shut down the equipment in the lab? Did she send in her final job application? She began having difficulty breathing. She was able to take only short, shallow breaths, and her hands and arms were tingling. She could feel her heart pounding and her body shaking. Terrified, Graciela suddenly fell to the ground. She wondered if she were having a heart attack. A friend saw Graciela fall, rushed to her side, and called an ambulance.

At the hospital doctors ran an EKG test to record the activity of Graciela's heart. They also ran a number of other stress tests. Fortunately, the tests indicated that Graciela's heart was healthy and she had not had a heart attack. The consensus was that Graciela suffered a panic attack, a period of symptoms that can include shortness of breath, irregularities in heartbeat, and other autonomic symptoms accompanied by intense fear. Recurrent panic attacks are one of the criteria for a diagnosis of panic disorder.

*****

Graciela's experience illustrates that both physiological symptoms, such as shortness of breath and increased heart rate, and emotional symptoms, such as the experience of fear, can accompany anxiety disorders such as panic disorder. As you read this chapter, consider how elements of Graciela's experience reveal the role of the nervous system in stress and immune responses, and the experience of anxiety. In addition to information about panic disorder and other anxiety disorders, this chapter includes sections on stress, obsessive-compulsive disorder, and two neurodevelopmental disorders: autism spectrum disorder and attention-deficit/hyperactivity disorder.

The chapter begins with a description of stress, a physiological reaction that many people experience as part of their daily lives. Next, we will explore some of the disorders that can include elements of a chronic or pathological stress response: posttraumatic stress disorder, anxiety disorders, and obsessive-compulsive disorder. The final sections include information about two neurodevelopmental disorders: autism spectrum disorder and attention-deficit/hyperactivity disorder. The figure below displays parts of the limbic system, which will be of particular relevance to us as we study many of these disorders.

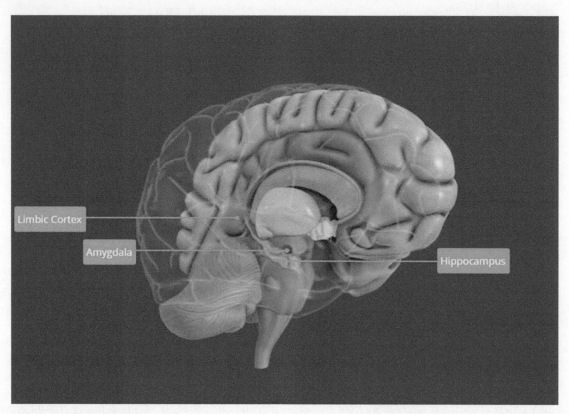

Structures of the limbic system.

Stress

Aversive stimuli can harm people's health. Many harmful effects are produced not by the stimuli themselves but by our reactions to them. Walter Cannon, the physiologist who criticized the James-Lange theory described in Chapter 11, introduced the term **stress** to refer to the physiological reaction caused by the perception of aversive or threatening situations.

The word *stress* was borrowed from engineering, in which it refers to the action of physical forces on mechanical structures. The word can be a noun or a verb, and the noun can refer to situations or the individual's response to them. When we say that someone was subjected to stress, we really mean that someone was exposed to a situation that elicited a particular reaction in that person: a **stress response.**

The physiological responses that accompany the negative emotions prepare us to threaten rivals or fight them, or to run away from dangerous situations. Walter Cannon introduced the phrase **fight-or-flight response** to refer to the physiological reactions that prepare us for the strenuous efforts required by fighting or running away. Usually, once we have fought with an adversary or run away from a dangerous situation, the threat is over, and our physiological condition can return to normal. The fact that the physiological responses may have adverse long-term effects on our health is unimportant as long as the responses are brief. But sometimes, the threatening situations are continuous rather than episodic,

Figure 17.1 Control of Secretion of Stress Hormones

The diagram illustrates control of the secretion of glucocorticoids by the adrenal cortex and of catecholamines by the adrenal medulla.

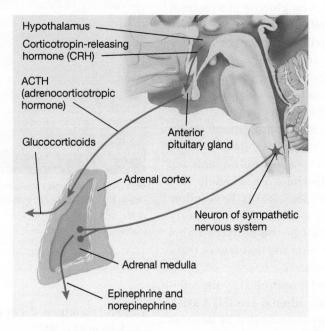

producing a more or less continuous stress response. And as we will see in the section on posttraumatic stress disorder, sometimes threatening situations are so severe that they trigger responses that can last for months or years.

Physiology of the Stress Response

LO 17.1 **Compare the SAM system and HPA axis in coordinating a stress response.**

As we saw in Chapter 11, emotions consist of behavioral, autonomic, and endocrine responses. The latter two components, the autonomic and endocrine responses, are the ones that can have adverse effects on health. (The behavioral components can, too, if, say, a person rashly gets into a fight with someone who is much bigger and stronger.) Because threatening situations generally call for vigorous activity, the autonomic and endocrine responses that accompany them are catabolic; that is, they help to mobilize the body's energy resources. The sympathetic branch of the autonomic nervous system is active, and the adrenal glands secrete epinephrine, norepinephrine, and steroid stress hormones. Because the effects of sympathetic activity are similar to those of the adrenal hormones, we will limit our discussion to the hormonal responses. The release of catecholamine stress hormones (epinephrine and norepinephrine) is controlled by the sympathetic adrenal-medullary system, while release of the glucocorticoid hormones is controlled by the hypothalamic pituitary adrenal axis.

SYMPATHETIC ADRENAL-MEDULLARY SYSTEM The release of catecholamine stress hormones is under the control of the **sympathetic adrenal-medullary system (SAM system).** In response to a stressful stimulus or environment, the hypothalamus and the sympathetic nervous system stimulate the adrenal medulla to release epinephrine and norepinephrine. Together, these catecholamine hormones initiate a rapid activation of the sympathetic nervous system (see Chapter 3 for review of sympathetic nervous system functions). (See Figure 17.1.)

Epinephrine affects glucose metabolism, causing the nutrients stored in muscles to become available to provide energy for strenuous exercise. Along with norepinephrine, the hormone also increases blood flow to the muscles by increasing the output of the heart. In doing so, it also increases blood pressure, which, over the long term, contributes to cardiovascular disease.

Besides serving as a stress hormone, norepinephrine is (as you know) secreted in the brain as a neurotransmitter. Some of the behavioral and physiological responses produced by aversive stimuli appear to be mediated by noradrenergic neurons. For example, microdialysis studies have found that stressful situations increase the release of norepinephrine in the hypothalamus, frontal cortex, and lateral basal forebrain (Cenci et al., 1992; Yokoo et al., 1990). Montero et al. (1990) found that destruction of the noradrenergic axons that ascend from the brain stem to the forebrain prevented the rise in blood pressure that is normally produced by social isolation stress. The stress-induced release of norepinephrine in the brain is controlled by a pathway from the central nucleus of the amygdala to the locus coeruleus, the nucleus of the brain stem that contains norepinephrine-secreting neurons (Van Bockstaele et al., 2001).

HYPOTHALAMIC PITUITARY ADRENAL AXIS The other stress-related hormone is *cortisol,* a steroid secreted by the adrenal cortex. Cortisol is called a **glucocorticoid** because it has profound effects on glucose metabolism. In addition, glucocorticoids help to break down protein and convert it to glucose, help to make fats available for energy, increase blood flow, and stimulate behavioral responsiveness, presumably by affecting the brain. They decrease the sensitivity of the gonads to luteinizing hormone (LH), which suppresses the secretion of the sex steroid hormones. In fact, Singer and Zumoff (1992) found that the blood level of testosterone in male hospital residents (doctors, not patients) was severely depressed, presumably because of the stressful work schedule they were obliged to follow. Glucocorticoids have other physiological effects, too, some of which are only poorly understood. Almost every cell in the body contains glucocorticoid receptors, which means that few of them are unaffected by these hormones.

The release of glucocorticoid is controlled by the activity of the **hypothalamic pituitary adrenal axis (HPA axis).** The secretion of glucocorticoids is controlled by neurons in the paraventricular nucleus of the hypothalamus (PVN), whose axons terminate in the median eminence, where the hypothalamic capillaries of the portal blood supply to the anterior pituitary gland are located. (The pituitary portal blood supply was described in Chapter 3.) The neurons of the PVN secrete a peptide called **corticotropin-releasing hormone (CRH),** which stimulates the anterior pituitary gland to secrete **adrenocorticotropic hormone (ACTH).** ACTH enters the general circulation and stimulates the adrenal cortex to secrete glucocorticoids. (See Figure 17.1.)

CRH (also called CRF, or corticotropin-releasing factor) is also secreted within the brain, where it serves as a neuromodulator/neurotransmitter, especially in regions of the limbic system that are involved in emotional responses, such as the periaqueductal gray matter, the locus coeruleus, and the central nucleus of the amygdala. The behavioral effects produced by an injection of CRH into the brain are similar to those produced by aversive situations; thus, some elements of the stress response appear to be produced by the release of CRH by neurons in the brain. For example, intracerebroventricular injection of CRH decreases the amount of time a rat spends in the center of a large open chamber (which is considered an anxiety-like behavior, Britton et al., 1982), enhances the acquisition of a classically conditioned fear response (Cole and Koob, 1988), and increases the startle response elicited by a sudden loud noise (Swerdlow et al., 1986). On the other hand, intracerebroventricular injection of a CRH antagonist *reduces* the anxiety caused by a variety of

Survivors of concentration camps, who were subjected to long-term stress, have had generally poorer health later in life than other people of the same age.

stressful situations (Heinrichs et al., 1994; Kalin et al., 1988; Skutella et al., 1994).

The secretion of glucocorticoids does more than help an animal react to a stressful situation: It helps the animal to survive. If a rat's adrenal glands are removed, the rat becomes much more susceptible to the effects of stress. In fact, a stressful situation that a normal rat would take in its stride might be fatal to one whose adrenal glands have been removed. And physicians know that if an adrenalectomized person is subjected to stressors, he or she must be given additional amounts of glucocorticoid (Tyrell and Baxter, 1981).

Health Effects of Long-Term Stress

LO 17.2 **Describe the negative health outcomes associated with chronic stress.**

Many studies of people who have been subjected to chronic or repeated stressful situations have found evidence of ill health. For example, survivors of concentration camps, who were subjected to long-term stress, have had generally poorer health later in life than other people of the same age (Cohen, 1953). Drivers of subway trains that injure or kill people are more likely to suffer from illnesses several months later (Theorell et al., 1992). Air traffic controllers, especially those who work at busy airports where the danger of collisions is greatest, show a greater incidence of high blood pressure, which gets worse as they grow older (Cobb and Rose, 1973). (See Figure 17.2.) They also are more likely to suffer from ulcers or diabetes.

Figure 17.2 Stress and Hypertension

The graph shows the incidence of hypertension in various age groups of air traffic controllers at high-stress and low-stress airports.

(Based on data from Cobb and Rose, 1973.)

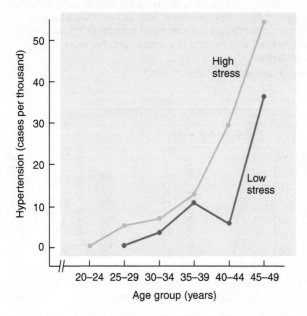

Figure 17.3 Stress and Healing of Wounds

The graph shows the percentage of caregivers and control participants whose wounds had healed as a function of time after the biopsy was performed.

(Based on data from Kiecolt-Glaser et al., 1995.)

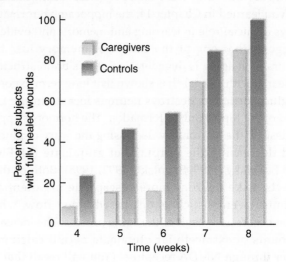

A pioneer in the study of stress, Hans Selye suggested that most of the harmful effects of stress were produced by the prolonged secretion of glucocorticoids (Selye, 1976). Although the short-term effects of glucocorticoids are essential and often beneficial, the long-term effects of sustained glucocorticoid exposure are damaging. These effects include increased blood pressure, damage to muscle tissue, steroid diabetes, infertility, inhibition of growth, inhibition of the inflammatory responses, and suppression of the immune system. High blood pressure can lead to heart attacks and stroke. Inhibition of growth in children who are subjected to prolonged stress prevents them from attaining their full height. Inhibition of the inflammatory response makes it more difficult for the body to heal itself after an injury, and suppression of the immune system makes an individual vulnerable to infections. Long-term administration of steroids to treat inflammatory diseases often produces cognitive deficits and can even lead to *steroid psychosis*, whose symptoms include profound distractibility, anxiety, insomnia, depression, hallucinations, and delusions (de Kloet et al., 2005; Lewis and Smith, 1983).

A growing collection of research suggests that impaired regulation of the HPA axis is involved in many of the harmful effects of long-term stress (McEwen, 2006). **Allostasis** is a term to describe the process of responding to stimuli and regaining and maintaining homeostasis. Allostasis may include a change in the set point of a system to respond to stimuli that are outside the range of typical homeostatic functioning (McEwen and Wingfield, 2010; Sterling & Eyer, 1988). Related, **allostatic load** refers to the cumulative

and collective wear and tear on body systems when there is too much stress response or when the stress response is not turned off. Allostatic load has been implicated in the negative health effects of prolonged or exaggerated stress response in stress and anxiety disorders. Fortunately, interventions such as physical activity and social integration can help restore healthy HPA axis regulation (McEwen & Gianaros, 2010).

The adverse effects of stress on healing were demonstrated in a study by Kiecolt-Glaser et al. (1995), who performed punch biopsy wounds in the participants' forearms, a harmless procedure that is used often in medical research. The participants were people who were providing long-term care for relatives with Alzheimer's disease—a situation that is known to cause stress—and control participants of the same approximate age and family income. The investigators found that wound healing took significantly longer in the caregivers (48.7 days versus 39.3 days). (See Figure 17.3.) A subsequent study (Kiecolt-Glaser et al., 2005) found that the wounds of couples who displayed high levels of hostile behavior healed more slowly than those of couples with more friendly interactions. A similar study found impaired wound healing among students during an exam period, compared to summer vacation (Marucha et al., 1998).

Effects of Stress on the Brain

LO 17.3 **Compare the effects of long-term glucocorticoid exposure and early nurturing experiences on the brain in response to stress.**

Stress can have long-lasting effects on the brain. This section will explore some of the research documenting brain changes following exposure to stress, as well as the unique contributions of early life stressors and new research on stress resilience.

Sapolsky and his colleagues have investigated one rather serious long-term effect of stress: brain damage. As you learned in Chapter 14, the hippocampal formation plays a crucial role in learning and memory, and evidence suggests that one of the causes of memory loss that occurs with aging is degeneration of this brain structure. Research with animals has shown that long-term exposure to glucocorticoids destroys neurons located in the CA1 field of the hippocampal formation. The hormones appear to destroy the neurons by decreasing the entry of glucose and decreasing the reuptake of glutamate (McEwen and Sapolsky, 1995; Sapolsky, 1992, 1995). Both of these effects make neurons more susceptible to potentially harmful events, such as decreased blood flow, which often occurs as a result of the aging process. The increased amounts of extracellular glutamate permit calcium to enter through NMDA receptors. (You will recall that the entry of excessive amounts of calcium can kill neurons.) Perhaps, then, the stressors to which people are subjected throughout their lives increase the likelihood of memory problems as they grow older. In fact, Lupien et al. (1996) found that elderly people with elevated blood levels of glucocorticoids learned a maze more slowly than did those with normal levels.

Even brief exposure to stress can have adverse effects on normal brain functioning. Diamond and his colleagues (Diamond et al., 1999; Mesches et al., 1999) placed rats individually in a Plexiglas box and then placed the box in a cage with a cat for 75 minutes. Although the cat could not harm the rats, the cat's presence (and odor) elicited a stress response; the stressed rats' blood glucocorticoid concentration increased to approximately five times its normal level. The investigators found that this short-term stress affected the functioning of the animals' hippocampi. The stressed rats' ability to learn a spatial task was impaired, and primed-burst potentiation (a form of long-term potentiation) was impaired in hippocampal slices taken from stressed rats. (See Figure 17.4.) A study by Thomas et al. (2007) found that acute stress diminished the long-term survival of hippocampal neurons produced by the process of neurogenesis. As we saw in Chapter 16, impaired hippocampal neurogenesis appears to play a role in the development of depression.

Uno et al. (1989) found that if long-term stress is intense enough, it can even cause severe brain damage in young primates. The investigators studied a colony of vervet monkeys housed in a primate center in Kenya. They found that some monkeys died, apparently from stress. Vervet monkeys have a hierarchical society, and monkeys near the bottom of the hierarchy are picked on by the others; thus, they are almost continuously subjected to stress. (Ours

---

Figure 17.4 Acute Stress, Glucocorticoid Level, Synaptic Plasticity, and Learning

The graphs show the effects of acute stress caused by exposing a rat to the sight and smell of a cat. The stress raised the glucocorticoid level (corticosterone, in the case of a rat), impaired the development of primed-burst potentiation (PBP, a form of long-term potentiation) in slices taken from these animals, and interfered with learning of a spatial task that requires the hippocampus.

(Based on data from Diamond et al., 1999.)

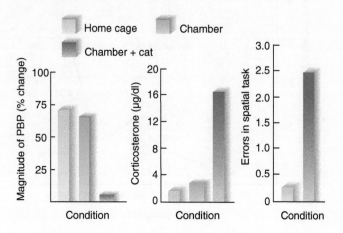

---

is not the only species with social structures that cause a stress reaction in some of its members.) The deceased monkeys had gastric ulcers and enlarged adrenal glands, which are signs of chronic stress. Upon examination of their brains, researchers discovered that neurons in the CA1 field of the hippocampal formation were completely destroyed. Severe stress appears to cause brain damage in humans as well; Jensen et al. (1982) found evidence of brain degeneration in CT scans of people who had been subjected to torture. Stress early in life also appears to affect brain development. van Harmelen et al., (2010) found that episodes of emotional maltreatment during childhood were associated with an average 7.2 percent reduction in the volume of the dorsomedial prefrontal cortex. (See Figure 17.5.) You will read more about the effects of early life stress on brain development in the next section on prenatal stress.

Several studies have confirmed that the stress of chronic pain has adverse effects on the brain and on cognitive behavior. Apkarian et al. (2004b) found that each year of severe chronic back pain resulted in the loss of 1.3 cm³ of gray matter in the cerebral cortex, with the greatest reductions seen in the dorsolateral prefrontal cortex. In addition, Apkarian et al. (2004a) found that chronic back pain led to poor performance on a task that has been shown to be affected by prefrontal lesions.

PRENATAL STRESS Prenatal stress can cause long-lasting malfunctions in learning and memory by interfering

Figure 17.5 Exposure to Early Life Stress Reduces the Volume of the Dorsomedial Prefrontal Cortex

The volume of the dorsomedial prefrontal cortex was reduced 7.2 percent in people who experienced emotional maltreatment during childhood.

(Based on van Harmelen et al., 2010)

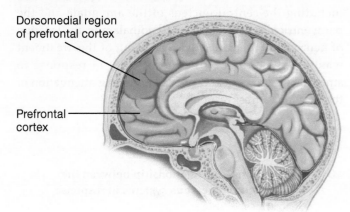

Figure 17.6 Prenatal Stress and the Amygdala

The graph shows volumes of nuclei of the amygdala in control rats and rats that had been subjected to prenatal stress.

(Based on data from Salm et al., 2004.)

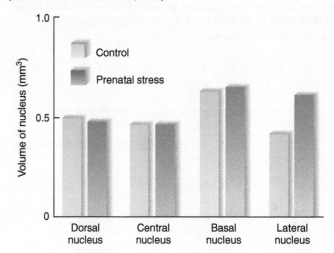

with normal development of the hippocampus. Son et al. (2006) subjected pregnant mice to stress caused by periodic restraint in a small chamber. They found that this treatment interfered with the establishment of hippocampal long-term potentiation in the offspring of the stressed females, along with impairments in a spatial learning task that requires the participation of the hippocampus. In humans, some studies have reported that prenatal and early life stress can reduce hippocampal volume in adulthood (Woon & Hedges, 2008).

Brunson et al. (2005) confirmed that stress early in life can cause the deterioration of normal hippocampal functions later in life. During the first week after birth the investigators placed female rats and their newborn pups in cages with hard floors and only a small amount of nesting material. When the animals were tested at 4–5 months of age, their behavior was normal. However, when they were tested at 12 months of age, the investigators observed impaired performance in the Morris water maze and deficient development of long-term potentiation in the hippocampus. They also found dendritic atrophy in the hippocampus, which might have accounted for the impaired spatial learning and synaptic plasticity.

Salm et al. (2004) found that mild prenatal stress can affect brain development and produce changes that last the animal's lifetime. Once a day during the last week of gestation, they removed pregnant rats from their cage and gave them an injection of a small amount of sterile saline—a procedure that lasted less than five minutes. This mild stress altered the development of the rat pups' amygdalae. The investigators found that the volume of the lateral nucleus of the amygdala, measured in adulthood, was increased by approximately 30 percent in the animals that sustained mild prenatal stress. (See Figure 17.6.) As previous experiments have shown, prenatal stress increases fearfulness in a novel environment (Ward et al., 2000). Presumably, the increased size of the lateral nucleus contributes to this fearfulness.

At least some of the effects of prenatal stress on the fetus appear to be mediated by the secretion of glucocorticoids. Barbazanges et al. (1996) subjected pregnant female rats to stress and later observed the effects of this treatment on their offspring once they grew up. They found that the prenatally stressed rats showed a prolonged secretion of glucocorticoids when they were subjected to restraint stress as adults. However, if the mothers' adrenal glands had been removed so that glucocorticoid levels could not increase during the stressful situation, their offspring reacted normally in adulthood. (The experimenters gave the adrenalectomized mothers controlled amounts of glucocorticoids to maintain them in good health.) (See Figure 17.7.)

RESILIENCE The news about stress and the brain is not all bad, however. Researchers are increasingly interested in studying resilience and plasticity in the brain. The vast majority of individuals exposed to early life or long-term stress maintain healthy brain and psychological functioning. Factors such as the presence of various protective hormones (such as testosterone, neuropeptide Y, and a hormone called DHEA that mediates negative effects of excess cortisol) and controlled exposure to stress-related stimuli can promote resilience in the event of stress. Researchers are actively

Figure 17.7 Prenatal Stress and Glucocorticoids in Adulthood

The graph shows the effects of prenatal stress and glucocorticoid level on the stress response of adult rats. Adrenalectomy of the mother before she was subjected to stress prevented the development of an elevated stress response in the offspring during adulthood.

(Based on data from Barbazanges et al., 1996.)

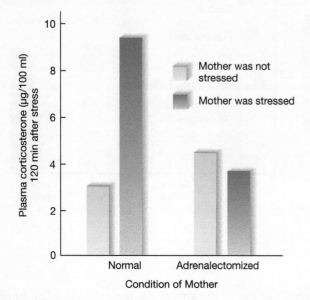

investigating brain changes, gene expression, and endocrine function to evaluate the brain basis for resilience (Russo et al., 2012). (See Figure 17.8.)

In research with laboratory animals, a study by Fenoglio et al. (2006) found that some experiences that

Figure 17.8 Factors Related to Stress Resilience

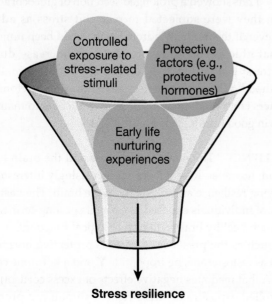

occur during early life can *reduce* reactivity to stressful situations in adulthood. Fenoglio et al. removed rat pups from their cage, handled them for 15 minutes, and then returned them to their cage. Their mother immediately began licking and grooming the pups. This nurturing behavior activated several regions of the pups' brains, including the central nucleus of the amygdala and the paraventricular nucleus of the hypothalamus, the location of neurons that secrete CRH. The result of this treatment was to reduce the production of CRH in response to stressful stimuli, which conferred a lifelong attenuation of the hormonal stress response.

Psychoneuroimmunology

LO 17.4 **Summarize the relationship between the immune and nervous systems in response to stress.**

As we have seen, long-term stress can be harmful to one's health and can even result in brain damage. The most important cause of these effects is an elevated level of glucocorticoids, but high blood pressure caused by epinephrine and norepinephrine also plays a contributing role. In addition, the stress response can impair the functions of the immune system, which protects us from assault by viruses, microbes, fungi, and other types of parasites. Study of the interactions between the immune system and behavior (mediated by the nervous system) is called **psychoneuroimmunology.** Some research in this field is described in the following section.

THE IMMUNE SYSTEM The immune system is one of the most complex systems of the body. Its function is to protect us from infection, and because infectious organisms have developed devious tricks through the process of evolution, our immune system has evolved devious tricks of its own. The description we provide here is abbreviated and simplified, but it presents some of the important elements of the system.

The immune system derives from white blood cells that develop in the bone marrow and in the thymus gland. Some of the cells roam through the blood or lymphatic system; others reside permanently in one place. Two types of specific immune reaction occur when the body is invaded by foreign organisms, including bacteria, fungi, and viruses: *chemically mediated* and *cell-mediated* reactions. Chemically mediated immune reactions involve antibodies. Infectious microorganisms have unique proteins on their surfaces, called **antigens.** These proteins serve as the invaders' calling cards, identifying them to the immune system. Through exposure to the microorganisms, the immune system learns to recognize these proteins. The result of this learning is the development of special lines of cells that produce specific

antibodies—proteins that recognize antigens and help to kill the invading microorganisms.

One type of antibody is released into the circulation by **B-lymphocytes** (or B cells), which receive their name from the fact that they develop in bone marrow. These antibodies, called **immunoglobulins,** are chains of protein. Each type of immunoglobulin (there are five of them) is identical except for one end, which contains a unique receptor. A particular receptor binds with a particular antigen, just as a molecule of a hormone or neurotransmitter binds with its receptor. When the appropriate line of B-lymphocytes detects the presence of an invading bacterium, the cells release their antibodies, which bind with the antigens present on the surface of the invading microorganisms. The antigens either kill the invaders directly or attract other white blood cells, which then destroy them. (See Figure 17.9a.)

The other type of defense by the immune system, cell-mediated immune reactions, is produced by **T- lymphocytes** (or T cells), which originally develop in the thymus gland. These cells also produce antibodies, but the antibodies remain attached to the outside of their membrane. T-lymphocytes primarily defend the body against fungi, viruses, and multicellular parasites. When antigens bind with their surface antibodies, the cells either directly kill the invaders or signal other white blood cells to come and kill them. (See Figure 17.9b.)

The reactions illustrated in Figure 17.9 are much simplified; actually, both chemically mediated and cell-mediated immune reactions involve several different types of cells. The communication between these cells is accomplished by **cytokines,** chemicals that stimulate cell division. The cytokines that are released by certain white blood cells when an invading microorganism is detected (principally *interleukin-1* and *interleukin-2)* cause other white blood cells to proliferate and direct an attack against the invader. The primary way in which glucocorticoids suppress specific immune responses is by interfering with the messages conveyed by the cytokines (Sapolsky, 1992).

NEURAL CONTROL OF THE IMMUNE SYSTEM   As we will see in the next section, the stress response can increase the likelihood of contracting infectious diseases. What is the physiological explanation for these effects? One answer, probably the most important one, is that stress increases the secretion of glucocorticoids, and as we saw, these hormones directly suppress the activity of the immune system.

Earlier in this chapter, you read about the results of studies of chronic stress on wound healing in caregivers of patients with Alzheimer's disease. Additional research in this population has revealed the relationship between stress and immune function. A direct relationship between stress and the immune system was demonstrated by Kiecolt-Glaser et al. (1987). Using several different laboratory tests, these investigators found that caregivers of family members with Alzheimer's disease, who certainly underwent considerable stress, showed weaker immune systems. One measure of the quality of a person's immune response is the amount of antibodies produced in response to a vaccination. Glaser et al. (2000) found that people taking care of spouses with Alzheimer's disease

Figure 17.9 Immune Reactions

(a) Chemically mediated reaction. The B-lymphocyte detects an antigen on a bacterium and releases a specific immunoglobulin. (b) Cell-mediated reaction. The T-lymphocyte detects an antigen on a bacterium and kills it directly or releases a chemical that attracts other white blood cells.

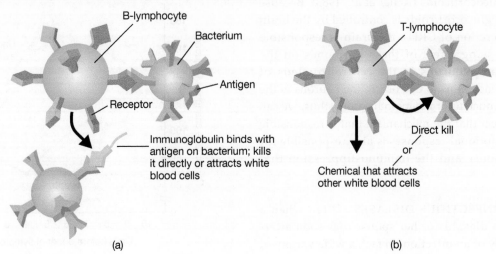

(a)   (b)

Figure 17.10 Effect of Stress on Immune Function

The graph shows levels of antibodies produced in response to a pneumococcal bacterial vaccine in the blood of controls and former and current caregivers of spouses with Alzheimer's disease.

(Based on data from Glaser, R., Sheridan, J., Malarkey, W. B., MacCallum, R. C., and Kiecolt-Glaser, J. K., Chronic stress modulates the immune response to a pneumococcal pneumonia vaccine, *Psychosomatic Medicine*, 2000, 62, 804–807.)

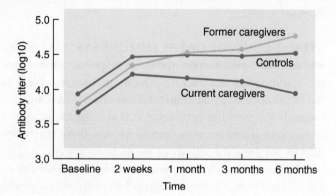

maintained lower levels of IgG antibodies after receiving a pneumococcal bacterial vaccine. (See Figure 17.10.) Bereavement, another source of stress, also suppresses the immune system. Schleifer et al. (1983) tested the husbands of women with breast cancer and found that their immune response was lower after their wives died. Knapp et al. (1992) even found that when healthy participants imagined themselves reliving unpleasant emotional experiences, the immune response measured in samples of their blood was decreased. Finally, people facing the psychological stress of undergoing surgery (Ahlers et al., 2008), taking an academic exam (Paik et al., 2000), or perhaps even experiencing Facebook-induced social stress (Campisi et al., 2012) display various degrees of immune suppression.

Several studies indicate that the suppression of the immune response by stress is largely (but not entirely) mediated by glucocorticoids (Keller et al., 1983). Because the secretion of glucocorticoids is controlled by the brain (through its secretion of CRH), the brain is responsible for the suppressing effect of these hormones on the immune system. Neurons in the central nucleus of the amygdala send axons to CRH-secreting neurons in the paraventricular nucleus of the hypothalamus; thus, we can reasonably expect that the mechanism that is responsible for negative emotional responses is also responsible for the stress response and the immunosuppression that accompanies it.

STRESS AND INFECTIOUS DISEASES Often when a married person dies, his or her spouse dies soon afterward, frequently of an infection. In fact, a wide variety of

stress-producing events in a person's life can increase the susceptibility to illness. For example, Glaser et al. (1987) found that medical students were more likely to contract acute infections and to show evidence of suppression of the immune system during the time that final examinations were given.

Stone et al. (1987) attempted to determine whether stressful events in people's daily lives might predispose them to upper respiratory infection. If a person is exposed to a microorganism that might cause such a disease, the symptoms do not occur for several days; that is, there is an incubation period between exposure and signs of the actual illness. Thus, the authors reasoned that if stressful events suppressed the immune system, one might expect to see a higher likelihood of respiratory infections several days after such stress. To test their hypothesis, they asked volunteers to keep a daily record of desirable and undesirable events in their lives over a 12-week period. The volunteers also kept a daily record of any discomfort or symptoms of illness.

The results were as predicted: During the three- to five-day period just before showing symptoms of an upper respiratory infection, people experienced an increased number of undesirable events and a decreased number of desirable events in their lives. (See Figure 17.11.)

Stone et al. (1987) suggest that the effect is caused by decreased production of a particular immunoglobulin that is present in the secretions of mucous membranes,

Figure 17.11 Role of Desirable and Undesirable Events on Susceptibility to Upper Respiratory Infections

The graph shows mean percentage change in frequency of undesirable and desirable events during the 10-day period preceding the onset of symptoms of upper respiratory infections.

(Based on data from Stone et al., 1987.)

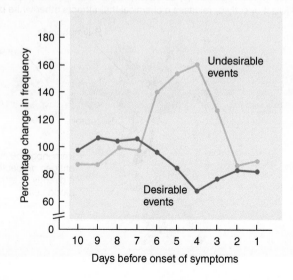

including those in the nose, mouth, throat, and lungs. This immunoglobulin, IgA, serves as the first defense against infectious microorganisms that enter the nose or mouth. They found that IgA is associated with mood; when a person is unhappy or depressed, IgA levels are lower than normal. Other studies have reported reductions in IgA associated with stress induced by academic exams, with reductions lasting as long as two weeks beyond the end of the stressor (Deinzer at al., 2000, Deinzer & Schüller, 1998). The results suggest that the stress caused by undesirable events may, by suppressing the production of IgA, lead to an increase in the likelihood of upper respiratory infections.

The results of the study by Stone et al. were confirmed by an experiment by Cohen et al. (1991). The investigators found that participants who were given nasal drops containing cold viruses were much more likely to develop colds if they reported stressful experiences during the past year and if they said they felt threatened, out of control, or overwhelmed by events. (See Figure 17.12.)

Figure 17.12 Colds and Psychological Stress

The graph shows the percentage of volunteers with colds as a function of an index of psychological stress.

(Based on data from Cohen et al., 1991.)

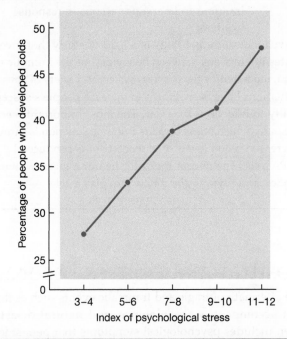

Section Review

Stress

LO 17.1 Compare the SAM system and HPA axis in coordinating a stress response.

The SAM system consists of hypothalamic and sympathetic nervous system activation of the adrenal medulla to release epinephrine and norepinephrine. These hormones contribute to glucose metabolism and increased blood pressure. The HPA axis consists of activation of the hypothalamus, resulting in release of corticotropin-releasing hormone (CRH). CRH activates the anterior pituitary to release adrenocorticotropic hormone (ACTH). ACTH causes the adrenal glands to release glucocorticoids which contribute to glucose metabolism, stimulate behavioral responsiveness, increase blood flow, and result in suppressed secretion of sex steroid hormones. Altogether activation of the SAM system and HPA axis contribute to generating a stress response to enable an individual to respond to the stressor (often by fighting or fleeing).

LO 17.2 Describe the negative health outcomes associated with chronic stress.

Although increased levels of epinephrine and norepinephrine can raise blood pressure, most of the harm to health comes from glucocorticoids. Prolonged exposure to high levels of these hormones can lead to hypertension, damage muscle tissue, lead to infertility, inhibit growth, inhibit the inflammatory response, and suppress the immune system. These effects can contribute to increased incidence of ulcers, diabetes, heart attack, stroke, increased wound-healing time, and growth inhibition in children.

LO 17.3 Compare the effects of long-term glucocorticoid exposure and early nurturing experiences on the brain in response to stress.

Prolonged glucocorticoid exposure can damage the hippocampus and acute stress can impair hippocampal functioning. Exposure to stress during prenatal or early postnatal life can affect brain development including impaired hippocampus function and increased size of the amygdala. Stress also decreases the survival rate of hippocampal neurons produced by adult neurogenesis. These changes appear to predispose animals to react more to stressful situations. In humans the stress of chronic pain can cause loss of cerebral gray matter, especially in the prefrontal cortex, with accompanying deficits in behaviors that involve the prefrontal cortex. Early life exposure to nurturing behavior activated several regions of rat pups' brains, including the central nucleus of the amygdala and the paraventricular nucleus of the hypothalamus, the location of neurons that secrete CRH. The result of this treatment was to reduce the production of CRH in response to stressful stimuli, which conferred a lifelong attenuation of the hormonal stress response.

LO 17.4 **Summarize the relationship between the immune and nervous systems in response to stress.**

Psychoneuroimmunology is a field of study that investigates interactions between behavior and the immune system, mediated by the nervous system. A variety of stressful situations have been shown to increase people's susceptibility to infectious diseases. The most important mechanism by which stress impairs immune function is through increased blood levels of glucocorticoids produced by the HPA axis. The neural input to the bone marrow, lymph nodes, and thymus gland may also play a role.

Thought Question

As part of a college mentoring program, you have agreed to mentor a first-year student during their first semester at your school. As an experienced student, you may have noticed that you and your friends are more likely to get sick during stressful points in the semester—when exams or projects are competing for your time and attention. You know that the release of glucocorticoids is likely responsible for increased risk of infections during these times. Being a good mentor, you want to share this information with your mentee and help them avoid getting sick. Write an e-mail to your mentee explaining how glucocorticoids can put them at risk of getting sick. Make suggestions to your mentee to help them avoid or minimize the risk of immune suppression during their first year in college.

Posttraumatic Stress Disorder

The aftermath of tragic and traumatic events such as those that accompany wars, violence, and natural disasters often includes psychological symptoms that persist long after the stressful events are over. According to the DSM-5, **posttraumatic stress disorder (PTSD)** consists of the "development of characteristic symptoms following exposure to one or more traumatic events" (American Psychiatric Association, 2013, p. 288). The likelihood of developing PTSD is increased if the traumatic event involved danger or violence from other people, such as assault, rape, or wartime experiences (Yehuda and LeDoux, 2007). Although men are exposed to traumatic events more often than women are, women are more likely to develop PTSD after being exposed to such events (Fullerton et al., 2001).

The lifetime prevalence of PTSD is 8.7 percent in the United States.

The lifetime prevalence of PTSD is 8.7 percent in the United States (American Psychiatric Association, 2013; Kessler et al., 2005); however rates of approximately 0.5–1 percent are reported in Europe and most Asian, African, and Latin American countries (Hinton and Lewis-Fernandez, 2011). The onset and severity of PTSD varies across cultures, and culture may influence the expression of PTSD symptoms (Hinton and Lewis-Fernandez, 2011).

Symptoms

LO 17.5 **List the symptoms of PTSD.**

The symptoms of PTSD include recurrent dreams or recollections of the traumatic event, feelings that the traumatic event is recurring ("flashback" episodes), and intense psychological distress. These dreams, recollections, or flashback episodes can lead the person to avoid thinking about the traumatic event, which often results in diminished interest in social activities, feelings of detachment from others, suppressed emotional feelings, and a sense that the future is bleak and empty. Other psychological symptoms include difficulty falling or staying asleep, irritability, outbursts of anger, difficulty in concentrating, and heightened reactions to sudden noises or movements. As this description indicates, people with PTSD have impaired mental health functioning. They also tend to have generally poor physical health (Zayfert et al., 2002). (See Table 17.1.)

Heritability

LO 17.6 **Describe the roles of genetic and environmental factors in the development of PTSD.**

The risk for PTSD depends on both genetic and environmental factors. Kolassa et al. (2010) studied 424 survivors of the genocide in the Rwanda. They found that the likelihood

Table 17.1 Symptoms of PTSD

Recurring memories, dreams, or flashbacks related to the traumatic event that cause distress

Avoiding stimuli related to the traumatic event

Changes in mood or thoughts related to the traumatic event, such as memory loss related to the event, increased negative emotions (e.g., fear, anger, guilt), decreased positive emotions, and decreased participation in significant activities or social interactions

Physiological reactions (e.g., increased heart rate or breathing) to stimuli related to the traumatic event

Increased irritability, hypervigilance and increased startle response, anger, aggression, self-destructive behavior, problems concentrating, and insomnia

Source: Based on American Psychiatric Association, 2013.

of developing PTSD increased with the number of traumatic events the person had experienced. (See Figure 17.13.) They also found that people with a particular allele of the gene responsible for the production of COMT, the enzyme that destroys catecholamines present in the interstitial fluid, were more likely to develop PTSD. This allele (the Val158Met polymorphism) is associated with slower destruction of catecholamines, which supports the conclusion from other research that these neurotransmitters are associated with the deleterious effects of stress.

Twin studies have shown that the overlap between PTSD and panic disorder, generalized anxiety disorder, and depressive disorder is at least partly a result of shared genetic factors (Nugent et al., 2008). Presumably, these genetic factors make some people more sensitive to the effects of stress. Evidence from twin studies suggests that genetic factors also play a role in a person's susceptibility to develop PTSD. In fact, genetic factors influence not only the

likelihood of developing PTSD after being exposed to traumatic events but also the likelihood that the person will be involved in such an event (Stein et al., 2002). For example, people with a genetic predisposition toward irritability and anger are more likely to be assaulted, and those with a predisposition toward risky behavior are more likely to be involved in accidents. A few studies have identified specific genes as possible risk factors for developing PTSD. These genes include those responsible for the production of dopamine D_2 receptors, dopamine transporters, and 5-HT transporters (Nugent et al., 2008).

Brain Changes

LO 17.7 Describe changes in the brain associated with PTSD.

As we saw in the previous subsection, studies with laboratory animals have shown that prolonged exposure to stress can cause brain abnormalities, particularly in the hippocampus and amygdala. At least two MRI studies have found evidence of hippocampal damage in veterans with combat-related posttraumatic stress disorder (Bremner et al., 1995; Gurvits et al., 1996). In the study by Gurvits et al., the volume of the hippocampal formation was reduced by over 20 percent, and the loss was proportional to the amount of combat exposure the veteran had experienced. Lindauer et al., (2005) found that police officers with PTSD had a smaller hippocampus than those who had also been exposed to trauma but had not developed the disorder.

An intriguing study by Gilbertson et al. (2002) suggests that at least part of the reduction in hippocampal volume seen in people with PTSD may *predate* the exposure to stress. In other words, a smaller hippocampus may be a predisposing factor in the acquisition of PTSD. Gilbertson et al., studied 40 pairs of monozygotic twins in which only one member went to Vietnam and experienced combat during the Vietnam War. Almost half of the men who experienced combat developed PTSD. As expected, the hippocampal volumes of these men were smaller than those of the men who did not develop PTSD after their combat experience. In addition, a smaller hippocampus was associated with more severe PTSD. The interesting fact

Figure 17.13 Prevalence of PTSD and Traumatic Events

This graph shows the prevalence of PTSD in survivors of the Rwanda genocide as a function of the number of traumatic events they had suffered.

(Based on data from Kolassa et al., 2010.)

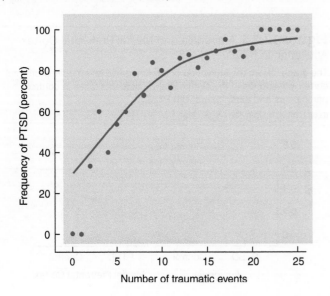

is that the twin brothers of the PTSD patients who stayed home *also* showed smaller-than-average hippocampal volumes. Given that monozygotic twins are genetically identical and usually have very similar brains, this finding suggests that a person with a small hippocampus is more likely to develop PTSD after exposure to psychological trauma. (See Figure 17.14.)

What role might the hippocampus play in a person's susceptibility to developing PTSD? One possibility is that the hippocampus, which is involved in contextual learning, participates in recognition of the context in which a traumatic event occurs. The hippocampus then aids in distinguishing safe from dangerous contexts (Yehuda and LeDoux, 2007). Consider a person who has been attacked by another person. The sight of other people who even slightly resemble the attacker or situations that even slightly resemble the one in which the attack occurred might then activate the amygdala and trigger an emotional response. However, a normally functioning hippocampus would detect the difference between the present context and the one associated with the attack and inhibit the activity of the amygdala.

You read a few paragraphs ago that most people who are exposed to a potentially traumatic event manage to suppress their emotional reaction. What brain mechanisms suppress the emotional reaction and enable a person to recover? As we saw in Chapters 11 and 16, the prefrontal cortex can exert an inhibitory effect on the amygdala and suppress emotional reactions. For example, the medial prefrontal cortex plays an essential role in the extinction of conditioned emotional responses. In fact, Milad et al. (2004) found that the medial prefrontal cortex was thicker in people who showed rapid extinction of a conditioned emotional response. And as we also saw earlier, van Harmelen et al. (2010) found a reduction in the volume of the ventromedial prefrontal cortex in adults who had sustained emotional maltreatment during childhood.

Several studies have found evidence that the amygdala is responsible for emotional reactions in people with PTSD and that the prefrontal cortex plays a role in these reactions in people without PTSD by inhibiting the activity of the amygdala (Rauch et al., 2006). For example, a functional-imaging study by Shin et al. (2005) found that, when shown pictures of faces with fearful expressions, people with PTSD show greater activation of the amygdala and smaller activation of the prefrontal cortex than did people without PTSD. In fact, the symptoms of the people with PTSD were positively correlated with the activation of the amygdala and negatively correlated with the activation of the medial prefrontal cortex. (See Figure 17.15.)

A growing body of research is investigating the relationship between traumatic brain injury (TBI) and PTSD. As described in Chapter 15, TBI is defined as "a blow or jolt to the head that disrupts brain function resulting in a brief loss or alternation of consciousness" (also known as a concussion; Simmons and Matthews, 2012, p. 613). Individuals involved in combat, motor vehicle accidents, or sports injuries may sustain TBI that can cause injury to axons and contribute to neuropsychiatric symptoms. PTSD and TBI are found to co-occur in many individuals, particularly those involved in military combat. PTSD and TBI share several common features such as anxiety and increased vigilance (Kaplan et al., 2010). Overlapping brain regions in the frontal cortex and changes in BDNF *(brain-derived neurotrophic factor)* may be involved in both TBI and PTSD (Kaplan et al., 2010; Simmons and Matthews, 2012).

Figure 17.14 Hippocampal Volumes of Pairs of Monozygotic Twins

The graph shows that the size of the hippocampus of twins not exposed to combat was similar to the size of their combat-exposed co-twins whether or not the co-twins had PTSD. These results suggest that hippocampal size is a genetically determined trait that predates the exposure to combat.

(Based on data from Gilbertson et al., 2002.)

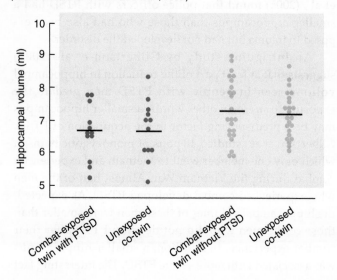

Figure 17.15 Amygdala and Medial Prefrontal Cortex Activation in PTSD

The graph shows the activation of the amygdala and medial prefrontal cortex in response to the sight of happy or fearful faces in control participants and participants with PTSD.

(Based on data from Shin et al., 2005.)

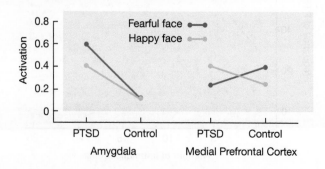

Treatment

LO 17.8 Summarize treatments for PTSD.

Many individuals display resilience in the face of trauma. Although many people are exposed to potentially traumatic events during their lives, most people recover rapidly and do not develop PTSD (Kessler et al., 1995). For example, Rothbaum and Davis (2003) reported that two weeks after having been raped, 92 percent of the individuals they studied showed symptoms that met the criteria for PTSD. However, within 30 days, the symptoms in most of the victims had subsided. The most common treatments for PTSD are cognitive behavior therapy, group therapy, and antidepressants. Boggio et al. (2010) reported on the results of a clinical trial of transcranial magnetic stimulation (TMS) of the dorsolateral prefrontal cortex in 30 patients with PTSD. They found that 10 sessions of stimulation of the left or right dlPFC significantly reduced the symptoms of PTSD and that the beneficial effects were still seen three months later. (See Figure 17.16.) Treatment with SSRIs resulted in reduced symptoms, improved cognitive function, and increased hippocampal volume in patients with PTSD (Bossini et al., 2007; Vermetten et al., 2003). In addition, psychotherapy for PTSD is associated with decreased amygdala activity and increased activity in the prefrontal cortex, dorsal anterior cingulate cortex, and hippocampus (Thomaes et al., 2014).

Some treatment strategies focus on *preventing* PTSD following a traumatic event. In a recent review of preventative pharmacological therapies, Searcy et al. (2012) described studies that included administration of cortisol to patients immediately after experiencing trauma, with the goal of providing additional negative feedback

Figure 17.16 Transcranial Magnetic Stimulation and PTSD

The graph shows the effects of TMS of the dorsolateral prefrontal cortex on symptoms of PTSD.

(Based on data from Boggio et al., 2010.)

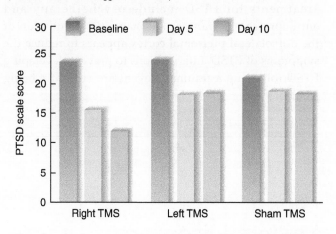

to the HPA axis to *reduce* its activity. This counterintuitive strategy appeared to be effective, and patients receiving cortisol were subsequently less likely to meet criteria for PTSD than patients receiving a placebo. In the same review, Searcy et al., (2012) also reported on the effectiveness of blocking catecholamine stress hormones (epinephrine or norepinephrine) and enhancing GABAergic activity using drug administration immediately following exposure to a traumatic event. Although the results are currently limited to a few studies, it appears that administrating drugs to manipulate stress response immediately after a traumatic event may be a promising treatment development for PTSD (Searcy et al., 2012).

Section Review

Posttraumatic Stress Disorder

LO 17.5 List the symptoms of PTSD.

Symptoms of PTSD include recurrent dreams or recollections of the event; feelings that the traumatic event is recurring ("flashback" episodes); and intense psychological distress, such as difficulty falling or staying asleep, irritability, outbursts of anger, difficulty in concentrating, and heightened reactions to sudden noises or movements.

LO 17.6 Describe the roles of genetic and environmental factors in the development of PTSD.

The risk for developing PTSD depends on both genetic and environmental factors. Environmental factors can include number of traumatic events experienced, and danger or violence from other people, such as assault, rape, or wartime experiences. Predisposing genetic factors appear to involve differences in the genes for D_2 receptors, dopamine transporters, and 5-HT transporters. Decreased hippocampal volume is a predisposing factor for the development of PTSD.

LO 17.7 Describe changes in the brain associated with PTSD.

Reduced volume and damage to the hippocampus is associated with PTSD. The prefrontal cortex of people who are resistant to the development of PTSD following severe stress appears to inhibit the amygdala. The prefrontal cortex appears to be hypoactive in people with PTSD. TBI and PSTD are found to co-occur and may involve overlapping brain changes.

LO 17.8 Summarize treatments for PTSD.

Treatments for PTSD include psychotherapy and antidepressants. Transcranial magnetic stimulation of the dorsolateral prefrontal cortex appears to reduce the symptoms of PTSD. Interventions to prevent developing PTSD following a traumatic event are currently being studied.

Thought Question

As an intern in a community mental health organization, your supervisor has asked you to help design educational materials for PTSD. Your supervisor tells you that some community members do not believe that PTSD has a biological basis. Because of this belief, many people do not seek treatment. Write an e-mail to your supervisor describing promotional materials you would design explaining the brain changes associated with PTSD. In your e-mail, include information about how therapeutic treatment can produce changes in the brain.

Anxiety Disorders

Anxiety disorders are characterized by unrealistic, unfounded fear and anxiety. With a lifetime prevalence of approximately 28 percent, anxiety disorders are the most common psychiatric disorders. In addition, anxiety disorders contribute to the occurrence of depressive and substance abuse disorders (Tye et al., 2011). This section describes four anxiety disorders with evidence for contributing biological factors: panic disorder, agoraphobia, generalized anxiety disorder, and social anxiety disorder. Although obsessive-compulsive disorder has traditionally been classified as an anxiety disorder, it has different symptoms from the other anxiety disorders and involves different brain regions, so it is discussed separately in the next section.

The symptoms of agoraphobia include intense fear or anxiety about leaving home, being in open spaces, or being in enclosed spaces or in lines or crowds.

Andrew Lever/Shutterstock

Symptoms

LO 17.9 List the symptoms of anxiety disorders.

People with **panic disorder** suffer from episodic attacks of acute anxiety—periods of acute and unremitting terror that grip them for variable lengths of time, from a few seconds to a few hours. The prevalence of this disorder is approximately 3–5 percent among adults in the United States (Schumacher et al., 2011); however, rates are lower in Asian, African, and Latin American countries (approximately 0.1–0.8 percent; Lewis-Fernández et al., 2010). Cultural differences and expectations are involved in the experiences of panic disorder (American Psychiatric Association, 2013). Women are approximately twice as likely as men to suffer from panic disorder, and this difference emerges in early adolescence (American Psychiatric Association, 2013). Some research has associated differences in the COMT gene with panic disorder in females; however, many factors are likely involved (Domschke et al., 2007).

Panic attacks include many physical symptoms, such as shortness of breath, clammy sweat, irregularities in heartbeat, dizziness, faintness, and feelings of unreality. The victim of a panic attack often feels that he or she is going to die and often seeks help in a hospital emergency room. Between panic attacks many people with panic disorder suffer from **anticipatory anxiety**—the fear that another panic attack will strike them.

This anticipatory anxiety is a symptom of another anxiety disorder: **agoraphobia** (*agora* means "open space"). The symptoms of agoraphobia include intense fear or anxiety about leaving home, being in open spaces, or being in enclosed spaces or in lines or crowds. People with agoraphobia may avoid these situations and experience fear or anxiety about these situations that is out of proportion to the actual threat or danger they pose. Agoraphobia can be severely disabling; some people with this disorder have stayed inside their homes for years, afraid to venture outside where they might have a panic attack in public.

The primary characteristics of **generalized anxiety disorder** are excessive anxiety and worry, difficulty in controlling these symptoms, clinically significant signs of distress and disruption of people's lives. The prevalence of generalized anxiety disorder is approximately 3 percent, and the incidence is approximately two times greater in women than in men. People of European descent and individuals from developed countries experience generalized anxiety disorder more frequently than those of non-European descent or from developing countries (Lewis-Fernández et al., 2010).

Social anxiety disorder (also called *social phobia*) is a persistent, excessive fear of being exposed to the scrutiny of other people that leads to avoidance of social situations in which the person is called on to perform (such as speaking or performing in public). If such situations are unavoidable, the person experiences intense anxiety and distress. The prevalence of social anxiety disorder, which is almost equally likely in men and women, is approximately 5 percent. In the United States, non-Hispanic Caucasian individuals experience higher rates of social anxiety disorder than persons of Asian, Latino, African American, and Afro-Caribbean descent (Lewis-Fernández et al., 2010). The experience of social anxiety disorder differs by culture. In Japan and Korea, individuals may experience taijin kyofusho or anxiety that the person is making others uncomfortable. Research suggests that both taijin kyofusho and social anxiety disorders symptoms can be effectively treated with drugs that increase activity in the serotonin system, suggesting shared neural networks (Stein, 2009). (See Table 17.2.)

Table 17.2 Symptoms of Anxiety Disorders

Panic Disorder	Agoraphobia	Generalized Anxiety Disorder	Social Anxiety Disorder
Panic attacks, consisting of physiological symptoms, intense discomfort, and intense fear with a rapid onset within a few minutes	Fear or anxiety related to situations, such as being in a crowd or a place from which escape is difficult, or being outside of a safe place and alone	Excessive anxiety and worry across many different situations and contexts	Fear or anxiety in situations that can include evaluation by others
Persistent worry about the occurrence of panic attacks	Fear of the situation is disproportionate to the actual context	Worry that is difficult to control	Social situations are avoided
Changes in behavior, such as avoiding places in which panic attacks have occurred	Avoidance of the situations that cause fear or anxiety	Restlessness, fatigue, problems with memory or concentration, tension, and insomnia	Intense fear in social situations that cannot be avoided

Source: Based on American Psychiatric Association, 2013.

Heritability

LO 17.10 Describe the roles of genetic and environmental factors in the development of anxiety disorders.

Family studies and twin studies indicate that panic disorder, generalized anxiety disorder, and social anxiety disorder all have a hereditary component (Hettema et al., 2001; Merikangas and Low, 2005). Genetic investigations indicate that variations in the gene that encodes production of the BDNF protein may play a role in anxiety disorders. BDNF regulates neuronal survival and differentiation during development, plays a role in long-term potentiation and memory, and is associated with anxiety and depression (Yu et al., 2009). A particular allele of the BDNF gene (Val66Met) impairs extinction of conditioned fear memory in both humans and mice, and results in atypical activity of frontal cortex–amygdala circuitry. This allele does not normally occur in mice, but it can be inserted into their genome. Soliman et al., (2010) found that the presence of the Val66Met allele altered the circuitry of the vmPFC and impaired the extinction of a conditioned fear response in both mice and humans. In addition, the presence of this allele decreased the activity of the vmPFC during extinction.

Panic attacks can be triggered in people with a history of panic disorder by a variety of treatments that activate the autonomic nervous system, such as through injections of lactic acid (a by-product of muscular activity), yohimbine (an α_2 adrenoreceptor antagonist), or doxapram (a drug used by anesthesiologists to increase breathing rate) or by breathing air containing an elevated amount of carbon dioxide (Stein and Uhde, 1995). Lactic acid and carbon dioxide both increase heart rate and rate of respiration, just as exercise does; yohimbine has direct pharmacological effects on the nervous system.

Panic attacks can be triggered in people with a history of panic disorder by a variety of treatments that activate the autonomic nervous system.

Brain Changes

LO 17.11 Describe changes in the brain associated with anxiety disorders.

Functional-imaging studies suggest that the amygdala and the cingulate, prefrontal, and insular cortexes are involved in anxiety disorders. Fischer et al. (1998) witnessed an unexpected panic attack in a participant while her regional cerebral blood flow was being measured by a PET scanner. They observed decreased activity in the right orbitofrontal cortex and anterior cingulate cortex. Pfleiderer et al. (2007) also observed a panic attack in a participant undergoing fMRI scanning and saw increased activity in the amygdala. Phan et al. (2005) found that people with social anxiety disorder showed increases in the activation of the amygdala when they looked at pictures of faces with angry, disgusted, or fearful expressions. In addition, the activation of the amygdala was positively correlated with the severity of the people's symptoms. Monk et al. (2008) found that adolescents with generalized anxiety disorder showed increased activation of the amygdala and decreased activation of the ventrolateral prefrontal cortex while looking at angry faces. They also found evidence that activation of the ventromedial prefrontal cortex (vmPFC) suppressed amygdala activation in healthy control participants but not in those with anxiety disorder. (As you will recall from Chapter 11, the vmPFC plays a critical role in extinction and inhibition of fear and anxiety.) Stein et al. (2007) found that college students with a high level of anxiety (but without a diagnosis of one of the anxiety disorders) showed increased activation of the amygdala and the insular cortex, both of which correlated positively with students' anxiety measures.

Tye et al. (2011) found that optogenetic stimulation of the terminals of neurons of the basolateral nucleus of the amygdala that formed synapses with neurons in the central nucleus caused an immediate termination of anxious behavior of mice. Conversely, optogenetic inhibition of these same terminals induced anxious behaviors. Optogenetic methods, described in Chapter 5, hold the promise of discovery of the neural circuits involved in the development and control of anxiety.

Treatment

LO 17.12 Summarize treatments for anxiety disorders.

Anxiety disorders are sometimes treated with benzodiazepines. As we just saw, increased activity of the amygdala is a common feature of the anxiety disorders. The amygdala contains a high concentration of $GABA_A$ receptors, which are the target of the benzodiazepines. (See Figure 17.17.) Paulus et al. (2005) found that administration of a benzodiazepine (lorazepam) decreased the activation of both the amygdala

Figure 17.17 Benzodiazepines Bind to GABA$_A$ Receptors

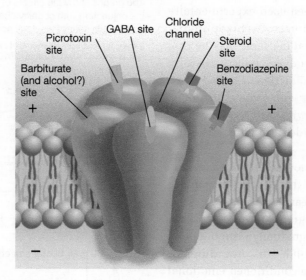

and the insula of participants looking at emotional faces. Administration of flumazenil, a benzodiazepine antagonist (having an action opposite that of benzodiazepines), produces panic in patients with panic disorder but not in control participants (Nutt et al., 1990).

Benzodiazepines are often used for emergency medical treatment of anxiety disorders because the therapeutic effects of these drugs have a rapid onset. However, they are less appropriate for long-term treatment. They cause sedation, they induce tolerance and withdrawal symptoms, and they have a potential for abuse. For these reasons, researchers have been seeking other drugs to treat anxiety disorders. Benzodiazepines exert their effects by interacting with GABA$_A$ receptors at a specific binding site (Sigel and Buhr, 1997). Chemicals that activate one of the known binding sites on this receptor, the neurosteroid binding site, enhance the activity of the GABA$_A$ receptor. During anxiety attacks, the synthesis of neurosteroids—and hence the activity of the GABA$_A$ receptor—is suppressed. A recently developed drug, XBD173, enhances the synthesis of neurosteroids and hence increases the activity of the GABA$_A$ receptor. Tests with human patients have shown that the drug reduces panic and does not produce sedation or withdrawal symptoms after seven days of treatment (Nothdurfter et al., 2011). Thus, this drug appears to be a promising candidate for treatment of anxiety disorders.

As we saw in Chapter 16, serotonin appears to play a role in depression. Much evidence suggests that serotonin plays a role in anxiety disorders, too. Even though the symptoms of the anxiety disorders discussed in this subsection are very different from those of obsessive-compulsive disorder (described in the next section), specific serotonin reuptake inhibitors (SSRIs; such as fluoxetine), which serve as potent serotonin agonists, have become the first-line medications for treating all of these disorders—preferably in combination with cognitive behavior therapy (Asnis et al., 2001; Ressler and Mayberg, 2007). Figure 17.18 shows the effect of fluvoxamine, an SSRI, on the number of panic attacks in patients with panic disorder. (See Figure 17.18.)

Figure 17.18 Fluvoxamine and Panic Disorder
The graph shows the effects of fluvoxamine (an SSRI) on the severity of panic disorder.

(Based on data from Asnis et al., 2001.)

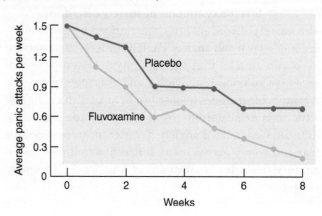

As we also saw in Chapter 16, administration of indirect agonists of the NMDA receptor that attach to the glycine binding site have been used experimentally to successfully treat the symptoms of schizophrenia. Preliminary research suggests that the same may be true for anxiety disorders. Several studies have successfully used D-cycloserine (DCS) in conjunction with cognitive behavior therapy to treat patients with anxiety disorders. For example, studies have shown that DCS facilitates treatment of social anxiety disorder and panic disorder. (See Figure 17.19.)

In the treatment of anxiety disorders, cognitive behavior therapy often uses procedures that desensitize patients to the objects or situations they fear. For example, Ressler et al. (2004) used a computer program to expose their patients to a virtual glass elevator, gradually bringing them higher and higher from the ground. This procedure appears to work by extinguishing a conditioned emotional response. In fact, a study by Walker et al. (2002) found that injections of D-cycloserine facilitated the extinction of a conditioned emotional response in rats. The drug had no effect on performance of a conditioned emotional response unless it was administered along with extinction training. Injections of the drug by itself had no effect. Presumably, D-cycloserine exerts its therapeutic effect by augmenting the ability of cognitive behavior therapy to extinguish fear responses.

Figure 17.19 D-Cycloserine and Anxiety Disorders

The graphs show the effects of D-cycloserine (DCS) and placebo in conjunction with cognitive behavior therapy on the symptoms of acrophobia (fear of heights), social phobia, and panic disorder.

(Based on data from Ressler et al., 2004 [acrophobia], Guastella et al., 2010b [social phobia], and Otto et al., 2010 [panic disorder]).

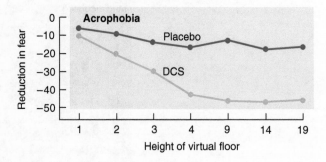

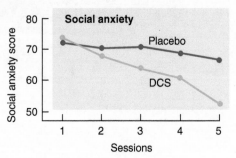

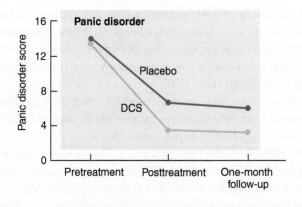

Section Review

Anxiety Disorders

LO 17.9 List the symptoms of anxiety disorders.
The anxiety disorders are characterized by unrealistic, unfounded fear and anxiety. Panic disorder is characterized by panic attacks that include physical symptoms of excessive autonomic activation and anticipatory anxiety. Agoraphobia includes intense fear or anxiety in unfamiliar situations or situations from which escape would be difficult. Generalized anxiety disorder includes excessive fear and worry across many different situations. Social anxiety disorder includes fear and worry in social situations.

LO 17.10 Describe the roles of genetic and environmental factors in the development of anxiety disorders.
Family and twin studies support a genetic component to anxiety disorders. Genes for BDNF likely play a role in anxiety disorders. Environmental factors contributing to the experience of anxiety disorders are supported by laboratory studies of lactic acid and carbon dioxide used to induce panic attacks.

LO 17.11 Describe changes in the brain associated with anxiety disorders.
Functional-imaging and optogenetic studies suggest that increased activity in the amygdala and decreased activity

in the prefrontal cortex are involved in anxiety disorders. Other research suggests that the cingulate and insular cortexes are also involved.

LO 17.12 Summarize treatments for anxiety disorders.
Anxiety disorders can be treated with benzodiazepines, SSRIs, cognitive behavioral therapy, densensitization procedures, and D-cycloserine

Thought Question

Most reasonable people would agree that a person with a mental disorder cannot be blamed for his or her thoughts and behaviors. For example, most of us would sympathize with someone whose life is disrupted by panic attacks, and we would not see their plight as a failure of will power. After all, whether these disorders are caused by traumatic experiences or brain abnormalities (or both), the afflicted person has not chosen to experience these symptoms. But what about less dramatic examples: Should we blame people for their shyness or hostility or other maladaptive personality traits? If, as many psychologists believe, people's personality characteristics are largely determined by their heredity (and thus by the structure and chemistry of their brains), what are the implications for our concepts of "blame" and "personal responsibility"?

Obsessive-Compulsive Disorder

As the name implies, people with an **obsessive-compulsive disorder (OCD)** suffer from **obsessions**—persistent and involuntary thoughts, images, or urges that will not leave them—and **compulsions**—behaviors that they cannot keep from performing. The incidence of obsessive-compulsive disorder is 1–2 percent both in the United States and internationally. Females are slightly more likely than males to have this diagnosis. The symptoms of OCD most commonly begin in young adulthood (Robbins et al., 1984).

Symptoms

LO 17.13 List the symptoms of OCD.

Obsessions include concern or disgust with bodily secretions, dirt, germs, and the like; fear that something terrible

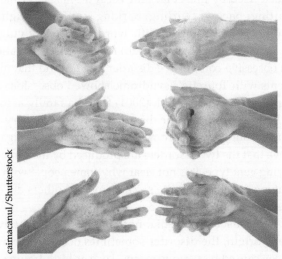

Some people with obsessive-compulsive disorder will wash their hands hundreds of times a day, even if their hands become covered with painful sores.

might happen; or a need for symmetry, order, or exactness. Most compulsions fall into one of four categories: *counting, checking, cleaning,* and *avoidance.* For example, people might repeatedly check burners on the stove to see that they are off and windows and doors to be sure that they are locked. Some people will wash their hands hundreds of times a day, even if their hands become covered with painful sores. Other people meticulously clean their house or endlessly wash, dry, and fold their clothes. Some become afraid to leave home because they fear contamination, and refuse to touch other members of their family. If they do accidentally become "contaminated," they usually have lengthy purification rituals.

Obsessions are seen in a variety of mental disorders, including schizophrenia. However, unlike people with schizophrenia, people with obsessive-compulsive disorder recognize that their thoughts and behaviors are irrational. Compulsions often become more and more demanding until they interfere with people's careers and daily lives. Although OCD is often associated with the other anxiety disorders, it is now believed to more closely align with other disorders that feature dysfunctional thoughts and repetitive behaviors such as hoarding or trichotillomania (hair-pulling disorder) (American Psychiatric Association, 2013). (See Table 17.3.)

Some investigators believe that the compulsive behaviors seen in OCD are forms of species-typical behaviors—for example, grooming, cleaning, and attention to sources of potential danger—that are released from normal control mechanisms by a brain dysfunction (Rapoport and Wise, 1988). Fiske and Haslam (1997) suggest that the behaviors seen in OCD are simply pathological examples of typical human behaviors to develop and practice social rituals. For example, people perform cultural rituals to mark transitions or changes in social status, to diagnose or treat illnesses, to restore relationships with deities, or to ensure the success of hunting or planting. Consider the following scenario (from Fiske and Haslam, 1997):

Table 17.3 Symptoms of Obsessive-Compulsive Disorder

Obsessive-Compulsive Disorder
Obsessions: Recurring and unwanted concerns, thoughts, or urges that can cause anxiety or distress; attempts may be made to ignore or suppress the obsessions, often by performing a compulsive behavior
Compulsions: Repetitive behaviors performed in response to an obsession; compulsions prevent or decrease anxiety or distress related to the obsessions
Obsessions and compulsions take time away from other activities and reduce quality of life for the individual

Source: Based on American Psychiatric Association, 2013.

Imagine that you are traveling in an unfamiliar country. Going out for a walk, you observe a man dressed in red, standing on a red mat in a red-painted gateway.... He utters the same prayer six times. He brings out six basins of water and meticulously arranges them in a symmetrical configuration in front of the gateway. Then he washes his hands six times in each of the six basins, using precisely the same motions each time. As he does this, he repeats the same phrase, occasionally tapping his right finger on his earlobe. Through your interpreter, you ask him what he is doing. He replies that there are dangerous polluting substances in the ground, ... [and that] he must purify himself or something terrible will happen. He seems eager to tell you about his concerns. (p. 225)

Why is the man acting this way? Is he a priest following a sacred ritual, or does he have obsessive-compulsive disorder? Without knowing more about the rituals followed by the man's culture, we cannot say. Fiske and Haslam compared the features of OCD and other psychological disorders in descriptions of rituals, work, or other activities in 52 cultures. They reported that the features of OCD were found in rituals in these cultures. The features of other psychological disorders were much less common. On the whole, the evidence suggests that the symptoms of OCD represent an exaggeration of typical human behavior.

Zhong and Liljenquist (2006) found that students at Northwestern University in the United States, apparently unknowingly consider cleansing rituals to "wash away their sins." The investigators had the participants recall in detail either an ethical or an unethical deed they had committed in the past. Later, they were asked to complete some word fragments by filling in letters where blanks occurred. Some word fragments could be made into words that did or did not pertain to cleansing. For example, W—H, SH–ER, and S–P could be *wash, shower,* and *soap,*

or they could be *wish, shaker,* and *step.* The participants who had described a misdeed were much more likely to think of cleansing-related words. And when offered a free gift—either a pencil or an antiseptic wipe—participants who described a misdeed were more likely to choose the antiseptic wipe.

Heritability

LO 17.14 **Describe the roles of genetic and environmental factors in the development of OCD.**

Evidence indicates that hereditary factors play at least some part in the development of obsessive-compulsive disorder. Several studies have found a greater concordance for obsessions and compulsions in monozygotic twins than in dizygotic twins (Hettema et al., 2001). Family studies have found that OCD is associated with a neurological disorder that appears during childhood (Pauls and Leckman, 1986; Pauls et al., 1986). This disorder, **Tourette's syndrome,** is characterized by muscular and vocal tics: facial grimaces, squatting, pacing, twirling, barking, sniffing, coughing, grunting, or repeating specific words (especially vulgarities). Leonard et al. (1992a, 1992b) found that many patients with obsessive-compulsive disorder had tics and that many patients with Tourette's syndrome showed obsessions and compulsions. Grados et al. (2001) found a family association between OCD and tic disorders (a broad category that includes Tourette's syndrome). Both groups of investigators believe that the two disorders are produced by the same underlying genotype. It is not clear why some people with this genotype develop Tourette's syndrome and others develop obsessive-compulsive disorder.

As with schizophrenia, not all cases of OCD have a genetic origin; the disorder sometimes occurs after brain damage caused by various means, such as birth trauma, encephalitis, and head trauma (Berthier et al., 1996; Hollander et al., 1990). In particular, the symptoms appear to be associated with damage to or dysfunction of the basal ganglia, cingulate gyrus, and prefrontal cortex (Giedd et al., 1995; Robinson et al., 1995).

Tic disorders (including OCD) can be caused by a group A β-hemolytic streptococcal infection (Kawikova et al., 2010; Perlmutter et al., 1998). This infection can trigger several autoimmune diseases, in which the patient's immune system attacks and damages certain tissues of the body, including the valves of the heart, the kidneys, and—in this case—parts of the brain. Figure 17.20 shows the parallel course of a child's symptoms and the level of antistreptococcal DNA-B in her blood, which indicates the presence of an active infection.

The symptoms of OCD appear to be produced by damage to the basal ganglia. Bodner et al., (2001) report the case of a 25-year-old man whose untreated sore throat developed into an autoimmune disease that produced obsessions and compulsions. The investigators found antibodies to type A β-hemolytic streptococcus, and MRI scans indicated abnormalities in the basal ganglia. An MRI study of 34 children with streptococcus-associated tics or OCD by Giedd et al., (2000) found an increase in the size of the basal ganglia that they attributed to an autoimmune inflammation of this region.

Brain Changes

LO 17.15 Describe changes in the brain associated with OCD.

Several functional-imaging studies have found evidence of increased activity in the frontal lobes and caudate

Figure 17.20 OCD and Streptococcal Hemolytic Infection

The graph shows the parallel course of a child's symptoms and the level of antistreptococcal DNA-B in her blood, which indicates the presence of an active infection. This relationship provides evidence that a group A β-hemolytic streptococcal infection can produce tics and the symptoms of OCD, presumably by affecting the basal ganglia.

(Based on data from Perlmutter et al., 1998.)

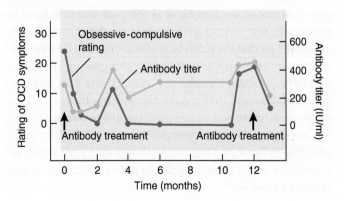

nucleus in patients with OCD. A review by Whiteside et al. (2004) found that functional-imaging studies consistently found increased activity of the caudate nucleus and the orbitofrontal cortex. Guehl et al., (2008) inserted microelectrodes into the caudate nuclei of three patients with OCD who were being evaluated for neurosurgery. They found that two of the patients, who reported the presence of obsessive thoughts during the surgery, showed increased activity in neurons in the caudate nucleus. The third patient, who did not report obsessive thoughts, showed a lower rate of neural activity.

A review by Saxena et al. (1998) described several studies that measured regional brain activity in patients with OCD before and after successful treatment with drugs or cognitive behavior therapy. In general, the improvement in a patient's symptoms was correlated with a reduction in the activity of the caudate nucleus and orbitofrontal cortex. The fact that cognitive behavioral therapy and drug therapy produced similar results is especially remarkable: It indicates that very different procedures may bring about physiological changes that alleviate a serious mental disorder.

Treatment

LO 17.16 Summarize treatments for OCD.

Three drugs are regularly used to treat the symptoms of OCD: clomipramine, fluoxetine, and fluvoxamine. These effective antiobsessional drugs are specific blockers of 5-HT reuptake; thus, they are serotonergic agonists. In general, serotonin has an inhibitory effect on species-typical behaviors, which has tempted several investigators to speculate that these drugs alleviate the symptoms of obsessive-compulsive disorder by reducing the strength of innate tendencies for counting, checking, cleaning, and avoidance behaviors that may underlie this disorder. Brain regions that have been implicated in OCD, including the orbitofrontal cortex and the basal ganglia, receive input from serotonergic terminals (El Mansari and Blier, 1997; Lavoie and Parent, 1990).

The importance of serotonergic activity in inhibiting compulsive behaviors is underscored by three interesting compulsions: trichotillomania, onychophagia, and acral lick dermatitis. *Trichotillomania* is compulsive hair pulling. People with this disorder (almost always females) often spend hours each night pulling hairs out one by one, sometimes eating them (Rapoport, 1991). *Onychophagia* is compulsive nail biting, which in its extreme can cause severe damage to the ends of the fingers. (For those who are sufficiently agile, toenail biting is not uncommon.) Double-blind studies have shown that both of these disorders can be treated successfully by clomipramine, the drug of choice for OCD (Leonard et al., 1992a).

Acral lick dermatitis is a disease of dogs, not humans. Some dogs will continuously lick at a part of their body, especially their wrist or ankle (called the *carpus* and the *hock*). The licking removes the hair and often erodes away the skin as well. The disorder seems to be genetic; it is seen almost exclusively in large breeds such as Great Danes, Labrador retrievers, and German shepherds, and it runs in families. A double-blind study found that clomipramine reduces this compulsive behavior (Rapoport et al., 1992).

We saw in the previous subsection that an NMDA receptor agonist, d-cycloserine, appears to be useful in treating the symptoms of a variety of anxiety disorders. This drug appears to help in the treatment of the symptoms of OCD as well. A double-blind study by Wilhelm et al. (2008) found that compared with patients who received a placebo, patients who received d-cycloserine along with sessions of cognitive behavior therapy showed a greater decrease in their obsessive symptoms and retained this improvement after the sessions ended. Presumably, the drug facilitated the extinction of the maladaptive thoughts and behaviors, just as it facilitates the extinction of conditioned emotional responses in patients with anxiety disorders. (See Figure 17.21.)

Some patients with severe OCD have been successfully treated with *cingulotomy*—surgical destruction of specific fiber bundles in the subcortical frontal lobe, including the cingulum bundle (which connects the prefrontal and cingulate cortexes with the limbic cortex of the temporal lobe) and a region that contains fibers that connect the basal ganglia with the prefrontal cortex (Ballantine et al., 1987; Mindus et al., 1994). These operations have a reasonably good success rate (Dougherty et al., 2002). Another reasonably successful surgical procedure, *capsulotomy*, destroys a region of a fiber bundle (the *internal capsule*) that connects the caudate nucleus with the medial prefrontal cortex (Rück et al., 2008). Brain lesions cannot be undone, so such procedures must be considered only as a last resort. As Rück et al. report, some patients suffer from adverse side effects after surgery, such as problems of planning, apathy, or difficulty inhibiting socially inappropriate behavior.

As we saw in Chapter 15, deep brain stimulation (DBS) has been found to be useful in treating the symptoms of Parkinson's disease. Because OCD, like Parkinson's disease, appears to involve abnormalities in the basal ganglia, several clinics have tried to use DBS of the basal ganglia or fiber tracts connected with them to treat this disorder. This form of therapy appears to reduce the symptoms of OCD in some patients (Abelson et al., 2005; Larson, 2008). Le Jeune et al. (2010) found that DBS of the subthalamic nucleus, which plays an integral role in the cortical–basal ganglia circuitry, reduces the symptoms of OCD. One of the more modern forms of psychosurgery is destruction of the internal capsule. Goodman et al. (2010) found that DBS of the internal capsule reduced the symptoms of OCD in four of six patients with severe, treatment-resistant OCD. A significant benefit of DBS is that, unlike psychosurgical procedures that destroy brain tissue, it is reversible: If no benefit is obtained from the stimulation, the electrodes can be removed.

As we saw in Chapters 8 and 14, the principal parts of the basal ganglia, the caudate nucleus and the putamen, receive information from the cerebral cortex. As this information is processed by the basal ganglia, it flows through two pathways before it passes to the thalamus and is sent back to the cortex. The *direct pathway* is excitatory, and the *indirect pathway* is inhibitory. (See Figure 17.22.) Saxena et al. (1998) suggest that the symptoms of OCD may be a result of overactivity of the direct pathway. They propose that one of the functions of this pathway is control of previously learned behavior sequences that have become automatic so that they can be executed rapidly. The orbitofrontal cortex, which is involved in recognizing situations that have personal significance, can activate this pathway and the behaviors that it controls. The inhibitory indirect pathway is involved in suppressing these automatic behaviors, permitting the person to switch to other, more adaptive behaviors. Thus, obsessive-compulsive behavior could be a result of an imbalance between the direct and indirect pathways.

Figure 17.21 D-Cycloserine and OCD

The graph shows the effects of D-cycloserine and placebo in conjunction with cognitive behavior therapy on the symptoms of obsessive-compulsive behavior.

(Based on data from Wilhelm et al., 2008.)

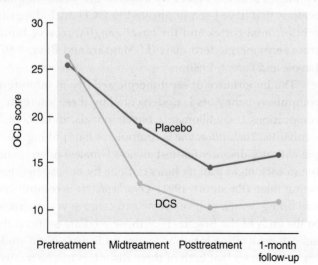

Figure 17.22 Direct and Indirect Pathways in the Basal Ganglia (a) The locations of the components of the basal ganglia and associated structures. (b) The major connections of the basal ganglia and associated structures. Excitatory connections are shown as black lines; inhibitory connections are shown as red lines.

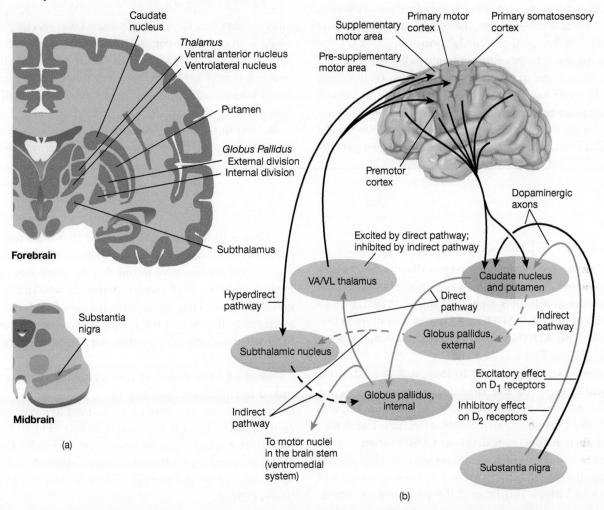

Section Review

Obsessive-Compulsive Disorder

LO 17.13 List the symptoms of OCD.

Obsessive-compulsive disorder (OCD) is characterized by obsessions—unwanted thoughts—and compulsions—uncontrollable behaviors, especially those involving cleanliness and attention to danger.

LO 17.14 Describe the roles of genetic and environmental factors in the development of OCD.

OCD has a heritable basis and is related to Tourette's syndrome, a neurological disorder characterized by tics and vocalizations. It can also be caused by brain damage at birth, encephalitis, and head injuries, especially when the basal ganglia are involved. A type A β-hemolytic streptococcus infection can stimulate an autoimmune attack—presumably on the basal ganglia—that produces symptoms of OCD.

LO 17.15 Describe changes in the brain associated with OCD.

Functional imaging indicates that people with obsessive-compulsive disorder tend to show increased activity in the orbitofrontal cortex, cingulate cortex, and caudate nucleus. Drug treatment or cognitive behavior therapy that successfully reduces the symptoms of OCD generally reduces the activity of the orbitofrontal cortex and caudate nucleus.

LO 17.16 Summarize treatments for OCD.

The most effective drugs for treating OCD are SSRIs such as clomipramine, fluoxetine, and fluvoxamine. Three other compulsions—hair pulling, nail biting, and (in dogs) acral lick syndrome—are also suppressed by clomipramine. In conjunction with cognitive behavior therapy, D-cycloserine, which acts as an indirect agonist at NMDA receptors, also appears to reduce the symptoms of OCD. Some investigators believe that clomipramine and related drugs alleviate the symptoms of OCD by increasing the activity of serotonergic pathways that play an inhibitory role in species-typical behaviors. In severe cases of OCD that do not respond to other treatments, surgical procedures such as cingulotomy and capsulotomy may provide relief. Deep brain stimulation with implanted electrodes has been shown to be effective in some patients and, unlike cingulotomy and capsulotomy, has the benefit of being reversible.

Thought Question

Imagine that you have a relative who was recently diagnosed with obsessive-compulsive disorder. You learn that your loved one is struggling to decide which treatment strategy is best for them. Your relative calls you to ask about which treatment strategies have brain-based evidence to support them. To help your relative be informed in making this difficult decision, briefly outline the treatments and explain their effects in the nervous system.

Autism Spectrum Disorder

The following sections of this chapter discuss two neurodevelopmental disorders: autism spectrum disorder (ASD) and attention-deficit/hyperactivity disorder (ADHD). Characteristics of ASD and ADHD are present very early in life. Both ASD and ADHD have a higher prevalence among males. Our focus first will be on ASD.

Parents typically expect to love and cherish their child and to be loved and cherished in return. Unfortunately, some infants are born with a disorder that impairs their ability to return their parents' affection. The symptoms of **autism spectrum disorder (ASD)** (often simply referred to as *autism*) include a failure to develop typical social relations with other people, impaired development of communicative ability, and the presence of repetitive, stereotyped behaviors, fixated interests, or inflexible adherence to routines Most people with ASD display cognitive impairments. The syndrome was named and characterized by Kanner (1943), who chose the term (*auto*, "self," *-ism*, "condition") to refer to the child's apparent self-absorption.

The prevalence of ASD is approximately 1 percent in both the United States and other countries (Brugha et al., 2011). The disorder is four times more common in males than in females. However, if only cases of autism with intellectual disability are considered, the ratio falls to 2:1, and if only cases of high-functioning autism are considered (those with average or above-average intelligence and reasonably good communicative ability), the ratio rises to approximately 7:1 (Fombonne, 2005). These data suggest that the social impairments are much more common in males, but the cognitive and communicative impairments are more evenly shared by males and females. A related diagnosis, *Rett syndrome* is a genetic neurological syndrome seen in girls that accompanies an arrest of normal brain development that occurs during infancy.

At one time, clinicians believed that ASD was more prevalent in families with higher socioeconomic status, but more recent studies have found that the frequency of diagnosis is the same in all socioeconomic classes. The reported incidence of ASD has increased in the past two decades, but evidence indicates that the apparent increase is a result of heightened awareness of the disorder and broadening of the diagnostic criteria.

Studies have failed to find evidence that autism is linked to childhood immunization with vaccines. In fact, the investigator who originally claimed to have obtained evidence for a linkage between immunization and autism was found guilty of dishonesty by the U.K. General Medical Council, and the article that first made this claim was retracted by the journal that published it, *The Lancet* (Dwyer, 2010).

Autism spectrum disorder is four times more common in males than in females.

Symptoms

LO 17.17 List the symptoms of ASD.

According to the DSM-5, a diagnosis of autism spectrum disorder requires the presence of two broad categories of symptoms: "persistent impairment in reciprocal social communication and social interaction", as well as "restricted, repetitive patterns of behavior, interests, or activities. These symptoms are present from early childhood and limit or impair everyday functioning" (American Psychiatric Association, 2013, p. 67). Social impairments are the first symptoms to emerge. Infants with ASD may appear ambivalent to being held, or they may arch their backs when picked up, as if they do not want to be held. They do not look or smile at their caregivers. If they are ill, hurt, or tired, they will not look to someone else for comfort. As they get older, they do not enter into social relationships with other children and will avoid eye contact with people. In severe cases, individuals with ASD may not seem to recognize the existence of other people.

The language development of people with autism spectrum disorder may be abnormal, delayed, or nonexistent. People with ASD often echo what is said to them, and they may refer to themselves as others do—in the second or third person. For example, they may say, "You want some milk?" to mean "I want some milk." They may learn words and phrases by rote, but they fail to use them productively and creatively. Those who do acquire reasonably good language skills may talk about their own preoccupations without understanding other people's interests. People with ASD may interpret other people's speech literally. For example, when a person with ASD is asked, "Can you pass the salt?," the response might simply be "Yes"—and not because they are trying to be funny or sarcastic.

People with autism spectrum disorder may show unusual interests and behaviors. For example, they may show stereotyped movements, such as flapping their hand back and forth or rocking back and forth. They may become obsessed with investigating objects, sniffing them, feeling their texture, or moving them back and forth. They may become attached to a particular object and insist on carrying it around with them. They may become preoccupied in lining up objects or in forming patterns with them, oblivious to everything else that is going on around them. Individuals with ASD often insist on following precise routines and may become upset when they are hindered from doing so. They show no make-believe play and are not interested in stories that involve fantasy. Although many people with ASD have impaired cognitive abilities, not everyone with this diagnosis does. Some individuals with ASD may be physically adept and graceful. Some have exceptional but isolated skills, such as the ability to multiply two four-digit numbers very quickly, without apparent effort. (See Table 17.4.)

Table 17.4 Symptoms of Autism Spectrum Disorder

Autism Spectrum Disorder
Deficits in communication and social interaction across many situations
Limited or repetitive behaviors, interests, or activities
Symptoms are present in childhood

Source: Based on American Psychiatric Association, 2013.

Heritability

LO 17.18 Describe the roles of genetic and environmental factors in the development of ASD.

Evidence indicates that autism spectrum disorder is strongly heritable. The best evidence for genetic factors comes from twin studies. These studies indicate that the concordance rate for ASD in monozygotic twins is approximately 70–90 percent, while the rate in dizygotic twins studied so far is approximately 5–10 percent (Sebat et al., 2007). A study by Ozonoff et al. (2011) found that an infant with an older sibling with ASD has an 18.7 percent likelihood of developing the disorder. Having multiple older siblings with ASD increased the risk to 32.2 percent. Genetic studies indicate that ASD can be caused by a wide variety of rare mutations, especially those that interfere with neural development and communication (Betancur et al., 2009).

The fact that autism spectrum disorder is highly heritable is presumptive evidence that the disorder is a result of structural or biochemical abnormalities in the brain. In addition, a variety of medical disorders—especially those that occur during prenatal development—can produce the symptoms of autism. Evidence suggests that approximately 10 percent of all cases of ASD have definable biological causes, such as rubella (German measles) during pregnancy, prenatal thalidomide, encephalitis caused by the herpes virus, and tuberous sclerosis, a genetic disorder that causes the formation of benign tumors in many organs, including the brain (DeLong, 1999; Fombonne, 2005; Rapin, 1999). Ploeger et al. (2010) suggest that interference with a particular stage of prenatal development can cause ASD. Early organogenesis is a stage of embryonic development that occurs during days 20–40 after fertilization. During this stage, major organs are beginning to develop, and factors that interfere with typical development can cause many abnormalities, including limb deformities, malformations of the skull and face, and brain pathologies. In the 1960s, many pregnant women took thalidomide, a drug that suppressed the symptoms of morning sickness. Unfortunately, it was discovered later that this drug caused severe birth defects—including autism spectrum disorder. Because most women knew when they had taken thalidomide, the time of drug exposure could be correlated with the development of autism in the women's children. It turned out that the sensitive period, during which exposure to thalidomide was most likely to cause the development of autism, was 20 to 36 days postfertilization, which coincides with the stage of early organogenesis. Presumably, drug-induced interference with typical brain development at this time set the stage for later development of ASD.

Brain Changes

LO 17.19 Describe changes in the brain associated with ASD.

Evidence indicates significant changes in the development of the brains of children with autism spectrum disorder. Courchesne et al. (2005, 2007) note that in ASD, although the brain is, on average, slightly smaller at birth, it begins to grow unusually quickly, and by two to three years of age it is about 10 percent larger than the brain of an age-matched, typically-developing child. Following this early spurt, grown in the brain of a person with ASD slows down, so by adolescence it is only about 1–2 percent larger than normal.

Not all parts of the brain show the same pattern of growth in autism spectrum disorder. The regions that appear to be most involved in the functions that are impaired in autism show the greatest growth early in life and the slowest growth between early childhood and adolescence. For example, the frontal cortex and temporal cortex grow quickly during the first two years of life but then show little or no increase in size during the next four years in ASD, whereas these two regions grow by 20 percent and 17 percent, respectively, in typically-developing brains. However, the growth pattern of some regions of the cerebral cortex, such as the striate cortex and extrastriate cortex, are relatively typical in the brains of individuals with ASD. The amygdala also shows an unusual pattern of growth during development. By four years of age it is larger in children with ASD. By the time of early adulthood it is the same size as the amygdala of typically-developing people but contains fewer neurons (Schumann and Amaral, 2006).

The brains of people with autism also show changes in white matter. In a study of the brains of people with autism, Herbert et al. (2004) found that the volume of white matter containing short-range axons was increased but that the volume of white matter containing long-range axons that connect distant regions of the brain was not. Courchesne et al. (2005, 2007) suggest that the production of excessive numbers of neurons early in development may cause the development of such a large number of short-range axons that the development of long-range axons is inhibited. The apparent hyperconnectivity of local regions of the cerebral cortex might possibly account for the exceptional isolated talents and skills shown by some people with ASD.

Frith et al., (1991) suggest that some of the social impairments of autism spectrum disorder stem from changes in the brain that prevent people from forming a "theory of mind." That is, they are unable "to predict and explain the behavior of other humans in terms of their mental states" (p. 448). They cannot infer the thoughts, feelings, and intentions of other people from their emotional expressions, tone of voice, and behavior.

Researchers have employed structural- and functional-imaging methods to investigate the neural basis of the three categories of symptoms in autism spectrum disorder. For example, Castelli et al. (2002) showed typically-developing volunteers and high-functioning people with ASD animations that depicted two triangles interacting in various goal-directed ways (for example, chasing or fighting) or in a way that suggested that one triangle was trying to trick or coax the other. For example, one typically-developing volunteer described an animation in this way: "Triangles cuddling inside the house. Big wanted to persuade little to get out. He didn't want to . . . cuddling again" (p. 1843). People with ASD were able to accurately describe the goal-directed interactions of the triangles, but they had difficulty accurately describing the "intentions" of a triangle trying to trick or coax the other. In other words, they had difficulty forming a theory of mind. Functional imaging during presentation of the animations showed normal activation of early levels of the visual association cortex (the extrastriate cortex), but activation of the superior temporal sulcus (STS) and the medial prefrontal cortex was much lower among people with autism. (See Figure 17.23.) Previous research has shown that the STS plays an important role in detection of stimuli that indicate the actions of another individual (Allison et al., 2000).

The lack of interest in or understanding of other people by people with autism spectrum disorder is reflected in the response to the sight of the human face. As we saw in Chapter 6, the fusiform face area (FFA), in the extrastriate cortex, is involved in the recognition of individual faces. A functional-imaging study by Schultz (2005) found little or no activity in the FFA of adults with autism spectrum disorder looking at pictures of human faces. (See Figure 17.24.) People with ASD have difficulty recognizing facial expressions of emotion or the direction of another person's gaze and have low rates of eye contact with other people. In autism, it seems likely that the FFA fails to respond to the sight of the human face because very little time may be spent studying other people's faces and hence expertise in interpersonal interactions does not develop. Grelotti et al. (2005) reported the case of a boy with ASD who had an extreme interest in Digimon cartoon characters. Functional imaging showed no activation of the FFA when the boy viewed photos of faces, but photos of Digimon characters evoked strong activation of this region. This case supports the conclusion that the failure of the sight of faces to activate the FFA in people with autism is caused by of lack of interest in or experience with faces, not by abnormalities in the FFA.

Figure 17.23 Theory of Mind

The graph shows relative activation of specific brain regions of adults with autism and control participants viewing a "theory of mind" animation of two triangles moving interactively with implied intentions. STS = superior temporal sulcus.

(Based on data from Castelli et al., 2002.)

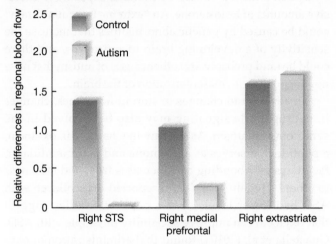

Regions with Significant Increase in Cerebral Blood Flow

A study by Pelphrey et al. (2002) found that people with autism spectrum disorder who were asked to identify the emotions shown in photographs of faces failed to look at other people's eyes, which are informative in making judgments of emotion. This tendency likely contributes to impairment in analyzing social information. The abnormal development of the amygdala in people with autism may be at least partly responsible for the low rates of eye contact with other people and difficulty in assessing other people's emotional state.

Many investigators have noted that the presence of repetitive, stereotyped behavior and obsessive preoccupations with particular subjects in autism spectrum disorder resemble the symptoms of obsessive-compulsive disorder. As we saw earlier in this chapter, the symptoms of OCD appear to be related to increased activity of the caudate nucleus. Research suggests that the same may be true for the behavioral symptoms of autism. Several studies have observed increased volume of the caudate nucleus in autism (Langen et al., 2007; Sears et al., 1999). In fact, Hollander et al., (2005) found that the volume of the right caudate nucleus was positively correlated with ratings of repetitive behavior in patients with ASD. (See Figure 17.25.)

Chapters 8 and 11 described the role of a circuit of *mirror neurons* in the perception of emotions and behavioral intentions. This circuit is activated when we see another person produce an expression of emotion or perform a goal-directed action, and feedback from this activity helps us to understand what the person feels or is trying to accomplish. In other words, the mirror neuron system may be involved in our ability to understand what people are trying to do and to empathize with their emotions.

Iacoboni and Dapretto (2006) suggest that the social deficits seen in autism may be a result of abnormal development of the mirror neuron system. In fact, a functional-imaging study by Dapretto et al. (2006) observed deficient activation in the mirror motor neuron system of children with ASD, and a structural MRI study by Hadjikhani et al. (2006) found that the cerebral cortex in the mirror neuron system was thinner in people with ASD. A study by Senju et al. (2007) even found that children with autism failed to yawn when they saw a video of other people yawning. Typically-developing volunteers showed an increased rate of yawning during or immediately after seeing videos that depicted yawning but not those that depicted other kinds of mouth movements. Presumably, the mirror neuron system is involved in this type of imitation.

Figure 17.24 Fusiform Face Area and Autism

Scans show activation of the fusiform face area in typically-developing peers, but not in people with autism while looking at pictures of human faces.

(Based on Schultz, R. T. International Journal of Developmental *Neuroscience*, 2005, *23*, 125–141.)

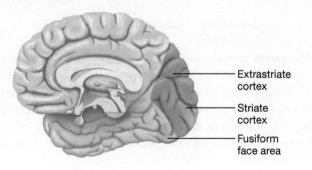

Extrastriate cortex

Striate cortex

Fusiform face area

Figure 17.25 Caudate Nucleus and Stereotyped Behavior in Autism

The graph shows repetitive behavior scores of people with autism spectrum disorder as a function of the volume of the right caudate nucleus. Larger volumes are associated with higher scores.

(Adapted from Hollander et al., 2005.)

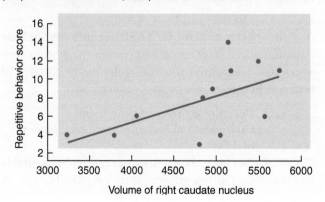

Baron-Cohen (2002) noted that the behavioral characteristics of people with autism spectrum disorder appear to be exaggerations of the traits that tend to be associated with males. As we saw, the incidence of ASD is four times more prevalent in males. Baron-Cohen hypothesized that these disorders may be a reflection of an "extreme male brain." For example, he noted that on average, females are better than males at inferring the thoughts or intentions of others, are more sensitive to facial expressions, are more likely to respond empathetically to the distress of others, and are more likely to share with others and take turns with them. On average, males are less likely to display these characteristics, and they are more likely to compete with their peers, to engage in rough-and-tumble play, and to establish dominance hierarchies. Males also tend to show more interest in toy vehicles, weapons, and building blocks and in pursuits such as engineering, metal-working, and computer programming and are generally better at map reading. In other words, males generally exhibit more interest in working with physical objects and logical systems than with social relations. According to Baron-Cohen, people with ASD show an exaggerated pattern of masculine interests and behaviors. For example, the lack of interest in other people and an obsession with counting and lining-up objects in a row that is seen in many people with autism are seen as extreme examples of masculine traits.

We saw in Chapter 10 that sexual differentiation of the brain is largely controlled by exposure to prenatal androgens. Auyeung et al. (2009) used two tests that measure symptoms of autism spectrum disorder to assess the behavior of typically-developing children whose mothers had undergone amniocentesis (removal of a small amount of amniotic fluid during pregnancy). Auyeung et al. found a significant positive correlation in both males and females between fetal testosterone levels and scores on these tests.

In addition, Knickmeyer et al. (2006) found that females with congenital adrenal hyperplasia, who were exposed to abnormally high levels of androgens during fetal development, had a greater number of traits associated with autism. Even if Baron-Cohen's hypothesis is correct, we cannot conclude that autism is caused by prenatal exposure to excessive amounts of testosterone. An "extreme masculine brain" could be caused by genetic abnormalities that increase the sensitivity of a developing brain to androgens, and there could be (and probably are) other causes of autism that have nothing to do with masculinization of the brain.

In addition to changes in steroid hormones, changes in neuropeptide signaling may also be involved in the symptoms of autism. As we saw in Chapter 10, oxytocin, a peptide that serves as a hormone and neuromodulator, facilitates pair bonding and increases trust and closeness to others. Modahl et al. (1998) reported that children with ASD had lower levels of this peptide. Studies suggest that oxytocin can improve sociability of people with ASD. Guastella et al. (2010a) found that administration of oxytocin increased the performance of adolescent males with ASD on a test of emotional recognition. Andari et al. (2010) found that oxytocin improved the performance of adults with ASD on a computerized ball-toss game that required social interactions with fictitious partners. Other researchers have suggested that changes in the genetic code for the oxytocin receptor may underlie social deficits in ASD (Campbell et al., 2011).

New treatment approaches to autism have begun to focus on brain-based changes. Several research groups are pursuing development of oxytocin-based interventions (Gordon et al., 2013; Preti et al., 2014) or deep brain stimulation of the prefrontal cortex (Enticott et al., 2014) as new avenues of treatment for autism.

Section Review

Autism Spectrum Disorder

LO 17.17 List the symptoms of ASD.
Autism spectrum disorder (ASD) symptoms include impaired social interaction and communication as well as restricted, repetitive interests, activities or patterns of behavior. Symptoms are present early in life.

LO 17.18 Describe the roles of genetic and environmental factors in the development of ASD.
Genetic studies have shown that autism is highly heritable but that many different genes are responsible for its development. ASD can also be caused by events that interfere with prenatal development, such as prenatal thalidomide exposure or maternal infection with rubella.

LO 17.19 Describe changes in the brain associated with ASD.
MRI studies indicate that the brains of babies who are later diagnosed with ASD show abnormally rapid growth until two to three years of age and then grow more slowly than the brains of unaffected children. The amygdala follows a similar pattern of development. Regions of the brain involved in higher-order processes such as communicative

functions and interpretation of social stimuli develop more quickly in people with ASD but then fail to continue to develop normally. People with ASD tend not to pay attention to other people's faces, as reflected in the lack of activation of the fusiform face area when they do so, and their ability to perceive emotional expressions on other people's faces is impaired. The volume and connectivity of white matter in the brain is changed in ASD. Activation of the STS and prefrontal cortex in tasks requiring theory of mind is different in ASD. Reduced activation of the mirror neuron system may be involved in ASD. Increased activity in the caudate nucleus may be involved in some of the behavioral symptoms of ASD. Reduced levels of the neuropeptide oxytocin or changes in the oxytocin receptor may also be involved in social symptoms of ASD.

Thought Question

Have you heard about research suggesting that childhood immunizations are associated with the development of autism? Have you heard (before reading this chapter) that the publication that reported this research and its principal author were discredited? Why do you think that many parents are still fearful about having their children immunized?

Attention-Deficit/ Hyperactivity Disorder

Some children have difficulty concentrating, remaining still, and working on a task. At one time or another, most children exhibit these characteristics. But children with **attention-deficit/hyperactivity disorder (ADHD)** display these symptoms so often that they interfere with the children's ability to learn. Symptoms of ADHD can affect individuals in both childhood and adulthood.

Symptoms

LO 17.20 **List the symptoms of ADHD.**

ADHD is the most common behavior disorder that shows itself in childhood. It is usually first discovered in the classroom, where children are expected to sit quietly and pay attention to the teacher or work steadily on a project. Some children's inability to meet these expectations then becomes evident. They have difficulty withholding a response, act without reflecting, often show reckless and impetuous behavior, and let interfering activities intrude into ongoing tasks.

According to the DSM-5, the diagnosis of ADHD requires the presence of six or more of nine symptoms of inattention and/or six or more of nine symptoms of hyperactivity and impulsivity that have persisted for at least six months. Symptoms of inattention include such things as "often had difficulty sustaining attention in tasks or play activities" or "is often easily distracted by extraneous stimuli," and symptoms of hyperactivity and impulsivity include such things as "often runs about or climbs excessively in situations in which it is inappropriate" or "often interrupts or intrudes on others (e.g., butts into conversations or games)" (American Psychiatric Association, 2013, pp. 73–74).

ADHD can be very disruptive of a child's education and that of other children in the same classroom. The prevalence of ADHD is approximately 5 percent of children in most cultures (American Psychiatric Association, 2013). Boys are about 10 times more likely than girls to receive a diagnosis of ADHD, but in adulthood the ratio is approximately 2 to 1, which suggests that many girls with this disorder fail to be diagnosed. Because the symptoms can vary—some children's symptoms are primarily those of inattention, some are those of hyperactivity, and some show mixed symptoms—most investigators believe that this disorder has more than one cause. Diagnosis is often difficult because the symptoms are not well defined. ADHD is often associated with aggression, conduct disorder, learning disabilities, depression, anxiety, and low self-esteem. Approximately 60 percent of children with ADHD continue to display symptoms of this disorder into adulthood, at which time a disproportionate number develop antisocial personality disorder and may be diagnosed with a substance abuse disorder (Ernst et al., 1998). Adults with ADHD are also more likely to show cognitive impairments and lower occupational attainment than would be predicted by their education (Seidman et al., 1998).

Suzanne Tucker/Shutterstock

Children with ADHD have difficulty withholding a response, act without reflecting, and often show reckless and impetuous behavior.

Table 17.5 Symptoms of Attention-Deficit/Hyperactivity Disorder

A persistent pattern of inattention and/or hyperactivity-impulsivity that interferes with functioning or development

Inattention: Decreased attention to details; makes careless mistakes or fails to follow directions or complete activities; has difficulty in organization; avoids activities that require sustained attention; easily distracted, forgetful; often loses things

Hyperactivity and impulsivity: Fidgets or squirms, leaves seat when sitting is expected, runs or climbs when inappropriate, talks excessively, interrupts or responds before question is finished, has difficulty waiting

Symptoms are present in childhood

Source: Based on American Psychiatric Association, 2013.

According to Sagvolden and his colleagues (Sagvolden and Sergeant, 1998; Sagvolden et al., 2005), the impulsive and hyperactive behaviors that are seen in children with ADHD are the result of a *delay of reinforcement gradient* that is steeper than normal. As we saw in Chapter 13, the occurrence of an appetitive stimulus can reinforce the behavior that just preceded it. For example, a piece of food can reinforce the lever press that a rat just made, and a smile can reinforce a person's attempts at conversation. Reinforcing stimuli are most effective if they immediately follow a behavior: The longer the delay, the less effective the reinforcement. Sagvolden and Sergeant suggest that deficiencies in dopaminergic transmission in the brains of people with ADHD increase the steepness of their delay of reinforcement gradient, which means that immediate reinforcement is even more effective in these children, but even slightly delayed reinforcement loses its potency. (See Figure 17.26.)

Figure 17.26 Hypothetical Delay of Reinforcement Gradient in ADHD

The graph illustrates different delay of reinforcement gradients as a function of time. Sagvolden and Sergeant (1998) hypothesize that a steeper gradient is responsible for the impulsive behavior of children with ADHD.

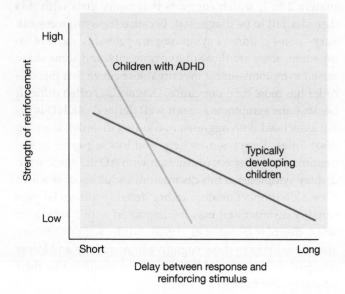

Why would a steeper delay of reinforcement gradient produce the symptoms of ADHD? According to Sagvolden and his colleagues, for people with a steep gradient, reinforcement with a short delay will be even more effective, thus producing overactivity. On the other hand, these people will be less likely to engage in behaviors that are followed by delayed reinforcement, as many of our behaviors (especially classroom activities) are. In support of this hypothesis, Sagvolden et al. (1998) trained typically-developing boys and boys with ADHD on an operant conditioning task. When a signal was present, responses would be reinforced every 30 seconds with coins or small prizes. When the signal was not present, responses were never reinforced. The typically-developing boys learned to respond only when the signal was present. When the signal was off, they waited patiently until it came on again. In contrast, the boys with ADHD showed impulsive behavior—intermittent bursts of rapid responses whether the signal was present or not. According to the investigators, this pattern of responding was what would be expected by a steep delay of reinforcement gradient.

Heritability

LO 17.21 Describe the roles of genetic and environmental factors in the development of ADHD.

There is strong evidence from both family studies and twin studies that hereditary factors play an important role in determining a person's likelihood of developing ADHD. The estimated heritability of ADHD is high, ranging from 75 percent to 91 percent (Thapar et al., 2005).

Good evidence that the levels of dopamine in the human prefrontal cortex have effects on behavior comes from studies of people with two different variants of the gene for an enzyme that affects dopamine levels in the brain. COMT (catechol-O-methyltransferase) is an enzyme that breaks down catecholamines (including dopamine and norepinephrine) in the extracellular fluid. Although reuptake is the primary means of removing catecholamines from the synapse, COMT also plays a role in deactivating these neurotransmitters after they are released. Mattay et al. (2003) noted that the clinical effects of amphetamine (which are similar to those of methylphenidate) are variable. In some people, amphetamine increases positive mood and facilitates performance on cognitive tasks, but in other people it has the opposite effect. Mattay et al. tested the effect of amphetamine on tasks that made demands on working memory in people with two different variants of the COMT gene. They found that people with the *val-val* variant, who have lower brain levels of catecholamines, performed better when they were given low doses of amphetamine. In contrast, administration of amphetamine to people with the *met-met* variant, who have higher brain levels of catecholamines, actually impaired their performance. Presumably, the first group was pushed up the U-shaped curve, and the second group, already around the top of the curve, was pushed down the other side. (See Figures 17.27 and 17.28.)

Brain Changes

LO 17.22 **Describe changes in the brain associated with ADHD.**

We saw in the previous section that the brains of children with autism develop differently from those of typically-developing children. Castellanos et al. (2002) have reported decreased total brain volume among children with ADHD compared to typically-developing peers. A study by Shaw et al., (2007) found differences in the development of the brains of children with ADHD as well. The investigators found that cortical growth was delayed in children with ADHD. In fact, the cortical thickness of the brains of children with ADHD at age 10.5 years was about the same as

that of the brains of unaffected children at 7.5 years. Ultimately, the growth of the brains of the children with ADHD caught up with those of unaffected children.

The symptoms of ADHD resemble those produced by damage to the prefrontal cortex: distractibility, forgetfulness, impulsivity, poor planning, and hyperactivity (Aron et al., 2004). As we saw in Chapter 13, the prefrontal cortex plays a critical role in short-term memory. We use short-term memory to remember what we have just perceived, to remember information that we have just recalled from long-term memory, and to process ("work on") all of this information. For this reason, short-term memory is often referred to as *working memory*. The prefrontal cortex uses working memory to guide thoughts and behavior, regulate attention, monitor the effects of our actions, and organize plans for future actions (Arnsten, 2009). Damage or abnormalities in the neural circuits that perform these functions give rise to the symptoms of ADHD.

The most common treatment for ADHD is administration of methylphenidate (Ritalin), a drug that inhibits the reuptake of dopamine. Amphetamine, another dopamine agonist, also reduces the symptoms of ADHD, but this drug is used much less often. As we saw in Chapter 16, the fact that dopamine antagonists were discovered to reduce the positive symptoms of schizophrenia suggested the hypothesis that schizophrenia is caused by overactivity of dopaminergic transmission. Similarly, the fact that methylphenidate, a dopamine *agonist,* alleviates the symptoms of ADHD has suggested the hypothesis that this disorder is caused by *underactivity* of dopaminergic transmission. As we saw in Chapter 13, normal functioning of the prefrontal cortex is impaired by low levels of dopamine receptor stimulation in this region, so the suggestion that

Figure 17.27 Interactions Between Amphetamine and COMT Alleles in Working Memory

The graph shows the differential effects of amphetamine on the performance on a working-memory task of people with two different variants of the gene for the COMT enzyme. The performance of people with the val-val variant was enhanced by amphetamine, and the performance of people with the met-met variant was reduced.

(Based on data from Mattay et al., 2003.)

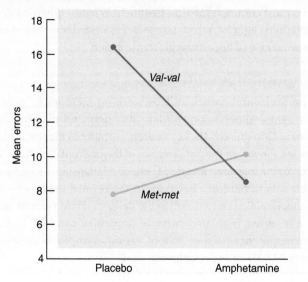

Figure 17.28 An Inverted U Curve

The graph illustrates an inverted U-curve function, in which low and high values of the variable on the horizontal axis are associated with low values of the variable on the vertical axis and moderate values are associated with high values. Presumably, the relationship between brain dopamine levels and the symptoms of ADHD follow a function like this one.

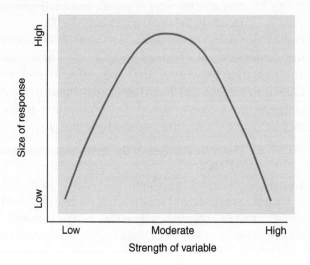

abnormalities in dopaminergic transmission play a role in ADHD seems reasonable.

Berridge et al. (2006) administered methylphenidate to rats and established a moderate dose that improved their performance on tasks that required attention and working memory—tasks that involve the participation of the prefrontal cortex. They used microdialysis to measure the release of dopamine and norepinephrine and found that the drug increased the levels of both of these neurotransmitters in the prefrontal cortex but not in other brain regions. A follow-up study by Devilbiss and Berridge (2008) found that a moderate dose of methylphenidate increased the responsiveness of neurons in the prefrontal cortex. A high dose of methylphenidate profoundly *suppressed* neural activity.

Many studies have shown that the effect of dopamine levels in the prefrontal cortex on the functions of this region follow an inverted U-shaped curve. (See Figure 17.28.) Graphs of many behavioral functions have an inverted U shape. For example, moderate levels of motivation increase performance on most tasks, but very low levels fail to induce a person to perform, and very high levels tend to make people nervous and interfere with their performance. The dose-response curve for the effects of methylphenidate also follow an inverted U-shaped function, which is why Berridge et al. tested different doses of the drug to find a dose that optimized the animals' performance. Clinicians have found the same to be true for the treatment of ADHD: Doses that are too low are ineffective, and doses that are too high produce increases in activity level that disrupt children's attention and cognition.

We mentioned that Berridge et al. (2006) found that methylphenidate increased the level of both dopamine and norepinephrine in the prefrontal cortex. It appears that both of these effects improve the symptoms of ADHD. Drugs that block α_2 receptors (one of the families of receptors that respond to norepinephrine) impair performance of monkeys on working-memory tasks and produce the symptoms of ADHD. Conversely, drugs that stimulate these receptors improve performance (Arnsten and Li, 2005). Evidence suggests that optimal levels of both dopamine and norepinephrine in the prefrontal cortex facilitate the functions of this region, and the effects of methylphenidate on both of these neurotransmitters is responsible for the drug's therapeutic effects.

Most investigators believe that ADHD is caused by abnormalities in a network of brain regions that involves the striatum (caudate nucleus and putamen) as well as the prefrontal cortex, which has reciprocal connections with the striatum. Functional-imaging studies lend support to this hypothesis. Studies have reported decreased activation of the caudate nucleus (Durston et al., 2003; Rubia et al., 1999; Vaidya et al., 2005) or medial prefrontal cortex (Rubia et al., 1999; Tamm et al., 2004) while participants with ADHD were performing tasks that required careful attention and the ability to inhibit a response. Given the importance of dopaminergic innervation of both regions, this provides additional support to the idea that abnormalities in dopaminergic transmission may be responsible for the alterations in brain functions observed in ADHD.

Section Review

Attention-Deficit/Hyperactivity Disorder

LO 17.20 List the symptoms of ADHD.
Children with ADHD show symptoms of inattention, hyperactivity, and impulsivity.

LO 17.21 Describe the roles of genetic and environmental factors in the development of ADHD.
Family and twin studies indicate a heritable component in this disorder. Molecular genetic studies have found an association between ADHD and different alleles for COMT, an enzyme that deactivates monoamines. Evidence suggests that a steeper delay of reinforcement gradient may account for impulsiveness and hyperactivity.

LO 17.22 Describe changes in the brain associated with ADHD.
Growth of the brains of children with ADHD follows that of the brains of unaffected children, but the rate of growth is slower. Most investigators believe that ADHD is caused by abnormalities in a network of brain regions that involves the striatum and the prefrontal cortex. Functional-imaging studies have shown hypoactivation of these structures in the brains of people with ADHD while they are performing tasks that require careful attention and the ability to inhibit a response. The most common medical treatment is methylphenidate, a dopamine agonist, which suggests this disorder is caused by *underactivity* of dopaminergic transmission.

Thought Question

The prefrontal cortex utilizes working memory to guide thought and behavior, regulate attention, and plan for the future. Dopamine is the key neurotransmitter in the prefrontal cortex. However, the performance of the prefrontal cortex and dopamine follow an inverted U-shape relationship. Dopamine also acts to reinforce behavior in the reward center of our brain. Explain how a defect in the delay in reinforcement and the inverted U-shaped curve of dopamine can lead to the development of a spectrum of various symptoms ranging from ADHD and schizophrenia.

Chapter Review Questions

1. Describe the physiological responses to stress and their effects on health.

2. Discuss psychoneuroimmunology and the interactions between the immune system and stress.

3. Discuss posttraumatic stress disorder.

4. Describe the symptoms and possible causes of panic disorder.

5. Describe the symptoms and possible causes of obsessive-compulsive disorder.

6. Describe the symptoms and possible causes of autism spectrum disorder.

7. Describe the symptoms and possible causes of attention-deficit/hyperactivity disorder.

Chapter 18
Substance Abuse

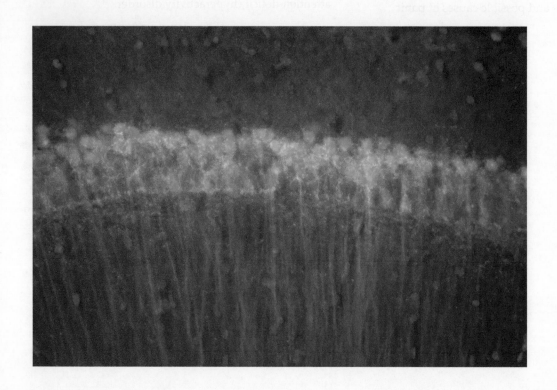

Chapter Outline

Learning Objectives

LO 18.1 Describe the features of positive reinforcement that all drugs of abuse share, including their general neural mechanisms.

LO 18.2 Explain how negative reinforcement can contribute to the development of substance abuse, including physical dependence, craving, and relapse.

LO 18.3 Summarize the evidence for a role of heredity in alcohol abuse.

LO 18.4 Summarize the evidence for a role of heredity in nicotine abuse.

LO 18.5 Summarize the evidence for a role of heredity in stimulant abuse.

LO 18.6 Describe the effects and roles of reinforcement and physical dependence in opiate abuse.

LO 18.7 Describe the effects and role of reinforcement in stimulant abuse.

LO 18.8 Describe the effects and roles of reinforcement and physical dependence in nicotine abuse.

LO 18.9 Describe the effects and roles of reinforcement and physical dependence in alcohol abuse.

LO 18.10 Describe the effects and role of reinforcement in cannabis abuse.

LO 18.11 Summarize the research for effective treatment for opiate abuse.

LO 18.12 Summarize the research for effective treatment for stimulant abuse.

LO 18.13 Summarize the research for effective treatment for nicotine abuse.

LO 18.14 Summarize the research for effective treatment for alcohol abuse.

LO 18.15 Describe the implications for brain stimulation treatments in substance abuse.

After abusing prescription opiates for several years, John was beginning to feel that he might be able to get his life back together. He had started using OxyContin (oxycodone) several years ago. At first, he tried it because he was curious. His father had an OxyContin prescription for back pain, and John and his friends stole a few pills for themselves and to sell to other friends. Taking one or two pills at a time, John felt relaxed and happy.

Initially, he took the pills orally, but after several months, friends at a party showed John how to break down the pills into powder and snort them. With this new way of taking the drug, John could use less of the drug and experience a more intense feeling than before. In the following months, John and his friends began snorting OxyContin more frequently. Stealing a few pills from his father's prescription was no longer an option, and John began buying OxyContin once every few weeks from someone in his neighborhood. John's use escalated, and soon he was buying OxyContin weekly.

Becoming such a frequent user, John began to go into debt to keep up his habit. He began looking for ways to get more pills. He did favors for friends in return for OxyContin and sold his belongings for more pills. He began to spend hours

making elaborate plans to secure a supply of the drug. He visited three doctors complaining of nonexistent back pain, seeking a prescription. One of his acquaintances mentioned to John that instead of snorting two pills, he could inject one capsule's worth of powder and experience the same high. John was nervous about injecting the drug, but his growing craving for the drug eventually motivated him to try it. Someone else told John to try heroin because it was cheaper. He began using heroin instead and substituting other opiate drugs such as Percocet or Vicodin whenever he could find them.

The hours spent trying to secure drugs, avoid being caught when using them, and the many under their influence, all began to add up. John was unable to maintain his commitments at work and to his family and friends. He lost his job and began fighting with his family constantly. One night, after a fight, John injected some heroin, got in his car, and drove away. He drove off the road, hitting a tree. He destroyed his car, sustained moderate injuries, and was arrested for driving under the influence (based on Lankenau et al., 2012). At his court hearing, the judge gave John the choice of jail time or a drug rehabilitation program. He chose the latter.

Soon after starting the program, he realized he was relieved to have been caught and to have an opportunity to stop the cycle of opiate use he had been trapped in. He was surprised that under the supervision of a physician he was prescribed and administered another opiate drug, methadone, as part of his treatment program. Methadone helped reduce his withdrawal symptoms and allowed him to focus on other aspects of his treatment. The counselors in his program told him to avoid his old neighborhood and avoid contact with his old acquaintances. He followed their advice. He had been clean for eight weeks, he had a job, and he began to repair his relationships with his family. He was doing well, but every now and then, despite his best intentions, he found himself thinking about how much his missed using opiates.

Then one day, while coming home from work, he looked up to see a billboard with an antidrug advertisement on it. The poster, produced by an antidrug agency, showed a giant, graphic image of heroin, needles, and pills. John was seized with a sudden, intense compulsion. He closed his eyes, trying to will the feeling away, but all he could think about was the feeling of using opiates.

*****

Substance abuse poses serious problems to our species. Consider the negative outcomes caused by the abuse of one of our oldest drugs, alcohol: vehicle accidents, fetal alcohol syndrome, cirrhosis of the liver, Korsakoff's syndrome, and increased risk of heart disease and stroke. Smoking (addiction to nicotine) increases the risk of lung cancer, heart attack, and stroke, and women who smoke give birth to smaller, less healthy babies. Cocaine abuse can cause psychotic behavior, brain damage, and death from overdose; competition for lucrative and illegal markets disrupts neighborhoods and communities, subverts political and judicial systems, and causes many violent deaths. The use of designer drugs exposes users to unknown dangers of untested and often contaminated products, as several people discovered when they acquired Parkinson's disease after taking a synthetic opiate that was tainted with a neurotoxin. (This unfortunate event was described in the opening case of Chapter 5.) People who use drugs intravenously increase their risk of contracting human immunodeficiency virus (HIV), hepatitis, or other infectious diseases. What makes using these drugs so attractive to so many people?

Part of the answer, as you might have predicted from what you have learned about the physiology of reinforcement in Chapter 13, is that all of these substances stimulate brain mechanisms responsible for positive reinforcement, which is common to drugs in the category *drugs of abuse*. In addition, most drugs in this category reduce or eliminate unpleasant feelings, some of which are produced by the drugs themselves. The immediate effects of these drugs

Table 18.1 Symptoms of Substance Use Disorders

Repeated use of the substance that results in tolerance to its effects
Craving for the substance
Intentions to reduce use of the substance
Large amounts of time are spent seeking or using the substance, or recovering from its effects
Continued use of substance despite significant problems in work, school, family or social interactions related to its use
Continued use even in dangerous situations or when substance worsens physical or psychological symptoms

Source: Based on American Psychiatric Association, 2013.

are more powerful than the knowledge that in the long term, there may be negative consequences. As a category, drugs of abuse include licit (legal, e.g., nicotine, alcohol), illicit (illegal, e.g., heroin), prescription (e.g., oxycodone), nonprescription (e.g., inhalants), naturally derived (present in a plant, animal or fungus e.g., marijuana), and synthetic (made by humans through a chemical process e.g., methamphetamine) substances.

John's case includes many features of substance abuse that will be explored in this chapter. For example, rates of substance abuse in general are higher among men; however, some research suggests that rates of prescription drug abuse may be similar among men and women (Greenfield et al., 2010). Abuse of prescription painkillers increased over 25 percent in the five years between 2005 and 2010. In 2010, oxycodone manufacturers changed the formula of the pills to make it more difficult to crush the pills or dissolve them to be snorted or injected. This change appeared to reduce the number of people abusing the drug (Butler et al., 2013).

John's experience demonstrates many of the diagnostic criteria for a *substance use disorder* (American Psychiatric Association, 2013). (See Table 18.1.) Substance use disorders are characterized by impaired control over the use of the substance (such as taking increasing amounts of the drug); a desire to reduce the amount of the drug used or unsuccessful attempts to cut back; large amounts of time spent obtaining the drug; drug craving; failure to meet educational, occupational, or family obligations; continued use even after experiencing interpersonal problems related to use of the drug; failure to stop using the drug despite problems related to its use; and experiencing tolerance and withdrawal (American Psychiatric Association, 2013).

In this chapter, we will examine common features associated with substance abuse. The chapter concludes with a closer examination of some specific types of drugs that are commonly abused, followed by treatment options. The chapter opening figure displays the ventral tegmental area and nucleus accumbens that play critical roles in substance abuse.

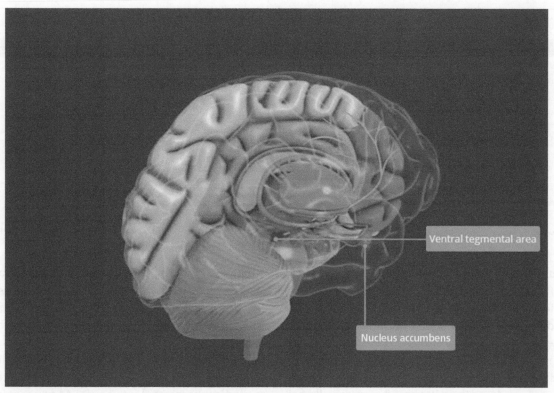

Shown here are regions of the brain that play a role in substance abuse.

Common Features of Substance Abuse

The term *addiction* has fallen out of favor with many researchers and clinicians. Although addiction is sometimes used to refer to severe problems related to compulsive or habitual behaviors ranging from drug use to gambling, many experts disagree on what features define addiction and the term typically has a negative connotation. Instead, many professionals (as well as the American Psychiatric Association—the organization responsible for diagnostic criteria for mental disorders) have adopted the term *substance abuse*. This term has a more neutral connotation and is more consistent with a *medical model*. The criteria described in Table 18.1 correspond to diagnosis with *substance use disorder*. Although the terminology differs somewhat from *substance abuse*, this diagnosis corresponds with the pattern of behaviors we will describe as substance abuse in this chapter.

The medical model emphasizes biological causes (including physiological and genetic factors) that underlie compulsive behaviors, such as substance abuse. This model typically emphasizes biologically-based treatments such as using pharmacological interventions to treat symptoms or change behavior. These treatments may be combined into a biopsychosocial approach as one element among many in a comprehensive treatment plan designed to reduce drug-taking behavior (Center for Substance Abuse Treatment, 1997). In this chapter, we will focus on exploring the biological aspects of substance abuse.

The use of medication to treat pain and human suffering traces back thousands of years. Long ago, people discovered that many substances found in nature—primarily leaves, seeds, and roots of plants but also some animal products—had medicinal qualities. They discovered herbs that helped to prevent infections, that promoted healing, that calmed an upset stomach, that reduced pain, or that helped to provide a night's sleep. They also discovered *recreational drugs*—drugs that produced pleasurable effects when eaten, drunk, or smoked. The most universal recreational drug, and perhaps the first one that our ancestors discovered, is ethyl alcohol. Yeast spores are present everywhere, and these microorganisms can feed on sugar solutions and produce alcohol as a by-product. Undoubtedly, people in many different parts of the world discovered the pleasurable effects of drinking liquids that had been left alone for a while, such as the juice that had accumulated in the bottom of a container of fruit. The juice may have become sour and bad-tasting because of the action of bacteria, but the effects of the alcohol encouraged people to experiment, which led to the development of a wide variety of fermented beverages.

Our ancestors also discovered other recreational drugs. Some of them were consumed only locally; others became so popular that their cultivation as commercial crops spread

Table 18.2 Commonly Abused Drugs

Drug	Neurotransmitter System	Sites of Action
Ethyl alcohol	Glutamate/GABA	NMDA receptor (indirect antagonist), GABA$_A$ receptor (indirect agonist)
Barbiturates/benzodiazepines	GABA	GABA$_A$ receptor (indirect agonist)
Cannabis (marijuana)	Cannabinoid	CB1 cannabinoid receptor (agonist)
Nicotine	Acetylcholine	Nicotinic ACh receptor (agonist)
Opiates (heroin, morphine, prescription analgesics)	Opioid	μ and δ opiate receptor (agonist)
Phencyclidine (PCP) and ketamine	Glutamate	NMDA receptor (indirect antagonist)
Cocaine	Monoamines	Blocks reuptake of dopamine (and serotonin and norepinephrine)
Amphetamine and methamphetamine	Dopamine	Causes release of dopamine (by running dopamine transporters in reverse)

Source: Adapted from Hyman, S. E., and Malenka, R. C., Addiction and the brain: The neurobiology of compulsion and its persistence, *Nature Reviews: Neuroscience*, 2001, 2, 695–703.

throughout the world. For example, people in Asia discovered the effects of the sap of the opium poppy and the beverage made from the leaves of the tea plant, people in India discovered the effects of the smoke of cannabis, people in South America discovered the effects of chewing coca leaves and making a drink from coffee beans, and people in North America discovered the effects of the smoke of the tobacco plant. Many of the drugs they discovered were actually poisons that served to protect the plants from animals (primarily insects) that ate them. Although the drugs were toxic in sufficient quantities, our ancestors learned how to take these drugs in amounts that would not make them ill—at least, not right away. The effects of these drugs on their brains kept them coming back for more. Table 18.2 lists some of the most commonly abused drugs and indicates their sites of action in the central nervous system.

Positive Reinforcement

LO 18.1 **Describe the features of positive reinforcement that all drugs of abuse share, including their general neural mechanisms.**

Drugs that lead to dependency must first reinforce people's behavior. As we saw in Chapter 13, positive reinforcement refers to the effect that certain stimuli have on the behaviors that preceded them. If, in a particular situation, a behavior is regularly followed by an appetitive stimulus (one that the organism will tend to approach), then that behavior will become more frequent in that situation. For example, if a hungry rat accidentally bumps into a lever and receives some food, the rat will eventually learn to press the lever. What actually seems to happen is that the occurrence of an appetitive stimulus activates a reinforcement mechanism in the brain that increases the likelihood of the most recent response (the lever press) in the present situation (the chamber that contains the lever).

Most drugs of abuse have reinforcing effects. (There is one exception—hallucinogens). That is, their effects include activation of the reinforcement mechanism. This activation

strengthens the response that was just made. Particularly, if the drug was taken by a fast-acting route such as injection or inhalation, the last response will be the act of taking the drug, so that response will be reinforced. This form of reinforcement is powerful and immediate and works with a wide variety of species. For example, a rat or a monkey will quickly learn to press a lever that controls a device that injects cocaine through a plastic tube inserted into a vein. As you saw in the case of John at the beginning of the chapter, changing the route of administration can change the abuse potential of a drug. Snorting, smoking, or injecting a drug automatically increases the abuse potential of the drug compared to using a slower route of administration, such as taking a drug orally, because more of the drug enters the brain more rapidly and activates the reinforcement pathway more strongly. (See Figure 18.1.)

ROLE IN SUBSTANCE ABUSE When appetitive stimuli occur, they usually do so because we just did something to

Figure 18.1 Route of Administration and Abuse Potential

The graph shows the concentration of cocaine in blood plasma after intravenous injection, inhalation, oral administration, and sniffing.

(Adapted from Feldman, R. S., Meyer, J. S., and Quenzer, L. F. Principles of Neuropsychopharmacology. Sunderland, MA: Sinauer Associates, 1997; after Jones, R. T. NIDA Research Mono-graphs, 1990, 99, 30–41.)

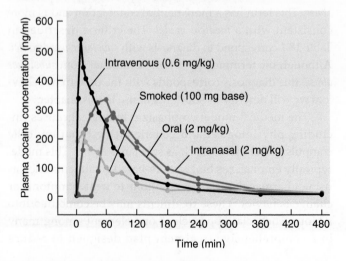

make them happen—and not because an experimenter was controlling the situation. The effectiveness of a reinforcing stimulus is greatest if it occurs immediately after a response. If the reinforcing stimulus is delayed, it becomes considerably less effective. The reason for this fact is found by examining the function of operant conditioning: learning about the consequences of our own behavior. Normally, causes and effects are closely related in time; we engage in one behavior and receive a corresponding consequence, good or bad. The consequences of the actions teach us whether to repeat that action, and events that follow a response by more than a few seconds were probably not caused by that response.

As we saw in Chapter 4, many individuals who use drugs recreationally prefer heroin to morphine not because heroin has a *different* effect, but because it has a more *rapid* effect. In fact, heroin is converted to morphine as soon as it reaches the brain. But because heroin is more lipid soluble, it passes through the blood–brain barrier more rapidly, and its effects on the brain are felt sooner than those of morphine. The most potent reinforcement occurs when drugs produce sudden changes in the activity of the reinforcement mechanism; slow changes are much less reinforcing. A person taking a drug recreationally typically seeks a sudden "rush" produced by a fast-acting drug. (As we will see later, the use of methadone to treat opiate abuse and nicotine patches to treat tobacco abuse are based on this phenomenon.)

Earlier, we posed the question of why people expose themselves to the risks associated with abusing reinforcing drugs. Do people choose to become dependent on a drug that produces pleasurable effects in the short term but also produces powerful aversive effects in the long term: loss of employment and social status, legal problems and possible imprisonment, damage to health, and even premature death? The answer is that, as we saw, our reinforcement mechanism evolved to deal with the *immediate* effects of our behavior. The immediate reinforcing effects of a drug can, for some individuals, overpower the recognition of the long-term aversive effects. Fortunately, most people are able to resist the short-term effects; only a minority of people who try highly-reinforcing drugs go on to abuse them. Although cocaine has one of the highest abuse potentials of all recreational drugs, only about 15 percent of people who use it, escalate their use of the drug to the point of substance abuse (Wagner and Anthony, 2002). As we will see later, particular brain mechanisms are responsible for inhibiting behavior that has unfavorable long-term consequences.

If a drug is taken by a slow-acting route, reinforcement can also occur, but the process is somewhat more complicated. If a person takes a pill and several minutes later experiences a feeling of euphoria, he or she will certainly remember swallowing the pill. The recollection of this behavior will activate some of the same neural circuits involved in actually swallowing the pill, and the reinforcement mechanism, now active because of the effects of the drug, will

reinforce the behavior. Other cognitive processes contribute to the reinforcement, too, such as the expectation that euphoric effects will occur. Perhaps someone said, "Take one of these pills; you'll get a great high!" But if a nonhuman animal is administered one of these pills, its behavior is unlikely to be reinforced. By the time the euphoric effect occurs, the animal will be doing something other than ingesting the drug. Without the ability to associate the effects of the drug with an earlier behavior and thus activate circuits involved in the performance of that behavior, the delay between the behavior and the reinforcing effect of the drug prevents the animal from learning to take the drug.

NEURAL MECHANISMS As we saw in Chapter 13, all natural reinforcers that have been studied so far (such as food for a hungry animal, water for a thirsty one, or sexual contact) have one physiological effect in common: They cause the release of dopamine in the nucleus accumbens (White, 1996). This effect is not the *only* effect of reinforcing stimuli, and even aversive stimuli can trigger the release of dopamine (Salamone, 1992). But although there is much that we do not yet understand about the neural basis of reinforcement, the release of dopamine appears to be a *necessary* (but not *sufficient*) condition for positive reinforcement to take place.

Role of the Mesolimbic Pathway Drugs that are abused—including amphetamine, cocaine, opiates, nicotine, alcohol, PCP, and cannabis—trigger the release of dopamine in the nucleus accumbens (NAC), as measured by microdialysis (Di Chiara, 1995). Different drugs stimulate the release of dopamine in different ways. The details of the ways in which particular drugs interact with the mesolimbic dopaminergic system are described later, in sections devoted to specific categories of drugs. (See Figure 18.2.)

The fact that the reinforcing properties of drugs involve the same brain mechanisms as natural reinforcers indicates that these drugs take advantage of brain mechanisms that normally help us adapt to our environment. It appears that the process of substance abuse begins in the mesolimbic dopaminergic system and then produces long-term changes in other brain regions that receive input from these neurons (Kauer and Malenka, 2007). The first changes appear to take place in the ventral tegmental area (VTA). Saal et al. (2003) found that a single administration of a variety of commonly abused drugs (including cocaine, amphetamine, morphine, alcohol, and nicotine) increased the strength of excitatory synapses on dopaminergic neurons in the VTA in mice. This change appears to result from insertion of additional AMPA receptors into the postsynaptic membrane of the DA neurons (Mameli et al., 2009). As we saw in Chapter 13, this process, normally mediated by glutamatergic NMDA receptors, is the neural basis of many forms of learning. A single injection of a reinforcing drug produces synaptic strengthening in the VTA that lasts for about five days. If an animal receives cocaine for about two weeks, the changes in the VTA persist.

Figure 18.2 Activation of the Mesolimbic Dopamine Pathway Is Necessary for Reinforcement

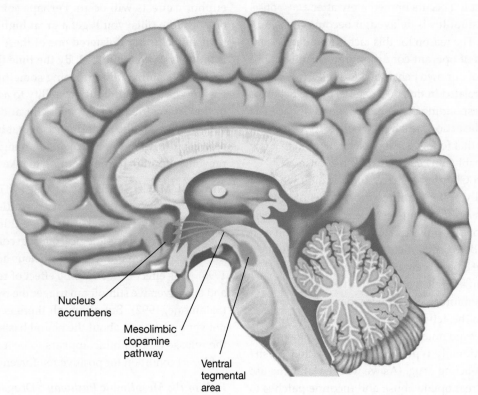

Nucleus accumbens

Mesolimbic dopamine pathway

Ventral tegmental area

Role of the Striatum As a result of the changes in the VTA, increased activation is seen in a variety of regions that receive dopaminergic input from the VTA, including the ventral striatum, which includes the NAC, and the dorsal striatum, which includes the caudate nucleus and putamen. Synaptic changes that are responsible for the compulsive behaviors that characterize substance abuse occur only after continued use of a drug. The most important of these changes appears to occur in the dorsal striatum. We saw in Chapter 13 that the basal ganglia (which include the dorsal striatum) play a critical role in operant conditioning, and substance abuse involves just that.

At first, the person using the drug experiences the pleasurable effects of the drug, reinforcing the behaviors that cause the drug to be delivered to the brain (procuring the drug, taking necessary steps to prepare it, then swallowing, smoking, sniffing, or injecting it). Eventually, these behaviors become habitual, and the impulse to perform them becomes difficult to resist. The early reinforcing effects that take place in the ventral striatum (namely, in the NAC) encourage drug-taking behavior, but the changes that make the behaviors become habitual involve the dorsal striatum. As we saw in Chapter 8, an important role of the dorsal striatum is establishment of automatic behaviors—the type of behaviors that are impaired in people with Parkinson's disease, which is caused by disruption of dopaminergic input to this region.

Studies with monkeys performing a response reinforced by infusion of cocaine over a long period of time show a progression of neural changes, beginning in the ventral striatum (in the NAC) and continuing upward to the dorsal striatum as the behavior becomes more automatic and habitual (Letchworth et al., 2001; Porrino et al., 2004, 2007).

Connections Between Mesolimbic Pathway and Striatum An experiment by Belin and Everitt (2008) suggests that the neural changes responsible for chronic drug use follow a dorsally cascading set of reciprocal connections between the striatum and the ventral tegmental area. Anatomical studies show that neurons in the ventral NAC project to the VTA, which sends dopaminergic projections back to a more dorsal region of the NAC, and so on. This back-and-forth communication continues, connecting increasingly dorsal regions of the striatum, all the way up to the caudate nucleus and putamen. Belin and Everitt found that bilateral infusions of a dopamine antagonist into the dorsal striatum of rats suppressed responding to a light that had been associated with infusions of cocaine, but that unilateral infusions had no effect. They also found that a unilateral lesion of the NAC had no effect on responding. However, they found that a lesion of the NAC on one side of the brain combined with infusion of a dopamine antagonist into the dorsal striatum on the other side of the brain suppressed responding to the

Figure 18.3 Establishment of Neural Changes in the Dorsal Striatum

The graph shows the effects of infusing various amounts of a drug that blocks dopamine receptors into the dorsal striatum contralateral to a lesion of the nucleus accumbens.

(Based on data from Belin and Everitt, 2008.)

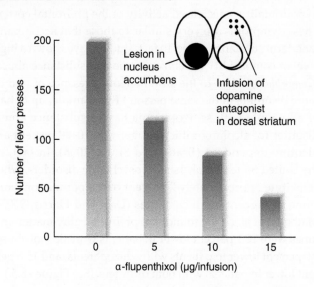

Figure 18.4 Dopamine Release Stimulated by Methylphenidate

The scatter plot shows that increases in the release of dopamine in the putamen (part of the dorsal striatum) are associated with increased craving in people who abuse cocaine.

(Based on data from Volkow et al., 2011.)

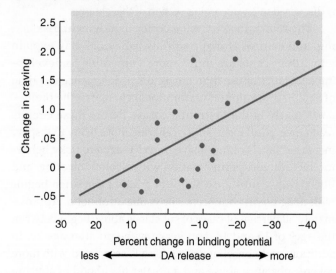

light. (See Figure 18.3.) Further support for the critical role of the dorsal striatum in automatic, habitual or compulsive behaviors was provided by a study with rats that found that infusion of a dopamine antagonist into the dorsal striatum suppressed lever presses that had been reinforced by the illumination of a light that had been paired with intravenous injections of cocaine (Vanderschuren et al., 2005). These results suggest that the control of compulsive drug-taking behavior is established by interactions between the ventral and dorsal striatum that are mediated by dopaminergic connections between these regions and the VTA.

Functional-imaging studies by Volkow and her colleagues (reviewed by Volkow et al., 2011) provide evidence that substance abuse involves the dorsal striatum in humans, as well as in other animals. The investigators found that when people who abuse cocaine are given an injection of methylphenidate (a drug with effects like those of cocaine or amphetamine), they show a much smaller release of dopamine in the NAC or dorsal striatum than do nonusers. However, when this group of people was shown a video of people smoking cocaine, they showed an increased release of dopamine in the dorsal striatum. Thus, the response to the drug itself is diminished in people who abuse the drug, but the response to cues associated with the drug is augmented—in the dorsal striatum. (See Figure 18.4.)

Altogether, the release of dopamine in the NAC leads to acquisition of the drug-taking behavior, but changes in the dorsal striatum are responsible for the establishment of the compulsive drug-taking habit. In addition, in individuals who abuse the drug, dopamine is released in the dorsal striatum not by the drug itself but by stimuli associated with procuring and taking the drug, including places where the drug was taken and people with whom it was taken. So when people first take a drug of abuse, they experience pleasurable effects. If they continue to take the drug, their compulsion to take the drug is not motivated by the pleasurable effects, but by drug-related cues that give rise to the urge to perform drug-seeking behaviors. As Volkow and her colleagues note, individuals who abuse substances are aroused and motivated when they are seeking a drug but are withdrawn and apathetic when they are in a drug-free environment, engaged in activities not related to drug taking.

Dopamine Receptors The alterations that occur in the NAC and later in the dorsal striatum include changes in dopamine receptors on the medium spiny neurons, which are the source of axons that project from both of these regions to other parts of the brain. Increases are seen in dopamine D_1 receptors, which cause excitation and facilitate behavior, and decreases are seen in dopamine D_2 receptors, which cause inhibition and suppress behavior. A study by Witten et al. (2010) found that one of the neural changes in the NAC caused by cocaine intake involves acetylcholinergic interneurons. ACh neurons comprise less than 1 percent of the neurons in the NAC, but these neurons have a powerful effect on the activity of the medium spiny neurons located there. Witten et al. found that cocaine increased the firing of the interneurons, and that inhibiting the firing of these neurons by optogenetic methods blocked the reinforcing effect of cocaine.

Role of the Prefrontal Cortex Most people who try drugs like cocaine or oxycodone do not progress to substance abuse (Volkow and Li, 2005). The likelihood of developing substance abuse is a function of heredity, age (adolescents are most vulnerable), and environmental factors (such as access to drugs and the occurrence of stressful life events). The role of heredity is discussed in an upcoming section of this chapter.

The role of the prefrontal cortex in judgment, risk taking, and control of inappropriate behaviors may explain why adolescents are much more vulnerable to developing substance abuse than are adults. Adolescence is a time of rapid and profound maturational change in the brain—particularly in the prefrontal cortex. Before these circuits reach their adult form, adolescents are more likely to display increased levels of impulsive, novelty-driven, risky behavior, including experimentation with alcohol, nicotine, and illicit drugs. Substance abuse in adults most often begins with drug use in adolescence or young adulthood. Approximately 50 percent of cases of substance abuse begin between the ages of 15 and 18, and very few begin after age 20. In addition, early onset of drug-taking is associated with more severe substance abuse and a greater likelihood of abusing multiple substances (Chambers et al., 2003). In fact, Tarter et al. (2003) found that 10- to 12-year-old boys who scored the lowest on tests of behavioral inhibition had an increased risk of developing substance abuse by age 19. Some regions of the prefrontal cortex have inhibitory connections with the striatum, and increased activity of these regions is correlated with resistance to substance abuse. Presumably, the increased vulnerability of adolescents to substance abuse is related to the relative immaturity of inhibitory mechanisms of their prefrontal cortex. The final development of neural circuits involved in behavioral control and judgment, along with the maturity that comes from increased experience, apparently helps people emerging from adolescence to resist the temptation to abuse drugs.

People with a long history of substance abuse not only show the same deficits on tasks that involve the prefrontal cortex as do people with lesions of this region, they also show structural abnormalities of this region. For example, Franklin et al. (2002) reported an average decrease of 5–11 percent in the gray matter of various regions of the prefrontal cortex of people who abused cocaine Thompson et al. (2004) found decreases in the gray matter volume of the cingulate cortex and limbic cortex of people who abused methamphetamine and Ersche et al. (2011) found similar decreases in the brains of people who abused cocaine. de Ruiter et al. (2011) found evidence of loss of behavioral control caused by decreased activation of the dorsomedial PFC in both heavy smokers and pathological gamblers, which supports the assertion of some investigators that pathological gambling should be regarded as a form of addiction (Thomas et al., 2011). Zhang et al. (2011) found decreased gray matter in the prefrontal cortex that was proportional to the amount of

people's lifetime tobacco use. The results of these studies do not permit us to determine whether abnormalities in the prefrontal cortex predispose people to develop substance abuse or whether drug taking causes these abnormalities (or both).

As we saw in Chapter 16, the negative and cognitive symptoms of schizophrenia appear to be a result of hypofrontality—decreased activity of the prefrontal cortex. These symptoms are very similar to those that accompany long-term substance abuse. In fact, studies have shown a high level of comorbidity of schizophrenia and substance abuse. (*Comorbidity* refers to the simultaneous presence of two or more disorders in the same person.) For example, up to half of all people with schizophrenia have a substance abuse disorder (of alcohol or illicit drugs), and 70–90 percent are nicotine dependent (Brady and Sinha, 2005). In fact, in the United States, smokers with psychiatric disorders, who constitute approximately 7 percent of the population, consume 34 percent of all cigarettes (Dani and Harris, 2005). Mathalon et al. (2003) found that prefrontal gray matter volumes were 10.1 percent lower in patients with alcohol abuse, 9.0 percent lower in patients with schizophrenia, and 15.6 percent lower in patients with both disorders. (See Figure 18.5.)

Weiser et al. (2004) administered a smoking questionnaire to a random sample of adolescent military recruits each year. Over a 4- to 16-year follow-up period, they found that, compared with nonsmokers, the prevalence of hospitalization for schizophrenia was 2.3 times higher in recruits

Figure 18.5 Alcoholism, Schizophrenia, and Prefrontal Gray Matter

The graph shows the volume of gray matter in the prefrontal cortex of healthy controls, patients who abuse alcohol, patients with schizophrenia, and patients comorbid for both disorders.

(Based on data from Mathalon et al., 2003.)

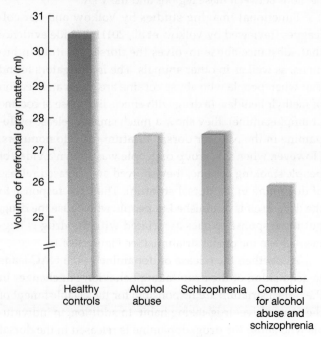

Figure 18.6 Smoking and Schizophrenia

The graph shows the prevalence of schizophrenia during a 4- to 16-year follow-up period as a function of number of cigarettes smoked each day at age 18.

(Based on data from Weiser et al., 2004.)

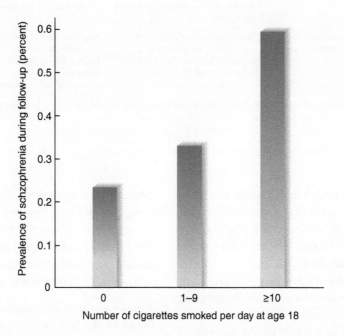

Number of cigarettes smoked per day at age 18

who smoked at least 10 cigarettes per day. (See Figure 18.6.) These results suggest that abnormalities in the prefrontal cortex may be a common factor in schizophrenia and substance abuse disorders. Again, research has not yet determined whether preexisting abnormalities increase the risk of these disorders or whether the disorders cause the abnormalities.

Neuropeptides   Two peptides, *orexin* and *MCH*, play a crucial role in the reinforcing effects of drugs. As we saw in Chapters 9 and 12, orexin (also called *hypocretin*) plays an important role in control of sleep stages and food-seeking behavior. Orexin is synthesized in neurons in the lateral hypothalamus and released in many parts of the brain, including those that play a role in reinforcement, such as the VTA, NAC, and dorsal striatum. Administration of reinforcing drugs or presentation of stimuli associated with them activate orexinergic neurons, and infusion of orexin into the VTA reinstates drug seeking that was previously extinguished. (Relapse—resumption of drug-seeking—is discussed later in this chapter.) In addition, infusing a drug that blocks orexin receptors into the VTA also blocks cocaine seeking elicited by drug-related cues and prevents the learning of a *conditioned place preference*—preference for a place where a reinforcing drug was previously administered (Aston-Jones et al., 2009; Kenney, 2011; Scharf et al., 2010).

The second peptide, MCH (*melanin-concentrating hormone*), is also synthesized in the lateral hypothalamus, and as we saw in Chapter 12, stimulates hunger and reduces

metabolic rate. MCH receptors are found in several places in the brain, including the NAC, where they are found on neurons that also contain DA receptors. Chung et al. (2009) found that stimulating both DA receptors and MCH receptors increased firing of NAC neurons, and that administering a drug that blocks MCH receptors decreased the effectiveness of cocaine or cocaine-related cues to alter the animals' behavior. A targeted mutation against the MCH receptor gene had the same effect. Cippitelli et al. (2010) found that MCH played a similar role in alcohol intake.

Negative Reinforcement

LO 18.2   **Explain how negative reinforcement can contribute to the development of substance abuse, including physical dependence, craving, and relapse.**

Have you ever had a headache, muscle ache, or other injury or illness that caused you pain or made you uncomfortable? How did you change your behavior to reduce the pain or discomfort? Maybe you took a pain reliever for your headache or illness, or got a massage for your sore muscle. If whatever you did worked to alleviate the pain, your decision to do so would certainly be reinforced.

A behavior that turns off (or reduces) an aversive stimulus will be reinforced. This phenomenon is known as **negative reinforcement.** For example, consider the following scenario: A man driving a car hears an annoying noise coming from the dash. He looks everywhere for the source of the

Table 18.3 Positive and Negative Reinforcement and Punishment

	To *Increase* the Behavior	To *Decrease* the Behavior
Add something to the environment	**Positive reinforcement:** Smoking (inhaling nicotine) makes you feel more alert. You will smoke more in the future.	**Positive punishment:** Smoking makes you feel nauseous. You will smoke less in the future.
Remove something from the environment	**Negative reinforcement:** Smoking makes your craving for a cigarette go away. You will smoke more in the future.	**Negative punishment:** To smoke, you must go outside, even on cold or rainy days, and leave the comfort of your home, school or office. You will smoke less in the future.

sound and eventually hits the dash with his hand. The noise ceases. The next time the car makes that sound, he immediately hits the dash again. The unpleasant noise (the aversive stimulus) is terminated when the man hits the dash (the response), so the response is reinforced.

Negative reinforcement should not be confused with *punishment*. Both phenomena involve aversive stimuli, but negative reinforcement makes a behavioral response more likely, while punishment makes it less likely. In the context of behavior, *positive* means adding something to the learning environment and *negative* means taking something away. *Reinforcement* means increasing the likelihood of a behavior occurring in the future, and *punishment* means decreasing the likelihood of a behavior occurring in the future. (See Table 18.3.)

Negative reinforcement could explain the acquisition of chronic drug use under some conditions. If a stressed person is suffering from some unpleasant feelings and then takes a drug that eliminates these feelings, the person's drug-taking behavior is likely to be reinforced. For example, alcohol can relieve feelings of anxiety. A person who finds him- or herself in a situation that arouses anxiety might find that having a drink or two makes him or her feel much better. In fact, people often anticipate this effect and begin drinking before the situation actually occurs.

PHYSICAL DEPENDENCE People who abuse a drug often become physically dependent on the drug; that is, they show *tolerance* and *withdrawal symptoms*. As we saw in Chapter 4, tolerance is the decreased sensitivity to a drug that comes from its continued use; the user must take larger and larger amounts of the drug for it to be effective. Once a person has taken a drug regularly enough to develop

tolerance, that person will generally exhibit withdrawal symptoms if he or she stops taking the drug. Withdrawal symptoms are primarily the opposite of the effects of the drug itself. For example, the effects of heroin—euphoria, constipation, and relaxation—lead to the withdrawal effects of dysphoria, diarrhea, and agitation.

Tolerance Most investigators believe that tolerance is produced by the body's attempt to compensate for the unusual condition of repeated presence of a drug in the body. The drug disturbs normal homeostatic mechanisms in the brain, and in reaction these mechanisms begin to produce effects opposite to those of the drug, partially compensating for the disturbance. Because of these compensatory mechanisms, the user must take increasing amounts of the drug to achieve the effects that were produced when he or she first started taking the drug. These mechanisms also account for the symptoms of withdrawal: When the person stops taking the drug, the compensatory mechanisms make themselves felt, unopposed by the action of the drug.

Withdrawal Although positive reinforcement seems to be what provokes drug taking in the first place, reduction of withdrawal effects could certainly play a role in maintaining someone's pattern of repeated drug use. The withdrawal effects are unpleasant, but as soon as the person takes some of the drug, these effects go away, producing negative reinforcement and contributing to continued use of the drug.

CRAVING Why do people crave drugs? Why does craving occur even after a long period of abstinence? Even after going for months or years without taking a drug, a person who previously abused a drug might sometimes experience intense craving that leads to relapse. Taking a drug over an extended period of time must produce some long-lasting changes in the brain that increase a person's likelihood of relapsing. Understanding this process might help clinicians to devise therapies that will assist people in breaking their drug dependence once and for all.

A taste of food can provoke hunger, which is why we refer to tidbits we eat before a meal as "appetizers." For a person with a history of substance abuse, a small dose of the drug has similar effects: It increases craving, or "appetite," for the drug. In addition, through the process of classical conditioning, stimuli that have been associated with drugs in the past can also elicit craving. For example, someone who is physically dependent on alcohol and sees a liquor bottle is likely to feel the urge to take a drink. In the past, agencies that sponsored anti-drug programs sometimes prepared posters illustrating the dangers of substance abuse that featured drug paraphernalia: syringes, needles, piles of white powder, and so on. Possibly, these posters did succeed in reminding people who did not use drugs that they should avoid them. But we do know that their effect on people who were trying to break a drug habit was exactly the opposite of what was intended. As we saw in the case at the beginning of this chapter, John saw a poster that pictured drug paraphernalia, and this sight provoked an urge to take the drug again. For this reason, this strategy is no longer used in campaigns against drug addiction.

RELAPSE One of the ways in which craving has been investigated in laboratory animals is through the *reinstatement model* of drug seeking. Animals are first trained to make a response (for example, pressing a lever) that is reinforced by intravenous injections of a drug such as cocaine. Next, the response is extinguished by providing injections of a saline solution rather than the drug. Once the animal has stopped responding, the experimenter administers a "free" injection of the drug (drug reinstatement procedure) or presents a stimulus that has been associated with the drug (cue reinstatement procedure). In response to these stimuli, the animals begin responding at the lever once more (Kalivas et al., 2006). Presumably, this kind of relapse (reinstatement of a previously extinguished response) is a good model for the craving that motivates drug-seeking behavior in a person who has chronically used the drug. (See Figure 18.7.)

Extinction To understand the process of reinstatement (and the craving that underlies it), let's first consider what happens during extinction. As we saw in Chapter 11, extinction is a form of learning. An animal does not forget to make a particular response; it learns not to make it. The ventromedial prefrontal cortex (vmPFC) plays a critical role in this process. For example, we saw in Chapter 11 that lesions of the vmPFC impair the extinction of a conditioned emotional

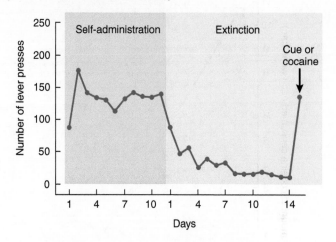

Figure 18.7 The Reinstatement Procedure: A Model of Relapse

The graph shows the acquisition of lever pressing for injections of a reinforcing drug during the self-administration phase and the extinction of lever pressing when the drug was no longer administered. A "free" shot of the drug or presentation of a cue associated with the drug during acquisition will reinstate responding.

(Based on data from Kalivas et al., 2006.)

response, that stimulation of this region inhibits conditioned emotional responses, and that extinction training activates neurons located there.

Studies with rats indicate that different regions of the prefrontal cortex exert facilitatory and inhibitory effects on drug-related responding by means of excitatory and inhibitory connections with the brain's reinforcement system. These effects appear to be responsible for extinction and reinstatement. Peters et al. (2008) found that stimulation of the vmPFC with an infusion of AMPA, a glutamate agonist, blocked reinstatement of responding normally produced by a free shot of cocaine or the presentation of a stimulus associated with cocaine reinforcement. That is, activation of the vmPFC inhibited responding. McFarland et al. (2003) found that reinstatement of lever pressing for infusions of cocaine was abolished by injecting a GABA agonist into the dorsal anterior cingulate cortex (dACC), a region of the dorsal PFC that has excitatory connections with the NAC. That is, inhibition of the dACC prevented the reinstatement of the response. These results indicate that the dACC plays a role in craving and the vmPFC plays a role in its suppression.

Volkow et al. (1992) found that during abstinence, the activity of the medial prefrontal cortex of people who abused cocaine was lower than that of non-cocaine-using participants. In addition, when people who use cocaine are performing tasks that normally activate the prefrontal cortex, their medial prefrontal cortex is less activated than that of control participants, and they perform more poorly on the tasks (Bolla et al., 2004; Garavan and Stout, 2005). In fact, Bolla et al. found that the amount of activation of the medial prefrontal cortex

Figure 18.8 Cocaine Intake and the Medial Prefrontal Cortex

The graph shows the relative activation of the medial prefrontal cortex as a function of the amount of cocaine normally taken each week by people who abused the drug.

(Based on data from Bolla et al., 2004.)

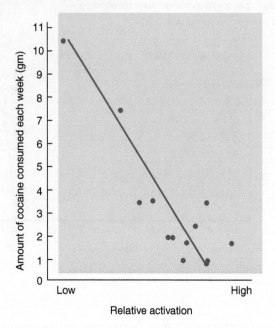

Relative activation

Figure 18.9 Social Stress and Cocaine Intake

The graph shows the cocaine intake of control rats and rats subjected to isolation stress early in life.

(Based on data from Kosten et al., 2000.)

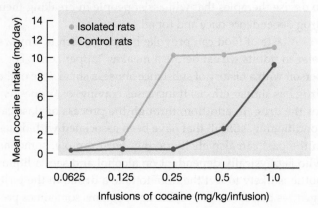

was inversely related to the amount of cocaine that the people normally took each week: The lower the brain activity, the more cocaine the person took. (See Figure 18.8.)

Stress As we have just seen, the presence of drug-related stimuli can trigger craving and drug-seeking behavior. In addition, clinicians have long observed that stressful situations can cause relapse. These effects have been observed in rats that had previously learned to self-administer cocaine or heroin. For example, Covington and Miczek (2001) paired naïve rats with rats that had been trained to become dominant. After being defeated by the dominant rats, the socially stressed rats became more sensitive to the effects of cocaine and showed bingeing—self-administration of larger amounts of the drug. Kosten et al. (2000) showed that stress that occurs early in life can have long-lasting effects on

drug-taking behavior. They stressed infant rats by isolating them from their mother and littermates for one hour per day for eight days. When these rats were given the opportunity in adulthood to access cocaine, they readily acquired the habit and took more of the drug than did control rats that had not been stressed. (See Figure 18.9.)

An important link between stressful experiences and drug craving is provided by corticotropin-releasing hormone, or CRH. (This peptide is also referred to as corticotropin-releasing factor, or CRF.) As we saw in Chapter 17, CRH plays an important role in development of adverse effects on health produced by stress and on the development of anxiety disorders. Just as administration of a drug or exposure to stimuli previously associated with drug-taking behavior can cause relapse, so can stressful experiences (Shalev et al., 2010). For example, administration of CRH can reinstate drug-taking behavior, and administration of a drug that blocks CRH receptors can reduce the likelihood of relapse from drugs or drug cues. CRH receptors in the VTA appear to be particularly important. For example, infusion of CRH into the VTA causes relapse, and infusion of a CRH receptor antagonist prevents reinstatement of drug-taking by a stressful stimulus (Z. Wang et al., 2007).

Section Review

Common Features of Substance Abuse

LO 18.1 Describe the features of positive reinforcement that all drugs of abuse share, including their general neural mechanisms.

Positive reinforcement occurs when a behavior is regularly followed by an appetitive stimulus—one that an

organism will approach. Drugs of abuse produce positive reinforcement; they reinforce drug-taking behavior. Laboratory animals will learn to make responses that result in the delivery of these drugs. The faster a drug produces its effects, the more quickly physical dependence will be established. All drugs that produce positive reinforcement stimulate the release of dopamine in the NAC, a structure that plays an important role in reinforcement. Neural changes that begin in the VTA and NAC eventually involve the dorsal striatum, which plays a critical role in operant conditioning. Orexin and MCH also play a role in the establishment of drug-taking behavior. The activity of inhibitory circuits in the prefrontal cortex promotes resistance to substance abuse. The susceptibility of adolescents to the abuse potential of drugs may be associated with the relative immaturity of the prefrontal cortex.

LO 18.2 Explain how negative reinforcement can contribute to the development of substance abuse, including physical dependence, craving, and relapse.

Negative reinforcement occurs when a behavior is followed by the reduction or termination of an aversive stimulus and can be responsible for initiating or maintaining drug use. The reduction of unpleasant withdrawal symptoms due to physical dependence by a dose of the drug undoubtedly plays a role in maintaining drug use, but it is not the sole cause of craving.

Craving—the urge to take a drug to which one has become physically dependent upon—cannot be completely explained by withdrawal symptoms, because it can occur even after a person has refrained from taking the drug for a long time. In laboratory animals a "free" shot of cocaine or presentation of stimuli previously associated with cocaine reinstates drug-seeking behavior as a model of relapse. The vmPFC plays an inhibitory role in reinstatement, and the dACC plays a facilitatory role. Long-term substance abuse is associated with decreased activity of the prefrontal cortex and decreased volume of prefrontal gray matter, which may impair people's judgment and ability to inhibit inappropriate responses, such as further drug taking. Stressful stimuli—even those that occur early in life—increase susceptibility to substance abuse. Release of CRH in the VTA plays an important role in this process.

Thought Question

Explain what it means to say that drugs of abuse "hijack" the reinforcement system.

Heredity

Not everyone is equally likely to abuse drugs. Many people drink alcohol moderately, and the majority of people who use drugs such as cocaine and heroin use them without becoming physically dependent on them. Evidence indicates that both genetic and environmental factors play a role in determining a person's likelihood of consuming drugs and of that use escalating to substance abuse. In addition, there are both general factors (such as likelihood of taking and abusing any of a number of drugs) and specific factors (such as likelihood of taking and abusing a particular drug).

Tsuang et al. (1998) studied 3,372 male twin pairs to estimate the genetic contributions to substance abuse. They found strong general genetic and environmental factors: Abusing any category of drug was associated with abusing drugs in all other categories: sedatives, stimulants, opiates, marijuana, and psychedelics. Abuse of marijuana was especially influenced by family environmental factors. Abuse of every category except psychedelics was influenced by genetic factors specific to that category. Abuse of heroin had a particularly strong unique genetic factor. Another study of male twin pairs found a strong common genetic factor for the use of all categories of drugs and found in addition that shared environmental factors had a stronger effect on use than on abuse (Kendler et al., 2003). In other words, environment plays a strong role in

influencing a person to try a drug and perhaps continue to use it recreationally, but genetics plays a stronger role in determining whether the person's use then develops into substance abuse.

Goldman et al. (2005) reviewed twin studies that attempted to measure the heritability of various types of substance abuse and similar behaviors, such as gambling. As you will see in Figure 18.10, the authors included pathological gambling. The following section will explore genetic contributions to abuse of alcohol, nicotine, and stimulants such as cocaine.

Figure 18.10 Heritability of Substance Abuse and Problem Gambling
(Adapted from Goldman et al., 2005.)

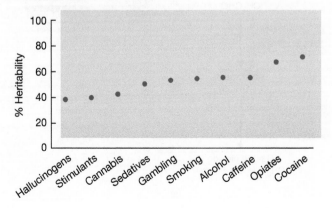

Alcohol

LO 18.3 **Summarize the evidence for a role of heredity in alcohol abuse.**

The genetic basis of alcohol abuse has received more attention than abuse of other drugs. Alcohol consumption is not distributed equally across the population; in the United States, 10 percent of the people drink 50 percent of the alcohol (Heckler, 1983). Many twin and adoption studies confirm that the primary reason for this disparity is genetic.

A susceptibility to alcohol abuse could conceivably be caused by differences in the ability to digest or metabolize alcohol or by differences in the structure or biochemistry of the brain. There is evidence that variability in the genes responsible for the production of alcohol-metabolizing enzymes play a role in susceptibility to alcohol abuse. A particular variant of this gene, which is especially prevalent in eastern Asia, is responsible for a reaction to alcohol intake that most people find aversive and that discourages further drinking (Goldman et al., 2005). (See Figure 18.11.) However, most investigators believe that differences in brain physiology—for example, brain changes that control sensitivity to the reinforcing effects of drugs or sensitivity to various environmental stressors—are more likely to play a role. For example, increased sensitivity to environmental stressors might encourage the use of alcohol as a means to reduce stress-related anxiety.

Nicotine

LO 18.4 **Summarize the evidence for a role of heredity in nicotine abuse.**

Investigators have also focused on the possibility that susceptibility to substance abuse may involve differences in functions of specific neurotransmitter systems. Nicotinic ACh receptors that contain the α5 subunit, found on neurons in the medial habenula, play a role in inhibiting the reinforcing effects of nicotine. Genetic studies found that a particular allele of the gene responsible for the production of this receptor is associated with increased susceptibility to nicotine abuse and consequent development of lung cancer (Bierut, 2008). A study by Kuryatov et al. (2011) found that the presence of this allele reduces the sensitivity of the α5 ACh receptors, and hence reduces the inhibitory effect of large doses of nicotine. The result would be increased susceptibility to the reinforcing effects of nicotine.

Stimulants

LO 18.5 **Summarize the evidence for a role of heredity in stimulant abuse.**

Renthal et al. (2009) performed a genome-wide analysis of the effects of cocaine on genetic material in the mouse DNA. They found that cocaine turned on hundreds of genes, many of which were already known to be involved in the behavioral effects of the drug. One of their most interesting discoveries was that cocaine turns on the genes that produce *sirtuins*,

---

Figure 18.11 Alcohol Metabolism

(a) There are two steps in the breakdown of alcohol; inactivity of alcohol dehydrogenase results in the accumulation of a toxic intermediate product that makes people feel ill and avoid alcohol. (b) Each person has two chromosomes with the gene for alcohol-metabolizing enzymes. Two copies (homozygous) of the active form of the gene results in normal metabolism of alcohol. Two copies of the inactive form of the gene results in impaired alcohol metabolism and an aversive reaction. One copy of the inactive gene (heterozygous) results in intermediate alcohol metabolism.

(Source: Based on Meyer, J. S., and Quenzer, L. F., *Psychopharmacology: drugs, the brain, and behavior*, Sunderland, MA: Sinauer Associates, 2005.)

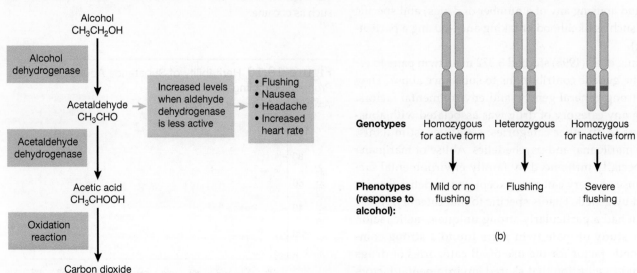

proteins that play important regulatory roles in cells. They also found that a sirtuin agonist increased the reinforcing effects of cocaine and that a sirtuin antagonist decreased it. As other investigators have noted, their approach holds promise for discovering the molecular biology of drugs of abuse and identifying potential treatments for people who abuse them.

Section Review

Heredity

LO 18.3 Summarize the evidence for a role of heredity in alcohol abuse.

While both environmental and genetic factors influence likelihood of developing substance abuse disorders, twin studies support a specific genetic contribution to maintaining substance use. Some individual genes have been shown to affect abuse of particular drugs. For example, variations in the genes for alcohol dehydrogenase play a role in susceptibility to alcohol abuse.

LO 18.4 Summarize the evidence for a role of heredity in nicotine abuse.

Variations in the gene for the α5 ACh receptor affect the likelihood of nicotine abuse. Genes that produce sirtuins modify responsiveness to the abuse potential of cocaine.

LO 18.5 Summarize the evidence for a role of heredity in stimulant abuse.

Genes that produce sirtuins modify responsiveness to the abuse potential of cocaine.

Thought Question

Can you think of any genetic factors besides the ones described in the previous section that might affect a person's susceptibility to drug abuse? For example, what kinds of individual differences might affect the likelihood that a person tries a drug, likes the effects of the drug, or does not go on to use a drug repeatedly?

Commonly Abused Drugs

People have been known to abuse an enormous variety of drugs, including alcohol, barbiturates, opiates, tobacco, amphetamine, cocaine, cannabis, designer drugs, hallucinogens such as LSD, PCP, and volatile solvents such as glues, gasoline, ether, and nitrous oxide. We will restrict our discussion to the most important of these drugs in terms of popularity and potential for abuse. Some drugs, such as caffeine, are both popular and reinforcing, but because they do not normally cause intoxication, impair health, or interfere with productivity, they will not be discussed here. (Chapter 4 did discuss the behavioral effects and site of action of caffeine.) This chapter will not include information about the wide variety of hallucinogenic drugs such as LSD or PCP. Although some people enjoy the effects of hallucinogens, other people find them frightening and LSD use does not normally lead to abuse. Animals do not readily self-administer hallucinogens, and there is little evidence of physical dependence, even with repeated use. PCP (phencyclidine) acts as an indirect antagonist at the NMDA receptor, which means that its effects overlap with those of alcohol. Rather than including a separate section on this drug, we have chosen to say more about alcohol, which is abused far more than any of the hallucinogenic drugs. This section will describe the abuse of opiates, stimulants, nicotine, alcohol, and cannabis.

Opiates

LO 18.6 Describe the effects and roles of reinforcement and physical dependence in opiate abuse.

Opium, derived from the opium poppy, has been eaten and smoked for centuries. Many prescription pain relievers (such as OxyContin, described in the case study at the beginning of this chapter) contain synthetic opiates, and many designer drugs are synthetic opiates (such as the failed batch created in the case study at the beginning of Chapter 5).

DESCRIPTION Opiate abuse has several high personal and social costs. Not only is opiate abuse illegal (of either illicit forms such as heroin, or misuse of prescription drugs), but due to tolerance, a person must take increasing amounts of the drug to achieve a "high." The habit thus becomes

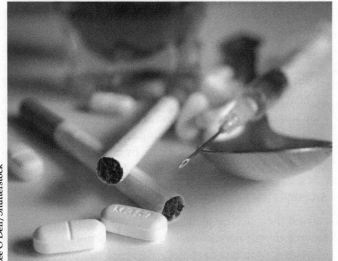

Opiates, stimulants, nicotine, alcohol, and cannabis cause intoxication, impair health, or interfere with productivity.

Lee O'Dell/Shutterstock

Figure 18.12 Opiate Effects

Opiate receptors in the nucleus accumbens and ventral tegmental area are involved in reinforcing effects of opiates. Receptors in the preoptic area are involved in hypothermia. Receptors in the periaqueductal gray matter are primarily responsible for analgesia, and receptors in the reticular formation are responsible for sedation.

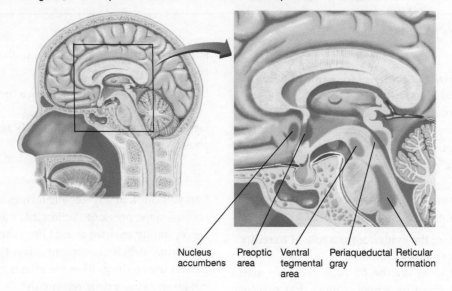

Nucleus accumbens — Preoptic area — Ventral tegmental area — Periaqueductal gray — Reticular formation

more and more expensive, and some people may resort to crime to obtain enough money to support escalating use of the drug. Many opiates can be taken intravenously using needles; and at present, a substantial percentage of people who inject drugs such as heroin have been exposed to hepatitis or HIV via contaminated syringes. If a pregnant woman becomes physically dependent on opiates, the fetus will also become dependent on the drug, which easily crosses the placental barrier. A newborn must be given opiates immediately after birth and then weaned off the drug with gradually decreasing doses to prevent or reduce withdrawal symptoms. The uncertainty about the strength of a given batch of synthetic opiates makes it possible for a user to receive an unusually large dose of the drug, with possibly fatal consequences. And some of the substances used to dilute opiates are themselves toxic.

REINFORCEMENT As we saw earlier, laboratory animals will self-administer opiates. When an opiate is administered systemically, it stimulates opiate receptors located on neurons in various parts of the brain and produces a variety of effects, including analgesia, hypothermia (lowering of body temperature), sedation, and reinforcement. Opiate receptors in the periaqueductal gray matter are primarily responsible for the analgesia, those in the preoptic area are responsible for the hypothermia, and those in the mesencephalic reticular formation are responsible for the sedation. As we shall see, opiate receptors in the VTA and the NAC appear to play a role in the reinforcing effects of opiates. (See Figure 18.12.)

As we saw in Chapter 4, there are three major types of opiate receptors: μ (mu), δ (delta), and κ (kappa). Evidence suggests that μ receptors and δ receptors are responsible for

reinforcement and analgesia and that stimulation of κ receptors produces aversive effects. Evidence for the role of μ receptors comes from a study by Matthes et al. (1996), who performed a targeted mutation against the gene responsible for production of the μ opiate receptor in mice. These animals, when they grew up, were completely insensitive to the reinforcing or analgesic effects of morphine, and they showed no signs of withdrawal symptoms after having been given increasing doses of morphine for six days. (See Figure 18.13.)

As we saw earlier, reinforcing stimuli cause the release of dopamine in the NAC. Injections of opiates are no exception to this general rule; Wise et al. (1995) found that the level of dopamine in the NAC increased by 150–300 percent while a rat was pressing a lever that delivered intravenous injections of heroin. Rats will also press a lever that delivers injections of an opiate directly into the VTA (Devine and Wise, 1994) or the NAC (Goeders et al., 1984). In other words, injections of opiates into both ends of the mesolimbic dopaminergic system are reinforcing.

The release of endogenous opioids may even play a role in the reinforcing effects of some drugs. Studies have shown that administration of naloxone (a drug that blocks opiate receptors), reduces the reinforcing effects of alcohol in both humans and laboratory animals. In fact, the use of opiate blockers is an approved treatment for alcohol abuse.

PHYSICAL DEPENDENCE Several studies have investigated the neural systems that are responsible for the development of tolerance and subsequent withdrawal effects of opiates. Maldonado et al. (1992) made rats physically dependent on morphine and then injected naloxone into various regions of the brain to determine whether the sudden

Figure 18.13 Effects of a Targeted Deletion of the µ Opiate Receptor

The graphs show a lack of response to morphine in mice with targeted mutations against the µ opiate receptor. (a) Latency to tail withdrawal from a hot object (a measure of analgesia). (b) Wet-dog shakes (a prominent withdrawal symptom in rodents) after being withdrawn from long-term morphine administration. (c) Conditioned place preference for a chamber associated with an injection of morphine (a measure of reinforcement).

(Based on data from Matthes et al. 1996.)

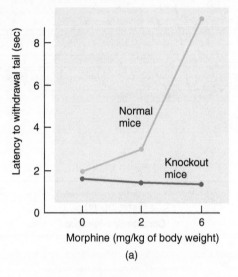

(a)

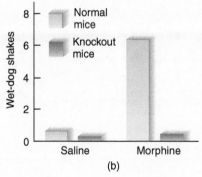

(b)

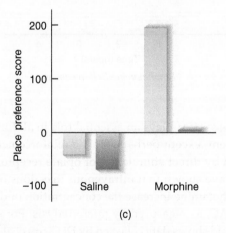

(c)

blocking of opiate receptors would stimulate symptoms of withdrawal. This technique—administering a drug of abuse for a prolonged interval and then blocking its effects with an antagonist—is referred to as **antagonist-precipitated withdrawal.** The investigators found that the most sensitive site was the locus coeruleus, followed by the periaqueductal gray matter. Injection of naloxone into the amygdala produced a weak withdrawal syndrome. Using a similar technique (first infusing morphine into various regions of the brain and then precipitating withdrawal by giving the animals an injection of naloxone), Bozarth (1994) confirmed the role of the locus coeruleus and the periaqueductal gray matter in the production of withdrawal symptoms.

A single dose of an opiate decreases the firing rate of neurons in the locus coeruleus, but if the drug is administered chronically, the firing rate will return to normal. Then, if an opiate antagonist is administered (to precipitate withdrawal symptoms), the firing rate of these neurons increases dramatically, which increases the release of norepinephrine in the regions that receive projections from this nucleus (Koob, 1996; Nestler, 1996). In addition, lesions of the locus coeruleus reduce the severity of antagonist-precipitated withdrawal symptoms (Maldonado and Koob, 1993). A microdialysis study by Aghajanian et al. (1994) found that antagonist-precipitated withdrawal caused an increase in the level of glutamate, the major excitatory neurotransmitter, in the locus coeruleus.

Stimulants

LO 18.7 Describe the effects and role of reinforcement in stimulant abuse.

Cocaine and amphetamine have similar behavioral effects, because both act as potent dopamine agonists. However, their sites of action are different. Cocaine binds with and deactivates the dopamine transporter proteins, thus blocking the reuptake of dopamine after it is released by the terminal buttons. Amphetamine also inhibits the reuptake of dopamine, but its most important effect is to directly stimulate the release of dopamine from terminal buttons. *Methamphetamine* is chemically related to amphetamine but is considerably more potent. Freebase cocaine (crack cocaine), a particularly potent form of the drug, is smoked and thus enters the blood supply of the lungs and reaches the brain very quickly. Because its effects are so potent and so rapid, it is probably the most effective reinforcer of all available drugs.

DESCRIPTION When people take cocaine, they become euphoric, active, and talkative. They say that they feel powerful and alert. When people abuse the drug, obtaining it becomes an obsession to which they devote more and more time and money. Laboratory animals, which will quickly learn to self-administer cocaine intravenously, also act excited and show intense exploratory activity. After receiving the drug for a day or two, rats start showing stereotyped movements, such as grooming, head bobbing, and persistent locomotion (Geary, 1987).

Figure 18.14 Dopamine Transporters, Methamphetamine Abuse, and Parkinson's Disease

The scans show concentrations of dopamine transporters from a control participant, a participant who had previously abused methamphetamine, and a participant with Parkinson's disease. Decreased concentrations of dopamine transporters indicate loss of dopaminergic terminals.

(Based on McCann, U. D., Wong, D. F., Yokoi, F., et al. *Journal of Neuroscience*, 1998, *18*, 8417–8422.)

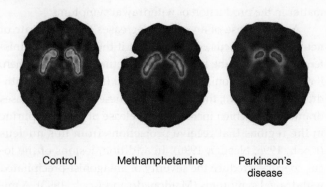

Control   Methamphetamine   Parkinson's disease

Figure 18.15 Release of Dopamine in the Nucleus Accumbens

The graphs show dopamine concentration in the nucleus accumbens, measured by microdialysis, during self-administration of intravenous cocaine or amphetamine by rats.

(Based on data from Di Ciano et al., 1995.)

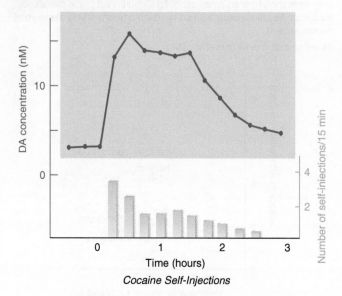

Cocaine Self-Injections

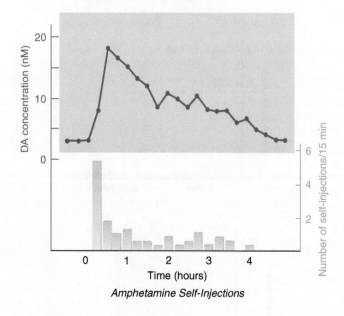

Amphetamine Self-Injections

One of the alarming effects of cocaine and amphetamine seen in people who abuse these drugs regularly is psychotic behavior: hallucinations, delusions of persecution, mood disturbances, and repetitive behaviors. These symptoms so closely resemble positive symptoms of schizophrenia that even a trained mental health professional cannot distinguish them unless he or she knows about the person's history of substance abuse. However, these symptoms decrease when people stop taking the drug. As we saw in Chapter 16, the fact that these symptoms are provoked by dopamine agonists and reduced by drugs that block dopamine receptors suggests that overactivity of dopaminergic synapses is responsible for the positive symptoms of schizophrenia.

Some evidence suggests that the use of stimulant drugs may have adverse long-term effects on the brain. For example, in a PET study McCann et al. (1998) discovered that people with a history of methamphetamine abuse showed a decrease in the numbers of dopamine transporters in the caudate nucleus and putamen, despite the fact that they had abstained from the drug for approximately three years. The decreased number of dopamine transporters suggests that the number of dopaminergic terminals in these regions is diminished. As the authors noted, these people might have an increased risk of Parkinson's disease as they get older. (See Figure 18.14.) Studies with laboratory animals have also found that methamphetamine can damage terminals of serotonergic axons and trigger death of neurons through apoptosis in the cerebral cortex, striatum, and hippocampus (Cadet et al., 2003).

REINFORCEMENT If rats or monkeys are given continuous access to a lever that permits them to self-administer cocaine, they can self-inject so much cocaine that they die. As a result, researchers who study this drug must limit animals' access to the drug. As we have seen, the mesolimbic dopamine system plays an essential role in all forms of reinforcement, except perhaps for the reinforcement that is mediated by direct stimulation of opiate receptors. Many studies have shown that intravenous injections of cocaine and amphetamine increase the concentration of dopamine in the NAC, as measured by microdialysis. For example, Figure 18.15 shows data collected by Di Ciano et al. (1995) in a study with rats that learned to press a lever that delivered intravenous injections of cocaine or amphetamine. The colored bars at the base of the graphs indicate the animals' responses, and the line graphs indicate the level of dopamine in the NAC.

Nicotine

LO 18.8 **Describe the effects and roles of reinforcement and physical dependence in nicotine abuse.**

Although its use is common, nicotine is a drug of abuse, and it accounts for more deaths than the other drugs described so far in this chapter.

DESCRIPTION The combination of nicotine and other substances in tobacco smoke is carcinogenic and leads to cancer of the lungs, mouth, throat, and esophagus. Approximately one-third of the adult population of the world smokes, and smoking is one of the few causes of death that is rising in developing countries. The World Health Organization estimates that 50 percent of the people who begin to smoke as adolescents and continue smoking throughout their lives will die from smoking-related diseases. Tobacco use is the leading cause of preventable death in developed countries (Dani and Harris, 2005). In the United States alone, tobacco abuse kills more than 430,000 people each year (Chou and Narasimhan, 2005). Worldwide, stroke is the second leading cause of death and lung cancer is the fifth (Lozano et al., 2013). Both of these causes of death are negatively influenced by smoking. Smoking by pregnant women also has negative effects on the health of their fetuses—potentially worse than those of cocaine (Slotkin, 1998).

The abuse potential of nicotine should not be underestimated; many people continue to smoke even when doing so causes serious health problems. For example, Sigmund Freud, whose theory of psychoanalysis stressed the importance of insight in changing one's behavior, was unable to stop smoking even after most of his jaw had been removed because of the cancer that this habit had caused (Brecher, 1972). He suffered severe pain and, as a physician, realized that he should have stopped smoking. He did not, and cancer finally killed him.

REINFORCEMENT Nicotine has a very high abuse potential. In a review of the literature, Stolerman and Jarvis (1995) note that smokers tend to smoke regularly or not at all; few can smoke just a little. Nineteen out of 20 smokers smoke every day, and only 60 out of 3,500 smokers questioned smoke fewer than five cigarettes per day. Forty percent of people continue to smoke after having their larynx removed (which is usually performed to treat throat cancer). More than 50 percent of heart attack survivors continue to smoke, and about 50 percent of people continue to smoke after surgery for lung cancer. Of those who attempt to quit smoking by enrolling in a special program, 20 percent manage to abstain for one year. The record is much poorer for those who try to quit on their own: One-third manage to stop for one day, one-fourth abstain for one week, but only 4 percent manage to abstain for six months.

Ours is not the only species willing to self-administer nicotine; so will laboratory animals (Donny et al., 1995).

Nicotine stimulates nicotinic acetylcholine receptors. It also increases the activity of dopaminergic neurons of the meso-limbic system (Mereu et al., 1987) and causes dopamine to be released in the NAC (Damsma et al., 1989). Figure 18.16 demonstrates the effects of two injections of nicotine or saline on the extracellular dopamine level of the NAC, measured by microdialysis.

Injection of a nicotinic agonist directly into the VTA will reinforce a conditioned place preference (Museo and Wise, 1994). Conversely, injection of a nicotinic antagonist into the VTA will block the ability of nicotine to cause the release of dopamine in the nucleus accumbens and reduce the reinforcing effect of intravenous injections of nicotine (Corrigall et al., 1994; Gotti et al., 2010). But although nicotinic receptors are found in both the VTA and the NAC, Corrigall et al. found that injections of a nicotinic antagonist in the NAC have no effect on reinforcement. Consistent with these findings, Nisell et al. (1994) found that infusion of a nicotinic antagonist into the VTA will prevent an intravenous injection of nicotine from triggering the release of dopamine in the NAC. Infusion of the antagonist into the NAC will not have this effect. Thus, the reinforcing effect of nicotine appears to be caused by activation of nicotinic receptors in the VTA.

Researchers have discovered a pathway in the brain that *inhibits* the reinforcing effects of nicotine. Neurons in the medial habenula, a region of the midbrain, contain a special type of nicotinic ACh receptor that includes an α5 subunit. The neurons that contain these receptors send their axons to the interpeduncular nucleus, located in the midline of the midbrain, caudal to the medial habenula. This pathway appears to be part of a system that inhibits the reinforcing effects of nicotine. Fowler et al. (2011) prepared a targeted mutation against the gene responsible for synthesis of α5 ACh receptors

---

Figure 18.16 Nicotine and Dopamine Release in the Nucleus Accumbens

The graph shows changes in dopamine concentration in the nucleus accumbens, measured by microdialysis, in response to injections of nicotine or saline. The arrows indicate the time of the injections.

(Based on data from Damsma et al., 1989.)

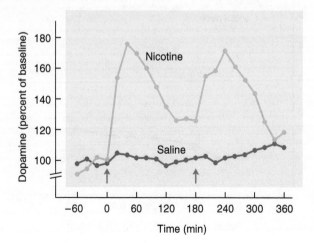

in the medial habenula of mice. They found that the knockout increased self-administration of high doses of nicotine. They also found that the procedure decreased the ability of nicotine to activate the interpeduncular nucleus, and that disruption of activity in this nucleus increased nicotine self-administration. The medial habenula-interpeduncular nucleus circuit appears to protect the animals (and presumably, our own species) against intake of large quantities of nicotine. A control mouse will increase its response rate when the amount of nicotine contained in each injection increases—up to a point, that is. Eventually, larger injections will suppress the animal's response rate so that it will not receive too much nicotine. But if α5 ACh receptors in the habenula are deactivated, this inhibitory effect does not occur. (See Figure 18.17.)

Role of Cannabinoid Receptors Studies have found that the endogenous cannabinoids play a role in the reinforcing effects of nicotine. *Rimonabant*, a drug that blocks cannabinoid CB1 receptors, reduces nicotine self-administration and nicotine-seeking behavior in rats (Cohen et al., 2005), apparently by reducing the release of dopamine in the NAC (De Vries and Schoffelmeer, 2005). By blocking CB1 receptors, rimonabant decreases the reinforcing effects of nicotine. As we saw in Chapter 12, rimonabant was used for antiobesity therapy for a short time but was withdrawn from the market because of dangerous side effects. Clinical trials have found that rimonabant appears to help prevent relapse in people who are trying to quit smoking, but it is not approved for this purpose, either. However, the effects of the drug in humans and laboratory animals suggest that craving for nicotine, like the craving for food, is enhanced by the release of endocannabinoids in the brain.

Figure 18.17 Effect of Knockout of the α5 ACh Receptor Gene in Mice

The graph shows that mice with a targeted mutation against α5 ACh receptors in the medial habenula self-administer increasing doses of nicotine, whereas control mice limit their intake.

(Based on data of Fowler et al., 2011.)

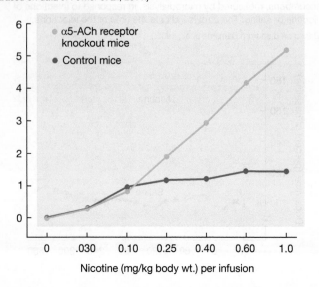

Nicotine (mg/kg body wt.) per infusion

PHYSICAL DEPENDENCE The nicotinic ACh receptor exists in three states. When a burst of ACh is released by an acetylcholinergic terminal button, the receptors open briefly, permitting the entry of calcium. (Most nicotinic receptors serve as heteroreceptors on terminal buttons that release another neurotransmitter. The entry of calcium stimulates the release of that neurotransmitter.) Within a few milliseconds, the enzyme AChE has destroyed the acetylcholine, and the receptors either close again or enter a desensitized state, during which they bind with, but do not react to, ACh. Normally, few nicotinic receptors enter the desensitized state. However, when a person smokes, the level of nicotine in the brain rises slowly and stays steady for a prolonged period because nicotine, unlike ACh, is not destroyed by AChE. At first, nicotinic receptors are activated, but the sustained low levels of the drug convert many nicotinic receptors to the desensitized state. Thus, nicotine has dual effects on nicotinic receptors: activation and then desensitization. In addition, probably in response to desensitization, with repeated use of the drug the number of nicotinic receptors increases (Dani and De Biasi, 2001).

Most smokers report that their first cigarette in the morning brings the most pleasure, presumably because the period of abstinence during the night has allowed many of their nicotinic receptors to enter the closed state and become sensitized again. The first dose of nicotine in the morning activates these receptors and has a reinforcing effect. After that, a large proportion of the smoker's nicotinic receptors become desensitized again; as a consequence, most smokers say that they smoke less for pleasure than to relax and gain relief from nervousness and craving. If smokers abstain for a few weeks, the number of nicotinic receptors in their brains returns to normal. However, as the high rate of relapse indicates, craving continues, which means that other changes in the brain must have occurred.

Cessation of smoking after long-term use causes withdrawal symptoms, including anxiety, restlessness, insomnia, and inability to concentrate (Hughes et al., 1989). Like the withdrawal symptoms of other drugs, these symptoms may increase the likelihood of relapse, but they do not explain why people become dependent to the drug in the first place.

Patient N. is a [38-year-old man who] started smoking at the age of 14. At the time of his stroke, he was smoking more than 40 unfiltered cigarettes per day and was enjoying smoking very much. . . . [H]e used to experience frequent urges to smoke, especially upon waking, after eating, when he drank coffee or alcohol, and when he was around other people who were smoking. He often found it difficult to refrain from smoking in situations where it was inappropriate, e.g., at work or when he was sick. He was aware of the health risks of smoking before his stroke but was not particularly concerned about those risks. Before his stroke, he had never tried to stop smoking, and he had had no intention of doing so. N. smoked his last cigarette on the evening before his stroke. When asked about his reason for quitting smoking, he stated simply, "I forgot that I was a smoker." When asked to elaborate, he said that he did not forget the fact that he was a smoker but rather that "my body forgot the urge to smoke." He felt no urge to smoke during his hospital stay, even though he had the opportunity to go outside to smoke. His wife was surprised by the fact that he did not want to smoke in the hospital, given the degree of his prior craving. N. recalled how his roommate in the hospital would frequently go outside to smoke and that he was so disgusted by the smell upon his roommate's return that he asked to change rooms. He volunteered that smoking in his dreams, which used to be pleasurable before his stroke, was now disgusting. N. stated that, although he ultimately came to believe that his stroke was caused in some way by smoking, suffering a stroke was not the reason why he quit. In fact, he did not recall ever making any effort to stop smoking. Instead, it seemed to him that he had spontaneously lost all interest in smoking. When asked whether his stroke might have destroyed some part of his brain . . . that made him want to smoke, he agreed that this was likely to have been the case (Naqvi et al., 2007, p. 548).

The case of patient N. below demonstrates an unusual exception to this phenomenon.

As Naqvi et al. (2007) report, Mr. N. sustained a stroke that damaged his insula. In fact, several other patients with insular damage had the same experience. Naqvi et al. identified 19 cigarette smokers with damage to the insula and 50 smokers with brain damage that spared this region. Of the 19 patients who had damage to the insula, 12 "quit smoking easily, immediately, without relapse, and without persistence of the urge to smoke" (Naqvi et al., 2007, p. 545). One patient with insula damage quit smoking but still reported feeling an urge to smoke. Figure 18.18 shows computer-generated images of brain damage that showed a statistically significant correlation with disruption of smoking. As you can see, the insula, which is colored red, showed the highest association with cessation of smoking.

Other studies have corroborated the report by Naqvi et al. (Hefzy et al., 2011). In addition, Forget et al. (2010) found that infusion of an inhibitory drug into the insula of rats reduced the reinforcing effects of nicotine. (See Figure 18.19.) As mentioned earlier, Zhang et al. (2011) found decreased gray matter in the frontal cortex of smokers, which may be at least partly responsible for the difficulty that smokers have in breaking their habit. These investigators also found that the insula was *larger* in smokers, which is consistent with the apparent role of the insula in nicotine addiction.

Figure 18.18 Damage to the Insula and Smoking Cessation

The diagram shows the regions of the brain (shown in red) where damage was most highly correlated with cessation of smoking.

(From Naqvi, N. H., Rudrauf, D., Damasio, H., and Bechara, A., Damage to the insula disrupts addiction to cigarette smoking, *Science*, 2007, *315*, 531–534. By permission.)

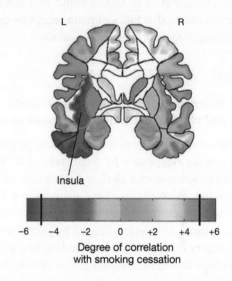

One of the several deterrents to cessation of smoking is the fact that overeating and weight gain frequently occur when people stop smoking. As mentioned earlier in this chapter and in Chapter 12, eating and a reduction in metabolic rate are stimulated by the release of MCH and orexin in the brain. Jo et al. (2005) found that nicotine inhibits MCH neurons, thus suppressing appetite. When people try to quit smoking, they are often discouraged by the fact that the

Figure 18.19 Effects of Inactivation of the Insula on Reinstatement of Drug-Seeking Behavior in Rats

Rats were trained to work for injections of nicotine, and then the behavior was extinguished. The graph shows that inactivation of the insula substantially reduced drug-seeking behavior elicited by nicotine or cues previously associated with nicotine.

(Based on data of Forget et al., 2010.)

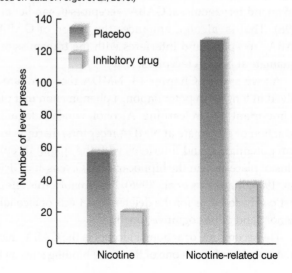

absence of nicotine in their brains releases their MCH neurons from this inhibition, increasing their appetite. Nicotine also stimulates the release of orexin, which, as we saw earlier in this chapter, is involved in drug-seeking behavior (Huang et al., 2011). Orexin is released in many parts of the brain, but one region may play an especially important role in smoking: the insula. Hollander et al. (2008) found that infusion of a drug into the insula that blocks orexin receptors decreased the responding of rats for injections of nicotine.

Alcohol

LO 18.9 Describe the effects and roles of reinforcement and physical dependence in alcohol abuse.

Alcohol has enormous costs to society. A large percentage of deaths and injuries caused by motor vehicle accidents are related to alcohol use, and alcohol contributes to violence and aggression. People who abuse alcohol often lose their jobs, their homes, and their families; many die of cirrhosis of the liver, exposure, or diseases caused by poor living conditions and injury or neglect of their bodies. Understanding the physiological and behavioral effects of this drug is an important issue.

DESCRIPTION   At low doses, alcohol produces mild euphoria and has an *anxiolytic* effect—that is, it reduces the discomfort of anxiety. At higher doses, it produces incoordination and sedation. In studies with laboratory animals, the anxiolytic effects manifest themselves as a release from the punishing effects of aversive stimuli. For example, if an animal is given electric shocks whenever it makes a particular response (say, one that obtains food or water), it will stop doing so. However, if it is then given some alcohol, it will begin making the response again (Koob et al., 1984). This phenomenon explains why people often do things they normally would not when they have had too much to drink; the alcohol removes the inhibitory effect of social controls on their behavior.

Alcohol has two major sites of action in the nervous system, acting as an indirect antagonist at NMDA receptors and an indirect agonist at GABA$_A$ receptors (Chandler et al., 1998). That is, alcohol enhances the action of GABA at GABA$_A$ receptors and interferes with the transmission of glutamate at NMDA receptors.

As we saw in Chapter 13, NMDA receptors are involved in long-term potentiation, a phenomenon that plays an important role in learning. Alcohol, which antagonizes the action of glutamate at NMDA receptors, disrupts long-term potentiation and interferes with the spatial receptive fields of place cells in the hippocampus (Givens and McMahon, 1995; Matthews et al., 1996). Presumably, this effect at least partly accounts for the deleterious effects of alcohol on memory and other cognitive functions.

The second site of action of alcohol is the GABA$_A$ receptor. Alcohol binds with one of the many binding sites on this receptor and increases the effectiveness of GABA in opening the chloride channel and producing inhibitory postsynaptic potentials. Proctor et al. (1992) recorded the activity of single neurons in the cerebral cortex of slices of rat brains. They found that the presence of alcohol significantly increased the postsynaptic response produced by the action of GABA at the GABA$_A$ receptor. As we saw in Chapter 4, the anxiolytic effect of the benzodiazepines is caused by their action as indirect agonists at the GABA$_A$ receptor. Because alcohol has this effect also, we can surmise that the anxiolytic effect of alcohol is a result of this action of the drug. The sedative effect of alcohol also appears to be exerted at the GABA$_A$ receptor. Suzdak et al. (1986) discovered a drug (Ro15-4513) that reverses alcohol intoxication by blocking the alcohol binding site on this receptor. Although the behavioral effects of alcohol are mediated by their action on GABA$_A$ receptors and NMDA receptors, high doses of alcohol have other, potentially fatal effects on all cells of the body, including destabilization of cell membranes.

As you have read previously, prenatal exposure to alcohol can have effects on the developing nervous system. Ikonomidou et al. (2000) found that exposure of the immature rat brain to alcohol triggered widespread cell death through apoptosis. The investigators exposed immature rats to alcohol at different times during the period of brain growth and found that different regions were vulnerable to the effects of the alcohol at different times. Apparently, both of alcohol's actions at GABA and glutamate receptors trigger apoptosis. To confirm this mechanism, Ikonomidou et al. found that administration of a GABA$_A$ agonist (phenobarbital, a barbiturate) or an NMDA antagonist (MK-801) to seven-day-old rats caused brain damage by means of apoptosis. (See Figure 18.20.)

REINFORCEMENT   Alcohol produces both positive and negative reinforcement. The positive reinforcement manifests itself as mild euphoria. As we saw earlier, *negative reinforcement* is caused by the termination of an aversive stimulus. If a person feels anxious and uncomfortable, then an anxiolytic drug that relieves this discomfort provides at least a temporary escape from an unpleasant situation.

The negative reinforcement provided by the anxiolytic effect of alcohol is probably not enough to explain the drug's abuse potential. Other drugs, such as the benzodiazepines (for example Valium or Ativan), are even more potent anxiolytics than alcohol, yet such drugs are abused less often. It is probably the unique combination of stimulating and anxiolytic effects—of positive and negative reinforcement—that makes alcohol so difficult for some people to resist.

Alcohol, like other drugs of abuse, increases the activity of the dopaminergic neurons of the mesolimbic system and increases the release of dopamine in the NAC as measured by microdialysis (Gessa et al., 1985; Imperato and Di Chiara, 1986). The release of dopamine appears to be related to the *positive* reinforcement that alcohol can produce. An injection

Figure 18.20 Early Exposure to Alcohol and Apoptosis

The photomicrographs of sections of rat brain show degenerating neurons (black spots). Exposure to alcohol during the period of rapid brain growth causes cell death by inducing apoptosis. These effects are mediated by the actions of alcohol as an NMDA antagonist and a GABA$_A$ agonist. MK-801, an NMDA antagonist, and phenobarbital, a GABA$_A$ agonist, also induce apoptosis.

(From Ikonomidou, C., Bittigau, P., Ishimaru, M. J., et al., Ethanol-induced apoptotic neurodegeneration and fetal alcohol syndrome, *Science*, 2000, *287*, 1056–1060. By permission.)

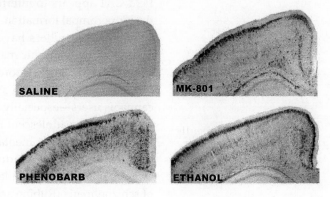

of a dopamine antagonist directly into the NAC decreases alcohol intake in rats (Samson et al., 1993), as does the injection of a drug into the VTA that decreases the activity of the dopaminergic neurons there (Hodge et al., 1993). In a double-blind study, Enggasser and de Wit (2001) found that haloperidol, an antipsychotic drug that blocks DA receptors, decreased the amount of alcohol that participants subsequently drank. Presumably, the drug reduced the reinforcing effect of the alcohol. In addition, individuals who normally feel stimulated and euphoric after having a drink reported a reduction in these effects after taking haloperidol.

Opiate receptors appear to be involved in a reinforcement mechanism that does not directly involve dopaminergic neurons. The reinforcing effect of alcohol is at least partly caused by its ability to trigger the release of the endogenous opioids. Several studies have shown that the opiate receptor blockers such as naloxone block the reinforcing effects of alcohol in a variety of species, including rats, monkeys, and humans (Altschuler et al., 1980; Davidson et al., 1996; Reid, 1996). In addition, endogenous opioids may play a role in alcohol craving. Heinz et al. (2005) found that one to three weeks of abstinence increased the number of μ opiate receptors in the NAC. The greater the number of receptors, the more intense the craving was. Presumably, the increased number of μ receptors increased the effects of endogenous opiates on the brain and served as a contributing factor to the craving for alcohol. (See Figure 18.21.)

PHYSICAL DEPENDENCE Withdrawal from long-term alcohol intake (like that of heroin, cocaine, amphetamine, and nicotine) decreases the activity of mesolimbic neurons and their release of dopamine in the NAC (Diana et al., 1993). If an indirect antagonist for NMDA receptors is then administered, dopamine secretion in the NAC recovers. The

evidence suggests the following sequence of events: Some of the acute effects of a single dose of alcohol are caused by the antagonistic effect of the drug on NMDA receptors. Long-term suppression of NMDA receptors causes upregulation—a compensatory increase in the sensitivity of the receptors. Then, when alcohol intake suddenly ceases, the increased activity of NMDA receptors inhibits the activity of ventral tegmental neurons and the release of dopamine in the NAC.

Although the effects of opiate withdrawal are often exaggerated, those produced by barbiturate or alcohol withdrawal are serious and can even be fatal. The increased sensitivity of NMDA receptors as they rebound from the suppressive effect of alcohol can trigger seizures that are considered to be a medical emergency and are usually treated with benzodiazepines. Confirming the cause of these reactions, Liljequist (1991) found that seizures caused by alcohol withdrawal could be prevented by giving mice a drug that blocks NMDA receptors.

Cannabis

LO 18.10 **Describe the effects and role of reinforcement in cannabis abuse.**

Another drug that people regularly self-administer is THC, the active ingredient in marijuana. THC is produced by the marijuana plant or it can be created synthetically. Synthetic cannabinoids such as K2 or Spice were implicated in nearly 30,000 emergency room visits in 2010, doubling the number from 2001 (Substance Abuse and Mental Health Services Administration). Synthetic cannabinoids were made illegal in the United States in 2012.

DESCRIPTION As you learned in Chapter 4, the site of action of the endogenous cannabinoids in the brain is the

Figure 18.21 Cravings for Alcohol and μ Opiate Receptors

The drawings of the results of PET scans show the presence of μ opiate receptors in the dorsal striatum of detoxified patients diagnosed with alcohol abuse and healthy control participants. The graph shows the relative alcohol craving score as a function of relative numbers of μ opiate receptors.

(Based on data from Heinz et al., 2005.)

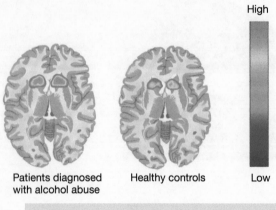

Patients diagnosed with alcohol abuse   Healthy controls

High

Low

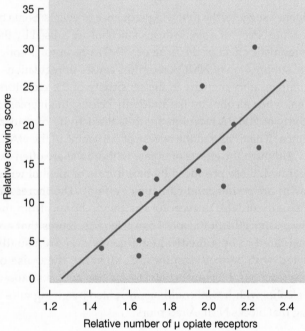

CB1 receptor. The endogenous ligands for the CB1 receptor, anandamide and 2-AG, are lipids. Administration of a drug that blocks CB1 receptors abolishes the "high" produced by smoking marijuana (Huestis et al., 2001).

As we saw in Chapter 4, the hippocampus contains a large concentration of CB1 receptors. Marijuana produces memory impairment. Evidence indicates that the drug does so by disrupting the normal functions of the hippocampus, which plays such an important role in memory. Pyramidal cells in the CA1 region of the hippocampus release endogenous cannabinoids, which provide a retrograde signal that inhibits GABAergic neurons that normally inhibit them. In this way the release of endogenous cannabinoids facilitates the activity of CA1 pyramidal cells and facilitates long-term potentiation (Kunos and Batkai, 2001).

We might expect that facilitating long-term potentiation in the hippocampus would enhance its memory functions. However, the reverse is true; Hampson and Deadwyler (2000) found that the effects of cannabinoids on a spatial memory task were similar to those produced by hippocampal lesions. Thus, excessive activation of CB1 receptors in field CA1 appears to interfere with normal functioning of the hippocampal formation.

Some researchers have reported a troubling finding associated with chronic marijuana use (Le Bec et al., 2009; Minozzi et al., 2010; Moore et al., 2007): The incidence of psychotic disorders such as schizophrenia is increased in cannabis users—especially those who have used cannabis frequently. The adolescent brain appears to be particularly vulnerable to developmental effects of marijuana exposure. THC exposure during adolescence in rodents results in impaired performance on later tasks that model symptoms of schizophrenia (Rubino and Parolaro, 2014). Keep in mind that a correlational study cannot prove the existence of a cause-and-effect relationship. It is possible that people who are already more likely to develop psychotic symptoms are also more likely to use cannabis. However, statistical adjustments suggest that a cause-and-effect relationship between cannabis use and psychosis cannot be ruled out.

REINFORCEMENT   THC, like other drugs that are abused, has a stimulating effect on dopaminergic neurons. Chen et al. (1990) injected rats with low doses of THC and measured the release of dopamine in the NAC by means of microdialysis. Sure enough, they found that the injections caused the release of dopamine. (See Figure 18.22.) Chen et al. (1993) found that local injections of small amounts of THC into the VTA had no effect on the release of dopamine in the NAC. However, injection of THC into the NAC *did* cause dopamine release there. Thus, the drug appears to act directly on

Figure 18.22 THC and Dopamine Secretion in the Nucleus Accumbens

The graph shows changes in dopamine concentration in the nucleus accumbens, measured by microdialysis, in response to injections of THC or an inert placebo.

(Based on data from Chen et al., 1990.)

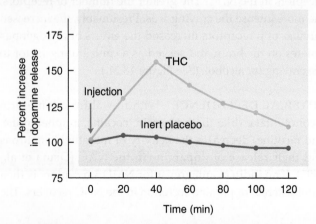

dopaminergic terminal buttons—presumably on presynaptic heteroreceptors, where it increases the release of dopamine.

A variety of laboratory animals, including mice, rats, and monkeys, will self-administer drugs that stimulate CB1 receptors, including THC (Maldonado and Rodriguez de Fonseca, 2002). A targeted mutation that blocks the production of CB1 receptors abolishes the reinforcing effect not only of cannabinoids but also of morphine and heroin (Cossu et al., 2001). This mutation also decreases the reinforcing effects of alcohol and the acquisition of self-administration of cocaine (Houchi et al., 2005; Soria et al., 2005). In addition, rimonabant, the CB1 receptor antagonist, decreases the reinforcing effects of nicotine.

The primary reinforcing component of marijuana, THC, is one of approximately 70 different chemicals produced only by the cannabis plant. Another chemical, *cannabidiol (CBD)*, plays an entirely different role. Unlike THC, which produces anxiety and psychotic-like behavior in large doses, CBD has antianxiety and antipsychotic effects. THC is a partial agonist of cannabinoid receptors, whereas CBD is an antagonist. Also unlike THC, CBD does not produce psychotropic effects: It is not reinforcing, and it does not produce a "high." In recent years, levels of THC in marijuana have increased greatly, while levels of CBD have decreased. During the past decade, the numbers of people who seek treatment for cannabis abuse has also increased (Morgan et al., 2010). Morgan and her colleagues recruited 94 people who used marijuana regularly for a study on the effects of THC and CBD. The investigators measured the concentration of THC and CBD in a sample of their marijuana and in a sample of their urine. They found that people smoking their customary marijuana with low levels of CBD and high levels of THC paid more

Figure 18.23 Effects of Varying Ratios of CBD and THC in Marijuana

The graph shows that smoking marijuana with high levels of CBD decreases the pleasantness of photographs associated with marijuana smoking.

(Based on data of Morgan et al., 2010.)

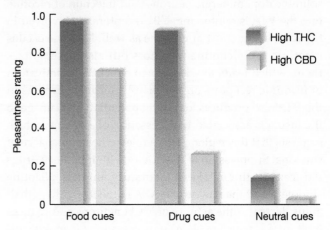

attention to photographs of cannabis-related stimuli and said that they liked them better than those smoking their customary marijuana with higher levels of CBD. Both groups gave high ratings to food-related photographs, so CBD had no effect on their interest in food. (See Figure 18.23.) A study by Ren et al. (2009) found that an injection of CBD reduced heroin-seeking behavior in rats, even up to two weeks later, which indicates that the effects of this drug are not limited to marijuana. CBD did not affect the animals' intake of heroin, but it did decrease the reinforcing effect of stimuli that had previously been associated with heroin.

Section Review

Commonly Abused Drugs

LO 18.6 Describe the effects and roles of reinforcement and physical dependence in opiate abuse.

Opiates produce analgesia, hypothermia, sedation, and reinforcement. Opiate receptors in the periaqueductal gray matter are responsible for the analgesia, those in the preoptic area for the hypothermia, those in the mesencephalic reticular formation for the sedation, and those in the VTA and NAC at least partly for the reinforcement. A targeted mutation in mice indicates that μ opiate receptors are responsible for analgesia, reinforcement, and withdrawal symptoms. The release of the endogenous opioids may play a role in the reinforcing effects of natural stimuli or even other drugs such as alcohol. The symptoms that are produced by antagonist-precipitated withdrawal from opiates can be elicited by injecting naloxone into the periaqueductal gray matter

and the locus coeruleus, which implicates these structures in these symptoms.

LO 18.7 Describe the effects and role of reinforcement in stimulant abuse.

Cocaine inhibits the reuptake of dopamine by terminal buttons, and amphetamine causes the dopamine transporters in terminal buttons to run in reverse, releasing dopamine from terminal buttons. Besides producing alertness, activation, and positive reinforcement, cocaine and amphetamine can produce psychotic symptoms that resemble positive symptoms of schizophrenia. The reinforcing effects of cocaine and amphetamine are mediated by an increase in dopamine in the NAC. Chronic methamphetamine abuse is associated with reduced numbers of dopaminergic axons and terminals in the striatum (revealed as a decrease in the numbers of dopamine transporters located there).

LO 18.8 Describe the effects and roles of reinforcement and physical dependence in nicotine abuse.

Nicotine does not cause intoxication and is readily available and legal. The craving for nicotine is extremely motivating. Nicotine stimulates the release of DA from mesolimbic dopaminergic neurons, and injection of nicotine into the VTA is reinforcing. CB1 receptors are involved in the reinforcing effect of nicotine as well. Nicotine excites nicotinic acetylcholine receptors but also desensitizes them, which leads to withdrawal effects. The activation of nicotinic receptors on presynaptic terminal buttons in the VTA also produces long-term potentiation. Damage to the insula is associated with cessation of smoking, which suggests that this region plays a role in the maintenance of smoking. Suppression of its activity with inhibitory drugs reduces nicotine intake in laboratory animals. Nicotine stimulation of the release of GABA in the lateral hypothalamus decreases the activity of MCH neurons and reduces food intake, which explains why cessation of smoking often leads to weight gain. Infusion of an orexin antagonist in the insula suppresses nicotine intake. Activity of a circuit from the medial habenula to the interpeduncular nucleus does the same. This effect depends on the presence of neurons with α5 ACh receptors in the habenula.

LO 18.9 Describe the effects and roles of reinforcement and physical dependence in alcohol abuse.

Alcohol has positively reinforcing effects and, through its anxiolytic action, has negatively reinforcing effects as well. It serves as an indirect antagonist at NMDA receptors and an indirect agonist at $GABA_A$ receptors. It stimulates the release of dopamine in the NAC. Withdrawal from long-term alcohol abuse can lead to seizures, an effect that seems to be caused by compensatory upregulation of NMDA receptors. Release of endogenous opioids also plays a role in the reinforcing effects of alcohol. Increases in the numbers of μ opiate receptors during abstinence from alcohol may intensify craving.

LO 18.10 Describe the effects and role of reinforcement in cannabis abuse.

The active ingredient in cannabis, THC, stimulates receptors whose natural ligand is anandamide. THC, like other drugs of abuse, stimulates the release of dopamine in the NAC. The presence of cannabidiol (CBD) in marijuana has a protective effect against dependence on cannabis. The CB1 receptor is responsible for the physiological and behavioral effects of THC and the endogenous cannabinoids. A targeted mutation against the CB1 receptor reduces the reinforcing effect of alcohol, cocaine, and the opiates as well as that of the cannabinoids. Blocking CB1 receptors also decreases the reinforcing effects of nicotine. Cannabinoids produce memory deficits by acting on inhibitory GABAergic neurons in the CA1 field of the hippocampus. Accumulating studies indicate that cannabis use is associated with an increased incidence of schizophrenia.

Thought Question

Although executives of tobacco companies used to insist that cigarettes were not addictive and asserted that people smoked simply because of the pleasure the act gave them, research indicates that nicotine is indeed a potent drug of abuse. Why do you think it took so long to recognize this fact?

Treatment for Substance Abuse

There are many reasons for engaging in research on the neuroscience of substance abuse, including an academic interest in the nature of reinforcement and the pharmacology of psychoactive drugs. But most researchers hope that the results of their research will contribute to the development of ways to treat and—better yet—prevent substance abuse. The incidence of substance abuse is high and research has not yet solved the problem. However, progress is being made.

A variety of therapeutic interventions have been developed. When selecting a therapeutic intervention, two important considerations are to first determine whether the intervention is supported by research demonstrating efficacy and then to assess the quality and quantity of the research supporting the treatment. Strategies, such as contingency management (a form of behavioral intervention using vouchers or rewards for reduced substance use), cognitive therapies, family therapies, agonist replacement for opiates and nicotine, and opiate antagonists for alcohol paired with behavioral interventions, are supported by research as effective treatments for substance abuse (Carroll and Onken, 2014; Carroll and Rounsaville, 2014).

Despite development of a wide range of interventions, successful treatment of substance abuse is challenging. Approximately 40–60 percent of individuals are abstinent one year after a substance abuse intervention (McLellan et al., 2000). It is important to also keep in mind that people have different goals for treatment, ranging from complete abstinence to reduced use of a drug. The remainder of this section will include summaries of some of the empirically-supported interventions for substance abuse that are known to interact with brain mechanisms responsible for substance abuse. This is not an exhaustive list, and research is underway to develop new and potentially more effective treatments.

Opiates

LO 18.11 **Summarize the research for effective treatment for opiate abuse.**

One treatment for opiate abuse is methadone maintenance. Methadone is a potent opiate, just like morphine or heroin. If it were available in a form suitable for injection, it would be abused. (Methadone clinics must control their stock of methadone carefully to prevent it from being stolen and sold.) Methadone maintenance programs administer the drug to their patients in an oral form, which they must consume in the presence of the personnel supervising this procedure. Because the oral route of administration increases the opiate level in the brain slowly, the drug does not produce a high, the way an injection of opiates will. In addition, because methadone is long lasting, the patient's opiate receptors remain occupied for a long time, which means that an injection of heroin has little effect. Of course, a very large dose of heroin will still produce a "rush," so the method is not foolproof.

A newer drug, *buprenorphine*, shows promise of being an even better therapeutic agent for opiate abuse treatment than methadone (Vocci et al., 2005). Buprenorphine is a partial agonist for the μ opiate receptor. You will recall from Chapter 16 that a partial agonist is a drug that has a high affinity for a particular receptor but activates that receptor less than the normal ligand does. This action reduces the effects of a receptor ligand in regions of high concentration and increases it in regions of low concentration, as shown in Figure 16.13. Buprenorphine blocks the effects of opiates and itself produces only a weak opiate effect. Unlike methadone, it has little value on the illicit drug market. A randomized placebo-controlled trial compared the effectiveness of buprenorphine and buprenorphine plus naloxone in people recovering from opiate abuse (Fudala et al., 2003). People in the two drug-treatment groups reported less craving than those in the control group. The proportion of people who continued to be abstinent was 17.8 percent for people treated with buprenorphine, 20.7 percent for people treated with the combination of the two drugs, and only 5.8 percent for people receiving a placebo. (See Figure 18.24.) After one month, all subjects were given buprenorphine plus naloxone for 11 months. The percentage of people who abstained (indicated by the absence of opiates in urine samples) ranged from 35.2 to 67.4 percent at various times during the 11-month period.

A major advantage of buprenorphine, besides its efficacy, is the fact that it can be used in office-based treatment. The addition of a small dose of naloxone ensures that the combination drug has no abuse potential—and will, in fact, cause withdrawal symptoms if it is used by a person who is currently abusing an opiate.

As we saw, opiate receptor blockers such as naloxone and naltrexone interfere with the action of opiates. Emergency rooms always have one of these drugs available to treat patients who have taken an overdose of heroin, and

Figure 18.24 Buprenorphine as a Treatment for Opiate Abuse

The graph shows the effects of treatment with buprenorphine, buprenorphine + naloxone, and a placebo on opiate craving in people being treated for opiate abuse.

(Based on data from Fudala et al., 2003.)

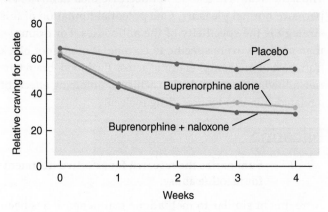

many lives have been saved by these means. But although an opiate antagonist will block the effects of heroin, the research reviewed earlier in this chapter suggests that it should *increase* the craving for heroin.

Stimulants

LO 18.12 **Summarize the research for effective treatment for stimulant abuse.**

As we saw earlier, the reinforcing effects of cocaine and amphetamine are primarily a result of the sharply increased levels of dopamine that these drugs produce in the NAC. Drugs that block dopamine receptors certainly block the reinforcing effects of cocaine and amphetamine, but they also produce dysphoria and anhedonia. People will not tolerate the unpleasant feelings these drugs produce, so they are not useful treatments for cocaine and amphetamine abuse. Drugs that *stimulate* dopamine receptors can reduce a person's dependence on cocaine or amphetamine, but these drugs have just as much abuse potential as the drugs they replace and have the same deleterious effects on health.

An interesting approach to cocaine addiction was suggested by a study by Carrera et al. (1995), who conjugated cocaine to a foreign protein and managed to stimulate rats' immune systems to develop antibodies to cocaine. The antibodies bound with molecules of cocaine and prevented them from crossing the blood–brain barrier. As a consequence, these "cocaine-immunized" rats were less sensitive to the activating effects of cocaine, and brain levels of cocaine in these animals were lower after an injection of cocaine. Since this study was carried out, animal studies with vaccines against cocaine, heroin, methamphetamine, and nicotine have been carried out, and several human clinical trials with vaccines for cocaine and nicotine have taken place (Cerny and Cerny, 2009; Carroll et al., 2011; Hicks et al., 2011; Stowe et al., 2011). The results of these animal studies and human trials are promising, and more extensive human trials are in progress. Theoretically, at least, treatment of substance abuse with immunotherapy should interfere only with the action of an abused drug and not with the normal operations of people's reinforcement mechanisms. Thus, the treatment should not decrease their ability to experience normal pleasure. One potential limitation of this strategy is the specificity of the antibodies. For example, if an antibody were specific to cocaine, it might not block transport of methamphetamine across the blood–brain barrier, allowing an individual to achieve reinforcing effects of a related, but not identical, drug molecule.

Nicotine

LO 18.13 **Summarize the research for effective treatment for nicotine abuse.**

A treatment similar to methadone maintenance has been used successfully as an adjunct to treatment for nicotine abuse. Chewing gum and transdermal patches that release nicotine are available for smoking-cessation treatment. Both methods maintain a sufficiently high level of nicotine in the brain to decrease a person's craving for nicotine. Once the behavioral habit of smoking has subsided, the dose of nicotine can be decreased to wean the person from the drug. Carefully controlled studies have shown that nicotine maintenance therapy, and not administration of a placebo, is useful in treatment for nicotine dependence (Raupach and van Schayck, 2011). However, nicotine maintenance therapy is most effective if it is part of a counseling program.

One of the limitations of a smoking cessation intervention that includes only nicotine maintenance is that this procedure does not provide an important nonnicotine component of smoking: the sensations produced by the action of cigarette smoke on the airways. As we saw earlier in this chapter, stimuli associated with the administration of drugs of abuse play an important role in sustaining substance abuse. Smokers who rate the pleasurability of puffs of normal and denicotinized cigarettes within seven seconds, which is less time than it takes for nicotine to leave the lungs, enter the blood, and reach the brain, reported that puffing denicotinized cigarettes produced equally strong feelings of euphoria and satisfaction and reductions in the urge to smoke. Furthermore, blocking the sensations of cigarette smoke on the airways by first inhaling a local anesthetic diminishes smoking satisfaction. Denicotinized cigarettes are not a completely adequate substitute for normal cigarettes, because nicotine itself, not just the other components of smoke, makes an important contribution to the sensations felt in the airways. In fact, trimethaphan, a drug that blocks nicotinic receptors but does not cross the blood–brain barrier, decreases the sensory effects of smoking and reduces satisfaction. Because trimethaphan does not interfere with the effects of nicotine on the brain, this finding indicates that the central effects of nicotine are not

sufficient by themselves to maintain nicotine abuse. Instead, the combination of an immediate cue from the sensory effects of components of cigarette smoke on the airways and a more delayed, and more continuous, effect of nicotine on the brain serves to make smoking so difficult to stop (Naqvi and Bechara, 2005; Rose, 2006).

As we saw earlier in this chapter, studies with laboratory animals have found that the endogenous cannabinoids are involved in the reinforcing effects of nicotine as well as those of marijuana. A recent clinical trial reported that rimonabant, a CB1 receptor antagonist, was effective in helping smokers to quit their habit (Henningfield et al., 2005). One significant benefit of the drug was a decrease in the weight gain that typically accompanies cessation of smoking and often discourages people who are trying to quit. As we saw in Chapter 12, the endocannabinoids stimulate eating, apparently by increasing the release of MCH and orexin. Blocking CB1 receptors abolishes this effect and helps to counteract the effects of withdrawal from nicotine on these neurons. But the problem with rimonabant is that some clinical trials have found that the drug can cause anxiety and depression, which provoked the withdrawal of its approval as an antiobesity medication.

Another drug, *varenicline,* has been approved for therapeutic use to treat nicotine dependence. Varenicline was developed especially as a treatment for nicotine abuse. The drug serves as a partial agonist for the nicotinic receptor, just as buprenorphine serves as a partial agonist for the μ opiate receptor. As a partial nicotinic agonist, varenicline maintains a moderate level of activation of nicotinic receptors but prevents high levels of nicotine from providing excessive levels of stimulation. Figure 18.25 shows the effects of treatment with varenicline and bupropion on continuous abstinence rates of smokers enrolled in a randomized, double-blind, placebo-controlled study (Nides et al., 2006). By the end of the 52-week treatment program, 14.4 percent of the smokers

Figure 18.25 Varenicline as a Treatment for Smoking
The graph shows the percentage of people who smoked that were treated with varenicline, bupropion, or placebo that abstained from cigarette smoking.

(Based on data from Nides et al., 2006.)

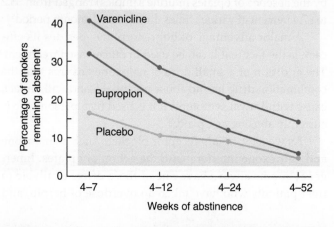

treated with varenicline were still abstinent, compared with 6.3 percent and 4.9 percent of the smokers who received bupropion and placebo, respectively.

Alcohol

LO 18.14 Summarize the research for effective treatment for alcohol abuse.

As mentioned earlier, several studies have shown that opiate antagonists decrease the reinforcing value of alcohol in a variety of species, including our own. This finding suggests that the reinforcing effect of alcohol—at least in part—is produced by the secretion of endogenous opioids and the activation of opiate receptors in the brain. A study by Davidson et al. (1996) illustrates this effect. The investigators arranged a double-blind, placebo-controlled study with 16 college-age men and women to investigate the effects of naltrexone on social drinkers. None of the participants were abusing alcohol, and pregnancy tests ensured that the women were not pregnant. They gathered around a table in a local restaurant/bar for three two-hour drinking sessions, two weeks apart. For several days before the meeting, they swallowed capsules that contained either naltrexone or an inert placebo. The results showed that naltrexone increased the amount of time to take the first sip and to take a second drink and that the blood alcohol levels of the naltrexone-treated participants were lower at the end of the session. In general, the people who had taken naltrexone found that their drinks did not taste very good—in fact, some of them asked for a different drink after taking the first sip.

These results are consistent with reports of the effectiveness of naltrexone as an adjunct to programs designed to treat alcohol abuse. For example, O'Brien et al. (1996) reported the results of two long-term programs using naltrexone along with more traditional behavioral treatments. Both programs found that administration of naltrexone significantly increased the likelihood of success. As Figure 18.26 shows, naltrexone decreased the participants' craving for alcohol and increased the number of participants who abstained from alcohol. Currently, many treatment programs are using a sustained-release form of naltrexone to help treat alcoholism, and results with the drug have been encouraging (Gastfriend, 2011).

One more drug has shown promise for treatment of alcohol abuse. As we saw earlier in this chapter, alcohol serves as an indirect agonist at the $GABA_A$ receptor and an indirect antagonist at the NMDA receptor. *Acamprosate,* an NMDA-receptor antagonist that has been used in Europe to treat seizure disorders, was tested for its ability to stop seizures induced by withdrawal from alcohol. The researchers discovered that the drug had an unexpected benefit: Patients who received the drug were less likely to start drinking again (Wickelgren, 1998). Several double-blind studies have confirmed the therapeutic benefits of acamprosate, but these benefits appear to be modest (Rösner et al., 2010).

Figure 18.26 Naltrexone as a Treatment for Alcoholism
The graphs show mean craving score and proportion of patients who abstained from drinking while receiving naltrexone or a placebo.
(Based on data from O'Brien et al., 1996.)

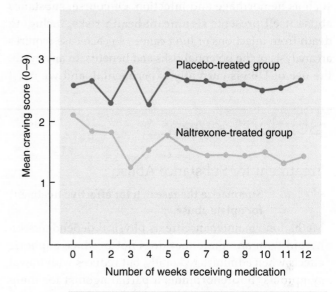

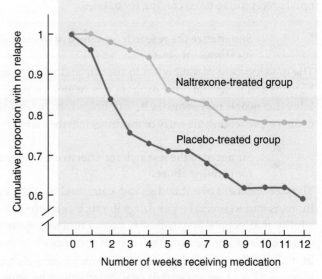

Brain Stimulation

LO 18.15 Describe the implications for brain stimulation treatments in substance abuse.

A novel approach to substance abuse is currently being investigated. As we saw in Chapters 13, 16, and 17, deep brain stimulation (DBS) has been shown to have therapeutic effects on the symptoms of Parkinson's disease, depression, anxiety disorders, and obsessive-compulsive disorder. A review by Luigjes et al. (2011) reported that seven animal studies have investigated the effectiveness of DBS of the NAC, subthalamic nucleus (STN), dorsal striatum, habenula, medial PFC, and hypothalamus. Eleven studies with human participants have targeted the NAC or the STN with DBS. So far, the authors report, the NAC appears to be the most promising target. For example, Mantione et al. (2010) used DBS to stimulate the NAC of a 47-year-old male who smoked. The investigators reported that the man effortlessly stopped smoking and lost weight (he was obese).

Deep brain stimulation is not a procedure to take lightly. It involves brain surgery, which runs a risk of complications such as hemorrhage and infection. Of course, substance abuse itself presents significant health risks, including death from infections or lung cancer, so each case requires an analysis of the potential risks and benefits. In any event, the use of DBS is currently experimental, and we must consider the strong possibility that such a dramatic procedure will produce placebo effects. (Yes, surgical procedures are susceptible to placebo effects.) A less invasive procedure, transcranial magnetic stimulation (TMS), is also being investigated as a treatment for substance abuse. For example, Amiaz et al. (2009) applied TMS over the left dorsolateral PFC of people who smoked. The treatment reduced tobacco use (verified by urinalysis), but the therapeutic effects eventually diminished over time.

Section Review

Treatment for Substance Abuse

LO 18.11 Summarize the research for effective treatment for opiate abuse.
Methadone maintenance treats physical dependence on heroin with an opiate that does not produce euphoric effects when administered orally, but reduces withdrawal symptoms. Buprenorphine, a partial agonist for the μ opiate receptor, reduces craving for opiates.

LO 18.12 Summarize the research for effective treatment for stimulant abuse.
The development of antibodies to cocaine and nicotine in humans and to several other drugs in rats creates the possibility that people may someday be immunized against drugs of abuse, preventing the entry of the drugs into the brain.

LO 18.13 Summarize the research for effective treatment for nicotine abuse.
The development of antibodies to cocaine and nicotine in humans and to several other drugs in rats creates the possibility that people may someday be immunized against drugs of abuse, preventing the entry of the drugs into the brain. Nicotine-containing gum and transdermal patches help smokers to reduce withdrawal symptoms of nicotine. However, sensations from the airways produced by the presence of cigarette smoke play an important role in nicotine abuse, and oral and transdermal nicotine administration do not provide these sensations. Rimonabant, a CB1 receptor antagonist, aids in smoking cessation and reduces the likelihood of weight gain, but it may produce adverse emotional effects. Bupropion, an antidepressant drug, has also been shown to help smokers stop their habit. Varenicline, a partial agonist for the nicotinic receptor, may be even more effective.

LO 18.14 Summarize the research for effective treatment for alcohol abuse.
The most effective pharmacological adjuncts to treatment for alcohol abuse appear to be opiate antagonists that reduce the drug's reinforcing effects. Acamprosate, an NMDA-receptor antagonist, appears to facilitate treatment of alcohol abuse as well.

LO 18.15 Describe the implications for brain stimulation treatments in substance abuse.
Deep brain stimulation of the NAC and STN and TMS of the prefrontal cortex show promise as a treatment for substance abuse.

Thought Question

A friend has recently asked you for advice about helping a family member who is interested in treatment for alcohol abuse. Your friend is curious about how some of the pharmacological treatments for alcohol abuse work. In an e-mail to your friend, explain how one or more pharmacological treatments for alcohol abuse work.

Chapter Review Questions

1. Describe two common features of substance abuse: positive and negative reinforcement.

2. Describe the neural mechanisms responsible for craving and relapse.

3. Review the neural basis of the reinforcing effects and withdrawal effects of opiates.

4. Discuss the role of heredity in nicotine abuse.

5. Discuss the molecular biology of drug abuse and the hereditary role of sirtuins in stimulant drugs.

6. Discuss the contribution and effect of dopamine in reinforcement and its role in substance abuse.

7. Explain the neuro-physiological basis of physical alcohol dependence.

8. Discuss the drugs of choice that may help to quit smoking.

Glossary

2-deoxyglucose (2-DG) (*dee ox ee gloo kohss*)   A sugar that enters cells along with glucose but is not metabolized.

α-melanocyte-stimulating hormone (α-MSH)   A neuropeptide that acts as an agonist at MC4 receptors and inhibits eating.

α-synuclein   A protein normally found in the presynaptic membrane, where it is apparently involved in synaptic plasticity. Abnormal accumulations are apparently the cause of neural degeneration in Parkinson's disease.

absence seizure   A type of seizure disorder often seen in children; characterized by periods of inattention, which are not subsequently remembered; also called *petit mal* seizure.

absorptive phase   The phase of metabolism during which nutrients are absorbed from the digestive system; glucose and amino acids constitute the principal source of energy for cells during this phase, and excess nutrients are stored in adipose tissue in the form of triglycerides.

accessory olfactory bulb   A neural structure located in the main olfactory bulb that receives information from the vomeronasal organ.

accommodation   Changes in the thickness of the lens of the eye, accomplished by the ciliary muscles, that focus images of near or distant objects on the retina.

acetylcholine (ACh) (*a see tul koh leen*)   A neurotransmitter found in the brain, spinal cord, and parts of the peripheral nervous system; responsible for muscular contraction.

acetylcholinesterase (AChE) (*a see tul koh lin ess ter ace*)   The enzyme that destroys acetylcholine soon after it is liberated by the terminal buttons, thus terminating the postsynaptic potential.

actin   One of the proteins (with myosin) that provide the physical basis for muscular contraction.

action potential   The brief electrical impulse that provides the basis for conduction of information along an axon.

activational effect (of hormone)   The effect of a hormone that occurs in the fully developed organism; may depend on the organism's prior exposure to the organizational effects of hormones.

acute anterior poliomyelitis (*poh lee oh my a lye tis*)   A viral disease that destroys motor neurons of the brain and spinal cord.

adenosine   A neuromodulator that is released by neurons engaging in high levels of metabolic activity; may play a primary role in the initiation of sleep.

adenosine triphosphate (ATP) (*ah den o seen*)   A molecule of prime importance to cellular energy metabolism; its breakdown liberates energy.

adrenal medulla   The inner portion of the adrenal gland, located atop the kidney, controlled by sympathetic nerve fibers; secretes epinephrine and norepinephrine.

adrenocorticotropic hormone (ACTH)   A hormone released by the anterior pituitary gland in response to CRH; stimulates the adrenal cortex to produce glucocorticoids.

advanced sleep phase syndrome   A 4-hour advance in rhythms of sleep and temperature cycles, apparently caused by a mutation of a gene (*per2*) involved in the rhythmicity of neurons of the SCN.

affective blindsight   The ability of a person who cannot see objects in his or her blind field to accurately identify facial expressions of emotion while remaining unconscious of perceiving them; caused by damage to the visual cortex.

afferent axon   An axon directed toward the central nervous system, conveying sensory information.

affinity   The readiness with which two molecules join together.

agonist   A drug that facilitates the effects of a particular neurotransmitter on the postsynaptic cell.

agoraphobia   A fear of being away from home or other protected places.

agouti-related protein (AGRP)   A neuropeptide that acts as an antagonist at MC4 receptors and increases eating.

agrammatism   One of the usual symptoms of Broca's aphasia; a difficulty in comprehending or properly employing grammatical devices, such as verb endings and word order.

akinetopsia   Inability to perceive movement, caused by damage to area V5 (also called MST) of the visual association cortex.

all-or-none law   The principle that once an action potential is triggered in an axon, it is propagated, without decrement, to the end of the fiber.

allele   The nature of the particular sequence of base pairs of DNA that constitutes a gene; for example, the genes that code for blue or brown iris pigment are different alleles of a particular gene.

allostasis   The process of responding to stimuli and regaining and maintaining homeostasis, including a change in the set point of a system to respond to stimuli that are outside the range of typical homeostatic functioning.

allostatic load   The cumulative and collective wear and tear on body systems when there is too much stress response or when the stress response is not turned off.

allylglycine   A drug that inhibits the activity of GAD and thus blocks the synthesis of GABA.

alpha activity   Smooth electrical activity of 8–12 Hz recorded from the brain; generally associated with a state of relaxation.

alpha motor neuron   A neuron whose axon forms synapses with extrafusal muscle fibers of a skeletal muscle; activation contracts the muscle fibers.

alprazolam   An indirect agonist for the GABAA receptor; part of the benzodiazepine class of drugs.

Alzheimer's disease   A degenerative brain disorder of unknown origin; causes progressive memory loss, motor deficits, and eventual death.

amacrine cell (*amm a krine*)   A neuron in the retina that interconnects adjacent ganglion cells and the inner processes of the bipolar cells.

AMPA receptor   An ionotropic glutamate receptor that controls a sodium channel; when open, it produces EPSPs.

amphetamine   An antagonist at dopamine and norepinephrine transporters that causes them to run in reverse, releasing these neurotransmitters into the synapse.

AMPT   A drug that blocks the activity of tyrosine hydroxylase and thus interferes with the synthesis of the catecholamines.

ampulla (*am pull uh*)   An enlargement in a semicircular canal; contains the cupula.

amusia (*a mew zia*)   Loss or impairment of musical abilities, produced by hereditary factors or brain damage.

amygdala (*a mig da la*)   A structure in the interior of the rostral temporal lobe, containing a set of nuclei; part of the limbic system.

amyloid plaque (*amm i loyd*)   An extracellular deposit containing a dense core of β-amyloid protein surrounded by degenerating axons and dendrites and activated microglia and reactive astrocytes.

amyotrophic lateral sclerosis (ALS)   A degenerative disorder that attacks the spinal cord and cranial nerve motor neurons.

anandamide (*a nan da mide*)   The first cannabinoid to be discovered and probably the most important one.

androgen (*an dro jen*)   A male sex steroid hormone. Testosterone is the principal mammalian androgen.

androgen insensitivity syndrome   A condition caused by a congenital lack of functioning androgen receptors; in a person with XY sex chromosomes, causes the development of a female with testes but no internal sex organs.

anomia   Difficulty in finding (remembering) the appropriate word to describe an object, action, or attribute; one of the symptoms of aphasia.

anorexia nervosa   A disorder that most frequently afflicts young women; exaggerated concern with being overweight that leads to excessive dieting and often compulsive exercising; can lead to starvation.

antagonist   A drug that opposes or inhibits the effects of a particular neurotransmitter on the postsynaptic cell.

antagonist-precipitated withdrawal   Sudden withdrawal from long-term administration of a drug caused by cessation of the drug and administration of an antagonistic drug.

anterior   With respect to the central nervous system, located near or toward the head.

anterior cingulate cortex   A region of the cerebral cortex associated with the perception of unpleasant stimuli, including pain and thirst

anterior pituitary gland   The anterior part of the pituitary gland; an endocrine gland whose secretions are controlled by the hypothalamic hormones.

anterograde   In a direction along an axon from the cell body toward the terminal buttons.

anterograde amnesia   Amnesia for events that occur after some disturbance to the brain, such as head injury or certain degenerative brain diseases.

anterograde labeling method (*ann ter oh grade*)   A histological method that labels the axons and terminal buttons of neurons whose cell bodies are located in a particular region.

anti-Müllerian hormone   A peptide secreted by the fetal testes that inhibits the development of the Müllerian system, which would otherwise become the female internal sex organs.

antibody   A protein produced by a cell of the immune system that recognizes antigens present on invading microorganisms.

anticipatory anxiety   A fear of having a panic attack; may lead to the development of agoraphobia.

antigen   A protein present on a microorganism that permits the immune system to recognize the microorganism as an invader.

antisense oligonucleotide (*oh li go new klee oh tide*)   Modified strand of RNA or DNA that binds with a specific molecule of mRNA and prevents it from producing its protein.

anxiety disorder   A psychological disorder characterized by tension, overactivity of the autonomic nervous system, expectation of an impending disaster, and continuous vigilance for danger.

anxiolytic (*angz ee oh lit ik*)   An anxiety-reducing effect.

AP5 (2-amino-5-phosphonopentanoate)   A drug that blocks the glutamate binding site on NMDA receptors.

aphasia   Difficulty in producing or comprehending speech not produced by deafness or a simple motor deficit; caused by brain damage.

apolipoprotein E (ApoE) (*ay po lye po proh teen*)   A glycoprotein that transports cholesterol in the blood and plays a role in cellular repair; presence of the E4 allele of the ApoE gene increases the risk of late-onset Alzheimer's disease.

apomorphine (*ap o more feen*)   A drug that blocks dopamine autoreceptors at low doses; at higher doses, blocks postsynaptic receptors as well.

apoptosis (*ay po toe sis*)   Death of a cell caused by a chemical signal that activates a genetic mechanism inside the cell.

apraxia   Difficulty in carrying out purposeful movements, in the absence of paralysis or muscular weakness.

apraxia of speech   Impairment in the ability to program movements of the tongue, lips, and throat required to produce the proper sequence of speech sounds.

arachnoid granulation   Small projections of the arachnoid membrane through the dura mater into the superior sagittal sinus; CSF flows through them to be reabsorbed into the blood supply.

arachnoid membrane (*a rak noyd*)   The middle layer of the meninges, located between the outer dura mater and inner pia mater.

arcuate fasciculus   A bundle of axons that connects Wernicke's area with Broca's area; damage causes conduction aphasia.

arcuate nucleus   A nucleus in the base of the hypothalamus that controls secretions of the anterior pituitary gland; contains NPY-secreting neurons involved in feeding and control of metabolism.

area postrema (*poss tree ma*)   A region of the medulla where the blood–brain barrier is weak; poisons can be detected there and can initiate vomiting.

astrocyte   A glial cell that provides support for neurons of the central nervous system, provides nutrients and other substances, and regulates the chemical composition of the extracellular fluid.

asymmetrical division   Division of a progenitor cell that gives rise to another progenitor cell and a neuron, which migrates away from the ventricular zone toward its final resting place in the brain.

atropine (*a tro peen*)   A drug that blocks muscarinic acetylcholine receptors.

attention-deficit/hyperactivity disorder (ADHD)   A disorder characterized by uninhibited responses, lack of sustained attention, and hyperactivity; first shows itself in childhood.

aura   A sensation that precedes a seizure; its exact nature depends on the location of the seizure focus.

autism spectrum disorder (ASD)   A chronic disorder whose symptoms include failure to develop normal social relations with other people, impaired development of communicative ability, lack of imaginative ability, and repetitive, stereotyped movements.

autonomic nervous system (ANS)   The portion of the peripheral nervous system that controls the body's vegetative functions.

autoradiography   A procedure that locates radioactive substances in a slice of tissue; the radiation exposes a photographic emulsion or a piece of film that covers the tissue.

autoreceptor   A receptor molecule located on a presynaptic neuron that responds to the neurotransmitter released by that neuron.

axon   The long, thin, cylindrical structure that conveys information from the soma of a neuron to its terminal buttons.

axonal varicosity   An enlarged region along the length of an axon that contains synaptic vesicles and releases a neurotransmitter or neuromodulator.

axoplasmic transport   An active process by which substances are propelled along microtubules that run the length of the axon.

β-amyloid (Aβ)   A protein found in excessive amounts in the brains of patients with Alzheimer's disease.

β-amyloid precursor protein (APP)   A protein produced and secreted by cells that serves as the precursor for β-amyloid protein.

B-lymphocyte   A white blood cell that originates in the bone marrow; part of the immune system.

basal ganglia   A group of subcortical nuclei in the telencephalon, the caudate nucleus, the globus pallidus, and the putamen; important parts of the motor system.

basal nucleus A nucleus of the amygdala that receives information from the lateral nucleus and sends projections to the ventromedial prefrontal cortex and the central nucleus.

basilar membrane (*bazz i ler*) A membrane in the cochlea of the inner ear; contains the organ of Corti.

behavioral neuroscientist A scientist who studies the physiology of behavior, primarily by performing physiological and behavioral experiments with laboratory animals.

belt region The first level of auditory association cortex; surrounds the primary auditory cortex.

benign tumor (*bee nine*) A noncancerous (literally, "harmless") tumor; has a distinct border and cannot metastasize.

benzodiazepine (*ben zoe dy azz a peen*) A category of anxiolytic drugs; an indirect agonist for the GABAA receptor.

beta activity Irregular electrical activity of 13–30 Hz recorded from the brain; generally associated with a state of arousal.

bicuculline (*by kew kew leen*) A direct antagonist for the GABA binding site on the GABAA receptor.

bilingual The ability to communicate fluently in two langauges.

binding site The location on a receptor protein to which a ligand binds.

binge-eating A disorder that includes bouts of excessive eating.

bipolar cell A bipolar neuron located in the middle layer of the retina, conveying information from the photoreceptors to the ganglion cells.

bipolar disorder A serious mood disorder characterized by cyclical periods of mania and depression.

black widow spider venom A poison produced by the black widow spider that triggers the release of acetylcholine.

blindsight The ability of a person who cannot see objects in his or her visual field to accurately reach for them while remaining unconscious of perceiving them; caused by damage to cortical regions involved in conscious perception of visual stimuli.

blood–brain barrier A semipermeable barrier between the blood and the brain produced by the cells in the walls of the brain's capillaries.

botulinum toxin (*bot you lin um*) An acetylcholine antagonist; prevents release by terminal buttons.

brain stem The "stem" of the brain, from the medulla to the midbrain, excluding the cerebellum.

bregma The junction of the sagittal and coronal sutures of the skull; often used as a reference point for stereotaxic brain surgery.

brightness One of the perceptual dimensions of color; intensity.

Bruce effect Termination of pregnancy caused by the odor of a pheromone in the urine of a male other than the one that impregnated the female; first identified in mice.

bulimia nervosa Bouts of excessive hunger and eating, often followed by forced vomiting or purging with laxatives; sometimes seen in people with anorexia nervosa.

buspirone (*BuSpar*) A 5-HT1A partial agonist.

calcarine fissure (*kal ka rine*) A fissure located in the occipital lobe on the medial surface of the brain; most of the primary visual cortex is located along its upper and lower banks.

CaM-KII Type II calcium-calmodulin kinase, an enzyme that must be activated by calcium; may play a role in the establishment of long-term potentiation.

CART Cocaine- and amphetamine-regulated transcript; a peptide neurotransmitter found in a system of neurons of the arcuate nucleus that inhibit feeding.

caspase A "killer enzyme" that plays a role in apoptosis, or programmed cell death.

cataplexy (*kat a plex ee*) A symptom of narcolepsy; complete paralysis that occurs during waking.

catecholamine (*cat a kohl a meen*) A class of amines that includes the neurotransmitters dopamine, norepinephrine, and epinephrine.

cauda equina (*ee kwye na*) A bundle of spinal roots located caudal to the end of the spinal cord.

caudal "Toward the tail"; with respect to the central nervous system, in a direction along the neuraxis away from the front of the face.

caudal block The anesthesia and paralysis of the lower part of the body produced by injection of a local anesthetic into the cerebrospinal fluid surrounding the cauda equina.

caudate nucleus A telencephalic nucleus, one of the input nuclei of basal ganglia; involved with control of voluntary movement.

central nervous system (CNS) The brain and spinal cord.

central nucleus The region of the amygdala that receives information from the basal, lateral, and accessory basal nuclei and sends projections to a wide variety of regions in the brain; involved in emotional responses.

central sulcus The sulcus that separates the frontal lobe from the parietal lobe.

cerebellar cortex The cortex that covers the surface of the cerebellum.

cerebellar peduncle (*pee dun kul*) One of three bundles of axons that attach each cerebellar hemisphere to the dorsal pons.

cerebellum (*sair a bell um*) A major part of the brain located dorsal to the pons, containing the two cerebellar hemispheres, covered with the cerebellar cortex; an important component of the motor system.

cerebral achromatopsia (*ay krohm a top see a*) Inability to discriminate among different hues; caused by damage to area V8 of the visual association cortex.

cerebral aqueduct A narrow tube interconnecting the third and fourth ventricles of the brain, located in the center of the mesencephalon.

cerebral cortex The outermost layer of gray matter of the cerebral hemispheres.

cerebral hemisphere (*sa ree brul*) One of the two major portions of the forebrain, covered by the cerebral cortex.

cerebrospinal fluid (CSF) A clear fluid, similar to blood plasma, that fills the ventricular system of the brain and the subarachnoid space surrounding the brain and spinal cord.

cerebrovascular accident A "stroke"; brain damage caused by occlusion or rupture of a blood vessel in the brain.

chlorpromazine (*klor proh ma zeen*) A drug that reduces the symptoms of schizophrenia by blocking dopamine D2 receptors.

cholecystokinin (CCK) (*coal i sis toe ky nin*) A hormone secreted by the duodenum that regulates gastric motility and causes the gallbladder (cholecyst) to contract; appears to provide a satiety signal transmitted to the brain through the vagus nerve.

choline acetyltransferase (ChAT) (*koh leen a see tul trans fer ace*) The enzyme that transfers the acetate ion from acetyl coenzyme A to choline, producing the neurotransmitter acetylcholine.

chorda tympani A branch of the facial nerve that passes beneath the eardrum; conveys taste information from the anterior part of the tongue and controls the secretion of some salivary glands.

choroid plexus The highly vascular tissue that protrudes into the ventricles and produces cerebrospinal fluid.

chromosome A strand of DNA, with associated proteins, found in the nucleus; carries genetic information.

cilium A hairlike appendage of a cell involved in movement or in transducing sensory information; found on the receptors in the auditory and vestibular system.

cingulate gyrus (*sing yew lett*) A strip of limbic cortex lying along the lateral walls of the groove separating the cerebral hemispheres, just above the corpus callosum.

circadian rhythm (*sur kay dee un* or *sur ka dee un*) A daily rhythmical change in behavior or physiological process.

circumlocution A strategy by which people with anomia find alternative ways to say something when they are unable to think of the most appropriate word.

clasp-knife reflex A reflex that occurs when force is applied to flex or extend the limb of an animal showing decerebrate rigidity; resistance is replaced by sudden relaxation.

classical conditioning A learning procedure; when a stimulus that initially produces no particular response is followed several times by an **unconditioned stimulus (US)** that produces a defensive or appetitive response (the **unconditioned response—UR**), the first stimulus (now called a **conditioned stimulus—CS**) itself evokes the response (now called a **conditioned response—CR**).

clonic phase The phase of a grand mal seizure in which the patient shows rhythmic jerking movements.

clozapine An atypical antipsychotic drug.

cocaine A drug that inhibits the reuptake of dopamine.

cochlea (*cock lee uh*) The snail-shaped structure of the inner ear that contains the auditory transducing mechanisms.

cochlear implant An electronic device surgically implanted in the inner ear that can enable a deaf person to hear.

cochlear nerve The branch of the auditory nerve that transmits auditory information from the cochlea to the brain.

cochlear nucleus One of a group of nuclei in the medulla that receive auditory information from the cochlea.

cognitive symptom A symptom of schizophrenia that involves cognitive deficits, such as difficulty in sustaining attention, deficits in learning and memory, poor abstract thinking, and poor problem solving.

color constancy The relatively constant appearance of the colors of objects viewed under varying lighting conditions.

complementary colors Colors that make white or gray when mixed together.

complex partial seizure A partial seizure, starting from a focus and remaining localized, that produces loss of consciousness.

compulsion The feeling that one is obliged to perform a behavior, even if one prefers not to do so.

computerized tomography (CT) The use of a device that employs a computer to analyze data obtained by a scanning beam of X-rays to produce a two-dimensional picture of a "slice" through the body.

conditioned emotional response A classically conditioned response that occurs when a neutral stimulus is followed by an aversive stimulus; usually includes autonomic, behavioral, and endocrine components such as changes in heart rate, freezing, and secretion of stress-related hormones.

conduction aphasia An aphasia characterized by inability to repeat words that are heard but the ability to speak normally and comprehend the speech of others.

cone One of the receptor cells of the retina; maximally sensitive to one of three different wavelengths of light and hence encodes color vision.

confocal laser scanning microscope A microscope that provides high-resolution images of various depths of thick tissue that contains fluorescent molecules by scanning the tissue with light from a laser beam.

congenital adrenal hyperplasia (CAH) (*hy per play zha*) A condition characterized by hypersecretion of androgens by the adrenal cortex; in females, causes masculinization of the external genitalia.

constructional apraxia Difficulty in drawing pictures or diagrams or in making geometrical constructions of elements such as building blocks or sticks; caused by damage to the right parietal lobe.

content word A noun, verb, adjective, or adverb that conveys meaning.

contralateral Located on the opposite side of the body.

convulsion A violent sequence of uncontrollable muscular movements caused by a seizure.

Coolidge effect The restorative effect of introducing a new female sex partner to a male that is in a refractory period.

core region The primary auditory cortex, located on a gyrus on the dorsal surface of the temporal lobe.

corpus callosum (*ka loh sum*) A large bundle of axons that interconnects corresponding regions of the association cortex on each side of the brain.

corpus luteum (*lew tee um*) A cluster of cells that develops from the ovarian follicle after ovulation; secretes estradiol and progesterone.

correctional mechanism In a regulatory process, the mechanism that is capable of changing the value of the system variable.

corticobulbar tract A bundle of axons from the motor cortex to the fifth, seventh, ninth, tenth, eleventh, and twelfth cranial nerves; controls movements of the face, neck, tongue, and parts of the extraocular eye muscles.

corticorubral tract The system of axons that travels from the motor cortex to the red nucleus.

corticospinal tract The system of axons that originates in the motor cortex and terminates in the ventral gray matter of the spinal cord.

corticotropin-releasing hormone (CRH) A hypothalamic hormone that stimulates the anterior pituitary gland to secrete ACTH (adrenocorticotropic hormone).

cranial nerve A peripheral nerve attached directly to the brain.

cross section With respect to the central nervous system, a slice taken at right angles to the neuraxis.

cryostat An instrument that produces very thin slices of body tissue inside a freezer chamber.

cupula (*kew pew luh*) A gelatinous mass found in the ampulla of the semicircular canals; moves in response to the flow of the fluid in the canals.

curare (*kew rahr ee*) A drug that blocks nicotinic acetylcholine receptors.

cutaneous sense (*kew tane ee us*) One of the somatosenses; includes sensitivity to stimuli that involve the skin.

cytochrome oxidase (CO) blob The central region of a module of the primary visual cortex, revealed by a stain for cytochrome oxidase; contains wavelength-sensitive neurons; part of the parvocellular system.

cytokine A category of chemicals released by certain white blood cells when they detect the presence of an invading microorganism; causes other white blood cells to proliferate and mount an attack against the invader.

cytoplasm The viscous, semiliquid substance contained in the interior of a cell.

cytoskeleton Formed of microtubules and other protein fibers, linked to each other and forming a cohesive mass that gives a cell its shape.

decerebrate Describes an animal whose brain stem has been transected.

decerebrate rigidity Simultaneous contraction of agonistic and antagonistic muscles; caused by decerebration or damage to the reticular formation.

decerebration A surgical procedure that severs the brain stem, disconnecting the hindbrain from the forebrain.

deep brain stimulation (DBS)   A surgical procedure that involves implanting electrodes in a particular region of the brain and attaching a device that permits the electrical stimulation of that region through the electrodes.

deep cerebellar nuclei   Nuclei located within the cerebellar hemispheres; receive projections from the cerebellar cortex and send projections out of the cerebellum to other parts of the brain.

defeminizing effect   An effect of a hormone present early in development that reduces or prevents the later development of anatomical or behavioral characteristics typical of females.

defensive behavior   A species-typical behavior by which an animal defends itself against the threat of another animal.

Deiters's cell (*dye terz*)   A supporting cell found in the organ of Corti; sustains the auditory hair cells.

delayed matching-to-sample task   A task that requires the subject to indicate which of several stimuli has just been perceived.

delayed sleep phase syndrome   A 4-hour delay in rhythms of sleep and temperature cycles, possibly caused by a mutation of a gene (*per3*) involved in the rhythmicity of neurons of the SCN.

delta activity   Regular, synchronous electrical activity of less than 4 Hz recorded from the brain; occurs during the deepest stages of slow-wave sleep.

delusion   A belief that is clearly in contradiction to reality.

dementia (*da men sha*)   A loss of cognitive abilities such as memory, perception, verbal ability, and judgment; common causes are multiple strokes and Alzheimer's disease.

dendrite   A branched, treelike structure attached to the soma of a neuron; receives information from the terminal buttons of other neurons.

dendritic spike   An action potential that occurs in the dendrite of some types of pyramidal cells.

dendritic spine   A small bud on the surface of a dendrite, with which a terminal button of another neuron forms a synapse.

dentate nucleus   A deep cerebellar nucleus; involved in the control of rapid, skilled movements by the corticospinal and rubrospinal systems.

deoxyribonucleic acid (DNA)   (*dee ox ee ry bo new clay ik*) A long, complex macromolecule consisting of two interconnected helical strands; along with associated proteins, strands of DNA constitute the chromosomes.

depolarization   Reduction (toward zero) of the membrane potential of a cell from its normal resting potential; membrane potential becomes more positive.

deprenyl (*depp ra nil*)   A drug that blocks the activity of MAO-B; acts as a dopamine agonist.

detector   In a regulatory process, a mechanism that signals when the system variable deviates from its set point.

deuteranopia (*dew ter an owe pee a*)   An inherited form of defective color vision in which red and green hues are confused; "green" cones are filled with "red" cone opsin.

developmental dyslexia   A reading difficulty in a person of normal intelligence and perceptual ability; of genetic origin or caused by prenatal or perinatal factors.

diazepam   An indirect agonist for the GABAA receptor; part of the benzodiazepine class of drugs.

diencephalon (*dy en seff a lahn*)   A region of the forebrain surrounding the third ventricle; includes the thalamus and the hypothalamus.

diffusion   Movement of molecules from regions of high concentration to regions of low concentration.

diffusion tensor imaging (DTI)   An imaging method that uses a modified MRI scanner to reveal bundles of myelinated axons in the living brain.

dihydrotestosterone (*dy hy dro tess tahss ter own*)   An androgen, produced from testosterone through the action of the enzyme 5α reductase.

direct agonist   A drug that binds with and activates a receptor.

direct antagonist   A synonym for receptor blocker.

direct dyslexia   A language disorder caused by brain damage in which the person can read words aloud without understanding them.

direct pathway (in basal ganglia)   The pathway that includes the caudate nucleus and putamen, the internal division of the globus pallidus, and the ventral anterior/ventrolateral thalamic nuclei; has an excitatory effect on movement.

doctrine of specific nerve energies   Müller's conclusion that, because all nerve fibers carry the same type of message, sensory information must be specified by the particular nerve fibers that are active.

dopamine (DA) (*dope a meen*)   A neurotransmitter; one of the catecholamines.

dopamine transporter   Proteins that remove dopamine from the synapse.

dorsal   "Toward the back"; with respect to the central nervous system, in a direction perpendicular to the neuraxis toward the top of the head or the back.

dorsal lateral geniculate nucleus (LGN)   A group of cell bodies within the lateral geniculate body of the thalamus; receives inputs from the retina and projects to the primary visual cortex.

dorsal root ganglion   A nodule on a dorsal root that contains cell bodies of afferent spinal nerve neurons.

dorsal root   The spinal root that contains incoming (afferent) sensory fibers.

dorsal stream   A system of interconnected regions of visual cortex involved in the perception of spatial location, beginning with the striate cortex and ending with the posterior parietal cortex.

dose-response curve   A graph of the magnitude of an effect of a drug as a function of the amount of drug administered.

Down syndrome   A disorder caused by the presence of an extra twenty-first chromosome, characterized by moderate to severe intellectual disability and often by physical abnormalities.

dronabinol   Cannabinoid receptor agonist.

dualism   The belief that the body is physical but the mind (or soul) is not.

duodenum   The first portion of the small intestine, attached directly to the stomach.

dura mater   The outermost of the meninges; tough and flexible.

efferent axon (*eff ur ent*)   An axon directed away from the central nervous system, conveying motor commands to muscles and glands.

electro-oculogram (EOG) (*ah kew loh gram*)   An electrical potential from the eyes, recorded by means of electrodes placed on the skin around them; detects eye movements.

electroconvulsive therapy (ECT)   A brief electrical shock, applied to the head, that results in a seizure; used therapeutically to alleviate severe depression.

electroencephalogram (EEG)   An electrical brain potential recorded by placing electrodes on the scalp.

electrolyte   An aqueous solution of a material that ionizes—namely, a soluble acid, base, or salt.

electromyogram (EMG) (*my oh gram*)   An electrical potential recorded from an electrode placed on or in a muscle.

electrostatic pressure   The attractive force between atomic particles charged with opposite signs or the repulsive force between atomic particles charged with the same sign.

embolus (*emm bo lus*) A piece of matter (such as a blood clot, fat, or bacterial debris) that dislodges from its site of origin and occludes an artery; in the brain an embolus can lead to a stroke.

emotional facial paresis Lack of movement of facial muscles in response to emotions in people who have no difficulty moving these muscles voluntarily; caused by damage to the insular prefrontal cortex, subcortical white matter of the frontal lobe, or parts of the thalamus.

encephalitis (*en seff a lye tis*) An inflammation of the brain; caused by bacteria, viruses, or toxic chemicals.

endocannabinoid (*en do can ab in oyd*) A lipid; an endogenous ligand for cannabinoid receptors, which also bind with THC, the active ingredient of marijuana.

endocrine gland A gland that liberates its secretions into the extracellular fluid around capillaries and hence into the bloodstream.

endogenous opioid (*en dodge en us oh pee oyd*) A class of peptides secreted by the brain that act as opiates.

endoplasmic reticulum Parallel layers of membrane found within the cytoplasm of a cell. Rough endoplasmic reticulum contains ribosomes and is involved with production of proteins that are secreted by the cell. Smooth endoplasmic reticulum is the site of synthesis of lipids and provides channels for the segregation of molecules involved in various cellular processes.

endplate potential The postsynaptic potential that occurs in the motor endplate in response to release of acetylcholine by the terminal button.

enkephalin (*en keff a lin*) One of the endogenous opioids.

enzymatic deactivation The destruction of a neurotransmitter by an enzyme after its release—for example, the destruction of acetylcholine by acetylcholinesterase.

enzyme A molecule that controls a chemical reaction, combining two substances or breaking a substance into two parts.

epidemiology The study of the distribution and causes of diseases in populations.

epinephrine (*epp i neff rin*) One of the catecholamines; a hormone secreted by the adrenal medulla; serves also as a neurotransmitter in the brain.

episodic memory Memory of a collection of perceptions of events organized in time and identified by a particular context.

estradiol (*ess tra dye ahl*) The principal estrogen of many mammals, including humans.

estrogen (*ess trow jen*) A class of sex hormones that cause maturation of the female genitalia, growth of breast tissue, and development of other physical features characteristic of females.

estrous cycle The female reproductive cycle of mammals other than primates.

estrus A period of sexual receptivity in many female mammals (excluding humans).

eszopiclone An indirect agonist for the GABAA receptor; used to treat insomnia.

evolution A gradual change in the structure and physiology of a species—generally producing more complex organisms—as a result of natural selection.

excitatory amino acid transporters Proteins that remove glutamate (and other excitatory amino acids) from the synapse.

excitatory postsynaptic potential (EPSP) An excitatory depolarization of the postsynaptic membrane of a synapse caused by the liberation of a neurotransmitter by the terminal button.

excitotoxic lesion (*ek sigh tow tok sik*) A brain lesion produced by intracerebral injection of an excitatory amino acid, such as kainic acid.

exocytosis (*ex o sy toe sis*) The secretion of a substance by a cell through means of vesicles; the process by which neurotransmitters are secreted.

experimental ablation The removal or destruction of a portion of the brain of a laboratory animal; presumably, the functions that can no longer be performed are the ones the region previously controlled.

extension A movement of a limb that tends to straighten its joints; the opposite of flexion.

extracellular fluid All body fluids outside cells: interstitial fluid, blood plasma, and cerebrospinal fluid.

extrafusal muscle fiber One of the muscle fibers that are responsible for the force exerted by contraction of a skeletal muscle.

extrastriate body area (EBA) A region of the visual association cortex located in the lateral occipitotemporal cortex; involved in perception of the human body and body parts other than faces.

extrastriate cortex (visual association cortex, or V2) A region of visual association cortex; receives fibers from the striate cortex and from the superior colliculi and projects to the inferior temporal cortex.

fastigial nucleus A deep cerebellar nucleus; involved in the control of movement by the reticulospinal and vestibulospinal tracts.

fasting phase The phase of metabolism during which nutrients are not available from the digestive system; glucose, amino acids, and fatty acids are derived from glycogen, protein, and adipose tissue during this phase.

fatal familial insomnia A fatal inherited disorder characterized by progressive insomnia.

fatty acid A substance derived from the breakdown of triglycerides, along with glycerol; can be metabolized by most cells of the body except for the brain.

fenfluramine (*fen fluor i meen*) A drug that stimulates the release of 5-HT.

fetal alcohol syndrome A birth defect caused by ingestion of alcohol by a pregnant woman; includes characteristic facial anomalies and faulty brain development.

fight-or-flight response A species-typical preparatory response to fighting or fleeing; thought to be responsible for some of the deleterious effects of stressful situations on health.

fissure A major groove in the surface of the brain, larger than a sulcus.

fixative A chemical such as formalin; used to prepare and preserve body tissue.

flexion A movement of a limb that tends to bend its joints; the opposite of extension.

flocculonodular lobe A region of the cerebellum; involved in control of postural reflexes.

fluorogold (*flew roh gold*) A dye that serves as a retrograde label; taken up by terminal buttons and carried back to the cell bodies.

fluoxetine (*floo ox i teen*) A drug that inhibits the reuptake of 5-HT.

follicle-stimulating hormone (FSH) The hormone of the anterior pituitary gland that causes development of an ovarian follicle and the maturation of an ovum.

forebrain The most rostral of the three major divisions of the brain; includes the telencephalon and diencephalon.

formalin (*for ma lin*) The aqueous solution of formaldehyde gas; the most commonly used tissue fixative.

fornix A fiber bundle that connects the hippocampus with other parts of the brain, including the mammillary bodies of the hypothalamus; part of the limbic system.

Fos (*fahs*) A protein produced in the nucleus of a neuron in response to synaptic stimulation.

functional imaging A computerized method of detecting metabolic or chemical changes in particular regions of the brain.

fourth ventricle   The ventricle located between the cerebellum and the dorsal pons, in the center of the metencephalon.

fovea (*foe vee a*)   The region of the retina that mediates the most acute vision of birds and higher mammals. Color-sensitive cones constitute the only type of photoreceptor found in the fovea.

free radical   A molecule with unpaired electrons; acts as a powerful oxidizing agent; toxic to cells.

frontal lobe   The anterior portion of the cerebral cortex, rostral to the parietal lobe and dorsal to the temporal lobe.

frontal section   A slice through the brain parallel to the forehead.

frontotemporal dementia   A mutation of the gene for tau protein causes degeneration of the frontal and temporal cortex, and subsequent dementia.

function word   A preposition, article, or other word that conveys little of the meaning of a sentence but is important in specifying its grammatical structure.

functional MRI (fMRI)   A functional imaging method; a modification of the MRI procedure that permits the measurement of regional metabolism in the brain, usually by detecting changes in blood oxygen level.

functionalism   The principle that the best way to understand a biological phenomenon (a behavior or a physiological structure) is to try to understand its useful functions for the organism.

fundamental frequency   The lowest, and usually most intense, frequency of a complex sound; most often perceived as the sound's basic pitch.

fusaric acid (*few sahr ik*)   A drug that inhibits the activity of the enzyme dopamine β-hydroxylase and thus blocks the production of norepinephrine.

fusiform face area (FFA)   A region of the visual association cortex located in the inferior temporal; involved in perception of faces and other complex objects that require expertise to recognize.

G protein   A protein coupled to a metabotropic receptor; conveys messages to other molecules when a ligand binds with and activates the receptor.

GABA   An amino acid; the most important inhibitory neurotransmitter in the brain.

GABA transporter   Proteins that remove GABA from the synapse.

galactosemia (*ga lak tow see mee uh*)   An inherited metabolic disorder in which galactose (milk sugar) cannot easily be metabolized.

gamete (*gamm eet*)   A mature reproductive cell; a sperm or ovum.

gamma motor neuron   A neuron whose axons form synapses with intrafusal muscle fibers.

ganglion cell   A neuron located in the retina that receives visual information from bipolar cells; its axons give rise to the optic nerve.

gap junction   A special junction between cells that permits direct communication by means of electrical coupling.

gene   The functional unit of the chromosome, which directs synthesis of one or more proteins.

generalization   A type of scientific explanation; a general conclusion based on many observations of similar phenomena.

generalized anxiety disorder   A disorder characterized by excessive anxiety and worry serious enough to cause disruption of a person's life.

generalized seizure   A seizure that involves most of the brain, as contrasted with a partial seizure, which remains localized.

genetic sex   Determined by presence of XX (female) or XY (male) chromosomes.

genome   The complete set of genes that compose the DNA of a particular species.

ghrelin (*grell in*)   A peptide hormone released by the stomach that increases eating; also produced by neurons in the brain.

glabrous skin (*glab russ*)   Skin that does not contain hair; found on the palms and the soles of the feet.

glia (*glee ah*)   The supporting cells of the central nervous system.

glioma (*glee oh mah*)   A cancerous brain tumor composed of one of several types of glial cells.

globus pallidus   A telencephalic nucleus; the primary output nucleus of the basal ganglia; involved with control of voluntary movement.

glucagon (*gloo ka gahn*)   A pancreatic hormone that promotes the conversion of liver glycogen into glucose.

glucocorticoid   One of a group of hormones of the adrenal cortex that are important in protein and carbohydrate metabolism, secreted especially in times of stress.

glucoprivation   A dramatic fall in the level of glucose available to cells; can be caused by a fall in the blood level of glucose or by drugs that inhibit glucose metabolism.

glutamate   An amino acid; the most important excitatory neurotransmitter in the brain.

glutamate excitotoxicity   Toxic overstimulation of the postsynaptic cell by excess glutamate.

glutamine synthase   Enzyme that breaks down glutamate into its precursor glutamine.

glycerol (*gliss er all*)   A substance (also called glycerine) derived from the breakdown of triglycerides, along with fatty acids; can be converted by the liver into glucose.

glycogen (*gly ko jen*)   A polysaccharide often referred to as *animal starch*; stored in liver and muscle; constitutes the short-term store of nutrients.

Golgi apparatus (*goal jee*)   A complex of parallel membranes in the cytoplasm that wraps the products of a secretory cell.

Golgi tendon organ   The receptor organ at the junction of the tendon and muscle that is sensitive to stretch.

gonad (rhymes with *moan ad*)   An ovary or testis.

gonadotropic hormone   A hormone of the anterior pituitary gland that has a stimulating effect on cells of the gonads.

gonadotropin-releasing hormone (GnRH) (*go nad oh trow pin*)   A hypothalamic hormone that stimulates the anterior pituitary gland to secrete gonadotropic hormone.

grand mal seizure   A generalized, tonic-clonic seizure, which results in a convulsion.

gyrus (plural: **gyri**) (*jye russ, jye rye*)   A convolution of the cortex of the cerebral hemispheres, separated by sulci or fissures.

hair cell   The receptive cell of the auditory apparatus.

hallucination   Perception of a nonexistent object or event.

Hebb rule   The hypothesis proposed by Donald Hebb that the cellular basis of learning involves strengthening of a synapse that is repeatedly active when the postsynaptic neuron fires.

hemicholinium-3   An antagonist at the choline transporter.

hemorrhagic stroke   A cerebrovascular accident caused by the rupture of a cerebral blood vessel.

heroin   Agonist for opiate receptor.

herpes simplex virus   A form of herpes virus used for anterograde transneuronal tracing, which labels a series of neurons that are interconnected synaptically.

hertz (Hz)   Cycles per second.

hindbrain   The most caudal of the three major divisions of the brain; includes the metencephalon and myelencephalon.

histamine A neurotransmitter synthesized from the amino acid histidine; plays an important role in maintenance of wakefulness and arousal.

homeostasis (*home ee oh stay sis*) The process by which the body's substances and characteristics (such as temperature and glucose level) are maintained at their optimal level.

horizontal cell A neuron in the retina that interconnects adjacent photoreceptors and the outer processes of the bipolar cells.

horizontal section A slice through the brain parallel to the ground.

hormone A chemical substance that is released by an endocrine gland that has effects on target cells in other organs.

hue One of the perceptual dimensions of color; the dominant wavelength.

huntingtin (Htt) A protein that may serve to facilitate the production and transport of brain-derived neurotrophic factor. Abnormal huntingtin is the cause of Huntington's disease.

Huntington's disease An inherited disorder that causes degeneration of the basal ganglia; characterized by progressively more severe uncontrollable jerking movements, writhing movements, dementia, and finally death.

hyperdirect pathway An excitatory pathway from the pre-SMA to the subthalamic nucleus that increases the activity of the GPi and appears to play a role in preventing or quickly stopping movements that are being initiated by the direct pathway.

hyperpolarization An increase in the membrane potential of a cell, relative to the normal resting potential; membrane potential becomes more negative.

hypnagogic hallucination (*hip na gah jik*) A symptom of narcolepsy; vivid dreams that occur just before a person falls asleep; accompanied by sleep paralysis.

hypofrontality Decreased activity of the prefrontal cortex; believed to be responsible for the negative symptoms of schizophrenia.

hypothalamic pituitary adrenal axis (HPA axis) A circuit that is activated as part of the stress response; results in the release of glucocorticoids.

hypothalamus The group of nuclei of the diencephalon situated beneath the thalamus; involved in regulation of the autonomic nervous system, control of the anterior and posterior pituitary glands, and integration of species-typical behaviors.

hypovolemia (*hy poh voh lee mee a*) Reduction in the volume of the intravascular fluid.

idazoxan A drug that blocks presynaptic noradrenergic α2 receptors and hence acts as an agonist, facilitating the synthesis and release of norepinephrine.

immunocytochemical method A histological method that uses radioactive antibodies or antibodies bound with a dye molecule to indicate the presence of particular proteins of peptides.

immunoglobulin An antibody released by B-lymphocytes that binds with antigens and helps to destroy invading microorganisms.

incus The "anvil"; the second of the three ossicles.

indirect agonist A drug that attaches to a binding site on a receptor and facilitates the action of the receptor; does not interfere with the binding site for the principal ligand.

indirect antagonist A drug that attaches to a binding site on a receptor and interferes with the action of the receptor; does not interfere with the binding site for the principal ligand.

indirect pathway (in basal ganglia) The pathway that includes the caudate nucleus and putamen, the external division of the globus pallidus, the subthalamic nucleus, the internal division of the globus pallidus, and the ventral anterior/ventrolateral thalamic nuclei; has an inhibitory effect on movement.

inferior colliculi Protrusions on top of the midbrain; part of the auditory system.

inferior temporal cortex The highest level of the ventral stream of the visual association cortex; involved in perception of objects, including people's bodies and faces.

informed consent The process in which researchers must inform any potential participant about the nature of the research, how any data will be collected and stored, and what the anticipated benefits and costs of participating will be.

ingestive behavior (*in jess tiv*) Eating or drinking.

inhalation Administration of a vaporous substance into the lungs.

inhibitory postsynaptic potential (IPSP) An inhibitory hyperpolarization of the postsynaptic membrane of a synapse caused by the liberation of a neurotransmitter by the terminal button.

insertional plaque The point of attachment of a tip link to a cilium.

insufflation Administration of a substance by sniffing or snorting; drug is absorbed through the mucous membranes of the nose.

insular cortex (*in sue lur*) A sunken region of the cerebral cortex that is normally covered by the rostral superior temporal lobe and caudal inferior frontal lobe.

insulin A pancreatic hormone that facilitates entry of glucose and amino acids into the cell, conversion of glucose into glycogen, and transport of fats into adipose tissue.

internal division of the globus pallidus (GPi) A division of the globus pallidus that provides inhibitory input to the motor cortex via the thalamus; sometimes stereotaxically lesioned to treat the symptoms of Parkinson's disease.

interneuron A neuron located entirely within the central nervous system.

interposed nuclei A set of deep cerebellar nuclei; involved in the control of the rubrospinal system.

interstitial fluid The fluid that bathes the cells, filling the space between the cells of the body (the "interstices").

intracellular fluid The fluid contained within cells.

intracerebral administration Administration of a substance directly into the brain.

intracerebroventricular (ICV) administration Administration of a substance into one of the cerebral ventricles.

intrafusal muscle fiber A muscle fiber that functions as a stretch receptor, arranged parallel to the extrafusal muscle fibers, thus detecting changes in muscle length.

intramuscular (IM) injection Injection of a substance into a muscle.

intraparietal sulcus (IPS) The end of the dorsal stream of the visual association cortex; involved in perception of location, visual attention, and control of eye and hand movements.

intraperitoneal (IP) injection (*in tra pair i toe nee ul*) Injection of a substance into the *peritoneal cavity*—the space that surrounds the stomach, intestines, liver, and other abdominal organs.

intravascular fluid The fluid found within the blood vessels.

intravenous (IV) injection Injection of a substance directly into a vein.

ion A charged molecule. *Cations* are positively charged, and *anions* are negatively charged.

ion channel A specialized protein molecule that permits specific ions to enter or leave cells.

ionotropic receptor (*eye on oh trow pik*) A receptor that contains a binding site for a neurotransmitter and an ion channel that opens when a molecule of the neurotransmitter attaches to the binding site.

ipsilateral Located on the same side of the body.

ischemic stroke A cerebrovascular accident caused by occlusion of a blood vessel and interruption of the blood supply to a region of the brain.

James-Lange theory A theory of emotion that suggests that behaviors and physiological responses are directly elicited by situations and that feelings of emotions are produced by feedback from these behaviors and responses.

kainate receptor (*kay in ate*) An ionotropic glutamate receptor that controls a sodium channel; stimulated by kainic acid.

ketamine A drug that binds with a noncompetitive binding site of the NMDA receptor and serves as an indirect antagonist.

kinesthesia Perception of the body's own movements.

kisspeptin A peptide produced by neurons in the arcuate nucleus of the hypothalamus under the control of leptin receptors; essential for initiation of puberty and maintenance of reproductive ability.

koniocellular sublayer (*koh nee oh sell yew lur*) One of the sublayers of neurons in the dorsal lateral geniculate nucleus found ventral to each of the magnocellular and parvocellular layers; transmits information from short-wavelength ("blue") cones to the primary visual cortex.

Korsakoff's syndrome Permanent anterograde amnesia caused by brain damage resulting from chronic alcohol abuse or malnutrition.

l-DOPA (*ell dope a*) The levorotatory form of DOPA; the precursor of the catecholamines; often used to treat Parkinson's disease because of its effect as a dopamine agonist.

lamella A layer of membrane containing photopigments; found in rods and cones of the retina.

lateral Toward the side of the body, away from the middle.

lateral corticospinal tract The system of axons that originates in the motor cortex and terminates in the contralateral ventral gray matter of the spinal cord; controls movements of the distal limbs.

lateral fissure The fissure that separates the temporal lobe from the overlying frontal and parietal lobes.

lateral geniculate nucleus A group of cell bodies within the lateral geniculate body of the thalamus that receives fibers from the retina and projects fibers to the primary visual cortex.

lateral group The corticospinal tract, the corticobulbar tract, and the rubrospinal tract.

lateral lemniscus A band of fibers running rostrally through the medulla and pons; carries fibers of the auditory system.

lateral nucleus A nucleus of the amygdala that receives sensory information from the neocortex, thalamus, and hippocampus and sends projections to the basal, accessory basal, and central nucleus of the amygdala.

lateral occipital complex (LOC) A region of the extrastriate cortex, involved in perception of objects other than people's bodies and faces.

lateral ventricle One of the two ventricles located in the center of the telencephalon.

Lee-Boot effect The slowing and eventual cessation of estrous cycles in groups of female animals that are housed together; caused by a pheromone in the animals' urine; first observed in mice.

leptin A hormone secreted by adipose tissue; decreases food intake and increases metabolic rate, primarily by inhibiting NPY-secreting neurons in the arcuate nucleus.

lesion study A synonym for experimental ablation.

Lewy body Abnormal circular structures with a dense core consisting of α-synuclein protein; found in the cytoplasm of nigrostriatal neurons in people with Parkinson's disease.

ligand (*lye gand* or *ligg and*) A chemical that binds with the binding site of a receptor.

limbic cortex Phylogenetically old cortex, located at the medial edge ("limbus") of the cerebral hemispheres; part of the limbic system.

limbic system A group of brain regions including the anterior thalamic nuclei, amygdala, hippocampus, limbic cortex, and parts of the hypothalamus, as well as their interconnecting fiber bundles.

lipoprivation A dramatic fall in the level of fatty acids available to cells; usually caused by drugs that inhibit fatty acid metabolism.

lithium A chemical element; lithium carbonate is used to treat bipolar disorder.

locus coeruleus (LC) (*sa roo lee us*) A dark-colored group of noradrenergic cell bodies located in the pons near the rostral end of the floor of the fourth ventricle; involved in arousal and vigilance.

long-term potentiation (LTP) A long-term increase in the excitability of a neuron to a particular synaptic input caused by repeated high-frequency activity of that input.

lordosis A spinal sexual reflex seen in many four-legged female mammals; arching of the back in response to approach of a male or to touching the flanks, which elevates the hindquarters.

loss of function Said of a genetic disorder caused by a recessive gene that fails to produce a protein that is necessary for good health.

loudness A perceptual dimension of sound; corresponds to intensity.

LSD A drug that stimulates 5-HT2A receptors.

luteinizing hormone (LH) (*lew tee a nize ing*) A hormone of the anterior pituitary gland that causes ovulation and development of the ovarian follicle into a corpus luteum.

lysosome (*lye so soam*) An organelle surrounded by membrane; contains enzymes that break down waste products.

macroelectrode An electrode used to record the electrical activity of large numbers of neurons in a particular region of the brain; much larger than a microelectrode.

magnetic resonance imaging (MRI) A technique whereby the interior of the body can be accurately imaged; involves the interaction between radio waves and a strong magnetic field.

magnetoencephalography A procedure that detects groups of synchronously activated neurons by means of the magnetic field induced by their electrical activity; uses an array of superconducting quantum interference devices, or SQUIDs.

magnocellular layer One of the inner two layers of neurons in the dorsal lateral geniculate nucleus; transmits information necessary for the perception of form, movement, depth, and small differences in brightness to the primary visual cortex.

major depressive disorder (MDD) A serious mood disorder that consists of unremitting depression or periods of depression that do not alternate with periods of mania.

malignant tumor A cancerous (literally, "harm-producing") tumor; lacks a distinct border and may metastasize.

malleus The "hammer"; the first of the three ossicles.

mammillary bodies (*mam i lair ee*) A protrusion of the bottom of the brain at the posterior end of the hypothalamus, containing some hypothalamic nuclei; part of the limbic system.

masculinizing effect An effect of a hormone present early in development that promotes the later development of anatomical or behavioral characteristics typical of males.

MDMA A drug that serves as a noradrenergic and serotonergic agonist, also known as "ecstasy"; has excitatory and hallucinogenic effects.

mechanoreceptor A sensory neuron that responds to mechanical stimuli: for example, those that produce pressure, stretch, or vibration of the skin or stretch of muscles or tendons.

medial Toward the middle of the body, away from the side.

medial forebrain bundle A fiber bundle that runs in a rostral-caudal direction through the basal forebrain and lateral hypothalamus; electrical stimulation of these axons is reinforcing.

medial geniculate nucleus A group of cell bodies within the medial geniculate body of the thalamus; receives fibers from the auditory system and projects fibers to the primary auditory cortex.

medial nucleus of the amygdala (*a mig da la*) A nucleus that receives olfactory information from the olfactory bulb and accessory olfactory bulb; involved in the effects of odors and pheromones on reproductive behavior.

medial preoptic area (MPA) An area of cell bodies just rostral to the hypothalamus; plays an essential role in male sexual behavior.

median preoptic nucleus A small nucleus situated around the decussation of the anterior commissure; plays a role in thirst stimulated by angiotensin.

medulla oblongata (*me doo la*) The most caudal portion of the brain; located in the myelencephalon, immediately rostral to the spinal cord.

Meissner's corpuscle A touch-sensitive cutaneous receptor, important in detecting edge contours or Braille-like stimuli, especially by fingertips.

melanin-concentrating hormone (MCH) A peptide neurotransmitter found in a system of lateral hypothalamic neurons that stimulate appetite and reduce metabolic rate.

melanocortin 4 receptor (MC4R) A receptor found in the brain that binds with α-MSH and agouti-related protein; plays a role in control of appetite.

melanopsin (*mell a nop sin*) A photopigment present in ganglion cells in the retina whose axons transmit information to the SCN, the thalamus, and the olivary pretectal nuclei.

melatonin (*mell a tone in*) A hormone secreted during the night by the pineal body; plays a role in circadian and seasonal rhythms.

membrane A structure consisting principally of lipid molecules that defines the outer boundaries of a cell and also constitutes many of the cell organelles, such as the Golgi apparatus.

membrane potential The electrical charge across a cell membrane; the difference in electrical potential inside and outside the cell.

meninges (singular: meninx) (*men in jees*) The three layers of tissue that encase the central nervous system: the dura mater, arachnoid membrane, and pia mater.

meningioma (*men in jee oh ma*) A benign brain tumor composed of the cells that constitute the meninges.

meningitis (*men in jy tis*) An inflammation of the meninges; can be caused by viruses or bacteria.

menstrual cycle (*men strew al*) The female reproductive cycle of most primates, including humans; characterized by growth of the lining of the uterus, ovulation, development of a corpus luteum, and (if pregnancy does not occur), menstruation.

Merkel's disk A touch-sensitive cutaneous receptor, important for detection of form and roughness, especially by fingertips.

mesencephalic locomotor region A region of the reticular formation of the midbrain whose stimulation causes alternating movements of the limbs normally seen during locomotion.

mesencephalon (*mezz en seff a lahn*) The midbrain; a region of the brain that surrounds the cerebral aqueduct; includes the tectum and the tegmentum.

mesocortical system (*mee zo kor ti kul*) A system of dopaminergic neurons originating in the ventral tegmental area and terminating in the prefrontal cortex.

mesolimbic system (*mee zo lim bik*) A system of dopaminergic neurons originating in the ventral tegmental area and terminating in the nucleus accumbens, amygdala, and hippocampus.

messenger ribonucleic acid (mRNA) A macromolecule that delivers genetic information concerning the synthesis of a protein from a portion of a chromosome to a ribosome.

metabotropic glutamate receptor (*meh tab a troh pik*) A category of metabotropic receptors that are sensitive to glutamate.

metabotropic receptor (*meh tab oh trow pik*) A receptor that contains a binding site for a neurotransmitter; activates an enzyme that begins a series of events that opens an ion channel elsewhere in the membrane of the cell when a molecule of the neurotransmitter attaches to the binding site.

metastasis (*meh tass ta sis*) The process by which cells break off of a tumor, travel through the vascular system, and grow elsewhere in the body.

methadone Agonist for opiate receptor.

methamphetamine An antagonist at dopamine and norepinephrine transporters that causes them to run in reverse, releasing these neurotransmitters into the synapse.

methylphenidate (*meth ul fen i date*) A drug that inhibits the reuptake of dopamine.

microdialysis A procedure for analyzing chemicals present in the interstitial fluid by extracting them through a small piece of tubing made of a semipermeable membrane that is implanted in the brain.

microelectrode A very fine electrode, generally used to record activity of individual neurons.

microglia The smallest of glial cells; they act as phagocytes and protect the brain from invading microorganisms.

microtome (*my krow tome*) An instrument that produces very thin slices of body tissues.

microtubule (*my kro too byool*) A long strand of bundles of protein filaments arranged around a hollow core; part of the cytoskeleton and involved in transporting substances from place to place within the cell.

midbrain The mesencephalon; the central of the three major divisions of the brain.

midsagittal plane The plane through the neuraxis perpendicular to the ground; divides the brain into two symmetrical halves.

mirror neurons Neurons located in the ventral premotor cortex and inferior parietal lobule that respond when the individual makes a particular movement or sees another individual making that movement.

mitochondrion An organelle that is responsible for extracting energy from nutrients.

mitral cell A neuron located in the olfactory bulb that receives information from olfactory receptors; axons of mitral cells bring information to the rest of the brain.

moclobemide (*mok low bem ide*) A drug that blocks the activity of MAO-A; acts as a noradrenergic agonist.

monism (*mahn ism*) The belief that the world consists only of matter and energy and that the mind is a phenomenon produced by the workings of the nervous system.

monoamine (*mahno a meen*) A class of amines that includes indolamines, such as serotonin, and catecholamines, such as dopamine, norepinephrine, and epinephrine.

monoamine hypothesis A hypothesis that states that depression is caused by a low level of activity of one or more monoamine systems.

monoamine oxidase (MAO) (*mahn o a meen*) A class of enzymes that destroy the monoamines: dopamine, norepinephrine, and serotonin.

monosynaptic stretch reflex A reflex in which a muscle contracts in response to its being quickly stretched; involves a sensory neuron and a motor neuron, with one synapse between them.

morphine Agonist for opiate receptor.

motor association cortex The region of the frontal lobe rostral to the primary motor cortex; also known as the premotor cortex.

motor endplate The postsynaptic membrane of a neuromuscular junction.

motor learning Learning to make a new response.

motor neuron   A neuron located within the central nervous system that controls the contraction of a muscle or the secretion of a gland.

motor unit   A motor neuron and its associated muscle fibers.

muscarine   An agonist for the metabotropic acetylcholine receptor

muscarinic receptor (*muss ka rin ic*)   A metabotropic acetylcholine receptor that is stimulated by muscarine and blocked by atropine.

muscimol (*musk i mawl*)   A direct agonist for the GABA binding site on the GABAA receptor.

mutation   A change in the genetic information contained in the chromosomes of sperm or eggs, which can be passed on to an organism's offspring; provides genetic variability.

myelin sheath   (*my a lin*)   A sheath that surrounds axons and insulates them, preventing messages from spreading between adjacent axons.

myofibril   An element of muscle fibers that consists of overlapping strands of actin and myosin; responsible for muscular contractions.

myosin   One of the proteins (with actin) that provide the physical basis for muscular contraction.

Müllerian system   The embryonic precursors of the female internal sex organs.

naloxone (*na lox own*)   A drug that blocks opiate receptors.

narcolepsy (*nahr ko lep see*)   A sleep disorder characterized by periods of irresistible sleep, attacks of cataplexy, sleep paralysis, and hypnagogic hallucinations.

natural selection   The process by which inherited traits that confer a selective advantage (increase an animal's likelihood to live and reproduce) become more prevalent in a population.

negative afterimage   The image seen after a portion of the retina is exposed to an intense visual stimulus; consists of colors complementary to those of the physical stimulus.

negative feedback   A process whereby the effect produced by an action serves to diminish or terminate that action; a characteristic of regulatory systems.

negative reinforcement   The removal or reduction of an aversive stimulus that is contingent on a particular response, with an attendant increase in the frequency of that response.

negative symptom   A symptom of schizophrenia characterized by the absence of behaviors that are normally present: social withdrawal, lack of affect, and reduced motivation.

neocortex   The phylogenetically newest cortex, including the primary sensory cortex, primary motor cortex, and association cortex.

neostigmine (*nee o stig meen*)   A drug that inhibits the activity of acetylcholinesterase.

neoteny   A slowing of the process of maturation, allowing more time for growth; an important factor in the development of large brains.

neural adhesion protein   A protein that plays a role in brain development; helps to guide the growth of neurons.

neural integration   The process by which inhibitory and excitatory postsynaptic potentials summate and control the rate of firing of a neuron.

neural tube   A hollow tube, closed at the rostral end, that forms from ectodermal tissue early in embryonic development; serves as the origin of the central nervous system.

neuraxis   An imaginary line drawn through the center of the length of the central nervous system, from the bottom of the spinal cord to the front of the forebrain.

neuroethics   An interdisciplinary field devoted to understanding implications of and developing best practices in ethics for neuroscience research.

neurofibrillary tangle (*new row fib ri lair y*)   A dying neuron containing intracellular accumulations of abnormally phosphorylated tau-protein filaments that formerly served as the cell's internal skeleton.

neurogenesis   Production of new neurons through the division of neural stem cells; occurs in the hippocampus and olfactory bulb and appears to play a role in learning.

neuromodulator   A naturally secreted substance that acts like a neurotransmitter except that it is not restricted to the synaptic cleft but diffuses through the extracellular fluid.

neuromuscular junction   The synapse between the terminal buttons of an axon and a muscle fiber.

neurosecretory cell   A neuron that secretes a hormone or hormone-like substance.

neurons   Nerve cells; the information-processing and information-transmitting cells of the nervous system.

neuropeptide Y (NPY)   A peptide neurotransmitter found in a system of neurons of the arcuate nucleus that stimulate feeding, insulin and glucocorticoid secretion, decrease the breakdown of triglycerides, and decrease body temperature.

neurotransmitter-dependent ion channel   An ion channel that opens when a molecule of a neurotransmitter binds with a postsynaptic receptor.

neurotransmitter   A chemical that is released by a terminal button; has an excitatory or inhibitory effect on another neuron.

nicotine   An agonist for the ionotropic acetylcholine receptor.

nicotinic receptor   An ionotropic acetylcholine receptor that is stimulated by nicotine and blocked by curare.

nigrostriatal system (*nigh grow stry ay tul*)   A system of neurons originating in the substantia nigra and terminating in the neostriatum (caudate nucleus and putamen).

nitric oxide synthase   An enzyme responsible for the production of nitric oxide (NO).

NMDA receptor   A specialized ionotropic glutamate receptor that controls a calcium channel that is normally blocked by Mg^{2+} ions; involved in long-term potentiation.

node of Ranvier   (*raw vee ay*)   A naked portion of a myelinated axon between adjacent oligodendroglia or Schwann cells.

noncompetitive binding   Binding of a drug to a site on a receptor; does not interfere with the binding site for the principal ligand.

norepinephrine (NE) (*nor epp i neff rin*)   One of the catecholamines; a neurotransmitter found in the brain and in the sympathetic division of the autonomic nervous system.

norepinephrine transporter   Proteins that remove norepinephrine from the synapse.

nucleolus   (*new clee o lus*)   A structure within the nucleus of a cell that produces the ribosomes.

nucleus (plural: *nuclei*)   An identifiable group of neural cell bodies in the central nervous system. Or a structure in the central region of a cell, containing the nucleolus and chromosomes.

nucleus accumbens (NAC)   A nucleus of the basal forebrain near the septum; receives dopamine-secreting terminal buttons from neurons of the ventral tegmental area and is thought to be involved in reinforcement and attention.

nucleus of the solitary tract   A nucleus of the medulla that receives information from visceral organs and from the gustatory system.

nucleus paragigantocellularis (nPGi)   A nucleus of the medulla that receives input from the medial preoptic area and contains neurons whose axons form synapses with motor neurons in the spinal cord that participate in sexual reflexes in males.

nucleus raphe magnus   A nucleus of the raphe that contains serotonin-secreting neurons that project to the dorsal gray matter of the spinal cord and is involved in analgesia produced by opiates.

ob mouse   A strain of mice whose obesity and low metabolic rate are caused by a mutation that prevents the production of leptin.

obsession An unwanted thought or idea with which a person is preoccupied.

obsessive-compulsive disorder (OCD) A mental disorder characterized by obsessions and compulsions.

obstructive hydrocephalus A condition in which all or some of the brain's ventricles are enlarged; caused by an obstruction that impedes the normal flow of CSF.

occipital lobe (*ok sip i tul*) The region of the cerebral cortex caudal to the parietal and temporal lobes.

olfactory bulb The protrusion at the end of the olfactory nerve; receives input from the olfactory receptors.

olfactory epithelium The epithelial tissue of the nasal sinus that covers the cribriform plate; contains the cilia of the olfactory receptors.

olfactory glomerulus (*glow mare you luss*) A bundle of dendrites of mitral cells and the associated terminal buttons of the axons of olfactory receptors.

oligodendrocyte (*oh li go den droh site*) A type of glial cell in the central nervous system that forms myelin sheaths.

olivocochlear bundle A bundle of efferent axons that travel from the olivary complex of the medulla to the auditory hair cells on the cochlea.

ondansetron 5-HT3 receptor antagonist.

operant conditioning A learning procedure whereby the effects of a particular behavior in a particular situation increase (reinforce) or decrease (punish) the probability of the behavior; also called *instrumental conditioning*.

opium Agonist for opiate receptor.

opsin (*opp sin*) A class of protein that, together with retinal, constitutes the photopigments.

optic chiasm (*kye az'm*) An X-shaped connection between the optic nerves, located below the base of the brain, just anterior to the pituitary gland.

optic disk The location of the exit point from the retina of the fibers of the ganglion cells that form the optic nerve; responsible for the blind spot.

optic flow The complex motion of points in the visual field caused by relative movement between the observer and environment; provides information about the relative distance of objects from the observer and of the relative direction of movement.

optic nerve Bundles of axons from retinal ganglion cells exit the eye and convey information to the lateral geniculate nucleus.

optogenetic method The use of a genetically modified virus to insert light-sensitive ion channels into the membrane of particular neurons in the brain; can depolarize or hyperpolarize the neurons when light of the appropriate wavelength is applied.

oral administration Administration of a substance into the mouth so that it is swallowed.

orexin A peptide, also known as *hypocretin*, produced by neurons whose cell bodies are located in the hypothalamus; their destruction causes narcolepsy.

organ of Corti The sensory organ on the basilar membrane that contains the auditory hair cells.

organic sense A sense modality that arises from receptors located within the inner organs of the body.

organizational effect (of hormone) The effect of a hormone on tissue differentiation and development.

orthographic dysgraphia A writing disorder in which the person can spell regularly spelled words but not irregularly spelled ones.

osmometric thirst Thirst produced by an increase in the osmotic pressure of the interstitial fluid relative to the intracellular fluid, thus producing cellular dehydration.

osmoreceptor A neuron that detects changes in the solute concentration of the interstitial fluid that surrounds it.

ossicle (*ahss i kul*) One of the three bones of the middle ear.

oval window An opening in the bone surrounding the cochlea that reveals a membrane, against which the baseplate of the stapes presses, transmitting sound vibrations into the fluid within the cochlea.

ovarian follicle A cluster of epithelial cells surrounding an oocyte, which develops into an ovum.

overtone The frequency of complex tones that occurs at multiples of the fundamental frequency.

OVLT (organum vasculosum of the lamina terminalis) A circumventricular organ located anterior to the anteroventral portion of the third ventricle; served by fenestrated capillaries and thus lacks a blood–brain barrier.

oxycodone Agonist for opiate receptor.

oxytocin (*ox ee tow sin*) A hormone secreted by the posterior pituitary gland; causes contraction of the smooth muscle of the milk ducts, the uterus, and the male ejaculatory system; also serves as a neurotransmitter in the brain.

Pacinian corpuscle (*pa chin ee un*) A vibration-sensitive cutaneous receptor, important in detecting vibration from an object being held.

panic disorder A disorder characterized by episodic periods of symptoms such as shortness of breath, irregularities in heartbeat, and other autonomic symptoms, accompanied by intense fear.

parabelt region The second level of auditory association cortex; surrounds the belt region.

parahippocampal cortex A region of limbic cortex adjacent to the hippocampal formation that, along with the perirhinal cortex, relays information between the entorhinal cortex and other regions of the brain.

parahippocampal place area (PPA) A region of limbic cortex on the medial temporal lobe; involved in perception of particular places ("scenes").

parasympathetic division The portion of the autonomic nervous system that controls functions that occur during a relaxed state.

paraventricular nucleus (PVN) A nucleus of the hypothalamus located adjacent to the dorsal third ventricle; contains neurons involved in control of the autonomic nervous system and the posterior pituitary gland.

parietal lobe (*pa rye i tul*) The region of the cerebral cortex caudal to the frontal lobe and dorsal to the temporal lobe.

parietal reach region A region in the medial posterior parietal cortex that plays a critical role in control of pointing or reaching with the hands.

parkin A protein that plays a role in ferrying defective or misfolded proteins to the proteasomes; mutated parkin is a cause of familial Parkinson's disease.

Parkinson's disease A neurological disease characterized by tremors, rigidity of the limbs, poor balance, and difficulty in initiating movements; caused by degeneration of the nigrostriatal system.

partial agonist A drug that has a very high affinity for a particular receptor but activates that receptor less than the normal ligand does; serves as an agonist in regions of low concentration of the normal ligand and as an antagonist in regions of high concentrations.

partial seizure A seizure that begins at a focus and remains localized, not generalizing to the rest of the brain.

parturition (*par tew ri shun*) The act of giving birth.

parvocellular layer One of the four outer layers of neurons in the dorsal lateral geniculate nucleus; transmits information necessary for perception of color and fine details to the primary visual cortex.

PCP Phencyclidine; a drug that binds with the PCP binding site of the NMDA receptor and serves as an indirect antagonist.

PCPA A drug that inhibits the activity of tryptophan hydroxylase and thus interferes with the synthesis of 5-HT.

peptide A chain of amino acids joined together by peptide bonds. Most neuromodulators, and some hormones, consist of peptide molecules.

peptide YY3–36 (PYY) A peptide released by the gastrointestinal system after a meal in amounts proportional to the size of the meal.

perception The conscious experience and interpretation of information from the senses.

perceptual learning Learning to recognize a particular stimulus.

perfusion (*per few zhun*) The process by which an animal's blood is replaced by a fluid such as a saline solution or a fixative in preparing the brain for histological examination.

periaqueductal gray matter (PAG) The region of the midbrain that surrounds the cerebral aqueduct; plays an essential role in various species-typical behaviors, including female sexual behavior.

peripheral nervous system (PNS) The part of the nervous system outside the brain and spinal cord, including the nerves attached to the brain and spinal cord.

perirhinal cortex A region of limbic cortex adjacent to the hippocampal formation that, along with the parahippocampal cortex, relays information between the entorhinal cortex and other regions of the brain.

persistent Müllerian duct syndrome A condition caused by a congenital lack of anti-Müllerian hormone or receptors for this hormone; in a male, causes development of both male and female internal sex organs.

PHA-L Phaseolus vulgaris leukoagglutinin; a protein derived from kidney beans and used as an anterograde tracer; taken up by dendrites and cell bodies and carried to the ends of the axons.

phagocytosis (*fagg o sy toe sis*) The process by which cells engulf and digest other cells or debris caused by cellular degeneration.

phantom limb Sensations that appear to originate in a limb that has been amputated.

pharmacokinetics The process by which drugs are absorbed, distributed within the body, metabolized, and excreted.

phase difference The difference in arrival times of sound waves at each of the eardrums.

phenylketonuria (PKU) (*fee nul kee ta new ree uh*) A hereditary disorder caused by the absence of an enzyme that converts the amino acid phenylalanine to tyrosine; the accumulation of phenylalanine causes brain damage unless a special diet is implemented soon after birth.

pheromone (*fair oh moan*) A chemical released by one animal that affects the behavior or physiology of another animal; usually smelled or tasted.

phonetic reading Reading by decoding the phonetic significance of letter strings; "sound reading."

phonological dysgraphia A writing disorder in which the person cannot sound out words and write them phonetically.

phonological dyslexia A reading disorder in which a person can read familiar words but has difficulty reading unfamiliar words or pronounceable nonwords.

photopigment A protein dye bonded to retinal, a substance derived from vitamin A; responsible for transduction of visual information.

photoreceptor One of the receptor cells of the retina; transduces photic energy into electrical potentials.

phototherapy Treatment of seasonal affective disorder by daily exposure to bright light.

physical dependence Compensatory changes following repeated use of a drug that result in withdrawal symptoms when the drug is no longer taken.

pia mater The inner layer of the meninges that clings to the surface of the brain; thin and delicate.

pineal gland (*py nee ul*) A gland attached to the dorsal tectum; produces melatonin and plays a role in circadian and seasonal rhythms.

pitch A perceptual dimension of sound; corresponds to the fundamental frequency.

place code The system by which information about different frequencies is coded by different locations on the basilar membrane.

placebo (*pla see boh*) An inert substance that is given to an organism in lieu of a physiologically active drug; used experimentally to control for the effects of mere administration of a drug.

pons The region of the metencephalon rostral to the medulla, caudal to the midbrain, and ventral to the cerebellum.

pontine nucleus A large nucleus in the pons that serves as an important source of input to the cerebellum.

population EPSP An evoked potential that represents the EPSPs of a population of neurons.

positive symptom A symptom of schizophrenia evident by its presence: delusions, hallucinations, or thought disorders.

positron emission tomography (PET) A functional imaging method that reveals the localization of a radioactive tracer in a living brain.

posterior With respect to the central nervous system, located near or toward the tail.

posterior parietal cortex The highest level of the dorsal stream of the visual association cortex; involved in perception of movement and spatial location.

posterior pituitary gland The posterior part of the pituitary gland; an endocrine gland that contains hormone-secreting terminal buttons of axons whose cell bodies lie within the hypothalamus.

postganglionic neuron Neurons of the autonomic nervous system that form synapses directly with their target organ.

postsynaptic membrane The cell membrane opposite the terminal button in a synapse; the membrane of the cell that receives the message.

postsynaptic potential Alterations in the membrane potential of a postsynaptic neuron, produced by liberation of neurotransmitter at the synapse.

postsynaptic receptor A receptor molecule in the postsynaptic membrane of a synapse that contains a binding site for a neurotransmitter.

posttraumatic stress disorder (PTSD) A psychological disorder caused by exposure to a situation of extreme danger and stress; symptoms include recurrent dreams or recollections; can interfere with social activities and cause a feeling of hopelessness.

predation Attack of one animal directed at an individual of another species on which the attacking animal normally preys.

prefrontal cortex The region of the frontal lobe rostral to the motor association cortex.

preganglionic neuron The efferent neuron of the autonomic nervous system whose cell body is located in a cranial nerve nucleus or in the intermediate horn of the spinal gray matter and whose terminal buttons synapse upon postganglionic neurons in the autonomic ganglia.

premotor cortex A region of motor association cortex of the lateral frontal lobe, rostral to the primary motor cortex.

presenilin (*pree sen ill in*) A protein produced by a faulty gene that causes β-amyloid precursor protein to be converted to the abnormal short form; may be a cause of Alzheimer's disease.

presynaptic facilitation The action of a presynaptic terminal button in an axoaxonic synapse; increases the amount of neurotransmitter released by the postsynaptic terminal button.

presynaptic inhibition The action of a presynaptic terminal button in an axoaxonic synapse; reduces the amount of neurotransmitter released by the postsynaptic terminal button.

presynaptic membrane   The membrane of a terminal button that lies adjacent to the postsynaptic membrane and through which the neurotransmitter is released.

primary auditory cortex   The region of the superior temporal lobe whose primary input is from the auditory system.

primary motor cortex   The region of the posterior frontal lobe that contains neurons that control movements of skeletal muscles.

primary somatosensory cortex   The region of the anterior parietal lobe whose primary input is from the somatosensory system.

primary visual cortex or striate cortex   The region of the posterior occipital lobe whose primary input is from the visual system.

prion (*pree on*)   A protein that can exist in two forms that differ only in their three-dimensional shape; accumulation of misfolded prion protein is responsible for transmissible spongiform encephalopathies.

progenitor cells   Cells of the ventricular zone that divide and give rise to cells of the central nervous system.

progesterone (*pro jess ter own*)   A steroid hormone produced by the ovary that maintains the endometrial lining of the uterus during the later part of the menstrual cycle and during pregnancy; along with estradiol it promotes receptivity in female mammals with estrous cycles.

projection fiber   An axon of a neuron in one region of the brain whose terminals form synapses with neurons in another region.

prolactin   A hormone of the anterior pituitary gland, necessary for production of milk; also facilitates maternal behavior.

proprioception   Perception of the body's position and posture.

prosody   The use of changes in intonation and emphasis to convey meaning in speech besides that specified by the particular words; an important means of communication of emotion.

prosopagnosia (*prah soh pag no zha*)   Failure to recognize particular people by the sight of their faces.

protanopia (*pro tan owe pee a*)   An inherited form of defective color vision in which red and green hues are confused; "red" cones are filled with "green" cone opsin.

proteasome   An organelle responsible for destroying defective or degraded proteins within the cell.

pseudorabies virus   A weakened form of a pig herpes virus used for retrograde transneuronal tracing, which labels a series of neurons that are interconnected synaptically.

psychoneuroimmunology   The branch of neuroscience involved with interactions among environmental stimuli, the nervous system, and the immune system.

punishing stimulus   An aversive stimulus that follows a particular behavior and thus makes the behavior become less frequent.

pure alexia   Loss of the ability to read without loss of the ability to write; produced by brain damage.

pure word deafness   The ability to hear, to speak, and (usually) to read and write without being able to comprehend the meaning of speech; caused by damage to Wernicke's area or disruption of auditory input to this region.

pursuit movement   The movement that the eyes make to maintain an image of a moving object on the fovea.

putamen   A telencephalic nucleus; one of the input nuclei of the basal ganglia; involved with control of voluntary movement.

pyramidal tract   The portion of the corticospinal tract on the ventral border of the medulla.

pyridoxine dependency (*peer i dox een*)   A metabolic disorder in which an infant requires larger-than-normal amounts of pyridoxine (vitamin B6) to avoid neurological symptoms.

rabies   A fatal viral disease that causes brain damage; usually transmitted through the bite of an infected animal.

radial glia   Special glia with fibers that grow radially outward from the ventricular zone to the surface of the cortex; provide guidance for neurons migrating outward during brain development.

raphe nuclei (*ruh fay*)   A group of nuclei located in the reticular formation of the medulla, pons, and midbrain, situated along the midline; contain serotonergic neurons.

rate code   The system by which information about different frequencies is coded by the rate of firing of neurons in the auditory system.

rate law   The principle that variations in the intensity of a stimulus or other information being transmitted in an axon are represented by variations in the rate at which that axon fires.

rebound phenomenon   The increased frequency or intensity of a phenomenon after it has been temporarily suppressed; for example, the increase in REM sleep seen after a period of REM sleep deprivation.

receptive field   That portion of the visual field in which the presentation of visual stimuli will produce an alteration in the firing rate of a particular neuron.

receptor blocker   A drug that binds with a receptor but does not activate it; prevents the natural ligand from binding with the receptor.

receptor potential   A slow, graded electrical potential produced by a receptor cell in response to a physical stimulus.

reconsolidation   A process of consolidation of a memory that occurs subsequent to the original consolidation that can be triggered by a reminder of the original stimulus; thought to provide the means for modifying existing memories.

red nucleus   A large nucleus of the midbrain that receives inputs from the cerebellum and motor cortex and sends axons to motor neurons in the spinal cord.

reduction   A type of scientific explanation; a phenomenon is described in terms of the more elementary processes that underlie it.

reflex   An automatic, stereotyped movement that is produced as the direct result of a stimulus.

refractory period (*ree frak to ree*)   A period of time after a particular action (for example, an ejaculation by a male) during which that action cannot occur again.

reinforcing stimulus   An appetitive stimulus that follows a particular behavior and thus makes the behavior become more frequent.

release zone   A region of the interior of the presynaptic membrane of a synapse to which synaptic vesicles attach and release their neurotransmitter into the synaptic cleft.

REM sleep   A period of desynchronized EEG activity during sleep, at which time dreaming, rapid eye movements, and muscular paralysis occur; also called *paradoxical sleep.*

REM sleep behavior disorder   A neurological disorder in which the person does not become paralyzed during REM sleep and thus acts out dreams.

reserpine (*ree sur peen*)   A drug that interferes with the storage of monoamines in synaptic vesicles.

resting potential   The membrane potential of a neuron when it is not being altered by excitatory or inhibitory postsynaptic potentials; approximately –70 mV in the giant squid axon.

reticular formation   A large network of neural tissue located in the central region of the brain stem, from the medulla to the diencephalon.

reticulospinal tract   A bundle of axons that travels from the reticular formation to the gray matter of the spinal cord; controls the muscles responsible for postural movements.

retina   The neural tissue and photoreceptive cells located on the inner surface of the posterior portion of the eye.

retinal (*rett i nahl*)   A chemical synthesized from vitamin A; joins with an opsin to form a photopigment.

retinal disparity The fact that points on objects located at different distances from the observer will fall on slightly different locations on the two retinas; provides the basis for stereopsis.

retrograde In a direction along an axon from the terminal buttons toward the cell body.

retrograde amnesia Amnesia for events that preceded some disturbance to the brain, such as a head injury or electroconvulsive shock.

retrograde labeling method A histological method that labels cell bodies that give rise to the terminal buttons that form synapses with cells in a particular region.

reuptake The reentry of a neurotransmitter just liberated by a terminal button back through the presynaptic membrane, thus terminating the postsynaptic potential.

rhodopsin (*roh dopp sin*) A particular opsin found in rods.

ribosome (*ry bo soam*) A cytoplasmic structure, made of protein, that serves as the site of production of proteins translated from mRNA.

rimonabant A drug that blocks CB1 receptors.

rod One of the receptor cells of the retina; sensitive to light of low intensity.

rostral "Toward the beak"; with respect to the central nervous system, in a direction along the neuraxis toward the front of the face.

round window An opening in the bone surrounding the cochlea of the inner ear that permits vibrations to be transmitted, via the oval window, into the fluid in the cochlea.

rubrospinal tract The system of axons that travels from the red nucleus to the spinal cord; controls independent limb movements.

Ruffini corpuscle A touch-sensitive cutaneous receptor, important in detecting stretching or static force against the skin, important in proprioception.

saccadic movement (*suh kad ik*) The rapid, jerky movement of the eyes used in scanning a visual scene.

saccule (*sak yule*) One of the vestibular sacs.

sagittal section (*sadj i tul*) A slice through the brain parallel to the neuraxis and perpendicular to the ground.

saltatory conduction Conduction of action potentials by myelinated axons. The action potential appears to jump from one node of Ranvier to the next.

satiety mechanism A brain mechanism that causes cessation of hunger or thirst, produced by adequate and available supplies of nutrients or water.

saturation One of the perceptual dimensions of color; purity.

scanning electron microscope A microscope that provides three-dimensional information about the shape of the surface of a small object by scanning the object with a thin beam of electrons.

schizophrenia A serious mental disorder characterized by disordered thoughts, delusions, hallucinations, and often bizarre behaviors.

Schwann cell A cell in the peripheral nervous system that is wrapped around a myelinated axon, providing one segment of its myelin sheath.

seasonal affective disorder (SAD) A mood disorder characterized by depression, lethargy, sleep disturbances, and craving for carbohydrates during the winter season when days are short.

seasonality effect The increased incidence of schizophrenia in people born during late winter and early spring.

second messenger A chemical produced when a G protein activates an enzyme; carries a signal that results in the opening of the ion channel or causes other events to occur in the cell.

secretase (*see cre tayss*) A class of enzymes that cut the β-amyloid precursor protein into smaller fragments, including β-amyloid.

seizure disorder The preferred term for epilepsy.

selective advantage A characteristic of an organism that permits it to produce more than the average number of offspring of its species.

selective serotonin reuptake inhibitor (SSRI) An antidepressant drug that primarily inhibits the reuptake of serotonin.

semantic dementia Loss of semantic memories caused by progressive degeneration of the neocortex of the lateral temporal lobes.

semantic memory A memory of facts and general information.

semicircular canal One of the three ringlike structures of the vestibular apparatus that detect changes in head rotation.

sensation The process in which specialized cells of the nervous system detect environmental stimuli and transduce their energy into receptor potentials.

sensitization An increase in the effectiveness of a drug that is administered repeatedly.

sensory association cortex Those regions of the cerebral cortex that receive information from the regions of primary sensory cortex.

sensory neuron A neuron that detects changes in the external or internal environment and sends information about these changes to the central nervous system.

sensory receptor A specialized neuron that detects a particular category of physical events.

sensory transduction The process by which sensory stimuli are transduced into slow, graded receptor potentials.

serotonin (5-HT) (*sair a toe nin*) An indolamine neurotransmitter; also called 5-hydroxytryptamine.

serotonin and norepinephrine reuptake inhibitor (SNRI) An antidepressant drug that primarily inhibits the reuptake of norepinephrine and serotonin.

serotonin transporter Proteins that remove serotonin from the synapse.

set point The optimal value of the system variable in a regulatory mechanism.

sex chromosome The X and Y chromosomes, which determine an organism's genetic sex. Typically, XX individuals are female, and XY individuals are male.

sexually dimorphic behavior A behavior that has different forms or that occurs with different probabilities or under different circumstances in males and females.

sexually dimorphic nucleus (SDN) A nucleus in the preoptic area that is much larger in males than in females; first observed in rats; plays a role in male sexual behavior.

sham lesion A placebo procedure that duplicates all the steps of producing a brain lesion except the one that actually causes the brain damage.

simple partial seizure A partial seizure, starting from a focus and remaining localized, that does not produce loss of consciousness.

sine-wave grating A series of straight parallel bands varying continuously in brightness according to a sine-wave function, along a line perpendicular to their lengths.

single-unit recording Recording of the electrical activity of a single neuron.

skeletal muscle One of the striated muscles attached to bones.

sleep apnea (*app nee a*) Cessation of breathing while sleeping.

sleep attack A symptom of narcolepsy; an irresistible urge to sleep during the day, after which the person awakens feeling refreshed.

sleep paralysis A symptom of narcolepsy; paralysis occurring just before a person falls asleep.

sleep-related eating disorder A disorder in which the person leaves his or her bed and seeks out and eats food while sleep-walking, usually without a memory for the episode the next day.

social anxiety disorder A disorder characterized by excessive fear of being exposed to the scrutiny of other people that leads to avoidance of social situations in which the person is called on to perform.

sodium–potassium pump A protein found in the membrane of all cells that extrudes sodium ions from and transports potassium ions into the cell.

soma The cell body of a neuron, which contains the nucleus.

somatic nervous system The part of the peripheral nervous system that controls the movement of skeletal muscles or transmits somatosensory information to the central nervous system.

somatotopic organization A topographically organized mapping of parts of the body that are represented in a particular region of the brain.

spatial frequency The relative width of the bands in a sine-wave grating, measured in cycles per degree of visual angle.

spinal cord The cord of nervous tissue that extends caudally from the medulla.

spinal nerve A peripheral nerve attached to the spinal cord.

spinal root A bundle of axons surrounded by connective tissue that occurs in pairs, which fuse and form a spinal nerve.

sporadic disease A disease that occurs rarely and is not obviously caused by heredity or an infectious agent.

SRY The gene on the Y chromosome whose product instructs the undifferentiated fetal gonads to develop into testes; official name is *sex-determining region Y*.

stapes (*stay peez*) The "stirrup"; the last of the three ossicles.

status epilepticus A condition in which a patient undergoes a series of seizures without regaining consciousness.

stereotaxic apparatus A device that permits a surgeon to position an electrode or cannula into a specific part of the brain.

stereotaxic atlas A collection of drawings of sections of the brain of a particular animal with measurements that provide coordinates for stereotaxic surgery.

stereotaxic surgery (*stair ee oh tak sik*) Brain surgery using a stereotaxic apparatus to position an electrode or cannula in a specified position of the brain.

steroid A chemical of low molecular weight, derived from cholesterol. Steroid hormones affect their target cells by attaching to receptors found within the nucleus.

stimulus-response learning Learning to automatically make a particular response in the presence of a particular stimulus; includes classical and instrumental conditioning.

stress A general, imprecise term that can refer either to a stress response or to a situation that elicits a stress response.

stress response A physiological reaction caused by the perception of aversive or threatening situations.

striate cortex (*stry ate*) **(primary visual cortex, or V1)** The primary visual cortex.

striated muscle Skeletal muscle; muscle that contains striations.

subarachnoid space The fluid-filled space that cushions the brain; located between the arachnoid membrane and the pia mater.

subcortical region The region located within the brain, beneath the cortical surface.

subcutaneous (SC) injection Injection of a substance into the space beneath the skin.

subfornical organ (SFO) A small organ located in the confluence of the lateral ventricles, attached to the underside of the fornix; contains neurons that detect the presence of angiotensin in the blood and excite neural circuits that initiate drinking.

subgenual anterior cingulate cortex (subgenual ACC) A region of the medial prefrontal cortex located below the "knee" at the front of the corpus callosum; plays a role in the symptoms of depression.

sublaterodorsal nucleus (SLD) A region of the dorsal pons, just ventral to the locus coeruleus, that contains REM-ON neurons; part of the REM flip-flop.

sublingual administration (*sub ling wul*) Administration of a substance by placing it beneath the tongue.

submissive behavior A behavior shown by an animal in response to threat behavior by another animal; serves to prevent an attack.

substantia nigra A darkly stained region of the tegmentum that contains neurons that communicate with the caudate nucleus and putamen in the basal ganglia.

subthalamic nucleus A nucleus located ventral to the thalamus, an important part of the subcortical motor system that includes the basal ganglia; a target of deep-brain stimulation for treatment of Parkinson's disease.

subventricular zone (SVZ) A layer of progenitor cells located just inside the ventricular zone; thicker in mammals with large brains.

sulcus (plural: sulci) (*sul kus, sul sigh*) A groove in the surface of the cerebral hemisphere, smaller than a fissure.

superior colliculi (*ka lik yew lee*) Protrusions on top of the midbrain; part of the visual system.

superior olivary complex A group of nuclei in the medulla; involved with auditory functions, including localization of the source of sounds.

superior sagittal sinus A venous sinus located in the midline just dorsal to the corpus callosum, between the two cerebral hemispheres.

supersensitivity The increased sensitivity of neurotransmitter receptors; caused by damage to the afferent axons or long-term blockage of neurotransmitter release.

supplementary motor area (SMA) A region of motor association cortex of the dorsal and dorsomedial frontal lobe, rostral to the primary motor cortex.

suprachiasmatic nucleus (SCN) (*soo pra ky az mat ik*) A nucleus situated atop the optic chiasm. It contains a biological clock that is responsible for organizing many of the body's circadian rhythms.

surface dyslexia A reading disorder in which a person can read words phonetically but has difficulty reading irregularly spelled words by the whole-word method.

symmetrical division Division of a progenitor cell that gives rise to two identical progenitor cells; increases the size of the ventricular zone and hence the brain that develops from it.

sympathetic adrenal-medullary system (SAM system) A circuit that is activated as part of the stress response; results in the release of catecholamines.

sympathetic division The portion of the autonomic nervous system that controls functions that accompany arousal and expenditure of energy.

sympathetic ganglia Nodules that contain synapses between preganglionic and postganglionic neurons of the sympathetic nervous system.

sympathetic ganglion chain One of a pair of groups of sympathetic ganglia that lie ventrolateral to the vertebral column.

synapse A junction between the terminal button of an axon and the membrane of another neuron.

synaptic cleft The space between the presynaptic membrane and the postsynaptic membrane.

synaptic vesicle (*vess i kul*) A small, hollow, beadlike structure found in terminal buttons; contains molecules of a neurotransmitter.

system variable A variable that is controlled by a regulatory mechanism, for example, temperature in a heating system.

T-lymphocyte   A white blood cell that originates in the thymus gland; part of the immune system.

tardive dyskinesia   A movement disorder that can occur after prolonged treatment with antipsychotic medication, characterized by involuntary movements of the face and neck.

target cell   The type of cell that is directly affected by a hormone or other chemical signal.

targeted mutation   A mutated gene (also called a "knockout gene") produced in the laboratory and inserted into the chromosomes of mice; fails to produce a functional protein.

tau protein   A protein that normally serves as a component of microtubules, which provide the cell's transport mechanism and cytoskeleton.

Tay-Sachs disease   A heritable, fatal, metabolic storage disorder; lack of enzymes in lysosomes causes accumulation of waste product and swelling of cells of the brain.

tectorial membrane (*tek torr ee ul*)   A membrane located above the basilar membrane; serves as a shelf against which the cilia of the auditory hair cells move.

tectospinal tract   A bundle of axons that travels from the tectum to the spinal cord; coordinates head and trunk movements with eye movements.

tectum   The dorsal part of the midbrain; includes the superior and inferior colliculi.

tegmentum   The ventral part of the midbrain; includes the periaqueductal gray matter, reticular formation, red nucleus, and substantia nigra.

temporal lobe (*tem por ul*)   The region of the cerebral cortex rostral to the occipital lobe and ventral to the parietal and frontal lobes.

terminal button   The bud at the end of a branch of an axon; forms synapses with another neuron; sends information to that neuron.

testosterone (*tess tahss ter own*)   The principal androgen found in males.

thalamus   The largest portion of the diencephalon, located above the hypothalamus; contains nuclei that project information to specific regions of the cerebral cortex and receive information from it.

THC   The active ingredient in marijuana; activates CB1 receptors in the brain.

therapeutic index   The ratio between the dose that produces the desired effect in 50 percent of the animals and the dose that produces toxic effects in 50 percent of the animals.

therapeutic lag   The period of time between beginning an antidepressant treatment and experiencing therapeutic effects, usually several weeks.

theta activity   EEG activity of 3.5–7.5 Hz that occurs intermittently during early stages of slow-wave sleep and REM sleep.

third ventricle   The ventricle located in the center of the diencephalon.

thought disorder   Disorganized, irrational thinking.

threat behavior   A species-typical behavior that warns another animal that it may be attacked if it does not flee or show a submissive behavior.

threshold of excitation   The value of the membrane potential that must be reached to produce an action potential.

thrombus   A blood clot that forms within a blood vessel, which may occlude it.

tiagabine   A GABA transporter antagonist.

timbre (*tim ber or tamm ber*)   A perceptual dimension of sound; corresponds to complexity.

tip link   An elastic filament that attaches the tip of one cilium to the side of the adjacent cilium.

tolerance   A decrease in the effectiveness of a drug that is administered repeatedly.

tonic phase   The first phase of a grand mal seizure, in which all of the patient's skeletal muscles are contracted.

tonotopic representation (*tonn oh top ik*)   A topographically organized mapping of different frequencies of sound that are represented in a particular region of the brain.

topical administration   Administration of a substance directly onto the skin or mucous membrane.

Tourette's syndrome   A neurological disorder characterized by tics and involuntary vocalizations and sometimes by compulsive uttering of obscenities and repetition of the utterances of others.

toxic gain of function   Said of a genetic disorder caused by a dominant mutation that involves a faulty gene that produces a protein with toxic effects.

transcortical sensory aphasia   A speech disorder in which a person has difficulty comprehending speech and producing meaningful spontaneous speech but can repeat speech; caused by damage to the region of the brain posterior to Wernicke's area.

transcranial magnetic stimulation (TMS)   Stimulation of the cerebral cortex by means of magnetic fields produced by passing pulses of electricity through a coil of wire placed next to the skull; interferes with the functions of the brain region that is stimulated.

transduction   See *sensory transduction*.

transmissible spongiform encephalopathy (TSE)   A contagious brain disease whose degenerative process gives the brain a spongelike appearance; caused by accumulation of misfolded prion protein.

transmission electron microscope   A microscope that passes a focused beam of electrons through thin slices of tissue to reveal extremely small details.

treatment-resistant depression   A major depressive disorder whose symptoms are not relieved after trials of several different treatments.

tricyclic antidepressant   A class of drugs used to treat depression; inhibits the reuptake of norepinephrine and serotonin but also affects other neurotransmitters; named for the molecular structure.

triglyceride (*try gliss er ide*)   The form of fat storage in adipose cells; consists of a molecule of glycerol joined with three fatty acids.

tritanopia (*try tan owe pee a*)   An inherited form of defective color vision in which hues with short wavelengths are confused; "blue" cones are either lacking or faulty.

tryptophan depletion procedure   A procedure involving a low-tryptophan diet and a tryptophan-free amino acid "cocktail" that lowers brain tryptophan and consequently decreases the synthesis of 5-HT.

tuberomammillary nucleus (TMN)   A nucleus in the ventral posterior hypothalamus, just rostral to the mammillary bodies; contains histaminergic neurons involved in cortical activation and behavioral arousal.

tumor   A mass of cells whose growth is uncontrolled and that serves no useful function.

tumor initiating cell   Cells that originate from transformations of neural stem cells, rapidly proliferate, and give rise to a glioma.

Turner syndrome   The presence of only one sex chromosome (an X chromosome); characterized by lack of ovaries but otherwise normal female sex organs and genitalia.

tympanic membrane   The eardrum.

ubiquitin   A protein that attaches itself to faulty or misfolded proteins and thus targets them for destruction by proteasomes.

umami (*oo mah mee*)   The taste sensation produced by glutamate.

utricle (*you trih kul*)   One of the vestibular sacs.

vagus nerve (*vay guss*) The largest of the cranial nerves, conveying efferent fibers of the parasympathetic division of the autonomic nervous system to organs of the thoracic and abdominal cavities.

Vandenbergh effect The earlier onset of puberty seen in female animals that are housed with males; caused by a pheromone in the male's urine; first observed in mice.

ventral "Toward the belly"; with respect to the central nervous system, in a direction perpendicular to the neuraxis toward the bottom of the skull or the front surface of the body.

ventral anterior nucleus (of thalamus) A thalamic nucleus that receives projections from the basal ganglia and sends projections to the motor cortex.

ventral corticospinal tract The system of axons that originates in the motor cortex and terminates in the ipsilateral ventral gray matter of the spinal cord; controls movements of the upper legs and trunk.

ventral root The spinal root that contains outgoing (efferent) motor fibers.

ventral stream A system of interconnected regions of visual cortex involved in the perception of form, beginning with the striate cortex and ending with the inferior temporal cortex.

ventral tegmental area (VTA) A group of dopaminergic neurons in the ventral midbrain whose axons form the mesolimbic and mesocortical systems; plays a critical role in reinforcement.

ventricle (*ven trik ul*) One of the hollow spaces within the brain, filled with cerebrospinal fluid.

ventricular zone (VZ) A layer of cells that line the inside of the neural tube; contains progenitor cells that divide and give rise to cells of the central nervous system.

ventrolateral nucleus (of thalamus) A thalamic nucleus that receives projections from the basal ganglia and sends projections to the motor cortex.

ventrolateral nucleus A nucleus of the thalamus that receives inputs from the cerebellum and sends axons to the primary motor cortex.

ventrolateral periaqueductal gray matter (vlPAG) A region of the dorsal midbrain that contains REM-OFF neurons; part of the REM flip-flop.

ventrolateral preoptic area (vlPOA) A group of GABAergic neurons in the preoptic area whose activity suppresses alertness and behavioral arousal and promotes sleep.

ventromedial group The vestibulospinal tract, the tectospinal tract, the reticulospinal tract, and the ventral corticospinal tract.

ventromedial nucleus of the hypothalamus (VMH) A large nucleus of the hypothalamus located near the walls of the third ventricle; plays an essential role in female sexual behavior.

ventromedial prefrontal cortex (vmPFC) The region of the prefrontal cortex at the base of the anterior frontal lobes, adjacent to the midline.

vergence movement The cooperative movement of the eyes, which ensures that the image of an object falls on identical portions of both retinas.

vermis The portion of the cerebellum located at the midline; receives somatosensory information and helps to control the vestibulospinal and reticulospinal tracts through its connections with the fastigial nucleus.

vesicle ACh transporter Proteins in the vesicle membrane that pump acetylcholine into a vesicle.

vesicle GABA transporter Proteins in the vesicle membrane that pump GABA into a vesicle.

vesicle glutamate transporter Proteins in the vesicle membrane that pump glutamate into a vesicle.

vesicle monoamine transporter Proteins in the vesicle membrane that pump monoamine neurotransmitters into a vesicle.

vesicle transporter Proteins in the vesicle membrane that pump neurotransmitter into a vesicle.

vestibular ganglion A nodule on the vestibular nerve that contains the cell bodies of the bipolar neurons that convey vestibular information to the brain.

vestibular sac One of a set of two receptor organs in each inner ear that detect changes in the tilt of the head.

vestibulospinal tract A bundle of axons that travels from the vestibular nuclei to the gray matter of the spinal cord; controls postural movements in response to information from the vestibular system.

vigabatrin Prevents the breakdown of GABA by blocking the enzyme GABA aminotransferase.

visual agnosia (*ag no zha*) Deficits in visual perception in the absence of blindness; caused by brain damage.

visual pathway The pathway of visual processing from the retina to the lateral geniculate nucleus to striate and extrastriate cortical regions.

visual word-form area (VWFA) A region of the fusiform gyrus on the base of the temporal lobe that plays a critical role in whole-word recognition.

volitional facial paresis Difficulty in moving the facial muscles voluntarily; caused by damage to the face region of the primary motor cortex or its subcortical connections.

voltage-dependent ion channel An ion channel that opens or closes according to the value of the membrane potential.

volumetric thirst Thirst produced by hypovolemia.

vomeronasal organ (VNO) (*voah mer oh nay zul*) A sensory organ that detects the presence of certain chemicals, especially when a liquid is actively sniffed; mediates the effects of some pheromones.

Whitten effect The synchronization of the menstrual or estrous cycles of a group of females, which occurs only in the presence of a pheromone in a male's urine.

whole-word reading Reading by recognizing a word as a whole; "sight reading."

withdrawal symptom The appearance of symptoms opposite to those produced by a drug when the drug is administered repeatedly and then suddenly no longer taken.

Wolffian system The embryonic precursors of the male internal sex organs.

zeitgeber (*tsite gay ber*) A stimulus (usually the light of dawn) that resets the biological clock that is responsible for circadian rhythms.

zolpidem An indirect agonist for the GABAA receptor; used to treat insomnia.

References

Abelson, J. L., Curtis, G. C., Sagher, O., Albucher, R. C., et al. Deep brain stimulation for refractory obsessive-compulsive disorder. *Biological Psychiatry*, 2005, *57*, 510–516.

Abizaid, A., Liu, Z. W., Andrews, Z. B., Shanabrough, M., et al. Ghrelin modulates the activity and synaptic input organization of midbrain dopamine neurons while promoting appetite. *Journal of Clinical Investigation*, 2006, *116*, 3229–3239.

Abrevalo, E., Shanmugasundararaj, S., Wilkemeyer, M. F., Dou, X., et al. An alcohol binding site on the neural cell adhesion molecule L1. *Proceedings of the National Academy of Sciences, USA*, 2008, *105*, 371–375.

Adair, J. C., and Barrett, A. M. Spatial neglect: Clinical and neuroscience review. *Annals of the New York Academy of Science*, 2008, *1142*, 21–43.

Adamantidis, A., Carter, M. C., and de Lecea, L. Optogenetic deconstruction of sleep–wake circuitry in the brain. *Frontiers in Molecular Neuroscience*, 2010, *2*, 1–9.

Adams, D. B., Gold, A. R., and Burt, A. D. Rise in female-initiated sexual activity at ovulation and its suppression by oral contraceptives. *New England Journal of Medicine*, 1978, *299*, 1145–1150.

Adams, R. B., and Kleck, R. E. Effects of direct and averted gaze on the perception of facially communicated emotion. *Emotion*, 2005, *5*, 3–11.

Adams, R. D. The anatomy of memory mechanisms in the human brain. In *The pathology of memory*, edited by G. A. Talland and N. C. Waugh. New York: Academic Press, 1969.

Adey, W. R., Bors, E., and Porter, R. W. EEG sleep patterns after high cervical lesions in man. *Archives of Neurology*, 1968, *19*, 377–383.

Adler, C. M., Malhotra, A. K., Elman, I., Goldberg, T., et al. Comparison of ketamine-induced thought disorder in healthy volunteers and thought disorder in schizophrenia. *American Journal of Psychiatry*, 1999, *156*, 1646–1649.

Adolphs, R. Neural systems for recognizing emotion. *Current Opinion in Neurobiology*, 2002, *12*, 169–177.

Adolphs, R., Damasio, H., Tranel, D., Cooper, G., et al. A role for somatosensory cortices in the visual recognition of emotion as revealed by three-dimensional lesion mapping. *Journal of Neuroscience*, 2000, *20*, 2683–2690.

Adolphs, R., Gosselin, F., Buchanan, T. W., Tranel, D., et al. A mechanism for impaired fear recognition after amygdala damage. *Nature*, 2005, *433*, 68–72.

Adolphs, R., and Tranel, D. Intact recognition of emotional prosody following amygdala damage. *Neuropsychologia*, 1999, *37*, 1285–1292.

Adolphs, R., Tranel, D., Damasio, H., and Damasio, A. Impaired recognition of emotion in facial expressions following bilateral damage to the human amygdala. *Nature*, 1994, *372*, 669–672.

Adolphs, R., Tranel, D., Damasio, H., and Damasio, A. Fear and the human amygdala. *Journal of Neuroscience*, 1995, *15*, 5879–5891.

Adolphs, R., Tranel, D., Hamann, S., Young, A. W., et al. Recognition of facial emotion in nine individuals with bilateral amygdala damage. *Neuropsychologia*, 1999, *37*, 1111–1117.

Advokat, C., and Kutlesic, V. Pharmacotherapy of the eating disorders: A commentary. *Neuroscience and Biobehavioral Reviews*, 1995, *19*, 59–66.

Agarwal, N., Pacher, P., Tegeder, I., Amaya, F., et al. Cannabinoids mediate analgesia largely via peripheral type 1 cannabinoid receptors in nociceptors. *Nature Neuroscience*, 2007, *10*, 870–879.

Aghajanian, G. K., Kogan, J. H., and Moghaddam, B. Opiate withdrawal increases glutamate and aspartate efflux in the locus coeruleus: An in vivo microdialysis study. *Brain Research*, 1994, *636*, 126–130.

Aharon, I., Etcoff, N., Ariely, D., Chabris, C. F., et al. Beautiful faces have variable reward value: fMRI and behavioral evidence. *Neuron*, 2001, *32*, 537–551.

Ahlers, O., Nachtigall, I., Lenze, J., Goldmann, A., et al. Intraoperative thoracic epidural anaesthesia attenuates stress-induced immunosuppression in patients undergoing major abdominal surgery. *British Journal of Anaesthesia*, 2008, *101*(6), 781–787.

Aktas, O., Kieseier, B., and Hartung, H.-P. Neuroprotection, regeneration and immunomodulation: Broadening the therapeutic repertoire in multiple sclerosis. *Trends in Neuroscience*, 2009, *33*, 140–152.

Alain, C., He, Y., and Grady, C. The contribution of the inferior parietal lobe to auditory spatial working memory. *Journal of Cognitive Neuroscience*, 2008, *20*, 285–295.

Albrecht, D. G. Analysis of visual form. Doctoral dissertation, University of California, Berkeley, 1978.

Alexander, G. M. An evolutionary perspective of sex-typed toy preferences: Pink, blue, and the brain. *Archives of Sexual Behavior*, 2003, *32*, 7–14.

Alexander, G. M., and Hines, M. Sex differences in response to children's toys in nonhuman primates (Cercopithecus aethiops sabaeus). *Evolution and Human Behavior*, 2002, *23*, 467–479.

Alexander, M. P., Fischer, R. S., and Friedman, R. Lesion localization in apractic agraphia. *Archives of Neurology*, 1992, *49*, 246–251.

Alirezaei, M., Watry, D. D., Flynn, C. F., Kiosses, W. B., et al. Human immunodeficiency virus-1/surface glycoprotein 120 induces apoptosis through RNA-activated protein kinase signaling in neurons. *Journal of Neuroscience*, 2007, *27*, 11047–11055.

Allebrandt, K. V., Teder-Laving, M., Akylo, M., Pichler, I., et al. CLOCK gene variants associate with sleep duration in two independent populations. *Biological Psychiatry*, 2010, *67*, 1040–1047.

Allen, L. S., and Gorski, R. A. Sexual orientation and the size of the anterior commissure in the human brain. *Proceedings of the National Academy of Sciences, USA*, 1992, *89*, 7199–7202.

Allison, T., Puce, A., and McCarthy, G. Social perception from visual cues: Role of the STS region. *Trends in Cognitive Science*, 2000, *4*, 267–278.

Allman, J. M. *Evolving Brains*. New York: Scientific American Library, 1999.

Almer, G., Hainfellner, J. A., Brücke, T., Jellinger, K., et al. Fatal familial insomnia: A new Austrian family. *Brain*, 1999, *122*(1), 5–16.

Altschuler, H. L., Phillips, P. E., and Feinhandler, D. A. Alterations of ethanol self-administration by naltrexone. *Life Sciences*, 1980, *26*, 679–688.

Amano, T., Unal, C. T., and Paré, D. Synaptic correlates of fear extinction in the amygdala. *Nature Neuroscience*, 2010, *13*, 489–494.

Amaral, D. G. The amygdala, social behavior, and danger detection. *Annals of the New York Academy of Sciences*, 2003, *1000*, 337–347.

Amaral, D. G., Price, J. L., Pitkänen, A., and Carmichael, S. T. Anatomical organization of the primate amygdaloid complex. In *The amygdala: Neurobiological aspects of emotion, memory, and mental dysfunction*, edited by J. P. Aggleton. New York: Wiley-Liss, 1992.

Ambady, N., and Rosenthal, R. Thin slices of expressive behavior as predictors of interpersonal consequences: A meta-analysis. *Psychological Bulletin*, 1992, *111*(2), 256.

American Psychiatric Association. *Diagnostic and Statistical Manual of Mental Disorders (DSM-5®)*. Washington, DC: American Psychiatric Association, 2013.

Amiaz, R., Levy, D., Vainiger, D., Grunhaus, L., et al. Repeated high-frequency transcranial magnetic stimulation over the dorsolateral prefrontal cortex reduces cigarette craving and consumption. *Addiction*, 2009, *104*, 653–660.

Anand, B. K., and Brobeck, J. R. Hypothalamic control of food intake in rats and cats. *Yale Journal of Biology and Medicine*, 1951, *24*, 123–140.

Ancoli-Israel, S., and Roth, T. Characteristics of insomnia in the United States: Results of the 1991 National Sleep Foundation survey. *Sleep*, 1999, *22*, S347–S353.

Andari, E., Duhamel, J. R., Zalla, T., Herbrecht, E., et al. Promoting social behavior with oxytocin in high-functioning autism spectrum disorders. *Proceedings of the National Academy of Sciences, USA*, 2010, *107*, 4389–4394.

Anders, S., Birbaumer, N., Sadowski, B., Erb, M., et al. Parietal somatosensory association cortex mediates affective blindsight. *Nature Neuroscience*, 2004, *7*, 339–340.

Anderson, A. K., and Phelps, E. A. Intact recognition of vocal expressions of fear following bilateral lesions of the human amygdala. *Neuroreport*, 1998, *9*, 3607–3613.

Anderson, A. K., and Phelps, E. A. Expression without recognition: Contributions of the human amygdala to emotional communication. *Psychological Science*, 2000, *11*, 106–111.

Anderson, S., Barrash, J., Bechara, A., and Tranel, D. Impairments of emotion and real-world complex behavior following childhood- or adult-onset damage to ventromedial prefrontal cortex. *Journal of the International Neuropsychological Society*, 2006, *12*, 224–235.

ann het Rot, M., Collins, K. A., Murrough, J. W., Perez, A. M., et al. Safety and efficacy of repeated-dose intravenous ketamine for treatment-resistant depression. *Biological Psychiatry*, 2010, *67*, 139–145.

Annese, J., Gazzaniga, M. S., and Toga, A. W. Localization of the human cortical visual area MT based on computer aided histological analysis. *Cerebral Cortex*, 2005, *15*, 1044–1053.

Anonymous. Effects of sexual activity on beard growth in man. *Nature*, 1970, *226*, 867–870.

Anzai, A., Peng, X., and Van Essen, D. C. Neurons in monkey visual area V2 encode combinations of orientations. *Nature Neuroscience*, 2007, *10*, 1313–1321.

Apkarian, A. V., Sosa, Y., Krauss, B. R., Thomas, P. S., et al. Chronic pain patients are impaired on an emotional decision-making task. *Pain*, 2004a, *108*, 129–136.

Apkarian, A. V., Sosa, Y., Sonty, S., Levy, R. M., et al. Chronic back pain is associated with decreased prefrontal and thalamic gray matter density. *Journal of Neuroscience*, 2004b, *24*, 10410–10415.

Arancio, O., Kandel, E. R., and Hawkins, R. D. Activity-dependent long-term enhancement of transmitter release by presynaptic 3′, 5′-cyclic GMP in cultured hippocampal neurons. *Nature*, 1995, *376*, 74–80.

Arcelus, J., Mitchell, A. J., Wales, J., and Nielsen, S. Mortality rates in patients with anorexia nervosa and other eating disorders: A meta-analysis of 36 studies. *Archives of General Psychiatry*, 2011, *68*(7), 724–731.

Archer, J. Testosterone and aggression. *Journal of Offender Rehabilitation*, 1994, *5*, 3–25.

Arendt, J., Deacon, S., English, J., Hampton, S., et al. Melatonin and adjustment to phase-shift. *Journal of Sleep Research*, 1995, *4*, 74–79.

Arnason, B. G. Immunologic therapy of multiple sclerosis. *Annual Review of Medicine*, 1999, *50*, 291–302.

Arnott, S. T., Binns, M. A., Grady, C. L., and Alain, C. Assessing the auditory dual-pathway model in humans. *Neuroimage*, 2004, *22*, 401–408.

Arnsten, A. F. The emerging neurobiology of attention deficit hyperactivity disorder: The key role of the prefrontal association cortex. *Journal of Pediatrics*, 2009, *54*, I-S43.

Arnsten, A. F. T., and Li, B.-M. Neurobiology of executive functions: Catecholamine influences on prefrontal cortical functions. *Biological Psychiatry*, 2005, *57*, 1377–1384.

Aron, A. R., Robbins, T. W, and Poldrack, R. A. Inhibition and the right inferior frontal cortex. *Trends in Cognitive Science*, 2004, *8*, 170–177.

Aronson, B. D., Bell-Pedersen, D., Block, G. D., Bos, N. P. A., et al. Circadian rhythms. *Brain Research Reviews*, 1993, *18*, 315–333.

Arora, S., Anubhuti. Role of neuropeptides in appetite regulation and obesity–a review. *Neuropeptides*, 2006, *40*(6), 375–401.

Arrasate, M., Mitra, S., Schweitzer, E. S., Segal, M. R., et al. Inclusion body formation reduces levels of mutant huntingtin and the risk of neuronal death. *Nature*, 2004, *431*, 747–748.

Arroyo, S., Lesser, R. P., Gordon, B., Uematsu, S., et al. Mirth, laughter and gelastic seizures. *Brain*, 1993, *116*, 757–780.

Artmann, H., Grau, H., Adelman, M., and Schleiffer, R. Reversible and non-reversible enlargement of cerebrospinal fluid spaces in anorexia nervosa. *Neuroradiology*, 1985, *27*, 103–112.

Aschoff, J. Circadian rhythms: General features and endocrinological aspects. In *Endocrine rhythms*, edited by D. T. Krieger. New York: Raven Press, 1979.

Asnis, G. M., Hameedi, F. A., Goddard, A. W., Potkin, S. G., et al. Fluvoxamine in the treatment of panic disorder: A multi-center, double-blind, placebo-controlled study in outpatients. *Psychiatry Research*, 2001, *103*, 1–14.

Astafiev, S. V., Shulman, G. L., Stanley, C. M., Snyder, A. Z., et al. Functional organization of human intraparietal and frontal cortex for attending, looking, and pointing. *Journal of Neuroscience*, 2003, *23*, 4689–4699.

Aston-Jones, G., and Bloom, F. E. Activity of norepinephrine-containing locus coeruleus neurons in behaving rats anticipates fluctuations in the sleep-waking cycle. *Journal of Neuroscience*, 1981, *1*, 876–886.

Aston-Jones, G., Smith, R. J., Moorman, D. E., and Richardson, K. A. Role of lateral hypothalamic orexin neurons in reward processing and addiction. *Neuropharmacology*, 2009, *56*, 112–121.

Aston-Jones, G., Rajkowski, J., Kubiak, P., and Alexinsky, T. Locus coeruleus neurons in monkey are selectively activated by attended cues in a vigilance task. *Journal of Neuroscience*, 1994, *14*, 4467–4480.

Attia, E., Haiman, C., Walsh, T., and Flater, S. T. Does fluoxetine augment the inpatient treatment of anorexia nervosa? *American Journal of Psychiatry*, 1998, *155*, 548–551.

Audero, E., Mlinar, B., Baccini, G., Skachokova, Z. K., Corradetti, R., and Gross, C. Suppression of serotonin neuron firing increases aggression in mice. *The Journal of Neuroscience*, 2013, *33*(20), 8678–8688.

Aurora, R. N., Zak, R. S., Maganti, P. K., Auerbach, S. H., et al. Best practice guide for the treatment of REM sleep behavior disorder (RBD). *Journal of Clinical Sleep Medicine*, 2010, *6*, 85–95.

Auyeung, B., Baron-Cohen, S., Ashwin, E., Knickmeyer, R., et al. Fetal testosterone predicts sexually differentiated childhood behavior in girls and in boys. *Psychological Science*, 2009, *20*, 144–148.

Avenet, P., and Lindemann, B. Perspectives of taste reception. *Journal of Membrane Biology*, 1989, *112*, 1–8.

Avila, M. T., Weiler, M. A., Lahti, A. C., Tamminga, C. A., et al. Effects of ketamine on leading saccades during smooth-pursuit eye movements may implicate cerebellar dysfunction in schizophrenia. *American Journal of Psychiatry*, 2002, *159*, 1490–1496.

Aziz-Zadeh, L., Cattaneo, L., Rochat, M., and Rizzolatti, G. Covert speech arrest induced by rTMS over both motor and nonmotor left hemisphere frontal sites. *Journal of Cognitive Neuroscience*, 2005, *17*, 928–938.

Baddeley, A. D. Memory: Verbal and visual subsystems of working memory. *Current Biology*, 1993, *3*, 563–565.

Bagatell, C. J., Heiman, J. R., Rivier, J. E., and Bremner, W. J. Effects of endogenous testosterone and estradiol on sexual behavior in normal young men. *Journal of Clinical Endocrinology and Metabolism*, 1994, *7*, 211–216.

Bai, F. L., Yamano, M., Shiotani, Y., Emson, P. C., et al. An arcuato-paraventricular and dorsomedial hypothalamic neuropeptide Y-containing system which lacks noradrenaline in the rat. *Brain Research*, 1985, *331*, 172–175.

Baier, B., Karnath, H.-O., Dieterich, M, Birklein, F., et al. Keeping memory clear and stable—The contribution of human basal ganglia and prefrontal cortex to working memory. *Journal of Neuroscience*, 2010, *30*, 9788–9792.

Bailey, C. H., Kandel, E. R., and Si, K. The persistence of long-term memory: A molecular approach to self-sustaining changes in learning-induced synaptic growth. *Neuron*, 2004, *44*, 49–57.

Bailey, J. M., and Pillard, R. C. A genetic study of male sexual orientation. *Archives of General Psychiatry*, 1991, *48*, 1089–1096.

Bailey, J. M., Pillard, R. C., Neale, M. C., and Agyei, Y. Heritable factors influence sexual orientation in women. *Archives of General Psychiatry*, 1993, *50*, 217–223.

Baizer, J. S., Ungerleider, L. G., and Desimone, R. Organization of visual inputs to the inferior temporal and posterior parietal cortex in macaques. *Journal of Neuroscience*, 1991, *11*, 168–190.

Bak, T. H., O'Donovan, D. G., Xuereb, J. H., Boniface, S., et al. Selective impairment of verb processing associated with pathological changes in Brodman areas 44 and 45 in the motor neurone disease-dementia-aphasia syndrome. *Brain*, 2001, *124*, 103–120.

Baker, C. I., Behrman, M., and Olson, C. R. Impact of learning on representation of parts and wholes in monkey inferotemporal cortex. *Nature Neuroscience*, 2002, *5*, 1210–1216.

Baker, M. Light tools. *Nature Methods*, 2011, *8*, 19–22.

Baldessarini, R. J. *Chemotherapy in Psychiatry*. Cambridge, Mass.: Harvard University Press, 1977.

Baldo, J. V., Wilkins, D. P., Ogar, J., Willock, S., et al. Role of the precentral gyrus of the insula in complex articulation. *Cortex*, 2011, *47*, 800–807.

Ballantine, H. T., Bouckoms, A. J., Thomas, E. K., and Giriunas, I. E. Treatment of psychiatric illness by stereotactic cingulotomy. *Biological Psychiatry*, 1987, *22*, 807–819.

Bandell, M., Macpherson, L. J., and Patapoutian, A. From chills to chilis: Mechanisms for thermosensation and chemesthesis via thermoTRPs. *Current Opinion in Neurobiology*, 2007, *17*, 490–497.

Banks, M. S., Aslin, R. N., and Letson, R. D. Sensitive period for the development of human binocular vision. *Science*, 1975, *190*, 675–677.

Bao, A. M., and Swaab, D. F. Sexual differentiation of the human brain: relation to gender identity, sexual orientation and neuropsychiatric disorders. *Frontiers in Neuroendocrinology*, 2011, *32*(2), 214–226.

Barbazanges, A., Piazza, P. V., Le Moal, M., and Maccari, S. Maternal glucocorticoid secretion mediates long-term effects of prenatal stress. *Journal of Neuroscience*, 1996, *16*, 3943–3949.

Barclay, C. D., Cutting, J. E., and Kozlowski, L. T. Temporal and spatial factors in gait perception that influence gender recognition. *Perception and Psychophysics*, 1978, *23*, 145–152.

Bard, F., Cannon, C., Barbour, R., Burke, R. L., et al. Peripherally administered antibodies against amyloid beta-peptide enter the central nervous system and reduce pathology in a mouse model of Alzheimer disease. *Nature Medicine*, 2000, *6*, 916–919.

Baron-Cohen, S. The extreme male brain theory of autism. *Trends in Cognitive Science*, 2002, *6*, 248–254.

Bartels, A., and Zeki, S. The neural basis of romantic love. *Neuroreport*, 2000, *27*, 3829–3834.

Bartels, A., and Zeki, S. The neural correlates of maternal and romantic love. *Neuroimage*, 2004, *21*, 1155–1166.

Bartness, T. J., Powers, J. B., Hastings, M. H., Bittman, E. L., et al. The timed infusion paradigm for melatonin delivery: What has it taught us about the melatonin signal, its reception, and the photoperiodic control of seasonal responses? *Journal of Pineal Research*, 1993, *15*, 161–190.

Bartolomeo, P., Bachoud-Lévi, A. C., and Denes, G. Preserved imagery for colours in a patient with cerebral achromatopsia. *Cortex*, 1997, *33*(2), 369–378.

Basbaum, A. I., and Fields, H. L. Endogenous pain control mechanisms: Review and hypothesis. *Annals of Neurology*, 1978, *4*, 451–462.

Basbaum, A. I., and Fields, H. L. Endogenous pain control systems: Brainstem spinal pathways and endorphin circuitry. *Annual Review of Neuroscience*, 1984, *7*, 309–338.

Basheer, R., Strecker, R. E., Thakkar, M. M., and McCarley, R. W. Adenosine and sleep–wake regulation. *Progress in Neurobiology*, 2004, *73*, 379–396.

Batterham, R. L., Cowley, M. A., Small, C. J., Herzog, H., et al. Gut hormone PYY3–36 physiologically inhibits food intake. *Nature*, 2002, *418*, 650–654.

Batterham, R. L., ffytche, D. H., Rosenthal, J. M., Zelaya, R. O., et al. PYY modulation of cortical and hypothalamic brain areas predicts feeding behaviour in humans. *Nature*, 2007, *450*, 106–109.

Baugh, C. M., Stamm, J. M., Riley, D. O., Gavett, B. E., et al. Chronic traumatic encephalopathy: Neurodegeneration following repetitive concussive and subconcussive brain trauma. *Brain Imaging and Behavior*, 2012, *6*(2), 244–254.

Bautista, D. M., Jordt, S.-E., Nikai, T., Tsuruda, P. R., et al. TRPA1 mediates the inflammatory actions of environmental irritants and proalgesic agents. *Cell*, 2006, *124*, 1269–1282.

Bautista, D. M., Siemens, J., Glazer, J. M., Tsuruda, P. R., et al. The menthol receptor TRPM8 is the principal detector of environmental cold. *Nature*, 2007, *448*, 204–208.

Bayley, P. J., Frascino, J. C., and Squire, L. R. Robust habit learning in the absence of awareness and independent of the medial temporal lobe. *Nature*, 2005, *436*, 550–553.

Bayley, P. J., Hopkins, R. O., and Squire, L. R. The fate of old memories after medial temporal lobe damage. *Journal of Neuroscience*, 2006, *26*, 13311–13317.

Beamer, W., Bermant, G., and Clegg, M. T. Copulatory behaviour of the ram, Ovis aries. II: Factors affecting copulatory satiation. *Animal Behavior*, 1969, *17*, 706–711.

Bean, N. J. Modulation of agonistic behavior by the dual olfactory system in male mice. *Physiology and Behavior*, 1982, *29*, 433–437.

Bean, N. J., and Conner, R. Central hormonal replacement and home-cage dominance in castrated rats. *Hormones and Behavior*, 1978, *11*, 100–109.

Beauvois, M. F., and Dérouesné, J. Phonological alexia: Three dissociations. *Journal of Neurology, Neurosurgery and Psychiatry*, 1979, *42*, 1115–1124.

Beauvois, M. F., and Dérouesné, J. Phonological alexia: Three dissociations. *Journal of Neurology, Neurosurgery and Psychiatry*, 1979, *42*, 1115–1124.

Beauvois, M. F., and Dérouesné, J. Lexical or orthographic dysgraphia. *Brain*, 1981, *104*, 21–45.

Bechara, A., Tranel, D., Damasio, H., Adolphs, R., et al. Double dissociation of conditioning and declarative knowledge relative to the amygdala and hippocampus in humans. *Science*, 1995, *269*, 1115–1118.

Beckstead, R. M., Morse, J. R., and Norgren, R. The nucleus of the solitary tract in the monkey: Projections to the thalamus and brainstem nuclei. *Journal of Comparative Neurology*, 1980, *190*, 259–282.

Beecher, H. K. *Measurement of Subjective Responses: Quantitative Effects of Drugs*. New York: Oxford University Press, 1959.

Beecher, M. D., & Brenowitz, E. A. Functional aspects of song learning in songbirds. *Trends in Ecology & Evolution*, 2005, *20*(3), 143–149.

Beeman, E. A. The effect of male hormone on aggressive behavior in mice. *Physiological Zoology*, 1947, *20*, 373–405.

Begenisic, T., Baroncelli, L., Sansevero, G., Milanese, M., et al. Fluoxetine in adulthood normalizes GABA release and rescues hippocampal synaptic plasticity and spatial memory in a mouse model of Down syndrome. *Neurobiology of Disease*, 2014, *63*, 12–19.

Behrman, M., Avidan, G., Gao, F., and Black, S. Structural imaging reveals anatomical alterations in inferotemporal cortex in congenital prosopagnosia. *Cerebral Cortex*, 2007, *17*, 2354–2363.

Beidler, L. M. Physiological properties of mammalian taste receptors. In *Taste and smell in vertebrates*, edited by G. E. W. Wolstenholme. London: J. & A. Churchill, 1970.

Beitz, A. J. The organization of afferent projections to the midbrain periaqueductal gray of the rat. *Neuroscience*, 1982, *7*, 133–159.

Belichenko, N. P., Belichenko, P. V., Kleschevnikov, A. M., Salehi, A., et al. The "Down syndrome critical region" is sufficient in the mouse model to confer behavioral, neurophysiological, and synaptic phenotypes characteristic of Down syndrome. *Journal of Neuroscience*, 2010, *29*, 5938–5948.

Belin, D., and Everitt, B. J. Cocaine seeking habits depend upon dopamine-dependent serial connectivity linking the ventral with the dorsal striatum. *Neuron*, 2008, *57*, 432–441.

Belin, P., Fecteau, S., and Bédard, C. Thinking the voice: Neural correlates of voice perception. *Trends in Cognitive Sciences*, 2004, *8*, 129–135.

Bell, A. H., Hadj-Bouziane, F., Frihauf, J. B., Tootell, R. B. H., et al. Object representations in the temporal cortex of monkeys and humans as revealed by functional magnetic resonance imaging. *Journal of Neurophysiology*, 2009, *101*, 688–700.

Bell, A.P., and Weinberg, M. S. *Homosexualities: A Study of Diversity Among Men and Women*. New York: Simon and Schuster, 1978.

Bell, A. P., Weinberg, M. S., and Hammersmith, S. K. *Sexual Preference: Its Development in Men and Women*. Bloomington: Indiana University Press, 1981.

Bell, G. S., Neligan, A., and Sander, J. W. An unknown quantity-The worldwide prevalence of epilepsy. *Epilepsia*, 2014, *55*(7), 958–962.

Bellocchio, L., Lafenêtre, P., Cannich, A., Cota, D., et al. Bimodal control of stimulated food intake by the endocannabinoid system. *Nature Neuroscience*, 2010, *13*, 281–283.

Belnoue, L., Grosjean, N., Abrous, D. N., and Koehl, M. A critical time window for the recruitment of bulbar newborn neurons by olfactory discrimination learning. *Journal of Neuroscience*, 2011, *31*, 1010–1016.

Ben Mamou, C., Gamache, K., and Nader, K. NMDA receptors are critical for unleashing consolidated auditory fear memories. *Nature Neuroscience*, 2006, *9*, 1237–1239.

Benca, R. M. Diagnosis and treatment of chronic insomnia: a review. *Psychiatric Services*, 2014, *56*(3), 332–343.

Benchenane, K., López-Atalaya, J. P., Fernández-Monreal, M., Touzani, O., et al. Equivocal roles of tissue-type plasminogen activator in stroke-induced injury. *Trends in Neuroscience*, 2004, *27*, 155–160.

Bendor, D., and Wang, X. Cortical representations of pitch in monkeys and humans. *Current Opinion in Neurobiology*, 2006, *16*, 391–399.

Benington, J. H., Kodali, S. K., and Heller, H. C. Monoaminergic and cholinergic modulation of REM-sleep timing in rats. *Brain Research*, 1995, *681*, 141–146.

Bennett, D. A., Wilson, R. S., Schneider, J. A., Evans, D. A., et al. Education modifies the relation of AD pathology to level of cognitive function in older persons. *Neurology*, 2003, *60*, 1909–1915.

Benowitz, L. I., and Carmichael, S. T. Promoting axonal rewiring to improve outcome after stroke. *Neurobiology of Disease*, 2010, *37*, 259–266.

Benson, D. L., Colman, D. R., and Huntley, G. W. Molecules, maps and synapse specificity. *Nature Reviews: Neuroscience*, 2001, *2*, 899–909.

Ben-Tovim, D. I. Eating disorders: Outcome, prevention, and treatment of eating disorders. *Current Opinion in Psychiatry*, 2003, 16, 65–69.

Berenbaum, S. A., and Resnick, S. M. Early androgen effects on aggression in children and adults with congenital adrenal hyperplasia. *Psychoneuroendocrinology*, 1997, *22*, 505–515.

Bergasa, N. V. The pruritis of cholestasis. *Journal of Hepatology*, 2005, *43*, 1078–1088.

Bergh, C., Callmar, M., Danemar, S., Hölcke, M., et al. Effective treatment of eating disorders: Results at multiple sites. *Behavioral Neuroscience*, 2013, *127*(6), 878.

Berglund, H., Lindström, P., and Savic, I. Brain response to putative pheromones in lesbian women. *Proceedings of the National Academy of Sciences, USA*, 2006, *103*, 8269–8274.

Berkovic, S. F., Mulley, J. C., Scheffer, I. E., and Petrou, S. Human epilepsies: Interaction of genetic and acquired factors. *Trends in Neurosciences*, 2006, *29*, 391–397.

Bermant, G., and Davidson, J. M. *Biological Bases of Sexual Behavior*. New York: Harper & Row, 1974.

Bernhardt, P. C., Dabbs, J. M., Fielden, J. A., and Lutter, C. D. Testosterone changes during vicarious experiences of winning and losing among fans at sporting events. *Physiology and Behavior*, 1998, *65*, 59–62.

Berns, G. S., McClure, S. M., Pagnoni, G., and Montague, P. R. Predictability modulates human brain response to reward. *Journal of Neuroscience*, 2001, *21*, 2793–2798.

Berridge, C. W., Devilbiss, D. M., Andrzejewski, M. E., Arnsten, A. F. T., et al. Methylphenidate preferentially increases catecholamine neurotransmission within the prefrontal cortex at low doses that enhance cognitive function. *Biological Psychiatry*, 2006, *60*, 1111–1120.

Berson, D. M., Dunn, F. A., and Takao, M. Phototransduction by retinal ganglion cells that set the circadian clock. *Science*, 2002, *295*, 1070–1073.

Berthier, M., Kulisevsky, J., Gironell, A., and Heras, J. A. Obsessive-compulsive disorder associated with brain lesions: Clinical phenomenology, cognitive function, and anatomic correlates. *Neurology*, 1996, *47*, 353–361.

Berthier, M., Starkstein, S., and Leiguarda, R. Asymbolia for pain: A sensory-limbic disconnection syndrome. *Annals of Neurology*, 1988, *24*, 41–49.

Berthoud, H.-R., Shin, A. C., and Zheng, H. Obesity surgery and gut-brain communication. *Physiology and Behavior*, 2011, *105*, 106–119.

Bertolini, A., Ferrari, A., Ottani, A., Guerzoni, S., et al. Paracetamol: New vistas of an old drug. *CNS Drug Review*, 2006, *12*, 250–275.

Best, P. J., White, A. M., and Minai, A. Spatial processing in the brain: The activity of hippocampal place cells. *Annual Review of Neuroscience*, 2001, *24*, 459–486.

Betancur, C., Sakurai, T., and Buxbaum, J. D. The emerging role of synaptic cell-adhesion pathways in the pathogenesis of autism spectrum disorders. *Trends in Neuroscience*, 2009, *32*, 402–412.

Bettelheim, B. *The Empty Fortress*. New York: Free Press, 1967.

Beversdorf, D. Q., Ratcliffe, N. R., Rhodes, C. H., and Reeves, A. G. Pure alexia: Clinical-pathologic evidence for a lateralized visual language association cortex. *Clinical Neuropathology*, 1997, *16*, 328–331.

Bewernick, B. H., Hurlemann, R., Matusch, A., Kayser, S., et al. Nucleus accumbens deep brain stimulation decreases ratings of depression and anxiety in treatment-resistant depression. *Biological Psychiatry*, 2010, *67*, 110–116.

Bhattacharyya, K. B. *Eminent neuroscientists: Their lives and works*. Academic Publishers, Kolkata, 2011.

Bierut, L. J., Stitzel, J. A., Wang, J. C., Hinrichs, A. L., et al. Variants in nicotinic receptors and risk for nicotine dependence. *American Journal of Psychiatry*, 2008, *165*, 1163–1171.

Billings, L. M., Green, K. N., McGaugh, J. L., and LaFerla, F. M. Learning decreases Aβ*56 and tau pathology and amerliorates behavioral decline in 3xTg-AD mice. *Journal of Neuroscience*, 2007, *27*, 751–761.

Bisiach, E., and Luzzatti, C. Unilateral neglect of representational space. *Cortex*, 1978, *14*, 129–133.

Blackwell, B., Bloomfield, S., and Buncher, C. R. Demonstration to medical students of placebo responses and non-drug factors. *The Lancet*, 1972, *299*(7763), 1279–1282.

Blackwood, D. H., Fordyce, A., Walker, M. T., St. Clair, D. M., et al. Schizophrenia and affective disorders—Cosegregation with a translocation at chromosome 1q42 that directly disrupts brain-expressed genes: Clinical and P300 findings in a family. *American Journal of Human Genetics*, 2001, *69*, 428–433.

Blair, R. J. R. The amygdala and ventro-medial-prefrontal cortex: Functional contributions and dysfunction in psychopathy. *Philosophical Transactions of the Royal Society of London*, 2008, *363*, 2557–2565.

Blanchard, R. Fraternal birth order and the maternal immune hypothesis of male homosexuality. *Hormones and Behavior*, 2001, *40*, 105–114.

Blaustein, J. D., and Feder, H. H. Cytoplasmic progestin receptors in guinea pig brain: Characteristics and relationship to the induction of sexual behavior. *Brain Research*, 1979, *169*, 481–497.

Blaustein, J. D., and Olster, D. H. Gonadal steroid hormone receptors and social behaviors. In *Advances in comparative and environmental physiology, vol. 3*, edited by J. Balthazart. Berlin: Springer-Verlag, 1989.

Blest, A. D. The function of eyespot patterns in insects. *Behaviour*, 1957, *11*, 209–256.

Bleuler, E. *Dementia Praecox of the Group of Schizophrenia*, 1911. Translated by J. Zinkin. New York: International Universities Press, 1911/1950.

Bliss, T. V., and Lømo, T. Long-lasting potentiation of synaptic transmission in the dentate area of the anaesthetized rabbit following stimulation of the perforant path. *Journal of Physiology*, 1973, *232*, 331–356.

Blüher, S., Raschpichler, M., Hirsch, W., and Till, H. A case report and review of the literature of laparoscopic sleeve gastrectomy in morbidly obese adolescents: Beyond metabolic surgery and visceral fat reduction. *Metabolism*, 2013, *62*(6), 761–767.

Blundell, J. E., and Halford, J. C. G. Serotonin and appetite regulation: Implications for the pharmacological treatment of obesity. *CNS Drugs*, 1998, *9*, 473–495.

Bobrow, D., and Bailey, M. J. Is male homosexuality maintained via kin selection? *Evolution and Human Behavior*, 2001, *22*, 361–368.

Bodner, S. M., Morshed, S. A., and Peterson, B. S. The question of PANDAS in adults. *Biological Psychiatry*, 2001, *49*, 807–810.

Boeve, B. F., Silber, M. H., Saper, C. B., Ferman, T. J., et al. Pathophysiology of REM sleep behaviour disorder and relevance to neurodegenerative disease. *Brain*, 2007, *130*, 2770–2788.

Bogaert, A. F. Biological versus nonbiological older brothers and men's sexual orientation. *Proceedings of the National Academy of Sciences, USA*, 2006, *103*, 10771–10774.

Bogaert, A. F., and Skorska, M. Sexual orientation, fraternal birth order, and the maternal immune hypothesis: A review. *Frontiers in Neuroendocrinology*, 2011, *32*(2), 247–254.

Boggio, P. S., Rocha, M., Oliveira, M. O., Fecteau, S., et al. Noninvasive brain stimulation with high-frequency and low-intensity repetitive transcranial magnetic stimulation treatment for posttraumatic stress disorder. *Journal of Clinical Psychiatry*, 2010, *71*, 992–999.

Bohbot, V. D., Lerch, J., Thorndycraft, B., Iaria, G., et al. Gray matter differences correlate with spontaneous strategies in a human virtual navigation task. *Journal of Neuroscience*, 2007, *27*, 10078–10083.

Boksa, P. Animal models of obstetric complications in relation to schizophrenia. *Brain Research Reviews*, 2004, *45*, 1–17.

Bolla, K., Ernst, M., Kiehl, K., Mouratidis, M., et al. Prefrontal cortical dysfunction in abstinent cocaine abusers. *Journal of Neuropsychiatry and Clinical Neuroscience*, 2004, *16*, 456–464.

Bolwig, T. G. How does electroconvulsive therapy work? Theories on its mechanism. *Canadian Journal of Psychiatry*, 2011, *56*, 13–18.

Boodman, S. G. Hungry in the dark: Some sleepeaters don't wake up for their strange nighttime binges. *Washington Post*, September 7, 2004, HE01.

Booth, F. W., and Neufer, P. D. Exercise controls gene expression. *American Scientist*, 2005, *93*, 28–35.

Born, R. T., and Tootell, R. B. H. Spatial frequency tuning of single units in macaque supragranular striate cortex. *Proceedings of the National Academy of Sciences, USA*, 1991, *88*, 7066–7070.

Bornstein, B., Stroka, H., and Munitz, H. Prosopagnosia with animal face agnosia. *Cortex*, 1969, *5*, 164–169.

Borod, J. C., Koff, E., Yecker, S., Santschi, C., et al. Facial asymmetry during emotional expression: Gender, falence, and measurement technique. *Neuropsychologia*, 1998, *36*, 1209–1215.

Bossini, L., Tavanti, M., Lombardelli, A., Calossi, S., et al. Changes in hippocampal volume in patients with post-traumatic stress disorder after sertraline treatment.

Journal of Clinical Psychopharmacology, 2007, *27*(2), 233–235.

Bossy-Wetzel, E., Schwarzenbacher, R., and Lipton, S. A. Molecular pathways to neurodegeneration. *Nature Medicine*, 2004, *10*, S2–S9.

Bouchard, C., Tremblay, A., Despres, J. P., Nadeau, A., et al. The response to long-term overfeeding in identical twins. *New England Journal of Medicine*, 1990, *322*, 1477–1482.

Boulos, Z., Campbell, S. S., Lewy, A. J., Terman, M., et al. Light treatment for sleep disorders: Consensus report. 7: Jet-lag. *Journal of Biological Rhythms*, 1995, *10*, 167–176.

Bourne, J., and Harris, K. M. Do thin spines learn to be mushroom spines that remember? *Current Opinion in Neurobiology*, 2007, *17*, 381–386.

Bourque, C. W. Central mechanisms of osmosensation and systemic osmoregulation. *Nature Reviews: Neuroscience*, 2008, *9*, 519–531.

Boussaoud, D., Desimone, R., and Ungerleider, L. G. Visual topography of area TEO in the macaque. *Journal of Comparative Neurology*, 1991, *306*, 554–575.

Bouvier, S. E., and Engel, S. A. Behavioral deficits and cortical damage loci in cerebral achromatopsia. *Cerebral Cortex*, 2006, *16*, 183–191.

Bowers, D., Blonder, L. X., Feinberg, T., and Heilman, K. M. Differential impact of right and left hemisphere lesions on facial emotion and object imagery. *Brain*, 1991, *114*, 2593–2609.

Boyden, E. S., Zhang, F., Bamberg, E., Nagel, G., et al. Millisecond-timescale, genetically targeted optical control of neural activity. *Nature Neuroscience*, 2005, *8*, 1263–1268.

Bozarth, M. A. Physical dependence produced by central morphine infusions: An anatomical mapping study. *Neuroscience and Biobehavioral Reviews*, 1994, *18*, 373–383.

Brackett, N. L., Ferrell, S. M., Aballa, T. C., Amador, M. J., et al. An analysis of 653 trials of penile vibratory stimulation in men with spinal cord injury. *Journal of Urology*, 1998, *159*, 1931–1934.

Bradbury, M. W. B. *The Concept of a Blood–Brain Barrier*. New York: John Wiley & Sons, 1979.

Bradley, D. C., Maxwell, M., Andersen, R. A., Banks, M. S., et al. Mechanisms of heading perception in primate visual cortex. *Science*, 1996, *273*, 1544–1547.

Brady, K. T., and Sinha, R. Co-occurring mental and substance use disorders: The neurobiological effects of chronic stress. *American Journal of Psychiatry*, 2005, *162*, 1483–1493.

Brandon, N. J., Millar, J. K., Korth, C., Sive, H., et al. Understanding the role of DISC1 in psychiatric disease and during normal development. *Journal of Neuroscience*, 2009, *29*, 12768–12775.

Braun, A. R., Balkin, T. J., Wesensten, N. J., Gwadry, F., et al. Dissociated pattern of activity in visual cortices and their projections during human rapid eye movement sleep. *Science*, 1998, *279*, 91–95.

Braun, S. New experiments underscore warnings on maternal drinking. *Science*, 1996, *273*, 738–739.

Bray, G. A., Nielsen, S. J., and Popkin, B. M. Consumption of high-fructose corn syrup in beverages may play a role in the epidemic of obesity. *American Journal of Clinical Nutrition*, 2004, *79*, 537–543.

Brecher, E. M. *Licit and Illicit Drugs*. Boston: Little, Brown & Co., 1972.

Bredel, M. Translating biological insights into clinical endpoints in neuro-oncology. *Lancet Oncology*, 2009, *10*, 928–929.

Breedlove, S. M. Sexual differentiation of the brain and behavior. In *Behavioral endocrinology*, edited by J. B. Becker, S. M. Breedlove, and D. Crews. Cambridge, MA: MIT Press, 1992.

Breedlove, S. M. Sexual differentiation of the human nervous system. *Annual Review of Psychology*, 1994, *45*, 389–418.

Breier, A., Su, T.-P., Saunders, R., Carson, R. E., et al. Schizophrenia is associated with elevated amphetamine-induced synaptic dopamine concentrations: Evidence from a novel positron emission tomography method. *Proceedings of the National Academy of Sciences, USA*, 1997, *94*, 2569–2574.

Brem, S., Bach, S., Kucian, K., Guttorm, T. K., et al. Brain sensitivity to print emerges when children learn letter–speech sound correspondences. *Proceedings of the National Academy of Sciences, USA*, 2010, *107*, 7939–7964.

Bremner, J. D., Randall, P., Scott, T. M., Bronen, R. A., et al. MRI-based measurement of hippocampal volume in patients with combat-related posttraumatic stress disorder. *American Journal of Psychiatry*, 1995, *152*, 973–981.

Brenowitz, E. A. Comparative approaches to the avian song system. *Journal of Neurobiology*, 1997, *33*(5), 517–531.

Brennan, P. A., and Keverne, E. B. Something in the air? New insights into mammalian pheromones. *Current Biology*, 2004, *14*, R81–R89.

Brickner, R. M. *The Intellectual Functions of the Frontal Lobe: A Study Based Upon Observations of a Man After Partial Frontal Lobectomy*. New York: Macmillan, 1936.

Bridges, R. S., DiBiase, R., Loundes, D. D., and Doherty, P. C. Prolactin stimulation of maternal behavior in female rats. *Science*, 1985, *227*, 782–784.

Bridges, R. S., Rigero, B. A., Byrnes, E. M., Yang, L., et al. Central infusions of the recombinant human prolactin receptor antagonist, S179D-PRL, delay the onset of maternal behavior in steroid-primed, nulliparous female rats. *Endocrinology*, 2001, *142*, 730–739.

Bridges, R. S., Robertson, M. C., Shiu, R. P. C., Sturgis, J. D., et al. Central lactogenic regulation of maternal behavior in rats: Steroid dependence, hormone specificity, and behavioral potencies of rat prolactin and rat placental lactogen I. *Endocrinology*, 1997, *138*, 756–763.

Breitve, M. H., Chwiszczuk, L. J., Hynninen, M. J., Rongve, A., et al. A systematic review of cognitive decline in dementia with Lewy bodies versus Alzheimer's. *Alzheimer's Research and Therapy*, 2014, *6*, 53.

Britten, K. H., and van Wezel, R. J. Electrical microstimulation of cortical area MST biases heading perception in monkeys. *Nature Neuroscience*, 1998, *1*, 59–63.

Britton, D. R., Koob, G. F., Rivier, J., and Vale, W. Intraventricular corticotropin-releasing factor enhances behavioral effects of novelty. *Life Sciences*, 1982, *31*, 363–367.

Broberger, C., de Lecea, L., Sutcliffe, J. G., and Hökfelt, T. Hypocretin/orexin- and melanin-concentrating hormone-expressing cells form distinct populations in the rodent lateral hypothalamus: Relationship to the neuropeptide Y and agouti gene-related protein systems. *Journal of Comparative Neurology*, 1998, *402*, 460–474.

Broca, P. Remarques sur le siège de la faculté du langage articulé, suivies d'une observation d'aphemie (perte de la parole). *Bulletin de la Société Anatomique* (Paris), 1861, *36*, 330–357.

Brolin, R. E. Bariatric surgery and long-term control of morbid obesity. *Journal of the American Medical Association*, 2002, *288*, 2793–2796.

Brown, A. M., Tekkök, S. B., and Ransom, B. R. Energy transfer from astrocytes to axons: The role of CNS glycogen. *Neurochemistry International*, 2004, *45*, 529–536.

Brown, A. S. Prenatal infection as a risk factor for schizophrenia. *Schizophrenia Bulletin*, 2006, *32*, 200–202.

Brown, A. S., and Derkits, E. J. Prenatal infection and schizophrenia: A review of epidemiologic and translational studies. *American Journal of Psychiatry*, 2010, *167*, 261–280.

Brown, A. S., Hooton, J., Schaefer, C. A., Zhang, H., et al. Elevated maternal interleukin-8 levels and risk of schizophrenia in adult offspring. *American Journal of Psychiatry*, 2004, *161*, 889–895.

Brown, A. S., Schaefer, C. A., Wyatt, R. J., Begg, M. D., et al. Paternal age and risk of schizophrenia in adult offspring. *American Journal of Psychiatry*, 2002, *159*, 1528–1533.

Brown, R. E., Stevens, D. R., and Haas, H. L. The physiology of brain histamine. *Progress in Neurobiology*, 2001, *63*, 637–672.

Brown, S., Ingham, R. J., Ingham, J. C., Laird, A. R., and Fox, P. T. Stuttered and fluent speech production: An ALE meta-analysis of functional neuroimaging studies. *Human Brain Mapping*, 2005, *25*, 105–117.

Brown, T. H., Ganong, A. H., Kairiss, E. W., Keenan, C. L., et al. Long-term potentiation in two synaptic systems of the hippocampal brain slice. In *Neural models of plasticity: Experimental and theoretical approaches*, edited by J. H. Byrne and W. O. Berry. San Diego: Academic Press, 1989.

Brownell, H. H., Michel, D., Powelson, J., and Gardner, H. Surprise but not coherence: Sensitivity to verbal humor in right-hemisphere patients. *Brain and Language*, 1983, *18*, 20–27.

Brownell, H. H., Simpson, T. L., Bihrle, A. M., Potter, H. H., and Gardner, H. Appreciation of metaphoric alternative word meanings by left and right brain-damaged patients. *Neuropsychologia*, 1990, *28*, 173–184.

Brownell, W. E., Bader, C. R., Bertrand, D., and de-Ribaupierre, Y. Evoked mechanical responses of isolated cochlear outer hair cells. *Science*, 1985, *227*, 194–196.

Brugha, T. S., McManus, S., Bankart, J., Scott, F., et al. Epidemiology of autism spectrum disorders in adults in the community in England. *Archives of General Psychiatry*, 2011, *68*, 5, 459–465.

Brüning, J. C., Gautam, D., Burks, D. J., Gillette, J., et al. Role of brain insulin receptor in control of body weight and reproduction. *Science*, 2000, *289*, 2122–2125.

Brunson, K. L., Kramár, E., Lin, B., Chen, Y., et al. Mechanisms of late-onset cognitive decline after early-life stress. *Journal of Neuroscience*, 2005, *25*, 9328–9338.

Bu, G. Apolipoprotein E and its receptors in Alzheimer's disease: Pathways, pathogenesis and therapy. *Nature Reviews: Neuroscience*, 2010, *10*, 333–344.

Buccino, G., Riggio, L., Melli, G., Binkofski, F., et al. Listening to action-related sentences modulates the activity of the motor system: A combined TMS and behavioral study. *Cognitive Brain Research*, 2005, *24*, 355–363.

Buccino, G., Vogt, S., Ritzi, A., Fink, G. R., et al. Neural circuits underlying imitation learning of hand actions: An event-related fMRI study. *Neuron*, 2004, *42*, 323–334.

Buchsbaum, M. S., Gillin, J. C., Wu, J., Hazlett, E., et al. Regional cerebral glucose metabolic rate in human sleep assessed by positron emission tomography. *Life Sciences*, 1989, *45*, 1349–1356.

Buck, L. Information coding in the vertebrate olfactory system. *Annual Review of Neuroscience*, 1996, *19*, 517–544.

Buck, L., and Axel, R. A novel multigene family may encode odorant receptors: A molecular basis for odor recognition. *Cell*, 1991, *65*, 175–187.

Buckner, R. L., Snyder, A. Z., Shannon, B. J., LaRossa, G., et al. Molecular, structural, and functional characterization of Alzheimer's disease: Evidence for a relationship between default activity, amyloid, and memory. *Journal of Neuroscience*, 2005, *25*, 7709–7717.

Budka, H., Almer, G., Hainfellner, J. A., Brücke, T., et al. The Austrian FFI cases. *Brain Pathology*, 1998, *8*, 554.

Bueler, H., Aguzzi, A., Sailer, A., Grenier, R. A., et al. Mice devoid of PrP are resistant to scrapie. *Cell*, 1993, *73*, 1339–1347.

Buhmann, C., Glauche, V., Sturenburg, H. J., Oechsner, M., et al. Pharmocologically modulated fMRI-cortical responsiveness to levodopa in drug-naïve hemiparkinsonian patients. *Brain*, 2003, *126*, 451–461.

Bullivant, S. B., Sellergren, S. A., Stern, K., Spencer, N. A., et al. Women's sexual experience during the menstrual cycle: Identification of the sexual phase by noninvasive measurement of luteinizing hormone. *Journal of Sex Research*, 2004, *41*, 82–93.

Bunyard, L. B., Katzel, L. I., Busby-Whitehead, M. J., Wu, Z., et al. Energy requirements of middle-aged men are modifiable by physical activity. *American Journal of Clinical Nutrition*, 1998, *68*, 1136–1142.

Burri, A., Cherkas, L., Spector, T., and Rahman, Q. Genetic and environmental influences on female sexual orientation, childhood gender typicality and adult gender identity. *PloS one* 6.7 (2011): e21982.

Burt, R. K., Loh, Y., Cohen, B., Stefoski, D., et al. Autologous non-myeloablative haemopoetic stem cell transplantation in relapsing-remitting multiple sclerosis: A phase I/II study. *Lancet Neurology*, 2009, *8*, 244–253.

Busskamp, V., Duebel, J., Balya, D., Fradot, M., et al. Genetic reactivation of cone photoreceptors restores visual responses in retinitis pigmentosa. *Science*, 2010, *329*, 413–417.

Butler, S. F., Cassidy, T. A., Chilcoat, H., Black, R. A., et al. Abuse rates and routes of administration of reformulated extended-release oxycodone: Initial findings from a sentinel surveillance sample of individuals assessed for substance abuse treatment. *Journal of Pain*, 2013, *14*(4), 351–358.

Buxbaum, L. J., Glosser, G., and Coslett, H. B. Impaired face and word recognition without object agnosia. *Neuropsychologia*, 1999, *37*, 41–50.

Byne, W., Tobet, S., Mattiace, L. A., Lasco, M. S., et al. The interstitial nuclei of the human anterior hypothalamus: An investigation of variation with sex, sexual orientation, and HIV status. *Hormones and Behavior*, 2001, *40*, 85–92.

Cabanac, M., and Lafrance, L. Facial consummatory-responses in rats support the ponderostat hypothesis. *Physiology and Behavior*, 1991, *50*, 179–183.

Cadet, J. L., Jayanthi, S., and Deng, X. Speed kills: Cellular and molecular bases of methamphetamine-induced nerve terminal degeneration and neuronal apoptosis. *FASEB Journal*, 2003, *17*, 1775–1788.

Cahill, L., Babinsky, R., Markowitsch, H. J., and McGaugh, J. L. The amygdala and emotional memory. *Nature*, 1995, *377*, 295–296.

Calder, A. J., Keane, J., Manes, F., Anntoun, N., et al. Impaired recognition and experience of disgust following brain injury. *Nature Neuroscience*, 2000, *3*, 1077–1078.

Calder, A. J., Young, A. W., Rowland, D., Perrett, D. I., et al. Facial emotion recognition after bilateral amygdala damage: Differentially severe impairment of fear. *Cognitive Neuropsychology*, 1996, *13*, 699–745.

Calvo-Merino, B., Grèzes, J., Glaser, D. E., Passingham, R. E., et al. Seeing or doing? Influence of visual and motor familiarity in action observation. *Current Biology*, 2006, *16*, 1905–1910.

Campbell, D. B., Datta, D., Jones, S. T., Lee, E. B., et al. Association of oxytocin receptor (OXTR) gene variants with multiple phenotype domains of autism spectrum disorder. *Journal of Neurodevelopmental Disorders*, 2011, *3*(2), 101–112.

Campbell, R., Heywood, C. A., Cower, A., Regard, M., et al. Sensitivity to eye gaze in prosopagnosic patients and monkeys with superior temporal sulcus ablation. *Neuropsychologia*, 1990, *28*, 1123–1142.

Campbell, R., MacSweeney, M., and Waters, D. Sign language and the brain: A review. *Journal of Deaf Studies and Deaf Education*, 2007.

Campeau, S., Hayward, M. D., Hope, B. T., Rosen, J. B., et al. Induction of the c-fos proto-oncogene in rat amygdala during unconditioned and conditioned fear. *Brain Research*, 1991, *565*, 349–352.

Camperio-Ciani, A., Corna, F., and Capiluppi, C. Evidence for maternally inherited factors favouring male homosexuality and promoting female fecundity. *Proceedings of the Royal Society of London B*, 2004, *271*, 2217–2221.

Campfield, L. A., Smith, F. J., Guisez, Y., Devos, R., et al. Recombinant mouse ob protein: Evidence for a peripheral signal linking adiposity and central neural networks. *Science*, 1995, *269*, 546–549.

Campisi, J., Bynog, P., McGehee, H., Oakland, J. C., et al. Facebook, stress, and incidence of upper respiratory infection in undergraduate college students. *Cyberpsychology, Behavior, and Social Networking*, 2012, *15*(12), 675–681.

Cannon, M., Jones, P. B., and Murray, R. M. Obstetric complications and schizophrenia: Historical and meta-analytic review. *American Journal of Psychiatry*, 2002, *159*, 1080–1092.

Cannon, T. D., Thompson, P. M., van Erp, T. G., et al. Cortex mapping reveals regionally specific patterns of genetic and disease-specific gray-matter deficits in twins discordant for schizophrenia. *Proceedings of the National Academy of Sciences, USA*, 2002, *99*, 3228–3233.

Cannon, W. B. The James-Lange theory of emotions: A critical examination and an alternative. *American Journal of Psychology*, 1927, *39*, 106–124.

Cape, E. G., and Jones, B. E. Effects of glutamate agonist versus procaine microinjections into the basal forebrain cholinergic cell area upon gamma and theta EEG activity and sleep–wake state. *European Journal of Neuroscience*, 2000, *12*, 2166–2184.

Carew, T. J. Development assembly of learning in Aplysia. *Trends in Neuroscience*, 1989, *12*, 389–394.

Carleton, A., Accolla, R., and Simon, S. A. Coding in the mammalian gustatory system. *Trends in Neuroscience*, 2010, *33*, 326–334.

Carmichael, M. S., Humbert, R., Dixen, J., Palmisano, G., et al. Plasma oxytocin increases in the human sexual response. *Journal of Clinical Endocrinology and Metabolism*, 1987, *64*, 27–31.

Carney, D. R., Cuddy, A. J., & Yap, A. J. Power posing brief nonverbal displays affect neuroendocrine levels and risk tolerance. *Psychological Science*, 2010, *21*(10), 1363–1368.

Carpenter, C. R. Sexual behavior of free ranging rhesus monkeys (*Macaca mulatta*). I: Specimens, procedures and behavioral characteristics of estrus. *Journal of Comparative Psychology*, 1942, *33*, 113–142.

Carpenter, S. K., Cepeda, N. J., Rohrer, D., Kang, S. H., et al. Using spacing to enhance diverse forms of learning: Review of recent research and implications for instruction. *Educational Psychology Review*, 2012, *24*(3), 369–378.

Carr, C. E., and Konishi, M. Axonal delay lines for time measurement in the owl's brainstem. *Proceedings of the National Academy of Sciences, USA*, 1989, *85*, 8311–8315.

Carr, C. E., and Konishi, M. A circuit for detection of interaural time differences in the brain stem of the barn owl. *Journal of Neuroscience*, 1990, *10*, 3227–3246.

Carr, L., Iacoboni, M., Dubeau, M. C., Mazziotta, J. C., et al. Neural mechanisms of empathy in humans: A relay from neural systems for imitation to limbic areas. *Proceedings of the National Academy of Sciences, USA*, 2003, *100*, 5497–5502.

Carrera, M. R., Ashley, J. A., Parsons, L. H., Wirsching, P., et al. Suppression of psychoactive effects of cocaine by active immunization. *Nature*, 1995, *378*, 727–730.

Carroll, F. L., Blouch, B. E., Pidaparthi, R. R., Abraham, P., et al. Synthesis of mercapto (+) methamphetamine haptens and their use for obtaining improved epitope density on (+) methamphetamine conjugate vaccines. *Journal of Medical Chemistry*, 2011, *54*, 5221–5228.

Carroll, K. M., and Onken, L. S. Behavioral therapies for drug abuse. *American Journal of Psychiatry*, 2014, *162*, 8, 1452–1460.

Carroll, K. M., and Rounsaville, B. J. Bridging the gap: A hybrid model to link efficacy and effectiveness research in substance abuse treatment. *Psychiatric Services*, 2014, *54*, 3, 333–339.

Carroll, R. C., Lissin, D. V., von Zastrow, M., Nicolol, R. A., et al. Rapid redistribution of glutamate recep-tors contributes to long-term depression in hippocampal cultures. *Nature Neuroscience*, 1999, *2*, 454–460.

Carter, C. S. Hormonal influences on human sexual behavior. In *Behavioral endocrinology*, edited by J. B. Becker, S. M. Breedlove, and D. Crews. Cambridge, Mass.: MIT Press, 1992.

Carter, M. E., Yizhar, O., Chikahisa, S., Nguyen, H., et al. Tuning arousal with optogenetic modulation of locus coeruleus neurons. *Nature Neuroscience*, 2010, *13*, 1526–1533.

Cartoni, C., Yasumatsu, K., Ohkuri, T., Shigemura, M., et al. Taste preference for fatty acids is mediated by GPR40 and GPR120. *Journal of Neuroscience*, 2010, *30*, 8376–8382.

Cartwright, R. Sleepwalking violence: A sleep disorder, a legal dilemma, and a psychological challenge. *American Journal of Psychiatry*, 2004, *161*(7) 1149–1158.

Cash, S. S., Halgren, E., Dehghani, N., Rossetti, A. O., et al. The human K-complex represents an isolated cortical down-state. *Science*, 2009, *324*, 1084–1087.

Caspi, A., Sugden, K., Moffitt, T. E., Taylor, A., et al. Influence of life stress on depression: Moderation by a polymorphism in the 5-HTT gene. *Science*, 2003, *301*, 386–389.

Cassidy, S. B., Schwartz, S., Miller, J. L., and Driscoll, D. J. Prader-willi syndrome. *Genetics in Medicine*, 2011, *14*(1), 10–26.

Castellanos, F. X., Lee, P. P., Sharp, W., Jeffries, N. O., et al. Developmental trajectories of brain volume *Journal of American Medical Association* abnormalities in children and adolescents with attention-deficit/hyperactivity disorder. *Journal of American Medical Association*, 2002, *288*(14), 1740–1748.

Castelli, F., Frith, C., Happé, F., and Frith, U. Autism, Asperger syndrome and brain mechanisms for the attribution of mental states to animated shapes. *Brain*, 2002, *125*, 1839–1849.

Castelli, L., Perozzo, P., Zibetti, M., Crivelli, B., et al. Chronic deep brain stimulation of the subthalamic nucleus for Parkinson's disease: Effects on cognition, mood, anxiety and personality traits. *European Neurology*, 2006, *55*, 136–144.

Catani, M., Jones, D. K., and ffytche, D. H. Perisylvian language networks of the human brain. *Annals of Neurology*, 2005, *57*, 8–16.

Caterina, M. J., Leffler, A., Malmberg, A. B., Martin, W. J., et al. Impaired nociception and pain sensation in mice lacking the capsaicin receptor. *Science*, 2000, *288*, 306–313.

Cavaco, S., Anderson, S. W., Allen, J. S., Castro-Caldas, A., et al. The scope of preserved procedural memory in amnesia. *Brain*, 2004, *127*, 1863–1867.

Cecil, J. E., Francis, J., and Read, N. W. Relative contributions of intestinal, gastric, oro-sensory influences and information to changes in appetite induced by the same liquid meal. *Appetite*, 1998, *31*, 377–390.

Cenci, M. A., Kalen, P., Mandel, R. J., and Bjoerklund, A. Regional differences in the regulation of dopamine and noradrenaline release in medial frontal cortex, nucleus accumbens and caudate-putamen: A microdialysis study in the rat. *Brain Research*, 1992, *581*, 217–228.

Censor, N., Sagi, D., and Cohen, L. G. Common mechanisms of human perceptual and motor learning. *Nature Reviews Neuroscience*, 2012, *13*(9), 658–664.

Center for Substance Abuse Treatment. *A guide to substance abuse services for primary care clinicians*. Treatment Improvement Protocol (TIP) Series, No. 24. Chapter 5—Specialized Substance Abuse Treatment Programs. Rockville, MD: U.S. Substance Abuse and Mental Health Services Administration, 1997. Available from: http://www.ncbi.nlm.nih.gov/books/NBK64815/

Cerletti, U., and Bini, L. Electric shock treatment. *Bollettino ed Atti della Accademia Medica di Roma*, 1938, *64*, 36.

Cerny, E. H., and Cerny, T. Vaccines against nicotine. *Human Vaccines*, 2009, *5*, 200–205.

Chamberlain, M. C. Bevacizumab for the treatment of recurrent Glioblastoma. *Clinical Medicine Insights: Oncology*, 2011, *5*, 117–129.

Chambers, R. A., Taylor, J. R., and Potenza, M. N. Developmental neurocircuitry of motivation in adolescence: A critical period of addiction vulnerability. *American Journal of Psychiatry*, 2003, *160*, 1041–1052.

Chaminade, T., Meltzoff, A. N., and Decety, J. An fMRI study of imitation: Action representation and body schema. *Neuropsychologia*, 2005, *43*, 115–127.

Chan, J. L., Mun, E. C., Stoyneva, V., Mantzoros, C. S., et al. Peptide YY levels are elevated after gastric bypass surgery. *Obesity*, 2006, *14*, 194–198.

Chan, B. L., Witt, R., Charrow, A. P., Magee, A., et al. Mirror therapy for phantom limb pain. *New England Journal of Medicine*, 2007, *357*(21), 2206–2207.

Chandler, L. J., Harris, R. A., and Crews, F. T. Ethanol tolerance and synaptic plasticity. *Trends in Pharmacological Science*, 1998, *19*, 491–495.

Chaney, M. A. Side effects of intrathecal and epidural opioids. *Canadian Journal of Anaesthesia*, 1995, *42*, 891–903.

Changizi, M. A., Zhang, Q., Ye, H., and Shimojo, S. The structures of letters and symbols throughout human history are selected to match those found in objects in natural scenes. *American Naturalist*, 2006, *167*, E117–E139.

Chatterjee, S., and Callaway, E. M. Parallel colour-opponent pathways to primary visual cortex. *Nature*, 2003, *426*, 668–671.

Chemelli, R. M., Willie, J. T., Sinton, C. M., Elmquist, J. K., et al. Narcolepsy in orexin knockout mice: Molecular genetics of sleep regulation. *Cell*, 1999, *98*, 437–451.

Chen, A. J.-W., and D'Esposito, M. Traumatic brain injury: From bench to bedside to society. *Neuron*, 2010, *66*, 11–14.

Chen, G., Henter, I. D., and Manji, H. K. Presynaptic glutamatergic function in bipolar disorder. *Biological Psychiatry*, 2010, *67*, 1007–1009.

Chen, J., Marmer, R., Pulles, A., Paredes, W., et al. Ventral tegmental microinjection of delta⁹-tetrahydrocannabinol enhances ventral tegmental somatodendritic dopamine levels but not forebrain dopamine levels: Evidence for local neural action by marijuana's psychoactive ingredient. *Brain Research*, 1993, *621*, 65–70.

Chen, J., Paredes, W., Li, J., Smith, D., et al. Delta⁹-tetrahydrocannabinol produces naloxone-blockable enhancement of presynaptic basal dopamine efflux in nucleus accumbens of conscious, freely-moving rats as measured by intracerebral microdialysis. *Psychopharmacology*, 1990, *102*, 156–162.

Chen, Y.-C., Thaler, D., Nixon, P. D., Stern, C. E., et al. The functions of the medial premotor cortex. II: The timing and selection of learned movements. *Experimental Brain Research*, 1995, *102*, 461–473.

Chen, Y. W., and Dilsaver, S. C. Lifetime rates of suicide attempts among subjects with bipolar and unipolar disorders relative to subjects with other axis I disorders. *Biological Psychiatry*, 1996, *39*, 896–899.

Chimowitz, M. I., Lynn, M. J, Derdeyn, C. P., Turan, T. N., et al. Stenting versus aggressive medical therapy for intracranial arterial stenosis. *New England Journal of Medicine*, 2011, *365*, 993–1003.

Christensen, R., Kristensen, P. K., Bartels, E. M., Bliddal, H., et al. Efficacy and safety of the weight-loss drug rimonabant: A meta-analysis of randomised trials. *Lancet*, 2007, *370*, 1706–1713.

Ciocchi, S., Herry, C., Grenier, F., Wolff, S. B., et al. Encoding of conditioned fear in central amygdala inhibitory circuits, *Nature*, 2010, *468*, 277–282.

Cho, M. M., DeVries, A. C., Williams, J. R., and Carter, C. S. The effects of oxytocin and vasopressin on partner preferences in male and female prairie voles (*Microtus ochrogaster*). *Behavioral Neuroscience*, 1999, *113*, 1071–1079.

Chou, I.-H., and Narasimhan, K. Neurobiology of addiction. *Nature Neuroscience*, 2005, *8*, 1427.

Chou, T. C., Bjorkum, A. A., Gaus, S. E., Lu, J., et al. Afferents to the ventrolateral preoptic nucleus. *Journal of Neuroscience*, 2002, *22*, 977–990.

Chubb, J. E., Bradshaw, N. J., Soares, D. C., Porteous, D. J., et al. The DISC locus in psychiatric illness. *Molecular Psychiatry*, 2008, *13*, 36–64.

Chung, S., Hopf, F. W., Nagasaki, H., Li, S. Y., et al. The melanin-concentrating hormone system modulates cocaine reward. *Proceedings of the National Academy of Sciences, USA*, 2009, *106*, 6772–6777.

Cipolotti, L., and Warrington, E. K. Does recognizing orally spelled words depend on reading? An investigation into a case of better written than oral spelling. *Neuropsychologia*, 1996, *34*, 427–440.

Cippitelli, A., Karlsson, C., Shaw, J. L., Thorsell, A., et al. Suppression of alcohol self-administration and reinstatement of alcohol seeking by melanin-concentrating hormone receptor 1 (MCH1-R) antagonism in Wistar rats. *Psychopharmacology*, 2010, *211*, 367–375.

Ciuman, R. R. The efferent system or olivocochlear function bundle—fine regulator and protector of hearing perception. *International Journal of Biomedical Science: IJBS*, 2010, *6*(4), 276.

Clark, J. T., Kalra, P. S., Crowley, W. R., and Kalra, S. P. Neuropeptide Y and human pancreatic polypeptide stimulates feeding behavior in rats. *Endocrinology*, 1984, *115*, 427–429.

Clarke, S., Bellmann, A., Meuli, R. A., Assal, G., et al. Auditory agnosia and auditory spatial deficits following left hemispheric lesions: Evidence for distinct processing pathways. *Neuropsychologia*, 2000, *38*, 797–807.

Clemenson, G. D., Deng, W., and Gage, F. H. Environmental enrichment and neurogenesis: From mice to humans. *Current Opinion in Behavioral Sciences*, 2015, *4*, 56–62.

Cnattingius, S., Hultman, C. M., Dahl, M., and Sparen, P. Very preterm birth, birth trauma, and the risk of anorexia nervosa among girls. *Archives of General Psychiatry*, 1999, *56*, 634–638.

Cobb, S., and Rose, R. M. Hypertension, peptic ulcer, and diabetes in air traffic controllers. *Journal of the American Medical Association*, 1973, *224*, 489–492.

Coccaro, E. F., and Kavoussi, R. J. Fluoxetine and impulsive aggressive behavior in personality-disordered subjects. *Archives of General Psychiatry*, 1997, *54*, 1081–1088.

Coccaro, E. F., Silverman, J. M., Klar, H. M., Horvath, T. B., et al. Familial correlates of reduced central serotonergic system function in patients with personality disorders. *Archives of General Psychiatry*, 1994, *51*, 318–324.

Cohen, C., Kodas, E., and Griebel, G. CB_1 receptor antagonists for the treatment of nicotine addiction. *Pharmacology, Biochemistry and Behavior*, 2005, *81*, 387–395.

Cohen, E. A. *Human behavior in the concentration camp.* New York: W. W. Norton, 1953.

Cohen, S., Tyrrell, D. A. J., and Smith, A. P. Psychological stress and susceptibility to the common cold. *New England Journal of Medicine*, 1991, *325*, 606–612.

Cohen-Bendahan, C. C., Buitelaar, J. K., van Goozen, S. H. M., Orlebeke, J. F., et al. Is there an effect of prenatal testosterone on aggression and other behavioral traits? A study comparing same-sex and opposite-sex twin girls. *Hormones and Behavior*, 2005a, *47*, 230–237.

Cohen-Bendahan, C. C., van de Beek, C., and Berenbaum S. A. Prenatal sex hormone effects on child and adult-sex-typed behavior: Methods and findings. *Neuroscience and Biobehavioral Reviews*, 2005b, *29*, 353–384.

Colapinto, J. *As nature made him: The boy who was raised as a girl.* New York: HarperCollins, 2000.

Cole, B. J., and Koob, G. F. Propranolol antagonizes the enhanced conditioned fear produced by corticotropin releasing factor. *Journal of Pharmacology and Experimental Therapeutics*, 1988, *247*, 901–910.

Cole, J. Empathy needs a face. *Journal of Consciousness Studies*, 2001, *8*, 51–68.

Collaborative Research Group. A novel gene containing a trinucleotide repeat that is expanded and unstable on Huntington's disease chromosomes. *Cell*, 1993, *72*, 971–983.

Connellan, J., Baron-Cohen, S., Wheelwright, S., Batki, A., et al. Sex differences in human neonatal social perception. *Infant Behavior and Development*, 2000, *23*, 113–118.

Collins, S., McLean, C. A., and Masters, C. L. Gerstmann–Sträussler–Scheinker syndrome, fatal familial insomnia, and kuru: A review of these less common human transmissible spongiform encephalopathies. *Journal of Clinical Neuroscience*, 2001, *8*(5), 387–397.

Connolly, J. D., Andersen, R. A., and Goodale, M. A. fMRI evidence for a "parietal reach region" in the human brain. *Experimental Brain Research*, 2003, *153*, 140–145.

Conway, B. R., Moeller, S., and Tsao, D. Y. Specialized color modules in macaque extrastriate cortex. *Neuron*, 2007, *56*, 560–573.

Coolen, L. M. Neural control of ejaculation. *Journal of Comparative Neurology*, 2005, *493*, 39–45.

Coolen, L. M., Allard, J., Truitt, W. A., and McKenna, K. E. Central regulation of ejaculation. *Physiology and Behavior*, 2004, *83*, 203–215.

Coolen, L. M., and Wood, R. I. Testosterone stimulation of the medial preoptic area and medial amygdala in the control of male hamster sexual behavior: Redundancy without amplification. *Behavioural Brain Research*, 1999, *98*, 143–153.

Cooper, J. A. A mechanism for inside-out lamination in the neocortex. *Trends in Neurosciences*, 2008, *32*, 113–119.

Coover, G. D., Murison, R., and Jellestad, F. K. Subtotal lesions of the amygdala: The rostral central nucleus in passive avoidance and ulceration. *Physiology and Behavior*, 1992, *51*, 795–803.

Copeland, B. J., and Pillsbury, H. C. Cochlear implantation for the treatment of deafness. *Annual Review of Medicine*, 2004, *55*, 157–167.

Corey, D. P., Garcia-Añoveros, J., Holt, J. R., Kwan, K. Y., et al. TRPA1 is a candidate for the mechanosensitive transduction channel of vertebrate hair cells. *Nature*, 2004, *432*, 723–730.

Corkin, S., Amaral, D. G., González, R. G., Johnson, K. A., et al. H. M.'s medial temporal lobe lesion: Findings from magnetic resonance imaging. *Journal of Neuroscience*, 1997, *17*, 3964–3979.

Corkin, S., Sullivan, E. V., Twitchell, T. E., and Grove, E. The amnesic patient H. M.: Clinical observations and test performance 28 years after operation. *Society for Neuroscience Abstracts*, 1981, *7*, 235.

Corrigall, W. A., Coen, K. M., and Adamson, K. L. Self-administered nicotine activates the mesolimbic dopamine system through the ventral tegmental area. *Brain Research*, 1994, *653*, 278–284.

Corwin, J. T., and Warchol, M. E. Auditory hair cells: Structure, function, development, and regeneration. *Annual Review of Neuroscience*, 1991, *14*, 301–333.

Cossu, G., Ledent, C., Fattore, L., Imperato, A., et al. Cannabinoid CB_1 receptor knockout mice fail to self-administer morphine but not other drugs of abuse. *Behavioural Brain Research*, 2001, *118*, 61–65.

Cotman, C. W., Berchtold, N. C., and Christie, L.-A. Exercise builds brain health: Key roles of growth factor cascades and inflammation. *Trends in Neuroscience*, 2007, *30*, 464–472.

Cottingham, S. L., and Pfaff, D. Interconnectedness of steroid hormone-binding neurons: Existence and implications. *Current Topics in Neuroendocrinology*, 1986, *7*, 223–249.

Cottone, P., Sabino, V., Roberto, M., Bajo, M., et al. CRF system recruitment mediates dark side of compulsive eating. *Proceedings of the National Academy of Sciences, USA,* 2009, *106,* 20016–20020.

Courchesne, E., Pierce, K., Schumann, C. M., Redcay, E., et al. Mapping early brain development in autism. *Neuron,* 2007, *56,* 399–413.

Courchesne, E., Redcay, E., Morgan, J. T., and Kennedy, D. P. Autism at the beginning: Microstructural and growth abnormalities underlying the cognitive and behavioral phenotype of autism. *Development and Psychopathology,* 2005, *17,* 577–597.

Court, J., Bergh, C., and Södersten, P. Mandometer treatment of Australian patients with eating disorders. *Medical Journal of Australia,* 2008, *288,* 120–121.

Covington, H. E., and Miczek, K. A. Repeated social-defeat stress, cocaine or morphine: Effects on behavioral sensitization and intravenous cocaine self-administration "binges." *Psychopharmacology,* 2001, *158,* 388–398.

Cowey, A. The blindsight saga. *Experimental Brain Research,* 2010, *200,* 3–24.

Cowley, M. A., Smith, R. G., Diano, S., Tschöp, M., et al. The distribution and mechanism of action of ghrelin in the CNS demonstrates a novel hypothalamic circuit regulating energy homeostasis. *Neuron,* 2003, *37,* 649–661.

Cox, A., Rutter, M., Newman, S., and Bartak, L. A comparative study of infantile autism and specific developmental language disorders. I: Parental characteristics. *British Journal of Psychiatry,* 1975, *126,* 146–159.

Cox, D., Meyers, E., and Sinha, P. Contextually evoked object-specific responses in human visual cortex. *Science,* 2004, *304,* 115–117.

Cox, J. J., Reimann, F., Nicholas, A. K., Thornton, G., et al. An SCN9A channelopathy causes congenital inability to experience pain. *Nature,* 2006, *444,* 894–898.

Coyle, J. T. Glutamate and schizophrenia: beyond the dopamine hypothesis. *Cellular and Molecular Neurobiology,* 2006, *26*(4–6), 363–382.

Crane, G. E. Iproniazid (Marsilid) phosphate, a therapeutic agent for mental disorders and debilitating diseases. *Psychiatry Research Reports,* 1957, *8,* 142–152.

Creese, I., Burt, D. R., and Snyder, S. H. Dopamine receptor binding predicts clinical and pharmacological potencies of antischizophrenic drugs. *Science,* 1976, *192,* 481–483.

Criado, J. R., Sanchez-Alavez, M., Conti, B., Giacchino, J. L., et al. Mice devoid of prion protein have cognitive deficits that are rescued by reconstitution of PrP in neurons. *Neurobiology of Disease,* 2005, *19,* 255–265.

Crockett, M. J., Clark, L., Hauser, M. D., and Robbins, T. W. Serotonin selectively influences moral judgment and behavior through effects on harm aversion. *Proceedings of the National Academy of Sciences, USA,* 2010, *107,* 17433–17438.

Crow, T. J. How and why genetic linkage has not solved the problem of psychosis: Review and hypothesis. *American Journal of Psychiatry,* 2007, *164,* 13–21.

Cubelli, R. A selective deficit for writing vowels in acquired dysgraphia. *Nature,* 1991, *353,* 258–260.

Culebras, A., and Moore, J. T. Magnetic resonance findings in REM sleep behavior disorder. *Neurology,* 1989, *39,* 1519–1523.

Culham, J. C., and Kanwisher, N. Neuroimaging of cognitive functions in human parietal cortex. *Current Opinion in Neurobiology,* 2001, *11,* 157–163.

Culotta, E., and Koshland, D. E. NO news is good news. *Science,* 1992, *258,* 1862–1865.

Cummings, D. E. Ghrelin and the short- and long-term regulation of appetite and body weight. *Physiology and Behavior,* 2006, *89,* 71–84.

Cunningham, J. T., Beltz, T. G., Johnson, R. F., and Johnson, A. K. The effects of ibotenate lesions of the median preoptic on experimentally induced and circadian drinking behaviours in rats. *Brain Research,* 1992, *580,* 325–330.

Daban, C., Martinez-Aran, A., Cruz, N., and Vieta, E. Safety and efficacy of vagus nerve stimulation in treatment-resistant depression: A systematic review. *Journal of Affective Disorders,* 2008, *110,* 1–15.

Dabbs, J. M., and Morris, R. Testosterone, social class, and antisocial behavior in a sample of 4,462 men. *Psychological Science,* 1990, *1,* 209–211.

Dai, S.-S., Zhou, Y.-G., Li, W., An, J. H., et al. Local glutamate level dictates adenosine A_{2A} receptor regulation of neuroinflammation and traumatic brain injury. *Journal of Neuroscience,* 2010, *30,* 5802–5810.

Dallos, P. The active cochlea. *Journal of Neuroscience,* 1992, *12,* 4575–4585.

Damasio, A. R., and Damasio, H. The anatomic basis of pure alexia. *Neurology,* 1983, *33,* 1573–1583.

Damasio, A. R., and Damasio, H. Hemianopia, hemiachromatopsia, and the mechanisms of alexia. *Cortex,* 1986, *22,* 161–169.

Damasio, A. R., Damasio, H., and Van Hoesen, G. W. Prosopagnosia: Anatomic basis and behavioral mechanisms. *Neurology,* 1982, *32,* 331–341.

Damasio, A. R., Grabowski, T. J., Bechara, A., Damasio, H., et al. Subcortical and cortical brain activity during the feeling of self-generated emotions. *Nature Neuroscience,* 2000, *3,* 1049–1056.

Damasio, A. R., and Tranel, D. Nouns and verbs are retrieved with differentially distributed neural systems. *Proceedings of the National Academy of Sciences, USA,* 1993, *90,* 4957–4960.

Damasio, A. R., Yamada, T., Damasio, H., Corbett, J., et al. Central achromatopsia: Behavioral, anatomic, and physiologic aspects. *Neurology,* 1980, *30,* 1064–1071.

Damasio, H. Neuroimaging contributions to the understanding of aphasia. In *Handbook of neuropsychology, vol. 2,* edited by F. Boller and J. Grafman. Amsterdam: Elsevier, 1989.

Damasio, H., and Damasio, A. R. The anatomical basis of conduction aphasia. *Brain,* 1980, *103,* 337–350.

Damasio, H., Eslinger, P., and Adams, H. P. Aphasia following basal ganglia lesions: New evidence. *Seminars in Neurology,* 1984, *4,* 151–161.

Damasio, H., Grabowski, T., Frank, R., Galaburda, A. M., et al. The return of Phineas Gage: Clues about the brain from the skull of a famous patient. *Science,* 1994, *264,* 1102–1105.

Damsma, G., Day, J., and Fibiger, H. C. Lack of tolerance to nicotine-induced dopamine release in the nucleus accumbens. *European Journal of Pharmacology,* 1989, *168,* 363–368.

Dani, J. A., and De Biasi, M. Cellular mechanisms of nicotine addiction. *Pharmacology, Biochemistry, and Behavior,* 2001, *70,* 439–446.

Dani, J. A., and Harris, R. A. Nicotine addiction and comorbidity with alcohol abuse and mental illness. *Nature Neuroscience,* 2005, *8,* 1465–1470.

Daniele, A., Giustolisi, L., Silveri, M. C., Colosimo, C., et al. Evidence for a possible neuroanatomical basis for lexical processing of nouns and verbs. *Neuropsychologia,* 1994, *32,* 1325–1341.

Daniels, D., Miselis, R. R., and Flanagan-Cato, L. M. Central neuronal circuit innervating the lordosis-producing muscles defined by transneuronal transport of pseudorabies virus. *Journal of Neuroscience,* 1999, *19,* 2823–2833.

Dapretto, M., Davies, M. S., Pfeifer, J. H., Scott, A. A., et al. Understanding emotions in others: Mirror neuron dysfunction in children with autism spectrum disorders. *Nature Neuroscience,* 2006, *9,* 28–30.

Darwin, C. *The expression of the emotions in man and animals.* Chicago: University of Chicago Press, 1872/1965.

Davidson, D., Swift, R., and Fitz, E. Naltrexone increases the latency to drink alcohol in social drinkers. *Alcoholism: Clinical and Experimental Research,* 1996, *20,* 732–739.

Davidson, S., and Giesler, G. J. The multiple pathways for itch and their interactions with pain. *Trends in Neurosciences,* 2010, *33,* 550–558.

Davidson, S., Zhang, X., Khasabov, S. G., Simone, D. A., et al. Relief of itch by scratching: State-dependent inhibition of primate spinothalamic tract neurons. *Nature Neuroscience*, 2009, *12*, 544–546.

Davies, G., Welham, J., Chant, D., Torrey, E. F., et al. A systematic review and meta-analysis of Northern Hemisphere season of birth studies in schizophrenia. *Schizophrenia Bulletin*, 2003, *29*, 587–593.

Davis, F. G., Kupelian, V., Freels, S., McCarthy, B., et al. Prevalence estimates for primary brain tumors in the United States by behavior and major histology groups. *Neuro-oncology*, 2001, *3*(3), 152–158.

Davis, J. D., and Campbell, C. S. Peripheral control of meal size in the rat: Effect of sham feeding on meal size and drinking rate. *Journal of Comparative and Physiological Psychology*, 1973, *83*, 379–387.

Davis, J. O., and Bracha, H. S. Famine and schizophrenia: First-trimester malnutrition or second-trimester beriberi? *Biological Psychiatry*, 1996, *40*, 1–3.

Davis, J. O., Phelps, J. A., and Bracha, H. S. Prenatal development of monozygotic twins and concordance for schizophrenia. *Schizophrenia Bulletin*, 1995, *21*, 357–366.

Davis, M. The role of the amygdala in fear-potentiated startle: Implications for animal models of anxiety. *Trends in Pharmacological Sciences*, 1992, *13*, 35–41.

Daw, N. W. Colour-coded ganglion cells in the goldfish retina: Extension of their receptive fields by means of new stimuli. *Journal of Physiology (London)*, 1968, *197*, 567–592.

Dawson, T. M., and Dawson, V. L. Molecular pathways of neurodegeneration in Parkinson's disease. *Science*, 2003, *302*, 819–822.

Day, J. J., Roitman, M. F., Wightman, R. M., and Carelli, R. M. Associative learning mediates dynamic shifts in dopamine signaling in the nucleus accumbens. *Nature Neuroscience*, 2007, *10*, 1020–1028.

de Castro, J. M. The control of eating behavior in free-living humans. In *Neurobiology of food and fluid intake*, 2nd ed., edited by E. Stricker and S. Woods. New York: Plenum Publishers, 2004.

de Gelder, B. Towards the neurobiology of emotional body language. *Nature Reviews: Neuroscience*, 2006, *7*, 242–249.

de Gelder, B., Vroomen, J., Pourtois, G., and Weiskrantz, L. Non-conscious recognition of affect in the absence of striate cortex. *Neuroreport*, 1999, *10*, 3759–3763.

De Jonge, F. H., Louwerse, A. L., Ooms, M. P., Evers, P., et al. Lesions of the SDN-POA inhibit sexual behavior of male Wistar rats. *Brain Research Bulletin*, 1989, *23*, 483–492.

de Kloet, E. R., Joëls, M., and Holsboer, F. Stress and the brain: From adaptation to disease. *Nature Reviews: Neuroscience*, 2005, *6*, 463–475.

De Ocampo, J., Foldvary, N., Dinner, D. S., and Golish, J. Sleep-related eating disorder in fraternal twins. *Sleep Medicine*, 2002, *3*, 525–526.

de Ruiter, M. B., Oosterlaan, J., Veltman, D. J., van den Brink, W., et al. Similar hyporesponsiveness of the dorsomedial prefrontal cortex in problem gamblers and heavy smokers during an inhibitory control task. *Drug and Alcohol Dependence*, 2012, *121*, 81–89.

De Strooper, B. Aph-1, Pen-2, and nicastrin with presenilin generate an active γ-secretase complex. *Neuron*, 2003, *38*, 9–12.

De Valois, R. L., Albrecht, D. G., and Thorell, L. Cortical cells: Bar detectors or spatial frequency filters? In *Frontiers in Visual Science*, edited by S. J. Cool and E. L. Smith. Berlin: Springer-Verlag, 1978.

De Valois, R. L., and De Valois, K. K. *Spatial Vision*. New York: Oxford University Press, 1988.

De Valois, R. L., Thorell, L. G., and Albrecht, D. G. Periodicity of striate-cortex-cell receptive fields. *Journal of the Optical Society of America*, 1985, *2*, 1115–1123.

De Vries, T. J., and Schoffelmeer, A. N. M. Cannabinoid CB_1 receptors control conditioned drug seeking. *Trends in Pharmacological Sciences*, 2005, *26*, 420–426.

Deacon, S., and Arendt, J. Adapting to phase shifts. I: An experimental model for jet lag and shift work. *Physiology and Behavior*, 1996, *59*, 665–673.

Dealberto, M. J. Why are immigrants at increased risk for psychosis? Vitamin D insufficiency, epigenetic mechanisms, or both? *Medical Hypotheses*, 2007, *68*, 259–267.

Dean, P. Effects of inferotemporal lesions on the behavior of monkeys. *Psychological Bulletin*, 1976, *83*, 41–71.

Debanne, D., Gähwiler, B. H., and Thompson, S. M. Asynchronous pre- and postsynaptic activity induces associative long-term depression in area CA1 of the rat hippocampus in vitro. *Proceedings of the National Academy of Sciences*, USA. 1994, *91*, 1148–1152.

Debiec, J., Diaz-Mataix, L., Bush, D. E. A., Doyère, V., et al. The amygdala encodes specific sensory features of an aversive reinforcer. *Nature Neuroscience*, 2010, *13*, 536–537.

Dehaene, S. *Reading in the Brain: The Science and Evolution of a Human Invention*. New York: Viking, 2009.

Dehaene, S., Nakamura, K., Jobert, A., Kuroki, C., et al. Why do children make mirror errors in reading? Neural correlates of mirror invariance in the visual word form area. *NeuroImage*, 2010, *49*, 1837–1848.

Deinzer, R., Kleineidam, C., Stiller-Winkler, R., Idel, H., et al. Prolonged reduction of salivary immunoglobulin A (sIgA) after a major academic exam. *International Journal of Psychophysiology*, 2000, *37*(3), 219–232.

Deinzer, R., and Schüller, N. Dynamics of stress-related decrease of salivary immunoglobulin A (sIgA): Relationship to symptoms of the common cold and studying behavior. *Behavioral Medicine*, 1998, *23*(4), 161–169.

Dejerine, J. Contribution àl'étude anatomo-pathologique et clinique des différentes variétés de cécité verbale. *Comptes Rendus des Séances de la Société de Biologie et de Ses Filiales*, 1892, *4*, 61–90.

Del Cerro, M. C. R., Izquierdo, M. A. P., Rosenblatt, J. S., Johnson, B. M., et al. Brain 2-deoxyglucose levels related to maternal behavior-inducing stimuli in the rat. *Brain Research*, 1995, *696*, 213–220.

Delay, J., and Deniker, P. Le traitement des psychoses par une methode neurolytique derivée d'hibernothéraphie: Le 4560 RP utilisée seul une cure prolongée et continuée. *Comptes Rendus Congrès des Médecins Aliénistes et Neurologistes de France et des Pays de Langue Française*, 1952a, *50*, 497–502.

Delay, J., and Deniker, P. 38 cas des psychoses traitées par la cure prolongée et continuée de 4560 RP. *Comptes Rendus du Congrès des Médecins Aliénistes et Neurologistes de France et des Pays de Langue Française*, 1952b, *50*, 503–513.

Delgado, P. L., Charney, D. S., Price, L. H., Aghajanian, G. K., et al. Serotonin function and the mechanism of antidepressant action: Reversal of antidepressant induced remission by rapid depletion of plasma tryptophan. *Archives of General Psychiatry*, 1990, *47*, 411–418.

DeLisi, L. E., Szulc, K. U., Bertisch, H. C., Majcher, M., et al. Understanding structural brain changes in schizophrenia. *Dialogues in Clinical Neuroscience*, 2006, *8*(1), 71–78.

DeLoache, J. S., Uttal, D. H., and Rosengren, K. S. Scale errors offer evidence for a perception-action dissociation early in life. *Science*, 2004, *304*, 1027–1029.

DeLong, G. R. Autism: New data suggest a new hypothesis. *Neurology*, 1999, *52*, 911–916.

DelParigi, A., Tschöp, M., Heiman, M. L., Salbe, A. D., et al. High circulating ghrelin: A potential cause for hyperphagia and obesity in Prader-Willi syndrome. *Journal of Clinical Endocrinology and Metabolism*, 2002, *87*, 5461–5464.

Dement, W. C. The effect of dream deprivation. *Science*, 1960, *131*, 1705–1707.

Dement, W., & Kleitman, N. Cyclic variations in EEG during sleep and their relation to eye movements, body motility, and dreaming. *Electroencephalography and Clinical Neurophysiology*, 1957, *9*(4), 673–690.

Démonet, J.-F., Taylor, M. J., and Chaix, Y. Developmental dyslexia. *Lancet*, 2004, *363*, 1451–1460.

Deol, M. S., and Gluecksohn-Waelsch, S. The role of inner hair cells in hearing. *Nature*, 1979, *278*, 250–252.

Derdikman, D., and Moser, E. I. A manifold of spatial maps in the brain. *Trends in Cognitive Science*, 2010, *14*, 561–568.

Dérouesné, J., and Beauvois, M. F. Phonological processing in reading: Data from alexia. *Journal of Neurology, Neurosurgery, and Psychiatry*, 1979, *42*, 1125–1132.

Deurveilher, S., and Semba, K. Indirect projections from the suprachiasmatic nucleus to major arousal-promoting cell groups in rat: Implications for the circadian control of behavioural state. *Neuroscience*, 2005, *130*, 165–183.

Deutsch, J. A., and Gonzalez, M. F. Gastric nutrient content signals satiety. *Behavioral and Neural Biology*, 1980, *30*, 113–116.

Devane, W. A., Hanus, L., Breuer, A., Pertwee, R. G., et al. Isolation and structure of a brain constituent that binds to the cannabinoid receptor. *Science*, 1992, *258*, 1946–1949.

Devilbiss, D. M., and Berridge, C. W. Cognition-enhancing doses of methylphenidate preferentially increase prefrontal cortex neuronal responsiveness. *Biological Psychiatry*, 2008, *64*, 626–635.

Devine, D. P., and Wise, R. A. Self-administration of morphine, DAMGO, and DPDPE into the ventral tegmental area of rats. *Journal of Neuroscience*, 1994, *14*, 1978–1984.

Dhaka, A., Uzzell, V., Dubin, A. E., Mathur, J., et al. TRPV1 is activated by both acidic and basic pH. *Journal of Neuroscience*, 2009, *29*, 153–158.

Di Chiara, G. The role of dopamine in drug abuse viewed from the perspective of its role in motivation. *Drug and Alcohol Dependency*, 1995, *38*, 95–137.

Di Ciano, P., Coury, A., Depoortere, R. Y., Egilmez, Y., et al. Comparison of changes in extracellular dopamine concentrations in the nucleus accumbens during intravenous self-administration of cocaine or d-amphetamine. *Behavioural Pharmacology*, 1995, *6*, 311–322.

Di Marzo, V., and Matias, I. Endocannabinoid control of food intake and energy balance. *Nature Neuroscience*, 2005, *8*, 585–589.

Di Tomaso, E., Beltramo, M., and Piomelli, D. Brain cannabinoids in chocolate. *Nature*, 1996, *382*, 677–678.

Diamond, D. M., Park, C. R., Heman, K. L., and Rose, G. M. Exposing rats to a predator impairs spatial working memory in the radial arm water maze. *Hippocampus*, 1999, *9*, 542–552.

Diamond, M., and Sigmundson, H. K. Sex reassignment ar birth: Long-term review and clinical implications. *Archives of Pediatric and Adolescent Medicine*, 1997, *151*, 298–304.

Diana, M., Pistis, M., Carboni, S., Gessa, G. L., et al. Profound decrement of mesolimbic dopaminergic neuronal activity during ethanol withdrawal syndrome in rats: Electrophysiological and biochemical evidence. *Proceedings of the National Academy of Sciences, USA*, 1993, *90*, 7966–7969.

Diba, K., and Buzsáki, G. Forward and reverse hippocampal place-cell sequences during ripples. *Nature Neuroscience*, 2007, *10*, 1241–1242.

DiFiglia, M., Sena-Esteves, M., Chase, K., Sapp, E., et al. Therapeutic silencing of mutant huntingtin with siRNA attenuates striatal and cortical neuropathology and behavioral deficits. *Proceedings of the National Academy of Sciences, USA*, 2007, *104*, 17204–17209.

Dijk, D. J., Boulos, Z., Eastman, C. I., Lewy, A. J., et al. Light treatment for sleep disorders: Consensus report. 2: Basic properties of circadian physiology and sleep regulation. *Journal of Biological Rhythms*, 1995, *10*, 113–125.

Dixon, A. K. The effect of olfactory stimuli upon the social behaviour of laboratory mice *(Mus musculus L)*. Doctoral dissertation, Birmingham University, Birmingham, England, 1973.

Dixon, A. K., and Mackintosh, J. H. Effects of female urine upon the social behaviour of adult male mice. *Animal Behaviour*, 1971, *19*, 138–140.

Doetsch, F., and Hen, R. Young and excitable: The function of new neurons in the adult mammalian brain. *Current Opinion in Neuroscience*, 2005, *15*, 121–128.

Doidge, N. *The brain that changes itself.* New York: Penguin, 2007.

Dolan, R. P., and Schiller, P. H. Evidence for only depolarizing rod bipolar cells in the primate retina. *Visual Neuroscience*, 1989, *2*, 421–424.

Döme, P., Kapitány, B., Ignits, G., and Rihmer, Z. Season of birth is significantly associated with the risk of completed suicide. *Biological Psychiatry*, 2010, *68*, 148–155.

Domschke, K., Deckert, J., O'Donovan, M. C., and Glatt, S. J. Meta-analysis of COMT val158met in panic disorder: Ethnic heterogeneity and gender specificity. *American Journal of Medical Genetics Part B: Neuropsychiatric Genetics*, 2007, *144*(5), 667–673.

Dominguez, J. M., Gil, M., and Hull, E. M. Preoptic glutamate facilitates male sexual behavior. *Journal of Neuroscience*, 2006, *26*, 1699–1703.

Donny, E. C., Caggiula, A. R., Knopf, S., and Brown, C. Nicotine self-administration in rats. *Psychopharmacology*, 1995, *122*, 390–394.

Dorries, K. M., Adkins, R. E., and Halpern, B. P. Sensitivity and behavioral responses to the pheromone androsteneone are not mediated by the vomeronasal organ in domestic pigs. *Brain, Behavior, and Evolution*, 1997, *49*, 53–62.

Doty, R. L. Olfaction. *Annual Review of Psychology*, 2001, *52*, 423–452.

Dougherty, D. D., Baie, L., Gosgrove, G. R., Cassem, E. H., et al. Prospective long-term follow-up of 44 patients who received cingulotomy for treatment-refractory obsessive-compulsive disorder. *American Journal of Psychiatry*, 2002, *159*, 269–275.

Douglass, J., McKinzie, A. A., and Couceyro, P. PCR differential display identifies a rat brain mRNA that is transcriptionally regulated by cocaine and amphetamine. *Journal of Neuroscience*, 1995, *15*, 2471–2481.

Downing, P. E., Chan, A. Y., Peelen, M. V., Dodds, C. M., et al., Domain specificity in visual cortex. *Cerebral cortex*, 2005, *16*(10), 1453–1461.

Downing, P. E., Jiang, Y., Shuman, M., and Kanwisher, N. A cortical area selective for visual processing of the human body. *Science*, 2001, *293*, 2470–2473.

Drake, C. L., Roehrs, T., Richardson, G., Walsh, J. K., et al. Shift work sleep disorder: Prevalence and consequences beyond that of symptomatic day workers. *Sleep*, 2004, *27*, 1453–1462.

Drayna, D., Manichaikul, A., de Lange, M., Snieder, H., et al. Genetic correlates of musical pitch recognition in humans. *Science*, 2001, *291*, 1969–1972.

Dringenberg, H. C., Hargreaves, E. L., Baker, G. B., Cooley, R. K., et al. *p*-Chlorophenylalanine-induced serotonin depletion: reduction in exploratory locomotion but no obvious sensory-motor deficits. *Behavioural Brain Research*, 1995, *68*(2), 229–237.

Dronkers, N. F. A new brain region for coordinating speech articulation. *Nature*, 1996, *384*, 159–161.

Dube, M. G., Kalra, S. P., and Kalra, P. S. Food intake elicited by central administration of orexins/hypocretins: Identification of hypothalamic sites of action. *Brain Research*, 1999, *842*, 473–477.

Duchenne, G.-B. *The mechanism of human facial expression.* Translated by R. A. Cuthbertson. Cambridge, England: Cambridge University Press, 1990. (Original work published 1862.)

Duke, A. A., Bègue, L., Bell, R., and Eisenlohr-Moul, T. Revisiting the serotonin–aggression relation in humans: A meta-analysis. *Psychology Bulletin*, 2013, *139*(5), 1148–1172.

Dudek, S. M., and Bear, M. F. Homosynaptic long-term depression in area CA1 of hippocampus and effects of N-methyl-D-aspartate receptor blockade. *Proceedings of the National Academy of Sciences, USA*, 1992, 89, 4363–4367.

Dukelow, S. P., DeSouza, J. F., Culham, J. C., van den Berg, A. V., et al. Distinguishing subregions of the human MT+ complex using visual fields and pursuit eye movements. *Journal of Neurophysiology*, 2001, *86*, 1991–2000.

Dulac, C., and Axel, R. A novel family of genes encoding putative pheromone receptors in mammals. *Cell*, 1995, *83*, 195–206.

Dunlosky, J., Rawson, K. A., Marsh, E. J., Nathan, M. J., et al. Improving students' learning with effective learning techniques promising directions from cognitive and educational psychology. *Psychological Science in the Public Interest*, 2013, *14*(1), 4–58.

Dunn, A. L., Trivedi, M. H., Kampert, J. B., Clark, C. G., et al. Exercise treatment for depression: Efficacy and dose response. *American Journal of Preventive Medicine*, 2005, *28*, 1–8.

Dunn, M. Commentary on Lundholm et al. (2015): What came first, the steroids or the violence? *Addiction*, 2015, *110*(1), 109–110.

Durie, D. J. Sleep in animals. In *Psychopharmacology of sleep*, edited by D. Wheatley. New York: Raven Press, 1981.

Durston, S., Tottenham, N. T., Thomas, K. M., Davidson, M. C., et al. Differential patterns of striatal activation in young children with and without ADHD. *Biological Psychiatry*, 2003, *53*, 871–878.

Dutta, T. M., Josiah, A. F., Cronin, C. A., Wittenberg, G. F., et al. Altered taste and stroke: A case report and literature review. *Topics in Stroke Rehabilitation*, 2013, *20*(1), 78–86.

Duvarci, S., Popa, D., and Paré, D. Central amygdala activity during fear conditioning. *Journal of Neuroscience*, 2011, *31*, 289–294.

Dwyer, C. *Lancet* retracts MMR paper after GMC finds Andrew Wakefield guilty of dishonesty. *British Medical Journal*, 2010, *340*, c696.

Dykes, R. W. Parallel processing of somatosensory information: A theory. *Brain Research Reviews*, 1983, *6*, 47–115.

Eaton, W. W., Mortensen, P. B., and Frydenberg, M. Obstetric factors, urbanization and psychosis. *Schizophrenia Research*, 2000, *43*, 117–123.

Ebisawa, T., Uchiyama, M., Kajimura, N., Mishima, K., et al. Association of structural polymorphisms in the human period3 gene with delayed sleep phase syndrome. *EMBRO Reports*, 2001, *2*, 342–346.

Eden, G. F., and Zeffiro, T. A. Neural systems affected in developmental dyslexia revealed by functional neuroimaging. *Neuron*, 1998, *21*, 279–282.

Edwards, D. P., Purpura, K. P., and Kaplan, E. Contrast sensitivity and spatial-frequency response of primate cortical neurons in and around the cytochrome oxidase blobs. *Vision Research*, 1995, *35*, 1501–1523.

Egan, G., Silk, T., Zamarripa, F., Williams, J., et al. Neural correlates of the emergence of consciousness of thirst. *Proceedings of the National Academy of Sciences, USA*, 2003, *100*, 15241–15246.

Ehrsson, H. H., Spence, C., and Passingham, R. E. That's my hand! Activity in premotor cortex reflects feeling of ownership of a limb. *Science*, 2004, *305*, 875–877.

Ehrsson, H. H., Wiech, K., Weiskopf, N., Dolan, R. J., and Passingham, R. E. Threatening a rubber hand that you feel is yours elicits a cortical anxiety response. *Proceedings of the National Academy of Sciences, USA*, 2007, *104*, 9828–9833.

Eichenbaum, H., Otto, T., and Cohen, N. J. The hippocampus: What does it do? *Behavioral and Neural Biology*, 1992, *57*, 2–36.

Eichenbaum, H., Stewart, C., and Morris, R. G. M. Hippocampal representation in spatial learning. *Journal of Neuroscience*, 1990, *10*, 331–339.

Eippert, F., Bingel, U., Schoell, E. D., Yacubian, J., et al. Activation of the opioidergic descending pain control system underlies placebo analgesia. *Neuron*, 2009, *63*, 533–543.

Eisele, Y. S., Bolmont, T., Heikenwalder, M., Langer, F., et al. Induction of cerebral β-amyloidosis: Intracerebral versus systemic Aβ inoculation. *Proceedings of the National Academy of Sciences, USA*, 2009, *106*, 12926–12931.

Ekman, P. *The face of man: Expressions of universal emotions in a New Guinea village*. New York: Garland STPM Press, 1980.

Ekman, P. Facial expressions of emotion: An old controversy and new findings. *Philosophical Transactions of the Royal Society of London B*, 1992, *335*, 63–69.

Ekman, P., and Davidson, R. J. Voluntary smiling changes regional brain activity. *Psychological Science*, 1993, *4*, 342–345.

Ekman, P., and Friesen, W. V. Constants across cultures in the face and emotion. *Journal of Personality and Social Psychology*, 1971, *17*, 124–129.

Ekman, P., Levenson, R. W., and Friesen, W. V. Autonomic nervous system activity distinguished between emotions. *Science*, 1983, *221*, 1208–1210.

El Mansari, M., and Blier, P. In vivo electrophysiological characterization of 5-HT receptors in the guinea pig head of caudate nucleus and orbitofrontal cortex. *Neuropharmacology*, 1997, *36*, 577–588.

El Mansari, M., Sakai, K., and Jouvet, M. Unitary characteristics of presumptive cholinergic tegmental neurons during the sleep-waking cycle in freely moving cats. *Experimental Brain Research*, 1989, *76*, 519–529.

Elbert, T., Flor, H., Birbaumer, N., Knecht, S., et al. Extensive reorganization of the somatosensory cortex in adult humans after nervous system injury. *Neuroreport*, 1994, *5*, 2593–2507.

Elbert, T., Pantev, C., Wienbruch, C., Rockstroh, B., et al. Increased cortical representation of the fingers of the left hand in string players. *Science*, 1995, *270*, 305–307.

Elias, C. F., Lee, C., Kelly, J., Aschkenasi, C., et al. Leptin activates hypothalamic CART neurons projecting to the spinal cord. *Neuron*, 1998a, *21*, 1375–1385.

Elias, C. F., Saper, C. B., Maratos-Flier, E., Tritos, N. A., et al. Chemically defined projections linking the mediobasal hypothalamus and the lateral hypothalamic area. *Journal of Comparative Neurology*, 1998b, *402*, 442–459.

Elias, M. Serum cortisol, testosterone and testosterone-binding globulin responses to competitive fighting in human males. *Aggressive Behavior*, 1981, *7*, 215–224.

Elmquist, J. K., Elias, C. F., and Saper, C. B. From lesions to leptin: Hypothalamic control of food intake and body weight. *Neuron*, 1999, *22*, 221–232.

Elsworth, J. D., Jentsch, J. D., Morrow, B. A., Redmond, D. E., et al. Clozapine normalizes prefrontal cortex dopamine transmission in monkeys subchronically exposed to phencyclidine. *Neuropsychopharmacology*, 2008, *33*, 491–496.

Endoh, M., Maiese, K., and Wagner, J. A. Expression of the neural form of nitric oxide synthase by CA1 hippocampal neurons and other central nervous system neurons. *Neuroscience*, 1994, *63*, 679–689.

Enggasser, J. L., and de Wit, H. Haloperidol reduces stimulant and reinforcing effects of ethanol in social drinkers. *Alcoholism: Clinical and Experimental Research*, 2001, *25*, 1448–1456.

Enticott, P. G., Fitzgibbon, B. M., Kennedy, H. A., Arnold, et al. A double-blind, randomized trial of deep repetitive transcranial magnetic stimulation (rTMS) for autism spectrum disorder. *Brain Stimulation*, 2014, *7*(2), 206–211.

Ernst, M., Zametkin, A. J., Matochik, J. A., Jons, P. H., et al. DOPA decarboxylase activity in attention deficit hyperactivity disorder adults: A [fluorine^{18}]flurodopa positron emission tomographic study. *Journal of Neuroscience*, 1998, *18*, 5901–5907.

Ernulf, K. E., Innala, S. M., and Whitam, F. L. Biological explanation, psychological explanation, and tolerance of homosexuals: A cross-national analysis of beliefs and attitudes. *Psychological Reports*, 1989, *248*, 183–188.

Ersche, K. D., Barnes, A., Jones, P. S., Morein-Zamir, S., et al. Abnormal structure of frontostriatal brain systems is associated with aspects of impulsivity and compulsivity in cocaine dependence. *Brain*, 2011, *134*, 2013–2024.

Ertelt, D., Small, S., Solodkin, A., Dettmers, C., et al. Action observation has a positive impact on rehabilitation of motor deficits after stroke. *NeuroImage*, 2007, *36*, T164–T173.

Eslinger, P. J., and Damasio, A. R. Severe disturbance of higher cognition after bilateral frontal lobe ablation: Patient EVR. *Neurology*, 1985, *35*, 1731–1741.

Esselink, R. A., de Bie, R. M., de Haan, R. J., Lenders, W. P. M., et al. Long-term superiority of subthalamic nucleus stimulation over pallidotomy in Parkinson's disease. *Neurology*, 2009, *73*, 151–153.

Everson, C. A., and Wehr, T. A. Nutritional and metabolic adaptations to prolonged sleep deprivation in the rat. *American Journal of Physiology*, 1993, *264*, R376–R387.

Fadiman, A. *The spirit catches you and you fall down*. New York: Farrar, Straus, and Giroux; 1997.

Farber, N. B., Wozniak, D. F., Price, M. T., Labruyere, J., et al. Age-specific neurotoxicity in the rat associated with NMDA receptor blockade: Potential relevance to schizophrenia? *Biological Psychiatry*, 1995, *38*, 788–796.

Farina, C., Weber, M. S., Meinl, E., Wekerle, H., et al. Glatiramer acetate in multiple sclerosis: Update on potential mechanisms of action. *Lancet Neurology*, 2005, *4*, 567–575.

Farlow, M., Murrell, J., Ghetti, B., Unverzagt, F., et al. Clinical characteristics in a kindred with early-onset Alzheimers disease and their linkage to a G→T change at position 2149 of amyloid precursor protein gene. *Neurology*, 1994, *44*, 105–111.

Farooqi, I. S., and O'Rahilly, S. Monogenic obesity in humans. *Annual Review of Medicine*, 2005, *56*, 443–458.

Farrell, M. J., Egan, G. F., Zamarripa, F., Shade, R., et al. Unique, common, and interacting cortical correlates of thirst and pain. *Proceedings of the National Academy of Sciences, USA*, 2006, *103*, 2416–2421.

Farroni, T., Johnson, M. H., Menon, E., Zulian, L., et al. Newborns' preference for face-relevant stimuli: Effects of contrast polarity. *Proceedings of the National Academy of Sciences, USA*, 2005, *102*, 17245–17250.

Feder, H. H. Estrous cyclicity in mammals. In *Neuroendocrinology of reproduction*, edited by N. T. Adler. New York: Plenum Press, 1981.

Feinle, C., Grundy, D., and Read, N. W. Effects of duodenal nutrients on sensory and motor responses of the human stomach to distension. *American Journal of Physiology*, 1997, *273*, G721–G726.

Feldman, R. P., and Goodrich, J. T. The Edwin Smith Surgical Papyrus. *Child's Nervous System*, 1999, *15*(6-7), 281–284.

Fenoglio, K. A., Chen, Y., and Baram, T. Z. Neuroplasticity of the hypothalamic-pituitary-adrenal axis early in life requires recurrent recruitment of stress-regulation brain regions. *Journal of Neuroscience*, 2006, *26*, 2434–2442.

Fernandez-Ruiz, J., Wang, J., Aigner, T. G., and Mishkin, M. Visual habit formation in monkeys with neurotoxic lesions of the ventrocaudal neostriatum. *Proceedings of the National Academy of Sciences, USA*, 2001, *98*, 4196–4201.

Ferris, C. F., Kulkarni, P., Sullivan, J. M., Harder, J. A., et al. Pup suckling is more rewarding than cocaine: Evidence from functional magnetic resonance imaging and three-dimensional computational analysis. *Journal of Neuroscience*, 2005, *25*, 149–156.

Fettiplace, R., and Hackney, C. M. The sensory and motor roles of auditory hair cells. *Nature Reviews: Neuroscience*, 2006, *7*, 19–29.

Fibiger, H. C. The dopamine hypothesis of schizophrenia and mood disorders: Contradictions and speculations. In *The mesolimbic dopamine system: From motivation to action*, edited by P. Willner and J. Scheel-Krüger. Chichester, England: John Wiley & Sons, 1991.

Field, T., Woodson, R., Greenberg, R., and Cohen, D. Discrimination and imitation of facial expressions in neonates. *Science*, 1982, *218*, 179–181.

Fietz, S. A., Kelava, I., Vogt, J., Wilsch-Bräuninger, M., et al. OSVZ progenitors of human and ferret neocortex are epithelial-like and expand by integrin signaling. *Nature Neuroscience*, 2010, *13*, 690–699.

Fieve, R. R. The clinical effects of lithium treatment. *Trends in Neurosciences*, 1979, *2*, 66–68.

Finger, S. *Origins of neuroscience: A history of explorations into brain function*. New York: Oxford University Press, 1994.

Finger, T. E., Danilova, V., Barrows, J., Bartel, D. L., et al. ATP signaling is crucial for communication from taste buds to gustatory nerves. *Science*, 2005, *310*, 1495–1499.

Firestein, S., Zufall, F., and Shepherd, G. M. Single odor-sensitive channels in olfactory receptor neurons are also gated by cyclic nucleotides. *Journal of Neuroscience*, 1991, *11*, 3565–3572.

Fischer, H., Andersson, J. L. R., Furmark, T., and Fredrikson, M. Brain correlates of an unexpected panic attack: A human positron emission tomographic study. *Neuroscience Letters*, 1998, *251*, 137–140.

Fisher, C., Byrne, J., Edwards, A., and Kahn, E. A psychophysiological study of nightmares. *Journal of the American Psychoanalytic Association*, 1970, *18*, 747–782.

Fisher, C., Gross, J., and Zuch, J. Cycle of penile erection synchronous with dreaming (REM) sleep: Preliminary report. *Archives of General Psychiatry*, 1965, *12*, 29–45.

Fischer, H. *A guide to U.S. military casualty statistics: Operation Inherent Resolve, Operation New Dawn, Operation Iraqi Freedom, and Operation Enduring Freedom*. Washington, DC: Congressional Research Service, August 7, 2015.

Fisher, S. E. Genetic susceptibility to stuttering. *New England Journal of Medicine*, 2010, *362*, 750–752.

Fiske, A. P., and Haslam, N. Is obsessive-compulsive disorder a pathology of the human disposition to perform socially meaningful rituals? Evidence of similar content. *Journal of Nervous and Mental Disease*, 1997, *185*, 211–222.

Fitzgerald, P. Repetitive transcranial magnetic stimulation and electroconvulsive therapy: Complementary or competitive therapeutic options in depression? *Australas Psychiatry*, 2004, *12*, 234–238.

Fitzpatrick, D., Itoh, K., and Diamond, I. T. The laminar organization of the lateral geniculate body and the striate cortex in the squirrel monkey (Saimiri sciureus). *Journal of Neuroscience*, 1983, *3*, 673–702.

Fitzsimons, J. T., & Moore-Gillon, M. J. Drinking and antidiuresis in response to reductions in venous return in the dog: Neural and endocrine mechanisms. *The Journal of physiology*, 1980, *308*(1), 403–416.

Flaum, M., and Andreasen, N. C. Diagnostic criteria for schizophrenia and related disorders: Options for DNS-IV. *Schizophrenia Bulletin*, 1990, *17*, 27–49.

Fleming, A. S., Corter, C., Stallings, J., and Steiner, M. Testosterone and prolactin are associated with emotional responses to infant cries in new fathers. *Hormones and Behavior*, 2002, *542*, 399–413.

Fleming, A. S., and Rosenblatt, J. S. Maternal behavior in the virgin and lactating rat. *Journal of Comparative and Physiological Psychology*, 1974, *86*, 957–972.

Flier, J. S. What's in a name? In search of leptin's physiologic role. *Journal of Clinical Endocrinology and Metabolism*, 1998, *83*, 1407–1413.

Flock, A. Physiological properties of sensory hairs in the ear. In *Psychophysics and physiology of hearing*, edited by E. F. Evans and J. P. Wilson. London: Academic Press, 1977.

Flood, J. F., and Morley, J. E. Increased food intake by neuropeptide Y is due to an increased motivation to eat. *Peptides*, 1991, *12*, 1329–1332.

Flores, R., Hirota, Y., Armstrong, B., Sawa, A., et al. DISC1 regulates synaptic vesicle transport via a lithium-sensitive pathway. *Neuroscience Research*, 2011, *71*, 71–77.

Flynn, F. W., and Grill, H. J. Insulin elicits ingestion in decerebrate rats. *Science*, 1983, *221*, 188–190.

Fogel, S. M., and Smith, C. T. The function of the sleep spindle: A physiological index of intelligence and a mechanism for sleep-dependent memory consolidation. *Neuroscience and Biobehavioral Reviews*, 2011, *35*, 1154–1165.

Fombonne, E. Epidemiology of autistic disorder and other pervasive developmental disorders. *Journal of Clinical Psychiatry*, 2005, *66* (Suppl. 10), 3–8.

Fontana, A., Gast, H., Reigh, W., Recher, M., et al. Narcolepsy: Autoimmunity, effector

T cell activation due to infection, or T cell independent, major histocompatibility complex class II induced neuronal loss? *Brain*, 2010, *133*, 1300–1311.

Forget, B., Pushparaj, A., and Le Foll, B. Granular insular cortex inactivation as a novel therapeutic strategy for nicotine addiction. *Biological Psychiatry*, 2010, *68*, 265–271.

Forno, L. S. Neuropathology of Parkinson's disease. *Journal of Neuropathology and Experimental Neurology*, 1996, *55*, 259–272.

Fort, O., Bassetti, C. L., and Luppi, P. H. Alternating vigilance states: New insights regarding neuronal networks and mechanisms. *European Journal of Neuroscience*, 2009, *29*, 1741–1753.

Foster, D. L., and Nagatani, S. Physiological perspectives on leptin as a regulator of reproduction: Role in timing puberty. *Biology of Reproduction*, 1999, *60*, 205–215.

Foundas, A. L., Bollich, A. M., Feldman, J., Corey, D. M., et al. M. Aberrant auditory processing and atypical planum temporale in developmental stuttering. *Neurology*, 2004, *63*, 1640–1646.

Fowler, C., Lu, Q., Johnson, P. M., Marks, M. J., et al. Habenular α5 nicotinic receptor subunit signaling controls nicotine intake. *Nature*, 2011, *471*, 597–601.

Frankle, W. G., Lombardo, I., New, A. S., Goodman, M., et al. Brain serotonin transporter distribution in subjects with impulsive aggressivity: A positron emission study with [¹¹C]McN 5652. *American Journal of Psychiatry*, 2005, *162*, 915–923.

Franklin, T. R., Acton, P. D., Maldjian, J. A., Gray, J. D., et al. Decreased gray matter concentration in the insular, orbitofrontal, cingulate, and temporal cortices of cocaine patients. *Biological Psychiatry*, 2002, *51*, 134–142.

Freed, C. R. Will embryonic stem cells be a useful source of dopamine neurons for transplant into patients with Parkinson's disease? *Proceedings of the National Academy of Sciences, USA*, 2002, *99*, 1755–1757.

Freedman, M. S., Lucas, R. J., Soni, B., von Schantz, M., et al. Regulation of mammalian circadian behavior by non-rod, non-cone, ocular photoreceptors. *Science*, 1999, *284*, 502–504.

Freedman, R. Psychiatrists' role in the health of the pregnant mother and the risk for schizophrenia in her offspring. *American Journal of Psychiatry*, 2010, *167*, 239–240.

Frendl, A., and Csiba, L. Pharmacological and non-pharmacological recanalization strategies in acute ischemic stroke. *Frontiers in Neurology*, 2011, *2*, 1–11.

Frenette, E. REM sleep behavior disorder. *Medical Clinics of North America*, 2010, *94*, 593–614.

Frey, S. H., Vinton, D., Norlund, R., and Grafton, S. T. Cortical topography of human anterior intraparietal cortex active during visually guided grasping. *Cognitive Brain Research*, 2005, *23*, 397–405.

Frey, U., Krug, M., Reymann, K. G., and Matthies, H. Anisomycin, an inhibitor of protein synthesis, blocks late phases of LTP phenomena in the hippocampal CA1 region in vitro. *Brain Research*, 1988, *452*, 57–65.

Frey, U., and Morris, R. G. Synaptic tagging and long-term potentiation. *Nature*, 1997, *385*, 533–536.

Fridricksson, F., Moss, J., Davis, B., Baylis, G. C., et al. Motor speech perception modulates the cortical language areas. *NeuroImage*, 2008, *41*, 605–613.

Fried, I., Katz, A., McCarthy, G., Sass, K. J., et al. Functional organization of human supplementary motor cortex studied by electrical stimulation. *Journal of Neuroscience*, 1991, *11*, 3656–3666.

Friedman, M. I., and Bruno, J. P. Exchange of water during lactation. *Science*, 1976, *191*, 409–410.

Friedman, M. I., Horn, C. C., and Ji, H. Peripheral signals in the control of feeding behavior. *Chemical Senses*, 2005, *30* (Suppl. 1), i182–i183.

Frisch, R. E. Body fat, menarche, fitness and fertility. In *Adipose tissue and reproduction*, edited by R. E. Frisch. Basel: S. Karger, 1990.

Frith, U., Morton, J., and Leslie, A. M. The cognitive basis of a biological disorder: Autism. *Trends in Neuroscience*, 1991, *14*, 433–438.

Fry, J. M. Treatment modalities for narcolepsy. *Neurology*, 1998, *50*, S43–S48.

Fu, H. J., Liu, B., Frost, J. L., and Lemere, C. A. Amyloid-beta immunotherapy for Alzheimer's disease. *CNS and Neurological Disorders: Drug Targets*, 2010, *9*, 197–206.

Fudala, P. J., Bridge, T. P., Herbert, S., Williford, W. O., et al. Office-based treatment of opiate addiction with a sublingual-tablet formulation of buprenorphine and naloxone. *New England Journal of Medicine*, 2003, *349*, 949–958.

Fukuwatari, T., Shibata, K., Igushi, K., Saeki, T., et al. Role of gustation in the recognition of oleate and triolein in anomic rats. *Physiology and Behavior*, 2003, *78*, 579–583.

Fullerton, C. S., Ursano, R. J., Epstein, R. S., Crowley, B., et al. Gender differences in posttraumatic stress disorder after motor vehicle accidents. *American Journal of Psychiatry*, 2001, *158*, 1485–1491.

Fulton, J. F. *Functional Localization in Relation to Frontal Lobotomy*. New York: Oxford University Press, 1949.

Funkiewiez, A., Ardouin, C., Caputo, E., Krack, P., et al. Long term effects of bilateral subthalamic nucleus stimulation on cognitive function, mood, and behaviour in Parkinson's disease. *Journal of Neurology, Neurosurgery, and Psychiatry*, 2004, *75*, 834–839.

Gagliardo, A., Ioalé, P., and Bingman, V. P. Homing in pigeons: The role of the hippocampal formation in the representation of landmarks used for navigation. *Journal of Neuroscience*, 1999, *19*, 311–315.

Gaillard, R., Naccache, L., Pinel, P., Clémenceau, S., et al. Direct intracranial, fMRI, and lesion evidence for the causal role of left inferotemporal cortex in reading. *Neuron*, 2006, *50*, 191–204.

Gajdusek, D. C. Unconventional viruses and the origin and disappearance of kuru. *Science*, 1977, *197*, 943–960.

Galen. *De usu partium*. Translated by M. T. May. Ithaca, N.Y.: Cornell University Press, 1968.

Gallassi, R., Morreale, A., Montagna, P., Cortelli, P., et al. Fatal familial insomnia: Behavioral and cognitive features. *Neurology*, 1996, *46*, 935–939.

Gallese, V., Fadiga, L., Fogassi, L., and Rizzolatti, G. Action recognition in the premotor cortex. *Brain*, 1996, *119*, 593–609.

Gangestad, S. W., and Thornhill, R. Human oestrus. *Proceedings of the Royal Society B*, 2008, *275*, 991–1000.

Garavan, H., and Stout, J. C. Neurocognitive insights into substance abuse. *Trends in Cognitive Sciences*, 2005, *9*, 195–201.

Garcia-Falgueras, A., and Swaab, D. F. A sex difference in the hypothalamic uncinate nucleus: Relationship to gender identity. *Brain*, 2008, *131*, 3132–3146.

Garcia-Velasco, J., and Mondragon, M. The incidence of the vomeronasal organ in 1000 human subjects and its possible clinical significance. *Journal of Steroid Biochemistry and Molecular Biology*, 1991, *39*, 561–563.

Gardner, H., Brownell, H. H., Wapner, W., and Michelow, D. Missing the point: The role of the right hemisphere in the processing of complex linguistic materials. In *Cognitive processing in the right hemisphere*, edited by E. Pericman. New York: Academic Press, 1983.

Gariano, R. F., and Groves, P. M. Burst firing induced in midbrain dopamine neurons by stimulation of the medial prefrontal and anterior cingulate cortices. *Brain Research*, 1988, *462*, 194–198.

Garrido, L., Eisner, F., McGettigan, C., Stewart, L., et al. Developmental phonagnosia: A selective deficit of vocal identity recognition. *Neuropsychology*, 2009, *47*, 123–131.

Gastfriend, D. T. Intramuscular extended-release naltrexone: current evidence. *Annals of the New York Academy of Sciences*, 2011, *1216*, 144–166.

Gauthier, I., Skudlarski, P., Gore, J. C., and Anderson, A. W. Expertise for cars and birds recruits brain areas involved in face recognition. *Nature Neuroscience*, 2000, *3*, 191–197.

Gauthier, I., Tarr, M. J., Anderson, A. W., Skudlarski, P., et al. Activation of the middle fusiform "face area" increases with expertise in recognizing novel objects. *Nature Neuroscience*, 1999, *2*, 568–573.

Gazzaniga, M. Forty-five years of split-brain research and still going strong. *Nature Reviews: Neuroscience*, 2005, *6*, 653–659.

Gazzaniga, M. S., and LeDoux, J. E. *The Integrated Mind*. New York: Plenum Press, 1978.

Geary, N. Cocaine: Animal research studies. In *Cocaine abuse: New directions in treatment and research*, edited by H. I. Spitz and J. S. Rosecan. New York: Brunner-Mazel, 1987.

Gentilucci, M. Grasp observation influences speech production. *European Journal of Neuroscience*, 2003, *17*, 179–184.

George, M. S., Parekh, P. I., Rosinsky, N., Ketter, T. A., et al. Understanding emotional prosody activates right hemisphere regions. *Archives of Neurology*, 1996, *53*, 665–670.

Gerashchenko, D., Blanco-Centurion, C., Greco, M. A., and Shiromani, P. J. Effects of lateral hypothalamic lesion with the neurotoxin hypocretin-2-saporin on sleep in Long-Evans rats. *Neuroscience*, 2003, *116*, 223–235.

Gerashchenko, D., Chou, T. C., Blanco-Centurion, C. A., Saper, C. B., and et al. Effects of lesions of the histaminergic tuberomammillary nucleus on spontaneous sleep in rats. *Sleep*, 2004, *27*, 1275–1281.

Gerashchenko, D., Kohls, M. D., Greco, M., Waleh, N. S., et al. Hypocretin-2-saporin lesions of the lateral hypothalamus produce narcoleptic-like sleep behavior in the rat. *Journal of Neuroscience*, 2001, *21*, 7273–7283.

Gerbino, L., Oleshansky, M., and Gershon, S. Clinical use and mode of action of lithium. In *Psychopharmacology: A generation of progress*, edited by M. A. Lipton, A. DiMascio, and K. F. Killam. New York: Raven Press, 1978.

Gerfen, C. R. Molecular effects of dopamine on striatal-projection pathways. *Trends in Neuroscience*, 2000, *23*(Suppl.), S64–S70.

Gerhand, S. Routes to reading: A report of a non-semantic reader with equivalent performance on regular and exception words. *Neuropsychologia*, 2001, *39*, 1473–1484.

Gerloff, C., Corwell, B., Chen, R., Hallett, M., et al. Stimulation over the human supplementary motor area interferes with the organization of future elements in complex motor sequences. *Brain*, 1997, *120*, 1587–1602.

Gershon, E. S., Bunney, W. E., Leckman, J., Van Eerdewegh, M., et al. The inheritance of affective disorders: A review of data and hypotheses. *Behavior Genetics*, 1976, *6*, 227–261.

Geschwind, N., Quadfasel, F. A., and Segarra, J. M. Isolation of the speech area. *Neuropsychologia*, 1968, *6*, 327–340.

Gessa, G. L., Muntoni, F., Collu, M., Vargiu, L., et al. Low doses of ethanol activate dopaminergic neurons in the ventral tegmental area. *Brain Research*, 1985, *348*, 201–204.

Getchell, T. V., Kwong, K., Saunders, C. P., Stromberg, A. J., et al. Leptin regulates olfactory-mediated behavior in *ob/ob* mice. *Physiology and Behavior*, 2006, *87*, 848–856.

Getz, L. L., and Carter, C. S. Prairie-vole partnerships. *American Scientist*, 1996, *84*, 55–62.

Ghilardi, J. R., Röhrich, H., Lindsay, T. H., Sevcik, M. A., et al. Selective blockade of the capsaicin receptor TRPV1 attenuates bone cancer pain. *Journal of Neuroscience*, 2005, *25*, 3126–3131.

Giedd, J. N., Rapoport, J. L., Garvey, M. A., Perlmutter, S., et al. MRI assessment of children with obsessive-compulsive disorder or tics associated with streptococcal infection. *American Journal of Psychiatry*, 2000, *157*, 281–283.

Giedd, J. N., Rapoport, J. L., Kruesi, M. J. P., Parker, C., et al. Sydenham's chorea: Magnetic resonance imaging of the basal ganglia. *Neurology*, 1995, *45*, 2199–2202.

Gilbertson, M. W., Shenton, M. E., Ciszewski, A., Kasai, K., et al. Smaller hippocampal volume predicts pathologic vulnerability to psychological trauma. *Nature Neuroscience*, 2002, *5*, 1242–1247.

Gillespie, P. G. Molecular machinery of auditory and vestibular transduction. *Current Opinion in Neurobiology*, 1995, *5*, 449–455.

Gillette, M. U., and McArthur, A. J. Circadian actions of melatonin at the suprachiasmatic nucleus. *Behavioural Brain Research*, 1995, *73*, 135–139.

Girardeau, G., Benchenane, K., Wiener, S. I., et al. Selective suppression of hippocampal ripples impairs spatial memory. *Nature Neuroscience*, 2009, *12*, 1222–1223.

Giussani, C., Roux, F. E., Lubrano, V., Gaini, S. M., et al. Review of language organisation in bilingual patients: What can we learn from direct brain mapping? *Acta Neurochirurgica*, 2007, *149*(11), 1109–1116.

Givens, B., and McMahon, K. Ethanol suppresses the induction of long-term potentiation in vivo. *Brain Research*, 1995, *688*, 27–33.

Glaser, R., Rice, J., Sheridan, J., Post, A., et al. Stress-related immune suppression: Health implications. *Brain, Behavior, and Immunity*, 1987, *1*, 7–20.

Glaser, R., Sheridan, J., Malarkey, W. B., MacCallum, R. C., et al. Chronic stress modulates the immune response to a pneumococcal pneumonia vaccine. *Psychosomatic Medicine*, 2000, *62*, 804–807.

Glaum, S. R., Hara, M., Bindokas, V. P., Lee, C. C., et al. Leptin, the obese gene product, rapidly modulates synaptic transmission in the hypothalamus. *Molecular Pharmacology*, 1996, *50*, 230–235.

Gloor, P., Olivier, A., Quesney, L. F., Andermann, F., et al. The role of the limbic system in experiential phenomena of temporal lobe epilepsy. *Annals of Neurology*, 1982, *12*, 129–144.

Goate, A. M. Monogenetic determinants of Alzheimer's disease: APP mutations. *Cellular and Molecular Life Sciences*, 1998, *54*, 897–901.

Godden, D. R., & Baddeley, A. D. Context-dependent memory in two natural environments: On land and underwater. *British Journal of psychology*, 1975, *66*(3), 325–331.

Godfrey, P. A., Malnic, B., and Buck, L. The mouse olfactory receptor gene family. *Proceedings of the National Academy of Sciences, USA*, 2004, *101*, 2156–2161.

Goeders, N. E., Lane, J. D., and Smith, J. E. Self-administration of methionine enkephalin into the nucleus accumbens. *Pharmacology, Biochemistry, and Behavior*, 1984, *20*, 451–455.

Goedert, M. Alpha-synuclein and neurodegenerative diseases. *Nature Review Neuroscience*, 2001, *2*, 492–501.

Goedert, M., and Spillantini, M. G. Tau mutations in fronto-temporal dementia FTDP-17 and their relevance for Alzheimer's disease. *Biochimica et Biophysica Acta*, 2000, *1502*, 110–121.

Goel, V., and Dolan, R. J. The functional anatomy of humor: Segregating cognitive and affective components. *Nature Neuroscience*, 2001, *4*, 237–238.

Goel, V., and Dolan, R. J. Social regulation of affective experience of humor. *Journal of Cognitive Neuroscience*, 2007, *19*, 1574–1580.

Golarai, G., Ghahremani, D. G., Whitfield-Gabrieli, S., Reiss, A., et al. Differential development of high-level visual cortex correlated with category-specific recognition memory. *Nature Neuroscience*, 2007, *10*, 512–522.

Golarai, G., Hong, S., Haas, B. W., Galaburda, A. M., et al. The fusiform face area is enlarged in Williams syndrome. *Journal of Neuroscience*, 2010, *30*, 6700–3712.

Golby, A. J., Gabrieli, J. D., Chiao, J. Y., and Eberhardt, J. L. Differential responses in the fusiform region to same-race and other-race faces. *Nature Neuroscience*, 2001, *4*, 845–850.

Goldberg, R. F., Perfetti, C. A., and Schneider, W. Perceptual knowledge retrieval activates sensory brain regions. *Journal of Neuroscience*, 2006, *26*, 4917–4921.

Golden, N. H., Ashtari, M., Kohn, M. R., Patel, M., et al. Reversibility of cerebral ventricular enlargement in anorexia nervosa, demonstrated by quantitative magnetic resonance imaging. *Journal of Pediatrics*, 1996, *128*(2), 296–301.

Goldey, K. L., and van Anders, S. M. Sexy thoughts: Effects of sexual cognitions on testosterone, cortisol, and arousal in women. *Hormones and Behavior*, 2011, *59*(5), 754–764.

Goldman, D., Oroszi, G., and Ducci, F. The genetics of addictions: Uncovering the genes. *Nature Reviews Genetics*, 2005, *6*, 521–532.

Goldstein, J. M., Seidman, L. J., Horton, N. J., Makris, N., et al. Normal sexual dimorphism of the adult human brain assessed by *in vivo* magnetic resonance imaging. *Cerebral Cortex*, 2001, *11*, 490–497.

Golgi, C. *Opera omnia, vols. I and II*. Milan: Hoepli, 1903.

Golombek, D. A., and Rosenstein, R. E. Physiology of circadian entrainment. *Physiological Reviews*, 2010, *90*, 1063–1102.

González. M. M., and Aston-Jones, G. Circadian regulation of arousal: Role of the noradrenergic locus coeruleus system and light exposure. *Sleep*, 2006, *29*, 1327–1336.

González, M. M., and Aston-Jones, G. Light deprivation damages monoamine neurons and produces a depressive behavioral phenotype in rats. *Proceedings of the National Academy of Sciences, USA*, 2008, *105*, 4898–4903.

Goodale, M. A., Meenan, J. P., Bülthoff, H. H., Nicolle, D. A., et al. Separate neural pathways for the visual analysis of object shape in perception and prehension. *Current Biology*, 1994, *4*, 604–610.

Goodale, M. A., and Milner, A. D. Separate visual pathways for perception and action. *Trends in Neuroscience*, 1992, *15*, 20–25.

Goodale, M. A., and Westwood, D. A. An evolving view of duplex vision: Separate but interacting cortical pathways for perception and action. *Current Opinion in Neurobiology*, 2004, *14*, 203–211.

Goodglass, H., and Kaplan, E. *Assessment of Aphasia and Related Disorders*. Philadelphia: Lea & Febiger, 1972.

Goodman, W. K., Foote, K. D., Greenberg, B. D., Ricciuti, N., et al. Deep brain stimulation for intractable obsessive compulsive disorder: Pilot study using a blinded, staggered-onset design. *Biological Psychiatry*, 2010, *67*, 535–542.

Gooley, J. J., Lu, J., Fischer, D., and Saper, C. B. A broad role for melanopsin in nonvisual photoreception. *Journal of Neuroscience*, 2003, *23*, 7093–7106.

Gooren, L. The biology of human psychosexual differentiation. *Hormones and Behavior*, 2006, *50*, 589–601.

Gordon, H. W., and Sperry, R. Lateralization of olfactory perception in the surgically separated hemispheres in man. *Neuropsychologia*, 1969, *7*, 111–120.

Gordon, I., Vander Wyk, B. C., Bennett, R. H., Cordeaux, C., et al. Oxytocin enhances brain function in children with autism.

Proceedings of the National Academy of Sciences, 2013, *110*(52), 20953–20958.

Gordon, I., Zagoory-Sharon, O., Leckman, J. F., and Feldman, R. Prolactin, oxytocin, and the development of paternal behavior across the first six months of fatherhood. *Hormones and Behavior*, 2010, *58*, 513–518.

Gosselin, N., Peretz, I., Noulhiane, M., Hasboun, D., et al. Impaired recognition of scary music following unilateral temporal lobe excision. *Brain*, 2005, *128*, 628–640.

Gottesman, I. I., and Bertelsen, A. Confirming unexpressed genotypes for schizophrenia. *Archives of General Psychiatry*, 1989, *46*, 867–872.

Gottesman, I. I., and Shields, J. *Schizophrenia: The epigenetic puzzle*. New York: Cambridge University Press, 1982.

Gottfried, J. A., Winston, J. S., and Dolan, R. J. Dissociable codes of odor quality and odorant structure in human piriform cortex. *Neurons*, 2006, *49*, 467–479.

Gotti, C., Guiducci, S., Tedesco, V., Corbioli, S., et al. Nicotinic acetylcholine receptors in the mesolimbic pathway: primary role of ventral tegmental area alpha6beta2* receptors in mediating systemic nicotine effects on dopamine release, locomotion, and reinforcement. *Journal of Neuroscience*, 2010, *30*, 5311–5325.

Gould, E., Beylin, A., Tanapat, P., Reeves, A., et al. Learning enhances adult neurogenesis in the hippocampal formation. *Nature Neuroscience*, 1999, *2*, 260–265.

Gouras, P. Identification of cone mechanisms in monkey ganglion cells. *Journal of Physiology*, 1968, *199*, 533–538.

Graber, G. C., and Kristal, M. B. Uterine distention facilitates the onset of maternal behavior in pseudopregnant but not in cycling rats. *Physiology and Behavior*, 1977, *19*, 133–137.

Gradinaru, V., Mogri, M., Thompson, Henderson, J. M., et al. Optical deconstruction of parkinsonian neural circuitry. *Science*, 2009, *324*, 354–359.

Grados, M. A., Riddle, M. A., Samuels, J. F., Liang, K.-Y., et al. The familial phenotype of obsessive-compulsive disorder in relation to tic disorders: The Hopkins OCD Family Study. *Biological Psychiatry*, 2001, *50*, 559–565.

Grafton, S. T. Contributions of functional imaging to understanding parkinsonian symptoms. *Current Opinion in Neurobiology*, 2004, *14*, 715–719.

Graybiel, A. M. Basal ganglia: New therapeutic approaches to Parkinson's disease. *Current Biology*, 1996, *6*, 368–371.

Graziano, M. S. A., and Aflalo, T. N. Mapping behavioral repertoire onto the cortex. *Neuron*, 2007, *56*, 239–251.

Gréco, B., Edwards, D. A., Zumpe, D., and Clancy, A. N. Androgen receptor and mating-induced Fos immunoreactivity are

co-localized in limbic and midbrain neurons that project to the male rat medial preoptic area. *Brain Research*, 1998, *781*, 15–24.

Greenblatt, D. J., Shader, R. I., Divoll, M., and Harmatz, J. S. Benzodiazepines: A summary of pharmacokinetic properties. *British Journal of Clinical Pharmacology*, 1981, *11* (S1), 11S–16S.

Greene, J. D., Sommerville, R. B., Nystrom, L. E., Darley, J. M., et al. An fMRI investigation of emotional engagement in moral judgment. *Science*, 2001, *293*, 2105–2108.

Greenfield, S. F., Back, S. E., Lawson, K., and Brady, K. T. Substance abuse in women. *The Psychiatric Clinics of North America*, 2010, *33*(2), 339–355.

Gregg, T. R., and Siegel, A. Brain structures and neurotransmitters regulating aggression in cats: Implications for human aggression. *Progress in Neuro-Psychopharmacology and Biological Psychiatry*, 2001, *25*, 91–240.

Grelotti, D. J., Gauthier, I., and Schultz, R. T. Social interest and the development of cortical face specialization: What autism teaches us about face processing. *Developmental Psychobiology*, 2002, *40*, 213–225.

Grelotti, D. J., Klin, A. J., Gauthier, I., Skudlarski, P., et al. fMRI activation of the fusiform gyrus and amygdala to cartoon characters but not to faces in a boy with autism. *Neuropsychologia*, 2005, *43*, 373–385.

Grill, H. J., and Kaplan, J. M. Caudal brainstem participates in the distributed neural control of feeding. In *Handbook of behavioral neurobiology, vol. 10: Neurobiology of food and fluid intake*, edited by E. Stricker. New York: Plenum Press, 1990.

Grill-Spector, K., Knouf, N., and Kanwisher, N. The fusiform face area subserves face perception, not generic within-category identification. *Nature Neuroscience*, 2004, *7*, 555–561.

Grill-Spector, K., and Malach, R. The human visual cortex. *Annual Review of Neuroscience*, 2004, *27*, 649–677.

Gropper, S. S., Simmons, K. P., Connell, L. J., and Ulrich, P. V. Changes in body weight, composition, and shape: A 4-year study of college students. *Applied Physiology, Nutrition, and Metabolism*, 2012, *37*(6), 1118–1123.

Gross, C. G. Visual functions of inferotemporal cortex. In *Handbook of sensory physiology, vol. 7: Central processing of visual information*, edited by R. Jung. Berlin: Springer-Verlag, 1973.

Grossman, E. D., Battelli, L., and Pascual-Leone, A. Repetitive TMS over posterior STS disrupts perception of biological motion. *Vision Research*, 2005, *45*, 2847–2853.

Grossman, E. D., and Blake, R. Brain activity evoked by inverted and imagined biological motion. *Vision Research*, 2001, *41*, 1475–1482.

Grossman, E. D., Donnelly, M., Price, R., Pickens, D., et al. Brain areas involved in perception of biological motion. *Journal of Cognitive Neuroscience*, 2000, *12*, 711–720.

Groves, D. A., and Brown, V. J. Vagal nerve stimulation: A review of its applications and potential mechanisms that mediate its clinical effects. *Neuroscience and Biobehavioral Reviews*, 2005, *29*, 493–500.

Grunhaus, L., Shipley, J. E., Eiser, A., Pande, A. C., et al. Sleep-onset rapid eye movement after electroconvulsive therapy is more frequent in patients who respond less well to electroconvulsive therapy. *Biological Psychiatry*, 1997, *42*, 191–200.

Guastella, A. J., Einfeld, S. L., Gray, K. M., Rinehart, N. J., et al. Intranasal oxytocin improves emotion recognition for youth with autism spectrum disorders. *Biological Psychiatry*, 2010a, *67*, 692–694.

Guastella, A. J., Richardson, R., Lovibond, P. F., Rapee, R. M., et al. A randomized controlled trial of D-cycloserine enhancement of exposure therapy for social anxiety disorder. *Biological Psychiatry*, 2010b, *63*, 544–549.

Guehl, D., Benazzouz, A., Aouizerate, B., Cuny, E., et al. Neuronal correlates of obsessions in the caudate nucleus. *Biological Psychiatry*, 2008, *63*, 557–562.

Guilleminault, C., Wilson, R. A., and Dement, W. C. A study on cataplexy. *Archives of Neurology*, 1974, *31*, 255–261.

Gulevich, G., Dement, W. C., and Johnson, L. Psychiatric and EEG observations on a case of prolonged (264 hours) wakefulness. *Archives of General Psychiatry*, 1966, *15*, 29–35.

Gunderson, E. W., Kirkpatrick, M. G., Willing, L. M., and Holstege, C. P. Intranasal substituted cathinone "bath salts" psychosis potentially exacerbated by diphenhydramine. *Journal of Addiction Medicine*, 2013, *7*(3), 163–168.

Guridi, J., and Obeso, J. A. The subthalamic nucleus, hemiballismus and Parkinson's disease: Reappraisal of a neurosurgical dogma. *Brain*, 2001, *124*, 5–19.

Gurvits, T. V., Shenton, M. E., Hokama, H., Ohta, H., et al. Magnetic resonance imaging study of hippocampal volume in chronic, combat-related posttraumatic stress disorder. *Biological Psychiatry*, 1996, *40*, 1091–1099.

Gutiérrez-Galve, L., Wheeler, Kingshott, C. A. M., Altmann, D. R., et al. Changes in the frontotemporal cortex and cognitive correlates in first-episode psychosis. *Biological Psychiatry*, 2010, *68*, 51–60.

Gutin, B., Owens, S., Okuyama, T., Riggs, S., et al. Effect of physical training and its cessation on percent fat and bone density of children with obesity. *Obesity Research*, 1999, *7*, 208–214.

Gvilia, I., Xu, F., McGinty, D., and Szymusiak, R. Homeostatic regulation of sleep: A role for preoptic area neurons. *Journal of Neuroscience*, 2006, *26*, 9426–9433.

Haarmeier, T., Their, P., Repnow, M., and Petersen, D. False perception of motion in a patient who cannot compensate for eye movements. *Nature*, 1997, *389*, 849–852.

Haas, R. H. Thiamin and the brain. *Annual Review of Nutrition*, 1988, *8*, 483–515.

Habib, M. The neurological basis of developmental dyslexia: An overview and working hypothesis. *Brain*, 2000, *123*, 2373–2399.

Hacke, W., Albers, G., Al-Rawi, Y., Bogousslavsky, J., et al. The desmoteplase in acute ischemic stroke trial (DIAS): A phase II MRI-based 9-hour window acute stroke thrombolysis trial with intravenous desmoteplase. *Stroke*, 2005, *36*, 66–73.

Hackett, R. A., Preuss, T. M., and Kaas, J. H. Architectonic identification of the core region in auditory cortex of macaques, chimpanzees, and humans. *Journal of Comparative Neurology*, 2001, *441*, 197–222.

Hadjikhani, N., and de Gelder, B. Seeing fearful body expressions activates the fusiform cortex and amygdala. *Current Biology*, 2003, *13*, 2201–2205.

Hadjikhani, N., Joseph, R. M., Snyder, J., and Tager-Flusberg, H. Anatomical differences in the mirror neuron system and social cognition network in autism. *Cerebral Cortex*, 2006, *16*, 1276–1282.

Hadjikhani, N., Liu, A. K., Dale, A. M., Cavanagh, P., et al. Retinotopy and color sensitivity in human visual cortical area V8. *Nature Neuroscience*, 1998, *1*, 235–241.

Hadjipanayis, C. G., and Van Meir, E. G. Tumor initiating cells in malignant gliomas: Biology and implications for therapy. *Journal of Molecular Medicine*, 2009, *87*, 363–374.

Häfner, H. Onset and early course as determinants of the further course of schizophrenia. *Acta Psychiatrica Scandinavica*, 2000, *102*, 44–48.

Häfner, H., Riecher-Rössler, A., An Der Heiden, W., et al. Generating and testing a causal explanation of the gender difference in age at first onset of schizophrenia. *Psychological Medicine*, 1993, *23*, 925–940.

Häfner, H., and an der Heiden, W. Course and outcome of schizophrenia. In *Schizophrenia* (Second ed.), edited by S. R. Hirsch and D. R. Weinberger. Oxford: Blackwell Scientific, 2003.

Häfner, H., Löffler, W., Maurer, K., Hambrecht, M., et al. Depression, negative symptoms, social stagnation and social decline in the early course of schizophrenia. *Acta Psychiatrica Scandinavica*, 1999, *100*, 105–118.

Häfner, H., Maurer, K., Löffler, W., an der Heiden, W., et al. Modeling the early course of schizophrenia. *Schizophrenia Bulletin*, 2003, *29*, 325–340.

Häfner, H., Maurer, K., Trendler, G., an der Heiden, W., et al. Schizophrenia and depression: Challenging the paradigm of two separate diseases-A controlled study of schizophrenia, depression and healthy controls. *Schizophrenia Research*, 2005, *77*, 11–24.

Hague, S. M., Klaffke, S., and Bandmann, O. Neurodegenerative disorders: Parkinson's disease and Huntington's disease. *Journal of Neurology, Neurosurgery, and Psychiatry*, 2005, *76*, 1058–1063.

Hahn, T. M., Breininger, J. F., Baskin, D. G., and Schwartz, M. W. Coexpression of AGRP and NPY in fasting-activated hypothalamic neurons. *Nature Neuroscience*, 1998, *1*, 271–272.

Hainer, V., Stunkard, A., Kunesova, M., Parizkova, J., et al. A twin study of weight loss and metabolic efficiency. *International Journal of Obesity and Related Metabolic Disorders*, 2001, *25*, 533–537.

Hajak, G., Clarenbach, P., Fischer, W., Haase, W., et al. Effects of hypnotics on sleep quality and day-time well-being: Data from a comparative multicentre study in outpatients with insomnia. *European Psychiatry*, 1995, *10* (Suppl. 3), 173S–179S.

Halaas, J. L., Gajiwala, K. D., Maffei, M., Cohen, S. L., et al. Weight-reducing effects of the plasma protein encoded by the obese gene. *Science*, 1995, *269*, 543–546.

Halassa, M. M., Florian, C., Fellin, T., Munoz, J. R., et al. Astrocytic modulation of sleep homeostasis and cognitive consequences of sleep loss. *Neuron*, 2009, *61*, 213–219.

Halgren, E., Walter, R. D., Cherlow, D. G., and Crandall, P. E. Mental phenomena evoked by electrical stimulation of the human hippocampal formation and amygdala. *Brain*, 1978, *101*, 83–117.

Halpern, M. The organization and function of the vomeronasal system. *Annual Review of Neuroscience*, 1987, *10*, 325–362.

Halsband, U., and Freund, H. J. Premotor cortex and conditional motor learning in man. *Brain*, 1990, *113*, 207–222.

Hamet, P., and Tremblay, J. Genetics and genomics of depression. *Metabolism: Clinical and Experimental*, 2005, *54*, 10–15.

Hamilton, L. D., and Meston, C. M. The effects of partner togetherness on salivary testosterone in women in long distance relationships. *Hormones and Behavior*, 2010, *57*, 198–202.

Hampson, R. E., and Deadwyler, S. A. Cannabinoids reveal the necessity of hippocampal neural encoding for short-term memory in rats. *Journal of Neuroscience*, 2000, *20*, 8932–8942.

Hansen, D. V., Lui, J. H., Parker, P. R., and Kriegstein, A. R. Neurogenic radial glia in the outer subventricular zone of human neocortex. *Nature*, 2010, *464*, 554–561.

Hardy, J. Amyloid, the presenilins and Alzheimer's disease. *Trends in Neuroscience*, 1997, *4*, 154–159.

Hardwick, R. M., Rottschy, C., Miall, R. C., and Eickhoff, S. B. A quantitative meta-analysis and review of motor learning in the human brain. *Neuroimage*, 2013, *67*, 283–297.

Harmon, L. D., and Julesz, B. Masking in visual recognition: Effects of two-dimensional filtered noise. *Science*, 1973, *180*, 1194–1197.

Harrar, V., and Spence, C. The taste of cutlery: How the taste of food is affected by the weight, size, shape, and colour of the cutlery used to eat it. *Flavour*, 2013, *2*(1), 1–13.

Harris, G. W., and Jacobsohn, D. Functional grafts of the anterior pituitary gland. *Proceedings of the Royal Society of London B*, 1951–1952, *139*, 263–267.

Harrison, Y., and Horne, J. A. Sleep loss impairs short and novel language tasks having a prefrontal focus. Journal of Sleep Research, 1998, *7*, 95–100.

Harrison, Y., and Horne, J. A. One night of sleep loss impairs innovative thinking and flexible making. Organizational Behavior and Human Decision Processes, 1999, *78*, 128–145.

Hart, B. L. Hormones, spinal reflexes, and sexual behaviour. In *Determinants of sexual behaviour*, edited by J. B. Hutchinson. Chichester, England: John Wiley & Sons, 1978.

Hartline, H. K. The response of single optic nerve fibers of the vertebrate eye to illumination of the retina. *American Journal of Physiology*, 1938, *121*, 400–415.

Harvey, S. M. Female sexual behavior: Fluctuations during the menstrual cycle. *Journal of Psychosomatic Research*, 1987, *31*, 101–110.

Haslinger, B., Erhard, P., Altenmüller, E., Schroeder, U., et al. Transmodal sensorimotor networks during action observation in professional pianists. *Journal of Cognitive Neuroscience*, 2005, *17*, 282–293.

Hattar, S., Liao, H.-W., Takao, M., Berson, D. M., et al. Melanopsin-containing retinal ganglion cells: Architecture, projections, and intrinsic photosensitivity. *Science*, 2002, *295*, 1065–1070.

Hattie, J., and Yates, G. *Visible learning and the science of how we learn*. Routledge: London, 2014.

Haubensak, W., Kunwar, P. S., Cai, H., Ciocchi, S., et al. Genetic dissection of an amygdala microcircuit that gates conditioned fear. *Nature*, 2010, *468*, 270–276.

Haug, H.-J. Prediction of sleep deprivation outcome by diurnal variation of mood. *Biological Psychiatry*, 1992, *31*, 271–278.

Hauk, O., Johnsrude, I., and Pulvermüller, F. Somatotopic representation of action words in human motor and premotor cortex. *Neuron*, 2004, *41*, 301–307.

Hauser, M. D. Right hemisphere dominance for the production of facial expression in monkeys. *Science*, 1993, *261*, 475–477.

Haverkamp, S., Wässle, H., Duebel, J., Kuner, T., et al. The primordial, blue-cone color system of the mouse retina. *Journal of Neuroscience*, 2005, *25*, 5438–5445.

Hawke, C. Castration and sex crimes. *American Journal of Mental Deficiency*, 1951, *55*, 220–226.

He, J., Ma, L., Kim, S., Nakai, J., and Yu, C. R. Encoding gender and individual information in the mouse vomeronasal organ. *Science*, 2008, *320*, 535–538.

He, W., Yasumatsu, K., Varadarajan, V., Yamada, A., et al. Umami taste responses are mediated by α-transducin and α-gustducin. *Journal of Neuroscience*, 2004, *24*, 7574–7680.

Hebb, D. O. *The Organization of Behaviour*. New York: Wiley-Interscience, 1949.

Heckert, J. The hazards of growing up painlessly. *The New York Times Magazine*, November 15, 2012, Retrieved from http://www.nytimes.com

Heckler, M. M. *Fifth special report to the U.S. Congress on alcohol and health*. Washington, DC: U.S. Government Printing Office, 1983.

Heeb, M. M., and Yahr, P. Cell-body lesions of the posterodorsal preoptic nucleus or posterodorsal medial amygdala, but not the parvicellular subparafascicular thalamus, disrupt mating in male gerbils. *Physiology and Behavior*, 2000, *68*, 317–331.

Heffner, H. E., and Heffner, R. S. Role of primate auditory cortex in hearing. In *Comparative perception, vol. II: Complex signals*, edited by W. C. Stebbins and M. A. Berkley. New York: John Wiley & Sons, 1990.

Hefzy, H., Silver, R. W., and Silver, B. The no smoking sign-Insular infarction. *Journal of Neuroimaging*, 2011, *213*, 435–450.

Heilman, K. M., Rothi, L., and Kertesz, A. Localization of apraxia-producing lesions. In *Localization in neuropsychology*, edited by A. Kertesz. New York: Academic Press, 1983.

Heilman, K. M., Watson, R. T., and Bowers, D. Affective disorders associated with hemispheric disease. In *Neuropsychology of Human Emotion*, edited by K. M. Heilman and P. Satz. New York: Guilford Press, 1983.

Heimer, L., and Larsson, K. Impairment of mating behavior in male rats following lesions in the preoptic-anterior hypothalamic continuum. *Brain Research*, 1966/1967, *3*, 248–263.

Heinrichs, M., Baumgartner, T., Kirshbaum, C., and Ehlert, U. Social support and oxytocin interact to suppress cortisol and subjective responses to psychosocial stress. *Biological Psychiatry*, 2003, *54*, 1389–1398.

Heinrichs, S. C., Menzaghi, F., Pich, E. M., Baldwin, H. A., et al. Anti-stress action of a corticotropin-releasing factor antagonist on behavioral reactivity to stressors of varying type and intensity. *Neuropsychopharmacology*, 1994, *11*, 179–186.

Heinz, A., Reimold, M., Wrase, J., Hermann, D., et al. Correlation of stable elevations in striatal μ-opioid receptor availability in detoxified alcoholic patients with alcohol craving. *Archives of General Psychiatry*, 2005, *62*, 57–64.

Helenius, P., Uutela, K., and Hari, R. Auditory stream segregation in dyslexic adults. *Brain*, 1999, *122*, 907–913.

Helmuth, L. Dyslexia: Same brains, different languages. *Science*, 2001, *291*, 2064–2065.

Hendrickson, A. E., Wagoner, N., and Cowan, W. M. Autoradiographic and electron microscopic study of retino-hypothalamic connections. *Zeitschrift für Zellforschung und Mikroskopische Anatomie*, 1972, *125*, 1–26.

Hendry, S. H. C., and Yoshioka, T. A neurochemically distinct third channel in the macaque dorsal lateral geniculate nucleus. *Science*, 1994, *264*, 575–577.

Henke, P. G. The telencephalic limbic system and experimental gastric pathology: A review. *Neuroscience and Biobehavioral Reviews*, 1982, *6*, 381–390.

Hennessey, A. C., Camak, L., Gordon, F., and Edwards, D. A. Connections between the pontine central gray and the ventromedial hypothalamus are essential for lordosis in female rats. *Behavioral Neuroscience*, 1990, *104*, 477–488.

Henningfield, J. E., Fant, R. V., Buchhalter, A. R., and Stitzer, M. L. Pharmacotherapy for nicotine dependence. *CA: A Cancer Journal for Clinicians*, 2005, *55*, 281–299.

Henry, M. L., Beeson, P. M., Stark, A. J., and Rapcsak, S. Z. The role of left perisylvian cortical regions in spelling. *Brain and Language*, 2007, *100*, 44–52.

Herbert, M. R., Ziegler, D. A., Makris, N., Filipek, P. A., et al. Localization of white matter volume increase in autism and developmental language disorder. *Annals of Neurology*, 2004, *55*, 530–540.

Herculano-Houzel, S., Collins, C. E., Wong, P., and Kaas, J. H. Cellular scaling rules for primate brains. *Proceedings of the National Academy of Sciences, USA*, 2007, *104*, 3562–3567.

Herholz, K. Neuroimaging in anorexia nervosa. *Psychiatry Research*, 1996, *62*, 105–110.

Hering, E. *Outlines of a Theory of the Light Sense*, 1905. Translated by L. M. Hurvich and D. Jameson. Cambridge, Mass.: Harvard University Press, 1965

Hetherington, A. W., and Ranson, S. W. Hypothalamic lesions and adiposity in the rat. *Anatomical Record*, 1942, *78*, 149–172.

Hettema, J. M., Neale, M. C., and Kendler, K. S. A review and meta-analysis of the genetic epidemiology of anxiety disorders. *American Journal of Psychiatry*, 2001, *158*, 1568–1578.

Heywood, C. A., and Cowey, A. The role of the "face-cell" area in the discrimination and recognition of faces by monkeys. *Philosophical Transactions of the Royal Society of London B*, 1992, *335*, 31–38.

Heywood, C. A., Gaffan, D., and Cowey, A. Cerebral achromatopsia in monkeys. *European Journal of Neuroscience*, 1995, *7*, 1064–1073.

Heywood, C. A., and Kentridge, R. W. Achromatopsia, color vision, and cortex. *Neurology Clinics of North America*, 2003, *21*, 483–500.

Hickok, G., Bellugi, U., and Klima, E. S. The neurobiology of sign language and its implications for the neural basis of language. *Nature*, 1996, *381*, 699–702.

Hickok, G., Wilson, M., Clark, K., Klima, E. S., et al. Discourse deficits following right hemisphere damage in deaf signers. *Brain and Language*, 1999, *66*, 233–248.

Hicks, M. J., De, B. P., Rosenberg, J. B., Davidson, J. T., et al. Cocaine analog coupled to disrupted adenovirus: A vaccine strategy to evoke high-titer immunity against addictive drugs. *Molecular Therapy*, 2011, *19*, 612–619.

Hideyama, T., Yamashita, T., Suzuki, T., Tsuji, S., et al. Induced loss of ADAR2 engenders slow death of motor neurons from Q/R site-unedited GluR2. *Journal of Neuroscience*, 2010, *30*, 11917–11925.

Hikosaka, O., Sakai, K., Miyauchi, S., Takino, R., et al. Activation of human presupplementary motor area in learning of sequential procedures: A functional MRI study. *Journal of Neurophysiology*, 1996, *76*, 617–621.

Hill, A. S., Sahay, A., and Hen, R. Increasing adult hippocampal neurogenesis is sufficient to reduce anxiety and depression-like behaviors. *Neuropsychopharmacology*, 2015.

Hill, J. O., Wyatt, H. R., Reed, G. W., and Peters, J. C. Obesity and the environment: Where do we go from here? *Science*, 2003, *299*, 853–855.

Hill, J. P., Hauptman, J., Anderson, J., Fujioka, K., et al. Orlistat, a lipase inhibitor, for weight maintenance after conventional dieting: A 1-year study. *American Journal of Clinical Nutrition*, 1999, *69*, 1108–1116.

Hillis, A. E., Newhart, M., Heidler, J., Barker, P. B., et al. Anatomy of spatial attention: Insights from perfusion imaging and hemispatial neglect in acute stroke. *Journal of Neuroscience*, 2005, *25*, 3161–3167.

Hillis, A. E., Work, M., Barker, P. B., Jacobs, M. A., et al. Re-examining the brain regions crucial for orchestrating speech articulation. *Brain*, 2004, *127*, 1479–1487.

Hines, M. Prenatal endocrine influences on sexual orientation and on sexually differentiated childhood behavior. *Frontiers in Neuroendocrinology*, 2011, *32*(2), 170–182.

Hines, M., Allen, L. S., and Gorski, R. A. Sex differences in subregions of the medial nucleus of the amygdala and the bed nucleus

of the stria terminalis of the rat. *Brain Research*, 1992, *579*, 321–326.

Hinton, D., and Lewis-Fernández, R. The cross-cultural validity of posttraumatic stress disorder: Implications for DSM-5. *Depression and Anxiety*, 2011, *28*(9), 783–801.

Hobson, J. A. *The dreaming brain*. New York: Basic Books, 1988.

Hochberg, L. R., Serruya, M. D., Friehs, G. M., Mukand, J. A., et al. Neuronal ensemble control of prosthetic devices by a human with tetraplegia. *Nature*, 2006, *442*, 164–171.

Hock, C., Konietzko, U., Streffer, J. R., Tracy, J., et al. Antibodies against β-amyloid slow cognitive decline in Alzheimer's disease. *Neuron*, 2003, *38*, 547–554.

Hodge, C. W., Haraguchi, M., Erickson, H., and Samson, H. H. Ventral tegmental microinjections of quinpirole decrease ethanol and sucrose-reinforced responding. *Alcohol: Clinical and Experimental Research*, 1993, *17*, 370–375.

Hoeft, F., Meyler, A., Hernandez, A., Juel, C., et al. Functional and morphometric brain dissociation between dyslexia and reading ability. *Proceedings of the National Academy of Sciences, USA*, 2007, *104*, 4234–4239.

Hofbauer, R. K., Rainville, P., Duncan, G. H., and Bushnell, M. C. Cortical representation of the sensory dimension of pain. *Journal of Neurophysiology*, 2001, *86*, 402–411.

Hofle, N., Paus, T., Reutens, D., Fiset, P., et al. Regional cerebral blood flow changes as a function of delta and spindle activity during slow wave sleep in humans. *Journal of Neuroscience*, 1997, *17*(12), 4800–4808.

Hofman, P. M., Van Riswick, J. G., and Van Opstal, A. J. Relearning sound localization with new ears. *Nature Neuroscience*, 1998, *1*(5), 417–421.

Hohman, G. W. Some effects of spinal cord lesions on experienced emotional feelings. *Psychophysiology*, 1966, *3*, 143–156.

Holden, C. The violence of the lambs. *Science*, 2000, *289*, 580–581.

Hollander, E., Anagnostou, E., Chaplin, W., Esposito, K., et al. Striatal volume on magnetic resonance imaging and repetitive behaviors in autism. *Biological Psychiatry*, 2005, *58*, 226–232.

Hollander, E., Schiffman, E., Cohen, B., Rivera-Stein, M. A., et al. Signs of central nervous system dysfunction in obsessive-compulsive disorder. *Archives of General Psychiatry*, 1990, *47*, 27–32.

Hollander, J. A., Lu, Q., Cameron, M. D., Kamenecka, T. M., et al. Insular hypocretin transmission regulates nicotine reward. *Proceedings of the National Academy of Sciences, USA*, 2008, *105*, 19480–19485.

Hollis, J. H., McKinley, M. J., D'Souze, M., Kampe, J., et al. The trajectory of sensory pathways from the lamina terminalis to the

insular and cingulate cortex: A neuroanatomical framework for the generation of thirst. *American Journal of Physiology*, 2008, *294*, R1390–R1401.

Holmes, G. The cerebellum of man. *Brain*, 1939, *62*, 21–30.

Holstege, G., Georgiadis, J. R., Paans, A. M. J., Meiners, L. C., et al. Brain activation during human male ejaculation. *Journal of Neuroscience*, 2003a, *23*, 9185–9193.

Holstege, G., Reinders, A. A. T., Panns, A. M. J., Meiners, L. C., et al. Brain activation during female sexual orgasm. Program No. 727.7. *2003 Abstract Viewer/Itinerary Planner*. Washington, DC: Society for Neuroscience, 2003b.

Holtzheimer, P. E., and Mayberg, H. S. Deep brain stimulation for psychiatric disorders. *Annual Review of Neuroscience*, 2011a, *34*, 289–307.

Holtzheimer, P. E., and Mayberg, H. S. Stuck in a rut: Rethinking depression and its treatment. *Trends in Neuroscience*, 2011b, *94*, 1–9.

Hong, C. C. H., Jin, Y., Potkin, S. G., Buchsbaum, M. S., et al. Language in dreaming and regional EEG alpha-power. *Sleep*, 1996, *19*, 232–235.

Hopf, H. C., Mueller-Forell, W., and Hopf, N. J. Localization of emotional and volitional facial paresis. *Neurology*, 1992, *42*, 1918–1923.

Hoppe, C. Controlling epilepsy. *Scientific American Mind*, 2006, *17*, 62–67.

Horne, J. A. A review of the biological effects of total sleep deprivation in man. *Biological Psychology*, 1978, *7*, 55–102.

Horne, J. A., and Minard, A. Sleep and sleepiness following a behaviourally "active" day. *Ergonomics*, 1985, *28*, 567–575.

Horowitz, R. M., and Gentili, B. Dihydrochalcone sweeteners. In *Symposium: Sweeteners*, edited by G. E. Inglett. Westport, CT.: Avi Publishing, 1974.

Horowitz, T. S., Cade, B. E., Wolfe, J. M., and Czeisler, C. A. Efficacy of bright light and sleep/darkness scheduling in alleviating circadian maladaptation to night work. *American Journal of Physiology*, 2001, *281*, E384–E391.

Horton, J. C., and Hubel, D. H. Cytochrome oxidase stain preferentially labels intersection of ocular dominance and vertical orientation columns in macaque striate cortex. *Society for Neuroscience Abstracts*, 1980, *6*, 315.

Houchi, H., Babovic, D., Pierrefiche, O., Ledent, C., et al. CB1 receptor knockout mice display reduced ethanol-induced conditioned place preference and increased striatal dopamine D2 receptors. *Neuropsychopharmacology*, 2005, *30*, 339–340.

Howard, J. D., Plailly, J., Grueschow, M., Haynes, J.-D., et al. Odor quality coding and categorization in human posterior piriform cortex. *Nature Neuroscience*, 2009, *12*, 932–938.

Howell, M. J., and Schenck, C. H. Treatment of nocturnal eating disorders. *Current Treatment Options in Neurology*, 2009, *11*, 333–339.

Howell, S., Westergaard, G., Hoos, B., Chavanne, T. J., et al. Serotonergic influences on life-history outcomes in free-ranging male rhesus macaques. *American Journal of Primatology*, 2007, *69*, 851–865.

Hu, W.-P., Li, J.-D., Zhang, C., Boehmer, L., et al. Altered circadian and homeostatic sleep regulation in prokineticin 2-deficient mice. *Sleep*, 2007, *30*, 247–256.

Huang, A. L., Chen, X., Hoon, M. A., Chandrashekar, J., et al. The cells and logic for mammalian sour taste detection. *Nature*, 2006, *442*, 934–938.

Huang, H., Xu, Y., and van den Pol, A. N. Nicotine excites hypothalamic arcuate anorexigenic proopiomelanocortin neurons and orexigenic neuropeptide Y neurons: Similarities and differences. *Journal of Neurophysiology*, 2011, *106*, 1191–1202.

Hubel, D. H., and Wiesel, T. N. Functional architecture of macaque monkey visual cortex. *Proceedings of the Royal Society of London B*, 1977, *198*, 1–59.

Hubel, D. H., and Wiesel, T. N. Brain mechanisms of vision. *Scientific American*, 1979, *241*, 150–162.

Huber, R., Ghilardi, M. F., Massimini, M., Ferrarelli, F., et al. Arm immobilization causes cortical plastic changes and locally decreases sleep slow wave activity. *Nature Neuroscience*. 2006, *9*, 1169–1176.

Huber, R., Ghilardi, M. F., Massimini, M., and Tononi, G. Local sleep and learning. *Nature*, 2004, *430*, 78–81.

Hublin, C. Narcolepsy: Current drug-treatment options. *CNS Drugs*, 1996, *5*, 426–436.

Hublin, C., Kaprio, J., Partinen, M., Heikkila, K., et al. Prevalence and genetics of sleepwalking: A population-based twin study. *Neurology*, 1997, *48*, 177–181.

Hudson, J. I., Hiripi, E., Pope, H. G., and Kessler, R. C. The prevalence and correlates of eating disorders in the National Comorbidity Survey Replication. *Biological Psychiatry*, 2007, *61*(3), 348–358.

Hudspeth, A. J., and Gillespie, P. G. Pulling springs to tune transduction: Adaptation by hair cells. *Neuron*, 1994, *12*, 1–9.

Huestis, M. A., Gorelick, D. A., Heishman, S. J., Preston, K. L., et al. Blockade of effects of smoked marijuana by the CB1-selective cannabinoid receptor antagonist SR131716. *Archives of General Psychiatry*, 2001, *58*, 322–328.

Hughes, J., Smith, T. W., Kosterlitz, H. W., Fothergill, L. A., et al. Identification of two related pentapeptides from the brain with potent opiate agonist activity. *Nature*, 1975, *258*, 577–579.

Hughes, J. R., Gust, S. W., Skoog, K., Keenan, R. M., et al. Symptoms of tobacco withdrawal: A replication and extension. *Archives of General Psychiatry*, 1989, *14*, 577–580.

Hull, E., and Dominguez, J. M. Sexual behavior in male rodents. *Hormones and Behavior*, 2007, *52*, 45–55.

Hulshoff-Pol, H. E., Schnack, H. G., Bertens, M. G., van Haren, N. E., et al. Volume changes in gray matter in patients with schizophrenia. *American Journal of Psychiatry*, 2002, *159*, 244–250.

Humphrey, A. L., and Hendrickson, A. E. Radial zones of high metabolic activity in squirrel monkey striate cortex. *Society for Neuroscience Abstracts*, 1980, *6*, 315.

Hunt, D. M., Dulai, K. S., Cowing, J. A., Julliot, C., et al. Molecular evolution of trichromacy in primates. *Vision Research*, 1998, *38*, 3299–3306.

Hussey, E., and Safford, A. Perception of facial expression in somatosensory cortex supports simulationist models. *Journal of Neuroscience*, 2009, *29*, 301–302.

Huszar, D., Lynch, C. A., Fairchild-Huntress, V., Dunmore, J. H., et al. Targeted disruption of the melanocortin-4 receptor results in obesity in mice. *Cell*, 1997, *88*, 131–141.

Hwa, J. J., Ghibaudi, L., Gao, J., and Parker, E. M. Central melanocortin system modulates energy intake and expenditure of obese and lean Zucker rats. *American Journal of Physiology*, 2001, *281*, R444–R451.

Hyman, S. E., and Malenka, R. C. Addiction and the brain: The neurobiology of compulsion and its persistence. Nature Reviews: Neuroscience, 2001, *2*, 695–703.

Iacoboni, M., and Dapretto, M. The mirror neuron system and the consequences of its dysfunction. *Nature Reviews: Neuroscience*, 2006, *7*, 942–951.

Iacoboni, M., Molnar-Szakacs, I., Gallese, V., Buccino, G., et al. Grasping the intentions of others with one's own mirror neuron system. *PLoS Biology*, 2005, *3*, e79.

Iacoboni, M., Woods, R. P., Brass, M., Bekkering, H., et al. Cortical mechanisms of human imitation. *Science*, 1999, *286*, 2526–2528.

Iaria, G., Petrides, M., Dagher, A., Pike, B., et al. Cognitive strategies dependent on the hippocampus and caudate nucleus in human navigation: Variability and change with practice. *Journal of Neuroscience*, 2003, *23*, 5945–5952.

Ibuka, N., and Kawamura, H. Loss of circadian rhythm in sleep-wakefulness cycle in the rat by suprachiasmatic nucleus lesions. *Brain Research*, 1975, *96*, 76–81.

Ikoma, A., Steinhoff, M., Ständer, S., Yosipovitch, G., et al. The neurobiology of itch. *Nature Reviews: Neuroscience*, 2006, *7*, 535–547.

Ikonomidou, C., Bittigau, P., Ishimaru, M. J., Wozniak, D. F., et al. Ethanol-induced apoptotic neurodegeneration and fetal alcohol syndrome. *Science*, 2000, *287*, 1056–1060.

Imperato, A., and Di Chiara, G. Preferential stimulation of dopamine-release in the accumbens of freely moving rats by ethanol. *Journal of Pharmacology and Experimental Therapeutics*, 1986, *239*, 219–228.

Imrey, P. B., Jackson, L. A., Ludwinski, P. H., England, A. C., et al. Outbreak of serogroup C meningococcal disease associated with campus bar patronage. *American Journal of Epidemiology*, 1996, *143*(6), 624–630.

Indersmitten, T., & Gur, R. C. Emotion processing in chimeric faces: Hemispheric asymmetries in expression and recognition of emotions. *The Journal of Neuroscience*, 2003, *23*(9), 3820–3825.

Insel, T. R. A neurobiological basis of social attachment. *American Journal of Psychiatry*, 1997, *154*, 726–735.

Insel, T. R., Wang, Z. X., and Ferris, C. F. Patterns of brain vasopressin receptor distribution associated with social organization in microtine rodents. *Journal of Neuroscience*, 1994, *14*, 5381–5392.

Inskip, H. M., Harris, E. C., and Barraclough, C. Lifetime risk of suicide for alcoholism, affective disorder and schizophrenia. *British Journal of Psychiatry*, 1998, *172*, 35–37.

Ishizuka, T., Murotani, T., and Yamatodani, A. modafinil activates the histaminergic system through the orexinergic neurons. *Neuroscience Letters*, 2010, *483*, 193–196.

Ito, M., Ishihara, A., Gokori, A., Matsushita, H., et al. Mechanism of the anti-obesity effects induced by a novel melanin-concentrating hormone 1-receptor antagonist in mice. *British Journal of Pharmacology*, 2010, *159*, 374–383.

Ito, T., Tiede, M., and Ostry, D. J. Somatosensory function in speech perception. *Proceedings of the National Academy of Sciences, USA*, 2009, *106*, 1245–1248.

Iversen, L. Cannabis and the brain. *Brain*, 2003, *126*, 1252–1270.

Iwata, M. Kanji versus Kana: Neuropsychological correlates of the Japanese writing system. *Trends in Neurosciences*, 1984, *7*, 290–293.

Izard, C. E. *The face of emotion*. New York: Appleton-Century-Crofts, 1971.

Jackson, M. E., Frost, A. S., and Moghaddam, B. Stimulation of prefrontal cortex at physiologically rele-vant frequencies inhibits dopamine release in the nucleus accumbens. *Journal of Neurochemistry*, 2001, *78*, 920–923.

Jacob, S., and McClintock, M. K. Psychological state and mood effects of steroidal chemosignals in women and men. *Hormones and Behavior*, 2000, *37*, 57–78.

Jacobs, B. L., and Fornal, C. A. Activity of serotonergic neurons in behaving animals. *Neuropsychopharmacology*, 1999, *21*, 9S–15S.

Jacobs, B. L., and McGinty, D. J. Participation of the amygdala in complex stimulus recognition and behavioral inhibition: Evidence from unit studies. *Brain Research*, 1972, *36*, 431–436.

Jacobs, G. H. Primate photopigments and primate color vision. *Proceedings of the National Academy of Sciences, USA*, 1996, *93*, 577–581.

Jacobsen, C. F., Wolfe, J. B., and Jackson, T. A. An experimental analysis of the functions of the frontal association areas in primates. *Journal of Nervous and Mental Disorders*, 1935, *82*, 1–14.

Jakobson, L. S., Archibald, Y. M., Carey, D., and Goodale, M. A. A kinematic analysis of reaching and grasping movements in a patient recovering from optic ataxia. *Neuropsychologia*, 1991, *29*, 803–809.

James, T. W., Culham, J., Humphrey, G. K., Milner, A. D., et al. Ventral occipital lesions impair object recognition but not object-directed grasping: An fMRI study. *Brain*, 2003, *126*, 2463–2475.

James, W. What is an emotion? *Mind*, 1884, *9*, 188–205.

Jaramillo, F. Signal transduction in hair cells and its regulation by calcium. *Neuron*, 1995, *15*, 1227–1230.

Jaynes, J. The problem of animate motion in the seventeenth century. *Journal of the History of Ideas*, 1970, *6*, 219–234.

Jeffress, L. A. A place theory of sound localization. *Journal of Comparative and Physiological Psychology*, 1948, *41*, 35–39.

Jensen, T., Genefke, I., and Hyldebrandt, N. Cerebral atrophy in young torture victims. *New England Journal of Medicine*, 1982, *307*, 1341.

Jentsch, J. D., Redmond, D. E., Elsworth, J. D., Taylor, J. R., et al. Enduring cognitive deficits and cortical dopamine dysfunction in monkeys after long-term administration of phencyclidine. *Science*, 1997, *277*, 953–955.

Jeon, T.-I., Zhu, B., Larson, J. L., and Osborne, T. F. SREBP-2 regulates gut peptide secretion through intestinal bitter taste receptor signaling in mice. *Journal of Clinical Investigation*, 2008, *118*, 3693–3700.

Jeste, D. V., Del Carmen, R., Lohr, J. B., and Wyatt, R. J. Did schizophrenia exist before the eighteenth century? *Comprehensive Psychiatry*, 1985, *26*, 493–503.

Jewett, D. C., Cleary, J., Levine, A. S., Schaal, D. W., et al. Effects of neuropeptide Y on food-reinforced behavior in satiated rats. *Pharmacology, Biochemistry, and Behavior*, 1992, *42*, 207–212.

Jo, Y.-H., Wiedl, D., and Role, L. W. Cholinergic modulation of appetite-related synapses in mouse lateral hypothalamic slice. *Journal of Neuroscience*, 2005, *25*, 11133–11144.

Jobard, G., Crivello, F., and Tzourio-Mazoyer, N. Evaluation of the dual route theory of reading: A metaanalysis of 35 neuroimaging studies. *NeuroImage*, 2003, *20*, 693–712.

Jobst, E. E., Enriori, P. J., and Cowley, M. A. The electrophysiology of feeding circuits. *Trends in Endocrinology and Metabolism*, 2004, *15*, 488–499.

Johanek, L. M., Meyer, R. A., Hartke, T., Hobelmann, J. G., et al. Psychophysical and physiological evidence for parallel afferent pathways mediating the sensation of itch. *Journal of Neuroscience*, 2007, *27*, 7490–7497.

Johansson, G. Visual perception of biological motion and a model for its analysis. *Perception and Psychophysics*, 1973, *14*, 201–211.

Johansson, R. S., and Flanagan, J. R. Coding and use of tactile signals from the fingertips in object manipulation tasks. *Nature Reviews Neuroscience*, 2009, *10*, 345–359.

Johnson, B. A., and Leon, M. Chemotopic odorant coding in a mammalian olfactory system. *Journal of Comparative Neurology*, 2007, *503*, 1–34.

Johnson, M. A. Subcortical face processing. *Nature Reviews: Neuroscience*, 2005, *6*, 766–774.

Johnson, M. K., Kim, J. K., and Risse, G. Do alcoholic Korsakoff's syndrome patients acquire affective reactions? *Journal of Experimental Psychology: Learning, Memory, and Cognition*, 1985, *11*, 22–36.

Jonas, P., Bischofberger, J., and Sandkühler, J. Corelease of two fast neurotransmitters at a central synapse. *Science*, 1998, *281*, 419–523.

Jones, B. E. Influence of the brainstem reticular formation, including intrinsic monoaminergic and cholinergic neurons, on forebrain mechanisms of sleep and waking. In *The diencephalon and sleep*, edited by M. Mancia and G. Marini. New York: Raven Press, 1990.

Jones, D. T., and Reed, R. R. Golf: An olfactory neuron specific-G protein involved in odorant signal transduction. *Science*, 1989, *244*, 790–795.

Jones, S. S., Collins, K., and Hong, H.-W. An audience effect on smile production in 10-month-old infants. *Psychological Science*, 1991, *2*, 45–49.

Jope, R. S., Song, L., Li, P. P., Young, L. T., et al. The phosphoinositide signal transduction system is impaired in bipolar affective disorder brain. *Journal of Neurochemistry*, 1996, *66*, 2402–2409.

Jornales, V. E., Jakob, M., Zamani, A., and Vaina, L. M. Deficits on complex motion perception, spatial discrimination and eye movements in a patient with bilateral occipital-parietal lesions. *Investigative Ophthalmology and Visual Science*, 1997, *38*, S72.

Jouvet, M. The role of monoamines and acetylcholine-containing neurons in the regulation of the sleep-waking cycle. *Ergebnisse der Physiologie*, 1972, *64*, 166–307.

Jouvet-Mounier, D., Astic, L., and Lacote, D. Ontogenesis of the states of sleep in rat, cat, and guinea pig during the first postnatal month. *Developmental Psychobiology*, 1970, *2*, 216–239.

Kaas, J. H., and Collins, C. E. The organization of sensory cortex. *Current Opinion in Neurobiology*, 2001, *11*, 498–504.

Kaas, J. H., Hackett, T. A., and Tramo, M. J. Auditory processing in primate cerebral cortex. *Current Opinion in Neurobiology*, 1999, *9*, 164–170.

Kales, A., Tan, T.-L., Kollar, E. J., Naitoh, P., et al. Sleep patterns following 205 hours of sleep deprivation. *Psychosomatic Medicine*, 1970, *32*, 189–200.

Kalin, N. H., Sherman, J. E., and Takahashi, L. K. Antagonism of endogenous CRG systems attenuates stress-induced freezing behavior in rats. *Brain Research*, 1988, *457*, 130–135.

Kalivas, P. W., Peters, J., and Knackstedt, L. Animal models and brain circuits in drug addiction. *Molecular Interventions*, 2006, *6*, 339–344.

Kane, M. D., Lipinski, W. J., Callahan, M. J., Bian, F., et al. Evidence for seeding of β-amyloid by intracerebral infusion of Alzheimer brain extracts in β-amyloid precursor protein-transgenic mice. *Journal of Neuroscience*, 2000, *20*, 3606–3611.

Kang, C., and Drayna, D. Genetics of speech and language disorders. *Annual Review of Genomics and Human Genetics*, 2011, *12*, 145–164.

Kanner, L. Autistic disturbances of affective contact. *The Nervous Child*, 1943, *2*, 217–250.

Kanwisher, N., and Yovel, G. The fusiform face area: A cortical region specialized for the perception of faces. *Philosophical Transactions of the Royal Society of London B*, 2006, *361*, 2109–2128.

Kaplitt, M. G., Feigin, A., Tang, C., Fitzsimons, H. L., et al. Amygdala central nucleus lesions: Effect on heart rate conditioning in the rabbit. *Physiology and Behavior*, 1979, *23*, 1109–1117.

Kaplan, G. B., Vasterling, J. J., and Vedak, P. C. Brain-derived neurotrophic factor in traumatic brain injury, post-traumatic stress disorder, and their comorbid conditions: Role in pathogenesis and treatment. *Behavioural Pharmacology*, 2010, *21*(5-6), 427–437.

Kaplitt, M. G., Feigin, A., Tang, C., Fitzsimons, H. L., et al. (2007). Safety and tolerability of gene therapy with an adeno-associated virus (AAV) borne GAD gene for Parkinson's disease: an open label, phase I trial. *The Lancet*, *369*(9579), 2097–2105.

Kapur, S. Psychosis as a state of aberrant salience: A framework linking biology, phenomenology, and pharmacology in schizophrenia. *American Journal of Psychiatry*, 2003,*160*, 13–23.

Karacan, I., Salis, P. J., and Williams, R. L. The role of the sleep laboratory in diagnosis and treatment of impotence. In *Sleep disorders: Diagnosis and treatment*, edited by R. J. Williams and I. Karacan. New York: John Wiley & Sons, 1978.

Karacan, I., Williams, R. L., Finley, W. W., and Hursch, C. J. The effects of naps on nocturnal sleep: Influence on the need for stage 1 REM and stage 4 sleep. *Biological Psychiatry*, 1970, *2*, 391–399.

Karlsgodt, K. H., Kochunov, P, Winkler, A. M., et al. A multimodal assessment of the genetic control over working memory. *Journal of Neuroscience*, 2010, *30*, 8197–8202.

Karlson, P., and Luscher, M. "Pheromones": A new term for a class of biologically active substances. Nature, 1959, *183*, 55–56.

Karlsson, M. P., and Frank, L. M. Awake replay of remote experiences in the hippocampus. Nature Neuroscience, 2009, *12*, 913–918.

Karnath, H.-O., Rüter, J., Mandler, A., and Himmelbach, M. The anatomy of object recognition–visual form agnosia caused by medial occipitotemporal stroke. *Journal of Neuroscience*, 2009, *29*, 5854–5862.

Kartsounis, L. D., Rudge, P., and Stevens, J. M. Bilateral lesions of CA1 and CA2 fields of the hippocampus are sufficient to cause a severe amnesic syndrome in humans. *Journal of Neurology, Neurosurgery and Psychiatry*, 1995, *59*, 95–98.

Katanoda, K., Yoshikawa, K., and Sugishita, M. A functional MRI study on the neural substrates for writing. *Human Brain Mapping*, 2001, *13*, 34–42.

Katzman, D. K., Christensen, B., Young, A. T., and Zipursky, R. B. Starving the brain: Structural abnormalities and cognitive impairment in adolescents with anorexia nervosa. *Seminars in Clinical Neuropsychiatry*, 2001, *2*, 146–152.

Kauer, J. A., and Malenka, R. C. Synaptic plasticity and addiction. *Nature Reviews: Neuroscience*, 2007, *8*, 844–858.

Kavoi, B., and Jameela, H. Comparative morphometry of the olfactory bulb, tract and stria in the human, dog and goat. *International Journal of Morphology*, 2011, *29*(3), 939–946.

Kawahara, Y., Ito, K., Sun, H., Aizawa, H., et al. RNA editing and death of motor neurons. *Nature*, 2004, *427*, 801.

Kawai, K., Sugimoto, K., Nakashima, Miura, H., et al. Leptin as a modulator of sweet taste sensitivities in mice. *Proceedings of the National Academy of Sciences, USA*, 2000, *97*, 11044–11049.

Kawauchi, H., Kawazoe, I., Tsubokawa, M., Kishida, M., et al. Characterization of melanin-concentrating hormone in chum salmon pituitaries. *Nature*, 1983, *305*, 321–323.

Kayama, Y., Ohta, M., and Jodo, E. Firing of "possibly" cholinergic neurons in the rat laterodorsal teg-mental nucleus during sleep and wakefulness. *Brain Research*, 1992, *569*, 210–220.

Kawikova, I., Grady, P. B. X., Tobiasova, Z., Zhang, Y., et al. Children with Tourette's syndrome may suffer immunoglobulin A dysgammaglobulinemia: Preliminary report. *Biological Psychiatry*, 2010, *67*, 679–683.

Kaye, W. H., Klump, K. L., Frank, G. K. W., and Strober, M. Anorexia and bulimia nervosa. *Annual Review of Medicine*, 2000, *51*(1), 299–313.

Kaye, W. H., Nagata, T., Weltzin, T. E., Hsu, G., et al. Double-blind placebo-controlled administration of fluoxetine in restricting- and restricting-purging-type anorexia nervosa. *Biological Psychiatry*, 2001, *49*, 644–652.

Keller, S. E., Weiss, J. M., Schleifer, S. J., Miller, N. E., et al. Stress-induced suppression of immunity in adrenalectomized rats. *Science*, 1983, *221*, 1301–1304.

Kelso, S. R., Ganong, A. H., and Brown, T. H. Hebbian synapses in hippocampus. *Proceedings of the National Academy of Sciences, USA*, 1986, *83*, 5326–5330.

Kempermann, G., Wiskott, L., and Gage, F. H. Functional significance of adult neurogenesis. *Current Opinion in Neurobiology*, 2004, *13*, 186–191.

Kendell, R. E., and Adams, W. Unexplained fluctuations in the risk for schizophrenia by month and year of birth. *British Journal of Psychiatry*, 1991, *158*, 758–763.

Kendler, K. S., Jacobson, K. C., Prescott, C. A., and Neale, M. C. Specificity of genetic and environmental risk factors for use and abuse/dependence of cannabis, cocaine, hallucinogens, sedatives, stimulants, and opiates in male twins. *American Journal of Psychiatry*, 2003, *160*, 687–695.

Kennedy, S. H., Konarski, J. Z., Segal, Z. V., et al. Differences in brain glucose metabolism between responders to CBT and venlafaxine in a 16-week randomized controlled trial. *American Journal of Psychiatry*, 2007, *164*, 778–788.

Kenney, P. J. Tobacco dependence, the insular cortex and the hypocretin connection. *Pharmacology, Biochemistry and Behavior*, 2011, *97*, 700–707.

Keonigs, M., Young, L., Adolphs, R., et al. Damage to the prefrontal cortex increases utilitarian moral judgments. *Nature*, 2007, *446*, 708–911.

Koepp, G. A., Manohar, C. U., McCrady-Spitzer, S. K., Ben-Ner, A., Hamann, D. J., Runge, C. F., & Levine, J. A. Treadmill desks: A 1-year prospective trial. *Obesity*, 2013. *21*(4), 705–711.

Kertesz, Andrew, Chapter 4 - The Anatomy of Jargon, In Jargonaphasia, edited by JASON W. BROWN, Academic Press, 1981, Pages 63-112, ISBN 9780121375805, http://dx.doi.org/10.1016/B978-0-12-137580-5.50010-0.

Kessler, R. C., Berglund, P., Demler, O., Jin, R., et al. The epidemiology of major depressive disorder: Results from the National Comorbidity Survey Replication (NCS-R), *Journal of the American Medical Association* 2003, *289*, 3095–3105.

Kessler, R. C., Lane, M. C., Shahly, V., and Stang, P. E. Accounting for comorbidity in assessing the burden of epilepsy among US adults: Results from the National Comorbidity Survey Replication (NCS-R). *Molecular Psychiatry*, 2005, *17*(7), 748–758.

Kessler, R. C., Sonnega, A., Bromet, E., Hughes, M., et al. Posttraumatic stress disorder in the National Comorbidity Survey. *Archives of General Psychiatry*, 1995, *52*, 1048–1060.

Kestler, L. P., Walker, E., and Vega, E. M. Dopamine receptors in the brains of schizophrenia patients: A meta-analysis of the findings. *Behavioral Pharmacology*, 2001, *12*, 355–371.

Kety, S. S., Rosenthal, D., Wender, P. H., and Schulsinger, K. F. The types and prevalence of mental illness in the biological and adoptive families of adopted schizophrenics. In *The transmission of schizophrenia*, edited by D. Rosenthal and S. S. Kety. New York: Pergamon Press, 1968.

Kety, S. S., Wender, P. H., Jacobsen, B., Ingraham, L. J., et al. Mental illness in the biological and adoptive relatives of schizophrenic adoptees: Replication of the Copenhagen Study in the rest of Denmark. *Archives of General Psychiatry*, 1994, *51*, 442–455.

Kew, J. J. M., Ridding, M. C., Rothwell, J. C., Passingham, R. E., et al. Reorganization of cortical blood flow and transcranial magnetic stimulation maps in human subjects after upper limb amputation. *Journal of Neurophysiology*, 1994, *72*, 2517–2524.

Keys, A., Brozek, J., Henschel, A., Mickelsen, O., and Taylor, H. L. *The biology of human starvation*. Minneapolis, Minn.: University of Minnesota Press, 1950.

Khateb, A., Fort, P., Pegna, A., Jones, B. E., et al. Cholinergic nucleus basalis neurons are excited by histamine in vitro. *Neuroscience*, 1995, *69*, 495–506.

Kiecolt-Glaser, J. K., Glaser, R., Shuttleworth, E. C., Dyer, C. S., et al. Chronic stress and immunity in family caregivers of Alzheimer's disease victims. *Psychosomatic Medicine*, 1987, *49*, 523–535.

Kiecolt-Glaser, J. K., Marucha, P. T., Malarkey, W. B., Mercado, A. M., et al. Slowing of wound healing by psychological stress. *Lancet*, 1995, 346, 1194–1196.

Kiecolt-Glaser, J. K., Loving, T. J., Stowell, J. R., Malarkey, W. B., et al. (2005). Hostile marital interactions, proinflammatory cytokine production, and wound healing. *Archives of General Psychiatry*, 62(12), 1377–1384.

Kim, J. S., Kornhuber, H. H., Schmid-Burgk, W., and Holzmüller, B. Low cerebrospinal fluid glutamate in schizophrenic patients and a new hypothesis on schizophrenia, *Neuroscience Letters*, 1980, 20(3): 379–382.

Kim, J. Y., Duian, X., Liu, C. Y., Jang, M. H., et al. DISC1 regulates new neuron development in the adult brain via modulation of AKT-mTOR signaling through KIAA1212. *Neuron*, 2009, 63, 761–773.

King, S., St-Hilaire, A., and Heidkamp, D. Prenatal factors in schizophrenia. *Current Directions in Psychological Science*, 2010, 19, 209–213.

Kingston, K., Szmukler, G., Andrewes, D., Tress, B., et al. Neuropsychological and structural brain changes in anorexia nervosa before and after refeeding. *Psychological Medicine*, 1996, 26, 15–28.

Kinnamon, S. C., and Cummings, T. A. Chemosensory transduction mechanisms in taste. *Annual Review of Physiology*, 1992, 54, 715–731.

Kinsley, C. H., and Bridges, R. S. Morphine treatment and reproductive condition alter olfactory preferences for pup and adult male odors in female rats. *Developmental Psychobiology*, 1990, 23, 331–347.

Kirkpatrick, B., Kim, J. W., and Insel, T. R. Limbic system fos expression associated with paternal behavior. *Brain Research*, 1994, 658, 112–118.

Kirsch, I. Specifying non-specifics: Psychological mechanism of the placebo effect. In *The placebo effect: An interdisciplinary exploration*, edited by A. Harrington. Cambridge: Harvard University Press, 1997.

Kitada, T., Asakawa, S., Hattori, N., Matsumine, H., et al. Mutations in the parkin gene cause autosomal recessive juvenile parkinsonism. *Nature*, 1998, 392, 605–608.

Kito, S., Hasegawa, T., and Koga, Y. Neuroanatomical correlates of therapeutic efficacy of low-frequency right prefrontal transcranial magnetic stimulation in treatment-resistant depression. *Psychiatry and Clinical Neuroscience*, 2011, 65, 175–182.

Klaur, J., Zhao, Z., Klein, G. M., Lo, E. H., et al. The neurotoxicity of tissue plasminogen activator. *Journal of Cerebral Blood Flow and Metabolism*, 2004, 24, 945–963.

Klein, D. A., and Walsh, B. T. Eating disorders: Clinical features and pathophysiology. *Physiology and Behavior*, 2004, 81, 359–374.

Kleschevnikov, A. M., Belichenko, P. V., Faizi, M., Jacobs, L. F., et al. Deficits in cognition

and synaptic plasticity in a mouse model of Down syndrome ameliorated by GABA$_B$ receptor antagonists. *Journal of Neuroscience*, 2012, 32(27), 9217–9227.

Klinge, C., Eippert, F., Röder, B., and Büchel, C. Corticocortical connections mediate primary visual cortex responses to auditory stimulation in the blind. *Journal of Neuroscience*, 2010, 30, 12798–12805.

Klunk, W. E., Engler, H., Nordberg, A., Bacskai, B. J., et al. Imaging the pathology of Alzheimer's disease: Amyloid-imaging with positron emission tomography. *Neuroimaging Clinics of North America*, 2003, 13, 781–789.

Knapp, P. H., Levy, E. M., Giorgi, R. G., Black, P. H., et al. Short-term immunological effects of induced emotion. *Psychosomatic Medicine*, 1992, 54, 133–148.

Knebelmann, B., Boussin, L., Guerrier, D., Legeai, L., et al. Anti-Muellerian hormone Bruxelles: A nonsense mutation associated with the persistent Muellerian duct syndrome. *Proceedings of the National Academy of Sciences, USA*, 1991, 88, 3767–3771.

Knecht, S., Breitenstein, C., Bushuven, S., Wailke, S., et al. Levodopa: Faster and better word learning in normal humans. *Annals of Neurology*, 2004, 56, 20–26.

Knecht, S., Drager, B., Deppe, M., Bobe, L., et al. Handedness and hemispheric language dominance in healthy humans. *Brain*, 2000, 123, 2512–2518.

Knickmeyer, R. C., Baron-Cohen, S., and Fane, B. A. Androgens and autistic traits: A study of individuals with congenital adrenal hyperplasia. *Hormones and Behavior*, 2006, 48, 1007–1008.

Knudsen, E. I. Instructed learning in the auditory localization pathway of the barn owl. *Nature*, 2002, 417(6886), 322–328.

Knutson, B., Adams, C. M., Fong, G. W., and Hommer, D. Anticipation of increasing monetary reward selectively recruits nucleus accumbens. *Journal of Neuroscience*, 2001, 21, RC159 (1–5).

Knutson, B., and Adcock, R. A. Remembrance of rewards past. *Neuron*, 2005, 45, 331–332.

Kobatake, E., Tanaka, K., and Tamori, Y. Long-term learning changes the stimulus selectivity of cells in the inferotemporal cortex of adult monkeys. *Neuroscience Research*, 1992, S17, S237.

Koenen, K. C., Harley, R., Lyons, M. J., Wolfe, J., et al. A twin registry study of familial and individual risk factors for trauma exposure and posttraumatic stress disorder. *Journal of Nervous and Mental Disease*, 2002, 190, 209–218.

Koenigs, M., Young, L., Adolphs, R., Tranel, D., et al. Damage to the prefrontal cortex increases utilitarian moral judgments. *Nature*, 2007, 446, 908–911.

Kohler, E., Keysers, C., Umiltà, M. A., Fogassi, L., et al. Hearing sounds, understanding actions: Action representation in mirror neurons. *Science*, 2002, 297, 846–848.

Kojima, M., Hosoda, H., Date, Y., Nakazato, M., et al. Ghrelin is a growth-hormone-releasing acylated peptide from stomach. *Nature*, 1999, 402, 656–660.

Kolassa, I. T., Kolassa, S., Ertl, V., Papassotiropoulos, A., et al. The risk of posttraumatic stress disorder after trauma depends on traumatic load and the catechol-o-methyltransferase Val(158)Met polymorphism. *Biological Psychiatry*, 2010, 67, 304–308.

Komisaruk, B. R., and Larsson, K. Suppression of a spinal and a cranial nerve reflex by vaginal or rectal probing in rats. *Brain Research*, 1971, 35, 231–235.

Komisaruk, B. R., and Steinman, J. L. Genital stimulation as a trigger for neuroendocrine and behavioral control of reproduction. *Annals of the New York Academy of Sciences*, 1987, 474, 64–75.

Kong, J., Shepel, N., Holden, C. P., Mackiewicz, M., et al. Brain glycogen decreases with increased periods of wakefulness: Implications for homeostatic drive to sleep. *Journal of Neuroscience*, 2002, 22, 5581–5587.

Koob, G. F. Drug addiction: The yin and yang of hedonic homeostasis. *Neuron*, 1996, 16, 893–896.

Koob, G. F., Thatcher-Britton, K., Britton, D., Roberts, D. C. S., et al. Destruction of the locus coeruleus or the dorsal NE bundle does not alter the release of punished responding by ethanol and chlordiazepoxide. *Physiology and Behavior*, 1984, 33, 479–485.

Kordower, J. H., Dodiya, H. B., Kordower, A. M., Terpstra, B., et al. Transfer of host-derived alpha synuclein to grafter dopaminergic neurons in rat. *Neurobiology of Disease*, 2011, 43, 552–557.

Korngold, C., Farrell, H. M., and Fozdar, M. The National Football League and chronic traumatic encephalopathy: Legal implications. *Journal of the American Academy of Psychiatry and the Law Online*, 2013, 41(3), 430–436.

Kornhuber, H. H. Cerebral cortex, cerebellum, and basal ganglia: An introduction to their motor functions. In *The neurosciences: Third study program*, edited by F. O. Schmitt and F. G. Worden. Cambridge, MA.: MIT Press, 1974.

Koroshetz, W. J., and Moskowitz, M. A. Emerging treatments for stroke in humans. *Trends in Pharmacological Sciences*, 1996, 17, 227–233.

Kortegaard, L. S., Hoerder, K., Joergensen, J., Gillberg, C., et al. A preliminary population-based twin study of self-reported eating disorder. *Psychological Medicine*, 2001, 31, 361–365.

Kosfeld, M., Heinrichs, M., Zak, P. J., Fischbacher, U., et al. Oxytocin increases trust in humans. *Nature*, 2005, *433*, 673–676.

Kosten, T., Miserendino, M. J. D., and Kehoe, P. Enhanced acquisition of cocaine self-administration in adult rats with neonatal isolation stress experience. *Brain Research*, 2000, *875*, 44–50.

Kourtzi, A., and Kanwisher, N. Activation in human MT/MST by static images with implied motion. *Journal of Cognitive Neuroscience*, 2000, *12*, 48–55.

Kovács, G., Vogels, R., and Orban, G. A. Selectivity of macaque inferior temporal neurons for partially occluded shapes. *Journal of Neuroscience*, 1995, *15*, 1984–1997.

Koylu, E. O., Couceyro, P. R., Lambert, P. D., and Kuhar, M. J. Cocaine and amphetamine-regulated transcript peptide immunohistochemical localization in the rat brain. *Journal of Comparative Neurology*, 1998, *391*, 115–132.

Kozlowski, L. T., and Cutting, J. E. Recognizing the sex of a walker from a dynamic point-light display. *Perception and Psychophysics*, 1977, *21*, 575–580.

Krack, P., Kumar, R., Ardouin, C., Dowsey, P. L., et al. Mirthful laughter induced by subthalamic nucleus stimulation. *Movement Disorders*, 16(5), 867–875.

Kramer, F. M., Jeffery, R. W., Forster, J. L., and Snell, M. K. Long-term follow-up of behavioral treatment for obesity: Patterns of weight regain among men and women. *International Journal of Obesity*, 1989, *13*, 123–136.

Kraut, R. E., and Johnston, R. Social and emotional messages of smiling: An ethological approach. *Journal of Personality and Social Psychology*, 1979, *37*, 1539–1553.

Kravitz, A. V., Freeze, B. S., Parker, P. R. L., Kay, K., et al. Regulation of parkinsonian motor behaviours by optogenetic control of basal ganglia circuitry. *Nature*, 2010, *466*, 622–626.

Kress, M., and Zeilhofer, H. U. Capsaicin, protons and heat: New excitement about nociceptors. *Trends in Pharmacological Science*, 1999, *20*, 112–118.

Kristensen, P., Judge, M. E., Thim, L., Ribel, U., et al. Hypothalamic CART is a new anorectic peptide regulated by leptin. *Nature*, 1998, *393*, 72–76.

Krolak-Salmon, P., Hénaff, M.-A., Vighetto, A., Bertrand, O., et al. Early amygdala reaction to fear spreading in occipital, temporal, and frontal cortex: A depth electrode ERP study in humans. *Neuron*, 2004, *42*, 665–676.

Kruijver, F. P. M., Zhou, J.-N., Pool, C. W., Hofman, M. A., et al. Male-to-female transsexuals have female neuron numbers in a limbic nucleus. *Journal of Clinical Endocrinology and Metabolism*, 2000, *85*, 2034–2041.

Krumhansl, C. L. Plink: "Thin slices" of music. *Music Perception: An Interdisciplinary Journal*, 2010, *27*(5) 337–354.

Kuffler, S. W. Neurons in the retina: Organization, inhibition and excitation problems. *Cold Spring Harbor Symposium on Quantitative Biology*, 1952, *17*, 281–292.

Kuffler, S. W. Discharge patterns and functional organization of mammalian retina. *Journal of Neurophysiology*, 1953, *16*, 37–68.

Kumar, K., Wyant, G. M., and Nath, R. Deep brain stimulation for control of intractable pain in humans, present and future: A ten-year follow-up. *Neurosurgery*, 1990, *26*, 774–782.

Kumpik, D. P., Kacelnik, O., and King, A. J. Adaptive reweighting of auditory localization cues in response to chronic unilateral earplugging in humans. *Journal of Neuroscience*, 2010, *30*, 4883–4894.

Kunos, G., and Batkai, S. Novel physiologic functions of endocannabinoids as revealed through the use of mutant mice. *Neurochemical Research*, 2001, *26*, 1015–1021.

Kunugi, H., Nanko, S., and Murray, R. M. Obstetric complications and schizophrenia: Prenatal underdevelopment and subsequent neurodevelopmental impairment. *British Journal of Psychiatry*, 2001, *40*, s25–s29.

Kupfer, D. J. REM latency: A psychobiologic marker for primary depressive disease. *Biological Psychiatry*, 1976, *11*, 159–174.

Kurata, K., and Hoffman, D. S. Differential effects of muscimol microinjection into dorsal and ventral aspects of the premotor cortex of monkeys. *Journal of Neurophysiology*, 1994, *71*, 1151–1164.

Kurihara, K. Recent progress in taste receptor mechanisms. In *Umami: A basic taste*, edited by Y. Kawamura and M. R. Kare. New York: Dekker, 1987.

Kuriki, S., Mori, T., and Hirata, Y. Motor planning center for speech articulation in the normal human brain. *Neuroreport*, 1999, *10*, 765–769.

Kuryatov, A., Berrettini, W., and Lindstrom, J. Acetylcholine receptor (AChR) α5 subunit variant associated with risk for nicotine dependence and lung cancer reduces (α4β2)$_2$α5 AChR function. *Molecular Pharmacology*, 2011, *79*, 119–125.

LaBar, K. S., LeDoux, J. E., Spencer, D. D., and Phelps, E. A. Impaired fear conditioning following unilateral temporal lobectomy in humans. *Journal of Neuroscience*, 1995, *15*, 6846–6855.

Lahti, A. C., Weiler, M. A., Michaelidis, T., Parwani, A., et al. Effects of ketamine in normal and schizophrenic volunteers. *Neuropsychopharmacology*, 2001, *25*, 455–467.

Lai, E. C., Jankovic, J., Krauss, J. K., Ondo, W. G., et al. Long-term efficacy of posteroventral pallidotomy in the treatment of Parkinson's disease. *Neurology*, 2000, *55*, 1218–1222.

Lai, Y.-Y., Kodama, T., Schenkel, E., and Siegel, J. M. Behavioral response and transmitter release during atonia elicited by medial medullary stimulation. *Journal of Neurophysiology*, 2010, *104*, 2024–2033.

Laitinen, L. V., Bergenheim, A. T., and Hariz, M. I. Leksell's posteroventral pallidotomy in the treatment of Parkinson's disease. *Journal of Neurosurgery*, 1992, *76*, 53–61.

Lambon Ralph, M. A., and Patterson, K. Generalization and differentiation in semantic memory. *Annals of the New York Academy of Science*, 2008, *1124*, 61–76.

Landsness, E. C., Goldstein, M. R., Peterson, M. J., Tononi, G., et al. Antidepressant effects of selective slow wave sleep deprivation in major depression: A high-density EEG investigation. *Journal of Psychiatric Research*, 2011, *45*, 1019–1026.

Landisman, C. E., and Ts'o, D. Y. Color processing in macaque striate cortex: Relationships to ocular dominance, cytochrome oxidase, and orientation. *Journal of Neurophysiology*, 2002, *87*, 3126–3137.

Lange, C. G. *Über gemüthsbewegungen*. Leipzig, Germany: T. Thomas, 1887.

Langen, M., Durston, S., Staal, W. G., Palmen, S. J. M. C., et al. Caudate nucleus is enlarged in high-functioning medication-naïve subjects with autism. *Biological Psychiatry*, 2007, *62*, 262–266.

Langston, J. W., Ballard, P., Tetrud, J., and Irwin, I. Chronic parkinsonism in humans due to a product of meperidine-analog synthesis. *Science*, 1983, *219*, 979–980.

Lankenau, S. E., Teti, M., Silva, K., Bloom, J. J., et al. Initiation into prescription opioid misuse amongst young injection drug users. *International Journal of Drug Policy*, 2012, *23*(1), 37–44.

Larson, P. S. Deep brain stimulation for psychiatric disorders. *Neurotherapeutics*, 2008, *5*, 50–58.

Laruelle, M., Abi-Dargham, A., Van Dyck, C. H., Gil, R., et al. Single photon emission computerized tomography imaging of amphetamine-induced dopamine release in drug-free schizophrenic subjects. *Proceedings of the National Academy of Sciences, USA*, 1996, *93*, 9235–9240.

Laschet, U. Antiandrogen in the treatment of sex offenders: Mode of action and therapeutic outcome. In *Contemporary sexual behavior: Critical issues in the 1970s*, edited by J. Zubin and J. Money. Baltimore: Johns Hopkins University Press, 1973.

Lau, H. C., Rogers, R. D., Haggard, P., and Passingham, R. E. Attention to intention. *Science*, 2004, *303*, 1208–1210.

Lavoie, B., and Parent, A. Immunohistochemical study of the serotoninergic innervation of the basal ganglia in the squirrel monkey. *Journal of Comparative Neurology*, 1990, *299*, 1–16.

Lavond, D. G., Kim, J. J., and Thompson, R. F. Mammalian brain substrates of aversive classical conditioning. *Annual Review of Psychology*, 1993, *44*, 317–342.

Lê, S., Cardebat, D., Boulanouar, K., Hénaff, M. A., et al. Seeing, since childhood, without ventral stream: A behavioural study. *Brain*, 2002, *125*, 58–74.

Le Bec, P.-Y., Fatséas, M., Denis, C., Lavie, E., et al. Cannabis et psychose: Recherche d'un lien de causalité à partir d'une revue critique systématique de la literature. *L'Encéphale*, 2009, *35*, 377–385.

Le Grand, R., Mondloch, C. J., Maurer, D., and Brent, H. P. Early visual experience and face processing. *Nature*, 2001, *410*, 890.

Le Grand, R., Mondloch, C. J., Maurer, D., and Brent, H. P. Expert face processing requires visual input to the right hemisphere during infancy. *Nature Neuroscience*, 2003, *6*, 1108–1112.

Le Jeune, F., Vérin, M., N'Diaye, K., Drapier, D., et al. Decrease of prefrontal metabolism after subthalamic stimulation in obsessive-compulsive disorder: A positron emission tomography study. *Biological Psychiatry*, 2010, *68*, 1016–1022.

LeDoux, J. E. Brain mechanisms of emotion and emotional learning. *Current Opinion in Neurobiology*, 1992, *2*, 191–197.

Lee, A., Clancy, S., and Fleming, A. S. Mother rats bar-press for pups: Effects of lesions of the mpoa and limbic sites on maternal behavior and operant responding for pup-reinforcement. *Behavioural Brain Research*, 2000, *108*, 15–31.

Lee, A. W., and Brown, R. E. Comparison of medial preoptic, amygdala, and nucleus accumbens lesions on parental behavior in California mice (*Peromyscus californicus*). *Physiology and Behavior*, 2007, *92*, 617–628.

Lee, J., Lin, L., and Robertson, T. The impact of media multitasking on learning. *Learning, Media and Technology*, 2012, *37*(1), 94–104.

Lee, M. S., Lee, H. Y., Lee, H. J., and Ryu, S. H. Serotonin transporter promoter gene polymorphism and long-term outcome of antidepressant treatment. *Psychiatric Genetics*, 2004, *14*, 111–115.

Lee, S. J., Desplats, P., Sigurdson, C., Tsigelny, I., et al. Cell-to-cell transmission of non-prion protein aggregates. *Nature Reviews: Neuroscience*, 2010, *6*, 702–706.

Lee, S.-J., Lim, H.-S., Masliah, E., and Lee, H.-J. Protein aggregate spreading in neurodegenerative diseases: Problems and perspectives. *Neuroscience Research*, 2011, *70*, 339–348.

Lehman, M. N., Silver, R., Gladstone, W. R., Kahn, R. M., et al. Circadian rhythmicity restored by neural transplant: Immunocytochemical characterization with the host brain. *Journal of Neuroscience*, 1987, *7*, 1626–1638.

Lehman, M. N., and Winans, S. S. Vomeronasal and olfactory pathways to the amygdala controlling male hamster sexual behavior: Autoradiographic and behavioral analyses. *Brain Research*, 1982, *240*, 27–41.

Leibenluft, E., Moul, D.E., Schwartz, P. J., Madden, P. A., et al. A clinical trial of sleep deprivation in combination with antidepressant medication. *Psychiatry Research*, 1993, *46*, 213–227.

Leiguarda, R. C., and Marsden, C. D. Limb apraxias: Higher-order disorders of sensorimotor integration. *Brain*, 2000, *123*, 860–879.

Leonard, C. M., Rolls, E. T., Wilson, F. A. W., and Baylis, G. C. Neurons in the amygdala of the monkey with responses selective for faces. *Behavioral Brain Research*, 1985, *15*, 159–176.

Leonard, H. L., Lenane, M. C., Swedo, S. E., Rettew, D. C., et al. Tics and Tourette's disorder: A 2- to 7-year follow-up of 54 obsessive-compulsive children. *American Journal of Psychiatry*, 1992a, *149*, 1244–1251.

Leonard, H. L., Lenane, M. C., Swedo, S. E., Rettew, D. C., et al. Tourette syndrome and obsessive-compulsive disorder. *Advances in Neurology*, 1992b, *58*, 83–93.

Lesser, R. Selective preservation of oral spelling without semantics in a case of multi-infarct dementia. *Cortex*, 1989, *25*, 239–250.

Letchworth, S. R., Nader, M. A., Smith, H. R., Friedman, D. P., et al. Progression of changes in dopamine transporter binding site density as a result of cocaine self-administration in rhesus monkeys. *Journal of Neuroscience*, 2001, *21*, 2799–2807.

LeVay, S. A difference in hypothalamic structure between heterosexual and homosexual men. *Science*, 1991, *253*, 1034–1037.

Levenson, R. W., Ekman, P., and Friesen, W. V. Voluntary facial action generates emotion-specific autonomic nervous system activity. *Psychophysiology*, 1990, *27*, 363–384.

Levine, J. A., Eberhardt, N. L., and Jensen, M. D. Role of nonexercise activity thermogenesis in resistance to fat gain in humans. *Science*, 1999, *283*, 212–214.

Levine, J. A., Lanningham-Foster, L. M., McCrady, S. K., Krizan, A. C., et al. Inter-individual variation in posture allocation: Possible role in human obesity. *Science*, 2005, *307*, 584–586.

Levine, M. S., Cepeda, C., and André, V. M. Location, location, location: Contrasting roles of synaptic and extrasynaptic NMDA receptors in Huntington's disease. *Neuron*, 2010, *65*, 145–147.

Levy, R. M., and Bredesen, D. E. Controversies in HIV-related central nervous system disease: Neuropsychological aspects of HIV-1 infection. In *AIDS clinical review 1989*, edited by P. Volberding, and M. A. Jacobson. New York: Marcel Dekker, 1989.

Lewis, D. A., Hashimoto, T., and Volk, D. W. Cortical inhibitory neurons and schizophrenia. *Nature Reviews: Neuroscience*, 2005, *6*, 312–324.

Lewis, D. A., and Smith, R. E. Steroid-induced psychiatric syndromes: A report of 14 cases and a review of the literature. *Journal of the Affective Disorders*, 1983, *5*, 19–32.

Lewis, E. B. Clusters of master control genes regulate the development of higher organisms. *Journal of the American Medical Association*, 1992, *267*, 1524–1531.

Lewis, M. B., and Bowler, P. J. Botulinum toxin cosmetic therapy correlates with a more positive mood. *Journal of Cosmetic Dermatology*, 2009, *8*, 24–26.

Lewis-Fernández, R., Hinton, D. E., Laria, A. J., Patterson, et al. Culture and the anxiety disorders: Recommendations for DSM-V. *Depression and Anxiety*, 27(2), 212–229.

LeWitt, P. A., Rezai, A. R., Leehey, M. A., Ojemann, S. G., et al. AAV2-GAD gene therapy for advanced Parkinson's disease: A double-blind, sham-surgery controlled, randomized trial. *Lancet Neurology*, 2011, *10*, 309–319.

Lewy, A. K., Lefler, B. J., Emens, J. S., and Bauer, V. K. The circadian basis of winter depression. *Proceedings of the National Academy of Sciences, USA*, 2006, *103*, 7414–7419.

Li, S. H., Lam, S., Cheng, A. L., & Li, X. J. (2000). Intranuclear huntingtin increases the expression of caspase-1 and induces apoptosis. *Human Molecular Genetics*, 9(19), 2859–2867.

Li, A.-J., and Ritter, S. Glucoprivation increases expression of neuropeptide Y mRNA in hindbrain neurons that innervate the hypothalamus. *European Journal of Neuroscience*, 2004, *19*, 2147–2154.

Li, M. R., and Cheung, B. M. Rise and fall of anti-obesity drugs. *World Journal of Diabetes*, 2011, *15*, 19–23.

Li, S., Cullen, W. K., Anwyl, R., and Rowan, M. J. Dopamine-dependent facilitation of LTP induction in hippocampal CA1 by exposure to spatial novelty. *Nature Neuroscience*, 2003, *5*, 526–531.

Li, X., Li, W., Wang, H., Cao, J., et al. Pseudogenization of a sweet-receptor gene accounts for cats' indifference toward sugar. *PLoS Genetics*, 2005, *1*, 27–35.

Li, Y. C., Kellendonk, C., Simpson, E. H., Kandel, E. R., et al. D2 receptor overexpression in the striatum leads to a deficit in inhibitory transmission and dopamine sensitivity in mouse prefrontal cortex. *Proceedings of the National Academy of Sciences, USA*, 2011, *108*, 12107–12012.

Lidberg, L., Asberg, M., and Sundqvist-Stensman, U. B. 5-Hydroxyindoleacetic acid levels in attempted suicides who have killed their children. *Lancet*, 1984, 2, 928.

Lidberg, L., Tuck, J. R., Asberg, M., Scalia-Tomba, G. P., et al. Homicide, suicide and CSF 5-HIAA. *Acta Psychiatrica Scandanavica*, 1985, 71, 230–236.

Lieberman, J. A. Dopamine partial agonists: A new class of antipsychotic. *CNS Drugs*, 2004, 18, 251–267.

Liepert, J., Bauder, H., Wolfgang, H. R., Miltner, W. H., et al. Treatment-induced cortical reorganization after stroke in humans. *Stroke*, 2000, 31, 1210–1216.

Liljequist, S. The competitive NMDA receptor antagonist, CGP 39551, inhibits ethanol withdrawal seizures. *European Journal of Pharmacology*, 1991, 192, 197–198.

Lim, M. M., Wang, Z., Olazábal, D. E., Ren, X., et al. Enhanced partner preference in a promiscuous species by manipulating the expression of a single gene. *Nature*, 2004, 429, 754–757.

Lim, M. M., and Young, L. F. Vasopressin-dependent neuronal circuits underlying pair bond formation in the monogamous prairie vole. *Neuroscience*. 2004, 125, 35–45.

Lin, J. S., Sakai, K., and Jouvet, M. Evidence for histaminergic arousal mechanisms in the hypothalamus of cat. *Neuropharmacology*, 1998, 27, 111–122.

Lin, L., Faraco, J., Li, R., Kadotani, H., Rogers, W., et al. The sleep disorder canine narcolepsy is caused by a mutation in the hypocretin (orexin) receptor 2. *Cell*, 1999, 98, 365–376.

Lindauer, R. J. L., Olff, M., van Meijel, E. P. M., Carlier, I. V. E., et al. Cortisol, learning, memory, and attention in relation to smaller hippocampal volume in police officers with posttraumatic stress disorder. *Biological Psychiatry*, 2005, 59, 171–177.

Lisk, R. D., Pretlow, R. A., and Friedman, S. Hormonal stimulation necessary for elicitation of maternal nest-building in the mouse (*Mus musculus*). *Animal Behaviour*, 1969, 17, 730–737.

Lisman, J. A mechanism for the Hebb and the anti-Hebb processes underlying learning and memory. *Proceedings of the National Academy of Sciences*, USA, 1989, 86, 9574–9578.

Liu, C., Zhang, W.-T., Tang, Y.-Y., Mai, X.-Q., et al. The visual word form area: Evidence from an fMRI study of implicit processing of Chinese characters. *NeuroImage*, 2008, 40, 1350–1361.

Liu, L., Wong, T. P., Pozza, M. F., Lingenhoehl, K., et al. Role of NMDA receptor subtypes in governing the direction of hippocampal synaptic plasticity. *Science*, 2004, 304, 1021–1023.

Liuzzi, F. J., and Lasek, R. J. Astrocytes block axonal regeneration in mammals by activating the physiological stop pathway. *Science*, 1987, 237, 642–645.

Livingstone, M. S., and Hubel, D. H. Anatomy and physiology of a color system in the primate visual cortex. *Journal of Neuroscience*, 1984, 4, 309–356.

Lledo, P. M., Hjelmstad, G. O., Mukherji, S., Soderling, T. R., et al. Calcium/calmodulin-dependent kinase II and long-term potentiation enhance synaptic transmission by the same mechanism. *Proceedings of the National Academy of Sciences*, USA, 1995, 92, 11175–11179.

Lo, E. H., Dalkara, T., and Moskowitz, M. A. Mechanisms, challenges and opportunities in stroke. *Nature Reviews Neuroscience*, 2003, 4(5), 399–414.

Logothetis, N. K., Pauls, J., and Poggio, T. Shape representation in the inferior temporal cortex of monkeys. *Current Biology*, 1995, 5, 552–563.

Löken, L. S., Wessberg, J., Morrison, I., McGlone, F., et al. Coding of pleasant touch by unmyelinated afferents in humans. *Nature Neuroscience*, 2009, 12, 547–548.

Lomber, S. G., and Malhotra, S. Double dissociation of "what" and "where" processing in auditory cortex. *Nature Neuroscience*, 2008, 11, 609–616.

Lømo, T. Frequency potentiation of excitatory synaptic activity in the dentate area of the hippocampal formation. *Acta Physiologica Scandinavica*, 1966, 68 (Suppl. 227), 128.

Longcamp, M., Anton, J.-L., Roth, M., and Velay, J.-L. Premotor activations in response to visually presented single letters depend on the hand used to write: A study on left-handers. *Neuropsychologia*, 2005, 43, 1801–1809.

Lozano, A. M., Mayberg, H. S., Giacobbe, P., Hamani, C., et al. Subcallosal cingulate gyrus deep brain stimulation for treatment-resistant depression. *Biological Psychiatry*, 2008, 64, 461–467.

Lu, J., Greco, M. A., Shiromani, P., and Saper, C. B. Effect of lesions of the ventrolateral preoptic nucleus on NREM and REM sleep. *Journal of Neuroscience*, 2000, 20, 3830–3842.

Lu, J., Zhang, Y.-H., Chou, T. C., Gaus, S. E., et al. Contrasting effects of ibotenate lesions of the paraventricular nucleus and subparaventricular zone on sleep–wake cycle and temperature regulation. *Journal of Neuroscience*, 2001, 21, 4864–4874.

Ludwig, D. S, Tritos, N. A., Mastaitis, J. W., Kulkarni, R., et al. Melanin-concentrating hormone overexpression in transgenic mice leads to obesity and insulin resistance. *Journal of Clinical Investigation*, 2001, 107, 379–386.

Luigjes, J., van den Brink, W., Feenstra, M., van den Munckhof, P., et al. Deep brain stimulation in addiction: A review of potential brain targets. *Molecular Psychiatry*, 2012, 17, 572–583.

Luo, M., Fee, M. S., and Katz, L. C. Encoding pheromonal signals in the accessory olfactory bulb of behaving mice. *Science*, 2003, 299, 1196–1201.

Lupien, S., Lecours, A. R., Schwartz, G., Sharma, S., et al. Longitudinal study of basal cortisol levels in healthy elderly subjects: Evidence for subgroups. *Neurobiology of Aging*, 1996, 17, 95–105.

Lüscher, C., Xia, H., Beattie, E. C., Carroll, R. C., et al. Role of AMPA receptor cycling in synaptic transmission and plasticity. *Neuron*, 1999, 24, 649–658.

Luzzi, S., Pucci, E., Di Bella, P., and Piccirilli, M. Topographical disorientation consequent to amnesia of spatial location in a patient with right parahippocampal damage. *Cortex*, 2000, 36, 427–434.

Lydon, J. P., DeMayo, F. J., Funk, C. R., Mani, S. K., et al. Mice lacking progesterone receptor exhibit pleitropic reproductive abnormalities. *Genes and Development*, 1995, 15, 2266–2278.

Lynch, G., Larson, J., Kelso, S., Barrionuevo, G., et al. Intracellular injections of EGTA block induction of long-term potentiation. *Nature*, 1984, 305, 719–721.

Lytton, W. W., and Brust, J. C. M. Direct dyslexia: Preserved oral reading of real words in Wernicke's aphasia. *Brain*, 1989, 112, 583–594.

Ma, W., Miao, Z., and Novotny, M. Induction of estrus in grouped female mice (*Mus domesticus*) by synthetic analogs of preputial gland constituents. *Chemical Senses*, 1999, 24, 289–293.

Ma, X., Zubcevic, L., Brüning, J. C., Ashcroft, F. M., et al. Electrical inhibition of identified anorexigenic POMC neurons by orexin/hypocretin. *Journal of Neuroscience*, 2007, 27, 1529–1533.

MacDonald, A. W., Carter, C. S., Kerns, J. G., Ursu, S., et al. Specificity of prefrontal dysfunction and context processing deficits to schizophrenia in never-medicated patients with first-episode psychosis. *American Journal of Psychiatry*, 2005, 162, 475–484.

MacLean, H. E., Warne, G. L., and Zajac, J. D. Defects of androgen receptor function: From sex reversal to motor-neuron disease. *Molecular and Cellular Endocrinology*, 1995, 112, 133–141.

MacLean, P. D. Psychosomatic disease and the "visceral brain": Recent developments bearing on the Papez theory of emotion. *Psychosomatic Medicine*, 1949, 11, 338–353.

MacSweeney, M., Capek, C. M., Campbell, R., and Woll, B. The signing brain: The neurobiology of sign language. *Trends in Cognitive Sciences*, 2008a, 12, 432–440.

MacSweeney, M., Waters, D., Brammer, M. J., Woll, B., et al. Phonological processing in deaf signers and the impact of age of first language acquisition. *NeuroImage*, 2008b, *40*, 1369–1379.

Madden, P. A. F., Heath, A. C., Rosenthal, N. E., and Martin, N. G. Seasonal changes in mood and behavior: The role of genetic factors. *Archives of General Psychiatry*, 1996, *53*, 47–55.

Madsen, P. L., Holm, S., Vorstrup, S., Friberg, L., et al. Human regional cerebral blood flow during rapid-eye-movement sleep. *Journal of Cerebral Blood Flow and Metabolism*, 1991, *11*, 502–507.

Magee, J. C., and Johnston, D. A synaptically controlled, associative signal for Hebbian plasticity in hippocampal neurons. *Science*, 1997, *275*, 209–213.

Maggard, M. A., Shugarman, L. R., Suttorp, M., Maglione, M., et al. Meta-analysis: Surgical treatment of obesity. *Annals of Internal Medicine*, 2005, *142*, 547–559.

Maguire, E. A., Frackowiak, R. S. J., and Frith, C. D. Recalling routes around London: Activation of the right hippocampus in taxi drivers. *Journal of Neuroscience*, 1997, *17*, 7103–7110.

Maguire, E. A., Gadian, D. G., Johnsrude, I. S., Good, C. D., et al. Navigation-related structural change in the hippocampi of taxi drivers. *Proceedings of the National Academy of Sciences, USA*, 2000, *97*, 4398–4403.

Maguire, E. A., Nannery, R., and Spiers, H. J. Navigation around London by a taxi driver with bilateral hippocampal lesions. *Brain*, 2006, *129*(11), 2894–2907.

Mahowald, M. W., and Schenck, C. H. Insights from studying human sleep disorders. *Nature*, 2005, *437*, 1279–1285.

Maj, M. Organic mental disorders in HIV-1 infection. *AIDS*, 1990, *4*, 831–840.

Mak, G. K., Enwere, E. K., Gregg, C., Pakarainen, T., et al. Male pheromone-stimulated neurogenesis in the adult female brain: Possible role in mating behavior. *Nature Neuroscience*, 2007, *10*, 1003–1011.

Makino, H., and Malinow, R. AMPA receptor incorporation into synapses during LTP: The role of lateral movement and exocytosis. *Neuron*, 2009, *64*, 381–390.

Maldonado, R., and Koob, G. F. Destruction of the locus coeruleus decreases physical signs of opiate withdrawal. *Brain Research*, 1993, *605*, 128–138.

Maldonado, R., and Rodriguez de Fonseca, F. Cannabinoid addiction: Behavioral models and neural correlates. *Journal of Neuroscience*, 2002, *22*, 3326–3331.

Maldonado, R., Stinus, L., Gold, L. H., and Koob, G. F. Role of different brain structures in the expression of the physical morphine-withdrawal syndrome. *Journal of*

Pharmacology and Experimental Therapeutics, 1992, *261*, 669–677.

Malhotra, A. K., Adler, C. M., Kennison, S. D., Elman, I., et al. Clozapine blunts N-methyl-D-aspartate antagonist-induced psychosis: A study with ketamine. *Biological Psychiatry*, 1997, *42*, 664–668.

Mallow, G. K. The relationship between aggression and cycle stage in adult female rhesus monkeys (*Macaca mulatta*). *Dissertation Abstracts*, 1979, *39*, 3194.

Mallucci, G., Dickinson, A., Linehan, J., Klöhn, P. C., et al. Depleting neuronal PrP in prion infections prevents disease and reverses spongiosis. *Science*, 2003, *302*, 871–874.

Malnic, B., Godfrey, P. A., and Buck, L. B. The human olfactory receptor gene family. *Proceedings of the National Academy of Sciences, USA*, 2004, *101*, 2584–2589.

Malnic, B., Hirono, J., Sato, T., and Buck, L. B. Combinatorial receptor codes for odors. *Cell*, 1999, *96*, 713–723.

Malsbury, C. W. Facilitation of male rat copulatory behavior by electrical stimulation of the medial preoptic area. *Physiology and Behavior*, 1971, *7*, 797–805.

Mameli, M., Halbout, B., Creton, C., Engblom, D., et al. Cocaine-evoked synaptic plasticity: Persistence in the VTA triggers adaptations in the NAC. *Nature Neuroscience*, 2009, *12*, 1039–1041.

Mancuso, K., Hauswirth, W. W., Li, Q., Connor, T. B., et al. Gene therapy for red-green colour blindness in adult primates. *Nature*, 2009, *461*, 784–787.

Mandiyan, V. S., Coats, J. K., and Shah, N. M. Deficits in sexual and aggressive behaviors in Cnga2 mutant mice. *Nature Neuroscience*, 2005, *8*, 1660–1662.

Mani, S. K., Blaustein, J. D., Allen, J. M., Law, S. W., et al. Inhibition of rat sexual behavior by antisense oligonucleotides to the progesterone receptor. *Endocrinology*, 1994, *135*(4), 1409–1414.

Manji, H. K., Moore, G. J., and Chen, G. Bipolar disorder: Leads from the molecular and cellular mechanisms of action of mood stabilisers. *British Journal of Psychiatry*, 2001, *178* (Suppl 41), S107–S109.

Manley, R. S., O'Brien, K. M., and Samuels, S. Fitness instructors' recognition of eating disorders and attendant ethical/liability issues. *Eating Disorders*, 2008, *16*, 103–116.

Mann, J. J., Malone, K. M., Diehl, D. J., Perel, J., et al. Positron emission tomographic imaging of serotonin activation effects on prefrontal cortex in healthy volunteers. *Journal of Cerebral Blood Flow and Metabolism*, 1996, *16*, 418–426.

Manning, L., and Campbell, R. Optic aphasia with spared action naming: A description

and possible loci of impairment. *Neuropsychologia*, 1992, *30*, 587–592.

Manns, J. R., Hopkins, R. O., and Squire, L. R. Semantic memory and the human hippocampus. *Neuron*, 2003, *38*, 127–133.

Mantione, M., van de Brink, W., Schuurman, P. R., and Denys, D. Smoking cessation and weight loss after chronic deep brain stimulation of the nucleus accumbens: Therapeutic and research implications: Case report. *Neurosurgery*, 2010, *66*, E218.

Mantyh, P. W. Connections of midbrain periaqueductal gray in the monkey. II: Descending efferent projections. *Journal of Neurophysiology*, 1983, *49*, 582–594.

Mao-Draayer, Y., and Panitch, H. Alexia without agraphia in multiple sclerosis: Case report with magnetic resonance imaging localization. *Multiple Sclerosis*, 2004, *10*, 705–707.

Maquet, P. Sleep function(s) and cerebral metabolism. *Behavioural Brain Research*, 1995, *69*, 75–83.

Maquet, P., Dive, D., Salmon, E., Sadzot, B., et al. Cerebral glucose utilization during sleep-wake cycle in man determined by positron emission tomography and [^{18}F]2-fluro-2-deoxy-D-glucose method. *Brain Research*, 1990, *413*, 136–143.

Margolin, D. I., and Goodman-Schulman, R. Oral and written spelling impairments. In *Cognitive neuropsychology in clinical practice*, edited by D. I. Margolin. New York: Oxford University Press, 1992.

Margolin, D. I., Marcel, A. J., and Carlson, N. R. Common mechanisms in dysnomia and post-semantic surface dyslexia: Processing deficits and selective attention. In *Surface dyslexia: Neuropsychological and cognitive studies of phonological reading*, edited by M. Coltheart. London: Lawrence Erlbaum Associates, 1985.

Margolin, D. I., and Walker, J. A. Personal communication, 1981.

Margolskee, R. G., Dyer, J., Kokrashvili, Z., et al. T1R3 and gustducin in gut sense sugars to regulate expression of Na$^+$ glucose cotransporter 1. *Proceedings of the National Academy of Sciences, USA*, 2007, *104*, 15075–15080.

Marinkovic, K., Dhond, R. P., Dale, A. M., Glessner, M., et al. Spatiotemporal dynamics of modality-specific and supramodal word processing. *Neuron*, 2003, *38*, 487–497.

Marrosu, F., Portas, C., Mascia, M. S., Casu, M. A., et al. Microdialysis measurement of cortical and hippocampal acetylcholine release during sleep–wake cycle in freely moving cats. *Brain Research*, 1995, *671*, 329–332.

Marshall, B. E., and Longnecker, D. E. General anesthetics. In *The pharmacological basis of therapeutics*, edited by L. S. Goodman, A. Gilman, T. W. Rall, A. S. Nies, and P. Taylor. New York: Pergamon Press, 1990.

Marshall, L., and Born, J. The contribution of sleep to hippocampus-dependent memory consolidation. *Trends in Cognitive Science*, 2007, *11*, 442–450.

Marson, L. Central nervous system neurons identified after injection of pseudorabies virus into the rat clitoris. *Neuroscience Letters*, 1995, *190*, 41–44.

Marson, L, and McKenna, K. E. A role for 5-hydroxytryptamine in descending inhibition of spinal sexual reflexes. *Experimental Brain Research*, 1992, *88*, 313–320.

Marson, L., and McKenna, K. E. CNS cell groups involved in the control of the ischiocavernosus and bulbospongiosus muscles: A transneuronal tracing study using pseudorabies virus. *Journal of Comparative Neurology*, 1996, *374*, 161–179.

Marson, L, and Murphy, A. Z. Identification of neural circuits involved in female genital responses in the rat: A dual virus and anterograde tracing study. *American Journal of Physiology*, 2006, *291*, 419–428.

Martinez, M., Campion, D., Babron, M. C., and Clergetdarpous, F. Is a single mutation at the same locus responsible for all affected cases in a large Alzheimer pedigree (FAD4)? *Genetic Epidemiology*, 1993, *10*, 431–435.

Martínez-Cué, C., Delatour, B., and Potier, M. C. Treating enhanced GABAergic inhibition in Down syndrome: Use of GABA α5-selective inverse agonists. *Neuroscience and Biobehavioral Reviews*, 2014, *46*, 218–227.

Martín-Murcia, F., Díaz, A. J. C., and Gonzalez, L. P. A case study of anorexia nervosa and obsessive personality disorder using third-generation behavioral therapies. *Clinical Case Studies*, 2011, *10*(3), 198–209.

Martins, I. J., Hone, E., Foster, J. K., Sünram-Lea, S. I., et al. Aoplipoprotein E, cholesterol metabolism, diabetes, and the convergence of risk factors for Alzheimer's disease and cardiovascular disease. *Molecular Psychiatry*, 2006, *11*, 721–736.

Marucha, P. T., Kiecolt-Glaser, J. K., and Favagehi, M. Mucosal wound healing is impaired by examination stress. *Psychosomatic Medicine*, 1998, *60*(3), 362–365.

Mas, M. Neurobiological correlates of masculine sexual behavior. *Neuroscience and Biobehavioral Reviews*, 1995, *19*, 261–277.

Masland, R. H. Neuronal diversity in the retina. *Current Opinion in Neurobiology*, 2001, *11*, 431–436.

Mathalon, D. H., Pfefferbaum, A., Lim, K. O., Rosenbloom, M. J., et al. Compounded brain volume deficits in schizophrenia-alcoholism comorbidity. *Archives of General Psychiatry*, 2003, *60*, 245–252.

Mathers, C. D., and Loncar, D. Projections of global mortality and burden of disease from 2002 to 2030. *PLoS Medicine*, 2006, *3*, e442.

Mathis, C. A., Klunk, W. E., Price, J. C., and DeKosky, S. T. Imaging technology for neurodegenerative diseases. *Archives of Neurology*, 2005, *62*, 196–200.

Matsuda, L. A., Lolait, S. J., Brownstein, M. J., Young, A. C., and Bonner, T. I. Structure of a cannabinoid receptor and functional expression of the cloned cDNA. *Nature*, 1990, *346*, 561–564.

Matsumoto, D., and Willingham, B. Spontaneous facial expressions of emotion of congenitally and noncongenitally blind individuals. *Journal of Personality and Social Psychology*, 2009, *96*, 1–10.

Matsunami, H., Montmayeur, J.-P., and Buck, L. B. A family of candidate taste receptors in human and mouse. *Nature*, 2000, *404*, 601–604.

Mattay, V. S., Goldberg, T. E., Fera, F., Hariri, A. R., et al. Catechol *O*-methyltransferase val_{159}-*met* genotype and individual variation in the brain response to amphetamine. *Proceedings of the National Academy of Sciences, USA*, 2003, *100*, 6186–6191.

Matteo, S., and Rissman, E. F. Increased sexual activity during the midcycle portion of the human menstrual cycle. *Hormones and Behavior*, 1984, *18*, 249–255.

Matthes, H. W. D., Maldonado, R., Simonin, F., Valverde, O., et al. Loss of morphine-induced analgesia, reward effect and withdrawal symptoms in mice lacking the μ-opioid-receptor gene. *Nature*, 1996, *383*, 819–823.

Matthews, D. B., Simson, P. E., and Best, P. J. Ethanol alters spatial processing of hippocampal place cells: A mechanism for impaired navigation when intoxicated. *Alcoholism: Clinical and Experimental Research*, 1996, *20*, 404–407.

Mattick, J. S. The hidden genetic program of complex organisms. *Scientific American*, 2004, *291*, 60–67.

Mattson, M. P., Haughey, N. J., and Nath, A. Cell death in HIV dementia. *Cell Death and Differentiation*, 2005, *12*, 893–904.

Maviel, T., Durkin, T. P., Menzaghi, F., and Bontempi, B. Sites of neocortical reorganization critical for remote spatial memory. *Science*, 2004, *305*, 96–99.

Mayberg, H. S. Targeted electrode-based modulation of neural circuits for depression. *Journal of Clinical Investigation*, 2009, *119*, 717–725.

Mayberg, H. S., Lozano, A. M., Voon, V., McNeely, H. E., et al. Deep brain stimulation for treatment-resistant depression. *Neuron*, 2005, *45*, 651–660.

Mayberg, H. S., Silva, J. A., Branna, S. K., et al. The functional neuroanatomy of the placebo effect. *American Journal of Psychiatry*, 2002, *159*, 728–737.

Mayer, D. J., and Liebeskind, J. C. Pain reduction by focal electrical stimulation of the brain: An anatomical and behavioral analysis. *Brain Research*, 1974, *68*, 73–93.

Mayers, A. G., and Baldwin, D. S. Antidepressants and their effect on sleep. *Human Psychopharmacology*, 2005, *20*, 533–559.

Mazur, A. Hormones, aggression, and dominance in humans. In *Hormones and aggressive behavior*, edited by B. B. Svare. New York: Plenum Press, 1983.

Mazur, A., and Booth, A. Testosterone and dominance in men. *Behavioral and Brain Sciences*, 1998, *21*, 353–397.

Mazur, A., and Lamb, T. Testosterone, status, and mood in human males. *Hormones and Behavior*, 1980, *14*, 236–246.

McCann, U. D., Wong, D. F., Yokoi, F., Villemagne, V., et al. Reduced striatal dopamine transporter density in abstinent methamphetamine and methcathinone users: Evidence from positron emission tomography studies with [^{11}C]WIN-35,428. *Journal of Neuroscience*, 1998, *18*, 8417–8422.

McCarley, R. W., and Hobson, J. A. The form of dreams and the biology of sleep. In *Handbook of dreams: Research, theory, and applications*, edited by B. Wolman. New York: Van Nostrand Reinhold, 1979.

McCaul, K. D., Gladue, B. A., and Joppa, M. Winning, losing, mood, and testosterone. *Hormones and Behavior*, 1992, *26*, 486–504.

McCleod, P., Dittrich, W., Driver, J., Perret, D., et al. Preserved and impaired detection of structure from motion by a "motion blind" patient. *Vision and Cognition*, 1996, *3*, 363–391.

McClintock, M. K. Menstrual synchrony and suppression. *Nature*, 1971, *229*, 244–245.

McClintock, M. K., and Adler, N. T. The role of the female during copulation in wild and domestic Norway rats (*Rattus norvegicus*). *Behaviour*, 1978, *67*, 67–96.

McConeghy, K. W., Hatton, J., Hughes, L., and Cook, A. M. A review of neuroprotection pharmacology and therapies in patients with acute traumatic brain injury. *CNS Drugs*, 2012, *26*(7), 613–636.

McEwen, B. Protective and damaging effects of stress mediators: Central role of the brain. *Dialogues in Clinical Neuroscience*, 2006, *8*(4), 367–381.

McEwen, B. S., and Gianaros, P. J. Central role of the brain in stress and adaptation: Links to socioeconomic status, health, and disease. *Annals of the New York Academy of Sciences*, 2010, *1186*(1), 190–222.

McEwen, B. S., and Sapolsky, R. M. Stress and cognitive function. *Current Biology*, 1995, *5*, 205–216.

McFarland, K., Lapish, C. C., and Kalivas, P. W. Prefrontal glutamate release in the core of the nucleus accumbens mediates cocaine-induced reinstatement of drug-seeking behavior. *Journal of Neuroscience*, 2003, *23*, 3531–3537.

McGrath, C. L., Glatt, S. J., Sklar, P., Le-Niculescu, H., et al. Evidence for genetic association of *RORB* with bipolar disorder. *BMC Psychiatry*, 2009, 9, 70.

McGrath, J. J., and Welham, J. L. Season of birth and schizophrenia: A systematic review and meta-analysis of data from the Southern Hemisphere. *Schizophrenia research*, 1999, 35(3), 237–242.

McGrath, J., Saari, K., Hakko, H., Jokelainen, J., et al. Vitamin D supplementation during the first year of life and risk of schizophrenia: A Finnish birth cohort study. *Schizophrenia Research*, 2004, 67(2), 237–245.

McGrath, J., Welham, J., and Pemberton, M. Month of birth, hemisphere of birth and schizophrenia. *British Journal of Psychiatry*, 1995, 167, 783–785.

McIver, B., Connacher, A., Whittle, I., Baylis, P., et al. Adipsic hypothalamic diabetes insipidus after clipping of anterior communicating artery aneurysm. *British Medical Journal*, 1991, 303, 1465–1467.

McKinley, M. J., Cairns, M. J., Denton, D. A., Egan, G., et al. Physiological and pathophysiological influences on thirst. *Physiology and Behavior*, 2004, 81, 795–803.

McKinley, M. J., Walker, L. L., Alexiou, T., et al. Osmoregulatory fluid intake but not hypovolemic thirst is intact in mice lacking angiotensin. *American Journal of Physiology*, 2008, 294, R1533–R1543.

McLaughlin, S. K., McKinnon, P. J., Robichon, A., Spickofsky, N., et al. Gustducin and transducin: A tale of two G proteins. *Ciba Foundation Symposiums*, 1993, 179, 196–200.

McLellan, A. T., Lewis, D. C., O'Brien, C. P., and Kleber, H. D. Drug dependence, a chronic medical illness: Implications for treatment, insurance, and outcomes evaluation. *Journal of the American Medical Association*, 2000, 284(13), 1689–1695.

Mechelli, A., Crinion, J. T., Noppeney, U., O'Doherty, J., et al. Neurolinguistics: Structural plasticity in the bilingual brain. *Nature*, 2004, 431(7010), 757–757.

Mechoulam, R., Ben-Shabat, S., Hanus, L., Ligumsky, M., et al. Identification of an endogenous 2-monoglyceride, present in canine gut, that binds to cannabinoid receptors. *Biochemical Pharmacology*, 1995, 50, 83–90.

Medcalf, R. Plasminogen activation-based thrombolysis for ischaemic stroke: The diversity of targets may demand new approaches. *Current Drug Targets*, 2011, 12, 1772–1781.

Mednick, S. A., Machon, R. A., and Huttunen, M. O. An update on the Helsinki influenza project. *Archives of General Psychiatry*, 1990, 47, 292.

Mednick, S., Nakayama, K., and Stickgold, R. Sleep-dependent learning: A nap is as good as a night. *Nature Neuroscience*, 2003, 6, 697–698.

Mehta, R. P., Rosowski, J. J., Voss, S. E., O'Neil, E., et al. Determinants of hearing loss in perforations of the tympanic membrane. *Otology and Neurotology*, 2006, 27 (2), 136.

Melges, F. T. *Time and the inner future: A temporal approach to psychiatric disorders.* New York: John Wiley & Sons, 1982.

Melzak, R. Phantom limbs. *Scientific American*, 1992, 266, 120–126.

Menco, B. P. M., Bruch, R. C., Dau, B., and Danho, W. Ultrastructural localization of olfactory transduction-components: The G protein subunit $G_{olf\alpha}$ and type III adenylyl cyclase. *Neuron*, 1992, 8, 441–453.

Menon, V., and Desmond, J. E. Left superior parietal cortex involvement in writing: Integrating fMRI with lesion evidence. *Cognitive Brain Research*, 2001, 12, 337–340.

Meredith, M. Chronic recording of vomeronasal pump activation in awake behaving hamsters. *Physiology and Behavior*, 1994, 56, 345–354.

Meredith, M., and O'Connell, R. J. Efferent control of stimulus access to the hamster vomeronasal organ. *Journal of Physiology*, 1979, 286, 301–316.

Meeren, H. K., van Heignsbergen, C. C., and de Gelder, B. Rapid perceptual integration of facial expression and emotional body language. *Proceedings of the National Academy of Sciences, USA*, 2005, 102, 16518–16523.

Mereu, G., Yoon, K.-W. P., Boi, V., Gessa, G. L., et al. Preferential stimulation of ventral tegmental area dopaminergic neurons by nicotine. *European Journal of Pharmacology*, 1987, 141, 395–400.

Merikangas, K. R., and Low, N. C. Genetic epidemiology of anxiety disorders. *Handbook of Experimental Pharmacology*, 2005, 169, 163–179.

Mesches, M. H., Fleshner, M., Heman, K. L., Rose, G. M., et al. Exposing rats to a predator blocks primed burst potentiation in the hippocampus *in vitro. Journal of Neuroscience*, 1999, 19, RC18 (1–5).

Meyer, M., Alter, K., Friederici, A. D., Lohmann, G., et al. FMRI reveals brain regions mediating slow prosodic modulations in spoken sentences. *Human Brain Mapping*, 2002, 17, 73–88.

Meyer-Bahlburg, H. F. L., Dolezal, C., Baker, S. W., and New, M. I. Sexual orientation in women with classical or non-classical congenital adrenal hyperplasia as a function of degree of prenatal androgen excess. *Archives of Sexual Behavior*, 2008, 37, 85–99.

Meyer-Bahlburg, H. F. L. Psychoendocrine research on sexual orientation: Current status and future options. *Progress in Brain Research*, 1984, 63, 375–398.

Meyer-Bahlburg, H. F. L. Gender and sexuality in classic congenital adrenal hyperplasia. *Endocrinology and Metabolism Clinics of North America*, 2001, 30, 155–171.

Meyer-Bahlburg, H. F. L. Gender identity outcome in female-raised 46, XY persons with penile agenesis, cloacal exstrophy of the bladder, or penile ablation. *Archives of Sexual Behavior*, 2005, 34, 423–438.

Michel, L., Derkinderen, P., Laplaud, D., Daumas-Duport, B., et al. Emotional facial palsy following striato-capsular infarction. *Journal of Neurology, Neurosurgery, and Psychiatry*, 2008, 79, 193–194.

Mieda, M., Williams, S. C., Sinton, C. M., Richardson, J. A., et al. Orexin neurons function in an efferent pathway of a food-entrainable circadian oscillator in eliciting food-anticipatory activity and wakefulness. *Journal of Neuroscience*, 2004, 24, 10493–10501.

Mignot, E. Genetic and familial aspects of narcolepsy. *Neurology*, 1998, 50, S16–S22.

Migues, P. V., Hardt, O., Wu, D. C., Gamache, K., et al. PKMζ maintains memories by regulating GluR2-dependent AMPA receptor trafficking. *Nature Neuroscience*, 2010, 13, 630–634.

Milad, M. R., Vidal-Gonzalez, I., and Quirk, G. J. Electrical stimulation of medial prefrontal cortex reduces conditioned fear in a temporally specific manner. *Behavioral Neuroscience*, 2004, 118, 389–394.

Milani, P., Gagliardi, S., Cova, E., and Cereda, C. SOD1 transcriptional and posttranscriptional regulation and its potential implications in ALS. *Neurology Research International*, 2011, 72, 1153–1159.

Mileykovskiy, B. Y., Kiyashchenko, L. I., and Siegel, J. M. Behavioral correlates of activity in identified hypocretin/orexin neurons. *Neuron*, 2005, 46, 787–798.

Millar, R. P. Roseweir, A. K., Tello, J. A., Anderson, R. A., et al. Kisspeptin antagonists: Unraveling the role of kisspeptin in reproductive physiology. *Brain Research*, 2010, 1364, 81–89.

Miller, G. Neurodegeneration: Could they all be prion diseases? *Science*, 2009, 326, 1337–1339.

Miller, J., Arrasate, M., Shaby, B. A., Mitra, S., et al. Quantitative relationships between huntingtin levels, poly-glutamine length, inclusion body formation, and neuronal death provide novel insight into Huntington's disease molecular pathogenesis. *Journal of Neuroscience*, 2010, 30, 10541–10550.

Miller, N. E. Understanding the use of animals in behavioral research: Some critical issues. *Annals of the New York Academy of Sciences*, 1983, 406, 113–118.

Miller, R. G., Mitchell, J. D., Lyon, M., and Moore, D. H. Riluzole for amyotrophic lateral sclerosis (ALS)/motor neuron disease (MND). *Amyotrophic Lateral Sclerosis and Other Motor Neuron Disorders*, 2003, 4, 191–206.

Miller, V. M., and Best, P. J. Spatial correlates of hippocampal unit activity are altered by lesions of the fornix and entorhinal cortex. *Brain Research*, 1980, *194*, 311–323.

Milner, A. D., Perrett, D. I., Johnston, R. S., and Benson, P. J. Perception and action in "visual form agnosia." *Brain*, 1991, *114*, 405–428.

Milner, B. Memory and the temporal regions of the brain. In *Biology of memory*, edited by K. H. Pribram and D. E. Broadbent. New York: Academic Press, 1970.

Milner, B., Corkin, S., and Teuber, H.-L. Further analysis of the hippocampal amnesic syndrome: 14-year follow-up study of H. M. *Neuropsychologia*, 1968, *6*, 317–338.

Mindus, P., Rasmussen, S. A., and Lindquist, C. Neurosurgical treatment for refractory obsessive-compulsive disorder: Implications for understanding frontal lobe function. *Journal of Neuropsychiatry and Clinical Neurosciences*, 1994, *6*, 467–477.

Minozzi, S., Davoli, M., Bargagli, A. M., Amato, L., et al. An overview of systematic reviews on cannabis and psychosis: Discussing apparently conflicting results. *Drug and Alcohol Review*, 2010, *29*, 304–317.

Mirenowicz, J., and Schultz, W. Importance of unpredictability for reward responses in primate dopamine neurons. *Journal of Neurophysiology*, 1994, *72*, 1024–1027.

Mirenowicz, J., and Schultz, W. Preferential activation of midbrain dopamine neurons by appetitive rather than aversive stimuli. *Nature*, 1996, *379*, 449–451.

Misanin, J. R., Miller, R. R., and Lewis, D. J. Retrograde amnesia produced by electroconvulsive shock after reactivation of a consolidated memory trace. *Science*, 1968, *160*, 554–555.

Mishkin, M. Visual mechanisms beyond the striate cortex. In *Frontiers in physiological psychology*, edited by R. W. Russell. New York: Academic Press, 1966.

Mitchell, J. E. Psychopharmacology of eating disorders. *Annals of the New York Academy of Sciences*, 1989, *575*, 41–49.

Mitler, M. M. Evaluation of treatment with stimulants in narcolepsy. *Sleep*, 1994, *17*, S103–S106.

Mittal, V. A., Ellman, L. M., and Cannon, T. D. Gene-environment interaction and covariation in schizophrenia: The role of obstetric complications. *Schizophrenia Bulletin*, 2008, *34*, 1083–1094.

Miyashita, Y. Cognitive memory: Cellular and network machineries and their top-down control. *Science*, 2004, *306*, 435–440.

Mizrahi, A., Crowley, J. C., Shtoyerman, E., and Katz, L. C. High-resolution in vivo imaging of hippocampal dendrites and spines. *Journal of Neuroscience*, 2004, *2*, 3147–3151.

Mizuno, Y., Kondo, T., Kuno, S., Nomoto, M., et al. Early addition of selegiline to L-DOPA treatment is beneficial for patients with

Parkinson disease. *Clinical Neuropharmacology*, 2010, *33*, 1–4.

Mochizuki, T., Crocker, A., McCormack, S., Yanagisawa, M., et al. Behavioral state instability in orexin knock-out mice. *Journal of Neuroscience*, 2004, *24*, 6291–6300.

Modahl, C., Green, L., Fein, D., Morris, M., et al. Plasma oxytocin levels in autistic children. *Biological Psychiatry*, 1988, *43*, 270–277.

Moghaddam, B., and Bunney, B. S. Differential effect of cocaine on extracellular dopamine levels in rat medial prefrontal cortex and nucleus accumbens: Comparison to amphetamine. *Synapse*, 1989, *4*, 156–161.

Molko, N., Cohen, L., Mangin, J. F., Chochon, F., et al. Visualizing the neural bases of a disconnection syndrome with diffusion tensor imaging. *Journal of Cognitive Neuroscience*, 2002, *14*, 629–636.

Mollon, J. D. "Tho' she kneel'd in that place where they grew. . .": The uses and origins of primate colour vision. *Journal of Experimental Biology*, 1989, *146*, 21–38.

Mombaerts, P. Molecular biology of odorant receptors in vertebrates. *Annual Review of Neuroscience*, 1999, *22*, 487–510.

Monaghan, D. T., and Cotman, C. W. Distribution of NMDA-sensitive L-3H-glutamate binding sites in rat brain as determined by quantitative autoradiography. *Journal of Neuroscience*, 1985, *5*, 2909–2919.

Money, J., and Ehrhardt, A. *Man & woman, boy & girl*. Baltimore, MD: Johns Hopkins University Press, 1972.

Monk, C. S., Telzer, E. H., Mogg, K., Bradley, B. P., et al. Amygdala and ventrolateral prefrontal cortex activation to masked angry faces in children and adolescents with generalized anxiety disorder. *Archives of General Psychiatry*, 2008, *65*, 568–576.

Monsonego, A., and Weiner, H. L. Immunotherapeutic approaches to Alzheimer's disease. *Science*, 2003, *302*, 834–838.

Montagna, P., Gambetti, P., Cortelli, P., and Lugaresi, E. Familial and sporadic fatal insomnia. *The Lancet Neurology*, 2003, *2*, 167–176.

Montero, S., Fuentes, J. A., and Fernandez-Tome, P. Lesions of the ventral noradrenergic bundle prevent the rise in blood pressure induced by social deprivation stress in the rat. *Cellular and Molecular Neurobiology*, 1990, *10*, 497–505.

Moore, D. J., West, A. B., Dawson, V. L., and Dawson, T. M. Molecular pathophysiology of Parkinson's disease. *Annual Review of Neuroscience*, 2005, *28*, 57–87.

Moore, D. R., and Shannon, R. V. Beyond cochlear implants: Awakening the deafened brain. *Nature Neuroscience*, 2009, *12*, 686–691.

Moore, G. J., Bebchuk, J. M., Wilds, I. B., Chen, G., et al. Lithium-induced increase in

human brain grey matter. *Lancet*, 2000, *356*, 1241–1242.

Moore, R. Y., and Eichler, V. B. Loss of a circadian adrenal corticosterone rhythm following suprachiasmatic lesions in the rat. *Brain Research*, 1972, *42*, 201–206.

Moore, R. Y., Speh, J. C., and Leak, R. K. Suprachiasmatic nucleus organization. *Cell Tissue Research*, 2002, *309*, 89–98.

Moore, T. H. M., Zammit, S., Lingford-Hughes, A., Barnes, T. R. E., et al. Cannabis use and risk of psychotic or affective mental health outcomes: A systematic review. *Lancet*, 2007, *370*, 319–328.

Moran, T. H. Gut peptides in the control of food intake. *International Journal of Obesity*, 2009, *33*, S7–S10.

Moran, T. H., Shnayder, L., Hostetler, A. M., and McHugh, P. R. Pylorectomy reduces the satiety action of cholecystokinin. *American Journal of Physiology*, 1989, *255*, R1059–R1063.

Moretto, G., Làdavas, E., Mattioli, F., and di Pellegrino, G. A psychophysiological investigation of moral judgment after ventromedial prefrontal damage. *Journal of Cognitive Neuroscience*, 2009, *22*, 1888–1899.

Morgan, C. J. A., Freeman, T. P., Schafer, G. L., and Curran, H. V. Cannabidiol attenuates the appetitive effects of δ9-tetrahydrocannabinol in humans smoking their chosen cannabis. *Neuropsychopharmacology*, 2010, *35*, 1879–1885.

Mori, E., Ikeda, M., Hirono, N., Kitagaki, H., et al. Amygdalar volume and emotional memory in Alzheimer's disease. *American Journal of Psychiatry*, 1999, *156*, 216–222.

Morris, J. A., Gobrogge, K. L., Jordan, C. L., and Breedlove, S. M. Brain aromatase: Dyed-in-the-wool homosexuality. *Endocrinology*, 2004, *145*, 475–477.

Morris, J. S., Frith, C. D., Perrett, D. I., Rowland, D., et al. A differential neural response in the human amygdala to fearful and happy facial expressions. *Nature*, 1996, *383*, 812–815.

Morris, N. M., Udry, J. R., Khan-Dawood, F., and Dawood, M. Y. Marital sex frequency and midcycle female testosterone. *Archives of Sexual Behavior*, 1987, *16*, 27–37.

Morris, R. G. M., Garrud, P., Rawlins, J. N. P., and O'Keefe, J. Place navigation impaired in rats with hippocampal lesions. *Nature*, 1982, *297*, 681–683.

Moscovitch, M., and Olds, J. Asymmetries in emotional facial expressions and their possible relation to hemispheric specialization. *Neuropsychologia*, 1982, *20*, 71–81.

Moscovitch, M., Winocur, G., and Behrmann, M. What is special about face recognition? Nineteen experiments on a person with visual object agnosia and dyslexia but normal face recognition. *Journal of Cognitive Neuroscience*, 1997, *9*, 555–604.

Mosharov, E. V., Larsen, K. R., Kanter, E., Phillips, K. A., et al. Interplay between cytosolic dopamine, calcium, and α-synuclein causes selective death of substantia nigra neurons. *Neuron*, 2009, *62*, 218–229.

Mosienko, V., Bert, B., Beis, D., Matthes, S., et al. Exaggerated aggression and decreased anxiety in mice deficient in brain serotonin. *Translational Psychiatry*, 2012, 2(5), e122.

Mountcastle, V. B. Modality and topographic properties of single neurons of cat's somatic sensory cortex. *Journal of Neurophysiology*, 1957, *20*, 408–434.

Mueser, K. T., Bellack, A. S., and Brady, E. U. Hallucinations in schizophrenia. *Acta Psychiatrica Scandinavica*, 1990, *82*, 26–29.

Mueser, K. T., Deavers, F., Penn, D. L., and Cassisi, J. Psychosocial treatments for schizophrenia. *Annual Review of Clinical Psychology*, 2013, *9*, 465–497.

Mueser, K. T., & McGurk, S. R. Schizophrenia. 9. *Lancet*, 2004, *363*, 2063–2072.

Mukhametov, L. M. Sleep in marine mammals. In *Sleep mechanisms*, edited by A. A. Borbély and J. L. Valatx. Munich: Springer-Verlag, 1984.

Münch, C., and Bertolotti, A. Self-propagation and transmission of misfolded mutant SOD1: Prion or prion-like phenomenon? *Cell Cycle*, 2011, *10*, 1711.

Murray, S. O., Boyaci, H., and Kersten, D. The representation of perceived angular size in human primary visual cortex. *Nature Neuroscience*, 2006, *9*, 429–434.

Murre, J. M. J., Graham, K. S., and Hodges, J. R. Semantic dementia: Relevance to connectionist models of long-term memory. *Brain*, 2001, *124*, 647–675.

Murrough, J. W., Iosifescu, D. V., Chang, L. C., Al Jurdi, R. K., et al. Antidepressant efficacy of ketamine in treatment-resistant major depression: A two-site randomized controlled trial. *American Journal of Psychiatry*, 2013, *170*(10), 1134–1142.

Museo, G., and Wise, R. A. Place preference conditioning with ventral tegmental injections of cystine. *Life Sciences*, 1994, *55*, 1179–1186.

Mushiake, H., Inase, M., and Tanji, J. Neuronal activity in the primate premotor, supplementary, and precentral motor cortex during visually guided and internally determined sequential movements. *Journal of Neurophysiology*, 1991, *66*, 705–718.

Myers, R. D., Wooten, M. H., Ames, C. D., and Nyce, J. W. Anorexic action of a new potential neuropeptide Y antagonist [D-Tyr^{27,36}, D-Thr^{32}]-NPY (27–36) infused into the hypothalamus of the rat. *Brain Research Bulletin*, 1995, *37*, 237–245.

Nachev, P., Kennard, C., and Husain, M. Functional role of the supplementary and pre-supplementary motor areas. *Nature Reviews: Neuroscience*, 2008, *9*, 856–869.

Nadeau, S. E. Impaired grammar with normal fluency and phonology. *Brain*, 1988, *111*, 1111–1137.

Nader, K. Memory traces unbound. *Trends in Neuroscience*, 2003, *26*, 65–72.

Naeser, M. A., Palumbo, C. L., Helm-Estabrooks, N., Stiassny-Eder, D., et al. Severe nonfluency in aphasia: Role of the medial subcallosal fasciculus and other white matter pathways in recovery of spontaneous speech. *Brain*, 1989, *112*, 1–38.

Nägerl, U. V., Köstinger, G., Anderson, J. C., Martin, K. A. C., et al. Protracted synaptogenesis after activity-dependent spinogenesis in hippocampal neurons. *Journal of Neuroscience*, 2007, *27*, 8149–8156.

Nakahara, D., Ozaki, N., Miura, Y., Miura, H., et al. Increased dopamine and serotonin metabolism in rat nucleus accumbens produced by intracranial self-stimulation of medial forebrain bundle as measured by in vivo microdialysis. *Brain Research*, 1989, *495*, 178–181.

Nair, S. G., Adams-Deutsch, R., Epstein, D. H., and Shaham, Y. The neuropharmacology of relapse to food seeking: Methodology, main findings, and comparison with relapse to drug seeking. *Progress in Neurobiology*, 2009, *89*, 18–45.

Nakamura, J., Endo, K., Sumida, T., and Hasegawa, T. Bilateral tactile agnosia: A case report. *Cortex*, 1998, *34*, 375–388.

Nakamura, K., Honda, M., Okada, T., Hanakawa, T., et al. Participation of the left posterior inferior temporal cortex in writing and mental recall of kanji orthography: A functional MRI study. *Brain*, 2000, *123*, 954–967.

Nakamura, T., and Gold, G. A cyclic nucleotide-gated conductance in olfactory receptor cilia. *Nature*, 1987, *325*, 442–444.

Nakazato, M., Mauakami, N., Date, Y., Kojima, M., et al. A role for ghrelin in the central regulation of feeding. *Nature*, 2001, *409*, 194–198.

Nambu, A. Seven problems on the basal ganglia. *Current Opinion in Neurobiology*, 2008, *18*, 595–604.

Nambu, A., Tokuno, H., and Takada, M. Functional significance of the cortico-subthalamo-pallidal "hyperdirect" pathway. *Neuroscience Research*, 2002, *43*, 111–117.

Nambu, T., Sakurai, T., Mizukami, K., Hosoya, Y., et al. Distribution of orexin neurons in the adult rat brain. *Brain Research*, 1999, *827*, 243–260.

Naqvi, N. H., and Bechara, A. The airway sensory impact of nicotine contributes to the conditioned reinforcing effects of individual puffs from cigarettes. *Pharmacology, Biochemistry and Behavior*, 2005, *81*, 821–829.

Naqvi, N. H., Rudrauf, D., Damasio, H., and Bechara, A. Damage to the insula disrupts addiction to cigarette smoking. *Science*, 2007, *315*, 531–534.

Nasir, J., Floresco, S. B., O'Kusky, J. R., Diewert, V. M., et al. Targeted disruption of the Huntington's disease gene results in embryonic lethality and behavioral and morphological changes in heterozygotes. *Cell*, 1995, *81*, 811–823.

Nassi, J. J., and Callaway, E. M. Parallel processing strategies of the primate visual system. *Nature Reviews: Neuroscience*, 2009, *10*, 360–372.

Nathans, J. The evolution and physiology of human color vision: Insights from molecular genetic studies of visual pigments. *Neuron*, 1999, *24*, 299–312.

Nauta, W. J. H. Hypothalamic regulation of sleep in rats: Experimental study. *Journal of Neurophysiology*, 1946, *9*, 285–316.

Nauta, W. J. H. Some efferent connections of the prefrontal cortex in the monkey. In *The frontal granular cortex and behavior*, edited by J. M. Warren and K. Akert. New York: McGraw-Hill, 1964.

Navakkode, S., Sajikuman, S., Sacktor, T. C., and Frey, J. U. Protein kinase Mζ is essential for the induction and maintenance of dopamine-induced long-term potentiation in apical CA1 dendrites. *Learning and Memory*, 2010, *17*, 605–611.

Nazir, T. A., Jacobs, A. M., and O'Regan, J. K. Letter legibility and visual word recognition. *Memory and Cognition*, 1998, *26*, 810–821.

Nef, P., Hermansborgmeyer, I., Artierespin, H., Beasley, L., et al. Spatial pattern of receptor expression in the olfactory epithelium. *Proceedings of the National Academy of Sciences, USA*, 1992, *89*, 8948–8952.

Nergårdh, R., Ammar, A., Brodin, U., Bergström, J., et al. Neuropeptide Y facilitates activity-based anorexia. *Psychoneuroendocrinology*, 2007, *32*, 493–502.

Nestler, E. J. Under siege: The brain on opiates. *Neuron*, 1996, *16*, 897–900.

Nestojko, J. F., Bui, D. C., Kornell, N., and Bjork, E. L. Expecting to teach enhances learning and organization of knowledge in free recall of text passages. *Memory & Cognition*, 2014, *42*(7), 1038–1042.

Nestor, P. J., Graham, N. L., Fryer, T. D., Williams, B. G., et al. Progressive non-fluent aphasia is associated with hypometabolism centered on the left anterior insula. *Brain*, 2003, *126*, 2406–2418.

Neumann, K., Preibisch, C., Euler, H. A., von Gudenberg, A. W., et al. Cortical plasticity associated with stuttering therapy. *Journal of Fluency Disorders*, 2005, *30*, 23–39.

Neumeister, A., Konstantinidis, A., Stastny, J., Schrarz, M. J., et al. Association between serotonin transporter gene promotor polymorphism (5HTTLPR) and behavioral responses to tryptophan depletion in healthy women with and without family history of depression. *Archives of General Psychiatry*, 2002, *59*, 613–620.

Neumeister, A., Nugent, A. C., Waldeck, T., Geraci, M., et al. Neural and behavioral responses to tryptophan depletion in unmedicated patients with remitted major depressive disorder and controls. *Archives of General Psychiatry*, 2004, *61*, 765–773.

New, A. S., Hazlett, E. A., Buchsbaum, M. S., Goodman, M., et al. Blunted prefrontal cortical [18]fluorodeoxyglucose positron emission tomography response to meta-chlorophenylpiperazine in impulsive aggression. *Archives of General Psychiatry*, 2002, *59*, 621–629.

New AS[1], Buchsbaum MS, Hazlett EA, Goodman M, et al. **Fluoxetine increases relative metabolic rate in prefrontal cortex in impulsive aggression.** *Psychopharmacology*, 2004 Nov;176(3-4):451-8. Epub 2004 May 25.

Newman, A. J., Supalla, T., Hauser, P. C., Newport, E., et al. Prosodic and narrative processing in American Sign Language: An fMRI study. *NeuroImage*, 2010, *52*, 669–676.

Nichelli, P., Grafman, J., Pietrini, P., Clark, K., et al. Where the brain appreciates the moral of a story. *NeuroReport*, 1995, *6*, 2309–2313.

Nicholl, C. S., and Russell, R. M. Analysis of animal rights literature reveals the underlying motives of the movement: Ammunition for counter offensive by scientists. *Endocrinology*, 1990, *127*, 985–989.

Nicoll, J. A. R., Wilkinson, D., Holmes, C., Steart, P., et al. Neuropathology of human Alzheimer disease after immunization with amyloid-β peptide: A case report. *Nature Medicine*, 2003, *9*, 448–452.

Nicoll, R. A., Alger, B. E., and Jahr, C. E. Enkephalin blocks inhibitory pathways in the vertebrate CNS. *Nature*, 1980, *287*, 22–25.

Nicoll, R. A., and Malenka, R. C. A tale of two transmitters. *Science*, 1998, *281*, 360–361.

Nides, M., Oncken, C., Gonzales, D., Rennard, S., et al. Smoking cessation with varenicline, a selective α4β2 nicotinic receptor partial agonist: Results from a 7-week, randomized, placebo- and bupropion-controlled trial with 1-year follow-up. *Archives of Internal Medicine*, 2006, *166*, 1561–1568.

Nili, U., Goldberg, H., Weizman, A., and Dudai, Y. Fear thou not: Activity of frontal and temporal circuits in moments of real-life courage. *Neuron*, 2010, *66*, 949–962.

Nilius, B., Owsianik, G., Voets, T., and Peters, J. A. Transient receptor potential cation channels in disease. *Physiological Review*, 2007, *87*, 165–217.

Nilsson, H. J., Levinsson, A., and Schouenborg, J. Cutaneous field stimulation (CFS): A new powerful method to combat itch. *Pain*, 1997, *71*, 49–55.

NINDS. Tissue plasminogen activator for acute ischemic stroke. The National Institute of Neurological Disorders and Stroke RT-PA stroke study group. *New England Journal of Medicine*, 1995, *333*, 1189–1191.

Nisell, M., Nomikos, G. G., and Svensson, T. H. Systemic nicotine-induced dopamine release in the rat nucleus accumbens is regulated by nicotinic receptors in the ventral tegmental area. *Synapse*, 1994, *16*, 36–44.

Nishino, S. Clinical and neurobiological aspects of narcolepsy. *Sleep Medicine*, 2007, *8*, 373–399.

Nishino, S., Ripley, B., Overeem, S., Lammers, G. J., et al. Hypocretin (orexin) deficiency in human narcolepsy. *Lancet*, 2000, *355*, 39–40.

Nissant, A., Bardy, C., Katagiri, H., Murray, K., et al. Adult neurogenesis promotes synaptic plasticity in the olfactory bulb. *Nature Neuroscience*, 2009, *12*, 728–730.

Niwa, M., Kamiya, A., Murai, R., Kubo, K., et al. Knockdown of DISC1 by in utero gene transfer disturbs postnatal dopaminergic maturation in the frontal cortex and leads to adult behavioral deficits. *Neuron*, 2010, *65*, 480–489.

Nobler, M. S., Oquendo, M. A., Kegeles, L. S., Malone, K. M., et al. Deceased regional brain metabolism after ECT. *American Journal of Psychiatry*, 2001, *158*, 305–308.

Norgren, R., and Grill, H. Brain-stem control of ingestive behavior. In *The physiological mechanisms of motivation*, edited by D. W. Pfaff. New York: Springer-Verlag, 1982.

Normandin, J., and Murphy, A. Z. Nucleus paragigantocellularis afferents in male and female rats: Organization, gonadal steroid receptor expression, and activation during sexual behavior. *Journal of Comparative Neurology*, 2008, *508*, 771–794.

Nothdurfter, C., Rammes, G., Baghai, T. C., Schüle, C., et al. TSPO (18 kDa) as a target for novel anxiolytics with a favourable side-effect profile. *Journal of Neuroendocrinology*, 2012, *24*, 82–92.

Novin, D., VanderWeele, D. A., and Rezek, M. Hepatic-portal 2-deoxy-D-glucose infusion causes eating: Evidence for peripheral glucoreceptors. *Science*, 1973, *181*, 858–860.

Novotny, M. V., Ma, W., Wiesler, D., and Zidek, L. Positive identification of the puberty-accelerating pheromone of the house mouse: The volatile ligands associating with the major urinary protein. *Proceedings of the Royal Society of London B*, 1999, *266*, 2017–2022.

Nowak, D. A., Berner, J., Herrnberger, B., Kammer, T., et al. Continuous theta-burst stimulation over the dorsal premotor cortex interferes with associative learning during object lifting. *Cortex*, 2009, *45*, 473–482.

Nugent, N. R., Amstadter, A. B., and Koenen, K. C. Genetics of post-traumatic stress disorder: Informing clinical conceptualizations and promoting future research. *American Journal of Medical Genetics Part C*, 2008, *148C*, 127–132.

Numan, M. Medial preoptic area and maternal behavior in the female rat. *Journal of Comparative and Physiological Psychology*, 1974, *87*, 746–759.

Numan, M. Motivational systems and the neural circuitry of maternal behavior in the rat. *Developmental Psychobiology*, 2007, *49*, 12–21.

Numan, M., and Numan, M. J. Projection sites of medial preoptic area and ventral bed nucleus of the stria terminalis neurons that express Fos during maternal behavior in female rats. *Journal of Neuroendocrinology*, 1997, *9*, 369–384.

Nutt, D. J., Glue, P., Lawson, C. W., and Wilson, S. Flumazenil provocation of panic attacks: Evidence for altered benzodiazepine receptor sensitivity in panic disorders. *Archives of General Psychiatry*, 1990, *47*, 917–925.

Oaknin, S., Rodriguez del Castillo, A., Guerra, M., Battaner, E., et al. Change in forebrain Na, K-ATPase activity and serum hormone levels during sexual behavior in male rats. *Physiology and Behavior*, 1989, *45*, 407–410.

Oberman, L. M., Winkielman, P., and Ramachandran, V. S. Face to face: Blocking facial mimicry can selectively impair recognition of emotional expressions. *Social Neuroscience*, 2007, *2*, 167–178.

Obler, L. K., and Gjerlow, K. *Language and the brain*. Cambridge, England: Cambridge University Press, 1999.

O'Brien, C. P., Volpicelli, L. A., and Volpicelli, J. R. Naltrexone in the treatment of alcoholism: A clinical review. *Alcohol*, 1996, *13*, 35–39.

Ockleford, E. M., Vince, M. A., Layton, C., and Reader, M. R. Responses of neonates to parents' and others' voices. *Early Human Development*, 1988, *18*, 27–36.

Oertel, D., and Young, E. D. What's a cerebellar circuit doing in the auditory system? *Trends in Neuroscience*, 2004, *27*, 104–110.

Ogawa, K., Nittono, H., and Hori, T. Brain potentials before and after rapid eye movements: An electrophysiological approach to dreaming in REM sleep. *Sleep*, 2005, *28(9)*, 1077–1082.

Ogawa, S., Olazabal, U. E., Parhar, I. S., and Pfaff, D. W. Effects of intrahypothalamic administration of antisense DNA for progesterone receptor mRNA on reproductive behavior and progesterone receptor immunoreactivity in female rat. *Journal of Neuroscience*, 1994, *14*, 1766–1774.

Ogden, C. L., Carroll, M. D., and Flegal, K. M. Epidemiologic trends in overweight and obesity. *Endocrinology and Metabolism Clinics of North America*, 2003, *32*, 741–760.

O'Keefe, J., and Bouma, H. Complex sensory properties of certain amygadala units in the freely moving cat. *Experimental Neurology*, 1969, 23, 384–98.

O'Keefe, J., and Dostrovsky, T. The hippocampus as a spatial map: Preliminary evidence from unit activity in the freely moving rat. *Brain Research*, 1971, 34, 171–175.

Olanow, C. W., Goetz, C. G., Kordower, J. H., Stoessl, A. J., et al. A double-blind controlled trial of bilateral fetal nigral transplantation in Parkinson's disease. *Annals of Neurology*, 2003, 54, 403–414.

Olausson, H., Lamarre, Y., Backlund, H., Morin, C., et al. Unmyelinated tactile afferents signal touch and project to insular cortex. *Nature Neuroscience*, 2002, 5, 900–904.

Olds, J. Commentary. In *Brain stimulation and motivation*, edited by E. S. Valenstein. Glenview, IL: Scott, Foresman, 1973.

Oleksenko, A. I., Mukhametov, L. M., Polyakova, I. G., Supin, A. Y., et al. Unihemispheric sleep deprivation in bottlenose dolphins. *Journal of Sleep Research*, 1992, 1, 40–44.

Oliveri, M., Turriziani, P., Carlesimo, G. A., Koch, G., et al. Parieto-frontal interactions in visual-object and visual-spatial working memory: Evidence from transcranial magnetic stimulation. *Cerebral Cortex*, 2001, 11, 606–618.

Olsson, A., Nearing, K. I., and Phelps, E. A. Learning fears by observing others: The neural systems of social fear transmission. *SCAN*, 2007, 2, 3–11.

Olszewski, P. K., Fredriksson, R., Olszewska, A. M., Stephansson, O., et al. Hypothalamic FTO is associated with the regulation of energy intake not feeding reward. *BMC Neuroscience*, 2009, 10, 129.

Omura, K., Tsukamoto, T., Kotani, Y., Ohgami, Y., et al. Neural correlates of phoneme-to-grapheme conversion. *Neuroreport*, 2004, 15, 949–953.

O'Neill, J., Pleydell-Vouverie, B., Dupret, D., and Csicsvari, J. Play it again: Reactivation of waking experience and memory. *Trends in Neuroscience*, 2010, 33, 220–229.

Opitz, B., and Friederici, A. D. Interactions of the hippocampal system and the prefrontal cortex in learning language-like rules. *NeuroImage*, 2003, 19, 1730–1737.

Opitz, B., and Friederici, A. D. Neural basis of processing sequential and hierarchical syntactic structures. *Human Brain Mapping*, 2007, 28, 585–592.

Orzel-Gryglewska, J. Consequences of sleep deprivation. *International Journal of Occupational Medicine and Environmental Health*, 2010, 23, 95–114.

Osaka, N., Osaka, M., Morishita, M., Kondo, H., et al. A word expressing affective pain activates the anterior cingulate cortex in the human brain: An fMRI study. *Behavioural Brain Research*, 2004, 153, 123–127.

Ossebaard, C. A., Polet, I. A., and Smith, D. V. Amiloride effects on taste quality: Comparison of single and multiple response category procedures. *Chemical Senses*, 1997, 22, 267–275.

Ostrowsky, K., Magnin, M., Tyvlin, P., Isnard, J., et al. Representation of pain and somatic sensation in the human insula: A study of responses to direct electrical cortical stimulation. *Cerebral Cortex*, 2002, 12, 376–385.

Otsuki, M., Soma, Y., Arai, T., Otsuka, A., et al. Pure apraxic agraphia with abnormal writing stroke sequences: Report of a Japanese patient with a left superior parietal haemorrhage. *Journal of Neurology, Neurosurgery, and Psychiatry*, 1999, 66, 233–237.

Otsuki, M., Soma, Y., Arihiro, S., Watanabe, Y., et al. Dystypia: Isolated typing impairment without aphasia, apraxia or visuospatial impairment. *European Neurology*, 2002, 47, 136–140.

Otto, M. W., Tolin, D. F., Simon, N. M., et al. Efficacy of D-cycloserine for enhancing response to cognitive-behavior therapy for panic disorder. *Biological Psychiatry*, 2010, 67, 365–370.

Overduin, J., Frayo, R. S., Grill, H. J., Kaplan, J. M., et al. Role of the duodenum and macronutrient type in ghrelin regulation. *Endocrinology*, 2005, 146, 845–850.

Owen, A. M., James, M., Leigh, P. N., Summers, B. A., et al. Fronto-striatal cognitive deficits at different stages of Parkinson's disease. *Brain*, 1992, 115, 1727–1751.

Ozonoff, S., Young, G. S., Carter, A., Messinger, D., et al. Recurrence risk for autism spectrum disorders: A baby siblings research consortium study. *Pediatrics*, 2011, 238, e1–e8.

Packard, M. G., and Teather, L. A. Double dissociation of hippocampal and dorsal-striatal memory systems by posttraining intracerebral injections of 2-amino-5-phosphonopentanoic acid. *Behavioral Neuroscience*, 1997, 111, 543–551.

Padberg, F., and Moller, H. J. Repetitive transcranial magnetic stimulation: Does it have potential in the treatment of depression? *CNS Drugs*, 2003, 17, 383–403.

Padwal, R. S., & Majumdar, S. R. Drug treatments for obesity: Orlistat, sibutramine, and rimonabant. *The Lancet*, 2007, 369(9555), 71–77.

Paik, I. H., Toh, K. Y., Lee, C., Kim, J. J., et al. Psychological stress may induce increased humoral and decreased cellular immunity. *Behavioral Medicine*, 2000, 26(3), 139–141.

Pallast, E. G. M., Jongbloet, P. H., Straatman, H. M., and Zeilhuis, G. A. Excess of seasonality of births among patients with schizophrenia and seasonal ovopathy. *Schizophrenia Bulletin*, 1994, 20, 269–276.

Papadimitriou, G. N., Christodoulou, G. N., Katsouyanni, K., and Stefanis, C. N. Therapy and prevention of affective illness by total sleep deprivation. *Journal of the Affective Disorders*, 1993, 27, 107–116.

Papassotiropoulos, A., Wollmer, M. A., Aguzzi, A., Hock, C., et al. The prion gene is associated with human long-term memory. *Human Molecular Genetics*, 2005, 14, 2241–2246.

Papez, J. W. A proposed mechanism of emotion. *Archives of Neurology and Psychiatry*, 1937, 38, 725–744.

Pardo, J. V., Sheikh, S. A., Schwindt, G. C., Lee, J. T., et al. Chronic vagus nerve stimulation for treatment-resistant depression decreases resting ventromedial prefrontal glucose metabolism. *NeuroImage*, 2008, 42, 879–889.

Paré, D., Quirk, G. J., and LeDoux, J. E. New vistas on amygdala networks in conditioned fear. *Journal of Neurophysiology*, 2004, 92, 1–9.

Park, Y.-U., Jeong, J., Lee, H., Mun, J. Y., et al. Disrupted-in-schizophrenia 1 (DISC1) plays essential roles in mitochondria in collaboration with mitofilin. *Proceedings of the National Academy of Sciences, USA*, 2010, 107, 17785–17790.

Parker, A. J. Binocular depth perception and the cerebral cortex. *Nature Reviews: Neuroscience*, 2007, 8, 379–391.

Parmentier, R., Ohtsu, H., Djebbara-Hannas, Z., Valatx, J.-L., et al. Anatomical, physiological, and pharmacological characteristics of histidine decarboxylase knock-out mice: Evidence for the role of brain histamine in behavioral and sleep–wake control. *Journal of Neuroscience*, 2002, 22, 7695–7711.

Pascoe, J. P., and Kapp, B. S. Electrophysiological characteristics of amygdaloid central nucleus neurons during Pavlovian fear conditioning in the rabbit. *Behavioural Brain Research*, 1985, 16, 117–133.

Pasterski, V. L., Geffner, M. E., Brain, C., Hindmarsh, P., et al. Prenatal hormones and postnatal socializtion by parents as determinants of male-typical toy play in girls with congenital adrenal hyperplasia. *Child Development*, 2005, 76, 264–278.

Pattatucci, A. M. L., and Hamer, D. H. Development and familiality of sexual orientation in females. *Behavior Genetics*, 1995, 25, 407–420.

Paulesu, E., Démonet, J.-F., Fazio, F., McCrory, E., et al. Dyslexia: Cultural diversity and biological unity. *Science*, 2001, 291, 2165–2167.

Pauls, D. L., and Leckman, J. F. The inheritance of Gilles de la Tourette's syndrome and associated behaviors. *New England Journal of Medicine*, 1986, *315*, 993–997.

Pauls, D. L., Towbin, K. E., Leckman, J. F., Zahner, G. E., et al. Gilles de la Tourette's syndrome and obsessive-compulsive disorder: Evidence supporting a genetic relationship. *Archives of General Psychiatry*, 1986, *43*, 1180–1182.

Paulus, M. P., Feinstein, J. S., Castillo, G., Simmons, A. N., et al. Dose-dependent decrease of activation in bilateral amygdala and insula by lorazepam during emotion processing. *Archives of General Psychiatry*, 2005, *62*, 282–288.

Pazzaglia, M., Smania, N., Corato, E., and Aglioti, S. M. Neural underpinnings of gesture discrimination in patients with limb apraxia. *Journal of Neuroscience*, 2008, *28*, 3030–3041.

Peck, B. K., and Vanderwolf, C. H. Effects of raphe stimulation on hippocampal and neocortical activity and behaviour. *Brain Research*, 1991, *568*, 244–252.

Pedersen, C. B., and Mortensen, P. B. Evidence of a dose-response relationship between urbanicity during upbringing and schizophrenia risk. *Archives of General Psychiatry*, 2001, *58*, 1039–1046.

Pedersen-Bjergaard, U., Host, U., Kelbaek, H., Schifter, S., et al. Influence of meal composition on postprandial peripheral plasma concentrations of vasoactive peptides in man. *Scandanavian Journal of Clinical and Laboratory Investigation*, 1996, *56*, 497–503.

Peigneux, P., Laureys, S., Fuchs, S., Collette, F., et al. Are spatial memories strengthened in the human hippocampus during slow wave sleep? *Neuron*, 2004, *44*, 535–545.

Pellerin, L., Bouzier-Sore, A.-K., Aubert, A., Serres, S., et al. Activity-dependent regulation of energy metabolism by astrocytes: An update. *Glia*, 2007, *55*, 1251–1262.

Pelleymounter, M. A., Cullen, M. J., Baker, M. B., Hecht, R., et al. Effects of the obese gene product on body weight regulation in ob/ob mice. *Science*, 1995, *269*, 540–543.

Pelphrey, K. A., Morris, J. P., Michelich, C. R., Allison, T., et al. Functional anatomy of biological motion perception in posterior temporal cortex: An fMRI study of eye, mouth and hand movements. *Cerebral Cortex*, 2005, *15*, 1866–1876.

Pelphrey, K. A., Sasson, N. J., Reznick, J. S., Paul, G., et al. Visual scanning of faces in autism. *Journal of Autism and Developmental Disorders*, 2002, *32*, 249–261.

Pelphrey, K. A., Singerman, J. D., Allison, T., and McCarthy, G. Brain activation evoked by perception of gaze shifts: The influence of context. *Neuropsychologia*, 2003, *41*, 156–170.

Penfield, W., and Perot, P. The brain's record of auditory and visual experience: A final summary and discussion. *Brain*, 1963, *86*, 595–697.

Penfield, W., and Rasmussen, T. *The cerebral cortex of man: A clinical study of localization.* Boston: Little, Brown & Co., 1950.

Perani, D., Saccuman, M. C., Scifo, P., Spada, D., et al. Functional specializations for music processing in the human newborn brain. *Proceedings of the National Academy of Sciences, USA*, 2010, *107*, 4758–4763.

Pereira, A. C., Huddleston, D. E., Brickman, A. M., Sosunov, A. A., et al. An *in vivo* correlate of exercise-induced neurogenesis in the adult dentate gyrus. *Proceedings of the National Academy of Sciences, USA*, 2007, *104*, 5638–5643.

Peretz, I., Blood, A. J., Penhune, V., and Zatorre, R. Cortical deafness to dissonance. *Brain*, 2001, *124*, 928–940.

Peretz, I., Cummings, S., and Dubé, M. P. The genetics of congenital amusia (tone deafness): A family-aggregation study. *American Journal of Human Genetics*, 2007, *81*, 582–588.

Peretz, I., Gagnon, L., and Bouchard, B. Music and emotion: Perceptual determinants, immediacy, and isolation after brain damage. *Cognition*, 1998, *68*, 111–141.

Peretz, I., and Zatorre, R. J. Brain organization for music processing. *Annual Review of Psychology*, 2005, *56*, 89–114.

Perez, M. A., Tanaka, S., Wise, S. P., Willingham, D. T., et al. Time-specific contribution of the supplementary motor area to intermanual transfer of procedural knowledge. *Journal of Neuroscience*, 2008, *28*, 9664–9669.

Perlmutter, S. J., Garvey, M. A., Castellanos, X., Mittleman, B. B., et al. A case of pediatric autoimmune neuropsychiatric disorders associated with streptococcal infectiohs. *American Journal of Psychiatry*, 1998, *155*, 1592–1598.

Perrett, D. I., Hietanen, J. K., Oram, M. W., and Benson, P. J. Organization and functions of cells responsive to faces in the temporal cortex. *Philosophical Transactions of the Royal Society of London B*, 1992, *335*, 23–30.

Pert, C. B., Snowman, A. M., and Snyder, S. H. Localization of opiate receptor binding in presynaptic membranes of rat brain. *Brain Research*, 1974, *70*, 184–188.

Peters, J., LaLumiere, R. T., and Kalivas, P. W. Infralimbic prefrontal cortex is responsible for inhibiting cocaine seeking in extinguished rats. *Journal of Neuroscience*, 2008, *28*, 6046–6053.

Petersen, S. E., Miezin, F. M., and Allman, J. M. Transient and sustained responses in four extrastriate visual areas of the owl monkey. *Experimental Brain Research*, 1988, *70*, 55–60.

Petkov, C. I., Kayser, C., Augath, M., and Logothetis, N. K. Functional imaging reveals nuberous fields in the monkey auditory cortex. *PLoS Biology*, 2006, *4*, 1213–1226.

Peuskens, H., Sunaert, S., Dupont, P., Van Hecke, P., et al. Human brain regions involved in heading estimation. *Journal of Neuroscience*, 2001, *21*, 2451–2461.

Peyrache, A., Khamassi, M., Benchenane, K., et al. Replay of rule-learning related neural patterns in the prefrontal cortex during sleep. *Nature Neuroscience*, 2009, *12*, 919–926.

Peyron, C., Faraco, J., Rogers, W., Ripley, B., et al. A mutation in a case of early onset narcolepsy and a generalized absence of hypocretin peptides in human narcoleptic brains. *Nature Medicine*, 2000, *6*(9), 991–997.

Peyron, R., Laurent, B., and Garcia-Larrea, L. Functional imaging of brain responses to pain: A review and meta-analysis. *Neurophysiology Clinics*, 2000, *30*, 263–288.

Pfaff, D. W., and Sakuma, Y. Deficit in the lordosis reflex of female rats caused by lesions in the ventromedial nucleus of the hypothalamus. *Journal of Physiology*, 1979, *288*, 203–210.

Pfaus, J. G., Kleopoulos, S. P., Mobbs, C. V., Gibbs, R. B., et al. Sexual stimulation activates *c-fos* within estrogen-concentrating regions of the female rat forebrain. *Brain Research*, 1993, *624*, 253–267.

Pfeifer, J. H., Iacoboni, M., Mazziotta, J. C., and Dapretto, M. Mirroring others' emotions relates to empathy and interpersonal competence in children. *NeuroImage*, 2008, *39*, 2076–2085.

Pfleiderer, B., Zinkirciran, S., Arolt, V., Heindel, W., et al. fMRI amygdala activation during a spontaneous panic attack in a patient with panic disorder. *World Journal of Biological Psychiatry*, 2007, *8*, 269–272.

Pfister, E. L., Kennington, L., Straubhaar, J., Wagh, S., et al. Five siRNAs targeting three SNPs may provide therapy for three-quarters of Huntington's disease patients. *Current Biology*, 2009, *19*, 774–778.

Phan, K. L., Fitzgerald, D. A., Nathan, P. J., and Tancer, M. E. Association between amygdala hyperactivity to harsh faces and severity of social anxiety in generalized social phobia. *Biological Psychiatry*, 2005, *59*, 424–429.

Phelps, E. A., Delgado, M. R., Nearing, K. I., and LeDoux, J. E. Extinction learning in humans: Role of the amygdala and vmPFC. *Neuron*, 2004, *43*, 897–905.

Phiel, C. J., and Klein, P. S. Molecular targets of lithium action. *Annual Review of Pharmacology and Toxicology*, 2001, *41*, 789–813.

Phillips, M. I., and Felix, D. Specific angiotensin II receptive neurons in the cat subfornical organ. *Brain Research*, 1976, *109*, 531–540.

Phillips, R. G., and LeDoux, J. E. Differential contribution of amygdala and hippocampus to cued and contextual fear conditioning. *Behavioral Neuroscience*, 1992, *106*, 274–285.

Piccirillo, J. F., Duntley, S., and Schotland, H. Obstructive sleep apnea. *Journal of the American Medical Association*, 2000, *284*, 1492–1494.

Pickles, J. O., and Corey, D. P. Mechanoelectrical transduction by hair cells. *Trends in Neuroscience*, 1992, *15*, 254–259.

Pijl, S., and Schwarz, D. W. F. Intonation of musical intervals by musical intervals by deaf subjects stimulated with single bipolar cochlear implant electrodes. *Hearing Research*, 1995a, *89*, 203–211.

Pijl, S., and Schwarz, D. W. F. Melody recognition and musical interval perception by deaf subjects stimulated with electrical pulse trains through single cochlear implant electrodes. *Journal of the Acoustical Society of America*, 1995b, *98*, 886–895.

Pike, K. M., Walsh, B. T., Vitousek, K., Wilson, G. T., et al. Cognitive behavior therapy in the posthospitalization treatment of anorexia nervosa. *American Journal of Psychiatry*, 2003, *160*, 2046–2049.

Pinkham, A. E., Brenhsinger, C., Kohler, C., Gur, R. E., et al. Actively paranoid patients with schizophrenia over attribute anger to neutral faces. *Schizophrenia Research*, 2011, *125*, 174–178.

Pitcher, D., Garrido, L., Walsh, V., and Duchaine, B. C. Transcranial magnetic stimulation disrupts the perception and embodiment of facial expressions. *Journal of Neuroscience*, 2008, *28*, 8929–8933.

Pitkänen, A., Savander, V., and LeDoux, J. E. Organization of intra-amygdaloid circuits: An emerging framework for understanding functions of the amygdala. *Trends in Neuroscience*, 1997, *20*, 517–523.

Pleim, E. T., and Barfield, R. J. Progesterone versus estrogen facilitation of female sexual behavior by intracranial administration to female rats. *Hormones and Behavior*, 1988, *22*, 150–159.

Ploeger, A., Raijmakers, M. E. J., van der Maas, H. L. J., and Galis, F. The association between autism and errors in early embryogenesis: What is the causal mechanism? *Biological Psychiatry*, 2010, *67*, 602–607.

Pobric, G., Jefferies, E., and Lambon Ralph, M. A. Anterior temporal lobes mediate semantic representation: Mimicking semantic dementia by using rTMS in normal participants. *Proceedings of the National Academy of Sciences, USA*, 2007, *104*, 20137–20141.

Pobric, G., Mashal, N., Faust, M., and Lavidor, M. The role of the right cerebral hemisphere in processing novel metaphoric expressions: A transcranial magnetic stimulation study. *Journal of Cognitive Neuroscience*, 2008, *20*, 1–12.

Poeppel, D. Pure word deafness and the bilateral processing of the speech code. *Cognitive Science*, 2001, *25*, 679–693.

Poggio, G. F., and Poggio, T. The analysis of stereopsis. *Annual Review of Neuroscience*, 1984, *7*, 379–412.

Pollio, G., Xue, P., Zanisi, M., Nicolin, A., and Maggi, A. Antisense oligonucleotide blocks progesterone-induced lordosis behavior in ovariectomized rats. *Molecular Brain Research*, 1993, *19*(1), 135–139.

Poizner, H., Feldman, A. G., Levin, M. F., Berkinblit, M. B., et al. The timing of arm-trunk coordination is deficient and vision-dependent in Parkinson's patients during reaching movements. *Experimental Brain Research*, 2000, *133*, 279–292.

Polymeropoulos, M. H., Higgins, J. J., Golbe, L. I., Johnson, W. G., et al. Mapping of a gene for Parkinson's disease to chromosome 4q21-q23. *Science*, 1996, *274*, 1197–1199.

Pomp, D., and Nielsen, M. K. Quantitative genetics of energy balance: Lessons from animal models. *Obesity Research*, 1999, *7*, 106–110.

Pompili, M., Mancinelli, I., Girardi, P., Ruberto, A., et al. Suicide in anorexia nervosa: A meta-analysis. *International Journal of Eating Disorders*, 2004, *36*, 99–103.

Popko, B. Myelin maintenance: Axonal support required. *Nature Neuroscience*, 2010, *13*, 275–277.

Popova, N. K. From genes to aggressive behavior: The role of serotonergic system. *BioEssays*, 2006, *28*, 495–503.

Poremba, A., Saunders, R. C., Crane, A. M., Cook, M., et al. Functional mapping of the primate auditory system. *Science*, 2003, *299*, 568–572.

Porkka-Heiskanen, T., Strecker, R. E., and McCarley, R. W. Brain site-specificity of extracellular adenosine concentration changes during sleep deprivation and spontaneous sleep: An *in vivo* microdialysis study. *Neuroscience*, 2000, *99*, 507–517.

Porrino, L. J., Lyons, D., Smith, H. R., Daunais, J. B., et al. Cocaine self-administration produces a progressive involvement of limbic, association, and sensorimotor striatal domains. *Journal of Neuroscience*, 2004, *24*, 3554–3562.

Porrino, L. J., Smith, H. R., Nader, M. A., and Beveridge, T. J. The effects of cocaine: A shifting target over the course of addiction. *Progress in Neuropsychopharmacology and Biological Psychiatry*, 2007, *31*, 1593–1600.

Porter, J., Craven, B., Khan, R. M., Chang, S.-J., et al. Mechanisms of scent-tracking in humans. *Nature Neuroscience*, 2007, *10*, 27–29.

Porter, K. R., McCarthy, B. J., Freels, S., Kim, Y., et al. Prevalence estimates for primary brain tumors in the United States by age, gender, behavior, and histology. *Neuro-oncology*, 2010, *12*(6), 520–527.

Posmontier, B. Sleep quality in women with and without postpartum depression. *Journal of Obstetric, Gynecoloic, and Neonatal Nursing*, 2008, *37*, 722–735.

Presidential Commission for the Study of Bioethical Issues. *Gray matters: Integrative approaches for neuroscience, ethics, and society.* Washington, DC: Author, 2014. http://www.bioethics.gov/sites/default/files/Gray%20Matters%20Vol%201.pdf.

Preti, A., Melis, M., Siddi, S., Vellante, M., et al. Oxytocin and autism: A systematic

review of randomized controlled trials. *Journal of Child and Adolescent Psychopharmacology*, 2014, *24*(2), 54–68.

Preti, G., Wysocki, C. J., Barnhart, K. T., Sondheimer, S. J., et al. Male axillary extracts contain pheromones that affect pulsitile secretion of luteinizing hormone and mood in women recipients. *Biology of Reproduction*, 2003, *68*, 2107–2113.

Price, E. O., Katz, L. S., Wallach, S. J. R., and Zenchak, J. J. The relationship of male–male mounting to the sexual preferences of young rams. *Applied Animal Behavior Science*, 1988, *21*, 347–352.

Price, D. B. Psychological and neural mechanisms of the affective dimension of pain. *Science*, 2000, *288*, 1769–1772.

Price, D. D., Finniss, D. G., and Benedetti, F. A comprehensive review of the placebo effect: Recent advances and current thought. *Annual Review of Psychology*, 2008, *59*, 565–590.

Price, L. H., and Heninger, G. R. Drug therapy: Lithium in the treatment of mood disorders. *New England Journal of Medicine*, 1994, *331*, 591–598.

Prince, J. E., Brignall, A. C., Cutforth, T., Shen, K., et al. Kirrel3 is required for the coalescence of vomeronasal sensory neuron axons into glomeruli and for male-male aggression. *Development*, 2013, *140*(11), 2398–2408.

Pritchard, T. C., Hamilton, R. B., Morse, J. R., and Norgren, R. Projections of thalamic gustatory and lingual areas in the monkey, *Macaca fascicularis. Journal of Comparative Neurology*, 1986, *244*, 213–228.

Proctor, W. R., Soldo, B. L., Allan, A. M., and Dunwiddie, T. V. Ethanol enhances synaptically evoked GABA$_A$ receptor-mediated responses in cerebral cortical neurons in rat brain slices. *Brain Research*, 1992, *595*, 220–227.

Provencio, I., Rodriguez, I. R., Jiang, G., Hayes, W. P., et al. A novel human opsin in the inner retinal *Journal of Neuroscience*, 2000, *20*, 600–605.

Prusiner, S. B. Novel proteinaceous infectious particles cause scrapie. *Science*, 1982, *216*, 136–144.

Pulvermüller, F., and Fadiga, L. Active perception: Sensorimotor circuits as a cortical basis for language. *Nature Reviews: Neuroscience*, 2010, *11*, 351–360.

Pulvermüller, F., Huss, M., Kherif, F., Moscoso del Prado Martin, F., et al. Motor cortex maps articulatory features of speech sounds. *Proceedings of the National Academy of Sciences, USA*, 2006, *103*, 7865–7870.

Qu, D., Ludwig, D. S., Gammeltoft, S., Piper, M., et al. A role for melanin-concentrating hormone in the central regulation of feeding behaviour. *Nature*, 1996, *380*, 243–247.

Quillen, E. W., Keil, L. C., & Reid, I. A. Effects of baroreceptor denervation on endocrine and drinking responses to caval constriction in dogs. *American*

Journal of Physiology-Regulatory, Integrative and Comparative Physiology, 1990, *259*(3), R618-R626.

Quirk, G. J., Muller, R. U., Kubie, J. L., and Ranck, J. B. The positional firing properties of medial entorhinal neurons: Description and comparison with hippocampal place cells. *Journal of Neuroscience*, 1992, *12*, 1945–1963.

Rahman, Q. The neurodevelopment of human sexual orientation. *Neuroscience & Biobehavioral Reviews*, 2005, *29*(7), 1057–1066.

Rahman, Q., and Hull, M. S. An empirical test of the kin selection hypothesis for male homosexuality. *Archives of Sex Behavior*, 2005, *34*, 461–467.

Raine, A., Meloy, J. R., Bihrle, S., Stoddard, J., et al. Reduced prefrontal and increased subcortical brain functioning assessed using positron emission tomography in predatory and affective murderers. *Behavioral Science and the Law*, 1998, *16*, 319–332.

Raine A, Lencz T, Bihrle S, LaCasse L, et al. Reduced Prefrontal Gray Matter Volume and Reduced Autonomic Activity in Antisocial Personality Disorder. *Arch Gen Psychiatry*, 2000, *57*(2), 119–127.

Rainville, P., Duncan, G. H., Price, D. D., Carrier, B., et al. Pain affect encoded in human anterior cingulate but not somatosensory cortex. *Science*, 1997, *277*, 968–971.

Rakic, P. Specification of cerebral cortical areas. *Science*, 1988, *241*, 170–176.

Rakic, P. Evolution of the neocortex: A perspective from developmental biology. *Nature Reviews Neuroscience*, 2009, *10*, 724–735.

Ramachandran, V. S., and Hirstein, W. The perception of phantom limbs. *Brain*, 1998, *121*, 1603–1630.

Ralph, M. R., and Lehman, M. N. Transplantation: A new tool in the analysis of the mammalian hypothalamic circadian pacemaker. *Trends in Neurosciences*, 1991, *14*, 362–366.

Ramakrishnan, K., and Scheid, D. C. Treatment options for insomnia. *American Family Physician*, 2007, *76*, 517–526.

Ramanathan, L., Gulyani, S., Nienhuis, R., and Siegel, J. M. Sleep deprivation decreases superoxide dismutase activity in rat hippocampus and brainstem. *Neuroreport*, 2002, *13*, 1387–1390.

Ramesh, V., Thakkar, M. M., Strecker, R. E., Basheer, R., et al. Wakefulness-inducing effects of histamine in the basal forebrain of freely moving rats. *Behavioural Brain Research*, 2004, *152*, 271–278.

Ramirez, I. Why do sugars taste good? *Neuroscience and Biobehavioral Reviews*, 1990, *14*, 125–134.

Ramus, F., Rosen, S., Dakin, S. C., Day, B. L., et al. Theories of developmental dyslexia: Insights from a multiple case study of dyslexic adults. *Brain*, 2003, *126*, 841–865.

Ranganath, C., DeGutis, J., and D'Esposito, M. Category-specific modulation of inferior temporal activity during working memory encoding and maintenance. *Cognitive Brain Research*, 2004, *20*, 37–45.

Rapcsak, S. Z., and Beeson, P. M. The role of the left posterior inferior temporal cortex in spelling. *Neurology*, 2004, *62*, 2221–2229.

Rapin, I. Autism in search of a home in the brain. *Neurology*, 1999, *52*, 902–904.

Rapoport, J. L. Recent advances in obsessive-compulsive disorder. *Neuropsychopharmacology*, 1991, *5*, 1–10.

Rapoport, J. L., Ryland, D. H., and Kriete, M. Drug treatment of canine acral lick: An animal model of obsessive-compulsive disorder. *Archives of General Psychiatry*, 1992, *49*, 517–521.

Rapoport, J. L., and Wise, S. P., Obsessive compulsive disorder: Evidence for basal ganglia dysfunction *Psychopharmacology Bulletin*, 1988, *24*, 380–384.

Rasmusson, D. D., Clow, K., and Szerb, J. C. Modification of neocortical acetylcholine release and electroencephalogram desynchronization due to brain stem stimulation by drugs applied to the basal forebrain. *Neuroscience*, 1994, *60*, 665–677.

Rattenborg, N. C., Lima, S. L., and Amlaner, C. J. Facultative control of avian unihemispheric sleep under the risk of predation. *Behavioural Brain Research*, 1999, *105*, 163–172.

Rauch, S. L., Shin, L. M., and Phelps, E. A. Neurocircuitry models of posttraumatic stress disorder and extinction: Human neuroimaging research-Past, present, and future. *Biological Psychiatry*, 2006, *60*, 376–382.

Rausch, J. L., Johnson, M. E., Fei, Y. J., Li, J. Q., et al. Initial conditions of serotonin transporter kinetics and genotype: Influence on SSRI treatment trial outcome. *Biological Psychiatry*, 2002, *51*, 723–732.

Raupach, T., and van Schayck, C. P. Pharmacotherapy for smoking cessation, *CNS Drugs*, 2011, *26*, 371–382.

Rauschecker, J. P., and Scott, S. K. Maps and streams in the auditory cortex: Nonhuman primates illuminate human speech processing. *Nature Neuroscience*, 2009, *12*, 718–724.

Rauschecker, J. P., and Tian, B. Mechanisms and streams for processing of "what" and "where" in auditory cortex. *Proceedings of the National Academy of Sciences, USA*, 2000, *97*, 11800–11806.

Ravussin, E., Valencia, M. E., Esparza, J., Bennett, P. H., et al. Effects of a traditional lifestyle on obesity in Pima Indians. *Diabetes Care*, 1994, *17*, 1067–1074.

Reber, P. J., and Squire, L. R. Encapsulation of implicit and explicit memory in sequence learning. *Journal of Cognitive Neuroscience*, 1998, *10*, 248–263.

Recer, P. Study: English is a factor in dyslexia. Washington, DC: Associated Press, 16 March 2001.

Rechtschaffen, A., and Bergmann, B. M. Sleep deprivation in the rat by the disk-over-water method. *Behavioural Brain Research*, 1995, *69*, 55–63.

Rechtschaffen, A., and Bergmann, B. M. Sleep deprivation in the rat: An update of the 1989 paper. *Sleep*, 2002, *25*, 18–24.

Rechtschaffen, A., Bergmann, B. M., Everson, C. A., Kushida, C. A., et al. Sleep deprivation in the rat. X: Integration and discussion of the findings. *Sleep*, 1989, *12*, 68–87.

Rechtschaffen, A., Gilliland, M. A., Bergmann, B. M., and Winter, J. B. Physiological correlates of prolonged sleep deprivation in rats. *Science*, 1983, *221*, 182–184.

Rechtschaffen, A, Kales, A (eds). *A manual of standardized terminology, techniques and scoring system for sleep stages of human subjects.* U.S. Public Health Service, U.S. Government Printing Office, Washington D.C. 1968

Reddrop, C., Moldrich, R. X., Beart, P. M., Farso, M., et al. Vampire bat salivary plasminogen activator (desmoteplase) inhibits tissue-type plasminogen activator-induced potentiation of excitotoxic injury. *Stroke*, 2005, *36*, 1241–1246.

Redgrave, P., Rodriguez, M., Smith, Y., et al. Goal-directed and habitual control in the basal ganglia: Implications for Parkinson's disease. *Nature Reviews: Neuroscience*, 2010, *11*, 760–772.

Reed, C. L., Caselli, R. J., and Farah, M. J. Tactile agnosia: Underlying impairment and implications for normal tactile object recognition. *Brain*, 1996, *119*, 875–888.

Reed, J. M., and Squire, L. R. Retrograde amnesia for facts and events: Findings from four new cases. *Journal of Neuroscience*, 1998, *18*, 3943–3954.

Regan, B. C., Julliot, C., Simmen, B., Vienot, F., et al. Fruits, foliage and the evolution of primate colour vision. *Philosophical Transactions of the Royal Society of London B*, 2001, *356*, 229–283.

Rehn, A. E., Van Den Buuse, M., Copolov, D., Briscoe, T., et al. An animal model of chronic placental insufficiency: Relevance to neurodevelopmental disorders including schizophrenia. *Neuroscience*, 2004, *129*, 381–391.

Reid, C. A., Dixon, D. B., Takahashi, M., Bliss, T. V. P., et al. Optical quantal analysis indicates that long-term potentiation at single hippocampal mossy fiber synapses is expressed through increased release probability, recruitment of new release sites, and activation of silent synapses. *Journal of Neuroscience*, 2004, *243*, 3618–3626.

Reid, L. D. Endogenous opioids and alcohol dependence: Opioid alkaloids and the propensity to drink alcoholic beverages. *Alcohol*, 1996, *13*, 5–11.

Reinehr, T., Roth, C. L., Schernthaner, G. H., Kopp, H. P., et al. Peptide YY and glucagon-like peptide-1 in morbidly obese patients before and after surgically induced weight loss. *Obesity Surgery*, 2007, *17*, 1571–1577.

Reiner, W. G. Gender identity and sex-of-rearing in children with disorders of sexual differentiation. *Journal of Pediatric Endocrinology and Metabolism*, 2005, *18*, 549–553.

Rempe, M. J., Best, J., and Terman, D. A mathematical model of the sleep/wake cycle. *Journal of Mathematical Biology*, 2010, *60*, 615–644.

Rempel-Clower, N. L., Zola, S. M., Squire, L. R., and Amaral, D. G. Three cases of enduring memory impairment after bilateral damage limited to the hippocampal formation. *Journal of Neuroscience*, 1996, *16*, 5233–5255.

Ren, Y., Whattard, J., Higuera-Matas, A., Morris, C. V., et al. Cannabidiol, a nonpsychotropic component of cannabis, inhibits cue-induced heroin seeking and normalizes discrete mesolimbic neuronal disturbances. *Journal of Neuroscience*, 2009, *29*, 14764–14769.

Renthal, W., Kumar, A., Xiao, G., Wilkinson, M., et al. Genome-wide analysis of chromatin regulation by cocaine reveals a role for sirtuins. *Neuron*, 2009, *62*, 335–348.

Ressler, K. J., and Mayberg, H. S. Targeting abnormal neural circuits in mood and anxiety disorders: From the laboratory to the clinic. *Nature Neuroscience*, 2007, *10*, 1116–1124.

Ressler, K. J., Rothbaum, M. O., Tannenbaum, L., Anderson, P., et al. Cognitive enhancers as adjuncts to psychotherapy: Use of D-cycloserine in phobic individuals to facilitate extinction of fear. *Archives of General Psychiatry*, 2004, *61*, 1136–1134.

Ressler, K. J., Sullivan, S. L., and Buck, L. A molecular dissection of spatial patterning in the olfactory system. *Current Opinion in Neurobiology*, 1994, *4*, 588–596.

Rétey, J. V., Adam, M., Honneger, E., Khatami, R., et al. A functional genetic variation of adenosine deaminase affects the duration and intensity of deep sleep in humans. *Proceedings of the National Academy of Sciences, USA*, 2005, *102*, 15676–15681.

Reynolds, D. V. Surgery in the rat during electrical analgesia induced by focal brain stimulation. *Science*, 1969, *164*, 444–445.

Rhees, R. W., Shryne, J. E., and Gorski, R. A. Onset of the hormone-sensitive perinatal period for sexual differentiation of the sexually dimorphic nucleus of the preoptic area in female rats. *Journal of Neurobiology*, 1990a, *21*, 781–786.

Rhees, R. W., Shryne, J. E., and Gorski, R. A. Termination of the hormone-sensitive period for differentiation of the sexually dimorphic nucleus of the preoptic area in male and female rats. *Developmental Brain Research*, 1990b, *52*, 17–23.

Rice, N. J., Valyear, K. F., Goodale, M. A., Milner, A. D., et al. Orientation sensitivity to graspable objects: An fMRI adaptation study. *NeuroImage*, 2007, *36*, T87–T93.

Rieber, N., Giel, K. E., Meile, T., Enck, P., et al. Psychological dimensions after laparoscopic sleeve gastrectomy: reduced mental burden, improved eating behavior, and ongoing need for cognitive eating control. *Surgery for Obesity and Related Diseases*, 2013, *9*(4), 569–573.

Riemann, D., Wiegand, M., and Berger, M. Are there predictors for sleep deprivation response in depressive patients? *Biological Psychiatry*, 1991, *29*, 707–710.

Rijntjes, M., Dettmers, C., Buchel, C., Kiebel, S., et al. A blueprint for movement: Functional and anatomical representations in the human motor system. *Journal of Neuroscience*, 1999, *19*, 8043–8048.

Riley, E. P., Infante, M. A., and Warren, K. R. Fetal alcohol spectrum disorders: An overview. *Neuropsychology Review*, 2011, *21*, 73–80.

Rilling, J. K., Glasser, M. F., Preuss, T. M., Ma, X., et al. The evolution of the arcuate fasciculus revealed with comparative DTI. *Nature Neuroscience*, 2008, *11*, 426–428.

Risch, N., Herrell, R., Lehner, T., Liang, K. Y., et al. Interaction between the serotonin transporter gene (*5-HTTLPR*), stressful life events, and risk of depression: A meta-analysis. *Journal of the American Medical Association*, 2009, *301*, 2462–2471.

Rissman, E. F., Early, A. H., Taylor, J. A., Korach, K. S., et al. Estrogen receptors are essential for female sexual receptivity. *Endocrinology*, 1997, *138*, 507–510.

Ritter, R. C., Brenner, L., and Yox, D. P. Participation of vagal sensory neurons in putative satiety signals from the upper gastrointestinal tract. In *Neuroanatomy and physiology of abdominal vagal afferents*, edited by S. Ritter, R. C. Ritter, and C. D. Barnes. Boca Raton, Fla.: CRC Press, 1992.

Ritter, S., Dinh, T. T., and Friedman, M. I. Induction of Fos-like immunoreactivity (Fos-li) and stimulation of feeding by 2, 5-anhydro-D-mannitol (2, 5-AM) require the vagus nerve. *Brain Research*, 1994, *646*, 53–64.

Ritter, S., Dinh, T. T., and Zhang, Y. Localization of hindbrain glucoreceptive sites controlling food intake and blood glucose. *Brain Research*, 2000, *856*, 37–47.

Ritter, S., and Taylor, J. S. Vagal sensory neurons are required for lipoprivic but not glucoprivic feeding in rats. *American Journal of Physiology*, 1990, *258*, R1395–R1401.

Rizzolatti, G., and Sinigaglia, C. The functional role of the parieto-frontal mirror circuit: Interpretations and misinterpretations. *Nature Reviews: Neuroscience*, 2010, *11*, 264–274.

Rizzolatti, R., Fogassi, L., and Gallese, V. Neurophysiological mechanisms underlying the understanding and imitation of action. *Nature Reviews: Neuroscience*, 2001, *2*, 661–670.

Rizzoli, S. O., and Betz, W. J. Synaptic vesicle pools. *Nature Reviews: Neuroscience*, 2005, *6*, 57–69.

Robbins, L. N., Helzer, J. E., Weissman, M. M., Orvaschel, H., et al. Lifetime prevalence of specific psychiatric disorders in three sites. *Archives of General Psychiatry*, 1984, *41*, 949–958.

Roberto, M., Madamba, S. G., Stouffer, D. G., Parsons, L. H., et al. Increased GABA release in the central amygdala of ethanol-dependent rats. *Journal of Neuroscience*, 2004, *24*(45), 10159–10166.

Roberts, S. C., Havlicek, J., Flegr, J., Mruskova, M., et al. Female facial attractiveness increases during the fertile phase of the menstrual cycle. *Biology Letters*, 2004, *271*, S270–S272.

Robertson, G. S., Pfaus, J. G., Atkinson, L. J., Matsumura, H., et al. Sexual behavior increases c-*fos* expression in the forebrain of the male rat. *Brain Research*, 1991, *564*, 352–357.

Robinson, D., Wu, H., Munne, R. A., Ashtari, M., et al. Reduced caudate nucleus volume in obsessive-compulsive disorder. *Archives of General Psychiatry*, 1995, *52*, 393–398.

Robinson, F. R. Role of the cerebellum in movement control and adaptation. *Current Opinion in Neurobiology*, 1995, *5*, 755–762.

Rodman, H. R., Gross, C. G., and Albright, T. D. Afferent basis of visual response properties in area MT of the macaque. I: Effects of striate cortex removal. *Journal of Neuroscience*, 1989, *9*, 2033–2050.

Rodman, H. R., Gross, C. G., and Albright, T. D. Afferent basis of visual response properties in area MT of the macaque. II: Effects of superior colliculus removal. *Journal of Neuroscience*, 1990, *10*, 1154–1164.

Roe, A. W., Parker, A. J., Born, R. T., and DeAngelis, G. C. Disparity channels in early vision. *Journal of Neuroscience*, 2007, *27*, 11820–11831.

Roeltgen, D. P., Rothi, L. H., and Heilman, K. M. Linguistic semantic apraphia: A dissociation of the lexical spelling system from semantics. *Brain and Language*, 1986, *27*, 257–280.

Roffwarg, H. P., Dement, W. C., Muzio, J. N., and Fisher, C. Dream imagery: Relation to rapid eye movements of sleep. *Archives of General Psychiatry*, 1962, *7*, 235–258.

Roffwarg, H. P., Muzio, J. N., and Dement, W. C. Ontogenetic development of human sleep-dream cycle. *Science*, 1966, *152*, 604–619.

Rogawski, M. A., and Wenk, G. L. The neuropharmacological basis for the use of memantine in the treatment of Alzheimer's disease. *CNS Drug Reviews*, 2003, *9*, 275–308.

Roland, P. E. Metabolic measurements of the working frontal cortex in man. *Trends in Neurosciences*, 1984, *7*, 430–435.

Rolls, E. T. Feeding and reward. In *The neural basis of feeding and reward*, edited by B. G. Hobel and D. Novin. Brunswick, ME: Haer Institute, 1982.

Rolls, E. T. Learning mechanisms in the temporal lobe visual cortex. *Behavioural Brain Research*, 1995, *66*, 177–185.

Rolls, E. T., and Baylis, G. C. Size and contrast have only small effects on the responses to faces of neurons in the cortex of the superior temporal sulcus of the monkey. *Experimental Brain Research*, 1986, *65*, 38–48.

Rolls, E. T., Murzi, E., Yaxley, S., Thorpe, S. J., et al. Sensory-specific satiety: Food-specific reduction in responsiveness of ventral forebrain neurons after feeding in the monkey. *Brain Research*, 1986, *368*, 79–86.

Rolls, E. T., Yaxley, S., and Sienkiewicz, Z. J. Gustatory responses of single neurons in the orbitofrontal cortex of the macaque monkey. *Journal of Neurophysiology*, 1990, *64*, 1055–1066.

Romanovsky, A. A. Thermoregulation: Some concepts have changed. Functional architecture of the thermoregulatory system. *American Journal of Physiology*, 2007, *292*, R37–R46.

Rosa, R. R., and Bonnet, M. H. Reported chronic insomnia is independent of poor sleep as measured by electroencephalography. *Psychosomatic Medicine*, 2000, *62*, 474–482.

Rose, J. D. Changes in hypothalamic neuronal function related to hormonal induction of lordosis in behaving hamsters. *Physiology and Behavior*, 1990, *47*, 1201–1212.

Rose, J. E. Nicotine and nonnicotine factors in cigarette addiction. *Psychopharmacology*, 2006, *184*, 274–285.

Roselli, C. E., Larkin, K., Resko, J. A., Stellflug, J. N., et al. The volume of a sexually dimorphic nucleus in the ovine medial preoptic area/anterior hypothalamus varies with sexual partner preference. *Endocrinology*, 2004, *145*, 478–483.

Rosenblatt, J. S., Hazelwood, S., and Poole, J. Maternal behavior in male rats: Effects of medial preoptic area lesions and presence of maternal aggression. *Hormones and Behavior*, 1996, *30*, 201–215.

Rosenthal, D. A program of research on heredity in schizophrenia. *Behavioral Science*, 1971, *16*, 191–201.

Rosenthal, N. E., Sack, D. A., Gillin, C., Lewy, A. J., et al. Seasonal affective disorder: A description of the syndrome and preliminary findings with light therapy. *Archives of General Psychiatry*, 1984, *41*, 72–80.

Rosenthal, N. E., Sack, D. A., James, S. P., Parry, B. L., et al. Seasonal affective disorder and phototherapy. *Annals of the New York Academy of Sciences*, 1985, *453*, 260–269.

Roses, A. D. A model for susceptibility polymorphisms for complex diseases: Apolipoprotein E and Alzheimer disease. *Neurogenetics*, 1997, *1*, 3–11.

Rösner, S., Hackl-Herrwerth, A., Leucht, S., Lehert, P., et al. Acamprosate for alcohol dependence. *Cochrane Database of Systematic Reviews*, 2010, Issue 9.

Roth, M., Decery, J., Raybaudi, M., Massarelli, R., et al. Possible involvement of primary motor cortex in mentally simulated movement: A functional magnetic resonance imaging study. *Neuroreport*, 1996, *7*, 1280–1284.

Roth, T., and Pravosudov, V. Tough times call for bigger brains. *Communicative and Integrative Biology*, 2009, *2*(3), 236.

Rothbaum, B. O., and Davis, M. Applying learning principles to the treatment of post-trauma reactions. *Annals of the New York Academy of Science*, 2003, *1008*, 112–121.

Rothman, S. M., and Olney, J. W. Excitotoxicity and the NMDA receptor. *Trends in Neurosciences*, 1987, *10*, 299–302.

Rozin, P., Dow, S., Moscovitch, M., and Rajaram, S. What causes humans to begin and end a meal? A role for memory for what has been eaten, as evidenced by a study of multiple meal eating in amnesic patients. *Psychological Science*, 1998, *9*(5), 392–396.

Rubia, K., Overmeyer, S., Taylor, E., Brammer, M., et al. Hypofrontality in attention deficit hyperactivity disorder during higher-order motor control: A study with functional MRI. *American Journal of Psychiatry*, 1999, *156*, 891–896.

Rubin, B. S., and Barfield, R. J. Priming of estrous responsiveness by implants of 17B-estradiol in the ventromedial hypothalamic nucleus of female rats. *Endocrinology*, 1980, *106*, 504–509.

Rubin, L. L., and Staddon, J. M. The cell biology of the blood–brain barrier. *Annual Review of Neuroscience*, 1999, *22*, 11–28.

Rubino, T., and Parolaro, D. Cannabis abuse in adolescence and the risk of psychosis: A brief review of the preclinical evidence. *Progress in Neuro-Psychopharmacology and Biological Psychiatry*, 2014, *52*, 41–44.

Rück, C., Karlsson, A., Steele, J. D., Edman, G., et al. Capsulotomy for obsessive-compulsive disorder. *Archives of General Psychiatry*, 2008, *65*, 914–922.

Rumpel, S., LeDoux, J., Zador, A., and Malinow, R. Postsynaptic receptor trafficking underlying a form of associative learning. *Science*, 2005, *308*, 83–88.

Rusak, B., and Morin, L. P. Testicular responses to photoperiod are blocked by lesions of the suprachiasmatic nuclei in golden hamsters. *Biology of Reproduction*, 1976, *15*, 366–374.

Russchen, F. T., Amaral, D. G., and Price, J. L. The afferent connections of the substantia innominata in the monkey, *Macaca fascicularis*. *Journal of Comparative Neurology*, 1986, *242*, 1–27.

Russell, G. F. M., and Treasure, J. The modern history of anorexia nervosa: An interpretation of why the illness has changed. *Annals of the New York Academy of Sciences*, 1989, *575*, 13–30.

Russell, M. J. Human olfactory communication. *Nature*, 1976, *260*, 520–522.

Russell, M. J., Switz, G. M., and Thompson, K. Olfactory influences on the human menstrual cycle. *Pharmacology, Biochemistry and Behavior*, 1980, *13*, 737–738.

Russo, S. J., Murrough, J. W., Han, M. H., Charney, D. S., et al. Neurobiology of resilience. *Nature Neuroscience*, 2012, *15*(11), 1475–1484.

Rutter, M. Cognitive deficits in the pathogenesis of autism. *Journal of Child Psychology and Psychiatry*, 1983, *24*, 513–531.

Ryba, N. J., and Tirindelli, R. A new multigene family of putative pheromone receptors. *Neuron*, 1997, *19*, 371–392.

Ryback, R. S., and Lewis, O. F. Effects of prolonged bed rest on EEG sleep patterns in young, healthy volunteers. *Electroencephalography and Clinical Neurophysiology*, 1971, *31*, 395–399.

Saal, D., Dong, Y., Bonci, A., and Malenka, R. C. Drugs of abuse and stress trigger a common synaptic adaptation in dopamine neurons. *Neuron*, 2003, *37*, 577–582.

Saayman, G. S. Aggressive behaviour in free-ranging chacma baboons (*Papio ursinus*). *Journal of Behavioral Science*, 1971, *1*, 77–83.

Sachar, E. J., and Baron, M. The biology of affective disorders. *Annual Review of Neuroscience*, 1979, *2*, 505–518.

Sackeim, H. A., Decina, P., Prohovnik, I., Malitz, S., et al. Anticonvulsant and antidepressant properties of electroconvulsive therapy: A proposed mechanism of action. *Biological Psychiatry*, 1983, *18*, 1301–1310.

Sackeim, H. A., and Gur, R. C. Lateral asymmetry in intensity of emotional expression. *Neuropsychologia*, 1978, *16*, 473–482.

Sacktor, T. C. PINing for things past. *Science Signaling*, 2010, *3*, pe9.

Sacktor, T. C. How does PKMζ maintain long-term memory? *Nature Reviews: Neuroscience*, 2011, *12*, 9–15.

Sadato, N., Pascualleone, A., Grafman, J., Ibanez, V., et al. Activation of the primary visual cortex by Braille reading in blind subjects. *Nature*, 1996, *380*, 526–528.

Saffran, E. M., Marin, O. S. M., and Yeni-Komshian, G. H. An analysis of speech perception in word deafness. *Brain and Language*, 1976, *3*, 209–228.

Saffran, E. M., Schwartz, M. F., and Marin, O. S. M. Evidence from aphasia: Isolating the components of a production model. In *Language production*, edited by B. Butterworth. London: Academic Press, 1980.

Sagvolden, T., Aase, H., Zeiner, P., and Berger, D. Altered reinforcement mechanisms in attention-deficit/hyperactivity disorder. *Behavioural Brain Research*, 1998, *94*, 61–71.

Sagvolden, T., Johansen, E. B., Aase, H., and Russell, V. A. A dynamic developmental theory of attention-deficit/hyperactivity disorder (ADHD) predominantly hyperactive/impulsive and combined subtypes. *Behavioral and Brain Sciences*, 2005, *28*, 397–419.

Sagvolden, T., and Sergeant, J. A. Attention deficit/hyperactivity disorder: From brain dysfunctions to behaviour. *Behavioural Brain Research*, 1998, *94*, 1–10.

Sahu, A., Kalra, P. S., and Kalra, S. P. Food deprivation and ingestion induce reciprocal changes in neuropeptide Y-concentrations in the paraventricular nucleus. *Peptides*, 1988, *9*, 83–86.

Sakai, F., Meyer, J. S., Karacan, I., Derman, S., et al. Normal human sleep: Regional cerebral haemodynamics. *Annals of Neurology*, 1979, *7*, 471–478.

Sakai, K. L., Noguchi, Y., Takeuchi, T., and Watanabe, E. Selective priming of syntactic processing by event-related transcranial magnet stimulation of Broca's area. *Neuron*, 2002, *35*, 1177–1182.

Sakuma, Y., and Pfaff, D. W. Facilitation of female reproductive behavior from mesencephalic central grey in the rat. *American Journal of Physiology*, 1979a, *237*, R279–R284.

Sakuma, Y., and Pfaff, D. W. Mesencephalic mechanisms for integration of female reproductive behavior in the rat. *American Journal of Physiology*, 1979b, *237*, R285–R290.

Sakuma, Y., and Pfaff, D. W. Convergent effects of lordosis-relevant somatosensory and hypothalamic influences on central gray cells in the rat mesencephalon. *Experimental Neurology*, 1980a, *70*, 269–281.

Sakuma, Y., and Pfaff, D. W. Excitability of female rat central gray cells with medullary projections: Changes produced by hypothalamic stimulation and estrogen treatment. *Journal of Neurophysiology*, 1980b, *44*, 1012–1023.

Sakurai, T. The neural circuit of orexin (hypocretin): Maintaining sleep and wakefulness. *Nature Reviews: Neuroscience*, 2007, *8*, 171–181.

Sakurai, T., Amemiya, A., Ishii, M., Matsuzaki, I., et al. Orexins and orexin receptors: A family of hypothalamic neuropeptides and G protein-coupled receptors that regulate feeding behavior. *Cell*, 1998, *20*, 573–585.

Sakurai, Y., Ichikawa, Y., and Mannen, T. Pure alexia from a posterior occipital lesion. *Neurology*, 2001, *56*, 778–781.

Sakurai, Y., Momose, T., Iwata, M., Sudo, Y., et al. Different cortical activity in reading of Kanji words, Kana words and Kana nonwords. *Cognitive Brain Research*, 2000, *9*, 111–115.

Sakurai, Y., Sakai, K., Sakuta, M., and Iwata, M. Naming difficulties in alexia with agraphia for kanji after a left posterior inferior temporal lesion. *Journal of Neurology, Neurosurgery, and Psychiatry*, 1994, *57*, 609–613.

Salamone, J. D. Complex motor and sensorimotor function of striatal and accumbens dopamine: Involvement in instrumental behavior processes. *Psychopharmacology*, 1992, *107*, 160–174.

Salas, J. C. T., Iwasaki, H., Jodo, E., Schmidt, M. H., et al. Penile erection and micturition events triggered by electrical stimulation of the mesopontine tegmental area. *American Journal of Physiology*, 2007, *294*, R102–R111.

Salm, A. K., Pavelko, M., Krouse, E. M., Webster, W., et al. Lateral amygdaloid nucleus expansion in adult rats is associated with exposure to prenatal stress. *Developmental Brain Research*, 2004, *148*, 159–167.

Salmelin, R., Schnitzler, A., Schmitz, F., and Freund, H. J. Single word reading in developmental stutterers and fluent speakers. *Brain*, 2000, *123*, 1184–1202.

Samson, H. H., Hodge, C. W., Tolliver, G. A., and Haraguchi, M. Effect of dopamine agonists and antagonists on ethanol reinforced behavior: The involvement of the nucleus accumbens. *Brain Research Bulletin*, 1993, *30*, 133–141.

Samuels, B. A., and Hen, R. Neurogenesis and affective disorders. *European Journal of Neuroscience*, 2011, *35*, 1152–1159.

Sanacora, G., Gueorguieva, R., Epperson, C. N., Wu, Y. T., et al. Subtype-specific alterations of gamma-aminobutyric acid and glutamate in patients with major depression. *Archives of General Psychiatry*, 2004, *61*, 705–713.

Sander, J. W., and Shorvon, S. D. Epidemiology of the epilepsies. *Journal of Neurology, Neurosurgery & Psychiatry*, 1996, *61*, 433–443.

Saper, C. B., Chou, T. C., and Scammell, T. E. The sleep switch: Hypothalamic control of sleep and wakefulness. *Trends in Neurosciences*, 2001, *24*, 726–731.

Saper, C. B., Fuller, P. M., Pedersen, N. P., Lu, J., et al. Sleep state switching. *Neuron*, 2010, *68*, 1023–1042.

Saper, C. B., Scammell, T. E., and Lu, J. Hypothalamic regulation of sleep and circadian rhythms. *Nature*, 2005, *437*, 1257–1263.

Sapolsky, R. M. *Stress, the aging brain and the mechanisms of neuron death*. Cambridge, MA: MIT Press, 1992.

Sapolsky, R. M. Social subordinance as a marker of hypercortisolism: Some unexpected subtleties. *Annals of the New York Academy of Sciences*, 1995, *771*, 626–639.

Sarem-Aslani, A., and Mullett, K. Industrial perspective on deep brain stimulation: History, current state, and future developments. *Frontiers in Integrative Neuroscience*, 2011, *5*.

Sassenrath, E. N., Powell, T. E., and Hendrickx, A. G. Perimenstrual aggression in groups of female rhesus monkeys. *Journal of Reproduction and Fertility*, 1973, *34*, 509–511.

Sato, N., Sakata, H., Tanaka, Y. L., and Taira, M. Navigation-associated medial parietal neurons in monkeys. *Proceedings of the National Academy of Sciences, USA*, 2006, *103*, 17001–17006.

Satterlee, J. S., Barbee, S., Jin, P., Krichevsky, A., et al. Noncoding RNAs in the brain. *Journal of Neuroscience*, 2007, *27*, 11856–11859.

Sauter, D. A., Eisner, F., Ekman, P., and Scott, S. K. Cross-cultural recognition of basic emotions through nonverbal emotional vocalizations. *Proceedings of the National Academy of Sciences, USA*, 2010, *107*, 2408–2412.

Savic, I., Berglund, H., Gulyas, B., and Roland, P. Smelling of odorous sex hormone-like compounds causes sex-differentiated hypothalamic activations in humans. *Neuron*, 2001, *31*, 661–668.

Savic, I., Berglund, H., and Lindström, P. Brain response to putative pheromones in homosexual men. *Proceedings of the National Academy of Sciences, USA*, 2005, *102*, 7356–7361.

Savic, I., Hedén-Blomqvist, E., and Berglund, H. Pheromone signal transduction in humans: What can be learned from olfactory loss. *Human Brain Mapping*, 2009, *30*, 3057–3065.

Sawchenko, P. E. Toward a new neurobiology of energy balance, appetite, and obesity: The anatomists weigh in. *Journal of Comparative Neurology*, 1998, *402*, 435–441.

Saxena, S., Brody, A. L., Schwartz, J. M., and Baxter, L. R. Neuroimaging and frontal-subcortical circuitry in obsessive-compulsive disorder. *British Journal of Psychiatry*, 1998, *173*, 26–37.

Saxton, T. K., Lyndon, A. C., Little, A. C., and Roberts, S. C. Evidence that androstadienone, a putative human chemosignal, modulates women's attributions of men's attractiveness. *Hormones and Behavior*, 2008, *54*, 597–601.

Scammell, T. E., Estabrooke, I. V., McCarthy, M. T., Chemelli, R. M., et al. Hypothalamic arousal regions are activated during modafinil-induced wakefulness. *Journal of Neuroscience*, 2000, *20*, 8620–8628.

Scammell, T. E., Gerashchenko, D. Y., Mochizuki, T., McCarthy, M. T., et al. An adenosine A2a agonist increases sleep and induces Fos in ventrolateral preoptic neurons. *Neuroscience*, 2001, *107*, 653–663.

Schaller, G., Schmidt, A., Pleiner, J., Woloszczuk, W., et al. Plasma ghrelin concentrations are not regulated by glucose or insulin: A double-blind, placebo-controlled crossover clamp study. *Diabetes*, 2003, *52*, 16–20.

Scharf, R., Sarhan, M., and DiLeone, R. J. Role of orexin/hypocretin in dependence and addiction. *Brain Research*, 2010, *1314*, 130–138.

Schein, S. J., and Desimone, R. Spectral properties of V4 neurons in the macaque. *Journal of Neuroscience*, 1990, *10*, 3369–3389.

Schenck, C. H., Bundlie, S. R., Ettinger, M. G., and Mahowald, M. W. Chronic behavioral disorders of human REM sleep: A new category of parasomnia. *Sleep*, 1986, *9*, 293–308.

Schenck, C. H., Hurwitz, T. D., Bundlie, S. R., and Mahowald, M. W. Sleep-related eating disorders: Polysomnographic correlates of a heterogeneous syndrome distinct from daytime eating disorders. *Sleep*, 1991, *14*, 419–431.

Schenck, C. H., Hurwitz, T. D., and Mahowald, M. W. REM-sleep behavior disorder: An update on a series of 96 patients and a review of the world literature. *Journal of Sleep Research*, 1993, *2*, 224–231.

Schenck, C. H., and Mahowald, M. W. Motor dyscontrol in narcolepsy: Rapid-eye-movement (REM) sleep without atonia and REM sleep behavior disorder. *Annals of Neurology*, 1992, *32*, 3–10.

Schenk, D., Barbour, R., Dunn, W., Gordon, G., et al. Immunization with amyloid-beta attenuates Alzheimer-disease-like pathology in the PDAPP mouse. *Nature*, 1999, *400*, 173–177.

Schenkein, J., and Montagna, P. Self management of fatal familial insomnia. 1: What is FFI? *Medscape General Medicine*, 2006a, *8*, 65.

Schenkein, J., and Montagna, P. Self management of fatal familial insomnia. 2: Case report. *Medscape General Medicine*, 2006b, *8*, 66.

Scherschlicht, R., Polc, P., Schneeberger, J., Steiner, M., et al. Selective suppression of rapid eye movement sleep (REMS) in cats by typical and atypical antidepressants. In *Typical and atypical antidepressants: Molecular mechanisms*, edited by E. Costa and G. Racagni. New York: Raven Press, 1982.

Schiffman, J., Ekstrom, M., LaBrie, J., Schulsinger, F., et al. Minor physical anomalies and schizophrenia spectrum disorders: A prospective investigation. *American Journal of Psychiatry*, 2002, *159*, 238–243.

Schiffman, J., Walker, E., Ekstrom, M., Schulsinger, F., et al. Childhood videotaped social and neuromotor precursors of schizophrenia: A prospective investigation, *American Journal of Psychiatry*, 2004, *161*, 2021–2027.

Schiffman, S. S. Intensification of sensory properties of foods for the elderly. *Journal of Nutrition*, 2000, *130*(4), 927S–930S.

Schiffman, S. S., Lockhead, E., and Maes, F. W. Amiloride reduces the taste intensity of Na^+ and Li^+ salts and sweeteners. *Proceedings of the National Academy of Sciences, USA*, 1983, *80*, 6136–6140.

Schiller, P. H. The ON and OFF channels of the visual system. *Trends in Neuroscience*, 1992, *15*, 86–92.

Schiller, P. H., and Malpeli, J. G. Properties and tectal projections of monkey retinal ganglion cells. *Journal of Neurophysiology*, 1977, *40*, 428–445.

Schiller, P. H., Sandell, J. H., and Maunsell, J. H. R. Functions of the ON and OFF channels of the visual system. *Nature*, 1986, *322*, 824–825.

Schleifer, S. J., Keller, S. E., Camerino, M., Thornton, J. C., et al. Suppression of lymphocyte stimulation following bereavement. *Journal of the American Medical Association*, 1983, *15*, 374–377.

Schloegl, H., Percik, R., Horstmann, A., Villringer, A., et al. Peptide hormones regulating appetite-Focus on neuroimaging studies in humans. *Diabetes/Metabolism Research and Reviews*, 2011, *27*, 104–112.

Schlosser, D. A., Pearson, R., Perez, V. B., and Loewy, R. L. Environmental risk and protective factors and their influence on the emergence of psychosis. *Adolescent Psychiatry*, 2012, *2*(2), 163–171.

Schmid, D., Held, K., Ising, M., Uhr, M., et al. Ghrelin stimulates appetite, imagination of food, GH, ACTH, and cortisol, but does not affect leptin in normal controls. *Neuropsychopharmacology*, 2005, *30*, 1187–1192.

Schmidt, M. H., and Schmidt, H. S. Sleep-related erections: Neural mechanisms and clinical significance. *Current Neurology and Neuroscience Reports*, 2004, *4*, 170–178.

Schmidt, M. H., Valatx, J.-L., Sakai, K., Fort, P., et al. Role of the lateral preoptic area in sleep-related erectile mechanisms and sleep generation in the rat. *Journal of Neuroscience*, 2000, *20*, 6640–6647.

Schneider, B., Muller, M. J., and Philipp, M. Mortality in affective disorders. *Journal of the Affective Disorders*, 2001, *65*, 263–274.

Schneider, P., Scherg, M., Dosch, H. G., Specht, H. L., et al. Morphology of Heschl's gyrus reflects enhanced activation in the auditory cortex of musicians. *Nature Neuroscience*, 2002, *5*, 688–694.

Schoenfeld, M. A., Neuer, G., Tempelmann, C., Schüssler, K., et al. Functional magnetic resonance tomography correlates of taste perception in the human primary taste cortex. *Neuroscience*, 2004, *127*, 347–353.

Schultz, R. T. Developmental deficits in social perception in autism: The role of the amygdala and fusiform face area. *International Journal of Developmental Neuroscience*, 2005, *23*, 125–141.

Schumacher, J., Kristensen, A. S., Wendland, J. R., Nöthen, M. M., et al. The genetics of panic disorder. *Medical Genetics*, 2011, *48*, 361–368.

Schumacher, J., Laje, G., Abou Jamra, R., Becker, T., et al. The DISC locus and schizophrenia: Evidence from an association study in a central European sample and from a meta-analysis across different European populations. *Human Molecular Genetics*, 2009, *18*, 2719–2727.

Schumann, C. M., and Amaral, D. G. Stereological analysis of amygdala neuron number in autism. *Journal of Neuroscience*, 2006, *26*, 7674–7679.

Schwartz, M. F., Marin, O. S. M., and Saffran, E. M. Dissociations of language function in dementia: A case study. *Brain and Language*, 1979, *7*, 277–306.

Schwartz, M. F., Saffran, E. M., and Marin, O. S. M. The word order problem in agrammatism. I: Comprehension. *Brain and Language*, 1980, *10*, 249–262.

Schwartz, S., Ponz, A., Poryazova, R., Werth, E., et al. Abnormal activity in hypothalamus and amygdala during humour processing in human narcolepsy with cataplexy. *Brain*, 2008, *131*, 514–522.

Schwartz, W. J., and Gainer, H. Suprachiasmatic nucleus: Use of ^{14}C-labelled deoxyglucose uptake as a functional marker. *Science*, 1977, *197*, 1089–1091.

Schwarzlose, R. F., Baker, C. I., and Kanwisher, N. Separate face and body selectivity on the fusiform gyrus. *Journal of Neuroscience*. 2005, *25*, 11055–11059.

Scott, K. The sweet and the bitter of mammalian taste. *Current Opinions in Neurobiology*, 2004, *14*, 423–427.

Scott, S. K., Blank, E. C., Rosen, S., and Wise, R. J. S. Identification of a pathway for intelligible speech in the left temporal lobe. *Brain*, 2000, *123*, 2400–2406.

Scott, T. R., and Plata-Salaman, C. R. Coding of taste quality. In *Smell and taste in health and disease*, edited by T. N. Getchell. New York: Raven Press, 1991.

Scoville, W. B., and Milner, B. Loss of recent memory after bilateral hippocampal lesions. *Journal of Neurology, Neurosurgery and Psychiatry*, 1957, *20*, 11–21.

Seagraves, M. A., Goldberg, M. E., Deny, S., Bruce, C. J., et al. The role of striate cortex in the guidance of eye movements in the monkey. *The Journal of Neuroscience*, 1987, *7*, 3040–3058.

Searcy, C. P., Bobadilla, L., Gordon, W. A., Jacques, S., et al. Pharmacological prevention of combat-related PTSD: A literature review. *Military Medicine*, 2012, *177*(6), 649–654.

Sears, L. L., Vest, C., Mohamed, S., Bailey, J., et al. An MRI study of the basal ganglia in autism. *Progress in Neuro-Psychopharmacology and Biological Psychiatry*, 1999, 23, 613–624.

Sebat, J., Lakshmi, B., Malhotra, D., Troge, J., et al. Strong association of de novo copy number mutations with autism. *Science*, 2007, 316, 445–449.

Seidman, L. J., Biederman, J., Weber, W., Hatch, M., et al. Neuropsychological function in adults with attention-deficit hyperactivity disorder. *Biological Psychiatry*, 1998, 44, 260–268.

Seidman, M. D., Seigel, B., Shah, P., Bowyer, S. M. Hemispheric Dominance and Cell Phone Use. *Journal of the American Medical Association Otolaryngol Head Neck Surg.* 2013, 139(5), 466–470.

Selye, H. *The stress of life.* New York: McGraw-Hill, 1976.

Semenza, C., and Zettin, M. Evidence from aphasia for the role of proper names as pure referring expressions. *Nature*, 1989, 342, 678–679.

Senju, A., Maeda, M., Kikuchi, Y., Hasegawa, T., et al. Absence of contagious yawning in children with autism spectrum disorder, *Biology Letters*, 2007, 3, 706–708.

Serrano, P., Friedman, E. L., Kenney, J., et al. PKMζ maintains spatial, instrumental, and classically conditioned long-term memories. *PLoS Biology*, 2008, 23, 2698–2706.

Sforza, E., Montagna, P., Tinuper, P., Cortelli, P., et al. Sleep-wake cycle abnormalities in fatal familial insomnia: Evidence of the role of the thalamus in sleep regulation. *Electroencephalography and Clinical Neurophysiology*, 1995, 94, 398–405.

Shafto, M. A., Burke, D. M., Stamatakis, E. A., Tam, P. P., et al. On the tip-of-the-tongue: Neural correlates of increased word-finding failures in normal aging. *Journal of Cognitive Neuroscience*, 2007, 19, 2060–2070.

Shalev, U., Erb, S., and Shaham, Y. Role of CRF and other neuropeptides in stress-induced reinstatement of drug seeking. *Brain Research*, 2010, 1314, 15–28.

Shallice, T. Phonological agraphia and the lexical route in writing. *Brain*, 1981, 104, 413–429.

Sham, P. C., O'Callaghan, E., Takei, N., Murray, G. K., et al. Schizophrenia following pre-natal exposure to influenza epidemics between 1939 and 1960. *British Journal of Psychiatry*, 1992, 160, 461–466.

Shammi, P., and Stuss, D. T. Humor appreciation: A role of the right frontal lobe. *Brain*, 1999, 122, 657–666.

Shannon, R. V. Understanding hearing through deafness. *Proceedings of the National Academy of Sciences, USA*, 2007, 104, 6883–6884.

Shapiro, L. E., Leonard, C. M., Sessions, C. E., Dewsbury, D. A., and Insel, T. R. Comparative neuroanatomy of the sexually dimorphic hypothalamus in monogamous and polygamous voles. *Brain Research*, 1991, 541, 232–240.

Sharp, D. J., Scott, S. K., and Wise, R. J. S. Retrieving meaning after temporal lobe infarction: The role of the basal language area. *Annals of Neurology*, 2004, 56, 836–846.

Shaw, P., Eckstrand, K., Sharp, W., Blumenthal, J., et al. Attention-deficit/hyperactivity disorder is characterized by a delay in cortical maturation. *Proceedings of the National Academy of Sciences, USA*, 2007, 10, 19649–19654.

Shaywitz, B. A., Shaywitz, S. E., Pugh, K. R., Mencl, W. E., et al. Disruption of posterior brain systems for reading in children with developmental dyslexia. *Biological Psychiatry*, 2002, 52, 101–110.

Shema, R., Haramati, S., Ron, S., et al. Enhancement of consolidated long-term memory by overexpression of protein kinase Mζ in the neocortex. *Science*, 2011, 331, 1207–1210.

Shen, K., and Meyer, T. Dynamic control of CaMKII translocation and localization in hippocampal neurons by NMDA stimulation. *Science*, 1999, 284, 162–166.

Shepherd, G. M. Discrimination of molecular signals by the olfactory receptor neuron. *Neuron*, 1994, 13, 771–790.

Sher, A. E. Surgery for obstructive sleep apnea. *Progress in Clinical Biology Research*, 1990, 345, 407–415.

Sherin, J. E., Elmquist, J. K., Torrealba, F., and Saper, C. B. Innervation of histaminergic tuberomammillary neurons by GABAergic and galaninergic neurons in the ventrolateral preoptic nucleus of the rat. *Journal of Neuroscience*, 1998, 18, 4705–4721.

Sherry, D. F., Jacobs, L. F., and Gaulin, S. J. C. Spatial memory and adaptive specialization of the hippocampus. *Trends in Neuroscience*, 1992, 15, 298–303.

Shi, S.-H., Hayashi, Y., Petralia, R. S., Zaman, S. H., et al. Rapid spine delivery and redistribution of AMPA receptors after synaptic NMDA receptor activation. *Science*, 1999, 284, 1811–1816.

Shifren, J. L., Braunstein, G. D., Simon, J. A., Casson, P. R., et al. Transdermal testosterone treatment in women with impaired sexual function after oophorectomy. *New England Journal of Medicine*, 2000, 343, 682–688.

Shik, M. L., and Orlovsky, G. N. Neurophysiology of locomotor automatism. *Physiological Review*, 1976, 56, 465–501.

Shima, K., and Tanji, J. Both supplementary and presupplementary motor areas are crucial for the temporal organization of multiple movements. *Journal of Neurophysiology*, 1998, 80, 3247–3260.

Shima, K., and Tanji, J. Neuronal activity in the supplementary and presupplementary motor areas for temporal organization of multiple movements. *Journal of Neurophysiology*, 2000, 84, 2148–2160.

Shimada, M., Tritos, N. A., Lowell, B. B., Flier, J. S., et al. Mice lacking melanin-concentrating hormone are hypophagic and lean. *Nature*, 1998, 396, 670–674.

Shimura, T., Yamamoto, T., and Shimokochi, M. The medial preoptic area is involved in both sexual arousal and performance in male rats: Re-evaluation of neuron activity in freely moving animals. *Brain Research*, 1994, 640, 215–222.

Shin, A. C., Zheng, H., Pistell, P. J., and Berthoud, H.-R. Roux-en-Y gastric bypass surgery changes food reward in rats. *International Journal of Obesity*, 2011, 35, 642–651.

Shin, L. M., Wright, C. I., Cannistraro, P. A., Wedig, M. M., et al. A functional magnetic resonance imaging study of amygdala and medial prefrontal cortex responses to overtly presented fearful faces in posttraumatic stress disorder. *Archives of General Psychiatry*, 2005, 62, 273–281.

Shipley, M. T., and Ennis, M. Functional organization of the olfactory system. *Journal of Neurobiology*, 1996, 30, 123–176.

Shmuelof, L, and Zohary, E. Dissociation between ventral and dorsal fMRI activation during object and action recognition. *Neuron*, 2005, 47, 457–470.

Shors, T. J. Saving new brain cells. *Scientific American*, 2009, 100, 46–54.

Shuto, Y., Shibasaki, T., Otagiri, A., Kuriyama, H., et al. Hypothalamic growth hormone secretagogue receptor regulates growth hormone secretion, feeding, and adiposity. *Journal of Clinical Investigation*, 2002, 109, 1429–1436.

Sidman, M., Stoddard, L. T., and Mohr, J. P. Some additional quantitative observations of immediate memory in a patient with bilateral hippocampal lesions. *Neuropsychologia*, 1968, 6, 245–254.

Siegel, J. Clues to the functions of mammalian sleep. *Nature*, 2005, 437, 1264–1271.

Siegel, J. M., and McGinty, D. J. Pontine reticular formation neurons: Relationship of discharge to motor activity. *Science*, 1977, 196, 678–680.

Siegel, R. M., and Andersen, R. A. Motion perceptual deficits following ibotenic acid lesions of the middle temporal area (MT) in the behaving monkey. *Society for Neuroscience Abstracts*, 1986, 12, 1183.

Sigel, E., and Buhr, A. The benzodiazepine binding site of GABA$_A$ receptors. *Trends in Pharmacological Sciences*, 1997, 18(4), 425–429.

Silber, M. H., Ancoli-Israel, S., Bonnet, M. H., Chokroverty, S., Grigg-Damberger, M. M., Hirshkowitz, M., … and Iber, et al. The visual scoring of sleep in adults. *J Clin Sleep Med*, 2007, 3(2), 121–131.

Silva, A. J., Paylor, R., Wehner, J. M., and Tonegawa, S. Impaired spatial learning in alpha-calcium-calmodulin kinase II mutant mice. *Science*, 1992, *257*, 206–211.

Silver, R., LeSauter, J., Tresco, P. A., and Lehman, M. N. A diffusible coupling signal from the transplanted suprachiasmatic nucleus controlling circadian locomotor rhythms. *Nature*, 1996, *382*, 810–813.

Silveri, M. C. Peripheral aspects of writing can be differentially affected by sensorial and attentional defect: Evidence from a patient with afferent dysgraphia and case dissociation. *Cortex*, 1996, *32*, 155–172.

Silverman, J.L., Yang, M., Lord, C., and Crawley, J. N. Behavioural phenotyping assays for mouse models of autism. Nature Reviews: *Neuroscience*, 2010, 11, 490–501.

Simmons, A. N., and Matthews, S. C. Neural circuitry of PTSD with or without mild traumatic brain injury: A meta-analysis. *Neuropharmacology*, 2012, *62*(2), 598–606.

Simpson, J. B., Epstein, A. N., and Camardo, J. S. The localization of dipsogenic receptors for angiotensin II in the subfornical organ. *Journal of Comparative and Physiological Psychology*, 1978, *92*, 581–608.

Sincich, L. C., Jocson, C. M., and Horton, J. C. V1 interpatch projections to V2 thick stripes and pale stripes. *Journal of Neuroscience*, 2010, *30*, 6963–6974.

Sindelar, D. K., Ste. Marie, L., Miura, G. I., Palmiter, R. D., et al. Neuropeptide Y is required for hyperphagic feeding in response to neuroglucopenia. *Endocrinology*, 2004, 145, 3363–3368.

Singer, C., and Weiner, W. J. Male sexual dysfunction. *Neurologist*, 1996, *2*, 119–129.

Singer, T., Seymour, B., O'Doherty, J., Kaube, H., et al. Empathy for pain involves the affective but not sensory components of pain. *Science*, 2004, *303*, 1157–1162.

Singer, F., & Zumoff, B. (1992). Subnormal serum testosterone levels in male internal medicine residents. *Steroids*, *57*(2), 86–89.

Singh, D., and Bronstad, P. M. Female body odour is a potential cue to ovulation. *Proceedings of the Royal Society of London B*, 2001, *268*, 797–801.

Sipos, A., Rasmussen, F., Harrison, G., Tynelius, P., et al. Paternal age and schizophrenia: A population based cohort study. *British Medical Journal*, 2004, *330*, 147–148.

Sipos, M. L., and Nyby, J. G. Concurrent androgenic stimulation of the ventral tegmental area and medial preoptic area: Synergistic effects on male-typical reproductive behaviors in house mice. *Brain Research*, 1996, *729*, 29–44.

Sirigu, A., Deprati, E., Ciancia, S., Giraux, P., et al. Altered awareness of voluntary action after damage to the parietal cortex. *Nature Neuroscience*, 2004, *7*, 80–84.

Skaggs, W. E., and McNaughton, B. L. Spatial firing properties of hippocampal CA1 populations in an environment containing two visually identical regions. *Journal of Neuroscience*, 1998, *18*, 8455–8466.

Skene, D. J., Lockley, S. W., and Arendt, J. Melatonin in circadian sleep disorders in the blind. *Biological Signals and Receptors*, 1999, *8*, 90–95.

Skutella, T., Criswell, H., Moy, S., Probst, J. C., et al. Corticotropin-releasing hormone (CRH) antisense oligodeoxynucleotide induces anxiolytic effects in rat. *Neuroreport*, 1994, *5*, 2181–2185.

Slater, M., Perez-Marcos, D., Ehrsson, H. H., and Sanchez-Vives, M. V. Inducing illusory ownership of a virtual body. *Frontiers in Neuroscience*, 2009, *3*, 214–220.

Slotkin, T. A. Fetal nicotine or cocaine exposure: Which one is worse? *Journal of Pharmacology and Experimental Therapeutics*, 1998, *22*, 521–527.

Small, M., Bailey-Davis, L., Morgan, N., and Maggs, J. Changes in eating and physical activity behaviors across seven semesters of college living on or off campus matters. *Health Education and Behavior*, 2013, *40*(4), 435–41.

Smith, C. N., and Squire, L. R. Medial temporal lobe activity during retrieval of semantic memory is related to the age of the memory. *Journal of Neuroscience*, 2009. *29*, 930–938.

Smith, G. P. Animal models of human eating disorders. *Annals of the New York Academy of Sciences*, 1989, *16*, 219–237.

Smith, J. T., Acohido, B. V., Clifton, D. K., and Steiner, R. A. KiSS-1 neurones are direct targets for leptin in the ob/ob mouse. *Journal of Neuroendocrinology*, 2006, *18*, 298–303.

Smith, M. D., Patterson, E., Wahed, A. S., Belle, S. H., et al. Relationship between surgeon volume and adverse outcomes after RYGB in Longitudinal Assessment of Bariatric Surgery (LABS) study. *Surgery for Obesity and Related Disorders*, 2010, *6*, 118–125.

Snyder, L. H., Batista, A. P., and Andersen, R. A. Intention-related activity in the posterior parietal cortex: A review. *Vision Research*, 2000, *40*, 1433–1441.

Snyder, S. H. *Madness and the brain*. New York: McGraw-Hill, 1974.

Soares, J. C., and Gershon, S. The lithium ion: A foundation for psychopharmacological specificity. *Neuropsychopharmacology*, 1998, *19*, 167–182.

Södersten, P., Bergh, C., and Zandian, M. Understanding eating disorders. *Hormones and Behavior*, 2006, *50*, 572–578.

Södersten, P., Nergårdh, R., Bergh, C., et al. Behavioral neuroendocrinology and treatment of anorexia nervosa. *Frontiers in Neuroendocrinology*, 2008, *29*, 445–462.

Sokol, R. J., Delaney-Black, V., and Nordstrom, B. Fetal alcohol spectrum disorder. *Journal of the American Medical Association*, 2003, *290*(22), 2996–2999.

Soliman, F., Glatt, C. E., Bath, K. G., Levita, L., et al. A genetic variant BDNF polymorphism alters extinction learning in both mouse and human. *Science*, 2010, *327*, 863–866.

Solomon, S. G., and Lennie, P. The machinery of colour vision. *Nature Reviews: Neuroscience*, 2007, *8*, 276–286.

Solstad, T., Boccara, C. N., Kropff, E., Moser, M. B., et al. Representation of geometric borders in the entorhinal cortex. *Science*, 2008, *322*, 1865–1868.

Solyom, L., Turnbull, I. M., and Wilensky, M. A case of self-inflicted leucotomy. *British Journal of Psychiatry*, 1987, *151*, 855–857.

Son, G. H., Geum, D., Chung, S., Kim, E. J., et al. Maternal stress produces learning deficits associated with impairment of NMDA receptor-mediated synaptic plasticity. *Journal of Neuroscience*, 2006, *26*, 3309–3318.

Soon, C. S., Brass, M., Heinze, H.-J., and Haynes, J.-D. Unconscious determinants of free decisions in the human brain. *Nature Neuroscience*, 2008, *11*, 543–545.

Soria, G., Mendizabal, V., Rourino, C., Robledo, P, et al. Lack of CB_1 cannabinoid receptor impairs cocaine self-administration. *Neuropsychopharmacology*, 2005, *30*, 1670–1680.

Sormani, M. P., Bruzzi, P., Comi, G., and Filippi, M. The distribution of the magnetic resonance imaging response to glatiramer acetate in multiple sclerosis. *Multiple Sclerosis*, 2005, *11*, 447–449.

Sotillo, M., Carretié, L., Hinojosa, J. A., Tapia, M., et al. Neural activity associated with metaphor comprehension: Spatial analysis. *Neuroscience Letters*, 2005, *373*, 5–9.

Sotres-Bayon, F., and Quirk, G. J. Prefrontal control of fear: More than just extinction, *Current Opinion in Neurobiology*, 2010, *20*, 231–235.

Sotthibundhu, A., Sykes, A. M., Fox, B., Underwood, C. K., et al. β-Amyloid$_{1-42}$ induces neuronal death through the p75 neurotrophin receptor. *Journal of Neuroscience*, 2008, *28*, 3941–3946.

South, E. H., and Ritter, R. C. Capsaicin application to central or peripheral vagal fibers attenuates CCK satiety. *Peptides*, 1988, *9*, 601–612.

Southwell, A. L., Ko, J., and Patterson, P. H. Intrabody gene therapy ameliorates motor, cognitive, and neuropathological symptoms in multiple mouse models of Huntington's disease. *Journal of Neuroscience*, 2009, *29*, 13589–13602.

Solyom, L., Turnbull, I. M., and Wilensky, M. A case of self-inflicted leucotomy. *British Journal of Psychiatry*, 1987, *151*, 855–857.

Spezio, M. L., Huang, P.-Y. S., Castelli, F., and Adolphs, R. Amygdala damage impairs eye contact during conversations with real people. *Journal of Neuroscience*, 2007, *27*, 3994–3997.

Spiers, H. J., Maguire, E. A., and Burgess, N. Hippocampal amnesia. *Neurocase*, 2001, *7*, 357–382.

Sprengelmeyer, R., Young, A. W., Calder, A. J., Karnat, A., et al. Loss of disgust: Perception of faces and emotions in Huntington's disease. *Brain*, 1996, *119*, 1647–1665.

Sprengelmeyer, R., Young, A. W., Pundt, I., Sprengelmeyer, A., et al. Disgust implicated in obsessive-compulsive disorder. *Proceedings of the Royal Society of London B*, 1997, *264*, 1767–1773.

Squire, L. R. Stable impairment in remote memory following electroconvulsive therapy. *Neuropsychologia*, 1974, *13*, 51–58.

Squire, L. R. Memory and the hippocampus: A synthesis from findings with rats, monkeys, and humans. *Psychological Review*, 1992, *99*, 195–231.

Squire, L. R., Shimamura, A. P., and Amaral, D. G. Memory and the hippocampus. In *Neural models of plasticity: Experimental and theoretical approaches*, edited by J. H. Byrne and W. O. Berry. San Diego: Academic Press, 1989.

St. George-Hyslop, P. H., Tanzi, R. E., Polinsky, R. J., Haines, J. L., et al. The genetic defect causing familial Alzheimer's disease maps on chromosome 21. *Science*, 1987, *235*, 885–890.

Stahl, S. M. *Antipsychotics and mood stabilizers: Stahl's essential psychopharmacology*. Cambridge, England: Cambridge University Press, 2008.

Stahl, S. M., Grady, M. M., Moret, C., and Briley, M. SNRIs: Their pharmacology, clinical efficacy, and tolerability in comparison with other classes of antidepressants. *CNS Spectrums*, 2005, *10*, 732–747.

Standing, L. Learning 10,000 pictures. *Quarterly Journal of Experimental Psychology*, 1973, *25*, 207–222.

Stanislavsky, C. *An actor prepares*. New York: Theater Arts/Routledge, 1936.

Starkey, S. J., Walker, M. P., Beresford, I. J. M., and Hagan, R. M. Modulation of the rat suprachiasmatic circadian clock by melatonin in-vitro. *Neuroreport*, 1995, *6*, 1947–1951.

Staubli, U., Larson, J., and Lynch, G. Mossy fiber potentiation and long-term potentiation involve different expression mechanisms. *Synapse*, 1990, *5*, 333–335.

Stebbins, W. C., Miller, J. M., Johnsson, L.-G., and Hawkins, J. E. Ototoxic hearing loss and cochlear pathology in the monkey. *Annals of Otology, Rhinology and Laryngology*, 1969, *78*, 1007–1026.

Steele, A. D., Emsley, J. G., Ozdinler, P. H., Lindquist, S., et al. Prion protein (PrPc) positively regulates neural precursor proliferation during developmental and adult mammalian neurogenesis. *Proceedings of the National Academy of Sciences, USA*, 2006, *203*, 3416–3421.

Steeves, J. K. E., Humphrey, G. K., Culham, J. C., Menon, R. A., et al. Behavioral and neuroimaging evidence for a contribution of color and texture information to scene classification in a patient with visual form agnosia. *Journal of Cognitive Neuroscience*, 2004, *16*, 955–965.

Stefanacci, L., and Amaral, D. G. Topographic organization of cortical inputs to the lateral nucleus of the macaque monkey amygdala: A retrograde tracing study. *Journal of Comparative Neurology*, 2000, *22*, 52–79.

Stefanatos, G. A., Gershkoff, A., and Madigan, S. On pure word deafness, temporal processing, and the left hemisphere. *Journal of the International Neuropsychological Society*, 2005, *11*, 456–470.

Stein, D. J. Social anxiety disorder in the West and in the East. *Annals of Clinical Psychiatry*, 2009, *21*, 109–117.

Stein, M. B., Jang, K. L., Taylor, S., Vernon, P. A., et al. Genetic and environmental influences on trauma exposure and post-traumatic stress disorder symptoms: A twin study. *American Journal of Psychiatry*, 2002, *159*, 1675–1681.

Stein, M. B., Simmons, A. N., Feinstein, J. S., and Paulus, M. P. Increased amygdala and insula activation during emotion processing in anxiety-prone subjects. *American Journal of Psychiatry*, 2007, *164*, 318–327.

Stein, M. B., and Uhde, T. W. The biology of anxiety disorders. In *American Psychiatric Press textbook of psychopharmacology*. Washington, DC: American Psychiatric Press, 1995.

Steinert, R. E., Meyer-Gerspach, A. C., and Beglinger, C. The role of the stomach in the control of appetite and the secretion of satiation peptides. *American Journal of Physiology-Endocrinology and Metabolism*, 2012, *302*(6), E666–E673.

Steinhausen, H. C. The outcome of anorexia nervosa in the 20th century. *American Journal of Psychiatry*, 2002, *159*, 1284–1293.

Steininger, R. L., Alam, M. N., Szymusiak, R., and McGinty, D. State dependent discharge of ruberomammillary neurons in the rat hypothalamus. *Sleep Research*, 1996, *25*, 28.

Stephan, F. K., and Nuñez, A. A. Elimination of circadian rhythms in drinking activity, sleep, and temperature by isolation of the suprachiasmatic nuclei. *Behavioral Biology*, 1977, *20*, 1–16.

Stephan, F. K., and Zucker, I. Circadian rhythms in drinking behavior and locomotor activity of rats are eliminated by hypothalamic lesion. *Proceedings of the National Academy of Sciences, USA*, 1972, *69*, 1583–1586.

Steriade, M. Arousal: Revisiting the reticular activating system. *Science*, 1996, *272*, 225–226.

Steriade, M. The corticothalamic system in sleep. *Frontiers in Bioscience*, 2003, *8*, d878–d899.

Steriade, M. Grouping of brain rhythms in corticothalamic systems. *Neuroscience*, 2006, *137*, 1087–1106.

Steriade, M., Paré, D., Datta, S., Oakson, G., et al. Different cellular types in mesopontine cholinergic nuclei related to ponto-geniculo-occipital waves. *Journal of Neuroscience*, 1990, *8*, 2560–2579.

Sterling, P., and Eyer, J. Allostasis: a new paradigm to explain arousal pathology. In *Handbook of life stress, cognition and health*, edited by S. Fisher and J. Reason. New York: John Wiley & Sons, 1988.

Sterman, M. B., and Clemente, C. D. Forebrain inhibitory mechanisms: Cortical synchronization induced by basal forebrain stimulation. *Experimental Neurology*, 1962a, *6*, 91–102.

Sterman, M. B., and Clemente, C. D. Forebrain inhibitory mechanisms: Sleep patterns induced by basal forebrain stimulation in the behaving cat. *Experimental Neurology*, 1962b, *6*, 103–117.

Stern, K., and McClintock, M. K. Regulation of ovulation by human pheromones. *Nature*, 1998, *392*, 177–178.

Stewart, L. Fractionating the musical mind: Insights from congenital amusia. *Current Opinion in Neurobiology*, 2008, *18*, 127–130.

Stewart, L., Walsh, V., Frith, U., and Rothwell, J. C. TMS produces two dissociable types of speech disruption. *Neuroimage*, 2001, *13*, 472–478.

Stinson, D., and Thompson, C. Clinical experience with phototherapy. *Journal of the Affective Disorders*, 1990, *18*, 129–135.

Stoeckel, L. E., Weller, R. E., Giddings, M., and Cox, J. E. Peptide YY levels are associated with appetite suppression in response to long-chain fatty acids. *Physiology and Behavior*, 2008, *93*, 289–295.

Stolerman, I. P., and Jarvis, M. J. The scientific case that nicotine is addictive. *Psychopharmacology*, 1995, *117*, 2–10.

Stone, A. A., Reed, B. R., and Neale, J. M. Changes in daily event frequency precede episodes of physical symptoms. *Journal of Human Stress*, 1987, *13*, 70–74.

Stone, J. M., Morrison, P. D., and Pilowsky, L. S. Glutamate and dopamine dysregulation in schizophrenia: A synthesis and selective review. *Journal of Psychopharmacology*, 2007, *21*, 440–452.

Storz, G., Altuvia, S., and Wassarman, K. M. An abundance of RNA regulators. *Annual Review of Biochemistry*, 2005, *74*, 199–217.

Stowe, G. N., Vendruscolo, L. F., Edwards, S., Schlosburg, J. E., et al. A vaccine strategy that induces protective immunity against heroin. *Journal of Medical Chemistry*, 2011, *54*, 5195–5204.

Stowers, L., Holy, T. E., Meister, M., Dulac, C., et al. Loss of sex discrimination of male-male aggression in mice deficient for TRP2. *Science*, 2002, *295*, 1493–1500.

Stowers, L., and Marton, T. F. What is a pheromone? Mammalian pheromones reconsidered. *Neuron*, 2005, *46*, 699–702.

Strange, P. G. Antipsychotic drug action: Antagonism, inverse agonism or partial agonism. *Trends in Pharmacological Science*, 2008, *29*, 314–321.

Stumbrys, T., Erlacher, D., & Schredl, M. Testing the involvement of the prefrontal cortex in lucid dreaming: A tDCS study. *Consciousness and Cognition*, 2013, 22(4), 1214–1222.

Stumpf, R. M., and Boesch, C. Does promiscuous mating preclude female choice? Female sexual strategies in chimpanzees (*Pan troglodytes verus*) of the Taï National Park, Côte d'Ivoire. *Behavioral Ecology and Sociobiology*, 2005, *57*, 511–524.

Sturgis, J. D., and Bridges, R. S. N-methyl-DL-aspartic acid lesions of the medial preoptic area disrupt ongoing parental behavior in male rats. *Physiology and Behavior*, 1997, *62*, 305–310.

Sturup, G. K. Correctional treatment and the criminal sexual offender. *Canadian Journal of Correction*, 1961, *3*, 250–265.

Styron, W. *Darkness visible: A memoir of madness*. New York: Random House, 1990.

Substance Abuse and Mental Health Services Administration, http://www.samhsa.gov/newsroom/press-announcements/201410161215.

Suddath, R. L., Christison, G. W., Torrey, E. F., Casanova, M. F., et al. Anatomical abnormalities in the brains of monozygotic twins discordant for schizophrenia. *The New England Journal of Medicine*, 1990, *322*, 789–794.

Sulik, K. K. Genesis of alcohol-induced craniofacial dysmorphism. *Experimental Biology and Medicine*, 2005, *230*, 366–375.

Sun, Y., Ahmed, S., and Smith, R. G. Deletion of ghrelin impairs neither growth nor appetite. *Molecular and Cellular Biology*, 2003, *23*, 7973–7981.

Sun, Y., Wang, P., Zheng, H., and Smith, R. G. Ghrelin stimulation of growth hormone release and appetite is mediated through the growth hormone secretagogue receptor. *Proceedings of the National Academy of Sciences, USA*, 2004, *101*, 4679–4684.

Suntsova, N., Guzman-Marin, R., Kumar, S., Alam, M. N., et al. The median preoptic nucleus reciprocally modulates activity of arousal-related and sleep-related neurons in the perifornical lateral hypothalamus. *Journal of Neuroscience*, 2007, *27*, 1616–1630.

Susser, E. S., and Lin, S. P. Schizophrenia after prenatal exposure to the Dutch Hunger Winter of 1944–1945. *Archives of General Psychiatry*, 1992, *49*, 983–988.

Susser, E. S., Neugebauer, R., Hoek, H. W., Brown, A. S., et al. Schizophrenia after prenatal famine: Further evidence. *Archives of General Psychiatry*, 1996, *53*, 25–31.

Sutherland, R. J., McDonald, R. J., and Savage, D. D. Prenatal exposure to moderate levels of ethanol can have long-lasting effects on hippocampal synaptic plasticity in adult offspring. *Hippocampus*, 1997, *7*, 232–238.

Suzdak, P. D., Glowa, J. R., Crawley, J. N., Schwartz, R. D., et al. A selective imidazobenzodiazepine antagonist of ethanol in the rat. *Science*, 1986, *234*, 1243–1247.

Suzuki, S., Ramos, E. J., Goncalves, C. G., Chen, C., et al. Changes in GI hormones and their effect on gastric emptying and transit times after Roux-en-Y gastric bypass in rat model. *Surgery*, 2005, *138*, 283–290.

Svennilson, E., Torvik, A., Lowe, R., and Leksell, L. Treatment of Parkinsonism by stereotactic thermolesions in the pallidal region. *Neurologica Scandanavica*, 1960, *35*, 358–377.

Swaab, D. F., Gooren, L. J. G., and Hofman, M. A. Brain research, gender, and sexual orientation. *Journal of Homosexuality*, 1995, *28*, 283–301.

Swaab, D. F., and Hofman, M. A. An enlarged suprachiasmatic nucleus in homosexual men. *Brain Research*, 1990, *537*, 141–148.

Swanson, L. W., Köhler, C., and Björklund, A. The limbic region. I: The septohippocampal system. In Handbook of Chemical Neuroanatomy, Vol. 5: Integrated Systems of the CNS, Part I, edited by A. Björklund, T. Hökfelt, and L. W. Swanson. Amsterdam: Elsevier, 1987.

Sweet, W. H. Participant in "Brain Stimulation in Behaving Subjects." Neurosciences Research Program Workshop, 1966.

Swerdlow, N. R. Are we studying and treating schizophrenia correctly? *Schizophrenia Research*, 2011, *130*, 1–10.

Swerdlow, N. R., Geyer, M. A., Vale, W. W., and Koob, G. F. Corticotropin-releasing factor potentiates acoustic startle in rats: Blockade by chlordiazepoxide. *Psychopharmacology*, 1986, *88*, 147–152.

Szwed, M., Cohen, L, Qiao, E., and Dehaene, S. The role of invariant line junctions in object and visual word recognition. *Vision Research*, 2009, *49*, 718–725.

Szymanski, M., Barciszewska, M. Z., Zywicki M., and Barciszewski, J. Noncoding RNA transcripts. *Journal of Applied Genetics*, 2003, *44*, 1–19.

Takahashi, K., Lin, J.-S., and Sakai, K. Characterization and mapping of sleep–waking specific neurons in the basal-forebrain and preoptic hypothalamus in mice. *Neuroscience*, 2009, *161*, 269–292.

Takahashi, K., Lin, J.-S., and Sakai, K. Neuronal activity of histaminergic tuberomammillary neurons during wake–sleep states in the mouse. *Journal of Neuroscience*, 2006, *26*, 10292–10298.

Takahashi, L. K. Hormonal regulation of sociosexual behavior in female mammals. *Neuroscience and Biobehavioral Reviews*, 1990, *14*, 403–413.

Takahashi, Y. K., Nagayama, S., and Mori, K. Detection and masking of spoiled food smells by odor maps in the olfactory bulb. *Journal of Neuroscience*, 2004, *24*, 8690–8694.

Tamietto, M., Castelli, L., Vighetti, S., Paola, P., et al. Unseen facial and bodily expressions trigger fast emotional reactions. *Proceedings of the National Academy of Sciences, USA*, 2009, *106*, 17661–17666.

Tamm, L., Menon, V., Ringel, J., and Reiss, A. L. Event-related fMRI evidence of frontotemporal involvement in aberrant response inhibition and task switching in attention-deficit/hyperactivity disorder. *Journal of the American Academy of Child and Adolescent Psychiatry*, 2004, *43*, 1430–1440.

Tan, L. H., Laird, A. R., Li, K., and Fox, P. T. Neuro-anatomical correlates of phonological processing of Chinese characters and alphabetic words: A meta-analysis. *Human Brain Mapping*, 2005, *25*, 83–91.

Tarr, M. J., and Gauthier, I. FFA: A flexible fusiform area for subordinate-level visual processing automatized by expertise. *Nature Neuroscience*, 2000, *3*, 764–769.

Tarter, R. E., Kirisci, L., Mezzich, A., Cornelius, J. R., et al. Neurobehavioral disinhibition in childhood predicts early age at onset of substance use disorder. *American Journal of Psychiatry*, 2003, *160*, 1078–1085.

Taub, E., Uswatte, F., King, D. K., Morris, D., et al. A placebo-controlled trial of constraint-induced movement therapy for upper extremity after stroke. *Stroke*, 2006, *37*, 1045–1049.

Tavera-Mendoza, L. E., and White, J. H. Cell defenses and the sunshine vitamin. *Scientific American*, 2007, *297*, 62–72.

Taxidis, J., Coombes, S., Mason, R., and Owen, M. R. Modeling sharp wave-ripple complexes through a CA3-CA1 network model with chemical synapses. *Hippocampus*, 2011, DOI: 10.1002/hipo.20930.

Taylor, M. J., Sen, S., and Bhagwagar, Z. Antidepressant response and the serotonin transporter gene-linked polymorphic region. *Biological Psychiatry*, 2010, *68*, 536–543.

Teff, K. L., Elliott, S. S., Tschöp, M., Kieffer, T. J., et al. Dietary fructose reduces circulating insulin and leptin, attenuates postprandial suppression of ghrelin, and increases triglycerides in women. *Journal of Clinical Endocrinology and Metabolism*, 2004, *89*, 2963–2972.

Teitelbaum, P., and Stellar, E. Recovery from the failure to eat produced by hypothalamic lesions. *Science*, 1954, *120*, 894–895.

Teng, E., and Squire, L. R. Memory for places learned long ago is intact after hippocampal damage. *Nature*, 1999, *400*, 675–677.

Terenius, L., and Wahlström, A. Morphine-like ligand for opiate receptors in human CSF. *Life Sciences*, 1975, 16, 1759–1764.

Terman, M. Evolving applications of light therapy. *Sleep Medicine Reviews*, 2007, *11*, 497–507.

Terracciano, A., Tanaka, T., Sutin, A. R., Sanna, S., et al. Genome-wide association scan of trait depression. *Biological Psychiatry*, 2010, *68*, 811–817.

Terry, R. D., and Davies, P. Dementia of the Alzheimer type. *Annual Review of Neuroscience*, 1980, *3*, 77–96.

Tetel, M. J., Celentano, D. C., and Blaustein, J. D. Intraneuronal convergence of tactile and hormonal stimuli associated with female reproduction in rats. *Journal of Neuroendocrinology*, 1994, *6*, 211–216.

Tetel, M. J., Getzinger, M. J., and Blaustein, J. D. Fos expression in the rat brain following vaginal-cervical stimulation by mating and manual probing. *Journal of Neuroendocrinology*, 1993, *5*, 397–404.

Thach, W. T. Correlation of neural discharge with pattern and force of muscular activity, joint position, and direction of intended movement in motor cortex and cerebellum. *Journal of Neurophysiology*, 1978, *41*, 654–676.

Thaker, G. K., and Carpenter, W. T. Advances in schizophrenia. *Nature Medicine*, 2001, *7*, 667–671.

Thakkar, M. M., Winston, S., and McCarley, R. W. Orexin neurons of the hypothalamus express adenosine A1 receptors. *Brain Research*, 2002, *944*, 190–194.

Thapar, A., O'Donovan, M., and Owen, M. J. The genetics of attention deficit hyperactivity disorder. *Human Molecular Genetics*, 2005, *14*, R275–R282.

Thase, M. E. Treatment issues related to sleep and depression. *Journal of Clinical Psychiatry*, 2000, *61*, 46–50.

Theorell, T., Leymann, H., Jodko, M., Konarski, K., et al. "Person under train" incidents: Medical consequences for subway drivers. *Psychosomatic Medicine*, 1992, *54*, 480–488.

Thiels, E., Xie, X. P., Yeckel, M. F., Barrionuevo, G., et al. NMDA receptor-dependent LTD in different subfields of hippocampus in vivo and in vitro. *Hippocampus*, 1996, *6*, 43–51.

Thielscher, A., and Pessoa, L. Neural correlates of perceptual choice and decision making during fear–disgust discrimination. *Journal of Neuroscience*, 2007, *27*, 2908–2917.

Thier, P., Haarmeier, T., Chakraborty, S., Lindner, A., et al. Cortical substrates of perceptual stability during eye movements. *Neuroimage*, 2001, *14*, S33–S39.

Thomaes, K., Dorrepaal, E., Draijer, N., Jansma, E. P., et al. Can pharmacological and psychological treatment change brain structure and function in PTSD? A systematic review. *Journal of Psychiatric Research*, 2014, *50*, 1–15.

Thomas, A. C., Allen, F. L., Phillips, H., and Karantzas, G. Gaming machine addiction: The role of avoidance, accessibility and social support. *Psychology of Addictive Behaviors*, 2013, *29*, 217–230.

Thomas, O., Avidan, G., Humphreys, K., Jung, K. J., et al. Reduced structural connectivity in ventral visual cortex in congenital prosopagnosia. *Nature Neuroscience*, 2009, *12*, 29–31.

Thomas, R. M., Hotsenpiller, G., and Peterson, D. A. Acute psychosocial stress reduces cell survival in adult hippocampal neurogenesis without altering proliferation. *Journal of Neuroscience*, 2007, *27*, 2734–2743.

Thompson, P. M., Hayashi, K. M., Simon, S. L., Geaga, J. A., et al. Structural abnormalities in the brains of human subjects who use methamphetamine. *Journal of Neuroscience*, 2004, *24*, 6028–6036.

Thompson, P. M., Vidal, C., Giedd, J. N., Gochman, P., et al. Mapping adolescent brain change reveals dynamic wave of accelerated gray matter loss in very early-onset schizophrenia. *Proceedings of the National Academy of Sciences, USA*, 2001, *98*, 11650–11655.

Thompson, S. M., Fortunato, C., McKinney, R. A., Müller, M., et al. Mechanisms underlying the neuropathological consequences of epileptic activity in the rat hippocampus in vitro. *Journal of Comparative Neurology*, 1996, *372*, 515–528.

Thomson, J. J. *Rights, restitution, and risk: Essays in moral theory.* Cambridge, MA: Harvard University Press, 1986.

Thorn, C. A., Atallah, H., Howe, M., and Graybiel, A. M. Differential dynamics of activity changes in dorsolateral and dorsomedial striatal loops during learning. *Neuron*, 2010, *66*, 781–795.

Thrasher, T. N. Role of forebrain circumventricular organs in body fluid balance. *Acta Physiologica Scandanavica*, 1989, *136* (Suppl. 583), 141–150.

Thuy, D. H. D., Matsuo, K., Nakamura, K., Toma, K., et al. Implicit and explicit processing of kanji and kana words and non-words studied with fMRI. *Neuroimage*, 2004, *23*, 878–889.

Timmann, D., Watts, S., and Hore, J. Failure of cerebellar patients to time finger opening precisely causes ball high-low inaccuracy in overarm throws. *Journal of Neurophysiology*, 1999, *82*, 103–114.

Tizzano, M., Gulbransen, B. D., Vanderbeuch, A., et al. Nasal chemosensory cells use bitter taste signaling to detect irritants and bacterial signals. *Proceedings of the National Academy of Sciences, USA*, 2010, *107*, 3210–3215.

Toh, K. L., Jones, C. R., He, Y., Eide, E. J., et al. An hPer2 phosphorylation site mutation in familial advanced sleep phase syndrome. *Science*, 2001, *291*, 1040–1043.

Tootell, R. B. H., Tsao, D., and Vanduffel, W. Neuro-imaging weighs in: Humans meet macaques in "primate" visual-cortex. *Journal of Neuroscience*, 2003, *23*, 3981–3989.

Topper, R., Kosinski, C., and Mull, M. Volitional type of facial palsy associated with pontine ischemia. *Journal of Neurology, Neurosurgery, and Psychiatry*, 1995, *58*, 732–734.

Tordoff, M. G., and Friedman, M. I. Hepatic control of feeding: Effect of glucose, fructose, and mannitol. *American Journal of Physiology*, 1988, *254*, R969–R976.

Tordoff, M. G., Hopfenbeck, J., and Novin, D. Hepatic vagotomy (partial hepatic denervation) does not alter ingestive responses to metabolic challenges. *Physiology and Behavior*, 1982, *28*, 417–424.

Tracy, J. L., and Robbins, R. W. The automaticity of emotion recognition. *Emotion*, 2008, *8*, 81–95.

Tranel, D., Gullickson, G., Koch, M., and Adolphs, R. Altered experience of emotion following bilateral amygdala damage. *Cognitive Neuropsychiatry*, 2006, *11*(3), 219–232.

Triarhou, L. C. The percipient observations of Constantin von Economo on encephalitis lethargica and sleep disruption and their lasting impact on contemporary sleep research. *Brain Research Bulletin*, 2006, *69*, 244–258.

Tronel, S., Fabre, An., Charrier, V., Oliet, S. H. R., et al. Spatial learning sculpts the dendritic arbor of adult-born hippocampal neurons. *Proceedings of the National Academy of Sciences, USA*, 2010, *107*, 7963–7968.

Trulson, M. E., and Jacobs, B. L. Raphe unit activity in freely moving cats: Correlation with level of behavioral arousal. *Brain Research*, 1979, *163*, 135–150.

Trussell, L. O. Synaptic mechanisms for coding timing in auditory neurons. *Annual Review of Physiology*, 1999, *61*, 477–496.

Tsacopoulos, M., and Magistretti, P. J. Metabolic coupling between glia and neurons. *Journal of Neuroscience*, 1996, *16*, 877–885.

Tsai, H.-C., Zhang, F., Adamantidis, A., Stuber, G. D., et al. Phasic firing in dopaminergic neurons is sufficient for behavioral conditioning. *Science*, 2009, *324*, 1080–1084.

Tsankova, N., Renthal, W., Kuman, A., and Nestler, E. J. Epigenetic regulation in psychiatric disorders. *Nature Neuroscience*, 2007, *8*, 355–367.

Tsao, D. Y., Freiwald, W. A., Tootell, R. B. H., and Livingstone, M. S. A cortical region consisting entirely of face-selective cells. *Science*, 2006, *311*, 670–674.

Tsao, D. Y., Vanduffel, W., Sasaki, Y., Fize, D., et al. Stereopsis activates V3A and caudal intraparietal areas in macaques and humans. *Neuron*, 2003, *39*, 555–568.

Tsuang, M. T., Gilbertson, M. W., and Faraone, S. V. The genetics of schizophrenia: Current knowledge and future directions. *Schizophrenia Research*, 1991, *4*, 157–171.

Tsuang, M. T., Lyons, M. J., Meyer, J. M., Doyle, T., et al. Co-occurrence of abuse of different drugs in men: The role of drug-specific and shared vulnerabilities. *Archives of General Psychiatry*, 1998, *55*, 967–972.

Tucker, M. A., Hirota, Y., Wamsley, E. J., Lau, H., et al. A daytime nap containing solely non-REM sleep enhances declarative but not procedural memory. *Neurobiology of Learning and Memory*, 2006, *86*, 241–247.

Tunik, E., Frey, S. H., and Grafton, S. T. Virtual lesions of the anterior intraparietal area disrupt goal-dependent on-line adjustments of grasp. *Nature Neuroscience*, 2005, *8*, 505–511.

Turkstra, L. S., and Flora, T. L. Compensating for executive function impairments after TBI: A single case study of functional intervention. *Journal of Communication Disorders*, 2002, *35*(6), 467–482.

Turner, S. M., Beidel, D. C., and Nathan, R. S. Biological factors in obsessive-compulsive disorders. *Psychological Bulletin*, 1985, *97*, 430–450.

Tye, K. M., Prakash, R., Kim, S.-Y., Fenno, L. E., et al. Amygdala circuitry mediating reversible and bidirectional control of anxiety. *Nature*, 2011, *471*, 358–362.

Tyrell, J. B., and Baxter, J. D. Glucocorticoid therapy. In *Endocrinology and metabolism*, edited by P. Felig, J. D. Baxter, A. E. Broadus, and L. A. Frohman. New York: McGraw-Hill, 1981.

Unger, J., McNeill, T. H., Moxley, R. T., White, M., et al. Distribution of insulin receptor-like immunoreactivity in the rat forebrain. *Neuroscience*, 1989, *31*, 143–157.

Ungerleider, L. G., and Mishkin, M. Two cortical visual-systems. In *Analysis of visual behavior*, edited by D. J. Ingle, M. A. Goodale, and R. J. W. Mansfield. Cambridge, MA: MIT Press, 1982.

Uno, H., Tarara, R., Else, J. G., Suleman, M. A., and Sapolsky, R. M. Hippocampal damage associated with prolonged and fatal stress in primates. *Journal of Neuroscience*, 1989, *9*, 1705–1711.

Urban, P. P., Wicht, S., Marx, J., Mitrovic, S., et al. Isolated voluntary facial paresis due to pontine ischemia. *Neurology*, 1998, *50*, 1859–1862.

Urgesi, C., Berlucchi, G., and Aglioti, S. M. Magnetic stimulation of extrastriate body area impairs visual processing of nonfacial body parts. *Current Biology*, 2004, *13*, 2130–2134.

Vaidya, C. J., Bunge, S. A., Dudukovic, N. M., Zalecki, C. A., et al. Altered neural substrates of cognitive control in childhood ADHD: Evidence from functional magnetic resonance imaging. *American Journal of Psychiatry*, 2005, *162*, 1605–1613.

Vaina, L. M. Complex motion perception and its deficits. *Current Opinion in Neurobiology*, 1998, *8*, 494–502.

Valcour, V., Sithinamsuwan, P., Letendre, S., and Ances, B. Pathogenesis of HIV in the central nervous system. *Current HIV/AIDS*, 2011, *8*, 54–61.

Valenstein, E. S. *Great and Desperate Cures: The Rise and Decline of Psychosurgery and Other Radical Treatments for Mental Illness*. New York: Basic Books, 1986.

Valenza, N., Ptak, R., Zimine, I., Badan, M., et al. Dissociated active and passive tactile shape recognition: A case study of pure tactile apraxia. *Brain*, 2001, *124*, 2287–2298.

Valyear, K. F., Culham, J. C., Sharif, N., Westwood, D., et al. A double dissociation between sensitivity to changes in object identity and object orientation in the ventral and dorsal visual streams: A human fMRI study. *Neuropsychologia*, 2006, *44*, 218–228.

Van Assche, K., Gutwirth, S., and Sterckx, S. Protecting dignitary interests of Biobank research participants: Lessons from *Havasupai Tribe v Arizona Board of Regents*. *Law, Innovation and Technology*, 2013, *5*(1), 54–84

Van Bockstaele, E. J., Bajic, D., Proudfit, H., and Valentino, R. J. Topographic architecture of stress-related pathways targeting the noradrenergic locus coeruleus. *Physiology and Behavior*, 2001, *73*, 273–283.

van de Poll, N. E., Taminiau, M. S., Endert, E., and Louwerse, A. L. Gonadal steroid influence upon sexual and aggressive behavior of female rats. *International Journal of Neuroscience*, 1988, *41*, 271–286.

Van den Top, M., Lee, K., Whyment, A. D., Blanks, A. M., et al. Orexigen-sensitive NPY/AGRP pacemaker neurons in the hypothalamic arcuate nucleus. *Nature Neuroscience*, 2004, *7*, 493–494.

Van Der Helm, E., Gujar, N., and Walker, M. P. Sleep deprivation impairs the accurate recognition of human emotions. *Sleep*, 2010, *33*(3), 335.

van der Lee, S., and Boot, L. M. Spontaneous pseudopregnancy in mice. *Acta Physiologica et Pharmacologica Neerlandica*, 1955, *4*, 442–444.

Van Goozen, S., Wiegant, V., Endert, E., Helmond, F., et al. Psychoendocrinological assessments of the menstrual cycle: The relationship between hormones, sexuality, and mood. *Archives of Sexual Behavior*, 1997, *26*, 359–382.

van Harmelen, A. L., van Tol, M. J., van der Wee, N. J., Veltman, D. J., et al. Reduced medial prefrontal cortex volume in adults reporting childhood emotional maltreatment. *Biological Psychiatry*, 2010, *68*, 832–838.

van Leengoed, E., Kerker, E., and Swanson, H. H. Inhibition of post-partum maternal behaviour in the rat by injecting an oxytocin antagonist into the cerebral ventricles. *Journal of Endocrinology*, 1987, *112*, 275–282.

van Os, J., and Kapur, S. Schizophrenia. *Lancet*, 2009, *374*, 635–645.

van Os, J., and McGuffin, P. Can the social environment cause schizophrenia? *British Journal of Psychiatry*, 2003, *182*, 291–292.

Vandenbergh, J. G., Whitsett, J. M., and Lombardi, J. R. Partial isolation of a pheromone accelerating puberty in female mice. *Journal of Reproductive Fertility*, 1975, *43*, 515–523.

Vandenbulcke, M., Peeters, R., Fannes, K., and Vandenberghe, R. Knowledge of visual attributes in the right hemisphere. *Nature Neuroscience*, 2006, *9*, 964–970.

Vanderschuren, L. J. M. J., Di Ciano, P., and Everitt, B. J. Involvement of the dorsal striatum in cue-controlled cocaine seeking. *Journal of Neuroscience*, 2005, *25*, 8665–8670.

Vanderwolf, C. H. The electrocorticogram in relation to physiology and behavior: A new analysis. *Electroencephalography and Clinical Neurophysiology*, 1992, *82*, 165–175.

Vangipuram, S. D., and Lyman, W. D. Ethanol alters cell fate of fetal human brain-derived stem and progenitor cells. *Alcohol Clinics: Experimental Research*, 2010, *34*, 1574–1583.

Varese, F., Smeets, F., Drukker, M., Lieverse, R., et al. Childhood adversities increase the risk of psychosis: A meta-analysis of patient-control, prospective- and cross-sectional cohort studies. *Schizophrenia Bulletin*, 2012, *38*, 661–671.

Vassar, R., Ngai, J., and Axel, R. Spatial segregation of odorant receptor expression in the mammalian olfactory epithelium. *Cell*, 1993, *74*, 309–318.

Vathy, I., and Etgen, A. M. Hormonal activation of female sexual behavior is accompanied by hypothalamic norepinephrine release. *Journal of Neuroendocrinology*, 1989, *1*(5), 383–388.

Vergnes, M., Depaulis, A., Boehrer, A., and Kempf, E. Selective increase of offensive behavior in the rat following intrahypothalamic 5,7-DHT-induced serotonin depletion. *Brain Research*, 1988, *29*, 85–91.

Vermetten, E., Vythilingam, M., Southwick, S. M., Charney, D. S., et al. Long-term treatment with paroxetine increases verbal declarative memory and hippocampal volume in posttraumatic stress disorder. *Biological Psychiatry*, 2003, *54*(7), 693–702.

Verney, E. B. The antidiuretic hormone and the factors which determine its release. *Proceedings of the Royal Society of London B*, 1947, *135*, 25–106.

Vgontzas, A. N., and Kales, A. Sleep and its disorders. *Annual Review of Medicine*, 1999, *50*, 387–400.

Viding, E., Jones, A. P., Frick, P. J., Moffitt, T. E., et al. Heritability of antisocial behaviour at 9: Do callous-unemotional traits matter? *Developmental Science*, 2008, *11*, 17–22.

Viding, E., Blair, R. J. R., Moffitt, T. E., and Plomin, R. Evidence for substantial genetic risk for psychopathy in 7-year olds. *Journal of Child Psychology and Psychiatry*, 2005, *46*, 592–597.

Victor, M., and Agamanolis, J. Amnesia due to lesions confined to the hippocampus: A clinical-pathological study. *Journal of Cognitive Neuroscience*, 1990, *2*, 246–257.

Vinckier, F., Dehaene, S., Jobert, A., Dubus, J. P., et al. Hierarchical coding of letter strings in the ventral stream: Dissecting the inner organization of the visual word-form system. *Neurons*, 2007, *55*, 143–156.

Virkkunen, M., De Jong, J., Bartko, J., and Linnoila, M. Psychobiological concomitants of history of suicide attempts among violent offenders and impulsive fire setters. *Archives of General Psychiatry*, 1989, *46*, 604–606.

Viviani, R., Sim, E. J., Lo, H., Beschoner, P., et al. Baseline brain perfusion and the serotonin transporter promoter polymorphism. *Biological Psychiatry*, 2010, *67*, 317–322.

Vocci, F. J., Acri, J., and Elkashef, A. Medication development for addictive disorders: The state of the science. *American Journal of Psychiatry*, 2005, *162*, 1431–1440.

Vogel, G. W., Buffenstein, A., Minter, K., and Hennessey, A. Drug effects on REM sleep and on endogenous depression. *Neuroscience and Biobehavioral Reviews*, 1990, *14*, 49–63.

Vogel, G. W., Thurmond, A., Gibbons, P., Sloan, K., et al. REM sleep reduction effects on depression syndromes. *Archives of General Psychiatry*, 1975, *32*, 765–777.

Vogel, G. W., Vogel, F., McAbee, R. S., and Thurmond, A. J. Improvement of depression by REM sleep deprivation: New findings and a theory. *Archives of General Psychiatry*, 1980, *37*, 247–253.

Volkow, N., and Li, T. K. The neuroscience of addiction. *Nature Neuroscience*, 2005, *8*, 1429–1430.

Volkow, N. D., Hitzemann, R., Wang, G.-J., Fowler, J. S., et al. Long-term frontal brain metabolic changes in cocaine abusers. *Synapse*, 1992, *11*, 184–190.

Volkow, N. D., Wang, G.-J., Fowler, J. S., Tomasi, D., et al. Addiction: Beyond dopamine reward circuitry. *Proceedings of the National Academy of Sciences, USA*, 2011, *108*, 15037–15042.

Volpe, B. T., LeDoux, J. E., and Gazzaniga, M. S. Information processing of visual stimuli in an "extinguished" field. *Nature*, 1979, *282*, 722–724.

vom Saal, F. S. Models of early hormonal effects on intrasex aggression in mice. In *Hormones and aggressive behavior*, edited by B. B. Svare. New York: Plenum Press, 1983.

vom Saal, F. S., and Bronson, F. H. Sexual characteristics of adult female mice are correlated with their blood testosterone levels during prenatal development. *Science*, 1980, *208*, 597–599.

von Békésy, G. *Experiments in Hearing*. New York: McGraw-Hill, 1960.

von Kriegstein, K., Eger, E. Kleinschmidt, A., and Giraud, A. L. Modulation of neural responses to speech by directing attention to voices or verbal content. *Cognitive Brain Research*, 2003, *17*, 48–55.

Vuilleumier, P., Armony, J. L., Driver, J., and Dolan, R. J. Distinct spatial frequency sensitivities for processing faces and emotional expressions. *Nature Neuroscience*, 2003, *6*, 624–631.

Waber, R. L., Shiv, B., Carmon, Z., and Ariely, D. Commercial features of placebo and therapeutic efficacy. *Journal of the American Medical Association*, 2008, *299*, 1016–1017.

Wager, T. D., Rilling, J. K., Smith, E. E., Sokolik, A., et al. Placebo-induced changes in fMRI in the anticipation and experience of pain. *Science*, 2004, *303*, 1162–1166.

Wagner, F. A., and Anthony, J. C. From first drug use to drug dependence: Developmental periods of risk for dependence upon marijuana, cocaine, and alcohol. *Neuropsychopharmacology*, 2002, *26*, 479–488.

Wahl, M., Lauterbach-Soon, B., Juing, P., et al. Human motor corpus callosum: Topography, somatotopy, and link between microstructure and function. *Journal of Neuroscience*, 2007, *27*, 12132–12138.

Wahlbeck, K., Forsén, T., Osmond, C., Barker, D. J. P., et al. Association of schizophrenia with low maternal body mass index, small size at birth, and thinness during childhood. *Archives of General Psychiatry*, 2001, *58*, 48–52.

Walker, D. L., Ressler, K. J., Lu, K. T., and Davis, M. Facilitation of conditioned fear extinction by systemic administration or intra-amygdala infusions of D-cycloserine as assessed with fear-potentiated startle in rats. *Journal of Neuroscience*, 2002, *22*, 2343–2351.

Walker, E. F., Lewine, R. R. J., and Neumann, C. Childhood behavioral characteristics and adult brain morphology in schizophrenia. *Schizophrenia Research*, 1996, *22*, 93–101.

Walker, E. F., Savoie, T., and Davis, D. Neuromotor precursors of schizophrenia. *Schizophrenia Bulletin*, 1994, *20*, 441–451.

Walker, P. A., and Meyer, W. J. Medroxyprogesterone acetate treatment for paraphiliac sex offenders. In *Violence and the violent individual*, edited by J. R. Hays, T. K. Roberts, and T. S. Solway. New York: SP Medical and Scientific Books, 1981.

Wallen, K. Desire and ability: Hormones and the regulation of female sexual behavior. *Neuroscience and Biobehavioral Reviews*, 1990, *14*, 233–241.

Wallen, K. Sex and context: Hormones and primate sexual motivation. *Hormones and Behavior*, 2001, *40*, 339–357.

Wallen, K., Eisler, J. A., Tannenbaum, P. L., Nagell, K. M., et al. Antide (Nal-Lys GnRH antagonist) suppression of pituitary-testicular function and sexual behavior in group-living rhesus monkeys. *Physiology and Behavior*, 1991, *50*, 429–435.

Wamsley, E. J., Tucker, M., Payne, J. D., Benevides, J. A., et al. Dreaming of a learning task is associated with enhanced sleep-dependent memory consolidation. *Current Biology*, 2010, *20*, 1–6.

Walsh, T., McClellan, J. M., McCarthy, S. E., Addington, A. M., et al. Rare structural variants disrupt multiple genes in neurodevelopmental pathways in schizophrenia. *Science*, 2008, *320*, 539–543.

Walsh, V., Carden, D., Butler, S. R., and Kulikowski, J. J. The effects of V4 lesions on the visual abilities of macaques: Hue discrimination and color constancy. *Behavioural Brain Research*, 1993, *53*, 51–62.

Walsh, V., Ellison, A., Battelli, L., and Cowey, A. Task-specific impairments and enhancements induced by magnetic stimulation of human visual area V5. *Proceedings in Biological Sciences*, 1998, *265*, 537–543.

Walters, E. E., and Kendler, K. S. Anorexia nervosa and anorexic-like syndromes in a population-based female twin sample. *American Journal of Psychiatry*, 1995, *152*, 64–71.

Wandell, B. A., Dumoulin, S. O., and Brewer, A. A. Visual field maps in human cortex. *Neuron*, 2007, *56*, 366–383.

Wang, Q., Charych, E. I., Pulito, V. L., Lee, J. B., et al. The psychiatric disease risk factors DISC1 and TNIK interact to regulate synapse composition and function. *Molecular Psychiatry*, 2010, *16*, 1006–1023.

Wang, Z., Faith, M., Patterson, F., Tang, K., et al. Neural substrates of abstinence-induced cigarette cravings in chronic smokers. *Journal of Neuroscience*, 2007, *27*, 14035–14040.

Wang, Z., Sindreu, C. B., Li, V., Nudelman, A., et al. Pheromone detection in male mice depends on signaling through type 3 adenylyl cyclase in the main olfactory epithelium. *Journal of Neuroscience*, 2006, *26*, 7375–7379.

Ward, H. E., Johnson, E. A., Salm, A. K., and Birkle, D. L. Effects of prenatal stress on defensive withdrawal behavior and corticotrophin releasing factor systems in rat brain. *Physiology and Behavior*, 2000, *70*, 359–366.

Ward, L., Wright, E., and McMahon, S. B. A comparison of the effects of noxious and innocuous counterstimuli on experimentally induced itch and pain. *Pain*, 1996, *64*, 129–138.

Warne, G. L., and Zajac, J. D. Disorders of sexual differentiation. *Endocrinology and Metabolism Clinics of North America*, 1998, *27*, 945–967.

Warren, J. E., Sauter, D. A., Eisner, F., Wiland, J., et al. Positive emotions preferentially engage an auditory–motor "mirror" system. *Journal of Neuroscience*, 2006, *26*, 13067–13075.

Watkins, K. E., Dronkers, N. F., and Vargha-Khadem, F. Behavioural analysis of an inherited speech and language disorder: Comparison with acquired aphasia. *Brain*, 2002a, *125*, 452–464.

Watkins, K. E., Smith, S. M., Davis, S., and Howell, P. Structural and functional abnormalities of the motor system in developmental stuttering. *Brain*, 2008, *131*, 50–59.

Watkins, K. E., Vargha-Khadem, F., Ashburner, J., Passingham, R. E., et al. MRI analysis of an inherited speech and language disorder: Structural brain abnormalities. *Brain*, 2002b, *125*, 465–478.

Webster, H. H., and Jones, B. E. Neurotoxic lesions of the dorsolateral pontomesencephalic tegmentum-cholinergic cell area in the cat. II: Effects upon sleep-waking states. *Brain Research*, 1988, *458*, 285–302.

Weinberg, S. M., Jenkins, E. A., Marazita, M. L., and Maher, B. S. Minor physical anomalies in schizophrenia: A meta-analysis. *Schizophrenia Research*, 2007, *89* (1–3), 72–85.

Weinberger, D. R. Schizophrenia and the frontal lobe. *Trends in Neurosciences*, 1988, *11*, 367–370.

Weinberger, D. R., and Wyatt, R. J. Brain morphology in schizophrenia: *In vivo* studies. In *Schizophrenia as a brain disease*, edited by F. A. Henn and H. A. Nasrallah. New York: Oxford University Press, 1982.

Weiner, R. D., and Krystal, A. D. The present use of electroconvulsive therapy. *Annual Review of Medicine*, 1994, *45*, 273–281.

Weintraub, S., Mesulam, M.-M., and Kramer, L. Disturbances in prosody: A right-hemisphere contribution to language. *Archives of Neurology*, 1981, *38*, 742–744.

Weiser, M., Reichenberg, A., Grotto, I., Yasvitzky, R., et al. Higher rates of cigarette smoking in male adolescents before the onset of schizophrenia: A historical-prospective cohort study. *American Journal of Psychiatry*, 2004, *161*, 1219–1223.

Weiskrantz, L., Warrington, E. K., Sanders, M. D., and Marshall, J. Visual capacity in the hemianopic field following a restricted occipital ablation. *Brain*, 1974, *97*, 709–728.

Welsh, D. K., Logothetis, D. E., Meister, M., and Reppert, S. M. Individual neurons dissociated from rat suprachiasmatic nucleus express independently phased circadian firing rhythms. *Neuron*, 1995, *14*, 697–706.

Weltzin, T. E., Hsu, L. K. G., Pollice, C., and Kaye, W. H. Feeding patterns in bulimia nervosa. *Biological Psychiatry*, 1991, *30*, 1093–1110.

Wernicke, C. *Der aphasische symptomenkomplex.* Breslau, Poland: Cohn & Weigert, 1874.

Westmark, P. R., Westmark, C. J., Wang, S., et al. Pin1 and PKMzeta sequentially control dendritic protein synthesis. *Science Signaling*, 2010, *3*, ra18.

Whalen, P. J., Kagan, J., Cook, R. G., Davis, F. C., et al. Human amygdala responsivity to masked fearful eye whites. *Science*, 2004, *306*, 2061.

Whalen, P. J., Rauch, S. L., Etcoff, N. L., McInerney, S. C., et al. Masked presentations of emotional facial expressions modulate amygdala activity without explicit knowledge. *Journal of Neuroscience*, 1998, *18*, 411–418.

Whipple, B., and Komisaruk, B. R. Analgesia produced in women by genital self-stimulation. *Journal of Sex Research*, 1988, *24*, 130–140.

White, F. J. Synaptic regulation of mesocorticolimbic dopamine neurons. *Annual Review of Neuroscience*, 1996, *19*, 405–436.

White, J. Autonomic discharge from stimulation of the hypothalamus in man. *Association for Research in Nervous and Mental Disorders*, 1940, *20*, 854–863.

Whiteside, S. P., Port, J. D., and Abramowitz, J. S. A meta-analysis of functional neuroimaging in obsessive-compulsive disorder. *Psychiatry Research: Neuroimaging*, 2004, *132*, 69–79.

Whitten, W. K. Occurrence of anestrus in mice caged in groups. *Journal of Endocrinology*, 1959, *18*, 102–107.

Whittle, S., Yap, M. B. H., Yücel, M., Fornita, A., et al. Prefrontal and amygdala volumes are related to adolescents' affective behaviors during parent-adolescent interactions. *Proceedings of the National Academy of Sciences*, 2008, *105*, 3652–3657.

Wickelgren, I. Drug may suppress the craving for nicotine. *Science*, 1998, *282*, 1797–1798.

Wicker, B., Keysers, C., Plailly, J., Royet, J. P., et al. Both of us disgusted in *My* insula: The common neural basis of seeing and feeling disgust. *Neuron*, 2003, *40*, 655–664.

Wiesner, B. P., and Sheard, N. *Maternal behaviour in the rat.* London: Oliver and Brody, 1933.

Wigren, H. K., Schepens, M., Matto, V., Sternberg, D., et al. Glutamatergic stimulation of the basal forebrain elevates extracellular adenosine and increases the subsequent sleep. *Neuroscience*, 2007, *147*, 811–823.

Wilhelm, S., Buhlmann, U., Tolin, D. F., Meunier, S. A., et al. Augmentation of behavior therapy with D-cycloserine for obsessive-compulsive disorder. *American Journal of Psychiatry*, 2008, *165*, 335–341.

Willer, C. J., Speliotes, E. K., Loos, R. J. F., Li, S., et al. Six new loci associated with body mass index highlight a neuronal influence on body weight regulation. *Nature Genetics*, 2009, *41*, 25–34.

Willesen, M. G., Kristensen, P., and Romer, J. Co-localization of growth hormone secretagogue receptor and NPY mRNA in the arcuate nucleus of the rat. *Neuroendocrinology*, 1999, *70*, 306–316.

Williams, D. L., Cummings, D. E., Grill, H. J., and Kaplan, J. M. Meal-related ghrelin suppression requires postgastric feedback. *Endocrinology*, 2003, *144*, 2765–2767.

Williams, J. R., Insel, T. R., Harbaugh, C. R., and Carter, C. S. Oxytocin centrally administered facilitates formation of a partner preference in female prairie voles (*Microtus ochrogaster*). *Journal of Neuroendocrinology*, 1994, *6*, 247–250.

Williams, R. Slowing the decline. *Nature*, 2010, *466*, s13–s14.

Williams, Z. M., and Eskandar, E. N. Selective enhancement of associative learning by microstimulation of the anterior caudate. *Nature Neuroscience*, 2006, *9*, 562–568.

Willingham, D. G., and Koroshetz, W. J. Evidence for dissociable motor skills in Huntington's disease patients. *Psychobiology*, 1993, *21*, 173–182.

Wilson, B. E., Meyer, G. E., Cleveland, J. C., and Weigle, D. S. Identification of candidate genes for a factor regulating body weight in primates. *American Journal of Physiology*, 1990, *259*, R1149–R1155.

Wilson, E. O. *Sociobiology: The new synthesis.* Cambridge, MA: Harvard University Press, 1975.

Winans, E. Aripiprazole. *American Journal of Health-system Pharmacy*, 2003, *60*, 2437–2445.

Winslow, J. T., Ellingoe, J., and Miczek, J. A. Effects of alcohol on aggressive behavior in squirrel monkeys: Influence of testosterone and social context. *Psychopharmacology*, 1988, *95*, 356–363.

Winslow, J. T., and Miczek, K. A. Social status as determinants of alcohol effects on aggressive behavior in squirrel monkeys (*Saimiri sciureus*). *Psychopharmacology*, 1985, *85*, 167–172.

Winslow, J. T., and Miczek, K. A. Androgen dependency of alcohol effects on aggressive behavior: A seasonal rhythm in high-ranking squirrel monkeys. *Psychopharmacology*, 1988, *95*, 92–98.

Wirz-Justice, A., Graw, P., Kraeuchi, K., Sarrafzadeh, A., et al. "Natural" light treatment of seasonal affective disorder. *Journal of Affective Disorders*, 1996, *37*, 109–120.

Wirz-Justice, A., and Van den Hoofdakker, R. H. Sleep deprivation in depression: What do we know, where do we go? *Biological Psychiatry*, 1999, *46*, 445–453.

Wise, M. S. Narcolepsy and other disorders of excessive sleepiness. *Medical Clinics of North America*, 2004, *99*, 597–610.

Wise, R. A., Leone, P., Rivest, R., and Leeb, K. Elevations of nucleus accumbens dopamine and DOPAC levels during intravenous heroin self-administration. *Synapse*, 1995, *21*, 140–148.

Wise, R. J., Greene, J., Buchel, C., and Scott, S. K. Brain regions involved in articulation. *Lancet*, 1999, *353*, 1057–1061.

Wisniewski, A. B., Migeon, C. J., Meyer-Bahlburg, H. F., Gearhart, J. P., et al. Complete androgen insensitivity syndrome: Long-term medical, surgical, and psychosexual outcome. *The Journal of Clinical Endocrinology and Metabolism*, 2000, *85*(8), 2664–2669.

Wise, S. P., and Rapoport, J. L. Obsessive compulsive disorder: Is it a basal ganglia dysfunction? *Psychopharmacology Bulletin*, 1988, *24*, 380–384.

Wissinger, B., and Sharpe, L. T. New aspects of an old theme: The genetic basis of human color vision. *American Journal of Human Genetics*, 1998, *63*, 1257–1262.

Witten, I., Lin, S.-C., Brodsky, M., Prakash, R., et al. Cholinergic interneurons control local circuit activity and cocaine conditioning. *Science*, 2010, *330*, 1677–1681.

Wolpaw, J. R., and McFarland, D. J. Control of a two-dimensional movement signal by a noninvasive brain–computer interface in humans. *Proceedings of the National Academy of Sciences, USA*, 2004, *101*, 17849–17854.

Wong, G. T., Gannon, K. S., and Margolskee, R. F. Transduction of bitter and sweet taste by gustducin. *Nature*, 1996, *381*, 796–800.

Wong, W. I., Pasterski, V., Hindmarsh, P. C., Geffner, M. E., et al. Are there parental socialization effects on the sex-typed behavior of individuals with congenital adrenal hyperplasia? *Archives of Sexual Behavior*, 2012, *42*(3), 381–391.

Wong-Riley, M. T. Personal communication, 1978. Cited by Livingstone, M. S., and Hubel, D. H. Thalamic inputs to cytochrome oxidase-rich regions in monkey visual cortex. *Proceedings of the National Academy of Sciences, USA*, 1982, *79*, 6098–6101.

Wood, E. R., Dudchenko, P. A., Robitsek, R. J., and Eichenbaum, H. Hippocampal neurons encode information about different types of memory episodes occurring in the same location. *Neuron*, 2000, *27*, 623–633.

Wood, R. I., and Newman, S. W. Mating activates androgen receptor-containing neurons in chemosensory pathways of the male Syrian hamster brain. *Brain Research*, 1993, *614*, 65–77.

Woodruff-Pak, D. S. Eyeblink classical conditioning in H. M.: Delay and trace paradigms. *Behavioral Neuroscience*, 1993, *107*, 911–925.

Woods, B. T. Is schizophrenia a progressive neurodevelopmental disorder? Toward a unitary pathogenetic mechanism. *American Journal of Psychiatry*, 1998, *155*, 1661–1670.

Woods, S. C., Lotter, E. C., McKay, L. D., and Porte, D. Chronic intracerebroventricular infusion of insulin reduces food intake and body weight of baboons. *Nature*, 1979, *282*, 503–505.

Woods, S. C., Lutz, T. A., Geary, N., and Langhans, W. Pancreatic signals controlling food intake: Insulin, glucagon and amylin. *Philosophical Transactions of the Royal Society B*, 2006, *361*, 1219–1235.

Woodworth, R. S., and Schlosberg, H. *Experimental psychology*. New York: Holt, Rinehart and Winston, 1954.

Wooley, S. C., and Garner, D. M. Controversies in management: Should obesity be treated? Dietary treatments for obesity are ineffective. *British Medical Journal*, 1994, *309*, 655–656.

Woolfe, A., Goodson, M., Goode, D. K., Snell, P., et al. Highly conserved non-coding sequences are associated with vertebrate development. *PLoS Biology*, 2005, *3*, e7.

Woon, F. L., and Hedges, D. W. Hippocampal and amygdala volumes in children and adults with childhood maltreatment-related posttraumatic stress disorder: A meta-analysis. *Hippocampus*, 2008, *18*(8), 729–736.

World Health Organization. Obesity and overweight. WHO Factsheet, January, 2015. http://www.who.int/mediacentre/factsheets/fs311/en/

Wu, J. C., and Bunney, W. E. The biological basis of an antidepressant response to sleep deprivation and relapse: Review and hypothesis. *American Journal of Psychiatry*, 1990, *147*, 14–21.

Wulff, K., Gatti, S., Wettstein, J. G., and Foster, R. G. Sleep and circadian rhythm disruption in psychiatric and neurodegenerative disease. *Nature Reviews: Neuroscience*, 2010, *11*, 1–11.

Wyart, C., Webster, W. W., Chen, J. H., Wilson, S. R., et al. Smelling a single component of male sweat alters levels of cortisol in women. *Journal of Neuroscience*, 2007, *27*, 1261–1265.

Wyatt, R. D. Pheromones and signature mixtures: Defining species-wide signals and variable cues for identity in both invertebrates and vertebrates. *Journal of Comparative Physiology A*. 2010, *196*, 685–700.

Wynne, K., Stanley, S., McGowan, B., and Bloom, S. Appetite control. *Journal of Endocrinology*, 2005, *184*, 291–318.

Wysocki, C. J. Neurobehavioral evidence for the involvement of the vomeronasal system in mammalian reproduction. *Neuroscience and Biobehavioral Reviews*, 1979, *3*, 301–341.

Xiao, Z., Lee, T., Zhang, J. X., Wu, Q., et al. Thirsty heroin addicts show different fMRI activations when exposed to water-related and drug-related cues. *Drug and Alcohol Dependence*, 2006, *83*, 157–162.

Xu, Y. Revisiting the role of the fusiform face area in visual expertise. *Cerebral Cortex*, 2005, *15*, 1234–1242.

Yadav, J. S., Wholey, M. H., Kuntz, R. E., Fayad, P., et al. Protected carotid-artery stenting versus endarterectomy in high-risk patients. *New England Journal of Medicine*, 2004, *351*, 1493–1501.

Yamanaka, A., Beuckmann, C. T., Willie, J. T., Hara, J., et al. Hypothalamic orexin neurons regulate arousal according to energy balance in mice. *Neuron*, 2003, *38*, 701–713.

Yan, L., and Silver, R. Resetting the brain clock: Time course and localization of mPER1 and mPER2 protein expression in suprachiasmatic nucleus during phase shifts. *European Journal of Neuroscience*, 2004, *19*, 1105–1109.

Yang, L., Scott, K. A., Hyun, J., Tamashiro, K. L., et al. Role of dorso-medial hypothalamic neuropeptide Y in modulating food intake and energy balance. *Journal of Neuroscience*, 2009, *29*, 179–190.

Yang, T., and Maunsell, J. H. R. The effect of perceptual learning on neuronal responses in monkey visual area V4. *Journal of Neuroscience*, 2004, *24*, 1617–1626.

Yang, T. T., Gallen, C. C., Ramachandran, V. S., Cobb, S., et al. Noninvasive detection of cerebral plasticity in adult human somatosensory cortex. *Neuroreport*, 1994, *5*, 701–704.

Yao, Y., Kelly, M. T., Sajikumar, S., Serrano, P., et al. PKM zeta maintains late long-term potentiation by N-ethylmaleimide-sensitive factor/GluR2-dependent trafficking of postsynaptic AMPA receptors. *Journal of Neuroscience*, 2008, *28*, 7820–7827.

Yates, W. R., Perry, P., and Murray, S. Aggression and hostility in anabolic steroid users. *Biological Psychiatry*, 1992, *31*, 1232–1234.

Yehuda, R., and LeDoux, J. Response variation following trauma: A translational neuroscience approach to understanding PTSD. *Neuron*, 2007, *56*, 19–32.

Yeo, J. A. G., and Keverne, E. B. The importance of vaginal-cervical stimulation for maternal behaviour in the rat. *Physiology and Behavior*, 1986, *37*, 23–26.

Yildiz, A., Tomishige, M., Vale, R. D., and Selvin, P. R. Kinesin walks hand-over-hand. *Science*, 2004, *303*, 676–678.

Yilmaz, A., Schultz, D., Aksoy, A., and Canbeyli, R. Prolonged effect of an anesthetic dose of ketamine on behavioral despair. *Pharmacology, Biochemistry and Behavior*, 2002, *71*, 341–344.

Yin, H. H., Mulcare, S. P., Hilário, M. R. F., Holloway, T., et al. Dynamic reorganization of striatal circuits during the acquisition and consolidation of a skill. *Nature Neuroscience*, 2009, *12*, 333–341.

Yokoo, H., Tanaka, M., Yoshida, M., Tsuda, A., et al. Direct evidence of conditioned fear-elicited enhancement of noradrenaline release in the rat hypothalamus assessed by intracranial microdialysis. *Brain Research,* 1990, *536,* 305–308.

Yost, W. A. Auditory image perception and analysis: The basis for hearing. *Hearing Research,* 1991, *56,* 8–18.

Young, A. W., Aggleton, J. P., Hellawell, D. J., Johnson, M., et al. Face processing impairments after amygdalotomy. *Brain,* 1995, *118,* 15–24.

Young, S. N., and Leyton, M. The role of serotonin in human mood and social interaction: Insight from altered tryptophan levels. *Pharmacology, Biochemistry and Behavior,* 2002, *71,* 857–865.

Youngren, K. D., Inglis, F. M., Pivirotto, P. J., Jedema, H. P., et al. Clozapine preferentially increases dopamine release in the rhesus monkey prefrontal cortex compared with the caudate nucleus. *Neuropsychopharmacology,* 1999, *20,* 403–412.

Yousseif, A., Emmanuel, J., Karra, E., Millet, Q., et al. Differential effects of laparoscopic sleeve gastrectomy and laparoscopic gastric bypass on appetite, circulating acyl-ghrelin, peptide YY3-36 and active GLP-1 levels in non-diabetic humans. *Obesity Surgery,* 2014, *24*(2), 241–252.

Yu, H., Wang, Y., Pattwell, S., Jing, D., et al. Variant BDNF Val66Met polymorphism affects extinction of conditioned aversive memory. *Journal of Neuroscience,* 2009, *29,* 4056–4064.

Yurgelun-Todd, D. Emotional and cognitive changes during adolescence. *Current Opinion in Neurobiology,* 2007, *17,* 251–257.

Zammit, S., Thomas, K., Thompson, A., Horwood, J., et al. Maternal tobacco, cannabis and alcohol use during pregnancy and risk of adolescent psychotic symptoms in offspring. *British Journal of Psychiatry,* 2009, *195,* 294–300.

Zandian, M., Ioakimidis, I., Bergh, C., and Södersten, P. Cause and treatment of anorexia nervosa. *Physiology and Behavior,* 2007, *92,* 293–290.

Zarate, C. A., Jaskaran, B. S., Carlson, P. J., Brutsche, N. E., et al. A randomized trial of a N-methyl-D-aspartate antagonist in treatment-resistant major depression. *Archives of General Psychiatry,* 2006, *63,* 856–864.

Zayfert, C., Dums, A. R., Ferguson, R. J., and Hegel, M. T. Health functioning impairments associated with posttraumatic stress disorder, anxiety disorders, and depression. *Journal of Nervous and Mental Disease,* 2002, *190,* 233–240.

Zeki, S. The representation of colours in the cerebral cortex. *Nature,* 1980, *284,* 412–418.

Zeki, S., Aglioti, S., McKeefry, D., and Berlucchi, G. The neurological basis of conscious color perception in a blind patient. *Proceedings of the National Academy of Sciences, USA,* 1999, *96,* 13594–13596.

Zenner, H.-P., Zimmermann, U., and Schmitt, U. Reversible contraction of isolated mammalian cochlear hair cells. *Hearing Research,* 1985, *18,* 127–133.

Zentner, M., and Kagan, J. Infants' perception of consonance and dissonance in music. *Infant Behavior and Development,* 1998, *21,* 483–492.

Zhang, A., Kindrat, A. N., Sharif-Naeini, R., and Bourque, C. W. Actin filaments mediate mechanical gating during osmosensory transduction in rat supraoptic nucleus neurons. *Journal of Neuroscience,* 2007, *27,* 4008–4013.

Zhang, C., Truong, K. K., and Zhou, Q.-Y. Efferent projections of prokineticin 2 expressing neurons in the mouse suprachiasmatic nucleus. *PLoS ONE,* 2009, *4,* e7151.

Zhang, F., Wang, L.-P., Brauner, M., Liewald, J. F., et al. Multimodal fast optical interrogation of neural circuitry. *Nature,* 2007, *446,* 633–639.

Zhang, G. C., Mao, L. M., Liu, X. Y., and Wang, J. Q. Long-lasting up-regulation of orexin receptor type 2 protein levels in the rat nucleus accumbens after chronic cocaine administration. *Journal of Neurochemistry,* 2007, *103,* 400–407.

Zhang, X., Salmeron, B. J., Ross, T. J., Geng, X., et al. Factors underlying prefrontal and insula structural alterations in smokers. *NeuroImage,* 2011, *54,* 42–48.

Zhao, Y. J., Wee, H. L., Au, W. L., Seah, S. H., et al. Selegiline use is associated with a slower progression in early Parkinson's disease as evaluated by Hoehn and Yahr stage transition times. *Parkinsonism and Related Disorders,* 2011, *17,* 194–197.

Zhong, C.-B., and Liljenquist, K. Washing away your sins: Threatened morality and physical cleansing. *Science,* 2006, *313,* 1451–1452.

Zhou, F. C., Zhang, J. K., Lumeng, L., and Li, T. K. Mesolimbic dopamine system in alcohol-preferring rats. *Alcohol,* 1995, *12,* 403–412.

Zigman, J. M., Nakano, Y., Coppari, R., Balthasar, N., et al. Mice lacking ghrelin receptors resist the development of diet-induced obesity. *Journal of Clinical Investigation,* 2005, *115,* 3564–3572.

Zihl, J., Von Cramon, D., Mai, N., and Schmid, C. Disturbance of movement vision after bilateral posterior brain damage. Further evidence and follow up observations. *Brain,* 1991, *114,* 2235–2252.

Zinman, L., and Cudkowicz, M. Emerging targets and treatments in amyotrophic lateral sclerosis. *Lancet Neurology,* 2011, *10,* 481–490.

Ziomkiewicz, A., Pawlowski, B., Ellison, P. T., Lipson, S. F., et al. Higher luteal progesterone is associated with low levels of premenstrual aggressive behavior and fatigue. *Biological Psychology,* 2012, *91*(3), 376–382.

Zlokovic, B. V. The blood–brain barrier in health and chronic neurodegenerative disorders. *Neuron,* 2008, *57,* 178–201.

Zola-Morgan, S., Squire, L. R., and Amaral, D. G. Human amnesia and the medial temporal region: Enduring memory impairment following a bilateral lesion limited to field CA1 of the hippocampus. *Journal of Neuroscience,* 1986, *6,* 2950–2967.

Zorrilla, E. P., Iwasaki, S., Moss, J. A., Chang, J., et al. Vaccination against weight gain. *Proceedings of the National Academy of Sciences, USA,* 2006, *103,* 12961–12962.

Zou, Z., Horowitz, L. F., Montmayeur, J.-P., Snapper, S., et al. Genetic tracing reveals a stereotyped sensory map in the olfactory cortex. *Nature,* 2001, *414,* 173–179.

Zubieta, J.-K., Bueller, J. A., Jackson, L. R., Scott, D. J., et al. Placebo effects mediated by endogenous opioid activity on μ-opioid receptors. *Journal of Neuroscience,* 2005, *25,* 7754–7762.

Zumpe, D., Bonsall, R. W., Kutner, M. H., and Michael, R. P. Medroxyprogesterone acetate, aggression, and sexual behavior in male cynomolgus monkeys (Macaca fascicularis). *Hormones and Behavior,* 1991, *25,* 394–409.

Zwiers, M. P., Van Opstal, A. J., and Cruysberg, J. R. M. A spatial hearing deficit in early-blind humans. *Journal of Neuroscience,* 2001, *21,* RC142 (1–5).

Credits

Figure and Table Credits

Chapter 1. p. 19: Galen. *De Usu Partium*. Translated by M. T. May. Ithaca, N.Y.: Cornell University Press, 1968. p. 387. **p. 21, Fig01-03:** Pearson Education. **p. 22, TBL01-01:** Pearson Education. **p. 24, Fig01-05:** Pearson Education. **p. 26, Fig01-06:** Pearson Education. **p. 26, Fig01-07:** Redrawn with permission Laurie Grace from "Genes, Peoples, and Languages" by L. L. Cavalli-Sforza, *Scientific American*, November 1991. Copyright © 1991. Reprinted by permission of Laurie Grace. **p. 27, Fig01-08:** Suzana Herculana-Houzel; Marino L, "A Comparison of Encephalization Between Odontocete Cetaceans and Anthropoid Primates." *Brain Behav Evol*. 1998;51(4):230-8.Copyright 2012, Karger Publishers, Basel, Switzerland. **p. 32, Fig01-10:** Pearson Education.

Chapter 2. p. 37, FigCO02-360: Pearson Education. **p. 38, Fig02-01:** Pearson Education. **p. 38, Fig02-02:** http://www.easynotecards.com/uploads/902/92/_5b4ca280_149581079e5__8000_00000194.JPG. **p. 39, Fig02-03:** Pearson Education. **p. 40, Fig02-04:** Pearson Education. **p. 40, Fig02-05:** Pearson Education. **p. 41, Fig02-06:** Pearson Education. **p. 42, Fig02-07:** Pearson Education. **p. 44, Fig02-08:** Pearson Education. **p. 44, Fig02-09:** Pearson Education. **p. 45, Fig02-10:** Pearson Education. **p. 46, Fig02-11:** Pearson Education. **p. 48, Fig02-12:** Pearson Education. **p. 48, Fig02-13:** Pearson Education. **p. 51, Fig02-15:** Pearson Education. **p. 52, UNFig02-01:** Pearson Education. **p. 53, Fig02-16:** Pearson Education. **p. 54, Fig02-17:** Pearson Education. **p. 54, Fig02-18:** Pearson Education. **p. 55, UNFig02-02:** Pearson Education. **p. 56, Fig02-19:** Pearson Education. **p. 56, Fig02-20:** Pearson Education. **p. 58, Fig02-21:** Pearson Education. **p. 59, Fig02-22:** Pearson Education. **p. 60, Fig02-24:** Pearson Education. **p. 61, Fig02-25:** Pearson Education. **p. 61, Fig02-26:** Pearson Education. **p. 62, Fig02-27:** Pearson Education. **p. 63, Fig02-28:** Pearson Education. **p. 64, Fig02-29:** Pearson Education. **p. 65, Fig02-30:** Pearson Education. **p. 66, Fig02-31:** Pearson Education. **p. 67, Fig02-32:** Pearson Education.

Chapter 3. p. 72, FigCO03-360: Pearson Education. **p. 73, Fig03-01:** Pearson Education. **p. 74, Fig03-02:** Pearson Education. **p. 75, Fig03-03:** Pearson Education. **p. 76, Fig03-04:** Pearson Education. **p. 77, Fig03-05:** Pearson Education. **p. 78, Fig03-06:** Pearson Education. **p. 79, Fig03-07:** Pearson Education. **p. 79, TBL03-01:** Pearson Education. **p. 81, Fig03-08:** Adapted from Rakic, P., "A Small Step for the Cell, A Giant Leap for Mankind: A Hypothesis of Neocortical Expansion During Evolution," *Trends in Neuroscience*, 1995, 18, 383–388. **p. 81, Fig03-09:** Based on http://tulane.edu/som/departments/psychiatry/fimh/upload/shonkoff2008.pdf. **p. 82, Fig03-10:** Based on http://www.nature.com/npp/journal/v35/n1/fig_tab/npp2009115f1.html. **p. 83, Fig03-11:** Pearson Education. **p. 85, Fig03-12:** Pearson Education. **p. 85, Fig03-13:** Pearson Education. **p. 86, Fig03-14:** Pearson Education. **p. 87, Fig03-15:** Pearson Education. **p. 88, Fig03-16:** Pearson Education. **p. 89, Fig03-17:** From Hofer, S., and Frahm, J. "Topography of the Human Corpus Callosum Revisited—Comprehensive Fiber Tractography Using Diffusion Tensor Magnetic Resonance Imaging." *NeuroImage*, 2006, 32, 989–994. Reprinted with permission. **p. 90, Fig03-18:** Pearson Education. **p. 90, Fig03-19:** Pearson Education. **p. 91, Fig03-20:** Pearson Education. **p. 91, Fig03-21:** Pearson Education. **p. 92, Fig03-22:** Pearson Education. **p. 93, Fig03-23:** Pearson Education. **p. 94, Fig03-24:** Pearson Education. **p. 95, Fig03-25:** Pearson Education. **p. 95, Fig03-26:** Pearson Education. **p. 97, Fig03-27:** Pearson Education. **p. 98, Fig03-28:** Pearson Education. **p. 99, Fig03-29:** Pearson Education. **p. 100, TBL03-02:** Pearson Education.

Chapter 4. p. 105, Fig04-01: Pearson Education. **p. 106, Fig04-02:** Pearson Education. **p. 106, Fig04-03:** Based on Feldman, R. S., Meyer, J. S., and Quenzer, L. F. *Principles of Neuropsychopharmacology*. Sunderland, MA: Sinauer Associates, 1997; after Jones, R. T. *NIDA Research Monographs*, 1990, 99, 30–41. **p. 107, Fig04-04:** Pearson Education.

p. 108, Fig04-05: Pearson Education. **p. 109, Fig04-06:** Pearson Education. **p. 112, Fig04-07:** Pearson Education. **Fig04-08:** Pearson Education. **p. 114, Fig04-07d:** Pearson Education. **p. 115, TBL04-01:** Pearson Education. **p. 116, Fig04-09:** Pearson Education. **p. 117, Fig04-10:** Pearson Education. **p. 118, TBL04-02:** Pearson Education. **p. 118, Fig04-11:** Pearson Education. **p. 119, Fig04-12:** Pearson Education. **p. 119, Fig04-13:** Pearson Education. **p. 120, TBL04-03:** Pearson Education. **p. 120, TBL04-04:** Pearson Education. **p. 121, Fig04-14:** Pearson Education. **p. 122, Fig04-15:** Pearson Education. **p. 123, Fig04-16:** Pearson Education. **p. 123, Fig04-17:** Pearson Education. **p. 124, Fig04-18:** Pearson Education. **p. 125, Fig04-19:** Pearson Education. **p. 125, Fig04-20:** Pearson Education. **p. 126, Fig04-21:** Pearson Education. **p. 127, TBL04-05:** Pearson Education. **p. 129, TBL04-06:** Pearson Education.

Chapter 5. p. 134, FigCO5-360: Pearson Education. **p. 137, Fig05-02:** Pearson Education. **p. 137, Fig05-03:** Pearson Education. **p. 141, Fig05-09:** Pearson Education. **p. 142, Fig05-10:** Pearson Education. **p. 143, Fig05-13:** Pearson Education. **p. 144, Fig05-14:** Pearson Education. **p. 145, Fig05-15:** Based on http://www.nlm.nih.gov/medlineplus/ency/imagepages/19237.htm. **p. 146, TBL05-01:** Pearson Education. **p. 148, Fig05-19:** Pearson Education. **p. 149, Fig05-20:** Pearson Education. **p. 153, Fig05-24:** Pearson Education. **p. 154, UNFIG05-02:** Based on Hausser, M., and Smith, S. L. *Nature*, 2007, 446, 617–619. **p. 154, UNFIG05-03:** Pearson Education. **p. 41, UNFIG05-04:** Pearson Education. **p. 154-141, TBL05-02:** Pearson Education. **p. 158, Fig05-27:** Pearson Education. **p. 159, TBL05-03:** Pearson Education. **p. 161, Fig05-28:** Pearson Education. **p. 162, TBL05-04:** Pearson Education.

Chapter 6. p. 165, FigCO6-360: Pearson Education. **p. 167, Fig06-02:** Pearson Education. **p. 168, Fig06-03:** Pearson Education. **p. 168, Fig06-04:** Pearson Education. **p. 169, TBL06-01:** Pearson Education. **p. 169, Fig06-05:** Pearson Education. **p. 170, Fig06-06:** Adapted from Dowling, J. E., and Boycott, B. B. *Proceedings of the Royal Society of London*, B, 1966, 166, 80–111. Copyright © 1966. Reprinted by permission of Highwire Press. **p. 170, Fig06-07:** Based on Dowling, J. E., and Boycott, B. B. *Proceedings of the Royal Society of London*, B, 1966, 166, 80–111. **p. 171, Fig06-08:** Pearson Education. **p. 172, Fig06-09:** Pearson Education. **p. 173, Fig06-10:** Pearson Education. **p. 175, Fig06-11:** Pearson Education. **p. 176, Fig06-12:** Pearson Education. **p. 176, Fig06-13b:** Based on Sincich and Horton, *Annual Review of Neuroscience*, 2005, 28, 303–326. **p. 177, Fig06-14:** Pearson Education. **p. 178, Fig06-15:** Pearson Education. **p. 180, Fig06-16:** Pearson Education. **p. 181, Fig06-17:** Pearson Education. **p. 182, Fig06-18:** Based on data from Dartnall, H. J. A., Bowmaker, J. K., and Mollon, J. D. *Proceedings of the Royal Society of London*, B, 1983, 220, 115–130. **p. 182, Fig06-19:** Pearson Education. **p. 183, Fig06-20:** Pearson Education. **p. 183, Fig06-21:** Pearson Education. **p. 185, Fig06-23:** Pearson Education. **p. 185, TBL06-02:** Pearson Education. **p. 189, Fig06-26:** Pearson Education. **p. 190, Buxbaum, L. J., Glosser, G., and Coslett, H. B. "Impaired Face and Word Recognition Without Object Agnosia." *Neuropsychologia*, 1999, 37, 41–50. **p. 191, Fig06-29:** Based on Schwarzlose, R. F., Baker, C. I., and Kanwisher, N. *Journal of Neuroscience*, 2005, 23, 11055–11059. **p. 195, Fig06-34:** Adapted from Astafiev, S. V., Shulman, G. L., Stanley, C. M., et al. *Journal of Neuroscience*, 2003, 23, 4689–4699. **p. 197, Fig06-35:** Based on Hubel, D. H., and Wiesel, T. N. *Journal of Physiology* [London], 1959, 148, 574–591. **p. 198, Fig06-36:** Pearson Education. **p. 199, Zihl, J., Von Cramon, D., Mai, N., and Schmid, C. "Disturbance of Movement Vision After Bilateral Posterior Brain Damage. Further Evidence and Follow Up Observations." *Brain*, 1991, 114, 2235–2252. **p. 200-187, TBL06-03:** Pearson Education.

Chapter 7. p. 204, FigCO7-360: Pearson Education. **p. 204, Fig07-01:** Pearson Education. **p. 205, Fig07-02:** Pearson Education. **p. 206,**

702

Fig07-03: Pearson Education. **p. 206, Fig07-04:** Pearson Education. **p. 207, Fig07-05:** Pearson Education. **p. 208, Fig07-06:** Pearson Education. **p. 209, Fig07-07:** Pearson Education. **p. 210, Fig07-08:** Pearson Education. **p. 211, Fig07-09:** Pearson Education. **p. 212, TBL07-01:** Pearson Education. **p. 214, Fig07-11:** Pearson Education. **p. 214, Fig07-12:** Pearson Education. **p. 215, Fig07-13:** Pearson Education. **p. 215, Fig07-14:** Pearson Education. **p. 216, Fig07-15:** Pearson Education. **p. 218, Fig07-17:** Pearson Education. **p. 219, Fig07-18:** Pearson Education. **p. 221, Fig07-19:** Pearson Education. **p. 222, Fig07-20:** Pearson Education. **p. 223, TBL07-02:** Pearson Education. **p. 224, TBL07-03:** Pearson Education. **p. 225,** Based on Olausson, H., Lamarre, Y., Backlund, H., Morin, C., et al. "Unmyelinated Tactile Afferents Signal Touch and Project to Insular Cortex." *Nature Neuroscience*, 2002, 5, 900–904. **p. 226, TBL07-04:** Pearson Education. **p. 227,** Ikoma, A., Steinhoff, M., Ständer, S., Yosipovitch, G., et al. "The Neurobiology of Itch." *Nature Reviews: Neuroscience*, 2006, 7, 535–547. **p. 228, Fig07-23:** Pearson Education. **p. 230, Fig07-25:** Adapted from Price, D. B. *Science*, 2000, 288, 1769–1772. **p. 231, TBL07-05:** Pearson Education. **p. 233, UNFig07.01:** Basbaum, A. I., and Fields, H. L. "Endogenous Pain Control Mechanisms: Review and Hypothesis." *Annals of Neurology*, 1978, 4, 451–462. **p. 233, Fig07-29:** Pearson Education. **p. 234, 07-30:** Based on From Wager, T. D., Rilling, J. K., Smith, E. E., Sokolik, A., Casey, K. L., Davidson, R. J., Kosslyn, S. M., Rose, R. M., and Cohen, J. D., "Placebo-induced Changes in fMRI in the Anticipation and Experience of Pain," *Science*, 2004, 303, 1162–1166. Copyright © American Association for the Advancement of Science. **p. 235,** Dutta, T. M., Josiah, A. F., Cronin, C. A., Wittenberg, G. F., & Cole, J. W. (2013). "Altered Taste and Stroke: A Case Report and Literature Review." *Topics in Stroke Rehabilitation*, 20(1), 78-86. **p. 236, Fig07-31:** Pearson Education. **p. 237, Fig07-32:** Pearson Education. **p. 238, Fig07-33:** Pearson Education. **p. 240, Fig07-34:** Pearson Education. **p. 241, Fig07-35:** Pearson Education. **p. 242, Fig07-36:** Pearson Education. **p. 242, Fig07-37:** Adapted from Malnic, B., Hirono, J., Sato, T., and Buck, L. B. *Cell*, 1999, 96, 713–723. Copyright © 1999 by Elsevier. Reprinted by permission of Elsevier. **p. 243, Fig07-38:** Adapted from Johnson & Leon, *Journal of Comparative Neurology* (2007), 503: 1–34. Copyright © 2007. Reprinted by permission of John Wiley & Sons, Inc.

Chapter 8. p. 248, Fig08-01: Pearson Education. **p. 248, Fig08-02:** Pearson Education. **p. 249, Fig08-03:** Pearson Education. **p. 250, Fig08-04:** Pearson Education. **p. 251, Fig08-05:** Pearson Education. **p. 253, Fig08-06:** Pearson Education. **p. 254, Fig08-07:** Pearson Education. **p. 256, Fig08-08:** Pearson Education. **p. 257, Fig08-09:** Pearson Education. **p. 257, Fig08-10:** Pearson Education. **p. 258, Fig08-11:** Pearson Education. **p. 259, Fig08-12:** Pearson Education. **p. 260, TBL08-01:** Pearson Education. **p. 260, Fig08-13:** Pearson Education. **p. 261,** Gerloff, C., Corwell, B., Chen, R., Hallett, M., et al. "Stimulation over the Human Supplementary Motor Area Interferes with the Organization of Future Elements in Complex Motor Sequences." *Brain*, 1997, 120, 1587–1602. **p. 261,** Sirigu, A., Deprati, E., Ciancia, S., Giraux, P., et al. "Altered Awareness of Voluntary Action After Damage to the Parietal Cortex." *Nature Neuroscience*, 2004, 7, 80–84. **p. 262, TBL08-02:** Pearson Education. **p. 263, Fig08-14:** Pearson Education. **p. 264, Fig08-15:** Pearson Education. **p. 265, Fig08-16:** Pearson Education. **p. 266, Fig08-17:** Pearson Education. **p. 266,** Holmes, G. "The Cerebellum of Man." *Brain*, 1939, 62, 21–30. **p. 268, Fig08-18:** Pearson Education. **p. 270, Fig08-19:** Pearson Education. **p. 270,** Rizzolatti, R., Fogassi, L., and Gallese, V. "Neurophysiological Mechanisms Underlying the Understanding and Imitation of Action." *Nature Reviews: Neuroscience*, 2001, 2, 661–670. p. 675. **p. 272, 08-22:** Pearson Education. **p. 274, Fig08-23:** From *Fundamentals of Human Neuropsychology*, by B. Kolb and I. Q. Whishaw. W. H. Freeman and Company. **p. 274, Fig08-24:** Pearson Education.

Chapter 9. p. 279, Fig09-02: Pearson Education. **p. 279, TBL09-01:** Based on: Silber et al., 2007. (From Horne, J. A. *Why We Sleep: The Functions of Sleep in Humans and Other Mammals*. Oxford, England: Oxford University Press, 1988.) **p. 280, Fig09-03:** Pearson Education. **p. 281, TBL09-02:** Pearson Education. **p. 281,** Melges, F. T. *Time and the Inner Future: A Temporal Approach to Psychiatric Disorders*. New York: John Wiley & Sons, 1982. **p. 281, Fig09-04:** Pearson Education. **p. 283, Fig09-05:** Based on Mukhametov, L. M., in *Sleep Mechanisms*, edited by A. A., Borbély and J. L., Valatx. Munich: Springer-Verlag, 1984. **p. 286, Fig09-06:** Data from Mednick, Nakayama, and Strickgold, "Sleep-dependent Learning: A Nap is as Good as a Night" *Nature Neuroscience*, 6, 2003. Nature Publishing Group. **p. 286, Fig09-07:** Based on data from Mednick, Nakayama, and Stickgold, 2003. **p. 287, Fig09-08:** Based on Wamsley, E. J., Tucker, M., Payne, J. D., et al. "Dreaming of a Learning Task Is Associated with Enhanced Sleep Dependent Memory Consolidation. *Current Biology*, 2010, 20, 1–6. **p. 288, Fig09-09:** Pearson Education. **p. 289, Fig09-10:** Based on Marrosu, F., Portas, C., Mascia, M. S., Casu, M. A., et al. "Microdialysis Measurement of Cortical and Hippocampal Acetylcholine Release During Sleep–wake Cycle in Freely Moving Cats." *Brain Research*, 1995, 671, 329–332. **p. 290, Fig09-11:** Adapted from Woolf, N. J. *Progress in Neurobiology*, 1991, 37, 475–524. **p. 290, Fig09-12:** From Aston-Jones, G., and Bloom, F. E. *The Journal of Neuroscience*, 1981, 1, 876–886. Copyright 1981, *The Society for Neuroscience*. **p. 291, Fig09-13:** Adapted from Cotman, C. W., and McGaugh, J. L. *Behavioral Neuroscience: An Introduction*. New York: Academic Press, 1980. **p. 291, Fig09-14:** Adapted from Trulson, M. E., and Jacobs, B. L. *Brain Research*, 1979, 163, 135–150. **p. 292, Fig09-15:** Adapted from Consolazione, A., and Cuello, A. C. "CNS Serotonin Pathways." In *Biology of Serotonergic Transmission*, edited by N. N. Osborne. Chichester: England: Wiley & Sons, 1982. **p. 292, Fig09-16:** Adapted From Mileykovskiy, B. Y., Kiyashchenko, L. I., and Siegel, J. M. *Neuron*, 2005, 46, 787–798. Reprinted by permission. **p. 293, Tbl09-03:** Pearson Education. **p. 294, Fig09-17:** Pearson Education. **p. 295, Fig09-18:** Pearson Education. **p. 295, Fig09-19:** From Porkka-Heiskanen, T., Strecker, R. E., Thakkar, M., et al. *Science*, 1997, 276, 1265–1268. Copyright 1997 by the American Association for the Advancement of Science. **p. 296, Fig09-20:** Pearson Education. **p. 296, Fig09-21:** Pearson Education. **p. 297, Fig09-22:** From Schwartz, S., Ponz, A., Poryazova, R., et al. *Brain*, 2008, 131, 514–522. Reprinted by permission. **p. 297, Fig09-23:** Pearson Education. **p. 301,** Schenck, C. H., Bundlie, S. R., Ettinger, M. G., and Mahowald, M. W. "Chronic Behavioral Disorders of Human REM Sleep: A New Category of Parasomnia." *Sleep*, 1986, 9, 293–308. **p. 301,** Boodman, S. G. "Hungry in the Dark: Some Sleepeaters Don't Wake Up for Their Strange Nighttime Binges." *Washington Post*, Sept. 7, 2004, HE01. **p. 303, Fig09-24:** Pearson Education. **p. 304, Fig09-26:** Pearson Education. **p. 305, Fig09-27:** Pearson Education. **p. 306, UNFIg19-01:** Pearson Education. **p. 307, Fig09-28:** Pearson Education. **p. 307, Fig09-29:** http://www.nature.com/nature/journal/v497/n7450_supp/full/497S10a.html?WT.ec_id=NATURE-20130523.

Chapter 10. p. 313, Fig10-01: Pearson Education. **p. 314, Fig10-02:** Pearson Education. **p. 316, Fig10-03:** Adapted from Spaulding, M. H., in *Contributions to Embryology*, Vol. 13. Washington, DC: Carnegie Institute of Washington, 1921. **p. 316, Fig10-04:** Pearson Education. **p. 317, Fig10-05:** Pearson Education. **p. 317, TBL10-01:** Pearson Education. **p. 319, Fig10-06:** http://sbi4u3.weebly.com/uploads/1/6/4/0/16403200/3972834_orig.jpg. **p. 320, Fig10-07:** Based on http://www.biolmoodanxietydisord.com/content/2/1/3/figure/F2. **p. 321, Fig10-09:** Pearson Education. **p. 321, Fig10-08:** Data from S. Craig Roberts, et al. "Female Facial Attractiveness Increases During the Fertile Phase of the Menstrual Cycle." *Proceedings of the Royal Society London* B (Suppl) 271, S270-S272 (2004) **Fig.2. p. 322, Fig10-10:** Based on Wallen, K. "Sex and Context: Hormones and Primate Sexual Motivation." *Hormones and Behavior*, 2001, 40, 339–357. **p. 324, Fig10-11:** Based on Hamilton and Meston 2010 paper: Hamilton, L. D., & Meston, C. M. (2010). "The Effects of Partner Togetherness on Salivary Testosterone in Women in Long Distance Relationships." *Hormones and Behavior*, 57(2), 198–202. **p. 324, Fig10-12:** Pearson Education. **p. 325, Fig10-13:** Pearson Education. **p. 325, TBL10.02:** Pearson Education. **p. 329, Fig10-14:** Based on http://www.personal.psu.edu/afr3/blogs/siowfa12/hypothalamus2.jpg. **p. 329, Fig10-15:** Pearson Education. **p. 335, Fig10-17:** Pearson Education. **p. 335, Fig10-18:** Based on Roselli, C. E., Larkin, K., Resko, J. A., Stellflug, J. N., et al. "The Volume of a Sexually Dimorphic Nucleus in the Ovine Medial Preoptic Area/Anterior Hypothalamus Varies with Sexual Partner Preference." *Endocrinology*, 2004, 145, 478–483. **p. 337, TBL10-03:** Pearson Education. **p. 340, Fig10-22:** Rosenblatt, J. S., Siegel, H. I., and Mayer, A. D. *Advances in the Study of Behavior*, 1979, 10, 225–310. Reprinted with permission. **p. 340, TBL10-04:** Pearson Education. **p. 341, Fig10-23:** Pearson Education.

Chapter 11. p. 347, Fig11-01: Pearson Education. p. 348, Fig11-02: Pearson Education. p. 348, Fig11-03: Pearson Education. p. 349, Fig11-04: Pearson Education. p. 350, Fig11-05: Pearson Education. p. 350, TBL11-01: Pearson Education. p. 351, Fig11-06: Based on data from Higley et al. 1996. p. 353, Fig11-07: Pearson Education. p. 354, Fig11-08: Based on data from Higley et al. 1996. p. 354, Holden, C. "The Violence of the Lambs." *Science*, 2000, 289, 580–581. p. 356, Fig11-09: Pearson Education. p. 357, Fig11-10: Based on van de Poll, N. E., Taminiau, M. S., Endert, E., and Louwerse, A. L. "Gonadal Steroid Influence Upon Sexual and Aggressive Behavior of Female Rats." *International Journal of Neuroscience*, 1988, 41, 271–286. p. 357, Fig11-11: Pearson Education. p. 357, Fig11-12: Pearson Education. p. 359, Fig11-13: Based on Winslow, J. T., and Miczek, K. A. "Androgen Dependency of Alcohol Effects on Aggressive Behavior: A Seasonal Rhythm in High-ranking Squirrel Monkeys." *Psychopharmacology*, 1988, 95, 92–98. p. 361, Eslinger, P. J., and Damasio, A. R. "Severe Disturbance of Higher Cognition after Bilateral Frontal Lobe Ablation: Patient EVR." *Neurology*, 1985, 35, 1731–1741. p. 362, Fig11-16: Pearson Education. p. 364, Fig11-17: Pearson Education. p. 364, TBL11-02: Based on Keonigs, M., Young, L., Adolphs, R., et al. "Damage to the Prefrontal Cortex Increases Utilitarian Moral Judgments." *Nature*, 2007, 446, 708–911. p. 366, Fig11-18: Pearson Education. p. 368, Fig11-19: Pearson Education. p. 368, Fig11-20: Based on Tamietto, M., Castelli, L., Vighetti, S., et al. "Unseen Facial and Bodily Expressions Trigger Fast Emotional Reactions." *Proceedings of the National Academy of Sciences*, USA, 2009, 106, 17661–17666. p. 369, Fig11-21: Pearson Education. p. 370, Fig11-24: From Whalen, P. J., Kagan, J., Cook, R. G., et al. *Science*, 2004, 306, 2061. Copyright 2004 American Association for the Advancement of Science. p. 371, Fig11-25: Adapted from Perrett, D. I., et al. *International Journal of Comparative Physiology* (1990), 4, 25-55. Copyright © 1990. Reprinted by permission of *International Society for Comparative Physiology*. p. 371, Fig11-26: From Adolphs, R., Damasio, H., Tranel, D., Cooper, G., and Damasio, A. R. *The Journal of Neuroscience*, 2000, 20, 2683–2690. p. 373, Duchenne, G.-B. *The Mechanism of Human Facial Expression*. Translated by R. A. Cuthbertson. Cambridge, England: Cambridge University Press, 1990. (Original work published 1862.). p. 374, Fig11-29: Based on Goel, V., and Dolan, R. J. "Social Regulation of Affective Experience of Humor." *Journal of Cognitive Neuroscience*,2007, 19, 1574–1580. p. 376, Fig11-30: Pearson Education. p. 377, Hohman, G. W. "Some Effects of Spinal Cord Lesions on Experienced Emotional Feelings." *Psychophysiology*, 1966, 3, 143–156. p. 377, Hohman, G. W. "Some Effects of Spinal Cord Lesions on Experienced Emotional Feelings." *Psychophysiology*, 1966, 3, 143–156. p. 377, Damasio, A. R., Grabowski, T. J., Bechara, A., Damasio, H., et al. "Subcortical and Cortical Brain Activity During the Feeling of Self-Generated Emotions." *Nature Neuroscience*, 2000, 3, 1049–1056.

Chapter 12. p. 383, Fig12-01: Pearson Education. p. 383, Fig12-02: Pearson Education. p. 384, Fig12-03: Pearson Education. p. 385, Fig12-04: Pearson Education. p. 386, Fig12-06: Pearson Education. p. 387, Fig12-07: Adapted from Thrasher, T. N. *Acta Physiologica Scandinavica*, 1989, 136, 141–150. p. 388, TBL12-01: Pearson Education. p. 389, Fig12-08: Pearson Education. p. 390, Fig12-09: Pearson Education. p. 390, Widget 12.3 Pearson Education. p. 392, Fig12-11: Pearson Education. p. 392, Fig12-12: Based on data from Cummings et al., 2001. p. 393, Fig12-13: Pearson Education. p. 395, Fig12-14: Based on http://stomachpicture.com/wp-content/uploads/2014/08/label-digestive-system-5.jpg. p. 395, Rozin, P., Dow, S., Moscovitch, M., & Rajaram, S. (1998). "What Causes Humans to Begin and End a Meal? A Role for Memory for What has been Eaten, as Evidenced by a Study of Multiple Meal Eating in Amnesic Patients." *Psychological Science*, 9(5), 392–396. p. 397, Fig12-15: Based on Batterham, R. L., ffytche, D. H., Rosenthal, J. M., Zelaya, R. O., et al. "PYY Modulation of Cortical and Hypothalamic Brain Areas Predicts Feeding Behaviour in Humans." *Nature*, 2007, 450, 106–109. p. 398, Fig12-16: Based on data from Wilson, B. E., Meyer, G. E., Cleveland, J. C., and Weigle, D. S. "Identification of Candidate Genes for a Factor Regulating Body Weight in Primates." *American Journal of Physiology*, 1990, 259, R1149–R1155. p. 400, Fig12-18: Pearson Education. p. 401, Fig12-19: Pearson Education. p. 402, Fig12-20: Pearson Education. p. 404, Fig12-21: Pearson Education. p. 405, Fig12-22: Pearson Education. p. 407, TBL12.02: Pearson Education. p. 407, Fig12-23: Based on Blüher, S., Raschpichler, M., Hirsch, W., and Till, H. "A Case Report and Review of the Literature of Laparoscopic Sleeve Gastrectomy in Morbidly Obese Adolescents: Beyond Metabolic Surgery and Visceral Fat Reduction," *Metabolism*, 2013, 62[6], 761–767.). p. 411, Fig12-26: Pearson Education. p. 412, TBL12-03: Pearson Education. p. 414, Martín-Murcia, F., Díaz, A. J. C., & Gonzalez, L. P. (2011). "A Case Study of Anorexia Nervosa and Obsessive Personality Disorder Using Third-generation Behavioral Therapies." *Clinical Case Studies*, 10(3), 198–209. p. 415, TBL12-04: Based on DSM-5, *American Psychiatric Association*, 2013. p. 416, Keys, A., Brozek, J., Henschel, A., Mickelsen, O., and Taylor, H. L. *The Biology of Human Starvation*. Minneapolis, Minn.: University of Minnesota Press, 1950. p. 417, Fig12-28: Data From from Södersten, P., Bergh, C., and Zandian, M. *Hormones and Behavior*, 2006, 50, 572–578).

Chapter 13. p. 419, FigCO13-360: Pearson Education. p. 422, Fig13-01: Pearson Education. p. 423, Fig13-02: Pearson Education. p. 423, Fig13-03: Pearson Education. p. 424, Fig13-04: Pearson Education. p. 425, Fig13-05: Adapted from Atkinson, R. C., & Shiffrin, R. M. (1968). "Human Memory: A Proposed System and Its Control Processes. In K. Spence (Ed.), *The Psychology of Learning and Motivation* (Vol. 2). Oxford, England: Academic Press. p. 426, TBL13-01: Pearson Education. p. 426, Fig13-06: http://www.human-memory.net/types.html diagram by Luke Mastin. p. 427, Fig13-07: Pearson Education. p. 428, Fig13-08: Pearson Education. p. 429, Fig13-09: Pearson Education. p. 430, Fig13-10: Pearson Education. p. 431, Fig13-11: Adapted from Swanson, L. W. *Brain Maps: Structure of the Rat Brain*. New York: Elsevier, 1992. p. 432, Fig13-12: Based on data from Phillips, R. G., and LeDoux, J. E. "Differential Contribution of Amygdala and Hippocampus to Cued and Contextual Fear Conditioning." *Behavioral Neuroscience*, 1992, 106, 274–285. p. 433, TBL13-02: Pearson Education. p. 436, Fig13-14: Pearson Education. p. 436, Fig13-15: Based on data from Kourtzi, A., and Kanwisher, N. "Activation in Human MT/MST by Static Images with Implied Motion." *Journal of Cognitive Neuroscience*, 2000, 12, 48–55. p. 437, Miyashita, Y. "Cognitive Memory: Cellular and Network Machineries and Their Top-down Control." *Science*, 2004, 306, 435–440. p. 439, Fig13-16: Pearson Education. p. 440, Fig13-17: Pearson Education. p. 440, Murre, J. M., J., Graham, K. S., and Hodges, J. R. "Semantic Dementia: Relevance to Connectionist Models of Long-term Memory." *Brain*, 2001, 124, 647–675. p. 441, Fig13-18: Pearson Education. p. 442, Fig13-19: Adapted from Eichenbaum, H. "A Cortical–hippocampal System for Declarative Memory," *Nature Reviews: Neuroscience*, 2000," 1, 41–50. Data from Eichenbaum et al. 1990. p. 444, Fig13-20: Pearson Education. p. 444-431, Based on Milner, B., Corkin, S., and Teuber, H.-L. "Further Analysis of the Hippocampal Amnesic Syndrome: 14-year Follow-up Study of H. M." *Neuropsychologia*, 1968, 6, 317–338. Mindus, P., Rasmussen, S. A., and Lindquist, C., Milner, B. "Memory and the Temporal Regions of the Brain." In *Biology of Memory*, edited by K. H. Pribram and D. E. Broadbent. New York: Academic Press, 1970. Corkin, S., Sullivan, E. V., Twitchell, T. E., and Grove, E. "The Amnesic Patient H. M.: Clinical Observations and Test Performance 28 years after Operation." *Society for Neuroscience Abstracts*, 1981, 7, 235. p. 446, Reed, J. M., and Squire, L. R. "Retrograde Amnesia for Facts and Events: Findings from Four New Cases." *Journal of Neuroscience*, 1998, 18, 3943–3954. p. 446, Fig13-21: Data from Bayley, P. J., Hopkins, R. O., and Squire, L. R. "The Fate of Old Memories after Medial Temporal Lobe Damage. *Journal of Neuroscience*, 2006, 26, 13311–13317. p. 447, Fig13-22: Pearson Education. p. 447, Fig13-23: "Developmental Studies of Visual Recognition of Incomplete Objects." *Perceptual and Motor Skills*, 1960, 11, 289–298. Reproduced with permission of Ammons Scientific Ltd. in the format Republish in a book via Copyright Clearance Center. p. 448, Bayley, P. J., Frascino, J. C., and Squire, L. R. "Robust Habit Learning in the Absence of Awareness and Independent of the Medial Temporal Lobe." *Nature*, 2005, 436, 550–553. p. 449, Fig13-24: http://thebrain.mcgill.ca/flash/i/i_07/i_07_cr/i_07_cr_oub/i_07_cr_oub_1a.jpg. p. 450, Fig13-25: From Bohbot, V. D., Lerch, J., Thorndycraft, B., et al. "Gray Matter Differences Correlate with Spontaneous Strategies in a Human Virtual Navigation task." *Journal of Neuroscience*, 2007, 27, 10078–10083. p. 451, Fig13-27:

Adapted from Wood, E. R., Dudchenko, P. A., Robitsek, R. J., and Eichenbaum, H. "Hippocampal Neurons Encode Information about Different Types of Memory Episodes Occurring in the Same Location," *Neuron*, 2000, 27, 623–633. **p. 453, Fig13-28:** Pearson Education. **p. 454, Fig13-29:** From Berger, T. W. "Long-term Potentiation of Hippocampal Synaptic Transmission Affects Rate of Behavioral Learning." *Science*, 1984, 224, 627–630. Copyright 1984 by the American Association for the Advancement of Science. **p. 454, Fig13-30:** Pearson Education. **p. 454, Fig13-31:** Pearson Education. **p. 455, Fig13-32:** Pearson Education. **p. 456, Fig13-33:** Pearson Education. **p. 457, Fig13-34:** Pearson Education. **p. 458, Fig13-35:** From Nägerl, U. V., Köstinger, G., Anderson, J. C., Martin, K. A. C., and Bonhoeffer, T. *Journal of Neuroscience*, 2007, 27, 8149–8156. Reproduced with permission of Society for Neuroscience in the format Republish in a book via Copyright Clearance Center.

Chapter 14. p. 462, FigCO14-360: Pearson Education. **p. 463, Fig14-01:** Pearson Education. **p. 465, Fig14-02:** Pearson Education. **p. 465, Fig14-03:** From Sotillo, M., Carretié, L., Hinojosa, J. A., Tapia, M., Mercado, F., López-Martín, S., and Albert, J. *Neuroscience Letters*, 2005, 373, 5–9. Copyright © 2005, with permission from Elsevier. **p. 466, Fig14-04:** From Giussani, C., Roux, F. E., Lubrano, V., Gaini, S. M., & Bello, L. (2007). "Review of Language Organisation in Bilingual Patients: What Can We Learn from Direct Brain Mapping?" *Acta Neurochirurgica*, 149, 1109-1116. **p. 467,** Weintraub, Mesulam, and Kramer (1981) . **p. 469, Fig14-06:** Pearson Education. **p. 469,** Obler, L. K., and Gjerlow, K. *Language and the Brain*. Cambridge, England: Cambridge University Press, 1999. **p. 470, Fig14-07:** Pearson Education. **p. 470,** Saffran, E. M., Schwartz, M. F., and Marin, O. S. M. "Evidence from Aphasia: Isolating the Components of a Production Model." In *Language Production*, edited by B. Butterworth. London: Academic Press, 1980. **p. 471,** Saffran, E. M., Schwartz, M. F., and Marin, O. S. M. "Evidence from Aphasia: Isolating the Components of a Production Model." In *Language Production*, edited by B. Butterworth. London: Academic Press, 1980. **p. 472, Fig14-08:** From Dronkers, N. F. "A New Brain Region for Coordinating Speech Articulation." *Nature*, 1996, 384, 159–161. Reprinted with permission. **p. 472,** Kertesz, Andrew, "Chapter 4: The Anatomy of Jargon." In *Jargonaphasia*, edited by Jason W., Brown, Academic Press, 1981. **p. 87. p. 473,** Wernicke, C. *Der Aphasische Symptomenkomplex*. Breslau, Poland: Cohn & Weigert, 1874. **p. 473,** Saffran, E. M., Marin, O. S. M., and Yeni-Komshian, G. H. "An Analysis of Speech Perception in Word Deafness." *Brain and Language*, 1976, 3, 209–228. **p. 474, Fig14-10:** Based on data from Scott, S. K., Blank, E. C., Rosen, S., and Wise, R. J. S. "Identification of a Pathway for Intelligible Speech in the Left Temporal Lobe." *Brain*, 2000, 123, 2400–2406. **p. 475, Fig14-12:** Pearson Education. **p. 476,** Geschwind, N., Quadfasel, F. A., and Segarra, J. M. "Isolation of the Speech Area." *Neuropsychologia*, 1968, 6, 327–340. **p. 477,** Margolin, D. I., Marcel, A. J., and Carlson, N. R. "Common Mechanisms in Dysnomia and Post-semantic Surface Dyslexia: Processing Deficits and Selective Attention." In *Surface Dyslexia: Neuropsychological and Cognitive Studies of Phonological Reading*, edited by M. Coltheart. London: Lawrence Erlbaum Associates, 1985. **p. 477, Fig14-13:** From Hauk, O., Johnsrude, I., and Pulvermüller, F. "Somatotopic Representation of Action Words in Human Motor and Premotor Cortex." *Neuron*, 2004, 41, 301–307. **p. 478, Fig14-15:** Pearson Education. **p. 480, Fig14-18:** From MacSweeney, M., Waters, D., Brammer, M.J., et al. "Phonological Processing in Deaf Signers and the Impact of Age of First Language Acquisition." *NeuroImage*, 2008, 40, 1369–1379. Reprinted by permission. **p. 481,** Watkins, K. E., Smith, S. M., Davis, S., and Howell, P. "Structural and Functional Abnormalities of the Motor System in Developmental Stuttering." *Brain*, 2008, 131, 50–59. **p. 481, Fig14-20:** From Neumann, K., Preibisch, C., Euler, H. A., von Gudenberg, A. W., Lanfermann, H., Gall, V., and Giraud, A.-L., "Cortical Plasticity Associated with Stuttering Therapy." *Journal of Fluency Disorders*, 2005, 30, 23–39. **p. 482, TBL14-01:** Pearson Education. **p. 484, Fig14-21:** Pearson Education. **p. 484, Fig14-22:** From Mao-Draayer Y, Panitch H. "Alexia without Agraphia In Multiple Sclerosis: Case Report with MRI Localization." *Multiple Sclerosis* 2004; 10: 705–707. **p. 485, Fig14-23:** Pearson Education. **p. 486, Fig14-24:** Pearson Education. **p. 486, Fig14-25:** Pearson Education. **p. 487, Fig14-26:** Pearson Education. **p. 487, TBL14-02:** Pearson Education. **p. 488, Fig14-27:** Pearson Education. **p. 488, Fig14-28:** Adapted from Devlin, J. T., Jamison, H. L., Gonnerman, L. M., and Matthews, P. M. "The Role of the Posterior Fusiform Gyrus in Reading," *Journal of Cognitive Neuroscience*, 2006, 18, 911–922. **p. 489,** Dehaene, S., Nakamura, K., Jobert, A., et al. "Why Do Children Make Mirror Errors in Reading? Neural Correlates of Mirror Invariance in the Visual Word form Area." *NeuroImage*, 2010, 49, 1837–1848. **p. 493, TBL14-03:** Pearson Education.

Chapter 15. p. 497, FigCO15-360: Pearson Education. **p. 498, Fig15-01:** Based on http://m.everythingmaths.co.za/science/lifesciences/grade-10/03-cell-division/images/5ed8b922531822fe190fa496d527e344.png. **p. 498, Fig15-02:** Courtesy of A. D'Agostino, Good Samaritan Hospital, Portland, Oregon. **p. 499, TBL15-01:** Pearson Education. **p. 500, TBL15-02:** Pearson Education. **p. 501, Fig15-04:** Pearson Education. **p. 502, Fig15-05:** Pearson Education. **p. 504, Fig15-06:** Pearson Education. **p. 505, Fig15-07:** Based on data from Hacke, W., Albers, G., Al-Rawi, Y., Bogousslavsky, J., et al. "The Desmoteplase in Acute Ischemic Stroke Trial (DIAS): A Phase II MRI-Based 9-hour Window Acute Stroke Thrombolysis Trial with Intravenous Desmoteplase." *Stroke*, 2005, 36, 66–73. **p. 506, Fig15-09:** Based on data of Chimowitz, M. I., Lynn, M. J, Derdeyn, C. P., et al. "Stending Versus Aggressive Medical Therapy for Intracranial Arterial Stenosis." *New England Journal of Medicine*, 2011, 365, 993–1003. **p. 507, Fig15-10:** Based on data from Taub, E., Uswatte, F., King, D. K., Morris, D., et al. "A Placebo-Controlled Trial of Constraint-Induced Movement Therapy for Upper Extremity After Stroke." *Stroke*, 2006, 37, 1045–1049. **p. 512, Fig15-13:** Pearson Education. **p. 513, TBL15-03:** Pearson Education. **p. 514,** Prusiner, S. B. "Novel Proteinaceous Infectious Particles Cause Scrapie." *Science*, 1982, 216, 136–144. **p. 514, Fig15-14:** Pearson Education. **p. 516, Fig15-16:** Pearson Education. **p. 518, Fig15-17:** Pearson Education. **p. 519, Fig15-18:** Pearson Education. **p. 520, Fig15-19:** Based on Okun, M. S. "Deep-brain Stimulation for Parkinson's Disease." *New England Journal of Medicine*, 2012, 367[16], 1529–1538. **p. 521, Fig15-21:** Based on http://www.nist.gov/mml/bmd/images/11MML010_huntingtons_disease_LR.jpg. **p. 525, Fig15-26:** Pearson Education. **p. 527, Fig15-28:** Based on data from Hock, C., Konietzko, U., Streffer, J. R., Tracy, J., et al. "Antibodies Against ß-amyloid Slow Cognitive Decline in Alzheimer's Disease." *Neuron*, 2003, 38, 547–554. **p. 530, Fig15-30:** Based on http://www.sundaytimes.lk/130602/uploads/brain-fever.jpg.

Chapter 16. p. 535, CO16-360: Pearson Education. **p. 536, Fig16-01:** Based on data from Häfner, H., Riecher-Rössler, A., An Der Heiden, W., et al. "Generating and Testing a Causal Explanation of the Gender Difference in Age at First Onset of Schizophrenia." *Psychological Medicine*, 1993, 23, 925–940. **p. 537, TBL16-01:** Pearson Education. **p. 538, Fig16-02:** Pearson Education. **p. 539, Fig16-03:** Based on data from Weinberger, D. R., and Wyatt, R. J. "Brain Morphology in Schizophrenia: In Vivo Studies." In *Schizophrenia as a Brain Disease*, edited by F. A., Henn and H. A. Nasrallah. New York: Oxford University Press, 1982. **p. 540, Fig16-04:** Based on data from Kendell, R. E., and Adams, W. "Unexplained Fluctuations in the Risk for Schizophrenia by Month and Year of Birth." *British Journal of Psychiatry*, 1991, 158, 758–763. **p. 542, TBL16-02:** Pearson Education. **p. 543, TBL16-03:** Adapted from Schiffman, J., Ekstrom, M., LaBrie, J., Schulsinger, F., et al. "Minor Physical Anomalies and Schizophrenia Spectrum Disorders: A Prospective Investigation." *American Journal of Psychiatry*, 2002, 159, 238–243. **p. 543, Fig16-05:** Based on data from Weinberger, D. R., and Wyatt, R. J. "Brain Morphology in Schizophrenia: In Vivo Studies." In *Schizophrenia as a Brain Disease*, edited by F. A., Henn and H. A. Nasrallah. New York: Oxford University Press, 1982. **p. 543, Fig16-06:** Based on data from Hulshoff-Pol, H. E., Schnack, H. G., Bertens, M. G., van Haren, N. E., et al. "Volume Changes in Gray Matter in Patients with Schizophrenia." *American Journal of Psychiatry*, 2002, 159, 244–250. **p. 546, Fig16-09:** Based on data from Laruelle, M., Abi-Dargham, A., Van Dyck, C. H., Gil, R., et al. "Single Photon Emission Computerized Tomography Imaging of Amphetamine-induced Dopamine Release in Drug-free Schizophrenic Subjects." *Proceedings of the National Academy of Sciences*, USA, 1996, 93, 9235–9240. **p. 547, Fig16-10:** Based on data from Jentsch, J. D., Redmond, D. E., Elsworth, J. D., Taylor, J. R., et al. "Enduring Cognitive Deficits and Cortical Dopamine

Dysfunction in Monkeys after Long-term Administration of Phency-clidine." *Science*, 1997, 277,953–955. **p. 548, Fig16-11:** Pearson Education. **p. 549, Fig16-12:** Pearson Education. **p. 549, Fig16-13:** Pearson Education. **p. 551,** Styron, W. *Darkness Visible: A Memoir of Madness.* New York: Random House, 1990, **pp. 52–53. p. 554, Fig16-14:** Pearson Education. **p. 554, Fig16-15:** Based on data from Zarate, C. A., Jaskaran, B. S., Carlson, P. J., Brutsche, N. E., et al. "A Randomized Trial of a N-methyl-D-aspartate Antagonist in Treatment-resistant Major Depression." *Archives of General Psychiatry*, 2006, 63,856–864. **p. 556, Fig16-16:** Based on Stahl, S. M. (2008). *Antipsychotics and Mood Stabilizers: Stahl's Essential Psychopharmacology.* Cambridge University Press. **p. 558, Fig16-18:** "Tracings of Brain Activity" from (a) Mayberg et al. (2005), (b) Kito et al. (2011), (c) Pardo et al. (2008), (d) Mayberg et al. (2002), (e) Kennedy et al. (2007), (f) Mayberg et al. (2002). **p. 560, Fig16-19:** Based on data from Caspi, A., Sugden, K., Moffitt, T. E., Taylor, A., et al. "Influence of Life Stress on Depression: Moderation by a Polymorphism in the 5-HTT Gene." *Science*, 2003, 301, 386–389. **p. 561, Fig16-21:** From Gillin, J. C., and Borbély, A. A. "Sleep: A Neurobiological Window on Affective Disorders," *Trends in Neurosciences*, 1985, 8, 537–542. **p. 562, Fig16-22:** Based on data from Landsness et al. 2001. **p. 562, Fig16-23:** Based on data from Wu, J. C., and Bunney, W. E. "The Biological Basis of an Antidepressant Response to Sleep Deprivation and Relapse: Review and Hypothesis." *American Journal of Psychiatry*, 1990, 147, 14–21. **p. 563, Fig16-24:** Based on data from González. M. M., and Aston-Jones, G. "Circadian Regulation of Arousal: Role of the Noradrenergic Locus Coeruleus System and Light Exposure." *Sleep*, 2006, 29, 1327–1336., Gonzalez and Aston-Jones, 2008. **p. 564, Fig16-25:** Based on data from Lewy, A. K., Lefler, B. J., Emens, J. S., and Bauer, V. K. "The Circadian Basis of Winter Depression." *Proceedings of the National Academy of Sciences*, USA, 2006, 103, 7414–7419.

Chapter 17. p. 568, CO17-360: Pearson Education. **p. 569, Fig17-01:** Pearson Education. **p. 571, Fig17-02:** Based on data from Cobb, S., and Rose, R. M. "Hypertension, Peptic Ulcer, and Diabetes in Air Traffic Controllers." *Journal of the American Medical Association*, 1973, 224, 489–492. **p. 571, Fig17-03:** Based on data from Kiecolt-Glaser, J. K., Marucha, P. T., Malarkey, W. B., Mercado, A. M., et al. "Slowing of Wound Healing by Psychological Stress." *Lancet*, 1995, 346, 1194–1196. **p. 572, Fig17-04:** Based on data from Diamond, D. M., Park, C. R., Heman, K. L., and Rose, G. M. "Exposing Rats to a Predator Impairs Spatial Working Memory in the Radial Arm Water Maze." *Hippocampus*, 1999, 9, 542–552. **p. 573, Fig17-05:** Pearson Education. **p. 573, Fig17-06:** Based on data from Salm, A. K., Pavelko, M., Krouse, E. M., Webster, W., et al. "Lateral Amygdaloid Nucleus Expansion in Adult Rats is Associated with Exposure to Prenatal Stress." *Developmental Brain Research*, 2004, 148, 159–167. **p. 574, Fig17-07:** Based on data from Barbazanges, A., Piazza, P. V., Le Moal, M., and Maccari, S. "Maternal Glucocorticoid Secretion Mediates Long-term Effects of Prenatal Stress." *Journal of Neuroscience*,1996, 16, 3943–3949. **p. 574, Fig17-08:** Pearson Education. **p. 575, Fig17-09:** Pearson Education. **p. 576, Fig17-10:** Based on data from Glaser, R., Sheridan, J., Malarkey, W. B., MacCallum, R. C., and Kiecolt-Glaser, J. K., "Chronic Stress Modulates the Immune Response to a Pneumococcal Pneumonia Vaccine," *Psychosomatic Medicine*, 2000, 62, 804–807. **p. 576, Fig17-11:** Based on data from Stone, A. A., Reed, B. R., and Neale, J. M. "Changes in Daily Event Frequency Precede Episodes of Physical Symptoms." *Journal of Human Stress*, 1987, 13, 70–74. **p. 577, Fig17-12:** Based on data from Cohen, S., Tyrrell, D. A. J., and Smith, A. P. "Psychological Stress and Susceptibility to the Common Cold." *New England Journal of Medicine*, 1991, 325, 606–612. **p. 578,** *Diagnostic and Statistical Manual of Mental Disorders, 5th Edition: DSM-5.* Copyright © 2013 American Psychiatric Association. P. 274. **p. 579, TBL17-01:** American Psychiatric Association, 2013. **p. 579, Fig17-13:** Based on data from Kolassa et al. 2010. **p. 580, Fig17-14:** Based on data from Gilbertson, M. W., Shenton, M. E., Ciszewski, A., Kasai, K., et al. "Smaller Hippocampal Volume Predicts Pathologic Vulnerability to Psychological Trauma." *Nature Neuroscience*, 2002, 5, 1242–1247. **p. 580, Fig17-15:** Based on data from Shin, L. M., Wright, C. I., Cannistraro, P. A., Wedig, M. M., et al. "A Functional Magnetic Resonance Imaging Study of Amygdala and Medial Prefrontal Cortex Responses to Overtly Presented Fearful Faces in Post-traumatic Stress Disorder." *Archives of General Psychiatry*, 2005, 62, 273–281. **p. 581, Fig17-16:** Based on data from Boggio,

P. S., Rocha, M., Oliveira, M. O., et al. "Noninvasive Brain Stimulation with High-frequency and Low-intensity Repetitive Transcranial Magnetic Stimulation Treatment for Posttraumatic Stress Disorder." *Journal of Clinical Psychiatry*, 2010, 71, 992–999. **p. 583, TBL17-02:** American Psychiatric Association, 2013. **p. 585, Fig17-17:** Pearson Education. **p. 585, Fig17-18:** Based on data from Asnis Asnis, G. M., Hameedi, F. A., Goddard, A. W., Potkin, S. G., et al. "Fluvoxamine in the Treatment of Panic Disorder: A Multi-center, Double-blind, Placebo-controlled Study in Outpatients." *Psychiatry Research*, 2001, 103, 1–14. **p. 586, Fig17-19:** Based on data from Ressler et al. 2004 [acrophobia], Guastella et al. 2010b [social phobia], and Otto et al. 2010 [panic disorder]. **p. 588,** Fiske, A. P., and Haslam, N. "Is Obsessive-compulsive Disorder a Pathology of the Human Disposition to Perform Socially Meaningful Rituals? Evidence of Similar Content." *Journal of Nervous and Mental Disease*, 1997, 185, 211–222., p. 211. **p. 588, TBL17-03:** Pearson Education. **p. 589, Fig17-20:** Based on data from Perlmutter, S. J., Garvey, M. A., Castellanos, X., et al. "A Case of Pediatric Autoimmune Neuropsychiatric Disorders Associated with Streptococcal Infections." *American Journal of Psychiatry*, 1998, 155, 1592–1598. **p. 590, Fig17-21:** Based on data from Wilhelm et al. 2008. **p. 591, Fig17-22:** Pearson Education. **p. 593, TBL17-04:** American Psychiatric Association, 2013. **p. 593,** *Diagnostic and Statistical Manual of Mental Disorders, 5th Edition: DSM-5.* Copyright © 2013 American Psychiatric Association. P. 274. **p. 594,** Frith, U., Morton, J., and Leslie, A. M. "The Cognitive Basis of a Biological Disorder: Autism." *Trends in Neuroscience*, 1991, 14, 433–438. **p. 594,** Castelli, F., Frith, C., Happé, F., and Frith, U. "Autism, Asperger Syndrome and Brain Mechanisms for the Attribution of Mental States to Animated Shapes." *Brain*, 2002, 125, 1839–1849. (p. 1843). **p. 595, Fig17-23:** Based on data from Castelli, F., Frith, C., Happé, F., and Frith, U. "Autism, Asperger Syndrome and Brain Mechanisms for the Attribution of Mental States to Animated Shapes. *Brain*, 2002, 125, 1839–1849. **p. 595, Fig17-24:** Pearson Education. **p. 595, Fig17-25:** Adapted from Hollander, E., Anagnostou, E., Chaplin, W., Esposito, K., et al. "Striatal Volume on Magnetic Resonance Imaging and Repetitive Behaviors in Autism." *Biological Psychiatry*, 2005, 58, 226–232. **p. 597,** American Psychiatric Association, 2013, **pp. 59–60. p. 598, TBL17-05:** American Psychiatric Association, 2013. **p. 598, Fig17-26:** Pearson Education. **p. 599, Fig17-27:** Based on data from Mattay et al. 2003. **p. 599, Fig17-28:** Pearson Education.

Chapter 18. p. 604, TBL18-01: American Psychiatric Association, 2013. **p. 605, CO18-360:** Pearson Education. **p. 606, TBL18-02:** Adapted from Hyman, S. E., and Malenka, R. C. "Addiction and The Brain: The Neurobiology of Compulsion and Its Persistence." *Nature Reviews: Neuroscience*, 2001, 2, 695–703. **p. 606, Fig18-01:** Adapted from Feldman, R. S., Meyer, J. S., and Quenzer, L. F. *Principles of Neuropsychopharmacology.* Sunderland, MA: Sinauer Associates, 1997; after Jones, R. T. NIDA Research Mono-graphs, 1990, 99, 30–41. **p. 608, Fig18-02:** Pearson Education. **p. 609, Fig18-03:** Based on data from Belin, D., and Everitt, B. J. "Cocaine Seeking Habits Depend upon Dopamine-dependent Serial Connectivity Linking the Ventral with the Dorsal Striatum." *Neuron*, 2008, 57, 432–441. **p. 609, Fig18-04:** Based on data from Volkow, N. D., Wang, G.-J., Fowler, J. S., et al. "Addiction: Beyond Dopamine Reward Circuitry." *Proceedings of the National Academy of Sciences*, USA, 2011, 108, 15037–15042. **p. 610, Fig18-05:** Based on data from Mathalon, D. H., Pfefferbaum, A., Lim, K. O., Rosenbloom, M. J., et al. "Compounded Brain Volume Deficits in Schizophrenia-alcoholism Comorbidity." *Archives of General Psychiatry*, 2003, 60, 245–252. **p. 611, Fig18-06:** Based on data from Weiser, M., Reichenberg, A., Grotto, I., Yasvitzky, R., et al. "Higher Rates of Cigarette Smoking in Male Adolescents Before the Onset of Schizophrenia: A Historical-prospective Cohort Study." *American Journal of Psychiatry*, 2004, 161, 1219–1223. **p. 612, TBL18-03:** Pearson Education. **p. 613, Fig18-07:** Based on data from Kalivas, P. W., Peters, J., and Knackstedt, L. "Animal Models and Brain Circuits in Drug Addiction." *Molecular Interventions*, 2006, 6, 339–344. **p. 614, Fig18-08:** Based on data from Bolla, K., Ernst, M., Kiehl, K., Mouratidis, M., et al. "Prefrontal Cortical Dysfunction in Abstinent Cocaine Abusers." *Journal of Neuropsychiatry and Clinical Neuroscience*, 2004, 16, 456–464. **p. 614, Fig18-09:** Based on data from Kosten, T., Miserendino, M. J. D., and Kehoe, P. "Enhanced Acquisition of Cocaine Self-administration in Adult Rats with Neonatal Isolation Stress Experience." *Brain Research*, 2000, 875, 44–50. **p. 615, Fig18-10:**

Adapted from Goldman, D., Oroszi, G., and Ducci, F. "The Genetics of Addictions: Uncovering the Genes." *Nature Reviews Genetics*, 2005, 6, 521–532. **p. 616, Fig18-11:** Based on Meyer, J. S., and Quenzer, L. F., *Psychopharmacology: Drugs, the Brain, and Behavior*, Sunderland, MA: Sinauer Associates, 2005. **p. 618, Fig18-12:** Pearson Education. **p. 619, Fig18-13:** Based on data from Matthes et al. 1996. **p. 620, Fig18-14:** Based on McCann, U. D., Wong, D. F., Yokoi, F., et al. *Journal of Neuroscience*, 1998, 18, 8417–8422. **p. 620, Fig18-15:** Based on data from Di Ciano, P., Coury, A., Depoortere, R. Y., Egilmez, Y., et al. "Comparison of Changes in Extracellular Dopamine Concentrations in the Nucleus Accumbens During Intravenous Self-administration of Cocaine or D-amphetamine." *Behavioural Pharmacology*, 1995, 6, 311–322. **p. 621, Fig18-16:** Based on data from Damsma, G., Day, J., and Fibiger, H. C. "Lack of Tolerance to Nicotine-induced Dopamine Release in the Nucleus Accumbens." *European Journal of Pharmacology*,1989, 168, 363–368. **p. 622, Fig18-17:** Based on data of Fowler, C., Lu, Q., Johnson, P. M., et al. "Habenular a5 Nicotinic Receptor Subunit Signaling Controls Nicotine Intake." *Nature*, 2011, 471, 597–601. **p. 622-609,** Republished with Permission of American Association for the Advancement of Science (AAAS) from, "Damage to the Insula Disrupts Addiction to Cigarette Smoking" by Naqvi, N. H., Rudrauf, D., Damasio, H., and Bechara A - *Science*, 2007, 315, 531–534. Permission conveyed through Copyright Clearance Center, Inc. **p. 623,** Republished with Permission of American Association for the Advancement of Science (AAAS) from, "Damage to the Insula Disrupts Addiction to Cigarette Smoking" by Naqvi, N. H., Rudrauf, D., Damasio, H., and Bechara A. *Science*, 2007, 315, 531–531. Permission conveyed through Copyright Clearance Center, Inc. **p. 623, Fig18-18:** From Naqvi, N. H., Rudrauf, D., Damasio, H., and Bechara, A., "Damage to the Insula Disrupts Addiction to Cigarette Smoking." *Science*, 2007, 315, 531–534. **p. 623, Fig18-19:** Based on data of Forget, B., Pushparaj, A., and Le Foll, B. "Granular Insular Cortex Inactivation as a Novel Therapeutic Strategy for Nicotine Addiction." *Biological Psychiatry*, 2010, 68, 265–271. **p. 626, Fig18-21:** Based on data from Heinz et al., 2005. **p. 626, Fig18-22:** Based on data from Chen et al., 1990. **p. 627, Fig18-23:** Based on data of Morgan, C. J. A., Freeman, T. P., Schafer, G. L., and Curran, H. V. "Camnnabidiol Attenuates the Appetitive Effects of Δ9-Tetrahydrocannabinol in Humans Smoking their Chosen Cannabis." *Neuropsychopharmacology*, 2010, 35, 1879–1885. **p. 629, Fig18-24:** Based on data from Fudala, P. J., Bridge, T. P., Herbert, S., Williford, W. O., et al. "Office-based Treatment of Opiate Addiction with a Sublingual-tablet Formulation of Buprenorphine and Naloxone." *New England Journal of Medicine*, 2003, 349, 949–958. **p. 630, Fig18-25:** Based on data from Nides, M., Oncken, C., Gonzales, D., Rennard, S., et al. "Smoking Cessation with Varenicline, a Selective a4ß2 Nicotinic Receptor Partial Agonist: Results from a 7-week, Randomized, Placebo- and Bupropion Controlled Trial with 1-year Follow-up." *Archives of Internal Medicine*, 2006, 166, 1561–1568. **p. 631, Fig18-26:** Based on data from O'Brien, C. P., Volpicelli, L. A., and Volpicelli, J. R. "Naltrexone in the Treatment of Alcoholism: A Clinical Review." *Alcohol*, 1996, 13, 35–39.

Photo Credits

Chapter 1 p. 015, CO-01: Vitstudio/Shutterstock. **p. 018, 01-01:** Jaroslav74/Shutterstock. **p. 019, Fig01-01:** Photo Researchers/Alamy. **p. 019, 01-02:** Ioannis Pantzi\Shutterstock. **p. 020, Fig01-02:** The Print Collector/Alamy. **p. 023, Fig01-04:** North Wind Picture Archives. **p. 025, 1-3:** Dimarion/Shutterstock. **p. 029, 01-04:** Everett Collection/Shutterstock. **p. 030, Fig01-09:** IndiaPicture/Alamy. **p. 032, Fig01-10a:** Steve Debenport/Getty Images. **p. 032, Fig01-10b:** Fotostorm/Getty Images. **p. 032, Fig01-10c:** Hero Images/Getty Images. **p. 032, Fig01-10d:** WavebreakMediaMicro/Fotolia.

Chapter 2 p. 035, CO-02: Juan Gaertner/Shutterstock. **p. 043, 2.3:** Designua/Shutterstock. **p. 049, 02-02:** Anya Ku/Shutterstock. **p. 050, 02-04:** Pearson Education Ltd. **p. 053, 02-06:** Vit Krajicek/123rf. **p. 054, 02-07:** Peter Lamb/123rf. **p. 065, 02-11:** Hung Chung Chih/Shutterstock.

Chapter 3 p. 70, CO-03: ktsdesign/Fotolia. **p. 089, Fig03-17:** From Hofer, S., and Frahm, J. NeuroImage, 2006, 32, 989–994. Reprinted with permission.

Chapter 4 p. 102, CO-04: Cultura Rm/Alamy. **p. 111, 04-01:** brozova/123rf.com. **p. 121, 04-03:** JPC-PROD/Shutterstock.

Chapter 5 p. 132, CO-05: Mark N. Miller/University of California, Sf/Getty Images. **p. 136, Fig05-01a:** Benno Roozendaal, University of California. **p. 136, Fig05-01b:** Benno Roozendaal, University of California. **p. 138, Fig05-04_new:** Pearson Education. **p. 139, Fig05-06:** Carlson, Neil. **p. 139, Fig05-07:** From Rockel, A. J., and Jones, E. G. *Journal of Comparative* Neurology, 1973, 147, 61–92. Reprinted with permission. **p. 139, Fig05-05:** Source: © Pearson Education, Inc. **p. 140, Fig05-08_new:** David Scharf/Science Source . **p. 141, Fig05-09b:** Courtesy Dr. William E. Armstrong. **p. 142, Fig05-11:** Courtesy of Kirsten Nielsen Ricciardi and Jeffrey Blaustein, University of Massachusetts. **p. 143, Fig05-12:** Courtesy of Yvon Delville, University of Massachusetts Medical School. **p. 145, Fig05-16:** Legacy Good Samaritan Health Center. **p. 145, Fig05-16:** Legacy Good Samaritan Health Center. **p. 145, Fig05-16:** Legacy Good Samaritan Health Center. **p. 145, Fig05-16:** Legacy Good Samaritan Health Center. **p. 145, Fig05-16:** Legacy Good Samaritan Health Center. **p. 146, Fig05-17:** Popova Olga/Fotolia. **p. 146, Fig05-18:** Figure 3; Wakana S, Jiang H, Nagae-Poetscher L. M., et al. "Fiber Tract-based Atlas of Human White Matter Anatomy." *Radiology* 2004;230:77-87. Radiological Society of North America. **p. 151, Fig05-21:** Courtesy of Marc Tetel, Skidmore College. **p. 151, Fig05-22:** Courtesy of the Brookhaven National Laboratory and the State University of New York, Stony Brook. **p. 152, UNF05-01:** From Shaywitz, B. A., et al. *Nature*, 1995, 373, 607–609. Reprinted with permission. **p. 152, 05-01:** Levent Konuk/Shutterstock. **p. 153, Fig5-24:** Kastner Lab, Princeton University. **p. 156, Fig05-25a:** Geert DeVries, University of Massachusetts. **p. 156, Fig05-25b:** David A. Morilak and Roland Ciaranello, Nancy Pritzker Laboratory of Developmental and Molecular Neurobiology, Stanford Univ. School of Medicine. **p. 158, Fig05-27a:** Pearson Education. **p. 158, Fig05-27b:** Pearson Education.

Chapter 6 p. 163, CO-06: Scenics & Science/Alamy. **p. 166, Fig06-01:** Pintos, © Bev Doolittle, The Greenwich Workshop, Inc. **p. 167, 06-01:** Andrea Danti/Shutterstock. **p. 169, 06-02:** designua/123RF. **p. 176, Fig06-13a:** From Sincich, L. C., and Horton, J. C. *Annual Review of Neuroscience*, Volume 28 © 2005, 303–326 by Annual Reviews www.annualreviews.org. **p. 177, 06-06:** Aliaksandr Mazurkevich\123RF. **p. 178, 06-07:** 123rf.com. **p. 184, Fig06-22:** Pearson Education. **p. 186, Fig06-24:** Figure 2 from Zeki, Semir, et al. "The Neurological Basis of Conscious Color Perception in a Blind Patient." *Proceedings of the National Academy of Sciences* 96.24 (1999): 14124-14129. Copyright (1999) National Academy of Sciences, U.S.A. **p. 189, Fig06-26:** From Harmon, L. D., and Julesz, B. Science, 1973, 180, 1191–1197. Copyright 1973 by the American Association for the Advancement of Science. Reprinted with permission. **p. 190, Fig06-27:** Bell, A. H., Hadj-Bouziane, F., Frihauf, J. B., Tootell, R. B., & Ungerleider, L. G. (2009). "Object Representations in the Temporal Cortex of Monkeys and Humans as Revealed by Functional Magnetic Resonance Imaging." *Journal of Neurophysiology*, 101(2)., **p. 191, Fig06-28:** Erich Lessing/Art Resource. **p. 192, Fig06-30a:** Ravi S., Menon, Melvyn A., Goodale, Jennifer K. E. Steeves, Jody C. Culham, A. David Milner, and G. Keith Humphrey, "Behavioral and Neuroimaging Evidence for a Contribution of Color and Texture Information to Scene Classification in a Patient with Visual Form Agnosia." *Journal of Cognitive Neuroscience*, 16:6 (July-August, 2004), Figure 6, pp. 958. © 2004 by the Massachusetts Institute of Technology. **p. 192, Fig06-30b:** Ravi S., Menon, Melvyn A., Goodale, Jennifer K. E. Steeves, Jody C. Culham, A. David Milner, and G. Keith Humphrey, "Behavioral and Neuroimaging Evidence for a Contribution of Color and Texture Information to Scene Classification in a Patient with Visual Form Agnosia." *Journal of Cognitive Neuroscience*, 16:6 (July-August, 2004), Figure 6, p. 958. © 2004 by the Massachusetts Institute of Technology. **p. 193, Fig06-31:** Golijeh Golaral, Department of Psychology, Stanford University. **p. 193, Fig06-32:** Farroni, T., Johnson, M.H., Mennon, E., Zulian, L., Faraguna, D., and Csibra, G. *Proceedings of the National Academy of Sciences*, USA, 2005, 102, 17245-17250. **p. 194, Fig06-33:** Source: Grelotti, D. J., Gauthier, I., & Schultz, R. T. (2002). "Social Interest and the Development of Cortical

Face Specialization: What Autism Teaches us About Face Processing." *Developmental Psychobiology*, 40(3),213–225. **p. 195, 06-09:** Veronica Lara/Shutterstock.

Chapter 7 p. 202, CO-07: C.J. Guerin/Science Source. **p. 211, Fig07-10:** Andreas Bastian/Agencja Fotograficzna Caro/Alamy. **p. 217, Fig07-16:** Claude Alain, Yu He, and Cheryl Grady, "The Contribution of the Inferior Parietal Lobe to Auditory Spatial Working Memory." *Journal of Cognitive Neuroscience*, 20:2 (February, 2008), Figure 3, pp. 292. © 2008 by the Massachusetts Institute of Technology. **p. 222, Fig07-21a:** Hudspeth, A.J. **p. 222, Fig07-21b:** Hudspeth, A.J. **p. 227, 7-3:** Alice Day/Shutterstock. **p. 229, Fig07-24a:** Nakamura, J., Endo, K., Sumida, T., and Hasegawa, T. Cortex, 1998, 34, 375–388. **p. 229, Fig07-24b:** Reed, C. L., Caselli, R. J., and Farah, M. J. Brain, 1996, 119, 875–888. Reprinted with permission. **p. 231, Fig07-26:** From Rainville, P., Duncan, G. H., Price, D. D., Carrier, Benoit, and Bushnell, M. C. *Science*, 1997, 277, 968–971. Copyright © American Association for the Advancement of Science. Reprinted with permission. **p. 232, Fig07-27:** Agnes Mengin/MediaforMedical/Alamy. **p. 235, 7-4:** WilleeCole/Shutterstock.

Chapter 8 p. 245, CO-08: Blickwinkel/Alamy. **p. 271, Fig08-20:** From Iacoboni, M., Molnar-Szakacs, I., Gallese, V., et al. *PLoS Biology*, 2005, 3, e79 . **p. 271, Fig08-21:** From Connolly, J.D., Andersen, R. A., and Goodale, M.A. Experimental Brain Research, 2003, 153, 140–145. Reprinted with permission Copyright Clearance Center.

Chapter 9 p. 275, CO-09: Bsip/Newscom. **p. 278, Fig09-01:** Muammer Mujdat Uzel/Getty Images . **p. 282, 09-01:** DavidEwingPhotography/Shutterstock. **p. 299, 09-03:** Monkey Business Images/Shutterstock. **p. 300, 09-04:** rSnapshotPhotos/Shutterstock. **p. 302, 9-7:** Helder Almeida/Shutterstock. **p. 304, Fig09-25:** Geert DeVries, University of Massachusetts.

Chapter 10 p. 310, CO-10: Jose Luis Calvo/Shutterstock. **p. 333, 10-4:** blojfo/Shutterstock. **p. 335, Fig10-19:** From Zhou, J.-N., Hofman, M. A., Gooren, L. J. G., and Swaab, D. F. "A Sex Difference in the Human Brain and Its Relation to Transsexuality." *Nature*, 1995, 378, 68–70. Reprinted with permission Copyright Clearance Center, Inc. **p. 338, Fig10-20:** Neil Carlson. **p. 339, Fig10-21:** Neil Carlson.

Chapter 11 p. 344, CO-11: Juan Gaertner/Shutterstock. **p. 360, Fig11-14:** Everett Collection Historical / Alamy. **p. 361, Fig11-15:** Nili reference: Nili, U., Goldberg, H., Weizman, A., & Dudai, Y. (2010). "Fear Thou Not: Activity of Frontal and Temporal Circuits in Moments of Real-life Courage." *Neuron*, 66(6), 2010 Elsevier Inc. Published by Elsevier Inc. **p. 362, 11-2:** set/Shutterstock. **p. 366, Fig11-18:** Paul Ekman Group, LLC. **p. 367, 11-3:** William Perugini/Shutterstock. **p. 369, Fig11-22:** From Vuilleumier, P., Armony, J. L., Driver, J., and Dolan, R. J. *Nature Neuroscience*, 2003, 6, 624–631. **p. 370, Fig11-24:** From Whalen, P. J., Kagan, J., Cook, R. G., et al. *Science*, 2004, 306, 2061. Copyright 2004 American Association for the Advancement of Science. **p. 373, Fig11-27:** Curtis, V., Aunger, R., and Rabie, T., Biology Letters, 2004, 271, S131–S133; Royal Society of London. Permission by Copyright Clearance Center. **p. 373, Fig11-28:** Hulton-Deutsch Collection/Historical/Corbis. **p. 378, Fig.11-31a:** Ariel Skelley/Getty Images . **p. 378, Fig.11-31b:** Christa Renee/Getty Images . **p. 378, Fig.11-31c:** Jennie Woodcock; Reflections Photolibrary/CORBIS.

Chapter 12 p. 380, CO-12: Don W. Fawcett/Science Source. **p. 385, Fig12-05:** From Egan. G., Silk, T., Zamarripa, F., et al. *Proceedings of the National Academy of Sciences*, USA, 2004, 100, 15241-15246. **p. 391, Fig12-10:** Elitravo/Fotolia. **p. 398, Fig12-17:** AP Photo/The Rockefeller University. **p. 392, 12-2:** ollyy/Shutterstock. **p. 403, 12-4:** Kesu/Shutterstock. **p. 403, 12-5:** Pearson Education. **p. 408, Fig12-24:** AP Photo/Michael Conroy. **p. 410, Fig12-25a:** From Licinto, J., Caglayan, S., Ozata, M., et al. *Proceedings of the National Academy of Sciences*, USA, 2004, 101, 4531-4536. **p. 410, Fig12-25b:** From Licinto, J., Caglayan, S., Ozata, M., et al. *Proceedings of the National Academy of Sciences*, USA, 2004, 101, 4531-4536. **p. 414, 12-8:** tommaso lizzul/Shutterstock. **p. 416, Fig12-27:** Source: © Pearson Education, Inc.

Chapter 13 p. 419, CO-13: Lculig/Shutterstock. **p. 421, 13-1:** Athanasia Nomikou/Shutterstock. **p. 425, 13-4:** Dudarev Mikhail/Shutterstock.

p. 445, 13-5: CLIPAREA | Custom media/Shutterstock. **p. 455, 13-6:** SubDural12.

Chapter 14 p. 460, CO-14: Photo Quest /Science Photo Library/Corbis. **p. 464, 14-1:** Balefire/Shutterstock. **p. 466, Fig14-04:** Figure 1 From Giussani, C., Roux, F. E., Lubrano, V., Gaini, S. M., & Bello, L. (2007). "Review of Language Organisation in Bilingual Patients: What can we Learn from Direct Brain Mapping? *Acta Neurochirurgica*, 149(11), 1109–1116. **p. 467, 14-2:** Golden Pixels LLC/Shutterstock. **p. 468, Fig14-05:** From Meyer, M., Alter, K., Friederici, A. D., Lohmann, G., and von Cramon, D. Y. Human Brain Mapping, 2002, 17, 73–88. Reprinted with permission. **p. 472, Fig14-08b:** From Dronkers, N. F., Nature, 1996, 384, 159–161. Reprinted with permission. **p. 474, Fig14-11:** From Pulvermuller, F., Huss, M., Kherif, F. et al. *Proceedings of the National Academy of Sciences*, USA, 2006, 103, 7865-7870. **p. 479, Fig14-16:** From Catani, M., Jones, D. K., and ffytche, D. H. *Annals of Neurology*, 2005, 57, 8–16. Reprinted with permission. **p. 480, Fig14-17:** From Iacoboni, M., Woods, R. P., Brass, M., Bekkering, H., Mazziotta, J. C., and Rizzolatti, G. Science, 1999, 286, 2526–2528. Copyright © 1999 by the American Association for the Advancement of Science. Reprinted with permission. **p. 481, Fig14-19:** From Brown, S., Ingham, R. J., Ingham, J. C., Laird, A. R., and Fox, P. T. Human Brain Mapping, 2005, 25, 105–117. Reprinted with permission. **p. 490, 14-3:** SHUTTR_US_Feb_13/Shutterstock.

Chapter 15 p. 495, CO-15: Science Source. **p. 498, Fig15-02:** Legacy Good Samaritan Health Center. **p. 499, Fig15-03a:** Legacy Good Samaritan Health Center. **p. 499, Fig15-03b:** Legacy Good Samaritan Health Center. **p. 499, Fig15-03c:** Legacy Good Samaritan Health Center. **p. 499, Fig15-03d:** Legacy Good Samaritan Health Center. **p. 506, Fig15-08:** From Stapf, C., and Mohr, J. P. *Annual Review of Medicine*, 2002, 53, 453–475. Reprinted with permission. **p. 509, Fig15-11a:** Figure 1 (p. 248) from Baugh, C. M., Stamm, J. M., Riley, D. O., Gavett, B. E., Shenton, M. E., Lin, A., . . . & Stern, R. A. (2012). "Chronic Traumatic Encephalopathy: Neurodegeneration Following Repetitive Concussive and Subconcussive Brain Trauma." *Brain Imaging and Behavior*, 6(2), 244–254. Permission by Copyright Clearance Center. **p. 509, Fig15-11b:** Figure 2 (p. 250) from Baugh, C. M., Stamm, J. M., Riley, D. O., Gavett, B. E., Shenton, M. E., Lin, A., . . . & Stern, R. A. (2012). "Chronic Traumatic Encephalopathy: Neurodegeneration Following Repetitive Concussive and Subconcussive Brain Trauma." *Brain Imaging and Behavior*, 6(2), 244–254. Permission by Copyright Clearance Center. **p. 511, Fig15-12:** Katherine K., Sulik. **p. 516, Fig15-15:** Dr. Don Born, University of Washington. **p. 522, Fig15-22:** Steven Finkbeiner, Gladstone Institute of Neurological esease and the University fo California, SF. **p. 523, Fig15-23:** Legacy Good Samaritan Health Center. **p. 524, Lisa F. Young/Shutterstock. **p. 525, Fig15-25:** D.J., Selkoe, Brigham and Women's Hospital, Boston. **p. 526, Fig15-27:** William Klunk, University of Pittsburgh Amyloid Imaging Group. **p. 528, Fig15-29:** Legacy Good Samaritan Health Center.

Chapter 16 p. 533, CO-16: Oleg Senkov/Shutterstock. **p. 536, lightpoet/Shutterstock. **p. 538, Kenneth Sponsler/Shutterstock. **p. 539, cabania/Shutterstock. **p. 544, Fig16-07:** D. R., Weinberger, C., Saint Elizabeth'd Hospital, Washington, DC. **p. 544, 123rf. **p. 552, Chamille White/Shutterstock. **p. 557, Fig16-17:** From Mayberg, H. S., Lozano, A. M., Voon, V., et al. *Neuron*, 2005, 45, 651–660. Reprinted with permission Elsevier Science and Technology Journals through Copyright Clearance Center. **p. 559, Monkey Business Images/Shutterstock **p. 561, Fig16-20:** Pereira, A. C., Huddleston, D. E., Brickman, A. M., et al. *Proceedings of the National Academy of Sciences*, USA, 2007, 104, 5638–5643. **p. 561, Mirkoni/Shutterstock.

Chapter 17 p. 566, CO-17: De Agostini Picture Library/Science Source. **p. 570, Gwoeii/Shutterstock. **p. 578, Steven Frame/Shutterstock. **p. 582, Andrew Lever/Shutterstock. **p. 584, InfinityPhoto/Shutterstock. **p. 587, caimacanul/Shutterstock. **p. 592, Dubova/Shutterstock. **p. 597, Suzanne Tucker/Shutterstock.

Chapter 18 p. 617, CO-18: Bsip/Newscom. **p. 617, Lee O'Dell/Shutterstock. **p. 625, Fig18-20:** From Ikonomidou, C., Bittigau, P., Ishimaru, M. J., et al. *Science*, 2000, 287, 1056–1060. By permission of American Association for the Advancement of Science.

SUBJECT INDEX

Note: Page numbers in **bold** refer to pages with definitions. Page numbers followed by *f* and *t* refer to figures and tables, respectively.

A

Abnormal fetal development, schizophrenia and, 542
Absence seizures, 502, **502**
Absorptive phase, eating and, **389**, 389–390, 390*f*
Acamprosate, 631
Accessory olfactory bulb, 324, **324**
Accommodation, 168, **168**
Acetaminophen, 128
Acetyl coenzyme A, 119
Acetylcholine, 62, **63**, 63–64, 117–120
    drugs that act on, 120*t*
    neurotransmitter production, storage, release, 119
    pathways, 117–119, 118*f*
    receptors, 119
    reuptake and destruction, 119–120, 119*f*
    sleep/waking cycle and, 289, 289*f*, 290*f*
    synthesis of, 119, 119*f*, 157
Acetylcholinesterase, 64, **64**, 119
Acetylcholinesterase inhibitors, 156, 527
Acquired dyslexias, 485–489
Acquired immune deficiency syndrome (AIDS), 531
Acral lick dermatitis, 590
Acrostics, 34
Actin, 248, **248**
Action potential, 39, 49, **49**, 52–55
    all-or-none law and, 55, **55**
    conduction of, 55–56, 55*f*
    ion channels and, **52**, 52–53, 53*f*
    permeability to ions and, 54, 54*f*
    rate law and, **55**, 55–56, 56*f*
    saltatory conduction and, 56, **56**, 56*f*
    voltage-dependent ion channels and, **53**, 53–54, 54*f*
Activational hormones, sexual orientation and, 333
Acute anterior poliomyelitis, **530**, 530–531
Adenosine
    sleep regulation and, **288**, 288–289, 288*f*
    sleep/wake transitions and, 295, 295*f*
Adenosine triphosphate (ATP), 42, **42**
Adipose tissue, long-term satiety and, 398–399
Adipsia, 387
Adoption studies. *See also* Genetics
    genetic contributions to behavior and, 160
    schizophrenia and, 537–539
Adrenal medulla, 100, **100**
Adrenaline, 123
Adrenocorticotropic hormone (ACTH), 570, **570**
Aducanumab, 528
Advanced sleep phase syndrome, 306, **306**
Affective blindsight, 368, **368**
Affective disorders, 551–564
    allele polymorphism and, 559–560
    antidepressants and, 553, 554*f*
    biological treatments and, 552–557
    bipolar disorder, 552, **552**
    circadian rhythms and, 560–564
    deep brain stimulation and, 556–557, 557*f*
    electroconvulsive therapy and, **555**, 555–556
    frontal cortex and, 557–558, 558*f*
    heritability and, 552
    ketamine and, 553–555, 554*f*
    lithium and, 555, **555**
    major depressive disorder, 552, **552**
    mania and, 552
    monoamine hypothesis and, 559, **559**
    neurogenesis and, 560, 561*f*
    pharmacological treatment and, 553–555
    REM sleep deprivation and, 561–562
    seasonal affective disorder and, 563, **563**
    serotonin transporter and, 559–560
    slow-wave sleep deprivation and, 562, 562*f*
    suicide risk and, 552
    total sleep deprivation and, 562–563
    transcranial magnetic stimulation and, 556
    treatment-resistant depression, **553**, 553–555

tryptophan depletion procedure and, 559, **559**
    vagus nerve stimulation and, 556, 556*f*
    zeitgebers and, 563–564
Afferent axons, 98, **98**, 143–144
Affinity, drug, 108, **108**
Aggression, 353–360
    alcohol and, 359, 359*f*
    anabolic steroids and, 358–359
    androgens and, 355–358
    defensive behaviors and, 353, **353**
    environment and, 358
    heredity and, 354
    hormonal control of, 355–359
    human research and, 354–355
    laboratory animal research and, 353–354
    neural circuitry and, 353, 353*f*
    predation and, 353, **353**
    serotonin and, 353–354, 354*f*, 355, 356*f*
    submissive behaviors and, 353, **353**
    threat behaviors and, 353, **353**
Agonists, 110, **110**
Agoraphobia, 582, **582**
Agouti-related protein, 402–403, **403**
Agrammatism, 470, 470–471
AIDS dementia complex, 531
Akinesia, 516
Akinetopsia, 199, **199**
Alcohol abuse, 624–625
    acamprosate and, 631
    aggressive behavior and, 359, 359*f*
    apoptosis and, 624, 625*f*
    characteristics of, 624
    developmental disorders and, 510
    dopamine and, 624–625
    heredity and, 616, 616*f*
    naltrexone and, 631, 631*f*
    opiate receptors and, 625, 626*f*
    physical dependence and, 625
    prefrontal gray matter and, 610, 610*f*
    prenatal exposure and, 624
    reinforcement and, 624–625
    schizophrenia and, 541
    sites of action and, 624
    treatment and, 631
Alcohol dehydrogenase, 616, 616*f*
All-or-none law, 55, **55**
Allele, 160, **160**
Allele polymorphism, 559–560
Allostasis, 571, **571**
Allostatic factors, sleep/wake transitions and, 293
Allostatic load, stress response and, 571, **571**
Allylglycine, 116, **116**
Alpha activity, 278, **278**
Alpha-melanocyte-stimulating hormone, **404**, 404–405
Alpha motor neurons, 247, **247**
Alprazolam (Xanax), 117, **117**
Alzheimer's disease, 352, **524**, 524–528, 524*f*
    amyloid plaques and, 524, **524**
    amyloid precursor protein and, **524**, 524–525, 525*f*
    apolipoprotein E and, 526, **526**
    brain trauma and, 509
    causes of, 526–527
    cognitive activity and, 527
    Down syndrome and, 512
    education level and, 526
    frontotemporal dementia and, 525, **525**
    immunization and, 527, 527*f*
    microscopic features of, **524**, 524–525, 525*f*
    neurofibrillary tangles and, 524, **524**
    presenilin genes and, 526, **526**
    secretases and, **524**, 524–525
    stress and, 575–576
    tau protein and, 524, **524**
    traumatic brain injuries and, 526
    treatment and, 527–528

AM1172, 129
Amacrine cells, retina, 169, **169**
American Sign Language, 479–480
Amino acid neurotransmitter systems
    GABA (gamma-aminobutyric acid), **116**, 116–117
    glutamate, **115**, 115–116
Amnesia, 444–451
    anterograde amnesia, 444, **444**, 444*f*, 445–446
    declarative memories and, 448
    hippocampus and, 444–446
    Korsakoff's syndrome and, 444, **444**
    motor learning and, 446–447
    nondeclarative memory and, 448
    perceptual learning and, 447
    relational learning and, 448–451
    retrograde amnesia, 444, **444**, 444*f*, 446, 446*f*
    spatial memory and, 448–451
    stimulus-response learning and, 446
AMPA receptors, 115, **115**, 427–428, 428*f*, **456**, 456–457
Amphetamines
    abuse of, 619–620
    dopamine and, 123, **123**, 545
AMPT (alpha-methyl-*p*-tyrosine), 121, **121**
Ampulla, 221, **221**
Amusia, 219, **219**
Amygdala
    classical conditioning and, 427, 427*f*
    development over lifespan, 362, 362*f*
    emotional perception and, 367–370, 369*f*
    eye fixations and, 370, 370*f*
    fear response and, 348, 348*f*, 351–352
    limbic system and, 89, **89**
    posttraumatic stress disorder and, 580, 580*f*
    prenatal stress and, 573, 573*f*
    of rat, 324, 325*f*
Amyloid plaques, 524, **524**
Amyloid precursor protein (APP), 524, **524**
Amyotrophic lateral sclerosis (ALS), 116, 522, **522**
Anabolic steroids, aggressive behavior and, 358–359
Analgesic brain stimulation, pain and, 232
Anandamide, 128, **128**
Anatomical directions, 73–75, 74*f*
    anterior, 73, **73**
    caudal, 73, **73**
    contralateral, 73, **73**
    dorsal, 73, **73**
    ipsilateral, 73, **73**
    lateral, 73, **73**
    medial, 73, **73**
    neuraxis, 73, **73**
    posterior, 73, **73**
    rostral, 73, **73**
    ventral, 73, **73**
Ancient world, behavioral neuroscience and, 19
Androgen insensitivity, 333–334
Androgen insensitivity syndrome, 315, **315**
Androgenization, aggressive behavior and, 355–357
Androgens, 317*t*
    activational effects and, 358
    aggressive behavior and, 355–358
    dominance and, 358
    masculinization and defeminization and, 321
    organizational effects and, 357–358
    sexual interest stimulation and, 323
    sexual orientation and, 333–334
Androstadienone (AND), 326
Anhedonia, 537
Animal research, ethical issues and, 28–29
Anomia, 471, **471**
Anomic aphasia, 476–477, 482*t*
Anorexia nervosa, 414, **414**, 415*t*. *See also* Eating disorders
Anosmia, 235
Antagonist-precipitated withdrawal, 619, **619**
Antagonists, 110, **110**